W9-BVF-435

Fundamentals of

Human Neuropsychology

Fundamentals of
Human Neuropsychology

fourth edition

Bryan Kolb ▪ Ian Q. Whishaw

University of Lethbridge

W. H. Freeman and Company

New York

A Series of Books in Psychology

Editors:

Richard C. Atkinson
Gardner Lindzey
Richard F. Thompson

Cover Image: "Children of the Brain" celebrates the living brain, the functions of its parts, and its infinite ability to learn and generate ideas. The sculpture was prepared under the direction of architect Galt Durnford for the cornerstone of the McConnell Pavillion of the Montreal Neurological Institute in 1953 and has Wilder Penfield's favorite quotation as its caption: "Where shall wisdom be found and where is the place of understanding?" (Job 28:20) The inspiration for the concept originates with a Shakespearian sonnet:

Look, what thy memory cannot contain
Commit to these waste blanks, and thou shall find
Those children nursed, delivered from thy brain
To take a new acquaintance from thy mind

A drawing of the children of the left hemisphere was penned on the back of a Christmas card sent by Cornelius Ariens Kappers to Penfield in 1932. Kappers may have learned of the children from Ludwig Edinger, an accomplished artist, under whom he studied in 1906. Penfield commissioned Hortense Douglas Cantlie, an artist who drew his surgical illustrations, to arrange the children to reflect more accurately the functions of the gyri of the human cortex. The babies of the pre- and postcentral gyrus are aligned, head down along the central fissure to represent the sensory and motor homunculi. Vision is represented by a child staring out of the occipital pole, just behind two children who form the angular gyrus. Audition is represented by the child of the superior temporal gyrus cupping its ear. The child of the inferior frontal gyrus pensively tips the index finger to its temple as if engrossed in thought. Although Penfield had a deep interest in speech, he did not ask the artist to draw the dominant hemisphere that appeared on the original card, thus, no infants denote speech areas. Perhaps some other inspiration resulted in the sculpture immortalizing the children of the hemisphere now widely associated with intuition, insight, and creativity. (After Feindel, W., "Children of the brain—A cerebral Christmas card." *Neuro-Image* 4:1–4, 1987. Photograph by Deborah Muirhead, with permission of the literary executors of the Wilder Penfield estate.)

Cover design and illustration created by Dennis Kendrick

Library of Congress Cataloging-in-Publication Data

Kolb, Bryan, 1947–
Fundamentals of human neuropsychology/Bryan Kolb and Ian Q. Whishaw.—4th ed.
p. cm.
Includes bibliographical references and index.
ISBN 0-7167-2387-5
1. Neuropsychology. 2. Human behavior. I. Whishaw, Ian Q., 1939– II. Title.
[DNLM: 1. Neuropsychology. 2. Brain—anatomy & histology. 3. Mental processes—physiology. 4. Nervous System Diseases—psychology. 5. Mental Disorders—physiopathology. WL 102 K814f 1995]
QP360.K64 1995
612.8—dc20
DNLM/DLC for Library of Congress 94-45039

Printed in the United States of America

Second printing 1996, RRD

Contents

Preface

When we began to write the first edition of this book in 1977, neuropsychology was a different field. Neuropsychologists who actually worked with people were few in number. Researchers working with humans and those working with nonhuman animals labored largely independently of one another. In addition, there was great interest in clinical applications of neuropsychological theory. The 1980s and 1990s have seen a dramatic change in the field. Cognitive scientists have become interested in the brain and have added a new dimension to neuropsychological studies and theorizing. In addition, the development of sophisticated scanning devices to measure blood flow, metabolic activity, and various types of electrical activity in the brain has provided a way for cognitive scientists and behavioral neuroscientists to investigate brain function in normal subjects. This new technology has had another somewhat unexpected effect, too. Clinical neuropsychologists have had to redefine their role in the diagnosis of cortical injury.

The fourth edition of this book reflects these changes in the field. We have continued to integrate human and nonhuman work, particularly the work on nonhuman primates, and we have included more discussion of issues in cognitive psychology. These issues are addressed especially in the new chapter on attention and consciousness, which are topics that in our wildest dreams would not have appeared in the first editions. We have also added a chapter specifically devoted to vision (that is, the occipital lobes). Work in vision has exploded, both clinically and experimentally, and it made sense to focus our attention on this topic.

One of the unavoidable trends over the first three editions was an increase in length as we tried to expand the text to cover the field as it developed. As we approached the fourth edition, we felt that it was important to shorten the book because it was becoming unmanageable. This shortening led to a major reorganization and the removal of several chapters. In our view, the current version of the book has a core of information (Parts Two and Three) that forms the basis of a course in human neuropsychology. Part One provides background information for those who are new to the study of the brain. The emphasis in Parts Two and Three is on the normal operation of the brain. Part Four presents a discussion of disorders of the brain and provides useful supplementary reading for the interested student, or for use in more ambitious courses. We feel that many chapters can be read at a number of levels, depending upon the reader's sophistication in the neurosciences. We find that beginning students have little interest in history, for example, but as their interest in certain problems increases, they find historical or other theoretical information more relevant.

Again, we must say that we are deeply indebted to those who have written us with advice and comments about how to improve the book, as well as to those from whom we have solicited advice. Of course, the improvements are due to their help, and the errors are attributable solely to us. We are especially indebted to Mel Goodale, Peter MacNeilage, Michael Peters, Glen Prusky, Laughlin Taylor, and John Vokey for their extensive comments on selected chapters. We again acknowledge the enthusiasm and faith of Buck

Rogers of W. H. Freeman and Company who, in 1978, was one of the few who believed that neuropsychology was going to emerge as a significant field of study. We also wish to acknowledge Jonathan Cobb, Susan Brennan, and Georgia Lee Hadler at W. H. Freeman for their enthusiastic support of yet another try to get things right! Finally, we are grateful to Adria Allen for her heroic achievement of typing the entire third edition into a word processor so that we could begin the revision, and for her continuing help in completing the manuscript.

Bryan Kolb and Ian Q. Whishaw

Fundamentals of
Human Neuropsychology

part one

Background

In principle, it would seem simple to study human brain function: one need only study the behavior of people with known brain damage, note the changes in their behavior after the damage, and from them infer the function of the region involved. Unfortunately, is not quite so simple. Certain significant background information must be understood before any conclusions about brain-behavior relations can be drawn. Thus, students of human neuropsychology must be familiar with basic principles of brain function to appreciate fully the nature of the neurological basis of complex cognitive processes.

Chapters 1 through 7 present background information about the history of neuroscience, the evolution of the brain, and the fundamental principles of brain anatomy and chemistry. The fundamental principles of the operation of the sensory and motor system are also discussed. These chapters are written for the beginning student with no previous course in neuroscience, neuroanatomy, or physiological psychology. Students who have had such a course and feel comfortable in their knowledge of these areas can either review the material or proceed directly to Part Two. We recommend that students use the glossary found at the end of the text when they encounter words unfamiliar to them. Throughout the book, words listed in the glossary are printed in boldface type the first time they are used in the text.

chapter one

The Development of Neuropsychology

As Oedipus approached the city of Thebes, his way was blocked by the Sphinx, who posed this riddle: "What walks on four legs in the morning, two legs at noon, and three legs in the evening?" Oedipus replied, "A human." This was correct and he was allowed to pass, because a person crawls as an infant, walks as an adult, and uses a cane when old. The riddle posed by the Sphinx is the riddle of human nature, and although Oedipus knew the direct answer to the riddle he perhaps also understood its deeper meaning: "What are humans?" The deeper meaning of the riddle of human nature is still unanswered, and the object of this book is to pursue the answer in the place where it should logically be found: the brain.

The term "neuropsychology" in its English version originated quite recently. According to Bruce, it was first used by William Osler and then later appeared as a subtitle in D. O. Hebb's 1949 book, *The Organization of Behavior: A Neuropsychological Theory*. Although neither defined nor used in the text itself, the term was probably intended to represent a study that combined the neurologist's common interests in brain function. By 1957, the term had become a recognized designation for a subfield of the neurosciences, when Heinrich Kluver, in the preface to *Behavior Mechanism in Monkeys,* suggested that the book would be of interest to neuropsychologists and others. (Kluver had not used the term in the 1933 preface to the same book.) The term was given wide publicity when it appeared in 1960 in the title of a collection of K. S. Lashley's writings—*The Neuropsychology of Lashley*—most of which were rat and monkey studies edited by Beach. Again neuropsychology was not used or defined in the text.

We define **neuropsychology** as the study of the relation between brain function and behavior. Although the study draws information from many disciplines—for example, anatomy, biology, biophysics, ethology, pharmacology, physiology, physiological psychology, and philosophy—its central focus is the development of a science of human behavior based on the function of the human brain.

Neuropsychology is strongly influenced by two traditional foci for experimental and theoretical investigations in brain research: the **brain hypothesis,** the idea that the brain is the source of behavior; and the **neuron hypothesis,** the idea that the unit of brain structure and function is the neuron. This chapter traces the development of these two ideas. We will see that although the science is new, its major ideas are not. Agreement that these are important ideas was not easily arrived at, however. For much of our past we humans have groped in the dark for concepts that would help to describe the brain's function. From time to time an idea is serendipitously formulated, is sometimes grasped, is sometimes examined, and is sometimes discarded only to be rediscovered later. Through this history we hope to encourage the reader to see that the science is not dogma but a dialogue about ideas.

A few terms that will be encountered in this history are defined here. It is usual to divide the brain into three general parts: the forebrain, the brainstem, and the spinal cord (see Figure 1.5).

The human **cortex** (bark), which is thought to mediate complex conscious behavior, is the largest portion of the forebrain; its **gyri** (wrinkles) are its most distinctive feature. The cortex consists of left and right **hemispheres** (half globes), which are connected by the **corpus callosum.**

The **brainstem** is covered by the cortex and helps to regulate body functions and the execution of movements; the **cerebellum,** with its distinctive gyral pattern, is a large structure in the brainstem that is involved in movement.

The **spinal cord** receives sensory input from the body and sends input to the muscles; all brain actions are produced through cells in the spinal cord that project to the muscles. **Neurons** are specialized cells consisting of a **cell body,** which contains the machinery for sustaining the life of the cell, and a **nucleus,** which contains the genetic material that determines cell shape and function. Cells may have numerous **dendrites** (branches); these are an extension of the wall of the cell body and receive input from other cells. Each cell has one **axon** that carries information from the cell to other cells (see Figure 1.6). Axons influence other cells by secreting chemicals onto them through a **synapse** (clasp) that usually does not directly touch the receiving cell.

THE BRAIN HYPOTHESIS

The Brain versus the Heart

Since earliest times people have believed that their behavior is controlled either by a soul, a spirit, a rational system, or by some part of the body. These beliefs are recorded in the historical records of many different cultures. We have also held a variety of views about the nature and location of the controlling body part. Among the earliest surviving recorded hypotheses were those of Alcmaeon of Croton (ca. 500 B.C.) and Empedocles (ca. 490–430 B.C.). Alcmaeon located mental processes in the brain and so subscribed to what is now called the brain hypothesis; Empedocles located them in the heart and so subscribed to what could be called the cardiac hypothesis.

The relative merits of those two hypotheses were debated for the next 2000 years. For example, among Greek philosophers, Plato (427?–347 B.C.) developed the concept of a tripartite soul and placed its rational part in the brain because that was the part of the body closest to the heavens. Aristotle (384–322 B.C.) had a good knowledge of brain structure and realized that, of all animals, humans have the largest brain relative to body size. Nevertheless, he decided that because the heart is warm and active it is the source of mental processes; the brain, because it is cool and inert, serves as a radiator to cool the blood (actually, it turns out that the blood cools the brain). He explained away the large size of the brain as evidence of a relation to intelligence by stating that humans' blood is richer and hotter than other animals' and so requires a larger cooling system.

Early Greek and Roman physicians such as Hippocrates (cs. 460–377 B.C.) and Galen (A.D. 129–ca. 199), influenced by their clinical experience, described some aspects of brain anatomy and argued strongly for the brain hypothesis. Before becoming the leading physican in Rome, Galen had spent 5 years as a surgeon to gladiators and was aware of the behavioral consequences of brain damage. He went to great pains to refute Aristotle. He pointed out that the nerves from the sense organs go to the brain, not to the heart. He did experiments to compare the effects of pressure on the heart and brain. He noted that pressure on the brain causes cessation of movement and even death, whereas pressure on the heart causes pain but does not arrest voluntary behavior.

The cardiac hypothesis has left its mark on our language. In literature as in everyday speech, matters of emotion are frequently referred to the heart: love is symbolized by an arrow piercing the heart; a person distressed by unrequited love is said to be heartbroken; an unenthusiastic person is said to not be putting his or her heart into it; an angry person is said to have boiling blood.

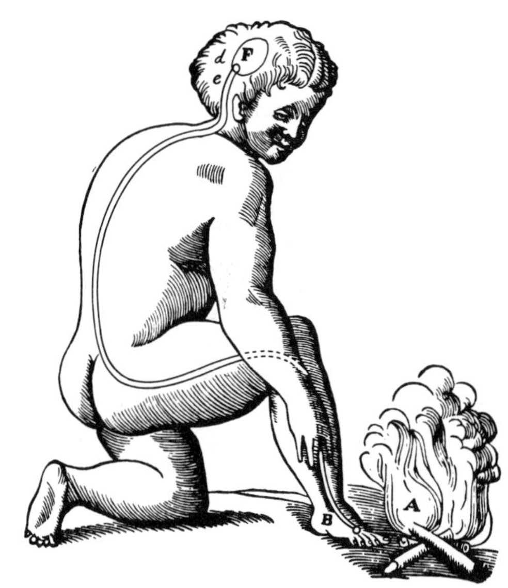

FIGURE 1.1. The concept of reflex originated with Descartes. In this example, heat from the flame causes a thread in the nerve to be pulled, releasing ventricular fluid through an opened pore. The fluid flows through the nerve, causing not only the foot to withdraw but also the eyes and head to turn to look at it, the hands to advance, and the whole body to bend to protect it. His concept was stimulated by the mechanical principles of displays used in water gardens fashionable in France in his day. A visitor in the gardens would step on a plate that mechanically caused statues to hide, appear, or squirt water. In fact, his use of the reflex concept was for behaviors that would today be considered more than reflexive, whereas what is held as reflexive today was not conceived of by Descartes. (From Descartes, 1664.)

Descartes: The Mind-Body Problem

Of course, simply knowing that the brain controls behavior is not enough; formulation of a complete hypothesis required knowledge of *how* the brain controls behavior. Modern thinking began with René Descartes (1596–1650), who replaced the Platonic concept of the tripartite soul with the idea of a unitary mind that is the reasoning or rational soul. Being nonmaterial and having no spatial extent, the mind is different from the body. Descartes was impressed by machines made in his time, such as statues in the water gardens of Paris. For example, when unknowing people stood before them, depressing a lever under the sidewalk, they received a spray of water in the face. Descartes proposed that the body is like these machines. It is material and thus clearly has spatial extent, and it responds reflexively to sensory changes by actions of the brain (Figure 1.1). Descartes argued that nonhuman animals have only bodies and no rational minds; thus their behavior can be explained mechanically as a series of reflex actions. He further proposed that human behavior requires the function of both mind and body, with the mind acting through the body to produce behavior.

In proposing that the mind and body are separate but can interact, Descartes originated the mind-body problem: How can a nonmaterial mind produce movements in a material body? Some dualists (those philosophers who hold that mind and body are separate) have argued that the two interact causally, but they cannot explain how. Other dualists avoid this problem by reasoning either that the mind and body function in parallel without interacting or that the body can affect the mind but the mind cannot affect the body. Thus, both dualist positions allow for theorizing about behavior without considering mind. Philosophers called monists avoid the mind-body problem by postulating that the mind and body are the same thing and either are both material or both nonmaterial. Clearly, the latter monist position might be an embarrassing one for a neuropsychologist!

There were two other logical consequences of Descartes's mind-body hypothesis. First, since the mind is indivisible, theories that subdivide brain function could not be correct. Second, since mind exists apart from the body, the functions of mind would require separate consideration. Thus, complete understanding of the body and how it worked would not bring complete understanding of human behavior. During the 19th century, physiologists would often describe the physiology of some newly discovered reflex system and then speculate about how the mind worked through it. (Even today, some scientists are challenged by the problem of mind—for example, see Eccles, *The Neurophysiological Basis of Mind: The Principles of Neurophysiology,* 1956.)

Most modern neuropsychologists assert that the body portion of the mind-body polarity is their proper domain of study. They say that the mind, although it may very well exist, cannot be studied by using conventional techniques. Some skeptics refer to the mind as the bogey in the brain, or the ghost in the machine, whereas psychologists refer to it as the little green man in the head. They argue, as does the philosopher Gilbert Ryle, that "mind" is simply a term for the brain and its activities and not a separate entity, just as "city" is a term for a collection of buildings and people.

Before Descartes there had been a belief, held by Galen and many subsequent writers, that mind is located in the fluid found in the hollows or ventricles of the brain rather than in the matter of the brain. This belief was reinforced in the 10th century when it came to be thought that the muscles are moved by being filled with a fluid, ventricular fluid being the prime candidate. In fact, some of the theories of how fluid in different ventricular cavities controls different aspects of behavior were quite elegant. Andreas Vesalius (1514–1564), however, discredited the ventricular theories. Vesalius dissected brains and noted that the relative size of the ventricles in animals and humans is the same. He concluded that since the rational human is distinguished by having the largest brain, it is the brain and not the ventricles that mediate mental processes. Descartes, therefore, located mental processes within brain tissue. He stated that the mind is in the **pineal body,** a small structure located in the brainstem, based on the logic that the pineal body is the only structure in the nervous system not composed of two bilaterally symmetrical halves and that it is located close to the ventricles. He proposed that the rest of the brain is not functioning neural tissue but is a covering cortex or bark that protects the important internal mechanisms. People later argued against Descartes's hypothesis by pointing out that when the pineal body was found to be damaged, there were no obvious changes in behavior. Today the pineal body is thought to be involved in controlling seasonal rhythms.

Gall and Spurzheim: The Phrenologists

The first global theory of how the brain works was the phrenological theory of Franz Josef Gall (1758–1828) and Johann Casper Spurzheim (1776–1832). Gall and Spurzheim made a number of important discoveries in neuroanatomy that alone give them a place in history. They proposed that the cortex and its gyri are composed of functioning cells that are connected with the brainstem and spinal cord. They found that the cortex projects to the spinal cord, and they recognized that the spinal cord contains cells that project to the muscles. Thus, the cortex could control behavior through its projections to the spinal cord. They also recognized that the two symmetrical hemispheres of the brain are connected by the corpus callosum and thus could interact with each other.

From this anatomical basis, Gall then proposed a theory of how the brain produces behavior, suggesting that different cortical areas have different functions. Gall's behavioral ideas began with observations made in his early youth. He noticed that students with good memories had large, protruding eyes. He thought it possible that a well-developed memory area of the brain located behind the eyes could cause them to protrude.

From this beginning, Gall and Spurzheim undertook to examine the external features of the skull and to correlate its bumps and depressions with what they thought to be important aspects of behavior. A bump on the skull indicated a well-developed underlying cortical gyrus and therefore a greater capacity for a particular behavior; a depression in the same area indicated an underdeveloped gyrus and a concomitantly reduced faculty. Thus, a person who had a high degree of what they called amativeness, would have a large bump in the area shown in Figure 1.2B, whereas a person with a low degree of this trait would have a depression in this same area.

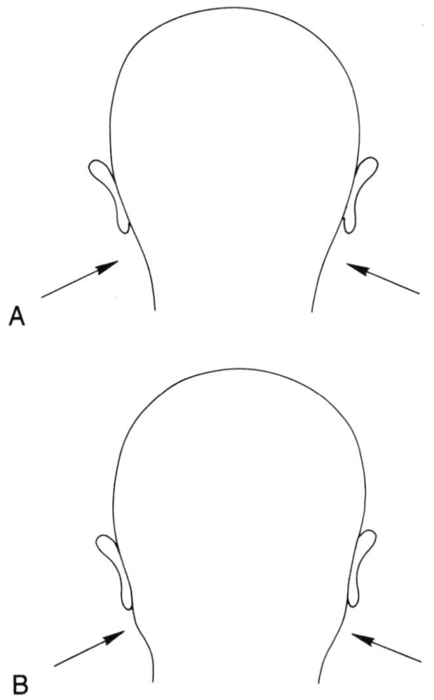

FIGURE 1.2. According to phrenologists, depressions (*A*) and bumps (*B*) on the skull indicate the size of the underlying area of brain and, when correlated with personality traits, indicate the part of the brain controlling the trait. Gall, examining a patient (who because of her behavior became known as "Gall's Passionate Widow"), found a bump at the back of her neck that he thought located the center for "amativeness" in the cerebellum (arrows in *B*). Flourens refuted this hypothesis by removing a dog's cerebellum to show that the cerebellum is involved in coordinating movement. As phrenology was popularized, bumps and depressions were indicated on the head in places that were no longer adjacent to the brain—as was the case with amativeness. (After Olin, 1910.)

Gall and Spurzheim identified a long list of behavioral traits, such as wit, inquiry, and faith. Many of these traits were borrowed from English or Scottish psychology. Each was assigned to a particular portion of the skull and, by inference, to the underlying portion of the brain. Figure 1.3 shows the resulting map they devised. Spurzheim called the study of the relationship between the skull's surface features and a person's faculties **phrenology.**

Gall and Spurzheim went to considerable effort to gather evidence for their theory, and Gall states that he devoted himself to observation and waited patiently for nature to bring her results to him. In developing his idea of the carnivorous instinct, Gall examined the skulls of meat- and plant-eating animals and detailed evidence from more than 50 species, including anecdotal evidence from his own lapdog. He studied human behavior, including accounts of a patricide and a murderer. He also examined the skulls of 25 other murderers. He included descriptions of people who delighted in witnessing death or torturing animals, or who historically were noted for cruelty and sadism, and he even considered evidence from numerous paintings and busts.

One might ask why it was that he made thousands of observations on this subject, and never found an exception. Gall's entire method was geared toward seeking confirmations. Statistical methods had not been invented, and so he never considered the possibility that his observations should meet certain standards or be tested in any objective way. Even when he made good observations that may have been subjected to more rigorous examination, he gave them little more weight than any anecdote. Gall also placed no emphasis on evidence from cases of brain damage. For example, he is credited with giving the first complete account of a relationship between left frontal brain damage and aphasia (see Figure 1.3),

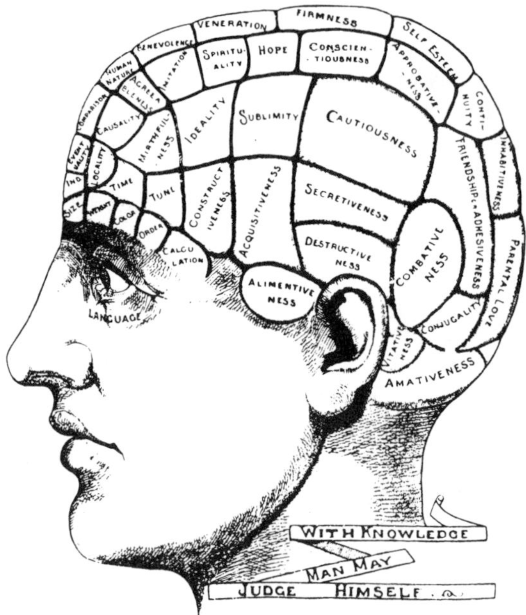

FIGURE 1.3. Originally Gall's system had 27 faculties. As phrenology (Spurzheim's name for the theory) expanded, the number of faculties increased. The figure shows the location of faculties according to Spurzheim. Language, indicated in the front of the brain (below the eye), actually derived from a case study of Gall's; a soldier had received a knife wound that penetrated the frontal lobe of his left hemisphere through the eye. The soldier became aphasic; he was thus the first comprehensive report of aphasia following left frontal damage.

yet he felt that this type of finding was not evidence per se but rather confirmation of a finding that was already established by the phrenological evidence.

Gall and Spurzheim's research was misguided for four reasons. First, the psychology of faculties bore little relation to real behavior: faculties such as faith, self-love, and veneration are impossible to define and to quantify objectively. The first breakthroughs in localization came only when researchers chose an objective behavior, such as speech, to correlate with an area of the brain. The second cause of the phrenologists' failure was their belief that the superficial features of the skull, the analysis of which they called cranioscopy, could be used to estimate brain size and shape. They failed to realize that the outer skull does not mirror the inner skull or the surface features of the cortex. Had they instead investigated the size of the convolutions or gyri, they might have discovered that the size of some gyri could be correlated with behavior. But they thought of gyral patterns as random wrinkles, such as those that might be found in a crumpled shirt, and so gave them no attention. The third problem was that phrenology invited quackery and thus, indirectly, ridicule by association. Because its followers devoted themselves to extremely superficial personality analysis, the entire endeavor was quickly brought into disrepute. In the eyes of the phrenologists' contemporaries, however, there was a more damning criticism, which was the fourth cause of their failure. Gall and Spurzheim had postulated that the brain is the organ of the mind, that personality characteristics are innate, and that the brain (or mind) is composed of independently functioning units. The prevailing opinion still reflected Descartes: the mind is nonmaterial and functions as a whole. Since these views are still held by many people today, it is possible to understand the hostility Gall and Spurzheim's ideas evoked nearly 200 years ago.

A historical remnant from the phrenology era is that the areas or lobes of the cortex are named after the bones of the skull; for example, the lobes in the front of the cortex are called frontal lobes and those on the back side are called the temporal lobes after the respective overlying bones. Additionally, despite the failure of scientific attempts to correlate appearance with various aspects of behavior, it is not uncommon to hear people accord virtues to others on the basis of their physical appearance. Readers may ask themselves how accurate they would be if asked to judge intelligence on the basis of photographs. Social psychologists have found that university students are not unwilling to make such judgments; they do so using the rule: beauty equals intelligence. In fairness to Gall, we may note that at least some of his science, inaccurate as it appears to have been, attempted an actual physical measurement.

Flourens: The First Experiments

Pierre Flourens (1794–1867), a French experimentalist, is generally credited with the demolition of phrenology. Flourens, who accepted the concept of a unified mind, buttressed philosophical arguments against Gall and Spurzheim with experimentation. Nor was he above using ridicule to discount them, as the following story from Flourens's book *Comparative Psychology* shows:

> The famous physiologist, Magendie, preserved with veneration the brain of Laplace. Spurzheim had the very natural wish to see the brain of a great man.
>
> To test the science of the phrenologist, Mr. Magendie showed him, instead of the brain of Laplace, that of an imbecile.
>
> Spurzheim, who had already worked up his enthusiasm, admired the brain of the imbecile as he would have admired that of Laplace. (Krech, 1962)

Flourens developed the technique of removing or lesioning parts of the brains of animals to study the changes produced in their behavior. His technique involved removing a small piece of cortex and then observing how the animal behaved and how it recovered from the loss of brain tissue. To search for different functions in the cortex, he varied the location from which he removed brain tissue. He found that after he removed pieces of cortex, animals first moved very little and failed to eat and drink, but with time they recovered to the point that they seemed normal. This pattern of loss and recovery held for all his experiments and so provided no support for the idea that different areas of the cortex had specialized functions. He concluded that there is no **localization of function** in the cortex but that all intellectual faculties reside there coextensively. He argued that loss of function is correlated with the extent of ablation of cortical tissue: if all tissue were removed all intellectual functions were gone; if sufficient tissue remained intact there was recovery of all function. He did find that other brain areas have specialized functions. For example, he found that the brainstem is important for breathing because animals died if it was damaged, and he found that the cerebellum coordinates locomotion. Gall had proposed that this area is the location of amativeness (see Figure 1.2).

In addition to his experimental contributions, Flourens gave neuropsychology a number of ideas. He was a strict Cartesian, even to the point of dedicating his book to Descartes. Flourens invested the cortex with the properties that Descartes had ascribed to the mind, including the functions of will, reason, and intelligence, and advocated that the only proper approach to understanding these functions is through introspection. He argued that although the cortex has mental functions it has no motor or sensory functions. The idea that there is uncommitted cortex (now called association cortex) available for higher functions is a Flourensian notion applied to a more circumscribed portion of the cortex. The idea that all functions could be recovered and taken over by undamaged portions of the cortex is frequently encountered in studies of functional recovery. Perhaps the most commonly encountered Flourensian idea is in pedagogy, where it is expressed as the assertion that most people never use more than 10% of the brain.

The conclusion that Flourens's experiments devastated Gall and Spurzheim was persuasive at the time, but is difficult to support in retrospect. Many of his experiments were performed with pigeons and chickens—animals with virtually no neocortex. His behavioral tests were assessments of activities such as eating and wing flapping and bore no relation to the faculties proposed for the cortex by Gall and Spurzheim. Many of the deficits from which his animals appeared to suffer may have been the result of postsurgical shock, brain swelling, or removal of far more tissue than the forebrain. Certainly subsequent workers who removed only the cortex did not find that pigeons lost all intellectual faculties as Flourens had defined them.

Broca: Localization of Language

Jean Baptiste Bouillaud (1796–1881), by supporting Gall's idea that language function is localized in the frontal lobe, provided the impetus for the study of brain function to take a new direction. On 21 February 1825 he read a paper before the Royal Academy of Medicine in France in which he argued from clinical studies that function is localized in the neocortex, and specifically that speech is localized in the frontal lobes just as Gall had suggested. (Gall had correlated the frontal cortex with language after studying a penetrating brain injury.) Observing that acts such as writing, drawing, painting, and fencing are carried out with the right hand, Bouillaud also suggested that the part of the brain that controls them might possibly be the left hemisphere. Why, he asked, should people not be left-brained for the movements of speech as well? A few years later, in 1836, Marc Dax read a paper in Montpellier, France, about a series of clinical cases demonstrating that disorders of speech were constantly associated with lesions of the left hemisphere. Dax's manuscript was published by his son in 1865.

Though neither Bouillaud's nor Dax's work had much impact when first presented, Ernest Auburtin, Bouillaud's son-in-law, took up Bouillaud's cause. At a meeting of the Anthropological Society of Paris in 1861, he reported the case of a patient who ceased to speak when pressure was applied to his exposed frontal lobe. He also gave the following description of another patient, with a challenge:

> For a long time during my service with M. Bouillaud I studied a patient, named Bache, who had lost his speech but understood everything said to him and replied with signs in a very intelligent manner to all questions put to him. This man, who spent several years at the Bicetre, is now at the Hospital for Incurables. I saw him again recently and his disease has progressed; slight paralysis has appeared but his intelligence is still unimpaired, and speech is wholly abolished. Without a doubt this man will soon die. Based on the symptoms that he presents we have diagnosed softening of the anterior lobes. If, at autopsy, these lobes are found to be intact, I shall renounce the ideas that I have just expounded to you. (Stookey, 1954)

Paul Broca (1824–1880), founder of the society, attended the meeting and heard Auburtin's challenge. Five days later he received a patient, Leborgne, who had lost his speech and was able to say only "tan" and utter an oath. He had paralysis on the right side of his body but in other respects seemed intelligent and normal. Broca invited Auburtin to examine Tan, as he came to be called, and together they agreed that if Auburtin was right, Tan should have a frontal lesion. Tan died on 17 April 1861, and the next day Broca submitted his findings to the Anthropological Society (this may be the fastest publication ever). The left frontal lobe was the focus of Tan's lesion. By 1863, Broca had collected eight more cases similar to Tan's and stated:

> Here are eight instances in which the lesion was in the posterior third of the third frontal convolution. This number seems to me to be sufficient to give strong presumptions. And the most remarkable thing is that in all the patients the lesion was on the left side. I do not dare draw conclusions from this. I await new facts. (Joynt, 1964)

It is usual to credit Broca with describing a behavioral syndrome (**aphasia**) that consists of an inability to speak despite the presence of intact vocal mechanisms and normal comprehension, correlating this syndrome with a part of the brain, and elaborating the concept of *cerebral dominance* of language in the left hemisphere, or, as he phrased it, "nous parlons avec l'hémisphère gauche." This is the beginning of the idea that the left and right hemispheres have different functions.

Largely because these contributions marked a change in the approach to analysis of brain function, they have been carefully scrutinized by historians. The clinical symptoms that Broca described were already known, as is demonstrated by Auburtin's account of the aphasic Bache—and Broca acknowledged this. Language and the frontal lobes had been correlated previously by Gall,

Bouillaud, and Auburtin, whose priority Broca recognized. Broca's anatomical analysis was criticized by Pierre Marie, who reexamined the brains of Broca's first two patients, Tan and Lelong, 25 years after Broca's death. Marie pointed out in his article, "The Third Left Frontal Convolution Plays No Particular Role in the Function of Language," that Lelong was probably a victim of a senile dementia, with general nonspecific atrophy of the brain common in senility, and was not aphasic, and that Tan had additional extensive damage in his posterior cortex that may have accounted for his aphasia. Broca had been aware of Tan's posterior damage but had concluded that, whereas the posterior damage contributed to his death, the anterior damage had occurred earlier, producing his aphasia. Finally, Dax was the first to suggest the doctrine of cerebral dominance. Broca also acknowledged this, although, according to Joynt, he was never able to establish to his own satisfaction that Dax had read a paper in Montpellier in 1836 in which he stated that speech was lateralized on the left.

There is substance to the details of all these criticisms; nevertheless, Broca's more enduring contribution was to lend his considerable prestige to the theory of localization of function, the clinical descriptions of brain-damage effects, and neuroanatomy and so to excite neuroscientists and the lay public alike. For this reason the anterior speech region is called **Broca's area** and the syndrome that results from its damage is called **Broca's aphasia.** (Broca used the term "aphemia" but it was criticized by Trousseau, who argued that it meant "infamy" and was thus inappropriate as a clinical designation. Trousseau suggested the word "aphasia," which Broca criticized as also inappropriate, since it meant "the state of a man who has run out of arguments;" but it nevertheless became accepted.)

Wernicke: Sequential Programming and Disconnection

Broca's description of aphasia as a condition resulting from left frontal lesions makes two rather simple points: (1) a behavior such as language is controlled by a specific brain area; and (2) destroying the area selectively destroys the behavior.

People who interpreted Broca in this way have been called strict localizationists. There were, however, many who disagreed with these points on both logical and clinical grounds. Among the most notable to dissent was Carl Wernicke (1848–1904). He made two findings that did not support strict localization: first, there is more than one language area; second, damage that spares a brain area could nevertheless produce deficits indistinguishable from those resulting from damage to the area.

Theodore Meynert (1833–1892) was the first to suggest that the cortex in the temporal lobe, behind Broca's area, is the part of the cortex that receives sensory projections from the ear and is thus the auditory cortex. He suspected a relation between hearing and speech and even described two cases of aphasic patients with lesions in this auditory projection area. It was his associate Wernicke, however, who subsequently described the details of this temporal lobe aphasia—or, as it has come to be called, **Wernicke's aphasia**—and placed it within a theoretical framework.

Wernicke described four major features of the aphasia that made it different from what Broca described: (1) there was damage in the first temporal gyrus, in what is now known as **Wernicke's area;** (2) there was no contralateral **hemiplegia** or paralysis; (3) the patients could speak fluently, but what they said was confused and made little sense—hence it was called **fluent aphasia;** and (4) although the patients were able to hear, they could not understand or repeat what was said to them.

Wernicke provided a model for how language is organized in the left hemisphere: it involves sequential programming of activity in his and Broca's language areas (Figure 1.4). Wernicke theorized that the sound images of objects are stored in Wernicke's area, whence they are sent over a pathway (later identified as the **arcuate fasciculus**) to Broca's area, where the representations of speech movements are retained. If the temporal lobe was damaged, speech movements could still be mediated by Broca's area but the

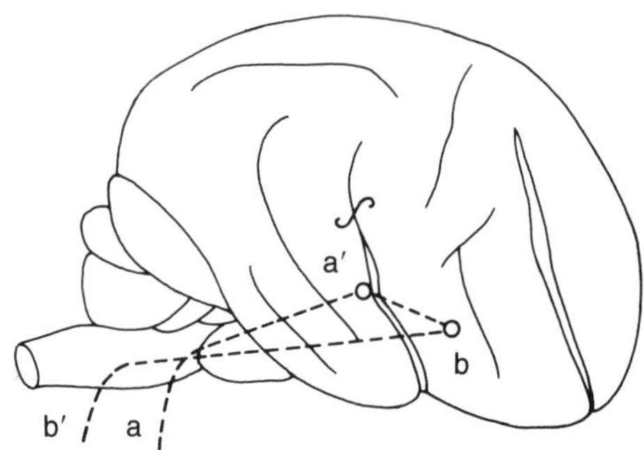

FIGURE 1.4. Wernicke's 1874 model showing how language is organized in the brain. Sounds enter the brain on the auditory pathway (a). Sound images are stored in Wernicke's area (a′) and are sent to Broca's word area (b) for articulation over the motor pathway (b′). Lesions on the pathway a-a′-b-b′ could produce different types of aphasia, depending on lesion location. It is curious that Wernicke drew all his language models on the right hemisphere and not the left, which is the dominant hemisphere for language, as Wernicke believed. It is amazing that his model was that of an ape, which could not speak, as Wernicke knew. (After Wernicke, 1874.)

speech would make no sense, because the person would be unable to monitor the words. Because damage to Broca's area produces loss of speech movements without the loss of sound images, Broca's aphasia is not accompanied by a loss of understanding.

Wernicke suggested that if the fibers connecting the two speech areas suffered damage (**disconnection**), but without damage to Broca's or Wernicke's area, a speech deficit would occur. Wernicke called such a disconnection **conduction aphasia:** both speech sounds and movements would be retained, as would comprehension, but speech would still be impaired because the person would not be able to judge the sense of the words that he or she heard uttered.

The analysis of brain lesion effects by subsequent neurologists was much influenced by Wernicke's concept of disconnection, because it provided a method of linking anatomy and behavior, which permitted prediction of new brain syndromes. Using this methodology, Dejerine in 1892 was able to describe a case in which **alexia,** loss of the ability to read, resulted from disconnecting the visual area from Wernicke's area. Wernicke's student Liepmann (1863–1925) was able to show that **apraxia,** an inability to make sequences of movements, followed disconnection of motor areas from sensory areas. Disconnection is an important idea because it predicts that a deficit that follows disconnection of an area can be identical to a deficit that follows damage to that area. As a result, strict localization of function becomes unworkable. Wernicke's speech model was revived by Norman Geschwind in the 1960s and is now sometimes referred to as the Wernicke-Geschwind model.

Fritsch and Hitzig: Electrophysiological Confirmation of Localization

The work of clinical neurologists such as Broca, Wernicke, and others indicated that behavior is somehow localized in the cortex. Although many researchers were excited by the idea, others maintained strong objections. A different approach that also supported functional localization was provided by development of the technique for electrically stimulating the brain. This involved placing a thin insulated wire, an electrode, just onto or into the cortex and passing a small electrical current through the uninsulated tip of the wire, thus exciting the cells near the electrode tip.

In 1870, Gustav Theodor Fritsch (1838–1929) and Eduard Hitzig (1838–1907) published their extraordinary paper, "On the Electrical Excitability of the Cerebrum." Hitzig had previously elicited eye movements by stimulating the temporal cortex of a man, and he may have derived the idea of stimulating the cortex from an observation made while dressing a wound, that mechanical irritation of the brain caused twitching in the contralateral limbs. Working in Hitzig's bedroom, the two performed successful preliminary experiments with a rabbit and then a dog in which they showed that stimulating the cortex could produce movements. Not only was the neocortex excitable, it was selectively excitable. Stimulating the frontal cortex produced movements on the opposite side of the body, whereas stimulation of the posterior neocortex produced no movement. Stimulation of restricted portions of the frontal cortex elicited movement of particular body parts—for example, neck, forelimb, hind limb (Figure 1.5)—which suggested that on the cortex there are centers or topographic representations of the different parts of the body. Fritsch and Hitzig summarized the interpretation of their findings in the conclusion to their 1870 paper:

> Furthermore, it may be concluded from the sum of all our experiments that, contrary to the opinions of Flourens and most investigators who followed him, the soul in no case represents a sort of total function of the whole cerebrum, the expression of which might be destroyed by mechanical means in toto, but not in its individual parts. Individual psychological functions, and probably all of them, depend for their entrance into matter or for their formation from it, upon circumscribed centers of the cerebral cortex. (Fritsch and Hitzig, 1960)

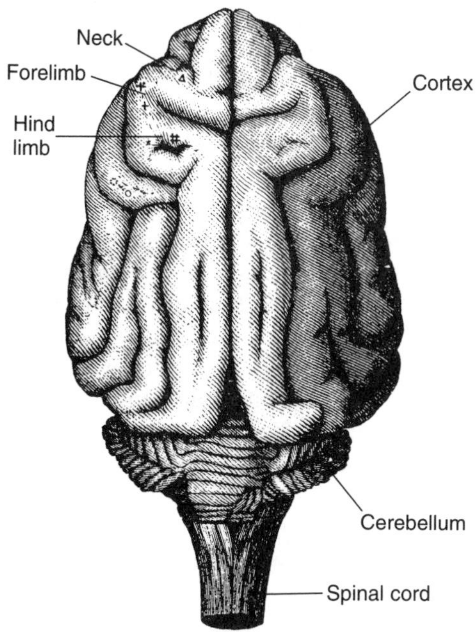

FIGURE 1.5. Drawing of the brain of a dog from Fritsch and Hitzig (1870). The areas from which movements of the opposite side of the body were evoked with electrical stimulation are restricted to the frontal cortex. Note that the cortex does not completely cover the brainstem and so the cerebellum can be seen.

The findings of Fritsch and Hitzig contributed to overthrowing three dicta that had been defended by Flourens: the cortex is unexcitable; it plays no role in producing movement; and function is not localized. Over the next few years David Ferrier (1843–1928) refined the stimulation technique and confirmed Fritsch and Hitzig's results in monkeys, dogs, cats, rabbits, guinea pigs, pigeons, fish, and frogs.

Although Fritsch and Hitzig may have stimulated the cortexes of wounded soldiers, the first experiment in which electrical stimulation of the cortex of a human was formally reported was performed in 1874 by R. Bartholow (1831–1904) in Cincinnati. Mary Rafferty, a patient in his care, had a cranial defect that exposed the posterior part of the cortex in each hemisphere. The following is an extract from his report of that experiment:

> Observation 3. *To test faradic reaction of the posterior lobes.* Passed an insulated needle into the left posterior lobe so that the non-insulated portion rested entirely in the substance of the brain. The other insulated needle was placed in contact with the dura mater, within one-forth of an inch of the first. When the circuit was closed, muscular contraction in the right upper and lower extremities ensued, as in the preceding observations. Faint but visible contraction of the left orbicularis palpebrarum [eyelid], and dilation of the pupils, also ensued. Mary complained of a very strong and unpleasant feeling of tingling in both right extremities, especially in the right arm, which she seized with the opposite hand and rubbed vigorously. Notwithstanding the very evident pain from which she suffered, she smiled as if much amused. (Bartholow, 1874)

Bartholow's publication caused such an outcry that he was forced to leave Cincinnati. Also, it is unlikely that he had stimulated the cortex, because in his account the electrodes were inserted about an inch into the brain tissue. Nevertheless, he had demonstrated that the electrical stimulation technique could be used with a conscious person, who could report the subjective sensations produced by stimulation. (The pain that Mary was reported to have suffered was not caused by stimulation of pain receptors in the brain—since there are none—but was probably a genuinely evoked sensation from brain stimulation.) It was not long before electrical stimulation was being used as standard part of many brain surgery procedures.

Goltz: Antilocalization

In his vigorous history of this period, Henry Head labeled Wernicke and others of his school the "diagram makers." This derogatory term was a reference to their oversimplification of the deficits that followed brain damage, as well as to their selection ("lop and twist," as he phrased it) of symptoms to fit their models. Head's criticisms were directed at the proliferation of maps and diagrams showing the supposed location of all types of functions. Head maintained that people persisted in concluding that because we have words for behaviors such as speech, eating, walking, and so forth, there must be one place in the brain that controls each behavior. Head preferred to argue that there are many forms of speech, eating, and walking, each of which is probably controlled by many different parts of the brain. Rather than review the complexities of the work throughout this period, it is perhaps more instructive to look at one dramatic kind of evidence brought forward in opposition to the theory of localization of function.

When Fritsch and Hitzig made their historical discovery that stimulation of a restricted portion of the neocortex resulted in specific movement, they concluded that that area of the cortex was necessary and sufficient for producing the movement. The experiments performed by Friedrich L. Goltz (1834–1902) in 1892 were intended specifically to test this idea.

Goltz argued that if a portion of the neocortex had a function, then removal of the cortex should lead to a loss of that function. He made very large lesions in three dogs, which removed the cortex and a good deal of underlying brain tissue, which he then studied for 57 days, 92 days, and 18 months, respectively. The dog that survived for 18 months was studied in the greatest detail. It was more active than a normal dog, alternated periods of sleep and waking (though these were shorter than normal), and panted when warm and shivered when cold. It walked well on uneven ground and was able to catch its balance when it slipped. If placed in an abnormal posture, it corrected its position. After hurting a hind limb on one occasion it trotted on three legs, holding up the injured limb. It was able to orient to touches or pinches on its body and snap at the object that touched it, although its orientations were not very accurate. If offered two portions of food—the first a piece of meat soaked in milk, the second a piece of meat soaked in bitter quinine—it accepted the first and rejected the second. It responded to light and sounds, although its response thresholds were elevated.

With reference to experiments of his time, Goltz stated that if stimulation of a particular portion of the brain were found to produce movement, and if the stimulated area were concluded to be a motor center, then it followed that removal of this area should abolish movement. This did not occur. In fact, decortication did not appear to completely eliminate any function, though it seemed to reduce all functions to some extent. This demonstration appeared to be a strong argument against localization of function and even seemed to question the role of the cortex in behavior.

Hughlings-Jackson: Hierarchical Organization

The fundamental difference between Goltz and those whom his experiments were intended to criticize was to be resolved by the **hierarchical**

organization concept of brain function proposed by the English neurologist John Hughlings-Jackson (1835–1911), who has been described as the founder of modern neurology.

Hughlings-Jackson thought of the nervous system as being organized in a number of layers arranged in a functional hierarchy. Each successively higher level would control more complex aspects of behavior but do so through the lower levels. Often Hughlings-Jackson described the nervous system as having three levels: the spinal cord, the brainstem, and the frontal cortex. But equally often he designated no particular anatomical area for a nervous system level. He had adopted the theory of hierarchy from the philosopher Herbert Spencer's argument that the brain evolved in a series of steps, each of which brought animals the capacity to engage in new behaviors. What Hughlings-Jackson did with the theory was novel. He suggested that diseases or damage that affected the highest levels would produce dissolution, the reverse of evolution: the animals would still have a repertory of behaviors, but those behaviors would be simpler, more typical of an animal that had not yet evolved the missing brain structure.

If the logic of this argument is followed, it becomes apparent how the results from Goltz's experiments can be reconciled with those of his opponents. Goltz's dogs were "low-level" dogs: they were able to walk and to eat, but if food had not been presented to them—had they been required to walk in order to find food—they may have failed and starved. Under the experimental conditions, walking would not have served a useful biological function. Similarly, all the other behaviors of the dogs were low-level behaviors. For example, they could regulate their body temperature by shivering and panting, but had they been placed in a situation requiring them to perform a complex series of acts to leave a cold or warm area for a neutral thermal zone, they may have failed and so would not have been able to thermoregulate behaviorally as normal dogs do. Hughlings-Jackson's concepts allowed the special role of the cortex in organizing purposeful behavior to be distinguished from the role of lower-level brain areas in supporting the more elementary components of behavior.

Hughlings-Jackson applied his concepts of hierarchical organization to many other areas of behavior, including language and aphasia. It was his view that every part of the brain is involved in language, with each part making some special contribution. The relevant question was not where language is localized but what unique contribution is made by each part of the cortex. Thus if, for example, the nondominant (the nonlanguage) hemisphere is not involved in language but in spatial organization, then damage to that hemisphere would be revealed not just in spatial disabilities but also in language impoverishment because spatial concepts cannot be employed. Hughlings-Jackson was particularly modern—so much so, in fact, that his ideas are receiving more serious consideration today than they did in his own time.

THE NEURON HYPOTHESIS

The second major influence on modern neuropsychology was the development of the neuron hypothesis: the idea that the nervous system is composed of discrete, autonomous cells, or units, that can interact but are not physically connected. The opposite position, known as the **nerve net hypothesis,** is that the nervous system is composed of a continuous network of interconnected fibers. At the cellular level, support for the neuron theory depended on the solutions to three problems: (1) How does the nervous system conduct information? (2) How is it constructed? (3) How is the nervous system itself interconnected and how is it interconnected with the muscles? These problems were solved in a series of steps that were closely linked with advances in making microscopes, understanding electricity, and developing techniques for recording the activity of cells.

Information Conduction

Early views of how the nervous system moves muscles involved some type of hydraulic theory requiring gas or liquid to flow through nerves into muscles. Such theories have been called *balloonist theories,* because movement was thought to be caused by the filling and emptying of muscles. Descartes espoused the balloonist hypothesis, for he argued that a fluid from the ventricles flows through nerves into muscles to make them move (see Figure 1.1). Francis Glisson in 1677 made a direct test of the balloon theory by immersing a man's arm in water and measuring the change in the water level when the muscles of the arm were contracted. Since the water level did not rise, Glisson concluded that no fluid entered the muscle. Swammerdam in Holland had reached the same conclusion from similar experiments on frogs, but his manuscript had lain unpublished for 100 years. (When students are asked if the water will rise when a muscle is contracted, many predict that it will.)

The impetus to adopt a theory of electrical conduction in neurons came from Stephen Gray, who in 1731 attracted considerable attention by demonstrating that the human body could be electrified. He showed that when a rod containing static electricity was brought close to the feet of a boy suspended by a rope, a grass-leaf electroscope (thin strip of conducting material) placed near the boy's nose was attracted to the boy's nose. It was only later, however, that Luigi Galvani (1737–1798) demonstrated that electrical stimulation of a frog's nerve could cause muscle contraction. In 1886, J. Bernstein developed the theory that the membrane of a nerve is polarized and that the action potential is a propagated depolarization of this membrane. Many of the details of ionic conduction were worked out by A. L. Hodgkin and A. F. Huxley, who received the Nobel Prize in physiology in 1963.

As successive findings brought hydraulic models of conduction into disfavor and more dynamic electrical models into favor, hydraulic theories of *behavior* were also critically reassessed. For example, Freud's theory of behavior, involving the different levels of id, ego, and superego, is very much a hydraulic model (for example, how much of each is there?). Although conceptually useful for a time, it had no impact on concepts of brain function, because it became clear that the brain does not function as a hydraulic system.

Nervous System Structure

Although it was widely believed that the nerves are hollow, fluid-containing tubes, the first cellular anatomist, Anton van Leeuwenhoek (1632–1723), examined nerves with a primitive microscope but was unable to find hollow tubes. He also described what he called "globules," but it is doubtful that these were cell bodies. They may have been either blobs of fat or optical aberrations (artifacts) produced by the crude microscopes of the day. From van Leeuwenhoek's time until the 1830s, when the achromatic microscope was developed to eliminate color distortions, the frequency of artifacts aroused a general distrust of microscope results. Through a series of observations with ever-improving microscopes, the various parts of a cell were eventually described. From these findings Theodor Schwann in 1839 enunciated the theory that cells are the basic structural unit of the nervous system. Ten years later Rudolf A. van Koelliker established that nerve fibers are linked to the cell body.

The earliest anatomists who tried to examine the substructure of the nervous system found a gelatinous white substance, almost a goo. Eventually it was discovered that if brain tissue were placed in alcohol or formaldehyde, water would be drawn out of the tissue and it could be made firm. It was then found that if the tissue were cut into thin sections many different structures could be seen.

An exciting development in neuroanatomy was the technique of staining, which allows different portions of the nervous system to be visualized. Various dyes were in common use in Germany for staining cloth. When these were applied to thinly cut tissue, some selectively stained the cell body, some stained the nucleus, and some stained the fatty covering around the nerve coming from the cell body. The most amazing cell stain came from the application of photographic techniques to nervous system tissue. Camillo Golgi in 1875 impregnated tissue with silver ni-

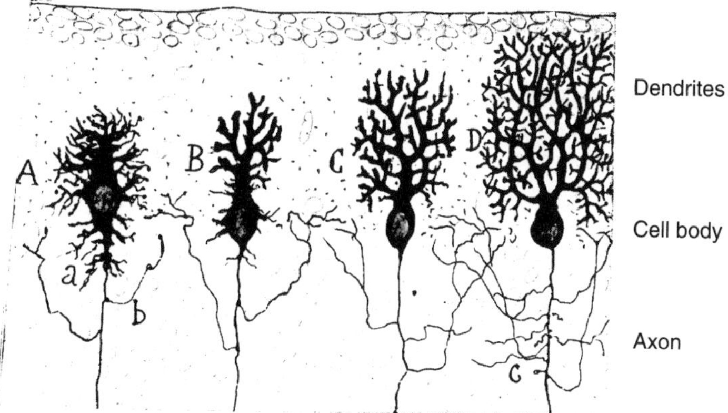

FIGURE 1.6. Successive phases (*A* to *D*) in the development of the branching of the cell of Purkinje from Ramón y Cajal (1937). The many dendrites in *A* are first pruned back and then grow to form an extensive arbor (*D*). The axon (c) is at first simple with only two collaterals (a and b), but becomes much more luxuriant (*D*).

trate and found that a few cells in their entirety—cell body, dendrites, and axons—became encrusted with silver. This allowed the entire neuron and all its processes to be visualized at one time. Golgi never described how he had been led to this remarkable discovery.

Microscopic examination revealed that, far from being a bowl of jelly, the brain is an enormously intricate substructure with components arranged in complex clusters, each of which is interconnected with many others. Psychologists who were separating behavior into parts by faculties could only have been encouraged by the details of the brain revealed by the anatomists. There was a genuine theoreticians' banquet on hand, and for every conceivable behavioral trait there was a newly discovered nucleus or pathway begging to be attached.

Nervous System Connections

So, how did the brain work? Was the brain a net of physically interconnected fibers, or a collection of discrete units? If it were an interconnected net, then it would follow that changes in one part would, by diffusion, produce changes in every other part. Since it would be difficult for a structure thus organized to localize function, a netlike structure would favor a holistic, or gestalt, type of brain function and psychology. Alternatively, a structure of discrete units would favor a psychology based on localization of function, since—at least theoretically—each cell could function autonomously.

The concept of a nerve net originated in 1855 with Franz von Leydig, who observed and described numerous interlacing fibrils in the nervous system of a spider. In 1883 Golgi suggested that axons, the fibers coming out of the cell body, are interconnected, forming an axonic net. Golgi claimed to have seen connections between cells, and he did not think that functions were localized.

This position was opposed by Santiago Ramón y Cajal (1852–1934), using Golgi's own silver staining technique. Cajal examined the brains of chicks as they developed and was able to see clearly that each nerve cell is an independent structure (Figure 1.6). Throughout a truly remarkable series of studies, he never saw connections. Golgi and Cajal jointly received the Nobel Prize in 1906; each in his acceptance speech argued his position on the neuron hypothesis, Golgi supporting the nerve net and Cajal supporting the neuron hypothesis.

In 1891, summarizing Cajal's work on nerve cells, Wilhelm Waldeyer coined the term "neuron hypothesis," the idea that neurons are not physically connected through their axons. Use of the electron microscope in the 20th century fully supports the neuron hypothesis.

Still, neurons must influence one another. Charles Scott Sherrington (1857–1952), an English physiologist, examined how nerves connect to muscles and first suggested how the connection is made. He theorized that neurons are connected by junctions, which he called synapses (from the Greek word meaning clasp). Later electron microscope studies were to confirm that synapses do not quite touch the cells with which they synapse. It then became generally thought that the synapses release chemicals to influence the next cell, and this was demonstrated later. In 1949, based on this principle, the Canadian psychologist Donald Hebb proposed a learning theory in which individual cells could, by being activated at the same time, grow synapses or strengthen existing synaptic connections between themselves so that they could become a functional unit (a semi-mini-nerve net, so to speak). He proposed that such a connection, the so-called **Hebb synapse,** is the structural basis of memory.

Many of the constituent concepts of the neuron hypothesis were formulated at roughly the same time as the developments in behavioral theory we reviewed earlier, and they occurred almost in parallel, seemingly without influencing how people thought behavior was produced. But the influence was there: knowing that the nervous system is composed of a uniform substance allowed it to be viewed as a single organ; knowing that it is electrically active led to experiments in which it was stimulated to produce behavior; knowing that some parts of the nervous system are composed of cell bodies and other parts of fibers permitted speculation about the relative effects of cell damage versus fiber damage; and being able to see subtle differences in cell structure under a microscope permitted the development of maps of cell arrangements, which seemed to correlate with the functional maps that came from studies of people with brain damage. Thus, although it may seem that behavior was effectively studied in ignorance of the brain's fine structure, actually it was not.

MODERN DEVELOPMENTS

Given the 19th-century developments in knowledge about brain structure and function—the brain and neuron hypotheses, the concept of the special nature of cortical function, and the concepts of localization of function and of disconnection—why did the science of neuropsychology not develop by 1900 rather than after 1949, when the term first appeared? There are several possible reasons. In the 1920s neurologists such as Henry Head rejected the classical approach of Broca, Wernicke, and others, arguing that their attempts to correlate behavior with anatomical sites represented approaches little better than those of the phrenologists. Then two world wars disrupted the development of science in many countries. In addition, psychologists, who traced their origins to philosophy rather than to biology, were not interested in physiological and anatomical approaches, directing their attention instead to behaviorism, psychophysics, and the psychoanalytical movement.

A number of modern developments have made a contribution to the growth of neuropsychology as an identifiable discipline in the neurosciences: neurosurgery; **psychometrics** (the method of measuring human abilities) and statistical analysis; and technological advances.

Neurosurgery

Penfield and Jasper have provided a brief but informative history of neurosurgery. Clearly, brain surgery was performed by prehistoric peoples, because skulls that had been subjected to surgery (the skulls show postsurgical healing) have been obtained from the Neolithic period in Europe and from the early Incas in Peru. It is likely that these early peoples found surgery to have a beneficial effect for some types of brain problems. Later, Hippocrates gave written directions for trephining (cutting a circular hole in the skull) on the side of the head opposite to the site of a local convulsion as a means of therapeutic intervention. Between the 13th and 19th centuries there were a number of attempts, some quite successful, to relieve various symptoms with surgery.

The modern era began once antisepsis, anesthesia, and the principle of localization of function were developed. In the 1880s, a number of surgeons reported the success of operations for the treatment of abscesses, tumors, and epilepsy-producing scars. Later, the Horsley-Clarke "stereotaxic device" was developed for holding the head in a fixed position, local anesthetic procedures were developed so that the patient could contribute to the success of surgery by responding to the effects of localized brain stimulation, and devices such as the **electroencephalograph** (**EEG**) and **pneumoencephalograph** were developed to locate the area of brain malfunction more precisely before surgery began. The value of the idea of localization of function should not be underestimated in this account. The first surgeons used signs of trauma on the skull as a means of localizing brain damage, but once it was realized that a variety of behavioral symptoms could be used to localize damage, surgeons had a clearer idea about where to make the surgical penetration.

The development of neurosurgery as a practical solution to some types of brain abnormality has had a profound influence on neuropsychology. In animal research the tissue removal or lesion technique was developed to the point that it became one of the most important sources of information about brain-behavior relationships. Yet in human research, most information came from patients with relatively poorly defined lesions; blood vessel damage included the brainstem as well as the cortex, and brain trauma produced lesions that were diffuse, irregular, or incomplete. Furthermore, patients lived for years after injury, and histological localization (localization of structures on a microscopic level) was thus impossible.

Neurosurgery provided a serendipitous solution. Surgical removal of cortical tissue in humans was as localized as that used in animal experiments. The surgeon drew a map of the lesion and sometimes even electrically stimulated the surrounding tissue, so the location of the lesion was known. Surgeons performed focal lesions, removed hemispheres, and cut the corpus callosum connecting the hemispheres, thus allowing for refined analysis of the contributions of different brain areas and their connections to behavior. In turn, information about behavior obtained from patients who had received surgery was very useful for diagnostic purposes in new patients.

Psychometrics and Statistical Evaluation

The first experiments on individual differences in psychological function were made by an astronomer, Friedrich Wilhelm Bessel, in 1796. Bessel had become curious about the dismissal of an assistant at the Greenwich observatory near London for being a second or so slower than his superior in observing stars and setting clocks. Bessel began a study of reaction time and found quite large variations among people. Individual differences were very much a part of Gall and Spurzheim's phrenology, but unlike their idea of localization of function, this feature of their science attracted little interest among neuroscientists. The problem was, how does one explain individual differences?

Charles Darwin's English cousin, Francis Galton, maintained a laboratory in London in the 1880s where for three pennies he measured physical features, perceptions, and reaction times with the goal of finding individual differences that could explain why some people were superior to others. Galton's elegant innovation was to apply the statistical methods of Quetlet, a Belgian statistician, to his results and so rank his subjects on a frequency distribution, the so-called bell-shaped curve (a graphical representation showing that some people perform well, some perform poorly, and most fall somewhere in between on almost every factor measured). This innovation was essential for the development of modern psychological tests. It was fitting that Galton's work was directed to describing individual differences, since Darwin's evolutionary theory of natural selection required that individual differences exist. To Galton's surprise, the perceptual and reaction time measures he used did not distinguish between the people he thought were average and those he thought were eminent.

French physician, biologist, and psychologist Alfred Binet came up with a solution to Galton's problem. Binet (1857–1911) was experimenting with a wide variety of measurements, including those of head size, facial features, and handwriting style, and was finding them to be inadequate for distinguishing mental differences. In 1904, the minister of public instruction commissioned Binet to develop tests to identify retarded children so that they could be singled out for special instruction. In collaboration with Théodore Simon, Binet produced what is now known as the 1905 Binet-Simon scale. The tests were derived empirically by administering questions to 50 normal 3- to 11-year-old children and some mentally retarded children and adults. The tests were designed to evaluate judgment, comprehension, and reason, which Binet thought were essential features of intelligence. The scale was revised in 1908; unsatisfactory tests were deleted, others were added, and the student population was increased to 300 children aged 3 to 13 years. From the tests a *mental level* was calculated: a score that 80% to 90% of normal children of a particular age attained. In 1916, Lewis Terman in the United States produced the Stanford-Binet test, in which the intelligence quotient (IQ)—mental age divided by chronological age times 100—was first used.

D. O. Hebb first gave IQ tests to brain-damaged people in Montreal, Canada, in 1940, with the resultant surprising discovery that lesions in the frontal lobes—until then considered the center of highest intelligence—did not decrease IQ scores. This counterintuitive finding identified the utility of such tests for assessing brain damage and effectively created a bond of common interest between neurology and psychology. Many of the clever innovations used for assessing brain function in various patient populations are strongly influenced by intelligence-testing methodology. Particularly notable is the fact that the tests are brief, are easily and objectively scored, and are standardized using statistical procedures. Many neuropsychologists use features of IQ scores to assess regional brain contributions to IQ, whereas others use IQ only as a measure of general psychological function to evaluate other test results. Although the concept of "mental testing" as it is used in many applications has been criticized a number of times, even harsh critics such as Gould feel that it has an appropriate use in neuropsychology. In fact, mental tests are themselves being modified by advances in neuropsychology.

Advances in Technology

Because advances in technology are so numerous, and because they are discussed elsewhere, they will not be detailed here. What should be remembered is the frequent statement, "Methods give the results." This was Flourens's exclamation when he advocated the experimental method rather than Gall's anecdotal and confirmatory approach. It was also Fritsch and Hitzig's statement when they overthrew Flourens's dogma on the electrical excitability of the cortex. Progress in science includes advancements in theory and methodology but also must include improvements in technology. In fact, in response to the question of why papers on methods are the most cited papers in science, one wag has declared that you cannot conduct an experiment with a theory. It was only through technological advance that the internal structure of neurons could be visualized, their electrical activity recorded, and their biochemical activity analyzed and modified. It is only through technology that the processes of disease, degeneration, and regeneration in the nervous system can be understood. In fact, methodology and results are often so intimately linked that they cannot be dissociated. For this reason, technological advances provide new opportunities to review old and well-established ideas, and old and well-established ideas should be thrown into the mill of technological innovation for confirmation or modification.

SUMMARY

This chapter sketches the history of two formative ideas in neuropsychology: the brain is the organ of the mind, and the cell is its functional unit. It was not enough to speculate that these statements are true; it was also necessary to demonstrate their truth experimentally.

This chapter also examines some early ideas of how the brain functions. Much of the debate focused on whether each function is localized in a particular part of the brain or many different brain areas are involved in a given function. The conclusion was that functions such as language involved a number of different brain areas.

Damaging the cortex extensively was found to leave intact surprisingly complex functions. The theory of hierarchical organization accounted for this by proposing that the brain evolved in steps, with each step adding a new level of complexity to behavior.

It was discovered that brain cells are autonomous but can work together as assemblies through existing synapses or by forming new synapses.

Surgery on humans provided clinical cases in which brain lesions were quite well localized, the development of statistics and behavioral tests allowed for better measures of behavior, and the development of technology continuously provided new ways of evaluating favored theories.

The thrust of this chapter is the history of the present science of neuropsychology. But we would like to emphasize that the history presented here is a bit selective, and many important people and many interesting stories had to be omitted. We leave the reader with the thought that to know history is to be able to replicate it, to advance it, and even to confound sphinxes with it.

REFERENCES

Bartholow, R. Experimental investigation into the functions of the human brain. *American Journal of Medical Sciences* 67:305–313, 1874.

Beach, F. A., D. O. Hebb, C. T. Morgan, and H. W. Nissen. *The Neuropsychology of Lashley*. New York, Toronto, and London: McGraw Hill, 1960.

Benton, A. L. Contributions to aphasia before Broca. *Cortex* 1:314–327, 1964.

Brazier, M. A. B. The historical development of neurophysiology. In J. Field, H. W. Magoun, and V. E. Hall, Eds. *Handbook of Physiology,* vol. 1. Washington, D.C.: American Physiological Society, 1959.

Broca, P. Sur le siege de la faculté du langage articule. *Bulletin of the Society of Anthropology* 6:377–396, 1865.

Broca, P. Remarks on the seat of the faculty of articulate language, followed by an observation of aphemia. In G. von Bonin, ed. *The Cerebral Cortex*. Springfield, Ill.: Charles C. Thomas, 1960.

Bruce, D. On the origin of the term "Neuropsychology." *Neuropsychologia* 23:813–814, 1985.

Clark, E., and C. D. O'Malley. *The Human Brain and Spinal Cord*. Berkeley and Los Angeles: University of California Press, 1968.

Descartes, R. *Traité de l'Homme*. Paris: Angot, 1664.

Eccles, J. C. *The Neurophysiological Basis of Mind: The Principles of Neurophysiology*. Oxford: Clarendon Press, 1956.

Finger, S. *Origins of Neuroscience*. New York: Oxford University Press, 1994.

Flourens, P. Investigations of the properties and the functions of the various parts which compose the cerebral mass. In G. von Bonin, ed. *The Cerebral Cortex*. Springfield, Ill.: Charles C. Thomas, 1960.

Fritsch, G., and E. Hitzig. On the electrical excitability of the cerebrum. In G. von Bonin, ed., *The Cerebral Cortex*. Springfield, Ill.: Charles C. Thomas, 1960.

Geschwind, N. *Selected Papers on Language and Brain*. Dordrecht, Holland; and Boston: D. Reidel Publishing Co., 1974.

Goltz, F. On the functions of the hemispheres. In G. von Bonin, ed. *The Cerebral Cortex*. Springfield, Ill.: Charles C. Thomas, 1960.

Gould, S. J. *The Mismeasure of Man*. New York: Norton, 1981.

Head, H. *Aphasia and Kindred Disorders of Speech*. London: Cambridge University Press, 1926.

Hebb, D. O. *The Organization of Behavior: A Neuropsychological Theory*. New York: Wiley, 1949.

Hebb, D. O., and W. Penfield. Human behavior after extensive bilateral removals from the frontal lobes. *Archives of Neurology and Psychiatry* 44:421–438, 1940.

Hughlings-Jackson, J. *Selected Writings of John Hughlings-Jackson,* J. Taylor, ed. vols. 1 and 2. London: Hodder, 1931.

Joynt, R. Paul Pierre Broca: His contribution to the knowledge of aphasia. *Cortex* 1:206–213, 1964.

Kluver, H. *Behavior Mechanisms in Monkeys*. Chicago: University of Chicago Press, 1933, 1957.

Krech, D. Cortical localization of function. In L. Postman, ed. *Psychology in the Making*. New York: Knopf, 1962.

Olin, C. H. *Phrenology*. Philadelphia: Penn Publishing Co., 1910.

Penfield, W., and H. Jasper. *Epilepsy and the Functional Anatomy of the Human Brain*. Boston: Little, Brown, 1954.

Ramón y Cajal, S. *Recollections of My Life*. Cambridge, Mass.: MIT Press, 1989.

Rothschuk, K. E. *History of Physiology*. Huntington, N.Y.: Robert E. Krieger, 1973.

Stookey, B. A note on the early history of cerebral localization. *Bulletin of the New York Academy of Medicine* 30:559–578, 1954.

Wernicke, C. *Der Aphasische Symptomenkomplex*. Breslau, Poland: M. Cohn and Weigert, 1874.

Young, R. M. *Mind, Brain and Adaption in the Nineteenth Century*. Oxford: Clarendon Press, 1970.

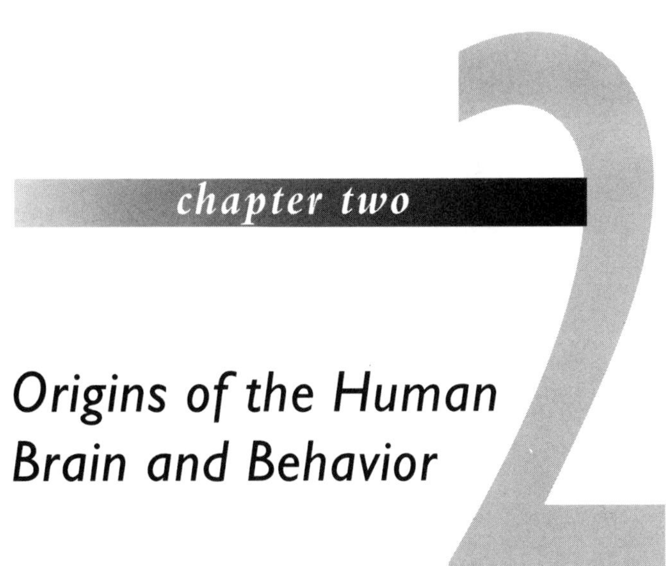

chapter two

Origins of the Human Brain and Behavior

> A badger recounts the story that God created all animals as embryos and called them before his throne, offering them the changes that they desired. They opted for specialized adult features, claws, teeth, hoofs, antlers, and so forth. But the human embryo, trusting God's judgment, accepted the way it was made. The creator was delighted and said that it would therefore remain an embryo until buried but would dominate the other embryos, and feel sorrow and feel joy. (White, 1958)

About 5 million years ago this embryo that walked upright diverged from an ancestral ape lineage. It was to become marked by two characteristics that distinguished it from other animals. First, it was bipedal and such a great traveler that its ancestors populated every habitable continent. Second, its brain underwent an unmatched evolution, increasing to about five times its original size. Although this book is about the functions of the human brain as it now exists, an important clue to understanding its present function is to consider its origins and the evolutionary forces that sculpted it. In this chapter we shall examine the origin of this special brain.

SPECIES COMPARISON
Why Study Nonhuman Animals?

To many people, human neuropsychology is a science that is independent of the study of animals. It is the study of the *human* brain and *human* behavior. This view assumes that both human neuroanatomy and human cognitive processes (that is, thinking) differ fundamentally from those of other animals. After all, humans talk, read, write, and do all sorts of things that monkeys and rats do not do. This line of reasoning is wrong for a number of reasons. Human and chimpanzee bodies are very similar, their brains are very similar, and their behavior is very similar. Thus, psychologists who work with chimps and other apes assume that the things they learn about them are applicable to the human brain and to human behavior.

It is surprising to some people that comparisons with other species, such as rats or cats, are also very informative. The evolutionary distance between humans and rats was once viewed as too great to allow valid generalizations. Indeed, Lockhart and several other authors have argued that the laboratory rat in particular is an indefensible choice for behavioral research. They point out that it has been bred for laboratory work and so for many purposes is a freak, an unnatural animal, and a degenerate compared with its wild cousins. Experimental research, however, provides no evidence that laboratory rats are degenerates. The behavior of the rat is extremely complex, most structures of the rat brain are much like those of the human brain, and many aspects of neocortical function in laboratory rats are remarkably similar to those of other mammals, including primates.

In emphasizing the utility of interspecies comparisons, we are not suggesting that other animals are merely little people in fur suits, without shoes and socks. We are emphasizing rather, that the similarities between humans and monkeys, rats, and other animals, suggest that the study of other animals can make an important contribution to the understanding of human brain-behavior relations. Behavior-brain comparisons across species provide insights that would be difficult to obtain by study of a single species, even one as interesting as humans. Additionally, behavior-brain relationships of other animals are interesting in themselves, as bird watchers, pet owners, and naturalists will confirm.

What questions can best be addressed through the study of nonhuman species? There are three primary lines of neuropsychological research in animals: (1) studies directed toward understanding the basic mechanisms of brain function; (2) studies designed to produce models of human neurological disorders; and (3) studies that aim to provide a description of the phylogenetic (evolutionary) development of the brain. We shall consider each of these separately in the following sections.

One purpose of cross-species comparisons in neuropsychology has been to arrive at an understanding of the basic mechanisms of brain function. An early example of this method is Harvey's investigation of the function of the heart. In establishing that the blood is transferred by the heart from veins to arteries, Harvey used the fish as a model. In the absence of a secondary circulation to the lungs, the passageway from veins to arteries could be seen. Harvey argued that the pulmonary circulation in mammals obscured our realization that the function of the heart is the same in all vertebrates. Similarly, in comparative behavioral work the species chosen for study depends on the nature of the question. For example, neurophysiologists may study the neural activity of giant nerve fibers in the squid because the nerve is so large and accessible. It is assumed that fundamental properties of these nerves are generalizable to mammals and presumably to humans.

The second goal of comparative work is to produce models of human neurological disorders. The aim is to produce the disorder, then manipulate numerous variables in order to understand the cause of the disorder and its course and ultimately to formulate a treatment. For example, a model of Parkinson's disease has been developed in the rat to seek the causes of this abnormal behavior in humans and to find treatments to eliminate them. The animals are really substitutes for humans, because it is assumed that similar principles underlie the cause and treatment of these disorders in humans and nonhumans alike.

The third rationale for using nonhuman species is to provide a neurology of mammalian behavior that emphasizes the phylogenetic development of the human brain. It is assumed that a study of the evolutionary development of the human brain is as important to understanding what humans are as a study of infants is to understanding what adults are. In addressing this question, however, some caution is necessary. Experiments with rats, cats, dogs, and rhesus monkeys do not permit inferences about evolutionary development because these animals do not form an evolutionary sequence: rats were never ancestral to cats, nor cats to monkeys. All these species evolved independently from some primitive mammalian ancestor, as shown in Figure 2.1. Furthermore, they have all been evolving for exactly the same length of time. The commonalities in their behavior and brain can only tell us that a common ancestor was the source of their similar features.

To do comparative work from a phylogenetic perspective, it is necessary to choose closely related species that constitute what Hodos and Campbell have termed a **quasi-evolutionary sequence.** Thus, a series of animals is used that includes the available living descendants of groups

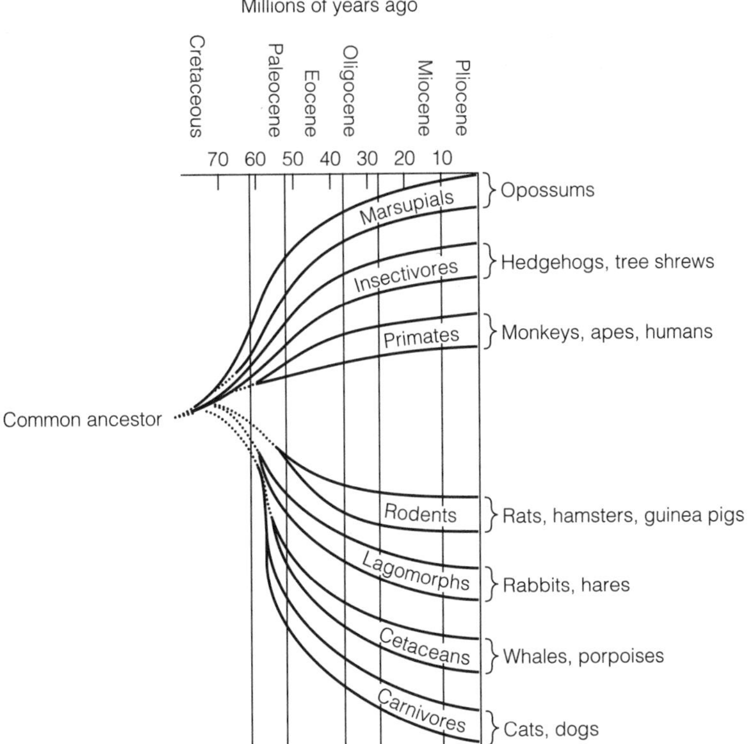

FIGURE 2.1. A phylogenetic tree showing the probable times of origin and affinities of the orders of mammals most commonly studied in comparative psychology and neuropsychology. Note that all contemporary species are the same evolutionary age. (After Young, 1962.)

that are believed to be ancestors of more advanced forms. For example, in the lineage to which humans belong, it is assumed that a number of present-day animals resemble a common ancestor closely enough to stand in for one. Notice from Figure 2.2 that when such a lineage is constructed and the brains of animals in the lineage are compared, structural differences are found that can be correlated with behavioral differences. Striate cortex is visual cortex, and its presence in tree shrews likely confers an ability to see branches, heights, and insects, which is not important to the ground-dwelling hedgehog. The large temporal lobe in the bush baby may be related to an ability to identify its highly varied diet of insects, fruits, leaves, and so forth. The large frontal lobes of the rhesus monkey are probably related to enabling its very complex group social life. The large parietal lobe of humans is probably a correlate of their abilities to make skilled movements.

Brain Size

Brain size presents a fascinating problem: What is it about size that is related to ability? The most obvious characteristic of the human brain is that it is larger than the brains of most other animals. It ranges in size from 1000 to 2000 g, with an average size of between 1300 and 1400 g; female brains weigh slightly less than those of males. The sex difference likely reflects both differences in body size and some functional differences produced by hormones. But how large is the human brain in relation to that of other animals? One might expect the human brain to be large because the human body is large. Likewise, the elephant

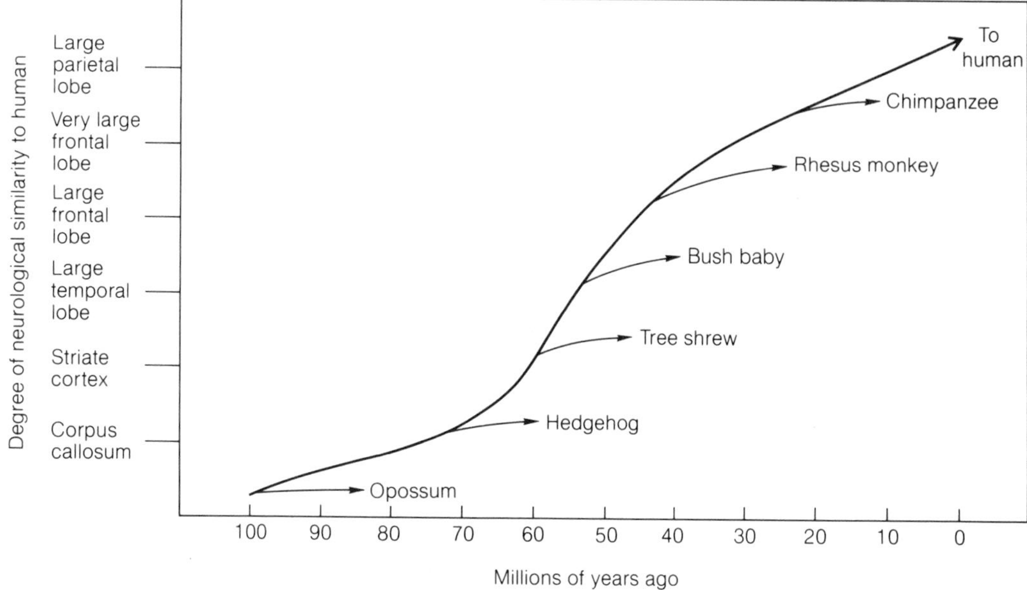

FIGURE 2.2. Phylogenetic relationships among the experimental subjects forming a quasi-evolutionary lineage. Notice that hedgehogs, tree shrews, bush babies, monkeys, and apes are living animals taken to be close approximations of the ancestors of humans. Note some of the brain changes that occurred at the branches in this lineage. (After Masterton and Skeen, 1972.)

would be expected to have a larger brain than humans, and indeed it is roughly three times larger.

Neuroanatomists long ago realized it is necessary to factor out body size. Jerison has developed what he terms the **encephalization quotient (EQ)**: the ratio of actual brain size to expected brain size. The expected brain size is a kind of average for living mammals that takes body size into account. Thus, the average or typical mammal (which incidentally is the cat) has an EQ of 1.0. If a hypothetical animal is twice as large as a cat and so is its brain, then its EQ is still 1.0. Animals that deviate from 1.0 have brains larger or smaller than would be expected for a mammal of that particular body size.

Table 2.1 summarizes the EQs for common laboratory animals and for humans. Notice that the rat's EQ is only 0.4, whereas the human's is 6.3. The rat's brain, then, is only 0.4 times as large as expected for the typical mammal of that body size, and the brain of a human is 6.3 times larger than expected. Note that the chimpanzee brain is about 2.5 times larger than predicted for a typical mammal of that body size (EQ = 2.48), but its EQ is still only about one-third as large as that of humans. The EQ makes it clear that the human brain really is larger than those of other primates. This high EQ is not unique to humans, however; the EQ of the dolphin is comparable, having a value of about 6.0. The EQ of an elephant (1.3), however, is only a little bigger than expected for an animal of its size.

Stephan and colleagues compared the brains of more than 60 species of mammals and found that although nearly all structures of the brain increase in size as the EQ increases, it is the cortex that shows the most dramatic increase. It would seem reasonable to suppose that if the human brain is different in some way, the difference would most

TABLE 2.1. Comparison of brain sizes of species most commonly studied in neuropsychology

Species	Brain volume (ml)	Encephalization quotient
Rat	2.3	0.40
Cat	25.3	1.01
Rhesus monkey	106.4	2.09
Chimpanzee	440.0	2.48
Human	1350.0	6.30

Note: Values estimated by using Jerison's formula [EQ = Ei/[12 × Pi(2/3)], where Ei = actual brain size of species "i," Pi = body size of species "i"] and body and brain values.
Source: From Blinkov and Glesner, 1968.

likely be found in the cortex. This possibility can be considered by comparing the human brain with the brains of other primates using a variety of measures of cortical structure, including volume and distribution of cortex and cell density.

Stephan and his coworkers have calculated what we will call a **cortical quotient (CQ)**: the ratio of actual neocortex to the expected neocortex of a typical mammal. (This index is an analogue of the encephalization quotient, except that it measures only the neocortex.) The CQ shows that the volume of the human neocortex is 3.2 times greater than the predicted volume for nonhuman primates in general and nearly 3 times greater than that predicted for a chimpanzee of the same body weight. These figures mean that the increase in neocortex volume from the apes to humans is greater than would be expected from the trends within the other primates.

The human cortex, and the cortex of other animals with big brains, is distinctive in another way. The cortex can be divided into areas that are specialized for audition, vision, movement, and so forth. Very simple animals have a minimum number of such areas—that is, one for each of the senses and one for movement—whereas more sophisticated animals have many areas. For example, the squirrel has 4 visual areas, the cat appears to have at least 12, and the owl monkey has as many as 14 (the actual number in humans is not known but is probably around 20). If each of these areas has a special function, as is supposed, then the growth of the human cortex is characterized not only by larger size but by many more functions as well.

We began this section by asking how brain size is related to ability. Although from a superficial point of view an increase in brain size might seem to be the distinctive correlate to the development of new abilities in species, it is likely that the development of new areas is much more important. The development of a new area is probably closely related to a new skill. Furthermore, the differences in behavior between individual animals is much more likely to be related to differences in sizes of brain regions than to total brain size. Although there has been and continues to be a good deal of debate about contemporary human brain size and intelligence, the effort in this respect is misplaced. The relevant anatomical unit of the brain is functional area, not brain size, and the relevant behavioral unit is specific skills, not general intelligence.

THE EVOLUTIONARY RECORD

There have been three major advances in the study of human evolution. First, the recent and sudden proliferation of **hominid** fossil discoveries has sparked new interest in human evolution, especially in the evolution of the human brain. By careful examination of the structure of bones, it is possible to make a **morphological reconstruction** of a specimen and compare it with other examples in extinct and living species. An example of a morphological reconstruction of Neanderthal, a precursor to modern humans in Europe, is shown in Figure 2.3. Although it was once suggested that these people were rather brutish, stooped characters, reconstructions demonstrate how similar to us they really were.

Second, the discovery of this fossil record has been matched by the development of new methods that add biochemical information to morpho-

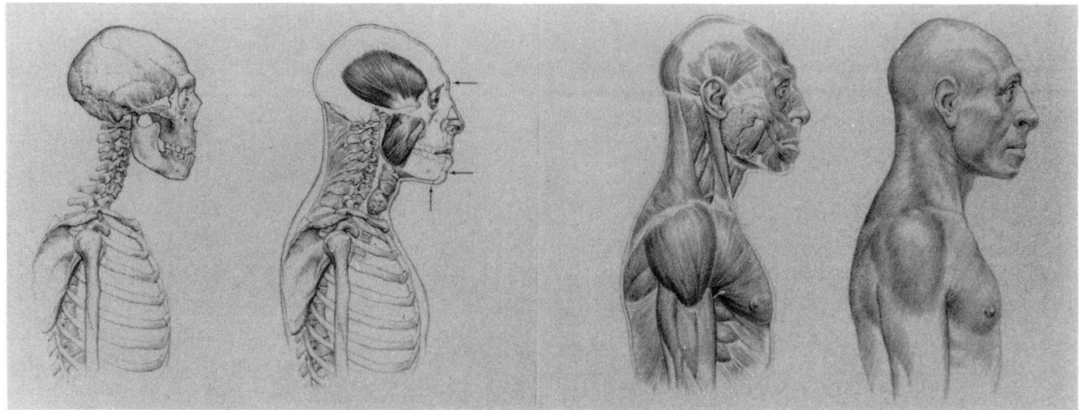

FIGURE 2.3. Reconstruction of the facial features of Neanderthal man. To the bare bones, temporal muscles and an outline of the skin are added. Arrows mark points where thickness is based on needle probes of humans or orangutans. Nose shape is based on projections from bony landmarks. The reconstruction is in striking contrast to previous depictions of Neanderthals as dull-witted and stooped. (Reconstruction by Jay Matternes. From B. Rensberger. Facing the past. *Science* 41–81, October 1981. Copyright © 1981. Reprinted with permission.)

logical descriptions. A problem with strictly morphological methods is that they may not permit a distinction between *homologous structures* of species (structures that have the same origin) and *analogous structures* (structures that look the same and have the same function but have different origins). For example, some Australian and European birds look similar and occupy similar biological niches. **Biochemical techniques** show these birds to be distinct species.

There are now a large number of such biochemical techniques. Here we mention three, in the order of their development. Proteins, such as hemoglobin or the albumin that transports nutrients in the blood, are more similar in closely related animals than in unrelated ones. The differences in protein amino acids between animals can be counted and compared to the known time of divergence of animals. This provides a molecular clock that can then be used to compare the ages of different species. For example, old- and new-world monkeys diverged from each other 30 million years ago. Their 24 differences in amino acids suggest a rate of one amino acid change every 1.25 million years. If this rate of change is applied to primates, it indicates that chimpanzees and humans diverged from each other about 5 million years ago.

Relatedness can also be determined by comparing strands of **deoxyribonucleic acid** (**DNA**), the genetic material from the nucleus of the cell, from different species. Using enzymes, DNA can be cut up into short segments. If the segments are placed in a synthetic gel and subjected to an electrical current they line up, longest to shortest, producing a signature of the owner. Signatures of various animals, and individuals, can be compared and calibrated using known time relationships (as above) to establish relatedness. Signatures of modern humans and chimpanzees suggest that they share 99% of their genes and are each other's closest relatives.

A third biochemical technique uses the DNA from **mitochondria**. Mitochondria are found in the cytoplasm of the cell and are passed from females to their offspring through the cytoplasm of the ovum. The DNA of mitochondria is analyzed in the way described above, but the analysis in mitochondria is simpler than in nuclear DNA. Mitochondrial analysis confirms a common ancestor for all modern humans within the last 200,000 years. Future techniques may include analyzing DNA from the Y chromosome, which permits tracking relationships through substances passed only between males.

Finally, new methods of behavioral analysis are beginning to disclose the evolutionary forces that sculpted modern humans. The behavioral studies are directed at humans and their proximate relatives (chimpanzees, gorillas, orangutans, and gibbons), as well as their more distant relatives (baboons and monkeys). Goodall's behavioral studies of chimpanzees paint a picture of a species so close to humans that one has the impression of looking into a mirror. These creatures occupy large territories that the males defend as a group. They wage war and kill neighbors to expand their territories. They are great travelers, ambulating along the ground, at a rate that humans have difficulty matching, for distances of 8 km or more a day. They are omnivores, eating vegetation, fruit, and insects, but they can also hunt cooperatively to catch monkeys, pigs, and other mammals. They have complex social groups within which family relations are important both for the individual and for the group structure. Finally, they have rich manual, facial, and vocal communication capabilities, and they construct and use tools for defense and to obtain food and water.

HUMAN ORIGINS

The story of our knowledge about human origins begins in 1859 with Darwin's publication of *Origin of Species*. Darwin carefully avoided the inflammatory subject of human ancestry, preferring to emphasize his studies of barnacles, extinct clams, and exotic animals from the faraway Galápagos Islands. His only reference to human evolution appears at the end of the book, where he states: "Light will be thrown on the origin of man and his history." That was enough! There was an immediate public preoccupation with our alleged ape ancestors, reputedly leading one Victorian lady to have said, "Descended from apes! My dear, we hope it is not true. But if it is, let us pray that it may not become generally known."

Our anatomical similarity to apes was difficult to ignore, and soon after *Origin of Species* appeared, T. H. Huxley showed that anatomically we are more similar to apes than apes are to monkeys. It was not until 1871 that Darwin concluded in his book *The Descent of Man* that humans descended from a "hairy, tailed quadruped, probably arboreal in its habits." In the following years the public belief emerged that being descended from apes need not be uncomfortable. It was wrongly presumed that humans are the pinnacle of a single lineage from extinct apelike animals, which were changed by the perfecting process of natural selection to become the very special product of evolution, *Homo sapiens sapiens*.

Episodic Evolution of Humankind

Darwin believed that evolution was gradual, being shaped largely by processes of **natural selection** and **sexual selection.** By natural selection Darwin meant that animals that accidentally developed skills that allowed them to exploit new habitats or niches would survive. By sexual selection he meant that if one sex found characteristics of the other appealing, then these characteristics would be selected for; for example, the appearance and size of the human sexes. The fossil record in Darwin's time was poorly documented, but the absence of gradual change in the record was of little concern to Darwin; he simply rejected fossils as a source of evidence for evolution.

A hundred years after Darwin, the fossil record is well documented and has given rise to a new theory, **punctated evolution.** This theory suggests that speciation occurs very rapidly, probably over a few hundred or a few thousand years. Most species exhibit little significant change during their tenure on earth. They disappear in the fossil record looking much the same as when they appeared in it.

Although life may have been on earth for some 650 million years, the fossil record shows that true mammals made their appearance only about 150 million years ago, and monkeylike mammals or primates first appeared only about 25 million years ago. This was perhaps truly the age of primates. Almost the entire land mass of the planet was covered by jungles. Biochemical techniques—largely involving the comparison of proteins and DNA in existing humans and the African apes, chimps, and gorillas—suggest that our ancestors diverged from the ape ancestors about 5 million years ago, and we appeared about 200,000 years ago.

We have noted that there have been theories that consider humans as the end product of a linear process of natural selection. The evidence shows, however, that the human family tree is

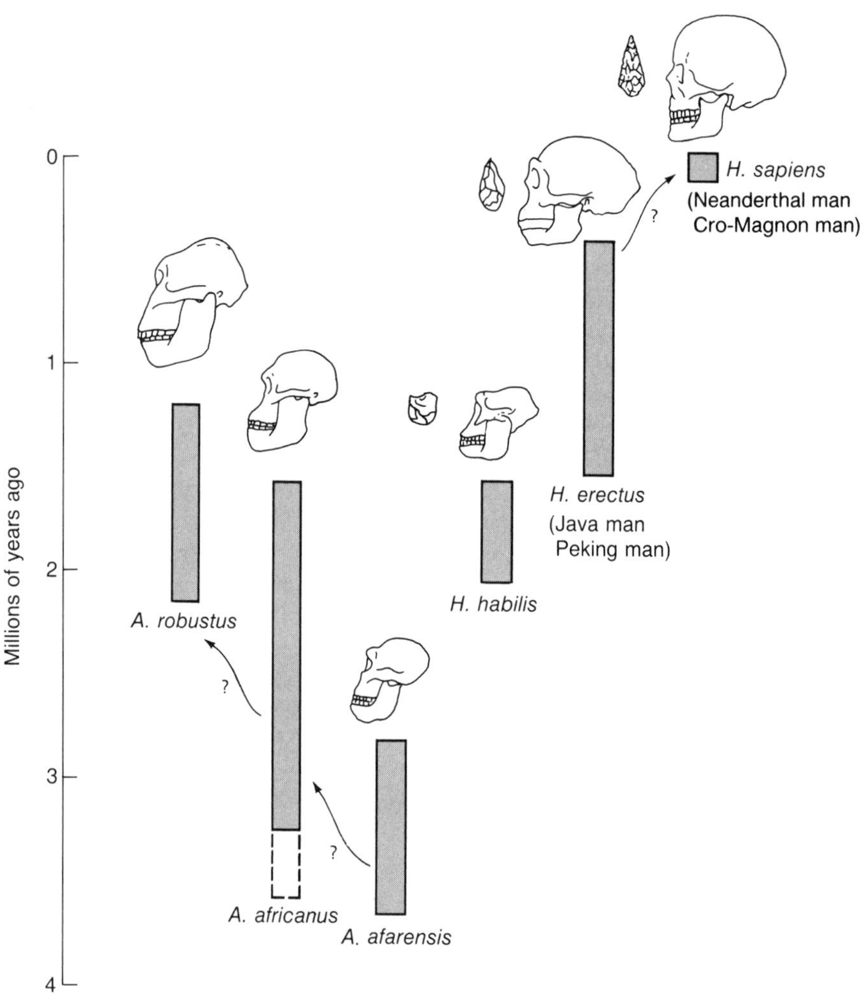

FIGURE 2.4. Summary of the recognized species of the human family. Question marks indicate that the proposed evolutionary relations are uncertain. Notice the development of tools by *Homo*. (After Stanley, 1981, and Johanson and Edey, 1981.)

really a bush with our species, the only surviving member, sitting alone on one branch. At the base of the bush lie the australopithecines, the ancestors to humans (Figure 2.4). One version of our evolution suggests that *Australopithecus* gave rise to humanlike animals or hominids, first *Homo habilis,* then *Homo erectus,* and then *Homo sapiens sapiens* (us). Other scenarios include many more representatives of *Homo,* many of which overlapped as do those in Figure 2.4, but let us consider only these four to see how our brain and behavior evolved.

Australopithecus: The East Side Story

Our likely ancestor is *Australopithecus* (*Australo* meaning southern, *pithecus* meaning ape) or an animal very like it. The name was coined by an Australian, R. A. Dart, for a find he made in South Africa (he was probably feeling homesick). These animals lived in eastern Africa and are the first to show a distinctly human characteristic: they walked upright. The conclusion that they walked upright is based on the description of numerous bones and on the discovery of fossilized footprints dated from 3.6 to 3.8 million years ago. The footprints feature a well-developed arch and big toe and point straight ahead, giving a pattern much more like that of humans than that of apes. Fossilized remains show that there were a number of distinct species (*A. afarensis, A. africanus,* and *A. robustus*) living in East Africa and Ethiopia. (For an enjoyable account of the discovery of the Ethiopian fossils, we recommend Johanson and Edey's book, *Lucy: The Beginnings of Humankind.*)

Why did *Australopithecus* suddenly appear? Coppens has advanced what he calls the east side theory. On the east side of the Great Rift valley in Africa there are many fossils of hominids stretching through millions of years, but there are no fossils of apes. On the west side of the rift valley, chimpanzees and gorillas currently live pretty much unchanged from what they were more than 15 million years ago. He proposes that about 8 million years ago there was a tectonic crisis (deformation of the earth's crust) that produced the Great Rift valley, leaving a wet jungle climate to the west and a much drier climate to the east. To the west the apes continued unchanged, while to the east the apes had to evolve rapidly to live in the mixture of trees and grass that formed their new brushwood habitat.

There are two versions of how this change took place. The *down-from-trees hypothesis* proposes that the trees being farther apart required apes to adopt bipedal locomotion. This change improved bipedal locomotion, reduced the area of body exposed to the sun, and resulted in the loss of body hair. The *water-baby hypothesis* proposed by A. Hardy suggests that there was a naked ape living along the ocean and it was forced to abandon its aquatic habitat when the ocean receded. This animal had become bipedal and lost its hair in order to swim and retained these features when it adapted to the land. Whichever story is correct, the ape changed to an upright posture, but continued to climb trees and adopted a much more varied diet. Brain size did not change much, and so changes in brain size could not have been due simply to adopting an upright posture and thus having the hands free.

Homo Habilis: The Omo Story

The oldest fossils to be designated as *Homo* are those found by Louis Leakey in the Olduvai Gorge in Tanzania in 1964, dated at about 1.75 million years old. The specimens bear a strong resemblance to *Australopithecus,* but Leakey argued that the dental pattern is more similar to modern humans and, more importantly, the animal apparently made simple stone tools, which were also found in the Olduvai Gorge. Leakey named the species *H. habilis* (that is, handyman).

Coppens has argued that the appearance of *Homo habilis* was related to climatic change. He studied a site on the Omo River that contained a continuous stratigraphic record starting 4 million years ago and ending 1 million years ago. The record indicated that 4 million years ago the climate was more humid and the vegetation was brushwood, whereas 1 million years ago it was less humid and the vegetation was savanna or grassland with only occasional trees. It was during this period that *Homo habilis* appeared with a larger brain and using tools.

It was once speculated that *Homo habilis* was a hunter-gatherer, with the males specializing in hunting and the females specializing in collecting nuts and digging for roots. The hunter-gatherer theory has had its influence on contemporary neuropsychology in suggesting that the better spatial skills of males is related to the fact that they had to be able to navigate long distances in search of prey, which they then killed by throwing spears. Females, confined to the home base, developed social and language skills that were important for instructing children and allowed them to maintain the social structure of the group.

This theory has some improbable features. Early hominids were not large: males were less than 5 feet tall and weighed about 100 pounds; females were smaller still. The animals on the savannas were much like the animals that live there today, and it is difficult to see how these early hominids could have been successful in hunting them. The animals are much too fast and dangerous, and furthermore the hominids would have been relatively defenseless and subject to predation from large cats and packs of dogs.

A more recent theory, suggested by Blumenschine and Cavallo, is that there was an ecological niche that a savanna hominid could occupy, that of a scavenger. Many animals would die as a result of age, hunger during droughts, or predation. These animals could be found on the open savanna, around water holes, or in trees where they had been placed by leopards. Their meat would be fresh for a day or two after death. A scavenger that could locate and butcher them quickly by daylight could compete with nocturnal scavengers such as jackals and large cats and so would have an ample source of food. It could do this by learning to read the environment and by watching the activity of vultures, predators, and animal herds. It would have to replace the sharp teeth, for tearing skin, and the strong jaws, for crushing bones to get at marrow, which other scavengers used, with sharp flakes of rock and hammers. It would also have to be a good carrier to retreat quickly to the safety of trees or rocks with the meat and bones. Importantly, scavenging, toolmaking, and butchering would have been a family affair. Children, with their keen eyesight, would have made an important contribution by locating carcasses, and the entire community would have been involved in toolmaking, butchering, and carrying.

There was a big difference in brain size between *Australopithecus* and *Homo habilis,* and it may well have been related to scavenging (see Figure 2.4). This life-style would have been very demanding on sensory, motor, and social skills. It would have required that scavengers be mobile to follow animals as they migrated with the change of seasons. It would have required good toolmaking skills because the meat and marrow would have been inaccessible without tools. The association of *Homo habilis* with the tools required for scavenging, stone flakes and hammers, but not with the tools used for hunting, provides strong support for the scavenging hypothesis.

Homo Erectus: The Traveler

Homo habilis is thought to have given rise to another species, *Homo erectus* ("upright human"), so named because of a mistaken notion that its predecessors were stooped. It first shows up in the fossil record about 1.6 million years ago and lasts until at least 400,000 years ago. *Homo erectus* has a pivotal position in this history. Its brain was significantly larger than that of any previous animal, and unlike the australopithecines and *H. habilis,* this creature was a traveler; its remains are found in East Africa as well as in Java (Java man) and China (Peking man).

Once a behavior has been changed to exploit a new habitat, other new sources of influence may come into play to encourage further change. A condition that could fortuitously lead to further developments is called a *preadaption.* Dean Falk (1990) has suggested that a change in venous blood flow (blood that is returning to the heart) around the brain removed a constraint that had to that point placed an upper limit on the growth of the brain of apes.

Although the brain makes up less than 2% of the body, it uses 25% of the body's oxygen and 70% of its glucose. As a result it generates a great deal of heat and is at risk of overheating under conditions of exercise or heat stress. Falk suggests that this risk of overheating places a limit on how big the brain can be and it is this constraint that has kept the brain of the chimpanzee at its current size. When examining the holes in the skull through which blood vessels pass, Falk noted that there was a change in pattern between those of the chimpanzees and the gracile (slender) forms of *Australopithecus* and the subsequent hominids. These hominids had holes suggesting that they had a widely dispersed venous flow from the brain. Falk speculates that this dispersed flow developed to serve as a radiator to help cool the brain. She suggests that it developed in response to the upright posture of the australopithecines and served to contribute toward cooling a body that was exposed to daytime savanna heat. Once this change occurred, however, it had the fortuitous effect of allowing the brain to grow larger in response to other kinds of pressure. The sequence of effects is as follows:

bipedalism ⟶ *development of a radiator*
⟶ *opportunity for brain expansion*

Once an upper limit to brain size was removed, many other influences could have led to brain growth, including social development, changes in food-gathering practices, and adaptations to a temperate climate as humans migrated into Europe. Humans are social, and increase in group size and the complexity of groups could have demanded a larger brain. Hominids did get bigger, and there is evidence that brain size can increase disproportionately to increases in body size. Hominids also changed diet, and changes in diet can change face and head structure, which may have contributed to increased brain size. From the beginning hominids were tool users, and changes in hand structure and more skilled movements may have contributed to an increase in brain size. As hominids moved north into colder climates, there were probably selective advantages for changes in limb and head size for the purposes of heat conservation. Rounder, larger bodies conserve heat better than oblong bodies, and they also serendipitously provide more volume. This development could have led to increased brain size (not surprisingly, the Eskimo have the largest brains of living human groups). Even mate selection could have contributed to increased brain size. There is evidence that males favor females who have more infantile facial features, and one such infantile facial feature is a greater head size relative to body size.

If one considers all the influences of preadaption and, except for brain size, the similarities between *Homo habilis* and *Homo erectus,* then it is possible to imagine that over about a million years *Homo habilis* simply increased its toolmaking skills to the point that it could become a hunter as well as a scavenger. This change would have been associated with its migration out of Africa and the increase in its brain size.

Homo Sapiens: The Eve Story

Up to about 60,000 years ago, Africa, Europe, and Asia were occupied by a variety of human species. The Neanderthal species occupied Europe. Neanderthal appeared very much like us, with a brain as large, but was stockier and stronger, apparently being built more for strength than for swiftness. Neanderthals apparently buried their dead with flowers, arguably the first evidence of religious belief.

According to the fossil record, modern humans, *Homo sapiens sapiens,* appeared in Asia and North Africa about 100,000 years ago and in Europe about 40,000 years ago. There are two explanations for what happened. One is that modern humans evolved in many different places, and the other is that they appeared suddenly and replaced all other hominids. The latter hypothesis currently appears to be gaining the most support both from biochemical and physical measurements.

Paleoanthropologists such as Thorne and Wolpoff argue that modern humans living in Asia have physical features that resemble ancient hominids who lived there as long as 500,000 years ago. Modern humans living in Europe have the physical features of ancient hominids who preceded them. Thus, Thorne and Wolpoff argue that modern humans evolved in many places at about the same rate. New adaptive genes, such as those that might have increased brain size, were disseminated throughout these diverse populations by migration, trade, and other social interactions. In support of their hypothesis, paleoanthropologists point out that there were no differences in the tools used by ancient and modern humans that would suggest that the modern humans would have an adaptive advantage over the indigenous humans.

Mitochondrial analysis of modern people by Cann and her coworkers suggests that all modern people came from an ancestral "Eve" who lived in Africa around 200,000 years ago. This ancestral stock divided into two groups, one of which remained in Africa, the other of which migrated. The analysis further suggests that modern humans did not simply migrate and develop into different races. Rather, modern humans migrated around the world and intermingled several times before developing into modern races. The kind of migration, intergroup contact, and intermingling that so typifies the last few centuries has apparently been the historical pattern for *Homo sapiens*.

There is considerable debate about what happened to indigenous people such as the Neanderthals with the arrival of modern humans. The biochemical measures give no evidence that these people intermingled with the local inhabitants, even though the archeological record indicates that they overlapped for a considerable period of time. Perhaps they intermingled but have no living descendants. If they did not intermingle, then that fact is hard to explain. Perhaps, as the best suggestion proposes, modern humans had such advanced language abilities that they were effectively separated from other species. If we consider the effects that Europeans have had on other human populations they encountered, then we can understand how the indigenous people were completely replaced. Within a few years of the Europeans' arriving in the Americas, the numbers of indigenous people were drastically reduced by new diseases and war, and in some places whole populations disappeared. Much the same thing happened in Tasmania. Thus, it is probable that the early history of *Homo* involved similar interactions.

The evolution of modern humans, from the time at which a creature appeared humanlike to the time at which it was morphologically identical to modern man, took nearly 4 million years. Thus, the evolution of the modern human and the modern human brain and its associated cognitive processes must be considered very rapid. Still, most of what has taken place in terms of changed human behavior has taken place recently. By 25,000 years ago modern humans were producing elaborate paintings on cave walls and carving ivory and stone figurines, providing the first human artistic relics. The tempo of change has quickened in the last 10,000 years. Agriculture and animal husbandry were established in the Middle East by 7000 B.C., followed by ideographic writing in the same region by 3000 B.C. The modern age really began in about A.D. 1500, and it was after this time that most of what we see around us today was invented or discovered. It is interesting, therefore, that most of what we associate with modern humans is of very recent origin, but the basic tools (the brain, free hands, and bipedal locomotion) have been with us for a very long time. We can only wonder why it took us so long to use our brain as we do now.

In conclusion, modern humans do not represent the final product of a gradual evolution, as was envisioned in Victorian times. Several species of hominid creatures have arisen and disappeared, and throughout much of our recent evolutionary history there has been more than one species of hominid alive at a time. None of these ancestors is alive today. Bipedalism was an important accomplishment, but it was not accompanied by an in-

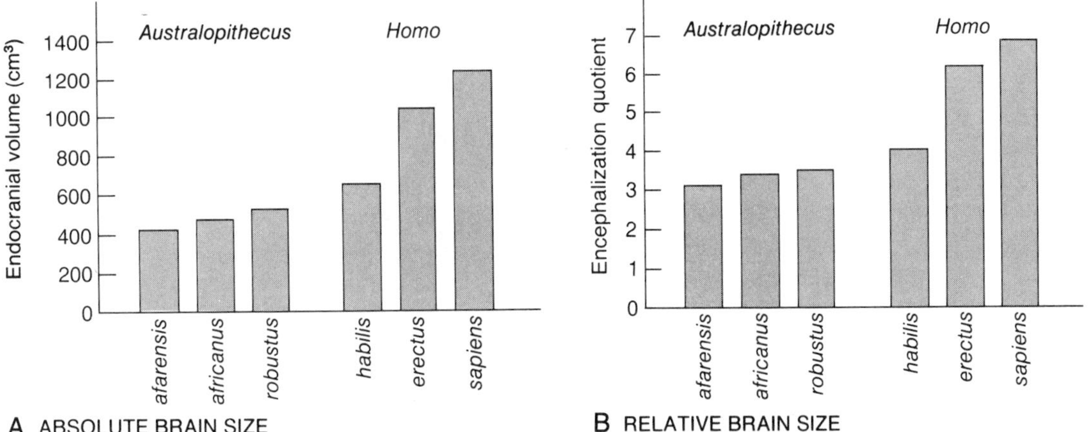

FIGURE 2.5. Endocranial volume (*A*) and encephalization quotients (*B*) for fossil hominids. Notice the sudden increase in brain size in *H. erectus*. (Data from McHenry, 1982.)

crease in brain size. That came later and was associated with the development of new behaviors.

Brain Evolution

Unlike skulls and other bones, soft tissues such as brains do not leave fossil records. Therefore the size and organization of a fossil's brain must be inferred from the shape, size and other features of the inside of the skull. A measure commonly used for such inferences is cranial capacity. The cranial capacity of a skull can provide a reasonable estimate of the size of an animal's brain. We must be wary of assuming that brain size is an index of intelligence, however. Although it is true that large-brained animals such as chimpanzees appear to be more intelligent than smaller-brained monkeys, animals are intelligent in different ways. Animals living in such different ecologies as treetops and water may not require the same size brain to generate their movements. Furthermore, there is considerable variation in the sizes of brains within a given species. Human brains range from about 1000 grams to nearly 2000 grams, with an unreliable correlation between size and apparent intelligence. This range indicates that modern brain size overlaps with that of all but our most ancient predecessors.

Nevertheless, despite these difficulties in interpreting brain size, one is still impressed with the dramatic change in cranial capacity between *A. afarensis* and *H. sapiens* (Figure 2.5). The brain of the early australopithecines was about the same size as that of a modern chimpanzee, about 400 g. None of the australopithecines developed particularly large brains, despite the species living for about 3 million years. The first toolmakers (*H. habilis*) had slightly larger brains, but even theirs were modest, measuring only one-half the size of our brain. The great expansion in brain size obviously occurred in *H. erectus,* because the brain shows an increase in size equal to that of the entire australopithecine brain. The factors that caused the dramatic increase in brain size in *H. erectus* and *H. sapiens* must have acted quickly. The sudden appearance of large-brained *H. erectus* implies that there probably was not a gradual selection of individuals with larger brains, but rather that having a larger brain must have conferred a decisive and immediate advantage.

Many explanations have been proposed for this change in brain size. *Prime mover theories* point to single causes. For example, it was once proposed that having free hands led to toolmaking and that led to having a larger brain. We now know that chimpanzees and many other animals use tools,

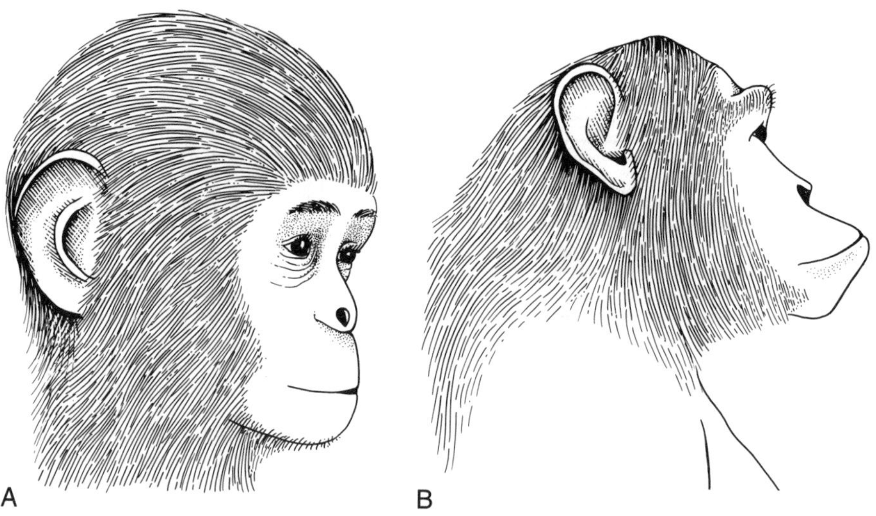

FIGURE 2.6. A juvenile (*A*) and adult (*B*) chimpanzee showing the greater resemblance of humans to the baby chimp and illustrating the principle of neoteny in human evolution. (After Gould, 1981.)

and the first upright apes did not have larger brains than other apes, which much weakens this argument. *General mover theories* point to many simultaneously acting causes (see above). Whatever the driving factors, any increase in brain size would have produced selective advantages manifested in increased abilities, and these in turn would have rapidly reinforced the trend.

It is possible to point to at least three mechanisms through which increases in brain size may have taken place. The first is **neoteny,** a process in which the rate of development slows down and juvenile stages of predecessors become the adult features of descendants. Because the head of infants is large relative to body size, this process would have led to "adult babies" with large brains. Many features of our anatomy link us with juvenile stages of primates, including a small face; vaulted cranium; large brain-to-body size ratio; unrotated big toe; upright posture; and primary distribution of hair on head, armpits, and pubic areas (Figure 2.6). We also retain behavioral features of infants, including exploration, play, and flexible behavior. An important part of the answer to the Sphinx's riddle about the nature of humans is that the adult who walks on two legs is sort of an infant chimpanzee.

A second cause could be related to increases in cortical areas that regulate more skillful behaviors. This process can be described by giving an imaginary example. Figure 2.7 shows the brain of a modern rat and indicates the various regions that are involved in movement and sensory processes. Let us suppose that our rat were to find it adaptive to adopt an arboreal habitat in which it made much more use of its forepaws for climbing and reaching for fruit. The skilled movements of the hand would require a larger representation in the cortex to mediate their action. Thus, the cortex would become comparatively larger to accommodate this larger representation, as is indicated in Figure 2.7B.

A third cause of brain size increase could be related to the development of new cortical areas. Let us suppose that our "skilled" rat needed new kinds of visual abilities to get around in its new

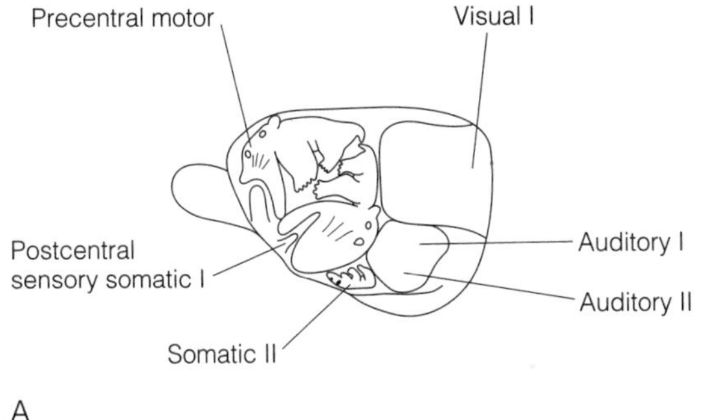

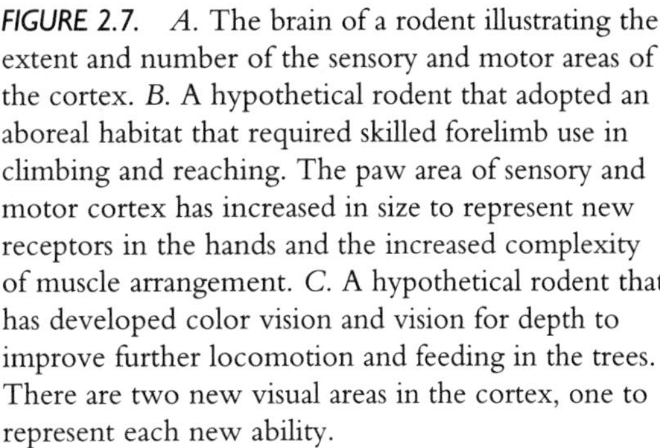

FIGURE 2.7. *A*. The brain of a rodent illustrating the extent and number of the sensory and motor areas of the cortex. *B*. A hypothetical rodent that adopted an aboreal habitat that required skilled forelimb use in climbing and reaching. The paw area of sensory and motor cortex has increased in size to represent new receptors in the hands and the increased complexity of muscle arrangement. *C*. A hypothetical rodent that has developed color vision and vision for depth to improve further locomotion and feeding in the trees. There are two new visual areas in the cortex, one to represent each new ability.

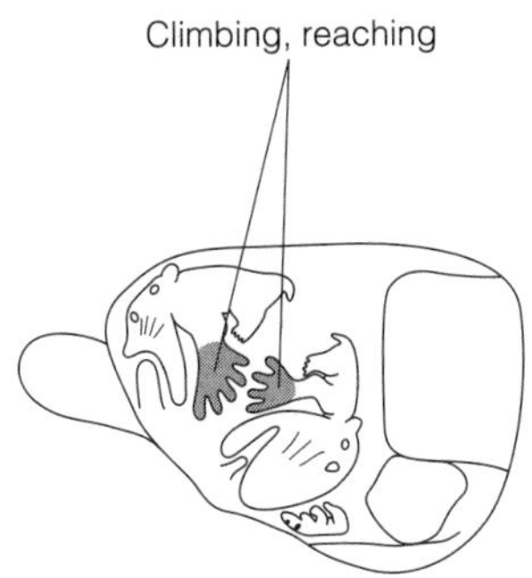

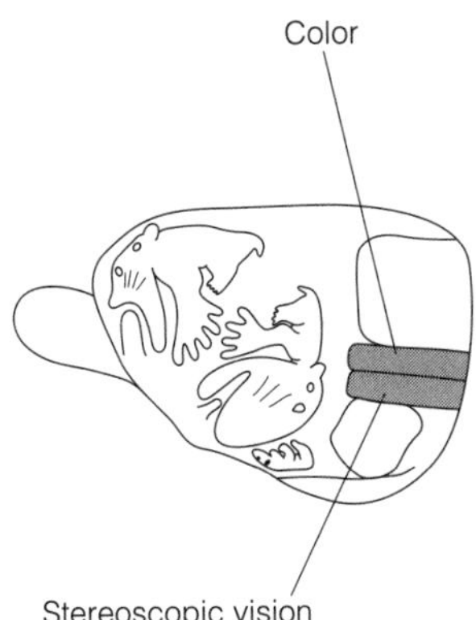

arboreal habitat. We could imagine that having good depth perception would be useful to allow it to jump from one small branch to another. To obtain depth perception some cells in each eye could become specialized for seeing the same object from different views, and these specialized cells could project a new area in the cortex that specialized in stereoscopic vision. We could also imagine that the skilled rat might encounter a particularly nutritious red fruit that it could get to eat before any other animals only if it had color vision: ergo new retinal cells and another new cortical area. This new motorically skilled and visually able rat would now have a much larger brain, as is shown in Figure 2.7C. If other new abilities were required, there would be still more areas and a still larger brain.

CONCLUSIONS

The divergence of the human brain from that of other living species has a history of at least 5 million years. The human brain has undergone a major expansion in the past 2 million years. This appears to have taken place in a number of quite quick steps that resulted in a number of humanlike animals being alive at one time. Climatic changes appear to be closely correlated with the appearance of new hominid species. Today's humans seem to have been around for only about

200,000 years, and they have replaced all of their predecessors. The general structure of the human brain is quite similar to that of other animals, even to very simple animals like rats. The way in which it differs is its size, especially the size of the neocortex. The larger size probably occurred in response to demands for many new skills rather than a demand for any single skill or ability. The increase in size in mammals generally and the primate lineage in particular is also associated with the appearance of new cortical areas for mediating new behavior.

REFERENCES

Beals, K. L., C. L. Smith, and S. M. Dodd. Brain size, cranial morphology, climate, and time machines. *Current Anthropology* 25:301–330, 1984.

Blinkov, S. M., and J. I. Glesner. *The Human Brain in Figures and Tables*. New York: Basic Books, 1968.

Blumenschine, R. J., and J. Q. Cavallo. Scavenging and human evolution. *Scientific American,* 90–96, October 1992.

Campbell, C. B. G., and W. Hodos. The concept of homology and the evolution of the nervous system. *Brain, Behavior and Evolution* 3:353–367, 1970.

Coppens, Y. The east side story: The origin of humankind. *Scientific American,* 88–95, May 1994.

Diamond, I. T., and K. L. Chow. Biological psychology. In S. Koch, ed. *Psychology: A Study of a Science,* vol. 4. New York: McGraw-Hill, 1962.

Falk, D. A reanalysis of the South African australopithecine natural endocasts. *American Journal of Physical Anthropology* 53:525–539, 1980.

Falk, D. Brain evolution in *Homo:* The "radiator" theory. *Behavioral and Brain Sciences* 13:344–368, 1990.

Goodall, J. *The Chimpanzees of Gombe*. Cambridge, Mass.: The Belknap Press of Harvard University Press, 1986.

Hodos, W., and C. B. G. Campbell. Scale naturae: Why there is no theory in comparative psychology. *Psychological Review* 76:337–350, 1969.

Holloway, R. L. Revisiting the South African Tuang australopithecine endocast: The position of the lunate sulcus as determined by the stereoplotting technique. *American Journal of Physical Anthropology* 56:43–58, 1981.

Jerison, H. J. *Evolution of the Brain and Intelligence*. New York: Academic Press, 1973.

Johanson, D., and M. Edey. *Lucy: The Beginnings of Humankind*. New York: Warner Books, 1982.

Jorde, L. B. Human genetic distance studies: Present status and future prospects. *Annual Review of Anthropology* 14:343–373, 1987.

Lockhart, R. B. The albino rat: A defensible choice or bad habit. *American Psychologist* 23:734–742, 1968.

McHenry, H. M. Fossils and the mosaic nature of human evolution. *Science* 190:425–431, 1975.

Passingham, R. E. *The Human Primate*. San Francisco: W. H. Freeman, 1982.

Sarnat, H. B., and M. G. Netsky. *Evolution of the Nervous System*. New York: Oxford University Press, 1974.

Stanley, S. M. *The New Evolutionary Timetable*. New York: Basic Books, 1981.

Stephen, H., R. Bauchot, and O. J. Andy. Data on the size of the brain and of various parts in insectivores and primates. In C. R. Noback and W. Montagna, eds., *The Primate Brain*. New York: Appleton, 1970, pp. 289–297.

Thorne, A., and M. H. Wolpoff. The multiregional evolution of humans. *Scientific American,* 76–83, April 1992.

White, T. H. *The Once and Future King*. London: Collins, 1958.

Young, J. Z. *The Life of Vertebrates*. New York: Oxford University Press, 1962.

chapter three

Organization of the Nervous System

3

> To say that the human cerebral cortex is the organ of civilization is to lay a very heavy burden on so small a mass of matter. One is reminded of Darwin's amazement that the wonderfully efficient and diversified behavior of an ant can be carried on with so small a brain, which is "not so large as the quarter of a small pin's head." The complexity of the human brain is as far beyond that of an ant as human conduct is higher than ant's behavior. (C. Juston Herrick, 1926)

The complexity of the brain's structure makes it difficult to relate its components to individual functions. The brain is composed of more than 180 billion cells, and more than 80 billion of these are directly engaged in information processing. Each cell receives up to 15,000 connections from other cells. If there were no order in this complexity, information would be incomprehensible. Fortunately, we can obtain some tentative answers about how this machinery works because it is possible to see some organization in the way things are arranged. Cells that are close together make most of their connections with one another. Thus they are arranged in assemblies, many of which are large enough to be identifiable on superficial examination.

Although the sizes and shapes of the brains of different people vary just as the features of faces do, the structures of the brain are common to all human beings. In fact, these structures seem to be common to all mammals. The anatomist Lorente de Nó, after examining the mouse brain through a microscope, remarked that its fine structure was little different from that of the human brain. Since many structures of the brain are common to most animals, including human beings, and because many human and animal behaviors are similar, it is possible to learn about the function of specific brain structures by relating anatomy to function.

ANATOMY OF THE NERVOUS SYSTEM

Neurons and Glia

The **germinal cells** (also called stem cells) of a developing embryo give rise to two primitive types of nervous system cells: **neuroblasts** and **spongioblasts** (a *blast* is an immature cell). The neuroblasts develop into **neurons** (from the Greek word for nerve), or nerve cells, which form

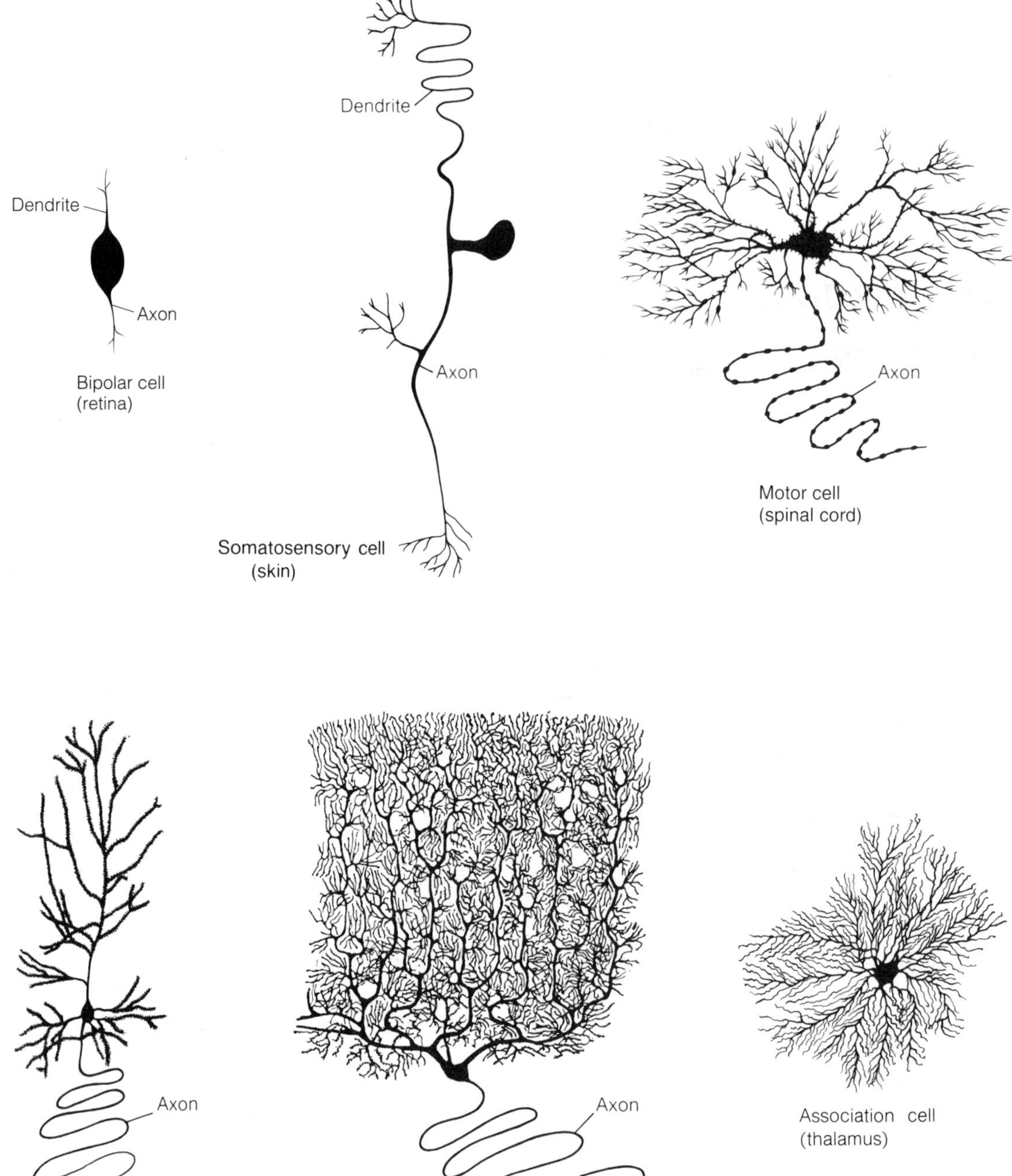

FIGURE 3.1. The nervous system is composed of neurons, or nerve cells, each of which is specialized as to function. The schematic drawings show the relative size, shape, and configuration of some neurons.

the functional units of the nervous system. The spongioblasts develop into **glial cells** (from *glia,* the Greek word for glue), which provide various types of support functions to neurons. These two types of cells, neurons and glia, make up the adult brain.

Figure 3.1 shows the relative size, shape, and location of some neurons. Note that very simple neurons consist of a cell body with a dendrite on one side and an axon on the other. Sensory cells that project from the body receptors into the spinal cord are modified so that the dendrite and axon are connected, which speeds conduction. Cells within the nervous system vary mainly in terms of their overall size and in the complexity of the dendritic processes. Table 3.1 summarizes some of the varied functions of glia.

Gray, White, and Reticular Matter

Different parts of the nervous system characteristically appear gray, white, or mottled and are called gray, white, or reticular matter, respectively. Areas where capillary blood vessels and cell bodies of neurons predominate constitute the **gray matter,** so named for its characteristic gray-brown color. From the cell body of each neuron, a process called an **axon** extends to form connections with neurons in other brain areas. These axons are generally covered with an insulating layer of glial cells. The glial cells are composed of a fatty substance (lipid) that gives them a white appearance, much as fat droplets in milk give it a white appearance. As a result, an area of the nervous system rich in axons covered with glial cells looks white and is consequently called **white matter.** An area of the nervous system where cell bodies and axons are mixed together is called **reticular matter** (from the Latin *rete,* meaning net) because of its mottled gray and white, or netlike, appearance.

TABLE 3.1. Glial cells and their function

Type	Function
Astroglia	Give structural support to and repair neurons
Oligodendroglia	Insulate and speed transmission of central nervous system neurons[a]
Schwann cells	Insulate and speed transmission of peripheral nervous system neurons
Microglia	Perform phagocytosis
Ependymal cells	Line the brain's ventricles and produce cerebrospinal fluid

[a] *Central nervous system neurons are found within the brain and spinal cord; peripheral nervous system neurons are found in the rest of the body.*

Nuclei and Tracts

A large number of cell bodies grouped together are called a **nucleus** (from the Latin *nux,* meaning nut) because of their collective appearance. This kind of grouping suggests that a nucleus will have a particular function, and this is the case. A large collection of axons from a nucleus is called a **tract** (from Old French, meaning path), or sometimes a fiber pathway. Tracts are involved in carrying information from one place to another; for example, the optic tract carries information from the eye into the brain. Since cell bodies are gray, nuclei are a distinctive gray; since glial cells make axons appear white, tracts are a distinctive white.

Staining

Because of their color, the larger nuclei and tracts of the brain can be seen in fresh brain tissue or brain tissue cut into thin sections, but the differences in appearance of smaller nuclei and tracts must be enhanced to make them visible. The technique of staining consists of placing brain tissue into dyes or certain biochemical agents. Because there are variations in the chemical composition of cells, their various parts can be colored selectively. Staining techniques aid immensely in differentiating brain tissue, and they are continually being refined. Stains now exist for coloring different parts of a cell, different kinds of cells, immature or mature cells, sick cells, and dead cells.

A Wonderland of Nomenclature

To the beginning student, the terminology used to label nuclei and tracts of the nervous system might seem chaotic. It is. Many structures have several names, often used interchangeably. For example, the **precentral gyrus** is variously referred to as the primary motor cortex, area 4, the motor strip, the motor homunculus, Jackson's strip, area pyramidalis, the somatomotor strip, gyrus precentralis, and M1 (it can be seen in Figure 3.6). Such proliferation of terminology is bothersome, but it is consoling to know that it reflects the culture and history of the neurosciences. Greek terminology is interchanged with English (mesencephalon for midbrain), Latin with English (fasciculus opticus for optic tract), and French for English (bouton termineau for synaptic knob). The neuroanatomist's imagination has sometimes strayed to body anatomy (mammillary bodies), to flora (amygdala, or almond), to fauna (hippocampus, or sea horse), and to mythology (Ammon's horn). Some terminology is a tribute to early pioneers: the fields of Forel, Rolando's fissure, and Deiters's nucleus. Other terms reflect color: substantia nigra (black substance), locus coeruleus (blue area), and red nucleus. The longest name is nucleus reticularis tegmenti pontis Bechterewi. Other labels are based on the consistency of tissue: substantia gelatinosa (gelatinous substance); some seem somewhat mystifying: substantia innominata (unnamable substance), zone incerta (uncertain area), nucleus ambiguus (ambiguous nucleus). Some terms are just technical, as with cell groups A-1 to A-10 (which, incidentally, were named only recently).

We attempt to use consistent and simple terms in this book, but in many cases alternative terms are widely used and so we have included them where necessary.

Approaches to the Study of Anatomy

Neuroanatomists study the structure of the brain using any of four main approaches: (1) comparative, (2) developmental, (3) cytoarchitectonic, and (4) biochemical.

The *comparative approach* consists of describing the brain's evolution from the primitive cord in simple wormlike animals to the large, complex "raveled knot" in the head of human beings. Since phyla of animals developed through stages from simple spongelike creatures to floating, swimming, crawling, walking, climbing, and flying creatures, the complexity of the nervous system can be correlated with each successive behavioral development. Thus, clues about function can be gained by correlating structure with the behavior of the animal in which the structure appears. Such analysis is not necessarily simple. The **limbic system,** a middle layer in the mammalian brain, first became quite large in amphibians and reptiles. Is its function to control new modes of locomotion, the orientation of the animals in a terrestrial world, new types of social behavior, or more advanced learning abilities? The answer is uncertain.

The comparative approach has yielded a key piece of information in neuropsychology: mammals can be distinguished from other animals by their large cortex, and this structure is particularly large in humans. It is understandable, then, that the cortex is thought to have an important function in conferring abilities unique to mammals, especially humans, and it thus receives proportionately more attention in neuropsychology—particularly human neuropsychology—than do other structures.

In the *developmental* (or ontogenetic) *approach* the changes in brain structure and size that occur during the development of an individual are described. Individual mammals pass through the same general phylogenetic stages as animal species do in their evolution; or, as it is sometimes stated, ontogeny recapitulates phylogeny. Thus again, the development of new structures can be correlated with emerging behaviors, much as is done in comparative studies. Additionally, the immature brain can often provide a simple version of the adult brain. Neuropsychologists widely assume that the neocortex is particularly immature in newborn infants. As a result, correlating the development of the neocortex with emerging complex and conscious behavior is viewed as a powerful method of uncovering its structural and functional relations.

Cytoarchitectonic analysis consists of describing the architecture of cells: their differences in structure, size, shape, and connections, and their distribution in different parts of the brain. The cytoarchitectonic approach has been used to particular advantage by neuroanatomists to produce various kinds of maps of the brain.

The most recent cytoarchitectonic technique is the *biochemical approach,* in which the brain's biochemical organization is studied. It is now clear that cells contain unique biochemical substances that allow them to play their special roles in intercellular communication or neurotransmission. Identifying these biochemical substances is of functional as well as anatomical importance. First, the activity of these systems can be related to different aspects of behavior. Second, abnormalities in the functioning of these systems can be related to types of abnormal behavior. When cells are active, grow, or make new connections, they change structurally. To achieve these changes a message must be sent from the genetic material in the nucleus to begin the process of making the new protein that is required. The "message" can be stained so that cells that are undergoing change can be visualized. This is useful in identifying cells that may be active in such processes as learning or in mediating recovery from brain damage.

ORIGIN AND DEVELOPMENT OF THE BRAIN

The nervous system can be viewed as evolving or developing in four somewhat general steps, as is shown diagrammatically in Figure 3.2. Embryologists have given rather cumbersome names to the developing brain regions, and since some of these names are also used to describe parts of the developed brain, they are also given in Figure 3.2.

The nervous system was first a segmented cord (or **spinal cord**) with fibers in each segment making connections to each segment of the body (Figure 3.2A). The nervous system of an earth-

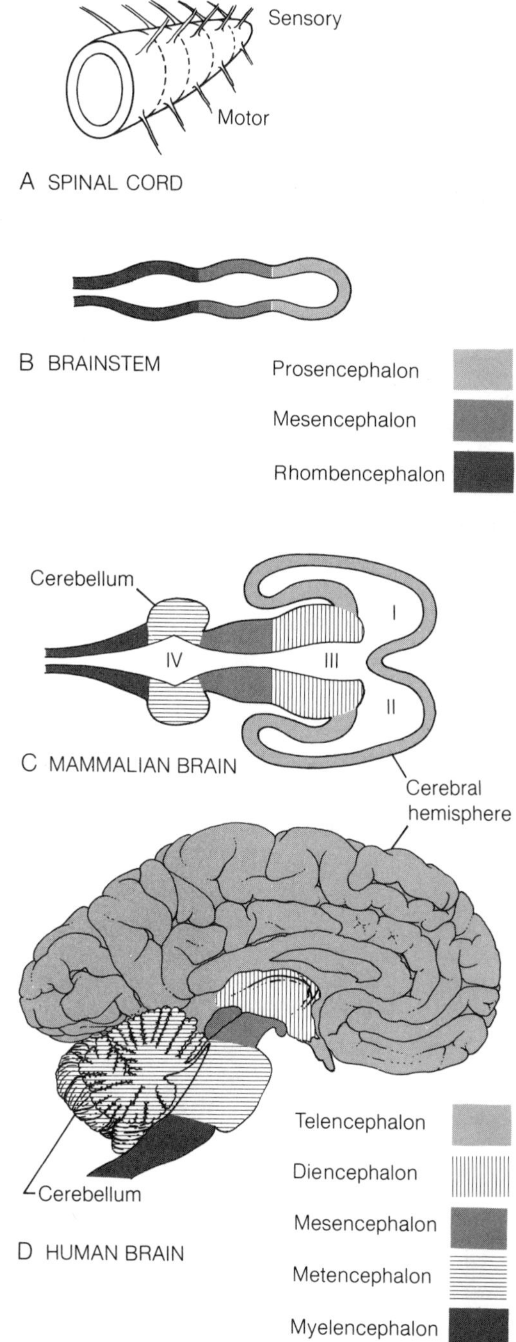

FIGURE 3.2. Steps in the development of the brain. *A*. Spinal cord. *B*. Brainstem. *C*. Mammalian brain, showing ventricles (I–V). *D*. Side view of the center of the human brain.

worm has organizational features something like this.

In more complex animals, one end of the animal specializes "to go first" and develops a variety of receptors (nose, eyes, ears) to tell where it is going (Figure 3.2B). A brain develops at the front end of the spinal cord to receive this information and to tell the rest of the body what to do. The brain of a fish is representative of this brain, and its equivalent in mammals is called the **brainstem.** This brain consists of three enlargements: the **prosencephalon** (front brain) is involved in olfaction, the **mesencephalon** (middle brain) is involved in vision and hearing, and the **rhombencephalon** (hindbrain) is involved in balance.

In mammals (Figure 3.2C), the prosencephalon develops to form the cerebral hemispheres (cortex and other structures), which are known as the **telencephalon** (endbrain). The remaining portion of the old prosencephalon is referred to as the **diencephalon** (between-brain). The back part of the brain also develops further as the cerebellum becomes larger. It is subdivided into the **metencephalon** (across-brain) and the **myelencephalon** (spinal brain). Note that the brain is still "hollow," and the hollows in each portion are referred to as **ventricles** (bladders). The ventricles are filled with fluid (**cerebrospinal fluid,** or **CSF**) and are numbered from I to IV.

The human brain is a more complex mammalian brain with most of the features of other mammalian brains and with especially large cerebral hemispheres (Figure 3.2D).

Table 3.2 summarizes the development of the brain from the stage of having three primary embryonic divisions to one of having five. In addition, the table shows some of the major brain structures found in each division of the mammalian brain.

TABLE 3.2. The divisions of the nervous system

Primitive brainstem divisions	Mammalian brain divisions	Portion of fully developed human brain	Functional divisions
Prosencephalon (forebrain)	Telencephalon (endbrain)	Neocortex Basal ganglia Limbic system Olfactory bulb Lateral ventricles	Forebrain
	Diencephalon (between-brain)	Thalamus Epithalamus Hypothalamus Pineal body Third ventricle	
Mesencephalon (midbrain)	Mesencephalon (midbrain)	Tectum Tegmentum Cerebral aqueduct	Brainstem
Rhombencephalon (hindbrain)	Metencephalon (across-brain)	Cerebellum Pons Fourth ventricle	
	Myelencephalon (spinal brain)	Medulla oblongata Fourth ventricle	
			Spinal cord

Orientation

Many structures of the brain are labeled according to their location relative to one another. Six conventional terms are used to indicate anatomical direction: *superior (top), lateral (side), medial (middle), ventral (bottom), anterior (front), and posterior (back).* Thus one structure can be said to lie superior, lateral, medial, ventral, anterior, or posterior to another. The nervous system is also arranged symmetrically and so consists of left and right sides. If two structures lie on the same side, they are said to be **ipsilateral;** if they lie on opposite sides, they are said to be **contralateral;** if one is on each side, they are said to be **bilateral.** Structures that are close to one another are said to be **proximal;** those far from one another are said to be **distal.** Finally, a projection that is approaching is said to be **afferent;** one that is leaving is said to be **efferent.**

The Spinal Cord

In a very simple animal, the body is a tube divided into segments. Within the body is a tube of nerve cells that is also divided into segments. Each segment receives fibers from sensory receptors of the part of the body adjacent to it and sends back fibers to the muscles of that part of the body. Each segment functions relatively independently, although fibers interconnect the segments and coordinate their activity.

This basic plan also holds for the human body. Figure 3.3A shows the segments of the human body. Each body segment, called a **dermatome** (meaning skin cut), encircles the body in a ring formation. Because mammals have limbs and human beings have an upright posture, the ring formation in humans is distorted into the pattern shown in Figure 3.3A. Note that as many as six segments are represented on the arm (if the person were on all fours, one can see how this pattern makes sense).

In the human spinal cord (Figure 3.3B), each segment of the cord is also linked with the organs and musculature of a specific body segment. There are 30 spinal cord segments: 8 cervical (C), 12 thoracic (T), 5 lumbar (L), and 5 sacral (S). The spinal cord segments connect with the body dermatomes of the same number.

Figure 3.3C shows a cross section of the spinal cord. Fibers entering the dorsal portion of the spinal cord carry information from the sensory receptors of the body. These fibers collect together as they enter the spinal cord, and this collection of fibers is referred to as a **dorsal root.** Fibers leaving the ventral portion of the spinal cord, carrying information from the spinal cord to the muscles, form a **ventral root.** The outer portion of the spinal cord consists of white matter or tracts, arranged so that with a few exceptions the dorsal tracts are motor and the ventral tracts are sensory. The inner portion of the cord, which has a butterfly shape, is gray matter; that is, it is composed largely of cell bodies.

François Magendie, a volatile and committed French experimental physiologist, reported in a three-page paper in 1822 that he had succeeded in cutting the dorsal and ventral roots of puppy dogs, animals in which the roots were sufficiently segregated to allow surgery. He found that sectioning of the dorsal roots was associated with loss of sensation and that sectioning of the ventral roots was associated with loss of movement. As early as 1811, the Scot Charles Bell, using anatomical information and the results from somewhat inconclusive experiments on rabbits, suggested somewhat different functions for each of the roots. Following Magendie's paper, Bell hotly disputed priority for the discovery, with at least some success. Magendie's experiment has been called the most important ever conducted on the nervous system, because it enabled neurologists for the first time to localize nervous system damage from the symptoms displayed by patients. Today the concept that the dorsal portion of the spinal cord is sensory and the ventral part is motor is called the **Bell-Magendie law** (one of the very few nervous system laws). Cuts to the dorsal roots are used to relieve pain that is otherwise resistant to treatment.

Because the cord and body have this segmental structure, rather good inferences can be made about the location of spinal cord damage or disease from changes in sensation or movement in

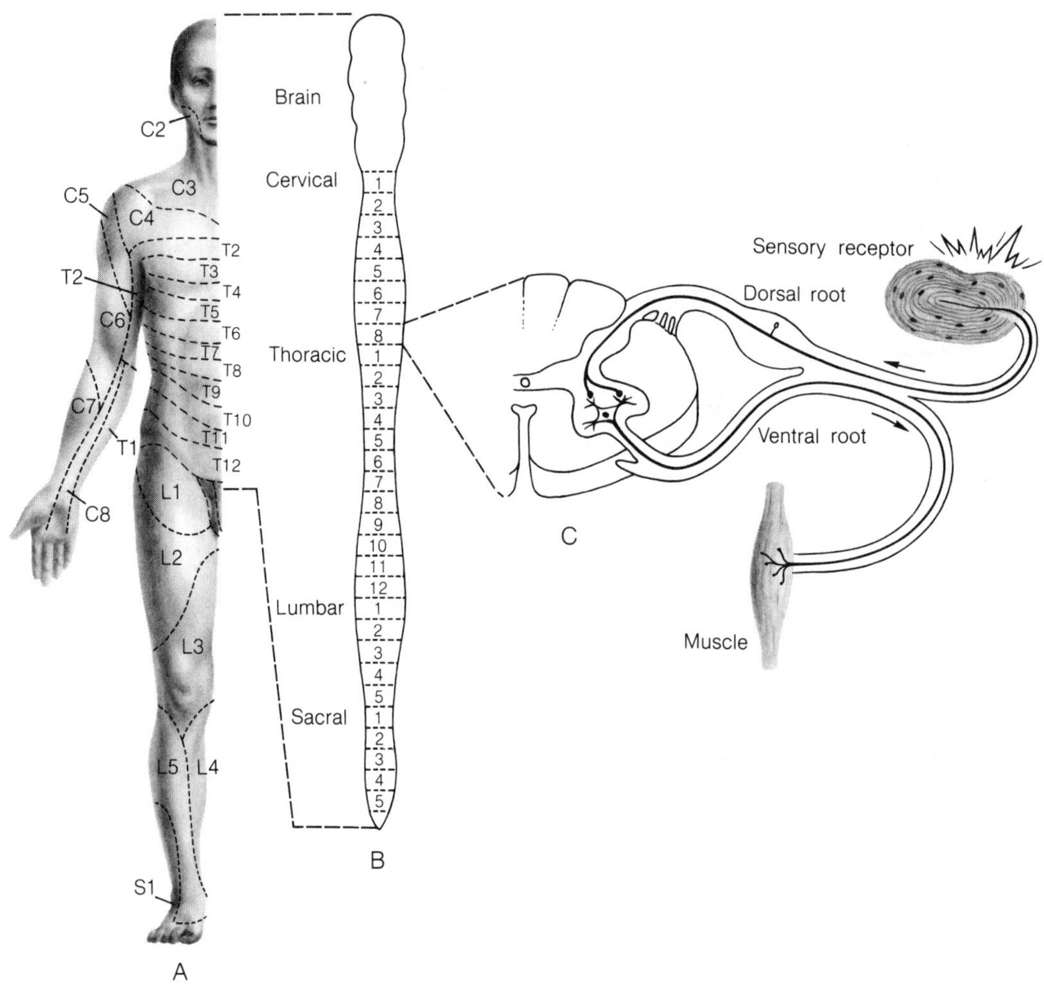

FIGURE 3.3. Relations between the dermatomes of the body and segments of the spinal cord. *A.* Body dermatomes. *B.* Spinal cord segments. *C.* Cross section through one segment of the spinal cord showing that sensory input from a dermatome arrives through the dorsal root, and motor output to the same body part goes through the ventral root.

particular body parts. The organs in the body are also arranged segmentally, but they appear not to have their own sensory representation within the brain. Pain in these organs is felt within the body portion of the dermatome and so is called **referred pain.** For example, pains in the heart are felt in the shoulder and arm, and kidney pain is felt in the back. A good knowledge of the location of referred pains can be used to diagnose problems within the body.

Spinal Cord Reflexes. The major thrust toward understanding spinal cord function came from the work of Sir Charles Sherrington and his students. Sherrington, a British physiologist, published a monumental summary of this research in 1906. Humans who have their spinal cord cut so that they no longer have control over their legs are called **paraplegic;** if the cut occurs higher on the cord so that they cannot use their arms either, they are called **quadraplegic.** Although it was once thought that the sectioned spinal cord had no function, it is now known that the spinal cord can mediate many reflexes as well as some more complex behaviors.

An understanding of some simplified circuitry through which the spinal cord produces reflexes stemmed from Sherrington's work. A pinprick to the skin damages the skin and stimulates pain **receptors** in the skin. Stimulating the receptor activates a pain neuron, which conducts the information to the spinal cord. There, the pain fibers activate **interneurons** that in turn activate *motor neurons.* The motor neurons synapse with muscles, and the muscles contract and flex the limb. This **withdrawal reflex** removes the limb from danger. If the stimulus is mild, only the distal portion of the limb is withdrawn, but if the stimulus is made successively stronger, the size of the movement increases until the whole limb is withdrawn. Tactile stimulation, such as light pressure on the skin, activates tactile and pressure receptors, which through interneurons and motor neurons will cause the limb to extend. This **extensor reflex** maintains contact with the stimulus; for example, the foot or hand touching a surface will maintain contact with the surface through this reflex.

The pain and tactile connections in the spinal cord go to many interneurons and many muscles on both sides of the body to produce the appropriate adjustments in many body parts. The spinal cord can also mediate more complex actions. If the body of a spinal animal is supported, then coordinated stepping can be elicited. Understanding the remaining abilities of the spinal cord led to enhanced survival rates for soldiers who suffered spinal cord damage in World War I.

Parallel Processing in the Spinal Cord. There are a number of different kinds of receptors in the body, including those for pain, temperature, pressure, and muscle and joint movement. The sizes of the fibers that come from each receptor are distinctive; generally, pain and temperature fibers are smaller and the other fibers are larger. Stimulating pain and temperature receptors usually produces **flexion** movements that bring the limb to the body; stimulating fine touch and pressure receptors usually produces **extension** movements that move it away from the body. Because the receptors, fibers, connections, and movements for each of these body senses are separate, each can be thought of as an independent sense. Since each sense produces a distinct movement, the senses can be thought of as being parallel systems; that is, each operates independently of the others.

The idea that there are multiple senses within what is usually thought of as the **somatosensory,** or body sense, **system** and that each has its own separate channel is applicable to many other senses and to the function of the brain more generally. Sensory systems can interact, however. It is common knowledge that itches or pains can be relieved by rubbing (activating fine touch and pressure receptors). Thus, it is proposed that there is a "gate" in the spinal cord that allows the fine touch and pressure pathway to block activity in the pain pathway. The gate is thought to consist of an inhibitory neuron in the spinal cord that, when activated by fine touch and pressure neurons, will inhibit pain neurons.

THE BRAINSTEM

A section of the human brain is shown in Figure 3.4. Many of the main structures of the brainstem can be seen in this figure. In general, the brainstem regulates many of the movements that animals make; it can respond to most sensory features of the environment and also regulates eating and drinking, body temperature, sleep and waking, and sexual behavior.

The Diencephalon

The diencephalon consists of the three thalamic structures: the thalamus (inner room or chamber); the epithalamus (upper room); and the hypothalamus (lower room).

The function of the **epithalamus** is not well understood, but one of its structures, the **pineal body,** seems to regulate body rhythms. Recall that Descartes, impressed by its solitary nature,

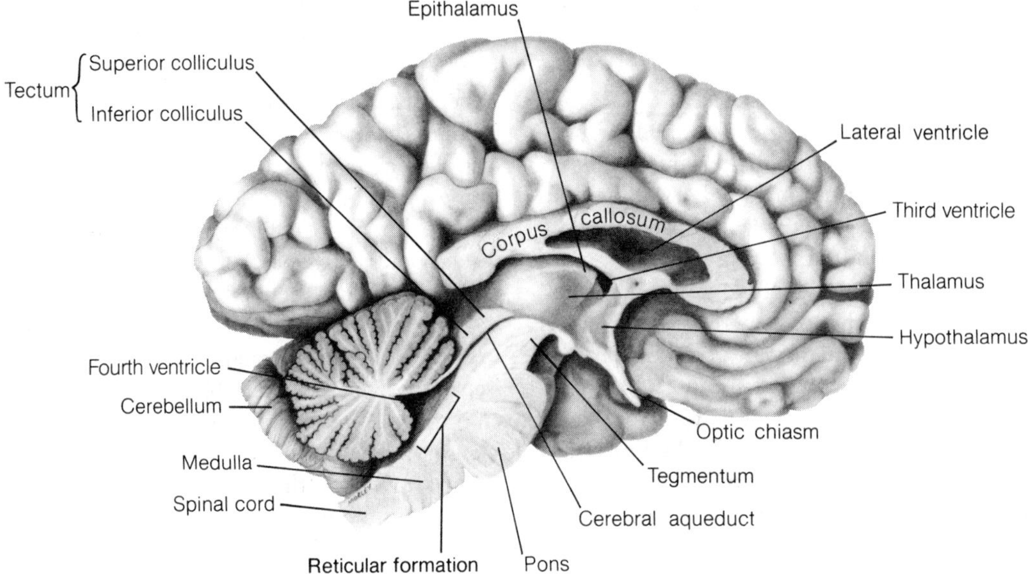

FIGURE 3.4. Medial view through the center of the brain showing structures of the brainstem.

suggested that the pineal body is the rendezvous between mind and matter and the source of the cerebral spinal fluid that powers movements.

The **thalamus** consists of a number of nuclei. All the sensory systems except olfaction (for example, vision, hearing, body senses) have relays in the thalamus on their way to the cortex. In addition, different parts of the cortex communicate with one another via relays through the thalamus.

The **hypothalamus** is composed of about 22 small nuclei, fiber systems that pass through it, and the **pituitary gland.** Although comprising only about 0.3% of the brain's weight, the hypothalamus is involved in nearly all aspects of behavior, including feeding, sexual behavior, sleeping, temperature regulation, emotional behavior, endocrine function, and movement.

The Midbrain

The **midbrain** consists of two main subdivisions: the **tectum,** or roof, which is the area lying above the cerebral aqueduct (part of the ventricular system), and the **tegmentum,** or floor, which lies below the aqueduct. The tectum consists primarily of two sets of bilaterally symmetical nuclei. The **superior colliculi** (upper hills) are the anterior pair. They receive projections from the retina of the eye and they mediate many visually related behaviors. The **inferior colliculi** (lower hills) are the posterior pair. They receive projections from the ear and they mediate many auditory-related behaviors. The tegmentum contains nuclei for some of the cranial nerves, and intermingled among these are a number of motor nuclei. Thus, following the plan of the spinal cord, the dorsal portion of the midbrain is sensory and the ventral portion is motor.

The Hindbrain

The **hindbrain** is organized in much the same way as the midbrain. Sensory nuclei of the **vestibular system** (the sensory system located in the inner ear that governs balance and orientation) overlie the fourth ventricle; beneath this ventricle are more motor nuclei of the cranial nerves. Overlying these is the very distinctive **cerebellum.**

The function of the cerebellum varies from one part of the structure to another, depending on the connections with the rest of the nervous system. Parts that receive most of their impulses from the vestibular system help to maintain the body's equilibrium, whereas parts receiving impulses mainly from the body senses are involved with postural reflexes and coordinating functionally related muscles. The major part of the cerebellum receives impulses from the neocortex and primarily controls skilled movements.

The surface of the cerebellum is marked by narrow folds, or folia, beneath which lies a thick cortex of gray matter covering a larger central mass of white matter. Within the white matter are several nuclei. The cerebellum is attached to the brainstem by three major fiber pathways in which all afferent fibers pass to its cortex and all efferent fibers originate in the underlying cerebellar nuclei and then pass on to other brain structures.

Damage to the cerebellum results in impairments of equilibrium, postural defects, and impairments of skilled motor activity. Injury or disease in the cerebellum, therefore, may break smooth movements into their jerky sequential components; ability to perform rapidly alternating movements may be impaired; and directed movements may overshoot their mark. In addition, muscle tone may be abnormal, so that movements are difficult to initiate.

Fibers from the spinal cord pass through the brainstem on their way to the forebrain, and fibers from the forebrain also connect with the brainstem and pass through it on their way to the spinal cord. This mixture of cells and fibers in the brainstem is referred to as the **reticular formation.**

The reticular formation is more commonly known as the **reticular activating system;** it obtained this designation in 1949 when Moruzzi and Magoun stimulated it electrically in anesthetized cats. They found that stimulation produced a waking pattern of electrical activity in the cat's cortex. As a result of their experiment, Moruzzi and Magoun proposed that the function of the reticular formation is to control sleeping and waking. Through the influence of these findings, the reticular formation gradually came to be known as the reticular activating system, the function of which was to maintain "general arousal" or "consciousness." It is now recognized that the various nuclei of the brainstem serve many functions and only a few are involved in waking and sleeping.

Cranial Nerves

There are 12 sets of **cranial nerves** lying within the brainstem; these convey sensory information from the specialized sensory systems of the head and control the special movements of muscle systems in the head; for example, movements of the eyes and tongue. A knowledge of the organization and function of the cranial nerves is important for neurological diagnosis. Table 3.3 summarizes the cranial nerves, their functions, and some of the more common symptoms that occur after damage to them.

THE FOREBRAIN

The **forebrain** is conventionally divided into five anatomical areas: (1) the cortex, (2) the limbic system, (3) the basal ganglia, (4) the thalamus, and (5) the olfactory bulbs and tract. The following sections will describe first the cortex and then the remaining structures. The cortex is closely related to and can expand its functions through the thalamus (through which it receives sensory information), the basal ganglia (which aid in the execution of movement), and the limbic system (which is involved in behaviors requiring memory).

The Cortex

The **cortex** or **neocortex** comprises most of the forebrain by volume. It consists of four to six layers of cells (or gray matter). The term "cortex" (from the Latin, meaning bark) is used to refer to any outer layer of cells. The terms "cortex" and "neocortex" are often used interchangeably, and so conventionally "cortex" refers to "neocortex"

TABLE 3.3. The cranial nerves

Number	Name	Functions	Method of examination	Typical symptoms of dysfunction
I	Olfactory	(s) Smell[a]	Various odors applied to each nostril	Loss of sense of smell (anosmia)
II	Optic	(s) Vision	Visual acuity, map field of vision	Loss of vision (anopsia)
III	Oculomotor	(m) Eye movement[a]	Reaction to light, lateral movements of eyes, eyelid movement	Double vision (diplopia), large pupil, uneven dilation of pupils, drooping eyelid (ptosis), deviation of eye outward
IV	Trochlear	(m) Eye movement	Upward and downward eye movements	Double vision, defect of downward gaze
V	Trigeminal	(s,m) Masticatory movements	Light touch by cotton baton; pain by pinprick; thermal by hot and cold tubes, corneal reflex by touching cornea; jaw reflex by tapping chin, jaw movements	Decreased sensitivity or numbness of face, brief attacks of severe pain (trigeminal neuralgia); weakness and wasting of facial muscles, asymmetrical chewing
VI	Abducens	(m) Eye movement	Lateral movements	Double vision, inward deviation of the eye
VII	Facial	(s,m) Facial movement	Facial movements, facial expression, test for taste	Facial paralysis, loss of taste over anterior two-thirds of tongue
VIII	Auditory vestibular	(s) Hearing	Audiogram tests hearing; stimulate by rotating patient or by irrigating the ear with hot or cold water (caloric test)	Deafness, sensation of noise in ear (tinnitus); disequilibrium, feeling of disorientation in space
IX	Glossopharyngeal	(s,m) Tongue and pharynx	Test for sweet, salt, bitter, and sour tastes on tongue; pharyngeal or gag reflex by touching walls of pharynx	Partial dry mouth, loss of taste (ageusia) over posterior third of tongue, anesthesia and paralysis of upper pharynx
X	Vagus	(s,m) Heart, blood vessels, viscera, movement of larynx and pharynx	Observe palate in phonation, palatal reflex by touching palate	Hoarseness, lower pharyngeal anesthesia and paralysis, indefinite visceral disturbance
XI	Spinal accessory	(m) Neck muscles and viscera	Movement, strength, and bulk of neck and shoulder muscles	Wasting of neck with weakened rotation, inability to shrug
XII	Hypoglossal	(m) Tongue muscles	Tongue movements, tremor, wasting or wrinkling of tongue	Wasting of tongue with deviation to side of lesion on protrusion

[a] *s and m refer to sensory or motor function (or both) of the nerve.*

unless otherwise indicated. The cortex has expanded the most during evolution; it comprises 80% of the human brain. The human neocortex has an area of up to 2500 cm^2 but a thickness of only 1.5 to 3.0 mm. The cortex is wrinkled; this wrinkling is nature's solution to the problem of confining the huge neocortical surface area within a skull that is still small enough to pass through the birth canal. Just as a crumpled sheet of paper can fit into a smaller box than a flat sheet, folding of the neocortex permits the relatively fixed volume of the skull to contain more neocortex.

Fissures, Sulci, and Gyri

The wrinkled surface of the neocortex consists of clefts and ridges. A cleft is called a **fissure** if it extends deeply enough into the brain to indent the ventricles, and a **sulcus** (plural sulci) is shallower. A ridge is called a **gyrus** (plural gyri).

Figure 3.5 shows the location of some of the more important fissures, sulci, and gyri of the brain. There is *some* variation in the location of these features on the two sides of a single individual's brain, and *substantial* variation in the loca-

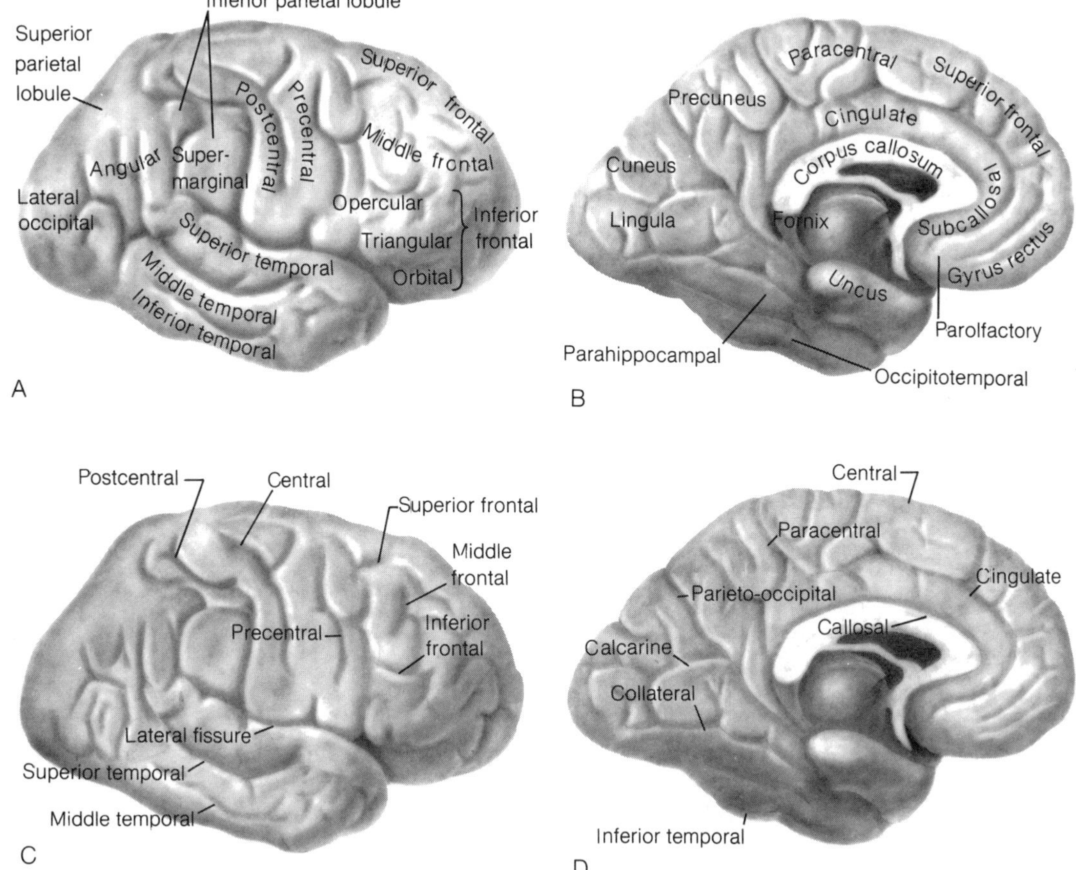

FIGURE 3.5. Gyri and sulci. Lateral (*A*) and medial (*B*) views of the gyri. Lateral (*C*) and medial (*D*) views of the sulci.

tion, size, and exact structure of the gyri and sulci in the brains of different individuals. The organization of cells in different gyri differs, with the change in organization between adjacent gyri usually occurring at the sulci. There is some evidence that gyri can be associated with specific functions. Two external features of the brain are relatively easy to locate: the **lateral fissure,** because it begins in a cleft on the anterior-inferior surface of the cortex, and the **central sulcus,** because it curves posteriorly as it reaches the medial longitudinal fissure separating the two hemispheres (see Figure 3.5C).

The Hemispheres and Lobes

As Figure 3.6 *(dorsal view)* shows, the cortex consists of two nearly symmetrical hemispheres, the left and the right, separated by the **medial longitudinal fissure.** Each hemisphere is subdivided into four lobes: frontal, parietal, temporal, and occipital. The **frontal lobes** have fixed boundaries: they are bounded posteriorly by the central sulcus, inferiorly by the lateral fissure, and medially by the **cingulate sulcus** just above a large interhemispheric band of fibers called the **corpus callosum.** The anterior boundary of the **parietal lobes** is the central sulcus, and their inferior boundary is the lateral fissure. The **temporal lobes** are bounded dorsally by the lateral fissure. The **occipital lobes** are separated from the parietal cortex medially by the **parieto-occipital sulcus.** On the lateral surface of the brain there are no definite boundaries between the occipital lobes and the parietal and temporal lobes.

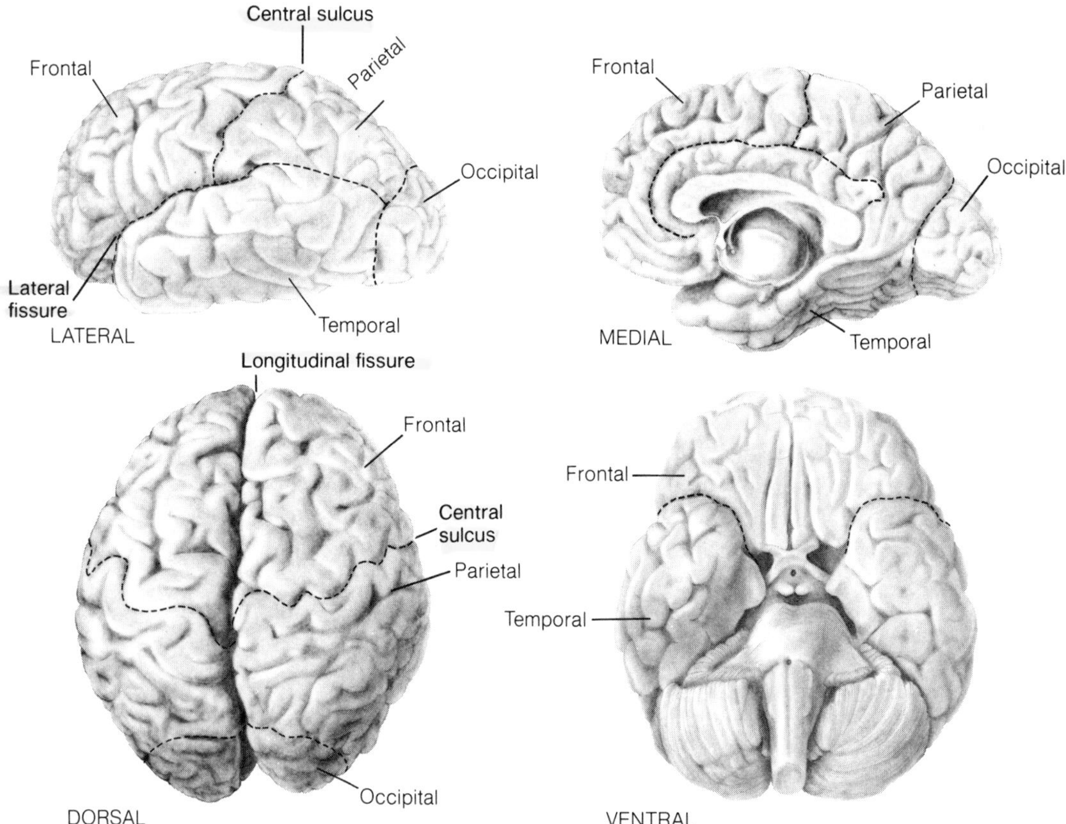

FIGURE 3.6. The location of the frontal, parietal, occipital, and temporal lobes of the brain.

As shown in Figure 3.5A, there are four major gyri in the frontal lobe: the superior frontal, middle frontal, inferior frontal, and precentral (which lies in front of the central sulcus). There are five major gyri in the parietal lobe: the superior and inferior, the postcentral (lying behind the central sulcus), and the supermarginal and angular (on either side of the lateral fissure). There are three gyri in the temporal lobe: the superior, middle, and inferior. Only the lateral gyrus is obvious in the occipital cortex in this lateral view.

TOPOGRAPHY OF THE NEOCORTEX

The several different kinds of maps that have been made of the neocortex are called **topographic maps.** These maps are constructed from information obtained by the application of specific research techniques:

1. **Projection maps** are constructed by tracing axons from the sensory systems into the brain and by tracing axons from the neocortex to the motor systems of the brainstem and spinal cord.

2. **Cytoarchitectonic maps** are constructed from study of the distribution of different types of cells in the neocortex.

3. **Functional maps** are constructed by studying the effects of brain damage, stimulating areas of the brain electrically and noting the elicited behavior, or recording electrical changes in response to sensory stimulation. Functional maps are also constructed by imaging techniques. These techniques monitor the ongoing activity of the brain as a subject engages in a behavior and so reveal what areas of the brain are active during that behavior.

Projection Maps

Figure 3.7 shows an example of a projection map constructed by tracing the route that axons take from sensory receptors to the neocortex, and by tracing the motor axons from the neocortex to motor neurons in the spinal cord. As the figure shows, the projections from the eye, the ear, and the body's somatosensory system can each be traced to a specific region of the neocortex; the visual system projects to the occipital lobe, the auditory system to the temporal lobe, and the somatosensory system to the parietal lobe. The major motor projection appears to originate in the precentral gyrus of the frontal lobe. These areas can be called **primary projection areas,** but it should be noted that the lateral view does not represent their entire extent, because they also project down into the gyri and fissures. The auditory zone, for example, is much larger within the lateral fissure. The primary projection areas of the neocortex are small relative to the total size of the cortex.

The primary sensory areas send projections into the areas adjacent to them, and the motor areas receive fibers from areas adjacent to them. Thus, the entire neocortex can be conceptualized as being divided into four fields: visual, auditory, body senses, and motor. Since areas of relatively direct projections are referred to as primary projection areas, the surrounding areas can be called **secondary projection areas.**

It is clear from this topography that the neocortex is highly organized. It is also clear why the posterior neocortex is considered to be largely sensory and the anterior neocortex to be largely motor. Finally, it is apparent why each of the lobes is thought to be associated with a particular general function:

Frontal lobes: motor

Parietal lobes: body senses

Temporal lobes: auditory function

Occipital lobes: visual functions

The areas that lie between the various secondary areas are higher-level association areas that mediate complex functions such as language, planning, memory, and attention.

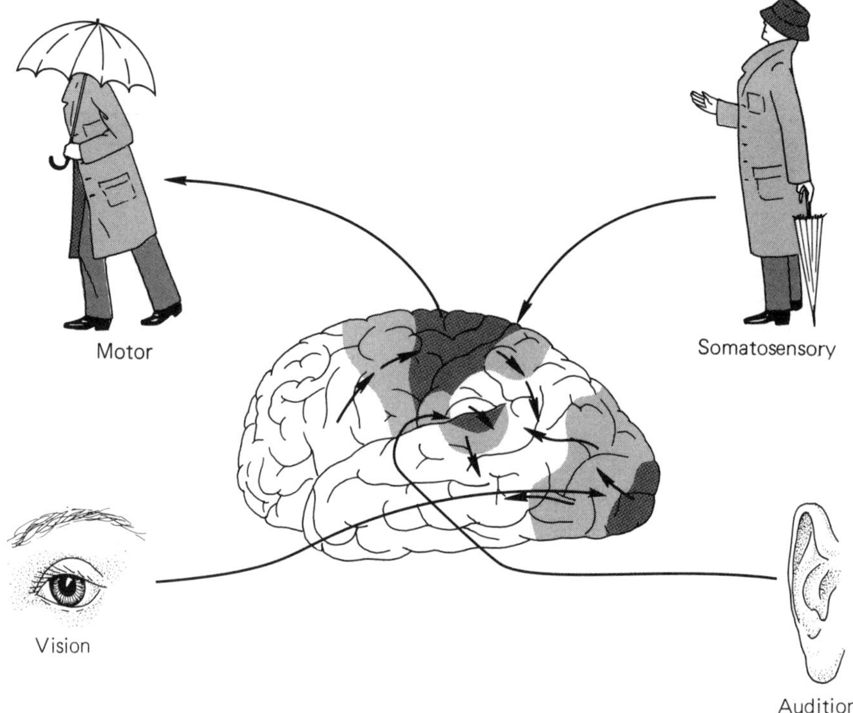

FIGURE 3.7. A projection map. The darkest shading indicates primary projection areas, which receive input from the sensory systems or project to spinal motor systems. The lightly shaded areas are secondary areas. The unshaded areas are higher-order association or tertiary areas.

Cytoarchitectonic Maps

The neurons of the neocortex are arranged in about six layers, as shown in Figure 3.8. The cell layers of the neocortex can be separated into three groups by function. (1) The bottom two layers, 5 and 6, send axons to other brain areas. Both the cells and the cell layers are large and distinctive in the motor cortex. (2) The fourth layer receives axons from other areas. This layer features large numbers of densely packed small cells in the primary areas of vision, somatosensation, and audition, which receive large projections from their respective sensory organs. (3) The first to third layers receive input mainly from the fourth layer and are quite well developed in the areas of cortex surrounding the primary areas. It is on such differences in cell distribution, as well as on differences in cell sizes and shapes, that cytoarchitectonic maps are based. For example, sensory areas have many layer 4 cells, motor areas have many layer 5 and 6 cells, and association areas have many layer 1, 2, and 3 cells.

Cytoarchitectonic maps are constructed by examining the neurons of the neocortex to identify regions that seem to have a unique organization. The many cytoarchitectonic maps of the neocortex differ chiefly in degree of complexity. The map presented in Figure 3.9 is known as **Brodmann's map.** It is by no means the simplest, but it is widely used.

In Brodmann's map, each of the areas is num-

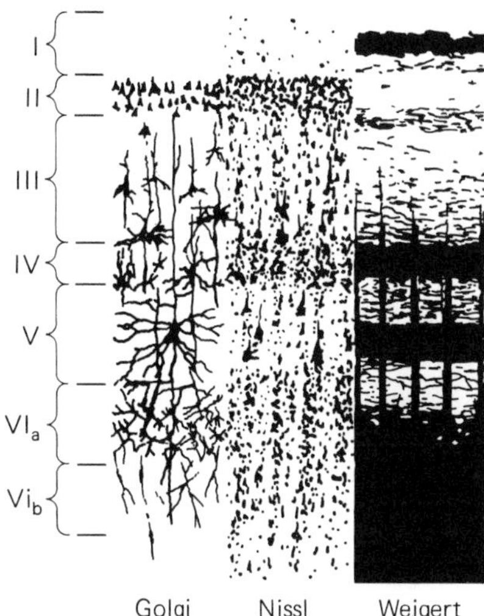

FIGURE 3.8. Structure of the cortex revealed through the use of three different stains. The Golgi stain penetrates only a few neurons but reveals all of their processes, the Nissl stain highlights only cell bodies, and the Weigert myelin stain reveals the location of axons. Note that these staining procedures highlight the different cell types of the cortex and reveal that it is composed of a number of layers, each of which contains typical cell types. (After Brodmann, 1909.)

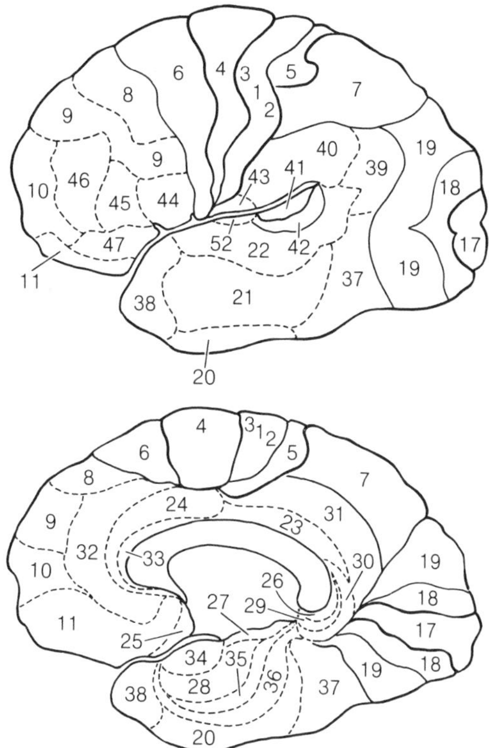

FIGURE 3.9. Brodmann's areas of the cortex. A few numbers are missing from the original sources, including 12–16 and 48–51. Some areas have histologically distinctive boundaries and are outlined with heavy solid lines; others, such as 6 and 18–19, have less distinctive boundaries and are outlined with light solid lines; the remaining areas have no distinct boundaries but gradually merge into one another and are outlined with dotted lines. (After Elliott, 1969.)

bered, but the numbers themselves have no special meaning. To do his analysis, Brodmann divided the brain at the central sulcus and then worked through each half in random order, numbering new conformations of cells as he found them. Thus, he found areas 1 and 2 in the posterior section, then switched to the anterior section and found areas 3 and 4, and then switched back again, and so on in this manner.

Table 3.4 summarizes some of the known relations between each of Brodmann's areas and its functions. The relation between structure and function is reasonably good. For example, area 17 corresponds to the primary visual projection area and areas 18 and 19 to the secondary visual projection areas. Area 4 is the primary motor cortex. Broca's area, which is thought to be related to articulating words, is area 44. Similar relations exist for other areas and functions.

One of the problems with Brodmann's map is that with the development of new techniques, such as single cell recording, single Brodmann areas have been found to really consist of two or more areas. For this reason, the map is continually being updated and now consists of a mixture of numbers, letters, and names.

Functional Maps

Of the many functional maps of the somatosensory and motor areas, the best known is by Pen-

TABLE 3.4. Functional areas and Brodmann cytoarchitectonic areas

Function	Brodmann area
Vision	
primary	17
secondary	18, 19, 20, 21, 37
Auditory	
primary	41
secondary	22, 42
Body senses	
primary	1, 2, 3
secondary	5, 7
Sensory, tertiary	7, 22, 37, 39, 40
Motor	
primary	4
secondary	6
eye movement	8
speech	44
Motor, tertiary	9, 10, 11, 45, 46, 47

field and his coworkers. During the course of brain surgery, they stimulated the brains of conscious people through thin wires, or electrodes, with low voltages of electric current. The protocol of such an experiment was to stimulate the cortical tissue briefly, observe whether the person made a movement or reported some sort of body sensation (such as an itch or tickle), record the location and response, and then move the stimulating electrode to repeat the procedure.

The results of several such experiments are shown diagrammatically in Figure 3.10. Areas that produced movement lie in the precentral gyrus in the primary motor-projection area. For both the motor and sensory areas there is a point-to-point relation between parts of the body and parts of the neocortex. Note that these distributions of the body on the cortex are distorted in the figure, the face and hands being far larger proportionately than other parts of the body. This topography is shown schematically by the cartoon people (or *homunculi*) drawn over the motor and sensory areas to indicate the parts of the body represented in different cortical areas.

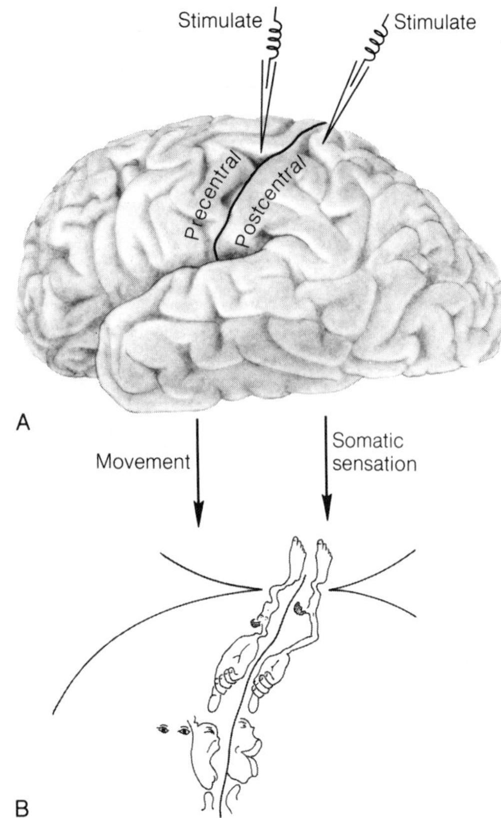

FIGURE 3.10. A functional map. *A.* Electrical stimulation is applied to the precentral or postcentral gyrus through small electrodes. *B.* Movement or sensation is produced at the locations shown by the homunculi, or "little men." (After Penfield and Jasper, 1954.)

The face and hands of the homunculi are larger because these body parts have more receptors, are capable of finer perceptions and movements than are other body areas, and so require proportionately more neocortex to represent them. The foot area lies in the longitudinal fissure (flexed up in Figure 3.10). The cortical representations of the eyes and mouth are actually not in the head region of the motor homunculus; they have their own areas just anterior to the head area.

The visual and auditory systems have a neocortical distribution as precise as that of the motor and somatosensory systems. The visual field (the area of the world the eyes see) is represented across the visual projection area in the occipital lobe, whereas the sensory area for sound, the basilar membrane, is represented in the primary auditory area of the temporal lobe. The taste area of the brain lies across a tongue-shaped area in the postcentral gyrus in Figure 3.10. The olfactory system has a representation in the ventrolateral anterior neocortex.

Cortical Connections

The various regions of the neocortex are interconnected by three types of axon projections: (1) relatively short connections between one gyrus and another, (2) longer connections between one lobe and another, and (3) interhemispheric connections, or **commissures,** between one hemisphere and another. Most of the interhemispheric connections link **homotopic areas,** or corresponding points, in the two hemispheres that are related to the midline of the body. Figure 3.11 shows the locations and names of some of these connections. The cortex also makes other types of connections with itself; cells in any area, for example, may send axons to cells in a subcortical area such as the thalamus, and the cells in the area of the thalamus may then send their axons to some other cortical area. These types of relations are more difficult to establish anatomically than are those based on direct connections. Yet the connections are of considerable functional interest, because damage to a pathway is often reflected in behavioral deficits as severe as those suffered following damage to the functional areas they connect. A glance at Figure 3.11 will show that it would be difficult indeed to damage any area of the cortex without damaging one or more of its interconnecting pathways.

The Limbic Lobe

During the evolution of the amphibians and reptiles, a number of three-layer cortical structures developed that sheath the periphery of the brainstem. With the subsequent growth of the neocortex they became sandwiched between the new brain and the old brain. Because of the evolutionary origin of these structures some anatomists have referred to them as the reptilian brain, but the term **limbic lobe** (from the Latin *limbus,* meaning border or hem), coined by Broca in 1878, is more widely recognized today. The limbic lobe is also referred to as the **limbic system** (which may very well be a misnomer). The limbic lobe consists of a number of structures, including the **hippocampus** (sea horse), **septum** (partition), and cingulate (girdle) gyrus, or **cingulate cortex,** which are interrelated (Figure 3.12). Nevertheless, the history of how the limbic "lobe" became the limbic "system" is one of the most interesting chapters of the neurosciences.

Initially, anatomists were impressed with the connections between the olfactory system and the limbic lobe. On this evidence it was suggested that the limbic structures were elaborated to deal with olfactory information, and so together they were called the **rhinencephalon,** or smell-brain. Because a number of experiments demonstrated that these limbic structures had little olfactory function, for a time their putative olfactory function lay in a scientific limbo. Then in 1937, Papez, in what was thought at the time to be a scientific tour de force, asked, "Is emotion a magic product, or is it a physiologic process which depends on an anatomic mechanism?" He suggested that emotion, which had no known anatomic substrate, is a product of the limbic lobe, which had no recognized function. He argued that the emotional brain consists of a circuit in which information flows from the mammillary bodies in the hypothalamus to the anterior thalamic nucleus to the cingulate cortex to the hippocampus and back to the mammillary bodies. Input could enter this circuit from other structures to be elaborated as emotion. For example, an idea ("It is dangerous to walk in the dark") from the neocortex could enter the circuit to be elaborated as fear ("I feel frightened in the dark") and ultimately to influence the hypothalamus to release a hormone that would be an appropriate companion for the idea and its emotional corollary.

Although there is evidence that the limbic lobe is related to emotion, it now receives considerable

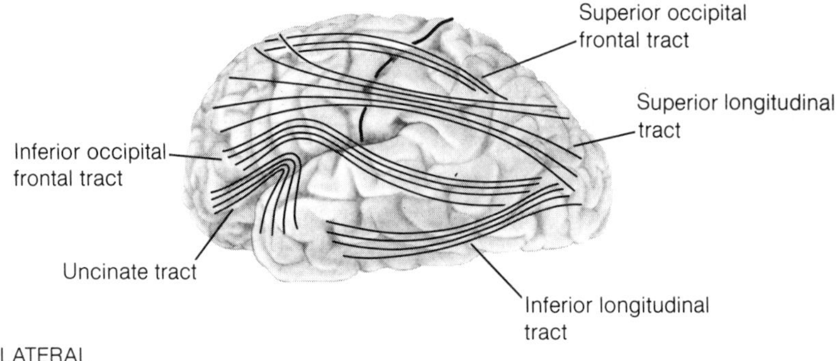

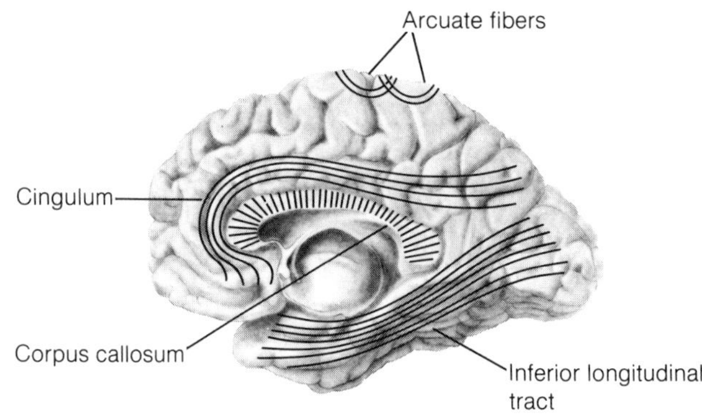

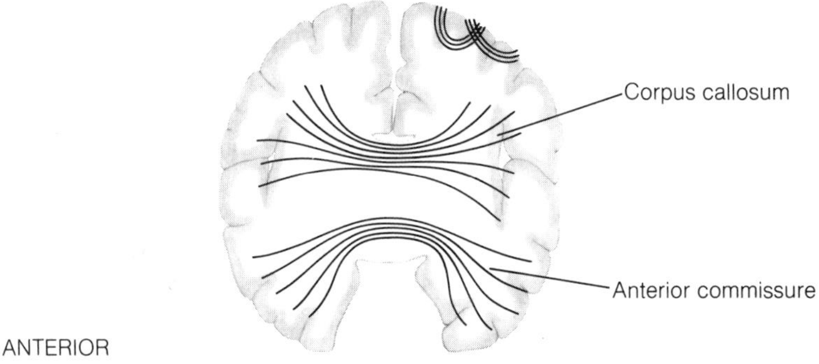

FIGURE 3.11. Connections between various regions of the cortex.

attention for the role that it plays in memory. For example, the perirhinal area (bordering the neocortex) is thought to be involved in recognition memory, the hippocampus in spatial memory, and the amygdala in emotional memory.

Basal Ganglia

The **basal ganglia** are a collection of nuclei lying mainly beneath the anterior regions of the neocortex (Figure 3.13). They include the **putamen**

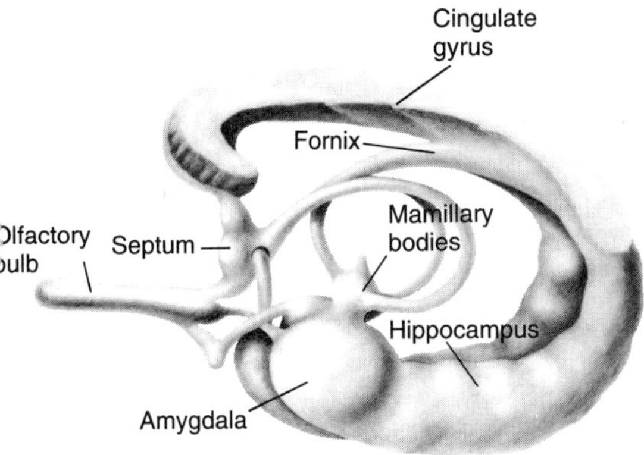

FIGURE 3.12. Model of the human limbic system and its major structures. (After Hamilton, 1976.)

(shell), the **globus pallidus** (pale globe), the **caudate nucleus** (tailed nucleus), and the **amygdala** (almond). These structures form a circuit with the cortex. The caudate nucleus receives projections from all areas of the neocortex and then projects through the putamen and globus pallidus to the thalamus and from there to the motor areas of the cortex. The basal ganglia also

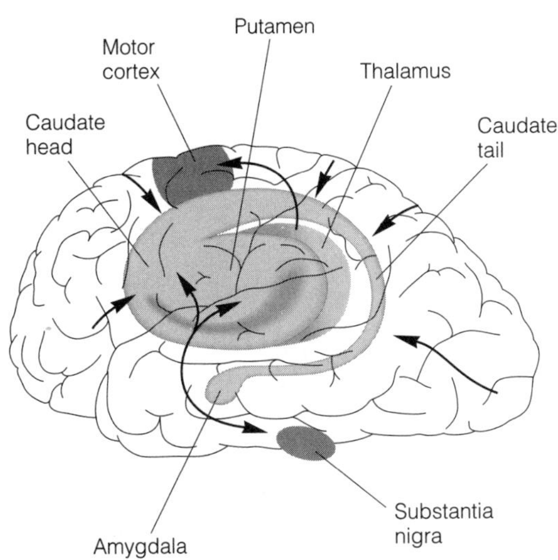

FIGURE 3.13. Relation between the basal ganglia and the cortex. Arrows indicate theoretical projections of various areas into basal ganglia structures.

have reciprocal connections with the midbrain, especially with a nucleus called the **substantia nigra** (black area). This projection provides the chemical dopamine to the basal ganglia; when dopamine is lost, a motor disorder called Parkinson's disease results.

The basal ganglia historically have been described as having three functions: (1) Damage to different portions of the basal ganglia can produce changes in posture, increases or decreases in muscle tone, and abnormal movements such as twitches, jerks, and tremors, and so the ganglia are thought to be involved in motor functions. (2) As a result of the kinds of deficits that occur, it is also thought that the basal ganglia sequence movements into a smoothly executed response, as occurs during talking. (3) The basal ganglia are also thought to support stimulus-response or habit learning.

The Thalamus

The thalamus can be divided into two areas, the ventral and dorsal thalami. The ventral thalamus provides a general input into the neocortex that may modulate the activity of the neocortex. The dorsal thalamus, or thalamus proper, is composed of a number of nuclei, each of which projects to a specific area of the neocortex, as shown in Figure 3.14. These nuclei route information from three sources to the cortex. (1) One group of nuclei relays information from sensory systems to their appropriate targets. For example, the lateral geniculate body (LGB) receives visual projections; the medial geniculate body (MGB) receives auditory projections; and the ventral-posterior lateral nuclei (VPL) receive touch, pressure, pain, and temperature projections from the body. In turn, the lateral geniculate body projects to area 17, the medial geniculate body projects to area 41, and the ventral posterior lateral nuclei project to Brodmann's areas 1, 2, and 3. The olfactory system has a projection through the dorsal medial nucleus (DM) to the neocortex. (2) Some nuclei relay information between cortical areas. A large area of the posterior cortex sends projections to and receives projections back from the pulvinar

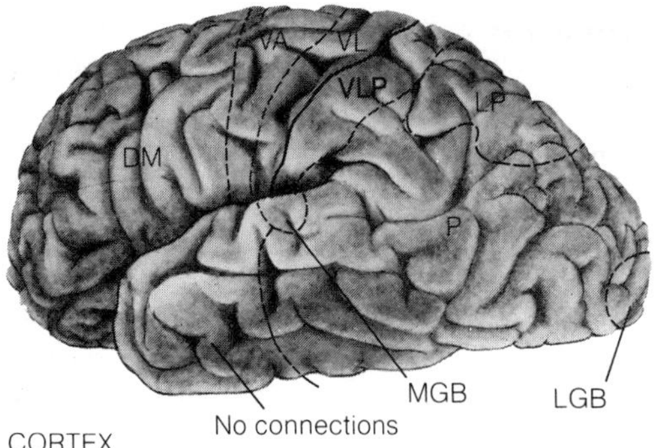

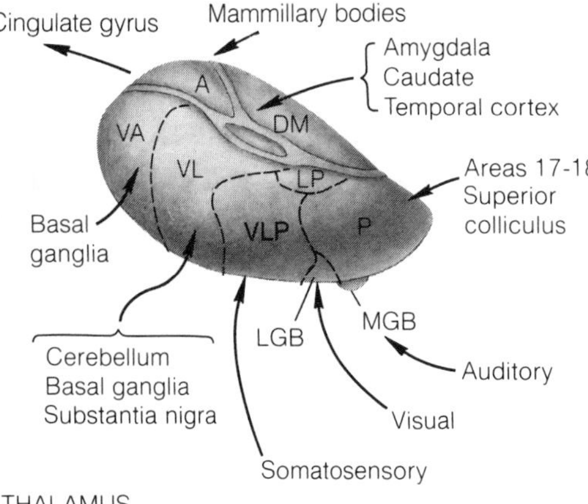

FIGURE 3.14. Relation between thalamic nuclei and various areas of the cortex to which they project. The arrows indicate the sources of input and output from the thalamus: anterior nucleus (A), dorsal medial nucleus (DM), ventral anterior nucleus (VA), ventral lateral nucleus (VL), lateral posterior nucleus (LP), ventral lateral posterior nucleus (VLP), pulvinar (P), lateral geniculate body (LGB), medial geniculate body (MGB).

(P). (3) The limbic cortex, basal ganglia, and cerebellum relay their projections to the cortex through the thalamus. The limbic system projects to the frontal cortex through DM, the basal ganglia project to the motor cortex through the ventral anterior nucleus (VA), and the cerebellum projects to the motor cortex through the ventral lateral nucleus (VL). This anatomy makes it clear that almost all the information that the cortex receives is first relayed through the thalamus.

THE CROSSED BRAIN

One of the most peculiar features of the organization of the brain is that each of its symmetrical halves responds to sensory stimulation from the contralateral side of the body or sensory world and controls the musculature on the contralateral side of the body (Figure 3.15). The visual system achieves this effect by crossing half the fibers of the optic tract and by reversing the image through the lens of the eye. Nearly all the fibers of the motor and somatosensory system cross. Projections from each ear go to both hemispheres, but there is substantial evidence that auditory excitation from one ear has a preferential route to the

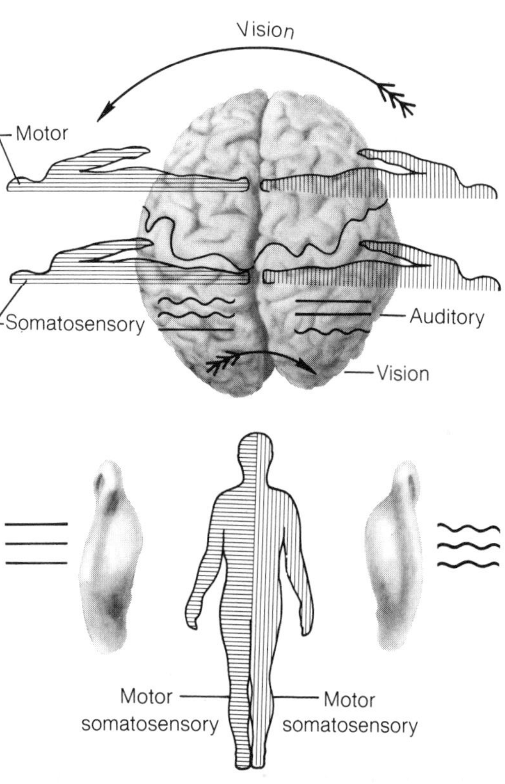

FIGURE 3.15. Schematic of the human brain from a dorsal view showing the projection of visual, auditory, and somatosensory input to contralateral areas of the cortex and the crossed projection of the motor cortex to the contralateral side of the body.

opposite hemisphere. As a result of this arrangement, along the center of the nervous system there are numerous crossings, or **decussations,** of sensory and motor fibers. Throughout the book, details of this anatomy will be described where they are relevant to discussions of the function of each of these systems. It is sufficient to say here that because of this arrangement, damage to one side of the brain generally causes sensory and motor impairments not to the same side of the body but to the opposite side.

THE VENTRICLES

Recall that the primitive spinal cord had the form of a tube with a hollow center. Figures 3.2B and 3.2C show that the central core of the brainstem and of the mammalian brain remain hollow. This cavity is filled with cerebrospinal fluid CSF, which is produced by the **choroid plexus,** a specialized cluster of glial cells found within the cavity. The cavity is larger in some portions of its length than in others; these enlargements are called ventricles. In the mammalian brain there are four ventricles, numbered I to IV, corresponding to the layout in Figure 1.2C. It is conventional to call the lateral ventricles the first (I) and second (II) ventricles, the ventricle in the diencephalon the third ventricle (III), and the ventricle in the metencephalon and myelencephalon the fourth ventricle (IV). The ventricle that was in the mesencephalon of the brainstem has become constricted and is called the cerebral aqueduct. The ventricles are distributed in the human brain exactly as in the mammalian brain.

BLOOD SUPPLY

The brain receives its blood supply from two **internal carotid arteries** and two **vertebral arteries,** one pair of which courses up each side of the neck. The internal carotid arteries enter the skull at the base of the brain, branching off into a number of smaller arteries and two major arteries, the **anterior cerebral artery** and the **middle cerebral artery,** which irrigate the anterior and middle portions of the cortex. The vertebral arteries enter at the base of the brain and then join together to form the basilar artery. After branching off into several smaller arteries that irrigate the cerebellum, the basilar artery gives rise to the **posterior cerebral artery,** which irrigates the medial temporal lobe and the posterior occipital lobe.

The distribution zones of the anterior, middle, and posterior cerebral arteries are shown in Figure 3.16. Note that if the hand is placed so that the wrist is on the artery trunk, the extended digits will give an approximate representation of the area of the cortex that is irrigated. These arteries irrigate not only the cortex but also subcortical structures. Thus, a disruption of blood flow to one of these arteries has serious consequences for subcortical as well as cortical structures. As we shall see in later chapters, the occurrence of both cortical and subcortical damage following vascular accident (stroke) is a major reason that studying stroke victims is such a difficult way to determine brain function.

The veins of the brain are classified as external and internal cerebral veins and cerebellar veins. The venous flow does not follow the course of corresponding arteries but instead follows a pattern of its own, eventually flowing into a system of venous sinuses, or cavities, that drain the dura mater.

PROTECTION

The brain and spinal cord are supported and protected from injury and infection in four ways. (1) The brain is enclosed in a thick bone, the skull, and the spinal cord is encased in a series of interlocking bony vertebrae. (2) Within these bony cases are three membranes: the outer *dura mater* (from the Latin, meaning hard mother), a tough double layer of collagenous fiber enclosing the brain in a kind of loose sack; the middle *arachnoid* (from the Greek, meaning resembling a spider's web), a very thin sheet of delicate collagenous connective tissue that follows the contours of the

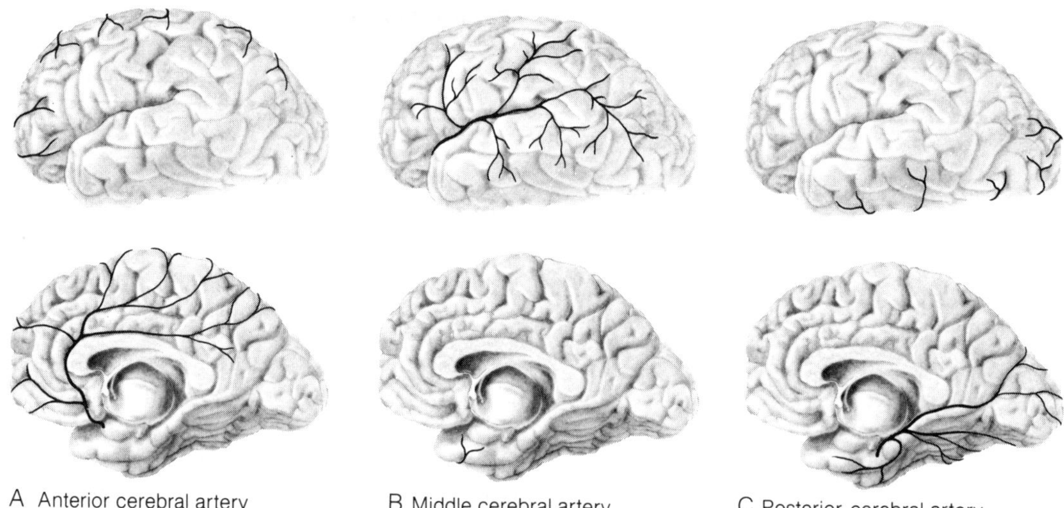

FIGURE 3.16. Distribution of the major cerebral arteries in the hemispheres: *top,* lateral view; *bottom,* medial view. Note that if you align your hand so that your wrist represents the artery, the extended digits will outline the area of cortex to which blood is distributed by each artery.

brain; and the inner *pia mater* (from the Latin, meaning soft mother), which is a moderately tough membrane of connective-tissue fibers made from reticular, elastic, and collagenous fibers that clings to the surface of the nervous tissue. (3) The brain is cushioned from shock and sudden changes of pressure by the cerebrospinal fluid, which fills the ventricles inside the brain and circulates around the brain beneath the arachnoid layer, in the subarachnoid space. This fluid is a colorless solution of sodium chloride and other salts and is made by a plexus of cells that protrudes into each ventricle. The CSF is made continually and flows from the ventricles, circulates around the brain, and is then absorbed by the venous sinuses of the dura mater. If the outflow is blocked, as occurs in a condition in infants called hydrocephalus, the ventricles enlarge in response to CSF pressure and produce an enlarged skull. The condition can be ameliorated by draining the ventricles through a tube. Although it is unlikely that the CSF nourishes the brain, it may play a role in excreting metabolic wastes from the brain. (4) The brain is protected from many chemical substances circulating in the rest of the body by the **blood-brain barrier.** This barrier consists of glial cells that are wrapped around blood vessels in such a way that access from the blood to the brain is prevented for many molecules.

REFERENCES

Brodmann, K. *Vergleichende Lokalisationlehr der Grosshirnrinde in ihren Prinzipien dargestellt auf Grund des Zellenbaues.* Leipzig: J. A. Barth, 1909.

Curtis, B. A., S. Jacobson, and E. M. Marcus. *An Introduction to the Neurosciences.* Philadelphia: Saunders, 1972.

Elliott, H. *Textbook of Neuroanatomy.* Philadelphia: Lippincott, 1969.

Everett, N. B. *Functional Neuroanatomy.* Philadelphia: Lea and Febiger, 1965.

Hamilton, L. W. *Basic Limbic System Anatomy of the Rat.* New York and London: Plenum, 1976.

Herrick, C. J. *Brains of Rats and Men.* Chicago: University of Chicago Press, 1926.

MacLean, P. D. Psychosomatic disease and the "visceral

brain'": Recent developments bearing on the Papez theory of emotion. *Psychosomatic Medicine* 11:338–353, 1949.

Papez, J. W. A proposed mechanism of emotion. *Archives of Neurology and Psychiatry* 38:724–744, 1937.

Passingham, R. E. Brain size and intelligence in man. *Brain Behavior and Evolution* 16:253–270, 1979.

Penfield, W., and E. Boldrey. Somatic motor and sensory representation in the cerebral cortex as studied by electrical stimulation. *Brain* 60:389–443, 1958.

Penfield, W., and H. H. Jasper. *Epilepsy and the Functional Anatomy of the Human Brain*. Boston: Little, Brown, 1954.

Ranson, S. W., and S. L. Clark. *The Anatomy of the Nervous System*. Philadelphia: Saunders, 1959.

Sarnat, H. B., and M. G. Netsky. *Evolution of the Nervous System*. New York: Oxford University Press, 1974.

Truex, R. C., and M. B. Carpenter. *Human Neuroanatomy*. Baltimore: Williams and Wilkins, 1969.

chapter four

4

Cellular Organization of the Nervous System

When male Grayling butterflies are ready to copulate, they fly upward toward females passing overhead. The male's response to females is not unerringly accurate, because sometimes the males fly toward other passing objects. This fact suggested to the ethologist Tinbergen that the most effective stimulus for releasing the male's approach response could be discovered with controlled experiments. Tinbergen made model butterflies, attached them to the line of a fishing rod, and "flew" them to determine which were the most effective in attracting males. Although the females are brightly colored and the males can see color, it was not an important feature of the stimulus. The males were attracted by dark, large, and irregularly moving stimuli. Furthermore, these characteristics were mutually reinforcing, which suggested to Tinbergen that the nervous system of male butterflies has a "pooling station" that integrates the different features of the stimulating object.

Tinbergen's experiments, although done with no knowledge or study of the butterfly's nervous system, still gave clues about how that system must work; thus, they are an example of excellent behavioral research. But knowledge of how the process of integration takes place involves knowing both the anatomical basis of the pooling station and its physiological activity. This story is applicable to neuropsychology. Much can be learned about people's behavior through careful observations and controlled experiments, but detailed knowledge of how the nervous system controls behavior is found in the study of the structure of cells and how they work. The following sections give a brief description of (1) the physical features of neurons and the techniques used to study them, and (2) the electrical activity of neurons and the techniques used to record their activity.

THE NEURON'S STRUCTURE

Neurons are cells that act as the integrating units of the nervous system, and although they share many characteristics of other cells in the body, they also have special characteristics that help them perform their functions.

Here are some generalizations about neurons and their functions. Neurons in the brain, once formed, do not regenerate, and unless they suffer lethal damage, most live as long as the person in which they are found. Each neuron is separated from physical contact with other neurons; it communicates across this separation using a language that is chemical. Neurons vary enormously in size and shape, the differences bearing evidence of each neuron's particular adaptation to its specialized function. Neurons are aggregated into communities, or nuclei, each of which makes a special contribution to behavior. Neurons change their behavior with experience: they learn, remember, and forget. Neurons can malfunction, causing disruptions in normal behavior. During development, far more neurons are created than will ultimately survive, and so cell death is a pronounced developmental stage in sculpting the adult brain. Neurons that leave the central nervous system (CNS), such as sensory neurons and motor neurons, retain the capacity to regenerate. In adults, the stem cells that originally gave rise to the brain's cells remain and retain the ability to generate new cells.

Figure 4.1 is a schematic drawing of a neuron. The neuron is enclosed in a specialized membrane. It has a **cell body,** or **soma** (Latin for body), in which there is a **nucleus** and other organelles. The size of the neuron is increased by branching filaments called **dendrites** (from the Greek, meaning tree) on which there are many

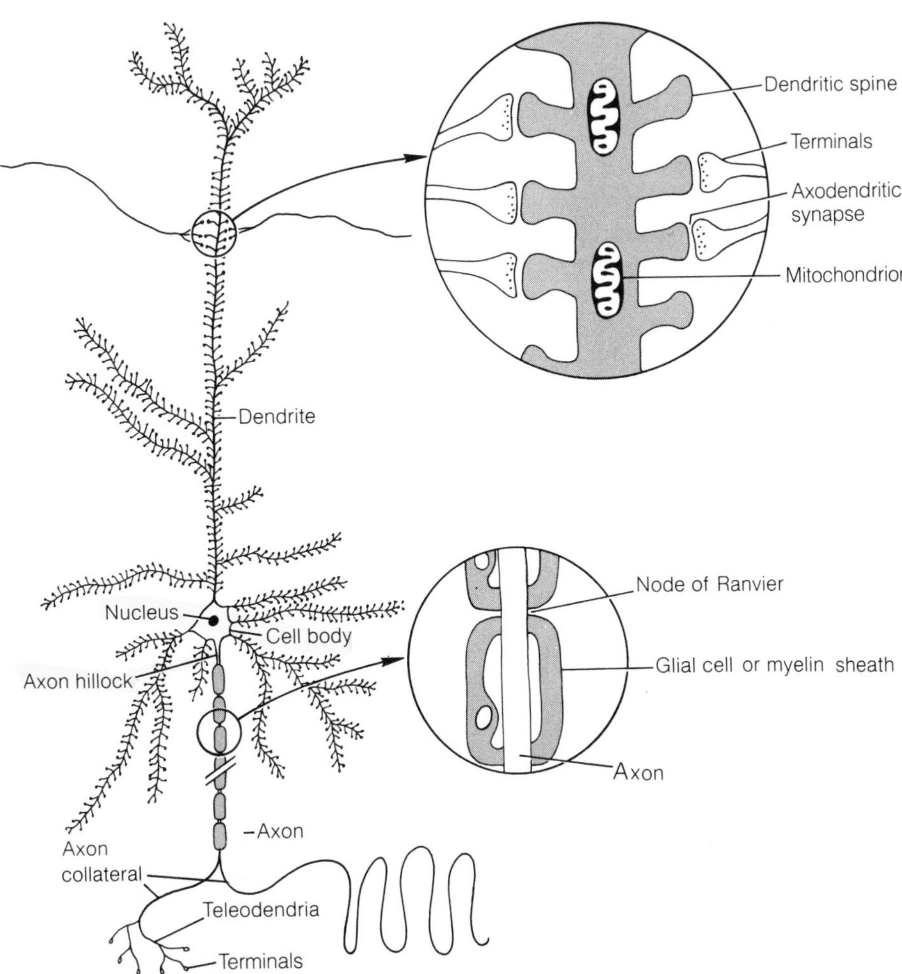

FIGURE 4.1. A typical neuron, showing some of its major physical features.

dendritic spines. The dendritic spines receive terminals or synapses from other neurons. The neuron has one process called an **axon** (from the Greek, meaning axle) that begins at an expansion of the cell wall called the **axon hillock.** The axon may divide into a number of **teleodendria,** each of which ends in a synapse. The axon is frequently coated with glial cells that make an insulating jacket or **myelin** sheath, leaving the axon exposed only at the glial junctions or **nodes of Ranvier.**

Neurons work in the following way (Figure 4.2). The dendrites collect information from many other neurons in the form of a change in electrical charge. When this charge exceeds a certain threshold, an electrical impulse beginning at the axon hillock is sent down the axon to its synapses. Since the impulse can only travel on the exposed membrane, it jumps from one node of Ranvier to the next. The synapses release a chemical known as a **transmitter substance** onto other cells, thereby changing their electrical charge and thus passing along the information. (The word "information" is used loosely to mean that we believe the activity of the cell is meaningful with respect to the behavior of the animal.)

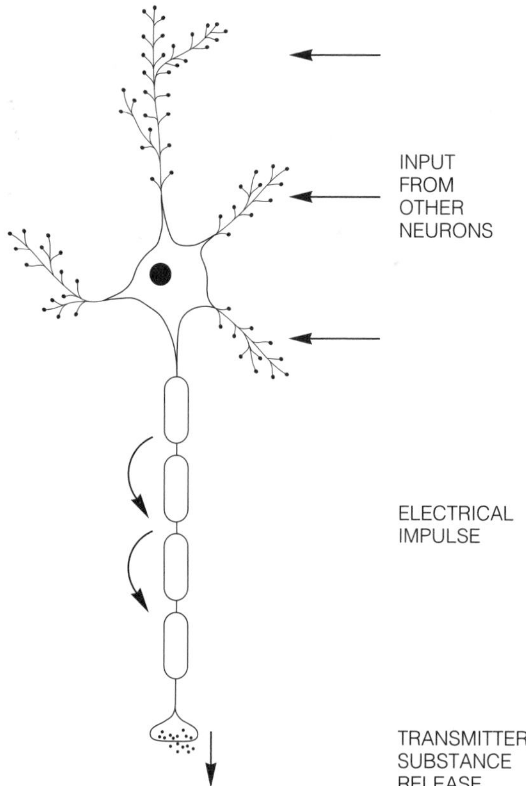

FIGURE 4.2. Sequence of steps in information conduction by a neuron. The input from other neurons produces an electrical charge on the dendrites that results in an action potential at the axon hillock. The action potential travels down the axon to release a transmitter substance at the synapse.

The Cell Membrane

The cell membrane surrounds the entire cell and consists of a double layer of molecules (Figure 4.3). Each molecule has a head and two tails. The heads are attracted to the water in the intracellular space and the tails are repelled by water, so the heads face outward and the tails inward. The membrane is semipermeable—that is, it acts as a barrier to the passage of many substances but allows a few substances to pass. Embedded within

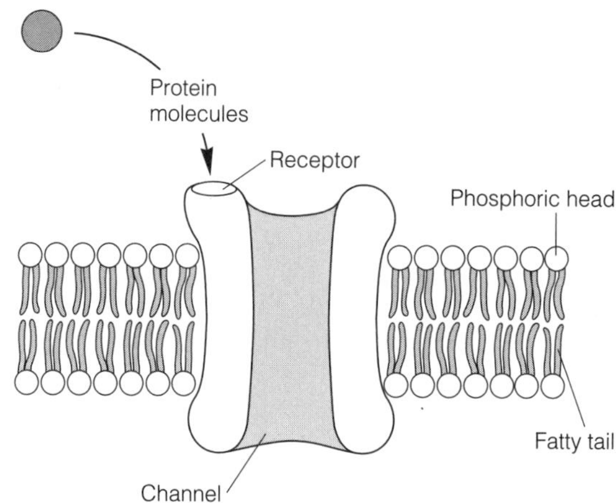

FIGURE 4.3. The cell membrane is made of bipolar molecules with heads pointing out and tails pointing in. Protein molecules are embedded in the membrane; these can contain receptors upon which chemicals can act and channels through which substances can pass.

the membrane are proteins. The proteins can contain **receptors** on which various chemicals can act or **channels** that allow substances to enter the cell, or they can actively transport substances across the cell membrane. Thus, the properties of the membrane and of the proteins allow the importing and exporting of substances and the changing of electrical charge.

The Cell Body

The cell body is the area of cytoplasm or semifluid substance filling the space outlined by the membrane. The cell body contains a variety of substances that determine its structure and function. The major physical features of the cell body are illustrated in Figure 4.4. An important function of the cell body and its constituents is the manufacture and transportation of proteins and other substances. Some of these proteins are destined to be secreted as transmitter substances, and others are required to maintain the cell.

The Nucleus

Each cell contains a nucleus, within which are **chromosomes** and a **nucleolus.** The chromosomes are composed of **deoxyribonucleic acid (DNA)**, which is the genetic material of the cell. The DNA contains the code for controlling the growth and development of the cell into its mature form. Once the cell is mature, it continues to produce the protein necessary to maintain its structure and to participate in its communication process. The cell can also respond to external signals (for example, hormones) to change its structure and function to enable new behaviors. The nucleolus produces material called **ribosomal ribonucleic acid (rRNA)**, which participates in the formation of protein.

The Endoplasmic Reticulum, Golgi Apparatus, and Lysomes

Extending throughout the cytoplasm is a network of membranelike tissue called the **endoplasmic reticulum (ER)**. Some ribosomes become attached to the ER, giving it a rough appearance, and so this part is called the rough ER. The rough ER is thought to make protein destined for export from the cell. The remaining part is called the smooth ER. When cells were first examined with a light microscope, a dense accumulation of ma-

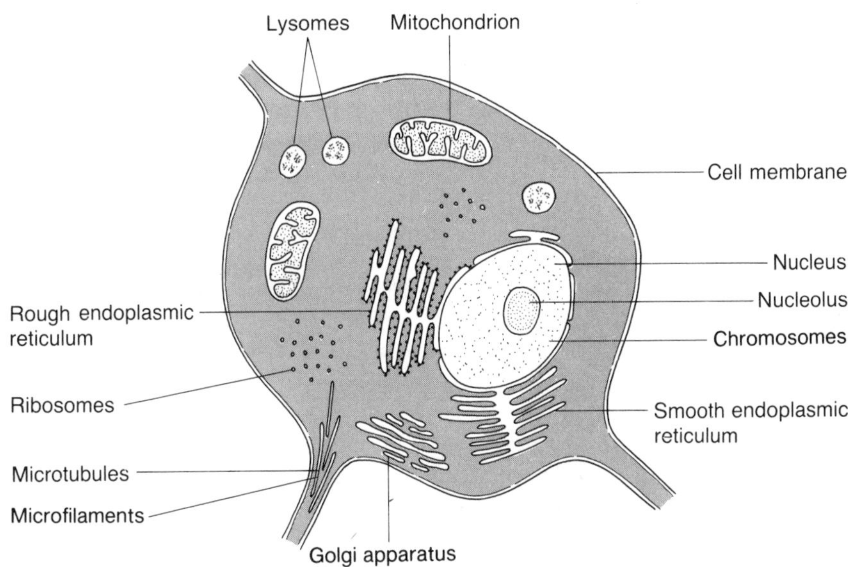

FIGURE 4.4. A typical cell body, showing some of its major features.

terial was seen around the nucleus. This was called **Nissl substance.** This substance had a great affinity for certain dyes, and so **Nissl stains** became very commonly used to stain nerve cells for microscopic examination. When the electron microscope was developed, examination of the Nissl substance showed that it was in fact rough ER. So Nissl stains allow the cell body to be seen because they stain its rich deposits of protein.

Examination of the cell with a light microscope shows a clump of material named the **Golgi apparatus.** Examination of the Golgi apparatus with an electron microscope shows it to be clusters of smooth ER that are thought to collect proteins from the rough ER and cover them with a membrane so that they form granules. The granules are transported to other parts of the cell or are exported from it.

The cell body contains *organelles* of various sizes that are shaped like sacks. These are called **lysomes** (from the Greek *lyso-,* meaning dissolution). Lysomes contain enzymes that degrade a wide variety of substances originating both inside and outside the cell. Lysomes may leave a residue called **lipofuscin granules,** which appear in cells in increasing concentration with aging.

Mitochondria

Most of the processes of the cell require energy, which is manufactured by the **mitochondria** (from the Greek *mito,* thread, and *chondrion,* granule). They have a characteristic cigar shape, with a smooth outer membrane and a folded internal one. It is thought that the mitochondria were originally primitive organisms that were incorporated into cells in a symbiotic relationship. Brain cells derive all their energy from glucose, which is extracted from the blood as it is needed (there are no mechanisms for glucose storage in the brain, and so deprivation of glucose results in rapid cell death). The mitochondria take up glucose and break it down to form **adenosine triphosphate (ATP)**, which is used by other components of the cell as an energy source. Another function of mitochondria is to store calcium, which is used in regulating the release of transmitter substances from the terminals. **Cytochrome oxydase** is a mitochondrial enzyme that can be stained. Areas of the brain that are metabolically very active have many mitochondria and thus can be highlighted with cytochrome oxydase staining procedures.

Microtubules and Microfilaments

Cells contain various small fiberlike structures in both the cell body and the cell processes. **Microtubules** of various sizes are thought to be involved in the transport of proteins from the cell body to the distal parts of the cell (orthograde transport) or from the distal cell elements to the cell body (retrograde transport). The substances are thought to be carried on the surface of the microtubules. There seem to be two transport systems: in one, some proteins can be seen to travel at 1 mm per day; in the second, other proteins travel at 100 mm per day or faster. These transport systems have been exploited to label neurons and their connections. A variety of chemicals and fluorescent dyes are carried by **microfilaments,** and if these agents are injected into tissue they will be picked up and transported on the microfilaments, thus labeling the cell when it is subsequently viewed with a microscope equipped with filters sensitive to these substances. The function of microfilaments is uncertain, but they may be involved in controlling the shape, movement, or fluidity of the cytoplasm.

Production of Protein

Proteins are essential to the cell's structure and function, and the structures described above participate in their formation (Figure 4.5). **Messenger RNA (mRNA)** is released into the cytoplasm by the DNA, whereas rRNA is released by the nucleolus. They combine into a polyribosome that forms the template for making protein. The protein attaches to the Golgi apparatus, where it is enclosed in a membrane. The protein is then exported to perform a variety of functions, such as contributing to the structure and function of the cell membrane, and it is also transported on the surface of microtubules to contribute to the structure and function of the cell membrane.

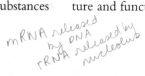

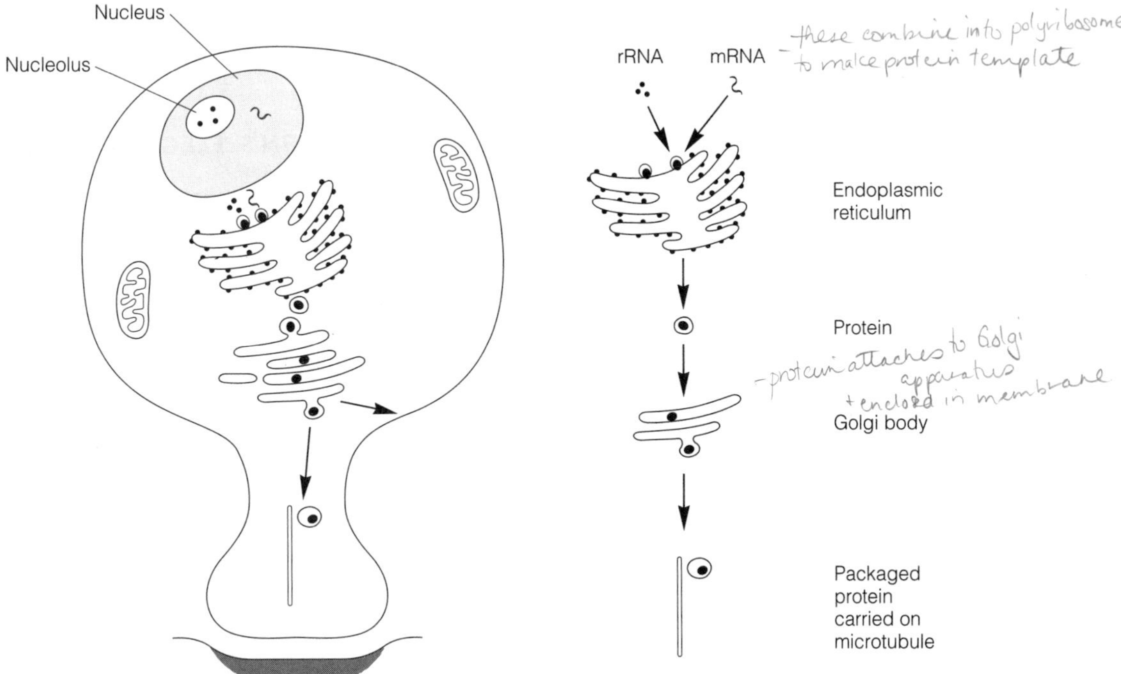

FIGURE 4.5. Steps in the formation and transport of protein.

The Dendrites

Dendrites are extensions of the cell body that increase the surface area and are specialized to receive information from other cells. The number of dendrites varies from neuron to neuron, with some having a few, others more than 20. Each dendrite can branch profusely. Dendrites vary from a few microns to millimeters in length and taper as they branch. Some dendrites have rough appendages called dendritic spines. These further expand the area of the cell and serve as locations on which the dendrites receive terminals from other cells.

A striking feature of dendrites is their ability to grow and change throughout the life of an animal. The growth of dendrites allows more connections from other neurons. These connections, in turn, may be the substrate for learning. It has been suggested that people who remain intellectually active have very long dendrites in old age (so there is some consolation in becoming a professor). By contrast, diseases that produce mental retardation or senility are associated with reduced dendritic length or spine number.

The Axon

The axon originates in the cell body at a transition point called the axon hillock. It transmits information that it receives from the dendrites and the cell to other cells. Each cell has only one axon, which can vary in length from a few microns to more than a meter. Most axons have branches called **collaterals.** At the end of the axon and its collaterals are fine terminations called teleodendria. The teleodendria end in little knobs, called terminals, which make junctions with other cells. The axons can grow new teleodendria and new terminals and so form the other half of the equation (with dendrites and spines) for mediating improved skills and learning. Because each neuron has only one axon, the cell can send only one message, but the collaterals and teleodendria allow that message to be sent to a number of destinations.

The Synapse

The synaptic terminals contain chemical substances that, when released, influence the activity of other cells. Some synaptic junctions may involve actual contact, but for most there is a small space between the terminal and its target. As illustrated by the seven inputs onto a pyramidal cell of the hippocampal formation (Figure 4.6), connections between neurons are not haphazard. Various cell groups target specific portions of a cell to which they connect. It is thought that synapses on the cell body are potentially more influential than those on the periphery because they are closer to the axon hillock from which the action potential originates.

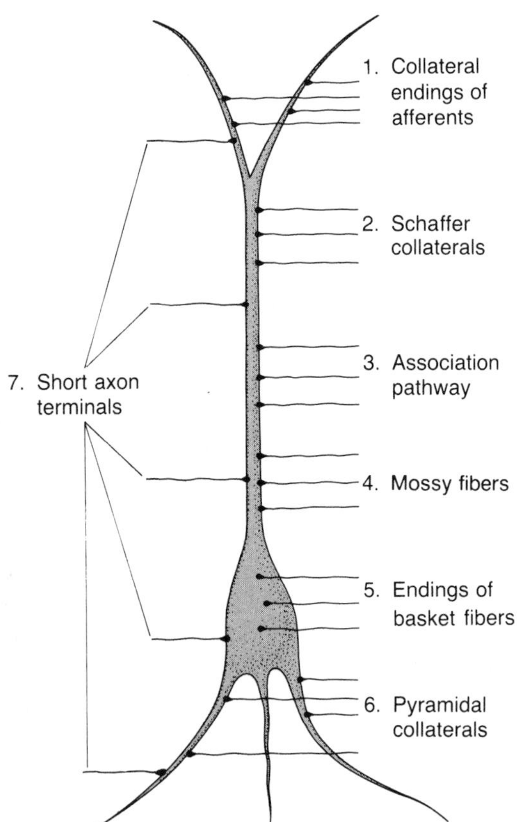

FIGURE 4.6. Segregation of inputs onto a single hippocampal pyramidal cell.

THE NEURON'S ELECTRICAL ACTIVITY

Much of the pioneering research done on the neuron's electrical activity, such as the work of Hodgkin and Huxley, used the giant axon of the squid, on the recommendation of the biologist Young. This axon measures up to a millimeter in diameter and is a hundred times larger than the axons of human nerve cells. The squid's axon is used to contract muscles that squirt water out the end of the squid's body, thereby propelling it through the water. Because effective propulsion requires all the muscles of the body to contract at the same time, the largest axons, which conduct information the fastest, connect to the most distant muscles. Because of its size, the giant axon is easily removed from the squid by dissection and is easy to use in experiments on electrical conduction in axons.

The Resting Potential

Neurons have a charge across their membranes. If the charge across the membrane is measured with an oscilloscope (a voltmeter with a TV screen for display) and if the membrane is otherwise left undisturbed, this charge will remain relatively constant at about -70 millivolts (mV) (the level varies between -55 and -90 mV in different animals). This charge is called the **resting potential,** and it is graphically illustrated in Figure 4.7. The following sections describe how the resting potential is produced and maintained.

Concentration and Electrostatic Gradients. Imagine the following experiment. If table salt is put into a glass of water, it will dissolve into sodium ions (Na^+) and chlorine ions (Cl^-). The sodium ions carry a positive charge and the chlorine ions a negative charge. Inequalities in the concentration of the ions in different places will cause the ions to flow down their **concentration gradient** until they are equally distributed. Inequalities in the

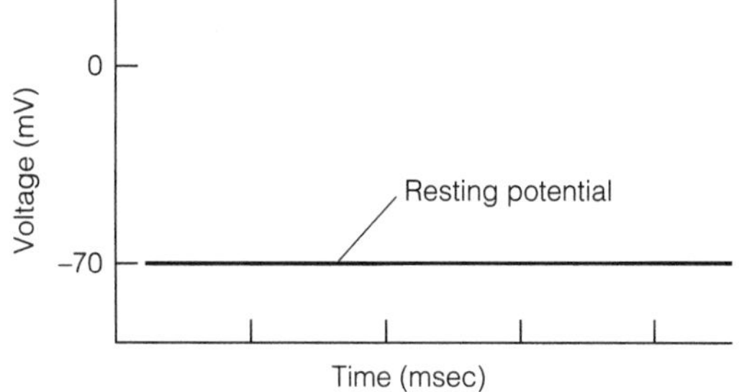

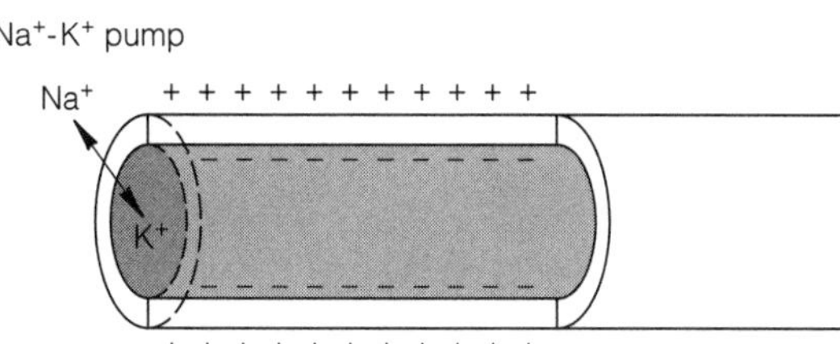

FIGURE 4.7. The nerve membrane, because of its permeability and through the action of the Na^+-K^+ pump, accumulates a charge, the inside of the membrane being negative with respect to the outside. This charge is about − 70 mV and is called the resting potential.

charges will cause the ions to flow down their **electrostatic gradient** until the charge is equal everywhere. In this example, the concentration and the charge of the ions are different properties of the same thing, and so the concentration of sodium and of chlorine will be equal everywhere and so will the electrostatic charge.

If a membrane, constructed of a material that prevents the ions from passing through, is placed down the center of the glass, then salt placed on one side of the membrane will stay there. If the membrane is modified so that only sodium can get through, the result is very interesting. The sodium ions will go through the barrier and attempt to diffuse down their concentration gradient to be distributed equally throughout the water on both sides of the membrane. To do so, the sodium ions would leave the chlorine ions behind but the chlorine ions, being negatively charged, attract the positively charged sodium ions back. This creates an electrostatic gradient for sodium that is different from its concentration gradient. The sodium ions reach a compromise in response to these two pressures. Most remain on the original side of the membrane to neutralize the charge of the chlorine ions, but some will diffuse across the barrier. Of these, a number, still attracted by the charge of the chlorine ions, remain on the outside surface of the membrane. Thus, the membrane has sodium ions on its outside surface and chlorine ions on its inside surface, which produces a transmembrane charge. This demonstration approximates what happens across a cell membrane.

The Contribution of the Cell Membrane. The membrane of a nerve axon separates two fluid compartments, the *intracellular* and the *extracellular,* each of which contains many ions. Of these, negatively charged organic (An^-) and chlorine ions (Cl^-) and positively charged potassium (K^+) and sodium ions (Na^+) are particularly important in electrical conduction. These ions would be equally distributed on both sides of the membrane if it did not act as a barrier to their easy passage. It does this in three ways:

1. It is impermeable to An^- ions because they are simply too large to pass through it; consequently, they are retained in the intracellular fluid.

2. It is semipermeable to Na^+, K^+, and Cl^-. Normally, K^+ passes more freely than Na^+ (Na^+, although smaller than K^+, is bound more strongly to water molecules, which add to its bulk). The permeability of the membrane also changes in certain situations, allowing these ions to pass more freely through it at certain times than at others. Each of these ions has its own channel through which it passes.

3. The membrane contains a pumping system, or *Na^+-K^+* pump, which exchanges intracellular Na^+ for extracellular K^+.

As a result of these three processes, there is a negative charge on the inside of the cell relative to the outside in the range of − 75 mV.

The Contribution of K^+ Ions. The concentrations of various substances in the intracellular fluid can be used to perform the following experiment. Remove the contents from the squid's giant axon. Place its normal concentration of An^- inside it. Then place the other chemicals of the extracellular fluid on either side of the membrane. Measure the voltage across the membrane by placing electrodes connected to a voltmeter on each side of it. At first, there is no charge across the membrane, but gradually a charge develops until the inside of the membrane is negative by about -75 mV relative to the outside. After this, there is no further change.

This charge develops in the manner described in the experiment above. Most K^+ ions remain within the axon to balance the negative charge of the An^-. Some leave the cell and remain on the outer surface of the cell membrane, attracted outward by their concentration gradient and inward by the electrostatic gradient. Figure 4.8 illustrates how a small amount of K^+ on the outside of the membrane produces a voltage difference. The cloud of positive (+) charges immediately outside the surface of the membrane represents the K^+ ions that have leaked across the membrane. The negative (−) charges immediately inside represent the An^- ions that could not cross the barrier. Note that the charge difference has accumulated only on the membrane; all other intracellular and extracellular fluid is in equilibrium.

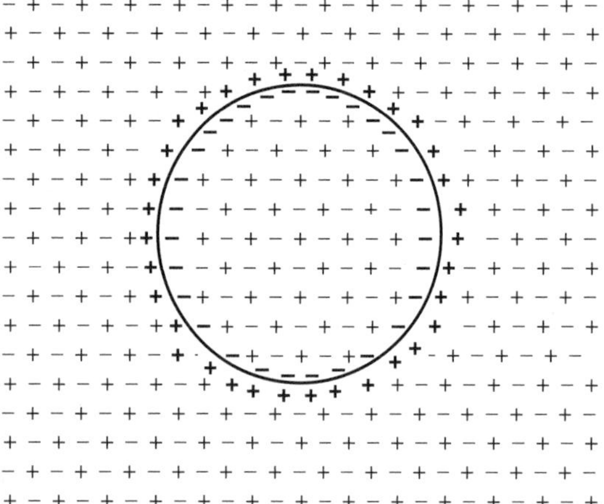

FIGURE 4.8. The net excess of positive charges outside the membrane of a nerve cell at rest represents a small fraction of the total number of ions inside and outside the cell.

Since some K^+ ions did pass through the barrier, it must contain holes large enough to let them pass but small enough to block the larger An^- ions. These holes are called *K^+ channels.* The existence of these channels has been confirmed in another way. If *tetraethylammonium (TEA)* is placed on a membrane, no K^+ ions escape; TEA attaches to and blocks the K^+ ion channels.

The Contribution of Na^+ Ions. In 1902, without performing an experiment, Julius Bernstein used an equation called the Nernst equation to predict the K^+ ion potential across the cell membrane. In the 1940s, when the experiment was performed, it only partly confirmed Bernstein's calculation. Something else was contributing to the nerve membrane charge.

The something else turned out to be Na^+ ions. Calculations of extracellular fluid concentrations show that there are more Na^+ ions in the extracellular fluid than there are in the intracellular fluid. Thus, the membrane controls the concentration of Na^+. Experimental work using TEA shows that the Na^+ ions do not pass through the K^+ ion channels, because TEA does not block their inward flow. This result suggests that Na^+ ions have their own channels, a conclusion confirmed by the finding that *tetrodotoxin (TTX)*—pufferfish poison—blocks the permeability of the membrane to Na^+ ions. As we have noted above, K^+ ions stop flowing out of the cell because their movement is opposed by the electrostatic pressure. Obviously, the inward flow of Na^+ ions can redress this situation. If there were no other checks, Na^+ ions would flow in, K^+ ions could then flow out, and the charge on the membrane would dissipate quickly.

Since the charge across the membrane does not dissipate, it is suggested that the membrane contains "pumps" that pump Na^+ ions back out of the cell. Present theory holds that there is a Na^+-K^+ pump that expels Na^+, exchanging three Na^+ ions for every two K^+ ions. The K^+ ions, of course, quickly leak back out, but the Na^+ ions apparently leak back in only slowly because the Na^+ channels are closed. The operation of the Na^+-K^+ pump requires energy, and it has been possible to demonstrate that its operation can be arrested with a metabolic poison such as ouabain.

To this point, we have not considered the contribution of Cl^-. Chlorine ions are free to cross the membrane passively. As a result, they respond to chemical and electrical gradients and do not affect the transmembrane potential established by the actively distributed Na^+ and K^+ ions.

Stimulation

The voltage on the membrane can be changed by electrically exciting the membrane or by blocking or opening channels with chemicals. Any influence or irritation that leads to a change in the voltage is called a **stimulus,** and the process, whether normal or abnormal, is called **stimulation.** In experimental situations, stimulation is usually provided by squirting chemicals onto neurons or giving brief electrical pulses to the neuron through small wires called stimulating electrodes.

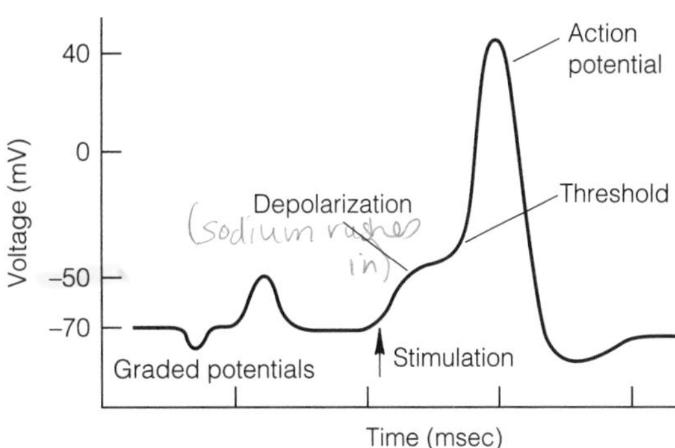

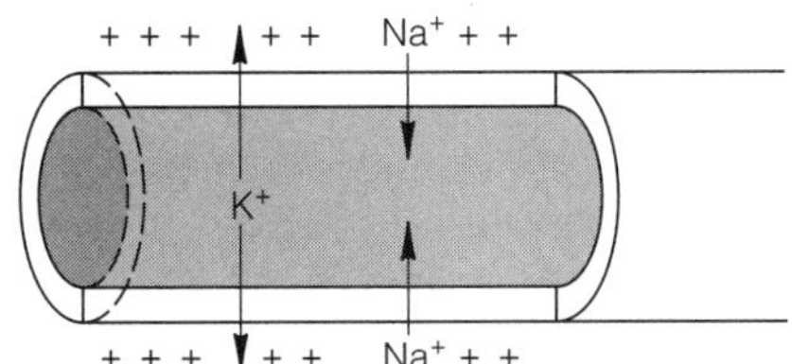

FIGURE 4.9. Stimulation of the membrane causes it to become more permeable to Na^+ ions. As a result the transmembrane potential declines, or depolarizes. At about -50 mV, its threshold, the membrane becomes completely permeable and its charge momentarily reverses. At this point K^+ ions flow out of the cell, restoring the transmembrane potential. This sequence of changes is represented by the peak on the graph called an action potential.

Graded Potentials

When an axon is stimulated, the voltage across the membrane changes. Depending on the type of stimulation, the transmembrane potential can increase or decrease (Figure 4.9). These **graded potentials** are brief, are restricted to the area of tissue stimulated, and are proportional to the intensity of stimulation. For a metaphor of a graded potential, imagine a stone dropped into a pond. Waves, proportional to the stone's size, will form around the stone's entry into the water and decay as they travel away.

If stimulation produces a change that decreases the transmembrane voltage toward 0 mV, the membrane is said to have become depolarized. If stimulation produces a change that increases the transmembrane voltage, the membrane is said to have become hyperpolarized. **Depolarization** is thought to be due to increased inward movement of Na^+ ions, whereas **hyperpolarization** is thought to be due to increased outward movement of K^+ ions or to increased inward movement of Cl^- ions.

The Action Potential

The neuron's membrane undergoes a dramatic change if stimulation is intense enough to cause the transmembrane voltage to depolarize to about -50 mV. At this voltage the membrane becomes completely permeable to Na^+, and Na^+ rushes into the cell until the voltage across the membrane falls through 0 mV and reverses to about +50 mV. The change in permeability is quite brief, about half a millisecond, after which the Na^+ channels are again closed. At the same time the membrane is also permeable to K^+ ions, which flow out of the cells balancing the inward flow of Na^+. Following this change the resting potential of the membrane is restored. The voltage at which the membrane undergoes this change is called its **threshold.** The sudden reversal of polarity and the restoration of the resting potential is called an **action potential.** The process is displayed graphically in Figure 4.9.

Gates and Channels

What triggers the action potential? The ion conductance channels for Na^+ are controlled by "gates" embedded in the channel (Figure 4.10A). These gates are sensitive to the voltage of the membrane and open when the membrane is depolarized. In Figure 4.10A, the charges across the membrane during a resting potential attract the charges on the gating molecule, thereby blocking the sodium channel. In Figure 4.10B, stimulation reverses the membrane charge. This reversal, in turn, repels the charge on the gating molecule, flipping open the gate to permit the inward flow of sodium ions. Thus, the transmembrane voltage acts as a stimulus for opening **voltage-sensitive channels** and producing an action potential.

The Nerve Impulse

When an action potential occurs in a region of the nerve membrane, it acts as a stimulus to open adjacent voltage-sensitive Na^+ channels. (These are channels that open in response to a change in voltage of the membrane.) Consequently, an action potential triggered at one end of an axon will travel along its length. (Action potentials can travel in either direction, but they normally begin at the cell body and travel away from it.) This moving action potential is called a **nerve impulse** (Figure 4.11). The rate at which the impulse travels along the axon, varying from 1 to 100 m/sec (meters per second), is quite slow, but neurons can sustain a wide range of firing rates. Usually they fire fewer than 100 times a second, but they can fire as frequently as 1000 times per second.

Saltatory Conduction

The nerve impulse does not travel at exactly the same speed in all neurons. At least two factors affect speed. One is resistance to current along the axon. Impulse speed increases as resistance decreases, and resistance is decreased most effectively by an increase in axon size. Therefore, large axons conduct at a faster rate than small ones. Were the nervous system to rely only on this factor, axons would have to be cumbersomely large.

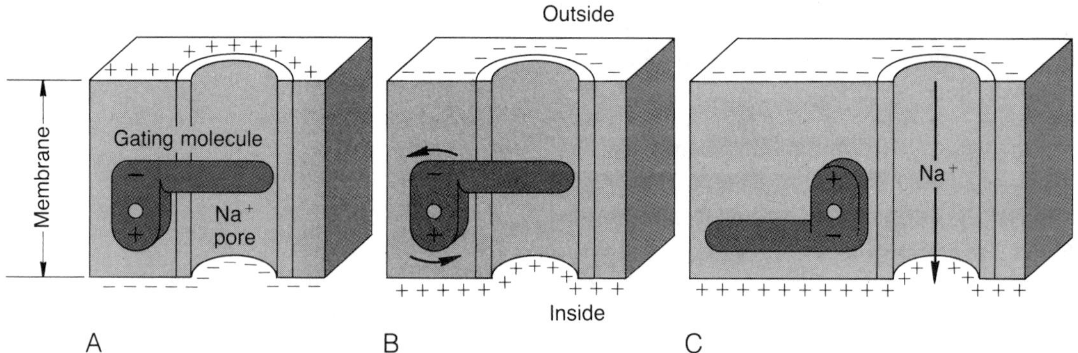

FIGURE 4.10. Hypothetical explanation for molecular events that underlie voltage-gated currents. *A.* Active membrane channel of a nerve cell at rest. *B.* Membrane changes during depolarization to open the gate. *C.* Na^+ ions freely cross the membrane.

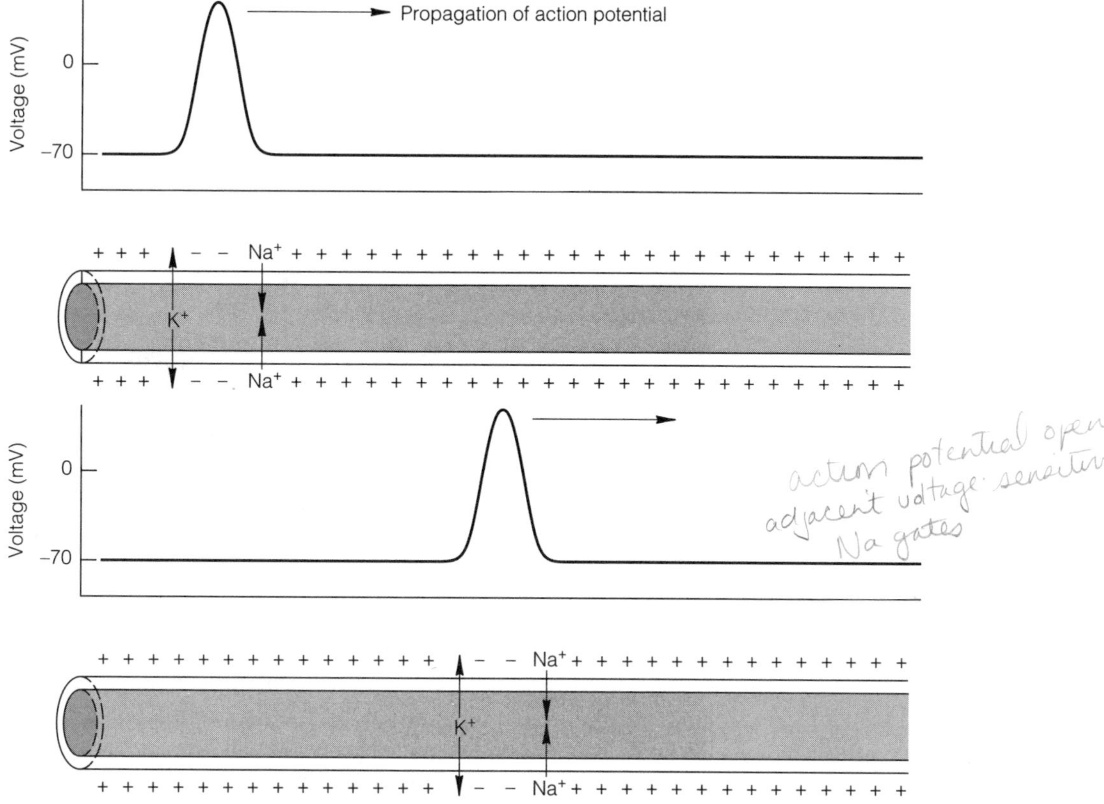

FIGURE 4.11. Because an action potential at one part of the axon opens adjacent voltage-sensitive Na^+ gates, the action potential is propagated along the axon.

Alternatively glial cells are used to speed impulse propagation.

Schwann cells in the peripheral nervous system and oligodendroglia in the central nervous system wrap around some axons, forming a compact sheath of myelin (from the Greek, meaning marrow) against the cell membrane. Between each glial cell the membrane of the axon is exposed, producing a gap called a node of Ranvier (Figure 4.12). In these myelinated axons the nerve impulse jumps along the axon from node to node, a type of conduction called **saltatory conduction** (from the Latin, meaning skip). Saltatory conduction is an extremely effective way of speeding the impulse because a small myelinated axon can conduct an impulse as rapidly as an unmyelinated axon 30 times as large.

The presence of myelin also conserves energy. Since myelin prevents current flow along most of the length of the axon, the metabolic processes required to maintain the resting potential need only be sustained at the nodes of Ranvier. Given the role of myelin, the devastating consequences of diseases that cause demyelination, such as multiple sclerosis or Guillain-Barre disease, can be appreciated.

The Origin of the Nerve Impulse

Dendrites have a membrane similar to the axon membrane and a similar resting potential, and they also undergo changes in potential when they are stimulated. But unlike axons, the dendrites do not have voltage-sensitive Na^+ channels and so

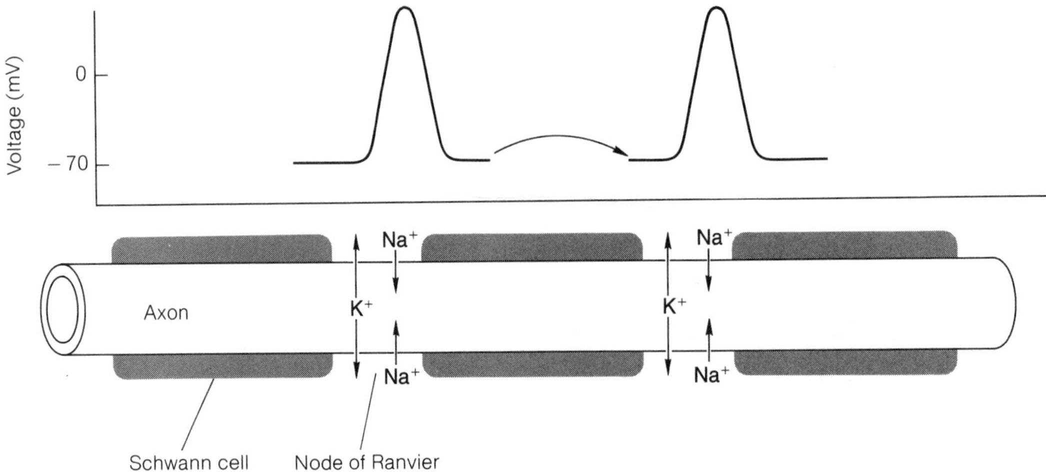

FIGURE 4.12. The nerve impulse jumps from one inter-Schwann cell space, called a node of Ranvier, to the next. This process, saltatory conduction, greatly speeds impulse transmission.

cannot produce action potentials. If a dendrite is stimulated, its voltage changes in proportion to the intensity of the stimulation; the change then spreads along the dendrite away from the point of stimulation, getting smaller with distance.

Dendritic responses have some interesting properties. If a dendrite is stimulated at two points in close proximity, the graded potentials will add; but if the two stimuli are given at widely separated points, the graded potentials will dissipate before they reach each other and will not add. Stimuli given at intermediate distances will produce additive graded potentials, but only at the points that receive the potentials from both sources. Also, the potentials will be smaller because they decay with distance. Similar rules apply when one stimulus hyperpolarizes the membrane and one depolarizes it, with the difference being that the graded potentials subtract. This tendency of adjacent graded potentials to add and subtract is called **spatial summation.**

If stimuli are given in rapid succession, the potentials will similarly add or subtract. The strength of the resulting graded potential will be determined by the strength of the two stimuli and the interval between them. If one stimulus hyperpolarizes the membrane and the other depolarizes it, the two stimuli will subtract, and the graded potential will decrease in size accordingly. This tendency of temporally adjacent graded potentials to add and subtract is called **temporal summation.**

Since there are thousands of synapses on the dendrites of a neuron, some of them exciting it and some inhibiting it, an action potential will occur only if the summed influence of the synapses is to lower the charge of the axon hillock's transmembrane to − 50 mV. Thus, the origin of axonal firing can be traced to the influence of graded potentials from the dendrites of the cell. Generally, the activity of the dendrites is constantly changing under the influence of inputs from many other cells, and only occasionally—under the influence of particular patterns of inputs—does cell firing occur.

Synaptic Transmission

Neurons communicate chiefly through the agency of the transmitters they release from their synapses. When the action potential reaches the synapse, calcium (Ca^{2+}) channels are opened in the synaptic membrane and inflowing calcium excites the release of the transmitter substance into the synaptic space. The transmitter attaches to receptors on the next neuron and, depending upon what kind of transmitter it is, depolarizes or hyperpolarizes that neuron.

THE BRAIN'S ELECTRICAL ACTIVITY

Because the activity of nerve cells has an electrochemical basis, it can be recorded with instruments sensitive to small changes in electrical activity. The several techniques for so recording the brain's electrical activity include (1) electroencephalographic (EEG) recording, (2) event-related potentials (ERP) recording, and (3) intracellular and extracellular unit recording. Relating each of these types of activity to behavior is used to determine the function of brain areas.

EEG Recording

A simple technique for recording the electrical activity of the brain was developed in the early 1930s by Hans Berger. He found that it was possible to record "brain waves" by placing a voltmeter across the skull. These waves, called **electroencephalograms (EEGs)**, have proved to be a valuable tool for studying sleep, for monitoring depth of anesthesia, for diagnosing epilepsy and brain damage, and for studying normal brain function.

To record EEG, a small metal disk is attached to the scalp to detect the electrical activity of neurons in the underlying brain area. These electrical changes are rather small, usually much less than a millivolt, but when amplified they can be displayed on an oscilloscope and written to paper on a chart recorder called an electroencephalograph.

Human EEG activity changes in a characteristic way during transitions from sleep to wakefulness (Figure 4.13). When a person is awake, the EEG pattern has a low voltage and a fast frequency. Rhythms become slower in frequency and larger in amplitude as a person goes through a transition to rest and then to sleep. Still slower waves occur during coma, anesthesia, or after brain trauma. Because of these patterns, EEG can be used to monitor sleep and waking behavior, to estimate the depth of anesthesia, to evaluate head injury, and to search for other brain abnormalities. EEG recording is routinely used for evaluation of **epilepsy.** In this condition, very abnormal spikes and waves can occur in the EEG, and these are associated with brief periods of loss of consciousness or involuntary movements. Using a number of recording electrodes and triangulation procedures, the source of the abnormal activity can be determined with EEG.

Event-Related Potentials

Event-related potentials (ERPs) consist of a brief change in the EEG signal in response to a sensory stimulus. For example, in response to a brief noise, the EEG pattern in the auditory cortex will change. The potentials are small and are hard to see in the background EEG activity, but if the stimulus is given repeatedly and the brain activity is averaged, the ERP becomes quite clear.

An example of an ERP is shown in Figure 4.14. Notice how the averaging procedure brings out the ERP's pattern. An ERP consists of a number of negative and positive waves that last for a few hundred milliseconds after the stimulus. These waves are labeled as positive (P) or negative (N) in relation to the time at which they occur; for example, P_4 is a positive wave occurring 400 msec after the auditory stimulus is given. The pattern of the ERP can be used to assess the normality of a brain area and also to analyze how it processes information. For example, an area of the brain that analyzes nouns will produce ERPs only when a subject hears nouns.

Single Cell Recording

If small insulated wires, or pipettes containing an ionized conducting solution, are inserted into the brain so that their tips are placed in or near a nerve cell, the changes in a single cell's electrical potential—that is, its activity—can be recorded relative to some indifferent electrode or ground. The technique requires amplification of the sig-

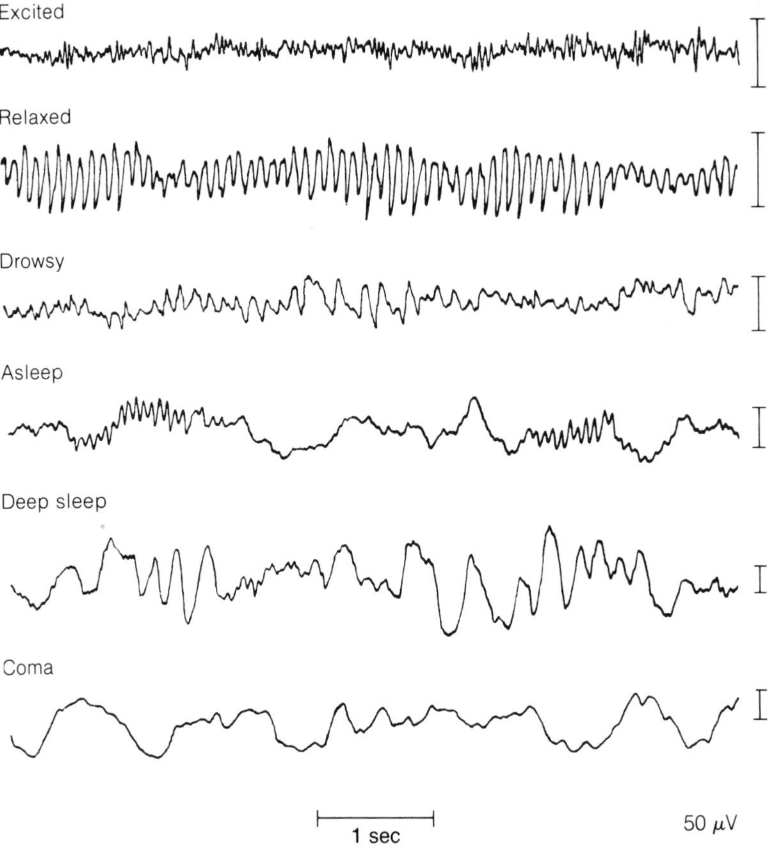

FIGURE 4.13. Characteristic EEG recorded during various behavioral states in humans. (After Penfield and Jasper, 1954.)

nal, which is displayed on an oscilloscope or played through a loudspeaker so that cell firing is heard as a beep or pop (when people talk about cell firing they are talking about these sounds). Examples of some action potentials that occur in rhythmic bursts are shown in Figure 4.15. Displayed along with the action potentials are graded potentials from the same cell. Notice how the rhythmic firing occurs each time the cell membrane depolarizes. The unit recording technique is the only way to determine what an individual cell is doing during a given behavior.

BRAIN IMAGING

The modern era of brain imaging began in the early 1970s, when Allan Cormack and Godfrey Hounsfield independently developed the principle of X-ray **computerized tomography,** usually referred to as the **CT scan.** This technique takes advantage of the fact that X rays reflect the relative density of the tissue through which they pass. Since areas rich in cells and areas rich in axons will have different densities, the CT scan can record the conformations of tissue. In a stan-

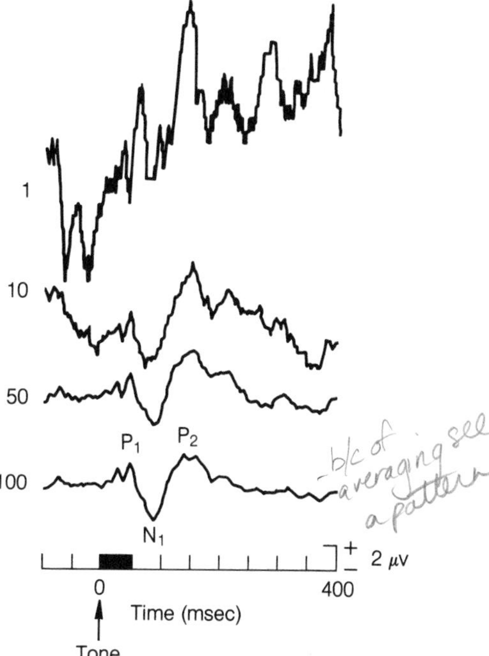

FIGURE 4.14. An illustration of the averaging process for auditory-cortex potentials. The number of repeated stimulations (a tone) included in the waveform is indicated on the left.

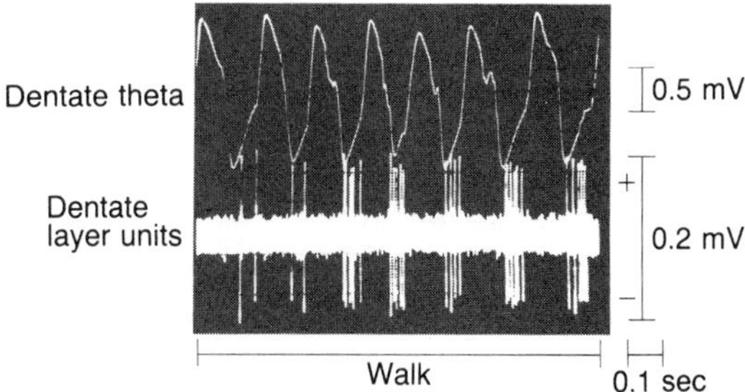

FIGURE 4.15. Dentate layer cells produce slow graded potentials called a theta rhythm, with action potentials occurring at the negative peak of the rhythm. The waves were recorded extracellularly from the hippocampus of a hopping rabbit. (Courtesy B. H. Bland.)

dard two-dimensional X ray such like that used to assess a bone fracture, the different brain structures are overlapping and are under very dense bone, and so it is very difficult to visualize individual brain structures. Cormack and Hounsfield recognized that if you pass a narrow X-ray beam through the same object at many different angles, it is possible to use computing and mathematical techniques to create a visual image of the brain. The development of the CT scan was remarkable in two respects. First, it changed the practice of neurology because there was a new way to look inside the head without using unpleasant, often dangerous, procedures. Second, the advent of the CT scan provoked others to use the clever mathematics and computer strategies to develop other types of image reconstructions (Figure 4.16). This has led to the development of several new imaging procedures.

Positron emission tomography (**PET**) was the first post-CT development. It became clear that if it were possible to reconstruct the density, and hence the anatomy, or neural areas, then it would also be possible to detect the location of a previously administered radioisotope. Thus, rather than pass X rays through the head, it is possible to detect positrons that are emitted from the brain. Positrons can be introduced into the brain by having subjects ingest glucose that contains a very short acting radioisotope of carbon, nitrogen, oxygen, or fluorine. The glucose is transported by the blood to the brain. The idea is that areas of the brain that are active will use more glucose, and hence become more radioactive, than less active areas. The radioisotopes have no deleterious effects because they have a very short life in the brain, on the order of minutes. One of the problems with PET is that the brain is always active, so it is necessary to subtract the brain's normal background activity from the activity measured during the test. A variation of the PET is **single-photon emission computerized tomography** (**SPECT**). SPECT takes advantage of the fact that certain commercially available tracers also emit photons, but they are not radioactive.

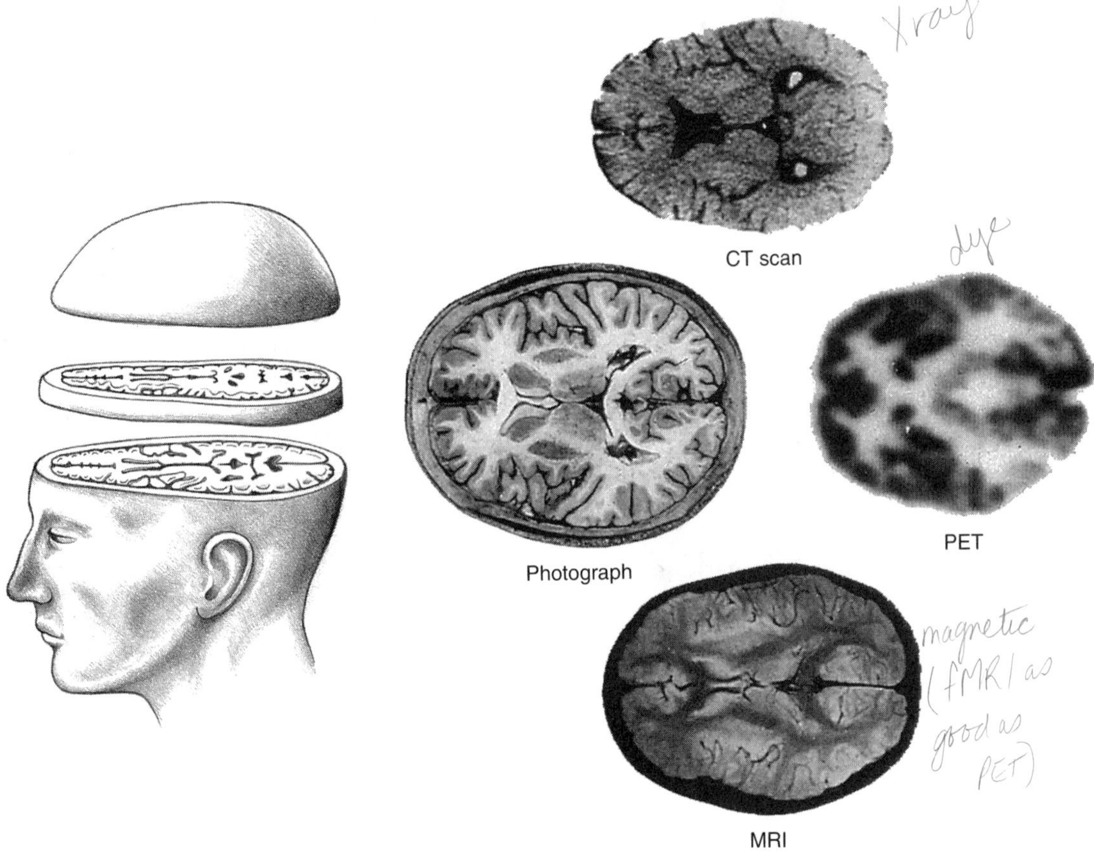

FIGURE 4.16. The four images at the right were created using four different techniques for imaging a slice of the brain. (After Posner and Raichle, 1994.)

SPECT is not as accurate as PET but does not require a cyclotron to make the tracers, which is a major advantage.

The second imaging development to come from the CT was **magnetic resonance imaging** (**MRI**). MRI is based on the principle that hydrogen atoms behave like spinning bar magnets in the presence of a magnetic field. Normally, atoms are pointed randomly in different directions, but when they are placed in a magnetic field, they line up in parallel as they orient themselves with respect to the field's lines of force. When radio waves are beamed across the atoms, they emit detectable radio waves that are characteristic of the number of atoms present (that is, their density) and their chemical environment. The development of the MRI had two important consequences. First, the images far surpass the best CT scan, so the image is more accurate. Second, the distribution of atoms such as oxygen varies with brain activity. It turns out that the amount of oxygen carried by the hemoglobin in the blood affects the magnetic properties of the blood. When neurons become more active, they release K^+, which is taken up by glial cells and released into blood vessels. The K^+ ions cause the blood vessels to dilate, thus increasing blood flow. MRI can detect the functionally induced changes in blood oxygenation. This procedure is known as **functional MRI or fMRI** and is an exciting development, since nothing needs to be injected into the brain. In addition, fMRI still gives an accurate structural map, which allows identification of the functionally active regions. fMRI is also more accurate than PET, with a resolution as good as 1 or 2 mm. Like PET, fMRI has a slow time resolution, so it is not possible to detect the activity of individual neurons, which lasts only milliseconds.

The latest major development in imaging is the neuromagnetic technique, which is known as the **magnetoencephalogram** (**MEG**). The MEG takes advantage of the fact that electrical currents of neurons generate tiny magnetic fields. Thus, MEG is another way of recording EEG or ERPs. The fact that these fields are so tiny presented a major technical obstacle, but this has now been overcome by the development of the superconducting quantum interference device (SQUID). One problem with measuring magnetic fields generated by the brain is that they are small relative to those of the earth or those generated by other electrical events outside the head. This is overcome by making tens or hundreds of measurements and then averaging them. Since MEG can locate the source of activity, an advantage that it has over other techniques is that it can record activity in the sulci, though it loses accuracy with depth of recording.

A relatively inexpensive way of imaging brain activity is to measure ERPs from many brain areas simultaneously. Since it is expected that specific brain areas will be responsive only to certain signals, the relative responses at different sites can be used to map brain function. A geodesic sensory net containing 64 to more than 100 electrodes is placed on a subject's head to detect ERPs simultaneously at many cortical sites (Figure 4.17). Using computerized techniques, the changes in signals at each electrode can be detected, subtracted from those that occur during resting conditions, and displayed graphically. By making maps of the ERPs at different times after the stimulus event, the relative times at which certain brain areas become active in processing informa-

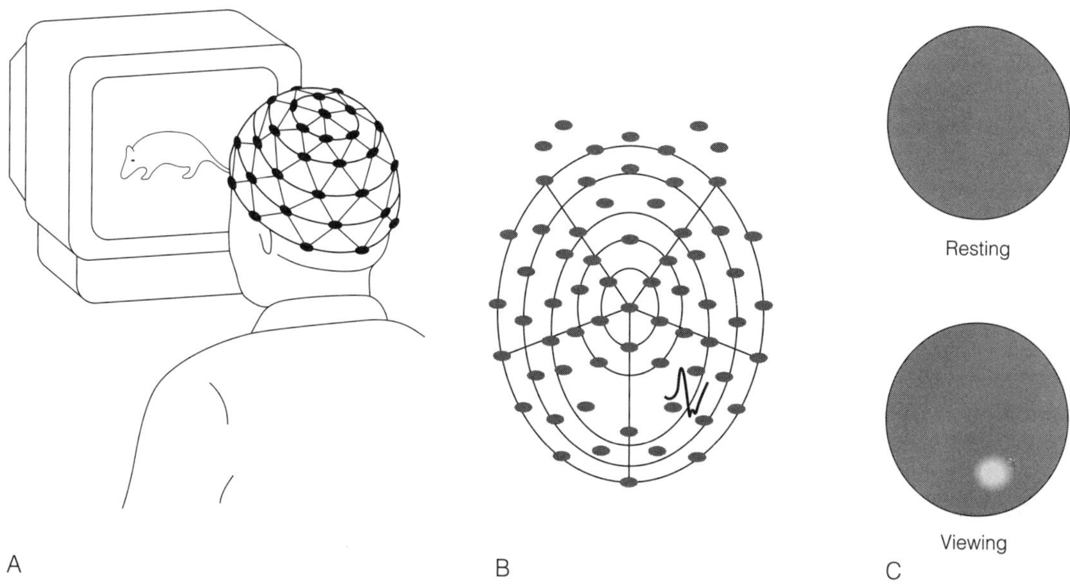

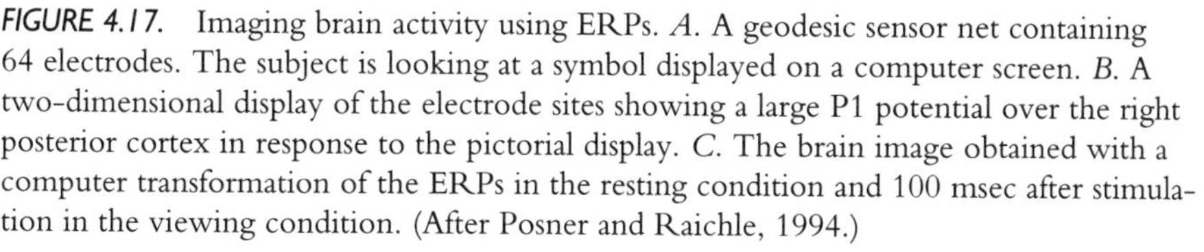
FIGURE 4.17. Imaging brain activity using ERPs. *A.* A geodesic sensor net containing 64 electrodes. The subject is looking at a symbol displayed on a computer screen. *B.* A two-dimensional display of the electrode sites showing a large P1 potential over the right posterior cortex in response to the pictorial display. *C.* The brain image obtained with a computer transformation of the ERPs in the resting condition and 100 msec after stimulation in the viewing condition. (After Posner and Raichle, 1994.)

tion can be determined. In the example shown in Figure 4.17, subjects are given a visual stimulus. A focus of ERPs is detected at about 100 msec over the right posterior cortex. By varying the content and modality of the stimulus, the relative involvement of brain areas can be mapped at different time intervals after the stimulus. Thus, a graphic depiction before and after stimulus presentation shows the relative area of the brain activated by the stimulus.

SUMMARY

We can see how the principles of cell activity determine behavior if we return to the opening description of the male Grayling butterfly. Recall Tinbergen's suggestion that in the male butterfly's nervous system there is a pooling station that integrates the different features (dark, large, and irregular) of a stimulus object to determine whether or not the male will approach it. Theoretically, all the male butterfly's behavior could be accounted for by the activity of one central neuron. The dendrites of that neuron would serve as the pooling station, and the axon would be the system that initiates an approach response. If three channels of input converge on the dendrites (one signaling darkness, one size, and one movement), simultaneous activity in the separate channels signaling dark, large, and irregular would produce graded potentials that, when summed, would trigger axonal firing and thus approach by the male butterfly. Activity in only one channel might not be sufficient to fire the neuron; activity in two channels might be sufficient to produce a response if input in each were particularly intense. At any rate, it can be seen that the dendrites in responding to each input could produce a nerve impulse on the axon and so determine whether approach is to occur.

This chapter describes the various parts of a neuron and illustrates how understanding the parts leads to an understanding of various aspects of brain function. The metabolic activity of the cell and the way that it manufactures the protein that it uses provides a number of ways to analyze the contribution of the cells to behavior. Neurons carry an electrical charge across their membranes, and other neurons, by secreting transmitter substances onto them, can change this electrical charge. These functions underlie the way cells communicate with one another and how they contribute to behavior. The structure of neurons and their electrical activity underlie a number of techniques for measuring brain activity, including single cell activity, EEG, and scans using ERPs and other techniques.

REFERENCES

Eccles, J. The synapse. *Scientific American* 212:56–66, Jan. 1965.

Hodgkin, A. L., and A. F. Huxley. Action potentials recorded from inside nerve fiber. *Nature* 144:710–711, 1939.

Kandel, E. R., and J. H. Schwartz. *Principles of Neural Science.* New York: Elsevier North Holland, 1991.

Katz, B. How cells communicate. In J. L. McGaugh, N. M. Weinberger, and R. H. Whalen, eds. *Psychobiology. Readings from Scientific American.* San Francisco: W. H. Freeman, 1972.

Penfield, W., and H. H. Jasper. *Epilepsy and the Functional Anatomy of the Human Brain.* Boston: Little, Brown, 1954.

Posner, M. I., and M. E. Raichle. *Images of Mind.* New York: W. H. Freeman, 1994.

Shepherd, G. M. *Neurobiology.* New York: Oxford University Press, 1983.

Sinclair, B. R., M. G. Seto, and B. H. Bland. Theta cells in the CA1 and dentate layers of the hippocampal formation: Relations to slow wave activity and motor behavior in the freely moving rabbit. *Journal of Neurophysiology* 48:1214–1225, 1982.

Tinbergen, N. *The Animal in Its World.* London: Allen & Unwin, 1972.

chapter five

5

The Biochemical Activity of the Brain

One of the most notable experiments ever performed on the nervous system was done by Otto Loewi in 1921. Loewi stimulated the vagus nerve to a frog's heart, causing the heart's rate of beating to decline. At the same time he washed the heart with a solution that he then collected. When he subsequently poured the solution onto a second heart, its rate of beating also declined. A substance had been liberated from the first heart that slowed the rate of the second. Loewi referred to this substance as *Vagusstoff* (vagus substance) and identified it as acetylcholine within a few years. Loewi was also able to stimulate the vagus to increase heart rate and, by collecting and applying the substance thus produced, to increase the rate of beating of a second heart. This substance turned out to be epinephrine. Although the experiment was initially difficult to replicate—it depends upon the stimulation, the kind of frog, the season, and so forth—the results were eventually obtained reliably and extended to rabbits, cats, and dogs. These pioneering experiments led to modern concepts of how nerves communicate with muscles and glands and eventually to the identification of substances that allow nerves to communicate with one another and of the rules that govern this communication. They also led to a scientific basis for *psychopharmacology,* the science of how drugs affect behavior through their action on the nervous system. A particular elegance of the experiments is that they embodied most of the procedures that were subsequently used to study neurotransmitters in the brain, including isolating a function, stimulating release of a transmitter, collecting and identifying the transmitter, and verifying its action.

THE SYNAPSE

It is now accepted that neurons communicate chiefly through the agency of the chemicals they release. These chemicals, known as **neurotransmitters,** are released by the synapses of one neuron onto the membrane of another neuron. Neurons can synthesize the transmitter and release it, and some can take it back up again for reuse.

Synapse Structure

Figure 5.1 is a diagram of a synapse. The membrane surrounding the terminal is called the **presynaptic membrane.** Penetrating the terminal

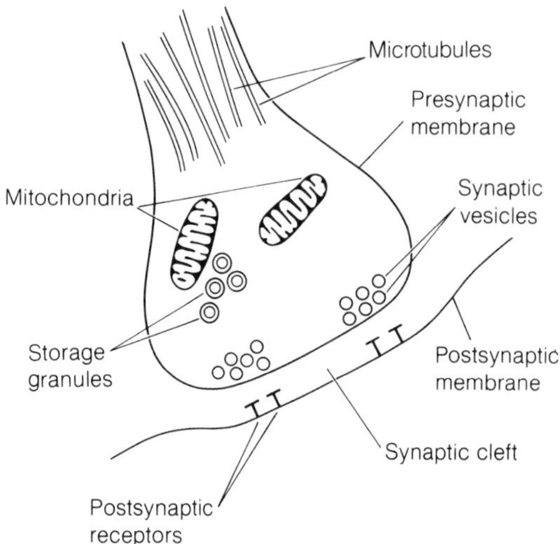

FIGURE 5.1. The major physical features of a synapse.

from the axon are microtubules, which may transport precursor chemicals for the manufacture of neurotransmitters into the terminal. There are mitochondria in the terminal that provide energy for its metabolic processes. In addition there can be two types of vesicles in the terminal: **storage granules,** which are presumed to be long-term storage sites for neurotransmitters, and **synaptic vesicles,** which hold neurotransmitters for immediate use. The terminal is separated from the **postsynaptic membrane** of the neuron with which it synapses by a very small space called the **synaptic cleft.** The postsynaptic membrane contains specialized proteins that act as **receptors** for the neurotransmitter.

Kinds of Synapses

There are differences in the shape of the terminals and the configuration of the junction that they make with neurons. There are also differences in the configuration and the size of the granules in the terminals. Finally, there are variations in the densities of the presynaptic and postsynaptic membranes at the point of the synapse. This diversity in size and density reflects the different functions of terminals. Although it is still not clear how the appearance of synapses relates to their function, some terminals inhibit the activity of cells with which they synapse, whereas others excite the cells with which they synapse. Figure 5.2 illustrates some of the differences in appearance of a glutamate synapse, thought to be excitatory, and a γ-aminobutyric acid (GABA) synapse, thought to be inhibitory. Note the differences in the shape of the vesicles, the width of the areas from which the vesicles are released and received, and the size of the synaptic spaces.

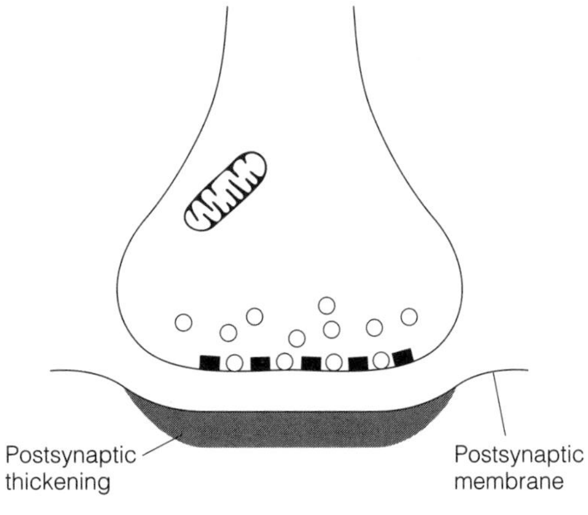

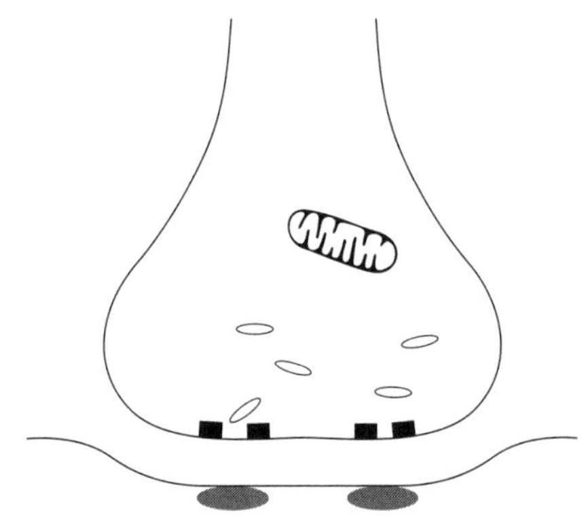

FIGURE 5.2. Physical differences in two kinds of synapses. The Type I synapse using glutamate as a transmitter is excitatory, and the Type II synapse using GABA as a transmitter is inhibitory.

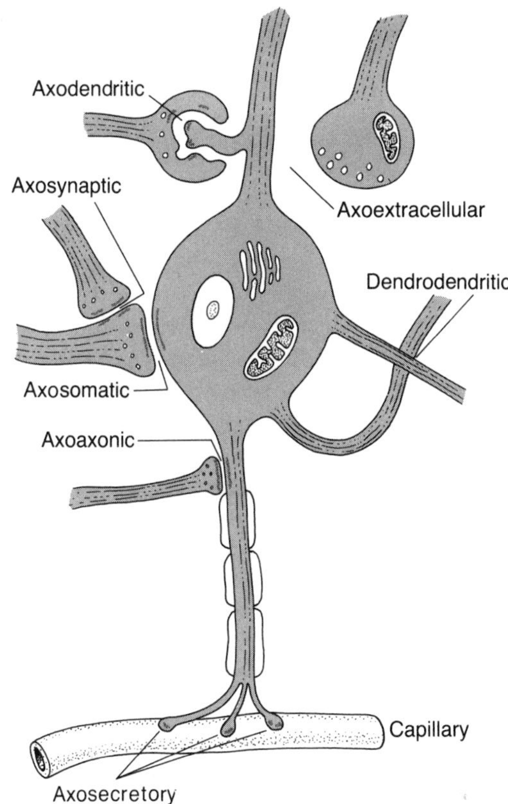

FIGURE 5.3. Types of synapses in the central nervous system.

The terminals of neurons make a wide variety of contacts with various portions of other neurons, but they are not limited to cell-to-cell contact. Examples of connections are shown in Figure 5.3. The various types of connections are given names depending upon the parts of the cell that are in contact; for example, axodendritic for an axon contacting a dendrite. Synapses can connect to dendrites, to the cell body, and to axons. These connections are called axodendritic, axosomatic, axoaxonic, and axosynaptic, depending upon the connection. Dendrites make contacts with one another—that is, dendrodendritic connections—and the tubular portions of axons may overlie other axons and dendrites, making contact in passing. There are also terminals that do not synapse with other neural elements, but instead secrete their transmitter chemical into the space outside the cell. These are called axoextracellular synapses. If the nervous system is thought of as a series of conduits for information, it can be appreciated that the variety of terminal locations provides many opportunities for unique or novel routes of communication. In addition to synapsing with other neural projections, terminals end on muscles and provide the route through which muscles are contracted. Additionally, they can end on capillaries, into which they may secrete hormones (axosecretory connections). In this way they can act as hormonal systems that distribute their transmitters throughout the body via the circulatory system.

The Steps in Synaptic Function

A number of steps are required for the synthesis of a neurotransmitter, its release, and its eventual disposition. By convention, these are broken down into the following seven steps (Figure 5.4). As will be discussed later, each of these steps is a biochemical event that potentially can be influenced in some way, thus altering function. Most of the effects of drug action occur at one of these steps:

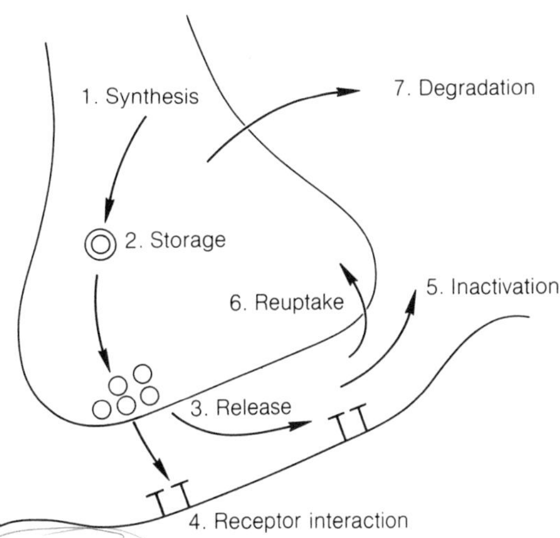

FIGURE 5.4. Steps in synaptic transmission in a generalized synapse.

1. *Synthesis.* The transmitter is either made in the cell body and transported to the synapse, or precursor chemicals, obtained from food or manufactured in the neuron, are transported down the axon into the terminal, where they are synthesized into the neurotransmitter.

2. *Storage.* The transmitter is stored in the terminal in one of several ways, at least one of which is in vesicles (shown as circles in Figure 5.4) available for release.

3. *Release.* When the nerve discharges, some of the vesicles release their contents into the synaptic cleft.

4. *Receptor interaction.* The released neurotransmitter crosses the synaptic cleft and binds weakly to specialized receptors on the postsynaptic membrane, where it initiates either depolarization or hyperpolarization of the postsynaptic membrane. In many systems more than one type of postsynaptic receptor may be sensitive to the neurotransmitter.

5. *Inactivation.* In some synapses the neurotransmitter is inactivated in the area of the synaptic cleft.

6. *Reuptake.* In other synapses the neurotransmitter is taken back up into the presynaptic neuron. In some synapses, both inactivation and reuptake may occur.

7. *Degradation.* The free neurotransmitter within the terminal may be degraded to control the neurotransmitter concentrations within the neuron.

TRANSMITTERS

Many different neurotransmitters are suspected to be active in the nervous system. As pointed out in the introduction to this chapter, acetylcholine was the first transmitter to be identified. Its identification was not that difficult because the acetylcholine synapse on the muscle is quite accessible. Acetylcholine was also the first transmitter substance to be identified in the central nervous system. The motor neurons that send axons to muscles also have collaterals in the spinal cord, and these synapses were also found to contain acetylcholine. This led to the general rule that all the synapses of a given neuron will have the same transmitter. Identifying transmitter substances in the brain is much more difficult because so many different synapses are in close proximity.

Proofs for Transmitter Function

The demonstration that a substance is a transmitter requires that a number of criteria be met. These criteria are very similar to those used by Otto Loewi to demonstrate that epinephrine and acetylcholine are the transmitters that regulate heart rate. They include the following:

1. The substance is shown to be present in the terminals.

2. The substance is released when the neuron fires.

3. Placing the substance on the innervated organ mimics the effect of nerve stimulation.

4. There is a chemical or an uptake mechanism present in the area of the synaptic cleft to inactivate the substance.

5. Destroying or inactivating the substance must block the effects of nerve stimulation.

At present, technology is simply unable to meet the rigor of all these demands, and so many chemicals that are strongly suspected of functioning as neurotransmitters can only be labeled putative (or supposed) transmitters. Nevertheless, quite a number of substances appear to be transmitters by at least some of these criteria.

Types of Transmitter Substances

There is evidence that at least 60 substances could be transmitters. These can be divided into three groups: (1) small molecules; (2) peptides, which are short chains of amino acids; and (3) gases.

There are nine small molecule transmitters, and these are sometimes referred to as the classical

TABLE 5.1. Classical neurotransmitters

Acetylcholine
Dopamine (DA)
Norepinephrine (NE)
Epinephrine
Serotonin (5-HT)
Histamine
γ-Aminobutyric acid (GABA)
Glycine
Glutamate

neurotransmitters. These are listed in Table 5.1. There are more than 50 short **peptides** (chains of **amino acids**) that are now grouped into 10 families. These substances include peptides that are also found in the gut and may play a role in the central control of feeding and drinking; hormones that are released from the hypothalamus; peptides that are released from the pituitary; and others (Table 5.2). Some peptides act like opiates; that is, they have pain-suppressing properties in addition to producing other opiatelike effects. The gases include nitric oxide (NO) and carbon monoxide (CO), which differ from the other transmitters in that they can diffuse through membranes and do not have clearly demarked cell membrane receptor targets.

There are some differences between the classical transmitters and the peptides. The classical transmitters, in addition to being smaller than the peptides, are synthesized from simpler substances or obtained directly from food. For example, acetylcholine is made in part from choline, which is obtained from the diet. Dopamine and norepinephrine are synthesized from the dietary amino acid tyrosine by minor editing. Serotonin is derived from the dietary amino acid tryptophan, and eating tryptophan-rich foods, such as bananas, has been shown to increase central serotonin activity. The amino acid glutamate, aspartate, and glycine are dietary amino acids obtained directly from protein in the diet. The synthesis of GABA requires only the removal of a carboxyl group (COOH) from glutamate. These transmitters also act in high concentrations, and their effects are relatively short lasting. Since they are made in the synapse, they can be replenished quickly after use.

TABLE 5.2. Some families of neuroactive peptides

Opioids: enkephalins, dynorphin
Neurohypophyseals: vasopressin, oxytocin
Secretins: gastric inhibitory peptide, growth hormone releasing factors
Insulins: insulin, insulin growth factors
Gastrins: gastrin, cholecystokinin
Somatostatins: pancreatic polypeptides

The peptides, by contrast, consist of two or more amino acids that are made by ribosomes in the cell body according to instructions from chromosomes in the nucleus. They must be transported from the cell body to the synapse. They are fractions of larger peptide molecules, are potent in small concentrations, and appear to have long-lasting actions. Once they are used, it takes some time for a renewed store to be transported back in.

Gases such as NO seem to be much more versatile in their transmitter functions. They can penetrate membranes readily and so can enter a cell to influence its function. Gases can also work backward: if a cell is excited it can release NO, which in turn affects the behavior of the cell that excited it; that is, it can instruct that cell to continue or stop firing.

It was originally believed that any one neuron would contain the same transmitter in all its terminals. It is now recognized that the neuroactive peptides may coexist in terminals with the classical neurotransmitters. It is unclear in these situations whether the peptides are acting like transmitters in the full sense or whether they have a modulatory effect on synaptic transmission.

There is no one-to-one relationship between transmitters and functions; any one transmitter can have many relations to behavior. All muscles are contracted by acetylcholine, but acetylcholine also acts in the sympathetic system and in the brain. In the sympathetic system, norepinephrine generally produces effects opposite to those of acetylcholine (for example, Otto Loewi's heart experiment); it also acts in the brain. GABA (inhibitory) and glutamate (excitatory) are found in almost all brain regions. Transmitter systems also appear to influence one another in that if the level of activity of one transmitter is changed, it in turn will change the activity of other transmitters. For example, all the major classes of drugs (see Table 5.3), except the major tranquilizers, have certain addictive properties. It is difficult to imagine that all the transmitters these drugs influence have rewarding properties. A more parsimonious theory suggests that these drugs have addictive effects because they either directly or indirectly influence a single transmitter substance that has rewarding properties. Since the major tranquilizers, in addition to blocking the rewarding effects of drugs, also block the neurotransmitter dopamine, dopamine is thought to be the transmitter that sustains reward.

RECEPTORS

Transmitters act on receptors located on the postsynaptic membrane. The receptors are proteins that face outward from the cell membrane to catch the transmitter. Receptors are thought to consist of two components: a binding site, which grasps the transmitter, and a channel that opens when the transmitter is bound, to let ions flow through the membrane. Figure 5.5A shows a diagram of an acetylcholine receptor. The receptor consists of five protein units, each of which is represented as a petal. Two of the units, called the alpha units, contain locations on which acetylcholine can bind, as is shown by the cutaway in Figure 5.5B. If acetylcholine occupies both of these sites, the conformation of the receptor is changed so that the channel is opened to allow Na^+ ions to enter and K^+ ions to leave.

Once receptors are activated they can produce

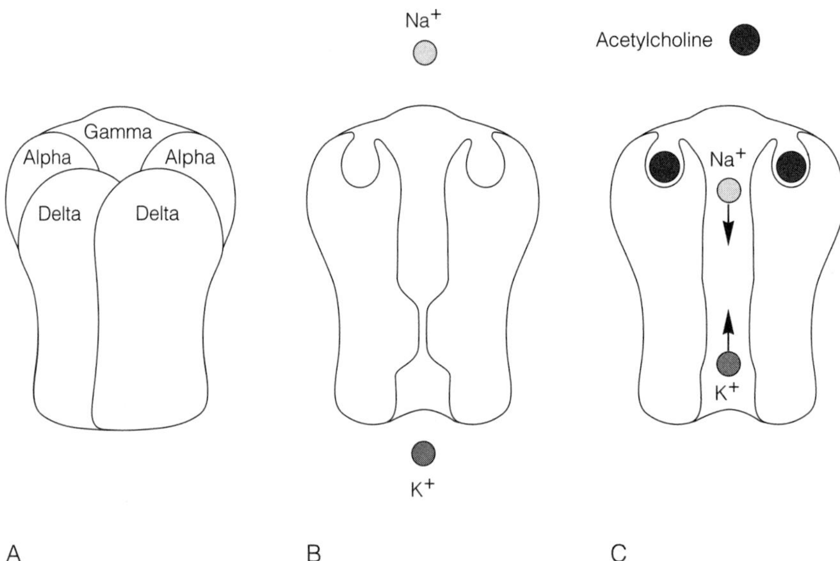

FIGURE 5.5. The acetylcholine receptor. *A.* The receptor consists of five protein units. *B.* Cross section through the alpha units that contain the receptor for acetylcholine. *C.* When acetylcholine binds to the receptors in both alpha units, a channel is opened to allow the passage of ions.

at least two effects. As illustrated in Figure 5.6, when a receptor is occupied by a transmitter, its conformation can change to allow ions to pass. If the voltage change that this causes is large enough adjacent Na^+ channels are excited so that they also allow ions to pass. Some receptors may also initiate a sequence of chemical changes within the cell. This activity in turn may regulate ion flow through a receptor on the membrane, or it may lead to changes in the number of receptors or may change other structures within the cell. The chemicals involved in this latter postsynaptic activity are called **second messengers.** (The first messenger is the neurotransmitter.) The first mechanism is clearly a way of producing an action potential, while the second can modify cells permanently, perhaps for such activities as learning.

Receptors sensitive to a given transmitter usu-

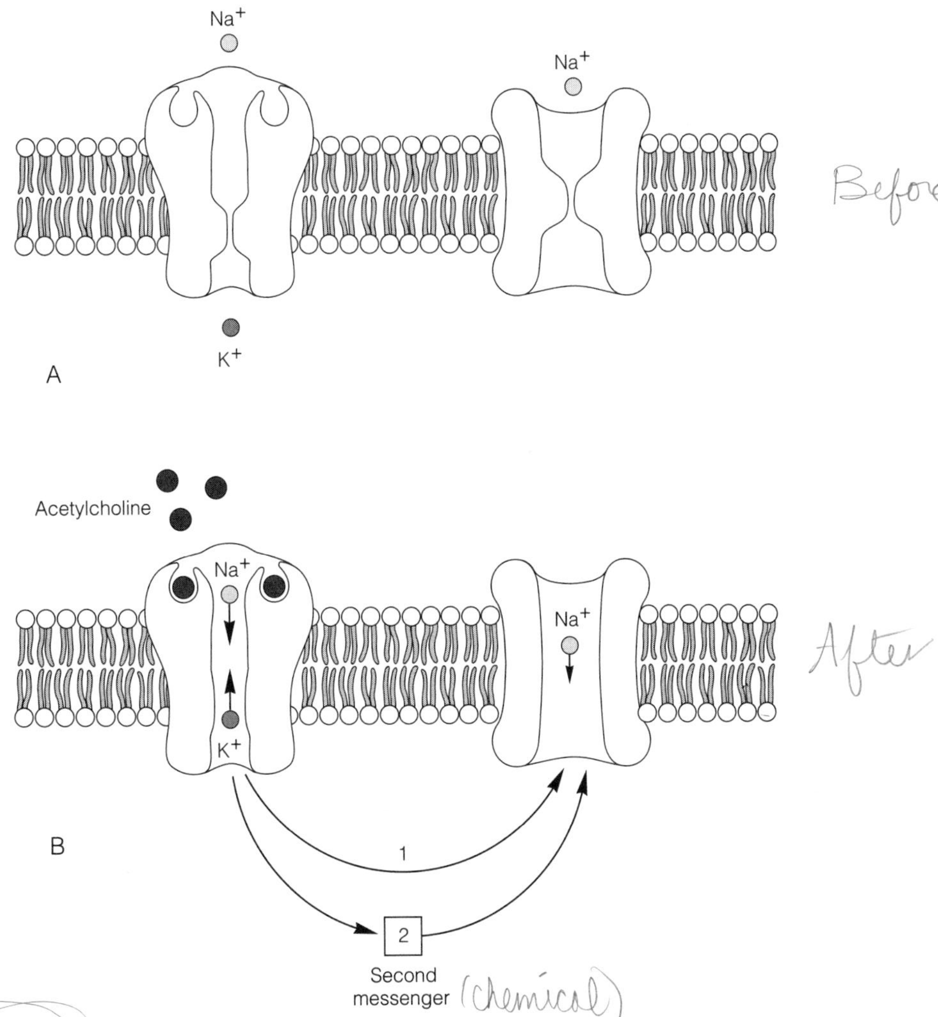

FIGURE 5.6. Two actions of receptors. Acetylcholine can bind to a receptor to open channels within that receptor. This voltage change can (1) induce adjacent voltage-regulated receptors to open, and/or (2) activate a second messenger that can in turn modify the cell membrane and its receptors.

ally take two or more forms. For example, on muscles the acetylcholine receptor is the nicotine receptor (because it is excited by nicotine), whereas in the brain most acetylcholine receptors are muscarine receptors (named for a mushroom derivative that activates them). The muscarine receptors are not sensitive to nicotine. Differences in receptor properties may be related to specific changes that the receptor can produce in the cell. Apart from their functional implications, receptor differences also have a pharmacological significance. A drug that blocks the function of a transmitter by acting upon one receptor may not influence that transmitter at its other receptor sites. For example, curare (a poison that South American Indians put on arrow tips) blocks acetylcholine nicotine receptors on muscles and produces death by suffocation because respiratory muscles are paralyzed. But curare has no effect on muscarine receptors, which are located on many other body organs. One explanation for some disease conditions is that they are related to an abnormality of a particular receptor. For example, there are at least five dopamine receptors, and one explanation of schizophrenia is that there is an excessive number of one of them, the D2 receptor.

DISTRIBUTION OF TRANSMITTERS

The distribution of neurotransmitters is determined in a number of ways. Samples of tissue can be taken from different brain areas and the concentrations of chemicals in the samples compared. This type of analysis gives only a relative measure of neurotransmitter distribution, and most neurotransmitters have been found in all regions of the brain, although in considerably varied concentrations. Generally it is not wise to conclude much about function from concentration differences; for example, a small quantity of neurotransmitter in one region may be just as important for a particular function as a large quantity in some other region.

Another technique for determining distribution is to stain the brain tissue with substances that interact with a neurotransmitter, its receptors, or some chemical closely related to the neurotransmitter's function. For example, norepinephrine and dopamine can be stained by exposing sections of tissue to formaldehyde vapor and then illuminating the tissue with ultraviolet light. Both transmitters fluoresce with a green color, but in distinguishably different shades. The presence of acetylcholine can be identified by staining tissue with a substance called butylthiocholine, which turns acetylcholinesterase, a chemical that breaks down acetylcholine, black. In most, but not all, brain sites, acetylcholinesterase indicates the presence of acetylcholine. New techniques are continually being developed to map the concentration and distribution of almost all neurotransmitter substances.

Neurochemical mapping procedures reveal that there are at least two types of distribution of transmitter substances. For the first type, there are cells containing the transmitter located in many different regions of the brain. The influence of these cells and their transmitter is mainly quite local. For the second type, neurons containing the transmitter are located in rather restricted nuclei but have axons that go to a wide range of brain areas. The origin and distribution of the dopamine, norepinephrine, and serotonin systems are examples of the second type. Their distribution in the rat is shown diagrammatically in Figure 5.7. Note that the cell bodies for each of these transmitters is restricted to a small brain region, but their axons project to most of the rest of the brain. These systems resemble hormone systems, except that the transmitters are carried from their origin by axons rather than by the bloodstream. Similar maps have been developed for other transmitter systems, including cholinergic and opioid systems, and generally the organization revealed in the rat (the favorite subject for this type of research) proves to be much the same for other animals, including humans.

MENTAL ILLNESS AND NEUROTRANSMITTERS

Since the last century it has been suggested that **psychosis**—an illness such as schizophrenia or

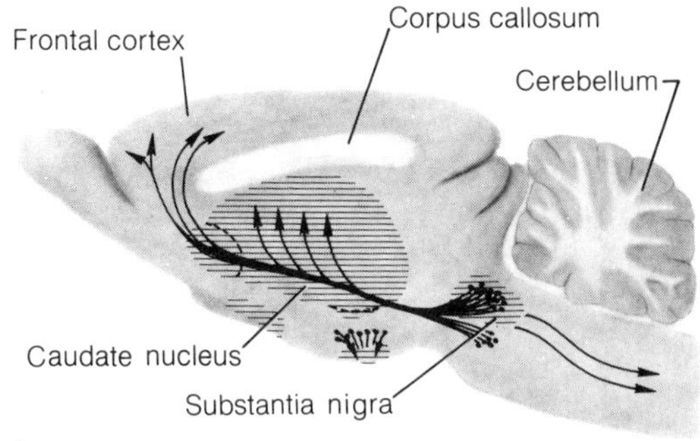

A DOPAMINE

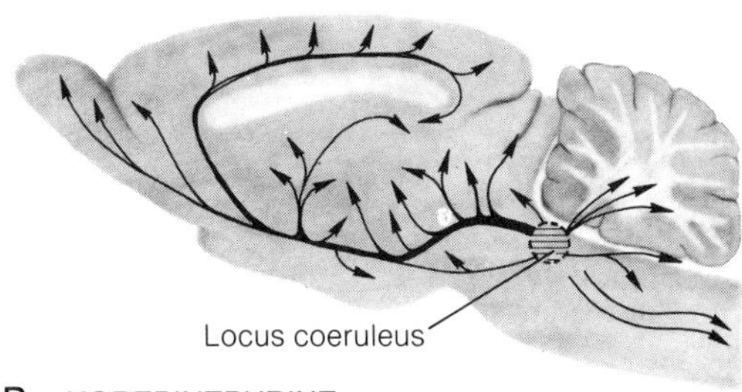

B NOREPINEPHRINE

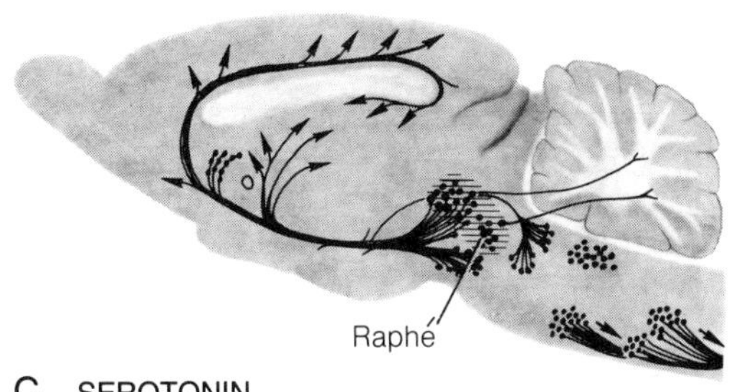

C SEROTONIN

FIGURE 5.7. Location of cell bodies, shown as black dots, and the projections of dopamine, norepinephrine, and serotonin pathways. (After Cooper, Bloom, and Roth, 1991.)

manic-depressive behavior in which there are disorganized thought processes—is the result of brain malfunction. It was variously proposed that psychoses are due to actual brain damage, ingestion of toxins that poison the brain, or synthesis by the brain itself of a toxin that causes it to malfunction. These ideas were reinforced by the observation that various chemical agents (for example, atropine), when ingested, produce behavior resembling that of psychosis. Then, in 1952, French physicians observed that a preanesthetic agent, chlorpromazine, had a tranquilizing effect on surgical patients. When tried on psychotic patients, it was found to have striking therapeutic action. By 1955 it was in use in North America and was probably instrumental in reducing the patient population of mental hospitals drastically (Figure 5.8). Since then many other antipsychotic drugs have been introduced, and an intense search for the mechanisms of their action has been under way. Because many psychoactive drugs are now thought to produce their effects by modifying synaptic activity, the rest of this chapter will describe some of the proposed influences of pharmacological agents on neurotransmitter systems.

DRUGS AND BARRIERS TO THEIR INFLUENCE

If the target of a drug is in the brain, it has a number of barriers to overcome before it gets there. Drugs are administered orally more often than by any other route. As is well known, alcohol administered by this method gets to the brain rather quickly. On the other hand, curare, a neuromuscular blocker that can cause death through respiratory muscle paralysis, has no effect when taken orally. If taken through the skin, however, curare's action is rapid. (For this reason South American Indians could kill animals with curare-tipped arrows and then eat the animals with impunity.) What is the basis for these differences?

Drugs taken by mouth reach the bloodstream by being absorbed through the stomach or small intestine, where absorption may be impaired by food in the system. The nature and form of a drug taken orally will also determine whether it will be absorbed and the rate of that absorption. If the drug is in a solid form it will not be absorbed if it cannot be dissolved by the gastric juices. In gen-

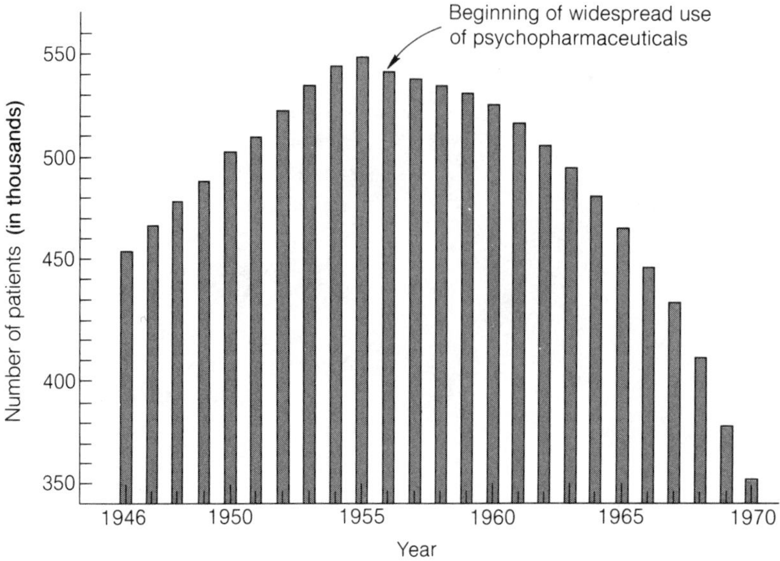

FIGURE 5.8. Numbers of resident patients in state and local government mental hospitals in the United States from 1946 through 1970. Note the dramatic decrease in the total patient population that began after 1955, when the therapeutic use of psychoactive drugs began. (After Efron, 1968.)

eral, if a drug is a weak acid it will be absorbed from the stomach, but if it is a weak base it will have to pass through the stomach—a process that may destroy it—before it is absorbed from the intestine. The characteristics of drugs that determine their absorption are usually summarized in standard reference sources, such as Gilman et al.

The gastrointestinal tract can be bypassed by inhaling the drug, allowing the blood to absorb it directly from the lungs; by injecting it into a muscle, allowing it to be absorbed by the blood; or by injecting it directly into the bloodstream. Usually, these methods require much smaller drug dosages than those required for oral administration. Once a drug is in the bloodstream, it will be diluted by a person's approximately 6 liters of circulating blood, and it is subject to further barriers. If it binds strongly to proteins it will be attached to blood proteins and stay in the circulatory system. If it is water-soluble but not fat-soluble it will pass into the extracellular fluid, and if it is fat-soluble it will also cross cell membranes and enter cells. The 35 or so liters of water in the extracellular and intracellular fluid will further dilute it.

The brain imposes another barrier, called the **blood-brain barrier.** In the body, there are pores in capillary membranes that allow substances to pass. In the brain, the capillaries are tightly joined together and covered on the outside by a fatty barrier called the **glial sheath,** which is provided by nearby astrocyte cells. Thus, a drug has to cross the capillary wall and penetrate the glial covering to pass out of the bloodstream and into the brain. The blood-brain barrier thus acts as an obstacle to some drugs, such as penicillin. If drugs that are destined for the brain will not cross the blood-brain barrier, they must be injected directly into the cerebrospinal fluid or into the brain tissue itself. The latter techniques are widely used on experimental animals but are unlikely to be used with humans because of the danger from possible complications.

Processes that are involved in eliminating drugs from the body will also influence drug action and duration of action. Drugs that are very fat-soluble may be taken up rapidly by fat cells and then be eliminated only slowly. Fast-acting anesthetics, for example, are very fat-soluble and their action on the brain is terminated quickly because they are absorbed by fat. Drugs are excreted or metabolized by the kidneys, liver, bile, sweat, milk, or through breath inhaled by the lungs. Their persistence in the body will be determined by the route through which they are eliminated and the efficiency of that route. The liver, for example, increases its metabolic capacity when challenged by alcohol, so that alcohol may be metabolized more quickly in drinkers than in abstainers. Some substances, particularly certain metals such as mercury, may not be excreted at all and, if administered repeatedly, may accumulate in the body until they have toxic effects. Drugs are usually manufactured with routes of administration and elimination in mind so that rates of absorption and duration of action can be controlled.

Most information concerning drug administration, absorption, elimination, and effects can be found in standard reference texts, such as Gilman et al. It is a good practice to consult these references before taking a drug or when dealing with patients who are receiving drugs.

CLASSIFICATION OF PSYCHOACTIVE DRUGS

It is possible to classify drugs using a number of systems: by the transmitter they influence, by their structure, or by their action. A widely used drug classification scheme was developed by the World Health Organization. According to this classification there are five major types of **psychoactive drugs,** grouped according to the effects they have on behavior (Table 5.3).

As pointed out earlier, drugs may intervene in the process of intercellular communication at any of a number of stages, but irrespective of its site of action a drug will have one of two effects: it will either increase or decrease the effectiveness of transmission at the synaptic junction. An example of how drugs can produce their effects by modulating neurotransmission is shown for the acetylcholine synapse at the neuromuscular junction (Figure 5.9). Choline, obtained from the diet, is converted by an enzyme called acetyl CoA into acetylcholine (ACh). Black widow spider venom causes ACh to be released from the synapse, whereas botulinum toxin (food poisoning) blocks its release. The receptors are stimulated by nicotine and blocked by curare. The breakdown of ACh into its constituent elements is blocked by eserine. These various effects also illustrate why poisoning with a drug like curare can be treated with eserine. Eserine, by blocking metabolism, increases the amount of ACh in the synaptic

TABLE 5.3. Classes of drugs that alter mood or behavior

1. *Sedative-Hypnotics (CNS depressants)*
   Barbiturates: phenobarbital (*Luminal*), pentobarbital (*Nembutal*), thiopental (*Pentothal*)
   Nonbarbiturate hypnotics: Methaqualone (*Quaalude*)
   Antianxiety agents (benzodiazapines): chlordiazepoxide (*Librium*), diazepam (*Valium*)
   Others: alcohol, bromide, paraldehyde, chloral hydrate, ether, halothane, chloroform
2. *Behavioral Stimulants and Convulsants*
   Amphetamines: *Dexedrine*
   Clinical antidepressants
   Monoamine oxidase (MAO) inhibitors: *Parnate*
   Tricyclic compounds: *Tofranil, Elavil*
   Cocaine
   Convulsants: strychnine, picrotoxin
   Caffeine
   Nicotine
3. *Narcotic Analgesics (Opiates)*
   Opium, heroin, morphine, codeine, *Percodan, Demerol*
4. *Antipsychotic Agents*
   Phenothiazines: chlorpromazine (*Thorazine*)
   Reserpine (*Serpasil*)
   Butyrophenones: haloperidol (*Haldol*)
   Lithium
5. *Psychedelics and Hallucinogens*
   LSD (lysergic acid diethylamide)
   Mescaline
   Psilocybin
   Substituted amphetamines: MDMA (Ecstasy)
   Tryptamine derivatives: bufotenine
   Phencyclidine
   Cannabis: marijuana, hashish, tetrahydrocannabinols

Note: Proprietary drug names in italics.
Source: After Julien, 1985.

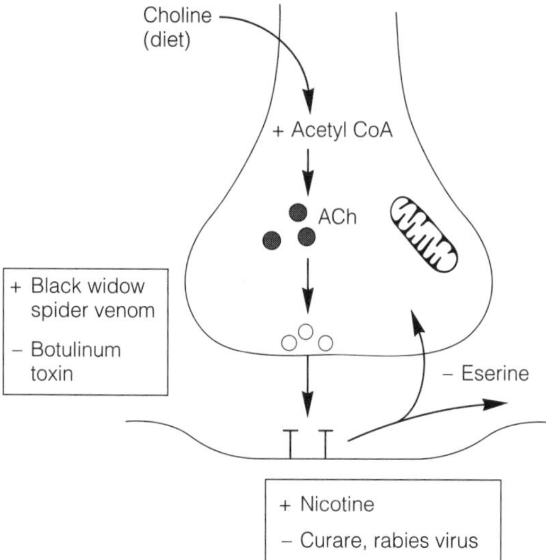

FIGURE 5.9. The synthesis of acetylcholine and the effects of some drugs in stimulating acetylcholine (+) or inhibiting acetylcholine (−) at the neuromuscular junction.

space, thus allowing it to overcome the effects of curare. One receptor disease, called myesthenia gravis, is caused by a reduction in the efficiency with which ACh receptors at the neuromuscular junction bind with ACh. Eserine is a treatment for this disease because it increases ACh.

Sedative-Hypnotics

Sedative-hypnotics are drugs that reduce anxiety at low doses, produce sedation at medium doses, and produce anesthesia or coma at high doses. Virtually any of these drugs, if given in the appropriate dose, can produce each of the effects illustrated in Figure 5.10. Sedative-hypnotics are a diverse group of drugs including barbiturates, benzodiazepines (known as minor tranquilizers, of which Valium is an example), and alcohol. They are widely used for their antianxiety actions, are effective in counteracting epilepsy, are used as anesthetics, and can be used to counteract the adverse effects of stimulants. It is thought that these drugs depress the activity of the systems that produce arousal or initiation of behavior. At low doses the sedative-hypnotics may depress the activity of norepinephrine synapses, but their precise mechanism of action is unknown. At higher doses they may block neurotransmission in many systems and thereby produce anesthesia or even coma. The benzodiazepines are thought to act by stimulating GABA function. Since GABA is an inhibitory transmitter, and since it is widely distributed in the brain, facilitating its activity can produce widespread inactivation of brain systems.

Because of the commonality of their actions on the nervous system, all the sedative-hypnotics are additive in effect. When taken together, the effects of two such drugs are often greater than would be predicted from the effects of either taken alone. The behavioral depression induced by these drugs is often followed by a period of hyperexcitability. After repeated administration, the hyperexcitability may be quite severe and can even result in convulsions and death. Prolonged use of sedative-hypnotics generally produces both dependence and tolerance. **Dependence** refers to the desire for or the necessity of continuing to take the drug. **Tolerance** refers to the decrease in response to the drug after it has been taken repeatedly. Tolerance can occur either because the body improves in its ability to metabolize the drug or because the nervous system becomes less re-

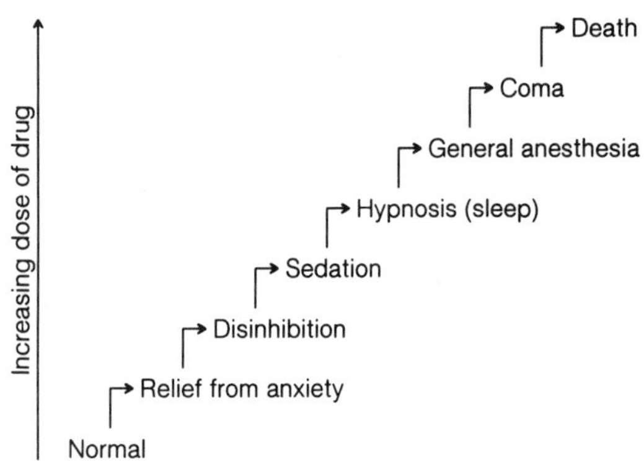

FIGURE 5.10. Continuum of behavioral sedation. How increasing doses of sedative-hypnotic drugs affect behavior. (After Julien, 1985.)

sponsive to it. Often withdrawal from drug abuse (alcoholism is a good example) is complicated by dependence, tolerance, and withdrawal symptoms. Sedative-hypnotics have been widely reported to impair memory, especially for recent events or ongoing events. A final characteristic of sedative-hypnotics is that they display good cross-dependence; that is, they can be substituted for one another. Many cases of drug dependence are complicated by multiple drug use in which a person may be taking a benzodiazepine such as Valium for anxiety, using alcohol, and also taking sleeping pills (barbiturates). The best treatment for chronic use is gradual withdrawal. For acute intoxication, stimulants may be helpful, but none specifically counteracts all depressant actions.

Stimulants

Stimulant drugs increase behavioral activity either by increasing motor activity or by counteracting fatigue. Stimulants are diverse drugs, with synergistic effects that differ from those described for sedative-hypnotics. They can be subdivided into four groups: behavioral stimulants, clinical antidepressants, convulsants, and general stimulants.

Behavioral stimulants include cocaine and the amphetamines, which are thought both to potentiate (augment) the release of dopamine and norepinephrine from the presynaptic membrane and to block the reuptake mechanism that reabsorbs dopamine back into the synapse after it has acted on the receptor. Both actions would increase not only the amount of dopamine available but also the duration of its availability for action on the receptors. Behavioral stimulants may also act on other amine synapses. The amphetamines have antidepressant properties, but their major clinical use is to counteract narcolepsy, an uncontrollable tendency to fall asleep. Amphetamines are also given to hyperactive children, whom they may help by prolonging their attention span.

Amphetamines produce cognitive arousal and counteract sleepiness when used in low doses. Repeated use creates tolerance and dependence. Tolerance levels can be remarkable: users who start with a 1 mg (milligram) dose may eventually take 1000 to 2000 mg per dose. If the drug is taken intravenously, known as "mainlining," tolerance and dependence occur more rapidly, and the user may display a condition of paranoid schizophrenia that is indistinguishable from the naturally occurring condition. Amphetamines also produce **sensitization,** a tendency to show greater behavioral response as a consequence of intermittent use of the drug (the opposite of tolerance). Hypothetically, sensitization can occur with as little as one experience with a drug and can last indefinitely. A review of some of the effects of amphetamines and the putative changes that underlie sensitization have been summarized by Robinson and Becker.

The antidepressants include desipramine, imipramine, fluoxetine (Prozac), and a number of other substances which also have stimulant properties. These drugs also act on dopamine, norepinephrine, and serotonin, thereby facilitating transmission by prolonging the time during which the neurotransmitter can act on the receptor. Some tricyclics, such as desipramine, have a more potent effect on norepinephrine reuptake, whereas others, such as imipramine and fluoxetine, more selectively block serotonin reuptake. The ability of cocaine to counteract depression was first documented by Sigmund Freud, but today the tricyclics, which are in some ways structurally similar to cocaine, are the treatment of choice for depression. Because some tricyclics are more effective than others in treating quite different depressive populations, their effects indicate that there may be at least two types of depression: one attributable to reduced norepinephrine transmission, the other to reduced serotonin transmission.

The *convulsants* include strychnine, picrotoxin, pentylenetetrazol, and bicuculline. Each acts on different transmitter systems and all produce behavioral seizures. Generally, although they have no clinical applications, they are used in experimental research.

General *cellular stimulants* include caffeine and nicotine. Caffeine inhibits an enzyme that ordinarily breaks down cyclic adenosine monophosphate (cyclic AMP). The resulting increase in cyclic AMP leads to an increase in glucose production within cells, thus making available more energy and allowing higher rates of cellular activity. Nicotine is known to stimulate the acetylcholine receptor at nerve-muscle junctions and then to leave a more long-lasting block on the junction. Both compounds are also thought to have a variety of other effects.

Narcotic Analgesics

The *narcotic analgesics,* such as heroin and morphine, although widely abused because of their addictive properties, are nevertheless among the most effective pain-relieving agents available. Their mechanism of action has been clarified recently by the discovery of endogenous opiatelike substances in the brain. It has been suggested that these naturally occurring opiate peptides are neurotransmitters in the brain, and that opiate drugs produce their effects by mimicking the postsynaptic stimulation of these neurotransmitters.

Antipsychotic Agents

The antipsychotic agents (often referred to as the major tranquilizers) are drugs that have been effective in treating schizophrenia; the most widely used of them is chlorpromazine. In fact there are two major classes of antipsychotic drugs: the **phenothiazines,** of which chlorpromazine is an example and which include many other -zine drugs, and the **butyrophenones,** of which haloperidol is the best known. Given the high incidence of schizophrenia, antipsychotic agents are continually being manufactured, and there may be as many as 2000 different drugs available. Although both classes of antipsychotics act on norepinephrine and dopamine systems, their antipsychotic action appears attributable to their action on dopamine. They are thought to reduce dopaminergic transmission by blocking the dopamine receptors.

The effectiveness of these drugs in treating schizophrenia has led to the "dopamine hypothesis of schizophrenia," which holds that some forms of schizophrenia may be related either to excessive levels of dopamine or to excessive numbers of dopamine receptors. This hypothesis should be viewed with caution. Neurotransmitter systems have complex interactions with one another, and it is quite possible that schizophrenia is caused by imbalances in any of a number of known or unknown systems that normally interact with dopamine transmission.

Psychedelics

The **psychedelic drugs** are a mixed group of agents that alter sensory perception and cognitive processes. There are at least three major groups of psychedelics. (1) Acetylcholine psychedelics either block or facilitate transmission in acetylcholine synapses. Drugs such as atropine block acetylcholine in the brain; others, such as muscarine, stimulate these receptors much as acetylcholine does, thus mimicking acetylcholine activity. (2) Norepinephrine psychedelics include mescaline and possibly cannabis. It is thought that they act by stimulating norepinephrine postsynaptic receptors. (3) Serotonin psychedelics include LSD (lysergic acid diethylamide) and psilocybin, which may mimic serotonin by stimulating postsynaptic receptors of serotonin synapses or may block the activity of serotonin neurons. In addition, these drugs may stimulate norepinephrine receptors.

NEUROTOXINS

There was little rain during the summer of 1987 in Prince Edward Island, Canada, and the streams leading into the ocean began to dry up and fill with seaweed. The seaweed was carried into the ocean and was eaten by mussels. In November and December, the mussels were eaten by more than 100 people, who became very ill. Some of them suffered enduring memory impairments but were otherwise cognitively intact. Postmortem examination of four of these people who died indicated that they had damage to the temporal lobes. The illness and brain damage are thought to have been caused by a chemical called *domoic acid,* which was made by the seaweed and to which the mussels were apparently impervious. The neurotoxin had entered the brains of people who had eaten the mussels and had selectively killed cells in the temporal lobes that are involved in memory.

What had happened was quickly understood because Olney and his coworkers, while investigating why monosodium glutamate ingested in food causes headaches, had found in 1971 that there are glutamatelike substances that bind to glutamate receptors and activate cells containing those receptors to the point that they die. These **neurotoxins** included *kainic acid, ibotenic acid,* and other substances. Domoic acid is related to these compounds and is the most potent of them all.

When these neurotoxins are injected directly into the brain, they bind to glutamate receptors and overstimulate the cell. Cells that have no glutamate receptors are, of course, impervious to the chemicals. For this reason they provide an experimental tool for selectively killing cells in restricted areas of the brain in order to examine their function. They also provide insight into other possible ways that brain damage can occur. It has been hypothesized, for example, that the brain might produce its own neurotoxins, resulting in regional self-destruction underlying a number of kinds of neurological conditions. Patients with Huntington's chorea are known to have degeneration of the caudate nucleus, and it has been suggested that the cells in their caudate nucleus die because this region of the brain produces a domoic acid-like substance that kills them.

This neurotoxic model provides yet another insight into endogenous brain damage. It has been known for a long time that **cerebral hypoxia** (brain oxygen starvation) and **cerebral ischemia** (loss of blood supply to a part of the brain) result in irreparable brain damage. Cerebral ischemia is seen in two common clinical situations, cardiac arrest and arteriosclerosis of the carotid or vertebro-basilar arteries. People who have experienced ischemia often show persistent memory deficits and other neurological symptoms. For a time it was thought that oxygen starvation (anoxia) per se was the cause of much of the damage. There were, however, some inconsistencies in this hypothesis, including the fact that the damage often appeared hours or days after circulation had been restored. It is now thought that the cells subjected to anoxia release excessive amounts of glutamate. Cells in the brain that appear particularly sensitive to anoxia, such as the CA1 cells of the hippocampus, have high concentrations of glutamate receptors. Thus, excessive glutamate release acting on the glutamate receptors has been hypothesized to be the causative agent in the death of these cells. If this is the case, then blocking glutamate receptors immediately after anoxia or a stroke should prevent cell death. A number of lines of experimental research indicate that glutamate-receptor blockade does retard cell death.

Another neurotoxin that receives wide experimental use is 6-hydroxydopamine (6-OHDA). It looks like dopamine and can be used to destroy dopamine cells selectively. In fact, depending upon how it is used, 6-OHDA can destroy dopamine cells, norepinephrine cells, or both. Thus, it is useful for experimental study of the role of these transmitters. If 6-OHDA is injected into the ventricles of the brain, it usually only destroys norepinephrine cells. If it is given in conjunction with a second compound, pargyline, a monoamine oxidase inhibitor, it also destroys dopamine cells. If desipramine, a norepinephrine uptake blocker, is also given to prevent 6-OHDA uptake into norepinephrine cells, then only dopamine cells are destroyed. The ability to remove dopamine cells from the brain selectively made it possible to produce an animal analogue of human Parkinson's disease, a disease characterized by the selective death of dopamine cells. More recently, it has been found that a synthetic morphine analogue, MPTP, accidentally created in an illicit drug factory, can also cause selective loss of dopamine cells in humans. Drug users who took it almost instantaneously acquired Parkinsonian symptoms. This substance, unlike 6-OHDA, does not have to be injected directly into the brain. The fact that a peripherally administered substance like MPTP can act as a neurotoxin has led to speculation that various chemicals in pollutants might have the capacity to act as neurotoxins as well. At about the same time that 6-OHDA was developed, it was also found that 5,7-dihydroxytryptamine (5,7-DHT) could be used in much the same way to destroy serotonergic neurons. Thus, it became clear that many substances might be found that could act as neurotoxins on many different systems.

The discovery of a variety of neurotoxins and a clarification of their actions opens many new possibilities for understanding how various kinds of brain damage occur. This broadens our perspective on how brain disease might progress, how environmental contaminants might affect the brain, and how some ingested substances might produce long-lasting behavioral changes. This also suggests new initiatives for preventative and remedial measures.

SUMMARY

Neurons communicate with one another by releasing chemicals at their terminals. These chemicals act on the receptors of other neurons to activate or inhibit them or to change their function in other ways. The synthesis, release, action, and reuptake of neurotransmitter substances are biochemical steps that can be influenced by drugs. Thus, understanding how neurotransmitters work also provides insights into normal behavior and into the mechanisms by which many drugs influence behavior. A large number of diseases and other neurological conditions may have their basis in the neurotransmitter malfunction. Their treatment is thus also facilitated by an understanding of neurotransmitter function.

REFERENCES

Cooper J. R., F. E. Bloom, and R. H. Roth. *The Biochemical Basis of Neuropharmacology*. New York: Oxford University Press, 1991.

Efron, D. H., ed. *Psychopharmacology: A Review of Progress*. Washington, D.C.: U.S. Department of Health, Education, and Welfare, 1968.

Gilman , A. G., L. S. Goodman, and A. Gilman, eds. *The Pharmacological Basis of Therapy*, 6th ed. New York: Macmillan, 1980.

Hokfelt, T. O., A Johansson, A. Ljungdahl, J. M. Jundberg, and M. Schultzberg. Peptidergic neurons. *Nature* (London) 284:515–521, 1980.

Julien, R. M. *A Primer of Drug Action*. New York: W. H. Freeman, 1985.

Kandel, E. R., and J. H. Schwartz. *Principles of Neural Science*. New York: Elsevier North Holland, 1991.

Olney, J. W., O. L. Ho, and V. Rhee. Cytotoxic effects of acidic and sulphur-containing amino acids on the infant mouse central nervous system. *Experimental Brain Research* 14:61–67, 1971.

Robinson, T. E., and J. B. Becker. Enduring changes in brain and behavior produced by chronic amphetamine administration: A review and evaluation of animal models of amphetamine psychosis. *Brain Research Reviews* 11:157–198, 1986.

Teitelbaum, J. S., R. J. Zatorre, S. Carpenter, D. Gendron, A. C. Evans, A. Gjedde, and N. R. Cashman. Neurologic sequelae of domoic acid intoxication due to the ingestion of contaminated mussels. *The New England Journal of Medicine* 322:1781–1787, 1990.

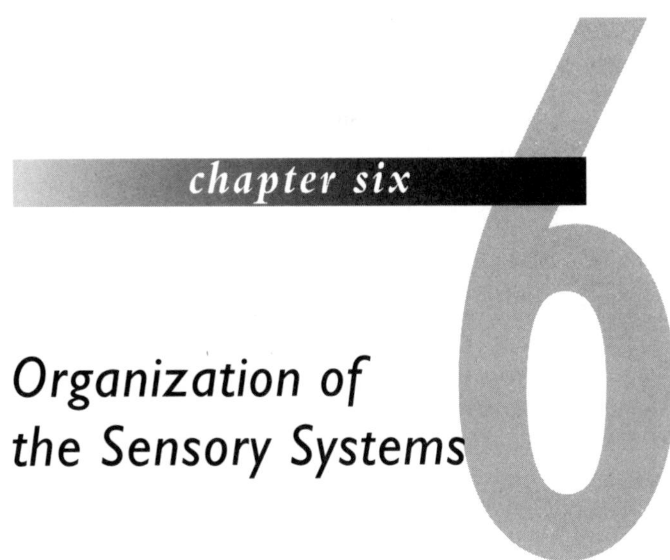

chapter six

Organization of the Sensory Systems

We believe that we see, hear, touch, and taste real things in a real world. Nevertheless, the only message our brain receives is the discharge passed along the neurons in the various sensory pathways. Although sensations such as vision and olfaction are different, the nerve discharges in the neurons of each sensory system are very similar, as are the neurons themselves. We now understand a lot about how nerves can turn energy such as light waves into nerve discharges, and we know the pathways those nerves take to the brain. We do not know how we end up thinking that one set of discharges represents what the world looks like and another set what it tastes like. Some philosophers have proposed that everything we know comes to us through our senses and, taken at face value, this seems reasonable. Nevertheless, we recognize that our senses can deceive us, and so other philosophers have proposed that we must have some innate knowledge about the world to be able to distinguish between real and imaginary sensations. Again, taken at face value, this also seems reasonable.

In this chapter we will summarize how sensory information reaches the cortex. We will place special emphasis on two features of sensory organization: (1) there are many submodalities in each of the sensory systems, and (2) each submodality is designed for a very specific function.

GENERAL PRINCIPLES OF THE SENSORY SYSTEMS

We are accustomed to thinking that there are five sensory systems (touch, taste, smell, vision, and hearing), but it is more accurate to state that there are five modalities through which we receive information. There are actually many submodalities or subsystems within each of these modalities. The submodalities are distinctive with respect to their receptors, the size of the fibers that go from the receptors to the brain, their connections within the brain, and the actions they produce.

Receptors

Receptors are specialized parts of cells that transduce, or convert, sensory energy (for example, light waves) into neural activity. The receptors in each sensory system are different, and so the sensory energy they can detect is different. For vision, light energy is converted into chemical energy in the receptors of the retina, and this chemical energy is in turn converted into neural activity. In the auditory system, sound waves are converted into a number of forms of mechanical energy that activate the receptors, and a neural discharge occurs. In the somatosensory system, mechanical energy in the form of touch, pressure, vibration, and so on, activates mechanoreceptors, which in turn generate neural activity. For taste and olfaction, various molecules carried by the air or contained in food fit themselves into receptors of various shapes to activate neural activity. For pain sensation, tissue must be damaged. It is thought that tissue damage releases a chemical called *neurokinin,* which in turn acts like a neurotransmitter to activate pain fibers.

In detecting energy, receptors act as filters. If we put flour into a sieve and shake it, the fine flour will go through and the coarse flour and lumps will not. Similarly, receptors of each sensory modality are designed to respond only to a narrow band of energy within the relevant energy spectrum. For audition the receptors of the human ear respond to sound waves between 20 and 20,000 Hz (cycles per second). Elephants can hear and produce sounds that are less than 20 Hz, and so humans cannot hear these sounds. Bats can hear and produce sounds that are as high as 120,000 Hz, and humans cannot hear these either. In fact, in comparison to many common animals, human sensory abilities are rather average. Even our pet dogs are marvels in comparison to us: they can detect odors we cannot detect, they can hear the ultrasounds emitted by rodents and bats, and they can see in the dark. (We can only hold up our superior color vision.) It is clear that each animal species has a special set of sensory system filters that produces an idiosyncratic representation of reality.

Receptive Fields

Receptors have a **receptive field,** which is the specific part of the world to which they respond. For some sensory systems the receptive field is fairly straightforward. For example, if the eyes are fixated, all the visible world that can be seen forms the receptive field for vision. If one eye is closed, the remaining world that can be seen by the open eye forms the receptive field for that eye. Within the eye is a cup-shaped retina that contains thousands of receptor cells. Because of the shape of the retina, each cell points in a particular direction, like a telescope pointing at a particular part of the sky, and the little part of the world from which each receptor receives light forms its receptive field. Of course, movements of the head or eyes can change the receptive field. The part of the skin on which a skin receptor is located forms its receptive field and generally consists of a few square millimeters of tissue. The receptive field for all tactile sensation consists of the entire body surface. Receptive fields not only sample sensory information but also, by contrast with what neighboring receptors detect, locate sensory events in space.

The olfactory sense is not very good at location: we do have two nostrils, but there is some question about how sensitive they are to the direction of odors. On the other hand, in the auditory system both ears hear most sounds, so that a sound is pinpointed not so much by differences in each ear's detection but by differences in loudness; that is, the ear closest to the sound hears it as loudest. That is why sounds directly in front of or behind us are sometimes difficult to locate. For taste, receptors for sweet substances are mainly on the tip of the tongue, receptors for bitter substances are mainly on the back of the tongue, and receptors for saltiness and sourness are along the tongue's margins. Hence, there are different receptive fields for tastes, but the locations of the fields may have more to do with deciding questions of ingestion than with pinpointing the food per se. The tip of the tongue is a good place for sweet receptors, because sweet foods are good to eat and can be swept into the mouth. Bitter foods, however, are usually poisonous, and so when they are detected on the back of the tongue they can be coughed out.

Cells in the central nervous system also have receptive fields. Thus, when the activity of a cell in the brain is being recorded, a stimulus must be moved around to find the part of the world (receptive field) to which the cell responds. It is by mapping the relation between the cells in the brain and the location of their receptive fields that the various sensory fields of the cortex can be mapped.

Rapidly and Slowly Adapting Receptors

Each sensory system answers questions such as, Is something there? and Is it still there? by dedicating subsystems to the questions. Receptors that detect whether something is there are easy to activate, but they also stop responding quickly. They are called rapidly adapting receptors. If you touch your arm very lightly with a finger you will immediately detect the touch, but if you then keep your finger still the sensation will fade as the receptors adapt. That is because the rapidly adapting hair receptors on the skin are designed to detect the movement of objects on the skin. If you push a little harder, you will be able to feel the touch for much longer because the receptors sensitive to pressure adapt more slowly to stimulation. In the visual system, receptors responsive to black and white have lower response thresholds and adapt more rapidly than do receptors sensitive to color. A dog with mainly black-white vision is thus sensitive to moving objects but has more difficulty detecting objects when they are still.

Localization and Identification

Sensory systems are designed to locate and identify stimuli. The receptive fields of individual receptors overlap. If one receptor is more activated by a stimulus than another, the object in question must be located more precisely in the receptive field of that receptor. Sensory systems must also answer questions such as, What is it? Detection of a stimulus is often determined by receptor density and overlap. Tactile receptors on the fingers are numerous compared with those on the back; therefore, the fingers can discriminate remarkably well. In the visual system the organization of receptors has two quite different arrangements to facilitate detection. In the fovea (a small area of the retina that provides color vision) the receptors (called cones) are small and densely packed to make fine discriminations in bright light. In the periphery of the retina the receptors for black-white vision are larger and more scattered, but large numbers of rods give their input to only a few neurons. The discrimination ability of rods is not good, but their ability to detect light (say, a lighted match at a distance of 2 miles on a dark night) is quite remarkable.

Neural Relays

Each sensory system requires three to four neurons, connected in sequence, to get information from the receptor cells to the cortex (for example, the visual and somatosensory systems have three, and the auditory system has four). When one considers the convergence of the sensory systems with each relay and their subsequent divergence when they reach the cortex, it becomes apparent that there must be a change in the code from level to level. This is illustrated in Figure 6.1 for the visual system. Lashley calculated that there are about 9 million rods and cones, 3.5 million bipolar cells, 0.2 million ganglion cells, 0.03 million lateral geniculate cells, and 0.6 million area-17 cells at the different levels in the rat's visual system. (These types of cells are discussed in detail in the later section on vision.) It seems quite obvious that there is not a straight-through, point-to-point correspondence between one relay and the next, but rather a recoding of activity in successive relays. Thus, our visual system—although sometimes compared to a camera because it has a lens,

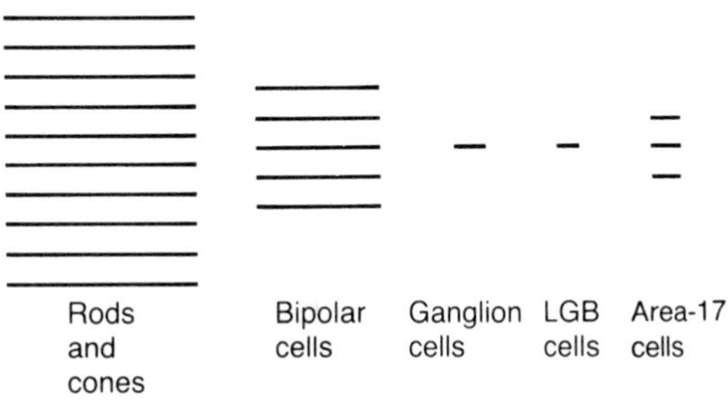

FIGURE 6.1. Diagrammatic representation of the numbers of cells at each level of the visual system. Both the length and the numbers of lines represent relative cell numbers.

an iris, and a retina for receiving light—is more like a TV camera, which turns pictures into waves that are later decoded in a TV set. Similarly, all the sensory submodalities turn energy into codes that are translated into perceptions in the brain.

Three important events can occur at the synapses between the neurons in the relays. First, a motor response can be produced. For example, axons from pain receptors first synapse in the spinal cord, where they can produce a withdrawal reflex. They next synapse in the brainstem, where they can produce whole limb or body movements, presumably withdrawal from the painful stimulus. Finally, they synapse in the thalamus, where, in conjunction with their connections in the cortex, they can produce anticipation and hence avoidance of the stimulus. Second, the message these systems carry can be modified. For example, descending impulses from the cortex can block or amplify its sensory signals. When we are excited by an activity such as playing a sport, for instance, we may not notice an injury. Later, thinking about the injury can make it seem much more painful. Third, systems can interact with one another. For example, we often rub the area around injuries to reduce their pain. Activating fine touch and pressure can apparently gate or block the transmission of information in pain pathways.

Information Coding

Once transduced, all sensory information from all sensory systems is coded by action potentials. The sensory information is conducted into the brain by bundles of axons, called *nerves* until they enter the brain or spinal cord and *tracts* thereafter, and every nerve carries the same kind of signal. How do action potentials code the differences in sensations, and how do they code the features of particular sensations? Parts of these questions seem easy to answer and other parts are very difficult. The presence of a stimulus can be coded by an increase or decrease in the discharge rate of a neuron, and the amount of change can code the intensity. Qualitative visual changes, such as a change from red to green, can be coded by activity in different neurons or even by different levels of discharge in the same neuron (that is, more activity = redder, less activity = greener).

What is less clear, however, is how we perceive such sensations as touch, sound, and smell as being different from one another. Part of the explanation is that the neural areas that process these sensations in the cortex are distinct. Another part is that we learn through experience to distinguish them. A third part is that each sensory system has a preferred link with certain kinds of movements, which ensures that the systems remain distinct at all levels of neural organization. For example, pain stimuli produce withdrawal responses, and fine touch and pressure stimuli produce approach responses. Of course, such distinctions are not always clear. There are people who can hear in color or identify smells by the sounds that they make. This ability is called **synesthesia,** or mixed senses. Anyone who has shivered upon hearing certain notes of a piece of music (or at the noise that chalk or fingernails can make on a blackboard) has "felt" sound.

Sensory Subsystems

We are used to thinking of the visual system as a single entity, but if we refer to Figure 6.2, we can see that it is really made up of a number of subsystems. We are aware of the operation of some of these subsystems, but we will not know of the operation of others until we learn about them. There is a pathway to the superoptic nucleus (1) of the hypothalamus that controls the daily rhythms of such behaviors as feeding and sleeping; a pathway to the pretectum (2) in the midbrain that controls pupillary responses to light; a pathway to the superior colliculus (3) in the midbrain that controls head orientation to objects; a pathway to the pineal body (4) that controls long-term circadian rhythms; a pathway to the accessory optic nucleus (5) that moves the eyes to compensate for head movements; a pathway to the visual cortex (6) that controls pattern perception, depth perception, color vision, and tracing of moving objects; and a pathway to the frontal cortex (7) that controls voluntary eye movements. The pathways to many of these "visual centers" are often more indirect than the illustration indicates, and they may involve other brain centers as well.

Just as there are many visual systems projecting into different brain regions, there are multiple subsystems projecting to the visual cortex. Thus, there are a number of parallel visual systems going through the visual cortex, each of which may have a rather specialized output. For example, the systems for pattern perception, color vision, depth perception, and visual tracking may be as independent from one another as are the systems that code hearing from those that code taste. The fact that they are in close anatomical proximity may not mean that they are functionally identical or interchangeable. Similarly, all of the sensory modalities contain subsystems that have specific roles.

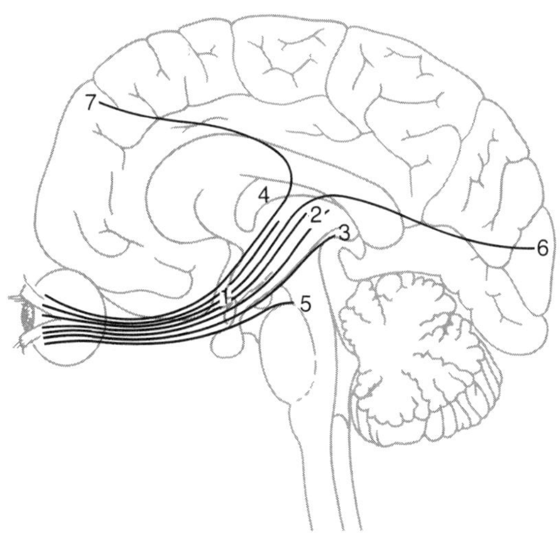

Visual system	Postulated function
1. Superoptic nucleus	Controls daily rhythms (sleep, feeding, etc.) in response to day-night cycles
2. Pretectum	Produces changes in pupil size in response to light-intensity changes
3. Superior colliculus	Head orienting, particularly to objects in peripheral visual fields
4. Pineal body	Long-term circadian rhythms
5. Acessory optic nucleus	Moves eyes to compensate for head movements
6. Visual cortex	Pattern perception, depth perception, color vision, tracking moving objects
7. Frontal eye fields	Voluntary eye movements

FIGURE 6.2. Schematic representation of visual subsystems. The numbers stand for brain structures, the lines for the individual pathways. Each pathway and each number represents a particular subsystem.

Multiple Representation

In most mammals, the neocortex represents the sensory field not once but a number of times (Figure 6.3). How many times a representation occurs depends upon the species of animal. Note that the squirrel in Figure 6.3 has 3 visual areas, whereas the owl monkey has 14. If each of these visual systems responds to one feature of the environment, then owl monkeys can see 11 kinds of things that squirrels cannot see (that is, assuming that the visual systems of both species have been mapped adequately). It is not clear what those 11 things might be since both species live in trees, have color vision, have good depth perception, and so on. Monkeys, however, make better use of their fingers, make use of facial expressions, and have a more varied diet than squirrels, and these differences might account for some of the monkey's additional functions. All mammals have at least one representation for each sensory system, and this is referred to as the primary area for that system. Additional areas are usually referred to as secondary areas because most of the information that reaches them is relayed through the primary area. Each additional representation is probably devoted to coding one specific aspect of a sensory modality.

VISION

Visual Receptors

A schematic illustration of the eye and its visual receptor surface, the retina, is presented in Figure 6.4. When light enters the eye, it is bent slightly by the cornea and then more profoundly by the lens so that images are focused on the receptors at the back of the eye. It then passes through the

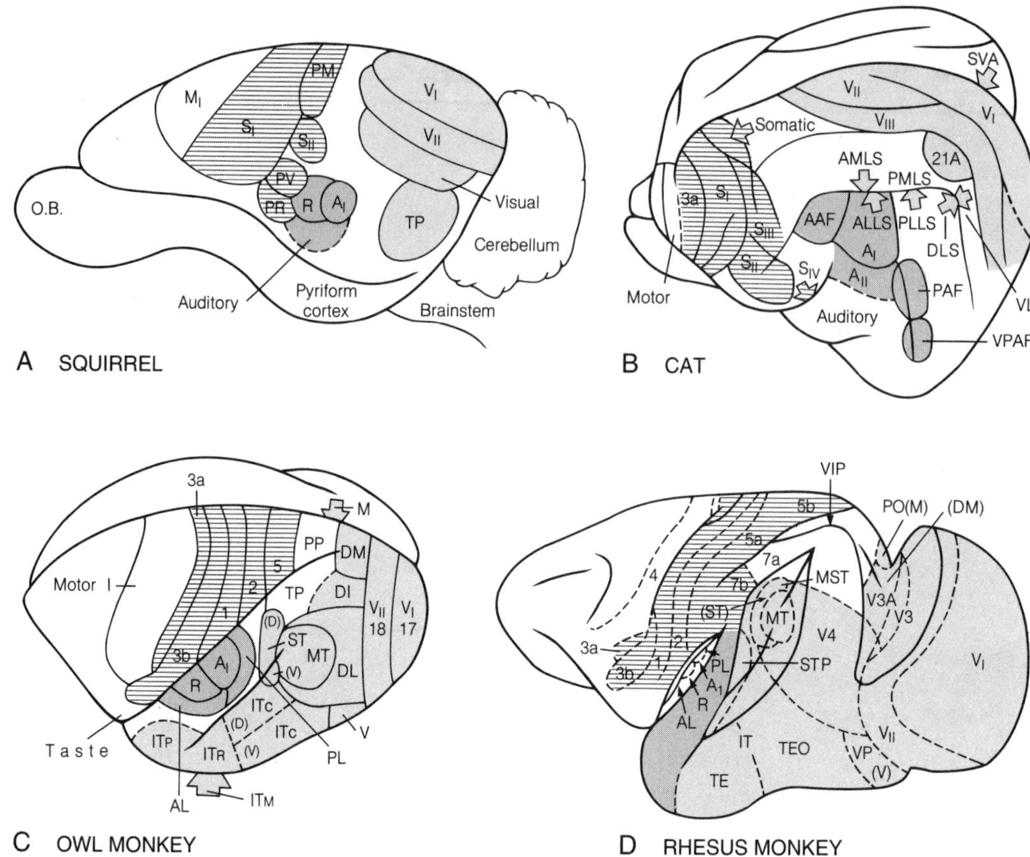

FIGURE 6.3. Subdivisions of sensory cortex in several extensively studied mammals. *A*. There are 5 somatic regions, 2 to 3 auditory regions, and 2 to 4 visual regions in the squirrel. *B*. Twelve visual areas, 4 somatic areas, and 5 auditory areas have been defined in the cat. *C*. To date, 14 visual areas, 4 auditory areas, and 5 somatic areas have been demonstrated in the owl monkey. *D*. Twelve visual areas, 4 auditory areas, and 8 somatic areas have been defined in the rhesus monkey. (After Kaas, 1987.)

photoreceptors to reflect from the **sclera** into the photoreceptors. The barrier provided by the retinal cells has little effect on our visual acuity for two reasons. First, the cells are relatively transparent and the photoreceptors are extremely sensitive; they can be excited by the absorption of a single photon of light. Second, many of the fibers forming the optic nerve skirt the central portion, or fovea, of the retina to facilitate light access to the receptors. Because of this, the fovea is seen as a depression on the retinal surface.

The retina contains two types of photoreceptive cells, rods and cones, both of which function to transduce light energy into action potentials. **Rods,** which are sensitive to dim light, are used mainly for night vision. **Cones** are better able to transduce bright light and are used for daytime vision. There are three types of cones, each type maximally responsive to wavelengths producing hues of red, blue, or yellow, and thus they mediate color vision. Rods and cones differ in their distribution across the retina; cones are packed

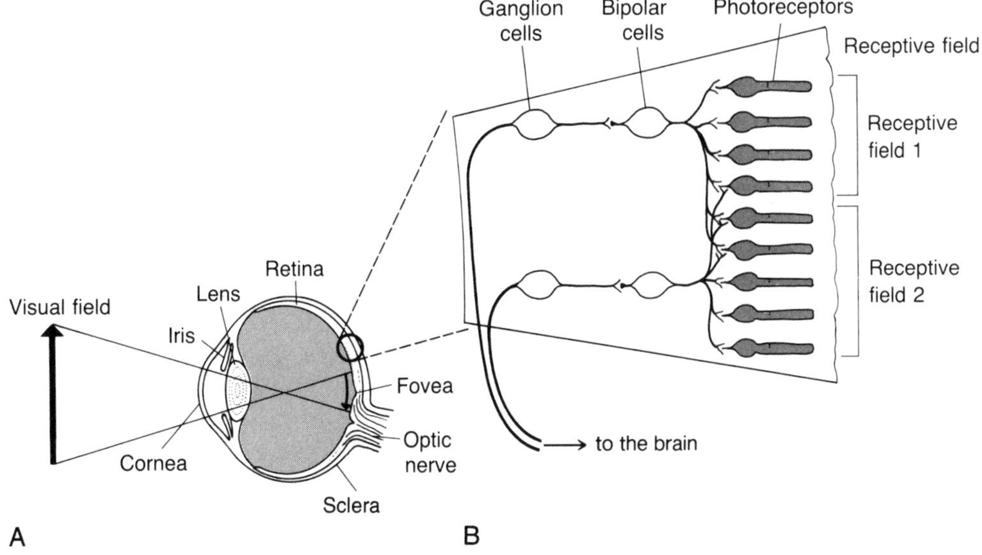

FIGURE 6.4. *A*. The anatomy of the eye. *B*. The anatomy of the retina.

together densely in the foveal region, and rods are more sparsely distributed in the periphery of the retina. Thus, to see in bright light it is best to look directly at things, and to see in dim light it is best to look slightly away.

The photoreceptive cells are connected to very simple cells called **bipolar cells,** in which the receptor cells induce graded potentials. The bipolar cells in turn induce action potentials in ganglion cells. As illustrated in Figure 6.4, it is the **ganglion cells** that send axons into the brain proper (the retina is actually part of the brain). In addition to the cells that relay information to the cortex, there are other cells in the retina—including horizontal and amacerine cells—that play a role in determining how cells in the retina code information.

Visual Pathways

The axons of ganglion cells leave the retina to form the optic nerve. Just before entering the brain the optic nerves partly cross, forming the **optic chiasm** (from the Greek letter χ). At this point about half the fibers from each eye cross, as illustrated in Figure 6.5A, in such a way that each visual half-field will be represented in the opposite hemisphere of the brain. Animals with eyes on the side of their head (rats, for example) have as many as 95% of their optic fibers crossing in order to ensure this crossed representation.

Having entered the brain, the ganglion cells divide, forming a number of separate pathways. The largest of these is the **geniculostriate system,** the projection that goes to the lateral geniculate nucleus or body (LGB) of the thalamus and then to layer 4 of the visual cortex. (Layer 4 of the visual cortex in primates is very large and has the form of a stripe across the visual cortex, hence the name striate or striped cortex.) The ganglion cells of the geniculostriate system synapse in the LGB. The LGB has six well-defined layers: layers 2, 3, and 5 receive fibers from the ipsilateral eye, and layers 1, 4, and 6 receive fibers from the contralateral eye. The topographic relation of the visual field is also maintained in the LGB, with the central portion representing the central visual field and the peripheral portions representing the peripheral visual field.

The LGB cells project mainly to area 17 of the visual cortex (there are thought to be smaller pro-

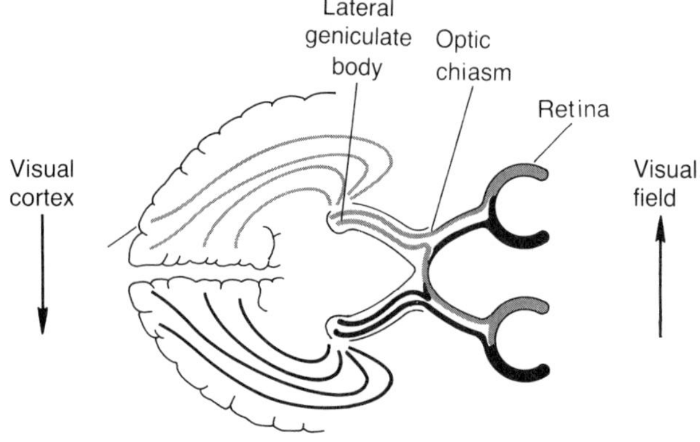

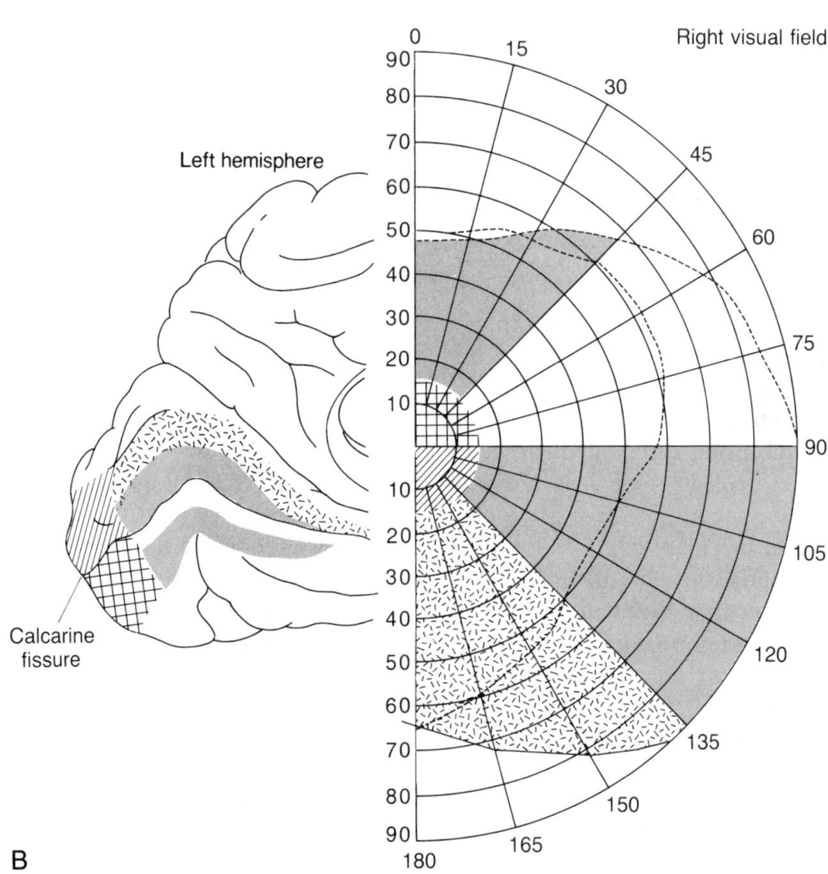

FIGURE 6.5. *A*. Projection of the visual system. Note that the visual fields are projected to the contralateral visual cortex. *B*. Projection of the right visual field on the left hemisphere (medial view). Note the relationship between the topography of the visual field and the topography of the cortex. (After Poggio, 1968.)

jections to other areas), where they are distributed in such a way that the visual field is again topographically represented. This representation, illustrated in Figure 6.5B, is quite easy to remember if one notes that it is upside down, inverted, and reversed. The central part of the visual field is represented at the back of the brain, and the peripheral part is represented toward the middle of the brain. The upper part of the visual field is represented below the calcarine fissure, and the lower part of the visual world is represented above the calcarine fissure. Figure 6.5 also shows that the visual input that strikes the left side of each retina, and therefore originates from the right side of the world, eventually goes to the left hemisphere.

Other visual pathways go to the superior colliculus, accessory optic nucleus, pretectum, and superoptic nucleus, as shown in Figure 6.6. Note also that the projections to the superior colliculus can reach the cortex through relays in the lateral posterior-pulvinar complex of the thalamus. Since the tectopulvinar pathway is the visual system in fish, amphibians, and reptiles, we can expect it to be capable of reasonably sophisticated vision.

Visual Cortex

The LGB is subdivided into two groups of cells on the basis of cell size, and size in turn is related to the kind of information the cells signal (Figure 6.7). Layers 5 and 6 are known as the **magnocellular layers,** because they are composed of large cells. They receive their input from large ganglion fibers called Y fibers. These fibers in turn receive their input from rods and are thus very sensitive to light but not to color. Layers 1 through 4 are known as the **parvocellular layers** because they are composed of smaller cells. They receive their input from small ganglion cells, each of which receives its input from one of the three kinds of cones. Thus, parvocellular cells are relatively less sensitive to light in general but are more sensitive to color. When these LGB cells project to layer 4 of the visual cortex they remain segregated. One zone in layer 4 receives input only from the parvocellular layer, and one receives input from the magnocellular layer. This segregation continues into the secondary areas; the various secondary areas are specialized for dif-

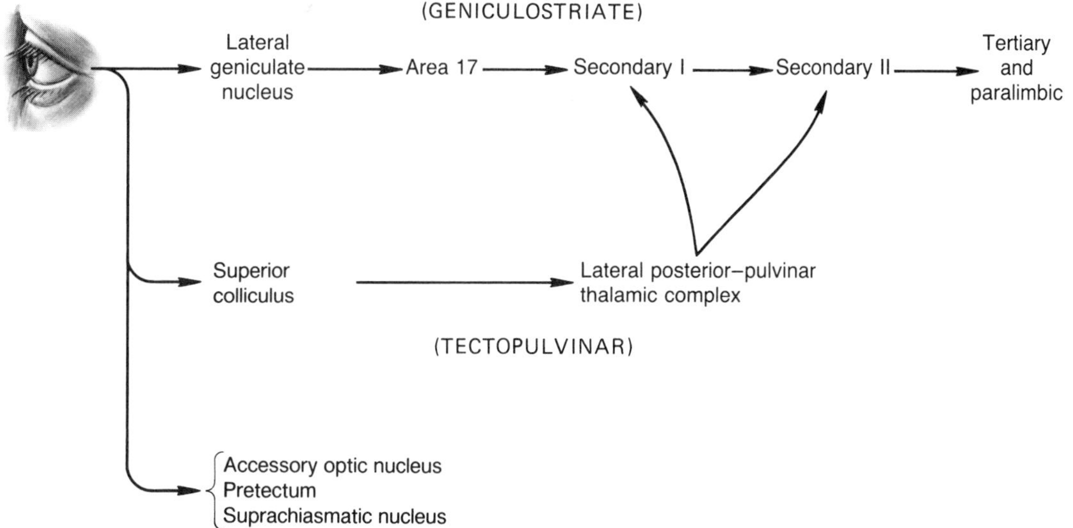

FIGURE 6.6. The connections of the visual system. One subsystem, the geniculostriate system, is specialized for pattern analysis; the other, the tectopulvinar system, is specialized for the detection of and orientation to visual stimuli.

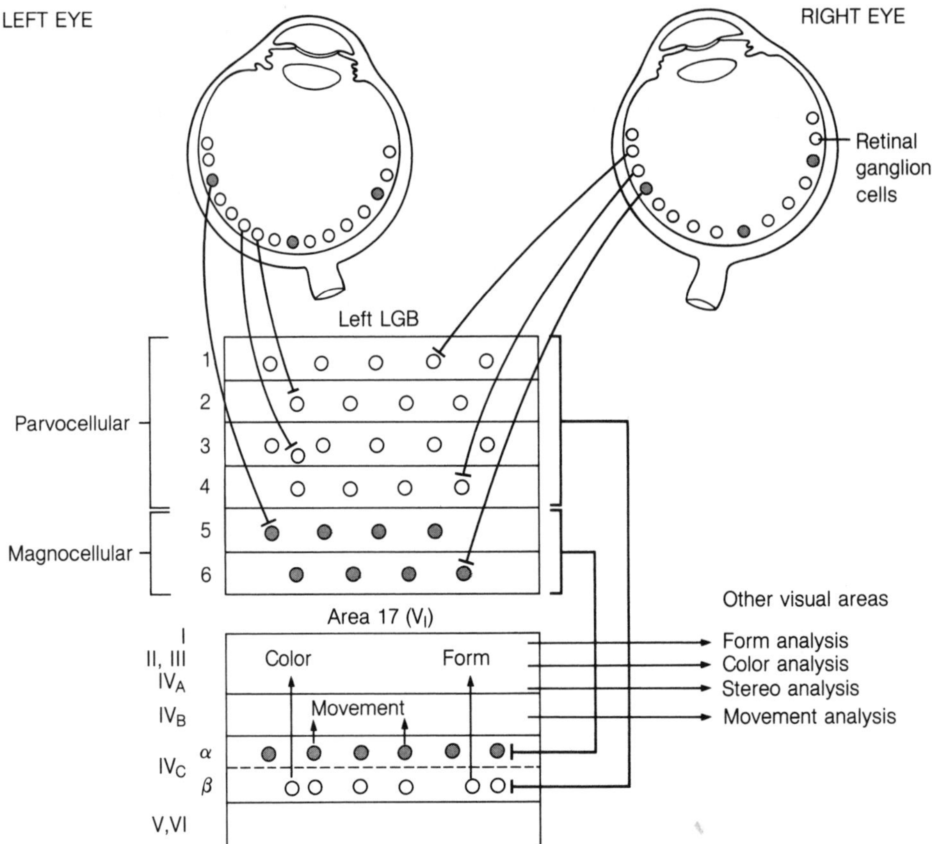

FIGURE 6.7. A schematic illustration showing that the primate visual system consists of several independent subdivisions that differ in their sensitivity to movement, color, depth, and shape. The parvocellular layers receive inputs from single cone types, whereas the magnocellular layers receive inputs from more than one cone type. The parvocellular and magnocellular layers project to different parts of layer 4 in area 17. In turn, these layers have different connections in the cortical columns, leading to segregation of color, form, and movement in other visual areas.

ferent kinds of vision (for example, shape, motion, and depth and color).

There are probably other subsystems within the geniculostriate system. The precise number of these retinal representations is not known for humans, but in monkeys there may be as many as 14 independently organized areas. The entire visual field is systematically represented in each of these independently organized areas. These visual representations are not mere copies of one another, because the size and organization of each field are different.

We have pointed out that the left visual field is represented in the right hemisphere and the right visual field is represented in the left hemisphere. How then are the two hemifields bound together to make a unified representation of the visual world? The answer is that the corpus callosum binds the hemifields. The midline of a representation in one hemisphere is connected to the midline of the representation in the other hemisphere. The rest of the fields are not connected.

Properties of Cells in Visual Areas

By using microelectrodes, neurophysiologists have recorded the activity of cells in anesthetized cats and monkeys while visual stimuli are presented on a screen placed in the animals' visual field. As we have noted, cells at each level of the visual system are responsive to a specific region of the visual field, known as the receptive field. Cells at each level of the visual system differ in two ways, however. First, the receptive fields tend to be larger at each succeeding level closer to the secondary cortex. Second, cells in different levels of the visual system respond to different properties of visual stimulation.

Generally, the farther along a cell is in the visual system, the more complex the visual stimulus must be to excite it. For example, cells in the retina are most responsive to spots of light falling in the center of their receptive fields. In some retinal cells this light rapidly increases the firing rate of the cell, and in others it inhibits all firing of the cell. In contrast, cells in area 17 are more responsive to bars of light of a particular orientation. Some cells are most responsive to bars of light oriented at 90° from the horizontal, whereas others are most responsive to bars oriented at other angles. Additionally, some cells are more sensitive to colors and others are more sensitive to motion and so forth.

Cells in the secondary areas require more complex stimuli, being most responsive to specific stimuli such as color and motion. Cells in some visual areas, such as the inferotemporal cortex, may require a very specific shape for maximum response (for example, a hand or a face), yet they can tolerate substantial changes in the size of the stimulus (**object constancy**), a characteristic that may be a physiological basis for constancy. These cells are sometimes referred to as grandmother cells, because it is hypothesized that they can have very specific responses for particular stimuli such as one's grandmother.

HEARING

Auditory Receptors

Sound consists of changes in air pressure; the frequency of pressure changes determines the frequency that we hear, and the amplitude of the pressure changes determines the loudness of the sound. The ear is composed of three portions, the outer, middle, and inner (Figure 6.8A). The outer ear consists of the pinna and the external ear canal. The pinna catches the waves of pressure and deflects them into the external ear canal, which amplifies the waves somewhat and directs them to the eardrum. When sound waves strike the eardrum it vibrates.

The middle ear contains three small bones or ossicles (the malleus, incus, and stapes) that are connected in series and that connect the eardrum to the round window. The vibration of the eardrum in turn vibrates the bones, producing an action like a piston that conveys and amplifies the vibrations of the eardrum to the round window.

In the inner ear is the cochlea, which is the portion of the ear that contains the sensory receptors. The cochlea is filled with fluid; floating in the middle of this fluid is a thin membrane called the basilar membrane. Embedded in a portion of the basilar membrane, called the organ of Corti, are hair cells. When the round window vibrates it sets up waves that travel through the fluid of the cochlea. The waves cause the basilar membrane to bend, and when the membrane bends the hair cells are stimulated, generating an action potential in those cells.

The basilar membrane is a not a uniform structure; it is narrow (100 μm [microns]) and thick near the round window and thinner and wider at its other end. It was Hermann von Helmholtz who in the late 1800s proposed that different portions of the basilar membrane resonate with different frequencies of sound because of this structure. Although von Helmholtz was not precisely correct, it was not until 1960 that George von Békésy was able to observe the basilar membrane directly to show that a traveling wave moves along it, starting at the oval window. He was able to place little grains on the basilar membrane and

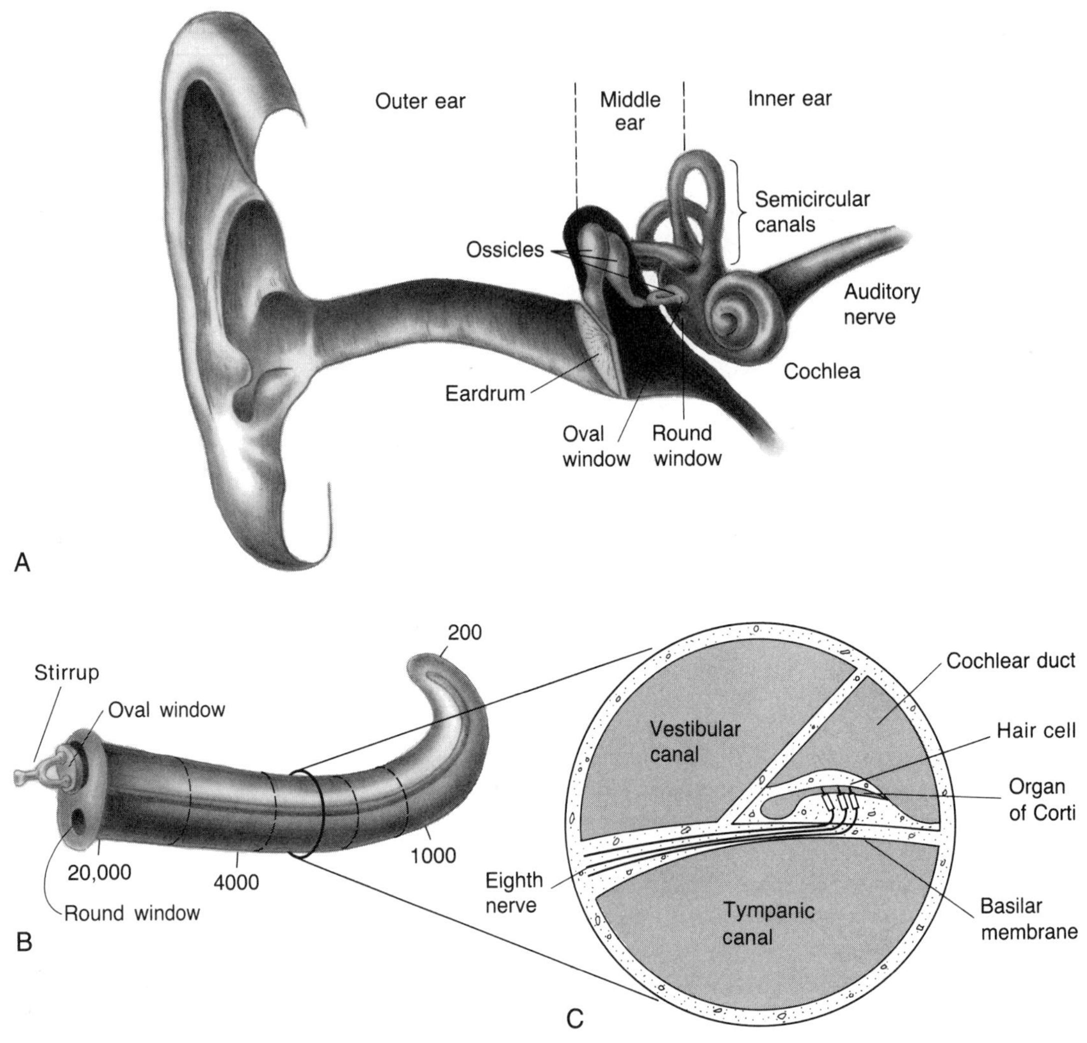

FIGURE 6.8. *A*. Anatomy of the ear. *B*. Anatomy of the cochlea and basilar membrane. The numbers represent frequencies to which the basilar membrane is maximally responsive. *C*. Cross section of the cochlea.

watch them jump in different places with different frequencies of vibration. Faster waves cause maximum peaks near the base of the basilar membrane, and slower frequencies cause maximum peaks near the apex. As a rough analogy, consider what happens when you shake a towel. If you shake it very quickly, the waves are very small and remain close to the portion of the towel that you are holding. But if you shake the towel slowly with a large movement, the waves reach their peak farther along the towel. The difference between the basilar membrane and the towel is that the basilar membrane is very short (33 mm) and there is only one peak. The hair cells in the organ of Corti are maximally disturbed at the point of the peak of the wave, resulting in the maximal neural response of hair cells at that point. A signal composed of many frequencies will cause several different points along the basilar membrane to vibrate and will excite hair cells at all these points.

As in the visual system, each of the receptor cells in the auditory system has its own receptive field, as does each cell in the higher auditory centers. The receptive field of the hair cells is not a point in space, as in the visual system, but rather a particular frequency of sound. Thus, in contrast to the retinotopic maps in the visual system, the auditory system is composed of tonotopic maps. By comparing the arrival of sound at each ear, sound can be located in space, and so the auditory system also has a map of space around the body on which it locates sound sources.

Auditory Pathways

The axons of the hair cells leave the cochlea to form the major part of the auditory nerve, the eighth cranial nerve. This nerve first projects to the level of the medulla in the lower brainstem, synapsing either in the dorsal or ventral cochlear nuclei or in the superior olivary nucleus. The axons of cells in these areas form the lateral lemniscus, which terminates in discrete zones of the inferior colliculus. Two distinct pathways emerge from the colliculus, coursing to the ventral and the dorsal medial geniculate bodies (Figure 6.9). The ventral region projects to the core auditory cortex (AI or Brodmann's area 41), and the dorsal region projects to the secondary regions, thus corresponding to the general pattern of multiple independent ascending pathways to the cortex. In contrast to the visual system, the projections of the auditory system provide both ipsilateral and contralateral inputs to the cortex, so that there is bilateral representation of each cochlear nucleus in the cortex. The majority of the input is contralateral, however, which is important in understanding the studies of cerebral asymmetry.

Auditory Cortex

In contrast to studies of the visual cortex and the somatosensory cortex, there has been relatively little research on the auditory cortex of primates. Most of the research has been done with cats, in which direct homologies to the human auditory cortex are uncertain. Nevertheless, there are sufficient data to provide a basis for general principles of auditory cortical organization in primates. There are several auditory areas in the cortex, because different regions of the medial geniculate nucleus project to independent tonotopically organized cortical zones in both cats and monkeys. These zones include the primary auditory cortex (AI or 41) and at least four other zones surrounding it.

In the human, the core area is within **Heschl's gyrus**, (Figure 6.10) and is surrounded by seven secondary areas (labeled a–g in the figure). Although the auditory cortex is normally thought of as being in the temporal lobe, it can be seen in Figure 6.10 that it actually extends into the parietal lobe, both into the parietal operculum, which is the parietal tissue on the upper side of the Sylvian fissure, and into the inferior parietal cortex, which is the parietal cortex at the posterior end of

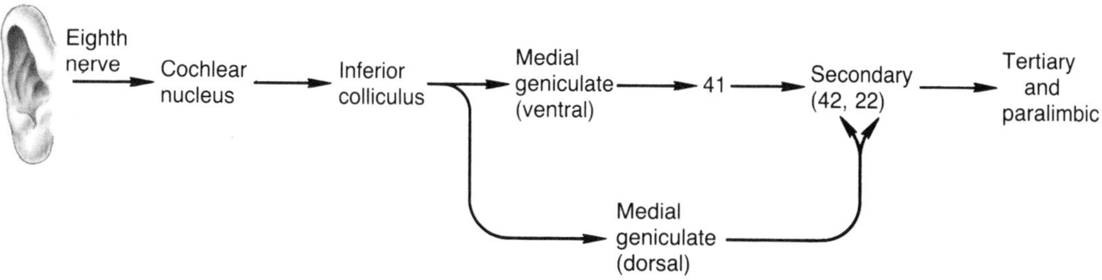

FIGURE 6.9. The major connections of the auditory system.

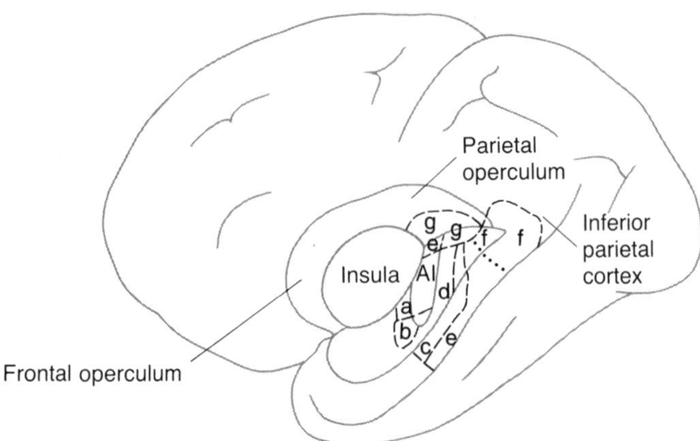

FIGURE 6.10. Representation of the auditory areas of the human brain. Dashed lines indicate borders between areas; solid lines indicate sulci. The lateral fissure has been schematically opened to illustrate the cortex within. The secondary areas are labeled a–g. (After Galaburda and Sanides, 1980.)

the Sylvian fissure. The tonotopic organization of each auditory area remains to be completely mapped, although in general it appears that in each subfield that has been mapped, low tones are represented toward the back and high tones more anteriorally.

There are species differences in the organization of the secondary cortex, as well as a marked anatomical asymmetry in humans that has not been described in cats or monkeys. In right-handed people the secondary cortex (known as the **planum temporale**) is larger on the left, whereas the primary cortex (Heschl's gyrus) is larger on the right.

Properties of Cells in the Auditory System

Microelectrode studies have shown that single neurons in the auditory system code the frequency (or pitch) of sounds, different neurons being maximally sensitive to different sound frequencies. In general, cells in subcortical nuclei are responsive to a broader band of frequencies than are cells higher in the system. Thus, a neuron in the cochlear nucleus may have a tuning curve with maximum sensitivity at 7000 Hz and partial sensitivity to frequencies between 1000 and 12,000 Hz, as compared with a neuron in AI, whose tuning curve is also maximally sensitive to 7000 Hz but is partially responsive to frequencies between only 5000 and 9000 Hz. In some of the secondary areas the specificity of frequency is reduced slightly, because the cells are also responsive both to very small differences in arrival time in the two ears (as little as 30 μs [microseconds, or 300 millionths of a second]) and to other special characteristics of sound such as harmonics. In humans it is likely that there are cells in the secondary auditory areas that are maximally sensitive to speech sounds (for example, da, la, ma), although this has not yet been demonstrated.

BALANCE

The inner ear also contains the receptor system that allows us to stay upright and keep our balance. This system is made up of two parts: (1) the **semicircular canals,** and (2) the **otolith organs,** the **utricle** and **saccule.** These receptors also contain hair cells that are bent when the head changes position. The three semicircular canals lie in different planes that are perpendicular to one another, and so they can respond to any movement of the head. The otolith organs detect linear acceleration of the head and are also responsive to the position of the head with respect to gravity. In addition the otoliths are sensitive to the static position of the head in space, whereas the semicircular canals are more sensitive to head movement. Fibers from the balance receptors project over the eighth nerve to a number of nuclei in the brainstem. These nuclei participate in maintaining balance while we move and also aid in controlling eye movements.

TOUCH

The visual and auditory systems are known as **exteroceptive** systems because they are sensitive to stimuli from the external environment. The somatosensory system or body sense system also has an exteroceptive function. In addition, however, it is **proprioceptive,** meaning that it provides information about the position of body segments relative to one another and the position of the body in space; it is also **interoceptive,** meaning that it records internal bodily events such as blood pressure. The somatosensory system is therefore not a single sensory system but a multiple one composed of several submodalities: (1) touch-pressure, which is sensation elicited by mechanical stimulation of the body surface; (2) position sense, or **kinesthesis,** which results from mechanical disturbances in the muscles and joints; this system has two subcomponents, the sense of static limb position and the sensation of limb movement; (3) heat and cold; and (4) pain, which is elicited by noxious stimulation.

Somatosensory Receptors

The somatosensory system has at least 20 different types of receptor cells, each transducing a different form of energy. Furthermore, the receptor surface of the somatosensory system is much larger than that of any other sense, because there are receptors in all body tissues except the brain itself. The basic organization of the receptors, however, is the same as in the two previously discussed systems, because the membrane potential of each is altered by a particular form of energy and because each has its own receptive field, which is an area of body tissue.

Hair Receptors. Hair receptors are located in hair follicles and are exquisitely sensitive to the bending of a hair. There are a number of types of hair receptors, each with distinctive morphological and physiological properties.

Touch Receptors. Touch receptors are quite varied in the spectrum of stimuli that excite them and in the morphology of their receptor specializations. They respond to stimulus characteristics such as vibration, skin indentation, and certain types of hair movements, with some receptors responding to the velocity of onset of stimulation and others to the duration of stimulation, or to moving stimuli. Touch receptors include Pacinian corpuscles, field receptors, Meissner's corpuscles, Merkel cell-neurite complexes, Ruffini endings, and mechanoreceptors.

Temperature Receptors. Temperature receptors (cold receptors and warm receptors) are sensitive to temperature change, showing a discharge that is related to skin temperature. Cold receptors are excited by decreases in skin temperature when the initial skin temperature ranges from approximately 15° to 40°C. Warm receptors respond maximally to increases in temperature in the approximate range of 30° to 48°C. Other types of receptors (some touch receptors and nociceptors) also respond to rapid temperature changes, but they are not specialized just for temperature changes as are the temperature receptors.

Nociceptors. Nociceptors, or pain receptors, are sensitive to mechanical or thermal stimuli that begin near levels that damage the tissue. In addition, some of these fibers respond to chemical stimuli. There are four types of nociceptors: mechanical nociceptors, mechanical and thermal nociceptors, deep pressure-pain receptors, and visceral afferents. The discharge of some of these receptors is associated with bright or sharp pain, which tells us where the pain is, and dull pain, which is more enduring and tells us we are still injured.

Joint Receptors. These receptors are responsive to the movements and positions of limbs. There are at least three types, including Ruffini endings, Paciniform corpuscles, and Golgi receptors.

Muscle and Tendon Receptors. These receptors are located in the muscles and tendons, responding primarily to stretch and contraction of these organs. They include muscle spindle receptors and Golgi tendon organs.

It should be apparent from our brief overview of the somatosensory receptors that the central representation of the information from all these receptors must be very complex indeed if there is to be a representation of all this information in the cortex, and if it is to be integrated to allow us a perception of touch.

Somatosensory Pathways

The somatosensory system can be seen as two subsystems, one for fine touch, pressure, and kinesthesis, the other for pain and temperature. Fibers that form the first system leave the receptors and ascend via the dorsal columns of the spinal cord to synapse in the cuneate and gracile nuclei of the lower brainstem. The fibers then cross to the opposite side of the brain to form the medial lemniscus, which terminates in the ventroposterior region of the ventrobasal thalamus (Figure 6.11). This thalamic nucleus then projects primarily to Brodmann's area 3-1-2, to form independent somatotopic maps.

In contrast to this pattern, the fibers of the pain and temperature system leave the receptors to synapse in the dorsal horn (the substantia gelatinosa) of the spinal cord. The cells in this area then cross over to the other side of the cord and form the lateral spinothalamic tract, which terminates primarily in the dorsal portions of the ventrobasal thalamus (ventroposterior oral and ventroposterior superior) as well as in the posterior thalamus. These nuclei project in turn to area 3-1-2. Thus, we see that there are multiple pathways to independent representations of the receptor surface in the somatosensory system, as was the case in other sensory systems.

Somatosensory Cortex

Like the other sensory systems, the somatosensory system is composed of a primary core area and a

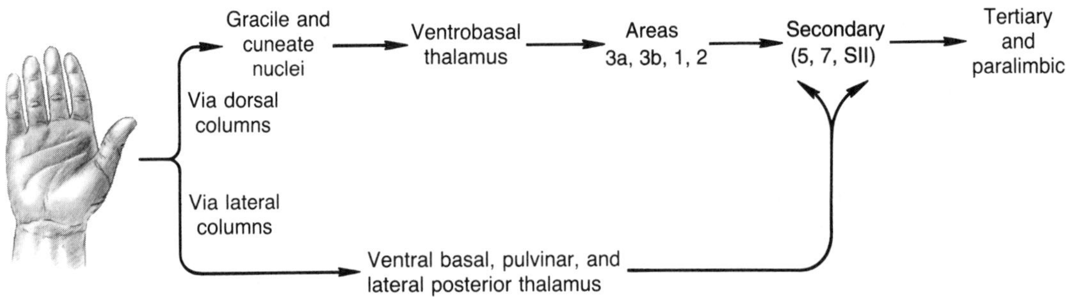

FIGURE 6.11. Major connections of the somatosensory system. The system has two major subdivisions that converge on the somatosensory cortex: one for fine touch, pressure, and kinesthesis; the other for pain and temperature.

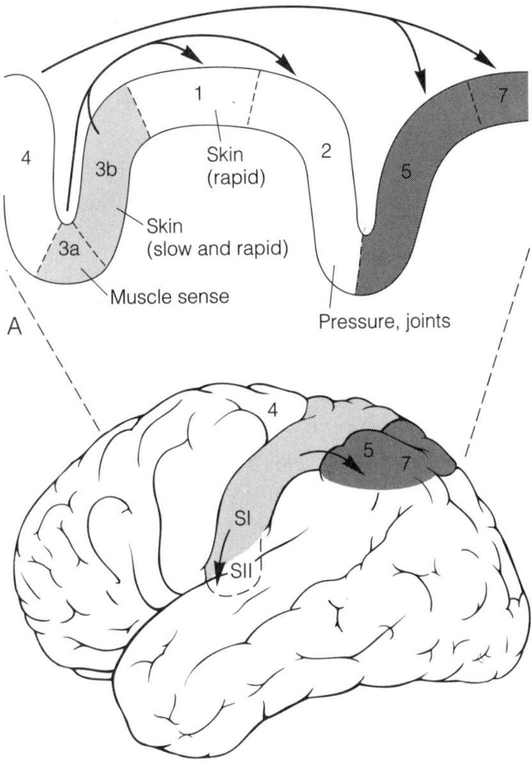

FIGURE 6.12. *A.* A section through SI (Brodmann's area 3-1-2) showing its subdivisions, the major response features of its cells, and interrelations. *B.* A lateral view of the human brain illustrating the locations of areas involved in somatosensation.

number of secondary areas. As illustrated in Figure 6.12, SI (somatosensory area I or Brodmann's area 3-1-2) forms the primary area, and it sends projections into SII and into areas 5 and 7. SI also sends projections into the adjacent motor cortex, area 4. Figure 6.12B shows a lateral section through these areas.

SI is made up of at least four areas, 3a, 3b, 1, and 2. Recording experiments show that each of these areas is dominated by responses to one type of body receptor, although there is overlap. Area 3a represents muscle sense (position and movement of muscles), area 3b represents slowly and rapidly adapting skin receptors, area 1 represents rapidly adapting skin receptors, and area 2 represents deep pressure and joint sense. Thus the body is represented at least four times in SI. Additionally, there are a number of other receptor types represented in each area, and so it is possible that there are still more body representation areas.

The somatotopic maps are disproportionate to the surface of the body (Figure 6.13) but proportionate to the subjective experience of sensitivity in different parts of the body. Thus the lips, tongue, hands, and fingers take up much more cortical area than the rest of the body and, of course, they are the most sensitive areas of the body. Therefore the somatotopic maps are at least partly maps of receptor distribution.

Species vary considerably in the distribution of receptors on the body surface, and therefore they

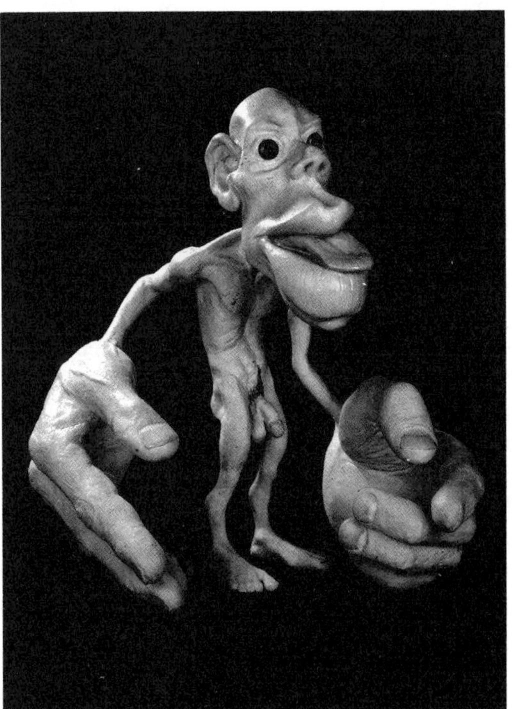

FIGURE 6.13. The misshapen appearance of this little man (or homunculus) reflects the disproportionate areas of the somatic sensory cortex devoted to different parts of the body. (After Bloom and Lazereson, 1988.)

also differ in their somatotopic maps. For example, the representation for the face of the rat, including the tactile hairs known as vibrissae, is very large relative to any other body part. The face and vibrissae of the rat are extremely sensitive, enabling rats to make tactile discriminations with only a single vibrissae. By contrast, an anteater, which uses its tongue to explore for ants, should have a truly impressive tongue representation on its cortex.

Properties of Cells in Somatosensory Areas

Microelectrode studies have suggested that at least five basic sensations are independently coded throughout the somatosensory system: light touch to the skin, deep pressure to the fascia below the skin, joint movement, pain, and temperature. Within the thalamus, cells are highly specific, any given cell being maximally responsive to only one mode of stimulation. Within the next higher level, in areas 3a and 3b of the cortex, the cells are just as specific to particular stimuli, but a given cell is responsive to a smaller region of skin. Thus, in the cortex there is increased discrimination of spatial location of the receptor surface.

In other cortical areas, including areas 1 and 2, receptive fields are larger and the properties of the cells are more complex in that they respond to edges and to objects. In addition some cells, especially in the hand region, have very complex properties, responding to the movement of stimuli in one direction or another or to the precise orientation of tactile stimuli on the skin surface. These neurons probably play some special role during movements of the hand designed to explore the shape of an object, and they also play a role in **stereognosis,** the ability to perceive a three-dimensional structure tactilely.

TASTE AND SMELL

The senses of taste and smell (or olfaction) do not have the extensive cortical representation that vision, audition, and touch do, and thus they do not appear as attractive (or perhaps as glamorous!) to neuroscientists for study. As a result there is far less known about these senses, even at the level of receptors, than about the other senses. Our discussion of these senses therefore will be limited, especially with respect to cortical contributions to taste and olfaction.

Receptors

In contrast to the other senses in which the stimuli are physical energy, the stimuli for taste and smell are chemical. There are specialized receptors in each system, as one would expect. For taste, the receptors are the taste buds, which are mistakenly believed by most people to be the bumps on the tongue. In fact, the bumps, called papillae, probably help the tongue grasp food; the taste buds lie buried around them. Saliva coats the tongue, and the chemicals in food are held in the saliva to be tasted. If the tongue is dry, the taste buds work poorly and food is difficult to taste. There are four different taste receptor types, each responding to a different chemical component of food: sweet, sour, salty, and bitter. The receptors for bitter lie exclusively at the back of the tongue and those for sweet at the front. Those for sour and salty are found on the sides. The taste specificity of particular receptors is not absolute because single fibers can respond to a variety of chemical stimuli. It appears likely that the perceived taste of any stimulus results from a pattern of firing of the entire population of taste receptors. Curiously, there are significant differences in the taste preferences both within and between species. For example, humans and rats both like sucrose and saccharin solutions, but dogs reject saccharin and cats are indifferent to both. Similarly, within the human species there are clear differences in taste thresholds. Older people generally have higher thresholds, largely because there is a dramatic reduction in the number of taste buds during aging. It is little wonder that children tolerate spices poorly: their taste is stronger. Furthermore, Bartoshuk has shown that there are absolute differences between adults: some people perceive certain tastes as strong and offensive, whereas others are indifferent to them.

The receptor surface for olfaction is the olfactory epithelium, which is located in the nasal cavity. The surface is composed of three cell types: receptor cells, supporting cells, and the cells below them, called basal cells. The receptor cells are covered by a layer of mucus in which receptor cilia are embedded. Thus, odors must pass through the mucus to reach the receptors, which means that changes in the properties of the mucus (such as when we have a cold) may influence how easily an odor can get to the receptors. The axons of the receptor cells form the olfactory tract. It is interesting to note that the area of the epithelium varies considerably across species. Estimates of its area are on the order of 2 or 4 cm^2 in humans, 18 cm^2 in dogs, and 21 cm^2 in cats. Such differences imply that there are interspecies differences in sensitivity to odors, which does seem to be true.

It is not clear how various odors produce different activity in the olfactory receptors. Individual receptors are not specific to single odors, and so it is likely that different proteins in the receptors are responsive to specific molecules of a given odor. Perhaps different receptors have different distributions of receptor proteins. Presumably it is the summed action of many receptors that leads to a particular pattern of neural activity that the olfactory system identifies as a particular odor.

Pathways

Three cranial nerves carry information from the tongue: the glossopharyngeal nerve (IX), the vagus nerve (X), and the chorda tympani branch of the facial nerve (VII). All three nerves enter the solitary tract, which forms the main gustatory nerve. There are two pathways originating in the solitary tract, as illustrated in Figure 6.14. One route goes to the ventroposterior medial nucleus of the thalamus, which in turn leads to two pathways—one to SI, and the other to a region just rostral to SII, in the insular cortex. The latter region is probably a pure taste area since it is not responsive to tactile stimulation. In contrast, the SI projection is sensitive to tactile stimuli and is probably responsible for the localization of tastes on the tongue. Those who enjoy wine are familiar with this distinction because wines are described not only by their gustatory qualities but also by the locations of flavors on the tongue. A second pathway of the solitary tract leads to the pontine taste area, which in turn projects to the lateral hypothalamus and amygdala. Both of these areas are involved in feeding, although the precise role of the taste information is uncertain.

The axons of the olfactory receptor cells synapse in the olfactory bulb, which is made up of several layers and may be seen as an analogue to the retina. Unlike the retina, however, little is known about the physiological organization of the olfactory bulb. The major output of the bulb

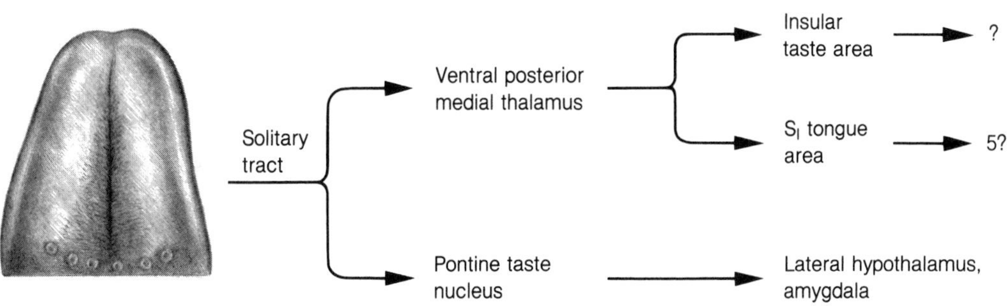

FIGURE 6.14. The major connections of the taste system.

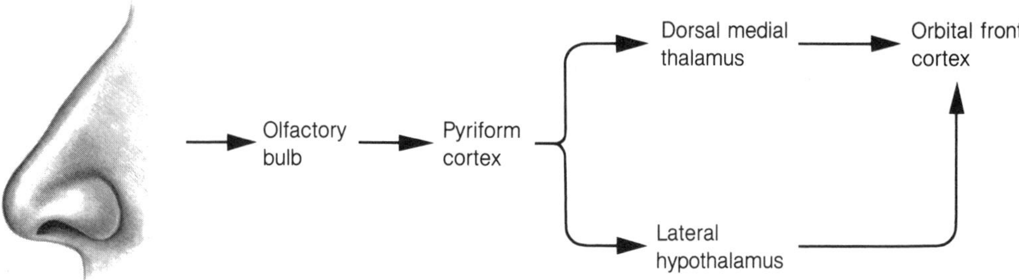

FIGURE 6.15. The major connections of the olfactory system.

is the lateral olfactory tract, which passes ipsilaterally to the pyriform cortex (Figure 6.15). The primary projection of the pyriform cortex is to the central portion of the dorsal medial nucleus of the thalamus, which in turn projects to the orbitofrontal cortex. Thus, the orbitofrontal cortex can be seen as the primary olfactory neocortex. There does not appear to be a secondary olfactory cortex. A second pyriform projection goes to the lateral hypothalamus, which in turn projects to the orbitofrontal cortex. Thus, as with the other sensory systems, there are two parallel routes for olfactory input to the cortex.

PERCEPTION

We have reviewed the basic organization of the sensory systems, illustrating the neural pathways from the receptors to the tertiary cortex and identifying some principles that govern the operation of the sensory systems. Our description is rather sterile, however, since our experiences of sensory stimuli are far richer than a mere description of the anatomy and physiology would lead us to believe. Our sensory impressions obviously are affected by our past experiences, the contexts in which they occur, our emotional state, and so on. There is certainly far more to the sensory systems than the transduction of physical energy into nervous activity. Our subjective experience of the physical energy is perception, and it is perception, rather than sensory transduction, that is of most interest to the neuropsychologist.

A

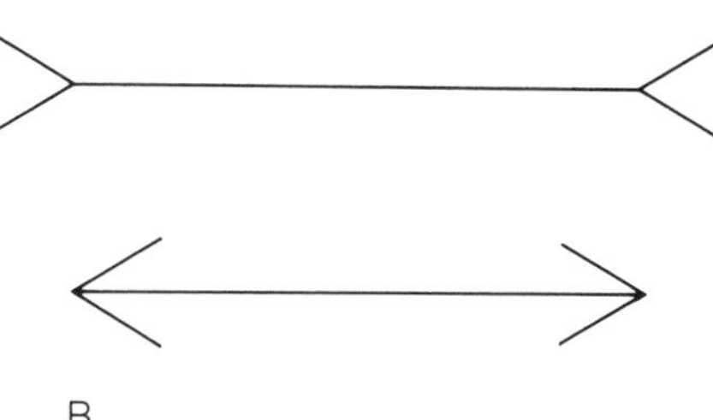

B

FIGURE 6.16. Demonstration of the distinction between sensation and perception. *A.* An ambiguous or reversible figure first described by Rubin. The figure can be seen as a vase or as two faces. *B.* The Müller-Lyer illusion: the top line appears longer than the bottom line because of contextual cues (the arrowheads).

The clearest proof that perception is more than sensation is the transformation of the same sensory stimulation into totally different perceptions and the fact that perceptions are affected by the context of the sensory input. The classic demonstration of the former effect is illustrated with such ambiguous figures as Rubin's vases (Figure 6.16A). The figure may be seen either as a vase or as two faces, and if one fixates on the center, the perceptions alternate even though the sensory stimulation remains constant. Similarly, the Müller-Lyer illusion in Figure 6.16B demonstrates the influence of context. The top line is perceived as longer than the bottom although both are the same length. The contextual cues (the arrowheads) alter the perception of line length. Ambiguous figures and illusions involve complex perceptual phenomena that are mediated by the neocortex. They also illustrate the complexity of perceptual phenomena and allow us some insight into the bases of cognitive processes.

REFERENCES

Bartoshuk, L. M. Gustatory system. In R. B. Masterton, ed. *Handbook of Behavioral Neurobiology,* vol. 1. New York: Plenum, 1978.

Bloom, F. E., and A. Lazerson. *Brain, Mind, and Behavior.* New York: W. H. Freeman, 1988.

Galaburda, A., and F. Sanides. Cytoarchitectonic organization of the human auditory cortex. *Journal of Comparative Neurology* 190:597–610, 1980.

Imig, T. J., M. A. Ruggero, L. M. Kitzes, E. Javel, and J. F. Brugge. Organization of auditory cortex in the owl monkey *(Aotus trivirgatus). Journal of Comparative Neurology* 171:111–128, 1977.

Kaas, J. H. The organization and evolution of neocortex. In S. P. Wise, ed. *Higher Brain Functions.* New York: John Wiley, 1987.

Kandel, E. R., and J. H. Schwartz. *Principles of Neural Science.* New York: Elsevier, 1991.

Lashley, K. S. The mechanisms of vision. XVI. The functioning of small remnants of the visual cortex. *Journal of Comparative Neurology* 70:45–67, 1939.

Livingston, M., and D. Hubel. Segregation of form, color, movement and depth: Anatomy, physiology, and perception. *Science* 240:740–749, 1988.

Masterton, R. B., ed. *Handbook of Behavioral Neurobiology,* vol. 1. New York: Plenum, 1978.

Merzenich, M. M., and J. F. Brugge. Representation of the cochlear partition on the superior temporal plane of the macaque monkey. *Brain Research* 50:276–296, 1973.

Poggio, G. F. Central neural mechanisms in vision. In V. B. Mountcastle, ed. *Medical Physiology.* St Louis: Mosby, 1968.

chapter seven

Organization of the Motor Systems

The first movements made by the newt *Amblystoma* (a small tailed amphibian) in its development are coiling movements of the whole body. The coiling is gradually modified until repeated alternating coils propel the animal through the water, thus allowing it to swim. The development of *Amblystoma,* however, does not stop with swimming, for it then grows first front limbs and then hind ones. At first its walking movements are secondary to swimming, its limbs being used only in conjunction with whole-body coiling. As the animal matures, the coiling diminishes in amplitude until the body is carried as a fixed trunk by the coordinated movements of the legs that support the animal's weight. This description of the ontogeny of *Amblystoma,* as given by Coghill, illustrates two developmental principles: animals develop from rostral to caudal, or nose to tail, and from proximal to distal, trunk to limbs, both physically and in terms of their movements.

We can follow this story a little further by considering how human infants develop the ability to reach for objects, as described by Twitchell (Figure 7.1). Before birth an infant's movements are whole-body movements, but after birth it gradually develops the grasping reaction, the ability to reach out with one limb and bring objects toward itself. The grasping reaction develops in a number of stages. Shortly after birth an infant can flex all the joints of an arm in such a way that it can scoop something toward its body, and this movement is executed with the help of other body movements. Between 1 and 4 months of age the infant can grasp objects that come in contact with its hands but can do so only by closing all the fingers of the hand simultaneously. Between 3 and 11 months it orients its hand toward, and gropes for, objects that have contacted it. Between 8 and 11 months it develops the "pincer grasp," using the index finger and thumb in opposition to each other. The development of the pincer grasp allows the infant to make a precise grasp as well as to manipulate small objects or objects located in hard-to-reach places. The infant's sequential development from whole-body movements, to limb movements, and finally, to independent digit movements, illustrates again the developmental principles described above.

Animals can swim, crawl, walk, jump and fly, as well as use parts of their bodies, such as the limbs and mouth, for more discrete manipulations. The theme presented in this chapter is that this diverse array of movements has a simple basis of organization. The motor system can be subdivided into

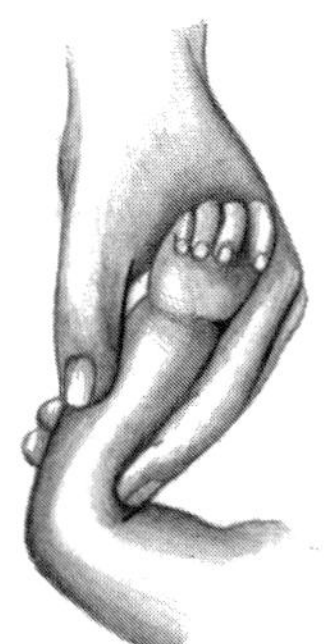

TRACTION RESPONSE (at birth)
S: Stretch shoulder adductors and flexors
R: All joints flex

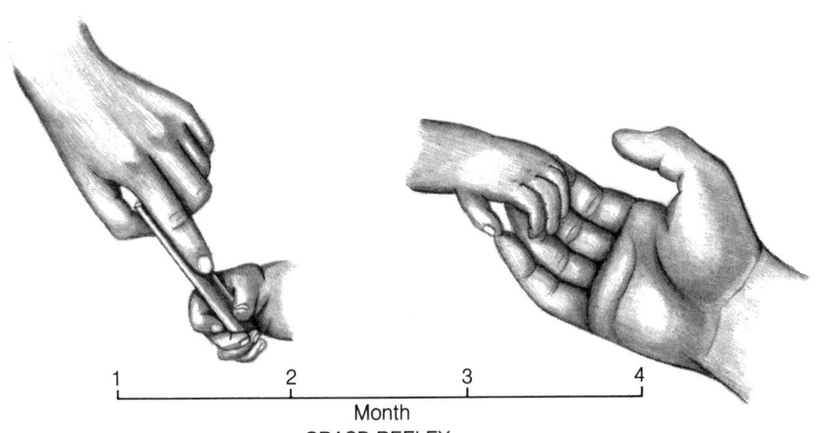

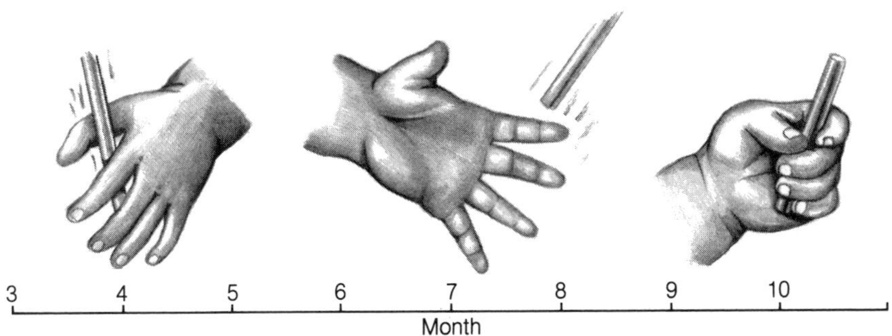

FIGURE 7.1. Evolution of the grasping response of infants. (After Twitchell, 1965.)

a number of subsystems, organized so that they can differentially control whole-body movements, independent movements of limbs, and independent movements of body parts such as the tongue and fingers. This organization can be seen in the evolution and development of movement and in the anatomical organization of the motor system. Primitive and infant animals can move only with whole-body movements, as fish do when they swim. More advanced and older animals move by making coordinated limb movements, as cattle or horses do when they walk. Many mammals, in addition to being able to make whole-body movements and coordinated limb movements, can make discrete movements of the limbs and digits to grasp objects. Finally, more fractionated or independent movements of the digits such as those used in the pincer grasp are especially characteristic of some primates and especially of humans. Brain injury can damage one or another of these subsystems, thus producing impairments that incapacitate trunk, limb, or hand movements.

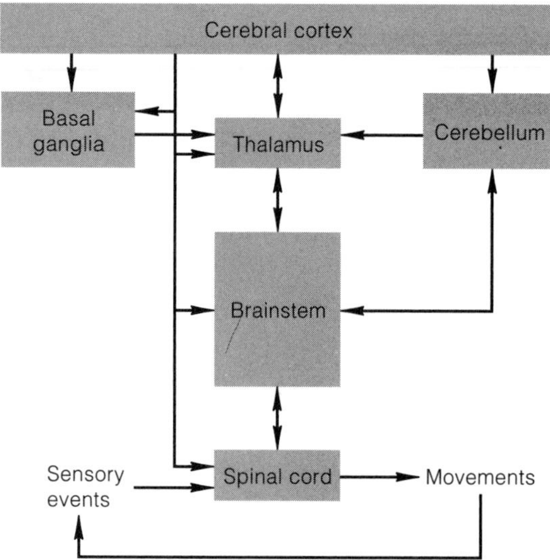

FIGURE 7.2. Diagram of the organization of the motor system showing its major structures and connections.

THE ANATOMY OF THE MOTOR SYSTEM

The motor system can be divided into a number of major components: the spinal cord, the brainstem, the cerebellum, the basal ganglia, and the neocortex. These components are organized hierarchically, but they also function in parallel and share many interconnections (Figure 7.2).

Our understanding of the motor system relies heavily on the work of Kuypers and his coworkers, who used an old, but ingeniously simple, procedure to disclose its organization. They traced motor fibers from muscles to their cells of origin in the spinal cord. Then they traced the fibers that connect with these spinal cord cells to their origins in various places in the brain. Their investigation revealed two major organizing principles of the motor system. First, two sets of pathways descend from the brain. The muscles of the fingers, arm, and shoulder are controlled by one set of pathways, and the trunk or axis of the body is controlled by a second set. The two sets of pathways are distinguished not only by their origins and routes, but also by the fact that the pathways that control hand and arm movements cross as they descend and control only the contralateral limbs, whereas the pathways that control trunk movements do not cross but branch to innervate both sides of the spinal cord. Second, some of the fibers in the crossed pathway make direct connections with motor neurons, and the digits are moved via these direct connections. In pursuing this story, we will describe first the spinal cord and then the projections to it from the brain; finally, we will describe the brain structures involved in movement.

THE SPINAL CORD

Structure of the Spinal Cord

The spinal cord has three functions: it contains the circuits for executing many reflexes, it contains programs for producing complex movements such as walking, and it relays information between the body and the brain. The spinal cord produces these actions by receiving projections from the sensory receptors of the body through its dorsal roots. Some of these projections synapse with motor neurons and interneurons to produce reflexes, whereas others project to the brain to participate in the production of more complex movements. In addition to sending and receiving large projections to and from the brain, the spinal cord has many connections between its segments.

The spinal cord can be subdivided functionally and anatomically into two rings, an inner and an outer. The inner ring is gray matter, a core of cells with a "butterfly" shape. The dorsal wings are called the **dorsal columns,** the ventral wings are called the **ventral columns,** and the area between these two columns is called the **intermediate zone** (Figure 7.3A). The cells in the dorsal columns are mainly sensory, while those in the intermediate zone and ventral columns are mainly motor. (The term "column" comes from the fact that these cells run the length of the spinal cord. In humans, because of their upright posture, the columns are also referred to as anterior and posterior rather than dorsal and ventral.) The outer ring is white matter, made up of fiber tracts running to and from the brain. The dorsal and ventral columns of gray matter subdivide the white matter into three *funiculi* (from the Latin for cord): the dorsal, the lateral, and the ventral funiculi. The dorsal funiculi carry sensory information to the brain, and the lateral and ventral funiculi mainly carry motor instructions from the brain.

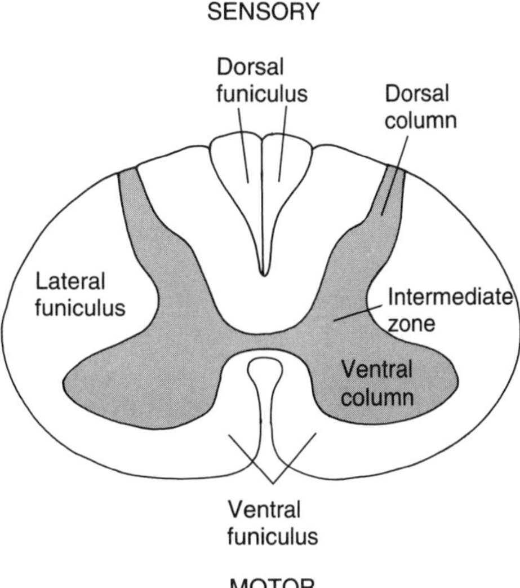

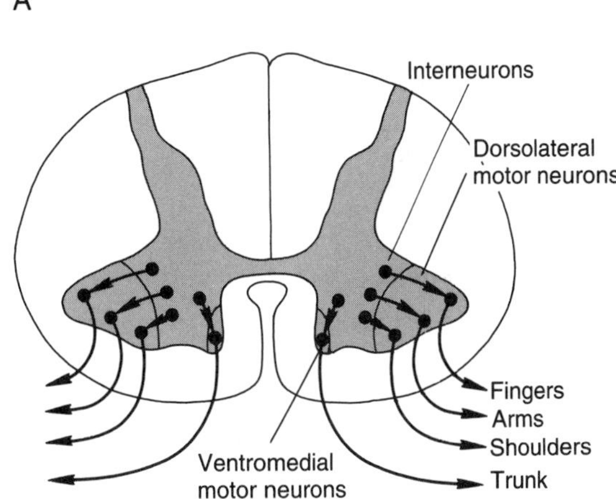

FIGURE 7.3. *A.* Major structures of the spinal cord. *B.* Topographic relation among interneurons, motor neurons, and the body locations to which motor neurons project.

Interneurons and Motor Neurons

The cells in the intermediate zone of the spinal cord are called **interneurons,** and they project to motor cells in the ventral column. The motor cells, called **motor neurons,** project to muscles (Figure 7.3B). All movements are produced via the motor neurons, and for this reason they are referred to as the final common path. As it turns out, very few other cells connect directly to motor neurons. They instead synapse first with the interneurons, which in turn synapse with the motor neurons.

There are two zones of motor neurons in the ventral columns: the lateral cell group is called the *dorsolateral cell group,* and the medial group is called the *ventromedial cell group* (Figure 7.3B). Motor neurons of the dorsolateral cell group innervate the musculature of the shoulders, hands, and digits. They are arranged in such a way that motor neurons innervating the digits are more dorsal and those innervating the arm and shoulders are more ventral. Motor neurons in the ventromedial cell group innervate the proximal musculature; that is, the musculature of the body midline or axis. The interneurons are similarly organized: the interneurons located in the dorsolateral portion of the intermediate zone connect to dorsolateral motor neurons, and the interneurons located in the ventromedial portion of the intermediate zone connect to ventromedial motor neurons. As a result, the dorsolateral interneurons eventually control distal musculature, and the ventromedial motor neurons eventually control proximal musculature.

In addition to the relation between motor neurons and body muscles, there is a distal-central organization of the motor neurons. More distally placed cells tend to produce extensor movements when active, and more centrally located cells tend to produce flexor movements. It is also suggested that the interneurons and motor neurons are arranged in pools that control specific muscle groups and perhaps even specific kinds of movements.

Projections to Interneurons and Motor Neurons

Each motor neuron receives thousands of terminals from other neurons, so to contract a muscle, a motor neuron must ultimately reflect the "majority opinion" from these various sources. Very little of the input onto a motor neuron is direct; rather, most comes indirectly through interneurons. There are three major sources of input: from the body, from the brain, and from other spinal cord segments. We will restrict our description to projections from the brain.

There are at least nine fiber projections from the brain, and each is probably involved in producing a different kind of movement. These projections can be divided into two major groups or systems (Figure 7.4A). The **lateral system** connects with dorsolateral interneurons and motor neurons. There are two major tracts in the lateral system: the lateral **corticospinal tract** (from cortex to spinal cord) and the **rubrospinal tract** (*rubro* for red, so from red nucleus of the midbrain to spinal cord). The **ventromedial system** connects with ventromedial interneurons and motor neurons. Its tracts include the vestibulospinal tracts, the reticulospinal tracts, and the tectospinal tracts from the brainstem, as well as the ventral

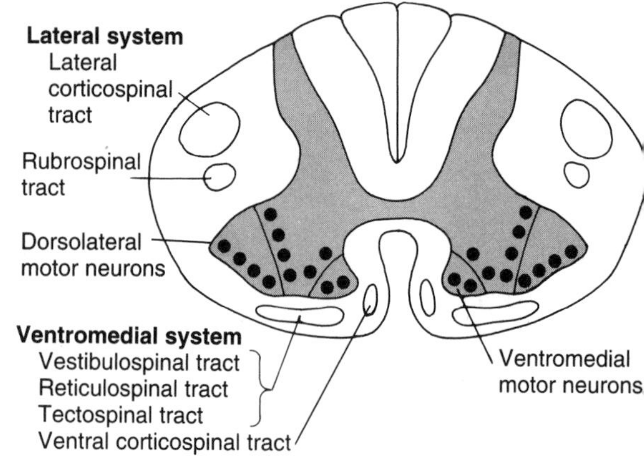

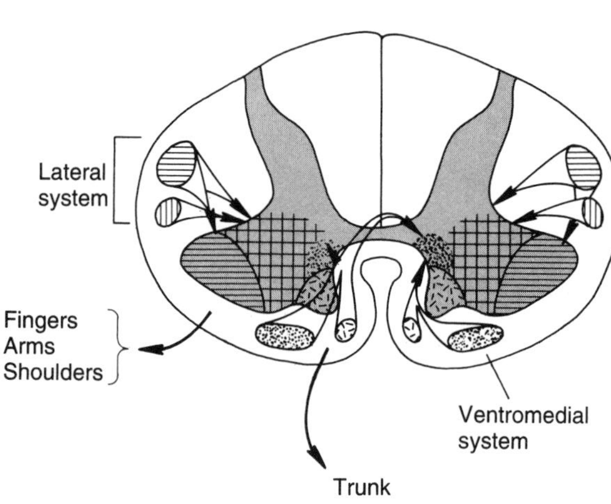

FIGURE 7.4. *A*. Location of the lateral and ventromedial systems and the interneurons and motor neurons of the ventral columns. *B*. Projection of the pathways of the lateral system and ventromedial system onto interneurons and motor neurons. Arrows indicate areas to which fiber tracts project.

corticospinal tract, which originates in the neocortex (Figure 7.4B). (It is noteworthy that the two systems are located in such a way that they have easy access to the neurons with which they connect as they pass down the spinal cord.) Because of their connections, the lateral system controls distal muscles and the ventromedial system controls proximal musculature.

The brainstem has a more complex architecture than the spinal cord, but the basic plan of the spinal cord can be recognized within the arrangement of its structures. The sensory and motor fibers of the spinal cord have their continuation in the sensory and motor fibers of the 12 cranial nerves that enter the brainstem. The spinal motor-neuron cell groups have their counterparts in the motor nuclei of the cranial nerves.

ORIGIN OF MOTOR TRACTS

As noted above, two systems project from the brain to the spinal cord. Each system contains at least one projection from the cortex and one from the brainstem. The cortex can control distal musculature through the lateral system and proximal musculature through the ventromedial system. The brainstem divides its projections in the same way. We will describe the cortical and brainstem levels of control separately.

Brainstem Origins of the Ventromedial System

The brainstem contains a number of nuclear groups that send fiber tracts to the brainstem motor nuclei and to the motor cells of the spinal cord through the ventromedial system. These structures produce many complex actions, including maintaining an upright posture; walking; controlling sleeping and waking; and controlling regulatory behaviors such as feeding, drinking, and sexual activity.

The tracts from the brainstem originate in the vestibular nuclei, the reticular formation, and the tectum. The vestibulospinal tract is the origin of information from the vestibular system of the middle ear, and it functions to maintain posture and balance. The tectospinal tract contains fibers that originate in the superior colliculus, the midbrain visual center. Its function is to produce orienting movements to visual stimuli. The reticulospinal tracts come from many cell groups in the reticular formation, which, in turn, receive projections from most of the sensory systems of the brainstem and spinal cord. The descending pathways of the reticulospinal tract are probably involved in producing various coordinated movements, including walking, swimming, and running.

The pathways of the ventromedial brain system are illustrated in Figure 7.5A. Note that, with the exception of the tectum, these pathways do not cross in the brainstem but do project bilaterally to medially located interneurons in the intermediate zone of the spinal cord. The axons of fibers in the ventromedial system give off a large number of collaterals to many interneurons in many spinal cord segments. This feature of their distribution, as well as their termination within the medially located interneurons of the spinal cord, suggests that they produce whole-body movements involving many muscle groups of the axial (trunk) and proximal body musculature. The fibers of the ventromedial system also project to the extraocular motor neurons in cranial nerves III, IV, and VI, as well as to the vagus (X), glossopharyngeal (IX), and spinal accessory (XI) nuclei. Through these nuclei these cranial nerves control eye and head movements, as well as some movements of the oral cavity.

The brainstem projection to the spinal cord also includes fibers from norepinephrinergic, serotonergic, and dopaminergic neurons. These projections are thought to be involved in the modulation of movement rather than in the production of movement per se.

Brainstem Origins of the Lateral System

The red nucleus and its associated rubrospinal tract first appears in animals that walk, suggesting that it plays a role in limb movement. Surprisingly, the red nucleus has become comparatively

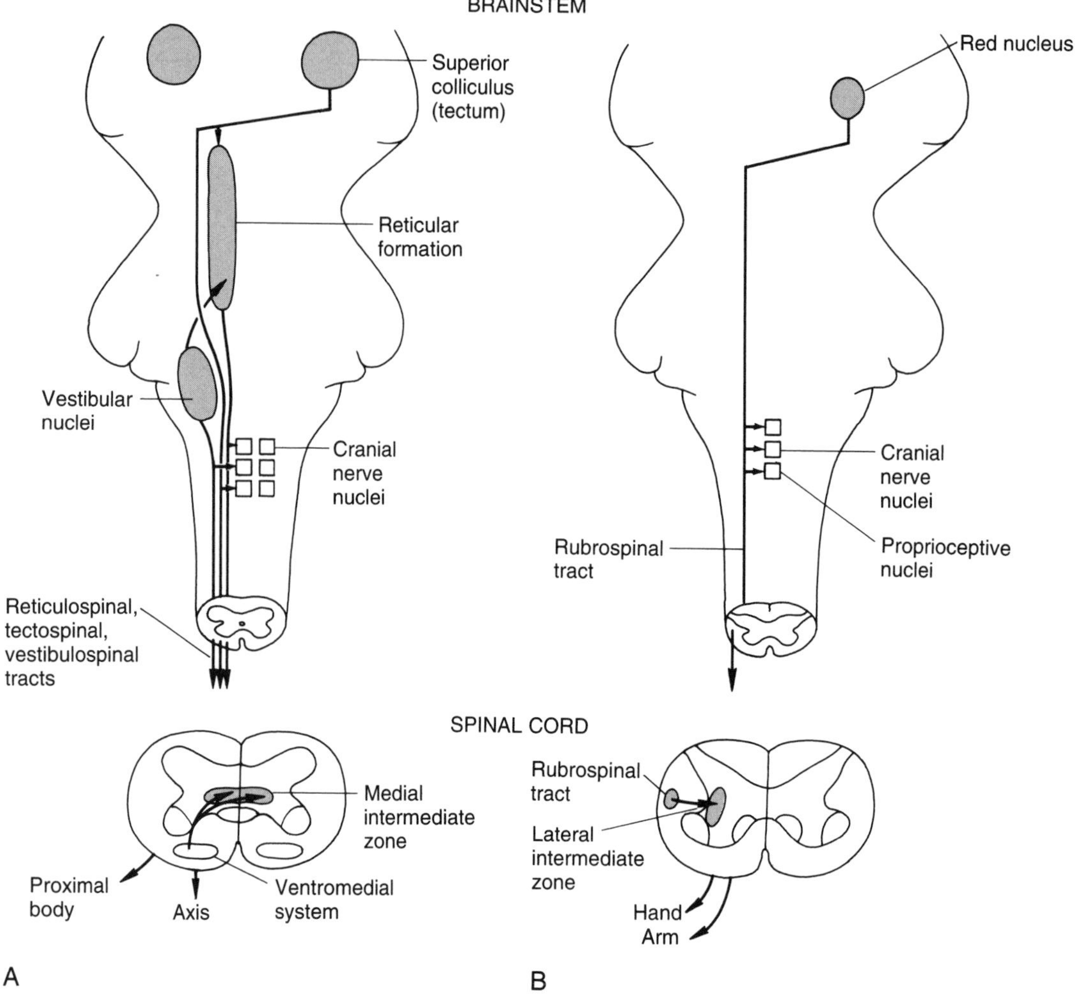

FIGURE 7.5. *A*. Brainstem structures that contribute fibers to the ventromedial system. *B*. Brainstem structures that contribute fibers to the lateral system. (After Ghez, 1991.)

smaller in primates, especially humans, and this suggests that its functions have been replaced in part by structures that are responsible for the skilled movements of these species.

The red nucleus of the midbrain sends its projection, the rubrospinal tract, through the lateral system of the spinal cord (Figure 7.5B). One of the notable features of the rubrospinal tract is that it crosses the midline to innervate the contralateral spinal cord. The red nucleus also sends projections to the cranial nuclei that control facial movements (the facial [VII] and hypoglossal [XII] nuclei). The rubrospinal fibers terminate on interneurons of the lateral portion of the intermediate zone of the spinal cord. They have fewer collaterals and make connections with fewer spinal cord segments than do fibers of the ventromedial system. Their organization and termination suggests that their function is to control independent movements of the distal musculature, such as movements of the hands, feet, arms, and legs. The rubrospinal tract also gives off collaterals to the sensory trigeminal nucleus (the fifth nerve, which receives fibers from the face), which in turn gives off collaterals to the dorsal column nuclei (nuclei that receive and relay proprioceptive input from the body). These connections suggest that the rubrospinal tract also has a modulatory action on sensory input from the body.

The Cortex

The motor areas of the cortex are unquestionably responsible for skilled movements. The cortex, mainly the motor areas 4 and 6 and the sensory area 3-1-2, send corticofugal fibers (*cortico* meaning cortex and *fugal* meaning flight) to brainstem motor nuclei and to interneurons and motor neurons of the spinal cord. The fibers that go to the motor nuclei are called **corticobulbar fibers,** and those that go to the spinal cord are called **corticospinal fibers.** Again there are two pathways to the spinal cord, one that crosses as part of the lateral system, and one that is uncrossed and is part of the ventromedial system. A diagram of the projections of the corticofugal pathways is shown in Figure 7.6. Figure 7.6A shows the route of the corticofugal component of the lateral system. The fibers of the lateral system end mainly on interneurons in the lateral part of the intermediate zone and on the laterally located motor neurons. Through these connections the projections control distal movements. Figure 7.6B shows the route of corticofugal fibers in the ventromedial system. These fibers terminate bilaterally on the most medially located interneurons and motor neurons. Through these connections they control proximal movements.

Motor Cortex and Movement

The cortex is topographically organized such that its different parts control different body parts. This topographical organization is represented by a homunculus in humans or by a corresponding cartoon in other animals. Kuypers and Brinkman and others have described the corticofugal projections in a number of animal species, but the projections in the monkey will serve the purposes of illustration (Figure 7.7). Here it can be seen that the trunk portion of the homunculus projects through the ventromedial system and the limb portion projects through the lateral system; these projections control proximal and distal movements, respectively.

There is some overlap in corticospinal connections in the spinal cord. Projections from the forelimb area project most densely to the interneurons and motor neurons of the cervical spinal cord to control limb movements. They also project to other levels of the spinal cord, however. This overlap might be significant in subserving movements that require the participation of many body parts.

The cortex also sends connections to many other areas of the brainstem, including the red nucleus and many of the nuclei in the ventromedial system. Through these connections the cortex can have some control over the motor function of these nuclei. There are also connections that go to the dorsal column nuclei and nuclei of the cranial nerves, which are relays for the body senses. Through these connections the cortex can modulate the sensory input that is coming from the body.

Species, Developmental, and Individual Differences

It is immediately obvious to anyone who observes the behavior of animals that there are striking differences in their movements. The following experiment shows that some of these differences can be accounted for by connections made by the descending motor pathways.

The corticospinal pathway can be sectioned selectively in the pyramids of the ventral brainstem (the pyramids are composed of the corticospinal fibers and are easy to reach surgically because of their superficial location). When this projection is cut, the terminations of the fibers can be determined by locating the degenerating terminals with the reduced-silver staining technique of Nauta and its modifications. Kuypers and others have studied terminal distribution in different species, and some of their results are illustrated in

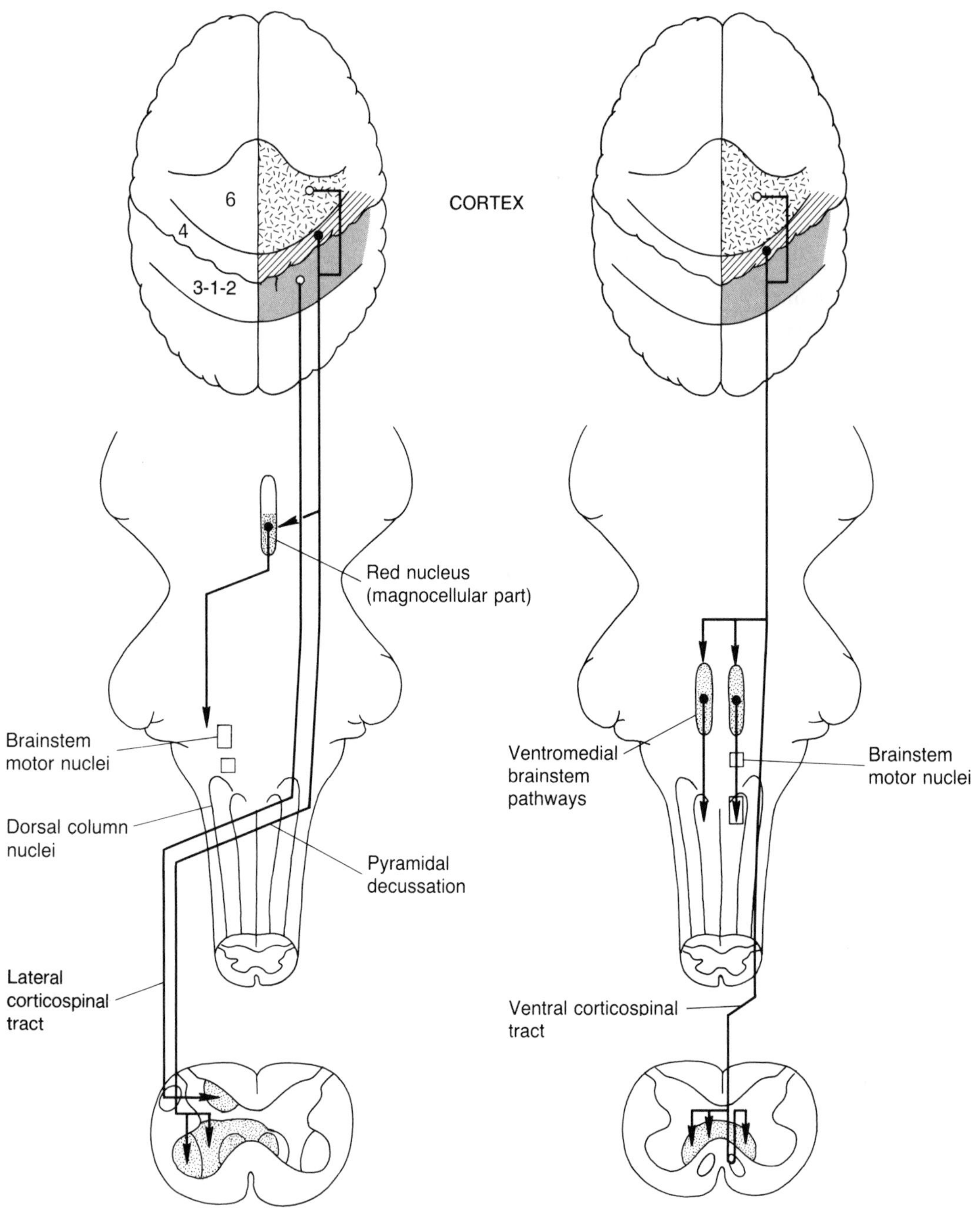

FIGURE 7.6. *A*. Corticospinal projections that contribute to the lateral system. *B*. Corticospinal projections that contribute to the ventromedial system. (After Ghez, 1991.)

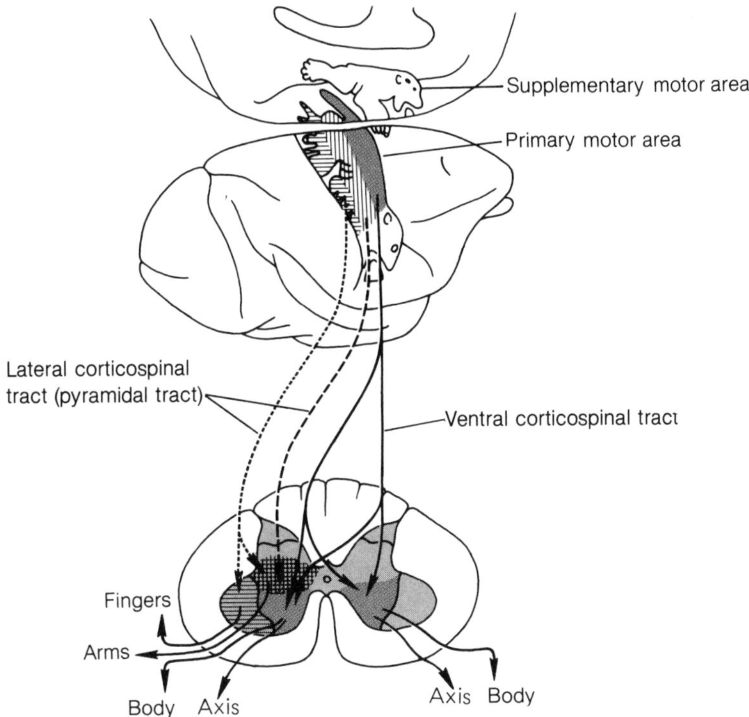

FIGURE 7.7. The relationship among primary motor cortex, descending tracts, spinal interneurons, motor neurons, and body musculature in the monkey. (After Lawrence and Kuypers, 1968.)

Figure 7.8. The opossum, which does not make use of extensive skilled limb movements, has terminals only in the dorsal columns. This suggests that in this species the corticospinal pathway is involved mainly in modulating sensations from the body. The cat has terminals in the intermediate zone containing interneurons. Cats can grasp objects with a paw but cannot make independent digit movements. The rhesus monkey additionally has terminals on the most laterally located motor neurons. Since it can make independent digit movements such as the pincer grasp, it is thought that these connections control independent digit movements. Finally, chimpanzees and humans have terminals on all motor neurons and interneurons. These connections are thought to convey further manipulatory skill to these species.

This same relationship between movement and connections of the corticospinal tract can be seen in development. Studies done on monkeys of different ages show that the corticospinal terminations are made gradually, and there is a concomitant development of skilled movements as they are made. In addition, studies on fiber diameter show that the thickest fibers, which are capable of the most rapid information conduction, make up only a small fraction of all the corticofugal fibers but make the most direct connections with motor neurons. These fibers also tend to mature and become functional last in development. These fibers have their origin in the digit area of the motor cortex and enable independent digit movements.

Examinations of corticofugal pathways in humans show that there is considerable variation

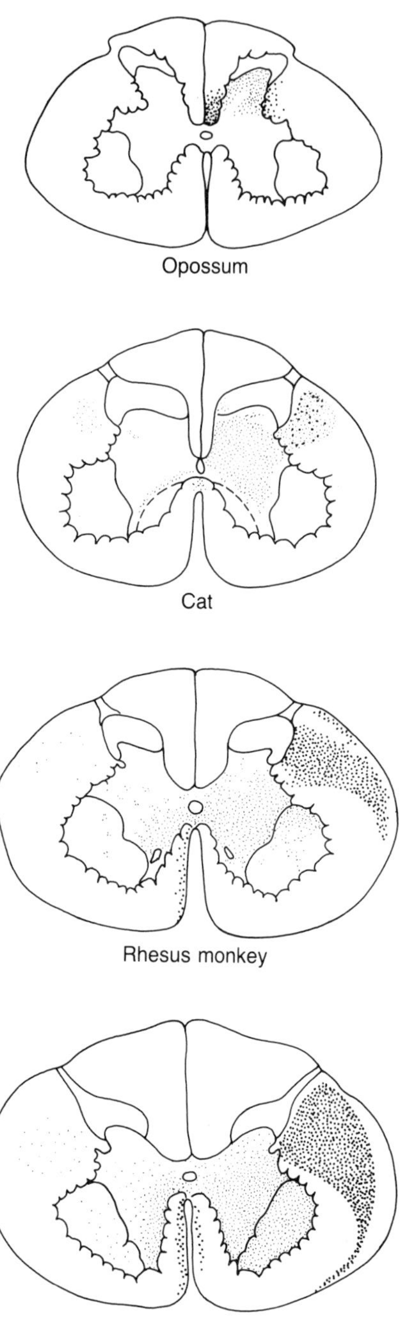

FIGURE 7.8. Distribution of corticospinal fibers (shown as gray areas) from the left hemisphere to the cervical portion of the spinal cord in the opossum, cat, rhesus monkey, and chimpanzee. (After Kuypers, 1981.)

among individuals. Nyberg-Hansen and Rinvik have described some of these variations, including no uncrossed corticospinal tract, no crossed corticospinal tract, and two crossed or two uncrossed corticospinal tracts. The functional significance of such variations is simply not known. Yakovlev and Rakic have examined the size of the corticospinal pathways and note that 80% of individuals have larger tracts on the right side of the spinal cord. In the remaining 20% the pattern is reversed. It might be thought that this asymmetry is related to handedness; that is, most people are right-handed and receive larger corticospinal projections on the right. This study, however, found that there is not a perfect relation between handedness and the size of the corticospinal pathways. Thus, at present, this anatomical bias has not been conclusively correlated with function.

Independence of Lateral and Ventromedial Systems

Behavioral evidence also supports the idea that the motor system is composed of different descending systems. This is illustrated by the following studies of animals and humans that have suffered brain damage. To analyze the contributions made by the lateral and ventromedial systems, Kuypers and coworkers studied rhesus monkeys, which have a motor anatomy quite similar to that of humans. In one group of monkeys they cut the fibers in the lateral system, and in the other group they cut the fibers in the ventromedial system.

After damage to the lateral system the animals took about 15 days to recover most of their movements. To eat, they were required reach through their cage bars for food. They were hesitant to extend their arms fully and often caught their fingers on the opening. Once they reached the food their fingers closed in concert, but weakly, and grasping was associated with a hooking movement of the whole arm. Gradually, the speed and strength of even these movements increased, yet the animals continued to display two striking deficits. First, they were unable to grasp food with the pincer grasp of the thumb and index finger opposed. Second, once they had grasped food with a whole-hand grip, they had difficulty in releasing it; to do so they rooted for it with their snouts. During locomotion, however, they had no difficulty in letting go of the bars of the cage. Thus their enduring deficit was in using the hand and digits for grasping and manipulating.

Other studies support the idea that the lateral system is involved in fine control of limb and digit movement. Beck and Chambers measured the functions of monkey limbs after lesions of the corticospinal tract. The monkeys showed slowed reaction times on two-choice tasks using the affected limb and showed greater loss of strength in flexion at the wrist than at the elbow or shoulder. Passingham and coworkers unilaterally removed the motor cortex (area 4) and the sensory cortex (area 3-1-2), from which the majority of corticospinal projections originate, in rhesus monkeys. After a period of recovery, the monkeys regained the ability to use the contralateral arm to climb and move around the cage and, with some prompting, to reach for food. But the monkeys were not able to use the pincer grasp to pick pieces of food out of a trough, although they could grasp food with whole-hand movements. Further impairment in reaching was revealed in the following way. The monkeys were required to insert one hand through a hole in a clear plastic wall and dislodge a piece of food attached to the wall on the other side. Thus, when the hand was inserted through the hole they had to turn it to the side, up, or down to reach the food. The monkeys were unable to rotate the wrist or elbow to reach the food in these tests. These experiments demonstrate not only that the cortex is necessary for individual finger movements, but also that it appears to be necessary for most skilled movements around individual joints.

The lesion experiments suggest that pathways of the ventromedial system are involved in whole-body movements. Animals with such lesions showed striking abnormalities in posture. They showed a prolonged inability to achieve upright posture and severe difficulty in moving the body or moving the limbs at the proximal joints. They also showed pronounced flexion of the head, limbs, and trunk, which lessened with recovery but did not disappear. When they were able to sit, they were unsteady and tended to slump forward with the shoulders elevated. Slight movements or sudden sounds made them fall, and when they started to fall, they failed to make corrective movements to support themselves. The animals had great difficulty in walking; they often veered off target and bumped into things. If the lateral system was spared, they retained the ability to use their limbs and hands.

Separate Systems in Humans

Many studies with humans who have sustained damage to the motor cortex or to the corticospinal projections give much the same results as those obtained with monkeys. Humans can perform arm movements when reaching, but independent movements of the digits are more severely impaired. For example Jeannerod has described human reaching as consisting of two components: (1) The *transportation component* involves movement of the limb to the object to be grasped. This movement is made mainly with the upper arm. (2) The *manipulation component* consists of forming the digits to grasp an object and then closing them on the object. This component begins while the hand is being transported to the target and consists of moving the digits away from the thumb to shape the hand into the size and shape of the object to be grasped.

Jeannerod presents two kinds of evidence that these two components of the grasp are independent. In a series of behavioral studies he demonstrated that by changing the size of the object as the hand is transported to it, the manipulation component can be changed independently of changes in the transport component. He also demonstrated that in patients with lesions of the pyramidal tract, the transport component of the reach is much less affected than the manipulatory component (Figure 7.9). Thus, in humans as in monkeys, the pyramidal tract seems to be essential for skilled hand and digit movements.

A very interesting behavioral result that supports the functional independence of proximal and distal movements is reported by Prablanc and

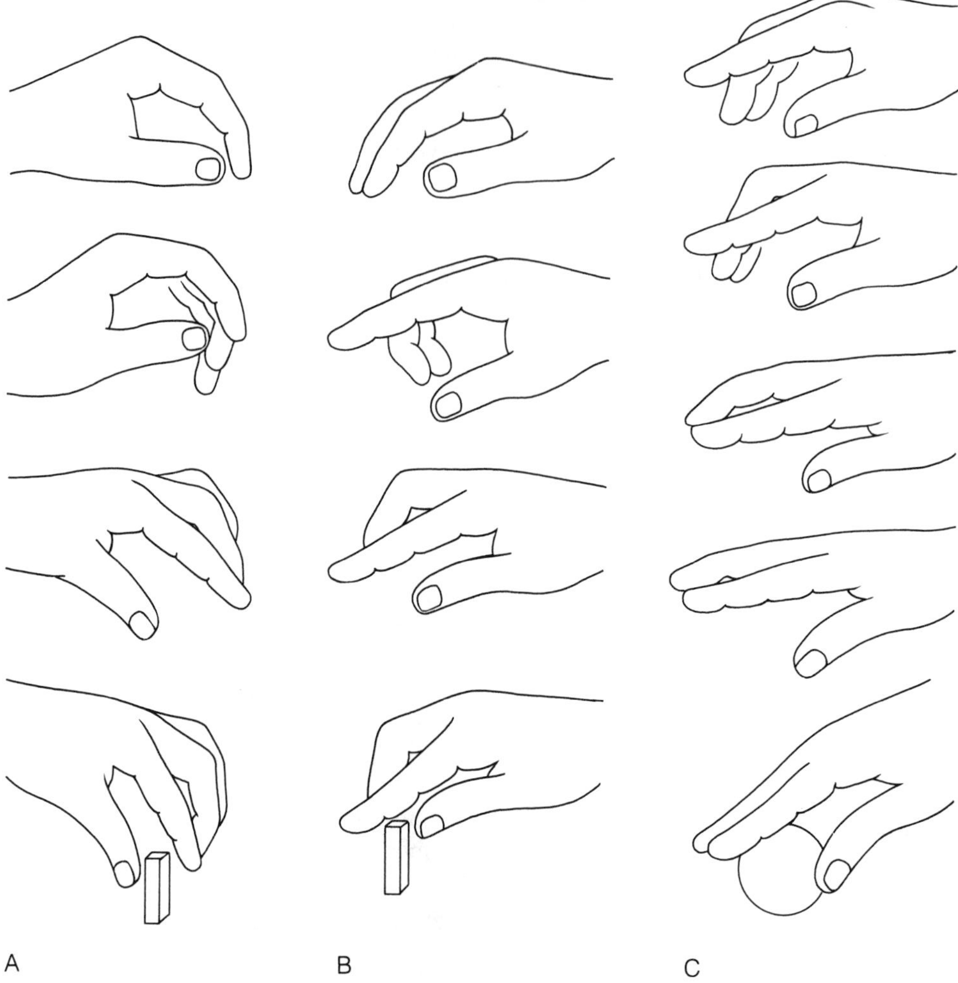

FIGURE 7.9. Patterns of finger movements in grasping with unaffected hand (*A*) and the hand affected with pyramidal tract damage (*B, C*). (After Jeannerod, 1988.)

coworkers (see Jeannerod). They had subjects wear prisms that displaced objects that were viewed. When subjects reached for the object, they reached to the location it was perceived to be and thus missed it. After a few reaching trials they adapted to the prisms and reached accurately. When the other hand was then tested, it needed to learn to locate the object in just the same way that the first hand had learned. There was no transfer from the training undergone by the first hand. Indeed, one hand could be trained with prisms that displaced the object in one direction while the other hand was trained with prisms that displaced the object in the other direction. If subjects were required to reach for the object with a stick held in their teeth, however, what they learned under the prisms condition transferred to both hands. This behavioral experiment suggests that mechanisms involved in motor learning of hand movements can be partially dissociated from systems controlling other movements. The experiment also demonstrates that what is learned with proximal movements can be generalized to distal movements.

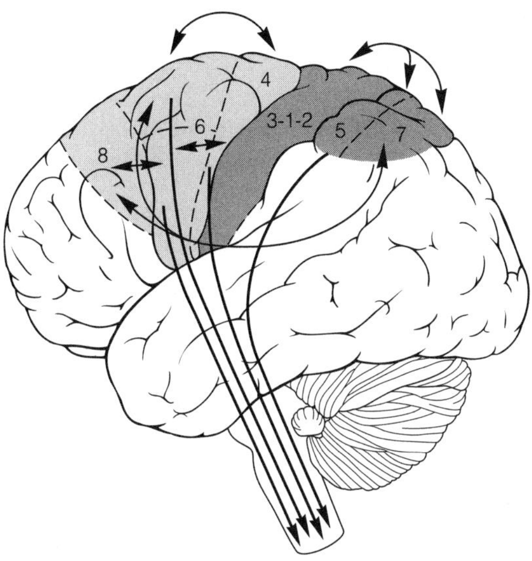

FIGURE 7.10. Emerging view of cortical motor systems. There are many reciprocal connections between sensory (3-1-2, 5, 7) and motor (8, 6, 4) areas. There are a number of separate descending pathways to the spinal cord.

SENSORY-MOTOR INTEGRATION

Cortical Organization

Until the 1950s, theories of how voluntary behavior are produced were quite simple. The motor cortex (area 4) was thought to send, through the pyramidal tract, signals that control motor neurons directly and so produce movement. Sectioning the pyramidal tract was predicted to result in the loss of all voluntary movement. When this was not found to be the case, the direct output model was gradually abandoned in almost every respect.

It has now been replaced by a hierarchical and parallel model (Figure 7.10). According to this model the cortical structures thought to be involved in movement include the primary motor cortex (area 4), the supplementary motor cortex (the dorsal portion of area 6), the premotor cortex (the ventral portion of area 6), the primary sensory cortex (area 3-1-2), and the posterior parietal cortex (areas 5 and 7). Some adjacent areas, including area 8, probably should also be included in this group. All these areas are sites of cells that send axons over the pyramidal tract to the spinal cord. They are also interconnected with one another to various degrees. They are hierarchically arranged, with input going from sensory cortex to parietal cortex to frontal cortex and from there to motor cortex.

Strick and his coworkers suggest that within this hierarchy there is also parallel control of movement. The major source of evidence supporting this model comes from anatomical studies. The organization of area 4, the supplementary motor cortex, and the premotor cortex has been found to be so similar that these structures should be considered parallel systems, each with a descending control over movement. The kinds of movements that each controls is not clear.

Using various tract tracing techniques, Galea and Darian-Smith have proposed that there are at least nine distinctive subsystems within the cortical spinal systems that originate in different areas and that are distinctive in terms of their other connections. Three of these projections come from area 4, and others come from the other sensory and motor cortical areas. Each of these systems seems distinct in terms of its connections to the thalamus, cerebellum, and other structures and in terms of its fibers and connections with the spinal cord. Each system is also thought to have substantial reciprocal connections with other areas. At present there are no behavioral data that could suggest functions for each of these systems, but potentially each could have a function of its own while at the same time interacting with other systems.

Sensory Contributions

Stimulus-response theories of behavior suggest that behaviors occur only in response to sensory stimulation. For complex movements, each response would serve as the stimulus for the next movement. Thus, motor learning was thought to consist of linking reflexes. In an influential paper published in 1951, Lashley argued that the movements involved in behaviors such as typing and playing the piano were simply too fast to depend upon sensory feedback. He suggested that there must be programs for sequences of movements that could be executed in the absence of feedback from each movement component.

Most people now accept Lashley's view, but evidence also shows that movement is still very dependent upon sensory feedback. This evidence is important in showing that motor impairments can come not only from damage to the motor cortex but also from damage to those portions of the nervous system thought to be mainly sensory in function. The following examples will illustrate this point.

Deafferentation is the procedure of removing somatosensory input by cutting the fibers that convey sensory information from the body to the brain. The major result of deafferentation studies is that there is a surprisingly wide range of movements that are possible in the absence of sensory information from one or more limbs, but there are also impairments. Rothwell and colleagues have examined the effects of deafferentation on the movements of the rhesus monkey. If only one forelimb is deafferented, the animal tends to neglect the limb and use its other limbs. If this behavior is prevented by binding the intact forelimb, the animal will learn to make very good use of the deafferented limb. If both forelimbs are deafferented, then after a period of recovery lasting a few weeks, very effective use is again possible. The animal can climb, walk, cling to the bars of its cage, and even reach for objects using the pincer grip. The capacity to make these movements does not need to be exercised before deafferentation. Rothwell's group deafferented preterm monkeys (removed from the uterus and replaced after surgery) and found that they displayed good postnatal development of movement. Of course, the monkeys do have vision, so it is possible that their movements are performed under visual guidance. To examine this possibility, Rothwell's group occluded the infant's eyes and found that they still displayed effective locomotion. They could even reach and use the pincer grasp, provided they were trained so that they knew there were objects they could reach for. These experiments demonstrate that there are central nervous system programs for movement that can operate in the absence of sensory stimulation feedback.

Nevertheless, as the following descriptions of the effects of deafferentation will slow, there are motor impairments in deafferented subjects. The importance of sensory information for normal walking in humans is demonstrated by the **ataxia** shown by people who suffer from a genetic disorder called *Friedreich's ataxia.* These people have degeneration of the dorsal funiculi, which contain the afferents conducting fine touch and pressure information from the body. They have little or no position sense and a poor sense of passive movement and vibration. When they walk, they support the body on a broad base, legs apart, and tend to shuffle, reel, and stagger. For humans, walking involves a bit of a balancing act; weight must be shifted from one leg to the other, and balancing is required as weight is carried forward on one limb. This balancing obviously requires afferent input, for ataxia does not lessen with time or practice. Thus, locomotion is more severely impaired in people than in monkeys, but the difference is due to the more complex mode of locomotion used by humans (monkeys walk with four feet on the ground) and not to the inability to produce movement.

Rothwell and coworkers have described the motor abilities of G. O., who was deafferented by a severe peripheral sensory disease. His motor power was unaffected, and he could produce a range of finger movements with accuracy. He could make individual finger movements and outline figures in the air with his eyes closed. He could move his thumb accurately through different distances and at different speeds, judge weights, and match forces with his thumb. He could also drive his old car but was unable to learn to drive a new car. Nevertheless, his hands were relatively useless to him in daily life. He was unable to write, to fasten shirt buttons, or to hold a cup. His difficulties lay in maintaining force for any length of time. He could begin movements quite normally but as he proceeded, the movement patterns gradually fell apart and became unrecognizable. This was best illustrated when he tried to carry a suitcase. He would quickly drop it unless he continually looked down at it to confirm that it was there. G. O.'s symptoms support the findings with monkeys in suggesting that sensory feedback is not required to generate a movement. His symptoms do suggest that sensory feedback is necessary to sustain a single movement or series of movements.

The impairments in digit use produced by deafferentation can also be as severe as, and very similar to, those that follow motor cortex damage. Leonard and her coworkers examined hand use in monkeys for 3 years following deafferentation. She found that although many whole-body movements recovered, fine movements of the digits used in grooming, scratching, and manipulation of food remained impaired. The monkeys were especially unable to oppose the index finger and thumb, the most sensitive points of their hands, and so had difficulty executing the fine movements required for the natural behaviors in which they engaged.

Cortical Stimulating and Recording

Early brain stimulation studies suggested that specific areas of the motor cortex control specific body parts. These experiments were performed using very low currents of stimulation and small electrodes. When body parts were mapped onto the cortex to show the relations between stimulation and movements, the human body was mapped out on the cortex as illustrated by Penfield's now very famous human homunculus. That is, if a digit area of the cortex was stimulated, that digit moved. This relationship led to the notion that movements are produced by relatively discrete descending projections of different parts of this homunculus to spinal motor neurons.

Early recording studies of the activity of cells in the motor cortex seemed to confirm this view. They showed that there is a close relation between the activation of certain muscles and specific regions of the motor cortex. In the best known of these studies, Evarts trained monkeys to move a lever by flexing or extending the wrist. He then stimulated the pyramidal tract in order to produce discharges that were conducted back to the motor cortex on corticospinal axons. If a cell from which he was recording in the motor cortex was activated by the retrograde discharge, then he could confirm that it was a cell that projected to the spinal cord. Subsequently, when the monkey moved the lever, Evarts found that cells in the arm area of the motor cortex discharged when the lever was moved and increased their discharge rate when the force required to move the lever was increased. Some of these cells also began to discharge before movement occurred, thus strongly indicating that they were involved in producing the movement, as opposed to responding to it. Thus, Evarts's study suggested that motor cortex cells are directly involved in producing the force exerted by specific muscles to move the wrist.

Subsequent work with monkeys shows that the situation is more complex than was suggested by these studies. First, Galea and Darian-Smith propose that rather than one homunculus, there may be as many as nine, three of which are in the primary motor cortex. Second, rather than stimulation eliciting a specific movement of a body part, movements appear to be more complex. Usually, stimulation of one finger area produces movements of a number of fingers, even with the lowest stimulation intensities. Additionally, finger movements can be obtained by stimulating at least two different areas of the primary motor cortex. Third, Schieber and Hibbard trained monkeys to make flexion and extension movements of each of their digits and of the wrist in response to visual cues. Then they recorded single cell activity in the digit and wrist areas of the motor cortex while the monkey made the different movements. They found that populations of cells in the motor cortex overlapped extensively. That is, cells in each of the digit zones and in the wrist zone discharged with most of the various digit and wrist movements. This result strongly suggests that movement of a digit is not produced just by the activity of cells in one digit area but by the action of many cells spread across all digit areas and the wrist area and perhaps even across a much larger cortical area.

If the motor cortex does not produce movements simply by activating appropriate muscles in the appropriate order, how does it produce movement? Georgopoulos and his coworkers have attempted to answer this question by observing the activity of populations of cells in the cortex. They suggest that the cortex does not order the contraction of muscles but orders the limb to move to a location in space. For example, they found that a typical neuron will fire during many hand movements, but its rate of firing will be highest when the hand moves in a given direction. The closer the hand movement is to this optimal trajectory, the higher the discharge rate. According to this account a population of cells is responsible for ordering movements to all possible spatial locations.

This position has been criticized by Fetz on two counts. He argues first that the movement-direction cells are found in too many places in the motor system (motor cortex, sensory cortex, basal ganglia, and so on) to all be direction cells, and second that they have been selected from a large population of cells, many of which have less interpretable discharges. Fetz suggests that these cells could just as well be coding muscle force; that is, moving a limb in one direction requires a pattern of muscular contractions that is different from the pattern required when the limb moves in another direction.

There are other potential explanations for the lack of specificity between cortical representation and movement. One of the oldest explanations of motor organization is that of ethologists who argue that movements are organized as action patterns. According to this view, animals, including humans, make a limited number of movements, and very few of these involve the movement of discrete body parts. The reader can confirm this by attempting a number of different finger movements: it is very difficult to move one finger while keeping others still. Ethologists argue that the movements made by members of a species are species-typical and are directed toward specific goals. When you pick up a small object, you use the pincer grip just as other humans, and many species of monkeys, do. The ethological approach suggests that what is coded in motor maps are species-typical movements, most of which involve the movements of many body parts; for example, shaping the hand to make a pincer grasp usually involves movements of a number of digits. These movements would require the simultaneous activity of the many parts of the motor system. The networks of cells coding action patterns would nevertheless be sufficiently plastic to allow those movements to be modified by learning.

A third idea, which requires none of the preorganization demanded by the action pattern approach, is the neural network approach. Neural networks are hypothetical or computer-simulated assemblies of cells organized in layers with mutual connections that allow them to learn to solve problems. Most of the cells in a network are active on each problem, but their pattern of activity differs from problem to problem. Once a neural network is organized through learning to produce movements, it will have the structure that a motor program gives, but it will have obtained that structure not from an innate organization but from the self-organization associated with learning. A problem with the neural network approach is that it does not account easily for the species-specific nature of movements. It is also possible that the motor program and neural net approaches are reconcilable. There may be an innately organized set of movements, that gives a neural network its starting position but still allows it a good deal of flexibility for learning new motor skills.

Lateralization of Movement Control

Although anatomy, stimulation, and single cell recording studies all point to a good deal of parallel processing in motor systems, other techniques of study provide evidence for their hierarchical organization.

It is well known that the motor cortex controls movements of the limbs on the opposite side of the body. In right-handed people, commands for those movements appear to come from the left hemisphere no matter which side of the body is moved. Evidence for this conclusion comes from the study of patients with brain injury, as well as from measures of regional cerebral blood flow (rCBF). If a person moves the right arm through a sequence of movements, then in the left hemisphere there is a large increase in rCBF in the motor cortex and lesser increases in the supplementary motor cortex and premotor cortex (Figure 7.11A). If the subject only rehearses the movement sequence, then in the left hemisphere increases in rCBF occur only in the supplementary motor cortex (Figure 7.11B). The increase in blood flow in the motor cortex is thought to be related to the movements themselves, whereas the increase in the association cortex and premotor cortex is thought to be related to the programming of the sequence of movements. There are no obvious increases in blood flow in the right hemisphere when the right hand is moved. When the subject moves the left hand through the sequence, then in the right hemisphere there is a large increase in cerebral blood flow in the motor cortex, but there are also increases in blood flow in the left hemisphere in the association cortex (Figure 7.11C). These changes suggest that the motor cortex in the right hemisphere is producing the movements, but they are being commanded from the association and motor areas of the left hemisphere. The commands are probably sent via the corpus callosum from the left hemisphere to the right hemisphere.

THE BASAL GANGLIA

The basal ganglia comprise a collection of nuclei in the forebrain that make connections with the midbrain, diencephalon, thalamus, and cortex (Figure 7.12). The basal ganglia make no direct connections to the spinal cord, but they have been traditionally considered part of the motor system. This tradition is based in large part on clinical observations that damage to various parts of the basal ganglia produces such change in movements as **akinesia** (an absence of spontaneous movements) and **hyperkinesia** (excessively slow or rapid involuntary movements). The basal ganglia have at least two functions in movement control. First, they form part of a circuit that links most of the neocortex with the motor cortex. This can be thought of as their public role because they participate in effective cortical function. But they also have a private role because in the absence of the cortex they still have functions, and direct damage to them when the cortex is present results in abnormalities not obtained from cortical damage.

The anatomical relationship between structures that make up the basal ganglia, including their afferent and efferent connections, and the cortex is shown in Figure 7.12. The architecture of these structures and their relationships to the cortex suggest that they form a loop that feeds into the association motor cortex. Projections from all parts of the cortex enter the neostriatum. The neostriatum then projects through the external and internal pallidum (also called the globus pallidus) and from there goes to the ventral-anterior and ventral-lateral thalamus and then terminates in the supplementary cortex. Thus, superficially at least, it appears that all parts of the cortex can exert a modulating influence of some sort on the motor cortex via the supplementary cortex.

The basal ganglia have reciprocal connections with the substantia nigra of the midbrain and receive terminals containing the neurotransmitter dopamine from the substantia nigra.

The two forms of motor abnormality that follow basal ganglia damage are almost opposites. The akinetic disorders such as Parkinson's disease, which results from the loss of dopamine, are characterized by muscular rigidity and difficulties in making movements. The hyperkinetic disorders such as Huntington's chorea are characterized by

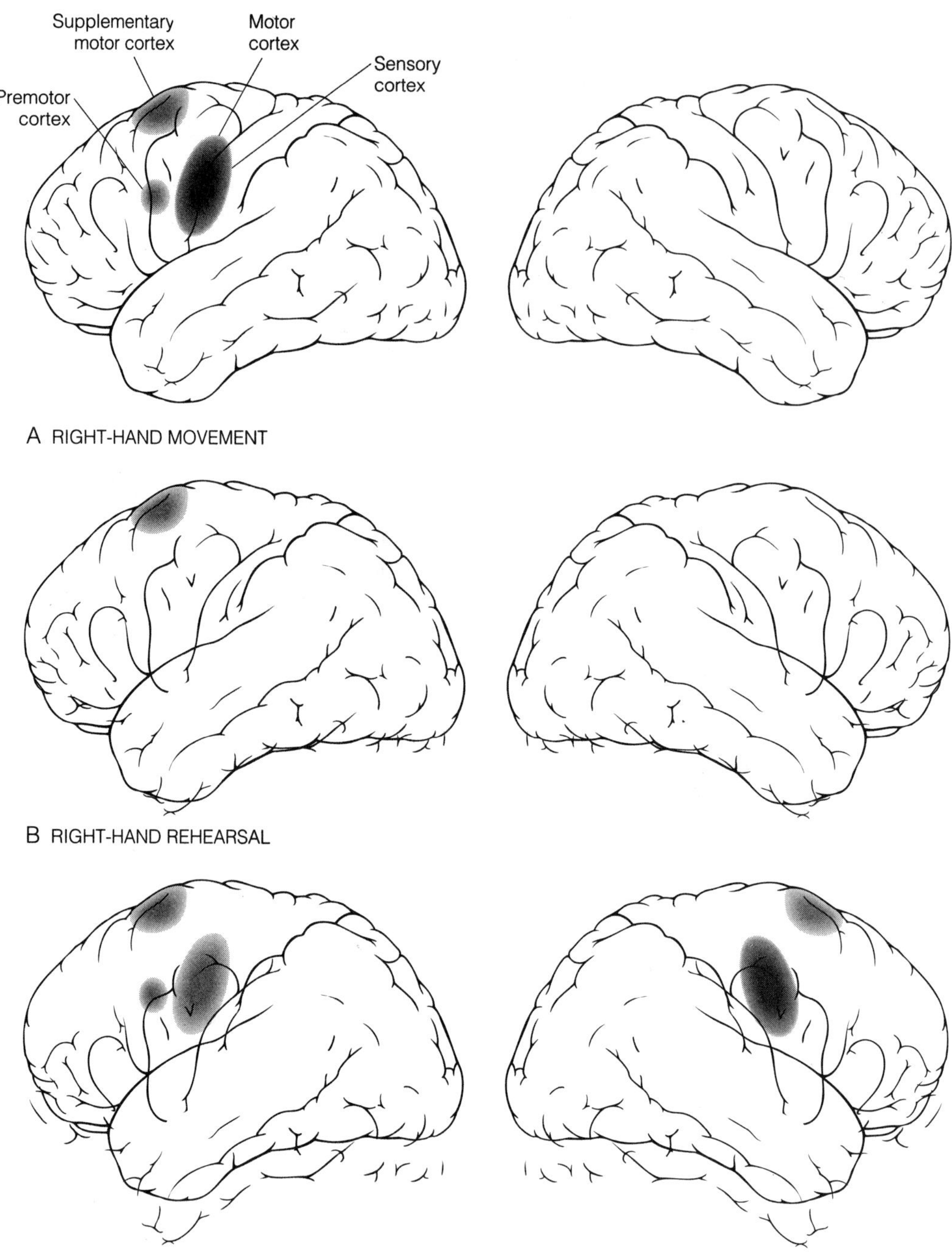

FIGURE 7.11. *A.* A sequence of movements with the right hand produces increases in blood flow in the supplementary motor cortex, premotor cortex, and motor cortex of the left hemisphere. *B.* Mental rehearsal of the movement of the right hand produces increases in blood flow in the supplementary motor cortex. *C.* A sequence of movements of the left hand produces increases in blood flow in the left motor cortex regions and in the motor cortex of the right hemisphere, suggesting that the left hemisphere commands the right hemisphere.

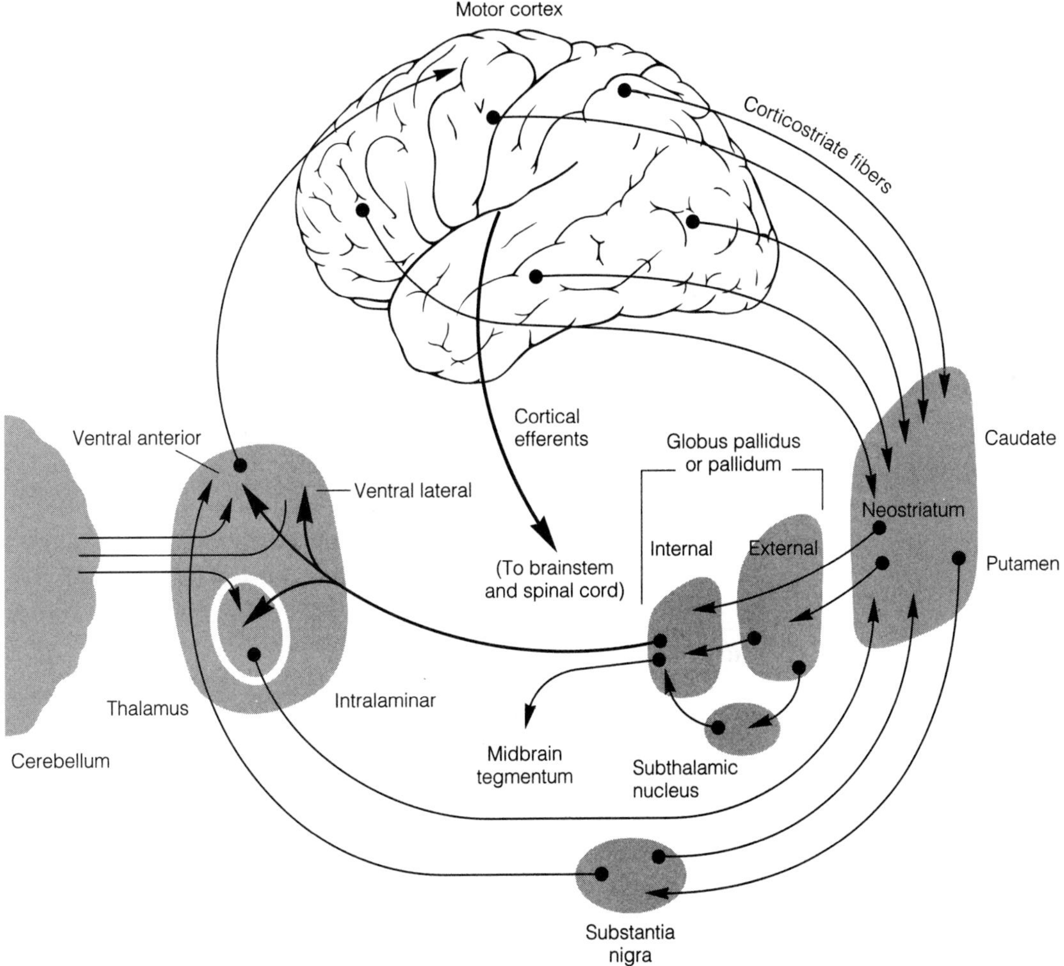

FIGURE 7.12. Circuitry showing the relation between the basal ganglia and the cortex. Note that projections from all parts of the cortex enter the basal ganglia but that only the premotor cortex receives projections from the basal ganglia via the circuit. (After DeLong, 1974.)

frequent involuntary movements. Surprisingly, the two types of disorders may be related. When Parkinson's patients receive medication, the side effects of the medication are involuntary movements similar to those of Huntington's chorea.

There are a number of proposals concerning the functions of the basal ganglia. None are entirely satisfactory and none exclude the others. Since damage to the basal ganglia produces motor abnormalities, they are seen as having motor functions. Since all areas of the neocortex project into the striatum and from there eventually project to the anterior neocortical regions involved in planning movements and sequencing movements, the basal ganglia are also seen as important for organizing and controlling complex movements. An example of a complex movement is reaching to grasp an object. The movement requires a number of joints to be activated together and that the hand be directed, in a controlled way, to a location in space. It also requires that a target of a certain size and shape be grasped. An inability to make such movements in severe Parkinson's disease, and the involuntary appearance of such movements in Huntington's chorea would be consistent with this view. Another theory of basal ganglia function stems from our understanding of the dopamine system. There is very large dopamine projection from the substantia nigra of the midbrain to the striatum. Dopamine, in addition to aiding the production of movements, is thought do mediate reward. The rewarding properties of drugs of abuse, such as cocaine or morphine, as well as the satisfaction that comes from eating and drinking, appear to depend on the integrity of the dopamine system. Thus, it is proposed that movements that are successful in accomplishing some goals are reinforced by the action of dopamine on the striatum. Movements selected in this way can more readily be activated in future similar situations. Since selecting movements that can be preferentially used in the future is learning, some people consider that the basal ganglia are important for motor learning. Thus, knowing what movement to make when one sees a light switch, shoe laces, or a door handle could be mediated by the basal ganglia. Some of the strategies and neural connections by which the basal ganglia perform such functions have been reviewed by Ann Graybiel and her coworkers.

Keele and Ivry have suggested that the underlying function of the basal ganglia may be to generate the forces that are necessary for normal movement. If the forces are too great or are delivered to both agonist and antagonist muscles at the same time, a condition of rigidity will result. If the forces are applied inconsistently, hyperkinetic disorders will result. They tested this idea by giving patients with basal ganglia disorders a force test. The subjects viewed a line on a TV screen. By pushing a button they could produce a second line on the screen. By varying the force of the button press, they could make the length of the second line match that of the first. After a number of practice trials, they were required to produce a button press of appropriate force without the aid of the priming line. Patients with basal ganglia disorders could not produce the appropriate force reliably, whereas patients with damage to the cortex or cerebellum were able to do the task. Potentially, observations such as those by Aldridge and coworkers that humans or animals with basal ganglia damage have difficulty in switching from one task to another and in sequencing movements could also be related to difficulties in generating the forces required to start or stop actions.

Damage to the basal ganglia also aggravates the effects of damage to the cortex. One of the most common causes of brain injury in humans is strokes in which blood vessels are occluded or damaged. Many people who have suffered strokes are paralyzed on one side of the body (hemiplegia) and are unable to recover movement of the contralateral arm. This impairment is often more severe than it should be if only the cortex were damaged. A cortical injury should impair mainly hand movement, but stroke patients frequently have no arm use at all. This difference can be accounted for by the additional damage done by vascular accidents. In addition to damaging the cortex, they usually also damage the underlying basal ganglia. The contributions of the basal ganglia to skilled movements have been neglected in descriptions of motor pathways. This is because it has not been determined how their more indirect connections eventually control movement. Nevertheless, studies using rats have demonstrated that severe impairments in limb use follow selective damage to cells in the caudate putamen or damage to dopamine projections to the caudate putamen, and the condition is greatly aggravated if it includes cortical injury. (See Whishaw and coworkers for a review of this work.)

CEREBELLAR ACCESS TO MOTOR SYSTEMS

The cerebellum is generally thought of as an important part of the motor system, but rather than sending projections directly to motor neurons or their interneurons, it projects to a number of nuclei that then join, either directly or indirectly, the lateral or ventromedial systems of the spinal cord (Figure 7.13).

The archicerebellum composes the entire cerebellum in fishes and is the first cerebellar structure to differentiate in the human fetus. In mammals it makes up the more medial and ventral portion of the cerebellum. Projections from the archicerebellum pass from the fastigial nucleus to the reticular formation and the vestibular nuclei. Tracts from these areas form part of the ventromedial projection of the spinal cord, which, as we have seen, is instrumental in controlling more proximal movements of the body, such as posture and locomotion. Tumors or damage to this area disrupt upright posture and walking but do not substantially disrupt other movements such as reaching, grasping, and finger movements. For example, a person with medial cerebellar damage may, when lying down, show few symptoms of such damage.

The paleocerebellum is the dominant cerebellar structure in quadrupeds from amphibians to mammals and seems closely related to the development and use of the limbs in locomotion. Projections from the nuclei of this area go to the red nucleus and possibly to the other brainstem nuclei as well. Thus, this system is probably involved in the control of limb movements through the lateral system and body movements through the ventromedial system. The predominant effect of damage to this area is an increase in rigidity of the limbs, which disrupts distal movement more than proximal movement.

The neocerebellum makes up the outermost lateral portion of the cerebellum. Although well developed in animals capable of nonsymmetrical limb movements, it shows its greatest development in primates. Projections from the lateral nuclei that serve this area go to the ventral thalamus and from there to the precentral motor cortex. Thus, this area has access to the corticospinal tract that controls more distal movements of the arms and fingers as well as proximal movements of the body. Damage to the neocerebellum produces weakness and a tendency to fatigue, difficulty in localizing or pointing to body parts correctly, and

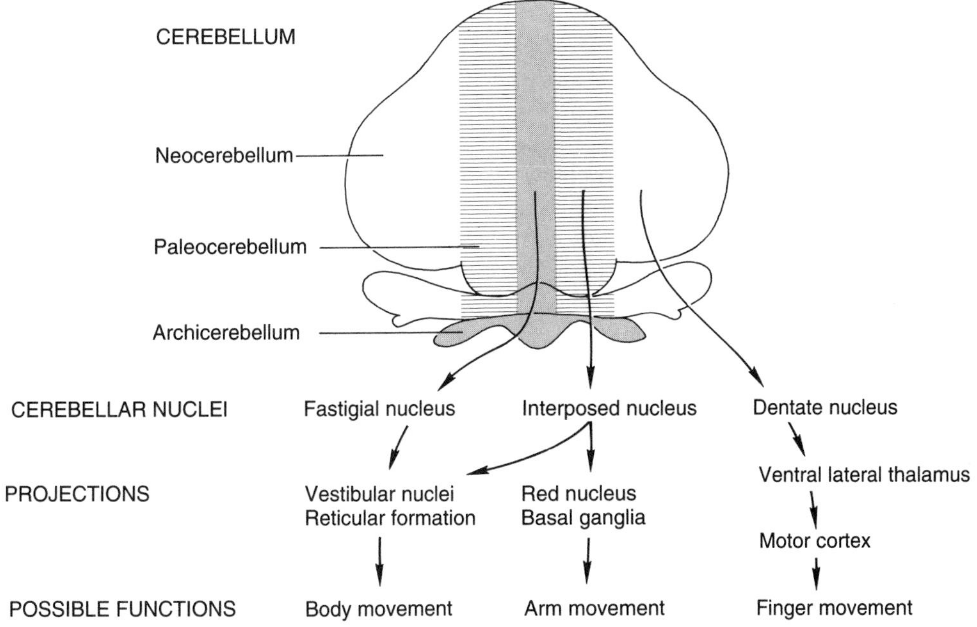

FIGURE 7.13. Projections from different cerebellar areas to spinal cord motor pathways and the routes they take in controlling various portions of the body musculature.

a variety of deficits in the control of the limbs, such as overshooting the mark when pointing, flailing at the joints, staggering, and an inability to carry out repeated rhythmic movements.

Although each of the areas of the cerebellum appears to be involved in moving specific body parts, the entire body is represented in each area. The entire body is also represented in the fastigial nucleus, the interposed nucleus, and again in the dentate nucleus. The architecture of the cerebellum itself is such that each of these body representations is interconnected. This organization may be related to the fact that movements of body parts seldom occur in isolation. For example, the movement of an arm, although executed by the paleocerebellum, often requires the adjustment of the hand and fingers and of the body.

Attempts to understand the functions of the cerebellum have centered around at least four major ideas: (1) its involvement in ensuring the accuracy of a specific movement, (2) its involvement in binding a number of individual movements into a complex coordinated movement, (3) its involvement in learning, and (4) its involvement in timing.

There is an extensive literature dating back more than 100 years that indicates that the cerebellum controls the accuracy of individual movements or the integration of a number of movements into a coordinated movement. Thach and his coworkers have reviewed much of this literature. They conclude that although movement impairments can be documented, it is not clear that the impairments adequately reveal the function of the cerebellum. They suggest that whereas individual movements or coordinated sequences of movements may be adequately produced by noncerebellar structures, such as the motor cortex, the cerebellum must make some additional contribution. They suggest that the cerebellum's function is in adjusting and fine-tuning movements. For example, the operations of skipping a rope, playing tennis, typing, shooting a basketball, or playing a musical instrument require slight adjustments from repetition to repetition so that they are performed precisely. Although the world record for shooting a basketball through a hoop is about 2500 consecutive successful shots, even most professional players have trouble making 10 shots in a row. After each miss, shooters must adjust their posture, aim, and their movement lest they continue to miss. These fine adjustments may be performed by the cerebellum and retained there for future use.

An experiment in which Thach and coworkers demonstrate such a function for cerebellar circuitry is shown in Figure 7.14. A subject throws a dart to a target. After a number of throws, spectacles containing wedge prisms are worn (Figure 7.14A). The prisms bend the light so that the subject, although looking directly at the target, has her eyes deviated to the left. When she initially throws the dart under the prism condition (Figure 7.14B), her throws are directed to the left (the direction in which her eyes are pointing). Since she can see the dart miss the mark, she adjusts each successive throw until accuracy is restored. When the spectacles are removed, throws are displaced to the right (reflecting the adjustments that she has learned). Again, with further practice the accuracy of throws is restored. Figure 7.14C shows the performance of a patient with damage to the olive (part of the cerebellar circuitry). Without the spectacles, dart throws are accurate. With the spectacles the throws are displaced but there is no correction. When the spectacles are removed throws are again accurate. Thus, the patient does not learn to throw accurately when wearing the prisms nor does the patient show an aftereffect when the prisms are removed. Thus, Thach and coworkers suggest that the function of the cerebellum is to ensure that movements are accurate in the many and varied situations in which they are used.

Keele and Ivry suggest that the underlying impairment in cerebellar disorders is a loss of timing. They propose that the cerebellum acts like a clock or pacemaker to ensure that movements are appropriately timed. They suggest that this timing function applies not only to movements but also

A Dart-throwing with prisms

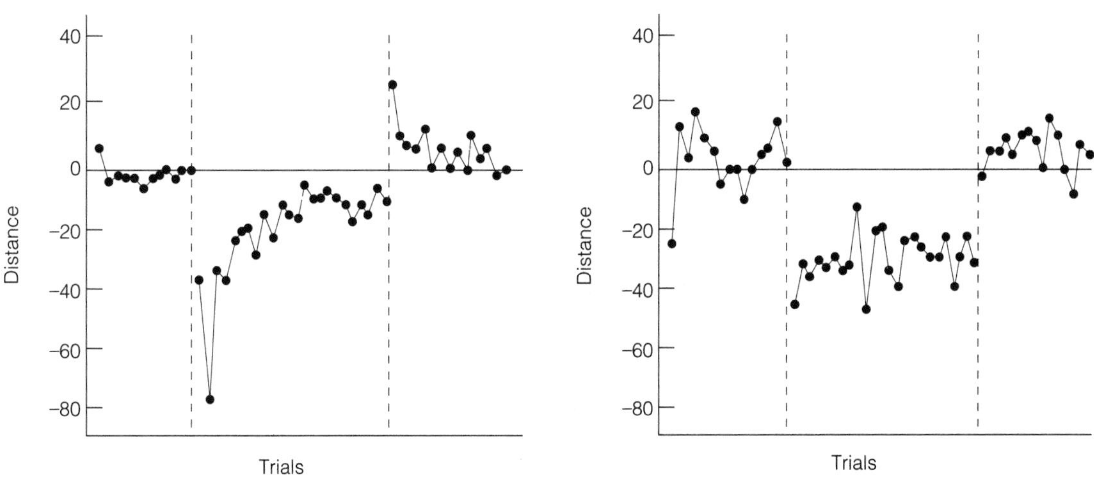

FIGURE 7.14. *A*. The task. A dart thrower wearing spectacles with prisms looks straight ahead although her eyes are deviated to the left. *B*. The normal subject throws the dart accurately without spectacles, throws to the left and then corrects the throws when wearing spectacles, and finally throws to the right and then corrects the throws when the spectacles are removed. *C*. A patient with damage to cerebellar circuitry fails to compensate when wearing spectacles, and shows no aftereffect when the spectacles are removed. (After Thach, Goodkin, and Keating, 1992.)

to other events. They have demonstrated this with two kinds of tests. In a motor test of timing, patients were asked to tap with a finger to keep time with a metronome. After a number of taps, the metronome was turned off and the patients were to continue to tap with the same beat. Patients with cerebellum damage, especially damage to the lateral cerebellum, were impaired on the task whereas patients with cortical or basal ganglia damage were not. In the perceptual task, patients were presented with two pairs of tones. The silent period between the first two tones was always the same, while that between the second two tones changed from trial to trial. The task for the patients was to tell whether the second silent period was longer or shorter than the first silent period. Patients with cerebellar damage were impaired at this task, whereas patients with cortical or basal ganglia damage could do the task. Thus the results of both tests suggest that the cerebellum can act as a clock to time movements or sensory events. This theory is not inconsistent with that of Thach in that both theories stress the involvement of the cerebellum in learning.

SUMMARY

The motor system comprises most of the brain and is made up of separate systems that produce whole-body movements, limb movements, and skilled hand and digit movements. Although movement can be produced in the absence of sensory input, skilled movements are normal only when sensory systems contribute. The spinal cord and brainstem code most of the elements of simple and complex movements, including reflexes and sequences of movements such as those used in walking. The motor cortex, in conjunction with the sensory cortex, is responsible for producing skilled movements, especially skilled movements of the arms, hands, and digits. The basal ganglia and the cerebellum play important roles in providing appropriate force, timing, and execution of skilled movements. One of the most striking features of the motor system is its redundancy: despite most kinds of damage, substantial movement ability is retained through undamaged portions of the motor system.

REFERENCES

Adkins, R. J., R. W. Morse, and A. L. Towe. Control of somatosensory input by cerebral cortex. *Science* 153:1020–1022, 1966.

Aldridge, J. W., K. C. Berridge, M. Herman, and L. Zimmer. Neuronal coding of serial order: Syntax of grooming in the neostriatum. *Psychological Science* 4:391–395, 1993.

Beck, C. H., and W. W. Chambers. Speed, accuracy, and strength of forelimb movement after unilateral pyramidotomy in rhesus monkeys. *Journal of Comparative and Physiological Psychology* 70:1–22, 1970.

Coghill, G. E. *Anatomy and the Problem of Behavior.* New York and London: Hafner, 1964.

DeLong, M. R. Motor functions of the basal ganglia: Single-unit activity during movement. In F. O. Schmitt and F. G. Worden, eds. *The Neurosciences: Third Study Program.* Cambridge, Mass.: MIT Press, 1974.

Evarts, E. V. Sensorimotor cortex activity associated with movements triggered by visual as compared to somesthetic inputs. In F. O. Schmitt and F. G. Worden, eds. *The Neurosciences, Third Study Program.* Cambridge, Mass.: MIT Press, 1974.

Fetz, E. E. Are movement parameters recognizably coded in the activity of single neurons? *Behavioral and Brain Sciences* 15:679–690, 1992.

Galea, M. P., and I. Darian-Smith. Multiple corticospinal neuron populations in the Macaque monkey are specified by their unique cortical origins, spinal terminations, and connections. *Cerebral Cortex* 4:166–194, 1994.

Georgopoulos, A. P., M. Taira, and A Lukashin. Cognitive neurophysiology of the motor cortex. *Science* 260:47–52, 1993.

Ghez, C. Introduction to the motor systems. In E. R. Kandel and J. H. Schwartz, eds. *Principles of Neural Science.* New York: Elsevier, 1991.

Graybiel, A. M., T. Aosaki, A. W. Flaherty, and M. Kimura. The basal ganglia and adaptive motor control. *Science* 265:1826–1831, 1994.

Groves, P. M. A theory of the functional organization of the neostriatum and the neostriatal control of voluntary movement. *Brain Research Reviews* 5:109–132, 1982.

Jeannerod, M. *The Neural and Behavioural Organization of Goal-Directed Movements.* Oxford: The Clarendon Press, 1988.

Kawashima, R., K. Yamada, S. Kinomura, T. Yamaguchi, H. Matsui, S. Yoshioka, and H. Fukuda. Regional cerebral blood flow changes of cortical motor areas and prefrontal areas in humans related to ipsilateral and contralateral hand movement. *Brain Research* 623:33–40, 1993.

Keele, S. W., and R. Ivry. Does the cerebellum provide a common computation for diverse tasks?: A timing hypothesis. In A. Diamond, ed. *The Development and Neural Bases of Higher Cognitive Functions, Annals of the New York Academy of Sciences* 608:197–211, 1991.

Kuypers, H. G. J. M. Anatomy of descending pathways. In V. B. Brooks, ed. *The Nervous System. Handbook of Physiology,* vol. VII. Bethesda, Md.: American Physiological Society, 1981.

Lashley, K. S. The problem of serial order in behavior. In L. A. Jeffress, ed. *Cerebral Mechanisms and Behavior.* New York: Wiley, 1951.

Leonard, C. M., D. S. Glendinning, T. Wilfong, B. Y. Cooper, and C. J. Vierck, Jr. Alterations of natural hand movements after interruption of fasciculus cuneatus in the macque. *Somatosensory and Motor Research* 9:61–75, 1991.

Nyberg-Hansen, R., and E. Rinvik. Some comments on the pyramidal tract, with special reference to its individual variations in man. *Acta Neurologica Scandinavia* 39:1–30, 1963.

Passingham, R. E., V. H. Perry, and F. Wilkinson. The long-term effects of removal of sensorimotor cortex in infant and adult rhesus monkeys. *Brain* 106:675–705, 1983.

Roland, P. E., B. Larsen, N. A. Lassen, and E. Skinhøj. Supplementary motor area and other cortical areas in organization of voluntary movements in man. *Journal of Neurophysiology* 43:539–560, 1980.

Rothwell, J. C., M. M. Traub, B. L. Day, J. A. Obeso, P. K. Thomas, and C. D. Marsden. Manual motor performance in a deafferented man. *Brain* 105:515–542, 1982.

Schieber, M. H., and L. S. Hibbard. How somatotopic is the motor cortex hand area? *Science* 261:489–492, 1993.

Thach, W. T., H. P. Goodkin, and J. G. Keating. The cerebellum and the adaptive coordination of movement. *Annual Reviews of Neuroscience* 15:403–442, 1992.

Twitchell, T. E. The automatic grasping response of infants. *Neuropsychologia* 3:247–259, 1965.

Whishaw, I. Q., W. T. O'Connor, and S. G. Dunnett. The contributions of motor cortex, nigrostriatal dopamine and caudate-putamen to skilled forelimb use in the rat. *Brain* 109:805–843, 1986.

Yakovlev, P. E., and P. Rakic. Patterns of decussation of bulbar pyramids and distribution of pyramidal tracts to two sides of the spinal cord. *Transactions of the American Neurological Association* 91:366–367, 1966.

part two

Cortical Organization

Human neuropsychology is interested primarily in the function of the human neocortex. In Part Two we begin by considering the general principles of neocortical function (Chapter 8). Chapters 9 and 10 then describe the fascinating division of function, almost unique to humans and certainly most elaborated in them, between the two cerebral hemispheres. This division not only has been an object of study in its own right but also has provided a key that opens new insights into cortical function. There has been a trend in neuropsychology to organize writings around the higher functions (for example, memory and language) rather than anatomical region. We believe that both approaches are essential. Thus, Chapters 11 through 14 describe the anatomical functions of each lobe of the cerebral hemispheres. (Part Three is organized around discussions of the higher functions.) Of course, the lobes do not work in isolation, and Chapter 15 describes their functional interrelationship.

To understand how the cortex functions, it is useful first to consider what processes are needed to account for our behavior. We have discussed the sensory systems and have seen that each sensory modality is composed of multiple pathways, allowing multiple routes for sensory information to access the cortex. There is much more to the analysis of sensory information, however, for we have not yet addressed those aspects of cerebral activity that encompass thought or cognition. One way to approach this topic is to ask what it is that a neural system must be able to do if we are to account for even simple aspects of cognition. We shall consider several such aspects before proposing how and where they might be performed.

We have seen that the inputs of the various sensory systems are independent, yet we experience a sensory event as a single percept. For example, when we touch a cat we have several concurrent sensations: the cat has fur with a particular texture; the cat's fur has color; the cat may be purring, meowing, or growling; and the cat has an odor. These pieces of sensory information are not perceived separately, but together as a single sensory experience. The ability to recognize concurrent sensory signals as a single percept is known as *cross-modal matching.* Cross-modal matching can occur with any combination of visual, auditory, and somatic stimuli; in each case the matching is assumed to occur in the cortex, where the inputs from different modalities overlap.

Each of our sensory systems produces a point-to-point representation of the receptor surface in the cortex. On the basis of this representation it should be possible to extract information about where the information is coming from. There are several characteristics of sensory processing that complicate this extraction. First, our sensory representations are biased. For example, the hands and face take up more space in the cortex than the back, and the fovea has a greater representation than the periphery of the retina. Thus, if spatial location were inferred directly from the sensory maps it would be distorted. Hence, it is necessary that our understanding of where things are, our "spatial map," be independent of this perceptual bias; we need a spatial coordinate system that gives us a faithful reproduction of space, independent of the proportional representation of the receptor surface. Besides the problem of bias, there is a difficulty with coding both location and content of sensory input in the same neurons. Neurons that are sensitive to color, for example, tend to respond to color regardless of where it might be, whereas neurons sensitive to location tend to respond to only a small region of the world. If the location neurons also coded pattern information, we would need redundancy throughout the visual field, which would be very inefficient. Third, we need a spatial coordinate system that guides motor responses independent of sensory content. That is, we need to be able to identify stimulus location without knowing what an object is. For instance, we can duck a low-flying missile, such as a snowball, even though we could not have identified what we ducked away from. In this case the details of the stimulus are irrelevant to the necessary motor response.

If we responded to all sensory stimulation, it would overwhelm us. We need a system that can filter information, responding only to the relevant portion of it. This filtering process, which is often referred to as selective attention, functions to select a small amount of information and to ignore most of the rest. For instance, as you read this page you ignore its shape, its color, the TV next door, the feel of your shoes, the taste in your mouth, and so on. If we were unable to ignore irrelevant inputs, we would find it very difficult to comprehend anything!

Attention is a double-edged sword, however, because once we have directed our attention to a particular configuration of stimuli, we need to be able to direct it elsewhere when it becomes appropriate. Thus, we need a mechanism that will allow shifts of attention and will do so at the right times. If we fail to shift we may be said to be perseverating, and if we shift attention too easily we may be too distractible.

Although our response to a sensory input may be immediate, it is often delayed, possibly for quite some time, especially if the response depends upon additional information. Consider the example of listening to a long joke. We make no response until the punch line, and we often need to store crucial information from the early part of the story to appreciate the humor. We encounter similar examples continually as we read a newspaper article, have a discussion, listen to music, compare the tastes of wines, and so on. An interesting characteristic of this storage system is that it needs to hold most information only for a short time. Indeed, it is obvious that we could not possibly store all that we experience, or even all that we filter out for our attention, or we soon would be overwhelmed with information. Hence, we must have some sort of filtering system that chooses the information for longer storage and perhaps even plays a role in the storage process.

Much of our sensory processing appears to be organized innately and requires little experience. Babies respond to touch, temperature, taste, and so on. Our perception of other sensory events, however, depends heavily upon experience, and at the extreme there is abstract information, such as language, that has meaning only because of learning. When we read the word "cat," for example, our experience with English allows us to identify the word and its meaning. Other configurations of letters such as "cta" are not processed in the same manner and are without meaning. This suggests that we have a store of words (sometimes called a *lexicon*) that we sift through to compare against the words we hear and read. Furthermore, the word "cat" has all sorts of meanings (both denotations and connotations) that are also stored. There must be parallel stores for other types of visual information, too—such as musical scores, international road signs, numbers, mathematical equations, and so on—which obviously are learned and have no intrinsic meaning to the nervous system. Further, such stores of abstract material are not restricted to the visual system. Stores must be present for aurally presented material, such as words, musical notes, and phrases.

Not all of our afferent input is external. We need mechanisms that register body movements and inform the sensory systems. For instance, if we are playing baseball and must run to catch a fly ball, the ball will appear to have two sources of movement: one is the ball's actual movement and the other is due to our head's movement back and forth as we run. In both cases the image of the ball is moving across the retina, but the cause is different. The fact that we can intercept the ball accurately (at least with practice!) implies that the brain can distinguish between the movement generated by the ball's velocity and the movement due to our head bobs. The process whereby this occurs is known as reafference. It appears that the motor systems "inform" the sensory systems of the movements that are made, which allows the sensory systems to subtract the movement from that of the object. The system can be fooled if there is no reafference, such as occurs when the body is moved by an external force. If you carefully move your eye by pressing your finger against the eyeball, the world appears to move. A similar movement of the eye made by the eye muscles results in no perceived movement, because of reafference.

Information that controls movements may arise directly from events and things currently present in the external world or from reafferences, or it may be "representational" in the sense that it is an internal representation of what was (and perhaps still is) in the external world. When behavior is guided by representation it is guided by a neural record that is independent of concurrent sensory input. This behavior may take several forms. A simple example is observing an object being placed in a drawer and then being able to retrieve it later, even though it is not visible. Our behavior is guided by a mental representation of the object in the drawer. As a more complex example, we may travel some distance to a favorite restaurant, taking a route that we have not previously taken. In this case the behavior is guided by an internalized representation of the restaurant and its location in some sort of "cognitive map" of the world. Internal representations are not simple, because they must encompass various types of information including both the spatial location of the sensory information and its nature (color, pitch, odor, and so forth). In the absence of representational information, behavior depends upon direct information, and people may be unable to plan ahead or to show any imagination.

Finally, if we are to make movements at the right time and place, we need a record of what movements have just occurred and a plan, or program, for what is to be done. The principal idea here is that it is only with the knowledge of what is ongoing that new units or series of units can be initiated. If you are sitting and wish to walk to another room, walking cannot be initiated until you have stood up. The initiation of walking requires feedback that standing has occurred and may also require inhibition of leg movements in order to stand. A further requirement may be that there is a plan of the movements that will be made, which can be called a prospective motor program. The idea here is that the movements can be organized in the correct order in advance and the motor program can be "read" by the brain to produce the correct movements in the right order.

It should be obvious by now that the complexity of human behavior requires considerably more processing of sensory information than simply recognizing patterns of input in the various sensory channels. Many other processes are involved, and these are largely cortical. It is tempting to try to assign discrete packets of cognitive activity to different pieces of cortical tissue, but this is fraught with problems, both because the complexity of the processes requires continual interaction of the different areas and because there are multiple solutions to different problems and various regions of the cortex may play greater or lesser roles in different strategies. Nevertheless, we can make some broad generalizations that will provide a basic framework for exploring the organization of the cortex.

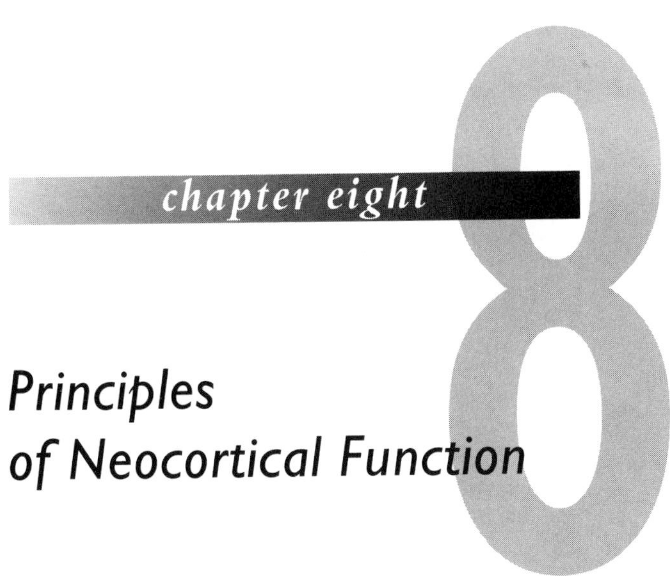

Principles of Neocortical Function

Mr. Higgins decided he should learn French so that he could enjoy French literature. After a year's intensive study Higgins was almost fluent in French, but it became clear to him that to really understand French, he was going to have to study Latin. Higgins had always been interested in Latin and so he plunged into it, only to find after a year's intense study that to master Latin, he really must study old Greek. Higgins was determined to learn French, and so he began a serious study of Greek. Alas, after a year's intense study of Greek, Higgins determined that he must now learn Sanskrit if he were to really appreciate Greek. This posed a problem, for there were few scholars of Sanskrit, but with a few months' effort, he managed to locate an old man in India who was a true scholar of Sanskrit. Excited at the possibility of soon learning French, Higgins moved to India to begin his study of Sanskrit. After six months the old man died. Demoralized because he did not yet have a good knowledge of Sanskrit, Higgins returned home and concluded that it was not possible to really learn French.

This story illustrates the difficulty of deciding what level of analysis can best explain behavior. The neuropsychologist obviously must study the basic structure and organization of the brain, especially the neocortex, and must keep abreast of the latest developments in neuroanatomy, neurochemistry, and neurophysiology. The problem is in knowing where to stop. Having a knowledge of the microstructure of mitochondria in the neuron may be fascinating and necessary for understanding how a neuron functions, but will this knowledge make it any easier to study the neurological control of language? There is, of course, no easy answer to this question; the neuropsychologist must avoid being trapped by Sanskrit but be aware of where French came from.

LEVELS OF FUNCTION FROM SPINAL CORD TO CORTEX

A metaphor for the relationship of the cortex to subcortical structures is that of a piano player to a piano. The cortex is the piano player who produces behavior by playing upon subcortical keys. This is an idea that can be dated to Herbert Spencer's mid–19th century speculation that each step in evolution added a new level of brain and a new level of behavioral complexity. This idea was adopted by Hughlings-Jackson and became a central focus of neurological theories of the 20th century.

The idea of functional levels of nervous system organization can be traced in part to early findings that the brain has a remarkable ability to survive after parts of it are destroyed. In this way the brain is not like a radio that stops functioning when one component is removed. This resiliency to damage was given popular exposure in 1700 by Du Verney. In a public demonstration he showed that when a nerve and muscle were dissected away from a frog, the nerve continued to function, because it produced muscle contractions when touched. In 1853, Pfluger demonstrated that a frog with only an intact spinal cord could survive and display quite complex responses. If acid was placed on the frog's right side, the right leg would reach up and remove the acid. If the right leg was restrained, then—after a number of ineffective efforts—the left leg would be used to remove the acid. Other workers, among them Ridi in 1810, demonstrated that if parts of the brainstem were intact, amphibians could walk, and in 1884 Fano studied the locomotor patterns of a tortoise with only a lower brainstem. These early experiments were followed by more systematic research into the capacities of different portions of the nervous system and into the details of their structure.

One such systematic study was done by Berridge on grooming in the rat. Rats (and other animals, including ourselves) begin by grooming the head and then work their way down the body. First, using their paws, rats rub the nose with symmetrical circular movements, then they sweep their paws across the face and behind the ears, and then they turn and begin to lick the body. This series of actions can be divided into as many as 50 linked movements. In examining this movement complex Berridge found that many levels of the nervous system are involved in producing the elements and the syntax of the behavior. That is, the behavior is not produced by one locus in the brain but depends upon many brain areas including the spinal cord, hindbrain, midbrain, diencephalon, basal ganglia, and cortex. The following sections describe some of the functions mediated by different anatomical levels of the nervous system (Figure 8.1). Parallel functions that may occur in humans will be noted as appropriate.

The Spinal Cord and Reflexes

Animals whose spinal cord is disconnected from the brain are unable to move voluntarily because the brain has no way to control the spinal neurons. Nonetheless, the spinal cord is intact and can mediate many reflexes, such as limb approach to a tactile stimulus and limb withdrawal from a noxious stimulus. The spinal cord also contains the circuitry to produce stepping responses and walking, provided that body weight is supported.

The Hindbrain and Postural Support

If the brain is injured such that the hindbrain and spinal cord are still connected but both are disconnected from the rest of the brain, the subject is called a **low decerebrate**. The sensory input into the hindbrain comes predominantly from the head and is carried over cranial nerves IV to XII. Most of these nerves also have motor nuclei in the hindbrain whose efferent fibers control muscles in the head and neck. Because relatively few interneurons in the spinal cord are located between sensory projections and motor projections, interneurons in the hindbrain have multiplied to form nuclei as well as more complex coordinating centers such as the cerebellum. Sensory input to the hindbrain is not limited to the cranial nerves, for the spinal somatosensory system has access to hindbrain motor systems, just as the hindbrain has access to spinal motor systems.

Low-decerebrate cats are described by Bazett and Penfield and by Bard and Macht in experiments in which the animals were kept alive for periods of weeks or months. The cats were generally inactive when undisturbed and showed no effective thermoregulatory ability, but they swallowed food placed on their tongues and so could be fed. If the animals were stimulated lightly in any of a variety of sensory modalities (such as touch, pain, sounds) they moved from their normal reclining position into a crouch. If the stimulation was stronger, they walked, somewhat unsteadily. These stimuli also elicited such affective

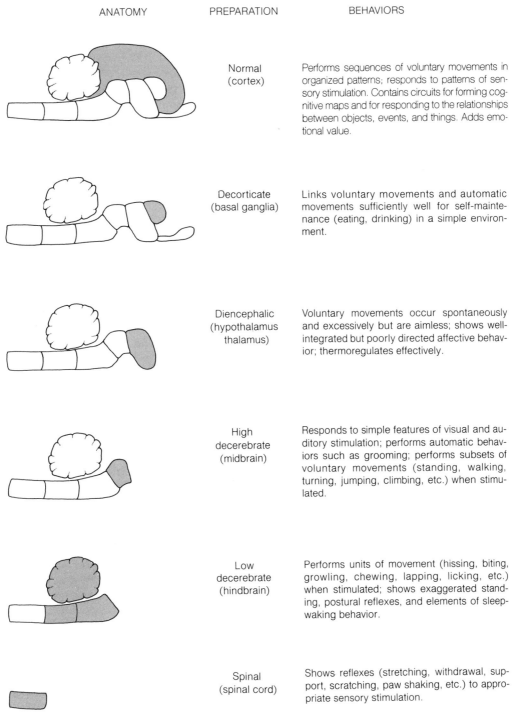

ANATOMY	PREPARATION	BEHAVIORS
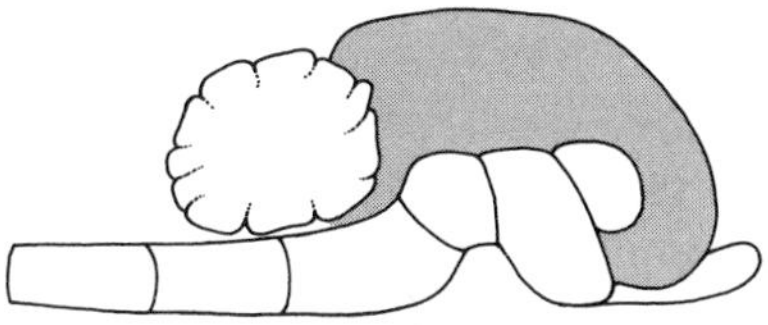	Normal (cortex)	Performs sequences of voluntary movements in organized patterns; responds to patterns of sensory stimulation. Contains circuits for forming cognitive maps and for responding to the relationships between objects, events, and things. Adds emotional value.
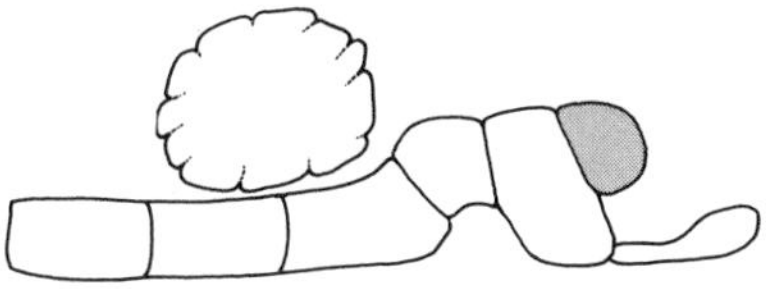	Decorticate (basal ganglia)	Links voluntary movements and automatic movements sufficiently well for self-maintenance (eating, drinking) in a simple environment.
	Diencephalic (hypothalamus thalamus)	Voluntary movements occur spontaneously and excessively but are aimless; shows well-integrated but poorly directed affective behavior; thermoregulates effectively.
	High decerebrate (midbrain)	Responds to simple features of visual and auditory stimulation; performs automatic behaviors such as grooming; performs subsets of voluntary movements (standing, walking, turning, jumping, climbing, etc.) when stimulated.
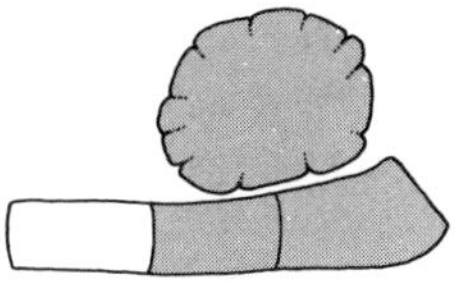	Low decerebrate (hindbrain)	Performs units of movement (hissing, biting, growling, chewing, lapping, licking, etc.) when stimulated; shows exaggerated standing, postural reflexes, and elements of sleep-waking behavior.
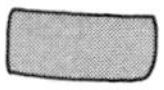	Spinal (spinal cord)	Shows reflexes (stretching, withdrawal, support, scratching, paw shaking, etc.) to appropriate sensory stimulation.

FIGURE 8.1. Behavior that can be supported by different levels of the nervous system. Shading indicates the highest remaining functional area.

behaviors of normal cats as biting, hissing, growling, and lashing of the tail.

One of the most characteristic aspects of behavior accorded by the hindbrain is a peculiar kind of stiffness called **decerebrate rigidity**. This is excessive muscle tone, particularly in the antigravity muscles (those that hold the body up), which are the body's strongest. Because of this rigidity, when an animal is placed in an upright position, its limbs extend and its head flexes upward. Sherrington refers to this rigidity as "exaggerated standing."

Against the background of decerebrate rigidity a number of *postural reflexes* can be elicited by changes in head position. If the head of a standing animal is pushed down toward the floor, the front limbs flex and the hind limbs extend; if the head is pushed up, the hind legs flex and the front legs extend. The first type of posture would be used by a normal cat looking under a couch, the second by a normal cat looking up onto a shelf. Turning the head to the side elicits extension of the limbs on the same side and flexion of the limbs on the opposite side of the body; this type of response occurs in a normal cat that has turned its head to look at some object and is prepared to pursue it. When the animals are placed on their sides, they extend their lower limbs (those in contact with the floor), and semiflex their upper limbs. This is a static reaction that represents the first stage of the **righting reflex**.

There are two types of sleep in normal animals: *quiet sleep,* characterized by muscle tone, and *active sleep,* characterized by an absence of muscle tone (these are commonly referred to as slow-wave sleep and dream sleep). Low-decerebrate animals are described as showing characteristics of both types of sleep at different times. Animals left undisturbed gradually lose their rigidity and subside or droop into a prone posture. Any mild stimulus such as a noise or a touch reinstates rigidity. This type of behavioral change seems analogous to quiet sleep. The animals also show a sudden collapse, accompanied by the loss of all body tone, which lasts from 15 sec to 12 min. This type of behavioral change seems analogous to active, or dream, sleep, particularly since some people with an illness called **narcolepsy** similarly collapse into active sleep. Thus, the neural centers producing sleep are located in the hindbrain.

The low-decerebrate animal's behavior, then, differs from that of the animal with spinal cord injury in a number of ways. First, responses such as tail lashing and biting are elicited by several (often cumulative) modes of stimulation. Such responses can be explained in the following way. In its simplest form tail lashing is a withdrawal reflex of the tail from adverse stimulation; it is a spinal reflex. Biting is a jaw reflex elicited by facial stimulation; it is mediated through the hindbrain by the sensory and motor components of the trigeminal (V) nerve. Because the sensory components of the spinal reflexes and hindbrain reflex circuits are linked to each other's motor components, pinching a cat's lip or tail can produce the same response—tail withdrawal (tail lashing) and biting. This principle of interlinking sensory and motor components of different levels is an organizational feature of all levels of brain function.

The behavioral changes seen in low-decerebrate animals are paralleled in people who are rendered comatose by brainstem damage of the type that essentially separates the lower brainstem from the rest of the brain. Barrett and his colleagues have documented a number of such cases. These people may alternate between states of consciousness resembling sleeping and waking, make eye movements to follow moving stimuli, cough, smile, swallow food, display decerebrate rigidity, and display postural adjustments when moved. When cared for, people with such brain damage may live for months or years with little change in their condition.

The Midbrain and Spontaneous Movement

The next level of brain organization can be seen in an animal that has an intact midbrain containing, in the tectum, the coordinating centers for vision (superior colliculus) and hearing (inferior colliculus) and, in the tegmentum, a number of motor nuclei, but lacks higher-center functioning. Damage that produces this condition is called **high decerebration**. Visual and auditory inputs allow the animal to perceive events at a distance, and so the high-decerebrate animal can respond to distant objects by moving toward them.

Bard and Macht report that high-decerebrate cats can walk, stand, resume upright posture when turned on their backs, and even run and climb when stimulated. Bignall and Schramm found that kittens decerebrated in infancy could orient to visual and auditory stimuli. The animals could even execute an attack response and pounce on objects at the source of a sound. In fact, Bignall and Schramm fed the cats by exploiting this behavior: they placed food near the source of the sound; attacking the sound source, the cats would then consume the food. Although the cats attacked moving objects, they gave no evidence of being able to see, for they bumped into things when they walked around. Woods has reported that high-decerebrate rats are active and make all the movements of normal rats; Grill and Norgren report that these rats are generally inactive and show normal locomotor abilities only when disturbed. Bignall and Schramm, as well as Woods, may have left some hypothalamic tissue intact, which would account for why their animals were more active than the animals observed in other studies.

These experiments demonstrate that all the components (or subsets) of **voluntary movements**—movements that take an animal from one place to another, such as turning, walking, climbing, and swimming—are present at the level of the midbrain. Normal animals use voluntary movements to provide for a variety of needs; for example, to find food, water, or a new home territory, or to escape a predator. These movements have also been variously called appetitive, instrumental, purposive, or operant. Voluntary movements, being executed through lower-level postural support and reflex systems, can also be elicited by lower-level sensory input; that is, a pinch or postural displacement can elicit turning, walking, or climbing. Thus, this new functional level is integrated with lower levels by both ascending and descending connections, exactly as the hindbrain and spinal levels are interconnected.

High-decerebrate animals can also effectively perform **automatic movements:** units of stereotyped behavior linked in a sequence. Grooming, chewing food, lapping water, and rejecting food are representative automatic behaviors of the rat. Generally, automatic behaviors (also variously called reflexive, consummatory, or respondent behaviors) are directed toward completing some sort of consummatory act and are not specifically directed toward moving an animal from one place to another. Grooming is an excellent example of an automatic behavior, since it consists of a large number of movements executed sequentially in an organized and quite stereotyped fashion. If a rat's fur is wet, it first shakes its back, then sits on its haunches and shakes its front paws, then licks water from them, wipes its snout rapidly with bilateral symmetrical movements, wipes its face with slight asymmetrical movements, and then turns to lick the fur on its body. Food rejection is similarly complex. If decerebrate rats are satiated and then given food, they perform a series of movements consisting of tongue flicks, chin rubbing, and paw shaking to reject the food. These behaviors are similar to the rejection behaviors made by normal rats in response to food they find noxious. If the animals are not sated, they will lap water and chew food brought to their mouths.

There are a number of accounts of infants born with large portions of the forebrain missing. One child studied by Gamper (Figure 8.2) had no brain present above the diencephalon and only a few traces of the diencephalon intact. This child was, therefore, anatomically equivalent to a high-decerebrate animal. The child showed many behaviors of newborn infants. It could sit up; it periodically slept and was wakeful; it could suck, yawn, stretch, cry, and follow visual stimuli with its eyes. However, the child showed little spontaneous activity and if left alone remained mostly in a drowsy state. Brackbill studied a similar child and found that in response to stimuli such as 60- to 90-dB (decibel) sounds it oriented in much the same way normal children do. Unlike normal

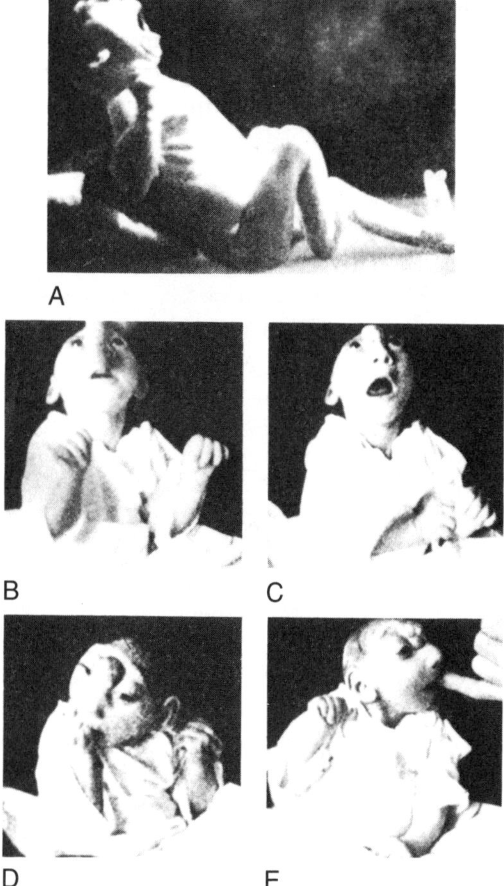

FIGURE 8.2. Instinctive behavior and oral automatisms in Gamper's mesencephalic human. *A.* Yawning with spreading of arms. *B.* Oral adversive movements after the lips are touched, with deviation of the eyes. *C.* Coordinated gaze and snapping movements after finger was removed from view. *D.* Spontaneous sucking of own hand. *E.* Oral adversion to the left side with deviation of head and eyes and tonic neck reflexes in the arms. (From E. Gamper, *Ztschr. ges. Neurol. Psychiat.* 104:49, 1926.)

children, however this child's responses did not change in size and did not habituate (gradually decrease in intensity) to repeated presentation. She concluded that the forebrain is not important in producing movements but is important in attenuating and inhibiting them. Generally, children born with such extensive brain abnormalities do not live long, and among those that live for a number of months there is no development of the complex behaviors seen in normal children. They appear to have the same behavioral capacities as high-decerebrate animals.

The Diencephalon and Affect and Motivation

The diencephalic animal, although lacking the basal ganglia and cerebral hemispheres, has an intact olfactory system, enabling it to smell odors at a distance. The hypothalamus and pituitary are also intact, and their control over hormonal systems no doubt integrates the body's physiology with the brain's activity. The hypothalamus is thought to be involved in **homeostasis;** that is, maintaining body temperature, chemical balance, energy reserves, and so forth. Diencephalic animals maintain normal body temperature, but they do not eat or drink well enough to sustain themselves. The diencephalon adds a dimension of affect and motivation to behavior in the sense that behavior becomes "energized" and sustained.

As we have mentioned, high-decerebrate animals show many of the component behaviors of rage, but the behaviors are not energetic, well integrated, or sustained. Cannon and Britton studied diencephalic cats and described what they called "quasi-emotional phenomena" (or sham rage) such as are usually seen in an infuriated animal; the behavior consists of lashing the tail, arching the trunk, making limb movements, displaying claws, snarling, and biting. Sympathetic signs of rage are present, including erection of the tail hair, sweating of the toe pads, dilation of the pupils, micturation, high blood pressure, high heart rate, and increases in epinephrine and blood sugar. These emotional attacks sometimes last for hours. Bard removed various amounts of forebrain and brainstem and found that for this sham rage to occur it was necessary to leave at least the posterior portion of the hypothalamus intact. Clinical reports indicate that similar sham emotional attacks can occur in people who have suffered hypothalamic lesions; that is, there are people who show unchecked rage or who literally laugh until they die.

One of the most pronounced features of the diencephalic animal's behavior is its constant activity; this has been observed by Sorenson and Ellison and by Grill and Norgren in rats and by Goltz in dogs. Since normal animals deprived of food and water become active, it is possible to argue that the diencephalic animal's hyperactivity is driven by a deficiency condition; that is, the animal is searching for food or water. Grill and Norgren, however, found that feeding the animals the same amount as control rats did not arrest hyperactivity.

These two examples of diencephalic behavior suggest that the diencephalon adds an energizing dimension to behavior that may justify labeling the behavior affective or motivated. Britain and Cannon, however, were aware of the inappropriateness of the rage behavior of the diencephalic cat, and so they called it sham rage to distinguish it from the directed rage of the normal cat. Perhaps the hyperactivity of the diencephalic animal should be called sham motivation to distinguish it from the goal-oriented behavior of the normal animal. In this sense the sham affect and sham motivation of the diencephalic animal are something like the exaggerated standing observed in low-decerebrate animals. Under appropriate forebrain control the behavior can be released for functional purposes, but in the absence of that control the behavior of the animal is excessive and seems inappropriate.

The Basal Ganglia and Self-Maintenance

Decortication is removal of the neocortex, leaving the basal ganglia and brainstem intact. Decorticate animals have been studied more closely than any others because they are able to maintain themselves without special care in laboratory conditions.

The first careful experiments were done by Goltz with decorticate dogs (see Chapter 1), but the most thorough studies have used rats as subjects. Within a day after surgery rats eat and maintain body weight on a wet mash diet and eat dry food and drink water brought in contact with the mouth. With a little training in drinking (holding the water spout to the mouth) they find water and become able to maintain themselves on water and laboratory chow. They have normal sleeping-waking cycles; run, climb, and swim; and even negotiate simple mazes. They can also sequence series of movements. For example, copulation involves a number of movements occurring sequentially and lasting for hours, yet the animals can perform the acts almost normally. Grooming also involves the sequential use of about 50 discrete movements, and it is also performed normally.

What is observed in the decorticate rat, and what is presumably conferred by the basal ganglia, is the ability to link automatic movements to voluntary movements so that the behaviors are biologically adaptive. A major portion of this linking probably involves inhibition or facilitation of voluntary movements. For example, the animal walks until it finds food or water and then inhibits walking to consume the food or water. Thus, the basal ganglia probably provide the circuitry required for the stimulus to inhibit movement so that ingestion can occur.

The Cortex

What the cortex *does* can also be ascertained by studying what the decorticate animal (with the neocortex alone removed or with the limbic system also removed) *cannot* do. All the elementary movements that animals might make seem to be part of their behavioral repertory after decortication. They can walk, eat, drink, mate, raise litters of pups, and so forth, in a seemingly adequate fashion.

There are, however, behaviors that decorticate animals seem unable to perform. They do not build nests, although they engage in some nest-building behaviors. They do not hoard food, although they might carry food around. They also have difficulty making skilled movements with the tongue and limbs, since they are unable to reach for food by protruding the tongue or by reaching with one forelimb. They can do pattern discriminations in different sensory modalities, but only if these are relatively simple. A series of experiments by Oakley shows that the animals can perform well in tests of classical conditioning, operant conditioning, approach learning, cue learning, and pattern discrimination. These experiments confirm that the cortex is not essential for learning per se. However, there are kinds of learning at which the animals fail. These include finding their way around in space and learning more complex pattern discriminations.

An instructive lesson that is obtained from studies of decortication is that the cortex does not add much in the way of new movements to an animal's behavioral repertory. What it appears to do is extend the usefulness of all behaviors or make them adaptive in many new situations. Thus, animals without a cortex can use their limbs for many purposes, but animals with a cortex can make more skilled and refined movements. Animals without a cortex can see and hear, but animals with a cortex can see and hear more complex patterns of stimuli.

THE STRUCTURE OF THE CORTEX

As the summary of the behaviors of animals without a cortex indicates, the cortex adds new dimensions to the analysis of sensory events and new levels of control to movements. What are the structural features of the cortex that permit this analysis?

We have already noted that the cortex can be divided by topographic maps (see Chapter 3), which are based upon various anatomical and functional criteria. The first complete cortical map of the human brain was published in 1905 by Campbell, and it was based upon both cell structure and myelin distribution. Soon after there were several alternative versions, the most notable by Brodmann. The various maps do not correspond exactly and they use different criteria and nomenclature. Furthermore, as new staining techniques are devised it is possible to subdivide and to redefine cortical areas in a truly bewildering manner, with estimates of the number of cortical areas in the human brain ranging from the approximately 50 of Brodmann to well over 200. Indeed, one neuroanatomical wag was quoted as concluding that "in cortical anatomy the gain is in the stain!"

One of the consistent themes in neuroanatomy over the last century is that cortical regions can be categorized as **primary sensory cortex, primary motor cortex,** and **association cortex.** Association cortex is usually also divided into **secondary cortex,** which elaborates information coming from primary areas, and higher-order areas, which may combine information from more than one system. This idea can be traced to Flechsig and his studies of the development of myelin in the cortex. Flechsig divided regions into (1) an early-myelinating primordial zone including the motor cortex and a region of visual, auditory, and somatosensory cortex; (2) a field of cortex bordering the primordial zone that myelinated next; and (3) a late-myelinating zone, which he called "association." Flechsig hypothesized psychological functions for his different zones, with the general idea being that the primary zones performed relatively simple sensory analyses while the association areas contained the highest mental functions. Flechsig's ideas greatly influenced neurological thinking of the 20th century.

Cortical Cells

There are two main categories of cortical nerve cells that can be easily distinguished in the cortex by the presence or absence of dendritic spines: spiny neurons and aspiny neurons. As their name suggests, their distinguishing feature is the presence or absence of dendritic spines.

Spiny neurons include **pyramidal cells,** which have cell bodies in the general shape of a pyramid, and spiny **stellate cells,** which are smaller, star-shaped interneurons. They are characterized by spines covering their dendrites. Spiny neurons are excitatory and are likely to use glutamate or aspartate as transmitters. Pyramidal cells, which constitute the largest population of cortical neurons (70%–85%), are the efferent projection neurons of the cortex. They are found in layers II, III, V, and VI. In general, the largest cells send their axons the farthest. The pyramidal cells of layer V are the largest, projecting to the brainstem and spinal cord. Those in layers II and III are smaller and project to other cortical regions (Figure 8.3).

Aspiny neurons have short axons, do not have dendritic spines, and are interneurons. They are quite diverse in appearance, with different types being named largely on the basis of the configuration of their axons and dendrites. For example, one type of aspiny stellate cell is called a basket cell because its axon projects horizontally, forming synapses that envelop the postsynaptic

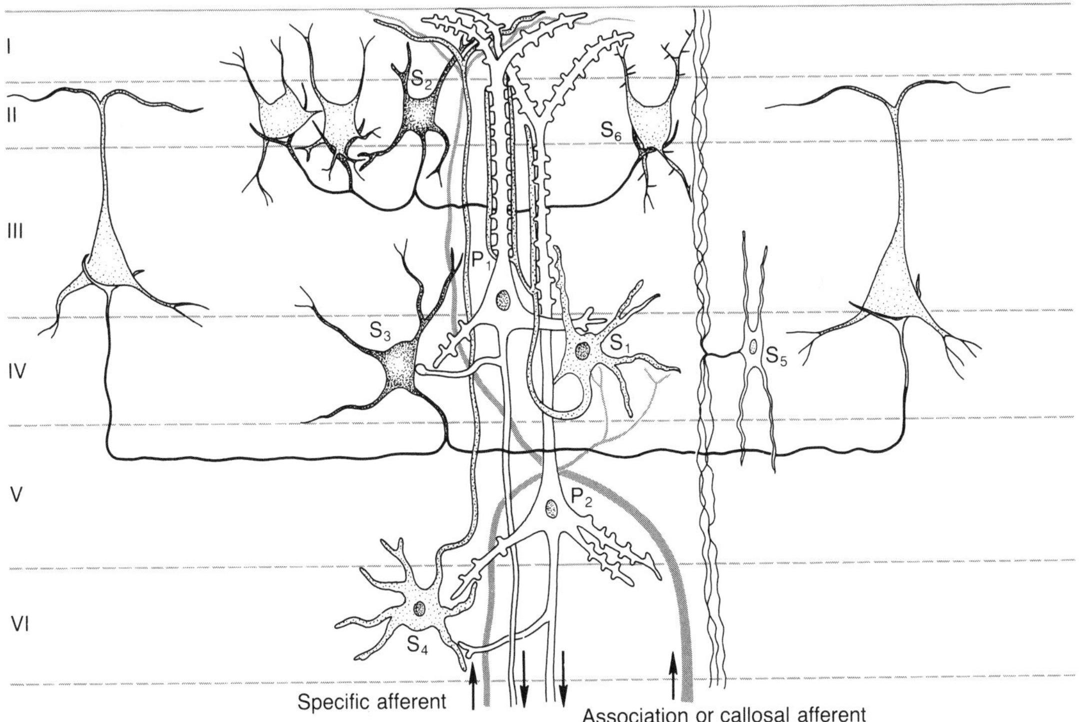

FIGURE 8.3. Illustration of the most important neocortical cell types. Pyramidal cells (P_1 and P_2) are found in layers III and V. The stellate cells are found throughout the cortex and include several types of cells (S_1–S_5). Thalamic afferents arrive in layer IV and synapse on stellate interneuron S_1. Associative or callosal afferents feed into the more superficial layers to synapse on interneurons or on the long apical (vertical) dendrites of pyramidal neurons. Basket stellate interneurons (S_2) establish connections within the superficial layers, probably functioning to inhibit the cells to which they project. Larger basket interneurons (S_3) located in the deeper layers may also spread inhibition laterally in the deeper layers. Fusiform (spindle-shaped) stellate cells (S_4) are located primarily in layer VI, sending excitatory axons vertically. Double bouquet-type stellate cells (S_5) may secure the spread of excitation over the entire depth of the cortex when layer IV is stimulated by incoming afferents. Spiny stellate cells are illustrated by S_6. Note that for simplicity the spines are not drawn on all of the pyramidal cells. (Direction of arrows indicate afferents [up] or efferents [down].) (Adapted from Szentagothai, 1969.)

cell like a basket. Despite differences in shape, all aspiny neurons are inhibitory and are likely to use GABA as a transmitter. Aspiny neurons also use many other transmitters; virtually every classical transmitter and neuropeptide has been colocalized with GABA in aspiny cells. Thus, not only are aspiny cells morphologically diverse, they show a remarkable chemical diversity as well.

Cortical Layers, Efferents, and Afferents

Each of the four to six layers of the cortex has different functions, different afferents (inputs), and different efferents (outputs). The cells of the middle layers of the cortex (especially in and around layer IV) comprise a zone of sensory analysis in that they receive projections from other areas of the cortex and other areas of the brain. The cells of layers V and VI comprise a zone of output in that they send axons to other cortical areas or other brain areas. Therefore, it is hardly surprising that the sensory cortex has a relatively large layer IV and a small layer V whereas the motor cortex has a relatively large layer V and a small layer IV. Figure 8.4 illustrates this difference and shows that although the different cortical layers can be distinguished in the cortex, the thickness of the layers also reflects their function.

Figure 8.4 also illustrates another feature of cortical organization: afferents to the cortex are of two general types: specific and nonspecific.

Specific afferents are those that terminate in relatively discrete regions of the cortex, usually in only one or two layers. These include projections from the thalamus as well as from the amygdala. Most of these projections terminate in layer IV, although projections from the amygdala and certain thalamic nuclei may terminate in the more superficial layers. The specific afferents bring information (such as sensory information) to an area of the cortex.

Nonspecific afferents are those that terminate diffusely over large regions of the cortex, in some cases over all of it. The norepinephrinergic projections from the brainstem, the cholinergic projections from the basal forebrain, and the projections from certain thalamic nuclei are examples of nonspecific afferents. Nonspecific afferents often terminate in many or all of the layers of the cortex and even release their transmitter substances into the extracellular space. They presumably serve some general function such as maintaining a level of tone or arousal so that the cortex can process information.

Cortical Columns, Spots, and Stripes

Most of the interactions between the layers of the cortex are with cells directly above or below, with relatively less interaction with cells more than a couple of millimeters on either side (see Figure 8-3). This vertical bias in cortical organization forms the basis for a second type of neocortical organization: the column.

There have been many terms for the vertical organization of the cortex, two of the most common being **column** and **module.** Although these terms are not always interchangeable, the idea is that groups of 150–300 neurons form little circuits ranging from about 0.5 to 2 mm wide, depending upon the cortical region. Evidence for some kind of modular unit comes from two principal sources. First, when the brain is cut horizontally and stained in special ways, it is possible to see patterns of spots or stripes in the cortex. Some examples will illustrate. If a radioactive amino acid is injected into one eye of a monkey, the radioactivity is transported across synapses to the primary visual cortex. The radioactivity is not evenly distributed across the cortex, however, as it goes only to places that connect with the affected eye (Figure 8.5A). Thus, the pattern of radioactivity seen in the primary visual cortex (area 17) is a series of stripes, much like those on a zebra. A different pattern is seen in the same visual cortex when a different technique is used, however. If the cortex is stained with cytochrome oxidase, which shows areas of high metabolic activity by staining mitochondria, the visual cortex appears to have spots, which are known as "blobs" (Figure 8.5B). These blobs are known to be involved in color perception. Curiously, if the same stain is applied to area 18, which is an adjacent visual region, the pattern of staining appears more like

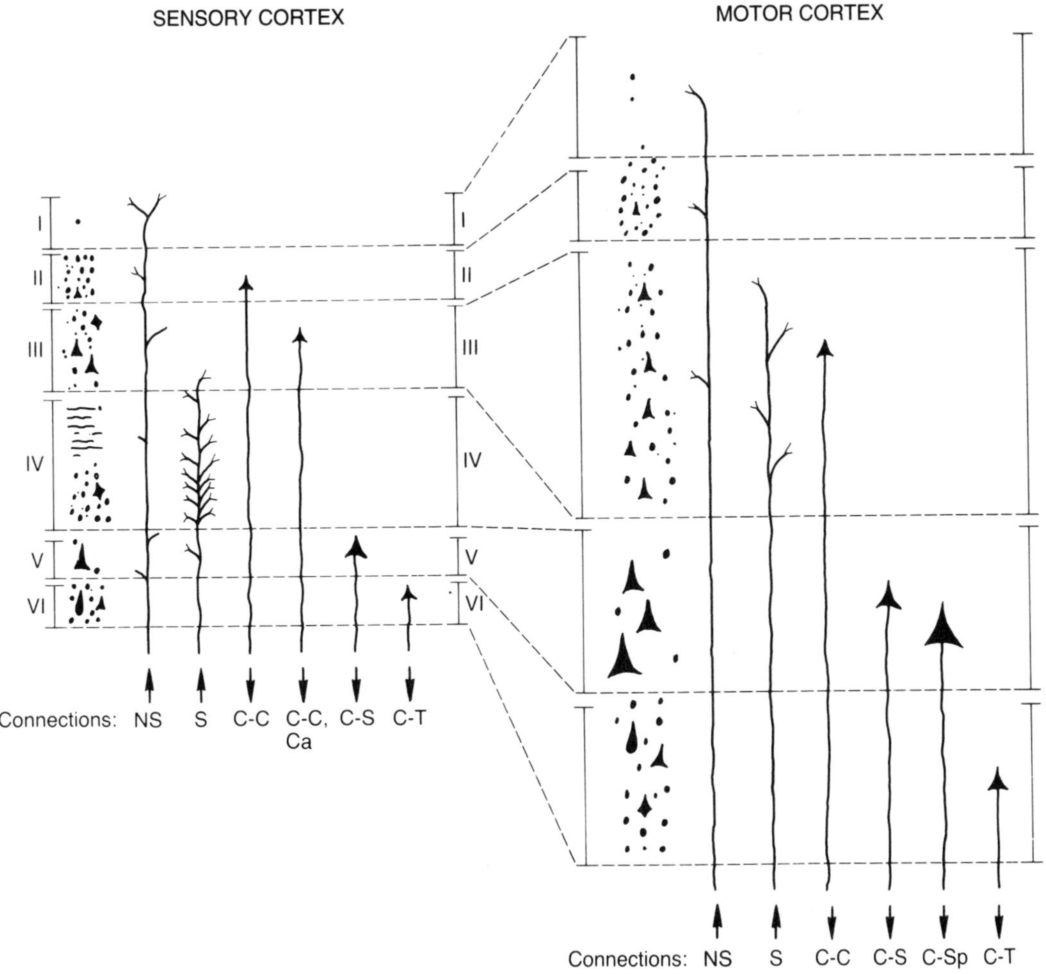

FIGURE 8.4. Schematic illustration of the neuronal elements of the sensory cortex and motor cortex. The sensory cortex is much thinner than the motor cortex, and the size of each layer is markedly different in the two. The specific (S) and nonspecific (NS) inputs to the cortex illustrate the different distribution of these afferents to the different laminae (layers). The outputs from the cortex arise from different layers, depending on the destination. Cortical-cortical (C-C) efferents arise from layers II and III, callosal (Ca) efferents arise from layer III, cortical-subcortical (C-S) and cortical-spinal (C-Sp) efferents arise from layer V, and cortical-thalamic (C-T) efferents arise from layer VI, as illustrated. (Direction of arrows at bottom of figure indicate afferents [up] or efferents [down].) (After Shepherd, 1979.)

stripes (Figure 8.5C) than like spots. Finally, if the primary somatosensory cortex of the rat is stained with a compound known as succinic dehydrogenase, the cortex shows a pattern of spots that are known as "barrels" (Figure 8.5D). Each of these barrels corresponds to one of the vibrissae on the face of the rat. As these examples illustrate, there appear to be many types of modules, and even the same stain shows a different modular organization in different regions.

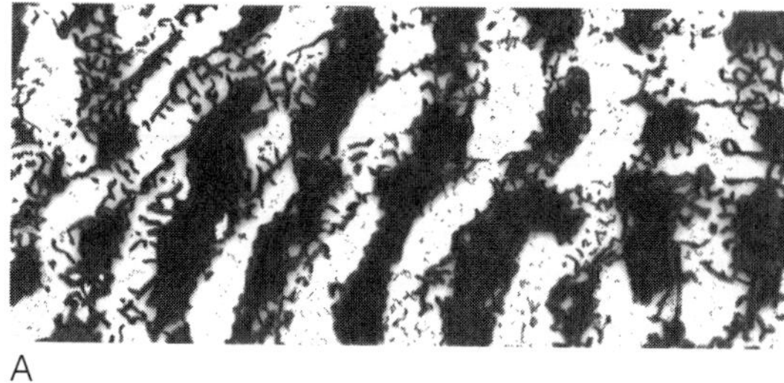

A

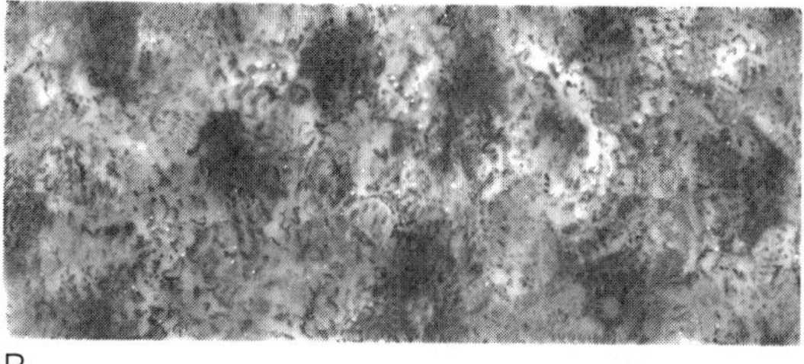

B

C

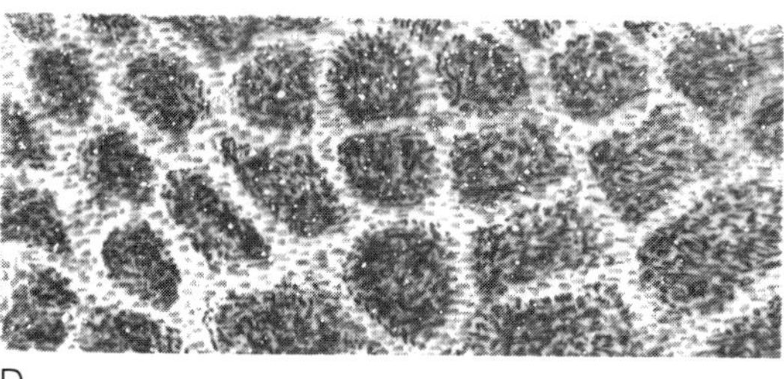

D

FIGURE 8.5. Examples of spots and stripes in the cortex. *A.* Ocular dominance columns in layer IV in the primary visual cortex (V1) of a rhesus monkey (autoradiograph after injection of radioactive proline into one eye). *B.* Blobs in layers II–III in V1 of a squirrel monkey (cytochrome oxidase histochemistry). *C.* Stripes in layers II–III in visual area V2 of a squirrel monkey (cytochrome oxidase histochemistry). *D.* Barrels in layer IV in the primary sensory cortex (SI) of a rat (succinic dehydrogenase histochemistry). (After Purves et al., 1992.)

A second way to demonstrate modular organization is shown physiologically in the sensory cortex. If a microelectrode is moved vertically through the sensory cortex from layer I to layer VI, all the neurons encountered appear to be very similar functionally. For example, if an electrode is placed in the somatosensory cortex and lowered vertically from layer I to layer VI, neurons in each layer are excited by a particular tactile stimulus (for example, a light touch) in a particular part of the body (for example, the left thumb). The cells of layer IV are activated earliest by an afferent input, as would be expected from the direct afferent connections to this layer. Cells of the other layers must have longer latencies, since they would have at least one more synapse on an interneuron in layer IV before receiving the sensory input. The pyramidal neurons of layer V are the last to be activated, again as would be expected because the efferents are there. The functional similarity of cells across all six layers at any point in the cortex suggests that the simplest functional unit of the cortex is a vertically oriented column of cells that composes a minicircuit. Groups of these columns may be organized in somewhat larger units as well. If an electrode samples the cells of area 17 (visual cortex), all the cells in a column will respond to a line of a given orientation (for example, 45°). If the electrode is moved laterally across the cortex, adjacent columns will be found to respond to successively different orientations (for example, 60°, 90°) until all orientations over 360° are sampled. The pattern will then repeat itself. Thus, in the visual cortex, columns are arranged in larger modules.

As interesting as cortical spots, stripes, and columns appear to be, there is considerable controversy over what the definition of a module might be and what the presence of a module means functionally. One problem is that although modules are apparent in primary sensory regions, they are less apparent in the association or motor cortex. Furthermore, if we are looking for a common definition of the dimensions of a module, then the stripes and spots are a problem since they differ greatly in size. Furthermore, closely related species often have a very different pattern of spots and stripes, which seems strange if they are fundamental units of cortical function. For example, although Old World monkeys have beautiful ocular dominance columns, these columns are not found in New World monkeys even though the visual abilities of the two groups are similar.

Zeki has suggested that the search for the basic module of cortical organization is akin to the physicist's search for the basic unit of all matter. There is an underlying assumption that the cortical module might be performing the same basic function throughout the cortex. In this view the expansion of the cortex would reflect an increase in the number of basic units, much as one would add chips to a computer. This notion has some appeal, but we are left wondering what the basic function and operation of the module might be. Recently, Purves and his colleagues have suggested a provocative view. They note that the spots and stripes on the cortex resemble the markings on the fur of many animals. They suggest that while these patterns may provide camouflage, disguise, or sexual attraction, these uses would not be one of the fur's fundamental purposes. Pursuing this analogy, they propose that some modular patterns may well reflect secondary functions of cortical organization. One possibility they suggest is that cortical modules may be an incidental consequence of the nature of synaptic processing in the cortex. In other words, as the cortex forms its intrinsic connections to process information, one efficient pattern of connectivity is the vertical module. In this view the module certainly reflects an important aspect of cortical organization, but is presence *reflects* cortical connectivity rather than *causing* it. If this is the case, then there must be an alternative way (or ways) of organizing cortical activity that does not require a constant module.

The conclusion we want to draw from this discussion is that there is clearly a vertical component to cortical organization, but the basic structure and function of the module is difficult to define at present. Nonetheless, it seems unlikely that there is a single way of organizing cortical connectivity across all species and cortical regions.

Multiple Representations: Mapping Reality

Early ideas about visual, auditory, and somatic function held that there are one or two representations of the external environment in the cortex and that these are responsible for our basic sensations. For example, when Penfield and his colleagues stimulated the motor and somatosensory strips of their patients at the Montreal Neurological Hospital, they found that it was possible to identify two regions of the parietal cortex that appeared to represent localized body parts such as the leg, hand, and face (see Figure 3.3). These regions, which were called homunculi, were seen as the areas of the cortex responsible for basic tactile sensations such as touch, pressure, and temperature. Subsequent investigations of nonhuman subjects led to the identification of analogous maps of the visual and auditory worlds as well, and it was generally believed that the rest of the human cortex is occupied with more complex functions that we might loosely call cognition.

This simple view of cortical organization began to be doubted during the late 1970s and 1980s, however, as more refined physiological and anatomical techniques began to reveal literally dozens of maps in each sensory modality, rather than just one or two. For example, depending upon the definition used, there are between 25 and 32 regions in the monkey cortex that could be implicated in visual functioning. Although the somatosensory and auditory maps may be less numerous, there still appear to be on the order of 10 to 15 maps in each of these modalities as well. The newly recognized regions are not duplicates of the original maps but rather are involved in the processing of different aspects of the sensory experience. For example, in vision there are areas specialized for analyzing basic features such as form, color, and movement. Furthermore, there are many psychological processes, such as visual object memory and visually guided movements, that require visual information. In addition to the demonstration of multiple maps, areas were identified that had functions in more than one modality (for example, vision and touch). These areas, known as **polymodal cortex** or **multimodal**

cortex, presumably function to combine characteristics of stimuli across different modalities. For example, we can identify visually objects that we have only touched, which implies some common perceptual system linking the visual and somatic systems.

There are three distinct regions of multimodal cortex, one in each of the parietal, temporal, and frontal lobes. The existence of these three areas implies that there is probably more than one process that requires polymodal information, although it is not known exactly what these processes might be.

One of the interesting implications of the discovery of so many cortical maps is that there is less and less cortex left over for the more complex functions. In fact, it is now clear that virtually all of the cortex behind the central fissure has some kind of sensory function. In addition, the frontal lobe receives connections from many of the maps, suggesting some type of sensory function in the frontal lobe as well.

A view is emerging that the cortex is fundamentally an organ of sensory perception and related processes. This idea has an interesting implication: animals with more cortex must have more sensory processing and a different perception of the world. Jerison has pursued this idea by suggesting that our knowledge of reality is directly related to the structure and number of our cortical maps. The more maps a brain has, the more of the external world is known to the animal and the more behavioral options available to it. For instance, animals such as rats and dogs, whose brains do not have a cortical region analyzing color, have a knowledge of the world that is colorless. This must limit the behavioral options of such animals, at least with respect to color. Similarly, although it is difficult for us to imagine, species that are not "smell blind" as we are, such as dogs, may know their world with object-specific olfactory images that are as useful to them as our visual images are to us. Following this line of reasoning, Jerison suggests that cortical maps determine reality for a given species. The more maps there are, the more complex the internal representation of the external world must be.

Cortical Systems: The Frontal Lobe, Paralimbic Cortex, and Subcortical Loops

The connections between cortical areas in a sensory system represent only a portion of the cortical connections. There are four other principal types: frontal lobe connections, paralimbic connections, subcortical loops, and other subcortical connections. We consider each of these in turn.

The frontal lobe can be subdivided into (1) the motor cortex, forming the motor homunculus; (2) the cortex just in front of the motor cortex, which is called the **premotor cortex;** and (3) the remaining cortex of the frontal lobe, which is known as the **prefrontal cortex.** Sensory regions do not connect directly with the motor cortex but may project to either the premotor or prefrontal cortex (Figure 8.6). Connections to the premotor cortex are involved in such things as the ordering of movements in time and the control of hand, limb, or eye movements with respect to specific sensory stimuli. Projections to the prefrontal cortex are involved in the control of movements in time and with respect to short-term memories of sensory information (see Chapter 16).

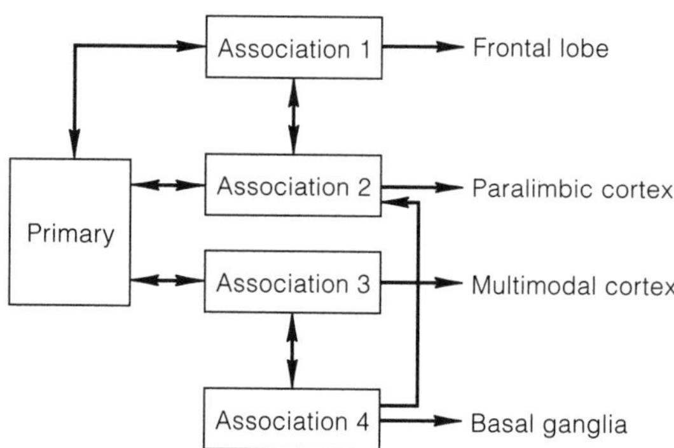

FIGURE 8.6. Schematic illustration of levels of organization in the cortex. The primary sensory cortex projects to sensory association regions that are interconnected. These regions project to several cortical targets—including the frontal lobe, paralimbic cortex, and multimodal cortex—and a subcortical target, the basal ganglia. There are several levels of association cortex, but for simplicity only a single level is illustrated here.

The **paralimbic cortex**, phylogenetically older cortex, is adjacent to limbic structures (Figure 8.7) and is composed of roughly three layers. It can be seen in two places: (1) on the medial surface of the temporal lobe, where it is known as *pyriform cortex, entorhinal cortex,* and *parahippocampal cortex;* and (2) just above the corpus callosum, where it is referred to as *cingulate cortex*. The paralimbic cortex has a special role in memory.

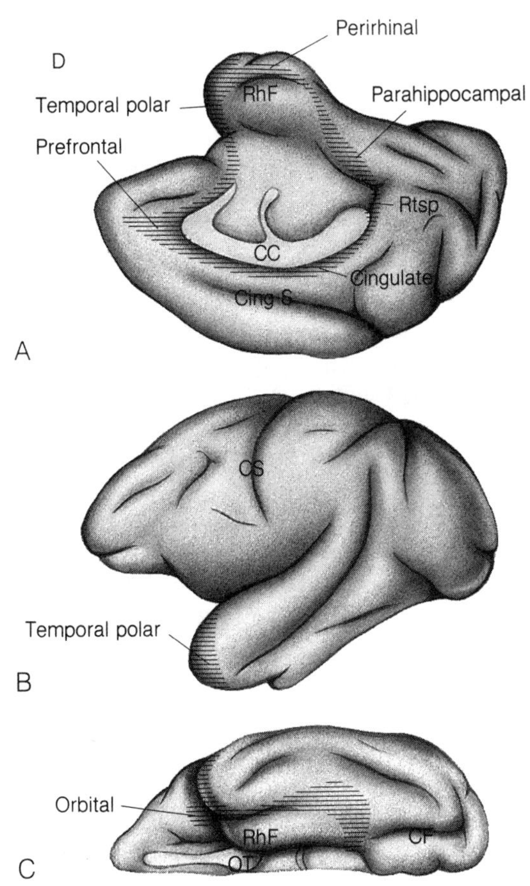

FIGURE 8.7. Diagram of the medial (*A*), lateral (*B*), and ventral (*C*) surfaces of the cerebral cortex of the rhesus monkey. Hatched areas identify the paralimbic areas in prefrontal, cingulate, retrosplenial (Rtsp), parahippocampal, and perirhinal cortex. Abbreviations: CC, corpus callosum; CF, calcarine fulcus; Cing S, cingulate sulcus; CS, central sulcus; RhF, rhinal fissure.

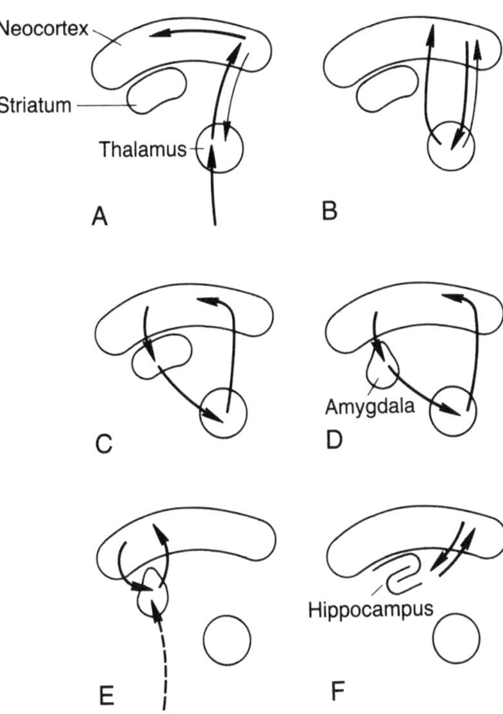

FIGURE 8.8. Schematic diagrams illustrating the cortical-subcortical feedback loops. *A* and *B* show two different thalamic loops. *C* shows the cortical-striatal-thalamic loop, *D* the cortical-amygdala-thalamic loop, *E* the cortical-amygdala loop, and *F* the cortical-hippocampal loop. Each of these feedback loops presumably functions to modify ongoing cortical activity. Thickness of the arrows represents the relative size of the connections. The dashed lines indicate various subcortical inputs to the amygdala.

The cortex receives all its sensory input from subcortical structures, either directly from the thalamus or indirectly through other structures, such as the tectum. Like cortical-cortical connections, most cortical-subcortical connections are reciprocal and thus can be conceived of as feedback loops (Figure 8.8). These include connections from the thalamus, amygdala, and hippocampus. In addition, there is an indirect loop with the striatum, which is connected with the thalamus. The specific functions of these loops are poorly understood, but they can be presumed to play some role in amplifying or modulating cortical activity. An example is the addition of affective tone to visual input by the amygdala. A ferocious dog may generate a strong affective response in us as it charges, in part because the amygdala adds affective tone to the visual input of the dog. Indeed, in the absence of the amygdala, laboratory animals appear to have absolutely no fear of threatening objects. We have seen cats whose amygdalas have been removed take leisurely strolls through rooms housing large monkeys, whereas no normal cat would even contemplate doing such a thing.

Cortical Connections: Reentry and the Binding Problem

We have seen that the cortex has multiple anatomically segregated and functionally specialized areas. How does this organization translate into our perception that things are unified and coherent? This problem is known as the **binding problem.** Stated differently, the binding problem asks how sensations in specific sensory channels (touch, vision, hearing, and so forth) can be combined so that they give the unified experience that we believe we have. More specifically, when you look at the face of a person, why does the shape, color, and size of the face combine to make a coherent representation?

There seem to be two possible solutions to this problem. One would be to have a high-order cortical center that receives input from all of the different cortical areas and integrates or binds them into a single perception. This has been a popular idea, but it is being abandoned because it is becoming clear that there is no such area. A second solution would be to interconnect all the different cortical areas, or some subset of them, so that information is somehow shared. This solution has some appeal because the cortex is characterized by a complicated pattern that has several interesting properties:

1. There is no area that could represent entire perceptual or mental states. Thus, not all cortical areas are connected with one another, and even within a sensory modality, not all cortical areas are connected. Various writers have tried to determine the rules of connectivity, but they are not simple and are beyond the scope of our discussion here (for details, see Felleman and van Essen; Pandya; Zeki). Suffice it to say that about 40% of the possible intercortical connections within a sensory modality are actually found.

2. All cortical areas have internal connections that connect units with similar properties. This feature is important, for it links neurons that are neighbors and synchronizes their activity.

3. One of the more remarkable aspects of cortical connectivity is a property known as **reentry.** When a given area A sends information to area B, area B reciprocates and sends a return message to area A (Figure 8.9). Reentry constitutes a mechanism whereby one cortical area can influence the area from which it receives input, and Zeki has suggested that an area could actually modify its inputs from another area before it even receives them! An important point is that the connections from areas A and B do not originate from the same regions, suggesting that they play different roles in influencing each other's activity.

The precise way in which intraareal connections, interareal connections, and reentry can solve the binding problem has been studied by computer modeling. The general idea of computer models is that the primary function of these connections is to correlate the activity within and between areas. The function of the correlation is to produce a globally coherent pattern, known as *integration,* over all areas of the perceptual system. The computer models show that integration can occur very quickly, on a time scale of 50 to 500 msec, which provides a way of binding the areas together briefly to form a unified percept. (This concept of cortical organization is likely to be foreign to many readers. We recommend Zeki's readable book for a longer discussion.)

Jerison considers the binding problem in another way. Recall that he considered the evolutionary expansion of cortical areas. This increase in areas has implications for a brain that has multi-

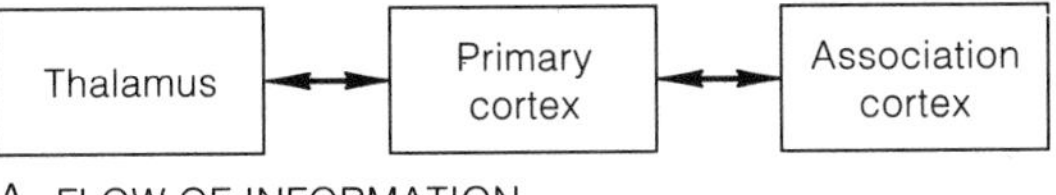

A FLOW OF INFORMATION

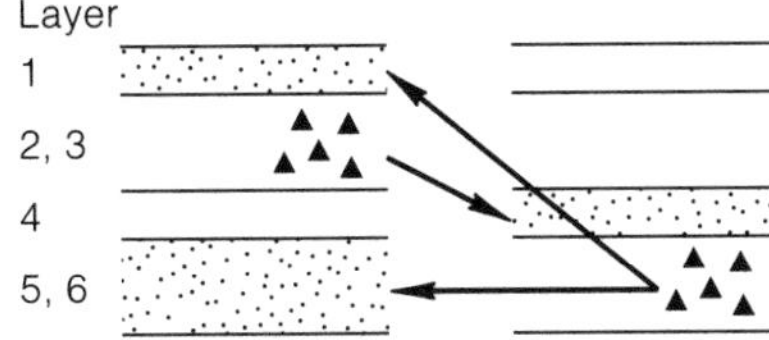

B REENTRY BETWEEN CORTICAL AREAS

FIGURE 8.9. *A*. The flow of information into the forebrain. Information from the thalamus goes to the primary cortex, which then projects to the association cortex. *B*. The principle of reentry. The cortical projection from the primary cortex arises from layers 2 and 3 and terminates in layer 4. There is a return connection (reentry) from layers 5 and 6 to layers 1 and 6. This principle of connectivity holds for all levels of cortical-cortical connectivity. The "higher" area is inferred from this pattern of connectivity.

ple neurosensory channels that are trying to integrate information into a single reality. Because so many different kinds of sensory information reach the cortex, it is somehow necessary to determine which information is about the same features in the external world. It would be useful to label them in some way. These labels would be created by the brain, and they would have to designate objects of the external world. Similarly, there would have to be some type of labels for a coordinate system of the external world in which objects would be located. In other words, the brain would have to create some type of labels of space and time. One could also imagine that some sensory information must be labeled in such a way that it might persist over time, and it would have to be possible to retrieve it when needed (that is, to remember it). Notice that these concepts of space, time, and memory are products of a particular kind of brain map and do not really exist in the information that is arriving to the cortex. Stated differently, knowledge of the world is constructed by the brain.

To Jerison, this knowledge is *mind*. Thus, as maps develop, the brain must also develop the mind to organize the maps in such a way as to produce knowledge of the external world. It is a small jump from this view to the idea that the next step in mental development is language. After all, language can be viewed as a way of representing knowledge.

Viewed in this way, one can see that the multiple maps in the human cortex provide a basis for our perception of the world as well as for our knowledge, or cognition, about the world. It should not be a surprise, therefore, that injuries to discrete cortical areas alter the way we perceive the world and the way we think about it. Indeed, we shall see that one form of sensory deficit is an **agnosia,** which literally means "not knowing."

FUNCTIONAL ORGANIZATION OF THE CORTEX

Hierarchical Model of Cortical Function

Fleshig first suggested that anatomical criteria could be used to delineate a hierarchy of cortical areas, but it was Luria who fully developed the idea in the 1960s. Luria divided the cortex into two functional units (Figure 8.10). The first, the posterior portion of the cortex, is the *sensory unit*. It receives sensory impressions, processes them, and stores them as information. The second, the anterior cortex (the frontal lobe), is the *motor unit*. It formulates intentions, organizes them into programs of action, and executes the programs. In both cortical units there is a hierarchical structure, with three cortical zones arranged functionally one above the other. The first zone corresponds to Fleshig's primary cortex; the second corresponds to the slower-developing cortex bordering the primary cortex, which Luria labeled as *secondary cortex;* and the third is the slowest-developing cortex, which Luria labeled as *tertiary cortex*.

Luria conceived of the cortex as working in the following way. Sensory input enters the primary sensory zones, is elaborated in the secondary zones, and is integrated in the tertiary zones of the sensory, or posterior, unit. For an action to be executed, activity from the posterior tertiary

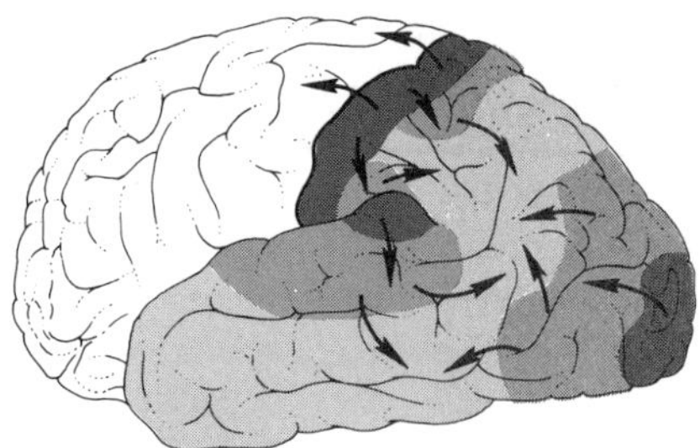

A The sensory unit

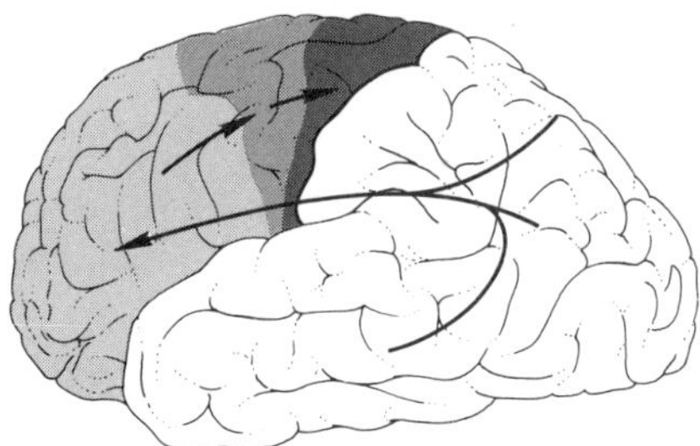

B The motor unit

FIGURE 8.10. *A.* The first functional unit of the cortex—the sensory unit. (Dark-shaded areas are primary zones; medium-shaded areas are secondary zones; light-shaded areas are tertiary zones.) Sensory input travels from primary to secondary to tertiary and is thereby elaborated from sensation into symbolic processes. *B.* The second functional unit of the cortex—the motor unit. Symbolic processes from the sensory unit are translated into intentions in the tertiary motor zones and then into patterns of action in the secondary and primary motor zones. (After A. R. Luria. © 1973. The Copyright Agency of the USSR. Reprinted with permission.)

sensory zones is sent to the tertiary zone of the motor, or frontal, unit; to the secondary zone; and then to the primary motor zone, where execution is initiated.

To give a very simplified example of how Luria's model of the cortex might function, say one were walking along and came upon a soccer game. In the primary visual area the actual perception of the movements of people and the ball would occur. In the secondary sensory zone, recognition that those activities constituted a soccer game would occur. In the tertiary zone the sounds and movements of the game would be synthesized into the realization that one team had scored and was ahead and that the game had a certain significance for league standings. This information would be passed on to the paralimbic cortex for processing as a memory and also passed on to the amygdala, where its emotional value would be assessed. These cortical events could then lead, in the tertiary zone of the frontal (motor) cortex, to formation of the intention or plan to play soccer. The programs to execute such a plan would be formulated in the secondary frontal zones. The actual movements to play the game would be initiated in the primary zone of the frontal cortex.

Using the example of a soccer game, we can also describe the effects of brain lesions. A lesion in the primary visual area would produce a blind spot in some part of the visual field, requiring the person to move his or her head backward and forward to see the entire game. A lesion in the secondary area might produce a perceptual deficit, making the person unable to recognize the activity as a soccer game. A lesion in the tertiary area might make it impossible to recognize the significance of the game in its abstract form; that is, that one team wins. Damage to the paralimbic cortex would leave no memory of the event, and damage to the amygdala would leave the person unresponsive to the event's significance. A lesion in the tertiary frontal area might prevent the formation of the intention to become a soccer player and join a club, buy a uniform, or get to practice on time. A lesion in the secondary frontal zone might make it difficult to execute the sequences of movements required in play. Finally, a lesion in the primary zone might make it difficult to execute the discrete movements required in the game; for example, kicking the ball.

Luria's theory was based upon three basic assumptions. First, it was assumed that the brain processes information serially. Thus, information from the receptors goes to the thalamus, then to the primary cortex, then to the secondary cortex, and finally to the tertiary sensory cortex. Similarly, the output goes from tertiary sensory to tertiary motor, then to secondary motor, and finally to primary motor. Second, it was assumed that the serial processing is hierarchical. That is, each level of processing adds complexity that is qualitatively different from the processing in the earlier levels. Furthermore, the tertiary cortex could be considered a "terminal station" insofar as it receives input from the lower areas and performs the highest forms of cognitive activity. Third, Luria's formulation was in accord with the common sense view that our perceptions of the world are a unified, coherent entity. If this is so, then it is entirely reasonable to assume that there must be some active process that creates this single percept, and naturally the simplest way to do this is to form it in the tertiary cortex.

The beauty of Luria's formulation is that it used the known anatomical organization of the cortex to provide a simple explanation for observations that Luria made daily in his clinic. The difficulty with Luria's model is that its basic assumptions have been questioned by new anatomical and physiological findings in the last decade. Consider the following problems.

First, a strictly hierarchical processing model requires that all cortical areas be linked serially, but this is not the case. We have seen that all cortical areas have reciprocal (reentrant) connections with the regions to which they connect. This means that there is not a simple "feed-forward" system arrangement. Furthermore, we noted earlier that only about 40% of the possible connections between different areas in a sensory modality are actually found. This means that there is no single area that receives input from all other areas. This presents a difficulty in actively forming a single percept in one area. Second, Zeki makes the interesting point that since a zone of cortex has connections with many cortical areas, it follows that each cortical zone is probably undertaking more than one operation, which is subsequently relayed to different cortical areas. In addition, it is likely that the results of the same operation are of interest to more than one cortical area, which would account for multiple connections. These principles can be seen in the primary visual cortex, which appears to make calculations related to color, motion, and form. These calculations are relayed to specific cortical regions for these processes. In addition, the same calculation may be sent to cortical as well as subcortical regions. The fact that cortical operations are relayed directly to subcortical areas is important because it implies that cortical processing can bypass Luria's motor hierarchy and go directly to subcortical motor structures. Furthermore, the fact that given cortical areas may do multiple calculations that are sent to multiple areas raises a question about what is hierarchical in the processing. Stated differently, can we assume that areas that are serially connected are actually undertaking more complicated operations? It would seem that an area such as the primary visual cortex, which is processing color, form, and movement, might be considered more complex than an area that processes only color. Finally, Luria assumed that his introspection about perception being a unitary phenomenon was correct. It appears, however, that it may not be. Thus, we may experience a single percept despite the fact that there is no single terminal area producing it. Indeed, this is the essence of the binding problem that we discussed earlier.

How, then, can we put this knowledge together in a meaningful way to see organization in the cortex? There seem to be two logical possibilities. One is that there is no hierarchical organization but rather some sort of nonordered neural network. As individuals gained experiences this network would become ordered and so produce perceptions, cognitions, and memory. Many neural network models of brain function propose that this is exactly what happens. This seems unlikely, however. A wealth of perceptual research suggests that the brain filters and orders sensory information in a very species-typical fashion.

The other possibility, suggested by Felleman and van Essen, is that cortical areas are hierarchically organized in some well-defined sense, with each area occupying a specific position relative to other areas, but with more than one area allowed to occupy a given hierarchical level. This type of processing can be seen as a parallel-hierarchical model. Felleman and van Essen proposed that the pattern of forward and backward connections could be used to determine hierarchical position.

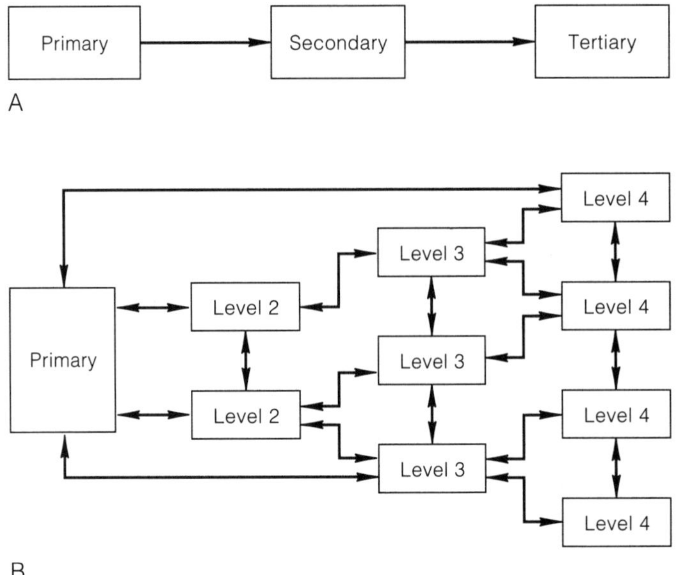

FIGURE 8.11. *A*. Luria's simple serial hierarchical model of cortical processing. *B*. Felleman and van Essen's distributed hierarchical model. In the latter model there are several levels of association areas. Areas at each level are interconnected with one another.

Thus, ascending (or forward) connections terminate in layer IV whereas descending (or feedback) connections avoid layer IV, usually terminating in the superficial and deep layers (see Figure 8.9). They also recognized a third type of connection, which is columnar in its distribution, terminating in all layers. This is less common but provides a basis for placing areas in the same location in the hierarchy.

By analyzing the patterns of connectivity between the visual, auditory, and somatosensory areas, Felleman and van Essen found evidence of what they called a distributed hierarchical system. Figure 8.11B shows a diagram of such a system. Notice that there are several levels of processing and that across the levels are interconnected processing streams that presumably represent different elements of the sensory experience. Note, too, that there are connections that skip levels and there is an expansion of the number of areas as the hierarchy unfolds.

A New Model of Cortical Function

The Felleman and van Essen model provides a relatively simple way of organizing sensory processing in the cortex. In addition, by adding the idea that the backward or lateral connections provide a basis for solving the binding problem, we have an explanation of our experience of a single, coherent perception of the world. Using their map (Figure 8.12), wiring diagrams of how to get from one area of the somatosensory system to the next (Figure 8.13) and from one area of the visual system to the next (Figures 8.13 and 8.14), and finally a chart of the functions of each of the areas (Table 8.1), it is possible to speculate about how information flows through and gets organized by the cortex.

To illustrate this new model, we will not use the example of playing soccer that we used to illustrate Luria's model, but we certainly invite the reader to attempt the exercise. We will start

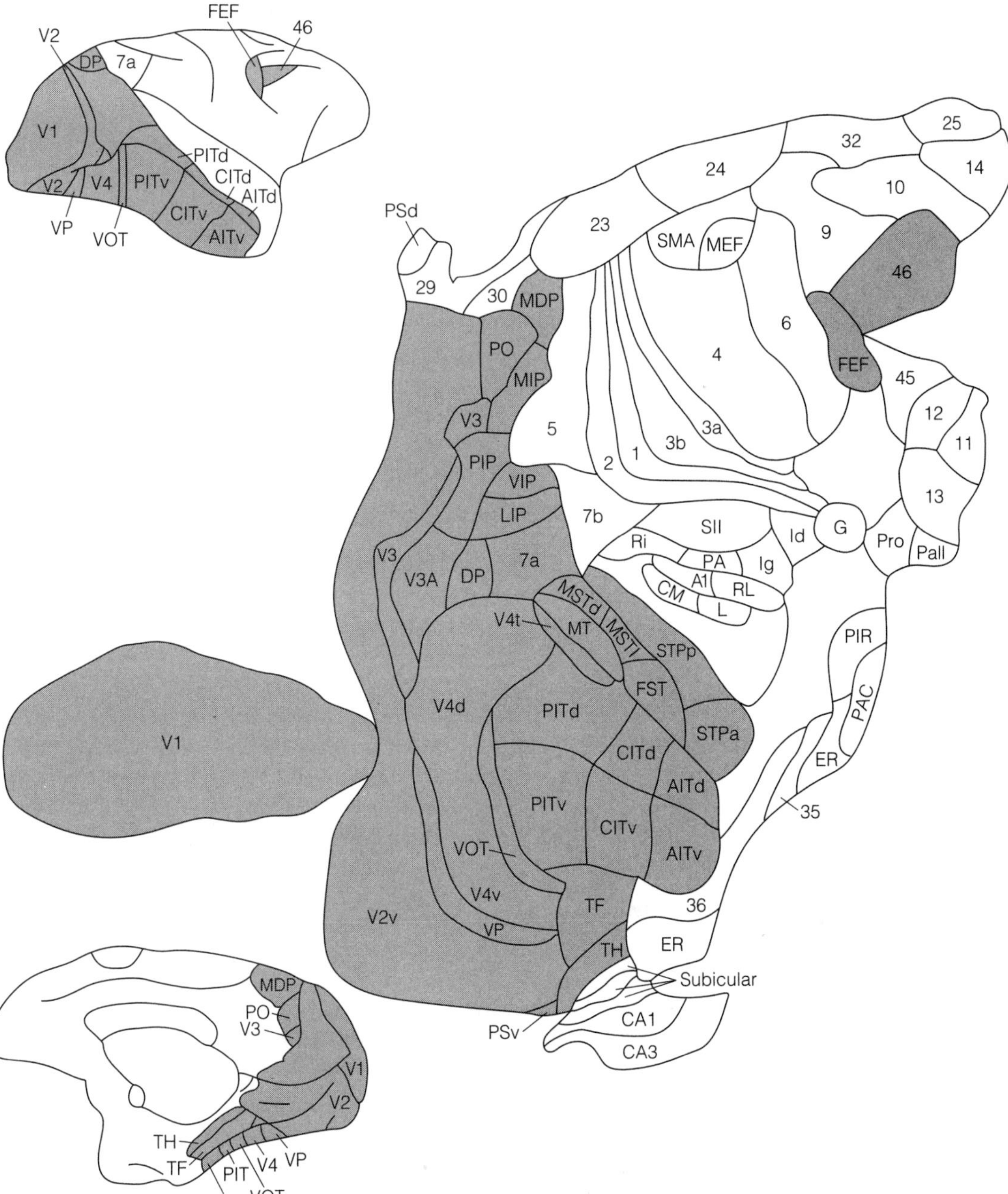

FIGURE 8.12. Map of cortical areas in the macaque. The cortex has been "flattened" so that all tissues hidden in sulci are visible. This map provides a perspective on the relative size of various cortical regions and on the amount of tissue dedicated to different functions. The locations of 32 visual areas are indicated with shading. The abbreviations are summarized in Table 8.1. (After Felleman and van Essen, 1991.)

TABLE 8.1. Summary of cortical areas in the monkey

Lobe	Structure	Name	Putative function
Occipital	V1	Visual area 1 (17)	Visual sorting
	V2	Visual area 2 (18)	Visual sorting
	V3	Visual area 3	Vision-dynamic form
	V3A	Visual area 3A	Vision-?
	V4	Visual area 4	Vision-color
	V4t	V4 transitional	Vision-?
	MT (V5)	Visual area 5	Motion
	VP	Ventral posterior visual	Vision-?
	VOT	Ventral occipital-temporal	Vision-?
Temporal	FST	Floor of superior temporal	Vision
	PITd	Posterior inferotemporal, dorsal	Vision
	PITv	Posterior inferotemporal, ventral	Vision
	CITd	Central inferotemporal, dorsal	Vision
	CITv	Central inferotemporal, ventral	Vision
	AITd	Anterior inferotemporal, dorsal	Vision
	AITv	Anterior inferotemporal, ventral	Vision
	STPp	Superior temporal polysensory, posterior	Polymodal
	STPa	Superior temporal polysensory, anterior	Polymodal
	FT	FT (hippocampal formation)	Memory
	TH	TH (hippocampal formation)	Memory
	AI	Primary auditory	Audition
	RL	Rostrolateral auditory	Audition
	CM	Caudomedial auditory	Audition
	L	Lateral auditory	Audition
	PA	Postauditory	Somato or auditory?
Hippocampus	ER	Entorhinal cortex	Memory and/or space
	35	Brodmann's 35	Memory and/or space
	36	Brodmann's 36	Memory and/or space
	Subicular	(Pre, post, sub)	Memory and/or space
	CA1	Ammon's horn, area 1	Memory and/or space
	CA3	Ammon's horn, area 3	Memory and/or space
Parietal	3a	Primary somatosensory	Cutaneous?
	3b	Primary somatosensory	Tactile; muscle, joint
	1	Somatosensory	Tactile-?
	2	Somatosensory	Vestibular
	SII	Secondary somatosensory map	Tactile patterns
	5	Secondary somatosensory (area PE)	Tactile patterns
	7a	Secondary visual (area PG)	Visuomotor guidance
	7b	Secondary somatosensory (area PF)	Visuomotor guidance
	MSTd	Medial superior temporal, dorsal	Visuomotor guidance
	MSTl	Medial superior temporal, lateral	Visuomotor guidance
	PO	Parietal-occipital	Visuomotor guidance
	PIP	Posterior intraparietal	Visuomotor guidance
	LIP	Lateral intraparietal	Visuomotor
	VIP	Ventral intraparietal	Visuomotor
	MIP	Medial intraparietal	Visuomotor
	MDP	Medial dorsal parietal	Visuomotor
	DP	Dorsal prelunate	Visuomotor

(continued)

TABLE 8.1. Summary of cortical areas in the monkey *(continued)*

Lobe	Structure	Name	Putative function
Frontal	4	Primary motor	Fine movements
	6	Secondary motor	Sequences
	SMA	Supplementary motor cortex	Bimanual movements
	MEF	Supplementary eye fields	Eye movements
	FEF	Frontal eye fields	Eye movements
	46	Dorsolateral prefrontal	Memory, movement, planning
	9, 10, 14	Dorsal prefrontal	Memory, movement, planning
	11, 12, 13	Orbital prefrontal	Emotion, memory
	25–32	Medial prefrontal	Memory, movement, planning
	G	Gustatory	Taste
	PRO	Prosiocortex	?
	PAL	Periallocortex	?
	PIR	Olfactory	Olfaction
	PAC	Olfactory	Olfaction
	ER	Olfactory	Olfaction
Cingulate	23, 24, 29, 30		Motivation, emotion, space, memory

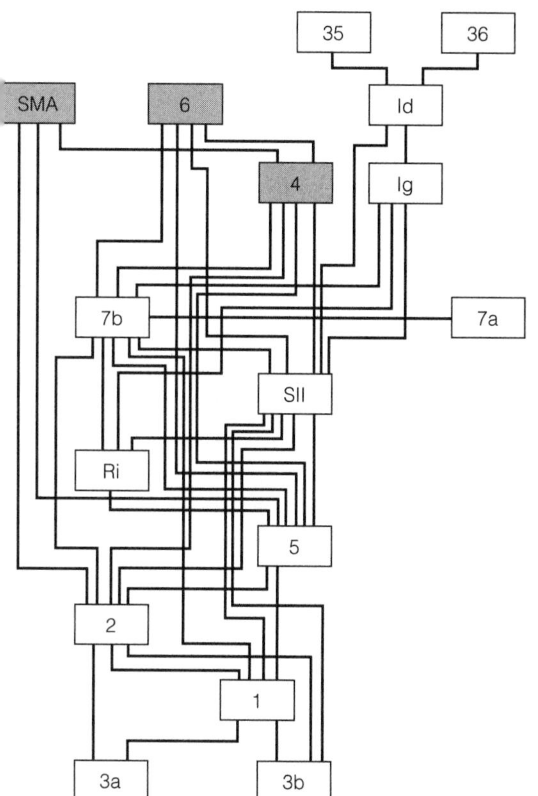

FIGURE 8.13. A proposed hierarchy for somatosensory and motor areas, based on 62 linkages among 10 somatosensory and 3 motor areas (shaded). Hierarchical assignments are based on the laminar information contained in Table 8.1. Also included in the hierarchy are connections with visual area 7a and with higher associational areas 35 and 36. Counting the highest level, there are 10 levels in the hierarchy, and possibly an 11th, depending on uncertainties with regard to interconnections among motor areas. (After Felleman and van Essen, 1991.)

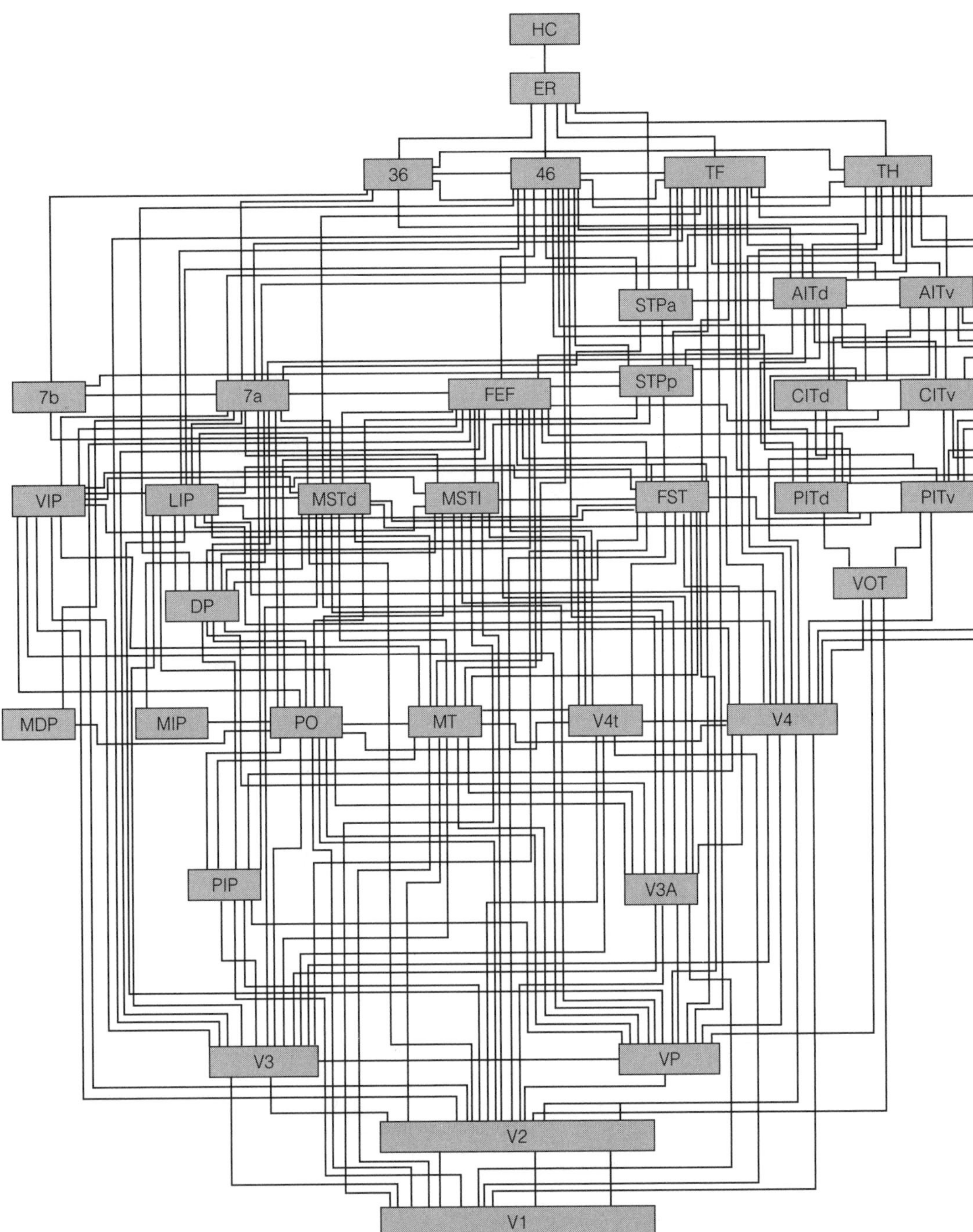

FIGURE 8.14. Hierarchy of visual areas. This hierarchy shows 32 visual cortical areas, plus several nonvisual areas (area 7b of somatosensory cortex, perirhinal area 36, the ER, and the hippocampal complex). These areas are connected by 187 linkages, most of which have been demonstrated to be reciprocal pathways. (After Felleman and van Essen, 1991.)

with some simpler examples, and since this information was obtained with rhesus monkeys, we will use some examples relevant to monkeys. Let us imagine that we set a monkey the task of reaching into a box in which, among other things, there are some jelly beans. If the monkey finds a jelly bean it is allowed to keep it, but if it takes something else it loses that object and has to wait as punishment before getting another trial. Thus, the monkey has to feel the objects until it finds a jelly bean and then it has to grasp it using a pincer grasp. From Table 8.1 we see that tactile information is first analyzed in area 3b of the somatosensory cortex and that the motor output to grasp comes from area 4 of the motor cortex. Although areas 3b and 4 are side by side on the map in Figure 8.12, the wiring diagram in Figure 8.13 shows that these areas are not connected. Figure 8.13 also shows that there are three streams that go to area 4. One goes through areas 1, 5, and SII (SII is important for pattern discriminations); one goes through areas 2 and 7b (possibly important for shape discrimination); and the third goes through areas 2 and SMA (which may be important for producing a series of movements). It is possible that this problem could be solved by only one of the three streams, but it could also be solved by all of them working together.

Here is a second problem. The monkey is presented with a TV screen that displays some jelly beans of various colors. If it touches a red jelly bean on the screen it receives a reward, but there is no reward for touching other jelly beans. Using the list of functions in Table 8.1, we can hypothesize that the monkey uses the color vision system, beginning in V1 (area 17), to identify the correct jelly bean, and uses area 4 of the motor system with which to point. Turning to the wiring diagram in Figure 8.14, we can imagine that the monkey must use the parvocellular system for color vision, which passes into V1 and then V2, and from there information must go to V4 (the color module of the visual system). We already know that area 7b will reach area 4; it is logical that this is at least one route.

The last jelly bean problem is still very simple. Consider what would happen if the correct jelly bean not only was red but also had to be large and moving. The monkey would now have to use area V4 (color), area V3 (dynamic form), and MT, or area V5 (motion), and have all this information converge on area 7b. But even this is a simple problem for a monkey (although the wiring diagram may be becoming a little complex for some of us). Let us give the monkey a problem that poses it a challenge: if on the last trial a large moving red jelly bean was correct, then on this trial a small green stationary jelly bean is correct. Now the monkey has to remember what it did on the last trial, and Table 8.1 tells us that the temporal cortex and perhaps even the hippocampus (HC) is required for memory. It is no longer sufficient to take a route to area 7a; the temporal cortical areas must also be involved. Now the solution to the problem requires activity in the occipital, parietal, temporal, and motor cortex almost simultaneously. Of course, that is not a problem; it is a simple matter to select a set of connections that could do the job. But now the question is whether that is how the monkey is doing it. When one thinks of all the areas and connections that are involved, the question is not so easily answered. Of course, the experimenter can always simplify the problem a little by creating a computer program that is regularly updated with areas, functions, and connections and that can generate solutions to problems such as the ones that we have posed here. Once we have done that we can begin to work on different problems, such as why monkeys are inordinately fond of red jelly beans.

SUMMARY

We made seven basic points in this chapter. First, the brain is organized in levels of function, beginning in the spinal cord and ending in the cortex. These levels can be demonstrated by studying animals with surgical removals of successively more brain tissue. Second, the cortex is composed of two basic types of neurons, spiny and aspiny, which are organized into about six layers. The layers can be considered sensory, motor, and associational. Third, the cortex has a vertical organization, which is referred to as a column or a module. Cortical modules can be seen in the spots and stripes visible in specific histological preparations. Fourth, there are multiple representations of sensory and motor functions in the cortex. One evolutionary change in mammals has been an increase in the number of representations. Fifth, one characteristic of cortical connectivity is reentry: each cortical area is reciprocally connected with many, but not all, other regions in a given sensory modality. Sixth, cortical activity is influenced by feedback loops not only from other cortical regions but also from subcortical forebrain regions such as the amygdala and hippocampus. Seventh, the cortex is functionally organized as a distributed hierarchical circuit.

REFERENCES

Bard, P., and M. B. Macht. The behavior of chronically decerebrate cats. In G. E. W. Wolstenholm, and C. M. O'Connor, eds. *Ciba Foundation Symposium on Neurological Basis of Behavior*. London: J. and A. Churchill, 1958.

Barrett, R., H. H. Merritt, and A. Wolf. Depression of consciousness as a result of cerebral lesions. *Research Publications of the Association for Research in Nervous and Mental Disease* 45:241–276, 1967.

Bazett, H. C., and W. G. Penfield. A study of the Sherrington decerebrate animal in the chronic as well as the acute condition. *Brain* 45:185–265, 1922.

Berridge, K. C., and I. Q. Whishaw. Cortex, striatum, and cerebellum: Control of serial order in a grooming sequence. *Experimental Brain Research* 90:275–290, 1992.

Brackbill, Y. The role of the cortex in orienting: Orienting reflex in an encephalic human infant. *Developmental Psychology* 5:195–201, 1971.

Felleman, D. J., and D. C. van Essen. Distributed hierarchical processing in the primate cerebral cortex. *Cerebral Cortex* 1:1–47, 1991.

Gallistel, C. R. *The Organization of Action*. Hillsdalle, N.J.: Lawrence Erlbaum Associates, 1980.

Gamper, E. In J. Field, H. W. Magoun, and V. E. Hall, eds. *Handbook of Physiology*, vol. 2. Washington, D.C.: American Physiological Society, 1959.

Goltz, F. On the functions of the hemispheres. In G. von Bonin, ed. *The Cerebral Cortex*. Springfield, Ill.: Charles C. Thomas, 1960.

Grill, H. J., and R. Norgren. Neurological tests and behavioral deficits in chronic thalamic and chronic decerebrate rats. *Brain Research* 143:299–312, 1978.

Grillner, S. Locomotion in the spinal cat. In R. B. Stein, ed. *Control of Posture and Locomotion*. New York: Plenum, 1973.

Jerison, H. J. *Brain Size and the Evolution of Mind*. New York: American Museum of Natural History, 1991.

Kuhn, R. A. Functional capacity of the isolated human spinal cord. *Brain* 73:1–51, 1950.

Le Brun Kemper, T., and A. M. Galaburda. Principles of cytoarchitectonics. In A. Peters and E. G. Jones, eds. *Cerebral Cortex*, vol. 1. New York: Plenum Press, 1985.

Luria, A. R. *The Working Brain*. Harmondsworth, England: Penguin, 1973.

Oakley, D. A. Cerebral cortex and adaptive behavior. In D. A. Oakley and H. C. Plotkin, eds. *Brain, Evolution and Behavior*. London: Methuen, 1979.

Pandya, D. N., and E. H. Yeterian. Architecture and connections of cortical association areas. In A. Peters and E. G. Jones, eds. *Cerebral Cortex*, vol. 4. New York: Plenum Press, 1985.

Penfield, W., and E. Boldrey. Somatic and motor sensory representation in the cerebral cortex of man as studied by electrical stimulation. *Brain* 60:389–443, 1937.

Purves, D., D. R. Riddle, and A.-S. LaMantia. Iterated patterns of brain circuitry (or how the brain gets its spots). *Trends in Neurosciences* 15:362–368, 1992.

Shepherd, G. M. *The Synaptic Organization of the Brain*, 2nd ed. New York: Oxford University Press, 1979.

Sherrington, C. S. *The Integrative Action of the Nervous System*. New Haven: Yale University Press, 1906.

Szentagothai, J. Architecture of the cerebral cortex. In H. H. Jasper, A. A. Ward, and A. Pope, eds. *Basic Mechanisms of the Epilepsies*. Boston: Little, Brown, 1969.

Tolman, E. C. *Behavior and Psychological Man*. Berkeley: University of California Press, 1961.

Tononi, G., O. Sporns, and G. M. Edelman. Reentry and the problem of integrating multiple cortical areas: Simulation of dynamic integration in the visual system. *Cerebral Cortex* 2:336–352, 1991.

Villablanca, J. R., C. E. Olmstead, and I. de Andres. Effects of caudate nuclei or frontal cortical ablations in kittens: Responsiveness to auditory stimuli and comparisons with adult-operated littermates. *Experimental Neurology* 61:635–649, 1978.

Whishaw, I. Q. The decorticate rat. In B. Kolb and R. Tees, eds. *The Neocortex of the Rat*. Cambridge, Mass.: MIT Press, 1989.

Woods, J. W. Behavior of chronic decerebrate rats. *Journal of Neurophysiology* 27:634–644, 1964.

Zeki, S. *A Vision of the Brain*. London: Blackwell Scientific, 1993.

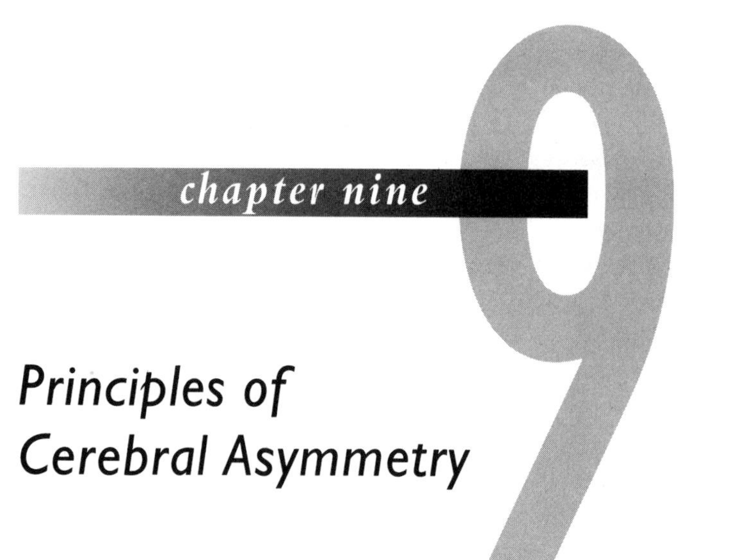

chapter nine

Principles of Cerebral Asymmetry

It has been more than 100 years since Marc Dax and Paul Broca discovered that damage to the left hemisphere produces an inability to talk but damage to the right hemisphere does not affect speech. Since then it has been generally accepted that the left hemisphere plays a special role in language, a role not shared by the right hemisphere. But language is not the only special function of the left hemisphere; at the beginning of this century Liepmann compared the movements of patients with lesions of either the left or the right hemisphere and demonstrated that the left hemisphere has a role in controlling movement that is not shared by the right. The special functions of the right hemisphere remained a mystery until comparatively recently, when the work of Zangwill, Hécaen, Milner, and others showed that it is more involved than the left in the analysis of the visuospatial dimensions of the world.

Although these findings appear to simplify the problem of understanding lateralization, the problem is complicated by the following three variables:

1. Laterality of function can be affected by environmental factors as well as genetically determined factors, such as gender and handedness; the cerebral organization of some left-handers and females appears to have less functional asymmetry than that of right-handers and males.

2. Laterality is relative, not absolute, because both hemispheres play a role in nearly every behavior; thus, although the left hemisphere is especially important for the production of language, the right hemisphere also has some language capabilities.

3. Whereas a functionally asymmetrical brain was once believed to be a uniquely human characteristic—one that suggested a straightforward relation between asymmetry and language—this idea has proved to be incorrect. There is evidence that certain songbirds, rats, cats, monkeys, and apes have a functionally and anatomically asymmetrical brain.

This chapter addresses the basic principles of cerebral asymmetry; the next chapter examines the factors that produce variations in the basic pattern of cerebral asymmetry. The answers to most questions about the nature of cerebral asymmetry are still incomplete, but our tentative answers take into account information about the brain's anatomical and functional asymmetry; the relation of hand preference and gender to asymmetry; the influence of culture and education on asymmetry; the nature of lateralized functions; and finally, the incidence of asymmetry in nonhumans.

ANATOMICAL ASYMMETRY IN THE HUMAN BRAIN

According to Hughlings-Jackson, Gratiolet first observed in the 1860s that the convolutions on the left hemisphere mature more rapidly than those on the right. Anatomical asymmetry was described again later in the 19th century by a number of authors, but these observations were largely ignored until the 1960s, when von Bonin reviewed the earlier literature and Geschwind and Levitsky described significant anatomical asymmetry in a large series of human brains. Geschwind and Levitsky reported that the planum temporale, which is the cortical area just posterior to the auditory cortex (Heschl's gyrus) within the Sylvian fissure, was larger on the left in 65% of the brains studied. On the average, the planum temporale in the left hemisphere was nearly 1 cm longer than in the right (Figure 9.1B). This report generated renewed interest in anatomical asymmetries in humans and other animals, and it put to rest the notion that the two hemispheres are structurally identical.

Many anatomical differences between the two hemispheres of the brain have now been reported (Table 9.1). The eight major differences can be summarized as follows:

1. The right hemisphere is slightly larger and heavier than the left, but there appears to be more gray matter in the left.

2. There is a marked asymmetry in the structure of the temporal lobes. Geschwind and

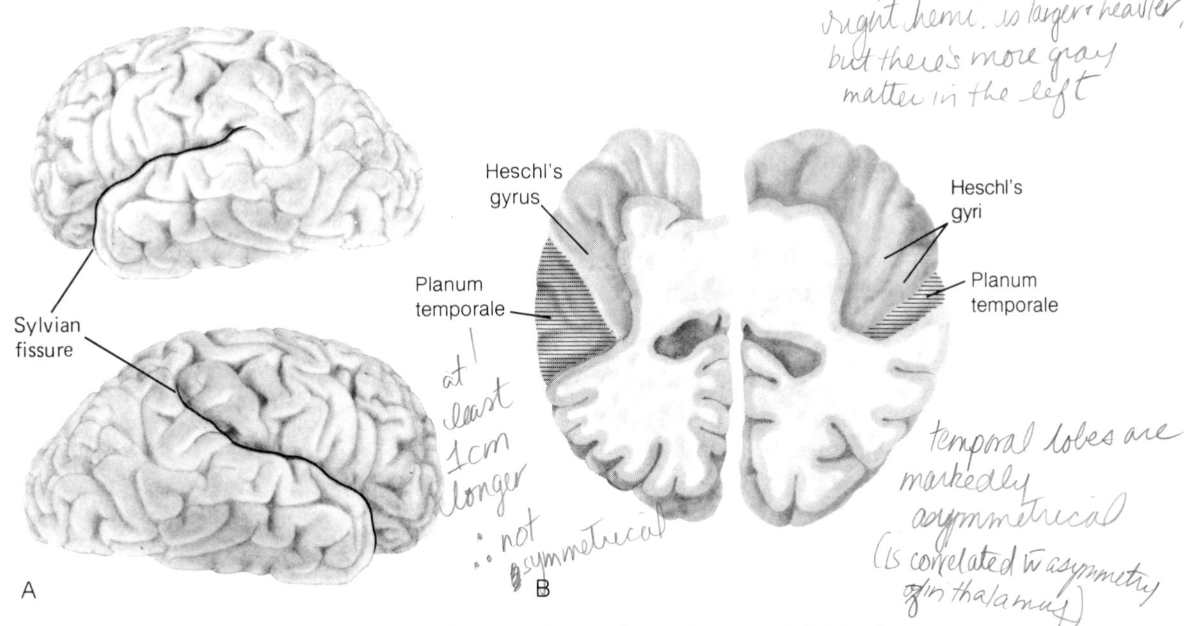

FIGURE 9.1. Anatomical differences between the two hemispheres are visible in the temporal lobes. *A.* The Sylvian fissure on the left *(top)* has a gentler slope than the fissure on the right. *B.* A knife has been moved along the Sylvian fissure of each hemisphere and through the brain, cutting away the top portion. The planum temporale (darkened area) is larger on the left than on the right.

TABLE 9.1. Summary of studies demonstrating anatomical asymmetry

Measure	Basic reference
Asymmetries favoring the left hemisphere	
Greater specific gravity	Von Bonin, 1962
Longer Sylvian fissure	Eberstaller, 1884; LeMay and Culebras, 1972; Heschl, 1878
Larger insula	Kodama, 1934
Doubling of cingulate gyrus	Eberstaller, 1884
Relatively more gray matter	Von Bonin, 1962; Gur et al., 1980
Larger planum temporale	Geschwind and Levitsky, 1968; Galaburda et al., 1978; Teszner et al., 1972; Witelson and Pallie, 1973; Wada et al., 1975; Rubens et al., 1976; Kopp et al., 1977
Larger lateral posterior nucleus	Eidelberg and Galaburda, 1982
Larger inferior parietal lobule	Lemay and Culebras, 1972
Larger area Tpt of temporoparietal cortex	Galaburda and Sanides, 1980
Wider occipital lobe	LeMay, 1977
Longer occipital horn of lateral ventricles	McRae et al., 1968; Strauss and Fitz, 1980
Larger total area of frontal operculum	Falzi et al., 1982
Asymmetries favoring the right hemisphere	
Heavier	Broca, 1865; Crichton-Browne, 1880
Longer internal skull size	Hoadley and Pearson, 1929
Doubling of Heschl's gyrus	von Economo and Horn, 1930; Chi et al., 1977
Larger medial geniculate nucleus	Eidelberg and Galaburda, 1982
Larger area of convexity of frontal operculum	Wada et al., 1975
Wider frontal lobe	LeMay, 1977

Levitsky's finding that the planum temporale is larger on the left has now been replicated by numerous other investigators, although the percentage of cases having a larger planum temporale on the left varies from 65% to 90% in different samples. In contrast, the primary auditory cortex of Heschl's gyrus is larger on the right, because there are usually two Heschl's gyri on the right and only one on the left (see Figure 9.1B). Thus, there is a complementary asymmetry in the temporal lobes that may provide an anatomical basis for the functional dissociation of the temporal lobes in language and in musical functions.

3. The asymmetry in the cortex of the temporal lobes is correlated with a corresponding asymmetry in the thalamus. Thus, Eidelberg and Galaburda found that the lateral posterior nucleus, which projects to the parietal cortex just caudal to the planum temporale, is larger on the left; whereas the medial geniculate nucleus, which projects to the primary auditory cortex, is larger on the right. This anatomical asymmetry complements an apparent functional asymmetry in the thalamus, the left thalamus being dominant for language functions.

4. The slope of the Sylvian fissure is different in the two sides of the brain, being gentler on the left than on the right (see Figure 9.1A). The region of the temporal-parietal cortex lying ventral to the Sylvian fissure therefore appears larger on the right.

5. The frontal operculum (Broca's area) is organized differently on the left and right. The area visible on the surface of the brain is about one-third larger on the right than on the left, whereas the area of cortex buried in the sulci of the region is greater on the left than the right. This asymmetry probably reflects the functional dissociation of the regions, the left side being involved in producing grammar in language and the right side possibly influencing tone of voice.

6. The distribution of various neurotransmitters is asymmetrical, in both the cortical and sub-

cortical regions. The particular asymmetries in the distribution of acetylcholine, GABA, norepinephrine, and dopamine are dependent on the structure under consideration. (See Falzi et al., Glick et al., and Oke et al.)

7. The right hemisphere extends farther anteriorly than the left, the left hemisphere extends farther posteriorly than the right, and the occipital horns of the lateral ventricles are five times more likely to be longer on the right than on the left. These asymmetries presumably reflect some gross difference in cerebral organization that has yet to be identified.

8. The details of anatomical asymmetry are affected by both sex and handedness, as we shall see in the next chapter.

Because these anatomical asymmetries of the cerebral hemispheres center primarily on the language areas, it is tempting to speculate that they evolved to subserve the production of language. Moreover, the presence of these asymmetries in preterm infants might be taken as support for the proposition that humans have an innate predisposition for language. It should be noted, however, that the brains of australopithecines share many of these asymmetries, but they did not have a vocal apparatus that would allow language as we conceive of it. Furthermore, some asymmetries, such as a heavier and larger right hemisphere and a longer Sylvian fissure, can also be seen in many nonhuman species. Finally, we caution that undue emphasis has been placed on finding anatomical asymmetries that can be associated with language. Enlarged areas in the left hemisphere must be balanced by smaller areas elsewhere on the same side or larger areas in other lobes on the contralateral hemisphere.

The emphasis upon the demonstration of gross morphological asymmetries in the human brain is a natural starting point in comparing the two hemispheres, but we must remember that the activities of the brain are carried out by neurons. It is reasonable, therefore, to ask if the structure of neurons might differ on the two sides of the brain. Identification of structural differences in the neurons in any two areas of the brain is a formidable task in view of the sheer number of neurons. Nonetheless, Scheibel and his colleagues have compared the dendritic fields of pyramidal cells in Broca's area (Figure 9.2; LOP), with those in the facial area of the motor cortex of the left hemisphere (LPC), and with homologous regions in the right hemisphere (ROP and RPC). Their results show that the neurons in each of these regions have a distinct pattern of branching. It can be seen that there are far more branches in cells in Broca's area than in the other areas. The degree or pattern of branching is important because each branch represents a potential location of enhancement or suppression of the graded potentials in the dendritic tree. Thus, more branch points allow more degrees of freedom with respect to the final activity of the cell. We must caution that Scheibel's data are from a small sample of brains ($n = 6$), but it is curious that five of the six brains were similar to the pattern shown in Figure 9.2. These five brains were from right-handers; the aberrant brain was from a non-right-hander!

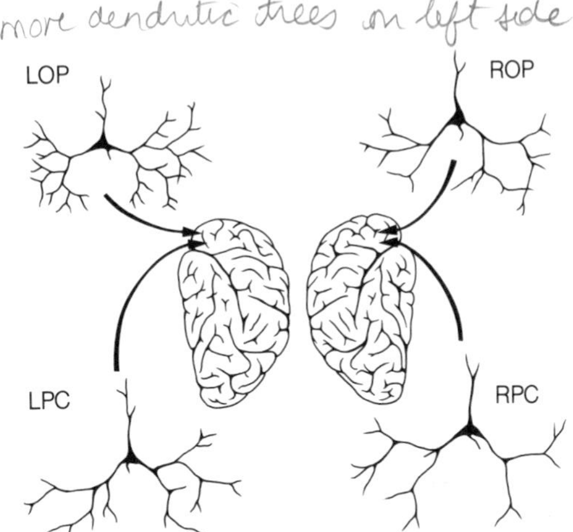

FIGURE 9.2. Schematic drawing emphasizing differences among the dendritic trees in the four areas: left triangularis-opercularis (LOP), right triangularis-opercularis (ROP), left precentral (LPC), and right precentral (RPC). (From Scheibel et al., 1985.)

ASYMMETRY IN NEUROLOGICAL PATIENTS

Cerebral asymmetry was first established by studying patients with neurological disease that was lateralized to one hemisphere. The improvement in neurosurgical treatment for neurological disorders, especially epilepsy, has provided a large source of subsequently healthy subjects who are usually very willing to participate in neuropsychological studies. Thus, a good deal is now known from these patients about both the lateralization and the localization of functions in the cerebral cortex, and it is information from these patients that forms the basis for a large part of the remainder of this book. In this section we consider the evidence demonstrating lateralization of function in these patients, emphasizing the study of patients with lateralized lesions and those undergoing commissurotomy, as well as of those who had one hemisphere anesthetized with intracarotid injections of sodium amobarbital.

Patients with Lateralized Lesions

The oldest method of investigating hemispheric specialization has been to study the effects of circumscribed unilateral lesions that occur as a result of strokes, surgery, and so forth, and to infer the function of the area from behavioral deficits. However, in order to conclude that the area has a special or lateralized function, it is also necessary to show that lesions in other areas of the brain do not produce a similar deficit.

The method that has proved strongest for demonstrating lateralization of function is one that Teuber calls double dissociation, an inferential technique premised on the following observations. It has been demonstrated consistently that lesions in the left hemisphere of right-handed patients can produce deficits in language functions (speech, writing, and reading) that do not follow lesions of the right hemisphere. Thus, the functions of the two hemispheres can be said to be dissociated. On the other hand, anecdotal and experimental evidence suggests that performance of spatial tasks, singing, playing musical instruments, and discriminating tonal patterns are more disrupted by right hemisphere than by left hemisphere lesions. Since right hemisphere lesions disturb tasks not disrupted by left hemisphere lesions and vice versa, the two hemispheres can be said to be doubly dissociated. A similar logic is used to localize functions within a hemisphere. That is, behavioral tests that are especially sensitive to damage to a specific locus and not to damage to others can be used to localize functions within a hemisphere, as illustrated in Table 9.2. Two hypothetical neocortical regions, 102 and 107, are doubly dissociated on tests of reading and writing: damage to area 102 disturbs reading, whereas damage to area 107 impairs writing. In principle, this logic can be extended to dissociate the functions of additional areas concurrently by triple dissociation, quadruple dissociation, and so on.

To illustrate the nature of lateralized functions in neurological cases, we contrast two patients from the Montreal Neurological Hospital, neither of whom was aphasic at the time of assessment (Figure 9.3). The first patient, P. G., was a 31-year-old man who had developed seizures over the course of 6 years prior to his surgery. At the time of his admission to the hospital his seizures were poorly controlled by medication, and subsequent neurological investigations revealed a large lesion, which turned out to be a tumor (a glioma), in the anterior part of the left temporal lobe. Preoperative psychological tests showed this man to be of superior intelligence, with the only significant deficits being on tests of verbal memory. Two weeks after surgery, psychological testing showed a general decrease in intelligence ratings and a further decrease in the verbal memory scores. Performance on other tests, including tests of recall of the Rey-Osterith figure (see Figures

TABLE 9.2. Hypothetical example of a double-dissociation behavioral test

Neocortical lesion site	Reading	Writing
102	Impaired	Normal
107	Normal	Impaired

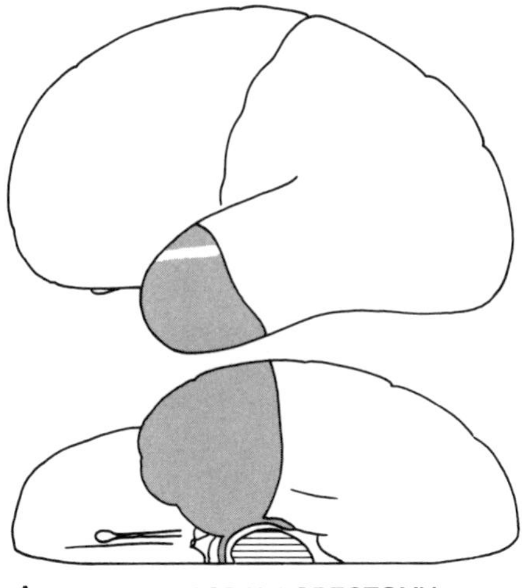

	Preoperative	Postoperative
Full scale IQ	123	109
Verbal IQ	122	103
Performance IQ	121	114
Memory quotient	96[a]	73[a]
Verbal recall	7.0[a]	2.0[a]
Nonverbal recall	10.5	10.5
Card sorting	6 categories	6 categories
Drawings: Copy	34/36	34/36
Recall	22.5/36	23.5/36

[a] *Significantly low score.*

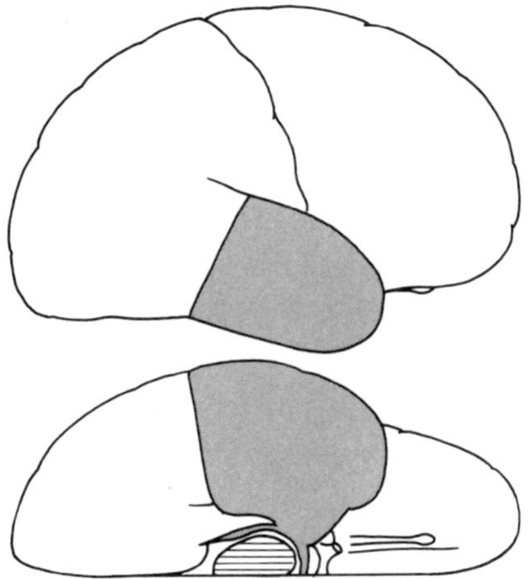

	Preoperative	Postoperative
Full scale IQ	114	103
Verbal IQ	115	115
Performance IQ	110	89[a]
Memory quotient	121	101
Verbal recall	16.0	12.0
Nonverbal recall	7.5	5.5[a]
Card sorting	3 categories	3 categories
Drawings: Copy	31/36	28/36[a]
Recall	11/36[a]	13/36[a]

[a] *Significantly low score.*

FIGURE 9.3. A comparison of psychological test results for a patient with a left temporal lobectomy (*A*) and a patient with a right temporal lobectomy (*B*) at the Montreal Neurological Hospital. The region removed is represented by the darkened zone, estimated by the surgeon at the time of operation. (Modified from Taylor, 1969.)

9.3A and 13.7C), were normal. The second patient, S. K., had a tumor (an astrocytoma) removed from the right temporal lobe. In contrast to the results from P. G., preoperative testing of S. K. showed a low score on the recall of the Rey-Osterith figure (see Figure 9.3B). Two weeks after surgery, repeat testing showed a marked decrease of the performance IQ rating and a decline of the nonverbal memory score, both on simple designs and on an alternate form of the Rey-Osterith figure. Comparison of these two patients provides a clear example of double dissociation: the patient with removal of the left temporal lobe was impaired only on verbal tests, whereas the patient with removal of the right temporal lobe was impaired only on nonverbal tests. Furthermore, both patients performed normally on many tests, providing evidence for localization, as well as lateralization, of function.

Patients with Commissurotomy

Epileptic seizures may begin in a restricted region of one hemisphere and then spread via the fibers of the corpus callosum to the homologous location in the opposite hemisphere. To prevent the spread of the seizure when medication has failed to impose control, the procedure of cutting the 200 million nerve fibers of the corpus callosum was performed in the early 1940s by William Van Wagnen, an American neurosurgeon. The procedure initially appeared to be too variable in its therapeutic outcome and was subsequently abandoned until the 1960s, when research by Myers and by Sperry with nonhuman species led to a reconsideration of the procedure. Two California surgeons, Joe Bogen and Philip Vogel, performed complete sections of the corpus callosum and of a smaller commissure known as the anterior commissure in a new series of about two dozen patients suffering from intractable epilepsy. The procedure was medically beneficial, leaving some patients virtually seizure-free afterward, with only rather minimal effects on their everyday behavior. More extensive psychological testing by Roger Sperry and his colleagues soon demonstrated, however, that these patients had a unique behavioral syndrome that has provided new insights into the nature of cerebral asymmetry.

Figure 9.4 illustrates the effect of commissurotomy on the normal function of the brain. After sectioning, the two hemispheres are independent; each receives sensory input from all sensory systems, and each can control the muscles of the body, but the two hemispheres can no longer communicate with each other. Because the functions in these separate cortexes or "split brains" are thus isolated, sensory information can be presented to one hemisphere and its function studied without the other hemisphere having access to the information.

From the numerous studies performed on split-brain patients it is now widely recognized that when the left hemisphere has access to information, it can initiate speech and hence communicate about the information. The right hemisphere apparently has reasonably good recognition abilities but is unable to initiate speech because it lacks access to the speech mechanisms of the left hemisphere. The following example helps to illustrate the phenomenon:

> Patient N. G., a California housewife, sits in front of a screen with a small black dot in the center. She is asked to look directly at the dot. When the experimenter is sure she is doing so, a picture of a cup is flashed briefly to the right of the dot. N. G. reports that she has seen a cup. Again she is asked to fix her gaze on the dot. This time, a picture of a spoon is flashed to the left of the dot. She is asked what she saw. She replies, "No, nothing." She is then asked to reach under the screen with her left hand and to select, by touch only, from among several items the one object that is the same as she has just seen. Her left hand manipulates each object and then holds up the spoon. When asked what she is holding, she says "pencil." (Springer and Deutsch, 1981, pp. 29–30)

The behavior of patient N. G. provides a clear demonstration of the behavior of the two hemispheres when they are not interacting. The picture of the cup was presented to the speaking left hemisphere, which could, of course, respond. The picture of the spoon was presented to the right hemisphere and, since the right hemisphere does not speak and the speaking left hemisphere was not connected to the right, N. G. failed to identify the picture correctly (Figures 9.5 and 9.6). The abilities of the right hemisphere are demonstrated when the left hand, which is controlled by the right hemisphere, was used to iden-

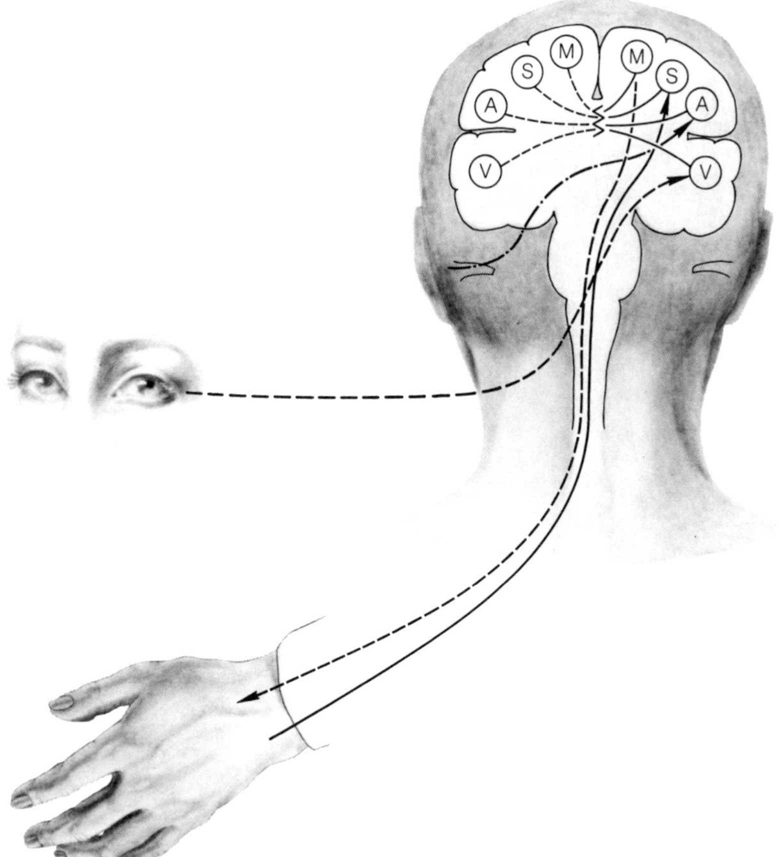

FIGURE 9.4. The effect of commissurotomy on connections between the hemispheres and to the sensory and motor systems. Note that although the connections between the visual (V), auditory (A), somatosensory (S), and motor (M) cortical regions and the receptors and effectors are unaffected, the connections between homotopic points in the two hemispheres are severed. Each hemisphere therefore functions independently of the other and without access to the other's sensations, thoughts, or actions.

tify the object. Finally, when asked what the still-out-of-sight left hand was holding, the left hemisphere did not know and incorrectly guessed "pencil."

The special capacities of the right hemisphere in facial recognition can also be demonstrated in the split-brain patient. Levy devised the chimeric figures test, which consists of faces and other patterns that have been split down the center and recombined (Figure 9.7). When the recombined faces were presented selectively to each hemisphere, the patients appeared to be unaware of the gross discordance between the two sides of the pictures. When asked to pick out the picture they had seen, they chose the face seen in the left visual field (that is, by their right hemisphere), demonstrating that the right hemisphere has a special role in the recognition of faces.

In summary, careful and sometimes ingenious studies of patients with commissurotomies have

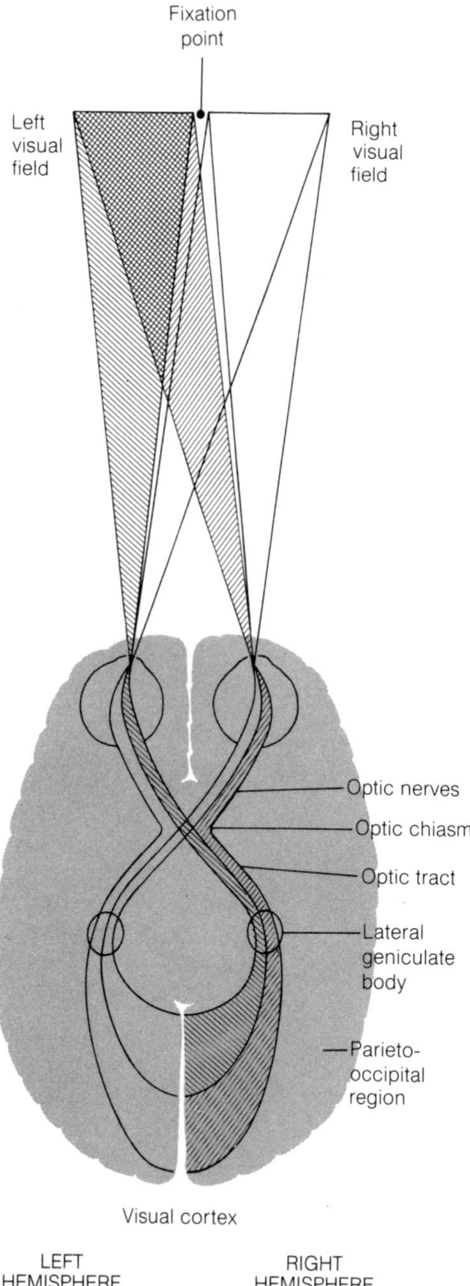

FIGURE 9.5. Visual pathways are crossed; thus visual fields (and not eyes) are represented in each hemisphere. All the field left of the fixation point (shaded region) is represented in the right visual cortex, and all the field right of the fixation point is represented in the left visual cortex.

provided clear evidence of the complementary specialization of the two cerebral hemispheres. It must be recognized, however, that as interesting as these patients are, they represent only a very small population and their two hemispheres are by no means normal. Most of these patients had focal

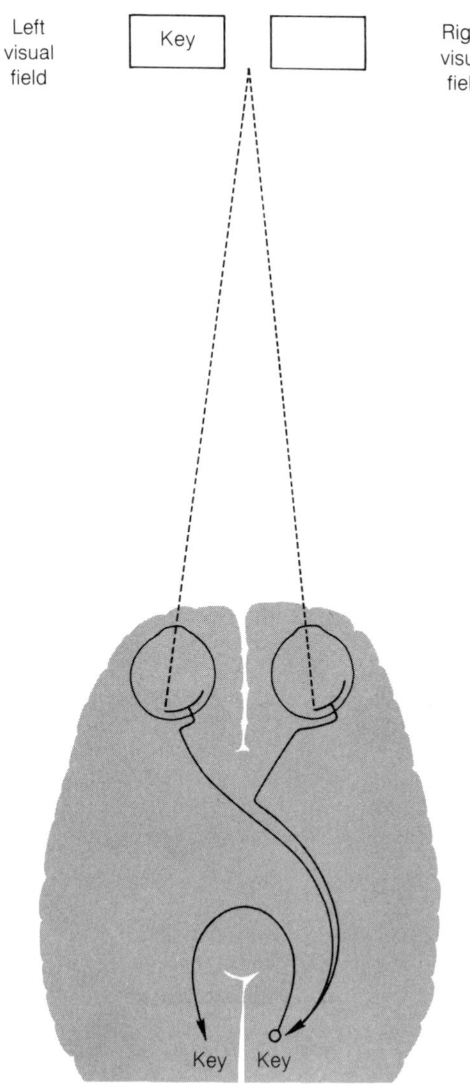

FIGURE 9.6. Visual input is transferred from the left visual field to the left visual cortex via the corpus callosum. Cutting the callosum would prevent such a transfer.

right visual cortex?

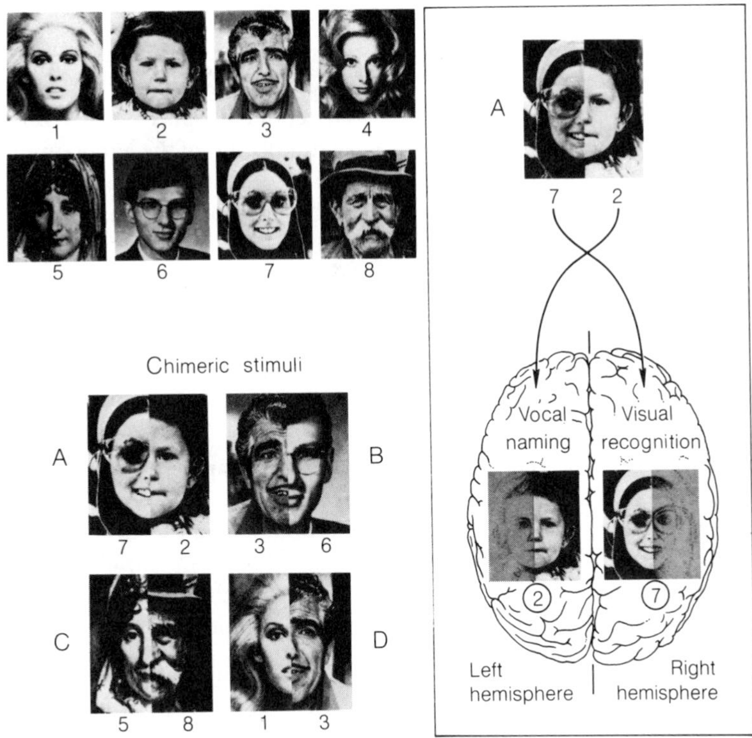

FIGURE 9.7. Composite faces used by Levy and coworkers to demonstrate the special role of the right hemisphere in facial recognition. Commissurotomy patients were shown the chimeric stimuli (composite pictures) *A* through *D*. When asked to choose the face they had seen from the array of original pictures, 1 through 8, the patients chose the face that was in the left visual field, as the right-hand side of the figure illustrates. (From J. Levy et al., 1972. Reprinted with permission of Oxford University Press, Oxford.)

lesions, which caused the initial seizure disorder, and some may have had brain damage early in life, leading to significant reorganization of cerebral function. Thus, generalizations and inferences must be made cautiously from these fascinating patients. We shall return to them in Chapter 16.

Brain Stimulation

In the early 1930s Wilder Penfield and his associates at the Montreal Neurological Institute pioneered the use of surgical treatment for epilepsy in patients whose seizures were poorly controlled by drug therapy. The logic of this procedure is to remove the region of cortex where the abnormal discharge originates. Since this is elective therapeutic surgery it can be planned for, and considerable care can be taken to ensure that areas of the cortex critical for the control of speech and movement are not damaged. To identify speech and movement areas and to localize the extent of the epileptogenic tissue, the surgeon stimulates the exposed cortex and records the responses of the conscious patient. Careful study of hundreds of patients in Montreal by Penfield and his students, and more recently by George Ojemann and his colleagues at the University of Washington, has provided clear evidence of cerebral asymmetry: stimulation of the left hemisphere can block the ability to speak, whereas stimulation of the right hemisphere seldom does so. The importance of this technique for neuropsychology cannot be underestimated. Following surgery, psychologists often have the opportunity to study patients and to correlate the results of cortical stimulation and psychological assessment; the work of Rasmussen and Brenda Milner at the Montreal Neurological Institute provides an excellent example of such collaboration.

Application of an electrical current to the cortex of a conscious patient has four general effects, three excitatory and one inhibitory. First, stimulation can produce localized movements, localized dysthesias (numbness or tingling in the skin), light flashes, or buzzing sensations. These effects are normally evoked from primary motor, somatosensory, visual, and auditory areas and pathways, respectively, and are produced by stimulation of either hemisphere with about the same frequency, a result that illustrates the often overlooked fact that the brain has symmetrical as well as asymmetrical functions. Second, stimulation can produce what Penfield called "interpretive" and "experiential" responses. These uncommon but often highly reliable phenomena include alterations in the interpretation of the patient's surroundings, such as déjà vu, fear and dreaming states, and the reproduction of visual or auditory aspects of specific previous experiences. That is, patients report specific "memories" in response to specific stimulation. These phenomena usually occur from tissue showing epileptogenic discharge, but there is an asymmetry in their occurrence: stimulation of the right temporal lobe produces these phenomena more frequently than stimulation of the left temporal lobe, which suggests that the right hemisphere has perceptual functions not shared by the left. Third, stimulation of the left frontal or temporal regions may accelerate the production of speech. Ojemann suggests that this acceleration may result from a type of "alerting response" and may occur in other cognitive processes, especially memory, although this is difficult to demonstrate unequivocally. Finally, stimulation blocks function. This effect is most evident in complex functions such as language and memory and is apparent only when current is applied while the patient is actively engaged in these behaviors. Stimulation of the same site in a quiet patient has no discernible effect. Disruption of speech is a well-documented effect of stimulation of the left hemisphere, but it is only recently that stimulation of the right hemisphere has been shown to disrupt behavior. Ojemann and his colleagues have reported that stimulation of the right hemisphere disrupts judgments of line orientation, labeling of facial expressions, and short-term memory for faces, the effects coming almost exclusively from the temporoparietal cortex: a result consistent with the presumed role of this cortex in visuospatial behavior.

In summary, stimulation of the cortex has proved to be a useful tool in demonstrating both localization and lateralization of function. The effect of disrupting stimulation can be quite localized, often changing as the site of stimulation is moved as little as a few millimeters, and it is often very reliable for individual patients. One additional intriguing aspect of data from cortical stimulation is that there is a great deal of variation from patient to patient in the exact location and extent of sites with particular effects on behavior. One can speculate that this variation forms a basis for individual differences in skills, since people presumably have different amounts of cortex devoted to particular functions. (See Ojemann for preliminary results of this type of analysis.)

Carotid Sodium Amobarbital Injection

Although language is usually located in the left hemisphere, a small percentage of people, most of them left-handed, have language represented in the right hemisphere. In the event of elective surgery, avoiding inadvertent damage to the speech zones requires that the surgeon be certain of their location. To achieve certainty in doubtful cases Wada and Rasmussen pioneered the technique of injecting sodium amobarbital into the carotid artery to produce a brief period of anesthesia of the ipsilateral hemisphere. (Injections are now normally made via a catheter inserted into the femoral artery.) This procedure results in an unequivocal localization of speech, because injection into the speech hemisphere results in an arrest of speech lasting up to several minutes, and as speech returns it is characterized by aphasic errors. Injection into the nonspeaking hemisphere may produce no, or only brief, speech arrest. The amobarbital procedure has the advantage that each hemisphere can be studied separately in the functional absence of the other, anesthetized one. Since the period of anesthesia lasts several minutes, it is possible to study a variety of functions, including memory and movement, to determine the capabilities of one hemisphere in the absence of the anesthetized one.

The test is always performed bilaterally, with the two cerebral hemispheres being injected on separate days to be sure that there is no residual drug effect from the injection of the first hemisphere at the time of injection of the opposite side. At the Montreal Neurological Hospital, where Wada initially developed the procedure, a small catheter is inserted, under X-ray control, well up into the internal carotid artery, and an angiogram is then carried out. The patient is given a dry run to familiarize him or her with the tests that will be done during and after the drug injection. This establishes a baseline performance level against which to compare the postinjection performance. The patient is then given a series of simple tasks, involving immediate and delayed memory for both verbal (sentences or words) and nonverbal (photographs of faces or objects) material, for the same purpose. Moments before the drug is injected, the supine patient raises both arms and wiggles the fingers and toes. The patient is asked to start counting from 1, and without warning the neurosurgeon injects the drug through the catheter over 2 to 3 sec. Within seconds, there are dramatic changes in behavior.

The contralateral arm falls to the bed with a flaccid paralysis and there is no response whatsoever to a firm pinch of the skin of the affected limbs. If the injected hemisphere is nondominant for speech, the patient may continue to count and carry out the verbal tasks while the temporary hemiparesis is present, although there is often a period of up to 20 to 30 sec during which the patient appears confused and is silent, but typically can resume speech with urging. When the injected hemisphere is dominant for speech, the patient typically stops talking and remains completely aphasic until recovery from the hemiparesis is well along, usually in 4 to 10 min. Speech is tested by asking the patient to name a number of common objects presented in quick succession, to count and recite the days of the week forward and backward, and to perform simple naming and spelling. In addition to aphasia and paresis, patients with anesthesia of either hemisphere are totally nonresponsive to visual stimulation in the contralateral visual field. For example, there is no reflexive blinking or orientation toward suddenly looming objects. Finally, injection of the speaking hemisphere not only produces contralateral hemiparesis but also renders the ipsilateral side unable to reproduce series of movements, a condition known as **apraxia**.

TABLE 9.3. Speech lateralization as related to handedness

Handedness	Number of cases	Speech representation (%)		
		Left	Bilateral	Right
Right	140	96	0	4
Left	122	70	15	15

Source: After Rasmussen and Milner, 1977.

The sodium amobarbital test, like direct brain stimulation, has been very useful in determining which hemisphere controls speech. Table 9.3 shows the relation between hand preference and the lateralization of cerebral speech processes for a large sample of patients ($n = 262$) who were studied by Rasmussen and Milner. As would be expected from the data on brain stimulation, there is a strong preponderance of left hemisphere speech representation: 96% of the right-handers and 70% of the left-handers show speech disturbance after sodium amobarbital injection into the left hemisphere and not after injection into the right. Curiously, 4% of the right-handed sample had their speech functions lateralized to the right cerebral hemisphere. Subsequent studies by Milner and Taylor have placed this figure around 1.7%, which is roughly the proportion of right-handed people who show aphasia from right hemisphere lesions. This reminds us that speech is sometimes found in the right hemisphere of right-handed people. The results for left-handed patients support the view that the pattern of speech representation is less predictable in left-handed and ambidextrous subjects than in right-handers, but that the majority of left-handers do have speech represented in the left hemisphere. It is interesting, however, that whereas none of the right-handers showed evidence of bilateral speech organization, in 15% of the non-right-handers there was some significant speech disturbance following injection of either side. These patients probably did not have a symmetrical duplication of language functions in the two hemispheres: injection of one hemisphere tended to disrupt naming (for example, names of the days of the week), whereas injection of the other hemisphere disrupted serial ordering (for example, ordering the days of the week). Hence, although people may have bilateral representation of speech, this representation is probably asymmetrical and need not imply that the person has "two left hemispheres." Further study of these patients probably would have revealed that visuospatial functions were bilaterally and asymmetrically represented as well, although this is mere conjecture on our part.

ASYMMETRY IN THE INTACT BRAIN

The study of neurological patients demonstrates a clear difference between the effects of lesions to the two hemispheres, particularly in the control of language. The reason for this difference is not so clear, however, as there are many problems in trying to make inferences about the functioning of the normal brain from clinical studies of the dysfunctioning brain. Just because a specific behavioral symptom is associated with damage to a particular brain area does not necessarily mean that the region once controlled the disrupted function. For example, the fact that 98% of right-handers have a disruption of language function with a left hemisphere stroke in the "language areas" does not mean that the function of the left hemisphere is language. Rather, it means that the left hemisphere executes instructions that are required for normal language functions. The question is what these functions are. One approach to this question is to study the normal brain and to try to make inferences about the function of its components from the behavior it produces. The most common approach is to take advantage of the anatomical organization of the sensory and motor systems to "trick" the brain into revealing its mode of operation. Such studies are often called **laterality** studies. Laterality studies are not without problems of their own, however, as we shall see.

Asymmetry in the Visual System

The organization of the visual system provides an opportunity to present each hemisphere selectively with specific visual information. Figure 9.6 shows the relation between each visual field and its field of projection in the visual cortex: visual stimuli in the left visual field are projected to the right visual cortex, whereas stimuli in the right visual field travel to the left visual cortex. By using a special instrument called a tachistoscope, visual information can be presented to each visual field independently. Subjects are asked to fixate on a center point marked by a dot or cross (see Figure 9.6). An image is then flashed in one visual field for about 50 msec—a time short enough to allow the image to be processed before the eyes can shift from the fixation point. By comparing the accuracy with which information from the two visual fields is processed, it is possible to infer which hemisphere is best suited to processing different types of information.

In the early 1950s Mishkin and Forgays first used the tachistoscopic procedure to demonstrate that normal right-handed subjects could identify English words presented to the right visual field more accurately than when the words were presented to the left visual field. Mishkin and

Forgays believed that acquired directional reading habits (that is, left to right in English) were responsible for this bias, but the studies with the Californian commissurotomy patients a decade later suggested another interpretation: information presented to only one visual field is processed most efficiently by the hemisphere that is specialized to receive it. Words presented to the left hemisphere, therefore, are processed more efficiently than words presented to the nonverbal right hemisphere. This conclusion was very important not only because it was consistent with the clinical inferences about cerebral specialization but also because it suggested that differences between the processing carried out by the right and left hemispheres were due to a fundamental difference in the perceptual processes of the two hemispheres.

The strongest evidence that visual-field differences in tachistoscopic studies are measuring functional asymmetries in the brain is that the asymmetries in tachistoscopic tasks are the same as those demonstrated with neurological patients. Thus, a right visual-field advantage is found with normal subjects in a variety of tasks using verbal material such as words and letters, and a left visual-field advantage is found for stimuli thought to be processed by the right hemisphere, including faces and other visuospatial stimuli (Table 9.4).

Asymmetry in the Auditory System

The auditory system is not as completely crossed as the visual—both hemispheres receive projections from each ear. However, the crossed connections do appear better developed and may have a preferred access to the cortex. Thus, sounds projected to the right ear are assumed to be processed primarily by the left hemisphere, and those to the left ear are processed primarily by the right hemisphere, as shown in Figure 9.8.

In the early 1960s Doreen Kimura studied patients while they performed dichotic listening tasks. Pairs of spoken digits (say, "two" and "six") were presented simultaneously, one of which was heard in each ear through headphones connected to a stereo tape recorder. Each patient was presented with three pairs of digits and then asked to recall as many of the six digits as possible, in any order. Kimura was interested in the auditory pro-

TABLE 9.4. Summary of relative asymmetry of function in studies of normal subjects

Function	Task	Left hemisphere dominance[a]	Right hemisphere dominance
Visual (tachistoscope)	Letters	1.2	1.0
	Words	1.5	1.0
	Two-dimensional point localization	1.0	1.2
	Dot and form enumeration	1.0	1.2
	Matching of slanted lines	1.0	1.1
	Stereoscopic depth perception	1.0	1.3
	Faces	1.0	1.2
Auditory (dichotic listening)	Words	1.9	1.0
	Nonsense syllables	1.7	1.0
	Backward speech	1.7	1.0
	Melodic pattern	1.0	1.2
	Nonspeech sounds (cough, laugh, etc.)	1.0	1.1
Manual	Skilled movements	1.0	1.0
	Free movements during speech	3.1	1.0
	Tactile dot (Braille)		Significantly higher

[a] *Numbers indicate the ratio of hemisphere dominance for each task.*
Source: Adapted from Kimura, 1973.

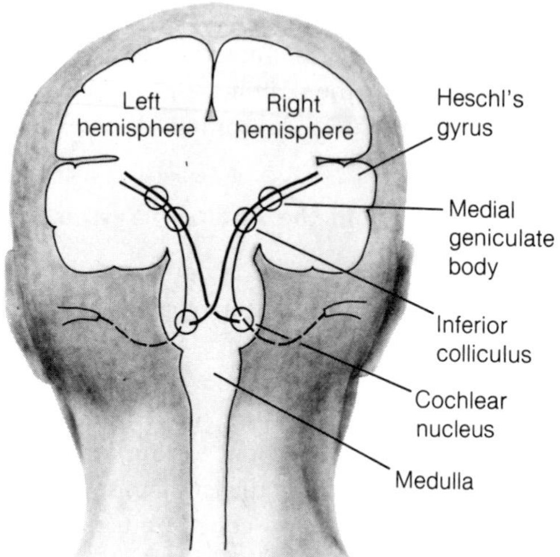

FIGURE 9.8. Auditory pathways from the ears to the cerebral auditory receiving areas in the right and left hemispheres are partially crossed. Although each hemisphere can receive input from both ears, the neural connections from one ear to the hemisphere on the opposite side are stronger than those to the hemisphere on the same side. When ipsilateral (same side) and contralateral (opposite side) inputs compete in the auditory neural system, it is thought that the stronger contralateral input inhibits or occludes the ipsilateral signals. (After Kimura, 1973.)

cessing capacities of patients with temporal lobe lesions, but she noticed that all subjects, regardless of lesion locus, recalled more digits that had been presented to the right ear than had been presented to the left. The right-ear advantage was also found in normal control subjects. This led Kimura to propose that when different stimuli are presented simultaneously to each ear, the pathway from the right ear to the speaking hemisphere has preferred access, and the ipsilateral pathway from the left ear is relatively suppressed. Thus, during a dichotic task, the stimulus to the left ear must travel to the right hemisphere and then across the cerebral commissures to the left hemisphere. This longer route via the left ear puts stimuli into this ear at a disadvantage, and words played to the right ear are recalled more accurately. Having found a right-ear advantage for the perception of dichotically presented speech stimuli, it was an obvious next step to search for tasks that gave a left-ear superiority. In 1964, Kimura reported just such an effect in the perception of melodies. Two excerpts of instrumental chamber music were played simultaneously through headphones, one to each ear. After each pair, four excerpts (including the two that had been played dichotically) were presented binaurally (to both ears), and the subject's task was to identify the two that had been heard previously. Amazingly, Kimura found a left-ear advantage for normal subjects on this task.

It should be noted that not all subjects show the expected ear advantages in dichotic studies, the effects are not large when they occur (seldom exceeding a twofold difference in accuracy in the two ears), and dichotic results are apparently affected by various contextual and practice effects. Nonetheless, the Kimura studies have played a seminal role in laterality research, since they complemented the results from the neurological literature. As a result, they opened up an entire field of research to anyone with imagination and a stereo tape recorder. More important, her experiments provided a noninvasive technique for identifying the hemisphere dominant for language, a question of special clinical importance, particularly in left-handed patients. Furthermore, the test has other clinical uses because patients with left temporal lobe damage are very poor at this task and patients with damage to the corpus callosum exhibit an almost complete inhibition of words presented to the left ear, even though they can recall words presented to this ear if there is no competing stimulus to the right ear.

The Kimura experiments are suggestive, for they imply that the left hemisphere is specialized for processing language-related sounds whereas the right hemisphere processes music-related sounds (Table 9.5). There is, however, another interpretation. It is possible that the asymmetry is related to some other feature of the temporal or spectral structure of the sounds, rather than language and music per se. Consider, for example, the finding by Papcun and colleagues. They showed that Morse code operators have a right-ear superiority for the perception of the code,

TABLE 9.5. Examples of ear advantages for various dichotic signals

Test	Basic reference
Tests showing a right-ear advantage	
Digits	Kimura, 1961
Words	Kimura, 1967
Nonsense syllables	Kimura, 1967
Formant transitions	Lauter, 1982
Backward speech	Kimura and Folb, 1968
Morse code	Papcun et al., 1974
Difficult rhythms	Natale, 1977
Tone used in linguistic decisions	Zurif, 1974
Tonal sequences with frequency transitions	Halperin et al., 1973
Ordering temporal information	Divenyi and Efron, 1979
Movement-related tonal signals	Sussman, 1979
Tests showing a left-ear advantage	
Melodies	Kimura, 1964
Musical chords	Gelfand et al., 1980
Environmental sounds	Curry, 1967
Emotional sounds and hummed melodies	King and Kimura, 1972
Tones processed independent of linguistic content	Zurif, 1974
Complex pitch perception	Sidtis, 1982
Tests showing no ear advantage	
Vowels	Blumstein et al., 1977
Isolated fricatives	Darwin, 1974
Rhythms	Gordon, 1970
Nonmelodic hums	van Lancker and Fromkin, 1973

Source: After Noffsinger, 1985.

even though the sounds are distinguished only by their *temporal* structure. Thus, this study might be taken as evidence that the left hemisphere is not specialized for language so much as for "something else." One possibility is the analysis of signals with a complex temporal microstructure. We shall return to this idea in our discussion of language.

Asymmetry in the Somatosensory System

Experiments on laterality in somatosensation have not been as popular as those in vision and audition. Nevertheless, the somatosensory system is almost completely crossed, a feature that allows an easy comparison of the two sides, just as in vision (Figure 9.9). By blindfolding subjects and requiring them to perform various tasks, such as reading Braille or handling objects separately with each hand, it is possible to identify differences in each hand's efficiency—differences that can be taken to imply functional asymmetry in cerebral organization.

One type of research has compared the performance of the left and right hands in the recognition of various shapes, angles, and patterns by testing each hand separately. The left hand of right-handed subjects is superior at nearly all tasks of this type. For example, Rudel and coworkers found that both blind and sighted subjects read Braille more rapidly with the left hand. Some children are actually fluent readers with the left hand but are totally unable to read with the right. Since Braille patterns are spatial configurations of dots, this observation is congruent with the proposal that the right hemisphere has a role in processing spatial information that is not shared by the left.

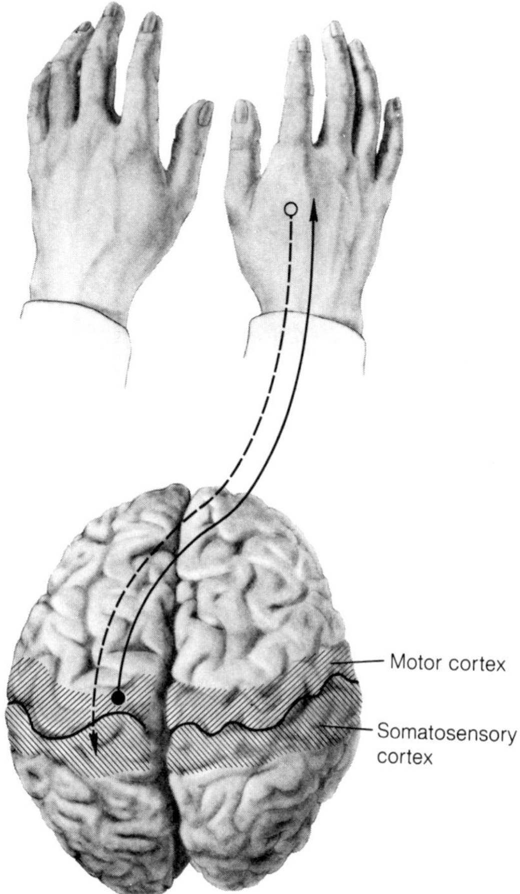

FIGURE 9.9. Somatosensory and motor pathways are almost wholly crossed; each hand is served primarily by the cerebral hemisphere on the opposite side.

A second type of somatosensory test employs an analogue of the dichotic procedure, the dichaptic test, which was used first by Witelson. She simultaneously presented to each hand a different, unfamiliar complex shape that could not be seen. The subjects felt the objects and then were allowed to look at an array of objects and select those they had previously touched. The results showed a left-hand (right hemisphere) superiority in the recognition of objects. More recently, Gibson and Bryden have been able to dissociate the performance of the left and right hands. In their experiment, subjects were dichaptically presented with cutouts of irregular shapes or letters made of sandpaper, which were moved slowly across the fingertips. Their subjects showed a right-hand advantage for identifying letters and a left-hand advantage for identifying irregular shapes.

Perhaps the most elegant somatosensory study was carried out by Nachson and Carmon in 1975. They presented subjects with two different tasks —one that they described as "spatial" and another described as "sequential." In these tasks the index, middle, and ring fingers were stimulated by tapered metal rods. Depending on the task, the subjects had to respond by pressing microswitches next to the rods. In the spatial task one finger was stimulated once, another twice, and third not at all. The subject's task was to indicate the pattern of stimulation by pressing the appropriate microswitches. In the sequential task, the three fingers were stimulated in random order and the subjects had to press the switches in the same sequence as they had been stimulated. With bimanual presentation, subjects made more errors with the left hand on the sequential task and more errors with the right hand on the spatial task. This result is important, for it implies that the left hemisphere has a special role in sequential analysis that presumably would be very important in the control of complex movement, a control that may be a special function of the left hemisphere.

Asymmetry in the Motor System

Although the motor system has a significant uncrossed component, clinical studies, first by Wyke and more recently by Kimura and others, have suggested that there is a functional asymmetry in the control of movement. Following the logic of the study of asymmetry in the intact sensory systems, it would seem reasonable to look for asymmetries in motor control. One difficulty that immediately confronts us, however, is that since there is an asymmetry in the accuracy of response to sensory input, the study of motor asymmetries is potentially confounded by the fact that the two sides do not start off equally. For example, if we found that the right hand reacts to verbal stimuli faster than the left, we would be unable to conclude that this is due to a motor asymmetry per se; it could be due entirely to the perceptual asymmetry. Therefore, two different types of experiments have been devised to assess motor asymmetries: (1) direct observation of motor asymmetry, and (2) interference tasks.

If there is an inherent asymmetry in the control of movement, it is possible that this asymmetry might be observable when people are engaged in other behaviors. For example, perhaps the right hand is more active during the performance of verbal tasks, which do not require a manual response, and the left hand is more active during the performance of nonverbal tasks, which also do not require a manual response. To examine this possibility Kimura and her students have done a number of intriguing experiments. It is a common observation that people often gesture when talking. By videotaping subjects talking or humming, Kimura was able to show that right-handed people tend to gesture with their right hands when talking but are equally likely to scratch, rub their nose, or touch their body with either hand. Kimura interpreted the observed gesturing with the limb contralateral to the speaking hemisphere to indicate a relation between speech and certain manual activities.

Since differences in gesturing, which favor the right hand in right-handed subjects, could simply reflect a difference in preferred hand rather than imply a functional asymmetry in motor control, another series of studies compared hand-movement asymmetries during analogous verbal and nonverbal tasks. The procedure involved videotaping right-handed subjects while they assembled blocks in three different types of tests. The first type, a "neutral task," required subjects to combine white blocks to form a 5-by-5 matrix. The second type, a "verbal task," required subjects to combine blocks with letters on them in a series of crossword-puzzle tasks. In the third type, a "nonverbal task," subjects did jigsaw puzzles with the same size blocks as in the preceding two types of tasks. Analysis of the movements showed that in the neutral task, subjects manipulated blocks with the right hand while supporting them with the left. Other movements seldom occurred. In the verbal task, most task-directed movements showed a right-hand preference. In the nonverbal task, by contrast, task-directed movements showed a leftward shift from the neutral condition, subjects now making far more movements with the left hand. These results suggest that the two hemispheres may have complementary roles in the control of movement—an asymmetry that is moderated by a native hand preference.

A second type of observed motor asymmetry has been reported in the performance of complex movements of the mouth. Wolf and Goodale have done single-frame analysis of videotaped mouth movements when people make verbal or nonverbal movements. Figure 9.10 illustrates their principal finding: the right side of the mouth opens wider and more quickly than the left for both verbal and nonverbal tasks. The location of the movement was an important factor in determining the size of the right bias, since movements embedded within a series showed a greater asymmetry than movements at the beginning. Goodale's observations support the idea that the left hemisphere has a special role in the selection, programming, and production of verbal and nonverbal oral movements. In view of claims that the left side of the face shows emotions more strongly than the right side, it would be interesting to use Goodale's technique to analyze the onset time of spontaneous facial expressions. It is reasonable to predict that if the right hemisphere is dominant in the control of facial expression, the onset would be sooner on the left side of the face. Goodale has shown that this is indeed the case.

A variety of laboratories have recently examined a well-known phenomenon that most people manifest: the difficulty of doing two complex tasks at the same time. If subjects are asked to balance a dowel on their left or right index fingers while talking, they are able to maintain the balance much longer with the left hand than with the right. Similar results are also reported for other complex tasks such as tapping a sequence of movements with the fingers; speaking interferes only with performance of the left hand. Perhaps the most interesting interference study we know

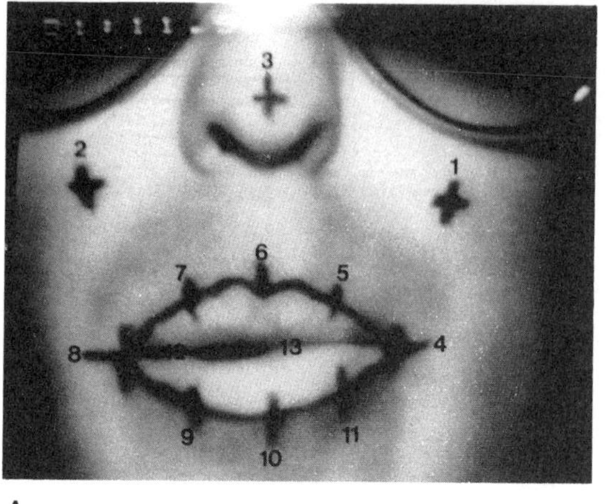

A

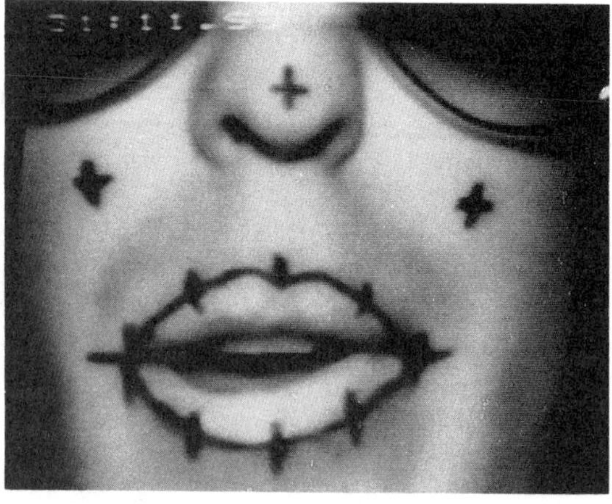

B

FIGURE 9.10. Successive video frames illustrating the mouth opening during the production of the syllable "ma" in the sequence "mabopi." Frame *B* occurred 67 msec after frame *A*. (Reprinted with permission from *Neuropsychologia* 25, Wolf and Goodale, Oral asymmetries during oral and nonoral movements of the mouth, copyright © 1987.)

of is an unpublished experiment by Hicks and Kinsbourne. They persuaded several unemployed musicians to come to their laboratory daily to play the piano. The task was to learn a different piece of music with each hand so that the two pieces could be played simultaneously. Once the musicians had mastered this very difficult task, the experimenters then asked them to speak or to hum while playing. Evidently, speaking disrupted playing with the right hand, and humming disrupted playing with the left.

As interesting as interference studies may be, interference effects are poorly understood and appear to be capricious. It is a common observation that as we become proficient at motor tasks we are less prone to interference effects. Consider the difficulty of talking while learning to play tennis; an interference paradigm of little challenge to a tennis professional. Interference studies provide a useful way to study the roles of the two hemispheres in the control movement, but much more work will be needed before we can identify the complementary roles of the two hemispheres. It will be necessary to identify which types of movements each hemisphere is especially good at controlling, since these movements will probably be resilient to interference effects. Further, there should be studies of the capacities of the hemispheres to produce simultaneous finger versus limb movements. Perhaps finger movements are more sensitive to interference effects when performed by the right hemisphere than by the left. Studies of interference effects are intriguing, however, since they may provide fresh insights into the organization of the motor systems.

What Do Laterality Studies Tell Us about Brain Function?

Laterality studies provide an important complement to the study of neurological patients and have served as the basis for much of the current theorizing about the nature of cerebral asymmetry. It should be recognized, however, that these studies are a very indirect measure of brain function and are far from being the ideal tools they are often assumed to be. Consider the following problems.

Measures of laterality do not correlate perfectly with invasive measures of cerebral asymmetry. For example, dichotic-listening studies show a right-ear bias for words in about 80% of right-handed subjects, but sodium amobarbital testing and brain stimulation show language to be represented in the left hemisphere in more than 95% of right-handers. What causes this discrepancy? There are several possibilities, one being that the test is measuring several things, only one of which is relative cerebral dominance. However, the behavioral tests may correlate with anatomical asymmetries more closely than the stimulation and sodium amobarbital data do. Thus, it is known that only about 75% to 80% of brains show a left-sided advantage in the posterior Sylvian area of right-handers, yet 99% of these brains show language in the left hemisphere in a sodium amobarbital test. Strauss and colleagues have proposed that there may be correlations between anatomy and behavior, and they present some preliminary data suggesting this. Unfortunately, we are still left with the question of why both the amobarbital test and brain-damage studies show a larger percentage of people with left hemisphere speech.

Measures of laterality do not correlate very highly with one another. We might expect that tachistoscopic and dichotic measures of laterality in the same subjects would be highly concordant, but they are not. Perhaps these tests are not really measuring the same things after all.

There is no simple way to correlate individual differences in the neural pathways to the cortex, or in the functional representations in the cortex, with individual performance on laterality tests. Individual differences in the brains of normal subjects almost certainly add a great deal of variability to the results, but there is currently no way to identify a systematic relationship between anatomy and performance.

The strategies that subjects adopt in laterality tasks can alter performance significantly. If subjects are instructed to pay particular attention to words entering the left ear in dichotic tasks, they can do so, abolishing the right-ear effect. Subjects can also enter tests with preconceived biases that may affect test performance. Finally, laterality effects may simply be a result of experiential, rather than biological, factors. Suspicion about laterality effects is reinforced by the observation that repeated testing of the same subjects does not always produce the same results.

Skepticism regarding the usefulness of laterality research reaches it peak in an insightful and provocative book by Efron. His thesis is that the apparent right-left difference in laterality studies can be explained entirely by the way in which the brain "scans" sensory input. Imagine the following experiment. Six numbers are presented for 100 msec in a line going from left to right. Three fall in each visual field such that 1, 2, and 3 fall in the left visual field and 4, 5, and 6 fall in the right visual field. The subject is asked to repeat the numbers that are seen. It turns out that the subjects tend to respond that the numbers were 4, 5, 6, 1, 2, 3. That is, it appears that the subjects are scanning, from left to right, the contents of the right visual field followed by the contents of the left visual field. Note that the apparent scanning has nothing to do with actually moving the eyes to read the numbers because the numbers are present for only 100 msec, which is not enough time for one eye movement. Thus, the scan is occurring after the stimuli have ended. One would predict that the longer it took to scan, the poorer the performance would be at the end of the scan because the information is decaying. Subsequent experiments have confirmed this expectation. Efron has done numerous experiments of this sort and has concluded that the brain has a tendency to scan information serially. If this is so, then it must necessarily examine some stimuli before others. If there is a tendency to examine stimuli in one visual half-field earlier than those in the other half-field, this would result in a left-right performance asymmetry without involving any hemispheric differences in processing capacity. Of course, there is still a bias in what is scanned first, but that is a different question. Efron does not argue that the two hemispheres are functionally and anatomically identical. He does argue that the evidence of laterality does not constitute an explanation and that we should be very skeptical when we read about descriptions of hemispheric "specialization." What, indeed, is actually lateralized?

MEASURES OF CEREBRAL BLOOD FLOW AND METABOLIC RATE

In 1890, Roy and Sherrington first postulated that when regions of the brain are functionally activated, the blood supply will increase correspondingly in these areas. The measurement of moment-to-moment variations in cerebral blood flow is difficult but is thought to be accurate, and measurements have been made since 1890 using some ingenious techniques. We noted in Chapter 4 that the invention of the CT scan led to the development of various brain imaging techniques, including PET and SPECT.

The use of both these techniques is still in its infancy, and a significant increase in resolution is required before effective mapping of the active cortex can be carried out. But with improved instrument resolution these procedures will become major techniques in the study of cerebral functioning, both of localization and of lateralization of functions (see the readable book by Posner and Raichle).

Localization of Function

Owing to the low resolution and slow speed of the imaging procedures used, cortical activation lasting only a few seconds will be missed by these techniques. Therefore, most studies to date have used simple tasks that are repeated over a period of several minutes. Nevertheless, the results are positive. Regional blood-flow measurements have been used to determine the normal resting pattern of activity of the brain when subjects are sitting still with their eyes closed and ears plugged. A highly reliable resting pattern emerges in which the frontal lobe receives relatively more blood than the rest of the hemisphere, roughly 15% more than the mean for the entire hemisphere. The pattern of cerebral activation changes markedly during basic auditory, visual, and tactile stimulation or during rhythmic movements. For example, auditory input bilaterally activates both superior temporal gyri, visual input activates the contralateral occipital cortex, and simple tactile object discrimination with the hand, mouth, or foot activates the corresponding part of the contralateral sensorimotor areas. Similarly, rhythmic movements of the hand, fingers, lips, and toes also activate the respective contralateral sensorimotor regions. Activation is not restricted to the primary sensory and motor regions, however; it is usually accompanied by activation in at least part of the frontal lobe. For example, rhythmic movements often activate the supplementary motor cortex, and tactile discrimination is associated with an increase in activity in the superior frontal sulcus, observations that are consistent with the proposed role of the frontal cortex in sensory processing and movement (see Chapter 14).

Blood Flow during Thinking

One of the most interesting findings with blood-flow and PET studies has come from the novel work of Roland and his colleagues, who have shown evidence of localization of cortical blood flow and cortical metabolic activity during specific types of thinking. In one study subjects were given three mental tasks to perform while regional blood flow was measured. In the first, the "50-3" task, the subjects started with the number 50 in their minds and then repeatedly subtracted 3 from the result. In the "jingle" task the subjects mentally jumped every second word in a nine-word jingle. In the "route-finding" task the subjects imagined that they started at their front door and then walked alternatively to the left or right each time they reached a corner. There were three major findings of this study. First, regional blood flow outside the primary sensory and motor areas was increased by thinking. Second, different types of thinking activated different cortical fields. There were changes in the frontal, temporal, and parietal cortex that were unique to each task, and, in addition, there were areas that were activated by one or two tasks. Areas of the prefrontal cortex of both hemispheres were activated by all tasks in all subjects, suggesting a role for the prefrontal cortex in organizing mental activity. An important point is that the primary and secondary auditory and somatosensory regions were never activated, suggesting that the observed changes were not a simple generalized increase in cerebral activity. Third, the results clearly show that thinking requires metabolic activity. What is curious is that the thinking required a *greater increase* in activity than Roland found in previous studies in which subjects made voluntary movements or processed sensory stimulation. (Is it any wonder that thinking is so much more tiring than watching TV?) Finally, there were asymmetries in this cerebral activity; although for most tasks there was a bilateral increase, the difference was in the relative level of activity in the two hemispheres.

Lateralization of Function

Brain imaging techniques have been used to identify asymmetries in cerebral functioning. As might be expected, there is an asymmetrical uptake of the tracers used when subjects either listen to or engage in conversation (Figure 9.11). For example, when a subject is listening to speech, both hemispheres show regional changes in cerebral activity especially within the auditory cortex, but the left hemisphere also shows increased activity in Broca's and Wernicke's areas. When speaking, subjects also show activity of the motor areas that represent the face and mouth, as well as activity of the supplementary motor cortex. Somewhat curiously, repetition of what has been called "automatic" speech, such as naming the days of the week over and over again, fails to produce an increase of activity in Broca's area, a result that would not have been predicted from the idea that this area is involved in producing movement or from the sodium amobarbital or stimulation studies discussed earlier. In contrast to the increase in uptake of tracer on the left side during speech perception, there is an increase in right-side uptake of tracer in the temporal lobe when subjects are played the tonal memory and timbre tests of the Seashore Musical Aptitude Test, a result consistent with Milner's demonstration that right temporal lobe lesions impair performance on these tests. Finally, Dabbs and others have found evidence that there may be an overall difference in blood flow to the two hemispheres: the right hemisphere receives slightly more blood flow than the left. This may be because the right hemisphere is larger, or it may occur for other reasons.

In summary, measures of regional blood flow and glucose uptake hold great promise for the future, once the instrumentation can be improved to enable faster and finer resolution. The cost of these procedures will remain prohibitive, however, and so it is likely that only a small number of laboratories will be able to perform this type of research. Further, it should be recognized that with the available technology, cognitive events that occur quickly (say, less than 45 sec in duration) cannot be measured.

ELECTRICAL RECORDING

The electrical activity of the brains of normal subjects can be recorded (as noted in previous chapters) by the EEG and MEG. These recordings can be related to different stimuli over time, and the electrical activity in the immediate pre- and post-stimulus periods can be correlated with the stimulus and response. *Event-related potentials* (ERPs) are an example of such recordings; they are transient voltage fluctuations generated in the brain in conjunction with sensory, motor, or cognitive events. ERPs include many of the components illustrated in Figure 4.14. These positive or negative peaks in the waves are known variously as P_1, N_1, P_3, and so on, or as P_{200}, P_{300}, and so on. The nomenclature can be confusing, since P_3 can also be written as P_{300}, in which case it is referring to the time after stimulus onset. The late-occurring wave (P_{300}) has received much attention because it appears to occur reliably when a person is actively processing ("attending to") incoming stimuli.

The basic assumption underlying ERP research is that some part of the neural activity producing the potentials has a functional role in the concurrent cognitive activity. The correlation between

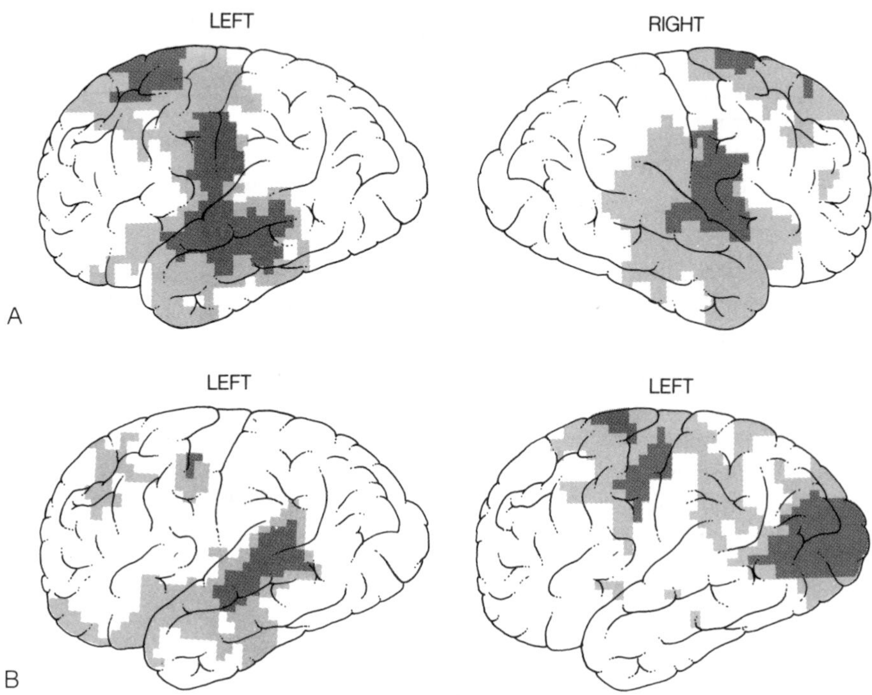

FIGURE 9.11. Relating brain function to regional blood flow. Because the pattern of blood flow varies with the behavioral task, the relative importance of different areas in different functions can be inferred: light shading indicates the average level of blood flow; dark shading indicates higher-than-average blood flow; the absence of shading indicates lower-than-average blood flow. *A.* Speaking activates the mouth-tongue-larynx of the motor and somatosensory cortex, the supplementary motor area, and the auditory cortex. These images, averaged from nine different subjects, show differences in the activity of the left and right hemispheres; in the left hemisphere the mouth area is more active, and the auditory cortex, including part of area 22, is considerably more active. *B.* Sensory perception changes the pattern of blood flow in the cortex, revealing the localization of areas that mediate the processing of sensory information. During the study shown on the right, the subject followed a moving object with his eyes, resulting in high activity in the visual cortex and frontal eye fields. During the study shown on the left, the same subject listened to spoken words, resulting in increased activity localized to the auditory cortex. Note that the position of the Sylvian and central fissures is approximate; the actual position could be determined only by opening the skull. The squared shapes are an artifact of the recording and averaging procedure and thus do not accurately indicate the shapes of areas in the brain. (Simplified from Lassen et al., 1978.)

ERP activity and language has proved to be a convenient experimental paradigm for evaluating ERP relationships with cognitive functions. Consider the following simple example. Helen Neville presented two different four-letter words tachistoscopically to the two visual fields, and the subjects' task was to recall the words. A control condition had subjects looking at unfocused words that could not be made out. There was a clear difference between the ERP amplitude (see the difference between N_1 and P_2 in Figure 9.12A) in the readable and unfocused conditions.

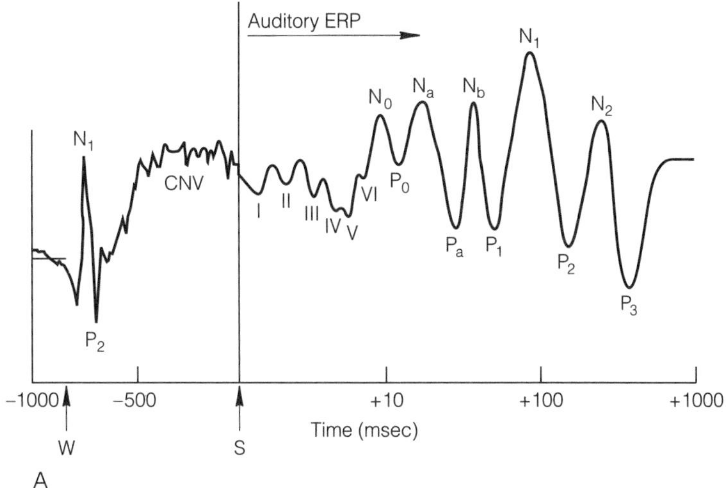

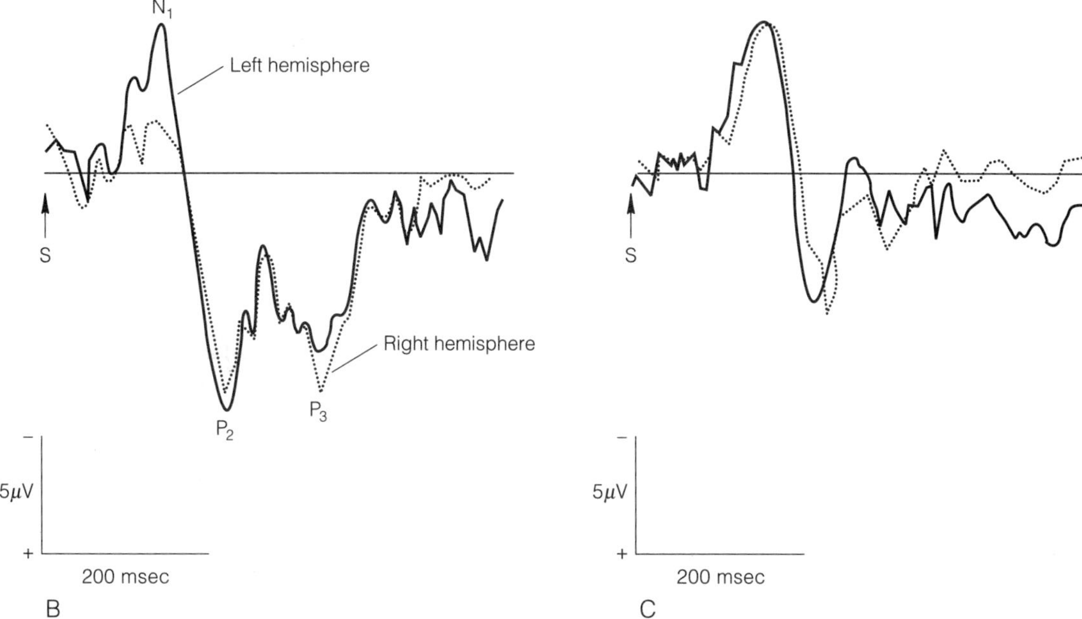

FIGURE 9.12. *A.* Idealized waveform of the auditory ERP—including the brainstem responses (waves I–VI); the mid-latency components (waves N_0, P_0, N_a, P_a, N_b); the long-latency "vertex potential" (waves P_1, N_1, P_2, N_2); and task-related endogenous components (N_2, P_3). The anticipated auditory signal is preceded by a slow negative shift (e.g., CNV). Note the logarithmic time base. (After Kutas and Hillyard, 1984.) ERPs from the left and right hemispheres of subject 1 to the presentation of pairs of words (*B*) and unfocused words (*C*). ERPs in *B* and *C* are from parietal electrodes (P_3 and P_4). (After Neville, 1980.)

This difference is taken as evidence of different cognitive processes at work in the two conditions.

There are three aspects of such ERP studies that deserve comment. First, it is clear that both hemispheres respond to the words. Second, although there is often an asymmetry in the magnitude of the response, the asymmetry is sometimes absent and is, at best, rather small. If the ERP is a valid measure of what is going on in the hemispheres, we might conclude that during the task there are a large number of information processing acts, and most of these are not lateralized in the brain, even when it is dealing with linguistic material. Third, our example showed differences in the ERPs between N_1 and P_2, but this is by no means the only place where ERPs reflect underlying processing; changes at P_3 and N_4 are also seen commonly.

In the past few years there have been two important advances in ERP studies. One of these is the development of recording systems that can process more than 100 channels concurrently. A second is the correlation of the electrical measures with MRIs of the same brains. This effectively allows the investigator to track processing in different regions of the brain simultaneously. Gevins has called this approach *event-related covariances* (ERCs). The idea is that ERPs in different regions are measuring event-related mass activities that should be related to one another over time. One could imagine that as information is processed in visual areas, there will be subsequent ERPs in areas of the frontal lobe receiving visual input.

We noted in Chapter 4 that neuromagnetic recordings (MEGs) are another way of inferring cortical activity. Like EEGs, MEGs can be averaged over time and correlated with cognitive processing, yielding *average evoked magnetic fields* (AEFs). Like ERPs, AEFs show a tendency toward asymmetry, but the more impressive result is that both hemispheres are involved in most cognitive processes. This work is still in its infancy, however, because the equipment costs are substantial. Nonetheless, it is likely to be a technique to be reckoned with over the next decade. For a useful review, see Hari.

WHAT IS LATERALIZED?

It is tempting to conclude that the functional asymmetries described thus far represent a large fundamental difference in the basic cognitive processes of the left and right cerebral hemispheres. However, before considering this issue we will summarize the data, since any theoretical statements are best considered in light of available information.

Table 9.6 summarizes the major data on cerebral lateralization and illustrates the range of functions lateralized principally in the left and right hemisphere. In right-handed people the left hemisphere has a greater role in language and in the control of complex voluntary movements than does the right hemisphere, and the right hemisphere has a greater role in the control of certain types of visuospatial abilities.

Theoretical Arguments

In recent years, a truly enormous number of proposals have been made on what is lateralized in the brain (see Allen for a readable summary). In general, there are two types of theories. One type proposes unique functions for each hemisphere; the other proposes some sort of cooperative interaction of the two hemispheres.

Unilateral Specialization Models. In its extreme form, this model states that only one hemisphere facilitates a given psychological process. For example, it has been argued since Broca that the left hemisphere alone performs language functions. Perhaps the most thorough modern version of the "left-for-language" theory is Lenneberg. A modification of the language theory is one proposed by Liepmann at the turn of the century. He proposed that the left hemisphere is specialized for some form of motor control, which would account for why both aphasia and apraxia are major symptoms of left hemisphere damage. Kimura extended this idea by proposing that although the left hemisphere mediates verbal function, it is specialized not for verbal function per se, but rather for certain kinds of motor function, both

TABLE 9.6. Summary of data on cerebral lateralization

Function	Left hemisphere	Right hemisphere
Visual system	Letters, words	Complex geometric patterns Faces
Auditory system	Language-related sounds	Nonlanguage environmental sounds Music
Somatosensory system	?	Tactile recognition of complex patterns Braille
Movement	Complex voluntary movement	Movements in spatial patterns
Memory	Verbal memory	Nonverbal memory
Language	Speech Reading Writing Arithmetic	Prosody?
Spatial processes		Geometry Sense of direction Mental rotation of shapes

Note: Functions of the respective hemispheres that are predominantly mediated by one hemisphere in right-handed people.

verbal and nonverbal. Kimura's argument is based on two premises. First, lesions of the left hemisphere disturb the production of voluntary movement—an impairment correlated with disturbance in speech. Second, Kimura proposes that verbal communication evolved from a stage that was primarily gestural, though with vocal concomitants, to one that is primarily vocal but that retains the capacity for manual communication. Since the neurological control of speech and language thus evolved out of a system of motor control of gesture, the left hemisphere is not specialized for language per se, but rather for motor control.

Several authors (for example, Efron) have suggested that it is not motor control per se that is located in the left hemisphere, but rather the capacity for fine resolution of stimuli in time. In other words, since the analysis and production of speech require fine discrimination over very short intervals, the left hemisphere might be specialized for temporal sequencing (organizing behavior and/or information over time). Elaborations of this idea have stressed the capacity of the left hemisphere to make fine discriminations in time, whether the stimuli are verbal or not (for example, Sergent). Most proposals of left hemisphere specializations have not been matched by similar concrete proposals for right hemisphere functions, although it is often said that the right hemisphere is specialized for "visuospatial functions." One exception is the temporal-discrimination hypotheses, which suggest that the right hemisphere specializes in grosser discriminations. For example, Sergent proposed that the right hemisphere is superior at recognizing faces because it is the grosser aspect of face stimuli (the gestalt) that is more important in recognition.

Rather than specifying different processing of specified psychological processes, other specialization models have focused on the idea that the two hemispheres might process information in distinctly different ways. The first clear proposal of this sort was made by Semmes in 1968. On the basis of her previous studies of World War II veterans suffering from penetrating brain injuries, she concluded that the left hemisphere functions as a collection of focalized regions, whereas the right hemisphere functions more diffusely, in a manner consistent with Lashley's notions of mass action and equipotentiality (see Chapter 8). Her logic was as follows. She had noticed that small lesions of the left hemisphere produced a wide variety of specific deficits (for example, impaired spelling and reading), the precise deficit depending on the locus of the lesion; similar-sized lesions within the right hemisphere were often without obvious effect. In contrast, large lesions of *either* hemisphere produced a large number of deficits. To account for these differences, Semmes argued that a person with a small lesion of the right hemisphere exhibits no deficits because specific functions are not localized in discrete regions in the right hemisphere, the functions being diffusely represented. A large lesion of the right hemisphere produces many more deficits than would be predicted from the total of smaller lesions because an entire functional field is removed. Large lesions of the left hemisphere produce many deficits simply because many small focal regions have been destroyed; in the left hemisphere the total is equal to the sum of the parts.

Semmes proposed that this differential organization of the two hemispheres is advantageous for efficient control of their respective functions. The diffuse organization of the right hemisphere is seen as advantageous for spatial abilities, since spatial analysis requires that different kinds of information (visual, auditory, tactile) be integrated into a single percept. Language functions are not integrated in the same manner but remain as individual units.

From these basic ideas about distinct functions of the two hemispheres has arisen the idea that the hemispheres represent two distinct modes of cognitive processing (for example, Levy, Sperry):

> The left hemisphere operates in a more logical, analytical, computer-like fashion, analyzing stimulus information input sequentially, abstracting out the relevant details to which it attaches verbal labels; the right hemisphere is primarily a synthesizer, more concerned with the overall stimulus configuration, and organizes and processes information in terms of gestalts or wholes. (Harris, 1978, p. 463)

Although these ideas have stimulated interest among philosophers and the general public, it is important to remember that they are based entirely upon inference and have jumped a long way from the data (such as those summarized in Table 9.6).

Interaction Models. All the various forms of interaction models share the common idea that both hemispheres have the capacity to perform all functions, but they do not. It is the specification of the reasons "why not" that has spawned numerous debates, experiments, and models. Consider some of the versions of the interaction model. First, there is the idea that the two hemispheres function simultaneously but work on different aspects of processing. This is a direct analogue to the multiple-channel idea of sensory processing. It is merely taken one step further so that the two hemispheres represent two more classes of sensory channels. Although this type of model is generally appealing, there has yet to be a satisfactory explanation of how the information is combined to provide a single percept or behavior. There is a group of models proposing that although the two hemispheres have the capacity to perform a given function, they inhibit or suppress each other's activity (for example, Kinsbourne, Moscovitch). Thus, the left hemisphere inhibits language processing in the right hemisphere, and the right hemisphere inhibits musical processing in the left. Developmentally, this type of model has some appeal because it appears that functions such as language can develop in the "wrong" hemisphere if the normally dominant hemisphere is damaged. Thus, if the language zones are damaged in infancy, language can develop in the right hemisphere. One difficulty with these models is that the physiological mechanisms of inhibition have not been clearly specified.

A third type of model is an information-processing model; such models may suggest either that the two hemispheres receive information preferentially and thus perform different analyses or that there is some mechanism enabling each hemisphere to "pay attention" to specific types of information, thus leading to different analyses (for example, Moscovitch). The details of these models are complex, based heavily on the information-processing theory of cognitive psychology. An interesting proposal of some of these models is that if one hemisphere is busy, it ought to be able to allocate other functions to the remaining hemisphere. A problem with the information-processing models is that they are necessarily vague on what physiological mechanisms might be responsible for selected attention.

In summary, the question of what is lateralized does not have a simple, nor a generally accepted, answer. There is no shortage of ideas and inferences. What is needed is more information about the nature of asymmetry and its origins, both developmentally and phylogenetically.

Preferred Cognitive Mode

From the previous theoretical arguments it is possible to speculate that individual differences in the behavior of normal subjects result, at least in part, from individual differences in how the cerebral hemispheres are organized and how functions are lateralized. Thus, subjects who are very logical, analytical, and verbal could be assumed to be more efficient in using their left hemispheres to solve problems in everyday life, whereas subjects who are predominantly concerned with wholes or general concepts could be assumed to be more efficient in using their right hemispheres. As an example (a tongue-in-cheek one), two professors, Alpha and Beta, are both excellent scholars, but they are totally different in how they work and think.

Alpha is meticulous and leaves no detail to chance; when learning new material he masters every detail and has total command of the topic. Alpha is verbal and can easily win debates with his quick thinking and elegant arguments. His writing is clear and concise, with flawless grammar and spelling. Alpha is athletic and is a nationally ranked tennis player. Curiously, he is only mediocre at other sports, but with prolonged practice he is able to master their details as well. Finally, Alpha's office is neat and tidy, with every item carefully placed in its correct location. On his desk is the project he is currently working on and nothing else.

Beta, on the other hand, appears to learn only the generalities of new material and seldom recalls the minute details. He grasps ideas quickly, however, and is often able to tie very diverse concepts into a meaningful picture. His thinking may appear muddled to those around him, for he has difficulty expressing his ideas, but given enough time he often impresses his colleagues with his insight into problems. His writing is poor in comparison with Alpha's, for he expresses himself with tortuous constructions and is plagued by grammatical and spelling errors about which he appears totally unconcerned. Nevertheless, Beta has a remarkable knack for asking the correct questions and tying together seemingly diverse literature. Like Alpha, Beta is athletic, but unlike Alpha, Beta acquires the general motor skills of new sports rapidly, although he has never been able to become a top participant in any event. Beta's office is messy and his desk is a pile of papers and books, because he works on several projects concurrently.

Alpha and Beta represent extremes of what could be described as left hemisphere and right hemisphere individuals, respectively. The fundamental difference between them is that each attacks problems by using what has been described as a different preferred cognitive mode. Alpha is analytical, logical, verbal, meticulous, whereas Beta is a synthesizer, more concerned with organizing concepts into meaningful wholes. Thus, in both the cognitive and the motor skills of Alpha and Beta, there is a basic difference that is assumed to reflect a fundamental difference in either brain organization or the "dominance" of one hemisphere over the other.

As intriguing as this analysis of Alpha and Beta might be, we caution that it is pure speculation, without empirical basis. It is probable that factors other than brain organization contribute to preferred cognitive mode. For example, a study by Webster and Thurber demonstrates that cognitive set can affect some tests of lateralization. They repeated Witelson and Pallie's dichaptic test (described earlier) but added an additional variable. One group (the gestalt group) was encouraged to learn the shapes by imagining the overall appearance, or gestalt; a second group (the analytic group) was encouraged to identify distinctive features of each shape and list them to themselves. This manipulation demonstrably influenced the degree of left-hand superiority, because the gestalt group had a significantly larger performance difference between the hands than did the analytic group. Although the basis for this effect is uncertain, it implies that strategies used by subjects can significantly influence tests of lateralization. Thus it seems reasonable to assume that differences in preferred cognitive mode may reflect socialization or environmental factors in addition to neuronal, biological, or constitutional factors. Nevertheless, the idea that individual differences in behavior result in part from individual differences in brain organization seems a provocative assumption worthy of serious study.

Measuring Behavior in Neuropsychology

It is appropriate at this point to discuss briefly the problem of measuring behavior. It might be thought that of all the procedures used in neuropsychology, the measurement of things or events might be the easiest to perform and replicate. This is not true. Many measurements are made to obtain inferences about some other processes. For example, in dichotic listening, if more words are recalled from the right ear than from the left, the inference is made that speech is lateralized to the left hemisphere. The assumptions underlying this inference are relatively simple, yet there are so many variables affecting the result that Bryden has found it necessary to devote an entire book to the problem. Perhaps, one may ask, if a more objective measure of something like brain size were used, would the results be clearer? This, however, seems unlikely. There appear to be so many different ways to measure objects that almost any result can be obtained. Consider the following.

Probably everyone has had the feeling that his or her feet are not exactly the same size. Often the difference manifests itself as greater discomfort in one foot when breaking in a new pair of shoes (we have never heard anyone suggest that the shoes might be different sizes). Foot size may be related to differences in brain organization. For example, people in medicine have known for a long time that damage to one hemisphere at an early age leads to smaller limbs in the contralateral side of the body (Figure 9.13). Jere and Jerome Levy attempted to measure differences in foot size in normal people in order to make inferences about cerebral organization. They measured foot size in 150 individuals. They found that signifi-

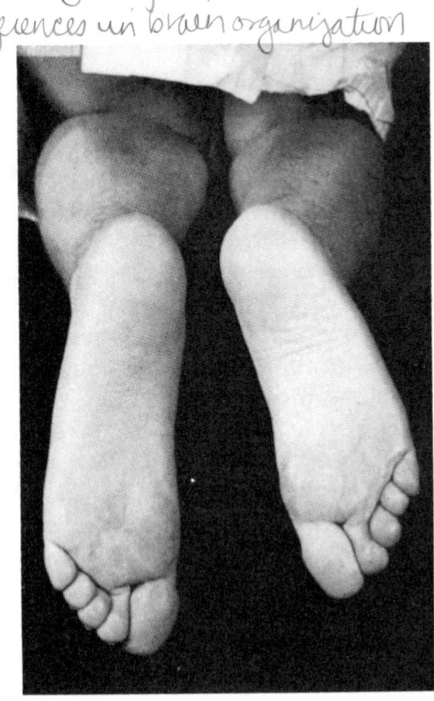

FIGURE 9.13. Growth asymmetry due to destruction of the left frontoparietal region at the time of birth. Such a case demonstrates that growth has a cortical control, quite aside from the effect of disuse, affecting limb size. (From W. Penfield and H. Jasper, Copyright © 1954. Reprinted with permission.)

cantly more right-handed females had larger left than right feet, whereas significantly more right-handed males had larger right than left feet. Just the opposite result was obtained with left-handed females and males. The Levys' measures were made by converting foot size to shoe size and then converting differences to a 7-point rating scale. A number of studies attempted to repeat the Levys' work. Mascie-Taylor and his coworkers measured foot size using "standard anthropometric technique" (described elsewhere as heel to longest toe with the subject seated and with the toenails cut). They found that the left foot was longer than the right in both sexes, confirming seven previous studies. There were no handedness effects. Peters and his coworkers measured the actual foot length from the heel to the longest toe in 365 seated subjects. They found no significant differences between the left and the right foot for any sex or handedness group, and they claimed partial support for their results from three other studies. Yanowitz and his colleagues traced the outline of 105 subjects' feet on a large sheet of paper. They found no differences in foot size with regard to sex or handedness. The final score on this series of studies is: one study for sex and handedness effects, eight studies for a left-foot effect, and two studies for no differences, with three additional studies in partial support for no differences. Of course, this story—like all good stories—has a sequel, but we refer the interested reader to Peters's review.

It might have been thought initially that measuring foot size is a relatively easy matter. This series of studies shows that it is not. Depending on the measuring device, the points across which length is measured, whether subjects are seated or standing, the time of day, and perhaps even shoe type worn before measurement, different results can be obtained. In many of the studies the importance of these variables was not recognized, and in others the procedure was not described in sufficient detail to permit exact replication. It is interesting that the most objective measure, photography, was not used in any of the studies (see Figure 9.13). A photographic record of the feet would have permitted reevaluation of the results at any time by investigators interested in the question of appropriate measurement.

There are perhaps three lessons that should be derived from this example (one of them is not that it is impossible to make measurements). The first is that if measuring something like feet is difficult, then inferring something about the brain from such measurements should be done with caution. The second is that there is nothing wrong with making multiple measurements. If they correlate then each is measuring the same thing; but if they do not, then either multiple factors are at work or some of the measures are not reliable. The third is that if a measurement is to be made, it should be the most meaningful one that can be made.

CONCLUDING REMARKS

We have shown how the two hemispheres of the human brain are both anatomically and functionally asymmetrical. Three important points must be emphasized before we consider variations in the "textbook pattern" of cerebral asymmetry in the next chapter, lest we leave the reader with three common misunderstandings.

First, many functions of the cerebral hemispheres are not asymmetrical, but symmetrical. In an examination in our undergraduate course in human neuropsychology we asked: In what ways is the human brain symmetrical? Thinking it to be a trick question, a majority of the students answered: "It isn't symmetrical, it's asymmetrical." This is wrong, of course, since many functions—especially of the primary sensory and motor areas—appear to be identical on the two sides of the brain. Furthermore, we must recognize that the functional differences between the two hemispheres are not absolute, but relative. Just because sodium amobarbital renders one hemisphere aphasic does not mean that language functions are only carried out in the aphasic hemisphere.

Second, cerebral *site* is at least as important in understanding brain function as cerebral *side*, a fact that is often overlooked when people theorize about cerebral organization. Thus, although the frontal lobes are asymmetrical, the functions of the two frontal lobes are more similar to each other than they are to those of the posterior cortex on the same side. In fact, it is often very difficult to localize lesions in neurological patients to one hemisphere in the absence of neurological data, even though the site (frontal as opposed to temporal or parietal) may be immediately obvious. Perhaps it is best to think of the functions of the cerebral cortex as being localized, and of hemispheric side as being only one step in localizing them.

Third, although it is tempting to conclude that the function of the left hemisphere is "language," the appropriate conclusion is that the left hemisphere is involved in processes that are necessary for certain aspects of language. Similarly, the right hemisphere appears to be specially involved in other types of processing, such as that required for visuospatial functions. While there has been a popularization of work on cerebral asymmetry and an extrapolation of neuropsychological results to the analysis of cultural and sex differences, to name only two, we must remember that it is a long inferential leap from the data available to explanations of what they mean. At present it is safe to conclude that we do not know what processes the two hemispheres are specialized to perform.

REFERENCES

Allen, M. Models of hemispheric specialization. *Psychological Bulletin* 93:73–104, 1983.

Amaducci, L., S. Sorbi, A. Albanese, and G. Gainotti. Choline acetyltransferase (ChAT) activity differs in right and left human temporal lobes. *Neurology* 31:799–805, 1981.

Blumstein, S., V. Tartter, D. Michel, B. Hirsch, and E. Leiter. The role of distinctive features in the dichotic perception of words. *Brain and Language* 4:508–520, 1977.

Bonin, B. von. Anatomical asymmetries of the cerebral hemispheres. In V. B. Mountcastle, ed. *Interhemispheric Relations and Cerebral Dominance.* Baltimore: Johns Hopkins Press, 1962.

Brandeis, D., and D. Lehmann. Event-related potentials of the brain and cognitive processes: Approaches and applications. *Neuropsychologia* 24:151–168, 1986.

Broca, P. Sur la faculté du langage articulé. *Bulletins et Mémoires de la Société D'Anthropologie de Paris* 6:377–393, 1865.

Bryden, M. P. *Laterality: Functional Asymmetry in the Intact Brain.* New York: Academic Press, 1982.

Carmon, A., Y. Harishanu, E. Lowinger, and L. Lavy. Asymmetries in hemispheric blood volume and cerebral dominance. *Behavioral Biology* 7:853–859, 1972.

Chi, J. G., E. C. Dooling, and F. H. Gilles. Left-right asymmetries of the temporal speech areas of the human fetus. *Archives of Neurology* 34:346–348, 1977.

Crichton-Browne, J. On the weight of the brain: Its component parts in the insane. *Brain* 2:42–67, 1880.

Cunningham, D. F. *Contribution to the Surface Anatomy of the Cerebral Hemispheres.* Dublin: Royal Irish Academy, 1892.

Curry, F. A comparison of left-handed subjects on verbal and nonverbal dichotic listening tasks. *Cortex* 3:343–352, 1967.

Dabbs, J. M. Left-right differences in cerebral blood flow and cognition. *Psychophysiology* 17:548–551, 1980.

Darwin, C. Ear differences and hemispheric specialization. In F. O. Schmitt and F. G. Worden, eds. *The Neurosciences: Third Study Program.* Cambridge, Mass.: MIT Press, 1974.

Divenyi, P., and R. Efron. Spectral versus temporal features in dichotic listening. *Brain and Language* 7:375–386, 1979.

Eberstaller, O. Zur Oberflächenanatomie der Grosshirnhemispharen. *Wien. Med. Blätter* 7:479–482, 542–582, 644–646, 1884.

Economo, C. V. von, and L. Horn. Über Windungsrelief, Masse and Rindenarchitektonik der Supratemporalfläche, ihre individuellen und ihre Seitenunterschiede. *Zeitschrift für Neurologie and Psychiatrie* 130:678–757, 1930.

Efron, R. *The Decline and Fall of Hemispheric Specialization.* Hillsdale, N.J.: Lawrence Erlbaum, 1990.

Eidelberg, D., and A. M. Galaburda. Symmetry and asymmetry in the human posterior thalamus. *Archives of Neurology* 39:325–332, 1982.

Falzi, G., P. Perrone, and L. A. Vignolo. Right-left asymmetry in anterior speech region. *Archives of Neurology* 39:239–240, 1982.

Galaburda, A. M., M. LeMay, T. L. Kemper, and N. Geschwind. Right-left asymmetries in the brain. *Science* 199:852–856, 1978.

Galaburda, A. M., and F. Sanides. Cytoarchitectonic organization of the human auditory cortex. *Journal of Comparative Neurology* 190:597–610, 1980.

Gelfand, S., S. Hoffmand, S. Waltzman, and N. Piper. Dichotic CV recognition at various interaural temporal onset asynchronies: Effect of age. *Journal of the Acoustical Society of America* 68:1258–1261, 1980.

Geschwind, N., and W. Levitsky. Left-right asymmetries in temporal speech region. *Science* 161:186–187, 1968.

Gevins, A. Distributed neuroelectric patterns of human neocortex during simple cognitive tasks. *Progress in Brain Research* 85:337–355, 1990.

Gibson, C., and M. P. Bryden. Dichaptic recognition of shapes and letters in children. *Canadian Journal of Psychology* 37:132–143, 1983.

Glick, S. D., D. A. Ross, and L. B. Hough. Lateral asymmetry of neurotransmitters in human brain. *Brain Research* 234:53–63, 1982.

Gordon, H. Hemispheric asymmetries in the perception of musical chords. *Cortex* 6:387–398, 1970.

Graves, R., H. Goodglass, and T. Landis. Mouth asymmetry during spontaneous speech. *Neuropsychologia* 20:371–381, 1982.

Gur, R. C., I. K. Packer, J. P. Hungerbuhler, M. Reivich, W. D. Obrist, W. S. Amarnek, and H. Sackheim. Differences in distribution of gray and white matter in human cerebral hemispheres. *Science* 207:1226–1228, 1980.

Halperin, Y., I. Nachson, and A. Carmon. Shift of ear superiority in dichotic listening to temporally patterned nonverbal stimuli. *Journal of the Acoutistical Society of America* 53:46–50, 1973.

Hampson, E., and D. Kimura. Hand movement asymmetries during verbal and nonverbal tasks. *Canadian Journal of Psychology* 38:102–125, 1984.

Hari, R. The neuromagnetic method in the study of the human auditory cortex. In F. Grandori, M. Hoke, and G. I. Romani, eds. *Auditory Evoked Magnetic Fields and Potentials. Advances in Audiology,* Vol. 6. Basel: Karger, 1990.

Harris, L. J. Sex differences in spatial ability: Possible environmental, genetic, and neurological factors. In M. Kinsbourne, ed. *Asymmetrical Function of the Brain.* Cambridge, Mass.: Cambridge University Press, 1978.

Heschl, R. L. *Über die vordere quere Schlafentwindung des Meschlichen Grosshirns.* Wien: Braumüller, 1878.

Hoadley, M. D., and K. Pearson. Measurement of internal diameter of skull in relation to "pre-eminence" of left hemisphere. *Biometrika* 21:94–123, 1929.

Kimura, D. Some effects of temporal-lobe damage on auditory perception. *Canadian Journal of Psychology* 15: 156–165, 1961.

Kimura, D. Left-right differences in the perception of melodies. *Quarterly Journal of Experimental Psychology* 16: 355–358, 1964.

Kimura, D. Functional asymmetry of the brain in dichotic listening. *Cortex* 3:163–178, 1967.

Kimura D. The asymmetry of the human brain. *Scientific American* 228:70–78, 1973.

Kimura D., and S. Folb. Neural processing of background sounds. *Science* 161:395–396, 1968.

King, F., and D. Kimura. Left-ear superiority in dichotic perception of vocal, non-verbal sounds. *Canadian Journal of Psychology* 26:111–116, 1972.

Kinsbourne, M. Eye and head turning indicates cerebral lateralization. *Science* 176:539–541, 1971.

Kinsbourne, M., and J. Cook. Generalized and lateralized effects of concurrent verbalization on a unimanual skill. *Quarterly Journal of Experimental Psychology* 23:341–345, 1971.

Kinsbourne, M., and R. E. Hicks. Functional cerebral space: A model for overflow, transfer and interference effects in human performance. In J. Requin, ed. *Attention and Performance,* vol. 7. New York: Academic Press, 1978.

Kodama, L. Beitrage zur Anatomie des Zentralnervensystems der Japaner. VIII. Insula Reil ii. *Folia Anatomica Japan* 12:423–444, 1934.

Kutas, M., and S. A. Hillyard. Event-related potentials in cognitive science. In M. S. Gazzaniga, ed. *Handbook of Cognitive Neuroscience.* New York: Plenum Press, 1984.

Lassen, N. A., D. H. Ingvar, and E. Skinhøj. Brain function and blood flow. *Scientific American* 239:62–71, 1978.

Lauter, J. Dichotic identification of complex sounds: Absolute and relative ear advantrages. *Journal of the Acoustical Society of America* 71:701–707, 1982.

LeMay, M. Asymmetries of the skull and handedness. *Journal of the Neurological Sciences* 32:243–253, 1977.

LeMay, M. Morphological aspects of human brain asymmetry. *Trends in Neurosciences* 5:273–275, 1982.

LeMay, M., and A. Culebras. Human brain-morphologic differences in the hemispheres demonstrable by carotid arteriography. *New England Journal of Medicine* 287: 168–170, 1972.

Levy, J., and J. M. Levy. Human lateralization from head to foot: Sex-related factors. *Science* 200:1291–1292, 1978.

Levy, J., and J. M. Levy. Foot-length asymmetry, sex, and handedness. *Science* 212:1418–1419, 1981.

Levy, J., C. Trevarthen, and R. W. Sperry. Perception of bilateral chimeric figures following hemispheric deconnection. *Brain* 95:61–78, 1972.

Mascie-Taylor, C. G. N., A. M. MacLarnon, P. M. Lanigan, and I. C. McManus. Foot-length asymmetry, sex, and handedness. *Science* 212:1416–1417.

McRae, D. L., C. L. Branch, and B. Milner. The occipital horns and cerebral dominance. *Neurology* 18:95–98, 1968.

Mishkin, M., and D. G. Forgays. Word recognition as a function of retinal locus. *Journal of Experimental Psychology* 43:43–48, 1952.

Moscovitch, M. Information processing and the cerebral hemispheres. In M. Gazzaniga, ed. *Handbook of Behavioral Neurobiology,* vol. 2. New York: Plenum Press, 1979.

Nachson, I., and A. Carmon. Hand preference in sequential and spatial discrimination tasks. *Cortex* 11:123–131, 1975.

Natale, M. Perception of nonlinguistic auditory rhythms by the speech hemisphere. *Brain and Language* 4:32–44, 1977.

Neville, H. Event-related potentials in neuropsychological studies of language. *Brain and Language* 11:300–318, 1980.

Noffsinger, D. Dichotic-listening techniques in the study of hemispheric asymmetries. In D. F. Benson and E. Zaidel, eds. *The Dual Brain.* New York: Guilford Press, 1985.

Ojemann, G. A. Brain organization for language from the perspective of electrical stimulation mapping. *Behavioral and Brain Sciences* 6:189–230, 1983.

Oke, A., R. Keller, I. Mefford, and R. N. Adams. Lateralization of norepinephrine in human thalamus. *Science* 200:1411–1413, 1978.

Papcun, G., S. Krashen, D. Terbeek, R. Remington, and R. Harshman. Is the left hemisphere organized for speech, language and/or something else? *Journal of the Acoustical Society of America* 55:319–327, 1974.

Penfield, W., and H. Jasper. *Epilepsy and the Functional Anatomy of the Human Brain.* Boston: Little, Brown, 1954.

Peters, M. Footedness: Asymmetries in foot preference and skill and neuropsychological assessment of foot movement. *Psychological Bulletin* 103:179–192, 1988.

Peters, M. B., B. Petries, and D. Oddie. Foot-length asymmetry, sex, and handedness. *Science* 212:1417–1418, 1981.

Posner, M. I., and M. E. Raichle. *Images of Mind.* New York: Scientific American Library, 1994.

Rasmussen, T., and B. Milner. The role of early left brain injury in determining lateralization of cerebral speech functions. *Annals of the New York Academy of Sciences* 299:355–369, 1977.

Roland, P. E., L. Eriksson, S. Stone-Elander, and L. Widen. Does mental activity change the oxidative metabolism of the brain? *Journal of Neuroscience* 7:2372–2389, 1987.

Roland, P. E., and L. Friberg. Localization of cortical areas activated by thinking. *Journal of Neurophysiology* 53:1219–1243, 1985.

Roland, P. E., E. Skinhøj, N. A. Lassen, and B. Larsen. The role of different cortical areas in man in the organization of voluntary movements in extrapersonal space. *Journal of Neurophysiology* 43:137–150, 1980.

Roy, C. S., and M. B. Sherrington. On the regulation of the blood supply of the brain. *Journal of Physiology* 11:85, 1890.

Rubens, A. B. Anatomical asymmetries of human cerebral cortex. In S. Harnad, R. W. Doty, L. Goldstein, J. Jaynes, and G. Krauthamer, eds. *Lateralization in the Nervous System.* New York: Academic Press, 1977.

Rubens, A. M., M. W. Mahowald, and J. T. Hutton. Asymmetry of the lateral (Sylvian) fissures in man. *Neurology* 26:620–624, 1976.

Rudel, R. G., M. B. Denckla, and E. Spalten. The functional asymmetry of Braille letter learning in normal sighted children. *Neurology* 24:733–738, 1974.

Scheibel, A. B., I. Fried, L. Paul, A. Forsythe, U. Tomiyasu, A. Wechsler, A. Kao, and J. Slotnick. Differentiating characteristics of the human speech cortex: A quantitative Golgi study. In D. F. Benson and E. Zaidel, eds. *The Dual Brain.* New York: Guilford Press, 1985.

Semmes, J. Hemispheric specialization: A possible clue to mechanism. *Neuropsychologia* 6:11–26, 1968.

Sergent, J. Role of the input in visual hemispheric asymmetries. *Psychological Bulletin* 93:481–512, 1983.

Sidtis, J. Predicting brain organization from dichotic listening performance: Cortical and subcortical functional asymmetries contribute to perceptual asymmetries. *Brain and Language* 17:287–300, 1982.

Springer, S. P., and G. Deutsch. *Left Brain, Right Brain,* 4th ed. New York: W. H. Freeman, 1993.

Squires, N. K., and C. Ollo. Human evoked potential techniques: Possible applications to neuropsychology. In H. J. Hannay, ed. *Experimental Techniques in Human Neuropsychology.* New York: Oxford University Press, 1986.

Strauss, E., and C. Fitz. Occipital horn asymmetry in children. *Annals of Neurology* 18:437–439, 1980.

Strauss, E., B. Kosaka, and J. Wada. The neurological basis of lateralized cerebral function: A review. *Human Neurobiology* 2:115–127, 1983.

Strauss, E., B. Kosaka, and J. Wada. Visual laterality effects and cerebral speech dominance determined by the carotid Amytal test. *Neuropsychologia* 23:567–570, 1985.

Taylor, L. B. Localisation of cerebral lesions by psychological testing. *Clinical Neurology* 16:269–287, 1969.

Teszner, D., A. Tzavaras, and H. Hécaen. L'asymetries droite-gauche du planum temporale: À-propos de l'etude de 100 cerveaux. *Revue Neurologique* 126:444–449, 1972.

Teuber, H.-L. Physiological psychology. *Annual Review of Psychology* 6:267–296, 1955.

Van Lancker, D., and V. Fromkin. Hemispheric specialization for pitch and "tone": Evidence from Thai. *Journal of Phonetics* 1:101–109, 1973.

Wada, J. A., R. Clarke, and A. Hamm. Cerebral hemispheric asymmetry in humans: Cortical speech zones in 100 adult and 100 infant brains. *Archives of Neurology* 32:239–246, 1975.

Wada, J., and T. Rasmussen. Intracarotid injection of sodium Amytal for the lateralization of cerebral speech dominance. *Journal of Neurosurgery* 17:266–282, 1960.

Webster, W. G., and A. D. Thurber. Problem solving strategies and manifest brain asymmetry. *Cortex* 14:474–484, 1978.

Witelson, S. F., and W. Pallie. Left hemisphere specialization for language in the newborn: Neuroanatomical evidence of asymmetry. *Brain* 96:641–646, 1973.

Wolf, M. E., and M. A. Goodale. Oral asymmetries during verbal and non-verbal movements of the mouth. *Neuropsychologia* 25:375–396, 1987.

Wyke, M. The effect of brain lesions on an arm-hand precision task. *Neuropsychologia* 6:125–134, 1968.

Zangwill, O. L. *Cerebral Dominance and Its Relation to Psychological Function*. Springfield, Ill.: Charles C. Thomas, 1960.

Zurif, E. Auditory lateralization. Prosodic and syntactic factors. *Brain and Language* 1:391–401, 1974.

chapter ten

10

Variations in Cerebral Asymmetry

Cerebral asymmetry is one of the most remarkable features of cerebral organization and continues to be a source of much theorizing in both the popular and the scientific literature. An important feature of cerebral asymmetry is the considerable individual variation in the pattern of left-right differences in both anatomical and functional asymmetry. By studying the nature of this variation, we may be able to separate the processes that are lateralized and gain insights into the nature of cerebral asymmetry.

INDIVIDUAL VARIATION IN ANATOMICAL ASYMMETRY

No two brains are alike. In fact, no two hemispheres are even grossly alike, as illustrated in Figure 10.1. Brains (and hemispheres) differ in their size, gyral patterns, distribution of gray and white matter, cytoarchitectonics, vascular patterns, neurochemistry, and so forth. The question is whether variations in anatomical organization are related in any meaningful way to factors such as handedness or gender, and whether variations are correlated with functional differences.

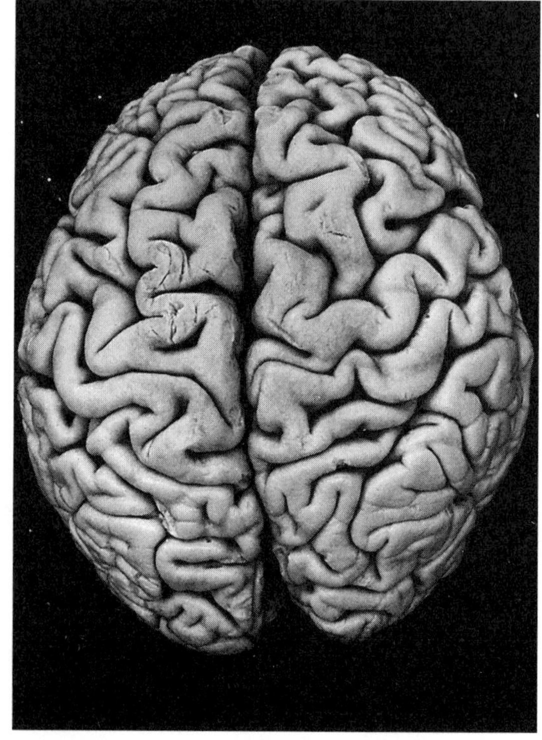

FIGURE 10.1. Photograph of a human brain taken from above. Notice that the two hemispheres appear very different.

Handedness

In 1985, Sandra Witelson thoroughly reviewed the evidence for a relation between anatomical asymmetries and handedness. She found that hand preference is correlated with right-left asymmetry in the parietal operculum, frontal cortex, occipital region, vascular patterns, and cerebral blood flow (Table 10.1). The overall conclusion is that in comparison with right-handers, a higher proportion of left-handers show no asymmetry or a reversal of the direction of anatomical asymmetry. Is this difference of functional significance? To answer this question, Ratcliffe and his colleagues correlated the asymmetry in the course of the Sylvian fissure, as revealed by carotid angiogram, with the results of carotid sodium amobarbital speech testing. They found that left- and right-handers with speech in the left hemisphere had a mean right-left difference of 27° in the angle formed by the vessels leaving the posterior end of the Sylvian fissure. Left- and right-handers with speech in the right hemisphere or with bilaterally represented speech had a mean difference of 0°. Thus, the anatomical asymmetry in their population was related to speech representation and not necessarily to handedness. In other words, the location of speech was a better predictor of individual variation in anatomical organization than was handedness.

Handedness may appear to be more closely related to anatomical anomalies because there is more variation in lateralization of speech in left-handers. A series of studies by Yakovlev and Rakic is germane. In a study of more than 300 cases, they found that in 80% of the cases the pyramidal tract descending to the right hand contains more fibers than does the same tract going to the left hand. Apparently, there are more fibers descending to the right hand both from the contralateral left hemisphere and from the ipsilateral right hemisphere than there are to the left hand. In addition, the contralateral tract from the left hemisphere crosses at a higher level in the medulla than does the contralateral tract from the right hemisphere. To date, data are only available for 11 left-handers, but the pattern is remarkably similar to that observed in the population at large: 9 of 11 (82%) of these cases had the typical right-side bias. Since two-thirds of these left-handers could have been expected to have speech localized on the left, there appears to be a closer relationship between locus of language and pyramidal tract

TABLE 10.1. Variations in anatomical asymmetry related to handedness

		Anatomical differences		
Measure	Handedness	Left larger (%)	Right larger (%)	No difference (%)
Blood volume	Right	25	62	13
	Left	64	28	8
Parietal operulum	Right	67	8	25
	Left	22	7	71
Frontal width	Right	19	61	20
	Left	27	40	33
Occipital width	Right	66	9	25
	Left	38	27	35
Occipital horns	Right	60	10	30
	Left	38	31	31

Source: Data from Hochberg and LeMay (1975), LeMay (1977), Carman et al. (1972), and McRae et al. (1968).

organization than between handedness and pyramidal tract organization.

A difficulty in accounting for variations in anatomical asymmetries is that there are both left- and right-handers in whom there is a marked dissociation between morphological and functional asymmetry. Thus, carotid sodium amobarbital testing may show speech to be in the left hemisphere, but the enlarged temporoparietal speech zone is inferred from other neurological studies to be in the right hemisphere. Consider also that a large percentage of the right-handed cases summarized in Table 10.1 do not show the expected asymmetries but have reversed asymmetries or no differences at all. These cases do pose a significant interpretation problem, and they suggest that other variables, still unknown, may also account for individual differences in both left- and right-handers.

One possible variable is that the connections of the two hemispheres may differ. To test this idea Witelson studied the hand preference of terminally ill subjects on a variety of unimanual tasks. She later did postmortem studies of their brains, paying particular attention to the size of the corpus callosum. She found that the cross-sectional area (Figure 10.2) was 11% greater in left-handed and ambidextrous people than in right-handed people, as summarized in Table 10.2. It remains to be determined whether the larger callosum of non-right-handers contains a greater total number of fibers, thicker axons, or more myelin. If the larger callosum is due to the number of fibers, the difference would represent some 25 million fibers! If Witelson's result is confirmed by others, it will imply that there is greater interaction between the hemispheres of left-handers and will suggest that the pattern of cerebral organization may be fundamentally different in left- and right-handers.

Gender

Less of the variation in anatomical asymmetry of the cerebral hemispheres can be associated with differences between males and females than with differences related to handedness. Although it is often stated that the cerebral hemispheres of females are less symmetrical than those of males, this conclusion is based largely on nonsignificant

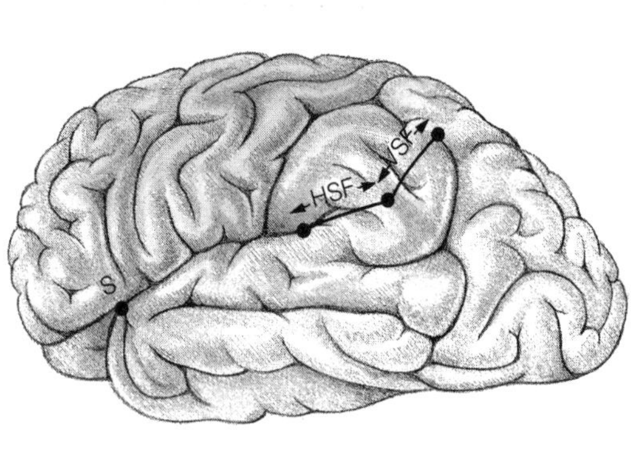

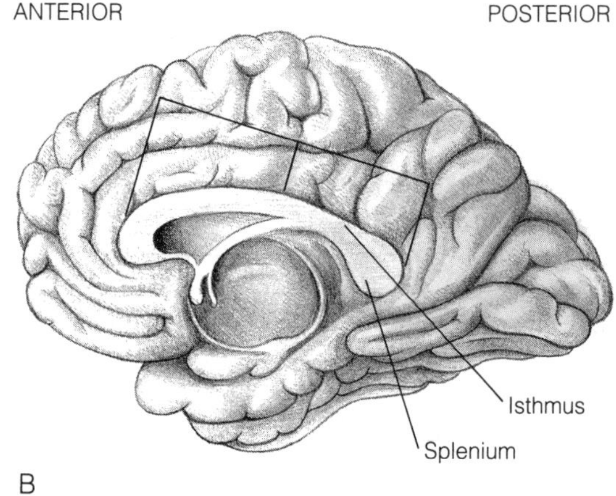

FIGURE 10.2. *A*. Side view of the human brain illustrating the measuring points on the Sylvian fissure. HSF refers to the horizontal portion; S refers to the beginning of the fissure; VSF refers to the vertical portion. *B*. The human corpus callosum shown in midsagittal section. The subdivisions that are typically measured are indicated: the entire length and cross-sectional area; the anterior and posterior halves; and the splenium.

TABLE 10.2. Summary of brain measures in four hand-sex groups

Group	n	Age (years)	Brain weight (g)	Callosal area (mm²)
Males				
RH	7	48	1442	672
MH	5	49	1511	801[a]
Females				
RH	20	51	1269	655
MH	10	49	1237	697[a]

Note: RH = consistently right-handed; MH = left-handed or ambidextrous.

[a] Differs significantly from other same-sex group.

Source: Simplified from Witelson, 1985.

trends or impressions. We are aware of only three statistically reliable differences related to gender in the cerebral hemispheres of humans. First, the asymmetry (left larger than right) in the planum temporale is seen more often in males than in females. In fact, a recent MRI study by Kulynych and colleagues found a large asymmetry in males (left 38% larger) but no asymmetry in females. This result is not found universally (for example, Aboitiz et al.), however, so we must interpret it with caution. Second, Witelson and Kigar quantified the slope of the Sylvian fissure with reference to various cortical landmarks (see Figure 10.2A). This led to a separate measure of the horizontal and vertical components of the Sylvian fissure. They found that although the horizontal component was longer in the left hemisphere of both sexes, men had a larger horizontal component in the left hemisphere than females. There was no difference in the right hemisphere. Thus, males have a larger asymmetry in the Sylvian fissure than females. Taken together, the results of the studies of the planum temporale and the Sylvian fissure suggest a sex difference in the organization of language-related functions. Third, de Lacoste-Utamsing and Holloway reported that the posterior part of the corpus callosum (the **splenium**) is significantly larger in females than in males (see Figure 10.2B). These callosal data have sparked considerable interest and controversy. In fact, this difference has received considerable publicity in the popular press, where it has been described as an established fact. *Time* magazine concluded that the difference is "possibly the basis for women's intuition." The controversy arises from the fact that the data have not been replicated by most others either doing postmortem examinations (see Witelson's data in Table 10.2) or using MRI scans. Wahlsten and Bishop reviewed 28 studies and concluded that there is no compelling evidence for any sex difference. Therefore, a cautious reading of the literature must lead to the conclusion that a sex difference is not yet established for the corpus callosum.

One of the most thorough studies of the callosum is being done by Witelson, who has been conducting an extensive study of the postmortem brains of individuals who have undergone neuropsychological testing before death. The advantage of her studies is that she is able to determine handedness and measure other cognitive functions that might then be correlated with morphology. She found that females do not have a larger callosum, or a larger splenium, even when size is corrected for brain weight, which is larger in males because they are larger overall. However, she did find that the relatively thin region just in front of the splenium (the isthmus) is relatively larger in females. In addition, she found that the callosal size decreases with chronological age in males but not in females. Furthermore, she found that callosal size in males, but not in females, varies with handedness. The interaction with sex, age, and handedness is instructive, since these variables are seldom controlled in postmortem studies. Future studies will need to control them carefully.

HANDEDNESS AND FUNCTIONAL ASYMMETRY

As the term *sinister*—usually used to mean wicked or evil, but originally meaning left-hand side in Latin—implies, left-handedness historically has been viewed as somewhat strange or unusual. The most commonly cited figure for left-handedness is 10%, representing the number of people who write with the left hand, but when other criteria are used, estimates range from 10% to 30%. The problem is that handedness is not absolute; some people are nearly totally left-handed, whereas others are ambidextrous (that is, they use either hand with equal facility). A rather useful distribution of handedness has been described by Annett (Table 10.3), who asked more than 2000 adults to indicate the hand they used to perform each of 12 different tasks. It can be seen that the evidence of left-handedness on Annett's tasks varied from a low of about 6% when cutting with scissors to a high of about 17% when dealing cards.

Theories of Hand Preference

The many theories put forward to account for hand preference can be categorized according to their environmental, anatomical, or genetic emphases.

Environmental Theories. There are three variations on an environmental theory of handedness, and they stress the utility of behavior, reinforcement, or accident, respectively. The first variation, the behavioral (sometimes called the theory of the Peloponnesian Wars, or the sword-and-shield hypothesis) is that a soldier who held his shield in his left hand better protected his heart and improved his chances of survival. Since the left hand was holding the shield, the right hand became more skilled in various movements and eventually was used for most tasks. According to a female-oriented variant of this theory, it is adaptive for a mother to hold an infant in her left hand so that it will be soothed by the rhythm of the mother's heart; the mother, like the soldier, then has the right hand free and so uses it for executing skilled movements. Such theories have difficulties, the most obvious being their failure to consider the possibility that right-handedness preceded, and thus is responsible for, the behavior. For example, MacNeilage and coworkers have proposed that feeding monkeys used their left hand to reach for fruit in trees and their right hand to hang on to the tree. Being stronger, the right hand eventually became the dominant hand in ground-dwelling primates, including humans.

The second variation on an environmental theory, that of reinforcement, has been elaborated by Collins. It is based on some ingenious experiments on "handedness" in mice: Collins raised mice in a world biased in such a way that the mice were forced to use either their left or right paws to obtain food located in a tube adjacent to the wall of their home cage. He found that the proportion of adult right- and left-pawed mice was directly related to which type of world they were raised in. Thus, he suggested, their preference was established by the contingencies of reinforcement from their environment. This view can be adapted to humans. The child's world is also right-handed in many ways, which reinforces the use of that hand. In addition, children in many countries were once forced to write with their right hands. Although emphasizing the potential importance of environmental factors, Collins's theory does not account for the difference between familial and nonfamilial handedness or the relation of handedness to cerebral dominance. It also seems to be contradicted by what happened when children were given their choice of hand in learning to write: the incidence of left-handed

TABLE 10.3. Summary of handedness in performing various tasks

Task	Left (%)	Either (%)	Right (%)
Dealing cards	17.02	3.32	79.66
Unscrewing jar	16.50	17.49	66.01
Shoveling	13.53	11.89	74.58
Sweeping	13.49	16.89	69.62
Threading needle	13.10	9.74	77.16
Writing	10.60	0.34	89.06
Striking match	9.95	8.74	81.31
Throwing ball	9.44	1.29	89.47
Hammering	9.22	2.54	88.24
Using toothbrush	9.18	8.49	82.33
Using racket	8.10	2.59	89.31
Using scissors	6.20	6.81	86.99

Note: Percentages based on 2321 respondents.
Source: Adapted from Annett, 1970.

writing rose only to 10%, which is the norm in most societies that have been studied.

According to the third variation on a theory of environmental influences on hand preference, there is a genetically determined bias toward being right-handed, but left-handed occurs through some cerebral deficit caused by accident. To account for the familial aspect of left-handedness Bakan and his colleagues have argued that there is a high probability of stressful births among left-handers, which increases the risk of brain damage and so maintains the incidence of left-handedness. This theory would predict that some consistent deficit in cognitive functioning in adult left-handers should result from their brain damage, but no such deficit has been shown. It could be argued that since the alleged damage occurs in infancy, the brain compensates in such a way that the only symptom that appears in adulthood is left-handedness, but this argument is hardly compelling support for the theory.

Anatomical Theories. Of the several anatomical theories of handedness, two, which are well documented, explain hand preference on the basis of anatomical asymmetry. In the first theory, right-handedness is attributed to enhanced maturation and ultimately greater development of the left hemisphere. Generalizing from this assumption, it is predicted that nonfamilial left-handers should show an asymmetry mirroring that of right-handers, whereas familial left-handers should show no anatomical asymmetry. These predictions are difficult to assess because no studies have specifically considered anatomical asymmetry with respect to handedness or to familial history and handedness. A major problem with this theory is that it simply pushes the question one step backward, asking not "why handedness?" but instead "why anatomical asymmetry?"

The second theory addresses this problem in part. As Morgan has pointed out, many animals have a left-sided developmental advantage that is not genetically coded. For example, there is a left-sided bias for the location of the heart, the size of the ovaries in birds, the control of birdsong, the size of the left temporal cortex in humans, the size of the left side of the skull in the great apes, and so on. This predominance of left-favoring asymmetries puts the more celebrated left hemisphere speech dominance in the more general perspective of all anatomical asymmetries. Since neither genetic evidence nor genetic theory accurately predicts these human asymmetries, Morgan assumes that they all result from some fundamental asymmetries in human body chemistry. The problem with Morgan's theory as applied to handedness is that it fails to explain left-handedness in the presence of other "normal" asymmetries such as the location of the heart.

Hormonal Theories. Geschwind and Galaburda proposed that cerebral asymmetry can be modified significantly during early life, leading to anomalous patterns of hemispheric organization. A central part of their theory is that one of the factors acting to alter cerebral organization during development is testosterone, the principal male hormone. Testosterone is known to have an effect on the development of the hypothalamus and cortex of nonhuman species, as well as on non-neural tissues, so it is reasonable to suggest that it has an effect on the human brain as well. Geschwind and Galaburda suggest that testosterone's effect is largely inhibitory, meaning that higher than normal levels of testosterone will slow development, possibly acting directly on the brain or indirectly through an action on genes. Central to the Geschwind-Galaburda theory is the idea that testosterone's inhibitory action occurs largely in the left hemisphere, thus allowing the right hemisphere to grow more rapidly. This leads to altered cerebral organization and, in some people, to left-handedness. A further feature of the theory is that testosterone also affects the immune system, leading to more diseases related to a malfunctioning immune system. (A parallel theory of the relation between the immune system and male afflictions has been proposed by Gualtieri and Hicks.)

The Geschwind-Galaburda theory has many details and arguments, which are beyond us here, but the theory has generated considerable research. Unfortunately, the bulk of the available evidence does not support the model (for a thorough review, see Bryden, McManus, and Bulman-Fleming). For example, in one study Grimshaw and colleagues studied handedness in children whose mothers had undergone amniocentesis, and from whom fetal levels of testosterone could be assessed. Increased testosterone levels did not result in increased left-handedness.

Genetic Theories. Of the many genetic models for handedness, most postulate a dominant gene or genes for right-handedness and a recessive gene or genes for left-handedness, but none of these models can accurately predict the probability of left-handedness.

The two best attempts to develop genetic models of handedness are those of Annett and of Levy and Nagylaki. Annett has proposed that there may be a gene for right-handedness but not for left-handedness. In the absence of the right-handed gene, the displayed handedness will be random. The incidence of right-handedness would be slightly higher in the group without the gene because of environmental factors predisposing the choice of the right hand. The theory proposed by Levy and Nagylaki is somewhat more complex. They propose a two-gene, four-allele model. That is, there is a gene for handedness and a gene for hemispheric representation of speech. The gene for left-handedness and the gene for having speech in the right hemisphere are both recessive.

Genetic theories have been criticized on a number of grounds (see Hardyck and Petrinovich), and none of these theories is totally satisfactory. For example, there is no attempt to differentiate between familial and nonfamilial left-handers.

From this review of theories of handedness, it is clear that we do not know why there is handedness, and we may never know. (To the multiplicity of theories of handedness we add our own: a man named Noah was disliked by his fellow townspeople because he was right-handed and they were southpaws and because he insisted on building an ark in the desert. A great flood came and everyone was drowned except Noah and his right-handed family. The rest is history.)

Cerebral Organization in Left-Handers

There appears to be a widespread belief in the neurological literature that cognitive functions are more bilaterally organized in left-handers than in right-handers. This conclusion probably arose from the aphasia literature, in which there are reports that aphasia occurs more often in left-handers than in right-handers with comparable damage, but that recovery from aphasia is more rapid and complete in the left-handers. Careful examination of the literature suggests, however, that these conclusions are based largely on compilations of scattered individual cases rather than on systematic studies of unselected cases. Two recent large-scale studies suggest that the well-known difference between cerebral organization in left- and right-handers may be wrong. First, in the previous chapter we discussed the sodium amobarbitol procedure and reported the data of Rasmussen and Milner. They found that 70% of left-handers appear to have language represented in the left hemisphere, 15% in the right hemisphere, and 15% bilaterally. Second, Kimura reported the incidence of aphasia and apraxia in a consecutive series of 520 patients selected only for unilateral brain damage. The frequency of left-handedness in her population was within the expected range, and these patients did not have a higher incidence of either aphasia or apraxia than right-handers. In fact, the incidence of aphasia was approximately 70% of the incidence in right-handers, exactly what would be predicted from the sodium amobarbitol studies. Thus, although a small proportion of left-handers may have bilateral speech or right hemisphere speech, the majority of left-handers do not.

It has been suggested that left-handers can be subdivided into two populations differing in cerebral organization: familial left-handers, who have a family history of left-handedness, and nonfamilial left-handers, who have no such family history. According to Hécaen and Sauguet, nonfamilial left-handed patients with unilateral lesions perform like right-handed patients on neuropsychological tests. In contrast, familial left-handers perform much differently, suggesting to Hécaen and Sauguet that they have a different pattern of cerebral organization.

In summary, we can find little evidence that the cerebral organization of speech or nonspeech functions in the 70% of left-handers with speech represented in the left hemisphere differs from the cerebral organization of these functions in right-handers. One caveat must be issued, however: there is a larger incidence of left-handedness among mentally defective children and children with various neurological disorders than is found in the general population. This is not surprising, however, because if the dominant hemisphere is injured at an early age, handedness and dominance can move under the control of what would normally be the nondominant hemisphere. Since there are so many more right-handed children, it would be expected by probability alone that more right-handed children with left hemisphere damage would switch to right hemisphere dominance than would switch in the reverse direction. That such switching can occur, however, cannot be used as grounds for predicting cognitive deficits or differences in cerebral organization in the general population of left-handers.

An additional question concerns the organization of the cerebral hemispheres in left-handers who have right hemisphere speech. It is reasonable to wonder if these people simply have a straight reversal of functions from one hemisphere to the other. Unfortunately, little is known about cerebral organization in people who have right hemisphere speech and otherwise normal brains.

SEX DIFFERENCES IN CEREBRAL ORGANIZATION

One of the most obvious sources of individual variation in the behavior of humans is gender: males and females behave differently. The question is whether any differences in cognitive behavior between males and females can be attributed to biological differences between the brains of the two sexes. There is substantial anecdotal and experimental evidence of such cognitive differences, and there have been several attempts to relate these to differences in brain organization. If any one principle can be abstracted to distinguish the sexes, it is that females tend to be more fluent than males in the use of language, and males tend to be better than females at spatial analysis. These differences have been attributed to the possibility of a difference between the sexes in the pattern of cerebral organization, but before considering the theories we shall review the data.

Evidence of Sex Differences

Evidence supporting the argument that there are significant sex differences in cerebral organization derive primarily from studies of normal subjects, laterality studies, cerebral blood-flow measurements, and neurological patients.

Normal Subjects. The place to start in the study of cognitive differences between males and females is with *The Psychology of Sex Differences,* a book published by MacCoby and Jacklin in 1974. In their thorough review of the literature to 1974 they found four reliable sex differences. First, girls have greater verbal ability than boys. At about age 11, the sexes begin to diverge, with female superiority increasing through high school and possibly beyond. Girls score higher on tasks involving both receptive and productive language and on high-level verbal tasks (analogies, comprehension of difficult written material, creative writing) as well as on lower-level measures (fluency). A simple demonstration of this sex difference can be seen when males and females are asked to fill in the blanks, as illustrated in Figure 10.3D. In this test the first letter of each of four words is provided. The task is to fill in missing letters to make a meaningful sentence. Females are much better at this task than males. Overall the magnitude of female superiority at verbal skills is small, in the range of one-quarter of a standard deviation.

Second, males excel in visual-spatial ability. This means that on tests of recall and detection of shapes, mental rotation of two- or three-dimen-

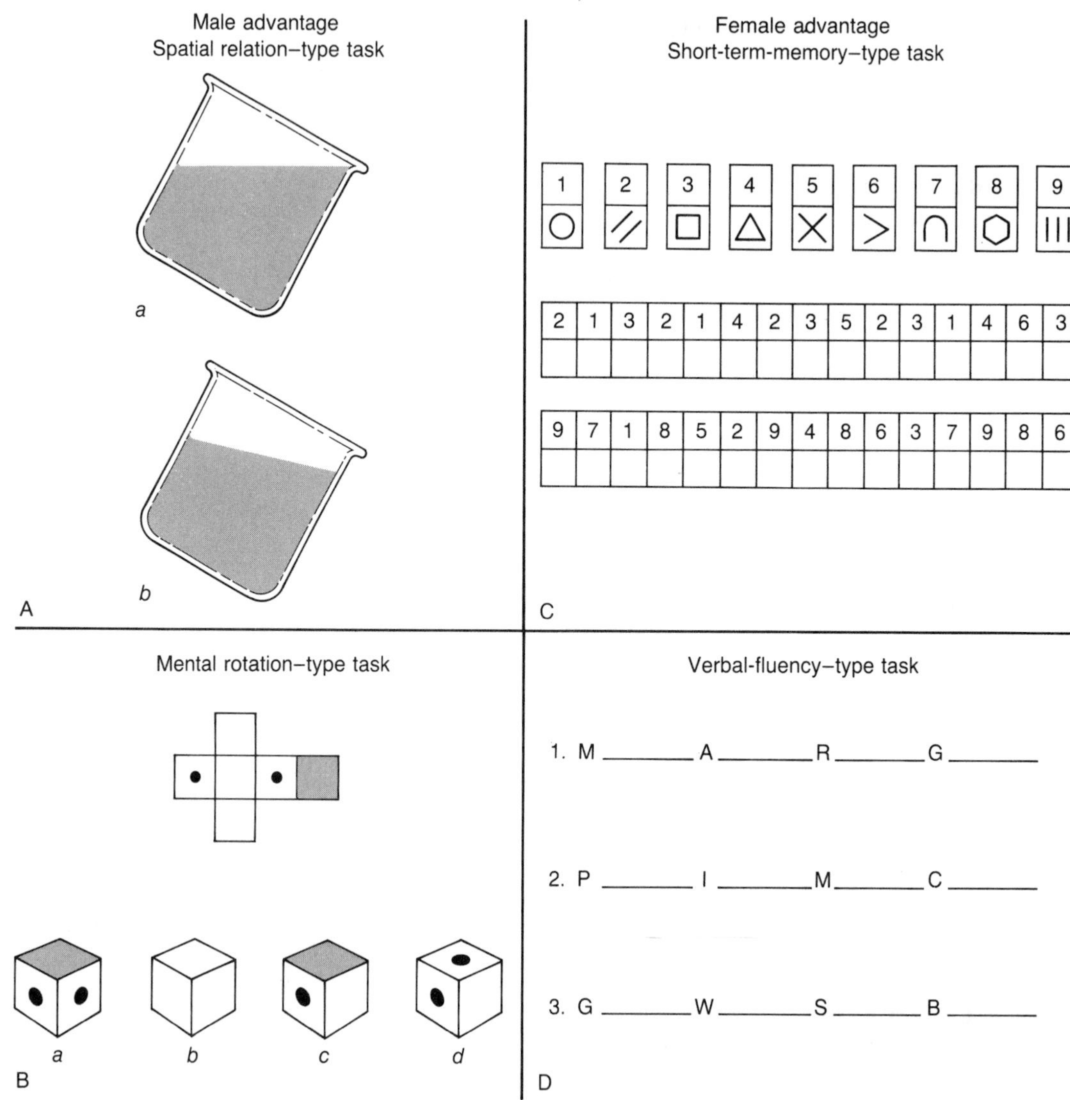

FIGURE 10.3. Examples of four types of tasks that reliably show sex-related differences. *A.* The top drawing shows a line drawn to indicate waterline in which the response indicates comprehension of the concept of horizontality of fluid level. The bottom illustration shows the line drawn incorrectly, indicating no comprehension of the concept. The bottom response is typical of about two-thirds of females. *B.* This task, which is similar to those in the spatial relations test of the Differential Aptitude Test, requires the subject to choose the one box from the bottom four that could be made from the plan above. Males typically find this task much easier than females. *C.* In this test the subject must fill in the empty boxes in the bottom rows with the appropriate symbols from the examples at the top. This is similar to the digit symbol test on the Wechsler intelligence tests. When given a larger number of boxes to fill in and a time limit of 90 sec, females complete 10%–20% more items than males. *D.* This test of verbal fluency requires the subject to fill in each blank to form words that make a sentence. Females are faster at this type of test than males.

sional figures, geometry, maze learning, map reading, aiming at and tracking objects, and geographical knowledge, males perform better on average than do females. Simple tests that can be used to demonstrate this sex difference are illustrated in Figure 10.3. For example, in the water level task (A) used by Thomas and coworkers, subjects are shown a tipped flask and asked to draw in the waterline. The researchers report that among 62 randomly chosen college men the error in estimating the angle of the water was about 2° off the horizontal. Of 91 women, 28 (31%) showed the same performance as men, whereas the remainder showed an error of 15° to 20°. In other words, although the men in his sample understood that the waterline remained horizontal, 69% of the women did not. In developmental studies Thomas and colleagues report that by 12 years of age most males indicate that the waterline is horizontal, but that females who perform in this way do so at a somewhat later age. Like the verbal advantage of females, the spatial advantage of males is small, the difference being only about 0.4 of a standard deviation.

Third, boys excel in mathematical ability. Although the two sexes are similar in their early acquisition of quantitative concepts and their mastery of arithmetic, beginning at about age 12 to 13 boys' mathematical skills increase faster than girls'. The better mathematical skills of boys is partly a function of the number of mathematics courses taken, since boys do take more courses, but this accounts for only part of the difference. Perhaps the most interesting studies on this issue have been done by Benbow and Stanley. In 1971 Julian Stanley founded the Study of Mathematically Precocious Youth. Over a 15-year period thousands of 12-year-old children have been given the Scholastic Aptitude Test Mathematics exam. Stanley's project was particularly interested in the children with the highest scores because they might be assumed to be least affected by extraneous factors such as social pressures. The curious thing they discovered is that the sex difference increased as the scores increased, That is, although the average score was only marginally higher for males than females, when they looked only at the children with the highest scores they found an enormous sex difference: there were 12 times as many "gifted" boys as girls. Furthermore, this ratio was found worldwide across different cultures, although the absolute scores varied with educational system. Benbow and Stanley have searched for, but have not found, support for a primarily environmental explanation of their data. The authors did find that mathematically gifted children are twice as likely as normal children to be left-handed or to have allergies, which suggests some physiological difference in these children. In addition, the authors point out that firstborn children are exposed to higher levels of prenatal hormones, and most of their mathematically gifted children are firstborns. Benbow concludes that there must be some biological factor that contributes to the sex difference but emphasizes that environmental factors may interact with the biology. Benbow and Stanley's research has proved controversial, and there is a continuing debate over the finding that males perform better at math.

Fourth, males are physically more aggressive than females. A sex difference is present as early as social play begins, at age 2 to 3 years, and remains through the college years. Studies with nonhuman primates and rodents show that the increased aggression in males is probably a result of the male hormone testosterone both pre- and postnatally. Castrating infant male rats or monkeys decreases aggression, and treating females with testosterone increases aggression.

The appearance of sex differences in the performance of what appear to be simple tests has important implications for neuropsychological assessment, since gender may be significant in predicting what normal performance levels should be. Consider the following example. We gave school-age children three tests widely used in neuropsychological assessment and found sex differences on two of the tests (Figure 10.4). On the Draw-a-Bicycle Test (we used a scoring system that looked for specific details like handlebars, pedals, and spokes) males performed better than females; on the Chicago Word-Fluency Test (the test requires the subject to write as many words

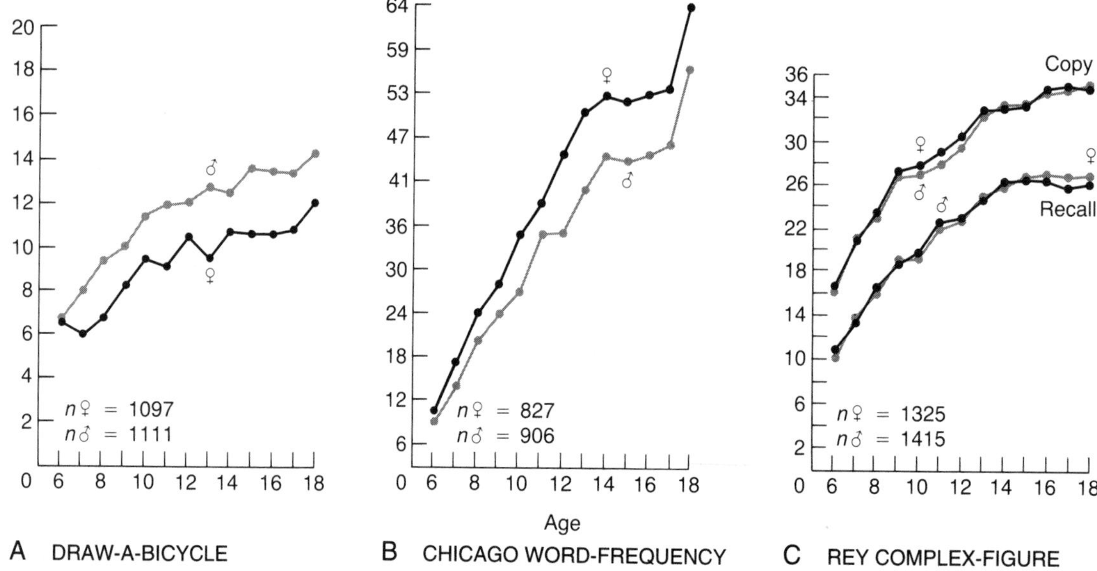

FIGURE 10.4. Performance of males and females of different ages on three neuropsychological tests. *A.* On the Draw-a-Bicycle Test, males obtain higher scores than females. *B.* On the Chicago Word-Fluency Test, females perform better than males. *C.* On the copy and recall of the Rey figure, there is no difference in performance between males and females. (Whishaw and Kolb, unpublished.)

beginning with "s" as possible in 5 min and as many four-letter words beginning with "c" as possible in 4 min), females performed better—at some ages by as much as 10 words—than males. On the copy and recall of the Rey figure (see Figure 13.7C), there was no sex difference. The appearance of reliable sex differences on these clinical tests implies that separate norms are necessary for the clinical assessment of males and females, although to date these separate norms have not been established for very many clinical tests.

The sex differences described by MacCoby and Jacklin have often been described as a "spatial" advantage for males and a "verbal" advantage for females, but more recent research has indicated that this dichotomy is too simple; there is a broader pattern of differences that cannot be labeled easily as verbal and spatial. Thus, females excel at both perceptual speed and visual memory (see Figure 10.3C), whereas males are better at perceptual closure (see Figure 13.7D), the disembedding of visual patterns from complex arrays (see Figure 13.7B), map-reading, and target-directed skills such as guiding or intercepting projectiles. The fact that females are superior at perceptual speed and visual memory is not predicted from a simple description of their superior abilities as "verbal," although males still appear to perform best at "spatial-type" tests. Finally, some researchers have been impressed by anecdotal evidence that males appear to excel at chess and musical composition. In Russia, where chess is a national pastime, no women have achieved grandmaster status, and women compete in separate tournaments. In music, women appear to be as competent in performing as men, but fewer excel in composition. It has been suggested that men have an advantage in these fields, as well as in mathematics, because all involve spatial ability. There may be substance to the argument that sex differences in chess and musical composition can be attributed to spatial factors, but it is also easy to suggest cultural and environmental reasons for why women have not excelled in these areas. For example, throughout life males have greater freedom of movement and receive more encouragement to compete in sports, and the differential in experiences that accrues to them as a result of these experiences could be reflected on spatial tests.

Laterality Studies. If the differences described above are physiological rather than cultural, one might expect to find a sex difference in the distribution of verbal and spatial functions between the hemispheres in laterality studies. The literature on sex-related differences in lateralization is characterized by inconsistencies, however. As Bryden emphasizes, procedural differences, small samples, and great variability plague this research, and it is difficult to be certain that observed differences truly reflect differences in laterality in the population. Nonetheless, he concludes that the majority of the verbal dichotic and verbal tachistoscopic studies that show any sex-related effects indicate a greater degree of lateralization in males. Furthermore, although sex-related differences are not as consistent on tests of spatial processing, there is some evidence that males are more lateralized on tests in both the visual and the tactile senses. We must emphasize, however, that sex differences in the degree or perceptual asymmetries can be profoundly influenced by the way in which the subjects approach the task. For example, women may tend to use verbal strategies to solve spatial problems and to encode spatial displays, and this may generate a laterality effect not because of a difference in cerebral lateralization of function between the sexes, but because of a difference in strategy or preferred cognitive mode used to solve the task. On the basis of the evidence to date, we must concur with Bryden that this alternative explanation seems reasonably plausible.

Cerebral Blood Flow. Some of the variation in studies of changes in cerebral blood flow during cognitive activity is apparently related to gender as well as to handedness. In 1982, Gur and his colleagues found that females and left-handers have a higher rate of cerebral blood flow and a greater percentage of fast-perfusing tissue (rapid blood exchange) than do right-handed males. All groups showed an increase in blood flow to the left hemisphere during verbal tasks and a complementary increase in blood flow to the right hemisphere during spatial tasks, but females and male left-handers showed reliably greater increases than right-handed males. The authors took these data to suggest possible differences in the distribution of gray and white matter in the two hemispheres of males and females, although confirmation of this hypothesis awaits postmortem studies. The authors failed to find support for a simple difference between verbal and spatial processing in the two sexes, however, because both sexes exhibited an increase in left hemisphere blood flow during the verbal task and in right hemisphere blood flow during the spatial task.

Neurological Patients. Although Lansdell first reported a sex-related difference in the effects of left and right temporal lobectomies in 1962, it was a series of papers by McGlone in the late 1970s and early 1980s that proved to be seminal for the study of sex differences in neurological patients. Her work led others to consider the possibility of at least two sex-related differences in neurological patients.

First, there appears to be a different pattern of results in the effects of lateralized lesions on the performance and verbal achievement subscales of the Wechsler Adult Intelligence Scale (WAIS) (see Chapter 25 for details of the WAIS). By using various statistical procedures with these data, Inglis and Lawson showed that although left and right hemisphere lesions differently affected verbal and performance subscales in males, left hemisphere lesions in females depressed both IQs equally, and right hemisphere lesions failed to depress either IQ (Figure 10.5). Thus, Inglis and Lawson found an equivalent effect of left hemisphere lesions on verbal IQ in both sexes, but males with right hemisphere lesions were more disrupted than females. This could imply a different right hemisphere organization in males and females. This seems unlikely, however, as there is

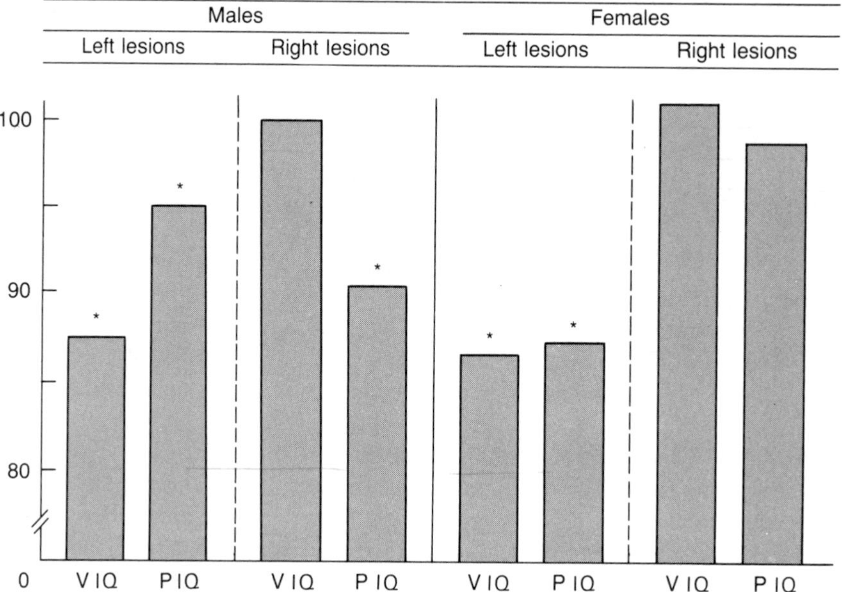

FIGURE 10.5. Summary of Inglis and Lawson's tabulation of studies reporting verbal and performance IQ scores in neurological patients. A clear sex difference emerged in which males with left hemisphere lesions exhibited a depression in verbal IQ (VIQ), whereas males with right hemisphere lesions exhibited a complementary deficit in performance IQ (PIQ). In contrast, females with right hemisphere lesions showed no significant depression in either IQ scale. The asterisks indicate scores that differ significantly from 100.

no evidence of a sex difference in a variety of symptoms commonly associated with right hemisphere damage. On the other hand, it could be that females are more likely than males to use verbal strategies (that is, a verbal cognitive mode) to solve the tests in the performance scale.

Second, work by Kimura has shown that the pattern of cerebral organization *within* each hemisphere may differ between the sexes. Although males and females were nearly as likely to be aphasic following left hemisphere lesions, males were likely to be aphasic and apraxic after damage to either the anterior or the posterior cortex, whereas females were far more likely to experience speech disorders and apraxia after anterior lesions than after posterior lesions (Figure 10.6). Kimura also reported data from a small sample of patients that suggest an analogous sex-related difference following right hemisphere lesions. Anterior, but not posterior, lesions in females impaired performance of the block design and object-assembly subtests of the WAIS, whereas males were equally affected on these tests by either anterior or posterior lesions. We have found parallel results in our studies of rats with prefrontal lesions: male rats with these lesions have much smaller deficits in various tests of spatial navigation than do female rats with similar lesions. This may suggest that there is a fundamental difference between the sexes in the intracerebral organization in mammals. In fact, in an anatomical study we were able to show a large difference in the dendritic organization of neurons in the prefrontal cortex of male and female rats. This sex difference was affected by treatments that either increased or decreased testosterone levels during development.

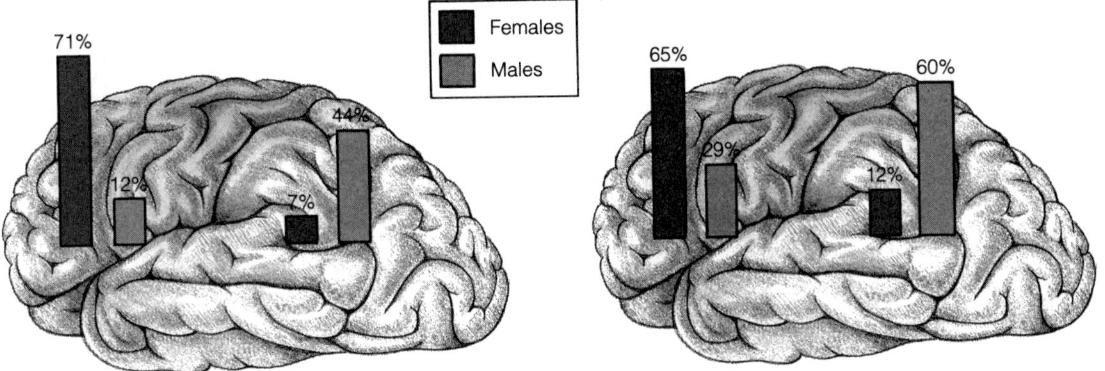

FIGURE 10.6. *A.* Apraxia, or difficulty in selecting hand movements, is associated with frontal damage to the left hemisphere in women and with posterior damage in men. It is also associated with difficulties in organizing speech. *B.* Aphasias, or speech disorders, occur most often in women when damage is to the front of the brain. In men, they occur more frequently when damage is in the posterior region. The data presented above derive from one set of patients. (After Kimura, 1992.)

Recently, Strauss and her colleagues reported a surprising result. They gave sodium amobarbital to 94 epileptic patients who were being considered for elective surgery after infant brain damage. It is well known that left hemisphere injury in infants leads to the shifting of language to the right hemisphere, so they anticipated this to happen in their cases with left hemisphere injury. The unexpected result was that there was a sex difference in the likelihood of cerebral reorganization following left hemisphere injury after 1 year of age: females were unlikely to show reorganization, whereas males appeared likely to shift language, perhaps as late as puberty. This unanticipated result suggests that the male brain may be more plastic after cortical injury, a conclusion that has important implications if it proves to be reliable.

Taken together, the data from neurological patients support the idea that unilateral cortical lesions have different effects in males and females. How the sexes differ in cerebral organization is simply not known at present. McGlone initially suggested that the female brain is functionally more symmetrical than the male brain, but this idea appears to be too simple to account for the data. Kimura's results suggest that there may be intrahemispheric differences in cerebral organization, but her studies need to be replicated by others. Further, there should be an examination of PET results to see if there is a different pattern of activation on specific tasks in males and females. Finally, we must be aware that apparent differences between the sexes, especially left-right ones, may reflect different strategies of problem solving in the two sexes rather than real neurological differences.

Explanation of Sex Differences

We can identify six explanations commonly advanced to account for sex differences: (1) differential brain organization, (2) hormonal effects on cerebral function, (3) genetic sex-linkage, (4) maturation rate, (5) environment, and (6) preferred cognitive mode.

Differential Brain Organization. In previous sections we considered sex differences in cerebral organization as inferred from studies of neurological patients, anatomy, and laterality studies. There is now good evidence that lesions affect males and females differently, but it has not been proved that this is due to differences in brain organization.

Hormonal Effects. There are clear sex differences in the neural control of a wide variety of reproductive and nonreproductive behavior patterns in most vertebrate species. In birds and mammals the presence of testosterone at critical times during development has unequivocal effects on the organization of both hypothalamic and forebrain structures, and it is believed that the observed morphological effects are responsible for the behavioral dimorphism. The influence of gonadal hormones on brain and behavioral development is often referred to as an *inductive* or *organizing* effect, and in the brain this organizing effect is said to lead to *sexual differentiation*. The actions of gonadal hormones (largely androgens) during development are permanent, but the mechanisms of action are still not well understood. It appears that androgens (typically "male" hormones) are converted into estradiol (normally "female" hormones) in the brain, and the binding of this estradiol to receptors leads to masculinization of the brain. Estradiol receptors have been found in the developing cortex of rodents and nonhuman primates, but they are not found in the adults. This suggests that the hormones may have an organizing effect on the brain of mammals only during development, although they can still influence neuronal function later in life.

Although the principal organizing action of hormones is assumed to occur during development, there are reasons to believe that there might be longer significant functional effects of hormones in adulthood. First, Hampson and Kimura have shown that the performance of women on certain tasks changes throughout the menstrual cycle as estrogen levels go up and down. High estrogen levels were associated with relatively depressed spatial ability as well as enhanced articulatory and motor capability. The effect of estrogen fluctuations during the menstrual cycle may be direct or indirect. It is known that catecholamine (for example, epinephrine and dopamine) levels are affected by estrogen and that catecholamine levels fluctuate during the estrous cycle in rats. In view of the importance of catecholamines in movement and other behaviors, it is obvious that estrogen could alter behavior through its stimulation of dopamine receptors in particular. There are dopamine receptors in the prefrontal cortex and medial temporal region, so there is a good possibility that estrogen could alter functioning in these regions.

There are also direct effects of estrogen on the structure of neurons. Woolley and her colleagues have shown that during the female rat's estrous cycle there are large changes in the number of dendritic spines on hippocampal neurons (Figure 10.7). This means that the number of synapses in the female rat's hippocampus goes up and down *in 4-day cycles!* There is little reason to believe that similar changes are not also occurring in the human brain. In a similar vein, Stewart and Kolb have found that female rats that have their ovaries removed in middle age show a dramatic increase in dendrites and spines of cortical neurons. Although these authors did not try to correlate such changes with cyclic fluctuations in the estrogen levels, their results are consistent with the general idea that estrogen has direct effects upon cerebral neurons in the adult animal.

There is also reason to believe that testosterone might affect cognition in adults. In the early part of this century it was believed that testosterone could reverse senescence, but there is little evidence that the hundreds of men given testicular implants actually benefited from this treatment (see an interesting book by Hamilton about this). Nonetheless, more recent evidence suggests that testosterone treatments may influence spatial cognition in older men. Janowsky and her colleagues gave retired men testosterone (or placebo) in scrotal patches and found a significant improvement in performance of spatial tasks but not in verbal or other cognitive measures. Interestingly, when the authors measured blood hormone levels they found a decrease in estradiol as well as an increase in testosterone. The low estradiol levels were correlated with the improved spatial performance. This would be predicted from Hamp-

FIGURE 10.7. Camera lucida drawings of dendrites of hippocampal pyramidal neurons from times of high (*A*) and low (*B*) levels of estrogen during the rats' estrous cycle. Notice that there are many fewer spines during the low period. (After Woolley et al., 1990.)

son's study of monthly fluctuations in women. In other words, it may not be that testosterone is so beneficial as that the suppression of estrogen is.

In summary, there is no question that gonadal hormones have significant effects on brain development and function. Although there is little direct evidence regarding how these effects might relate to the sex differences in cognitive function, there is good reason to suppose that at least some sex differences are related to gonadal hormones. Perhaps the most interesting possibility is that gonadal hormones alter the brain and make male and female brains more or less responsive in different environments. One way they have such an influence is by altering the susceptibility of cortical neurons to the influence of environmental stimuli. For example, Juraska has found that the exposure to gonadal hormones perinatally (that is, around birth) determines the later ability of environmental stimulation to alter dendritic growth. Furthermore, she has shown that the environmentally induced changes in the hippocampus and neocortex are affected differently by gonadal hormones. For instance, the female hippocampus is far more plastic in new environments than the male's, and this plasticity is dependent upon estrogen. This type of hormonally mediated selective effect of experience on the brain is important because it provides a route whereby experiential factors (including social factors) could influence the brain differently in males and females, leading to sex-related variations in the brain and behavior.

The fact that sex hormones are important to cerebral function in adults leads to an interesting possibility: the cognitive functions of the two sexes may diverge functionally at puberty and begin to converge again after menopause. We are unaware of any direct test of this hypothesis.

Genetic Sex-Linkage. A number of authors have proposed that the major factor in determining variation in spatial ability is genetic. It is postulated that a recessive gene on the X (female) chromosome is responsible. Every normal person has 46 chromosomes arranged in 23 pairs, one set from the father and one from the mother. The 23rd pair is composed of the sex chromosomes; if both are X, the child is female (XX), but if one is X and the other Y, the child is male (XY). If a gene for a particular trait is recessive, the trait will not be expressed in a female child unless the gene is present on both X chromosomes. However, the gene need be present only on one chromosome if the child is male. Thus, if a mother carries the gene on both of her X chromosomes, all of her sons will present the trait, but her daughters will show it only if the father also carries the recessive gene on his X chromosome. This hypothesis has generated a lot of interest and research, but a thorough review by Boles concludes that it has yet to be proved.

Maturation Rate. Developmental studies indicate that a fundamental difference in male and female cerebral maturation may help to account for the sex differences observed in adulthood. It has long been known that girls begin to speak sooner than boys; develop larger vocabularies during childhood; and, as children, use more complex linguistic constructions than boys. Further, the speech of young girls may be better enunciated than boys' speech, and girls are generally better readers than boys. Although developmental studies of laterality in children have yielded conflicting results, dichotic and tachistoscopic studies often indicate an earlier evolution of asymmetry in girls than in boys. Since it is well known that females attain physical maturity at an earlier age than males, it is reasonable to propose that the male brain matures more slowly than the female brain and that maturation rate is a critical determinant of brain asymmetry. That is, the more slowly a child matures, the greater the observed cerebral asymmetry. A study by Waber demonstrates just this finding. She reported that, regardless of sex, early-maturing adolescents performed better on tests of verbal abilities than of spatial ones, whereas late-maturing adolescents did the opposite. This study, then, implies that maturation rate may affect the organization of cortical function. Since, on average, females mature faster than males, superior spatial abilities in males may be directly related to their relatively slow development.

Environment. Probably the most influential psychological view of sex-related differences is that different environmental factors shape the behavior of males and females. For example, in the case of spatial ability, it is presumed that male children are expected to exhibit greater independence than females and thus to engage in activities such as exploring and manipulating the environment—activities that improve spatial skills. Harris considered all the research support for this argument and concluded that although a few studies can be found to support the view, the bulk of the evidence fails to do so. For example, in the study by Thomas and colleagues on the horizontality of a liquid (see Figure 10.3A), females who had failed the task were repeatedly shown a bottle half-filled with red water that was tilted at various angles. They were asked to adjust the "pretend waterline" by moving a disk, half red, half white, in a second bottle. Even when the subjects simply had to adjust the pretend waterline to match the visible real waterline, the women failed to show much improvement and were likely to state that "water is level when the bottle is upright but is inclined when the bottle is tilted." Males and females who perform correctly state that "water is always level." A priori, one would have expected females to have had as much experience as males with tilting vessels, and even if they had not, that special instruction would be helpful. This, however, does not seem to be the case. In conclusion, although environmental theories may be appealing, there is no evidence that the observed sex differences in verbal and spatial behaviors can be accounted for solely on the basis of environmental or social factors.

Preferred Cognitive Mode. We have mentioned several times that the strategies that males and females use to solve different tasks may be at least partly responsible for the observed sex differences. It may be that genetic, maturational, and environmental factors predispose males and females to prefer different modes of cognitive analysis. In other words, females develop in such a way that they prefer to solve problems primarily by using a verbal mode. Since this mode is less efficient at solving spatial problems, females exhibit an apparent deficit. By the same logic, females should do better than males at primarily verbal tasks. This proposition has yet to be thoroughly investigated.

Summary

There is evidence that at least four significant cognitive differences are sex-related: verbal differences, visuospatial differences, differences in mathematical ability, and differences in aggression. Although the causes of cognitive sex-related differences are unknown, it is likely that they are at least partly biological. Consider the following data. Harshman and his associates, in a very ambitious study of the interaction of sex and handedness in cognitive abilities, report a significant interaction between sex and handedness; that is, sex-related differences in verbal and visuospatial behavior varied as a function of handedness. (Recall that Witelson also found that callosal size varied by sex and handedness.) It is difficult to imagine how social or environmental factors alone could account for this type of result. It is thus very plausible to account for sex-related differences at least partly by neurological factors that may be modulated by the environment.

ENVIRONMENTAL EFFECTS ON ASYMMETRY

Environment is known to produce significant effects on brain growth in laboratory animals, and so it is reasonable to presume that different environments might affect the human brain differently and produce variation in the pattern of cerebral asymmetry. Two environmental variables would seem to be especially good candidates to consider: culture and literacy.

Cultural Effects on Asymmetry

Most studies of cultural differences have centered on the study of language. It has been proposed that non-European languages such as Japanese and Chinese might have more right hemisphere involvement since there seems to be more prosody (or song) to them. It has also been suggested that those who speak two or more languages may have a different pattern of language organization than those who speak only one. Laterality studies have lent some support to the idea that Asian and Native American languages may be represented more bilaterally in the brain. However, as we have seen, laterality studies can be influenced by many factors, such as strategy and task requirements, and so one would want to be very cautious about making inferences regarding cultural differences in brain organization from these studies. (See Uyehara and Cooper and Obler and colleagues for good discussions of the difficulties.)

Studies of neurological patients have provided no evidence for culturally or linguistically based differences in cerebral organization. A good example is a study by Rapport and coworkers. They evaluated the language functions of seven Chinese-English polyglots, whose mother tongue was Malay, Cantonese, or Hokkien. Their methods included using carotid sodium amobarbital, cortical stimulation, and clinical examination. They found that all these patients were left hemisphere dominant for both the Chinese and the English languages; there was no consistent evidence of increased participation by the right hemisphere for language functions. Although bilingual people probably have all languages located in the left hemisphere, this does not rule out the possibility that the language zones may be enlarged in the left hemisphere or may be slightly different in microorganization. Experience is known to alter somatosensory organization, so an analogous effect of experience on the language zones would seem to be a reasonable expectation. It is likely, however, that the major effects of language and environment on the brain are on the development of particular styles of problem solving (that is, cognitive mode), which are heavily dependent on culture, rather than on changes in cerebral asymmetry per se.

The writing system of the Japanese language provides an unusual opportunity to study cerebral organization because it is distinct from Indo-European languages in that it consists of two types of letters: phonograms (kana) and ideograms (kanji). Phonograms are analogous to English letters, since each phonogram represents a spoken sound. In contrast, the ideogram represents a unit of meaning, which may correspond to a word or words. It has been suggested that for reading the brain may process these two types of characters differently, and even that the right hemisphere might process kanji while the left hemisphere processes kana. There is little support for either idea. For example, in a large series of patients, Sugishita and his colleagues found no clear relationship between deficits in reading either script and locus of left hemisphere injury. In fact, most of their cases were impaired equally at both forms of reading.

Literacy, Hearing, and Asymmetry

Both education and congenital deafness have been alleged to alter hemispheric specialization.

The evidence that schooling changes cerebral organization is scanty and inconclusive, however, being based largely on laterality studies, which are difficult to interpret. Furthermore, illiterate aphasics do not appear to differ from educated ones. On the other hand, there is some evidence that congenital deafness may alter cerebral processing. Although left hemisphere damage produces aphasia in people who use American Sign Language (Ameslan), possibly because of the praxic requirements, there is evidence that congenitally deaf people may have abnormal patterns of cerebral organization. First, several laboratories have independently reported that congenitally deaf persons fail to show the usual right visual-field superiority in tasks of linguistic processing. This failure could be interpreted as evidence that if experience with auditory language is absent, lateralization of some aspect or aspects of nonauditory language functions is abolished. Or, these data could result from strategy differences that are due to different auditory experiences.

Second, Neville reported that during perception of line drawings, visual evoked potentials were significantly larger on the right in children with normal hearing and significantly larger on the left in deaf children who used Ameslan to communicate. Curiously, there was no asymmetry at all in children who could not sign but merely used pantomime to communicate. From the signers' left hemisphere effect for line drawings, Neville inferred that the deaf signers acquire their sign language much as normal children acquire verbal language: with their left hemisphere. Since sign language has a visuospatial component, however, certain visuospatial functions may have developed in the left hemisphere, producing an unexpected left hemisphere effect. The lack of asymmetry in nonsigners could mean that the absence of language experience somehow abolished certain aspects of cerebral asymmetry or, alternatively, that the expression of cerebral asymmetry depends on language experience. If the nonsigners learn Ameslan, and do so before puberty (the reasons are discussed below), they might develop an asymmetrical evoked-potential pattern similar to those of children who already sign.

Although congenital deafness may alter certain aspects of cerebral organization, Kimura, in reviewing 11 cases of signing disorders following brain damage, finds that the similarity with speakers is remarkable. She found that of 9 right-handed signers with left hemisphere lesions, all had a signing disorder. In 2 left-handers, one had a disorder with a left hemisphere lesion and one had a disorder with a right hemisphere lesion. These results are just what would be expected in a population of vocal communicators. Sign comprehension and writing comprehension were affected in much the same way as was signing, but reading was undisturbed. Kimura postulates that reading was spared because it is not syllabically based but is achieved by visual-to-visual matching. Kimura's review is instructive because it shows that the development of a language based on signs has the same anatomical basis as the development of regular vocal languages. This result strongly supports the idea that language has a preferential base and that this base is anatomically determined.

Finally, one piece of evidence pointing to early environment as a factor in asymmetry is based upon a study of Genie, an adolescent girl who endured nearly 12 years of extreme social and experiential deprivation and malnutrition. She was discovered at the age of $13\frac{1}{2}$, after having spent most of her life isolated in a small closed room, during which time she was punished for making any noise. After her rescue, Genie's cognitive development was rapid, although her language lagged behind other abilities. Results of her dichotic listening proved provocative for a right-handed person: although both ears showed normal hearing, there was a strong left-ear (hence right hemisphere) effect for both verbal and nonverbal (environmental) sounds. In fact, the right ear was nearly totally suppressed, a phenomenon characteristic of people with severe left hemisphere injury. Genie's right hemisphere appeared to be processing both verbal and nonverbal acoustic stimuli, as would be the case in people with a left hemispherectomy in childhood.

At least three explanations for Genie's abnormal lateralization are plausible. The first is that

TABLE 10.4. Summary of effects of hemidecortication on verbal and visuospatial abilities

	Left hemidecorticate	Right hemidecorticate
Intelligence	Low normal	Low normal
Language tests		
Single	Normal	Normal
Complex	Poor	Normal
Visuospatial tests		
Simple	Normal	Normal
Complex	Normal	Poor

disuse of the left hemisphere may simply have resulted in degeneration. This seems unlikely. The second is that in the absence of appropriate auditory stimulation the left hemisphere lost the ability to process linguistic stimuli. This is possible, since it is well known that without early exposure to foreign languages, adults have difficulty in learning many phoneme discriminations, even though they were able to make these discriminations as infants (see Werker and Tees). The third hypothesis is that Genie's left hemisphere was either being inhibited by the right hemisphere or by some other structure, or it was performing other functions. This remains to be shown.

Effects of Hemidecortication

If a person has life-threatening seizures resulting from severe infantile cerebral injury, the neocortex of an entire hemisphere may be surgically removed to control the seizures. Although most such surgery is performed during the patient's early adolescence, it is sometimes done in the first year of life, before speech has developed. These latter cases are particularly germane to the question of how cerebral lateralization develops. If the hemispheres vary functionally at birth, then the left and right hemispherectomies would be expected to produce different effects on cognitive abilities. If they do not vary at birth, then no cognitive differences would result from left or right hemidecortications.

The general results of recent studies of linguistic and visuospatial abilities in patients with unilateral hemidecortications support the conclusion that both hemispheres are functionally specialized, although both hemispheres appear to be capable of assuming some functions usually performed by the missing hemisphere. Table 10.4 summarizes these data. Notice that the left hemidecortication produces no severe deficits in visuospatial abilities. Yet the left hemisphere cannot completely compensate for the right hemisphere, as evidenced by the patients' difficulty in performing complex visuospatial tasks.

In an analysis of language abilities, Dennis and Whitaker found that, unlike right hemisphere removals, left hemisphere removals produced deficits in understanding auditory language when the meaning was conveyed by complex syntactic structure, particularly if the sentence contained an error (for example, "The tall guard wasn't shot by the armed robber"), and produced difficulty in determining sentence implication, integrating semantic and syntactic information to replace missing pronouns, and forming judgments of word interrelations in sentences. In an analysis of word comprehension, Dennis found that both hemispheres understand the meaning of words and both can spontaneously produce lists of names of things. When searching for words using different cues, however, the left hemisphere has an advantage over the right. Both hemispheres can name an object from its picture or from its description, but the left hemisphere can identify it on the basis of "rhymes with," whereas the right hemisphere is deficient in using this type of cue. In an analysis of reading skills, Dennis and her coworkers found that both hemispheres had almost equal ability in higher-order reading comprehension; however, the left hemisphere was superior to the right in reading and spelling unfamiliar words and in using sentence structure to achieve fluent reading. The left hemisphere also read prose passages with greater decoding accuracy, more fluency, and fewer errors that violated the semantic and syntactic structure of the sentence. The superiority of the left hemisphere seems to be its ability to manipulate and exploit language rules. The right

both hemis can do simple language tasks, but only left can use language rules hemisphere is not without its strengths in language, though. Performance was better with the right hemisphere in a task that required learning an association between nonsense words and symbols. In summarizing the studies on language Dennis suggests that if written language is thought of as a combination of meaning structure (morphology), sound structure (phonology), and picture structure (logography), then the isolated left hemisphere will show superior performance with morphology and phonology and inferior performance with logographic cues, whereas the isolated right hemisphere will show superior performance with logographic cues and inferior performance with morphological and phonological cues.

An almost analogous pattern of results is observed on tests of visuospatial function. Kohn and Dennis found that although patients with right hemisphere removals performed normally on simple tests of visuospatial functions such as drawing, they were significantly impaired on complex tests such as maze problems and map-reading.

To summarize, each hemisphere can assume some of the opposite hemisphere's functions if the opposite hemisphere is removed during development, but neither hemisphere is totally capable of mediating all of the missing opposite's functions. Thus, although the developing brain gives evidence of considerable plasticity, there is convincing evidence against equipotentiality: both hemispheres appear to have a processing capacity that probably has an innate structural basis. Furthermore, there seems to be a price for assuming new responsibilities. With few exceptions, patients undergoing hemidecortication are of below-average, or at best only average, intelligence, and they are often less than normally proficient at tests of the intact hemisphere's function.

Ontogeny of Asymmetry

Three general theoretical positions can be postulated to account for the ontogeny of cerebral specialization. We have called these (1) the maturation hypothesis, (2) the invariance (left-for-language) hypothesis, and (3) the parallel-development hypothesis. According to the maturation hypothesis, either hemisphere can be specialized for either language or nonlanguage functions, and the occurrence of specialization is entirely a matter of chance. According to the invariance hypothesis, the left hemisphere is special and is organized genetically to develop language skills; the right hemisphere is postulated to be a dumping ground for whatever is left over. According to the parallel-development hypothesis, both hemispheres, by virtue of their construction, play special roles, one hemisphere being destined to specialize in language and the other in nonlanguage functions.

Although there are fairly good arguments for each hypothesis, in our view a parallel-development theory that initially permits some flexibility, or equipotentiality, most usefully explains most of the available data. The cognitive functions of each hemisphere can be conceived as being hierarchical. Simple, or lower-level, functions are represented at the base of the hierarchy, corresponding to functions in primary, sensory, motor, language, or visuospatial areas. More complex, or higher-level, functions are represented farther up the hierarchy, the most complex being at the top; these functions are the most lateralized. At birth the two hemispheres overlap functionally because each is processing low-level behaviors. By age 5 the newly developing higher-order cognitive processes have very little overlap, and each hemisphere thus becomes increasingly specialized. By puberty each hemisphere has developed its own unique functions (Figure 10.8). Note that the cerebral hemispheres are not becoming more lateralized in development; rather, the developing cognitive functions are built on the lower functions, which are innately located in one hemisphere or the other.

All models of cerebral development must answer the question of how functions become restricted to one hemisphere rather than becoming bilateral. The parallel-development hypothesis answers that question. In a series of papers, Moscovitch emphasizes the possibility that one

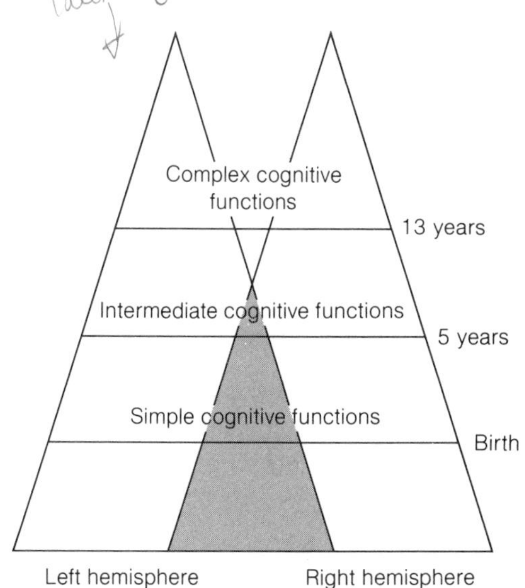

FIGURE 10.8. A model of the development of cognitive function in the left and right hemispheres of normal people. At the bottom of the pyramids cognitive functions are relatively simple (for example, for language, simple functions could include babbling and the use of simple nouns), and the functions of the two hemispheres overlap considerably. At the top of the pyramids, representing very complex functions, the functions of the two hemispheres do not overlap at all (for example, for language, complex functions could include the use of adult language structure). It is important to note that the hemispheres are not themselves becoming more lateralized with respect to a given function; rather, they are developing new functions that are more specialized. Since both hemispheres show functional overlap in the early years of life, each can adopt the functions of the other if brain damage has occurred at an early age.

hemisphere actively inhibits the other, thus preventing the contralateral hemisphere from developing similar functions. This active inhibition presumably develops at about age 5, as the corpus callosum becomes functional. Moscovitch proposes that this inhibitory process not only prevents the subsequent development of language processes in the right hemisphere, but also inhibits expression of the language processes already in the right hemisphere. Support for this idea comes from the observation that the right hemisphere of commissurotomy patients appears to have greater language abilities than expected from the study of normal patients, presumably because the right hemisphere is no longer subject to inhibition by the left. Furthermore, Netley reports that people born with no corpus callosum demonstrate little or no functional asymmetry as inferred from dichotic listening, suggesting that the absence of interhemispheric connection results in attenuated hemispheric differentiation. This phenomenon follows directly from the Moscovitch proposal.

ASYMMETRY IN NONHUMANS

It is implicitly assumed in many discussions of the nature of cerebral asymmetry and its role in behavioral diversity in humans that asymmetry is linked with specially human intellectual characteristics such as language. Asymmetry is not a uniquely human characteristic, however. In fact, it has been shown that certain elements of communicative vocalizations in frogs and salamanders are lateralized to the left side of the brain. Thus, an understanding of the origins and evolution of lateral asymmetries in the nonhuman brain is germane to any understanding of the nature of asymmetry in the human brain. A complete discussion is beyond the scope of this book, and we recommend a recent volume by Bradshaw and Rogers. We will highlight some of the most stimulating and robust data so far in birds, rodents, and nonhuman primates.

Asymmetry in Birds

Fernando Nottebohm reported a startling discovery in 1971. He severed the hypoglossal nerve in canaries and found a severe disruption in the birds' song after left lesions but not after right ones. Subsequent work in his lab, as well as many others, has shown that there are anatomical differences in the structures controlling birdsong in the two hemispheres and that many song-related regions are sexually dimorphic (that is, they are different in the two sexes). Curiously, although a left hemisphere dominance for song has been shown in many species of songbirds (and even chickens), it is not characteristic of all songbirds. Apparently the zebra finch has little anatomical or functional asymmetry, even though it sings. It may be that the lateralization is not for singing per se but for some other still unrecognized feature of bird vocalizations.

Nottebohm's discovery led to interest in the possibility of asymmetry in the visual system of birds because the optic nerves of most birds cross over almost completely at the optic chiasm. Thus, each hemisphere receives most input from a single eye. The beauty of this arrangement is that lateralization of visual function can be investigated by testing birds monocularly. Furthermore, birds have no corpus callosum and although there are other small commissures between the hemispheres, there is less interhemispheric transfer in birds than in mammals. Lateralization of visual function has now been shown for a range of visually guided functions in birds. According to Bradshaw and Rogers, the right-eye system is specialized for categorizing objects, such as food versus nonfood items, whereas the left-eye system is specialized to respond to the unique properties of each stimulus (color, size, shape, and so forth), including topographical information. Thus, the left hemisphere of birds appears to be specialized for categorizing objects and the right for processing topographical information. Research by Horn and his colleagues has also shown an asymmetry for memory formation in the chicken brain. Different synaptic and neurochemical changes occur in each hemisphere when the animals learn things. This presumably reflects some difference in the information processing by the two hemispheres. One curious asymmetry is in sleep. Birds spend much of their sleep time with only one hemisphere asleep, which presumably allows them to monitor the environment. On the other hand, it also means that there is a transient asymmetry in sensory processing, which might have significant implications for the animals. We note parenthetically that unilateral sleep also occurs in cetaceans (whales, dolphins) and seals, which would seem sensible in mammals that can drown!

In summary, studies of birds have revealed that lateralization takes many forms in the brain and is not a unique property of mammals. Indeed, Bradshaw and Rogers suggest that in view of the growing list of functional and structural asymmetries in birds, one begins to wonder whether it is not symmetry that needs to be explained.

Asymmetry in Rodents

Studies in rats and mice have focused on two rather different types of asymmetry. The first has emphasized postural and motor asymmetries such as paw preference and direction of movement. This form of lateralization is present in individuals and has been correlated with individual differences in the distribution of transmitters, especially dopamine. Unlike handedness in humans, most postural asymmetries in rodents are random across the population. Thus, although the neural bases of individual preferences may be relevant for understanding motor or postural asymmetries in humans, the directions of the asymmetries do not relate directly to human brain-behavior relationships.

The second form of lateralization is more interesting in the current context because it is seen in the population, much as we saw in birds. As in humans, there is an asymmetry in the anatomy of the two cerebral hemispheres, with the right hemisphere being larger. In addition, the cortex of the right hemisphere is thicker, especially in the visual and posterior parietal regions, and this difference is modulated by hormones. For example, several groups of researchers have seen a sex difference in the asymmetry: males have a greater difference than females. Furthermore, Stewart and Kolb showed that both prenatal stress and postnatal castration abolished the anatomical asymmetry in males, presumably due to alterations in the normal hormonal environment. Studies of functional correlates of the anatomical asymmetries have proved controversial. Nonetheless, evidence is accumulating to support the conclusion that the left hemisphere is specialized for the processing of species-specific calls, which has been interpreted as a specialization for the processing of series of stimuli over time (sequential processing). There have been claims that the right hemisphere is specialized for controlling emotional and spatial behavior, but this remains rather speculative. In an extensive study of motor, social, and spatial behavior of rats with left or right hemidecortications, we were completely unable to demonstrate any functional population asymmetry whatsoever. Although individual animals may use one hemisphere for particular functions, this result does not support the lateralization of emotional or spatial functions in rats. On the other hand, we have seen that hemidecortication in children produces far less asymmetry than might be expected, so perhaps more credence should be given to studies of small unilateral lesions.

One intriguing asymmetry in rodents is an apparent lateralization of the modulation of immune responses. For example, lesions in the left hemisphere of mice, but not in the right, suppress T-cell functions. This may be due to a lateralized control of the secretion of specific hormones, such as prolactin. It is not yet known if there are similar asymmetries in the control of immune functions in humans, although this has been hypothesized (see Kang and colleagues).

We noted earlier that stress may alter anatomical asymmetries in the cortex of rats, and many research groups have suggested that stress may also alter functional asymmetries. For example, Denneberg and his coworkers have hypothesized that specific experiences might alter the two hemispheres differentially during development. One could imagine that if different experiences differ in stress levels, then Denneberg's results could be explained by the lateralized responses to various stress-related hormones, such as glucocorticoids.

Asymmetry in Nonhuman Primates

One trend in primate brain evolution is for the Sylvian fissure to shift from an almost vertical orientation to a more horizontal orientation. This implies that there is an expansion of the parietal lobe, which pushes the Sylvian fissure down, especially in the left hemisphere. Thus, as with human brains, there is a greater upward slope in the Sylvian fissure on the right in apes and Old World monkeys. In addition, the right frontal lobe and left occipital lobe extend farther in the same species, again as in humans. Data for New World monkeys are more variable, but even here it appears that there is likely to be an asymmetry in the Sylvian fissure. The existence of asymmetries in the nonhuman primates is not to be interpreted as being identical to that in humans. Bradshaw and Rogers conclude that the asymmetries in the language-related parietal and temporal lobe structures are not fully developed until the arrival of hominids (that is, they are seen in fossil hominids and human brains). This suggests that the increased development of language-related structures in the posterior part of the brain did not occur until the advent of hominids.

Studies of hand preference in nonhuman primates have been very controversial. Studies in the 1960s by Mike Warren unequivocally failed to find any systematic hand preference in rhesus monkeys, and Warren concluded that observed preferences are task-dependent and are strongly affected by learning.

More recently, McNeilage and his colleagues have argued that because previous studies concentrated on particular types of movements, a hand preference in monkeys has been overlooked. Their basic premise is that as primates evolved there was a preference for reaching with one limb (the left) while supporting the body with the other (the right). As the prehensile hand developed and primates began to adopt a more upright posture, the need for a hand devoted to postural support diminished, and because this hand was free, it became specialized for manipulating objects. They later proposed that the hand specializations were accompanied by hemispheric specializations: a right hemisphere (left-hand) perceptuomotor specialization for unimanual predation (grasping fast-moving insects or small animals) and a left hemisphere specialization for whole-body movements. This hypothesis has been hotly debated. One of the significant difficulties is that studies of limb use in primates have been hampered by poor control of a myriad of confounding factors including species, age, sex, task difficulty, learning, sample sizes, and so forth. Nonetheless, evidence is accumulating in support of at least some components of the theory. For example, Ward's group has shown left-hand preferences for prey catching and food retrieval in prosimians and some Old World monkeys. One objection to the theory is that cerebral asymmetry must precede handedness, and it is not clear whether this is so and why it might have occurred.

If anything akin to cerebral asymmetry in humans is to be demonstrated in nonhuman primates, it seems reasonable to expect that tests of tactile, visual, and auditory perception would be a good place to start looking. Consider the following examples. Horster and Ettlinger trained 155 rhesus monkeys to make a tactile response in a task in which the subjects had to discriminate a cylinder from a sphere. The results showed that the 78 monkeys spontaneously using the left hand outperformed the 77 using the right hand. Thus, as in humans, the right hemisphere outperformed the left one, which suggests an asymmetry.

Hamilton and Vermeire took a different approach. They taught 25 split-brain monkeys to discriminate two types of visual stimuli that have shown lateralization in humans. In one task the animals had to discriminate between pairs of lines differing in slope by 15° (for example, 15° versus 30°, 105° versus 120°). For each pair, the more vertical line was designated as positive and the monkey received a food reward for choosing it. Each hemisphere was tested separately, and the results showed that most monkeys learned the line orientation discriminations faster with the left hemisphere. The second task required the animals to discriminate different monkey faces. The right hemisphere of most animals showed better discrimination and memory of the faces. There was no hemispheric difference in making a simple discrimination of black and white patterns. The curious thing about these results is that, a priori, the line-orientation task appears to be one in which humans would show a *right* hemisphere bias, rather than the left hemisphere bias shown by the monkeys. At any rate, it is safe to conclude that there appears to be evidence of hemispheric specialization for the processing of different types of visual information.

There is also evidence that the two hemispheres may differ in their production of facial expressions. Split-brain monkeys viewed videotapes of people, monkeys, other animals, and scenery, and the amount of time spent watching the recordings and the number of species-typical facial expressions made were recorded. The number of facial expressions elicited from the right hemisphere was greater than the number made when using the left hemisphere, which is what one would predict from studies of humans. In another study Hauser found that the left side of the monkey's face began to display facial expression before the right, and it was more expressive. Recall that a similar result was reported for humans.

Finally, there are many studies looking for asymmetries in auditory perception. In an early study Dewson removed the superior temporal gyrus (roughly equivalent to Wernicke's area in humans) in four rhesus monkeys, producing a lasting deficit on an auditory-visual task if the lesion was in the left hemisphere but not if it was in the right. The monkeys were required to press a panel that activated one of two acoustic stimuli, either a 1-kHz (kilohertz) tone or white noise. They were then presented with two panels, one green and one red. If the tone was heard, the monkeys pressed the red panel; if the white noise was heard, they pressed the green panel to receive the reward. Lesions on the left impaired performance of this task, but lesions to the analogous area on the right did not. The possibility of asymmetry in the auditory system was confirmed, however, by the work of Petersen and colleagues. They compared the ability of Japanese macaques to discriminate among communicatively relevant sounds and irrelevant sounds. The animals could discriminate relevant sounds presented to the right ear better than those presented to the left. The researchers suggested that the Japanese macaques engage in left hemisphere processing in a way that is analogous to that in humans. A further study by Heffner and Heffner supports this conclusion. They trained monkeys to discriminate between two forms of their "coo" vocalization. Then they removed the left or right superior temporal gyrus or the left or right parietal cortex. Removal of the left, but not the right, temporal cortex produced an impairment in performance on this task. Parietal lesions were without effect. Curiously, with training, the animals with left temporal lesions were able to relearn the task. When the remaining side was later removed, the animals had a permanent deficit in the task and were unable to relearn it.

Summary

The brains of nonhuman animals exhibit anatomical asymmetry, which may be analogous to that observed in humans. There are also functional asymmetries in perceptual processing and possibly in other functions. The demonstration of asymmetry in nonhuman brains implies that asymmetry in the human brain is not directly related either to handedness or to language. We are inclined to believe that the hemispheres of mammals are more likely to be specialized for the analysis of certain types of sensory information and perhaps for the control of certain categories of movements.

CONCLUDING REMARKS

The discovery of systematic relationships between normal variations in cerebral organization and individual differences in cognitive abilities represents one of the most challenging goals of neuropsychology. The complexity of the human brain makes the task difficult, but the problems are not intractable. Each of us has unique behavioral capacities as well as shortcomings (that is, "Achilles lobes"), which must surely be related to cerebral organization in some manner. Demonstrations of variations related to handedness imply that some variation is innate, although environmental variables almost certainly must modify cerebral organization. Finally, we must point out that although we have emphasized variations in the asymmetrical organization of the cerebrum, the individual variation within each hemisphere may be as large as that between the hemispheres.

REFERENCES

Aboitiz, F., A. B. Scheibel, and E. Zaidel. Morphometry of the Sylvian fissure and the corpus callousm, with emphasis on sex differences. *Brain* 115:1521–1541, 1992.

Annett, M. A classification of hand preference by association analysis. *British Journal of Psychology* 61:303–321, 1970.

Bakan, P., G. Dibb, and P. Reed. Handedness and birth stress. *Neuropsychologia* 11:363–366, 1973.

Benbow, C. P. Sex differences in mathematical reasoning ability in intellectually talented preadolescents: Their nature, effects, and possible causes. *Behavioral and Brain Sciences* 11:169–232, 1988.

Boles, D. B. X-linkage of spatial ability: A critical review. *Child Development* 51:625–635, 1980.

Bradshaw, J., and L. Rogers. *The Evolution of Lateral Asymmetries, Language, Tool Use, and Intellect.* New York: Academic Press, 1993.

Bryden, M. P., I. C. McManus, and M. B. Bulman-Fleming. Evaluating the empirical support for the Geschwind-Behan-Galaburda model of cerebral lateralization. *Brain and Cognition,* in press.

Carmon, A., Y. Harishanu, E. Lowinger, and S. Lavy. Asymmetries in hemispheric blood volume and cerebral dominance. *Behavioral Biology* 7:853–859, 1972.

Collins, R. L. Toward an admissible genetic model for the inheritance of the degree and direction of asymmetry. In S. Harnad, R. W. Doty, L. Goldstein, J. Jaynes, and G. Krauthamer, eds. *Lateralization of the Nervous System.* New York: Academic Press, 1977.

Curtiss, S. *Genie: a Psycholinguistic Study of a Modern-Day "Wild Child."* New York: Academic Press, 1978.

de Lacaste-Utamsing, C., and R. L. Holloway. Sexual dimorphism in the human corpus callosum. *Science* 216:1431–1432, 1982.

Dennenberg, V. H. Hemispheric laterality in animals and the effects of early experience. *The Behavioral and Brain Sciences* 4:1–50, 1981.

Dennis, M. Capacity and strategy for syntactic comprehension after left or right hemidecortication. *Brain and Language* 10:287–317, 1980.

Dennis, M. Language acquisition in a single hemisphere: Semantic organization. In D. Caplan, ed. *Biological*

Studies of Mental Processes. Cambridge, Mass.: MIT Press, 1980.

Dennis, M., M. Lovett, and C. A. Wiegel-Crump. Written language acquisition after left or right hemidecortication in infancy. *Brain and Language* 12:54–91, 1981.

Dennis, M., and H. A. Whitaker. Language acquisition following hemidecortication: Linguisitic superiority of the left over the right hemisphere. *Brain and Language* 3:404–433, 1976.

Dewson, J. H. Preliminary evidence of hemispheric asymmetry of auditory function in monkeys. In S. Harnad, R. W. Doty, L. Goldstein, J. Jaynes, and G. Krauthamer, eds. *Lateralization in the Nervous System.* New York: Academic Press, 1977.

Geschwind, N., and A. M. Galaburda. *Cerebral Lateralization: Biological Mechanisms, Associations, and Pathology.* Cambridge, Mass.: MIT Press, 1987.

Grimshaw, G. M., M. P. Bryden, and J. K. Finegan. Relations between prenatal testosterone and cerebral lateralization at age 10. *Journal of Clinical and Experimental Neuropsychology* 15:39–40, 1993.

Gualtieri, T., and R. E. Hicks. An immunoreactive theory of selective male affliction. *Behavioral and Brain Sciences* 8:427–477, 1985.

Gur, R. C., R. E. Gur, W. D. Obrist, J. P. Hungerbuhler, D. Younkin, A. D. Rosen, B. E. Skolnick, and M. Reivich. Sex and handedness differences in cerebral blood flow during test and cognitive activity. *Science* 217:659–660, 1982.

Hamilton, C. R., and B. A. Vermeire. Complementary hemispheric superiorities in monkeys. *Science* 242: 1691–1694, 1988.

Hamilton, D. *The Monkey Gland Affair.* London: Chatto & Windus, 1986.

Hampson, E. Variations in sex-related cognitive abilities across the menstrual cycle. *Brain and Cognition* 14:26–43, 1990.

Hampson, E., and D. Kimura. Sex differences and hormonal influences on cognitive function in humans. In J. B. Becker, S. M. Breedlove, and D. Crews, eds. *Behavioral Endocrinology.* Cambridge, Mass.: MIT Press, 1992.

Hardyck, C., and L. F. Petrinovich. Left-handedness. *Psychological Bulletin* 84:384–404, 1977.

Harshman, R. A., E. Hampson, and S. A. Berenbaum. Individual differences in cognitive abilities and brain organization, part I: Sex and handedness. Differences in ability. *Canadian Journal of Psychology* 37:144–192. 1983.

Hauser, M. D. Right hemisphere dominance for the production of facial expression in monkeys. *Science* 261:475–477, 1993.

Hécaen, H., M. DeAgostini, and A. Monzon-Montes. Cerebral organization in left-handers. *Brain and Language* 12:261–284, 1981.

Hécaen, H., and J. Sauguet. Cerebral dominance in left-handed subjects. *Cortex* 7:19–48, 1971.

Heffner, H. E., and R. S. Heffner. Temporal lobe lesions and perception of species-specific vocalizations by macaques. *Science* 226:75–76, 1984.

Hochberg, F. H., and M. LeMay. Arteriographic correlates of handedness. *Neurology* 25:218–222, 1975.

Horn, G. Neural basis of recognition memory investigated through an analysis of imprinting. *Philosophical Transactions of the Royal Society London B* 329:133–142, 1990.

Horster, W., and G. Ettlinger. An association between hand preferences and tactile discrimination performance in the rhesus monkey. *Neuropsychologica* 21:411–413, 1985.

Ifune, C. K., B. A. Vermeire, and C. R. Hamilton. Hemispheric differences in split-brain monkeys viewing and responding to videotape recordings. *Behavioral and Neural Biology* 41:231–235, 1984.

Inglis, J., and J. S. Lawson. A meta-analysis of sex differences in the effects of unilateral brain damage on intelligence test results. *Canadian Journal of Psychology* 36: 670–683, 1982.

Inglis, R., M. Rickman, J. S. Lawson, A. W. MacLean, and T. N. Monga. Sex differences in the cognitive effects of unilateral brain damage. *Cortex* 18:257–276, 1982.

Janowsky, J. S., S. K. Oviatt, and E. S. Orwoll. Testosterone influences spatial cognition in older men. *Behavioral Neuroscience* 108:325–332, 1994.

Juraska, J. Sex differences in developmental plasticity of behavior and the brain. In W. T. Greenough and J. M. Juraska, eds. *Developmental Neuropsychology.* New York: Academic Press, 1986.

Kang, D.-H., R. J. Davidson, C. L. Coe, R. E. Wheeler, A. J. Tomarken and W. B. Ershler. Frontal brain asymmetry and immune function. *Behavior Neuroscience* 105:860–869, 1991.

Kertesz, A., and N. Geschwind. Patterns of pyramidal decussation and their relationship to handedness. *Archives of Neurology* 24:326–332, 1971.

Kimura, D. Sex differences in cerebral organization for speech and praxic functions. *Canadian Journal of Psychology* 37:19–35, 1983.

Kimura, D. Sex differences in the brain. *Scientific American* 267(3):119–125, 1992.

Kolb, B., A. MacKintosh, I. Q. Whishaw, and R. J. Sutherland. Evidence for anatomical but not functional asymmetry in the hemidecorticate rat. *Behavioral Neuroscience* 98:44–58, 1984.

Kolb, B., and J. Stewart. Sex-related differences in dendritic branching of cells in the prefrontal cortex of rats. *Journal of Neuroendocrinology* 3:95–99, 1991.

Kolb, B., R. J. Sutherland, A. J. Nonneman, and I. Q. Whishaw. Asymmetry in the cerebral hemispheres of the rat, mouse, rabbit, and cat: The right hemisphere is larger. *Experimental Neurology* 78:348–359, 1982.

Lansdell, H. A sex difference in effect of temporal-lobe neurosurgery on design preference. *Nature* 194:852–854, 1962.

Levy, J. Possible basis for the evolution of lateral specialization of the human brain. *Nature* 224:614–615, 1969.

Levy, J., and T. Nagylaki. A model for the genetics of handedness. *Genetics* 72:117–128, 1972.

MacCoby, E., and C. Jacklin. *The Psychology of Sex Differences.* Stanford, Calif.: Stanford University Press, 1974.

McGlone, J. Sex differences in the cerebral organization of verbal function to patients with unilateral brain lesions. *Brain* 100:775–793, 1977.

McGlone, J. Sex differences in human brain asymmetry: A critical survey. *Behavioral and Brain Sciences* 3:215–263, 1980.

McKeever, W. F., H. W. Hoemann, V. A. Florina, and A. D. Van Deventer. Evidence of minimal cerebral asymmetries in the congenitally deaf. *Neuropsychologia* 14:413–423, 1976.

MacNeilage, P. F., M. G. Studdert-Kennedy, and B. Lindblom. Primate handedness reconsidered. *Behavioral and Brain Sciences* 10:247–303, 1987.

MacNeilage, P. F., M. G. Studdert-Kennedy, and B. Lindblom. Primate handedness: a foot in the door. *Behavioral and Brain Sciences* 11:737–746, 1988.

Manning, A. A., W. Gobel, R. Markman, and T. LaBrech. Lateral cerebral differences in the deaf in response to linguistic and nonlinguistic stimuli. *Brain and Language* 4:309–321, 1977.

Moscovitch, M. The development of lateralization of language functions and its relation to cognitive and linguistic development: A review and some theoretical speculations. In S. J. Segalowitz and F. A. Gruber, eds. *Language Development and Neurological Theory.* New York: Academic Press, 1977.

Netley, C. Dichotic listening of callosal agenesis and Turner's syndrome patients. In S. J. Segalowitz and F. A. Gruber, eds. *Language Development and Neurological Theory.* New York: Academic Press, 1977.

Neville, H. Electroencephalographic testing of cerebral specialization in normal and congenitally deaf children: A preliminary report. In S. J. Segalowitz and F. A. Gruber, eds. *Language Development and Neurological Theory.* New York: Academic Press, 1977.

Nottebohm, F. Brain pathways for vocal learning in birds: A review of the first 10 years. *Progress in Psychobiology and Physiological Psychology* 9:85–124, 1980.

Obler, L. K., R. J. Zatoree, L. Galloway, Jr., and J. Vaid. Cerebral lateralization in bilinguals: Methodological issues. *Brain and Language* 15:40–54, 1982.

Peters, M. Corpus callosum. *Canadian Journal of Psychology* 42:313–324, 1988.

Petersen, M. R., M. D. Beecher, S. R. Zoloth, D. B. Moody, and W. C. Stebbins. Neural lateralization: Evidence from studies of the perception of species-specific vocalizations by Japanese macaques *(Macada puscata).* *Science* 202:324–326, 1978.

Rapport, R. L., C. T. Tan, and H. A. Whitaker. Language function and dysfunction among Chinese- and English-speaking polyglots: Cortical stimulation. Wada testing, and clinical studies. *Brain and Language* 18:342–366, 1983.

Ratcliffe, G., C. Dila, L. Taylor, and B. Milner. The morphological asymmetry of the hemispheres and cerebral dominance for speech: A possible relationship. *Brain and Language* 11:87–98, 1980.

Stewart, J., and B. Kolb. The effects of neonatal gonadectomy and prenatal stress on cortical thickness and asymmetry in rats. *Behavioral and Neural Biology* 49:344–360, 1988.

Stewart, J., and B. Kolb. Dendritic branching in cortical pyramidal cells in response to ovariectomy in adult female rats: Suppression by neonatal exposure to testosterone. *Brain Research* 1994.

Sugishita, M., K. Otomo, S. Kabe, and K. Yunoki. A critical appraisal of neuropsychological correlates of Japanese ideogram (Kanji) and phonogram (Kana) reading. *Brain* 115:1563–1585, 1992.

Thomas, H., W. Jamison, and D. D. Hummel. Observation is insufficient for discovering that the surface of still water is invariantly horizontal. *Science* 191:173–174, 1973.

Tzavaras, A., G. Kaprinis, and A. Gatzoyas. Literacy and hemispheric specialization for language: Dichotic listening in illiterates. *Neuropsychologia* 19:565–570, 1981.

Uyehara, J. M., and W. C. Cooper, Jr. Hemispheric differences for verbal and nonverbal stimuli in Japanese- and English-speaking subjects assessed by Tsunoda's method. *Brain and Language* 10:405–417, 1980.

Waber, D. P. Sex differences in cognition: A function of maturation rate. *Science* 192:572–573, 1976.

Wada, J. A., R. Clarke, and A. Hamm. Cerebral asymmetry in humans: Cortical speech zones in 100 adult and 100 infant brains. *Archives of Neurology* 32:239–246, 1975.

Wahlsten, D., and K. M. Bishop. Sex differences in the

human corpus callosum. Unpublished manuscript, 1994.

Warren, J. M. Functional lateralization in the brain. *Annals of the New York Academy of Sciences* 299:273–280, 1977.

Wechsler, A. F. Crossed aphasia in an illiterate dextral. *Brain and Language* 3:164–172, 1976.

Witelson, S. F. Early hemisphere specialization and interhemispheric plasticity: An empirical and theoretical review. In S. J. Segalowitz and F. A. Gruber, eds. *Language Development and Neurological Theory*. New York: Academic Press, 1977.

Witelson, S. F. The brain connection: The corpus callosum is larger in left-handers. *Science* 229:665–668, 1985.

Witelson, S. F. Hand and sex differences in the isthmus and genu of the human corpus callosum. *Brain* 112: 799–835, 1989.

Witelson, S. F., and C. H. Goldsmith. The relationship of hand preference to anatomy of the corpus callosum in men. *Brain Research* 545:175–182, 1991.

Witelson, S. F., and D. L. Kigar. Sylvian fissure morphology and asymmetry in men and women: Bilateral differences in relation to handedness in men. *Journal of Comparative Neurology* 323:326–340, 1992.

Wittig, M. A., and A. C. Petersen. *Sex-Related Differences in Cognitive Functioning*. New York: Academic Press, 1979.

Woolley, C. S., E. Gould, M. Frankfurt, and B. S. McEwen. Naturally occurring fluctuation in dendritic spine density on adult hippocampal pyramidal neurons. *Journal of Neuroscience* 10:4035–4039, 1990.

Yakovlev, P. I., and P. Rakic. Patterns of decussation of bulbar pyramids and distribution of pyramidal tracts on two sides of the spinal cord. *Transactions of the American Neurological Association* 91:366–367, 1966.

chapter eleven

The Occipital Lobes

There is probably more known about the occipital lobes than about any other region of the cortex. This is largely because of the dominance of the sense of vision in humans and thus the great interest of researchers in how the brain processes visual information. Ramon y Cajal probably made the first systematic attempt to describe the organization of the visual system at the turn of the century. Shortly thereafter Brodmann described three occipital areas that appeared to support visual functions (his areas 17, 18, 19), but it was not until the clinical studies of World War I soldiers with gunshot wounds that there was any real progress in understanding the functional organization of the visual system. In the last 20 years, there have been major advances in our understanding of visual processing. The rapid progress is due in large part to new histological, behavioral, and physiological methods that have radically altered our view of the functioning of the occipital regions and the visual systems in general. Some of the new theoretical views remain controversial, but a consensus appears to be emerging on the general principles of occipital organization.

Although this chapter focuses on the occipital lobes, there is no clear anatomical division between the occipital, temporal, and parietal cortex. Thus, even though vision is the exclusive function of the occipital lobes, much of the remaining cortex also has visual functions that are closely associated with occipital areas (see Figure 8.12). In fact, for the primate brain it is obvious that more cortex is devoted to visual function than to any other activity. Felleman and van Essen illustrate that of the 32 cortical areas (of a total of about 70 in their scheme) that have visual functions in the monkey brain, only 9 are actually in the occipital lobe. The total surface area of the vision-related regions is about 55% of the whole cortical surface, which compares with 11% and 3% for the somatosensory and auditory regions, respectively. It is interesting that so little of the monkey cortex is involved in audition. This must certainly reflect a major difference between the brains of humans and monkeys, since we have a much larger auditory representation (see Chapter 6). Indeed, it is not too fanciful to speculate that with so little auditory cortex, it is not surprising that monkeys do not talk well!

The Felleman and van Essen map illustrates another interesting fact: the commonly used nomenclature of cortical anatomy is a smorgasbord. Some of the areas retain Brodmann's numbers (most of those with numerals), but many areas have other designations that are idiosyncratic at best. The important principle to extract at this point is that in addition to the occipital lobe, much of the parietal and temporal lobes have visual functions.

ANATOMY OF THE OCCIPITAL LOBES

The occipital lobes form the posterior pole of the cerebral hemispheres, lying under the occipital bone. On the medial surface of the hemisphere, the occipital lobe is distinguished from the parietal lobe by the parietal-occipital sulcus (Figure 11.1). There are no clear landmarks separating the occipital cortex from the temporal or parietal cortex on the lateral surface of the hemisphere, however, because the occipital tissue merges with the other regions. The lack of clear landmarks makes it difficult to define the extent of the occipital areas precisely and has led to much confusion over the exact boundaries. There are three clear landmarks within the visual cortex, however. The most prominent is the calcarine sulcus, which contains much of the primary cortex (see Figure 11.1). The calcarine fissure is interesting because it divides the upper and lower halves of the visual world, as illustrated in Figure 6.5. On the ventral surface of the hemisphere there are two gyri (lingual and fusiform). The lingual gyrus includes part of V2 and VP, whereas V4 is in the fusiform gyrus (see Figure 11.1).

Subdivisions of the Occipital Cortex

Brodmann originally divided the occipital lobe into three distinct anatomical regions (areas 17, 18, and 19), which until recently were seen as the visual regions of the cortex. More recent studies using imaging, physiological, and newer anatomical techniques have produced much finer subdivisions, although area 17 is still considered the primary visual area and is thus designated V1. We can now point to at least six different occipital regions, which are known as V1, V2, V3, V3A, V4, and V5 (Figure 11.2). Area V5 is also called MT. Area V3 is sometimes further subdivided into a dorsal (dV3) and a ventral (vV3 or VP) region. The division of V3 into two subparts is based upon the observation that the upper visual field is represented in VP and the lower visual field is represented in dV3. Previc has argued that the upper and lower fields may have different functions, one more specialized for visual search and recognition (upper) and one more specialized for visuomotor guidance (lower). This is an interesting concept and, if true, may apply to other visual regions as well.

One of the remarkable features of V1 is its complex laminar organization, which is probably the most distinct of all cortical areas. Although we usually say that the cortex has six layers, it is possible to see many more in V1, partly because layer 4 has four distinct layers. A surprising feature of V1 is that although it appears to be anatomically homogenous, it is possible to show that it is actually heterogeneous by staining V1 for an enzyme known as cytochrome oxidase (which is crucial in making energy available to cells). Hence, there are regions of cytochrome-rich areas, known as blobs, that are separated by interblob regions of little cytochrome activity (see Figure 8.5). It turns out that cells in the blobs are involved in color perception and the interblobs are involved in form and motion perception. The discovery that area V1 is functionally heterogeneous was unexpected. It means that a given cortical area may have more than one distinct function. It turns out that V2 is also heterogeneous when stained with cytochrome oxidase, but instead of blobs, there are stripes (see Figure 8.5). One type of stripes is thin (and they are thus called thin stripes); these are involved in color perception. Two other types, known as thick stripes and pale stripes, are involved in form and motion perception, respectively. Thus, we see that the heterogeneity of function observed in V1—and representing color, form, and motion—is preserved in V2, although it is organized in a different way.

When Felleman and van Essen compared the sizes of different visual areas, they found a 50-fold range. Areas V1 and V2 are the largest, with each occupying about 11% of the total area of the cortex. V4 is the next largest, at about 5%, and the

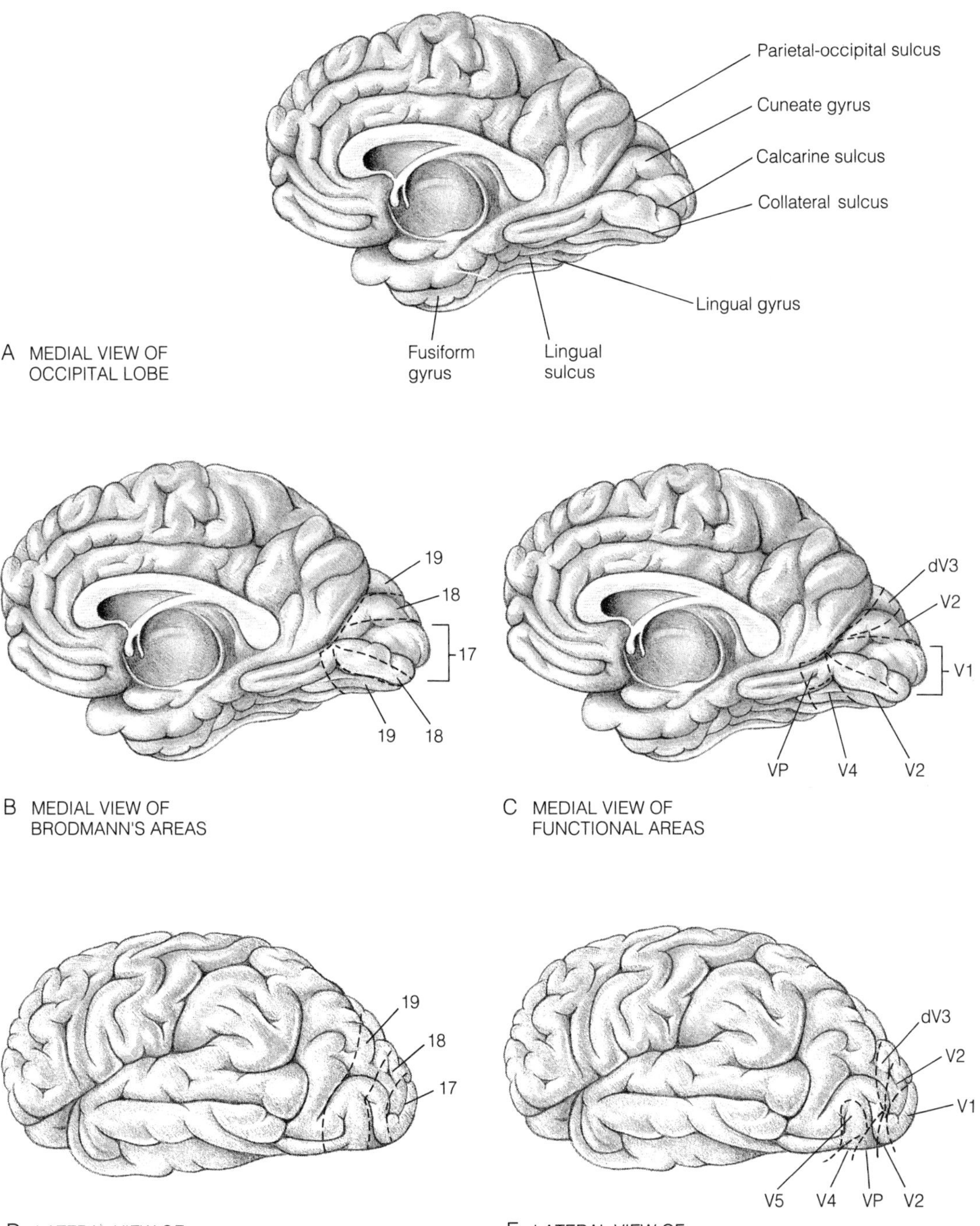

FIGURE 11.1. Gross anatomy of the occipital lobe. *A.* Medial view illustrating the major landmarks. *B.* Medial view of Brodmann's cytoarchitectonic areas. *C.* Medial view of functional areas. *D.* Lateral view of Brodmann's areas. *E.* Lateral view of functional areas.

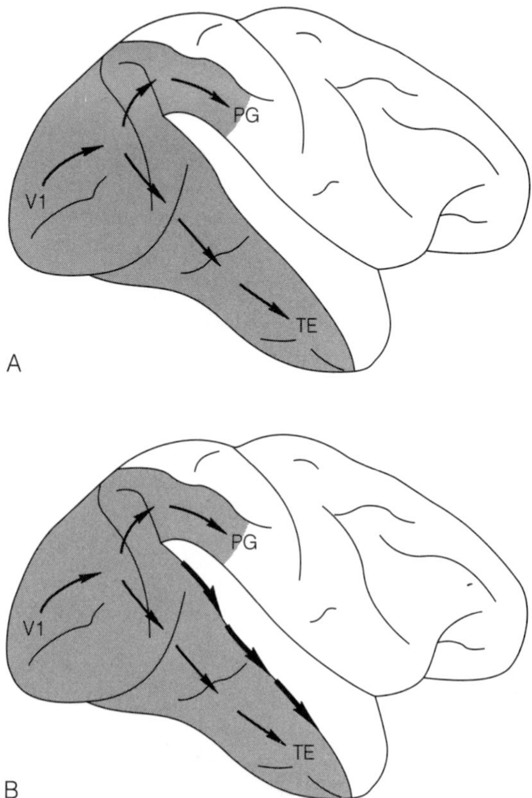

FIGURE 11.2. *A.* Ungerleider and Mishkin's summary of two visual streams of the rhesus monkey, one going to PG in the parietal cortex and one going to TE in the temporal cortex. *B.* Boussaoud, Ungerleider, and Desimone's illustration of a third visual pathway into the superior temporal sulcus.

remaining regions are much smaller. The relatively large sizes of V1, V2, and V4 are presumably related in some way to function, with the one commonality across all three areas being color, which is one of the key characteristics of primate vision. In addition, all three areas play some role in form detection.

Connections of the Visual Cortex

By the late 1960s the consensus was that the visual cortex is hierarchically organized with visual information proceeding from area 17 to area 18 to area 19. Each visual area was considered to provide some sort of elaboration on the processing of the previous area. This strictly hierarchical view is now known to be too simple. It is now thought that there is a distributed hierarchical process with multiple parallel pathways connected at each level, much as illustrated in Figure 8.11. There is still a hierarchy, but it contains a number of parallel and interconnecting pathways, each with relatively separate functions. The details of all the connections between the occipital areas and then on to the parietal, temporal, and frontal regions are bewildering, but it is possible to extract a few simple principles (see Figure 11.2). First, V1 is the primary area: it receives the largest input from the lateral geniculate nucleus of the thalamus and it projects to all other occipital regions. V1 is the first level in the hierarchy. Second, V2 also projects to all other occipital regions. V2 is the second level. Third, after V2 there are three distinct parallel pathways that emerge en route to the parietal cortex, superior temporal sulcus, and inferior temporal cortex (see Figure 11.2). The parietal pathway has a role in visual guidance of movement; the inferior temporal pathway is concerned with object perception (including color); and the superior temporal sulcus pathway is probably important in visual-spatial functions.

A THEORY OF OCCIPITAL LOBE FUNCTION

We have seen that areas V1 and V2 are heterogeneous in function; both have a segregation of processing for color, form, and motion. The heterogeneous functions of V1 and V2 are in contrast to the functions of the areas that follow. In a sense, V1 and V2 appear to work like little mailboxes into which different types of information are assembled before being sent on to the more specialized visual areas. From V1 and V2 there are three parallel pathways that are concerned with different attributes of vision. The information derived from the blob areas of V1 goes to V4, which can be considered a color area. Cells in V4 are not solely responsive to color, however, since some are also responsive to both form and color. The magnocellular input to V1, and then to V2, goes to V5, which is specialized to detect motion. Finally, there is an input to V3, which is concerned with what Zeki calls "dynamic form"—that is, the shape of objects in motion. Thus, we see that vision begins in the primary cortex (V1), which has multiple functions, and then continues in more specialized zones. It is not surprising to discover that selective lesions in areas V3, V4, and V5 produce quite specific deficits in visual processing. Damage to V4 renders a person able to see only in shades of gray. Curiously, patients not only fail to perceive colors, but they also cannot recall colors from before the injury, or even imagine colors. In a real sense the loss of V4 results in the loss of color cognition, or the ability to think about color. Similarly, a lesion in V5 produces an inability to perceive objects in motion. Objects at rest are perceived, but once the objects move, they vanish. In principle, a lesion of V3 will affect form perception, but since V4 also processes form it would require a rather large lesion of both V3 and V4 to eliminate form perception.

One of the important constraints on the functions of V3, V4, and V5 is that they all receive a major input from V1. People with lesions in V1 act as though they are blind, even though it can be shown that visual input can still get to higher levels—partly through small projections of the LGN to V2 and partly through projections from the colliculus to the thalamus (the pulvinar) to the cortex (the tecto-pulvinar system described in Chapter 6). The problem that people with V1 lesions appear to have is that they are not aware of the visual input and can be shown to have some aspects of vision only by special testing. Thus, when asked what they see, patients with V1 damage often reply that they see nothing. Nonetheless, they can act on visual information, indicating that they do indeed "see." Thus, V1 appears to be primary for vision in yet another sense: V1 must be functioning for the brain to make sense out of what the more specialized areas are doing. We must note, however, that there have been reports of people with significant V1 damage who are capable of some awareness of visual information, such as motion. Burbur and colleagues suggest that it may be integrity of V3 that allows this conscious awareness, but this remains a hypothesis.

Visual Functions Beyond the Occipital Lobe

Visual processing does not stop in secondary visual areas V3, V4, and V5. There are multiple visual regions in the parietal, temporal, and frontal lobes (see Figure 8.14). Functions have not been assigned to all of these additional visual regions, but it is possible to speculate on what their functions must be. To do this, we can divide visual phenomena into five general categories: vision for action, action for vision, visual recognition, visual space, and visual attention.

Vision for action refers to the visual processing required to direct specific movements. For example, when reaching for a particular object such as a cup, the fingers form a specific pattern that allows grasping of the cup. This is obviously a movement guided by vision, because people do not need to shape their hand consciously when they reach. In addition to grasping, there must be visual areas that guide all kinds of specific movements, including those of the eyes, head, and whole body. A single system could not easily guide all movements because the requirements are so different. Reaching to pick up a jelly bean requires a very different kind of motor control than ducking from a snowball, but both are visually guided. Furthermore, vision for action must be sensitive to movement of the target. Catching a moving ball requires specific information about the location, trajectory, speed, and shape of the object. Vision for action is thought to be a function of the parietal visual areas.

Action for vision is more of a "top-down" process in that a viewer actively searches for and attends selectively to only a portion of the target object (Figure 11.3). When we look at a visual stimulus we do not simply stare at it; rather, we scan the stimulus with numerous eye movements. These movements are not random but tend to focus upon important or distinct features of the stimulus. Thus, when we scan a face we make a lot of eye movements directed toward the eyes

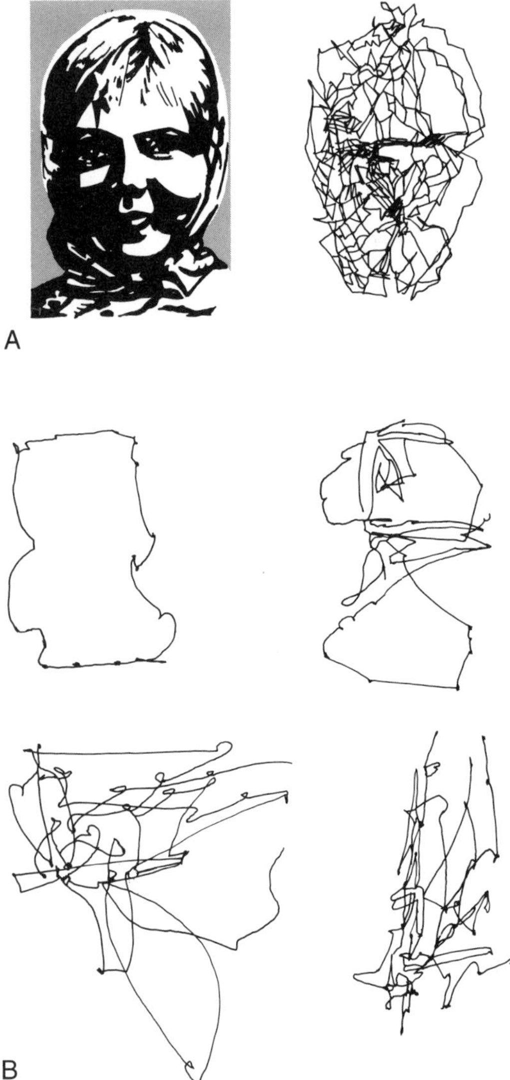

FIGURE 11.3. Eye movements during the examination of a visual stimulus. *A.* The concentration of eye movements (by a normal subject) to distinctive features of the face (eyes, nose, mouth); these movements are directed more at the left side of the photograph. *B.* The eye movements of a normal subject (*top*) examining a sphere (*left*) and a bust (*right*); (*bottom*) the eye movements of an agnosic subject examining the same shapes. Note the random movements of the agnosic subject. (From A. R. Luria, *The Working Brain.* Copyright © 1973, The Copyright Agency of the USSR. Reprinted with permission.)

and mouth. Curiously, we also make more eye scans directed to the left visual field (the right side of the person's face) than to the right visual field. This scanning bias may be important in the way we process faces, since it is not found in the scanning of other stimuli. People with deficits in action for vision are likely to have significant deficits in visual perception, although this has not been studied systematically. One interesting aspect of eye movements is that we often make them when we are thinking about particular types of visual information. For example, when people are asked to rotate objects mentally in order to answer simple questions about their appearance, they usually make many eye movements, especially to the left. Furthermore, when people are doing things in the dark, such as winding photographic film onto spools for processing, they also make many eye movements. Curiously, if the eyes are closed the movements stop. Indeed, it appears that it is easier to do many tasks in the dark if the eyes are closed. Since things are done tactilely in the dark it may be that there is interference by the visual system until the eyes are closed.

Visual recognition refers to the ability to recognize and understand visual information. For example, we can recognize specific faces and we can discriminate and interpret different expressions in those faces. Similarly, we can recognize letters or symbols and we can assign meaning to them. We can recognize different foods, tools, body parts, and so on. It is not reasonable to expect that we have different visual regions for each category of visual information, but we may have at least some specialization for biologically significant information, such as faces. Indeed, there are cells in the temporal cortex that appear to be highly specific in their preference for particular faces or hands. It is the visual areas in the temporal lobe that are specialized for visual recognition.

Visual space refers to the fact that visual information comes from specific locations in space. This information is needed to direct movements to objects in space and to assign meaning to them. But spatial location is not a unitary characteristic. Objects have location both relative to an individual (egocentric space) and relative to one another (allocentric space). The egocentric spatial properties are central to the control of actions toward objects. It therefore seems likely that this property is coded in systems related to vision for action. In contrast, the allocentric properties of objects are necessary for the construction of any type of memory of spatial location. A key feature of allocentric spatial coding is that it depends upon the identity of particular features of the world. Thus, it is likely to be associated with the regions involved in visual recognition. In summary, there is probably some form of spatial processing in both the parietal and temporal visual regions, but with very different functions.

Visual attention refers to the obvious fact that we cannot possibly process all the visual information available at any given time. This page has shape, color, texture, location, and so on, but the only really important characteristic is that it has words. Thus, when we read the page we select a specific aspect of visual input and attend to it selectively. In fact, neurons in the cortex show attentional properties of various kinds. For example, neurons may respond selectively to stimuli in particular places or at particular times or if a particular movement is to be executed. Independent mechanisms of attention are probably required for both the guidance of movements and the recognition of objects. Thus, there is likely to be some type of attentional processing associated with both parietal and temporal functions.

Visual Pathways Beyond the Occipital Lobe

In 1982 Ungerleider and Mishkin proposed that there are two broad streams of vision beyond the occipital lobe. First, they suggested that there is a dorsal stream that goes from V1 to the parietal visual areas. This system is concerned primarily with *where* visual information is located. Second, they proposed a ventral stream that goes from V1 to the temporal visual areas (see Figure 11.2). This system is concerned with *what* visual information is. The Ungerleider and Mishkin proposal was influential and appeared to be supported by the bulk of the anatomical and behavioral evidence. There is little doubt that humans and monkeys with parietal lobe lesions have difficulty in directing movements of the eyes and limbs to points in space. Similarly, there is no question that damage to the temporal lobe produces deficits in visual recognition and visual learning. Recently, Milner and Goodale have proposed a significant modification to the Ungerleider-Mishkin model.

Milner and Goodale argue that although the "where-what" model is superficially appealing, it cannot explain new behavioral evidence about the nature of the dorsal stream processing. Their proposal stems from observation of a patient who was blind but who nevertheless shaped her hand appropriately when asked to reach for objects. Her dorsal stream was intact, as revealed by the fact that she could see "unconsciously" location, size, and shape. On the other hand, other patients with dorsal stream damage consciously reported seeing objects but could not reach accurately or shape the hand appropriately when reaching. Goodale and Milner propose that rather than conceiving of the dorsal stream as a "where" system, it should be thought of as a set of systems for the on-line visual control of action. Their argument is based upon several new lines of evidence. First, they note that the predominant characteristic of the neurons in posterior parietal regions is that they are active during a combination of visual stimulation and associated behavior. For example, cells may be active only when a monkey reaches out to a particular object. Looking at an object in the absence of movement does not activate the neurons. Thus, these "visual" neurons are unique in that they are active only when the brain acts on visual information. Goodale and Milner suggest that these neurons therefore can be characterized as an interface between analysis of the visual world and motor action upon it. Obviously, the demands of action have important implications for what type of information must be sent to the parietal cortex. This would include information such as object shape, movement, and location. Each of these visual features is likely to be coded separately, and it turns out that there are at least three distinct pathways from V1 to the parietal cortex (Figure 11.4). One goes from V1 directly to V5 to parietal cortex, a second goes from V1 to

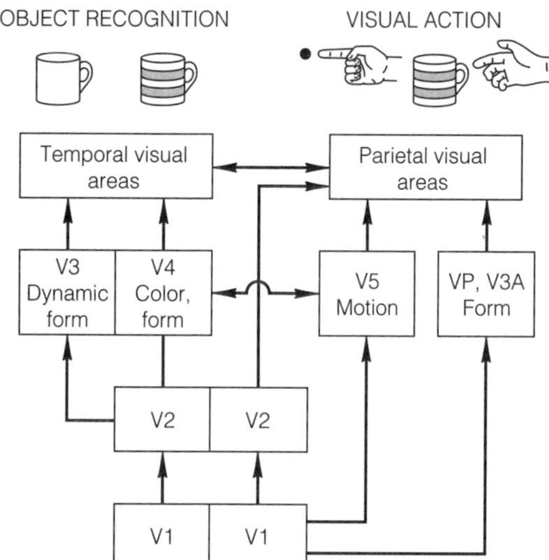

FIGURE 11.4. The main pathways of the two separate visual streams. V1 and V2 project to V3, V3A, V4, and V5, which then project to the temporal or visual areas. (After Goodale, 1993.)

V3 and V3A and then to parietal regions, and a third goes from V1 to V2 to the parietal cortex. These three pathways must certainly be functionally dissociable. Third, Goodale and Milner argue that most of the visual impairments associated with lesions to the parietal cortex can be characterized as visuomotor or orientational. (We return to this issue in the next chapter.)

The Goodale-Milner model is thus a new and different way of describing the functional division between the dorsal and ventral streams of visual processing. There is one additional wrinkle that must be added, however. It is now thought that there may be yet a third stream of visual processing. This stream originates from structures associated with both the parietal and temporal pathways and goes to a region of the temporal lobe that is buried in the superior temporal sulcus or STS (see Figure 11.2). This region is characterized by polysensory neurons, which means that the neurons are responsive to both visual and auditory or both visual and somatosensory input. The functions of this third stream remain vague at present, but the interaction of the parietal and temporal streams in the STS probably implies some sort of interaction between the "action" and "recognition" streams.

PET Studies of Dorsal and Ventral Streams

It is possible to identify regions associated with specific visual processes by measuring regional blood flow during the performance of visual tasks. Ungerleider and Haxby reviewed such studies, as summarized in Figure 11.5. In studies by Haxby and colleagues, subjects were given two tasks. In the first, the subjects indicated which of two faces was identical to a sample face. In the second, the subjects were asked to identify which of two stimuli had a dot (or square) in the same location as a sample. The results showed activation of the temporal regions for the facial stimuli and activation of the posterior parietal region for the location task. In addition, there was activation of frontal areas for the spatial task, supporting the idea that the frontal lobe plays a role in certain aspects of visual processing. One difficulty with interpretation of the spatial tasks is that subjects would have to make eye movements, which would activate regions in the dorsal stream, so it is not clear whether it was the spatial or the movement components that activated the parietal region. The important point, however, is that different regions were involved in the two tasks. A similar dissociation has been made between processes involved in detection of motion, color, and shape (Figure 11.5B). Detection of motion activates regions in the vicinity of V5, whereas detection of shape activates regions along the superior temporal sulcus and the ventral region of the temporal lobe. The perception of color is associated with activation of the region of the lingual gyrus, which is the location of V4. One study also found activation of a lateral occipital region, which is difficult to interpret in the light of lesion studies. This study had special attentional demands, which may be important in interpreting the observed activation.

In summary, studies of regional blood flow in normal subjects show results consistent with the

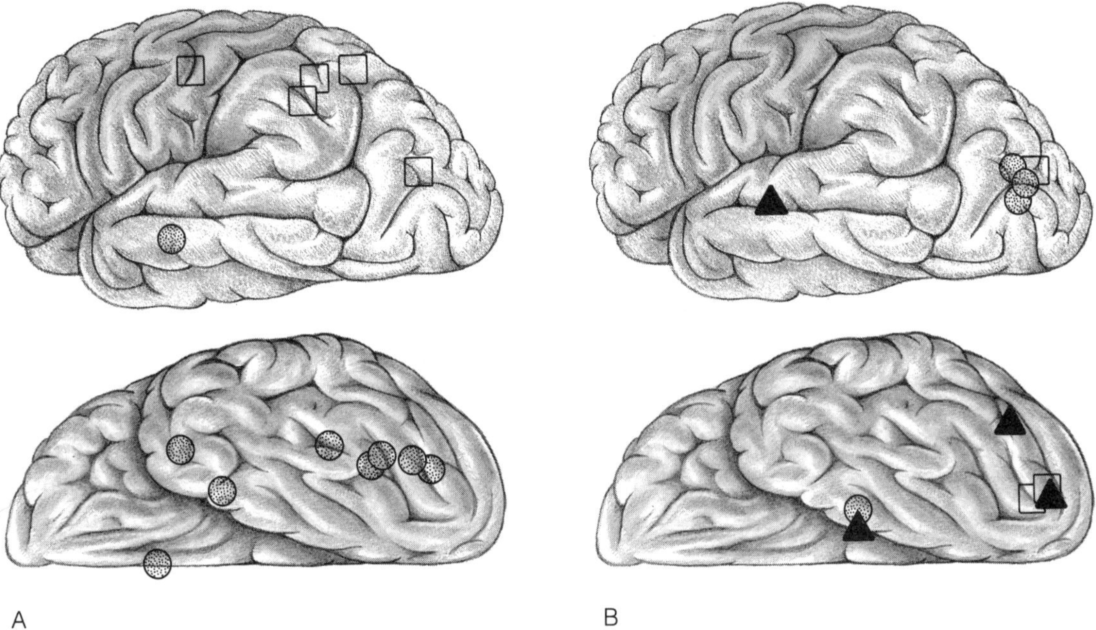

FIGURE 11.5. *A*. Summary of results of PET studies illustrating selective activation of cortical regions by tasks of facial recognition (circles) versus spatial location (squares). *B*. Selective activation of areas associated with perception of color (squares), motion (circles), and shape (triangles). (After Ungerleider and Haxby, 1994.)

general notion of two separate pathways, one to the parietal lobe and one to the temporal lobe. In addition, it is clear that there are separate visual functions in different temporal-occipital regions.

DISORDERS OF VISUAL PATHWAYS

Although we have been stressing the effects of specific injury to the cortex, there are various syndromes that occur from damage at different levels of the visual pathways from the retina to the cortex (Figure 11.6). Destruction of the retina or optic nerve of one eye produces monocular blindness, the loss of sight in that eye. A lesion of the medial region of the optic chiasm severs the crossing fibers, producing bitemporal **hemianopia**—loss of vision of both temporal fields. A lesion of the lateral chiasm results in a loss of vision of one nasal field, or nasal hemianopia. Complete cuts of the optic tract, lateral geniculate body, or area V1 will result in **homonymous hemianopia,** blindness of one entire visual field. Should this lesion be partial, as is often the case, quadrantic anopia occurs: destruction of only a portion of the visual field (Figures 11.6 and 11.7). Lesions of the occipital lobe often spare the central, or macular, region of the visual field, although the reason is uncertain. The most reasonable explanations are that this region receives a double vascular supply, from both the middle and the posterior cerebral arteries, making it more resilient to large hemispheric lesions; or that the foveal region of the retina projects to both hemispheres, so that even if one occipital lobe is destroyed, the other receives projections from the fovea. The former explanation is more likely. Macular sparing helps to differentiate lesions of the optic tract or thalamus from cortical lesions, since macular sparing occurs only after lesions (usually large) to the visual cortex. Macular sparing does not always occur, however, and many

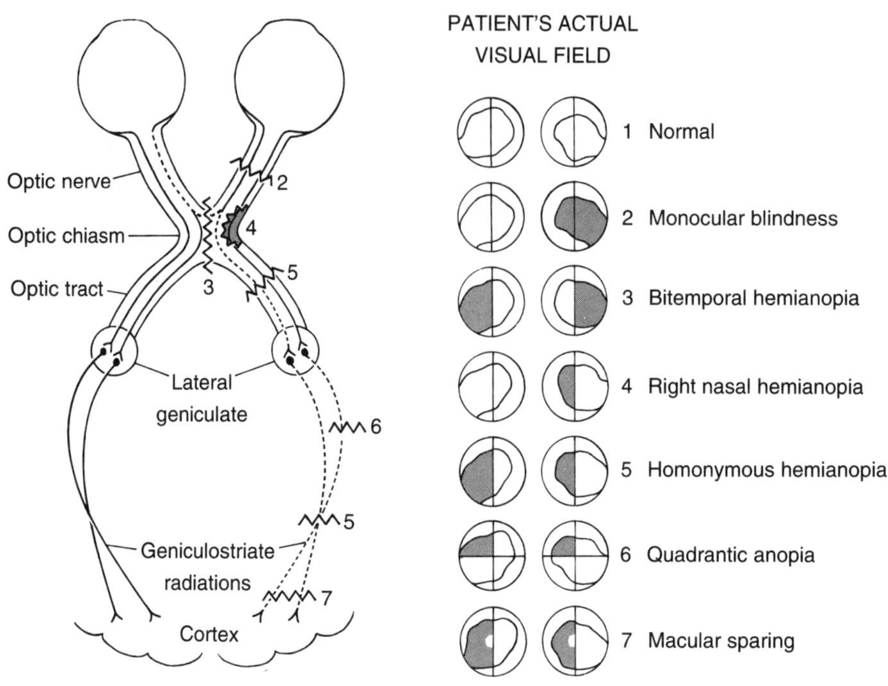

FIGURE 11.6. Visual defects following damage at different levels of the visual system as denoted by numbers. A darkened region in the visual field denotes a blind area. (After Curtis, 1972.)

people with visual cortex lesions have a complete loss of vision in one quarter or half of the fovea.

Small lesions of the occipital lobe often produce scotomas, small blind spots in the visual field (see Figure 11.7). A curious aspect of these defects is that people are often totally unaware of them, because of nystagmus (constant tiny involuntary eye movements) and "spontaneous filling in." Because the eyes are usually in constant motion, the scotoma moves about the visual field, allowing the brain to perceive all the information in the field. If the eyes are held still, the visual system actually completes objects, faces, and so on, resulting in a normal percept of the stimulus. The visual system may cover up the scotoma so successfully that its presence can be demonstrated to the patient only by "tricking" the visual system. This can be achieved by placing objects entirely within the scotoma and, without allowing the patient to shift gaze, asking what the object is. If no object is reported, the examiner moves the object out of the scotoma so that it suddenly "appears" in the intact region of the patient's visual field, thus demonstrating the existence of a blind region. A similar phenomenon can be demonstrated in one's own "blind spot." Stand beside a table, close one eye, stare at a spot on the table, and move a pencil along the table laterally, from directly below your nose to between 20 and 30 cm toward the periphery. Part of the pencil will vanish when you reach the blind spot. You can move the pencil through the blind spot slowly, and it will suddenly reappear on the other side.

DISORDERS OF CORTICAL FUNCTION

Research into selective disturbances of visual functions is rare and is limited mainly to case studies. The reason is that natural lesions seldom

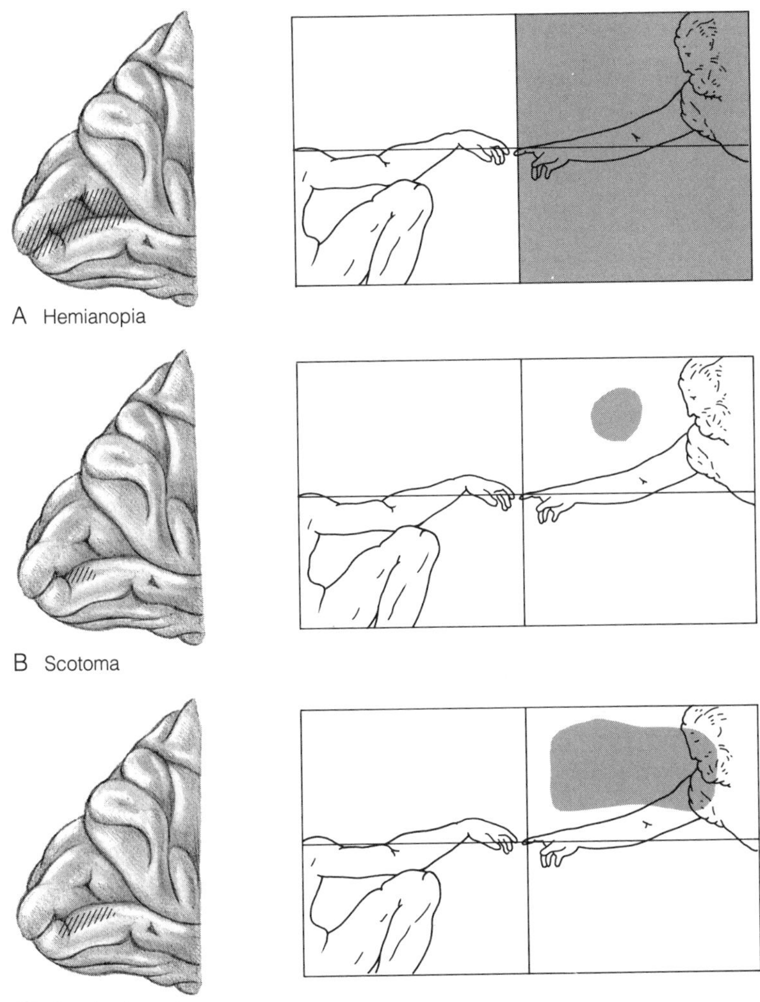

FIGURE 11.7. The consequences of lesions in V1. The shaded areas indicate the regions of visual loss. *A*. The effects of a complete lesion of V1 in the left hemisphere. There is a hemianopia affecting the right visual field. *B*. A small lesion of the lower lip of the calcarine fissure. There is a scotoma. *C*. A larger lesion of the lower lip of the calcarine fissure. There is a larger scotoma that affects most of the upper right visual quadrant.

respect the boundaries of specific areas. To get a feeling for the specific symptoms of injury to the visual cortex, we present several case histories, each with distinctly different symptoms and pathology. We begin with damage to V1 and then proceed along the hierarchies to higher areas and more complicated visual disturbances.

Case B. K.: V1 Damage and a Scotoma

One morning B. K. awoke to discover that he was hemianopic in the left visual field. Given a history of classic migraine, in which the aura was nearly always in the left visual field, it is likely that he had a migraine stroke. Within a few hours the lower field began to return, but the left upper quadrant was slow to show any change. A CT scan (Figure 11.8A) showed a clear infarct in the right occipital area. The size of a field defect is routinely measured with perimetry. This is a standardized method of measuring the size of a visual defect in which the subject fixates on a black dot in the center of a large white hemisphere. A small light is moved around the field and the task is to indicate when it can be seen. The brightness and size of the light can be varied, thus manipulating the difficulty of the task. The performance is mapped by indicating the area of "blindness" on a schematic diagram of the visual fields (Figure 11.8B). Size in the visual field is measured by visual angle, which is indicated in degrees. Thus, for B. K. the area of complete inability to perceive even a very large bright light is 6° up along the vertical midline and about 15° lateral along the horizontal midline. The area beyond this zone in the left upper quadrant does not have normal vision, however, since there is still an inability to perceive less bright lights in this area.

The nature of the visual defects can be illustrated best in the context of their poststroke evolution. For the first 2 to 3 days the field appeared dark, much as though a piece of smoked glass were blocking the view of the world beyond. On the fourth day, this darkness had disappeared and was replaced with "visual noise," called a scintillating scotoma, throughout much of the field, especially in the area of the scotoma. This noise is best described as being like colored "snow" on a TV screen. At about the same time, movement in the field was first perceived, as a traveling "wave" much like ripples on a pond. There was no perception of form or pattern. One curious phenomenon was first observed during perimetry testing 4 days after the stroke. If the stimulus light was moved into the blind field, it was not perceived until it moved into another quadrant. Curiously, however, B. K. immediately became aware (in hindsight) that the light had been present in the blind field and could accurately state where it entered the field. In other words, B. K. perceived location without being able to perceive content. (This phenomenon is known as blindsight and is discussed further in case D. B.) Over the ensuing 4 to 6 months the area of blindness decreased somewhat and acuity in the periphery improved significantly. Nonetheless, form vision remains poor in the left upper quadrant, outside the scotoma. The scintillating colored snow is still present, showing little change from the first few days after the stroke.

The visual phenomena observed by B. K. indicate that V1 (and perhaps V2) probably has an area of total cell death (the dense scotoma). The presence of poor form vision in the rest of the quadrant may reflect a loss of some but not all neurons in V1, possibly only those neurons that are especially sensitive to ischemia. The poor form vision might also be attributed to the fact that other visual areas, especially V2, remain intact. B. K.'s symptoms also show that other occipital areas are functional, because there is color and motion perception even though there is no form perception. Thus, B. K. can perceive accurately the color or motion of objects that he cannot identify. Those who are myopic (nearsighted) will have experienced a similar phenomenon: the colors of objects or lights can be appreciated, while the form is not recognizable. B. K.'s stroke thus indicates the presence of at least four independent visual functions: form (which is absent), and color, movement, and location (which are spared).

The loss of one quarter of the fovea leads B. K. to make a variety of visual errors. Immediately after the stroke he was able to read only with great difficulty. If one looks at a word, the fixation point is in the center of the word, so for B. K. half of the word is absent. Indeed, it was difficult to find the edge of the page because it was in the blind field. Normal reading returned as B. K. learned to direct his gaze slightly to the left and upward (probably about 2° in each direction), which allowed words to fall in the normal visual field. This "recovery" took about 6 weeks. Returning to playing squash and tennis was equally challenging, for once a ball entered the scotoma it was lost. Similarly, facial recognition was slower than it was before the stroke, because the information in the left visual field appears to be particularly important for face recognition.

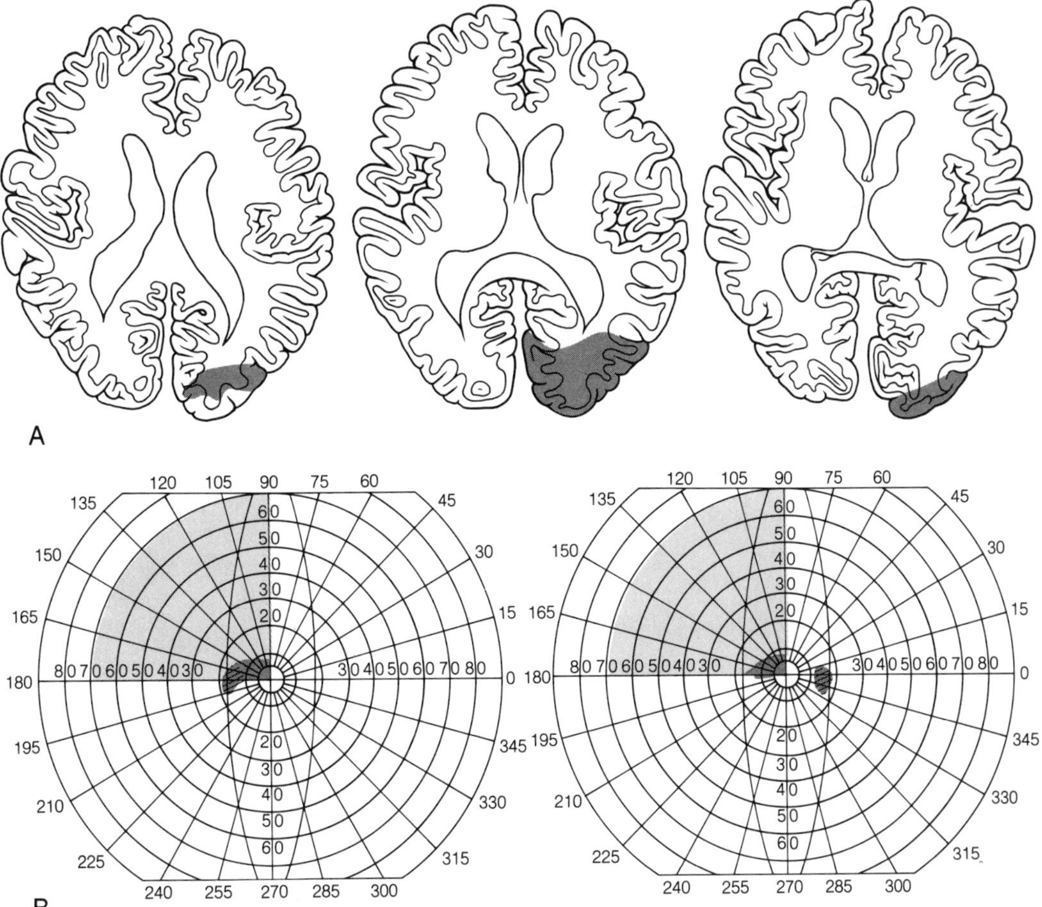

FIGURE 11.8. *A*. Schematic illustration of B. K.'s CT scan, showing the infarct in the right occipital area. *B*. Illustration of the visual fields of B. K. 6 months after the stroke. The shaded region shows the area of scotoma, the stippled region shows the area of reduced acuity, and the striped area shows the normal blind spot.

Case D. B.: V1 Damage and Blindsight

Case D. B. is one of the most extensively studied people with visual disturbance from an occipital lesion (see the detailed monograph by Weiskrantz). D. B.'s right calcarine fissure was removed surgically to excise an angioma, which is a collection of abnormal blood vessels. D. B. therefore has a hemianopia based on standard perimetry but has surprising visual capacities. When questioned about his vision in the left field, D. B. usually reports that he sees nothing. Occasionally he indicates that he had a "feeling" that a stimulus was "approaching" or was "smooth" or "jagged." But, according to Weiskrantz, he always stresses that he saw nothing in the sense of "seeing," that typically he was guessing, and that he was at a loss for words to describe any conscious perception. In spite of this, D. B. has some interesting visual capacities. First, when D. B. was asked to point to locations in the impaired field in which spots of light were turned on briefly, he was surprisingly accurate. His accuracy contrasts with his subjective impression that he saw nothing at all. Furthermore, he appears to be able to discriminate the orientation of lines, which he could not report "seeing." Thus, he can discriminate a difference in orientation of 10° between two successively presented gratings in his impaired field. Finally, D. B. can detect some forms of movement. When a vigorously moving stimulus was used, he reported "seeing" something. In this case he did not report actually seeing a visual stimulus but rather spoke of complex patterns of lines and grids. These may have been something like B. K.'s moving lines. In summary, D. B. has "cortical blindness" in which he reports no conscious awareness of "seeing" but still appears to be able to report the location of the objects he cannot perceive.

Case J. I.: V4 Damage and Color

Sacks and Wasserman report the touching story of J. I., an artist who suddenly became color-blind. In 1986 the man was in a car accident in which he sustained a concussion. His principal symptoms after the injury were that he could not distinguish any colors whatsoever, but his visual acuity had actually improved. "Within days . . . my vision was that of an eagle—I can see a worm wiggling a block away. The sharpness of focus is incredible." The impact of the color loss was far greater than one would have expected. J. I. could barely stand the pain of living in a world that was in shades of gray. He found the changed appearance of people unbearable, as their flesh was an abhorrent gray. He found foods disgusting in their grayish, dead appearance, and he had to close his eyes to eat. Flesh now appeared "rat-colored" to him. He could not even imagine colors any longer. The mental image of a tomato looked as black as its actual appearance. Even his dreams, which had once been in vivid colors, were now in black and gray. Detailed visual testing by Sacks and Wasserman, and later by Zeki, revealed that he was color-blind by the usual definitions, but this was attributed to specific damage to the occipital cortex. In addition, it did appear that his acuity had improved, especially at twilight or at night. Two years after his injury, J. I.'s despair had declined, and it actually appeared that he no longer could remember color well. This is very curious, because people who become blind through injury to the eyes or optic nerves do not lose their imagery or memory of color. There is little doubt that imagery and memory rely on the operation of at least some cortical structures necessary for the original perception.

Case L. M.: V5 Damage and Perception of Movement

Zihl and his colleagues report the case of a 43-year-old woman who had a bilateral posterior injury resulting from a vascular abnormality. Her primary chronic complaint was a loss of movement vision. For example, she had difficulty pouring tea into a cup because the fluid appeared to be frozen. In addition, she could not stop pouring because she could not see the fluid level rise. She found being in a room with other people disturbing because she could not see them moving; they would suddenly appear to be "here or there," but she did not see them in between. The results of other tests of visual function appeared essentially normal. She could discriminate colors, recognize objects, and read and write. This syndrome is especially intriguing because we would not believe intuitively that such a syndrome is likely! Loss of color or form vision fits with our everyday experience that people can be color-blind or myopic; loss of the ability to see moving objects is counterintuitive indeed. Case L. M. is important because she shows that the brain must analyze movement of form separately from the form itself.

Case D. F.: Occipital Damage and Visual Agnosia

Visual agnosia is the term coined by Sigmund Freud for the inability to combine individual visual impressions into complete patterns—thus, the inability to recognize objects or their pictorial representations, or to draw or copy them. Goodale, Milner, and their colleagues have studied extensively a 35-year-old visual agnosic who suffered carbon monoxide poisoning that resulted in bilateral damage to the lateral occipital region (mainly areas 18 and 19) and in the tissue at the junction of the parietal and occipital cortex. The principal deficit of D. F. is a profound inability to recognize line drawings of objects, which is known as visual-form agnosia. Thus, although D. F. could recognize many objects, she was unable to recognize drawings of them. Furthermore, although she could draw objects from memory, she had real difficulty in drawing objects and even more difficulty in copying line drawings (Figure 11.9). Thus, it appeared that D. F. had a serious defect in form perception. The remarkable thing about D. F., however, was her apparently nearly intact ability to guide hand and finger movements toward objects that she could not perceive. For example, although D. F. had a gross deficit in judging lines as horizontal or vertical, she could reach out and "post" a hand-held card into a slot at different orientations. Indeed, analysis of video records of D. F.'s reaching revealed that, like normal control subjects, D. F. began to orient the card correctly even as the hand was being raised from the start position of the task. In other words, D. F. could use visual form information to guide movements to objects (the dorsal stream), but she could not use visual information to recognize the same objects (the ventral stream).

Case V. K.: Parietal Damage and Visuomotor Guidance

Damage to the posterior parietal lobe produces a disorder known as optic ataxia, which refers to a deficit in visually guided hand movements that cannot be ascribed to motor, somatosensory, or visual field or acuity deficits. V. K. is a woman with bilateral hemorrhages in the occipital-parietal regions; her case is described by Jakobson and colleagues. Although she initially appeared to be virtually blind, her symptoms dissipated over a month, and she was left with disordered control of her gaze, an impairment in visual attention, and optic ataxia. (Collectively, these symptoms are known as Balint's syndrome.) She had good form and color vision and could recognize and name objects. V. K.'s ability to reach for objects was grossly impaired, however. Thus, in contrast to D. F., who was able to reach and orient her hand posture toward different objects that she could not perceive, V. K. was unable to coordinate reaching and grasping for objects that she could perceive. This difficulty was not merely one of being unable to direct movements in space, for she could point to objects. What she could not do was to form the appropriate hand postures for different object qualities. Taken together, cases D. F. and V. K. suggest that the mechanisms underlying the conscious perception of object form are dissociable from the mechanisms controlling visually guided movements to the same objects.

Cases D. and T.: Higher-Level Visual Processes

These two cases described by Campbell and colleagues illustrate a very intriguing dissociation of visual functions. Case D. has a right occipital-temporal lesion that is associated with a left upper quadrantanopia that extends into the lower quadrant. As would be expected from B. K., she had some initial difficulties in reading, but her language abilities were intact. Curiously, she was completely unable to recognize people by their faces and had difficulty identifying handwriting, including her own. The facial recognition deficit, which is known as prosopagnosia, is particularly interesting because prosopagnosics often cannot recognize even their own face in a mirror! Although D. could not recognize faces, she could make use of information in faces. For example, when given various tests of lipreading, she appeared completely normal. Furthermore, she could imitate the facial movements and expressions of another person.

Case T. provides an interesting contrast to D. This woman has a left occipital-temporal lesion with a right hemianopia. She had great difficulty reading (alexia) and was unable to name colors, even though she could discriminate them. In

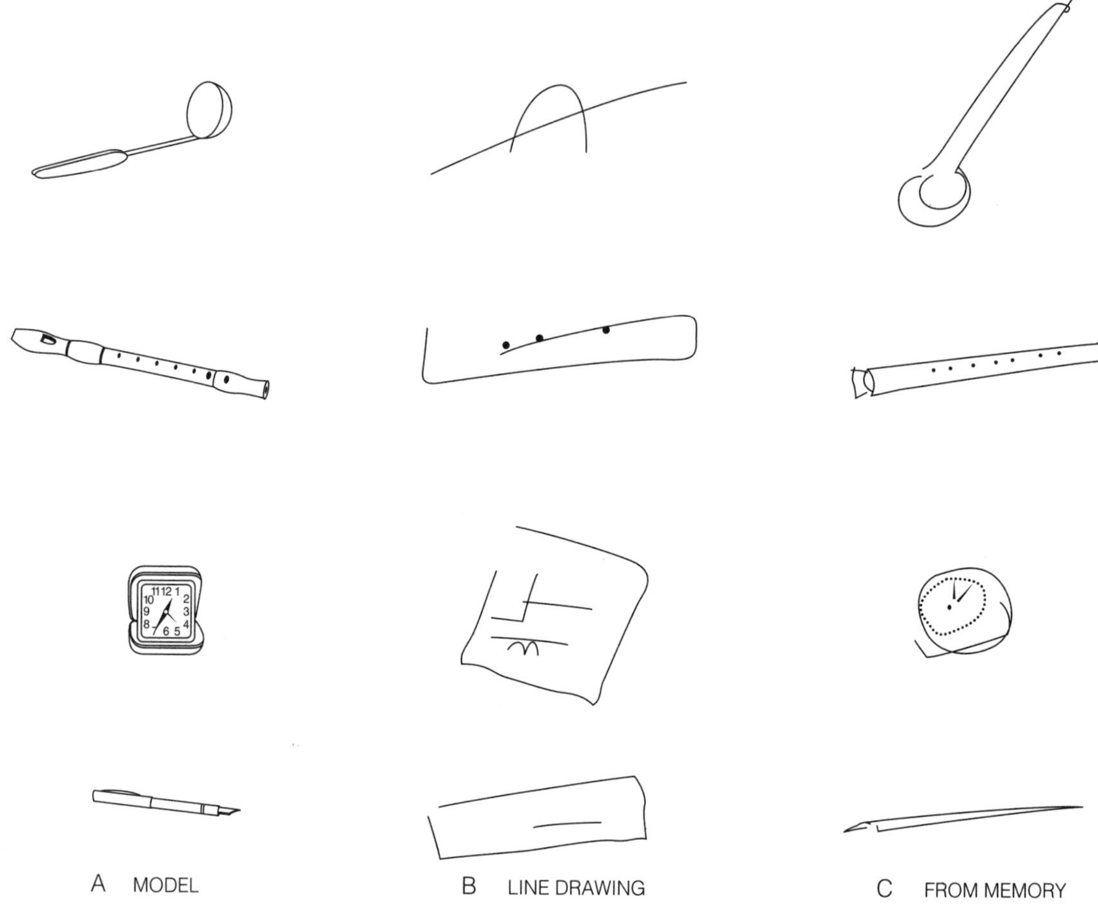

FIGURE 11.9. Samples of D. F.'s drawings. *A*. Examples of the original line drawings presented to D. F. *B*. Examples of D. F.'s drawings of the models. *C*. D. F.'s drawings based on memory of the models. Note that the drawings from memory are superior to the copies of the model line drawings.

contrast to D., T. had no difficulty in recognizing familiar faces but was impaired in lipreading.

Taken together, these two cases indicate that face identification and the extraction of speech information from faces do not call on the same cortical systems. In addition, the fact that D. has a lesion on the right and a deficit in face identification, and T. has a lesion on the left and a deficit in lipreading, suggests a relative asymmetry in some aspects of occipital lobe functions. It remains to be shown exactly what visual processes are impaired in the two cases or what the necessary lesions for deficits in facial recognition and lipreading might be.

Summary

Several principles can be extracted from the behavior and pathology of these few cases. First, there are clearly distinct syndromes of visual disturbance. Second, some of the symptoms can be taken as evidence of a fundamental dissociation between vision for guiding movements (the dorsal stream) and visual recognition (the ventral stream). Third, the dissociability of the symptoms in the various patients implies that our introspective view of a unified visual experience is false. In particular, the fact that objects can be seen when they are still but not when they are moving is particularly disturbing, because it seems to defy the common sense view that an object is identical when it is moving and still. Clearly the brain does not treat objects the same way in the two situations! Finally, we have at least suggestive evidence that there may be an asymmetry in occipital lobe functions.

VISUAL AGNOSIA

One of the difficulties in describing the symptomatology and pathology of agnosia is that there are a bewildering variety of patients and symptoms discussed in the neurological literature. Furthermore, as Farah has pointed out, there is no agreement on a taxonomy of agnosia, which makes classification of different patterns of symptoms very difficult. We shall separate visual agnosias into visual object agnosias and other agnosias.

Object Agnosia

The traditional way to classify object agnosia, which dates back to Lissauer in 1890, is to distinguish two broad forms of visual object agnosia: apperceptive agnosia and associative agnosia. **Apperceptive agnosia** refers to any failure of object recognition in which relatively basic visual functions (acuity, color, motion) are preserved. This category of agnosia has been applied to an extremely heterogeneous set of patients, but the fundamental deficit is an inability to develop a percept of the structure of an object or objects. In the simplest case, patients are simply unable to recognize, copy, or match simple shapes. Many patients have another unusual symptom, too, which is often referred to as simultagnosia. In this case patients can perceive the basic shape of an object, but they are unable to perceive more than one object at a time. Thus, if two objects are presented together, only one is perceived. Such patients often act as though they were blind, possibly because they are simply overwhelmed by the task at hand. Imagine trying to see the world one object at a time!

Apperceptive agnosia does not result from a restricted lesion but usually follows gross bilateral damage to the lateral parts of the occipital lobes, including regions sending outputs to the ventral stream. Such injuries are probably most commonly associated with carbon monoxide poisoning, which appears to produce neuronal death in "watershed" regions, or regions lying in the border areas between territories of different arterial systems.

Associative agnosia refers to an inability to recognize objects, despite an apparent perception of the object. Thus, the associative agnosic can copy a drawing rather accurately, indicating a coherent percept, but cannot identify it. This form of agnosia is therefore conceived as being at a "higher cognitive" level of processing that is associated with stored information about objects. In effect, this is a defect in memory that affects not only past knowledge about the object, but also the acquisition of new knowledge. Associative agnosias are more likely to be associated with damage to regions in the ventral stream that are farther along the processing hierarchy, such as the anterior temporal lobe.

Other Agnosias

We shall consider briefly three other forms of visual agnosia. The first is facial agnosia (or **prosopagnosia**). Patients with facial agnosia cannot recognize any previously known face, including their own as seen in a mirror or photograph. They can recognize people by face information, however, such as a birthmark, mustache, or characteristic hairdo. According to Damasio, most facial agnosics can tell human from nonhuman faces and can recognize facial expressions normally. All postmortem studies on facial agnosics have found bilateral damage, and imaging studies in living patients confirm the bilateral nature of the injury in most patients, with the damage centered in the region below the calcarine fissure at the occipital-temporal junction (see Figure 11.1). These results imply that the process of facial recognition is probably bilateral, but the contribution of each side is probably not equivalent (see below). In fact, patients with damage to the right fusiform and lingual areas (see Figure 11.1) have significant deficits in facial recognition, which tends to be slow and inaccurate. Such people do not have the all-pervasive deficit that includes their own face, however, as is found in cases of facial agnosia after bilateral injury.

A second form of agnosia is **alexia,** which is the inability to read. Alexia has often been seen as the complementary symptom to facial recognition deficits. Alexia is most likely to result from damage to the left fusiform and lingual areas. Either hemisphere can read letters, but only the left appears able to combine the letters to form lexical representations. Alexia can be conceived as a form of object agnosia, in which there is an inability to construct perceptual wholes from parts, or it may be a form of associative agnosia, in which case the word memory (the lexical store) is either damaged or inaccessible.

The final form of agnosia can be called visual-spatial agnosia. This term refers to a variety of disorders of spatial perception and orientation. One of the most disruptive forms is topographical disorientation, which is the inability to find one's way around familiar environments such as one's neighborhood. People with this deficit seem unable to recognize landmarks that would indicate the appropriate direction to travel. Most people with topographical disorientation have other visual deficits, especially defects in facial recognition. Thus, it is not surprising to find that the critical area for this disorder lies in the right medial occipital-temporal region, including the fusiform and lingual gyri.

A critical point in understanding the nature of visual agnosia is that the most commonly involved region is the tissue at the occipital-temporal border, which is part of the ventral visual stream. Note, however, that the different agnosias are at least partly dissociable, which means that there must be different streams of visual information processing in the ventral stream. It appears that visual agnosias do not result from damage to the dorsal stream.

ARE FACES SPECIAL?

Faces convey a wealth of social and affective information to humans. This importance of faces as visual stimuli has led several authors to postulate a special mode for the analysis of faces that is analogous to the left hemisphere's apparently innate predisposition for the analysis of words. Teuber suggested that when faces are encountered, they are analyzed by a special processing mechanism in the right hemisphere so that they are recognized in a manner analogous to the way words are recognized in the left hemisphere. One source of support for this idea comes from the observation that the perception of faces is strongly influenced by their orientation. For example, Yin found that the memory of photographs of faces was impaired in patients with right posterior lesions but that this handicap was reduced when the photographs were presented upside down or when other complex visual stimuli, such as houses, were used instead. Yin concluded that photographs of faces presented upright are processed by a special mechanism in the right hemisphere so that they are recognized in a manner analogous to word recognition. Because faces presented upside down do not stimulate the special mechanism, right posterior lesions do not affect the recognition of these stimuli.

The possibility that faces might be special raises several questions. First, if there is a special processing mechanism for faces, where is it located? Studies of monkeys have shown neurons in the temporal lobe that are specifically tuned to different faces, so the temporal lobe is a likely candidate. There is no evidence of an asymmetry in the temporal cortex of monkeys, but that does not preclude such an asymmetry in humans. Second, there is some doubt about the nature of the special perceptual mechanism. Teuber appears to have assumed it to be a mechanism devoted to combining features of facial stimuli into a whole, or gestalt, but it is uncertain how this mechanism would be specific for faces. In fact, a clever study by Diamond and Carey suggests that it is not specific to faces, because they found that dog experts, who could distinguish individual dog faces of the same breed, were just as sensitive to the inversion of dog photographs. These authors suggest that it is because we are experts at distinguishing the faces of humans (or dogs) that we are disturbed differentially when face photographs are inverted. The fact that children are poor at distinguishing faces and are relatively unaffected by inversion is consistent with this idea. Nonetheless, there is little doubt that faces are processed in a special way by the right hemisphere. We presented subjects with photographs of faces, as illustrated in Figure 11.10. Each of the two lower photographs is a composite of the left or the right side of the original face shown in the upper photograph. Asked to identify which of the composite photographs most resembled the original, normal subjects consistently matched the left side of the original photograph to its composite, whether or not the photographs were presented upright or inverted. Furthermore, patients with either right temporal or right parietal removals failed to match consistently either side of the face in either the upright or the inverted presentation.

The idea that faces are special is intriguing, but we believe that the data on facial perception and memory warrant a more parsimonious interpretation: the posterior part of the right hemisphere is specialized for the processing of complex visual patterns, whether they be faces, geometric patterns, or the like. Perception of faces is particularly sensitive to the effects of right posterior damage because faces are especially complex and because there are so many different faces, many of which superficially appear to be highly similar. Indeed, the uniqueness of individual human faces is based on very small differences, and mastery of the differentiation of faces requires considerable practice and possibly includes a genetic predisposition. In this regard, deficits in facial perception might result, in part, from deficits in the identification of the distinctive features used in differentiation, rather than in the flawed formation of an actual gestalt of a particular face. As we noted, if the normal pattern of visual scanning of faces is disrupted, recognition of faces might be impaired despite a relatively intact percept of a given face. Indeed, the difficulty that normal adults initially have in differentiating individuals of an unfamiliar race may imply that one must learn to scan the faces of different racial groups in particular ways to identify the cues necessary for accurate identification.

Finally, we consider the perception of our own face. This provides a unique example of visual perception, since our own image of our face comes largely from looking in a mirror, thus providing a reversed image, whereas others' image of our face comes from direct view. Inspection of Figure 11.10 illustrates the implications of this difference. The top photograph is the image that other people see of this woman and, since there is a left visual-field bias in our perception, most right-handers choose the bottom right as the picture most resembling the original. Consider the choice of the woman herself, however. Her common view of her face is the reverse of ours, and hence she is more likely to choose (and in fact did choose) the other composite photograph as most resembling her own face. One intriguing consequence of our biased self-facial image is our opinion of personal photographs. Many people complain about not being photogenic, that their photographs are never taken at the correct angle, that their hair wasn't just right, and so on. The problem may be rather different: we are accustomed to seeing ourselves in a reversed mirror image and hence when we view a photograph, we are biased to look at the side of our face that we do not normally perceive selectively. Indeed, we appear not to see ourselves as others see us.

VISUAL IMAGERY

Our ability to conjure up mental images is central to human thought. Indeed, imagery is crucial to many kinds of problem solving, such as mental arithmetic, map reading, and mechanical reason-

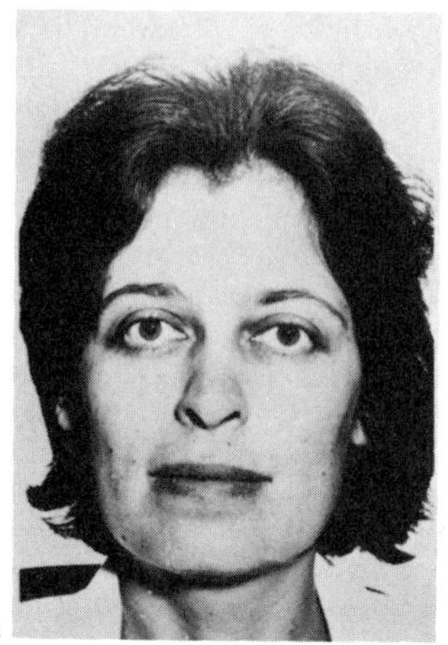

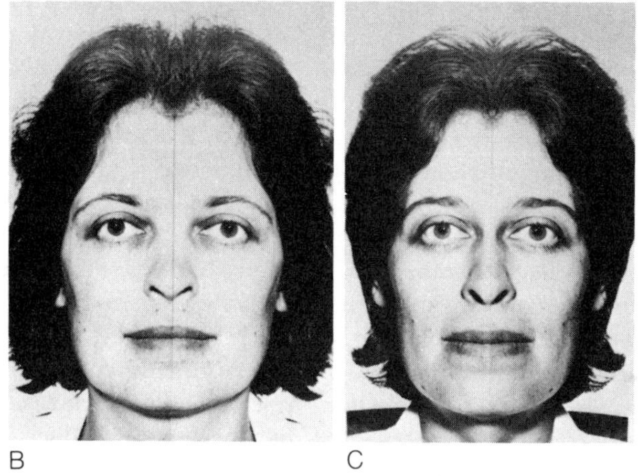

FIGURE 11.10. An example of the split-faces test. Subjects were asked which of the two bottom pictures, *B* or *C*, most closely resembles the top picture, *A*. Picture *C* was chosen by controls significantly more often than *B*. Picture *C* corresponds to that part of *A* falling in the subjects' left visual field. The woman in the picture chose *B*, which is the view she is accustomed to seeing in the mirror. (After Kolb, Milner, and Taylor, 1983.)

ing. We noted earlier that patients with damage to V4 lose color perception and also cannot imagine color. This suggests that at least some forms of imagery are dependent upon the same areas as initial perception of the image. Studies of cortical activity (EEG and ERP) and PET studies confirm the general idea that imagery shares cortical representation with visual perception. There are, however, a small group of patients reviewed by Farah who do not have visual impairments yet have deficits in image generation. Most of these people have damage in the posterior part of the left hemisphere, which suggests that there may be some region in this area that is necessary for image generation. Presumably this region acts in concert with the other visual areas to generate images in V1 and subsequently in other regions. A question that arises is whether a person with a lesion that produces visual agnosia might have the "image generation" area of the left hemisphere intact and so be able to generate images of things that cannot be perceived. This could be seen in the case of a patient who was unable to copy drawings or to recognize objects but who could nonetheless produce drawings of the objects from memory. Indeed, Behrmann and colleagues have described just such a patient, case C. K. The curious thing about C. K. is that although he cannot recognize objects, he can imagine them and can draw them in considerable detail from memory. This implies that there must be some dissociation between systems involved in object perception and the generation of images. We can conclude that neural structures mediating the perception and imagination of objects are unlikely to be completely independent, but it is clear that a deficit in object perception cannot be due simply to a loss of mental representations (that is, memory) of objects.

There has been considerable controversy over whether mental rotation of objects might be localized to some region of the right hemisphere. In her review of this literature Farah concludes that the studies have been "distressingly inconsistent." She proposes that mental rotation probably involves both hemispheres, with some degree of right hemisphere superiority. (For further reviews, see both Farah and Kosslyn.)

CONCLUSIONS

The function of the occipital lobe is vision. Separate anatomical regions within the occipital lobe are involved in the perception of form, movement, and color. Occipital structures are merely the beginning of visual processing because there are multiple visual systems that can be divided into at least two major routes, one going ventrally into the temporal lobe and one going dorsally into the parietal lobe. The ventral stream is most certainly involved with various aspects of stimulus recognition. The dorsal stream is for the guidance of movement in space. The representation of spatial information relies on the recognition of cues within the environment, which would therefore make visual-spatial recognition dependent upon processing in the ventral stream. An important aspect of the dorsal-ventral distinction in visual processing is that neither route is a single system. Rather, there are clearly dissociable subsystems involved in various functions. Finally, there is a suggestion that some occipital regions, especially those adjoining the temporal cortex, may be functionally asymmetrical. In particular, there appears to be some specialization for word recognition on the left and facial recognition on the right.

REFERENCES

Barbur, J. L., J. D. G. Watson, R. S. J. Frackowiak, and S. Zeki. Conscious visual perception without V1. *Brain* 116:1293–1302, 1993.

Behrmann, M., G. Winocur, and M. Moscovitch. Dissociation between mental imagery and object recognition in a brain-damaged patient. *Nature* 359:636–637, 1992.

Boussaoud, D., L. G. Ungerleider, and R. Desimone. Pathways for motion analysis: Cortical connections of the medial superior temporal and fundus of the superior temporal visual areas in the macaque. *Journal of Comparative Neurology* 296:462–495, 1990.

Campbell, R., T. Landis, and M. Regard. Face recognition and lipreading: A neurological dissociation. *Brain* 109:509–521, 1986.

Clarke, S., and J. Miklossy. Occipital cortex in man: Organization of callosal connections, related myelo- and cytoarchitecture, and putative foundaries of functional visual areas. *Journal of Comparative Neurology* 298:188–214, 1990.

Curtis, B. Visual system. In B. A. Curtis, S. Jacobson, and E. M. Marcus eds. *An Introduction to the Neurosciences.* Philadelphia and Toronto: W. B. Saunders, 1972.

Damasio, A. R., H. Damasio, and G. W. Van Hoesen. Prosopagnosia: Anatomical basis and behavioral mechanisms. *Neurology* 32:331–341, 1982.

Damasio, A. R., D. Tranel, and H. Damasio. Disorders of visual recognition. In F. Boller and J. Grafman, eds. *Handbook of Neuropsychology,* vol. 2. Elsevier: Amsterdam, 1989.

Diamond, R., and S. Carey. Why faces are and are not special: An effect of expertise. *Journal of Experimental Psychology: General* 15:107–117, 1986.

Farah, M. J. *Visual Agnosia.* Cambridge, Mass.: MIT Press, 1990.

Farah, M. J. The neurological basis of mental imagery: A componential analysis. *Cognition* 18:245–272, 1984.

Farah, M. J. The neuropsychology of mental imagery. In F. Boller and J. Grafman, eds. *Handbook of Neuropsychology,* vol. 2. Amsterdam: Elsevier, 1990.

Felleman, D. J., and D. C. van Essen. Distributed hierarchical processing in primate cerebral cortex. *Cerebral Cortex* 1:1–47, 1991.

Goodale, M. A. Visual pathways supporting perception and action in the primate cerebral cortex. *Current Opinion in Neurobiology* 3:578–585, 1993.

Goodale, M. A., D. A. Milner, L. S. Jakobson, and J. D. P. Carey. A neurological dissociation between perceiving objects and grasping them. *Nature* 349:154–156, 1991.

Jacobsen, L. S., Y. M. Archibald, D. P. Carey, and M. A. Goodale. A kinematic analysis of reaching and grasping movements in a patient recovering from optic ataxia. *Neuropsychologia* 29:803–809, 1991.

Kolb, B., B. Milner, and L. Taylor. Perception of faces by patients with localized cortical excisions. *Canadian Journal of Psychology* 37:8–18, 1983.

Kosslyn, S. M. Seeing and imaging in the cerebral hemispheres: A computational approach. *Psychological Review* 94:148–175, 1987.

Lissauer, H. Ein fall von seelenblindheit nebst einem Beitrage zur Theori derselben. *Archiv für Psychiatrie und Nervenkrankheiten* 21:222–270, 1890.

Luria, A. R. *The Working Brain.* New York: Penguin, 1973.

Meadows, J. C. Disturbed perception of colours associated with localized cerebral lesions. *Brain* 97:615–632, 1974.

Milner, A. D., and M. A. Goodale. Visual pathways to perception and action. *Progress in Brain Research* 95:317–337, 1993.

Milner, A. D., and M. A. Goodale. *The Visual Brain in Action.* Oxford: Oxford University Press, 1995.

Previc, F. H. Functional specialization in the lower and upper visual fields in humans: Its ecological origins and neurophysiological implications. *Behavioral and Brain Sciences* 13:519–575, 1990.

Sacks, O., and R. Wasserman. The case of the colorblind painter. *The New York Review of Books* 34:25–33, 1987.

Servos, P., M. A. Goodale, and G. K. Humphrey. The drawing of objects by a visual form agnosic: Contribution of surface properties and memorial representations. *Neuropsychologia* 31:251–259, 1993.

Ungerleider, L. G., and J. V. Haxby. "What" and "where" in the human brain. *Current Opinion in Neurobiology* 4:15–165, 1994.

Ungerleider, L. G., and M. Mishkin. Two cortical visual systems. In D. J. Ingle, M. A. Goodale, and R. J. W. Mansfield, eds. *Analysis of Visual Behavior.* MIT Press: Cambridge, Mass., 1982.

Weiskrantz, L. *Blindsight: A Case History and Implications.* Oxford: Oxford University Press, 1986.

Yin, R. K. Face recognition by brain-injured patients: A dissociable ability? *Neuropsychologia* 8:395–402, 1970.

Zeki, S. The visual image in mind and brain. *Scientific American* 267(3):68–76, 1992.

Zeki, S. *A Vision of the Brain.* Oxford: Blackwell, 1993.

Zihl, J., D. von Cramon, and N. Mai. Selective disturbance of movement vision after bilateral brain damage. *Brain* 106:313–340, 1983.

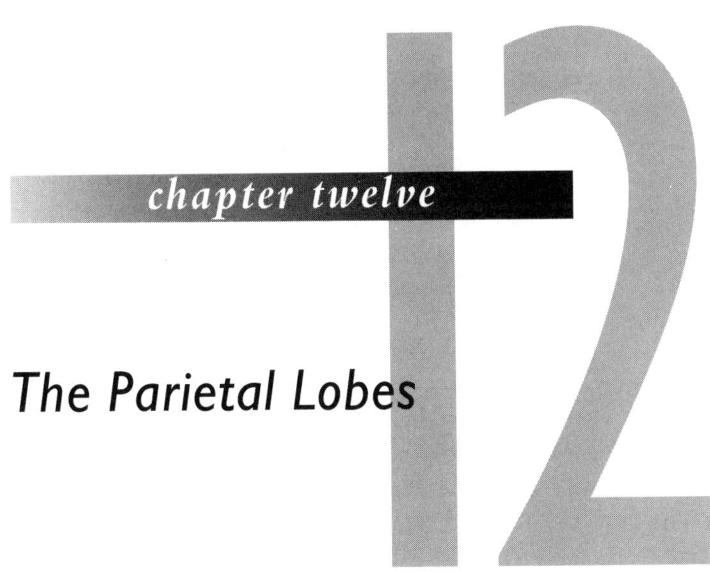

chapter twelve

The Parietal Lobes

The patient with a gross lesion of the parietal lobe presents a curious pattern of symptoms, including a failure to attend to any stimulation on one side of the world, a loss of ability to do arithmetic, an inability to read maps, and difficulty in reaching for objects. The interpretation of these abnormalities presents one of the most challenging puzzles in neuropsychology, in part because these symptoms are difficult to demonstrate in animal models of parietal lobe function. Common laboratory animals such as rats and cats have a very modest parietal "lobe," and although monkeys with parietal damage show many symptoms similar to those seen in human patients, symptoms related to language or spatial cognition are difficult to study in monkeys. Furthermore, the parietal lobes in the human brain have evolved to a much larger size, which might imply that humans will show some symptoms not seen in monkeys. In this chapter we will present a theoretical model of parietal lobe organization and then consider the major symptoms of parietal injury.

ANATOMY OF THE PARIETAL LOBES

Subdivisions of the Parietal Cortex

The parietal lobe is the region of cerebral cortex underlying the parietal skull bone. This area is roughly demarcated anteriorly by the central fissure, ventrally by the Sylvian fissure, dorsally by the cingulate gyrus, and posteriorly by the parietal-occipital sulcus. The principal regions of the parietal lobe include the postcentral gyrus (Brodmann's areas 1, 2, and 3), the superior parietal lobule (areas 5 and 7), the parietal operculum (area 43), the supramarginal gyrus (area 40), and the angular gyrus (area 39) (Figure 12.1). Together, the supramarginal gyrus and angular gyrus are often referred to as the inferior parietal lobe. The parietal lobe can be divided into two functional zones: an anterior zone including areas 1, 2, 3, and 43, and a posterior zone, which includes the remaining areas. The anterior zone is the somatosensory cortex; the posterior zone is referred to as the **posterior parietal cortex.**

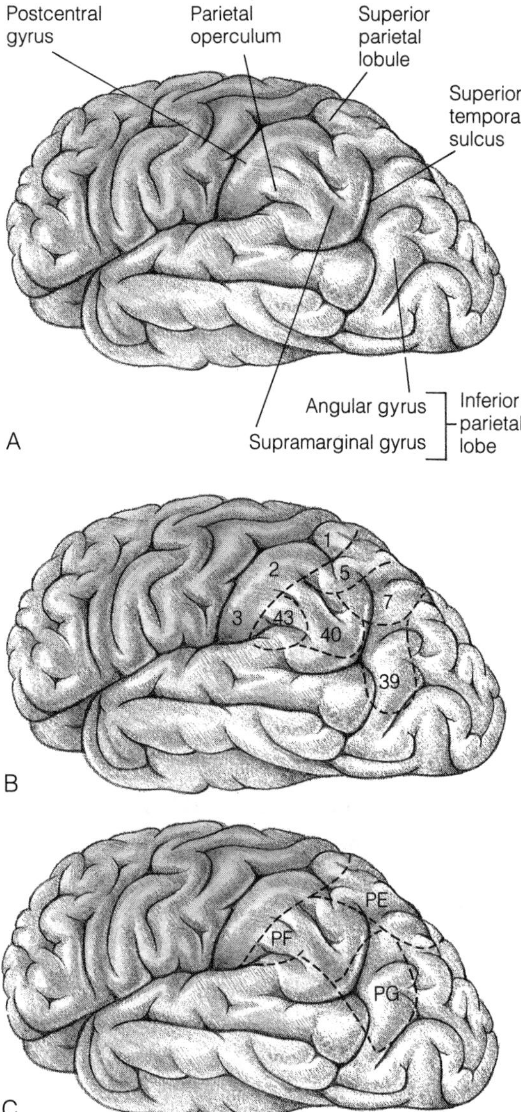

FIGURE 12.1. Gross anatomy of the parietal lobe. *A.* The major gyri and sulci. *B.* Brodmann's cytoarchitectonic regions. *C.* Von Economo's cytoarchitectonic regions.

The parietal lobes have undergone a major expansion in human evolution, largely in the inferior parietal region. This increase in size has made the comparison of various areas in the human brain with those in the monkey brain confusing, especially since Brodmann did not identify areas 39 and 40 in the monkey. This has led to debate over whether monkeys actually have regions homologous to areas 39 and 40. One solution to this problem is to consult another anatomist, von Economo. In von Economo's maps, in which parietal areas are called PA (parietal area A), PB, and so forth, there are three posterior parietal areas (PE, PF, PG) that he described in both humans and monkeys (Figure 12.1C). If we use this system, area PF is equivalent to area 7b and PE to area 5 in Felleman and van Essen's map (see Figure 8.12). Similarly, area PG in the monkey includes areas 7a, VIP, LIP, IPG, PP, MSTc, and MSTp. These latter areas are primarily visual (see Chapter 11).

An area of significant expansion in the human brain appears to be the polymodal portions of area PG and the adjoining polymodal cortex in the superior temporal sulcus (STS). Recall from Chapter 8 that polymodal cells are those that receive inputs from more than one modality. Those in PG respond to both somatosensory and visual inputs, whereas those in the STS respond to various combinations of auditory, visual, and somatosensory inputs. The increase in size of area PG and the STS is especially interesting because this region is anatomically asymmetrical in the human brain (see Figure 9.1). This asymmetry may reflect a much larger area PG (and possibly STS) on the right than on the left. If PG has a visual function and is larger in humans, especially in the right hemisphere, then we might expect unique visual symptoms after right parietal lesions, and this is indeed the case. Note, however, that PG is also larger on the left in the human than in the monkey, which would lead us to expect humans to have unique deficits after left hemisphere lesions. This too is the case.

Connections of the Parietal Cortex

The anterior parietal cortex has rather straightforward connections, which are illustrated in Felleman and van Essen's hierarchy (see Figure 8.13). There are projections from the primary somatosensory cortex to area PE, which has a tactile recognition function, as well as to motor areas including the primary motor cortex (area 4) and the supplementary motor and premotor regions. The motor connections must be important for providing sensory information about limb position in the control of movement (see Chapter 7).

Although more than 100 inputs and outputs of areas 5 and 7 in the monkey (PE, PF, and PG) have been described (see Figure 8.13), a few basic principles will summarize them (Figure 12.2):

1. Area PE (Brodmann's area 5) is basically a somatosensory area, receiving most of its connections from the primary somatosensory cortex. Its cortical outputs are to the primary motor cortex (area 4) and to the supplementary motor and premotor regions, as well as to PF. PE therefore plays some role in guiding movement by providing information about limb position.

2. Area PF (area 7b) has a heavy somatosensory input from the primary cortex (areas 1, 2, and 3) via PE. It also receives inputs from the motor and premotor cortex and a small visual input via PG. Its efferent connections are similar to those of PE, and these connections presumably provide some elaboration of similar information for the motor systems.

3. Area PG (area 7b and visual areas) receives more complex connections including visual, somaesthetic, proprioceptive, auditory, vestibular (balance), oculomotor (eye movement), and cingulate (motivational?). This region was described by MacDonald Critchley as the "parieto-temporo-occipital crossroads," which is apparent from the connectivity. It seems likely that its function reflects this intermodal mixing. This region is part of the dorsal stream of Ungerleider and Mishkin discussed in Chapter 11. It is assumed to have a role in controlling spatially guided behavior.

4. There is a close relationship between the posterior parietal connections and the prefrontal cortex (especially area 46; see Figures 8.12 and 8.14). Thus, there are connections between the posterior parietal cortex (PG and PF) and the

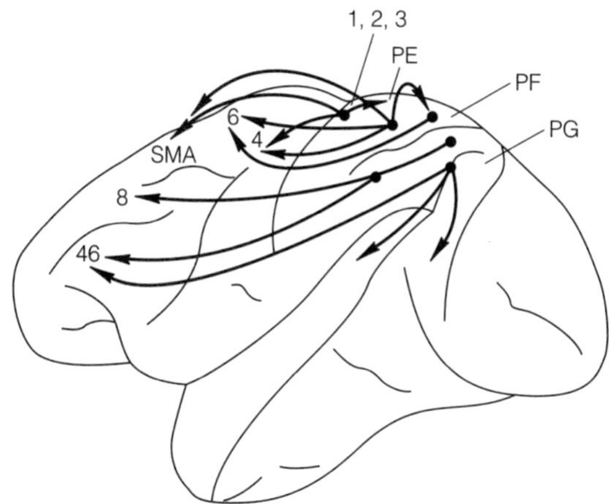

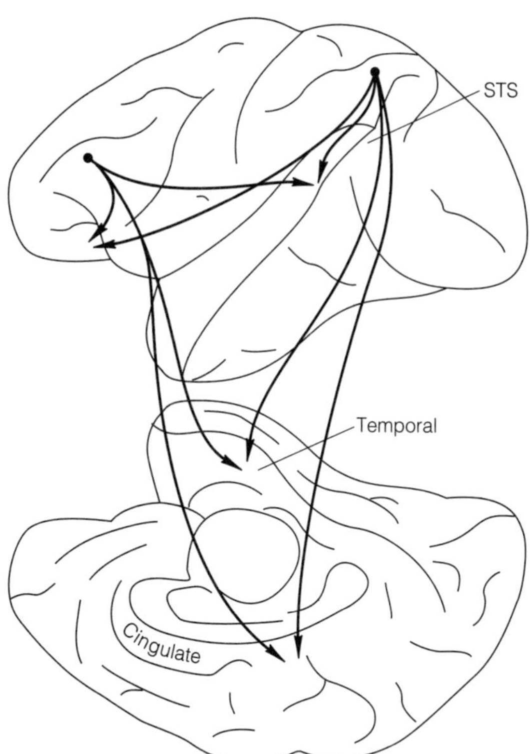

FIGURE 12.2. *A*. The major cortico-cortical projections of the parietal lobe. *B*. The posterior parietal and prefrontal projections to cingulate, orbital frontal, and temporal regions.

dorsolateral prefrontal region. Also, both prefrontal and posterior parietal regions project to the same areas of paralimbic cortex and temporal cortex as well as to the hippocampus and various subcortical regions. These connections emphasize a close functional relationship between the prefrontal cortex and the parietal cortex. This relationship probably has an important role in the control of spatially guided behavior.

A THEORY OF PARIETAL LOBE FUNCTION

If the anterior (somatosensory) and posterior parietal zones are considered as functionally distinct regions, two independent functions of the parietal lobes can be identified. One is concerned primarily with somatic sensations and perceptions; the other is specialized primarily for integrating sensory input from the somatic and visual regions and, to a lesser extent, from other sensory regions, mostly for the control of movement. We are concerned here mostly with the function of the posterior parietal zone, since the somatosensory functions have already been discussed in Chapter 6.

Imagine that you are having dinner with a friend in a restaurant. You are confronted with a set of cutlery, some dishes, a basket of bread, a glass of water, perhaps a glass of wine or a cup of coffee, a napkin, and of course your companion. Seemingly without effort you select various utensils and foods as you chat with your friend. If we analyze what is required to do all this, however, we see that your brain is faced with several complex tasks. For example, you must reach and grasp correctly a glass or cup or fork or piece of bread. Each of those movements is made to a different place and requires a different hand posture and/or limb movement. Your eyes and head must be directed to various places in space, and you must coordinate the movements of your limbs and your head to get food to your mouth. Furthermore, you must attend to certain objects and ignore others. (You do not take your companion's fork or drink!) You also must attend to the conversation of your friend and ignore other conversations around you. When you eat items from your plate, you must choose which one you want and select the correct utensil. It would be inappropriate to try to eat your peas with a knife. You must also make movements in the correct order. For example, you must cut your food before picking it up. Similarly, when you choose a bit of bread you must pick up a knife, get some butter, place the butter on the bread, and then eat the bread.

As we think about how the brain can manage the tasks we have presented, it seems obvious that there must be some sort of representation of the location of different objects around us, a sort of map of where things are. Furthermore, we assume that the map must be common to all our senses because we can move without apparent effort from visual to auditory to tactile information. On the basis of clinical observations of patients with parietal injury, it has been widely believed for at least 50 years that the parietal lobe plays a central role in the creation of this map. But what is the map? The commonly held introspective view is that real space must be mapped topographically because that is how it appears to us. That is, we take it for granted that the world around us is as we perceive it and thus that there must be some sort of unified spatial map. (This is a form of the binding problem discussed in Chapter 8.) Unfortunately, there is very little evidence for the existence of such a map in the brain. Rather, it seems likely that there is no single map, but a series of representations of space, which vary in two ways. First, different representations are used for different behavioral needs. Second, representations of space vary from very simple ones, which are applicable to the control of simple movements, to more abstract ones, which may represent information such as topographical knowledge. We consider each of these aspects of maps in turn.

Uses of Spatial Information

Goodale and Milner have emphasized that spatial information about the location of objects in the world is needed both to direct actions at those objects and to assign meaning and significance to them. In this sense spatial information is simply another property of visual information, much like form, motion, and color. However, just as form is coded in more than one way in visual processing, so is spatial information. The critical factor for both form and space is how the information is to be used.

Recall that form recognition is of two basic types. One is for object recognition and the other is for the guidance of movement. Spatial information can be thought of in the same way. The spatial information needed to determine the relationships between objects, independent of what the subject's behavior might be, is very different from the spatial information needed to guide eye, head, or limb movements to objects. In the latter case, the visuomotor control must be viewer-centered—that is, the location of an object and its local orientation and motion must be determined relative to the viewer. Furthermore, since the eyes, head, limbs, and body are constantly moving, computations about orientation, motion, and location must take place every time we wish to undertake an action. Details of object characteristics, such as color, are irrelevant to visuomotor guidance of the viewer-centered movements. That is, a detailed visual representation is not needed to guide hand action. Milner suggests that the brain operates on a "need to know" basis. Having too much information may be counterproductive for any given system. In contrast to the viewer-centered system, the object-centered system must be concerned with such properties of objects as size, shape, color, and relative location, so that the objects can be recognized when they are encountered in different visual contexts or from different vantage points. In this case the details of the objects themselves (color, shape) are important. Knowing where the red cup is relative to the green one requires identifying each of them.

The posterior parietal cortex is involved in the viewer-centered system. Since there are many different types of viewer-centered movements (eyes, head, limbs, body, and combinations of these), there must be separate control systems. Consider, for example, that the control of the eyes is based upon the optical axis of the eye, whereas the control of the limbs is probably based upon the position of the shoulders. They are very different types of movements. We have seen that there are many visual areas in the posterior parietal region (see Felleman and van Essen's map, Figure 8.12) and that there are multiple projections from the posterior parietal regions to the motor structures for the eyes (frontal eye fields, area 8) and limbs (premotor and supplementary motor). There are also connections to the prefrontal region (area 46) that have a role in short-term memory of the location of events in space.

The temporal lobe is involved in coding relational properties of objects. Part of this control is probably in the polymodal region of the superior temporal sulcus, and another part is in the hippocampal formation. We will return to the role of the temporal cortex later.

The role of the posterior parietal region in visuomotor guidance is confirmed by studies of neurons in the posterior parietal lobe of monkeys. The activity of these neurons is dependent upon the concurrent behavior of the animal with respect to visual stimulation. In fact, most neurons in the posterior parietal region are active both during sensory input *and* during movement. For example, there are cells that show only weak responses to stationary visual stimuli, but if the animal makes an active eye or arm movement toward the stimulus, *or even if it just shifts its attention to the object,* the discharge of the cells is strongly enhanced. Some cells are active when a monkey manipulates an object and also respond to the structural features of the object, such as size and orientation. That is, the neurons are sensitive to features of an object that determine the posture of the hand during manipulation. One characteristic common to all the posterior parietal neurons is their responsiveness to movements of the eyes and to the location of the eye in its socket. When cells are stimulated at the optimum spot in their receptive fields, they discharge at the highest rate when the eyes are in a particular position. This discharge appears to signal the size of the eye movement, which is known as a saccade, necessary to move the visual target to the fovea of the retina. In other words, these cells detect visual information and then move the eye to get the fine vision of the fovea to examine it. A curious aspect of many posterior parietal eye movement cells is that they are particularly responsive to visual stimuli that are behaviorally relevant, such as a cue signaling the availability of a reward. This has been interpreted as suggesting that these cells are affected by the "motivational" characteristics of information.

Stein summarizes the responses of posterior parietal neurons by emphasizing that they all share two important characteristics. First, they receive combinations of sensory, motivational, and related motor inputs. Second, their discharge is enhanced when the animal attends to, or makes a movement toward, a target. These neurons therefore are well suited to transform the necessary sensory information into commands for directing attention and guiding motor output.

It is not possible to study the activity of single cells in the human posterior parietal region, but ERPs in response to visual stimuli can be recorded. Thus, when a stimulus is presented in one visual field, activation would be expected in the opposite hemisphere, which receives information from the contralateral visual field. Hillyard has shown that when a visual stimulus is presented there is a large negative wave about 100–200 msec later in the posterior parietal region. The wave is larger than that seen in the occipital cortex and is largest in the hemisphere contralateral to the stimulus. There are two interesting characteristics of these waves that are reminiscent of neurons in monkeys. First, if the subject is asked to pay attention to a particular spot in one visual field, the ERP is largest when the stimulus is presented there rather than elsewhere. Second, there is a large parietal response 100–200 msec before eye movements. Roland has also shown that when subjects direct their attention to visual targets, blood flow increases preferentially in the posterior parietal region.

Taken together, the electrophysiological and blood-flow studies in monkeys and humans support the general idea that the posterior parietal region plays a significant role in directing movements in space and in detecting stimuli in space. One would predict, therefore, that posterior parietal lesions would impair the guidance of movements and perhaps the detection of sensory events.

The role of the superior parietal cortex in the control of eye movements has important implications for PET studies of visual processing. Recall from Chapter 11 that Haxby and colleagues showed that there was an increase in blood flow in the posterior parietal cortex when subjects identified different spatial locations. This was taken as evidence that the dorsal stream of processing is involved in "spatial processing." One difficulty with this interpretation, however, is that when people solve spatial tasks they move their eyes. The increased PET activation, therefore, could be due to the moving of the eyes, rather than to the processing of *where* the target actually was in space. Indeed, it has been claimed that when people solve problems in which they must rotate objects mentally, they move their eyes back and forth. These eye movements may reflect the ongoing activity of parietal circuits, but they also present a problem for PET studies. This possibility illustrates the practical difficulty of constructing watertight experimental designs in brain imaging studies.

Complexity of Spatial Information

The second aspect of spatial representation is complexity. Control of limb or eye movements is concrete and relatively simple, but there are other types of viewer-centered representations that are far more complex. For example, the concept of "left" and "right" is viewer-centered but need not require movement. Patients with posterior parietal lesions are impaired at distinguishing left from right. But there are even more complex relations. For example, we can create mental images of objects and manipulate them spatially. Patients with posterior parietal lesions are impaired at mental manipulations, too. Indeed, there is little doubt that parietal lesions interefere with various forms of complex spatial processing that do not appear to involve the dorsal visual stream's role in visuomotor guidance. Goodale and Milner suggest that these complex spatial deficits may arise from damage to the temporal-parietal polysensory regions that show such significant expansion in the human brain. (This is the third stream of processing illustrated in Figure 11.2.) Although this idea is still speculative, if it proves to be true we could expect—since this region shows a greater growth in the right hemisphere—to find greater deficits on such "spatial tasks" after right hemisphere lesions. This is the case.

Other Aspects of Parietal Function

There are three other parietal lobe symptoms that do not fit obviously into a simple view of the parietal lobe as a visuomotor control center. These include difficulties with arithmetic, mathematics, and certain aspects of language.

Luria has proposed that mathematics and arithmetic have a quasi-spatial nature. For example, addition and subtraction have spatial properties that are important to a correct solution. Consider the problem of subtracting 25 from 52. The "2" and "5" occupy different positions and have different meanings in the two numbers. There must be a "borrowing" of 10 from the 5 in 52 in order to do the subtraction, and so on. Viewed this way, the reason that parietal lobe patients have **acalculia** (an ability to do arithmetic) is because of the spatial nature of the task. Indeed, if parietal lobe patients are given simple problems like 6 − 4, they are usually able to do them because there are few spatial demands. Even when the problems are somewhat more difficult, such as 984 − 23, the patients have little problem. It is when more complex manipulations must be made that the patients' ability to do arithmetic breaks down, as in 983 − 24. We can speculate that in some ways this task is conceptually analogous to the mental manipulation of shapes except that it involves symbols. If so, this operation may be dependent upon the polysensory tissue at the left temporal-parietal junction.

Language has many of the same demands as arithmetic. The words "tap" and "pat" have the same letters, but the spatial organization is different. Similarly, "my son's wife" and "my wife's son" have identical words but very different meanings. These observations have led Luria and others to suggest that language can be seen as quasi-spatial. The patients may have a clear understanding of individual elements, but they are unable to understand the whole when the syntax becomes important. This, too, may be dependent upon the polysensory region at the temporal-parietal junction.

Summary

The posterior parietal lobe is thought to be a region that controls the visuomotor guidance of movements in egocentric (that is, viewer-centered) space. This is most obvious in the control of reaching and eye movements needed to grasp or manipulate objects. The eye movements are important, because they allow the visual system to attend to particular sensory cues in the environment. The polymodal region of the posterior parietal cortex is also important in various aspects of "mental space," which range from arithmetic and reading to the mental rotation and manipulation of visual images.

SOMATOSENSORY SYMPTOMS OF PARIETAL LOBE LESIONS

In this section we review the somatosensory symptoms associated with damage to the postcentral gyrus (areas 1, 2, 3a, and 3b) and the adjacent cortex (areas PE and PF).

Somatosensory Thresholds

Damage to the postcentral gyrus is typically associated with marked changes in somatosensory thresholds. The most thorough studies of these changes were made by Semmes and her colleagues on war veterans with missile wounds to the brain and by Corkin and her coworkers on patients who had undergone cortical surgery for relief of epilepsy. Both groups found that lesions of the postcentral gyrus produced abnormally high sensory thresholds, impaired position sense, and deficits in stereognosis. For example, in the Corkin study, patients performed poorly at detecting a light touch to the skin (pressure sensitivity), at determining if they were touched by one or two sharp points (two-point threshold), and at localizing points of touch on the skin on the side of the body contralateral to the lesion. If blindfolded, the patients also had difficulty in reporting whether the fingers of the contralateral hand were passively moved or not. Lesions of the postcentral gyrus may also produce a symptom that Luria called **afferent paresis.** Movements of the fingers are clumsy because the person has lost the necessary feedback about their exact position.

Somatoperceptual Disorders

The presence of normal somatosensory thresholds does not preclude the possibility of other types of somatosensory abnormalities. First, there is **astereognosis,** a disturbance that can be demonstrated in tests of tactile appreciation of object qualities, illustrated in Figure 12.3. In these tests, subjects are told to handle shapes or they have objects placed on the palm of the hand. The task is to match the original shape or object to one of several alternatives, which are also out of view.

A second somatoperceptual disorder, **simultaneous extinction,** can be demonstrated only by special testing procedures. The logic in this test is that a person is ordinarily confronted by an environment in which many sensory stimuli impinge on him or her simultaneously, yet the person is able to distinguish and perceive each of these individual sensory impressions. Thus, a task that presents stimuli one at a time represents an unnatural situation that may underestimate sensory disturbances or miss them altogether. Hence, in order to offer more complicated sensory stimulation, two tactile stimuli are presented simultaneously to homologous or heterologous body parts. The objective of such double simultaneous stimulation is to uncover those situations in which both of the stimuli would be reported if applied singly, but only one would be reported if both were applied together. A failure to report one stimulus is usually called **extinction.** Extinction is most commonly associated with damage to the somatic secondary cortex (areas PE and PF), especially in the right parietal lobe.

Blind Touch

We have seen evidence that patients can identify the location of a visual stimulus even though they deny "seeing" it. Paillard and his colleagues reported the case of a woman who appears to have a tactile analogue of blindsight. This woman had a

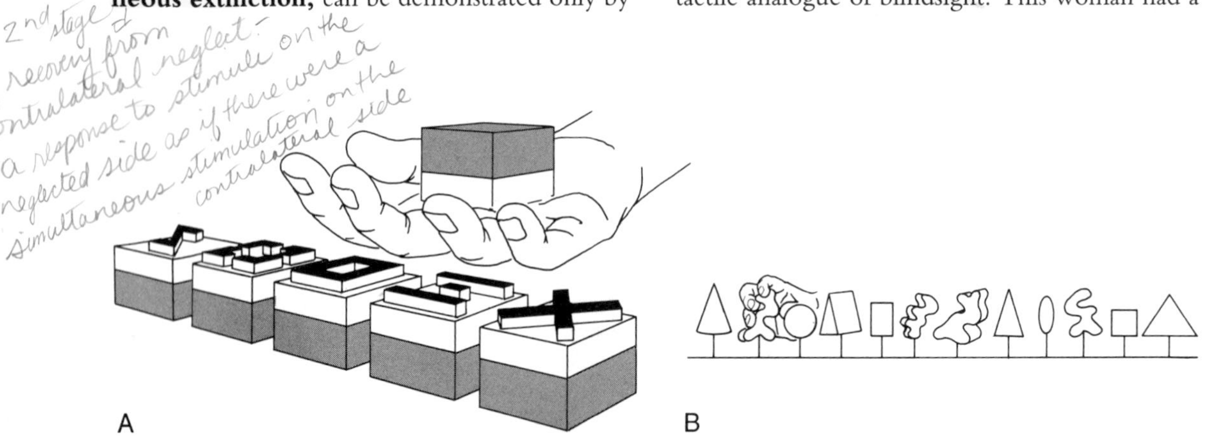

FIGURE 12.3. Examples of tests for tactile appreciation of objects. *A.* A pattern is placed on the subject's palm for 5 sec and then placed within the array. The task is to identify the original by handling all six patterns. *B.* A duplicate of one of the patterns is handled by the subject. The task is to identify, again by handling, the matching pattern in the array. (After Teuber, 1968.)

large lesion of areas PE, PF, and some of PG, resulting in a complete anesthesia of the right side of the body that was so severe that she was liable to cut or burn herself without being aware of it. Despite this, she was able to point with her left hand to locations on her right hand where she had been touched, even though she failed to report feeling the touch. Although this is a single case report, the phenomenon is clearly reminiscent of blindsight. The presence of a tactile analogue of blindsight is important because it suggests that there are two tactile systems, one of which is specialized for detection and the other for localization. This may be a general feature of sensory system organization.

Somatosensory Agnosias

There are two major types of somatosensory agnosias: astereognosis (from the Greek *stereo,* meaning solid)—the inability to recognize the nature of an object by touch; and **asomatognosia**—the loss of knowledge or sense of one's own body and bodily condition. Although astereognosis is essentially a disorder of tactile appreciation (see the previous discussion of somatoperceptual disorders), we include it here because it is often described clinically as an agnosia.

Asomatognosia is one of the most curious of all agnosias. It is an almost unbelievable syndrome—until one has actually observed a person neglecting part of his or her body or denying an obvious illness. There are a variety of different asomatognosias, including **anosognosia,** the unawareness or denial of illness; **anosodiaphoria,** indifference to illness; **autotopagnosia,** an inability to localize and name body parts; and **asymbolia for pain,** the absence of normal reactions to pain.

Asomatognosias may be for one or both sides of the body, although they are most commonly for the left side of the body and result from lesions in the right hemisphere. An exception is the autopagnosias, which usually result from lesions of the left parietal cortex. The most common example of this disorder is finger agnosia, a condition in which the person is unable to point to, or show the examiner, the various fingers of either hand.

SYMPTOMS OF POSTERIOR PARIETAL DAMAGE

The clinical literature describes a bewildering array of symptoms of posterior parietal injury. We will restrict our discussion here to the most commonly observed disorders.

Balint's Syndrome

In 1909, Balint described a patient who had a bilateral parietal lesion that was associated with rather peculiar visual symptoms. He had full visual fields and could recognize, use, and name objects, pictures, and colors normally. Nevertheless, the patient had three unusual symptoms. First, although he spontaneously looked straight ahead, when an array of stimuli was placed in front of him, he directed his gaze 35° to 40° to the right and perceived only what was lying in that direction. Thus, he could move his eyes but could not fixate on specific visual stimuli. Second, once his attention was directed toward an object, no other stimulus was noticed. With urging, he could identify other stimuli placed before him, but he would quickly relapse into his previous neglect. Balint concluded that the patient's field of attention was limited to one object at a time, a disorder that made reading very difficult because each letter was perceived separately. (This disorder is often referred to as simultagnosia.) Third, the patient had a severe deficit in reaching under visual guidance. Balint described this symptom as **optic ataxia.** He noted that the patient could still make movements directed toward the body accurately, presumably by using tactile or proprioceptive information, but could not make visually guided movements.

Although Balint's syndrome is quite rare, optic ataxia is a common symptom of posterior parietal lesions and can occur after unilateral lesions. Consider the following description of a patient of Damasio and Benton's:

> She consistently misreached for targets located in the nearby space, such as pencils, cigarettes, matches, ashtrays and cutlery. Usually she underreached by 2 to 5 inches, and then explored, by tact, the surface path leading to the target. This exploration, performed in one or two groping attempts, was often successful and led straight to the object. Occasionally, however, the hand would again misreach, this time on the side of the target and beyond it. Another quick tactually guided correction would then place the hand in contact with the object. . . . In striking contrast to the above difficulties was the performance of movements which did not require visual guidance, such as buttoning and unbuttoning of garments, bringing a cigarette to the mouth, or pointing to some part of her body. These movements were smooth, quick and on target. (Damasio and Benton, 1979, p. 171)

The deficits in eye gaze and visually guided reaching are most likely to result from lesions in the superior parietal region (area PE). Optic ataxia does not accompany lesions in the inferior parietal region, suggesting a clear functional dissociation of the two posterior parietal regions.

Contralateral Neglect and Other Symptoms of Right Parietal Lobe Lesions

A perceptual disorder following right parietal lesions was described by John Hughlings-Jackson in 1874. Not until the 1940s, however, was the effect of right parietal lesions clearly defined by Paterson and Zangwill. A classic paper by McFie and Zangwill, published in 1960, reviewed much of the previous work and described several symptoms of right parietal lesions, which are illustrated in the following patient.

Mr. P., a 67-year-old man, had suffered a right parietal stroke. At the time of our first seeing him (24 hours after admission), he had no visual-field defect or paresis. He did, however, have a variety of other symptoms:

1. Mr. P. neglected the left side of his body and of the world. When asked to lift up his arms, he failed to lift his left arm but could do so if one took his arm and asked him to lift it. When asked to draw a clock face, he crowded all the numbers onto the right side of the clock. When asked to read compound words such as "ice cream" and "football," he read "cream" and "ball." When he dressed, he did not attempt to put on the left side of his clothing (a form of dressing apraxia), and when he shaved, he shaved only the right side of his face. He ignored tactile sensation on the left side of his body. Finally, he appeared unaware that anything was wrong with him and was uncertain as to what all the fuss was about (anosagnosia). Collectively, these symptoms are referred to as contralateral neglect; we shall return to them shortly.

2. He was impaired at combining blocks to form designs (constructional apraxia) and was generally impaired at drawing freehand with either hand, copying drawings, or cutting out paper figures. When drawing, he often added extra strokes in an effort to make the pictures correct, but the drawings generally lacked accurate spatial relations. In fact, it is common for patients showing neglect to fail to complete the left side of the drawing, as illustrated in Figure 12.4.

3. He had a topographical disability, being unable to draw maps of well-known regions from memory. He attempted to draw a map of his neighborhood, but it was badly distorted with respect to directions, the spatial arrangement of landmarks, and distances. Despite all these disturbances, Mr. P. knew where he was and what day it was, and he could recognize his family's faces. He also had good language functions: he could talk, read, and write normally.

The contralateral neglect observed in Mr. P. is one of the most fascinating symptoms of brain dysfunction. Typically there is neglect of visual, auditory, and somaesthetic (somatosensory) stimulation on the side of the body and/or space opposite to the lesion, which may be accompanied by denial of the deficit. Recovery passes through

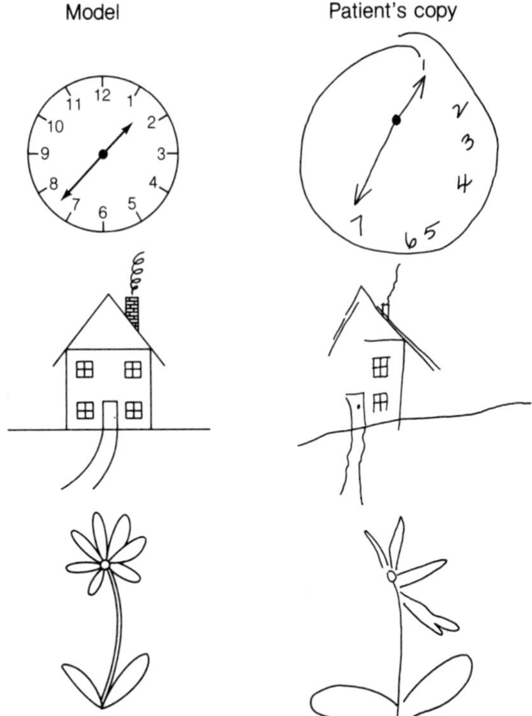

FIGURE 12.4. Drawings copied by a patient with contralateral neglect. (From F. E. Bloom and A. Lazerson. *Brain, Mind, and Behavior,* 2nd ed. New York: W. H. Freeman, p. 300. Copyright © 1988.)

two stages. The first, **allesthesia,** is characterized by the person's beginning to respond to stimuli on the neglected side, but doing so as if the stimuli were on the good side. The person responds to and orients to visual, tactile, or auditory stimuli on the left side of the body as if they were on the right. The second stage, which we noted earlier, is simultaneous extinction: the person responds to stimuli on the hitherto neglected side unless both sides are stimulated simultaneously, in which case he or she notices only the stimulation on the side ipsilateral to the lesion.

Neglect presents several obstacles to understanding. For example, what is the location of the lesion that produces this effect? Figure 12.5A is a composite drawing of the region damaged (as inferred from brain scans) in 13 patients with neglect as described by Heilman and Watson. The area of most overlap (Figure 12.5B) among the lesions was the inferior parietal lobule. It should be noted, however, that neglect is occasionally observed following lesions to the frontal lobe and cingulate cortex, as well as to subcortical structures including the superior colliculus and lateral hypothalamus. It is not clear, however, whether the same phenomenon results from these various lesions.

A second problem is why neglect occurs at all. There are two main theories: (1) that neglect is caused by defective sensation or perception, and (2) that it is caused by defective attention or orientation. The strongest argument favoring the

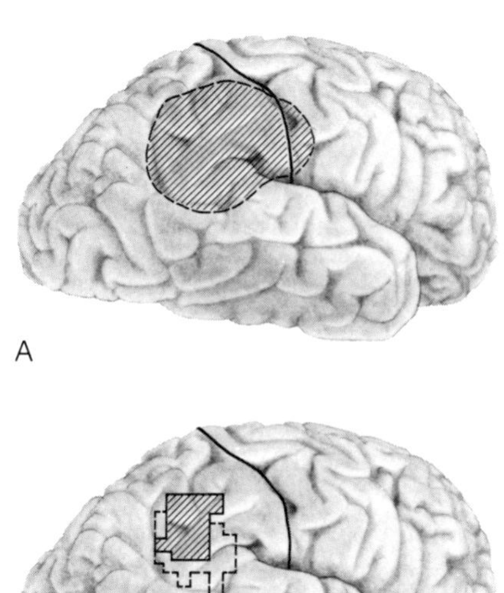

FIGURE 12.5. *A*. Composite drawing of the region damaged (as inferred from brain scans) in 13 patients with contralateral neglect as described by Heilman and Watson. The area of greatest overlap is the right inferior parietal lobule. *B*. Composite drawing of the region of overlap among lesions producing deficits in Warrington and Taylor's test of recognition of objects seen in unfamiliar views. The shaded region is the one of maximal overlap. Note the similarity between *A* and *B*.

theory of defective sensation is that a lesion to the parietal lobes, which receive input from all the sensory regions, can disturb the integration of sensation. Denny-Brown and Chambers termed this function *morphosynthesis* and its disruption *amorphosynthesis*. A current elaboration of this view hypothesizes that neglect follows right parietal lesion because the integration of the spatial properties of stimuli becomes disturbed. As a result, although stimuli are perceived, their location is uncertain to the nervous system and they are consequently ignored. The neglect is thought to be unilateral because in the absence of right hemisphere function, it is assumed that the left hemisphere is capable of some rudimentary spatial synthesis that prevents neglect of the right side of the world. This rudimentary spatial ability cannot compensate, however, for the many other behavioral deficits resulting from right parietal lesions.

Critchley and, later, others have suggested that neglect results from an inability to attend to input that has in fact been registered. This view has been elaborated most recently by Heilman and Watson. They propose that neglect is manifested by a defect in orienting to stimuli; the defect results from the disruption of a system whose function is to "arouse" the individual when new sensory stimulation is present.

Another common symptom of right parietal lobe lesion has been described by Warrington and her colleagues: patients with right parietal lesions, although able to recognize objects shown in familiar views, are badly impaired at recognizing objects shown in unfamiliar ones. For example, a side-view photograph of a bucket is recognized easily; a top-view photograph of the same bucket is recognized only with great difficulty (Figure 12.6). Warrington concludes that the deficit is not in forming a gestalt, or concept, of "bucket," but rather in perceptual classification—the mechanism for categorizing information as being part of the idea "bucket." Such allocation can be seen as a type of a spatial matching in which the common view of an object must be rotated spatially to match the novel view. Warrington and Taylor suggested that the focus for this deficit is roughly the inferior parietal lobule, the same region proposed as the locus of contralateral neglect (see Figure 12.5B).

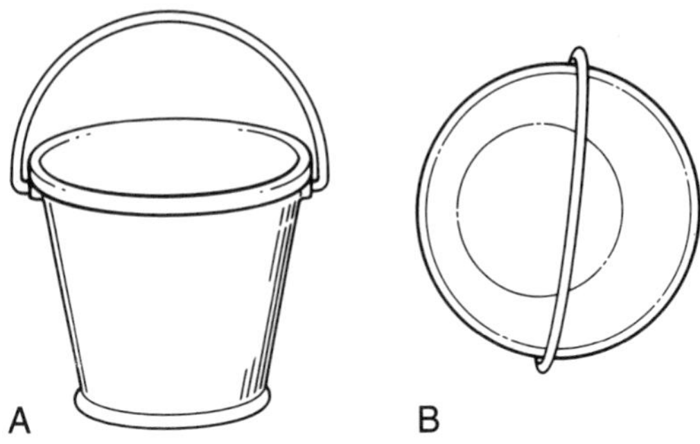

FIGURE 12.6. Drawing of a bucket in familiar (*A*) and unfamiliar (*B*) views. Patients with right parietal lesions have difficulty in recognizing objects in unfamiliar views such as this one.

The Gerstmann Syndrome and Other Left Parietal Symptoms

In 1924, Josef Gerstmann described a patient with an unusual symptom following a left parietal stroke: finger agnosia. The patient was unable to name or indicate recognition of the fingers on either hand. This discovery aroused considerable interest, and over the ensuing years other symptoms were reported to accompany finger agnosia, including right-left confusion, **agraphia** (inability to write) and acalculia (inability to perform mathematical operations). These four symptoms collectively became known as the Gerstmann syndrome. Gerstmann and others argued that these symptoms accompanied a circumscribed lesion in the left parietal lobe, roughly corresponding to the angular gyrus (area PG). If these four symptoms occurred as a group, the patient was said to demonstrate the Gerstmann syndrome, and the lesions could be localized in the angular gyrus. It seems doubtful that the Gerstmann syndrome is a useful diagnostic tool in routine investigations, but all of the symptoms can be associated with left parietal lesions.

There are various other symptoms of left parietal lesions, many of which are illustrated in the following case history.

On 24 August 1975, Mr. S., an 11-year-old boy, suddenly had a seizure, which was characterized by twitching on the right side of the body, particularly the arm and face. He was given anticonvulsant medication and was symptom-free until 16 September 1975, when he began to write upside down and backward, at which time he was immediately referred to a neurologist, who diagnosed a left parietal malignant astrocytoma. Careful neuropsychological assessment revealed a number of symptoms characteristic of left parietal lesions. (1) Mr. S. had several symptoms of disturbed language function: he was unable to write even his name (agraphia), had serious difficulties in reading (dyslexia), and spoke slowly and deliberately, making many errors in grammar (dysphasia). (2) He was unable to combine blocks to form designs and had difficulties learning a sequence of novel movements of the limbs, suggestive of apraxia (see below). (3) He was very poor at mental arithmetic (dyscalculia) and could not solve even simple additions and subtractions. (4) He had an especially low digit span, being able to master the immediate recall of only three digits, whether they were presented orally or visually. (5) He was totally unable to distinguish left from right, responding at random on all tests of this ability. (6) He had right hemianopia, probably because his tumor had damaged the geniculostriate connections. As Mr. S.'s tumor progressed, movement of the right side of his body became disturbed, because the tumor placed pressure on the frontal lobe. By the end of October 1975 Mr. S. died, neither surgery nor drug therapy being able to stop the growth of the tumor.

The symptoms that Mr. S. exhibited resemble those of other patients we have seen with left parietal lesions. Curiously, he did not have finger agnosia, one of the Gerstmann symptoms, illustrating the point that even very large lesions do not produce the same effects in every patient.

Apraxia and the Parietal Lobe

Apraxia is a disorder of movement in which there is a loss of skilled movement that is not caused by weakness; an inability to move; abnormal tone or posture; intellectual deterioration; poor comprehension; or other disorders of movement such as tremor. There are many types of apraxia, but we shall focus upon two here: ideomotor apraxia and constructional apraxia. In ideomotor apraxia patients are unable to copy movements or to make gestures (for example, to wave "hello"). Patients with left posterior parietal lesions often have this form of apraxia. Kimura has shown that the deficits in such patients can be quantified by asking them to copy a series of arm movements such as those illustrated in Figure 12.7. Patients with left parietal lesions are grossly impaired at this task, whereas people with right parietal lobe lesions perform the task normally. We return to ideomotor apraxia in Chapter 23.

Constructional apraxia refers to a visuomotor disorder in which patients are unable to perform activities such as assembling, building, or drawing. The patients attempt the activity, but the spatial organization of the product is disordered. For example, patients with constructional apraxia cannot put together a puzzle. Constructional apraxia can occur after injury to either parietal lobe, although there is considerable debate over whether the symptoms are the same after left- and right-sided lesions (see the review by Benton). Nonetheless, constructional apraxia often occurs in patients with posterior parietal lesions.

Both ideomotor and constructional apraxia can be seen as disturbances of movement that result from a disruption of the parieto-frontal connections controlling movement. Mountcastle proposed that the posterior parietal cortex receives afferent signals not only of the tactile and visual representation of the world but also of the position and movement of the body. He proposed that the region uses this information to function as "a command apparatus for operation of the limbs, hands, and eyes within immediate extrapersonal space." Thus, the parietal lobe not only integrates

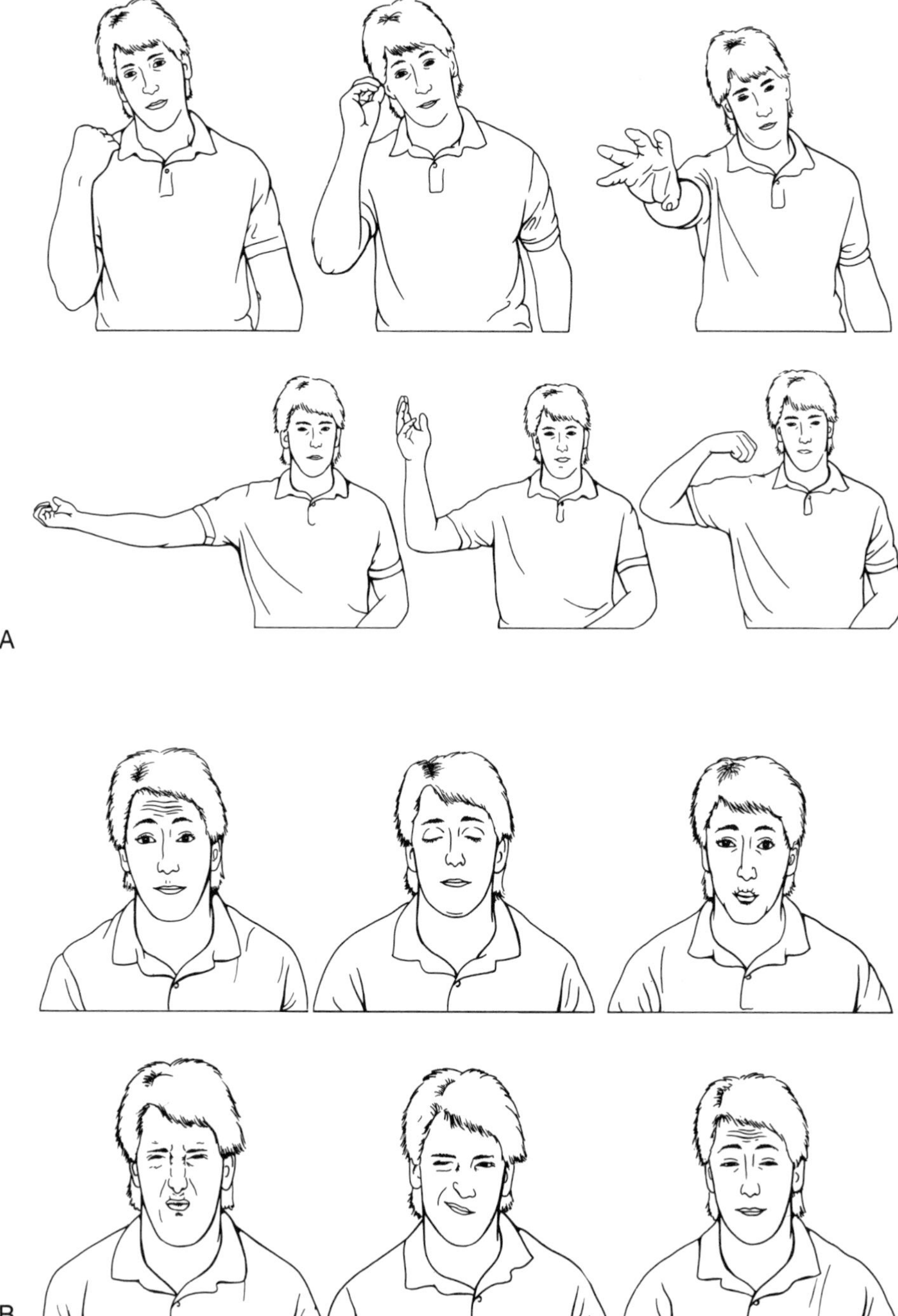

FIGURE 12.7. *A.* Examples of items of a serial arm-movement copying test. Subjects are asked to copy each of the series as accurately as they can. *B.* Examples of items from a serial facial-movement copying test.

sensory and spatial information to allow accurate movements in space, but also functions to direct or guide movements in the immediate vicinity of the body. Both ideomotor and constructional apraxia can be seen as examples of a dysfunction in this guidance.

Drawing

Although drawing deficits are known to occur following lesions to either hemisphere, it is generally believed that the deficits in drawing are greater after damage to the right hemisphere than after damage to the left, and that it is right parietal damage that has the greatest influence on drawing ability. This conclusion is consistent with the general idea that the right hemisphere plays a dominant role in spatial abilities, but it may not be correct. Rather, it appears that the disturbance in drawing is different after right and left hemisphere lesions. For example, Kimura and Faust asked a large sample of patients to draw a house and a man. Apraxic or aphasic left hemisphere patients did very poorly, producing fewer recognizable drawings and fewer lines than did right hemisphere patients. In contrast, right hemisphere patients tended to omit details from the left side of their drawings and to rotate the drawings on the page. Thus, although it is generally believed that drawing is impaired specifically by right parietal lesions, this conclusion may have been premature and based on a restricted, and possibly biased, sample of patients that excluded apraxic and aphasic patients. Drawing is a complex behavior that may require verbal as well as nonverbal (for example, spatial) processes. For instance, if asked to draw a bicycle many people will make a mental checklist of items to include (fenders, spokes, chain, and so on). In the absence of language, such people would be expected to draw less complete figures. Further, if patients are apraxic, there is likely to be a deficit in making the required movements. Similarly, the parts of a bicycle have a particular spatial organization. If spatial organization is poor, the drawing is likely to be distorted.

Spatial Attention

When we move about the world, we are confronted with a vast array of sensory information that cannot possibly all be treated equally by the nervous system. Thus, the brain must select certain information to process. Consider, for example, the sensory overload that occurs when we stop to chat with an old friend in a department store. There may be numerous other people around, and there will certainly be displays of various items to purchase. There may be competing sounds (others talking, music, cash registers), novel odors, and so on. Nonetheless, we can orient to a small sample of the incoming information and ignore most of the other input. In fact, we may do this to the exclusion of other, potentially more important, information. Cognitive psychologists refer to this selectivity of the sensory systems as *selective attention*. Thus, we are said to attend to particular stimuli. Recent work by Posner and his colleagues suggests that the parietal cortex may play a significant role in this process, especially for visual-spatial information.

In Posner's experiments, the subjects were asked to press a key as soon as a stimulus appeared. In addition, at the beginning of each trial they were given a visual cue intended to draw their attention to one side of the visual field or the other. On most trials the target was presented in the same field (valid trial), but on some it was in the opposite field (invalid trial). As might be expected, normal subjects were significantly faster on valid trials than on invalid ones. More important, however, is Posner's finding that patients with parietal lesions were nearly as good as normal subjects on valid trials but showed a marked impairment on invalid trials. In other words, if a stimulus was presented to the left on an invalid trial, patients with right parietal lesions were impaired, and if the stimulus was to the right on an invalid trial, patients with left parietal lesions were impaired. This result is not simply an example of contralateral neglect, because there is no asymmetry: both left and right parietal patients are impaired on appropriate trials.

Posner has proposed that one function of the parietal cortex is to allow shifts of attention from one stimulus to another, a process that he calls *disengagement*. Consider our example of dining with a friend. As we eat we shift from peas to bread and so on. We are disengaging each time we shift from one food to another.

Finally, we shall see in the next chapter that the temporal cortex may play a role in selecting both auditory stimuli and certain types of visual stimuli. It is likely that the parietal cortex selects visuospatial (and possibly auditospatial) information and the temporal cortex selects nonspatial information. The frontal lobe may play some greater, more general role in attention.

Disorders of Spatial Cognition

We use the term "spatial cognition" to refer to a broad category of abilities that involve mentally using or manipulating spatial properties of stimuli. This includes the ability to mentally manipulate images of objects and maps. The mental rotation tasks illustrated in Figures 10.3 and 19.11 provide good examples. Another would be the ability to follow an upside-down map. There is little doubt that posterior lesions, most likely including the region of PG and the polymodal cortex of the STS, produce deficits on rotation and map-reading tasks. Although it is widely assumed in the neuropsychological literature that the right hemisphere is "spatial" and that deficits in spatial cognition thus should be from right posterior lesions, the clinical evidence is far from convincing. Indeed, there is little doubt that both left and right hemisphere lesions produce deficits on spatial cognition tasks. There is an emerging view, however, that left and right hemisphere lesions have different effects on the performance of spatial cognition. For example, Corballis has suggested that mental rotation requires two different operations: first, the mental imaging of the stimulus, and second, the manipulation of the image. Newcombe and Ratcliff have suggested that the left hemisphere deficit may result from an inability to generate an appropriate mental image. In Chapter 11, we saw that visual imaging deficits result from left occipital lesions. In contrast, the right hemisphere deficit may represent an inability to perform operations on this mental image.

Deficits in the ability to use topographical information are more likely to be associated with damage to the right hemisphere than to the left. Such disorders include the loss of memory of familiar surroundings, the inability to locate items such as countries or cities on a map, and the inability to find one's way about the environment. Not surprisingly, such deficits are likely to be associated with other visual deficits (such as visual neglect or visual agnosia), but patients have been described with relatively specific disorders of topographical orientation. De Renzi concludes that injury to the right posterior hemisphere is a prerequisite for such disorders. Newcombe and Ratcliffe note that such disorders are often associated with injury to the right posterior cerebral artery and thus are likely to include right occipital-temporal and right hippocampal regions. When the parietal cortex is involved, it is most likely to be the inferior portion, probably including area PG and the STS.

Left and Right Parietal Lobes Compared

In a classic paper, McFie and Zangwill compared the symptoms of patients with left or right parietal lesions and found that although there were some overlapping symptoms, there was a clear asymmetry (Table 12.1). In addition, we have noted earlier that ideomotor apraxia is more likely to be associated with left parietal lesions.

One puzzling feature of the McFie and Zangwill study is that while there is clearly an asymmetry, there is little doubt that lesions to the two hemispheres produce some overlapping symptoms. Neuropsychological studies tend to emphasize the asymmetry of lesion effects, but the overlapping symptoms are important theoretically. Indeed, we noted earlier that both constructional apraxia and disorders of spatial cognition are poorly lateralized. Many theories of hemispheric asymmetry discussed in Chapter 9 do not predict

TABLE 12.1. Effects of left and right parietal lobe lesions compared

	Percentage of subjects with deficit[a]	
	Left (%)	Right (%)
Unilateral neglect	13	67
Dressing disability	13	67
Cube counting	0	86
Paper cutting	0	90
Topographical loss	13	50
Right-left discrimination	63	0
Weigl's sorting test	83	6

[a] *Note the small but significant overlap in symptoms of left and right lesions.*

Source: Based on data presented by McFie and Zangwill, 1960.

such ambiguity in symptom localization and tend to assume far greater dissociation of lesion effects than is actually observed in patients. One explanation for the overlapping symptoms is related to the concept of preferred mode of cognitive processing, which was introduced in Chapter 9. There we noted that many problems can be solved using either a verbal cognitive mode or a spatial nonverbal cognitive mode and that genetic, maturational, and environmental factors may predispose people to use different modes. For example, a complex spatial problem, such as reading an upside-down map, can be solved either directly, by "spatial cognition" (the directions to travel are intuited spatially), or indirectly, by "verbal cognition" (the spatial information is encoded into words and the problem is solved by being "talked" through step by step). There are people who are highly verbal and prefer the verbal mode even when it is less efficient; lesions of the left parietal lobe in these people would be expected to disturb functions that ordinarily are disrupted preferentially by right parietal lesions. Little direct evidence favors this explanation of functional overlap, but we believe it is a provocative idea that accounts in part for individual differences as well as for the apparent functional overlap revealed by lesion studies.

Summary of the Major Symptoms

Table 12.2 summarizes the major symptoms of lesions of the parietal lobe. Damage to the anterior parietal cortex, including area PE, produces deficits in various somatosensory functions. Damage to the posterior parietal regions produces most of the other disorders. The table also lists the regions most likely to be associated with the deficits, but there are few clear studies demonstrating anatomical dissociations of such deficits. One of the major difficulties in dissociating the regions is that it is rare for natural lesions in people to respect the anatomical boundaries and to involve only the neocortex. In addition, in contrast to the frontal and temporal lobes, which are often implicated in epilepsy and thus may be removed surgically, the parietal lobe is rarely epileptogenic, and so surgical removal is rare.

Clinical Neuropsychological Assessment

As we have seen, restricted lesions of the parietal cortex produce a wide variety of behavioral changes. It is logical to assume that behavioral tests used to evaluate brain damage in neurologically verified cases could be employed to predict the locus and extent of damage or dysfunction in new cases. (See Chapter 26 for more detail on the rationale of neuropsychological assessment.) In this section we briefly summarize a number of tests that have proved to be sensitive and valid predictors of brain injury (Table 12.3). Although these tests do not assess all the symptoms of parietal injury, they do evaluate a broad range of parietal lobe functions. It would be highly unusual for a person to perform normally on all these tests but show other symptoms of parietal lobe damage.

The two-point discrimination test assesses somatosensory thresholds. Recall that following lesions of the postcentral gyrus, the somatosensory threshold increases on the contralateral side of the body. The test requires the blindfolded subject to report whether he or she felt one or two points touch the skin (usually on the palm of the hand or the face). The distance between the points is at first very large (say, 3 cm) and is gradually reduced until the subject can no longer perceive two

TABLE 12.2. Summary of major symptoms of parietal lobe damage

Symptom	Most probable lesion site	Basic reference
Disorders of tactile function	Areas 1, 2, 3	Semmes et al., 1960 Corkin et al., 1970
Tactile agnosia	Area PE	Hécaen and Albert, 1978 Brown, 1972
Apraxia	Areas PF, PG, left	Heilman and Rothi, 1993 Geschwind, 1975 Kimura, 1980
Constructional apraxia	Area PG	Benton, 1990
Acalculia	Areas PG, STS	Levin et al., 1993
Impaired cross-modal matching	Areas PG, STS	Butters and Brody, 1968
Contralateral neglect	Area PG right	Heilman et al., 1993
Disorders of body image	Area PE?	Benton and Sivan, 1993
Right-left confusion	Areas PF, PG	Semmes et al., 1960
Disorders of spatial ability	Areas PE, PG?	Newcombe and Radcliff, 1990
Disorders of drawing	Area PG	Warrington et al., 1966 Kimura and Faust, 1987
Defects in eye movement	Areas PE, PF	Tyler, 1968
Misreaching	Areas 5, 7	Damasio and Benton, 1979

TABLE 12.3. Standardized clinical neuropsychological tests for parietal lobe damage

Function	Test	Basic reference
Somatosensory	Two-point discrimination	Corkin et al., 1970
Tactile form recognition	Seguin-Goddard Form Board Tactile patterns	Teuber and Weinstein, 1954 Benton et al., 1983
Contralateral neglect	Line bisection	Schenkenberg et al., 1980
Visual perception	Gollin Incomplete Figures Mooney Closure	Warrington and Rabin, 1970 Milner, 1980
Spatial relations	Right-left differentiation	Benton et al., 1983
Language		
Speech comprehension	Token	de Renzi and Faglioni, 1978
Reading comprehension	Token	
Apraxia	Kimura Box	Kimura, 1977

Note: These are standardized tests validated on large samples of patients with known localized brain damage.

points. In extreme cases the process is reversed: the distance must be increased to find when the subject first perceives two points.

The Seguin-Goddard Form Board is a test of tactile form recognition. The blindfolded subject manipulates 10 blocks of different shapes (star, triangle, and so forth) and attempts to place them in similarly shaped holes on a form board. When the test is completed, the form board and blocks are removed and the subject is asked to draw the board from memory. The precise locus of the lesion producing deficits on this test is controversial, and no claims have been proved. Nevertheless, research on tactile performance in monkeys with parietal lesions indicates that blindfolded tactile recognition is probably sensitive to lesions of areas PE and PF, whereas in humans the drawing part —a test of both memory and cross-modal matching—is probably sensitive to lesions in area PG.

A variety of tests of contralateral neglect have been devised, but we favor the one by Schenkenberg and colleagues because it is particularly sensitive. In this test the subject is asked to mark the middle of each of a set of 20 lines, each of which is a different length and is located at a different position on the page, some left of center, some in the middle, and some right of center. Patients showing neglect typically fail to mark the lines on the left side of the page.

Visual perceptual capacity is easily assessed by either the Mooney Closure Test or the Gollin Incomplete-Figures Test. In both tasks a series of incomplete representations of faces or objects is presented, and the subject must combine the elements to form a gestalt to identify the picture. These tests are especially sensitive to damage at the right parietal-temporal junction, presumably in regions of the ventral visual stream.

In the right-left differentiation test, a series of drawings of hands, feet, ears, and so on is presented in different orientations (upside down, rear view, and so forth), and the subject's task is to indicate whether the drawing is of the left or right body part. In a verbal variant of this test subjects are read a series of commands (for example, "Touch your right ear with your left hand"), which are to be carried out. Both of these tests are very sensitive to left parietal lobe damage, but caution is advised, because subjects with left frontal lobe damage are also often impaired at these tasks.

The token test is an easily administered test of language comprehension. Twenty tokens—four shapes (large and small circles, large and small squares) in each of five colors (white, black, yellow, green, red)—are placed in front of the subject. The test begins with simple tasks (for example, touching the white circle) and becomes progressively more difficult (for example, touching the large yellow circle and the large green square). A reading comprehension test can also be given by having the subject read the instructions out loud and then perform according to them. We have not considered language as a function of the parietal lobe, but the posterior speech zone

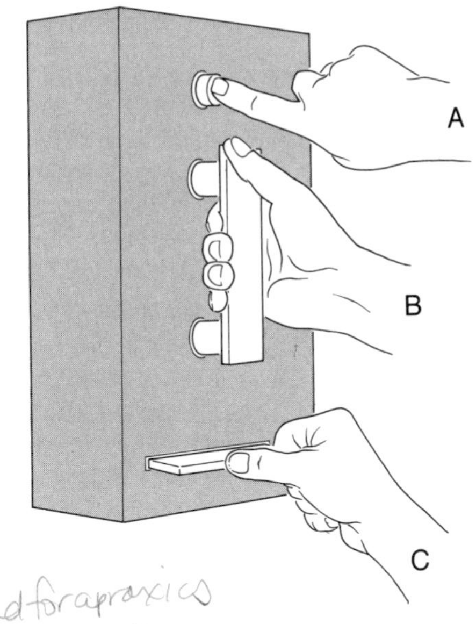

FIGURE 12.8. Kimura Box Test. Subjects are required to learn the movement series of (*A*) pushing the top button with the index finger, (*B*) pulling the handle as shown, and (*C*) pressing down on the bar with the thumb. Apraxic subjects are impaired at this task, and they may be unable to learn it at all, even with extended practice.

borders on area PG. Thus, injuries involving PG often include temporal speech-related cortex, and aphasia is observed.

It is unfortunate that there are no standardized tests of apraxia analogous to the token test for aphasia. However, the Kimura Box Test (Figure 12.8) is probably the best test currently available. The subject is required to make these consecutive movements of pushing a button with the index finger, pulling a handle with four fingers, and pressing a bar with the thumb. This test is done very poorly by apraxics, and many of them appear unable to perform this very simple series of movements even with extensive practice.

Together, these nine tests provide a simple, standardized, and thorough collection of tests of parietal lobe damage. In addition to these, there is a good series of tests in a "parietal lobe battery" described by Goodglass and Kaplan.

SUMMARY

The parietal lobe can be divided into three functional zones. The most anterior zones are primarily involved in somatosensory functions. The superior parietal region is primarily devoted to the visual guidance of movements of the hands and fingers, limbs, head, and eyes. This region can be conceived of as having a "spatial" function, although debate continues over what the nature of this spatial function actually is. The inferior parietal region has a role in processes related to spatial cognition and in what have been described as quasi-spatial processes, such as are used in arithmetic and reading.

REFERENCES

Andersen, R. A. Inferior parietal lobule function in spatial perception and visuomotor integration. *Handbook of Physiology* 5:483–518, 1987.

Balint, R. Seelenlahmung des "Schauens," optische Ataxie, raumliche Störung der Aufmerksamkeit. *Monatsschr. Psychiatr. Neurol.* 25:51–81, 1909.

Benton, A. L. Contructional apraxia. In F. Boller and J. Grafman, eds. *Handbook of Neuropsychology,* vol. 2. Amsterdam: Elsevier, 1990.

Benton, A. L., K. deS. Hamsher, N. R. Varney, and O. Spreen. *Contributions to Neuropsychological Assessment.* New York: Oxford University Press, 1983.

Benton, A. L., and A. B. Sivan. Disturbances of body schema. In K. M. Heilman and E. Valenstein, eds. *Clinical Neuropsychology,* 3rd ed. New York: Oxford University Press, 1993.

Butters, N., and B. A. Brody. The role of the left parietal lobe in the mediation of intra- and cross-modal associations. *Cortex* 4:328–343, 1968.

Corballis, M. C. Mental rotation: Anatomy of a paradigm. In M. Potegal, ed. *Spatial Abilities: Development and Physiological Foundations.* New York: Academic Press, 1900.

Corkin, S., B. Milner, and T. Rasmussen. Somatosensory thresholds. *Archives of Neurology* 23:41–58, 1970.

Critchley, M. *The Parietal Lobes.* London: Arnold, 1953.

Damasio, A. R., and A. L. Benton. Impairment of hand movements under visual guidance. *Neurology* 29:170–178, 1979.

de Renzi, E., and P. Faglioni. Normative data and screening power of a shortened version of the token test. *Cortex* 14:41–49, 1978.

Eidelberg, D. and A. M. Galaburda. Inferior parietal lobule: Divergent architectonic asymmetries in the human brain. *Archives of Neurology* 41:843–852, 1984.

Gerstmann, J. Some notes on the Gerstmann syndrome. *Neurology* 7:866–869, 1957.

Geschwind, N. The apraxias: Neural mechanisms of disorders of learned movement. *American Scientist* 63:188–195, 1975.

Goodale, M. A. Visual pathways supporting perception and action in the primate cerebral cortex. *Current Opinion in Neurobiology* 3:578–585, 1993.

Goodglass, H., and E. Kaplan. *The Assessment of Aphasia.* Philadelphia: Lea & Febiger, 1972.

Hécaen, H. Aphasic, apraxic, and agnosic syndromes in right and left hemisphere lesions. In P. Vincken and G. Bruyn, eds. *Handbook of Clinical Neurology,* vol. 4. Amsterdam: North-Holland, 1969.

Hécaen, H., and M. L. Albert. *Human Neuropsychology.* New York: John Wiley, 1978.

Heilman, K. M., and L. J. Gonzalez Rothi. Apraxia. In K. M. Heilman and E. Valenstein, eds. *Clinical Neuro-*

psychology, 3rd ed. New York: Oxford University Press,1993.

Heilman, K. M., R. T. Watson, and E. Valenstein. Neglect and related disorders. In K. M. Heilman and E. Valenstein, eds. *Clinical Neuropsychology,* 3rd ed. New York: Oxford University Press, 1993.

Hyvarinen, J. *The Parietal Cortex of Monkey and Man.* Berlin: Springer-Verlag, 1982.

Kimura, D. Acquisition of a motor skill after left hemisphere damage. *Brain* 100:527–542, 1977.

Kimura, D. Neuromotor mechanisms in the evolution of human communication. In H. D. Steklis and M. J. Raleigh, eds. *Neurobiology of Social Communication in Primates: An Evolutionary Perspective.* New York: Academic Press, 1980.

Kimura, D., and R. Faust. Spontaneous drawing in an unselected sample of patients with unilateral cerebral damage. In D. Ottoson, ed. *Duality and Unity of the Brain.* Wenner-Gren Center International Symposium Series (vol. 47). New York: MacMillan, 1987.

Levin, H. S., F. C. Goldstein, and P. A. Spiers. Acalculia. In K. M. Heilman and E. Valenstein, eds. *Clinical Neuropsychology,* 3rd ed. New York: Oxford University Press, 1993.

McFie, J., and O. L. Zangwill. Visual-constructive disabilities associated with lesions of the left cerebral hemisphere. *Brain* 83:243–260, 1960.

Milner, B. Complementary functional specializations of the human cerebral hemispheres. In R. Levy-Montalcini, ed. *Neurons, Transmitters, and Behavior.* Vatican City: Pontificiae Academiae Scientiarum Scripta Varia, 1980.

Milner, D. A., D. P. Carey, and M. Harvey. Visually guided action and the "need to know." *Behavioral and Brain Sciences* 17:213–214, 1994.

Mountcastle, V. B., J. C. Lynch, A. Georgopoulos, H. Sakata, and C. Acuna. Posterior parietal association cortex of the monkey: Command functions for operation within extra-personal space. *Journal of Neurophysiology* 38:871–908, 1975.

Newcombe, F., and G. Radcliff. Disorders of visuospatial analysis. In F. Boller and J. Grafman, eds. *Handbook of Neuropsychology,* vol. 2. Amsterdam: Elsevier, 1990.

Paterson, A., and O. L. Zangwill. Disorders of space perception association with lesions of the right cerebral hemisphere. *Brain* 67:331–358, 1944.

Posner, M. I., A. W. Inhoff, F. J. Friedrich, and A. Cohen. Isolating attentional systems: A cognitive-anatomical analysis. *Psychobiology* 15:107–121, 1987.

Posner, M. I., J. A. Walker, J. J. Friedrich, and R. D. Rafal. Effects of parietal lobe injury on covert orienting of visual attention. *Journal of Neuroscience* 4:1863–1874, 1984.

Schenkenberg, T., D. C. Bradford, and E. T. Ajax. Line bisection and unilateral visual neglect in patients with neurologic impairment. *Neurology* 30:509–517, 1980.

Semmes, J., and B. Turner. Effects of cortical lesions on somatosensory task. *Journal of Investigations in Dermatology* 69:181–189, 1977.

Semmes, J., S. Weinstein, L. Ghent, and H.-L. Teuber. *Somatosensory Changes after Penetrating Brain Wounds in Man.* Cambridge, Mass.: Harvard University Press, 1960.

Semmes, J., S. Weinstein, L. Ghent, and H.-L. Teuber. Correlates of impaired orientation in personal and extra-personal space. *Brain* 86:747–772, 1963.

Stein, J. F. The representation of egocentric space in the posterior parietal cortex. *Behavioral and Brain Sciences* 15:691–700, 1992.

Teuber, H.-L., and S. Weinstein. Performance on a formboard task after penetrating brain injury. *Journal of Psychology* 38:177–190, 1954.

Traverse, J., and Latto, R. Impairments in route negotiation through a maze after dorsolateral frontal, inferior parietal or premotor lesions in cynomolgus monkeys. *Behavioural Brain Research* 20:203–215, 1986.

Tyler, H. R. Abnormalities of perception with defective eye movements (Balint's syndrome). *Cortex* 4:154–171, 1968.

Warrington, E. K., M. James, and M. Kinsbourne. Drawing disability in relation to laterality of cerebral lesion. *Brain* 89:53–82, 1966.

Warrington, E. K., and P. Rabin. Perceptual matching in patients with cerebral lesions. *Neuropsychologia* 8:475–487, 1970.

Warrington, E. K., and A. M. Taylor. The contribution of the right parietal lobe to object recognition. *Cortex* 9:152–164, 1973.

Warrington, E. K., and L. Weiskrantz. An analysis of short-term and long-term memory defects in man. In J. A. Deutsch, ed. *The Physiological Basis of Memory.* New York: Academic Press, 1993.

chapter thirteen

The Temporal Lobes

In the late 19th century three major effects of temporal lobe lesions on behavior were documented. In 1874 Karl Wernicke described a language deficit, in 1888 Brown and Schaefer noted a disorder of affect and personality, and in 1899 Bekhterev reported memory impairment. It is only in recent years, however, that the functions of the temporal lobes—especially of the right hemisphere—have been elaborated upon. In this chapter we will review the anatomy of the temporal lobe, present a theoretical model of its function, describe the basic symptoms of damage to it, and briefly describe clinical tests of temporal lobe function.

ANATOMY OF THE TEMPORAL LOBES

Subdivisions of the Temporal Cortex

The temporal lobe comprises all the tissue that lies below the Sylvian fissure and anterior to the occipital and parietal cortex (Figures 13.1 and 13.2). Brodmann identified 10 temporal areas, but more recent anatomical studies have shown many more areas in the monkey (see Felleman and van Essen's map, Figure 8.12), so there are likely to be more areas in the human as well. We can divide the temporal regions on the lateral surface into those that are auditory (Brodmann's areas 41, 42, and 22 in Figure 13.1) and those that form the ventral visual stream on the lateral temporal lobe (areas 20, 21, 37, and 38 in Figure 13.1). The visual regions are often referred to as inferotemporal cortex or by von Economo's designation of TE. The sulci of the temporal lobe contain a lot of cortex, as can be seen in Figure 13.2. In particular, the Sylvian fissure contains tissue forming the *insula,* which includes the gustatory cortex as well as the auditory association cortex. The superior temporal sulcus (STS), which separates the superior and middle temporal gyri, also contains a significant amount of neocortex, which can be divided into many subregions (Figure 13.3). The cortex of the STS is multimodal, receiving input from auditory, visual, and somatic regions, as well as from the other two polymodal regions (frontal and parietal) and the paralimbic cortex.

The medial temporal region includes the hippocampus and surrounding cortex (uncus, subiculum, entorhinal cortex, perirhinal cortex) and the fusiform gyrus. The entorhinal cortex comprises Brodmann's area 28, and the perirhinal cortex is Brodmann's areas 35 and 36 (see Figures

8.12 and 13.3). Areas TH and TF are cortical areas at the posterior end of the temporal lobe and are often referred to as the parahippocampal cortex. The fusiform gyrus and inferior temporal gyrus are functionally part of the lateral temporal cortex.

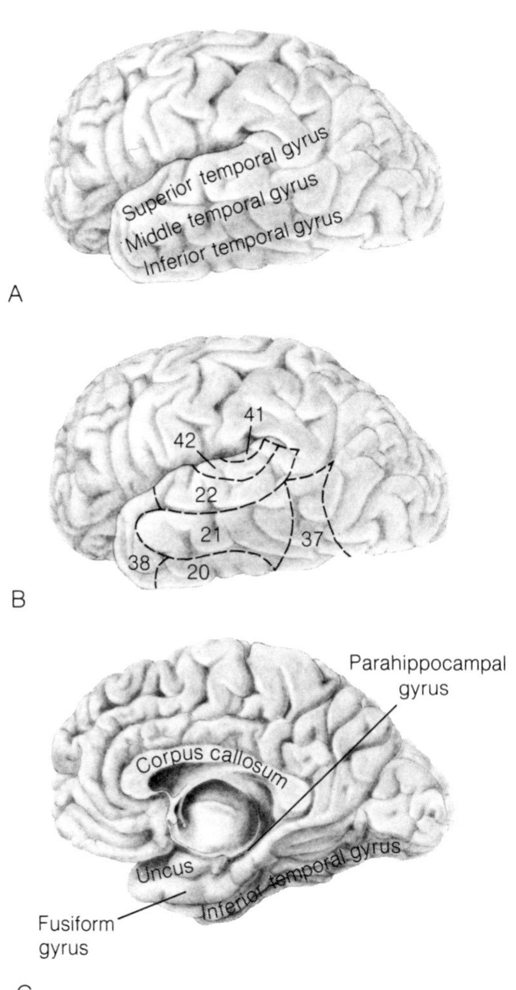

FIGURE 13.1. Gross anatomy of the temporal lobe. *A.* The three major gyri visible on the lateral surface of the temporal lobe. *B.* Brodmann's cytoarchitectonic zones on the lateral surface. Areas 20, 21, and 38 are referred to by von Bonin and Bailey's designation, TE. *C.* The gyri visible on a medial view of the temporal lobe. The uncus refers to the anterior extension of the hippocampal formation. The parahippocampal gyrus includes areas TF and TH.

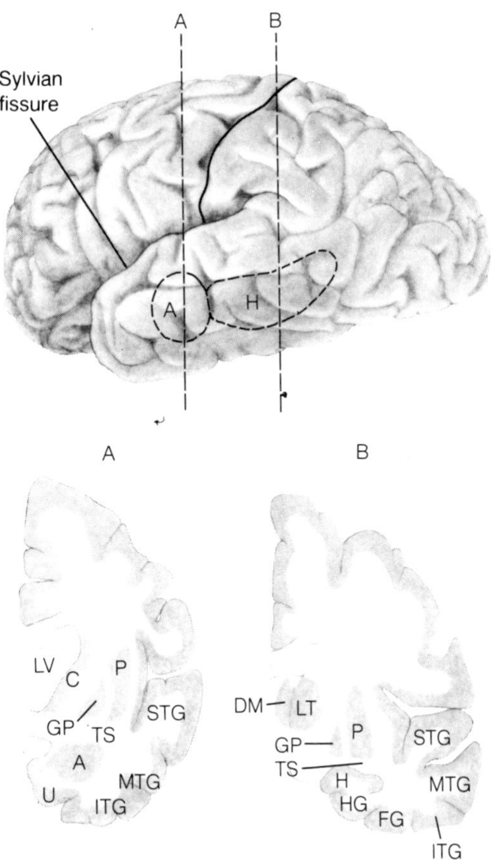

FIGURE 13.2. *Top:* Lateral view of the left hemisphere illustrating the relative positions of the amygdala (dashed circle) and hippocampus (dashed oval) buried deep in the temporal lobe. The dashed lines A and B indicate the approximate location of the sections in the bottom figure. *Bottom:* Frontal sections through the left hemisphere illustrating the cortical and subcortical regions of the temporal lobe. A, amygdala; C, caudate nucleus; DM, dorsomedial nucleus of the thalamus; FG, fusiform gyrus; GP, globus pallidus; H, hippocampus; HG, hippocampal gyrus; ITG, inferior temporal gyrus; LT, lateral thalamus; LV, lateral ventricle; MTG, middle temporal gyrus; P, putamen; STG, superior temporal gyrus; TS, temporal stem; U, uncus.

Connections of the Temporal Cortex

The temporal lobes are rich in internal connections, afferent projections from the sensory sys-

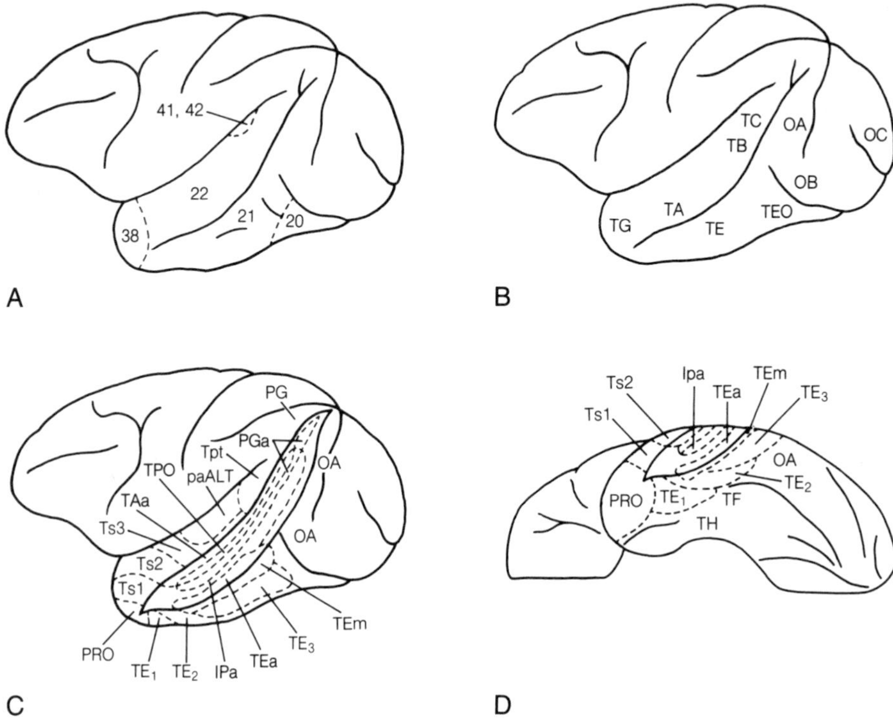

FIGURE 13.3. Cytoarchitectonic regions of the temporal cortex of the rhesus monkey. *A.* Brodmann's areas. *B.* von Bonin and Bailey's areas. *C., D.* Lateral and ventral views of Seltzer and Pandya's parcellation showing the multimodal areas in the superior temporal sulcus. The sulcus has been opened up to reveal many subareas on its banks. These are normally not visible from the surface.

tems, and efferent projections to the parietal and frontal association regions, limbic system, and basal ganglia. The neocortex of the left and right temporal lobes is connected via the corpus callosum to the archicortex via the anterior commissure.

Studies on the temporal-cortical connections of the monkey have revealed four distinct types of cortico-cortical connections, which are illustrated in Figure 13.4. The first is a hierarchical progression of connections from the primary and secondary auditory and visual areas, ending in the temporal pole. The visual projections form the ventral stream of visual processing. The second is a series of parallel projections from the visual and auditory association areas into the polymodal regions of the superior temporal sulcus. The third is a projection from the auditory and visual association areas into the medial temporal regions. This projection goes first to the perirhinal cortex, then to the entorhinal cortex, and finally into the hippocampal formation and/or the amygdala. The hippocampal projection is a major one, forming the **perforant pathway.** A disturbance of this projection results in a major dysfunction in hippocampal activity. Finally, the fourth is a series of parallel projections from the association areas to the frontal lobe. These four projection pathways presumably subserve different functions, which will become apparent in the next section. Briefly, the hierarchical sensory pathway probably subserves stimulus recognition; the polymodal pathway probably underlies stimulus categorization; the medial temporal projection is crucial to long-

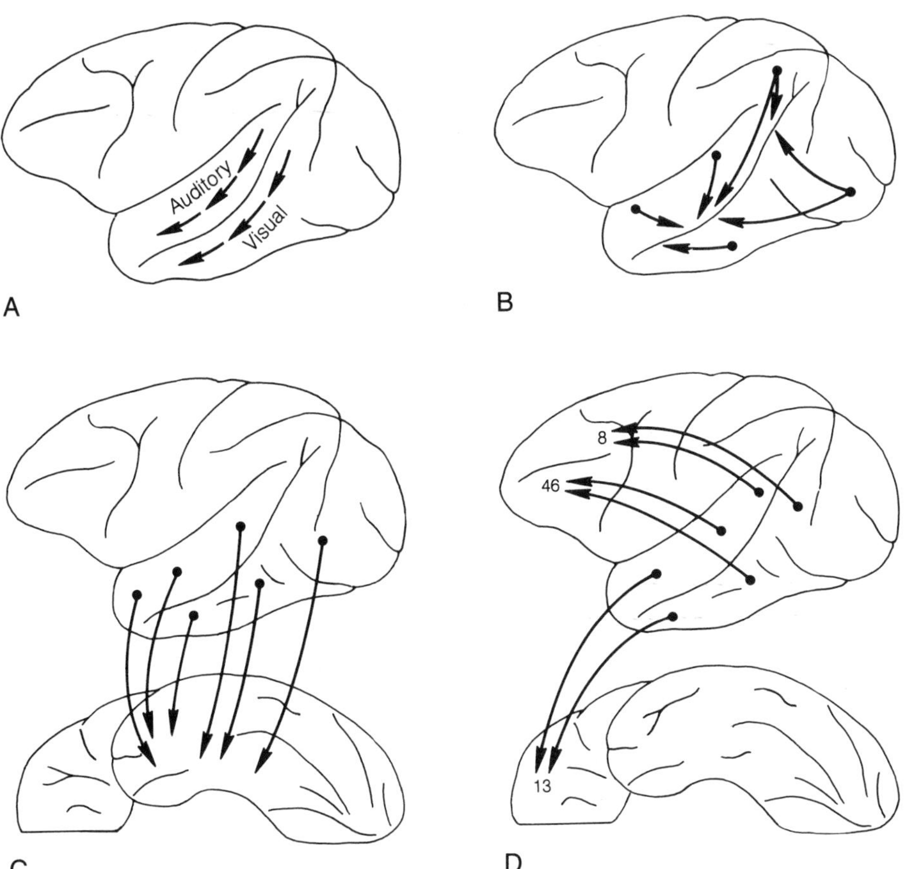

FIGURE 13.4. Summaries of the major intracortical connections of the temporal lobe. *A.* Auditory and visual information progresses from the primary regions toward the temporal pole, en route to the medial temporal regions. *B.* Auditory, visual, and somatic outputs go to the multimodal regions of the superior temporal sulcus. *C.* Auditory and visual information goes to the medial temporal region, including the amygdaloid formation and the hippocampal formation. *D.* Auditory and visual information goes to two prefrontal regions, one on the dorsolateral surface and one in the orbital region (area 13).

term memory; and the frontal lobe projection is necessary for various aspects of movement control, short-term memory, and affect.

A THEORY OF TEMPORAL LOBE FUNCTION

The temporal lobe does not have a unitary function, since it houses the primary auditory cortex, the secondary auditory and visual cortex, the limbic cortex, and the amygdala. On the basis of the cortical anatomy, we can identify three basic functions of the temporal cortex: one concerned primarily with the processing of auditory input, one specialized for visual object recognition, and one associated with long-term storage of sensory input. In addition, we can identify a function of the remaining temporal lobe region, the amygdala. The amygdala adds affective tone (that is, emotion) to sensory input and memories.

These functions are best understood by considering the analysis of sensory stimuli as they enter the nervous system. Consider the following example. You have gone for a hike in the woods. On your journey you notice that there are many different birds, and you decide to keep a mental note of which ones you encounter so that you can tell your sister, who is an avid birder. As you walk along you suddenly stop and back up—you have encountered a rattlesnake in the middle of the path. You decide to look for birds elsewhere!

What sensory processes were involved in your experience? First, as you searched for different birds you needed to be aware of specific colors, shapes, and sizes of birds that you might encounter. This is object recognition, which is the function of the ventral visual pathway in the temporal lobe. You also needed to be able to categorize the birds quickly, since they were often flying away, and you had to do so using information that varied in perspective from sighting to sighting (for example, lateral view versus rear view). This process of categorization is crucial to both perception and memory and is probably dependent upon the cortex in the STS. Categorization may require a form of directed attention because certain characteristics of stimuli are likely to play a more important role in classification than others. For example, classifying two different yellow birds requires that attention be directed away from color and focused upon shape, size, and other characteristics. Thus, damage to the temporal cortex leads to deficits in identifying and categorizing stimuli. There is no difficulty in locating the stimulus or in recognizing that a stimulus is present, however, because these are functions of the posterior parietal and primary sensory areas, respectively. As you walked along, you also may have heard birdsongs, and you needed to match songs with the visual input. This process of matching visual and auditory information is called **cross-modal matching.** It is also likely to involve the cortex of the STS. As you saw more and more birds, you had to keep some form of memory that you could later access. Furthermore, as you saw different birds you needed to access their names from your memory. These processes of long-term memory involve the entire ventral visual stream as well as the paralimbic cortex of the medial temporal region. When you encountered the snake you first heard the rattle, which alerted you and you stopped. As you scanned the ground you saw and identified the snake, and your heart rate and blood pressure rose. The affective response that you exhibited is a function of the amygdala. The association of sensory input and emotion is crucial for learning because stimuli become associated with their positive, negative, or neutral consequences, and behavior is modified accordingly. In the absence of this system all stimuli would be treated as equivalent. Consider the consequences of failing to associate the rattlesnake, which is poisonous, with the consequences of being bitten. Or consider being unable to associate good feelings (such as love) with a specific person. Laboratory animals with amygdala lesions become very placid and do not react emotionally to threatening stimuli. For example, monkeys that were previously terrified of snakes become indifferent to them. Finally, when you changed routes and went elsewhere you used the hippocampus. The hippocampus contains cells that code places in space; together, these cells allow us to navigate space and to remember where we are.

As we consider these general functions of the temporal lobes, we can see that the loss of these functions would have devastating consequences for behavior. There would be an inability to perceive or to remember events, including language, in the environment. There would be a loss of affect. Note, however, that an individual would be able to use the dorsal visual system to make visually guided movements and under some circumstances might actually appear rather normal.

ASYMMETRY OF TEMPORAL LOBE FUNCTION

The temporal lobes are sensitive to epileptiform abnormalities, and surgical removal of the abnormal temporal lobe is often of benefit in treating epilepsy. These facts have allowed neuropsychologists to study the complementary specialization of the temporal lobes. Comparison of the effects of left and right temporal lobectomy by Milner and her colleagues has revealed that specific memory defects vary according to which side the lesion is on: damage to the left temporal lobe is associated with deficits in verbal memory, damage to the right with deficits in nonverbal memory (for example, of faces). Similarly, left temporal lesions are associated with deficits in processing speech sounds, whereas right temporal lesions are associated with deficits in processing music. Little is known, however, about the relative role of the left and right temporal lobes in affective behavior. Nevertheless, a suggestion of asymmetry comes from unquantified clinical observations that left and right temporal lobe lesions appear to have different effects on personality, and that right, but not left, temporal lesions lead to impairments in interpretation of facial expression.

In reviewing the literature on the results of *unilateral* temporal lobectomy, one is often struck by the relatively minor effects of removal of such a large zone of the cerebral hemispheres. It is incorrect to assume from these studies, however, that removing both temporal lobes would merely add the symptoms of damage to those symptoms seen in unilateral temporal lobectomy. Bilateral temporal lobe removal produces dramatic effects on both memory and affect that are orders of magnitude greater than those observed following unilateral lesions. Thus, although the temporal lobes are relatively specialized in their functions, there is substantial functional overlap; do not be overly impressed by the apparent functional asymmetry.

SYMPTOMS OF TEMPORAL LOBE LESIONS

Eight principal symptoms are associated with disease of the temporal lobes: (1) disturbance of auditory sensation and perception, (2) disturbance of selective attention of auditory and visual input, (3) disorders of visual perception, (4) impaired organization and categorization of verbal material, (5) disturbance of language comprehension, (6) impaired long-term memory, (7) altered personality and affective behavior, and (8) altered sexual behavior. Table 13.1 summarizes the major symptoms of temporal lobe damage, lists the most probable lesion sites, and cites basic references.

Disorders of Auditory Perception

Damage to the primary visual or somatic cortex leads to a loss of conscious sensation, so it is reasonable to predict that bilateral damage to the auditory cortex will produce what can be called *cortical deafness*. Clinical evidence and evidence from laboratory animal studies do not support this prediction, however. In fact, there is little disruption of sensitivity to changes in sound frequency or intensity after either bilateral or unilateral auditory cortex lesions in any mammal studied. There are auditory perception deficits, however. First, Tallal and Piercy found that patients with lesions that included auditory cortex were impaired at discriminating 43-msec sounds of changing frequency but performed normally when the duration of the sounds was increased to 95 msec. A second, related impairment is observed in the judgment of the simultaneity of brief sounds. Cortical lesions appear to increase the time needed between sounds to discriminate the sounds. This impairment is presumably related to the common complaint among patients with left temporal lobe damage that people are talking too quickly. The problem is not so much the quickness of the speech but the inability to discriminate between sounds presented quickly—a difficulty commonly encountered by normal people during the acquisition of a new language. A third audioperceptual impairment is also related to the timing of auditory stimuli: the judgment of temporal order in sounds heard. If a normal subject is presented with two sounds, a temporal separation of only 50 to 60 msec is sufficient to identify which of the two sounds was presented first. Subjects with temporal lobe lesions may require as much as 500 msec between two sounds (a tenfold increase) to perform at the same level. Each of these audioperceptual impairments appears to be

TABLE 13.1. Summary of major symptoms of temporal lobe damage

Symptoms	Most probable lesion site	Basic reference
Disturbance of auditory sensation	Areas 41, 42, 22	Vignolo, 1969 Hécaen and Albert, 1978
Disturbance of selection of visual and auditory input	Areas TE, STS	Sparks et al., 1970 Dorff et al., 1965
Disorders of visual perception	Areas TE, STS, amygdala	Milner, 1968 Meier and French, 1968
Disorders of auditory perception	Areas 41, 42, 22	Samson and Zatorre, 1988 Swisher and Hirsch, 1972
Impaired organization and categorization of material	Areas TE, STS	Wilkins and Moscovitch, 1978 Read, 1981
Poor contextual use	Area TE	Milner, 1958
Disturbance of language comprehension	Area 22 left	Hécaen and Albert, 1978
Poor long-term memory	Areas TE, TF, TH, 28	Milner, 1970
Changes in personality and affect	Areas TE, plus amygdala	Blumer and Benson, 1975 Pincus and Tucker, 1974
Changes in sexual activity	Amygdala, plus ?	Blumer and Walker, 1975

more severe following left temporal lobe lesions than after right temporal lobe lesions—a result suggesting that these auditory skills are especially important in the discrimination of speech sounds.

Speech differs from other auditory input in several fundamental ways. First, the sounds of speech come largely from three restricted ranges of frequencies, which are known as *formants*. Figure 13.5A illustrates sound spectrograms of different two-formant syllables. The dark bars indicate the frequency bands seen in more detail in Figure 13.5B. Figure 13.5B shows that the syllables differ both in the onset frequency of the second (higher) formant and in the onset time of the consonant. Notice that vowel sounds are in a constant frequency band, but consonants show rapid changes in frequency. Second, the same speech sounds vary from one context in which they are heard to another, yet they are all perceived as being the same. Thus, the sound spectrogram of the letter "d" in English is different in the words "deep," "deck," and "duke," yet a listener perceives them to be the same. The auditory system must have a mechanism for categorizing sounds as being the same, and this mechanism must be affected by experience, since a major obstacle to learning foreign languages is the difficulty of learning the categories that are treated equivalently. Thus, a word's spectrogram is dependent on the words that precede and follow it. (There may be a parallel mechanism for musical categorization as well.) Third, speech sounds change very rapidly in relation to each other, and the sequential order of the sounds is critical to understanding. According to Liberman, we can perceive speech at rates of up to 30 segments per second, although normal speech is on the order of 8 to 10 segments per second. Speech perception at the higher rates is truly amazing, because it far exceeds the auditory system's ability to transmit all the speech as separate pieces of auditory information. For example, nonspeech noise is perceived as a buzz at a rate of only about 5 segments per second. Clearly, language sounds must be recognized and analyzed in a special way by the brain, much as the echolocation system of the bat is treated specially by the bat

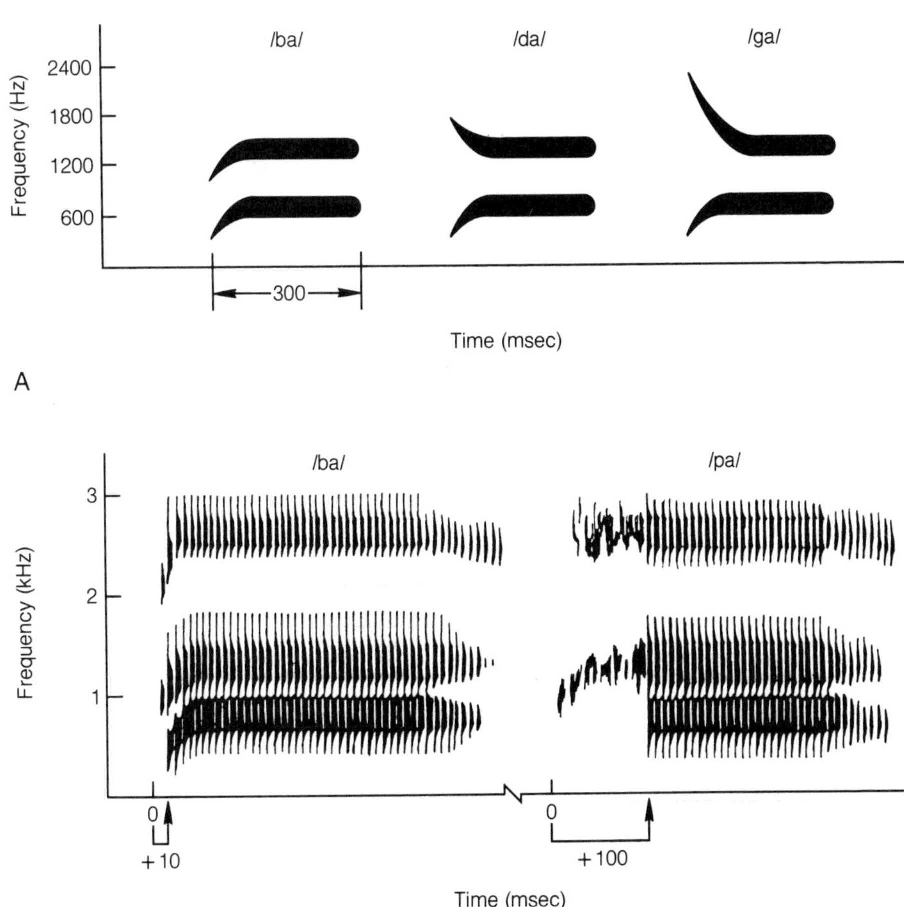

FIGURE 13.5. *A*. Schematic spectrograms of three different syllables, each made up of two formants. *B*. Spectrograms of syllables differing in voice onset time. (After Springer, 1979.)

brain. It is likely that the special mechanism for speech perception is in the left temporal lobe. This function may not be unique to humans, since studies in both monkeys and rats have shown specific deficits in the perception of species-typical vocalizations after temporal lesions.

The fact that left temporal lobe lesions alter the perception of speech sounds ought not to be surprising: it has been known since the time of Wernicke that lesions of the left temporal association cortex (primarily area 22) produce aphasia. The classical view of Wernicke's aphasia is that it is associated with disturbed recognition of words, the extreme form being "word deafness": an inability to recognize words as such despite intact hearing of pure tones.

Finally, there is an audioperceptual symptom that is specific to the right temporal lobe: the perception of certain characteristics of music. Musical sounds may differ from one another in three aspects: loudness, quality, and pitch. *Loudness* refers to the magnitude of a sensation as judged by a given individual. Loudness, although related to the intensity of a sound as measured in decibels, is in fact a subjective evaluation. In music, loudness is described by such terms as "very loud," "soft," "very soft," and so forth. *Quality* refers to the characteristic of a sound by which it can be distinguished from all other sounds of similar pitch and loudness. For example, we can distinguish the sound of a violin from that of a trombone even though they may play the same note at the same loudness. The French word *timbre* is normally used to describe this character of sound. *Pitch* refers to the position of a sound in a musical scale, as judged by the listener. Although pitch is clearly related to the frequency of the sound, there is more to it than that. Consider the note, middle C. This note can be described as a pattern of sound frequencies, as depicted in Figure 13.6. The amplitude of acoustic energy is conveyed by the darkness of the tracing in the figure. The lowest component of this note is the *fundamental frequency* of the sound pattern, which is 264 Hz, or middle C. The sound frequencies above the fundamental are known as *overtones* or *partials*. The overtones are generally simple multiples of the fundamental (for example, 2 × 264, or 528 Hz; 4 × 264, or 1056 Hz), as can be seen in Figure 13.6. Those overtones that are multiples of the fundamental are known as *harmonics*. Other sounds are called *transients*.

The classic view, dating back to Helmholtz in the late 1800s, held that pitch perception depends upon the fundamental frequency and the overtones provide timbre. This now appears to be incorrect. If the fundamental frequency is removed from a note with electronic filters, the overtones are sufficient to determine the pitch of the fundamental frequency—a phenomenon known as *periodicity pitch*. The ability to determine pitch from the overtones alone is probably due to the fact that the difference between the frequencies of the various harmonics is equal to the fundamental frequency (for example, 792 − 528 = 264 = the fundamental). Thus, the auditory system can determine this difference, and we perceive the fundamental frequency. It appears that it is the right temporal lobe that makes this periodicity pitch discrimination. For example, Zatorre found that

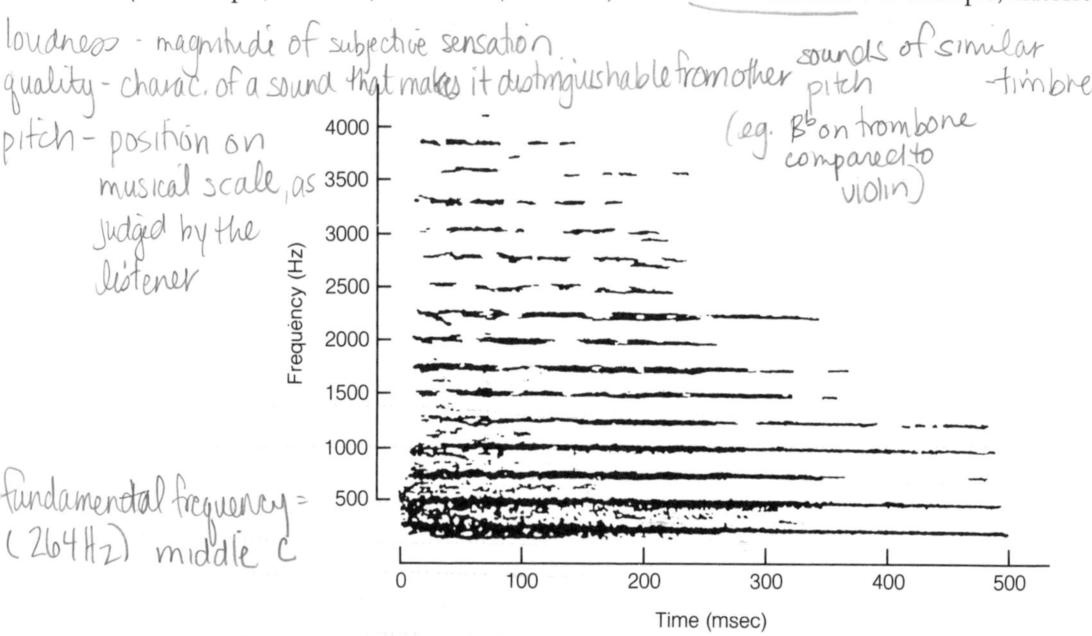

FIGURE 13.6. Spectrographic display of the steady-state portion of a middle C (264 Hz) played on a piano. Bands of acoustical energy are present at the fundamental frequency, as well as at integer multiples of the fundamental (harmonics). For complex tones at this fundamental frequency, the first five harmonics are dominant in the perception of pitch. (After Ritsma, 1967.)

patients with right temporal lobectomies, *which included the primary auditory cortex,* were impaired at making pitch discriminations when the fundamental was absent but were normal at making such discriminations when the fundamental was present. Right temporal lesions that spared the primary auditory cortex, or left temporal lobectomies, did not impair performance. Zatorre suggests that the right temporal lobe has a special function in extracting pitch from sound, regardless of whether the sound is speech or music. In the case of speech, the pitch will contribute to "tone" of voice, which is known as **prosody.**

There are a variety of other aspects of music that also may be specially processed in the right temporal lobe. The simplest would be timbre, and Milner did demonstrate that right temporal lesions impair the perception of timbre. In addition, there are more complex aspects of music, such as scales, chords, and progressions, all of which are constructed from single musical notes. Although speculative, it seems likely that we develop a "musical store" much as we develop a "syntactic store" of words. Thus, when we encounter a musical scale or progression, it is recognized as such. The mechanism of such a hypothetical store is unknown, but it may be a function of the right auditory association cortex.

In 1926 Henschen reported 16 patients who had deficits in musical perception but had no language deficit. Since preservation of musical abilities had been documented many times since the 1920s, Henschen concluded that the two functions are in the opposite sides of the brain. It seems unlikely that the brain is specifically designed to treat music and language differently; rather, certain characteristics of musical and language input are probably analyzed selectively by the two hemispheres. In a thoughtful review Brust concludes that current conceptions of the cerebral organization of music, including the view that increasing musical sophistication causes a shift in locus of musical processing, are oversimplifications. The door would seem wide open for imaginative studies of cerebral processing of musical perception and production in both brain-damaged and normal people. Recently, Zatorre and Halpern did such an experiment. They played a song familiar to English-speaking people (for example, "Jingle Bells") and at the same time presented the song lyrics on a screen. Two words in the text were capitalized, and the subject was instructed to indicate if the pitch corresponding to the second word was higher or lower than the first. For example, from "Jingle Bells," the subjects were given "Dashing through the SNOW in a one-horse open SLEIGH, o'er the fields we go, laughing all the way." The subject had to listen to the song and then indicate if the pitch of SLEIGH is higher or lower (it is higher). In a second task, the subjects were not played the song but were given only the lyrics. In this case, they had to rely on their own internal auditory image of the song. Patients with right temporal lobe lesions were impaired at both versions of the task, whereas those with left temporal lobe lesions performed as well as normal subjects. The authors conclude that their results support the idea that imagery arises from activation of a neural substrate shared with perceptual mechanisms and suggest that for music this mechanism is in the right temporal lobe.

Disorders of Visual Perception

Although individuals with temporal lobectomies do not normally have large defects in their visual fields, they do have deficits in visual perception. This was first demonstrated by Milner, who found that her patients with right temporal lobectomies were impaired in the interpretation of cartoon drawings in the McGill Picture-Anomalies Test. For example, in one item illustrating a monkey in a cage there is an oil painting on the wall of the cage—an obvious oddity or anomaly. But patients with right temporal lesions, although able to describe the contents of the picture accurately, were impaired at recognizing the anomalous character of this and other pictures. Similarly, on a test such as the Mooney Closure Test or tests requiring the discrimination of complex patterns (Figure 13.7), patients with temporal lobe damage perform very poorly. Probably one of the most interesting visual perceptual deficits is in facial perception and recognition. When Kolb and his associates presented patients with the split-faces test described in Chapter 11 (see Figure 11.10), they found that those with right temporal lobe resections failed to show a bias for that portion of the face falling in the left visual field, suggesting that these patients were perceiving faces abnormally. This conclusion is consistent with reports that patients with right temporal lobe damage are impaired at the recognition and recall of faces or photographs of faces. Furthermore, these patients do not appear able to perceive subtle social signals such as discreet but obvious glances at one's watch, a gesture often intended as a cue to break off a conversation. Presumably the patients fail to perceive the significance of the visual signal.

The description of deficits in visual perception in people with temporal lobe injury is consistent with the hypothetical role of the inferotemporal cortex in Ungerleider and Mishkin's ventral visual stream (see Chapter 11). There is an extensive literature showing that monkeys with inferotemporal lesions have severe and selective deficits in learning tasks that require the visual recognition of objects. Furthermore, it has long been known that inferotemporal cortex neurons in monkeys have selective characteristics, such as a preference

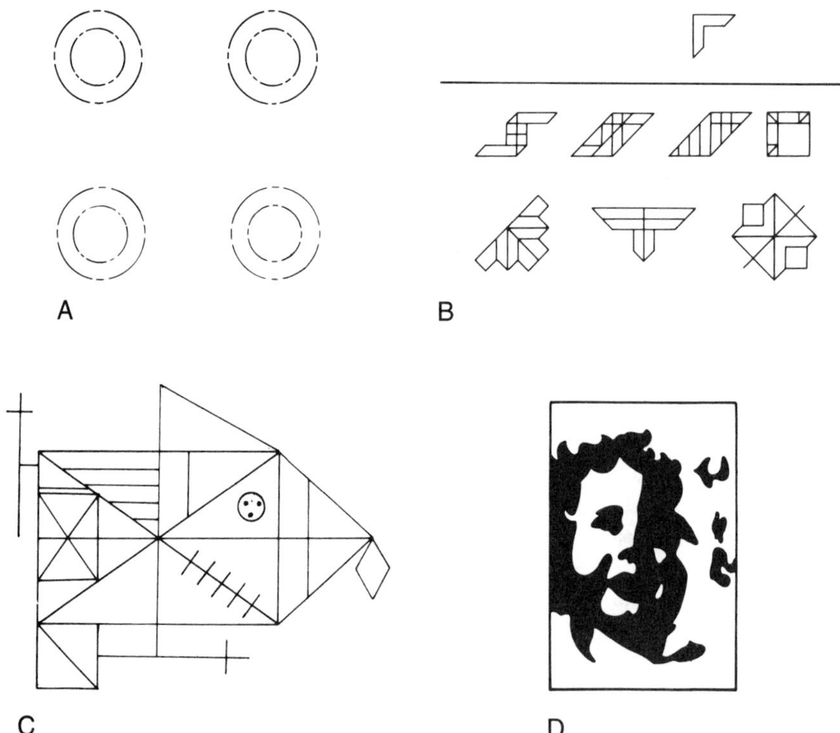

FIGURE 13.7. Examples of tests for visual disorders. *A.* Meier and French's test, in which the subject must identify the drawing that is different. *B.* Sample of the Gottschaldt Hidden-Figures Test. The task is to detect and trace the sample (upper drawing) in each of the figures below it. *C.* Rey Complex-Figure Test. The subject is asked to copy it as exactly as possible. *D.* Sample of the Mooney Closure Test. The task is to identify the face in the ambiguous shadows.

for faces or hands. These preferences may be quite specific. For example, Perrett and colleagues have shown that neurons in the STS may be responsive to particular faces seen head-on, faces viewed in profile, posture of the head, or even particular facial expressions. More recently, Perrett has also shown that some STS cells are maximally sensitive to primate bodies that are moving in a particular direction (Figure 13.8). This is quite remarkable because the basic configuration of the stimulus is identical as the body moves in different directions; it is only the direction that changes.

One problem with the identification of specialized temporal visual neurons is that it is impractical to have specific temporal cortex cells for every possible object feature in the world. Tanaka approached this problem by attempting to determine the features that are critical for the activation of neurons in the inferotemporal cortex of monkeys. He and his colleagues presented many three-dimensional animal and plant representations to find the effective stimuli for given cells. Then they tried to determine the necessary and sufficient properties of these cells. Tanaka found that most cells in area TE required rather complex features for their activation (Figure 13.9). These features contained a combination of characteristics such as orientation, size, color, and texture. Furthermore, he found that cells with similar, although slightly different, selectivity tended to cluster in columns (see Figure 13.9). Since the organization of the cortex has an important

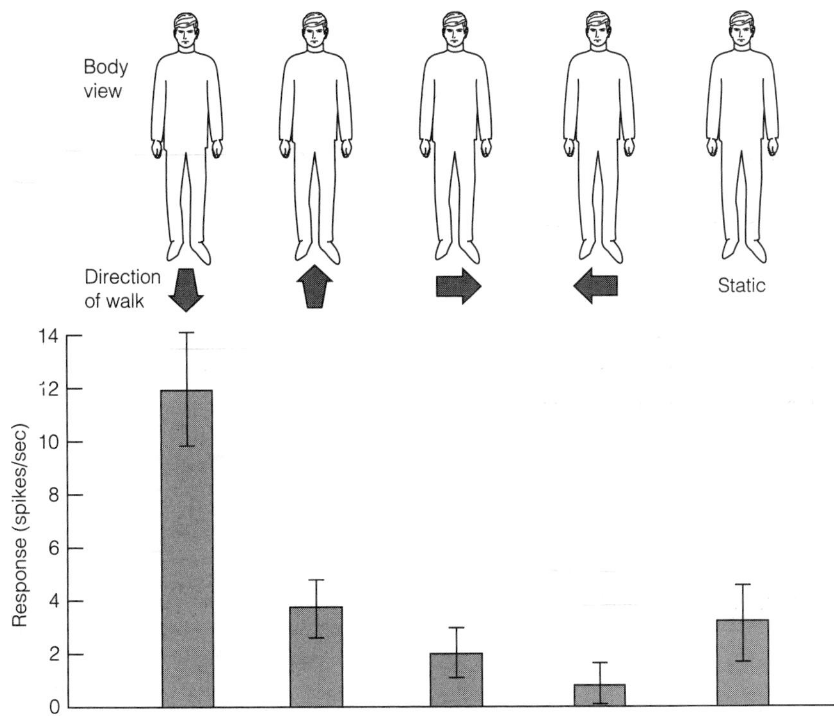

FIGURE 13.8. Neuronal sensitivity to direction of body movements. *Top:* Schematic representation of the front view of a body. *Bottom:* The histogram illustrates a greater neuronal response of STS neurons to the front view of a body when approaching the observing monkey compared with the same body views when moving away, to the right, to the left, and static. (After Perrett et al., 1990.)

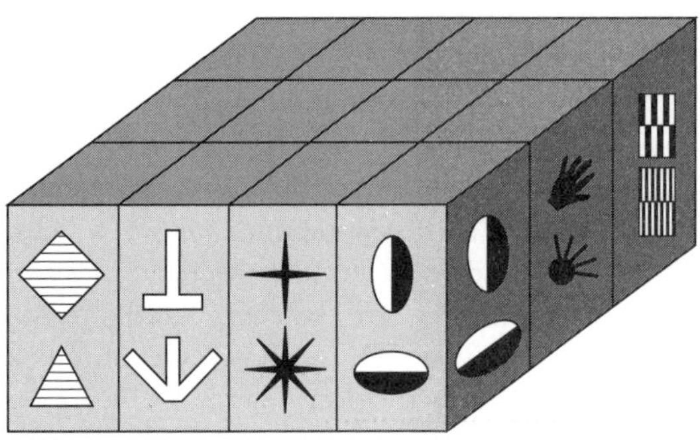

FIGURE 13.9. Schematic illustration of the columnar organization in area TE. Cells with similar but slightly different selectivity cluster in elongated vertical columns, perpendicular to the cortical surface.

vertical component (see Chapter 8), and since the neurons organized in columns in the temporal cortex are not identical in their stimulus selectivity, it seems likely that an object is not represented by the activity of a single cell but rather by the activity of many cells within a columnar module. This is an important finding because it provides an explanation for the phenomenon of stimulus equivalence—that is, the common observation that objects viewed at different orientations are the same object. Tanaka speculates that the representation of objects by multiple cells in a columnar module in which the selectivity varies from cell to cell and effective stimuli largely overlap can provide a way to minimize the effect of small changes in input images.

Tanaka and others have also described two other remarkable features of inferotemporal neurons in monkeys. First, the stimulus specificity of these neurons is altered by experience. Monkeys were trained to discriminate 28 complex shapes for a year. The stimulus preferences of inferotemporal neurons were then determined from a larger set of animal and plant models. In the trained monkeys, 39% of the inferotemporal neurons gave a maximum response to some of the stimuli used in training. This compared to only 9% of the neurons in naive monkeys. This result is exciting, because it shows that the temporal lobe's role in visual processing is not determined genetically but is subject to experience in the adult. One can speculate that this experience-dependent characteristic allows the visual system to adapt to different demands in a changing visual environment. This is an important feature for human visual recognition abilities that have very different demands in forests than in plains or urban environments. In addition, experience-dependent visual neurons ensure that we can identify visual stimuli that were never encountered in the evolution of our brain.

The second interesting feature of these neurons is that they may not only reflect the processing of visual input but also provide a mechanism for the internal representation of the images of objects. Fuster and Jervey first demonstrated that if monkeys were shown specific objects that were to be remembered, there were neurons in the inferotemporal cortex that continued to discharge during the "memory" period. These selective discharges of neurons may provide the basis of working memory for the stimuli. Furthermore, it has been proposed that the discharges of these neurons can provide the basis for imagery. That is, the discharge of groups of neurons that are selective for characteristics of particular objects may provide a mental image of the object in its absence. Jones has shown that right temporal lobe patients are poor at visual imagery. Recall, too, that Zatorre found right temporal lobe patients to be poor at musical imagery.

Disturbance of Selection of Visual and Auditory Input

People have a limited capacity to process the wealth of information in their environment and hence must select which inputs to process. This selectivity is generally not conscious, for the nervous system automatically scans input and selectively perceives the environment. (Conscious control can be exerted, of course, as when one searches for a mailbox to post a letter.) Selectivity in auditory perception is best illustrated by the problem of listening to two conversations simultaneously. Because it is impossible to process the two competing inputs concurrently, the auditory system adopts one of two strategies: either one conversation is ignored, or attention shifts back and forth from one conversation to the other. In either case there is a selection of input. Selective perception in the visual system operates similarly. For example, because it is not possible to watch all events of a gymnastics meet simultaneously, attention either is focused entirely on one event or is shifted from one event to another.

Let us now consider the person with temporal lobe damage. We shall see that selection of both auditory and visual input is impaired, which is ordinarily demonstrated only by special testing procedures. Selective attention to auditory input can be tested by using a technique called **dichotic listening.** Subjects are presented with two words or digits simultaneously, one to each ear. For normal subjects more of the words presented to the right ear will be reported; if tonal sequences are presented dichotically, there will be a left-ear advantage. Exploiting this technique in patients with temporal lobe lesions, Schulhoff and Goodglass have demonstrated that although the expected ear advantages are still present in both right and left sides, left temporal lobe lesions result in an overall drop in the number of tonal sequences recognized. One explanation for this effect is that the nervous system has difficulty focusing selectively on the input into one ear and attempts to process all the input concurrently; as a result, performance drops significantly. Analogous findings are reported for visual input. Dorff and colleagues presented two different visual stimuli simultaneously, one to each visual field. Damage to the left temporal lobe impaired recall of content of the right visual field, but damage to the right temporal lobe impaired recall of content of *both* visual fields. Again, it may be that the nervous system is now unable to focus on distinctive features of the stimuli to allow efficient perception and storage of the input. In the case of visual input, however, it is noteworthy that right temporal lesions produce bilateral deficits, whereas left temporal lesions produce unilateral ones. This difference implies that the right temporal lobe may have a greater role than the left in selective attention to visual input.

Categorization of Material

If one is asked to learn a list of words such as "dog, car, bus, apple, rat, lemon, cat, truck, orange," it is a common experience that the words will be categorized into three different classes—animals, vehicles, and fruit. If the list is later recalled, the items are likely to be recalled by category, and recall of the categories is likely to be used as an aid in recall of the items. The ability to organize material is especially important for language and memory. For example, it makes it possible to comprehend extended sentences, including both the meaning of individual sentences and the information that is inferred from them. Organization of sensory input appears to be a function of the temporal lobes. Patients with left temporal lobectomies are impaired in their ability to do this type of organization, even with single words or pictures of familiar objects. Thus, patients have difficulty in placing words or pictures into discrete categories, even when they are requested to, and they also have difficulty in using categories that most of us use automatically. For example, Milner has found that when these patients are given a category name (such as animal) and are asked to recall examplars of the category (such as dog, cat, rat), they have difficulty, even though they are fluent in other types of tests. Given that these patients have difficulty in relatively simple types of categorization tasks studied in the laboratory, one can imagine that their difficulty in spontaneous organization may represent a significant deficit in cognition, especially in memory for complex material.

Recently, neurolinguists have proposed that another type of categorization may occur in the left temporal lobe. Semantic categories are hierarchical categories in which a single word might belong to several categories simultaneously. For example, a duck belongs to the categories animal, bird, and waterfowl. Each of these categories represents a refinement of the previous one. Patients with posterior temporal lesions may show dysphasic symptoms in which they can recognize the broader categorization but have difficulty with the more specific one.

Using Contextual Information

The meaning of identical information can vary depending upon the context. For example, a word such as "fall" can refer to a season or to a tumble, depending upon the context. Similarly, context may be a major cue for facial recognition. Most of us have encountered someone completely out of context (for example, while in Paris we encounter a clerk from our neighborhood store at home) and have been unable to recall who the person is until the information about the context is provided. A more complex example of extracting meaning from context is found in social situations. The interpretation of events, and indeed our role in events, is dependent upon the social context. Thus, stimuli may be interpreted in one way when we are with our parents and in a different way when we are with our peers. This ability to use context as a key to the recognition of stimuli probably depends upon normal temporal lobe function, although data are rather sparse. In one study, Kolb and Taylor showed that temporal lobe patients found it difficult to choose correctly the facial expression appropriate for a faceless cartoon character when the only clue was the context (for example, surprise party, funeral, argument). Similarly, we described the deficit of patients with right temporal lobectomies in the McGill Picture-Anomalies Test (see the section on visual perceptual deficits, above). The only clue to the correct choice in the McGill anomalies is the context. Further studies are needed on both visual and auditory stimuli and context.

Memory

To many neuropsychologists the study of the temporal lobes is synonymous with the study of memory. In fact, in most physiological psychology and neuropsychology texts, index references to the temporal lobes lead one to a discussion of amnesia. The interest in the temporal lobes' function in memory was stimulated in the early 1950s by the discovery that bilateral removal of the medial temporal lobes, including the hippocampus and amygdala, resulted in amnesia for all events after the surgery (**anterograde amnesia**). It is now clear that both the medial temporal regions and the temporal neocortex are important for memory functions (see Chapter 16). Damage to the inferotemporal cortex specifically intereferes with conscious recall of information, the extent of the memory disturbance increasing in direct proportion to the amount of temporal lobe damaged. Lesions of the left temporal lobe result in impaired recall of verbal material, such as short stories and word lists, whether presented visually or aurally; lesions of the right temporal lobe result in impaired recall of nonverbal material, such as geometric drawings, faces, and tunes. Unlike parietal lobe lesions, however, temporal lobe lesions do not disturb the immediate recall of material such as strings of digits. Thus, the temporal and parietal lobes have complementary rather than redundant roles in memory.

The following two case histories demonstrate the role of the left and right temporal lobes in memory. Mr. B., a 38-year-old man, was suffering from an astrocytoma in the left temporal lobe. Prior to the onset he had been a successful executive in an oil company and was noted for his efficiency. As his tumor developed he became forgetful, and at the time of hospital admission his efficiency had dropped drastically; he had begun to forget appointments and other important events. Forgetfulness had become such a problem that he had begun to write notes to himself to cover his memory problem, but he often mislaid the notes, leading to even greater embarrassment. On formal tests of memory he had special difficulty in recalling short stories read to him a few minutes earlier. For example, in one test he was read the following story from the Wechsler Memory Scale and asked to repeat it as exactly as possible. "Anna Thompson of South Boston, employed as a scrub woman in an office building, was held up on State Street the night before and robbed of $15. She had four little children, the rent was due and they had not eaten for two days. The officers, touched by the woman's story, made up a purse for her." Mr. B. recalled: "A woman was robbed and went to the police station where they made her a new purse. She had some children too." This is very poor performance for a person of Mr. B.'s intelligence and education. On the other hand, his immediate recall of digits was good; he could repeat strings of seven digits accurately. Similarly, his recall of geometric designs was within normal limits, illustrating the asymmetry of memory functions, since his right temporal lobe was still intact.

Ms. C. illustrates the complement of Mr. B.'s syndrome. She was a bright 22-year-old college student who had an indolent tumor of the right temporal lobe. When we first saw her, following surgery, she complained of memory loss. She was within normal limits on formal tests of verbal memory, such as the story of Anna Thompson, but was seriously impaired on formal tests of visual memory, especially geometric drawings. For example, in one test she was shown geometric designs for 10 sec and then asked to draw them from memory. Ten minutes later she was asked to draw them again. She had difficulty with immediate recall (Figure 13.10), and after 10 min was unable to recall any of the drawings at all.

Affect and Personality

Although the temporal lobe has been known to be associated with disturbance of affect in humans for nearly 100 years, knowledge about the details of this role is still surprisingly fragmentary. Wilder Penfield and others reported that stimulation of the anterior and medial temporal cortex produces feelings of fear, an effect also occasionally obtained from stimulating the amygdala.

Temporal lobe epilepsy traditionally has been associated with personality characteristics in which there is an overemphasis on trivia and the petty details of daily life. Pincus and Tucker describe several symptoms of this personality, including pedantic speech, egocentricity, perseveration on discussion of personal problems (sometimes referred to as "stickiness," because one is stuck talking to the person), paranoia, preoccupation with religion, and proneness to aggressive outbursts. This constellation of behaviors produces what is described as *temporal lobe personality,* although very few people combine all these traits. Similar personality traits occur

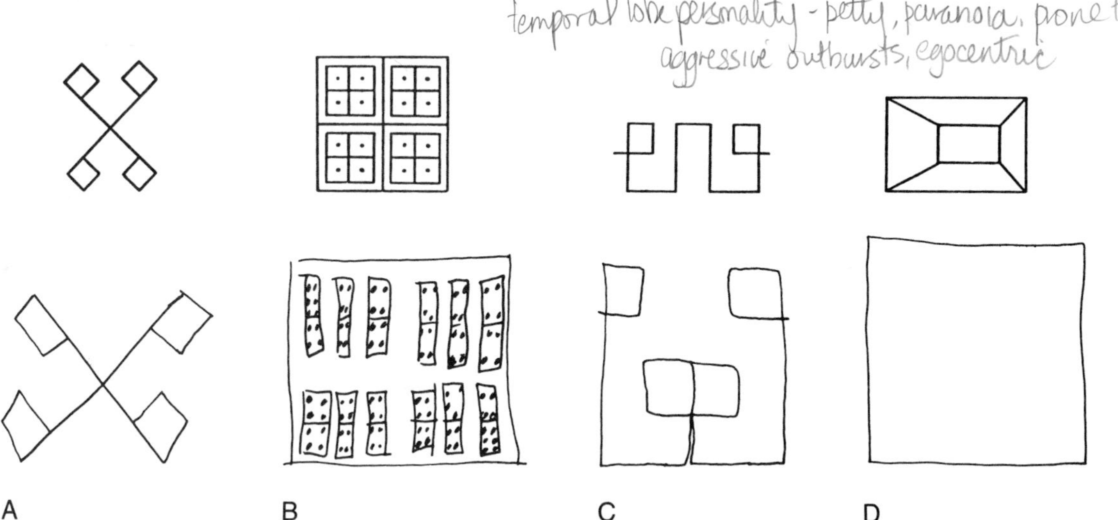

FIGURE 13.10. Illustration of impaired recall of geometric figures in the case of Ms. C. In each set shown (*A, B, C, D*) the top drawing is the original stimulus and the bottom drawing is Ms. C.'s sketch made immediately after viewing each figure for 10 seconds. Note that Ms. C.'s impairment is worse with the more complex figures. Ms. C. was unable to recall even the simplest figure 10 minutes after viewing it.

following temporal lobectomy. There appears to be a relative asymmetry in the symptoms, with right temporal lobectomy being more likely to be associated with these personality traits than left temporal lobectomy. This observation has not been quantified, however, and warrants further study. Finally, although temporal lobe epilepsy has long been linked anecdotally with psychosis-like episodes, Slater and associates in 1963 first demonstrated a statistical relationship between the occurrence of temporal lobe epilepsy and psychosis. Since no such relation has been described between temporal lobectomy and epilepsy, it has been suggested that chronic abnormal electrical activity may produce abnormalities in either the biochemistry or the normal electrophysiology of the brain, leading to psychotic behavior.

Clinical Neuropsychological Assessment of Temporal Lobe Damage

A number of standardized assessment tools have proved to be sensitive and valid predictors of temporal lobe injury (Table 13.2). Like clinical neuropsychological tests of parietal lobe function, these tests do not assess all possible temporal lobe symptoms, but it would be highly unusual for a person to perform normally on all these tests if there were damage to either temporal lobe.

Auditory and visual processing capacity can be assessed using dichotic listening and the McGill Picture-Anomalies Test, as described earlier in the chapter. The picture-anomalies task is not as sensitive an indicator today as it was when first used in the 1950s, perhaps because television viewing has made the average person more sophisticated in visual perceptual abilities. Nevertheless, a poor score on this test almost invariably denotes right temporal abnormality.

The best test of general verbal memory ability is the revised Wechsler Memory Scale. However, because the Wechsler memory quotient is affected by nonspecific disorders of attention, two subtests—paired associates and logical stories—are often used as a purer measure of verbal memory capacity. The paired-associates subtest requires a subject to learn a series of word pairs (for example, north-south, cabbage-pen) such that when one word is read (north, cabbage) its paired-associate word (south, pen) can be recalled. An example of the logical memory test was presented earlier in the chapter, in reference to Mr. B.'s verbal memory defect.

The Rey Complex-Figure Test has proved to be one of the best for evaluating nonverbal memory function of the right temporal lobe (see Figure 13.7C). A printed copy of a complex geometric pattern is placed before the subject with the instructions, "Copy the drawing as accurately as you can." Forty-five minutes later the subject is asked to reproduce as much of the figure as he or she can remember. Although the scoring criteria provide an objective measure of nonverbal memory, the test has the drawback that depressed or poorly motivated subjects may perform poorly,

TABLE 13.2. Standardized clinical neuropsychological tests for temporal lobe damage

Function	Test	Basic reference
Auditory processing capacity	Dichotic words and melodies	Sparks et al., 1970
Visual processing capacity	McGill Picture Anomalies	Milner, 1958
Verbal memory	Revised Wechsler Memory Scale; logical stories and paired associates	Milner, 1975
Nonverbal memory	Rey Complex Figure	Taylor, 1969
Language	Token	de Renzi and Faglioni, 1978

not because there is right temporal lobe damage, but because they refuse to try to recall the figure. There is no easy solution to this problem, since all tests of nonverbal memory are subject to this complication.

Finally, a deficit in language comprehension could be the result of a lesion in any of the language zones of the left hemisphere (that is, in the parietal, temporal, or frontal lobes); there is currently no neuropsychological assessment tool that can localize the area of damage within the left hemisphere. For this reason we once again recommend the token test as the test of choice for language comprehension.

SUMMARY

The temporal lobes are specialized for the analysis of both auditory and visual information. The auditory analysis has special features that allow processing of speech, which is characterized by its speed, and music. The visual analysis forms the ventral stream of visual processing, which is specialized for recognition of form. The medial temporal cortex plays an important role in long-term memory. The one subcortical region of the temporal lobes, the amygdala, adds affective tone to stimuli, which is crucial for recognition of the importance of particular stimuli.

REFERENCES

Blumer, D., and D. F. Benson. Personality changes with frontal and temporal lesions. In D. F. Benson and F. Blumer, eds. *Psychiatric Aspects of Neurologic Disease.* New York: Grune & Stratton, 1975.

Chedru, F., V. Bastard, and R. Efron. Auditory micropattern discrimination in brain damaged patients. *Neuropsychologia* 16:141–149, 1978.

de Renzi, E., and P. Faglioni. Normative data and screening power of a shortened version of the token test. *Cortex* 14:41–49, 1978.

Dorff, J. E., A. F. Mirsky, and M. Mishkin. Effects of unilateral temporal lobe removals on tachistoscopic recognition in the left and right visual fields. *Neuropsychologia* 3:39–51, 1965.

Fuster, J. M., and J. P. Jervey. Neuronal firing in the inferotemporal cortex of the monkey in a visual memory task. *Journal of Neuroscience* 2:361–375, 1982.

Geschwind, N. Disconnexion syndromes in animals and man. *Brain* 88:237–294, 585–644, 1965.

Hécaen, H., and M. L. Albert. *Human Neuropsychology.* New York: John Wiley, 1978.

Kolb, B., B. Milner, and L. Taylor. Perception of faces by patients with localized cortical excisions. *Canadian Journal of Psychology* 37:8–18, 1983.

Kolb, B., and L. Taylor. Facial expression and the neocortex. *Society for Neuroscience Abstracts* 14:219, 1988.

Lackner, J. R., and H.-L. Teuber. Alterations in auditory fusion thresholds after cerebral injury in man. *Neuropsychologia* 11:409–415, 1973.

Liberman, A. On finding that speech is special. *American Psychologist* 37:148–167, 1982.

Meier, M. S., and L. A. French. Lateralized deficits in complex visual discrimination and bilateral transfer of reminiscence following unilateral temporal lobectomy. *Neuropsychologia* 3:261–272, 1968.

Milner, B. Psychological defects produced by temporal lobe excision. *Research Publications of the Association for Research in Nervous and Mental Disease* 38:244–257, 1958.

Milner, B. Visual recognition and recall after right temporal lobe excision in man. *Neuropsychologia* 6:191–209, 1968.

Milner, B. Memory and the medial temporal regions of the brain. In K. H. Pribram and D. E. Broadbent, eds. *Biological Bases of Memory.* New York: Academic Press, 1970.

Penfield, W., and H. H. Jasper. *Epilepsy and the Functional Anatomy of the Human Brain.* Boston: Little, Brown, 1959.

Perrett, D. I., M. H. Harries, P. J. Benson, A. J. Chitty, and A. J. Mistlin. Retrieval of structure from rigid and biological motion: An analysis of the visual responses of neurones in the macaque temporal cortex. In A. Blake and T. Troscianko, eds. *AI and the Eye.* New York: John Wiley, 1990.

Perrett, D. I., P. Smith, D. D. Potter, A. J. Mistlin, A. S. Head, A. D. Milner, and M. A. Jeeves. Neurons responsive to faces in the temporal cortex: Studies of functional organization, sensitivity to identity and relation to perception. *Human Neurobiology* 3:197–208, 1984.

Pincus, J. H., and G. J. Tucker. *Behavioral Neurology.* New York: Oxford University Press, 1974.

Read, D. E. Solving deductive-reasoning problems after unilateral temporal lobectomy. *Brain and Language* 12:116–127, 1981.

Ritsma, R. Frequencies dominant in the perception of pitch of complex sounds. *Journal of the Acoustical Society of America* 42:191–198, 1967.

Samson, S., and R. J. Zatorre. Discrimination of melodic and harmonic stimuli after unilateral cerebral excisions. *Brain and Cognition* 7:348–360, 1988.

Schulhoff, C., and H. Goodglass. Dichotic listening: Side of brain injury and cerebral dominance. *Neuropsychologia* 7:149–160, 1969.

Sidtis, J. J. Music, pitch perception, and the mechanisms of cortical hearing. In M. S. Gazzaniga, ed. *Handbook of Cognitive Neuroscience*. New York: Plenum Press, 1984.

Sparks, R., H. Goodglass, and B. Nickel. Ipsilateral versus contralateral extinction in dichotic listening from hemispheric lesions. *Cortex* 6:249–260, 1970.

Swisher, L., and I. J. Hirsch. Brain damage and the ordering of two temporally successive stimuli. *Neuropsychologia* 10:137–152, 1972.

Tanaka, K. Neuronal mechanisms of object recognition. *Science* 262:685–688, 1993.

Taylor, L. B. Localization of cerebral lesions by psychological testing. *Clinical Neurosurgery* 16:269–287, 1969.

Ungerleider, L. G., and M. Mishkin. Two cortical visual systems. In D. J. Ingle, M. H. Goodale, and R. J. W. Mansfield, eds. *The Analysis of Visual Behavior*. Cambridge, Mass.: MIT Press, 1982.

Vignolo, L. A. Auditory agnosia: A review and report of recent evidence. In A. L. Benton, ed. *Contributions to Clinical Neuropsychology*. Chicago: Aldine, 1969.

Wilkins, A., and M. Moscovitch. Selective impairment of semantic memory after temporal lobectomy. *Neuropsychologia* 16:73–79, 1978.

Wolberg, Z., and J. D. Newman. Auditory cortex of squirrel monkey: Response patterns of single cells to species-specific vocalizations. *Science* 175:212–214, 1972.

Zatorre, R. J. Musical perception and cerebral function: A critical review. *Music Perception* 2:196–221, 1984.

Zatorre, R. J., and A. R. Halpern. Effect of unilateral temporal-lobe excision on perception and imagery of songs. *Neuropsychologia* 31:221–232, 1993.

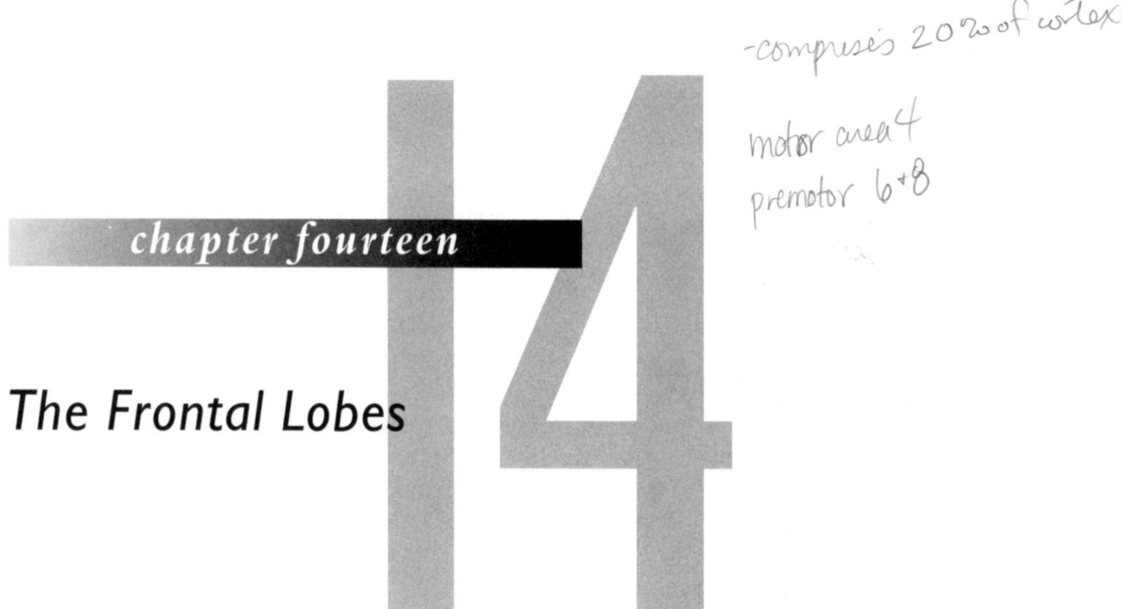

The Frontal Lobes

Historically, claims about the function of the frontal lobes have been extravagant and extreme. From the time of Gall until the 1930s, the frontal lobes were thought to be the seat of highest intellect. Functions as varied as "abstract behavior," foresight, intellectual synthesis, ethical behavior, affect, and self-awareness were proposed by a variety of writers. These proposed functions have proved difficult to define objectively or to study. Nonetheless, we are now in a position to provide a general theory of frontal lobe function and a survey of the most prominent symptoms of frontal lobe injury.

ANATOMY OF THE FRONTAL LOBES

The frontal lobes of the human brain comprise all the tissue in front of the central sulcus. This a vast area, representing 20% of the neocortex, and is made up of several functionally distinct regions that we shall group into three general categories: (1) motor, (2) premotor, and (3) prefrontal. The motor cortex is area 4. The premotor cortex includes areas 6 and 8. It can be divided into four areas: lateral area 6, or premotor cortex; medial area 6, or supplementary motor cortex; area 8, or the frontal eye field; and area 8A, or the supplementary eye field (Figure 14.1). In humans, the lateral premotor area has expanded as Broca's area (area 44) has developed. Prefrontal cortex is a peculiar name that derives from Rose and Woolsey's observation that the frontal lobes of all the mammalian species they examined had a region that received projections from the dorsomedial nucleus of the thalamus. They termed this region the prefrontal cortex. In primates the prefrontal cortex can be divided into three regions: (1) dorsolateral prefrontal cortex (areas 9, 46); (2) inferior (or ventral) prefrontal cortex (areas 11, 12, 13, 14); and (3) medial frontal cortex (areas 25, 32). One portion of the inferior frontal cortex (areas 11, 13, 14) is sometimes referred to as the orbital frontal cortex because of its relation to the orbit (or socket) of the eye. The medial frontal area is sometimes considered part of the anterior cingulate region rather than part of the prefrontal cortex. As in the temporal lobe, there are two areas in the frontal lobe that are multimodal and contain cells responsive to combinations of visual, auditory, and somatic stimuli. These areas are in the lateral premotor cortex (area 6) and in area 46 (Figure 14.2).

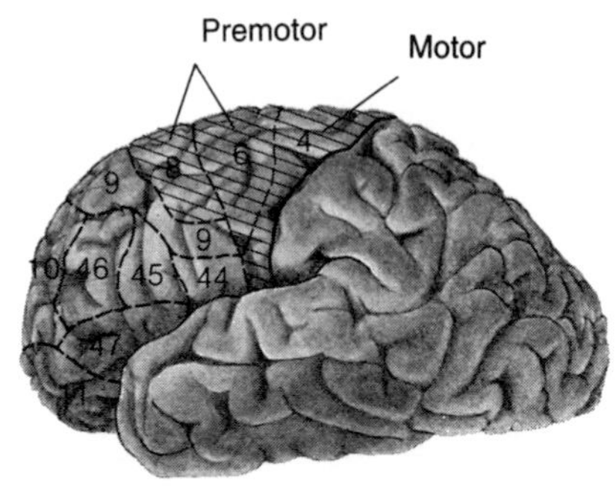

A LATERAL VIEW

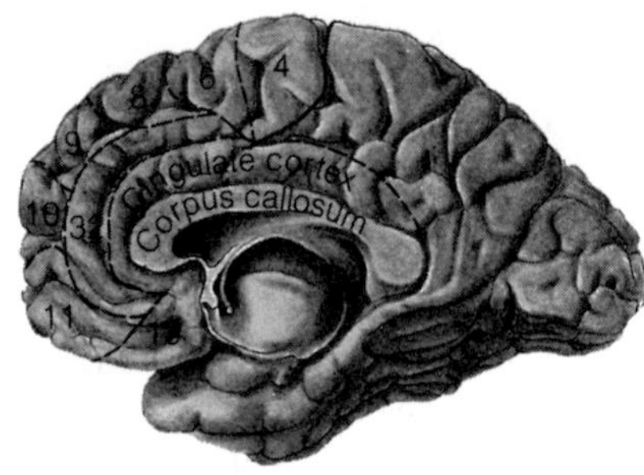

B MEDIAL VIEW

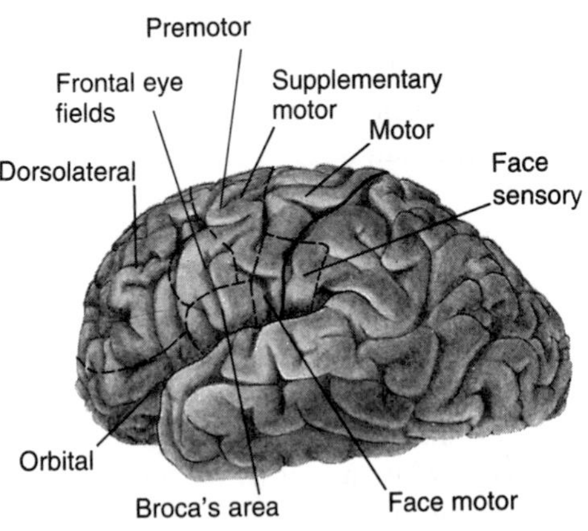

C FUNCTIONAL MAP

FIGURE 14.1. Lateral (*A*) and medial (*B*) views of Brodmann's cytoarchitectonic map of the frontal lobe. *C.* Approximate boundaries of functional zones of the frontal lobe. Note that area 6 contains two functional zones: the premotor cortex on the lateral surface and the supplementary motor cortex on the medial surface.

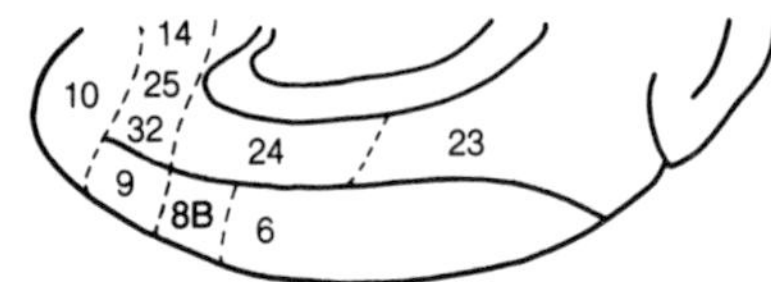

A

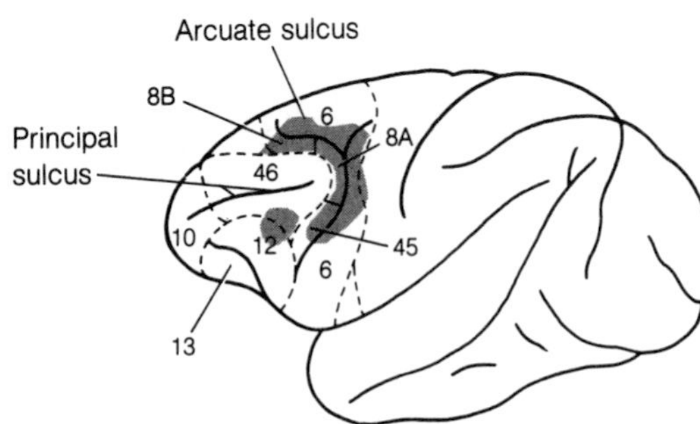

B

C

FIGURE 14.2. Medial (*A*), lateral (*B*), and ventral (*C*) views of Walker's cytoarchitectonic map of the frontal lobe of the rhesus monkey. There are two major sulci in the monkey frontal lobe, the principal sulcus and the arcuate sulcus. The shaded areas indicate the regions of multimodal cortex.

Connections of the Motor and Premotor Areas

The motor and premotor areas can be considered part of a functional system to control movements directly. There are several groups of connections in this system.

The motor cortex projects to the spinal motor neurons to control limb, hand, foot, and digit movements and to the appropriate cranial nerve motor neurons to control face movements. It also projects to other motor structures such as the basal ganglia and the red nucleus.

The premotor areas can influence movement directly via corticospinal projections or indirectly via projections to the motor cortex. The premotor regions also receive projections from the posterior parietal areas PE and PF. Thus, the premotor regions are connected to areas concerned with the execution of limb movements.

The frontal eye fields (areas 8 and 8A) receive projections from and send projections to regions involved in the control of eye movements. These regions thus receive visual input from posterior parietal region PG and the superior colliculus.

All of the premotor areas receive projections from the dorsolateral prefrontal cortex. This implies that this prefrontal area has some role in the control of limb and eye movements.

Connections of the Prefrontal Areas

The prefrontal areas can be viewed as the end points of the dorsal and ventral visual streams. In fact, Felleman and van Essen included prefrontal regions as part of the visual cortex (see Figure 8.12).

The dorsolateral prefrontal area (areas 9 and 46) receives its main inputs from the posterior parietal areas and the superior temporal sulcus. These connections are reciprocal. In addition, the dorsolateral cortex has extensive connections to regions to which the posterior parietal cortex also projects, including the cingulate cortex, basal ganglia, and superior colliculus (see Figure 12.2). The key to understanding the functions of the dorsolateral cortex is to be found in its relationship to the posterior parietal cortex (Figure 14.3).

The inferior frontal area (areas 11–14) receives its main afferents from the temporal lobe, including the auditory regions of the superior temporal gyrus, the visual regions of TE and the superior temporal sulcus, and amygdala. In addition, there are connections from the somatosensory cortex (area 43), gustatory cortex (in the insula), and olfactory regions of the pyriform cortex. The gustatory and olfactory connections are localized in the orbital cortex, and the visual, auditory, and somatosensory connections go largely to area 12. The inferior frontal area projects subcortically to the amygdala and hypothalamus; this provides a route for influencing the autonomic system, which controls changes in blood pressure, respiration, and so on. These changes are important in emotional responses.

The prefrontal regions receive a significant input from dopaminergic cells in the tegmentum. This input plays an important role in regulating how prefontal neurons react to stimuli, including stressful stimuli. Abnormalities in this projection play a central role in schizophrenia.

A THEORY OF FRONTAL LOBE FUNCTION

Imagine the following scenario. At the last moment you have invited friends for dinner. Since you have nothing to serve, you must go shopping after you leave work at 5:00 P.M. Before leaving, you prepare a list of items to buy. You are working under a time constraint because you must return home before your guests arrive and you need time to prepare. Since the items you need are not all at the same store, you must make an efficient plan of travel. You also must not be distracted by stores selling items you do not need (such as shoes) or by extended chats with store clerks or friends that you might encounter.

The task we have set ourselves is a bit rushed, but for most of us it offers little challenge. People with frontal lobe injury, however, cannot manage it. The fundamental requirements of the task that challenge frontal lobe patients are: (1) we must plan our behavior in advance and must select from many options; (2) in view of our time constraint, we must ignore stimuli and persist in the task at hand; and (3) we must keep track of what stores we have gone to and what items we have already purchased. We do not want to end up with four loaves of bread and no vegetables.

The behavioral requirements of this task can be described as the temporal organization of behavior, and this is the general function of the frontal

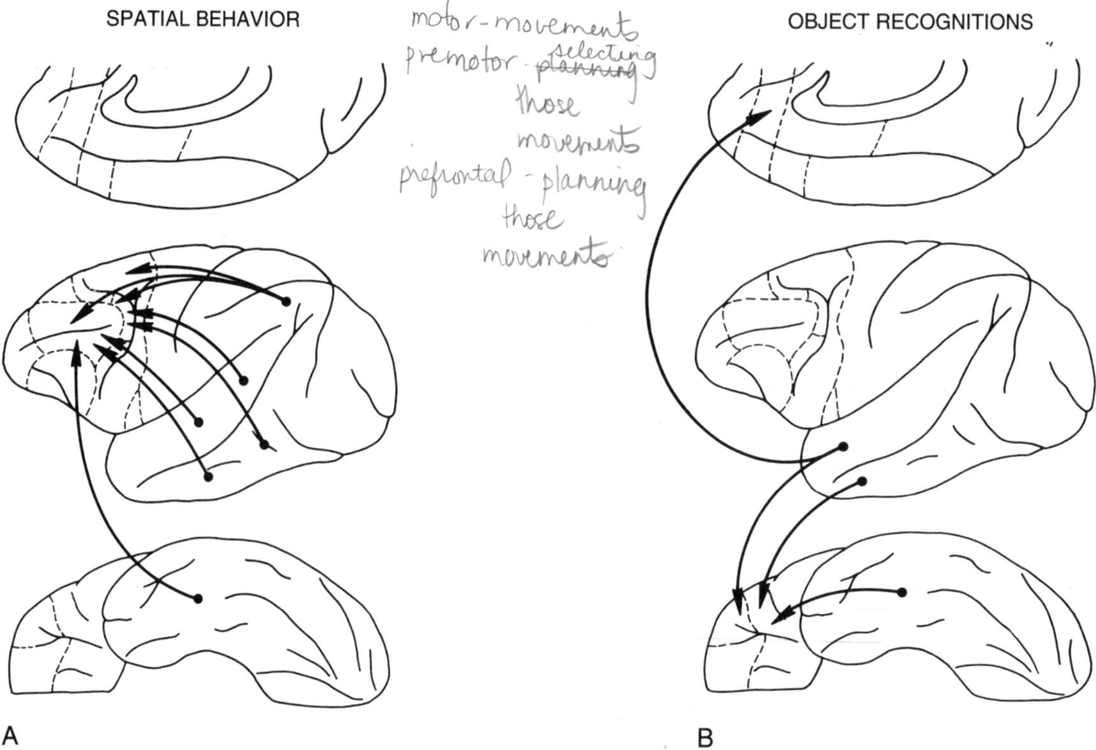

FIGURE 14.3. Schematic illustration of the cortico-cortical connections to the frontal lobe of the rhesus monkey. *A.* The connections to the dorsolateral surface. These include projections from posterior parietal as well as temporal regions. *B.* The connections to the inferior frontal region. These are from the temporal lobe. Connections from the insula and olfactory cortex are not shown.

lobe. The premotor and prefrontal regions contribute in different ways to this function, so we will consider them separately.

Functions of the Premotor Cortex

Whereas the motor cortex provides a mechanism for the execution of individual movements, the premotor cortex functions to select the movements to be executed. Consider the behavior of a resting dog. It may get up and respond to its owner's call, or it may get up for no apparent reason and wander about the yard. The former movements are made in response to a specific environmental cue, whereas the latter behavior can be conceived as being in response to an internal event. Passingham suggests that the premotor region functions primarily to choose behavior in response to external cues and the supplementary motor region makes a greater contribution when no such cues are available.

Just as we choose limb movements, we must select eye movements. This is the function of the frontal eye fields. Like limb movements, eye movements can be made to specific targets that are visible, or they can be made on the basis of internal cues. Thus, we can make eye movements to look at specific objects, or we can gaze around, seemingly without purpose. Passingham suggests that area 8 is specialized for stimulus-directed movements, whereas area 8A is responsible for internally driven movements.

The role of the premotor cortex in response selection was first shown in normal subjects by Roland and his colleagues. They compared the cerebral blood flow in subjects making either a repetitive movement of one finger or a complex sequence of 16 movements of the fingers of one hand. There was a larger increase in blood flow in the supplementary motor cortex *in both hemispheres* in the sequence task than in the repetitive task. There was, however, no increase in blood flow in the premotor region. Roland concluded that the supplementary motor region plays a special role in the selection and direction of motor sequences. An important aspect of Roland's experiment is that there was no external cue for the movements. That is, the production of the movement sequence was self-paced, or internally driven. Deiber and colleagues have shown that the premotor cortex is activated when movement sequences are paced externally by a cue. In their experiment the subjects performed one of two tasks. In the first, whenever a tone sounded they made a fixed movement, which was to move a joystick forward. In this case there was no response selection; the same response was made each time. In the second task, when the subjects heard the tone they randomly made one of four movements of the joystick (forward, backward, left, or right). This required a choice of movement. The results showed a significant effect of response selection: there was an increase in blood flow to both the premotor areas in the choice condition relative to the fixed condition. It is curious that both premotor regions were activated in the Deiber task, but a more recent experiment by Jenkins and colleagues may provide an explanation. These authors compared the performance of a prelearned sequence of finger movements to the learning of a sequence in which a tone indicated whether the sequence was correct or incorrect. The medial region was relatively more activated during the prelearned sequence, and the lateral region was more activated during the learning sequence. Passingham suggests that during the prelearned movement the cues were internal, whereas on the learning task the subjects had to attend to external cues.

Functions of the Prefrontal Cortex

The motor cortex is responsible for making movements. The premotor cortex selects movements. The prefrontal cortex controls the cognitive processes so that appropriate movements are selected at the correct time and place. This selection may be controlled by internalized information or may be made in response to context. We consider these aspects separately.

The internalized record of what has just occurred is independent of the existing sensory information and can be called **temporal memory** or **short-term memory.** We use temporal memory here to refer to a neural record of recent events. These events may be related to things or places and thus derive their information from the object-recognition or spatial streams of sensory processing. Recall that both streams project to the prefrontal cortex, although to different places. This suggests that there is temporal memory for both spatial and object information, although the memory will be localized in different places in the frontal cortex. The dorsolateral areas are especially involved in the selection of behavior based upon temporal memory. People whose temporal memory is defective become dependent upon environmental cues to determine their behavior. That is, behavior is not under the control of internalized knowledge but is controlled directly by external cues. One effect of this condition is that people with frontal lobe injuries have difficulty inhibiting behavior directed to external stimuli. In our dinner party example, frontal lobe patients would be expected to enter a shoe store or chat with friends as they responded to environmental cues that they encountered. Parenthetically, we have probably all experienced occasions upon which the organization of our behavior has failed as we were controlled by external cues rather than internalized information. How many times have we started to do something, been distracted by a question or some event, and then been unable to recall what we were doing? Sadly, this phenomenon increases with old age, which is not reassuring information about the state of one's prefrontal cortex!

Behavior is context-dependent. Hence, behavior that is appropriate at one moment may not be appropriate if there are subtle changes in the context. This is beautifully illustrated in Jane Goodall's graphic descriptions of the different behavioral patterns exhibited by chimpanzees. The make-up of the social group at any given time dictates the behavior of each chimpanzee. Given the presence and position of certain animals, a particular chimp may be bold and relaxed, whereas with a different mixture of animals the chimp is quiet and nervous. Further, it appears that an error in evaluating the context can have grievous consequences. It may be no accident that the frontal lobe has grown so large in primates that are so highly social. We can easily see the importance of social context when we reflect upon our behavior with our parents versus that with our closest friends. It is common experience that our tone of voice, the use of slang or swear words, and the content of conversations are quite different in the two contexts.

The choice of behaviors in context requires detailed sensory information, which is conveyed to the inferior frontal cortex from the temporal lobe. Of course, context also means affective context, and this contribution comes from the amygdala. People with inferior frontal lesions, which are relatively common in closed-head injuries, have difficulty with context, especially in social situations, and are notorious for making social gaffes.

Asymmetry of Frontal Lobe Function

In view of the functional asymmetry in the parietal and temporal association cortex, it could be expected that the frontal lobes are functionally asymmetrical. This is indeed the case. In keeping with the general complementary organization of the left and right hemispheres, the left frontal lobe has a preferential role in language-related movements, including speech, whereas the right frontal lobe plays a greater role in other movements such as facial expression. Like the asymmetry of the parietal and temporal lobes, the asymmetry of frontal lobe function is relative rather than absolute; studies of patients with frontal lesions indicate that both frontal lobes play a role in nearly all behavior. Thus, the laterality of function disturbed by frontal lobe lesions is far less striking than that observed from more posterior lesions. Nonetheless, as with the temporal lobe there is reason to believe that some effects of bifrontal lesions cannot be duplicated by lesions of either hemisphere alone. Table 14.1 summarizes a study comparing the behavioral effects of unilateral and bilateral lesions. People with bifrontal lesions are severely impaired at reporting the time of day and in decoding proverbs—effects seldom seen following unilateral frontal lesions.

TABLE 14.1. Relative frequency of defective performance on neuropsychological tests

	Percentage of group showing a deficit		
Test	Left (%)	Right (%)	Bilateral (%)
Verbal fluency	70	38	71
Verbal learning	30	13	86
Block construction	10	50	43
Design copying	10	38	43
Time orientation	0	0	57
Proverbs	20	25	71

Source: Adapted from Benton, 1968.

SYMPTOMS OF FRONTAL LOBE LESIONS

Our primary concern here is with the effects of unilateral lesions to the prefrontal cortex. In an effort to organize the symptoms conceptually, we have grouped them into eight major categories (Table 14.2). We do not mean to imply that the brain respects these categories but rather that the categories provide a conceptual framework within which to consider the symptoms.

Disturbances of Motor Function

We have grouped together impairments in a person's ability to make different types of movements.

Fine Movements, Speed, and Strength. Damage to the primary motor cortex is typically associated with a chronic loss of the ability to make fine, independent finger movements, presumably due to a loss of direct corticospinal projections onto motor neurons. In addition, there is a loss of speed and strength in both hand and limb movements in the contralateral limbs. The loss of strength is not merely a symptom of damage to area 4, because lesions restricted to the prefrontal cortex lead to a reduction in hand strength.

Movement Programming. In a classic paper in 1950, Lashley asked how movements are put together in a particular order. How is it, he asked, that a violinist can play an arpeggio so quickly and flawlessly? Clearly, each note is not "thought of" separately. Furthermore, how is it that during a tennis game a player can make very rapid movements, seemingly much too fast to have considered each movement itself? Lashley presumed that this function—serially ordering complex chains of behavior in relation to varying stimuli—must somehow be a function of the neocortex. Although he believed this behavior to be a function of the entire neocortex, it appears more likely to be a function of the frontal lobes.

Removal of the supplementary motor cortex results in a transient disruption of nearly all voluntary movements (including speech, if the removal is on the left). There is rapid recovery, however, and the only permanent disability appears to be in the performance of rapidly alternating movements with the hands or fingers. The

TABLE 14.2. Summary of major symptoms of frontal lobe damage

Most probable symptom	Lesion site	Basic reference
Disturbances of motor function		
Loss of fine movements	Area 4	Kuypers, 1981
Loss of strength	Areas 4, 6; dorsolateral	Leonard et al., 1988
Poor movement programming	Premotor	Roland et al., 1980
	Dorsolateral	Kolb and Milner, 1981
Poor voluntary eye gaze	Frontal eye fields	Guitton et al., 1982
Poor corollary discharge	Dorsolateral, premotor	Teuber, 1964
Broca's aphasia	Area 44	Brown, 1972
Loss of divergent thinking		
Reduced spontaneity	Orbital	Jones-Gotman and Milner, 1977
Poor strategy formation	Dorsolateral ?	Shallice and Evans, 1978
Environmental control of behavior		
Poor response inhibition	Prefrontal	Milner, 1964
Risk taking and rule breaking	Prefrontal	Miller, 1985
Impaired associative learning	Dorsolateral	Petrides, 1982
Poor temporal memory		
Poor recency memory	Dorsolateral	Milner, 1974
Poor frequency estimate	Dorsolateral	Smith and Milner, 1985
Poor self-order recall	Dorsolateral	Petrides and Milner, 1982
Poor delayed response	Dorsolateral	Freedman and Oscar-Berman, 1986
Impaired social behavior	Orbital; dorsolateral	Blumer and Benson, 1975
Altered sexual behavior	Orbital	Walker and Blumer, 1975
Impaired olfactory discrimination	Orbital	Potter and Butters, 1980
Disorders associated with damage to the face area	Face	Taylor, 1979

likely reason that relatively minor symptoms result from rather large supplementary motor lesions is that both the left and the right premotor cortexes participate in the control of movement. This idea is supported by observations that both left and right premotor areas show an increase in blood flow during unimanual tasks in humans; in monkeys, cells in both the left and the right areas show increased activity regardless of which hand is moving. There is also a bilateral projection from each supplementary motor cortex to the basal ganglia.

Further evidence favoring a role for the frontal cortex in movement programming comes from a study by Kolb and Milner. They asked patients with localized unilateral frontal lobectomies (most of which did not include the premotor cortex) to copy a series of arm or facial movements (see Figure 12.7). Although the patients had some mild impairment in copying the arm movements, it was small compared with the performance of patients with left parietal lobe lesions. In contrast, patients with both left and right frontal lobe damage were very poor at copying a series of facial movements. An analysis of the facial-movement task showed that the groups with frontal lobe lesions made more errors of sequence than normal controls or other groups of patients. In other words, patients with frontal lobe lesions had difficulty ordering the various components of the sequence into a chain of movements. The components were recalled correctly, but in the wrong order. To be sure, these patients made other sorts of errors as well, especially errors of memory in which items were not recalled. The reproduction of movement sequences requires temporal memory, and our impression is that the largest deficits come from dorsolateral lesions.

The observation that frontal injury severely disrupts the copying of facial but not arm movements implies that the frontal lobe may play a special role in the control of the face, perhaps even including the tongue. We shall see in the next section that patients with frontal lobe damage exhibit relatively little spontaneous facial expression—a result in accordance with the possible special role of the frontal lobe in the control of the face.

Voluntary Gaze. A number of studies using quite different procedures have been reported in which frontal lobe lesions produce alterations in voluntary eye gaze. For example, Teuber presented patients with an array of 48 patterns on a screen. The patterns could be distinguished by shape or color or both (Figure 14.4). At a warning signal a duplicate of one of the 48 patterns appeared in the center of the array, and the subject's task was to find the matching pattern and to identify it by pointing to it. Patients with frontal lobe lesions were impaired at finding the duplicate pattern.

Luria recorded patients' eye movements as they examined a picture of a complex scene. The eye-movement patterns of the patients with large frontal lobe lesions were quite different from those of normal control subjects or of patients with more posterior lesions. For example, if a normal control was asked about the age of the people in a picture, his or her eyes fixed on the

FIGURE 14.4. Visual search task used by Teuber (1964). The subject must locate a duplicate of the shape inside the central box.

heads; if asked how they are dressed, the eyes fixed on the clothing. Patients with large frontal lobe lesions tended to glance over the picture more or less at random, and a change in the question about the picture failed to alter the direction or the pattern of eye movements. Visual search in Luria's task would require internalized knowledge to direct the eyes.

Guitton and his colleagues examined a different type of oculomotor defect in frontal lobe patients. They studied the ability of patients to make voluntary eye movements toward or away from briefly appearing targets presented at random to the right or the left of a fixation point. Normally, if a stimulus cue is presented briefly in either visual field, a person will make a quick eye movement, called a saccade, toward the stimulus. Patients with frontal lobe lesions had no difficulty doing this, and so Guitton and his coworkers added a second feature to the task. Rather than make eye movements toward a target, the patients had to move their eyes to the same place in the opposite visual field. The task therefore required an inhibition of the normal saccade and a voluntary saccade to the similar point opposite. Patients with frontal lesions had two deficits on this variation of the task. First, although normal subjects failed to inhibit a short-latency response toward the cue in about 20% of the trials, patients with frontal lesions had much more difficulty. Second, following the initial saccade in the incorrect direction, normal subject had no difficulty in making a large corrective saccade toward the opposite field. In contrast, patients with frontal lesions, which included the frontal eye fields, had difficulty in executing the corrective response when the response had to be generated by the damaged hemisphere. In other words, they had difficulty in moving the eyes to the field contralateral to the frontal lesion. Corrective movements could be made normally in the field on the same side as the lesion.

The difficulty that patients with frontal lesions encounter in the visual-search task and the saccade task indicates the importance of the frontal cortex for certain aspects of oculomotor control. Only the study by Guitton and associates has localized the effect in the frontal eye fields, but it is likely that the most severe deficits in performing such tasks are associated with damage to those fields.

Corollary Discharge. If one pushes on the eyeball, the world appears to move. If one moves one's eyes, the world remains stable. Why? Teuber proposed that for a movement to take place there must be a signal to produce the movement and also a signal that the movement is going to occur. If the eyes are moved mechanically, there is no such signal and the world moves. However, when one moves the eyes, there is a signal that it will happen and the world stays still. This signal has been termed **corollary discharge,** or **reafference.**

Teuber argued that voluntary movements involve two sets of signals rather than one. There is the movement command, through the motor system, to effect the movements, and there is a signal (corollary discharge) from the frontal lobe to the parietal and temporal association cortex that presets the sensory system to anticipate the motor act. Thus, a person's sensory system can interpret changes in the external world in light of information about his or her movement. For example, when one is running, the external world remains stable even though the sense organs are in motion, because there is corollary discharge from the frontal lobe to the parietal-temporal cortex, signaling that the movements are occurring. A frontal lesion therefore not only can disturb the production of a movement but also can interfere with the message to the rest of the brain that a movement is taking place. By this indirect means, perception of the world by the posterior association cortex is altered.

There are two direct sources of evidence that the frontal lobe plays a role in corollary discharge: studies of cells in the frontal eye fields and experimental use of prisms on the eyes. Bizzi and Schiller, among others, have found that some cells in the frontal eye fields fire simultaneously with movements of the eyes. These cells cannot be causing the eyes to move, for to do so they would have to fire before the eye movements (just as to accelerate an automobile you must first depress the gas pedal). Rather, these cells must be monitoring the ongoing movement—a process suspiciously similar to what would be expected from a region involved in corollary discharge.

Further evidence comes from a beautiful experiment by Bossom. In the early 1960s, Held and others performed experiments by fitting prisms to the eyes of animals and humans. Whatever the subject saw was systematically displaced from its true location, all lines appearing subjectively curved and tilted, in keeping with the distortions imposed by the optics of the prism. After the prisms were worn for a few hours, the distortions and displacements diminished, and acts such as reaching for objects were performed normally. On abrupt removal of the prisms, the distortions were reinstated, requiring readaptation before perception was again normal. An important feature of these experiments was that passively sitting for a few hours did not produce the perceptual change; to induce the adaptation, the individual had to move about in the environment. This requirement implies that adaptation to the prism occurred in the motor system rather than in the sensory systems. With these experiments in mind, Bossom selectively removed the frontal, temporal, parietal, or occipital cortex in monkeys to see which lesion, if any, would disrupt prism adaptation. As one would predict from the work of Held, only frontal lesions impaired adaption to the distorting prisms; parietal, temporal, and occipital lesions did not. Teuber interprets this experiment as showing that corollary discharge is necessary for the adaptation to occur. In other words, the effects of movement must be monitored with respect to sensory input so that the brain can adjust the movements to make them accurate.

Speech. Speech is an example of movement selection. Words are responses generated in the context of both internal and external stimuli. Passingham argues that if the frontal lobe is a mechanism for selecting responses, then it must select words, too. He notes further that there are two speech zones in the frontal lobe: Broca's area, which he considers to be an extension of the lateral premotor area, and the supplementary speech area, which he considers to be an extension of the supplementary motor area. Viewed in this way, Broca's area is critically involved when a word must be retrieved on the basis of an object, word, letter, or meaning. That is, like the premotor area's role in other behaviors, Broca's area selects words on the basis of cues. In contrast, the supplementary speech area is required to retrieve words without external cues, which is also consistent with the general function of the supplementary motor area.

People with strokes involving Broca's area are impaired in their ability to use verbs and to produce appropriate grammar, a symptom known as agrammatism. People with strokes that include the supplementary speech area and extend into the left medial frontal region are often mute. The ability to speak usually recovers after a few weeks in people with unilateral lesions but not in those with bilateral lesions. This again supports the bilateral involvement of the supplementary motor areas in movement selection. The role of the supplementary motor region is corroborated by blood-flow studies done by Roland, who showed that when subjects recall the months of the year, which is done without external cues, there is activation of the medial premotor area.

Loss of Divergent Thinking

One of the clearest differences between the effects of parietal and temporal lobe lesions and the effects of frontal lobe lesions is in performance on standard intelligence tests. Posterior lesions produce reliable, and often large, decreases in IQ, but frontal lesions do not. The puzzle is why patients with frontal lobe damage appear to do such "stupid" things. Guilford has noted that traditional intelligence tests appear to measure what can be called **convergent thinking,** in the sense that there is just one correct answer to each question. Thus, definitions of words, questions about events, arithmetic problems, puzzles, and block designs, for example, are all looking for correct answers that are easily scored. There is, however, another type of intelligence that can be called **divergent thinking.** In this case the number and variety of responses to a single question are emphasized, rather than a particular answer. An example would be a question asking one to list the possible uses of a coat hanger. Zangwill suggested that frontal lobe injury might interfere with this sort of intelligence, rather than the type measured by standard IQ tests. There are several lines of evidence supporting his idea.

Behavioral Spontaneity. It has long been recognized that patients with frontal lobe lesions exhibit what Zangwill referred to as a "certain loss of spontaneity of speech" and a "difficulty in evoking appropriate words or phases." Subsequent studies by a variety of authors—Milner and, later, Ramier and Hécaen, among others—have been able to quantify this deficit. These researchers gave patients tests similar to the Thurstone Word-Fluency Test: patients were asked to write or to say, first, as many words starting with a given letter as they could think of in 5 min, then as many four-letter words starting with a given letter. Patients with frontal lobe lesions had a low output of words in this test, producing an average of 35 words total in Milner's sample. Although the principal locus of this defect appears to be in the left orbital-frontal region, lesions in the right orbital-frontal region may also produce a large reduction in verbal fluency. Again we see less asymmetry in the frontal lobes than one might expect. The following case is an example of low spontaneous verbal fluency resulting from a lesion of the right frontal lobe.

Mrs. P., a 63-year-old woman with a B.A. degree, was suffering from a large astrocytoma of the right frontal lobe. Her word fluency is reproduced in Figure 14.5A. Four features of frontal lobe damage are illustrated in her test performance. First, her total output of words is remarkably low: only eight words beginning with "s" and six words beginning with "c." (Control subjects of similar age and education produce a total of about 60 words in the same time period.) Second, we see rule breaking, which is a common characteristic of such patients on this test. We told her several times that the words starting with "c" could have only four letters. She replied. "Yes, yes, I know, I keep using more each time." Even though she understood the instructions, she could not organize her behavior to follow them successfully. Third, her writing was not fluid but rather jerky, much like that seen in a child learning to write, implying that her tumor had invaded area 4 or 6. Finally, Mrs. P. insisted on talking throughout the test—complaining that she simply could not think of any more words—and kept looking around the room for objects starting with the required letter.

A study by Jones-Gotman and Milner raises the question of whether this verbal-fluency deficit might have a nonverbal analogue. The researchers devised an ingenious experiment in which they asked patients to draw as many different drawings as they could in 5 min. The drawings were not supposed to be representational. The patients were then asked to draw as many different drawings as they could, but this time using only four lines (a circle was counted as a single line). The results showed a beautiful analogue to the verbal-fluency results. As can be seen in Figure 14.6, lesions in the right frontal lobe produced a very large decrease in the number of different drawings produced. Normal controls drew about 35 drawings, left frontal lobe patients about 24 drawings, and right frontal lobe patients about 15 drawings. This deficit appears to be related to an impoverished output; high perservation; and, in some cases, the drawing of nameable things (that is, representational drawings). As with verbal fluency, lesions in the orbital cortex or central face area appeared to produce a larger deficit than the more dorsal lesions.

The question arises of whether patients with frontal lobe lesions might actually show a reduced spontaneity of behavior in general. Such a finding would be consistent with the general idea that the frontal lobe selects appropriate behaviors on the basis of internal information. In the absence of this ability, people would appear to have little "spontaneous" behavior. With this in mind, Kolb and Milner recorded the spontaneous behavior of

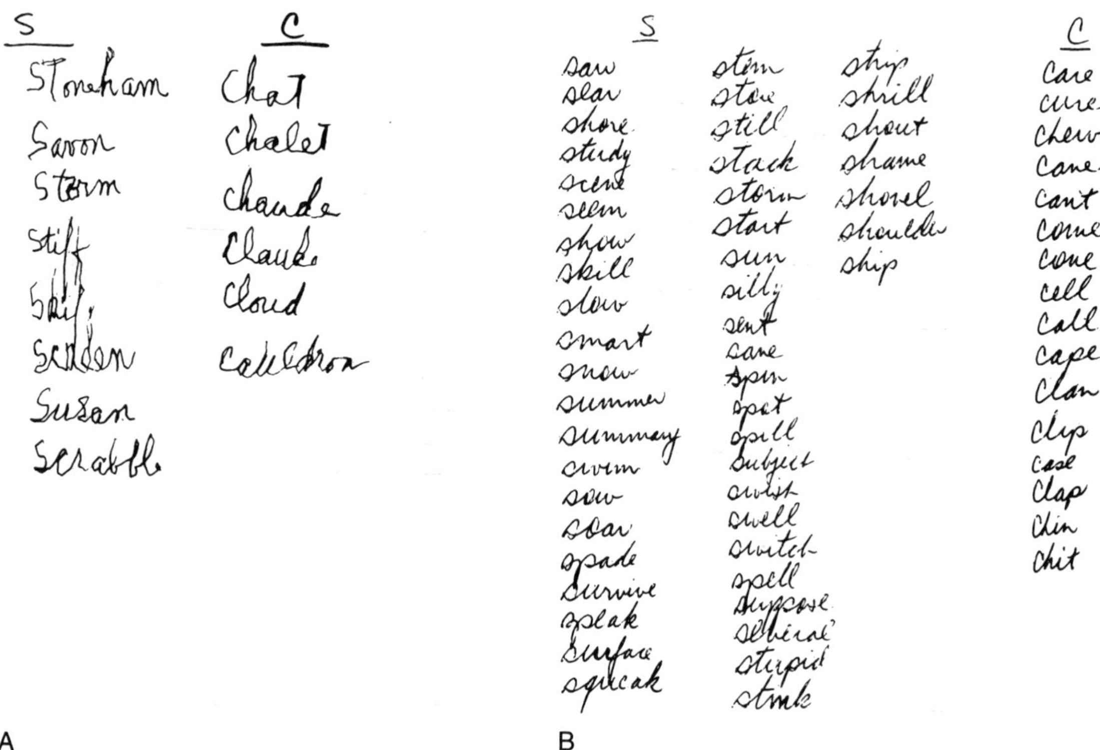

FIGURE 14.5. Word fluency. *A.* Mrs. P.'s lists. *B.* A normal control subject's lists. Both subjects were given 5 min to write as many English words as possible starting with the letter "s" and 4 min to write as many four-letter words as possible starting with the letter "c." Note Mrs. P.'s low output and her rule breaking in the four-letter "c" words. (Mrs. P. was multilingual, although English was her first language.)

frontal lobe patients. Patients with frontal lobe removals displayed fewer spontaneous facial movements and expressions than did normal controls or patients with more posterior lesions. In addition, there were dramatic differences in the number of words spoken by the patients during a neuropsychological interview: patients with left frontal removals rarely spoke, whereas patients with right frontal lesions were excessively talkative. Although the range of behaviors studied to date is small, there is reason to believe that frontal lobe patients have a general loss of spontaneous behavior. Frontal lobe patients characteristically appear lethargic or lazy: they often have difficulty getting out of bed in the morning, getting dressed, or initiating other daily activities such as going to work. One patient we saw is a particularly dramatic example. He was a prominent lawyer who suffered a midline meningioma in the frontal lobe. The tumor was removed surgically, but he was left with bilateral damage to the superior aspect of both frontal lobes. His IQ was still superior (over 140), and his memory for legal matters was unimpaired. Nonetheless he was unable to function in his profession because he could not get up in the morning to go to work, preferring to stay in bed and watch TV. When his wife forced him to get up and go to work, he was disruptive at the office because he could not concentrate on any law-related work. Rather, he was distracted by anything else going on in the office. Curiously, he remained an excellent resource for his colleagues,

lobotomies - seem lazy, but doesn't affect IQ

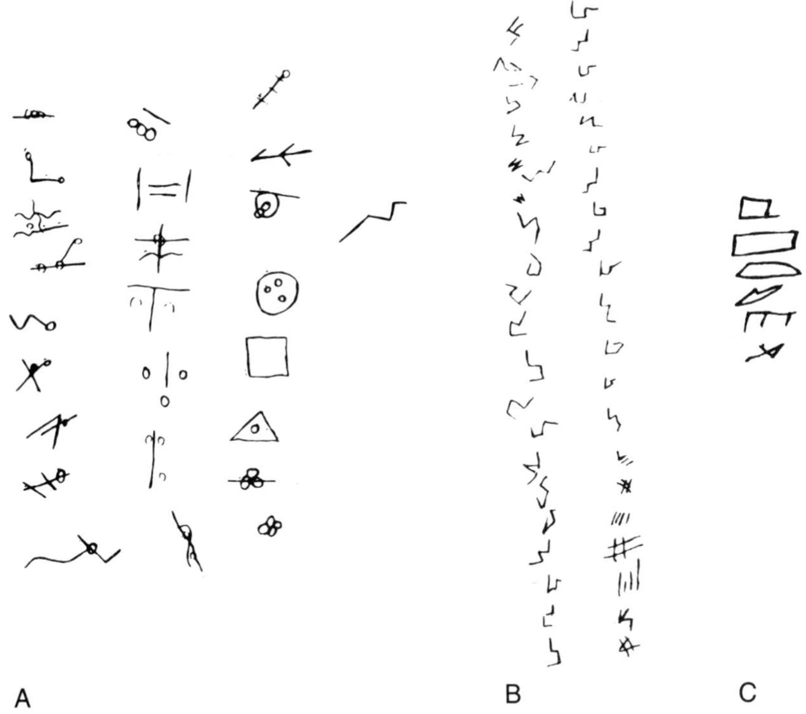

FIGURE 14.6. Design fluency. *A.* A normal subject's drawings. *B.* A frontal lobe patient's drawings showing perseveration. *C.* A frontal lobe patient's drawings showing lack of spontaneity.

who nonetheless found his behavior intolerable and consequently preferred to consult him by telephone!

Strategy Formation. Patients with frontal lobe lesions are especially impaired at developing novel cognitive plans or strategies for solving problems. For example, when Shallice and Evans asked subjects questions that required reasoning based upon general knowledge but for which no immediate obvious strategy was available, they found that frontal lobe patients did very poorly and often gave bizarre responses. In a later study, Shallice and Burgess gave patients a task very much like our dinner party problem. The subjects were given a list of six errands (for example, buy a brown loaf of bread) and an instruction to be at a particular place 15 min after starting. They were also to get answers to four questions (for instance, the price of a pound of tomatoes). They were not to enter shops except to buy something and were to complete the tasks as quickly as possible, without rushing. The frontal lobe patients found this simple task very difficult. They were inefficient, they broke rules (for example, entered unnecessary shops), and two of the three patients failed at least four of the tasks. Yet, when quizzed, all of the patients understood the task and attempted to comply. Similar difficulty with everyday problems is seen in a study by Smith and Milner. They asked subjects to estimate the average price of a particular object, such as a sewing machine. They suggested that to perform such a task one must develop a strategy that might involve deciding what is a typical sewing machine, judging the range of possible prices, and selecting a representative price for a machine of average quality. They found that patients with frontal lobe lesions—

bad at problem solving strategies / novel cognitive plans

especially right frontal lesions—were very poor at this task. In contrast, patients with temporal lobe damage who showed memory deficits on other tasks performed like controls on this task. Thus, it seems unlikely that a simple explanation of impaired memory will account for the poor performance of the frontal lobe patients.

Environment Control of Behavior: Impaired Response Inhibition and Inflexible Behavior

Perhaps the most commonly observed trait of frontal lobe patients is the difficulty they have in using information (feedback) from environmental cues to regulate or change their behavior. This manifests itself in a number of ways.

Response Inhibition. Patients with frontal lobe lesions consistently perseverate on responses in a variety of test situations, particularly those in which there are changing demands. The best example of this phenomenon is observed in the Wisconsin Card-Sorting Test, which has been studied extensively by Milner. Figure 14.7 shows the test material. The subject is presented with four stimulus cards, bearing designs that differ in color, form, and number of elements. The subject's task is to sort the cards into piles in front of one or another of the stimulus cards. The only help the subject is given is being told whether the choice is correct or incorrect.

The test works on this principle: the correct solution is, first, color; once the subject has figured out this solution, the correct solution then becomes, without warning, form. Thus, the subject must now inhibit classifying the cards on the basis of color and shift to form. Once the subject has succeeded at selecting by form, the correct solution again changes unexpectedly, this time to the number of elements. It will later become color again, and so on. Shifting response strategies is particularly difficult for people with frontal lesions, who may continue responding to the original stimulus (color) for as many as 100 cards until testing is terminated. Throughout this period they may comment that they know that color is no longer correct. They nevertheless continue to sort on the basis of color. For example, one person stated (correctly): "Form is probably the correct solution now so this [sorting to color] will be

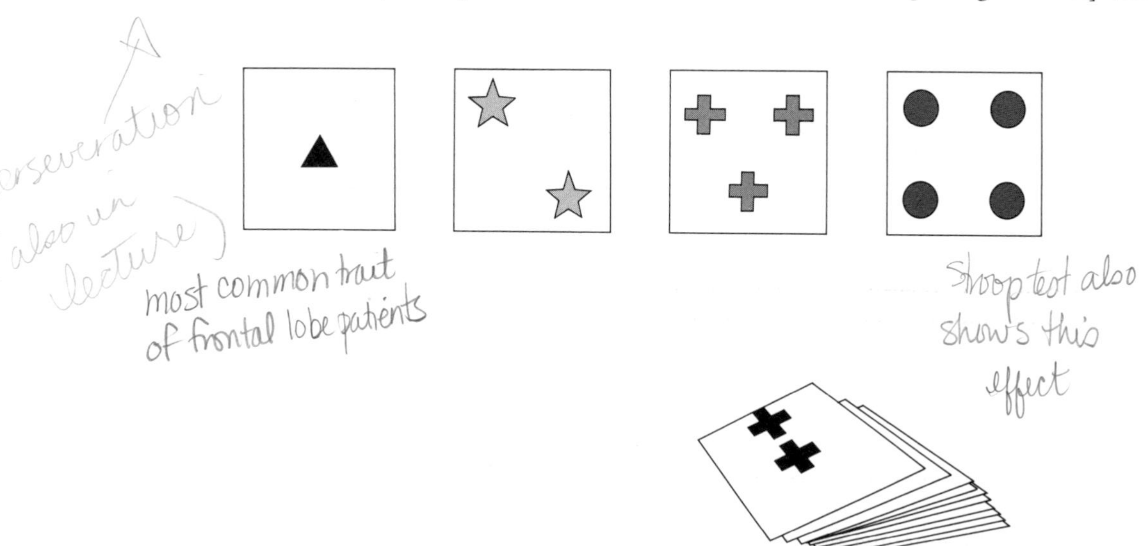

FIGURE 14.7. The Wisconsin Card-Sorting Test, showing test material as presented to the subject. (From B. Milner, Some effects of frontal lobectomy in man. In J. M. Warren and K. Akert, eds., *The Frontal Granular Cortex and Behavior,* 1964, p. 315. Copyright © 1964 by McGraw-Hill, Inc. Used with permission of McGraw-Hill Book Co.)

wrong, and this will be wrong, and wrong again." Such perservation is common on any task in which a frontal lobe patient is required to shift response strategies, demonstrating that the frontal lobe is necessary for flexibility in behavior. It is important to note that on card-sorting tasks the subjects must not be given any hint that they are to expect a change in the correct solution, because many frontal lobe patients improve dramatically when given this warning. The cue apparently allows enough flexibility in behavior to solve the problem.

It appears from Milner's work that the principal locus of this card-sorting effect is roughly around Brodmann's area 9 in the left hemisphere. Lesions elsewhere in the left frontal lobe, and often in the right, will also produce a deficit on this task, although a somewhat attenuated one.

Performance of the Stroop Test further demonstrates loss of response inhibition following frontal lobe damage. Subjects are presented with a list of color words (blue, green, red, and so forth), each word being printed in colored ink but never in the color denoted by the word (for example, the word "yellow" is printed in blue, green, or red ink). The subject's task is to name the color in which each word is printed as quickly as possible. Correct response requires the inhibition of reading the color name, an inhibition that is difficult for many control subjects. Perret found that patients with left frontal lesions were unable to inhibit reading the words and thus were impaired at this task.

Risk Taking and Rule Breaking. Frontal lobe patients are distinguished from other patients in their common failure to comply with task instructions. Milner found this to be especially common on tests of stylus-maze learning in which a buzzer indicated an error had occurred and subjects were to stop and start the maze over. Subjects with frontal lobe lesions tended to disregard the signal, thereby continuing the incorrect path and making more errors. This behavior is reminiscent of their inability to modify their responses in the card-sorting task. More recently, Miller gave subjects a task in which words had to be guessed on the basis of partial information. With each additional clue, the subject was assigned a successively lower point value for a correct answer, but points could be collected only if the answer was correct. An incorrect answer forfeited all the points for an item. Frontal lobe patients took more risks (and made more mistakes) than did other patients, and the risk taking was greatest in those frontal lobe patients who also had temporal lobe damage.

Associative Learning. It has often been claimed that patients with large frontal lobe lesions are unable to regulate their behavior in response to external stimuli. Thus, for example, Luria and Homskaya described patients with massive frontal lobe tumors who could not be trained to respond consistently with the right hand to a red light and with the left hand to a green light, even though the patients could indicate which hand was which and could repeat the instructions. In a related study, Petrides asked frontal lobe patients to learn arbitrary associations between colors and spatial locations or between colors and hand postures. For example, in the former test, patients were presented with six blue lights and six white index cards placed in a row on a table in front of them. Each light was associated with one and only one of the index cards, and the subjects' task was to learn which card was associated with which light. Damage to either the left or the right hemisphere resulted in poor performance on this task, as well as on an analogous task in which differently colored lights and six hand postures had to be associated in a similar way. Again, the behavioral impairments in the frontal lobe patients could not be attributed to a deficit in memory, since temporal lobe patients who performed poorly on other tests of memory performed normally at these tasks.

Like humans with frontal lobe lesions, monkeys with such lesions are impaired at learning arbitrary associations between a set of stimuli and a set of responses. In a monkey analogue of his associative-learning task, Petrides trained monkeys to make different movements of a lever when presented with different objects. In contrast to his control monkeys, who rapidly acquired the task, monkeys with premotor lesions were unable to learn it, although they were able to master unrelated tasks.

Poor Temporal Memory

Perhaps the single most important experimental discovery for understanding the functions of the frontal lobe was Jacobsen's finding that chimpanzees with frontal lobe lesions were impaired at the delayed-response test. In this task the animals observe a reward being placed under a plaque, in a well. The chimp's view is blocked for a few seconds and then it is allowed to retrieve the reward. Animals with prefrontal lesions perform at chance, even with extended practice. Although it is unlikely that the behavioral impairment is due to a single deficit, it is difficult to interpret the deficit without recourse to some sort of memory difficulty. Four additional experiments are especially germane here.

First, Passingham presented monkeys with a task in which the animals were required to open each of 25 doors to obtain a food reward. Food was behind each door only once per day, so the animals had to learn not to return to locations where the reward had been obtained already. He found that lesions in area 46 produced marked impairments in this task. Thus, whereas the normal monkeys developed a door-opening strategy that led to few repetitions, the lesioned animals were very inefficient, often returning to previously accessed doors (Figure 14.8A).

In the second experiment, Funahashi, Bruce, and Goldman-Rakic trained monkeys to fixate on a central spot of light while target lights were flashed in different parts of the visual field. The monkeys had to wait for the fixation spot to disappear before moving their eyes to the spot where the target light had been flashed. The researchers found that unilateral lesions in the principal sulcus (part of area 46) impaired the monkeys' ability to remember the location of the target in a restricted region of the contralateral visual field, as illustrated in Figure 14.8B. They interpret this result as showing that the principal sulcus contains a mechanism for guiding responses on the basis of stored information, which in this case is spatial.

The third experiment was one by Mishkin and his colleagues. They trained monkeys in a task known as delayed nonmatching to sample. In this test the monkey is confronted with an unfamiliar object, which it displaces to find a reward. After a delay the animal sees the same object paired with a new one. The monkey must recognize the object it saw earlier and move the new one instead in order to get a reward (Figure 14.8C). Monkeys with lesions of areas 10 and 32 are impaired at this task. Mishkin interprets this result as showing that this area of the frontal cortex participates in the short-term storage of object information.

FIGURE 14.8. Schematic illustrations of frontal lesions in monkeys (left side of each figure part). The gray areas represent lesion sites in three experiments (right side of each figure) showing a temporal memory deficit. *A*. Passingham's study: The task is to retrieve a food reward from each of 25 boxes, each of which is marked by a circle. Notice that the control animal seldom returns to a previously visited location, whereas the monkey with a sulcus principalis lesion makes numerous errors. *B*. Funahashi et al. study: The task is to fixate at the central point, and then after a brief delay moves the eyes to locate a target light flashed at one of the eight end points. Correct performance percentage is indicated by the relative positions of the lines along axes drawn through the central fixation point. The delay was 3 sec. Note that the monkey performed relatively poorly in one region of the visual field contralateral to the lesion. Lesions elsewhere in area 46 produced deficits in different regions of the visual field. *C*. Mishkin's study: The monkey is shown an object, which is displaced and a food reward obtained. The monkey is then presented with two objects after a short delay; the task is to obtain the reward, which is under the novel object. Monkeys with medial lesions are impaired at this task, which is nonspatial.

LESION SITE

EXPERIMENT

A

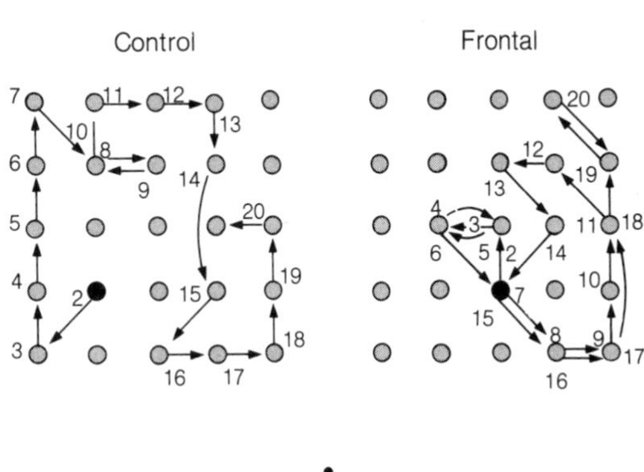

B

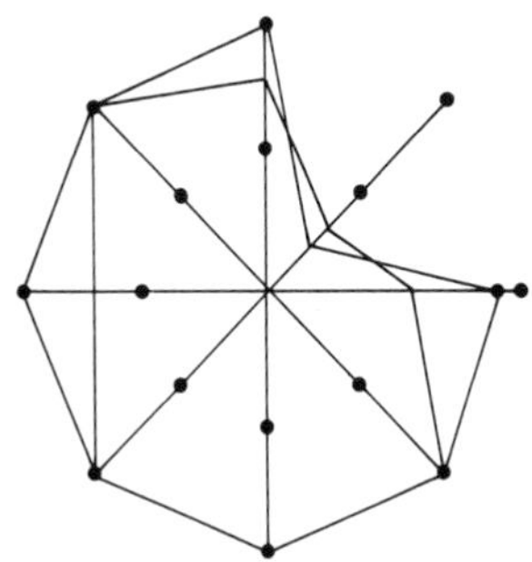

C

The final experiment was a 1991 study by Petrides in which monkeys were given two different tasks. In the first, the animals were presented with three objects and allowed to choose one for reward. The animals were then given a choice between the chosen object and one of the other objects, with the correct choice being the one that was not previously selected. In the second task, the animals were again presented with three objects and allowed one choice. On this task, however, they were then presented with the previously selected object and a novel object. In the first task the monkey must recall what it did with the objects. In the second task the monkey must recall only which object was seen before. Monkeys with dorsolateral lesions performed at chance on the first task but performed as well as controls on the second. This result suggests that the dorsolateral cortex plays a role in the monitoring of self-generated responses.

Taken together, these four experiments point to an unequivocal role of the frontal cortex in some type of short-term memory process, and to the fact that different regions of the prefrontal cortex are involved with the storage of different types of information. In view of the anatomical connections, it seems likely that area 46 plays a role in providing an internal representation of spatial information and that the medial regions play a similar role with object information. Further support for the role of area 46 can be found in electrophysiological studies showing cells in this area that are active during the delay intervals in delayed-response tests and whose activity ends abruptly when the animal responds. There are neurons that respond selectively to the spatial position of the cues, and one might expect to find similar neurons coding some features of objects as well.

Studies of temporal memory have taken a slightly different slant with human subjects. On the basis of earlier works by others, Corsi designed an ingenious test of memory for the order in which things have happened, which is often called recency memory. Subjects were shown a long series of cards, each card bearing two stimulus items, which were either words or pictures. On some cards a question mark appeared between the items, and the subjects' task was to indicate which of the two items had been seen more recently. Successful performance required the subjects to recall the order of presentation of the stimuli. On most test trials both the items had appeared previously, but on some, one item was new. In this case the task became one of simple recognition memory. Patients with frontal lobe lesions performed normally on the recognition trials, but they were impaired in judging the relative recency of two previously seen items. Further, there is relative asymmetry in the frontal lobes in this regard: the right frontal lobe appears more important for memory for nonverbal or pictorial recency; the left frontal lobe appears more important for verbal recency. In contrast, patients with temporal lobe lesions were impaired at the recognition test but not at the recency test. (This latter finding is curious, for it seems to be analogous to blindsight in that people who fail to recognize items can identify which was observed most recently. Might this suggest that there is a memory location system that is separate from a memory recognition system?)

Petrides and Milner designed an experiment that is conceptually similar to Passingham's self-ordering task in monkeys. Subjects were presented with stacks of cards on which were displayed an array of 12 stimuli, including words or drawings in parallel versions of the task. The stimuli in the array remained constant, but the position of each stimulus varied randomly from card to card. The subjects' task appeared rather simple: go through the stack and point to only one item on each card, taking care not to point to the same item twice. Thus, the subjects themselves initiated the plan to follow and determined the order of responding. Although the task appears easy to us, frontal lobe patients did not find it so: left frontal lobe lesions were associated with impaired performance of both verbal and nonverbal versions of the task, whereas right frontal lobe lesions were associated with poor performance only on the nonverbal test.

Petrides and Milner suggest that in contrast to the recency tests, the self-ordered tasks require subjects to organize and carry out a sequence of responses. From the moment the subjects begin to respond, they must constantly compare the responses they have made with those that still remain to be carried out. Hence, this type of task demands an accurate memory as well as an organized strategy. When questioned about their approach to the task at the end of testing, patients with frontal lesions were less likely than other subjects to report that they had used a particular strategy; and when they had, the strategy often appeared to be ill-defined and to have been used inconsistently. The deficit is unlikely to have been one of simple memory, since temporal lobe patients, who would have been expected to have defects of memory, performed normally at this task.

Impaired Social and Sexual Behavior

Social and sexual behaviors both require flexible responses that are highly dependent upon contextual cues. It is hardly surprising, therefore, that frontal lobe lesions would interfere with both of these behaviors.

One of the most obvious and striking effects of frontal lobe damage in humans is a marked change in social behavior and personality. Perhaps the most publicized example of personality change following frontal lobe lesions is that of Phineas Gage, first reported by Harlow in 1868. Gage was a dynamite worker and survived an explosion that blasted an iron tamping bar (about a meter long and 3 cm wide at its widest point) through the front of his head (Figure 14.9). After the accident

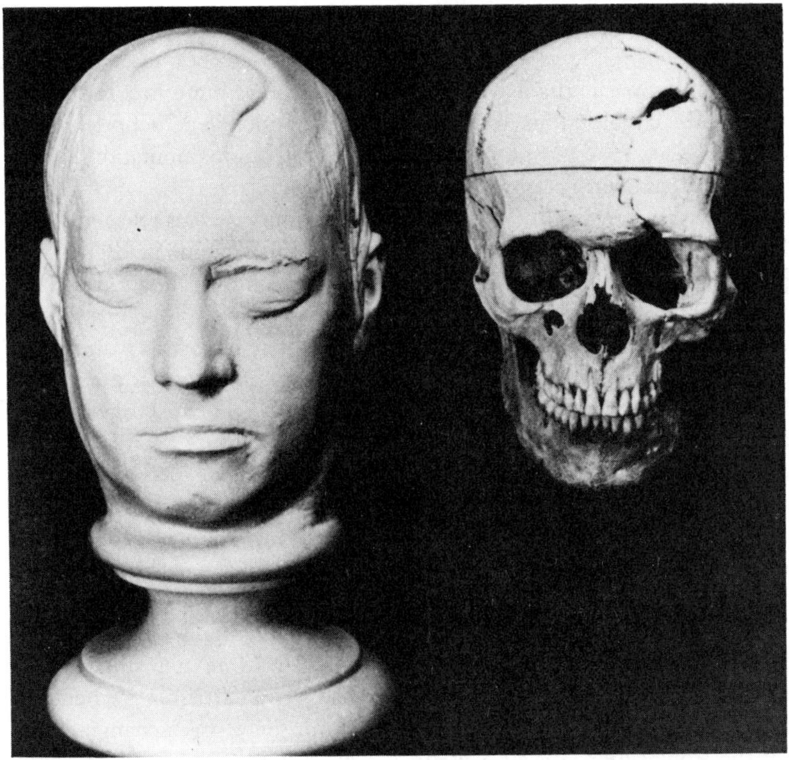

FIGURE 14.9. Bust and skull of Phineas Gage, showing the hole in the frontal bone made by the iron rod blown through his head. (From C. Blakemore, *Mechanics of the Mind.* Cambridge: Cambridge University Press, p. 3. Copyright © 1977. Reprinted with permission of Cambridge University Press.)

his behavior changed completely. He had been of average intelligence and was "energetic and persistent in executing all of his plans of operation." His personality after the injury is described as follows:

> The equilibrium or balance, so to speak, between his intellectual faculties and animal propensities seems to have been destroyed. He is fitful, irreverent, indulging at times in the grossest profanity, manifesting but little deference to his fellows, impatient of restraint or advice when it conflicts with his desires, at times pertinaciously obstinate, yet capricious and vacillating, devising many plans of operation, which are no sooner arranged than they are abandoned in turn for others appearing more feasible. A child in his intellectual capacity and manifestations, he has the animal passions of a strong man. (Blumer and Benson, 1975, p. 153)

Gage's injury affected primarily the left frontal lobe from the medial orbital region upward to the precentral region.

Although Gage's skull has been examined carefully, the first person with extensive frontal damage to undergo close scrutiny at autopsy was a furrier who fell 30 m from a window. He suffered a compound fracture of the frontal bones and severe injury to the right frontal lobe but, remarkably, was never unconscious and was confused only briefly. Before the fall the man had been good-natured and sociable, but afterward he became nasty and cantankerous. Autopsy, about a year after the accident, revealed deep scarring of the orbital part of both frontal lobes, although it was more extensive on the right.

From soon after the turn of the century until about 1950 there were many excellent psychiatric studies of the effect of brain lesions on personality. A consistent finding of this work (especially Kleist's, cited in Zangwill) was that damage to the orbital regions of the frontal lobe was associated with more dramatic changes in personality than dorsolateral lesions, although the latter also had significant effects. Although there are abundant clinical descriptions of the effects of frontal lobe lesions on personality, there are few systematic studies. At least two types of personality change have been clinically observed in such patients: Blumer and Benson have termed them **pseudodepression** and **pseudopsychopathy.** Patients classified as being pseudodepressed exhibit such symptoms as outward apathy and indifference, loss of initiative, reduced sexual interest, little overt emotion, and little or no verbal output. Patients classified as pseudopsychopathic exhibit immature behavior, lack of tact and restraint, coarse language, promiscuous sexual behavior, increased motor activity, and a general lack of social graces. Incontinence is not uncommon with large traumatic lesions and tumors in the frontal lobes. The following two case histories illustrate the psuedodepressed and pseudopsychopathic frontal personalities, respectively:

> At the age of 46, a successful salesman sustained a compound depressed fracture of the left frontal bone in a traffic accident. Treatment included debridement [surgical removal] and amputation of the left frontal pole. Recovery was slow, and 9 months after the injury he was referred for long-term custodial management. By this time, he had recovered motor function with only a minimal limp and slight hyperreflexia on the right side, had normal sensation, no evidence of aphasia, and normal memory and cognitive ability (IQ 118). Nonetheless, he remained under hospital care because of marked changes in personal habits.
>
> Prior to the accident, the patient had been garrulous, enjoyed people, had many friends and talked freely. He was active in community affairs, including Little League, church activities, men's clubs, and so forth. It was stated by one acquaintance that the patient had a true charisma, "whenever he entered a room there was a change in the atmosphere, everything became more animated, happy and friendly."
>
> Following the head injury, he was quiet and remote. He would speak when spoken to and made sensible replies but would then

lapse into silence. He made no friends on the ward, spent most of his time sitting alone smoking. He was frequently incontinent of urine, occasionally of stool. He remained unconcerned about either and was frequently found soaking wet, calmly sitting and smoking. If asked, he would matter-of-factly state that he had not been able to get to the bathroom in time but that this didn't bother him. Because of objectionable eating habits he always ate alone on the ward. His sleep pattern was reversed; he stayed up much of the night and slept during the day. He did not resent being awakened or questioned. He could discuss many subjects intelligently, but was never known to initiate either a conversation or a request. He could give detailed accounts of his life prior to the accident, of the hospitals he had been in, the doctors and treatment he had had, but there was an unreality to his conversation. When asked, he would deny illness, state emphatically that he could return to work at any time, and that the only reason he was not working was that he was being held in the hospital by the doctors. At no time did he request a discharge or weekend pass. He was totally unconcerned about his wife and children. Formerly a warm and loving father, he did not seem to care about his family. Eventually, the family ceased visiting because of his indifference and unconcern. (Blumer and Benson, 1975, pp. 156–157)

A 32-year-old white male was admitted for behavioral evaluation. History revealed that he had sustained a gunshot wound in Vietnam 5 years previously. A high-velocity missile had entered the left temple and emerged through the right orbit. Infection necessitated surgical removal of most of the orbital surface of the right frontal lobe. On recovery, he was neither paralyzed nor aphasic but suffered a remarkable change in personality.

Prior to injury he had been quiet, intelligent, proper, and compulsive. He was a West Point graduate and spent the ensuing years as a military officer attaining the rank of captain. Both as a cadet and later as an officer, he was known to be quiet, strict, and rigid. He was considered a good commander, trusted by his men, but never shared camaraderie with his troops or with his peers.

Subsequent to injury, he was outspoken, facetious, brash, and disrespectful. There was no evidence of self-pity, although he frequently made rather morbid jokes about his condition (for example, "dummy's head"). On admission to the hospital, he had just failed at an extremely simple job.

He was not aphasic but misused words in a manner that suggested inability to maintain specific meanings. For instance, when asked whether the injury had affected his thinking his response was, "Yeah—it's affected the way I think—it's affected my senses—the only things I can taste are sugar and salt—I can't detect a pungent odor—ha ha—to tell you the truth it's a blessing this way." When the examiner persisted, "How had it affected the way you think?" his response was "Yes—I'm not as spry on my feet as I was before." He was never incontinent, but did show a messiness in attire. His remarks to the nurses and other female personnel were open and frank but were never blatantly sexual. His premorbid IQ was reported at about 130. Present examination showed a full-scale IQ of 113. (Blumer and Benson, 1974, pp. 155–156)

Blumer and Benson are probably correct in their assertion that all the elements of these syndromes are observable only after bilateral frontal lobe damage. Nevertheless, some elements of these two rather different syndromes can be observed in most, if not all, persons with frontal lobe lesions. Pseudodepression appears most likely to follow lesions of the left frontal lobe, pseudopsychopathic behavior to follow lesions of the right frontal lobe.

Changes in sexual behavior are among the most difficult symptoms of frontal lobe damage to document properly, largely because of social taboos against investigating people's sex lives. To date, there are no such empirical studies, but there is anecdotal evidence that frontal lesions do alter libido and related behavior. Orbital frontal lesions may introduce abnormal sexual behavior (such as public masturbation) by reducing inhibitions, although the actual frequency of sexual behavior per se is not affected. On the other hand, dorsolateral lesions appear to reduce interest in sexual behavior, although the patients are still capable of the necessary motor acts and can perform sexually if led through the activity "step by step."

Several studies show that frontal lobe lesions in monkeys significantly alter social behavior. In one interesting study Butter and Snyder removed the dominant (so-called alpha) male from each of several groups of monkeys. They removed the frontal lobe from half of these alpha monkeys. When the animals were later returned to their groups, they all resumed the position of dominant male, but within a couple of days all the monkeys without frontal lobes were deposed and fell to the bottom of the group hierarchy.

Analogous studies of wild monkeys have shown similar results: monkeys with frontal lobe lesions fall to the bottom of the group hierarchy and eventually die, because they are helpless alone. It is not known exactly how the social behavior of these animals has changed, but there is little doubt that it is as dramatic as the changes in the social behavior of humans. The social interactions of monkeys are complex and involve a significant amount of context-dependent behavior; the behavior of a monkey will change depending upon the configuration of the proximal social group, and monkeys may lose this ability after frontal lobe lesions. There are likely to be additional components of this behavioral change, however, that relate to the interpretation of species-typical sensory cues, whether they be odors, facial expressions, or sounds.

Is There a Spatial Deficit?

We have indicated that a key to understanding the functions of the dorsolateral cortex is to be found in its relationship to the posterior parietal cortex. The posterior parietal cortex plays a central role in visuomotor guidance of movements in space, and the region of PG and the superior temporal sulcus plays some role in more complex spatial behavior such as mental rotation (see Chapter 12). These parieto-temporal regions provide a major input into the dorsolateral region, which implies some role of this area in spatially guided behavior. The precise role has been difficult to determine, however. It is clear that dorsolateral lesions impair short-term memory for the location of events, and this deficit presumably could interfere with the selection of behaviors with respect to places in space. Indeed, the delayed-response deficit, as well as the deficit in Passingham's task (see Figure 14.8), have spatial components. The role of the dorsolateral cortex in "spatial thinking" can be seen in a blood-flow study by Roland and Frieberg. They asked subjects to imagine walking along a familiar route and to take first a left turn, then a right, and so on taking alternate turns along the path. There was a major increase in blood flow in the dorsolateral region, suggesting a role for the dorsolateral cortex in the selection of spatially guided behaviors. Taken together, the blood-flow and lesion studies suggest that the frontal lobe has a role in selecting between different visual locations. Note, however, that there is little evidence favoring the role of the prefrontal cortex in topographic orientation or in the ability to mentally manipulate or organize spatial information.

Symptoms Associated with Damage to the Face Area

Over the years Taylor and his colleagues have accumulated some remarkable data from a small group of patients with localized surgical removals of the precentral and postcentral gyri, containing, respectively, the motor and sensory representations of the face (see Figure 14.1C). Unlike removal of cortical areas for the hand, removal of areas for the face is seldom associated with long-lasting somatosensory deficits on the face, even if both the sensory and motor representations are removed completely. This finding is in keeping with the evidence that the face is represented bilaterally in the cortex. There has been no systematic study of the facial motor abilities of patients with removal of both precentral and postcentral gyri, but Kolb and Milner found such patients able to perform facial-movement sequences normally. Furthermore, although these patients had difficulty in making individual facial movements in the initial postoperative period, especially on the side of the face contralateral to the lesion, they appeared to have regained normal voluntary facial control a month after surgery, although closer examination might have revealed subtle defects. In addition, their faces were expressive, and they displayed normal spontaneous facial expressions at frequencies well within normal limits.

In the immediate postoperative period patients with left hemisphere facial-area lesions are aphasic, being impaired at both language comprehension and production, as well as being alexic. However, these symptoms subside rapidly, probably having resulted from swelling and trauma associated with the surgical procedure. Within about 6 months to a year after surgery, only a slight residual expressive dysphasia remains. Yet these same patients are severely impaired at certain other language tests. In particular, they perform very poorly on tests of word fluency and are unable to make effective use of the phonetic elements of language.

In addition, these same patients are very poor spellers, occasionally writing words that are unrecognizable. Their low verbal fluency is complemented by a very low design fluency; patients with right facial-area lesions are worse at design fluency than even patients with very large anterior frontal lesions. This lack of spontaneity in verbal and design fluency is remarkable, considering the normal spontaneity of facial expressions noted above.

In summary, unilateral removal of the cortical area representing the face results in no significant chronic loss in sensory or motor control of the face (presumably because of the face's bilateral representation in the cortex) but does result surprisingly in chronic deficits in phonetic discrimination, spelling, verbal fluency, and design fluency. Taylor has preliminary data suggesting that these deficits may result primarily from damage to the precentral motor representation of the face, rather than from damage to the postcentral sensory representation. The origin of these deficits, however, is unexplained to date.

Clinical Neuropsychological Assessment of Frontal Lobe Damage

Considering the number and variety of symptoms associated with frontal lobe damage, surprisingly few standardized neuropsychological tests are useful for assessing frontal lobe function. The available tests (Table 14.3) are very good, however. As with the parietal and temporal lobe tests discussed in the previous two chapters, it would be highly unusual for a person to perform normally on all these tests if there were damage to either frontal lobe.

The Wisconsin Card-Sorting Test, described earlier, is the best available test of dorsolateral frontal cortex function. Briefly, the subject is told to sort the cards into piles in front of one or another of the stimulus cards bearing designs that differ in color, form, and number of elements. The correct solution shifts without the subject's knowledge once he or she has figured out each solution.

Recall that the Thurstone Word-Fluency Test (also referred to as the Chicago Word-Fluency Test) requires subjects to say or write as many words as possible beginning with a given letter in 5 min, and then as many four-letter words beginning with a given letter in 4 min. Although subjects with lesions anywhere in the prefrontal cortex are apt to do poorly on this test, subjects with facial-area lesions perform the worst, those with orbital lesions performing only slightly better. Performance is poorest, of course, when the lesion is in the left hemisphere.

The Gotman-Milner Design-Fluency Test (see Figure 14.6) is also very useful, although somewhat difficult to score. Subjects are asked to draw as many unnameable drawings as they can in 5 min. Frontal lobe patients will draw very few

TABLE 14.3. Standardized clinical neuropsychological tests for frontal lobe damage

Function	Test	Basic reference
Response inhibition	Wisconsin Card Sorting	Milner, 1964
	Stroop	Perret, 1974
Verbal fluency	Thurstone Word Fluency	Milner, 1964
		Ramier and Hécaen, 1970
Design fluency	Gotman-Milner Design Fluency	Jones-Gotman and Milner, 1977
Motor	Hand dynamometer	Taylor, 1979
	Finger tapping	Reitan and Davidson, 1974
	Sequencing	Kolb and Milner, 1981
Language comprehension		
Aphasia	Token	de Renzi and Faglioni, 1978
Spelling		Taylor, 1979
Phonetic discrimination		Taylor, 1979

items, draw nameable objects, or draw the same figure repeatedly. Like the verbal-fluency tests, the design-fluency task appears most sensitive to orbital injury.

Tests of motor function include tests of strength (hand dynamometer), finger-tapping speed, and movement sequencing. Strength and finger-tapping speed are significantly reduced contralateral to a lesion that is in the vicinity of the precentral or postcentral gyri. Motor sequencing can be assessed by using Kolb and Milner's facial-sequence test, although this test requires considerable practice to administer and scoring should be from videotaped records. Simpler tests of movement programming such as the Kimura Box Test (see Chapter 12) are not suitable because frontal lobe patients are unlikely to perform very poorly unless the lesion extends into the basal ganglia.

As in previous chapters, we recommend the token test as a quick screening test for aphasia, to be followed if necessary by more extensive aphasia testing (see Chapter 17). Although it is widely believed that damage to Broca's area results in deficits only in language production and not in comprehension, this is not strictly true. Left frontal lesions in the vicinity of Broca's area produce deficits in comprehension as well as in production. Spelling is seriously impaired by facial-area lesions and can be assessed by any standardized spelling test. Phonetic differentiation, a test described by Stitt and Huntington and used for neurological patients by Taylor, is another means of assessing facial-area function. A series of nonsense words, such as "agma," is presented and the subject's task is to identify the first consonant sound. This test proves difficult even for controls, but it is performed most poorly by subjects with facial-area damage, especially damage on the left side. However, frontal lobe lesions outside the facial area also may impair performance on this test significantly.

In the absence of language deficits it may prove difficult to localize frontal lobe damage in either the left or the right hemisphere with neuropsychological tests, presumably because the functions of the two frontal lobes overlap significantly. Clinical evaluation of personality as pseudodepressed or pseudopsychopathic (as discussed earlier) may prove useful in localizing the dysfunction to the left or the right hemisphere, respectively, but caution is advised. Unfortunately, no standardized quantitative measures of these symptoms are available.

OTHER ASPECTS OF FRONTAL LOBE FUNCTION

We have emphasized the results of anatomical and lesion studies in our analysis of frontal lobe function, with passing reference to electrophysiological work. Another way to investigate frontal lobe function is by inference from populations whose frontal lobes might reasonably be believed to be abnormal or at least unlike that of normal adults. This includes both people with diseases affecting the frontal lobe and children whose frontal lobes are not yet mature.

Diseases Affecting the Frontal Lobe

Many of the symptoms of frontal lobe injury are characteristic of people with psychiatric or neurological disorders, including especially schizophrenia (see Chapter 18), Parkinson's disease (see Chapter 20), and Korsakoff's disease (see Chapter 16). In each case there is reason to suppose that the frontal lobes are not functioning normally. Thus, in schizophrenia there is believed to be an abnormality in the mesocortical dopamine projection, which terminates largely in the frontal lobe; a decrease in blood flow to the frontal lobe; and possible frontal lobe atrophy. Schizophrenic patients perform poorly on all tests of frontal lobe function and exhibit abnormalities in the control of eye movements, but they perform relatively normally on tests of parietal lobe function. Parkinson's disease results from a loss of the dopamine cells of the substantia nigra. Although the primary projection of these cells is the caudate nucleus, there is a direct projection to the prefrontal cortex, too, and an indirect projection through the dorsomedial nucleus of the thalamus. Parkinson patients are characterized by a lack of facial expression similar to that seen in frontal lobe patients, and they are impaired at the Wisconsin Card-Sorting Test and at delayed response. Finally, patients with Korsakoff's disease suffer from alcohol-induced damage to the dorsomedial thalamus and may have a deficiency in catecholamines in the frontal cortex. Korsakoff patients perform poorly on the Wisconsin Card-Sorting Test, as well as on tests of spatial memory such as delayed response. In summary, it seems likely that a disturbance of frontal lobe function contributes significantly to the behavioral symptoms of schizophrenic, Parkinson, and Korsakoff patients.

Frontal Lobe Development

In a study of changes in synaptic density in the prefrontal cortex over a lifespan, Huttenlocher reported that synaptic density increased over the first year of life to a level well above adult levels, and then declined over the next 16 years (Figure 14.10). There was no change over the range between 16 and 72 years in his sample, and a slight decrease in a small sample of 74- to 90-year-old brains. The overproduction of synapses in the infant frontal cortex is typical of other cortical regions, appearing to be a general characteristic of brain development (see Chapter 21 for more details). It has been postulated that cells failing to make the essential functioning synaptic contacts undergo synaptic degeneration, thus eliminating unnecessary redundancy in the brain and improving the efficiency of processing. The slow maturation of the frontal lobe suggests that the temporal organization of behavior also may be slow to mature and may not reach maturity until late adolescence. It is difficult to correlate performance on neuropsychological tests with anatomical development because other parts of the brain are developing as well; also, one cannot be certain what role education might play in performance. Nevertheless, we have found that performance on tests such as the Wisconsin Card-Sorting Test and tests of verbal fluency do not reach adult levels until at least 12 years of age and possibly later for tests such as those of design fluency. Further, children do not appear to be socially mature until well into adolescence and are not recognized as legally competent in most jurisdictions until at least 16 years of age, suggesting that society recognizes the slow development of certain aspects of behavior.

Since one of the most complex aspects of social behavior in primates is its contextual dependence,

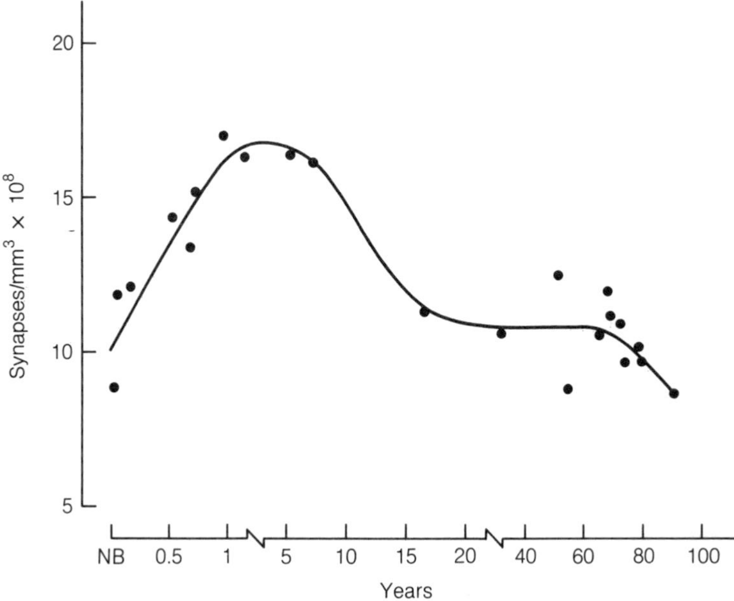

FIGURE 14.10. Synapse counts in layer 3 of the middle frontal gyrus of the human brain as a function of age. The number of synapses increases until 1 year of age and then decreases, reaching asymptote at about age 16. There is a further decline in old age, after about age 70. (After Huttenlocher, 1979.)

and given that adults with frontal lobe injuries are particularly poor at tasks that depend on recognizing context, we asked whether or not children would be able to judge correctly the emotion of people from the context of a situation. To do so, we took advantage of a test we devised to study adult frontal lobe patients. In this test subjects are presented with a series of cartoon situations depicting some emotion-laden situation such as a hold-up, a surprise party, or a funeral. The face of the key character is left blank, and the task is to choose the appropriate expression from a series of facial photographs. Our results showed that although children could match the emotions of people in different photographs as accurately as adults by about age 8, they performed as poorly as frontal lobe patients on the contextual test until about age 15. In conclusion, behaviors that would seem to be dependent upon the normal operation of the frontal lobe appear to be slow in developing, as would be predicted from the anatomical studies.

SUMMARY

The frontal lobe can be conceived as the end point for the spatial and object-recognition functions that are initiated in the occipital lobe. The frontal lobe's function in these processes is to select behaviors with respect to context and internalized knowledge. It is possible to subdivide the frontal lobe into three distinct functional zones: motor cortex, premotor cortex, and prefrontal cortex. The motor cortex is responsible for making movements. The premotor cortex selects movements. The prefrontal cortex controls the cognitive processes so that appropriate movements are selected at the correct time and place. The premotor cortex can be divided into two regions, the lateral area responsible for selecting behaviors in response to environmental cues and the supplementary area responsible for selecting behaviors on the basis of internalized knowledge. The prefrontal cortex can be divided into two general zones, a dorsolateral zone responsible for selecting behavior with respect to temporal memory and the inferior prefrontal region responsible for selecting behavior with respect to context, both current and that based upon knowledge.

REFERENCES

Benton, A. L. Differential effects of frontal lobe disease. *Neuropsychologia* 6:53–60, 1968.

Bizzi, E., and P. H. Schiller. Single unit activity in the frontal eye fields of unanesthetized monkeys during head and eye movement. *Experimental Brain Research* 10:151–158, 1970.

Blumer, D., and D. F. Benson. Personality changes with frontal and temporal lobe lesions. In D. F. Benson and D. Blumer, eds. *Psychiatric Aspects of Neurologic Disease.* New York: Grune & Stratton, 1975.

Bossom, J. The effect of brain lesions on adaptation in monkeys. *Psychonomic Science* 2:45–46, 1965.

Brown, J. *Aphasia, Apraxia and Agnosia.* Springfield, Ill.: Charles C. Thomas, 1972.

Bruce, C. J., and M. E. Goldberg. Physiology of the frontal eye fields. *Trends in Neuroscience* 7:436–441, 1984.

Butter, C. M., and D. R. Snyder. Alterations in aversive and aggressive behaviors following orbital frontal lesions in rhesus monkeys. *Acta Neurobiologiae Experimentalis* 32:525–565, 1972.

Deiber, M.-P., R. E. Passingham, J. G. Colebatch, K. J. Friston, P. D. Nixon, and R. S. J. Frackowiak. Cortical areas and the selection of movement. A study with positron emission tomography. *Experimental Brain Research* 84:393–402, 1991.

de Renzi, E., and P. Faglioni. Normative data and screening power of a shortened version of the token test. *Cortex* 14:41–49, 1978.

Drewe, E. A. Go–no-go learning after frontal lobe lesions in humans. *Cortex* 11:8–16, 1975.

Freedman, M., and M. Oscar-Berman. Bilateral frontal lobe disease and selective delayed response deficits in humans. *Behavioral Neuroscience* 100:337–342, 1986.

Funahashi, S., C. J. Bruce, and P. S. Goldman-Rakic. Perimetry of spatial memory representation in primate prefrontal cortex. *Society for Neuroscience Abstracts* 12:554, 1986.

Fuster, J. M. *The Prefrontal Cortex,* 2nd ed. New York: Raven Press, 1989.

Goldman-Rakic, P. S. Circuitry of the primate prefrontal cortex and regulation of behavior by representational memory. In F. Blum, ed. *Handbook of Physiology; Nervous System, Vol. V: Higher Functions of the Brain, Part 1.* Bethesda, Md.: American Physiological Society, 1987.

Guilford, J. P. *The Nature of Human Intelligence.* New York: McGraw-Hill, 1967.

Guitton, D., H. A. Buchtel, and R. M. Douglas. Disturbances of voluntary saccadic eye-movement mechanisms following discrete unilateral frontal-lobe removals. In G. Lennerstrand, D. S. Lee, and E. L. Keller, eds. *Functional Basis of Ocular Motility Disorders.* Oxford: Pergamon, 1982.

Held, R. Dissociation of visual function by deprivation and rearrangement. *Psychology Forschung* 31:338–348, 1968.

Huttenlocher, P. R. Synaptic density in human frontal cortex—developmental changes and effects of aging. *Brain Research* 163:195–205, 1979.

Jacobsen, C. F. Studies of cerebral function in primates. *Comparative Psychology Monographs* 13:1–68, 1936.

Jenkins, I. H., R. E. Passingham, P. D. Nixon, R. S. J. Frackowiak, and D. J. Brooks. The learning of motor sequences: A PET study. *European Journal of Neuroscience* (Suppl. 5):3215, 1992.

Jones-Gotman, M., and B. Milner. Design fluency: The invention of nonsense drawings after focal cortical lesions. *Neuropsychologia* 15:653–674, 1977.

Kolb, B., and B. Milner. Performance of complex arm and facial movements after focal brains lesions. *Neuropsychologia* 19:505–514, 1981.

Kolb, B., and B. Milner. Observations on spontaneous facial expression after focal cerebral excisions and after intracarotid injection of sodium Amytal. *Neuropsychologia* 19:514–515, 1981.

Kolb, B., and L. Taylor. Affective behavior in patients with localized cortical excisions: An analysis of lesion site and side. *Science* 214:89–91, 1981.

Kolb, B., L. Taylor, and B. Wilson. Developmental changes in the recognition and comprehension of facial expression: Implications for frontal lobe function. *Brain and Cognition* 20:74–84, 1992.

Kuypers, H. G. J. M. Anatomy of the descending pathways. In V. B. Brooks, ed. *The Nervous System, Handbook of Physiology,* vol 2. Baltimore: Williams and Wilkins, 1981.

Lashley, K. S. The problem of serial order in behavior. In F. A. Beach, D. O. Hebb, C. T. Morgan, and H. W. Nissen, eds. *The Neuropsychology of Lashley*. New York: McGraw-Hill, 1960.

Leonard, G., L. Jones, and B. Milner. Residual impairment in handgrip strength after unilateral frontal-lobe lesions. *Neuropsychologia* 26:555–564, 1988.

Luria, A. R. *The Working Brain.* New York: Penguin, 1973.

Luria, A. R., and E. D. Homskaya. Disturbance in the regulative role of speech with frontal lobe lesions. In J. M. Warren and K. Akert, eds. *Frontal Granular Cortex and Behavior.* New York: McGraw-Hill, 1964.

Miller, L. Cognitive risk taking after frontal or temporal lobectomy. I. The synthesis of fragmented visual information. *Neuropsychologia* 23:359–369, 1985.

Miller, L., and B. Milner. Cognitive risk taking after frontal or temporal lobectomy. II. The synthesis of phonemic and semantic information. *Neuropsychologia* 23:371–379, 1985.

Milner, B. Some effects of frontal lobectomy in man. In J. M. Warren and K. Akert, eds. *The Frontal Granular Cortex and Behavior.* New York: McGraw-Hill, 1964.

Milner, B., P. Corsi, and G. Leonard. Frontal cortex contribution to recency judgements. *Neuropsychologia* 29:601–618, 1991.

Milner, B., and M. Petrides. Behavioural effects of frontal-lobe lesions in man. *Trends in Neurosciences* 7:403–407, 1984.

Mishkin, M., and F. J. Manning. Non-spatial memory after selective prefrontal lesions in monkeys. *Brain Research* 143:313–323, 1978.

Passingham, R. E. Memory of monkeys *(Macaca mulatta)* with lesions in prefrontal cortex. *Behavioral Neuroscience* 99:3–21, 1985.

Passingham, R. E. *The Frontal Lobes and Voluntary Action.* Oxford: Oxford University Press, 1993.

Perret, E. The left frontal lobe of man and the suppression of habitual responses in verbal categorical behavior. *Neuropsychologia* 12:323–330, 1974.

Petrides, M. Motor conditional associative learning after selective prefrontal lesions in the monkey. *Behavioural Brain Research* 5:407–413, 1982.

Petrides, M. Functional specialization within the dorsolateral frontal cortex for serial order memory. *Proceedings of the Royal Society, London* B246:299–306, 1991.

Petrides, M., and B. Milner. Deficit on subject ordered tasks after frontal- and temporal-lobe lesions in man. *Neuropsychologia* 20:249–262, 1982.

Potter, H., and N. Butters. An assessment of olfactory deficits in patients with damage to prefrontal cortex. *Neuropsychologia* 18:621–628, 1980.

Ramier, A.-M., and H. Hécaen. Role respectif des atteintes frontales et de la lateralisation lésionnelle dans les deficits de la "fluence verbale." *Revue de Neurologie* 123:17–22, 1970.

Roland, P. E. Metabolic measurements of the working frontal cortex in man. *Trends in Neuroscience* 7:430–435, 1984.

Roland, P. E., and L. Friberg. Localization of cortical areas activated by thinking. *Journal of Neurophysiology* 53: 1219–1243, 1985.

Roland, P. E., B. Larsen, N. A. Lassen, and E. Skinhøj. Supplementary motor area and other cortical areas in organization of voluntary movements in man. *Journal of Neurophysiology* 43:118–136, 1980.

Rose, J. E., and C. N. Woolsey. The orbitofrontal cortex and its connections with the mediodorsal nucleus in rabbit, sheep and cat. *Research Publications of the Association of Nervous and Mental Disease* 27:210–232, 1948.

Semmes, J., S. Weinstein, L. Ghent, and H.-L. Teuber. Impaired orientation in personal and extrapersonal space. *Brain* 86:747–772, 1963.

Shallice, T., and P. Burgess. Deficits in strategy application following frontal lobe damage in man. *Brain* 114:727–741, 1991.

Shallice, T., and M. E. Evans. The involvement of the frontal lobes in cognitive estimation. *Cortex* 14:294–303, 1978.

Smith, M. L., and B. Milner. Differential effects of frontal-lobe lesions on cognitive estimation and spatial memory. *Neuropsychologia* 22:697–705, 1984.

Stitt, C., and D. Huntington. Some relationships among articulation, auditory abilities and certain other variables. *Journal of Speech and Learning Research* 12:576–593, 1969.

Taylor, L. Psychological assessment of neurosurgical patients. In T. Rasmussen and R. Marino, eds. *Functional Neurosurgery*. New York: Raven Press, 1979.

Teuber, H.-L. The riddle of frontal lobe function in man. In J. M. Warren and K. Akert, eds. *The Frontal Granular Cortex and Behavior*. New York: McGraw-Hill, 1964.

Teuber, H.-L. Unity and diversity of frontal lobe function. *Acta Neurobiologiae Experimentalis* 32:615–656, 1972.

Tyler, H.R. Disorders of visual scanning with frontal lobe lesions. In S. Locke, ed. *Modern Neurology*. London: J. and A. Churchill, 1969.

Walker, E. A., and D. Blumer. The localization of sex in the brain. In K. J. Zulch, O. Creutzfeldt, and G. C. Galbraith, eds. *Cerebral Localization*. Berlin and New York: Springer-Verlag, 1975.

Zangwill, O. L. Psychological deficits associated with frontal lobe lesions. *International Journal of Neurology* 5:395–402, 1966.

chapter fifteen

15

Disconnection Syndromes

Disconnection is the severing of the connections between two areas of the brain without damaging the areas themselves. The behavioral changes that result can be rather odd and are different from what could be expected if neither of the connected areas was damaged. Figure 15.1 presents Downer's experiment on a monkey that had received two forms of disconnection. All of the commissures connecting the two halves of the brain were cut. The amygdala on one side was removed. Downer then covered one of the animal's eyes with an occluder and presented objects to it. If the objects were presented to the eye ipsilateral to the hemisphere with the ablated amygdala, the animal appeared "tame," even if the objects were ones that are frightening to monkeys. If the objects were presented to the eye ipsilateral to the intact amygdala, the animals made their usual species-typical responses and appeared "wild." The results can be explained as follows. For an animal to display species-typical responses to a visual stimulus, the information must be projected from the eye to the visual cortex, through the temporal lobes to the amygdala, and from the amygdala to the brainstem and frontal cortex, where autonomic responses, movements, and facial expressions, respectively, are activated. When the commissures between the two halves of the brain are disconnected, visual information from an eye can project only to the ipsilateral hemisphere. If that hemisphere contains an intact amygdala, the circuit for activating species-typical behavior is complete and behavior will be normal. If the hemisphere does not have an intact amygdala, visual information will be disconnected from motor systems and will not be able to elicit species-typical behavior. Had the commissures not been cut, the experiment would not work because information from one hemisphere could cross to the other, and each eye thus would have access to the intact amygdala.

So far we have emphasized the importance of neocortical and subcortical regions in controlling various aspects of behavior. We have associated particular behavioral deficits with different brain lesions and from these deficits have tried to infer the function of the missing region. In looking at brain function in this way we have postponed discussion of the functions of the connections between various regions. In this chapter we consider these functions and the effects of cutting the cerebral connections. The cutting of the connections is called disconnection, and the ensuing behavioral effects are called *disconnection syndromes*. We

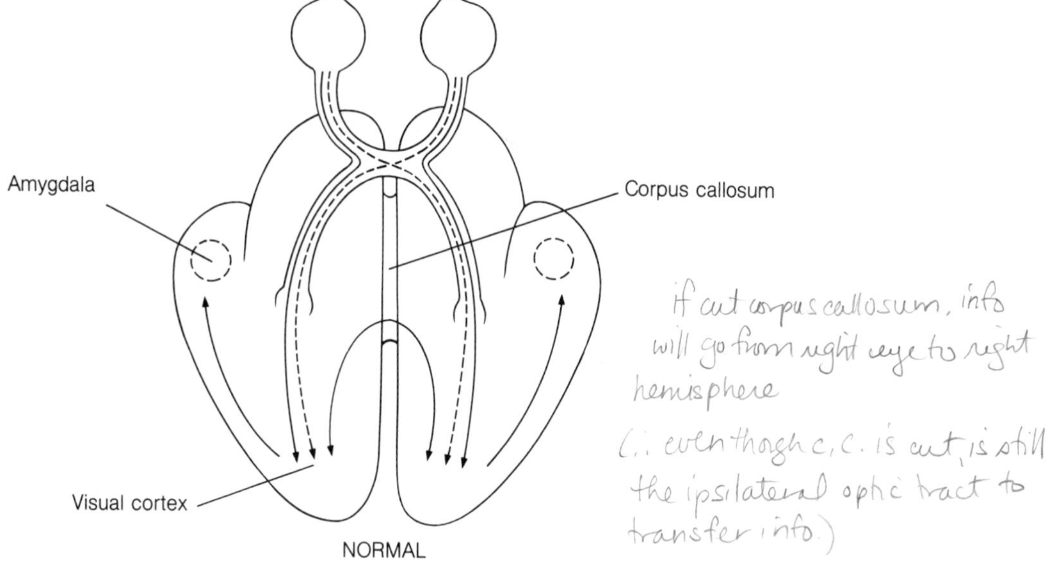

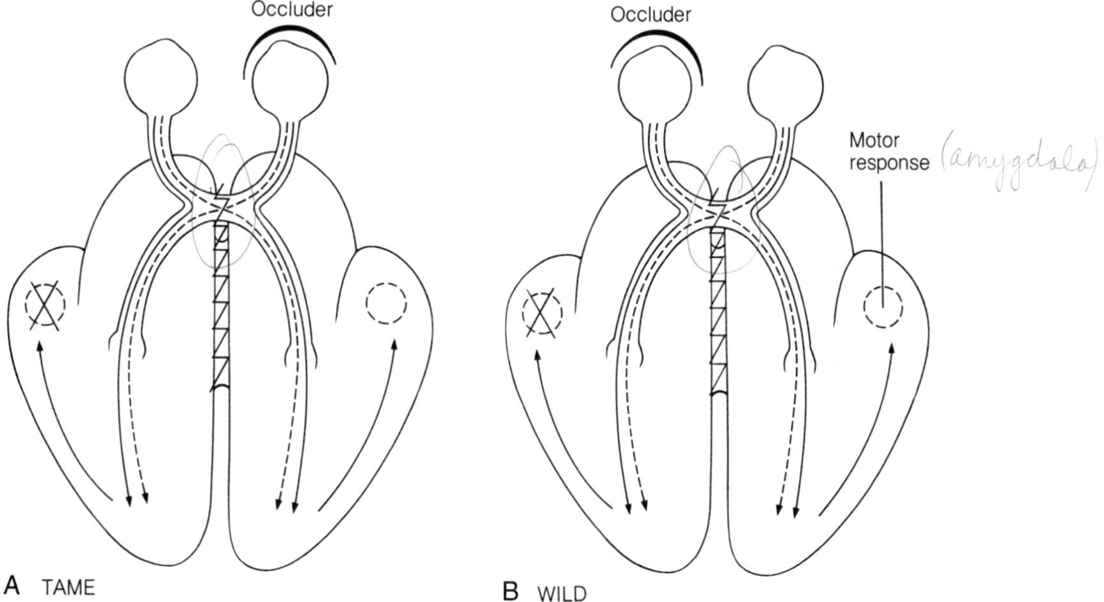

FIGURE 15.1. Downer's experiment. *A*. The commissures between the two halves of the brain are severed, the amygdala on the left is removed, and an occluder covers the right eye. The monkey displays no species-typical responses to visual stimuli and is described as "tame." *B*. The left eye is occluded; the monkey displays species-typical behavior in response to visual stimuli and is classified as "wild."

begin by reviewing the major connections at the cerebral hemispheres.

ANATOMY OF CEREBRAL CONNECTIONS

There are three major types of fiber connections of the neocortex: association, projection, and commissural fibers.

Association Fibers

Two types of association fibers can be distinguished: (1) long fiber bundles that connect distant neocortical areas, and (2) short subcortical U-fibers that connect adjacent neocortical areas. The long fiber bundles include the uncinate fasciculus, the superior longitudinal fasciculus, the cingulum, the inferior longitudinal fasciculus, and the inferior frontal-occipital fasciculus.

Projection Fibers

Projection fibers include ascending fibers from lower centers to the neocortex, such as projections from the thalamus, and descending fibers from the neocortex to the brainstem and spinal cord.

Commissural Fibers

Commissural fibers function primarily to join the two hemispheres and include principally the corpus callosum, the anterior commissure, and the hippocampal commissures. The corpus callosum (from the Latin *callus,* meaning hard body) provides the major connection of neocortical areas. In humans it is made up of 200 million to 800 million fibers, about half of which are unmyelinated and are quite small. Most, but not all, areas of the two hemispheres are connected. Figure 15.2 illustrates the patterns of connections between the hemispheres in a rhesus monkey. Most of area 17, primary visual cortex (V1), is devoid of interhemispheric connections, except for that portion representing the visual meridian. The lack of such connections has been explained in functional terms: this cortex represents the visual world topographically, and there is no need for one half of the representation to be connected to the other. The motor and sensory areas for distal portions of the limbs (mainly the hands and feet) also lack connections. It could be argued that since their essential function is to work independently of one another, connections are not necessary. Among the areas that do receive interhemispheric connections, the density of projections is not homogeneous. Areas of the cortex that represent the midline of the body—such as the central meridian of the visual fields, auditory fields, and trunk of the body on the somatosensory and motor representations—have the densest connections. The functional utility of this arrangement is that movements of the body or actions in central space require interhemispheric cooperation. A prominent working hypothesis concerning callosal function is the zipper hypothesis, which suggests that the corpus callosum knits together the representations of the midpoints of the body and space that are divided by the longitudinal fissure.

The connections of the corpus callosum appear to fall into three general classes. (1) Most of the projections are topographical. That is, they go to identical points in the contralateral hemisphere. Presumably, these projections knit the two areas together functionally. (2) A second group of projections go to areas to which the homotopic area on the contralateral side projects. Thus, projection zones within a hemisphere also maintain close relations with parallel zones in the contralateral hemisphere. (3) A third group of projections have a diffuse terminal distribution. It is possible that these projections alert the appropriate zones of one hemisphere that the other is active.

The location of fiber projections within the corpus callosum is quite precise. The pattern in the rhesus monkey is illustrated in Figures 15.2B and 15.2C. The anterior portion of the corpus callosum is called the **genu** (the knee), and it contains the fibers from the prefrontal cortex. Fibers through the body of the corpus callosum are, from front to back, from the premotor,

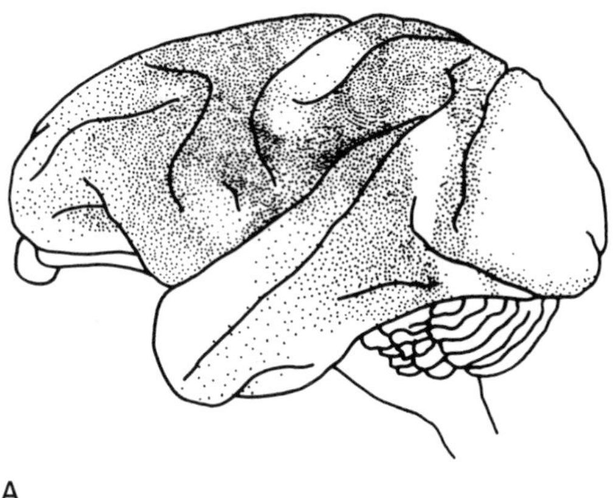

A

FIGURE 15.2. *A*. The stippled areas indicate regions of the cortex of a rhesus monkey that receive projections from the contralateral hemisphere. *B*. Locations (indicated by letters) in which a radioactive label was injected (PF, prefrontal cortex; PM, premotor cortex; M, motor cortex; S, sensory cortex; PP, posterior parietal cortex; ST, superior temporal gyrus; IT, inferotemporal cortex; V, occipital visual areas). *C*. Regions of the corpus callosum showing zones through which the label was transported after injections into the cortex (F, fornix; AC, anterior commissure; VHC, ventral hippocampal commissure; DHC, dorsal hippocampal commissure). (After Pandya and Seltzer, 1986.)

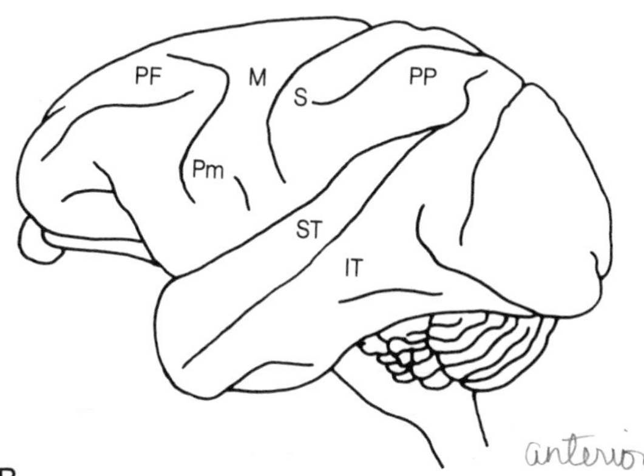

B

Pm
M
S
PP
ST
IT
PF
F
VHC
DHC
V
AC
Genu
Rostrum
Splenium

C

motor, somatosensory, and posterior parietal cortex. Fibers in the posterior portion or splenium are from the superior temporal, inferior temporal, and visual cortex.

The **anterior commissure** is much smaller than the corpus callosum and connects portions of the anterior temporal lobe, the amygdala, and the paleocortex of the temporal lobe surrounding the amygdala. In humans born with no corpus callosum (a condition called **agenesis of the corpus callosum**), the anterior commissure is greatly enlarged to connect far greater regions of the neocortex.

THE BEHAVIORAL EFFECTS OF DISCONNECTION

Colonnier recounts the interesting story in which Monsieur de la Peyronie in 1741 reviewed all the literature concerning areas claimed to be the seat of the soul and dismissed each claim in turn. Peyronie then went on to recount some of his own patients' cases, from which he claimed that "whereby it appears that the corpus callosum cannot be either compressed, sphacelated [affected with gangrene] or otherwise injured, but for both reason and all sensations are abolished" (Colonnier, p. 35), the corpus callosum must necessarily be the immediate seat of the soul. Colonnier then notes that by 1941 McCulloch and Garol reviewed the literature and concluded that few impairments could be found after callosum damage except perhaps in complicated symbolic activity.

The clinical effects of disconnection, however, were first seriously considered by Karl Wernicke in 1874 and were very much a part of early neurology. He predicted the existence of an aphasic syndrome (**conduction aphasia**) that would result from severing fiber connections between the anterior and posterior speech zones. Later, in 1892, J. Dejerine was the first to demonstrate a distinctive behavioral deficit resulting from pathology of the corpus callosum. In a series of papers published around 1900, Hugo Liepmann most clearly demonstrated the importance of severed connections as an underlying factor in the effects of cerebral damage. Having carefully analyzed the behavior of a particular patient, Liepmann predicted a series of disconnections of the neocortex that could account for the behavior. In 1906, after the patient died, Liepmann published the postmortem findings, which supported his hypothesis. He wrote extensively on the principle of disconnection, particularly about the idea that some apraxias might result from disconnection. He reasoned that if a patient were given a verbal command to use the left hand in a particular way, only the verbal left hemisphere would understand the command. To move the left hand, a signal would then have to travel from the left hemisphere through the corpus callosum to the right hemispheric region that controls movements of the left hand, as illustrated in Figure 15.3. Interrupting the portion of the corpus callosum that carries the command from the left hemisphere to the right would disconnect the right hemisphere's motor region from the command. Thus, although the subject would comprehend the command, the left hand would be unable to obey it (Figure 15.3B). This apraxia would occur in the absence of the weakness or incoordination of the left hand that would occur if there were a lesion in the motor cortex of the right hemisphere, which controls the actual movement of the left hand.

Liepmann's deduction, although brilliant, was ignored for a number of reasons. First, it was published in German and so was not widely read by English-speaking neurologists; Liepmann's papers have been translated into English only recently by Doreen Kimura. Second, except in the extremely unusual case of a patient with a natural lesion of only the corpus callosum, any observed behavioral deficits should be attributed to damage of gray matter itself without reference to connections. Third, a large number of animal studies consistently purported to demonstrate that no significant behavioral effects followed the cutting of the corpus callosum. Not until the late 1950s and 1960s did it become clear that the results from the animal studies could be attributed largely to crude behavioral testing.

An important series of papers by Myers and by Sperry in the early 1950s revived interest in the effects of disconnecting neocortical regions. They examined the behavioral effects of severing the corpus callosum of cats. Their work confirmed others' earlier observations that the animals were virtually indistinguishable from their surgically intact counterparts and indeed appeared normal under most tests and training conditions. Unlike the previous studies, however, their studies revealed that under special training procedures the animals could be shown to have severe deficits. Thus, if the sensory information were allowed separate access to each hemisphere, each could be shown to have its own independent perceptual, learning, and memory processes. The corpus callosum does indeed have an important function. This conclusion has been confirmed in the subsequent studies by Sperry and his colleagues on the effects of surgical disconnection of the cerebral hemispheres of humans for the treatment of intractable epilepsy (see Chapter 9).

The success of the Myers and Sperry experiments stimulated interest in other connections of the brain. Geschwind began to reassess the clinical effects of naturally occurring neocortical lesions as possibly indicating disconnection of various regions of the cerebral hemispheres. In parallel work, Mishkin began to construct animal models of human disconnection syndromes

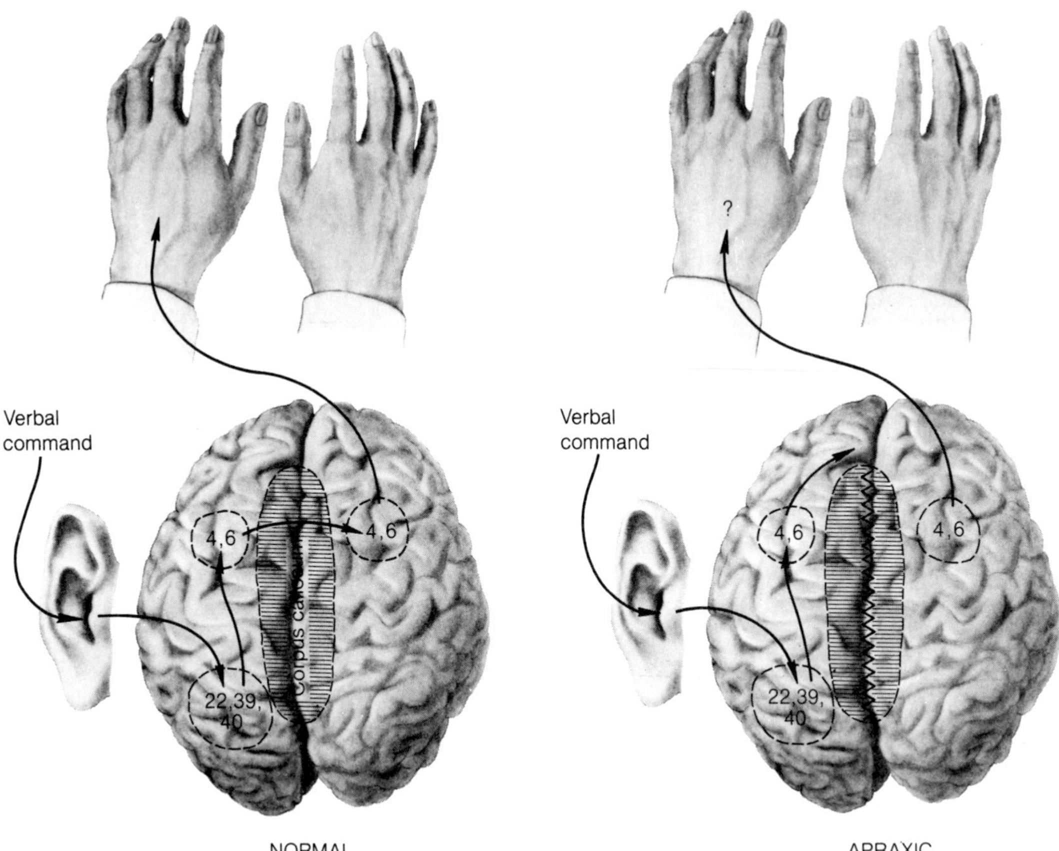

FIGURE 15.3. Liepmann's theory of apraxia resulting from lesions of the corpus callosum. (The jagged line in the bottom right illustration indicates section of the callosum.) The verbal command has no way of reaching the motor cortex (area 4) of the right hemisphere to move the left hand. Geschwind proposed that bilateral apraxia could result from a lesion disconnecting the posterior speech zone (areas 22, 39, 40) from the motor cortex of the left hemisphere. In this case the verbal command cannot gain access to either the left or right motor cortex.

by disconnecting related neocortical regions from one another. These researchers have demonstrated the critical interdependence of these regions.

In fact, the anatomical organization of the neocortex allows for relatively easy disconnection. First, the primary sensory areas have no direct connections between each other and so can be disconnected quite easily. Second, even in higher-order sensory zones, there are few if any direct connections between sensory systems, and so they can be disconnected easily. Third, since the hemispheres are in large part duplicate and are connected by only a few projection systems, they are easy to separate and are sometimes found separated congenitally. In the remainder of this chapter, we first discuss the work of Sperry on the "split-brain" patient, who provides an excellent model of disconnection syndromes. Next we reconsider Geschwind's reinterpretation of three classic symptoms of cortical damage (aphasia, apraxia, and agnosia) as disconnection syndromes. Finally, we briefly study Mishkin's animal model of disconnection in the visual system.

HEMISPHERIC DISCONNECTION

There are three conditions in which the hemispheres become completely separated. First, in humans, the interhemispheric fibers are sometimes cut as a therapy for epilepsy. Second, people are born with congenitally reduced or completely missing interhemispheric connections. Third, in animals, disconnections are performed to trace functional systems, to model human conditions, and to answer basic questions about interhemispheric development.

Epileptic seizures may begin in a restricted region of one hemisphere (most often the temporal lobes) and then spread via the fibers of the corpus callosum or anterior commissure to the homologous location in the opposite hemisphere. These seizures can usually be controlled by anticonvulsant medication, but in some cases the medication is of little value, and the seizures may actually become life-threatening because they recur often, sometimes several times in an hour. To relieve this seizure condition, the corpus callosum and anterior commissure can be surgically sectioned to prevent the spread of abnormal electrical activity from one hemisphere to the other. Patients who have received this treatment obtain substantial relief from their epilepsy and often show marked improvements in personal well-being, competency, and intelligence. The reason for a congenital lack of interhemispheric connections is not known. Interestingly, albinos of nearly all species and Siamese cats have peculiarities in fiber crossings, mostly a reduced number of uncrossed fibers in the visual system. A number of summaries of research on interhemispheric connections have been published, including one by Steele-Russell and colleagues in 1979 and another by Lepore and associates in 1986.

Commissurotomy

Commissurotomy is the surgical cutting of the cerebral commissures as an elective treatment for epilepsy. The surgeons Philip Vogel and Joe Bogen at the White Memorial Medical Center in Los Angeles reintroduced this technique, and the results of Sperry and his coworkers with their "split-brain" patients are now well known. As a result of the surgery each hemisphere receives fibers that allow it to see only the opposite side of the visual world. Likewise, each hemisphere predominantly receives information from the opposite side of the body and controls movements on the opposite side of the body. The surgery also isolates speech in those individuals with lateralized speech. Consequently, the dominant hemisphere (usually the left) is able to speak, and the nondominant hemisphere is not. Usually about a year or so is required for recovery from the surgical trauma. Within 2 years the typical patient is able to return to school, household duties, or work. A standard medical examination would not reveal anything unusual in the behavior of these patients, and their scores on standard tests are normal. The patients' everyday behavior appears similar to that of normal unified individuals.

Specific tests, however, can show differences between the functioning of split-brain patients and that of normal people. Each hemisphere can be shown to have its own sensations, percepts, thoughts, and memories that are not accessible to the other hemisphere. The usual test procedures involve presenting stimuli to one hemisphere and then testing each hemisphere for what transpired. For example, a person who is asked to touch an object out of view with one hand and then find a similar object with the other hand is unable to match the objects correctly. Odors presented to one nostril cannot be identified by the other, objects seen in one visual field cannot be recognized in the other, and so on. Although the hemispheres function independently, they both do so at a high level. High levels of function apply even to language skills. The nondominant hemisphere, although unable to speak, can understand instructions, read written words, match pictures to words, and go from written to spoken words. Language ability is best for nouns and poorer for verbs. The nondominant hemisphere also performs in a superior fashion on a variety of spatial tasks, including copying designs, reading faces, fitting forms into molds, and so on. The nondominant hemisphere also has a concept of self. It can recognize and identify social relations, pictures of the person, pictures of family members, acquaintances, pets and belongings, and historical and social figures. Each hemisphere also has a general awareness of body states such as those involved in hunger and fatigue.

Callosal Agenesis and Early Transections

Exceptions to the pattern of results obtained with adult commissurotomy patients are found in individuals who are born without a corpus callosum. These patients can perform interhemispheric comparisons of visual and tactile information. The interpretation of these results is that the patients have enhanced conduction in the remaining commissures (for example, for vision) and that they develop enhanced abilities to use their few uncrossed projections (for example, for tactile information). These patients do have deficits in some features of the tasks, however. There are a number of reports of poor transfer of information if stimuli are complex. Furthermore, nonspecific deficits in task performance have been reported in these patients. Lassonde presented pairs of stimuli to six patients with agenesis of the corpus callosum, asking them if the pairs were the same or different. Letters, numbers, colors, or forms were used. The pairs were presented one on top of the other in one visual field (intrahemispheric task), or one stimulus was presented in one visual field and the other stimulus in the other visual field (interhemispheric task). The acallosal group was equally accurate in identifying same-different pairs under both conditions. Their reaction times, however, were very slow for both forms of presentation. Lassonde suggests that the callosum participates in hemispheric activation as well as in transfer of information. Thus, the acallosal group has alternative ways of obtaining interhemispheric transfer of information but not of activation.

A particularly interesting question, using agenesis patients, has been discussed by Jeeves. This question concerns the development of language laterality and other asymmetries. One explanation of why language is lateralized to one hemisphere is that it gets a start there and then that hemisphere actively inhibits its development in the other hemisphere. In individuals with callosal agenesis, of course, the opportunity for such an inhibitory process to work is much reduced. Yet most of these people have language and other functions lateralized similarly to the general population. They also tend to be right-handed, as is the general population. This indicates that the corpus callosum and other commissures are not necessary for the development of asymmetries.

There are similarities in the effects of callosal agenesis and the effects of transections made early in life. Lassonde and coworkers compared the performance of five children aged 6 to 16 years on interhemispheric transfer of tactile information and motor learning. The younger children were found to be less affected by the transections than the older children. The researchers suggest that the younger children come to rely on ipsilateral pathways to obtain information and execute movements. That older children are more impaired suggests that if transections occur early it is possible that ipsilateral pathways make new connections, become functionally validated, or simply become more sensitive.

SYSTEMS DISCONNECTION

Sperry, Gazzaniga, and others have studied extensively the effects of hemispheric disconnection on behaviors related to both sensory and motor systems.

Olfaction

Unlike all the other senses, the olfactory system is not crossed. The input from the left nostril goes straight back to the left hemisphere, and the input anosmic - can't identify smells

from the right nostril goes to the right hemisphere. Fibers traveling through the anterior commissure join the olfactory regions in each hemisphere, just as fibers traveling through the corpus callosum join the motor cortex of each hemisphere.

If the anterior commissure is severed, odors presented to the right nostril cannot be named, because the speaking left hemisphere is disconnected from the information. Similarly, the right hemisphere has the information but has no control of speech. The olfactory function is still intact, however, because the patient can use the left hand to pick out an object, such as an orange, that corresponds to the odor smelled. In this case, no connection with speech is necessary, since the right hemisphere both contains the olfactory information and controls the left hand. If requested to use the right hand, the patient would be unable to pick out the object because the left hemisphere, which controls the right hand, is disconnected from the sensory information. Thus, the patient appears normal with one hand and anosmic with the other (Figure 15.4).

Vision

The visual system is crossed, so information flashed to one visual field travels selectively to the contralateral hemisphere. Recall that by using this fact researchers have demonstrated left and right visual-field superiorities for different types of input. For example, verbal material (such as words) is perceived more accurately when presented to the right visual field, presumably because the input travels to the left, speech, hemisphere. On the other hand, various types of visuospatial input produce a left visual-field superiority, since the right hemisphere appears to have a more important role in analyzing this information. Note, however, that the visual-field superiority observed in normal subjects is *relative*. That is, words presented to the left visual field, and hence right hemisphere, are sometimes perceived, although not as accurately or consistently as when they are presented to the right visual field. The relative effects occur because either hemisphere potentially has access to input to the opposite hemisphere via the corpus callosum,

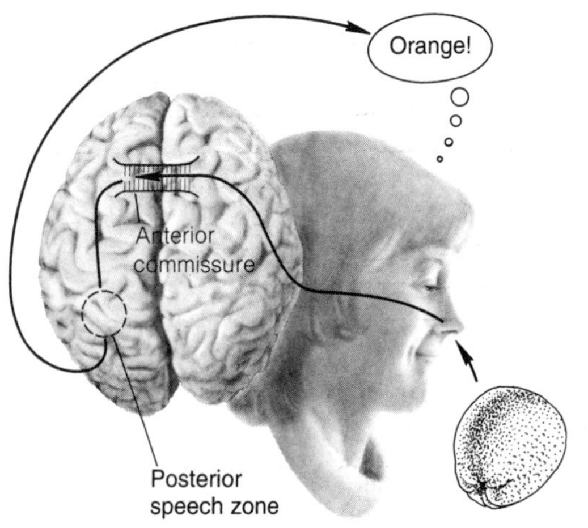

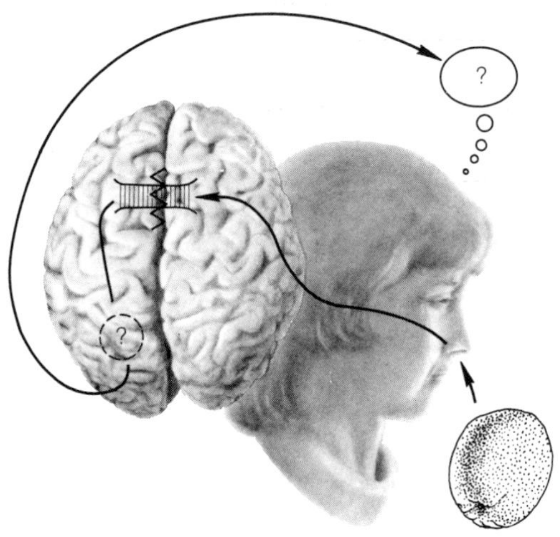

FIGURE 15.4. In the normal individual, olfactory input to the right nostril travels directly back into the right hemisphere and crosses the anterior commissure, thus gaining access to the left (speech) hemisphere. Anosmia results from section of the anterior commissure. (The jagged line indicates the lesion of the anterior commissure.) When the pathway is severed, the left hemisphere has no way of knowing what odor the right hemisphere perceived.

which joins the visual areas. In the commissurotomy patient there is no longer such access because the connection is severed. Since speech is housed in the left hemisphere of right-handed patients, visual information presented to the left visual field will be disconnected from verbal associations because the input goes to the right, nonlinguistic, hemisphere. Similarly, complex visual material presented to the right visual field will be inadequately processed, because it will not have access to the visuospatial abilities of the right hemisphere. It follows that if material is appropriately presented, it should be possible to demonstrate aphasia, agnosia, alexia, and **acopia** (the inability to copy a geometric design) in a patient who ordinarily exhibits none of these symptoms. This is indeed the case, as we will now demonstrate.

Consider the language-related deficits aphasia, alexia, and agnosia. If verbal material were presented to the left visual field, the commissurotomy patient would be unable to read it or to answer questions about it verbally, since the input is disconnected from the speech zones of the left hemisphere. Presentation of the same verbal material to the right visual field presents no difficulties, since the visual input projects to the verbal left hemisphere. Similarly, if an object is presented to the left visual field, the patient would be unable to name it and thus would appear to be either agnosic and aphasic. If presented to the right visual field, this same object would be correctly named, because the left visual cortex perceives the object and has access to the speech zones. Thus, we can see that the split-brain patient is aphasic, alexic, and agnosic if verbal material or an object requiring a verbal response is presented visually to the right hemisphere, but this person appears normal if material is presented to the left hemisphere.

A further deficit can be seen if the patient is asked to copy a complex visual figure. As discussed earlier, the right hemisphere is specialized for the perception of complex visual material. Since the right hemisphere controls the left hand we might predict that the left hand would be able to copy the figure but the right hand, deprived of the expertise of the right hemisphere, would be severely impaired. This is indeed the case: the left hand draws the figure well, whereas the right hand cannot and is thus acopic.

Somesthesis

Like the visual system, the somatosensory system is completely crossed. Sensations of touch in the left hand travel to the right hemisphere, and those in the right hand travel to the left hemisphere. An object placed in the left hand can be named because the tactile information projects to the right hemisphere, crosses to the left, and subsequently has access to the speech zones. Similarly, if a subject is blindfolded and the right hand is molded to form a particular shape, the left hand is able to copy the shape because the tactile information goes from the right hand to the left hemisphere, then across the corpus callosum to the right hemisphere, and the left hand forms the same shape.

If, however, the two hemispheres are disconnected from each other, the somatosensory functions of the left and right parts of the body become independent. For example, if some object is placed in the left hand of a blindfolded patient, who is then asked to choose the presented object from an array of objects, the left hand can pick out the object, but the right hand cannot. If an object is placed in a blindfolded patient's right hand, the patient can name it, but not if it is placed in the left hand because the sensory input is disconnected from the left (speech) hemisphere.

Disconnection effects can also be demonstrated without the use of objects. For example, if the patient is blindfolded and one hand is shaped in a particular way, the opposite hand is unable to mimic the posture. One hand has no way of "knowing" what the other hand is doing in the absence of input coming from the opposite hemisphere via the corpus callosum. If the patient is not blindfolded, however, he or she can find out what the opposite hand is doing simply by looking at it.

Audition

The auditory system is somewhat more complex than the other systems because it has both crossed and uncrossed connections. Although the left hemisphere appears to receive most of its input from the right ear, it also receives input from the left ear. Therefore, words played into the left ear can travel directly to the left hemisphere or can go to the right hemisphere and then to the left via the corpus callosum. In normal subjects dichotic-listening tasks clearly show that the contralateral input is preferred because words presented to the right ear are selectively perceived over words presented to the left ear. Remember, however, that this difference is relative, because some words presented to the left ear are also reported.

The bilateral anatomical arrangement just described appears to reduce the effects of disconnection, but nevertheless one effect has been demonstrated. In the dichotic-listening task, input from the left ear is totally suppressed; the patient reports only those words played to the right ear. That is, digits or words played to the right ear are reported, but no input to the left ear is reported. This is a little surprising, since words played to the left ear, even under these conditions, would be expected to attain some direct access to the left hemisphere. This direct access does not appear to occur.

Movement

Because the motor system is largely crossed, we might predict that disconnection of the hemispheres would induce several kinds of motor difficulties. First, on any task involving either a verbal command for the left hand to follow or verbal material for the left hand to write, a form of apraxia and agraphia could be expected, because the left hand would not receive instructions from the left hemisphere. That is, the left hand would be unable to obey the command (apraxia) or to write (agraphia). These disabilities would not be seen in the right hand because it has access to the speech hemisphere. Similarly, if the right hand were asked to copy a geometric design it might be impaired (acopia) because it is disconnected from the right hemisphere, which ordinarily has a preferred role in the drawing of this type of material. These symptoms of disconnection are in fact observed in commissurotomy patients, although the severity of the deficit declines significantly over time after surgery, possibly because the left hemisphere's ipsilateral control of movement is being used.

A second situation that might be expected to produce severe motor deficits in commissurotomy patients is one in which the two arms must be used in cooperation. Ordinarily, one hand is informed of what the other is doing via the corpus callosum. Preilowski and later Zaidel and Sperry examined the effect of disconnection of this type of bimanual cooperative movement. Patients were severely impaired at alternating tapping movements of the index fingers. Similarly, in a task similar to an Etch-a-Sketch, one requiring that a line inclined at an angle be traced, callosal patients did very poorly. This task requires the use of two cranks, one operated by each hand; one crank moves the tracing pen vertically, the other moves it horizontally. A high degree of manual cooperation is required to trace a diagonal line smoothly. If the hemispheres have been disconnected, this cooperation is severely retarded, because the left and right motor systems cannot gain information about what the opposite side is doing, except indirectly, by the patient's watching them.

Dramatic illustrations of conflict between hands can be seen in the following description:

> In one case the patient (W. J.) would repeatedly pick up a newspaper with his right hand and lay it down with his left hand. This would be performed several times until finally the left hand threw the newspaper on the floor. Another patient (R. Y.) was described by a physiotherapist: "He was buttoning his shirt with his right hand and the left hand was coming along just behind it undoing the buttons just as quickly as he could fasten them." However, as in the praxic impairments described earlier, instances of intermanual conflict were generally confined to the first postoperative months and again seemed related to the age of the patient and extent of extra-callosal damage. It is of interest to note that the

same patients while inhibiting these episodes of intermanual conflict were able to use their left hand in a purposeful and cooperative manner when "not thinking of what they were doing." For example, they could pour coffee out of a pot held in the right hand into a cup held by its handle with the left hand. The above mentioned peculiarities in motor functions were observed only in the complete split-brain patients. (Preilowski, 1975, p. 119)

The Problem of Partial Disconnection

Results from tests of callosal patients raise the question of whether a partial section of the corpus callosum would have as severe effects as a complete disconnection. Recently, surgeons have experimented with partial surgical disconnection of the hemispheres, hoping to attain the same clinical relief from seizures but with fewer neuropsychological side effects. Although the results are still preliminary, partial disconnection, in which the posterior part of the corpus callosum is left intact, appears to combine markedly milder effects than complete commissurotomy with the same therapeutic benefits. For example, Sperry and colleagues have found that patients with partial disconnection are significantly better at motor tasks such as the Etch-a-Sketch. Research on monkeys with partial commissurotomies suggests that the posterior portion of the corpus callosum (splenium) subserves visual transfer (as does the anterior commissure), whereas the region just in front of the splenium affects somatosensory transfer. The functions of the more anterior portions of the corpus callosum are largely unknown, but transfer of motor information is presumed to be one such function.

Conclusions

The results of studies on surgical disconnection of the hemispheres indicate that many symptoms, including aphasia, alexia, agnosia, agraphia, acopia, and apraxia, can be demonstrated in the *absence of any direct damage* to particular cytoarchitectonic or functional neocortical regions. They can also occur for one side of the body and not the other. Symptoms like aphasia, agnosia, and so forth can be thought of as resulting from *disconnection* of cortical regions rather than necessarily from damage *to* cortical regions. We shall return to this idea shortly.

LESION EFFECTS REINTERPRETED AS DISCONNECTION SYNDROMES

In 1965, Geschwind published a theoretically significant monograph, "Disconnexion Syndromes in Animals and Man," that tied together a vast amount of literature and anticipated many of the effects of callosal surgery. Geschwind's thesis was that certain types of behavioral deficits result from disconnections between the hemispheres, within a hemisphere, or a combination of both. The value of this monograph is not its review of the data, but rather its reintroduction of the concept first proposed by Dejerine and Liepmann nearly 70 years earlier, that disconnecting neocortical regions can cause a variety of neurological symptoms. To demonstrate the utility of the model, we will discuss only the three classic symptoms of left hemisphere damage: apraxia, agnosia, and alexia.

Apraxia

Early in this chapter we noted that if a lesion of the corpus callosum disconnected the left hand from the left hemisphere, that hand would be unable to respond to verbal commands and would be considered apraxic. Suppose, however, that the right hand is unable to respond to verbal commands. Geschwind speculated that this deficit results from a lesion in the left hemisphere that disconnects its motor cortex (which controls the right hand) from the speech zone; thus, the right hand could not respond to verbal commands and would be considered apraxic.

Although Geschwind's model can explain bilateral apraxia in some patients, it must be emphasized that disconnection is not the only cause of apraxia. Because the posterior cortex has direct access to the subcortical neural mechanisms of arm and body movements (see Chapter 7), parietal input need not go through the motor cortex except for control of finger movements. Further, as we noted earlier, patients with sections of the corpus callosum are initially apraxic but show substantial recovery despite a disconnection of the motor cortex of the left and right hemispheres.

Agnosia and Alexia

Geschwind theorized that agnosia and alexia can be produced by disconnecting the posterior speech area from the visual association cortex. They can be produced by a lesion that disconnects the visual association region on the left from the speech zone or by a lesion that disconnects the right visual association cortex from the speech zone by damaging the corpus callosum, as illustrated in Figure 15.5. Thus, the patient, although able to talk, is unable to identify words or objects because the visual information is disconnected from the posterior speech zone in the left hemisphere.

EXPERIMENTAL VERIFICATION OF DISCONNECTION EFFECTS

Disconnection can be used experimentally to demonstrate the function of various brain regions. We began this chapter with a discussion of Downer's ingenious experiment to demonstrate the effects of temporal lobectomy. Mishkin and others have disconnected different brain areas in animals to demonstrate the functional connections in the hierarchical organization of the visual system and, more recently, of the somatosensory system. This research clearly demonstrates the usefulness of the disconnection approach and has led to significant progress in our understanding of the sensory systems.

In the visual system, connections in each hemisphere run from area V1 to area V2 and to areas

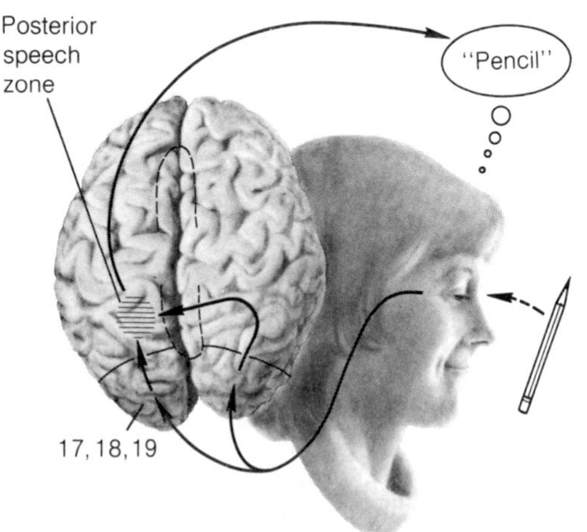

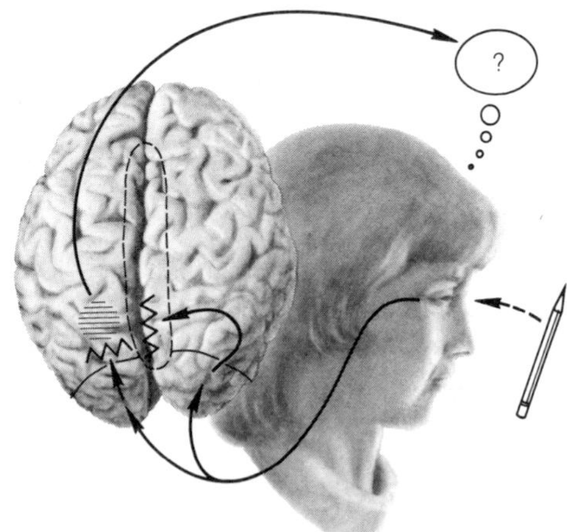

FIGURE 15.5. Geschwind's model of agnosia and alexia resulting from disconnection of the visual cortex from the posterior speech zone. (The jagged lines indicate the lesion of the pathways.) Normally, the visual input of both hemispheres travels to the posterior speech zone and association cortex, where it is processed to allow speech describing the written word or object. In the absence of the connection, processing of the visual input is no longer possible, and agnosia and alexia result.

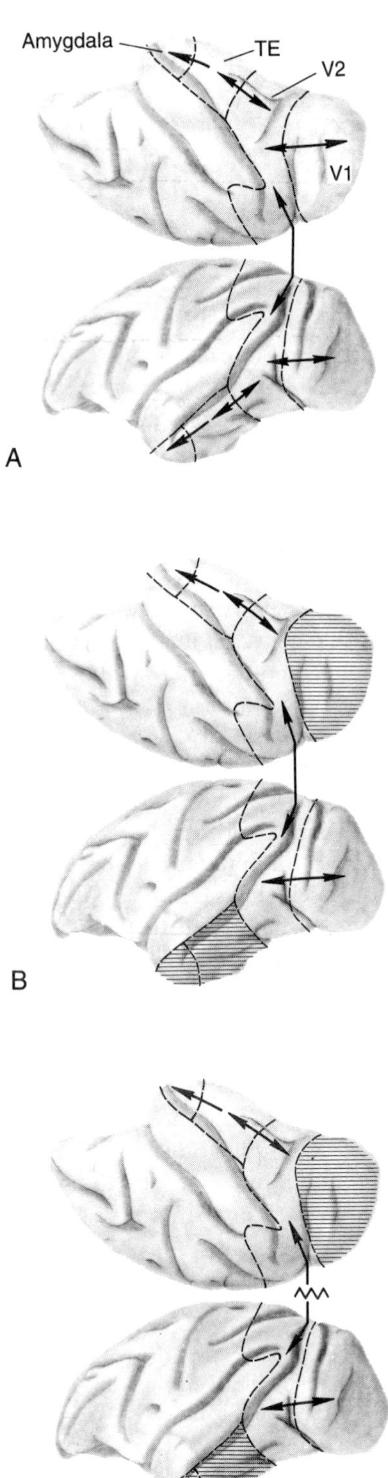

FIGURE 15.6. Disconnection effects in the visual system of monkeys. *A*. The visual system is intact. *B*. The left visual cortex still has access to the visual association cortex of the right hemisphere, and so vision is still possible. *C*. The intact components of the visual system are disconnected, producing major visual deficits. (After Mishkin, 1979.)

V3, V4, and V5 in the same hemisphere (Figure 15.6A). Connections from V3, V4, and V5 cross the corpus callosum to the analogous areas on the opposite side, as well as connecting with area TE on the same side. Area TE connects to the anterior temporal cortex (area 21) and the amygdala on the same side and connects via the anterior commissure to these structures on the opposite side. What would happen to vision if the connections were cut? This question has been addressed in experiments using monkeys.

Such experiments require that the monkeys first be tested to determine their visual capabilities. The easiest method is to teach the animal a visual discrimination, such as between a "+" and a "0." Food reinforcement is associated with one stimulus and not with the other. The monkey's task is to identify the correct stimulus and respond to it. Control monkeys learn this problem in 100 to 150 trials or fewer, and so if a monkey that has been lesioned fails to learn this problem in 1000 trials, it is assumed that it will not learn it at all; the lesion can be inferred to have some important effect on the monkey's ability to discriminate between visual stimuli.

By using tasks of this sort, Mishkin and others have demonstrated that bilateral lesions in areas V1, V2, or TE result in an impaired, or abolished, ability to solve visual-discrimination problems. Because unilateral lesions do not have such an effect, what seems to be necessary is one intact trio of areas V1, V2, and TE. There is, however, one constraint: the remaining regions must be connected. Thus, in Figure 15.6B, a lesion in area V1 on the right and in TE on the left does not disturb performance, since there is still an intact system that can be used. If the connection between the hemispheres is now severed, the neocortical areas are still intact but are not connected, and the result is failure on the visual-discrimination problem (Figure 15.6C). Clearly, the neocortical regions do not function properly if they are not connected to one another.

Mishkin first studied area TE, thinking it to be the final step in the neocortical visual system. More recently he has studied the problem of how visual stimuli might gain what he calls "motivational" or "emotional" significance. Monkeys with bilateral temporal lobectomies including the amygdala attach no significance to visual stimuli. That is, they will repeatedly taste nasty-tasting objects or place inedible objects in their mouths. In his 1965 paper Geschwind proposed that this symptom represents a disconnection of the amygdala from the visual system. That is, although an animal's visual sensory system might be intact, the animal would behave as if it were not because it is disconnected from another system that attaches meaning to visual information. Figure 15.7A illustrates the additional connections when the amygdala is included in an extended visual system. Area TE connects with the amygdala on the same side and connects with the amygdala on the opposite side via the anterior commissure.

To test Geschwind's proposal, Mishkin devised the experiment illustrated in Figures 15.7B and 15.7C. The amygdala was lesioned on the left and the inferior temporal cortex on the right. This arrangement left one complete system of areas V1, V2, TE, and the amygdala; using it, the monkey's performance on visual problems was normal, as would be expected. The anterior commissure was then cut, leaving all the necessary pieces of the system intact but disconnecting the intact amygdala from the neocortical portion of the system.

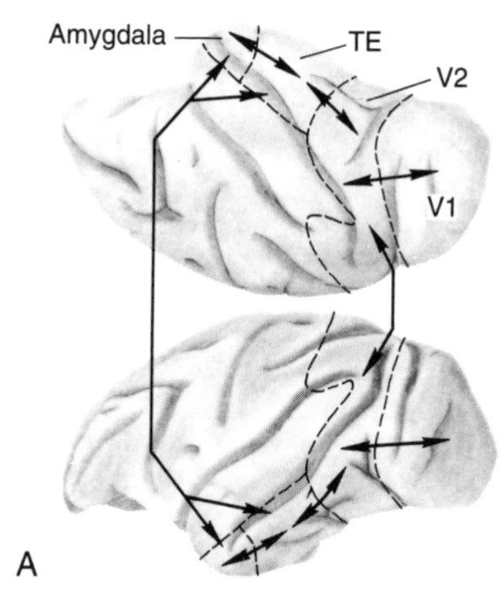

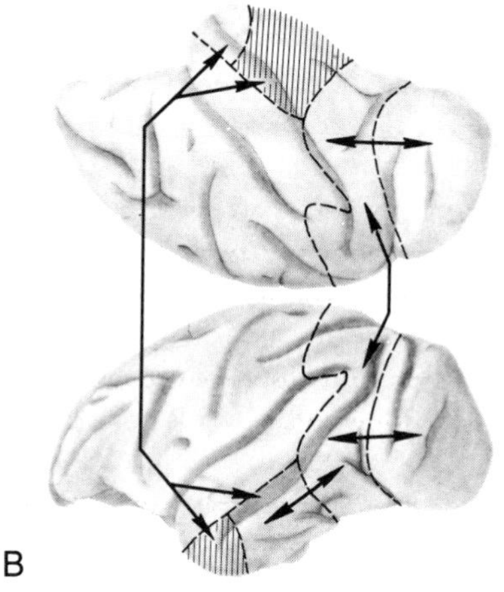

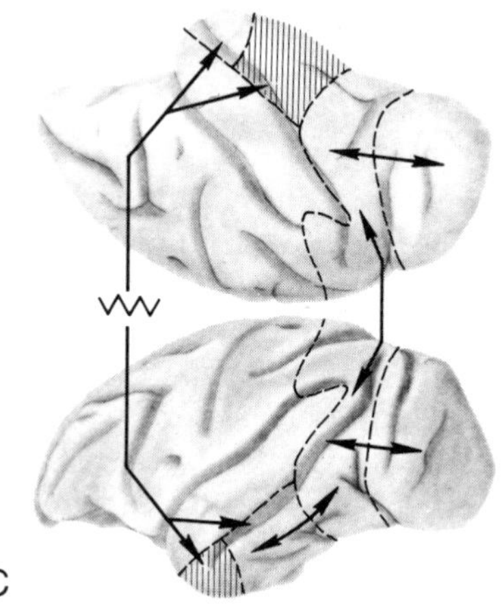

FIGURE 15.7. Disconnection of affect from visual input. *A.* The connections of the normal visual system, including the callosal and anterior commissural connections. *B.* Even if parts of the system are damaged, it can still function. *C.* If the anterior commissure is severed, visual input is separated from affect, resulting in visual deficits. (After Mishkin, 1979.)

Performance on visual problems instantly deteriorated, indicating that there was some interruption of the normal processing of visual material, as would be predicted from Geschwind's model.

In another application of the disconnection model to studying the visual system, Nakamura and Mishkin have shown blindness in monkeys after disconnection of the intact visual system from nonvisual regions. Monkeys received unilateral decortications in which the visual areas (in addition to the motor and limbic cortex) were spared. Then the cerebral commissures and contralateral optic tract were severed. Unexpectedly, the animals were blind! None of the animals showed any detectable reaction to visually presented stimuli, whether these were food, fearful objects, threats, or sudden movements. When placed in an unfamiliar environment, they bumped into obstacles and found food objects only by touching them accidentally on tactile exploration. Although some of the monkeys showed some recovery over time, others did not, remaining functionally blind even 2 years after surgery. Further experiments revealed that the visual cortex was still functioning electrophysiologically, yet the animals behaved as though it no longer functioned at all. The results point to an important role of the nonvisual cortex in visual perception and demonstrate the importance of studying the connections to, as well as the areas of, a functional system.

CONCLUSIONS

There are a number of issues we have not touched upon in this chapter that should be mentioned briefly in closing. There are significant species differences in the anatomy and functions of interconnecting hemispheric commissures. Some primitive marsupials do not have a corpus callosum. Some birds, although having interhemispheric commissures, seem to behave as might humans who have no corpus callosum. Sherry has reported that if an occluder is placed over the eye of a food-catching bird, the information it stores in its contralateral hemisphere about where its food is located is not accessible to the other eye. The animals apparently have separate memory stores for each eye. There are also suggestions that a variety of individual differences exist in callosal size and patterns. For example, Witelson reported that the corpus callosum is larger in left-handers than in right-handers.

We might also suggest that disconnection hypotheses could be applicable to interpretations of various developmental stages of infants. It is well known that myelination of fibers is one of the last events in the maturation of neural systems. Therefore, if certain connections have not matured while others have, features of behavior may very well parallel symptoms observed in disconnection cases. For example, during the course of development infants will extend their arms to reach for objects in the visual field of the limb. If the object moves across the visual midline, the hand will not follow it, but the other hand will be extended to grasp for it. A little later in development, the infant will follow the object with a hand even if the object crosses the midline. This behavior could be a result of hemispheric disconnection, attributable to immaturity or a lack of myelination of the interhemispheric pathways. Similarly, careful consideration of other behaviors displayed by infants could be interpreted in the same way. Mitchel has found that human infants younger than about 1 year are like split-brain patients in that they are unable to transfer information about objects obtained by touch. In the experiments, infants were conditioned to expect that someone would play "peek-a-boo" on one or the other side of their body, shortly after they were allowed to feel an object of a certain texture in one hand. Then they were allowed to feel the object in the other hand. If intermanual transfer occurred, it was expected that they would display the conditioned response, which they did not. Rudy and Stadler-Morris found that rats trained on a spatial-navigation task learned the task with one hemisphere at 22 days of age but could not learn it with the other. By the time they were 25 days old they did display interocular equivalence. The researchers suggest that the 22-day-old rat behaves like a split-brain animal.

infants < 1yr. old are like split brains (unable to transfer info)

Disconnections may be relevant to at least two other lines of inquiry. First, it has been reported that patients with schizophrenia have an enlargement of the corpus callosum. Observations of this effect have led Beaumont and Dimond to suggest that schizophrenics may show some abnormalities in the transfer of information between the hemispheres. Subsequently, a number of reports seem to confirm this suggestion. Schrift and coworkers, although finding evidence of interhemispheric transfer deficits, suggest that these may not be specific to schizophrenia and are difficult to dissociate from focal or hemispheric impairment. Second, people working with patients who have suffered head trauma have often been puzzled by the severe chronic impairments these patients may display even with only minimal direct brain injury. Gennarelli and his coworkers have suggested that the impairments may be due to diffuse axonal injury. Head trauma often causes twisting and shearing of the two hemispheres, which could result in a traumatic form of disconnection. Indeed, Fantie studied a group of university students with relatively mild closed-head injuries and no apparent deficits and found impairments in callosal transfer of tactile information.

Finally, many people have written about the implications of the split-brain cases to support theories of mind and concepts of individuality. We have not touched upon this issue. It is certainly the case that for dualists, who hold that the brain has a separate corresponding mental representation, there are compelling reasons to consider that there are two brains and two minds in split-brain individuals. For materialists, the philosophical implications are not so weighty. But for everyone, there is a challenge to understand how individuals with separated hemispheres function in a seemingly integrated way.

REFERENCES

Beaumont, J., and S. Dimond. Brain disconnection and schizophrenia. *British Journal of Psychiatry* 123:661–662, 1973.

Colonnier, M. Notes on the early history of the corpus callosum with an introduction to the morphological papers published in this Festschrift. In F. Lepore, M. Ptito, and H. H. Jasper, eds. *Two Hemispheres—One Brain*. New York: Alan R. Liss, 1986.

Downer, J. L. de C. Changes in visual gnostic functions and emotional behavior following unilateral temporal pole damage in the "split-brain" monkey. *Nature* 191:50–51, 1961.

Gazzaniga, M. S. *The Bisected Brain*. New York: Appleton-Century-Crofts, 1970.

Gennarelli, T. A., J. H. Adams, and D. I. Graham. Diffuse axonal injury—a new conceptual approach to an old problem. In A. Baethmann, K. G. Go, and A. Unterberg, eds. *Mechanisms of Secondary Brain Damage*. New York: Plenum, 1986.

Geschwind, N. Disconnexion syndromes in animals and man. *Brain* 88:237–294, 585–644, 1965.

Jeeves, M. A. Callosal agenesis: Neuronal and developmental adaptions. In F. Lepore, M. Ptito, and H. H. Jasper, eds. *Two Hemispheres—One Brain*. New York: Alan R. Liss, 1986.

Lassonde, M. The facilitatory influence of the corpus callosum on intrahemispheric processing. In F. Lepore, M. Ptito, and H. H. Jasper, eds. *Two Hemispheres—One Brain*. New York: Alan R. Liss, 1986.

Lassonde, M., H. Sauerwein, G. Geoffroy, and M. Decarie. Effects of early and late transection of the corpus callosum in children. *Brain* 109:953–967, 1986.

Lepore, F., M. Ptito, and H. H. Jasper, eds. *Two Hemispheres—One Brain*. New York: Alan R. Liss, 1986.

Mishkin, M. Analogous neural models for tactile and visual learning. *Neuropsychologia* 17:139–152, 1979.

Mitchel, G. F. Self-generated experience and the development of lateralized neurobehavioral organization in infants. *Advances in the Study of Behavior* 17:61–83, 1987.

Myers, R. E. Functions of the corpus callosum in interocular transfer. *Brain* 57:358–363, 1956.

Nakamura, R. K., and M. Mishkin. Blindness in monkeys following non-visual cortical lesions. *Brain Research* 188:572–577, 1980.

Pandya, D. N., and B. Seltzer. The topography of commissural fibers. In F. Lepore, M. Ptito, and H. H. Jasper, eds. *Two Hemispheres—One Brain*. New York: Alan R. Liss, 1986.

Preilowski, B. Bilateral motor interaction: Perceptual-motor performance of partial and complete "split-brain" patients. In K. J. Zulch, O. Creutzfeldt, and G. C. Galbraith, eds. *Cerebral Localization*. Berlin and New York: Springer-Verlag, 1975.

Rudy, J. W., and S. Stadler-Morris. Development of interocular equivalence in rats trained on a distal-cue navigation task. *Behavioral Neuroscience* 101:141–143, 1987.

Schrift, M. J., H. Bandla, P. Shah, and M. A. Taylor. Interhemispheric transfer in major psychoses. *Journal of Nervous and Mental Disease* 174:203–207, 1986.

Sherry, D. F. Food storage by birds and mammals. *Advances in the Study of Behavior* 15:153–183, 1985.

Sperry, R. W. Lateral specialization in the surgically separated hemispheres. In F. O. Schmitt and F. G. Worden, eds. *Neurosciences: Third Study Program*. Cambridge, Mass.: MIT Press, 1974.

Spiegler, B. J., and M. Mishkin. Evidence for the sequential participation of inferior temporal cortex and amygdala in the acquisition of stimulus-reward associations. *Behavioral Brain Research* 3:303–317, 1981.

Steele-Russell, I., M. W. Van Hof, and G. Berlucchi, eds. *Structure and Function of Cerebral Commissures*. London: Macmillan and Co., 1979.

Witelson, S. F. Wires of the mind: Anatomical variation in the corpus callosum in relation to hemispheric specialization and integration. In F. Lepore, M. Ptito, and H. H. Jasper, eds. *Two Hemispheres—One Brain*. New York: Alan R. Liss, 1986.

Zaidel, D., and R. W. Sperry. Some long term motor effects of cerebral commissurotomy in man. *Neuropsychologia* 15:193–204, 1977.

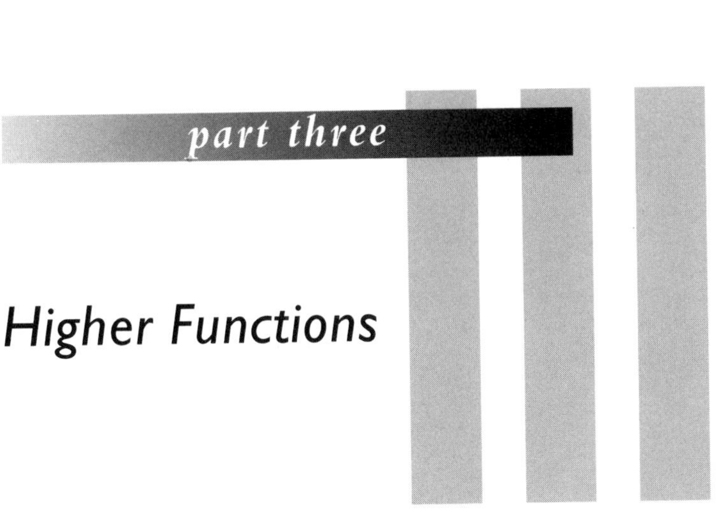

part three

Higher Functions

Just as there has been a long tradition in neurology of studying the lobes of the brain, so there has been a long tradition in psychology of studying hypothetical functions of memory, language, emotion, space, and attention. Chapters 16–20 examine brain function from the perspective of the psychologist with an interest in these functions. Much of the basic material has been introduced in Part Two, but the perspective should be sufficiently different and fresh to make the retelling of the tale worthwhile.

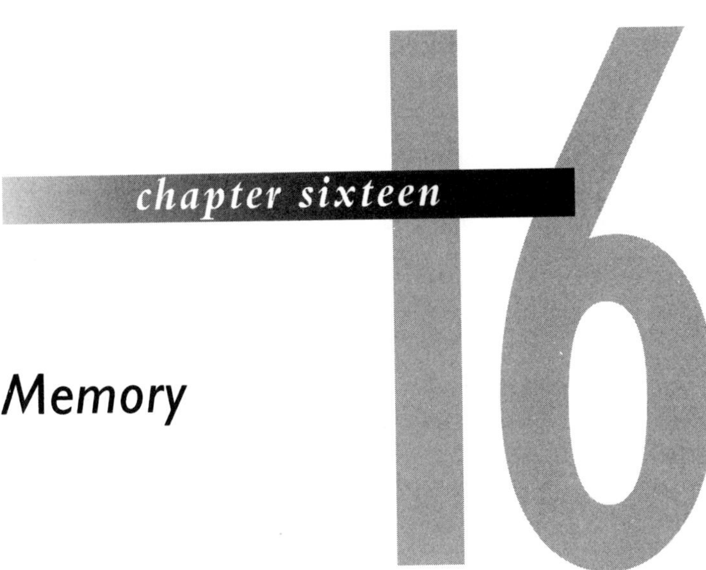

chapter sixteen

Memory

Psychologists began studying memory in the mid-19th century; the first monograph, Ebbinghaus's, was published in 1885. The 1880s have been described as a revolutionary decade for memory research because it marked the beginnings of the description of memory disorders. The 1980s have been described as a second decade of revolution by Schacter because it marks the realization that memory comes in many different forms. Accompanying the discovery of forms of memory have been new approaches to the investigation of the neural basis of memory. These include new theoretical developments, the increasing interest by cognitive psychologists in brain function, and the use of brain imaging techniques.

SOURCES OF MEMORY LOSS

We have all suffered **amnesia,** or memory loss. The most dramatic example of forgetting is infantile amnesia. Although the early years are generally regarded as being a time of critical importance in a child's development, they are not consciously remembered in adulthood. Of course, it is possible that the information is still there but can no longer be retrieved because the developing forebrain either disrupts the memory or blocks its retrieval. A more plausible explanation is that one memory system is used by infants and another one develops for adults. Memories seem to be lost because they are not stored in the new conscious adult system.

Adults also forget, as witnessed by people who turn up with no knowledge of their previous life but with intact skills and language. An acute form of amnesia is described by Fisher and Adams. In **transient global amnesia** the onset is sudden and includes an inability to form new memories as well as a loss of old memories, without apparent precipitating cause. This syndrome has been linked to concussion, migraine, hypoglycemia, and epilepsy, as well as to interruption of blood flow in the posterior cerebral artery from either a transient ischemic attack or an embolism. Transient global amnesia can be a one-time event, but Markowitsch suggests that there also can be permanent memory loss. Indeed, a thorough study by Mazzucchi and colleagues shows that there is a significant chronic memory loss in transient global amnesia; this is usually overlooked because of the dramatic recovery and because careful memory testing is seldom done.

transient global amnesia - sudden onset, retro + anterograde, no apparent cause -can be one time or can be permanent

Head injuries commonly produce a form of amnesia, the severity of the injury determining the characteristics of the amnesia. There is typically a transient loss of consciousness followed by a short period of confusion. The period forgotten generally shrinks over time, often leaving a residual amnesia of only a few seconds to a minute for events immediately preceding the injury. Duration of the posttraumatic amnesia varies. In one series of patients with severe head injuries, Whitty and Zangwill found that 10% had durations of less than 1 week, 30% had durations of 2 to 3 weeks, and the remaining 60% had durations of more than 3 weeks. Sometimes certain events, such as the visit of a relative or some unusual occurrence, are retained as "islands of memory" during this amnesic period. Posttraumatic amnesia commonly ends quite abruptly, often after a period of natural sleep.

Amnesia can also be produced by other manipulations. Memory loss often follows use of minor tranquilizers or alcohol. One therapy for depression, electroconvulsive shock, can produce memory loss, and the technique has been used extensively to model amnesia in animal experiments. Convulsive therapy with a drug called Metrazol was discovered by von Meduna in 1933. He thought that people with epilepsy could not be schizophrenic and so believed that drug-induced seizures could cure insanity. In 1937, Cerletti and Bini replaced Metrazol with electricity to produce **electroconvulsive shock therapy** (**ECT** or **ECS**). In ECT, 70V to 120V alternating current is passed from one side of the brain to the other through electrodes placed on the skull. The treatment can be effective for depression, but a side effect is an adverse effect on memory. In a 1982 review, Taylor and associates reached several conclusions about the nature of the memory loss: (1) bilateral ECT often induces memory changes, even with the standard number of treatments (eight or nine); (2) the effects of ECT on memory appear to be cumulative, greater effects being seen with successive treatments; (3) the majority of cognitive and memory defects appear to be entirely reversible, with a return to pretreatment levels of function or better within 6 to 7 months; (4) some subtle but persistent defects may be found some months after ECT, especially in personal or autobiographical material; and (5) the persistent defects tend to be irritating rather than seriously incapacitating. There have been claims that unilateral ECT has significantly less effect on memory than bilaterial ECT. It seems reasonable to expect that unilateral ECT on the left might preferentially disturb verbally mediated memory, whereas unilateral ECT on the right might preferentially disturb nonverbal memory.

Damage to restricted portions of the brain can also cause amnesia, which often takes very curious forms. For example, there are clinical reports of people who become amnesic for the meaning of nouns, but not verbs, and vice versa. There are other reports of people who become amnesic for animals, but not people, or who become amnesic for human faces but not for other objects.

There are also the everyday little amnesias: we forget people's names, faces, our keys, and so on. We also rapidly forget things that we do not need to know, such as telephone numbers we need but once. This kind of amnesia can become bothersome to people as they age and begin to suffer from "old timer's disease." This amnesia is often first characterized by amnesias for the names of people we do not often meet and items of information that we encounter in newspapers and in conversation. For some people, memory disorders of aging can become incapacitating, as occurs in Alzheimer's disease, which is characterized by the loss of many past memories and is accompanied by the loss of neurons and by other pathologies in the cortex.

What do all these examples demonstrate? They suggest that there are different kinds of memory, one of which begins at about 2 years of age. They suggest that memories can be lost and that recent memories are the most fragile. They suggest that memories for personal identity are different from memories for skills and language because amnesics can lose one but not the other. They suggest that the ability to form new memories can be lost while old memories are retained, but they also suggest that both kinds of memories can be lost and retained together. In an attempt to classify memory disorders, at least two approaches have been taken: the first suggests that there is a memory center in the brain, and the second suggests that there are many kinds of memories, each of which has its own brain location. The second approach has been gaining favor recently.

Before beginning an explanation of memory disorders, we will define a few terms. Amnesia for new information is called **anterograde amnesia.** Amnesia for previously learned information is called **retrograde amnesia.** Memory for things that are retained only for a short period of time, such as telephone numbers or directions to a store, is called **short-term memory.** Memory for things that are remembered for a long period of time, such as your own telephone number or the route to reach school, is called **long-term memory.** The search for the neural basis of memory is directed in large part toward these different processes.

NEUROPSYCHOLOGICAL INVESTIGATION OF MEMORY

The formal neuropsychological study of memory dates back to about 1915, when Karl Lashley embarked on a lifetime project to identify the neural locations of learned habits. In most of his experiments he either removed portions of the neocortex or made cuts of fiber pathways hoping to prevent transcortical communication between the sensory and motor regions of the cortex. After hundreds of experiments, Lashley was still unable to interfere with specific memories. In 1950, he concluded that "it is not possible to demonstrate the isolated localization of a memory trace anywhere in the nervous system. Limited regions may be essential for learning or retention of a particular activity, but the engram is represented throughout the region." (Lashley, 1950)

It turns out that Lashley was prophetic in this conclusion, but the study of memory was to take a decided detour. Only 3 years later, in 1953, a neurosurgeon named William Scoville inadvertently made one of the most influential findings in neuropsychology when he operated on the now-famous patient H. M. Bilateral removal of the medial temporal lobes in H. M. (Figure 16.1) made him amnesic for virtually all events *following* the operation. No one could have predicted from Lashley's extensive work that removal of any structure would result in a person remembering things from the distant past but not from the recent past! The surgery had interfered with the process of storing or retrieving new memories but had not touched previously stored memories. The case of H. M. revolutionized the study of the memory process and shifted the emphasis from a search for the location of memory to an analysis of the process of storing memories. Indeed, Scoville and Milner's description of H. M. is probably the second most influential observation ever made in neuropsychology, with only Broca's surpassing it. Because H. M. has been so influential we will begin with a short description of his case.

The Case of H. M.

In the 1950s, the importance of the temporal lobes in human memory was demonstrated in reports describing several patients with bilateral hippocampal damage. Scoville and Milner's patient H. M. is the most thoroughly studied, having been followed for more than 35 years. He was a motor winder by trade and had experienced generalized epileptic seizures that had grown progressively worse in frequency and severity despite very high doses of medication. On 23 August 1953, William Scoville performed a bilateral medial temporal lobe resection (see Figure 16.1) in an attempt to stop the seizures. Afterward H. M. experienced a severe anterograde amnesia that has persisted with little improvement to this day:

> H. M.'s IQ is above average (118 on the Wechsler Adult Intelligence Scale), and he performed normally on perceptual tests. H. M.'s memory for events prior to the surgery is good, as is his capacity to recall remote events such as incidents from his school days or jobs he held in his late teens or early twenties,

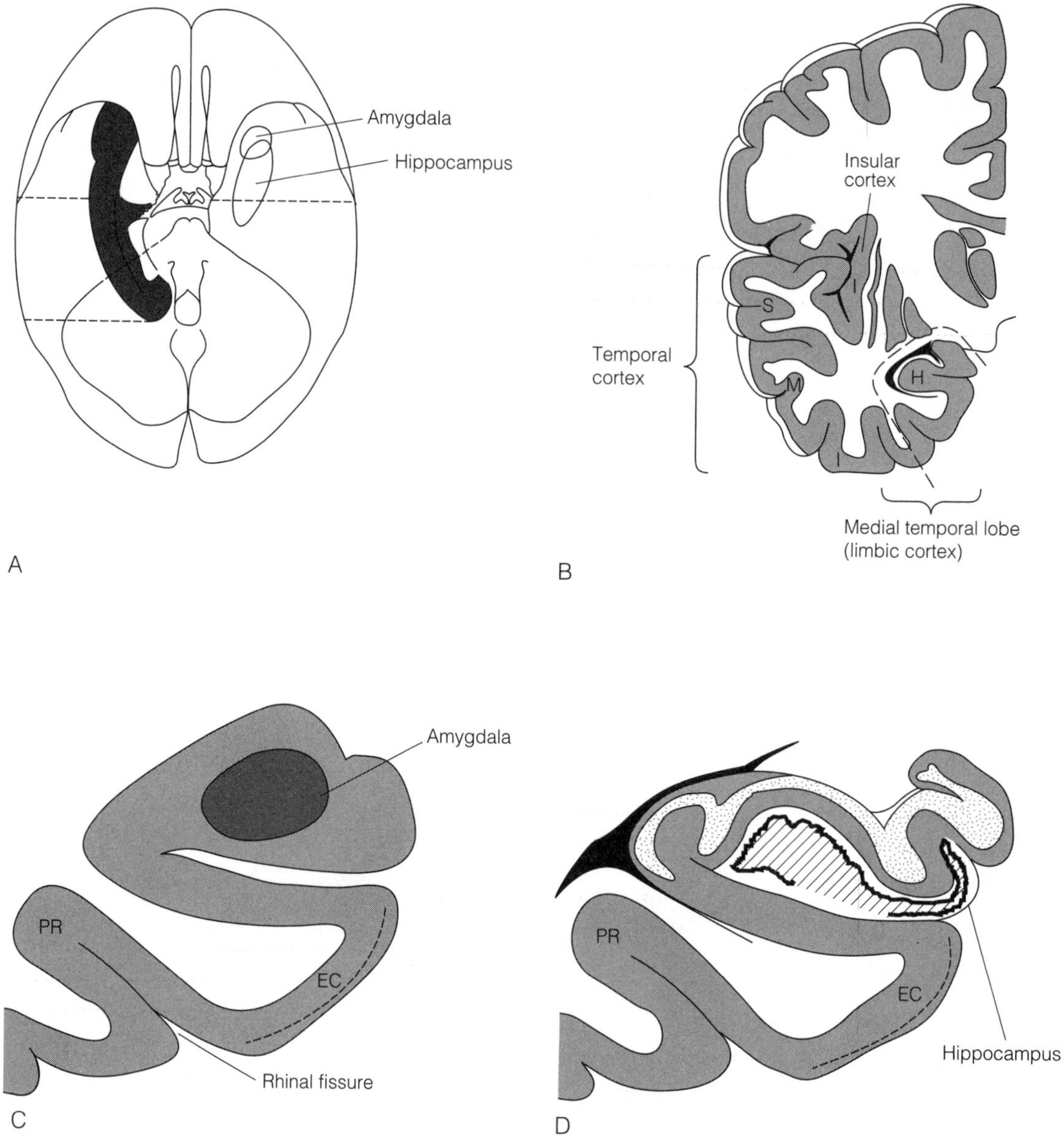

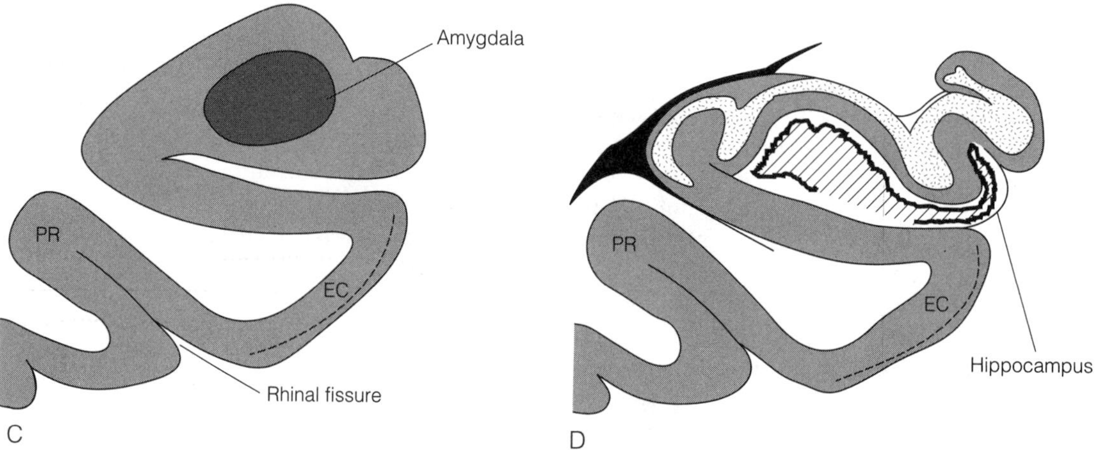

FIGURE 16.1. *A*. The left side of the figure shows the extent of H. M.'s lesion; the right side has been left intact to show the approximate location of the amygdala and hippocampus. *B*. A coronal section through the brain of one hemisphere at the level of the hippocampus (H) showing the location of the temporal neocortex (S, M, and I are superior, middle, and inferior temporal gyri) and the medial temporal limbic area. The dashed line indicates the approximate area of H. M.'s lesion. *C*. A coronal section through the anterior portion of the limbic area showing the location of the amygdala. *D*. A coronal section through the medial portion of the limbic area showing the location of the hippocampus. Note the location in *C* and *D* of the entorhinal cortex (EC) and perirhinal cortex (PR, the area around the rhinal fissure).

prior to his surgery. Socially, H. M. is quiet and well mannered. He dresses neatly but has to be reminded when to shave. He speaks in a monotone but articulates his words well and has a vocabulary in keeping with his above-average intelligence. His language comprehension is normal and he understands complex verbal material, including jokes, and he can engage in sophisticated conversations.

H. M.'s recall of personal events is interesting and enlightening, as witnessed by the following description. Notice his severe handicap in everyday life and his ability to remember some events but only after prolonged repetition.

H. M. has been cared for all this time by his mother, who usually accompanies him wherever he goes. It so happened, however, that in 1966 the mother was in Hartford Hospital, recovering from a minor operation, just when H. M. was about to leave for Boston. It was his father, therefore, who packed H. M.'s clothes for him and brought him to meet us at Dr. Scoville's office prior to the journey. The father had also taken the patient to visit his mother in the hospital that very morning, the third such visit within a week. Yet when we questioned H. M., he seemed not to remember any of these visits, although he expressed a vague idea that something might have happened to his mother. On the journey to Boston, he kept saying that he felt a little uneasy and wondered if something might be wrong with one of his parents, though he could not be sure which one. On being asked who had packed his bag for the trip, he said "Seems like it was my mother. But then that's what I'm not sure about. If there is something wrong with my mother, then it could have been my father." Despite our explaining the situation to him repeatedly during the journey, H. M. was never able to give a clear account of what had happened, and was still feeling "uneasy" when he reached Boston, wondering if something was "wrong" with one of his parents. Gradually, this uneasiness wore off, and although he was told repeatedly that he could telephone home any time he wished, he no longer seemed to know why he should do so. Next day he appeared completely unaware that there had been any question of illness in his family. When asked again who had packed his suitcase, he said "It must have been my mother. She always does these things." It seemed to us instructive how the emotional tone (one of concern and uneasiness), which was associated with the vague knowledge of his mother's illness, appeared to fade away nearly as rapidly as his knowledge of the events provoking it.

During three of the nights at the Clinical Research Center, the patient rang for the night nurse, asking her, with many apologies, if she would tell him where he was and how he came to be there. He clearly realized that he was in a hospital but seemed unable to reconstruct any of the events of the previous day. On another occasion he remarked "Every day is alone in itself, whatever enjoyment I've had, and whatever sorrow I've had." Our own impression is that many events fade for him long before the day is over. He often volunteers stereotyped descriptions of his own state, by saying that it is "like waking from a dream." His experience seems to be that of a person who is just becoming aware of his surroundings without fully comprehending the situation, because he does not remember what went before.

In December 1967 (eighteen months after the visit to Boston), H. M.'s father died suddenly, and H. M. is said to have become temporarily quite irritable and intractable, rushing out of the house in anger one evening. The cause of the anger was finding that some of his guns were missing. These had been prize possessions of which he often spoke and which he had kept in his room for many years, but an uncle had claimed them as his legacy after the father's death. The patient was upset by what to him was an inexplicable loss, but became calm when they were replaced in his room. Since then, he has been his usual even-tempered self. When questioned about his parents two months later, he seemed to be dimly aware of his father's death. In these and similar respects, he demonstrates some capacity to set up traces of constant features of his immediate environment. In this instance, the continued absence of one of his parents may have served as an unusually effective clue. Until then, H. M.'s entire life had been spent at home with his father and mother.

After his father's death, H. M. was given protected employment in a state rehabilitation center, where he spends week-days participating in rather monotonous work, programmed for severely retarded patients. A typical task is the mounting of cigarette lighters on the cardboard frames for display. It is characteristic that he cannot give us any description of his place of work, the nature of his job, or the route along which he is driven each day, to and from the center.

In contrast to the inability to describe a job after six months of daily exposure (except for weekends), H. M. is able to draw an accurate floor plan of the bungalow in which he has lived for the past eight years. He also seems to be familiar with the topography of the immediate neighborhood, at least within two or three blocks of his home, but is lost beyond that. His limitations in this respect are illustrated by the manner in which he attempted to guide us to his house, in June 1966, when we were driving him back from Boston. After leaving the main highway, we asked him for help in locating his house. He promptly and courteously indicated to us several turns, until we arrived at a street which he said was quite familiar to him. At the same time, he admitted that we were not at the right address. A phone call to his mother revealed that we were on the street where he used to live before his operation. With her directions we made our way to the residential area where H. M. now lives. He did not get his bearings until we were within two short blocks of the house, which he could just glimpse through the trees. (Milner et al., 1968, pp. 216–217)

Other Support for Medial Temporal Lobe Memory Function

The idea that the temporal lobes have some role in memory does not derive only from the case of H. M. The first suggestion that the temporal lobes might play a critical role in human memory was provided by Bekhterev in 1900. He reported a patient who had shown a severe memory impairment, and he demonstrated on autopsy a bilateral softening in the region of the uncus, hippocampus, and adjoining medial temporal cortex. In the 1950s, the importance of the temporal lobes in human memory was clearly demonstrated in reports describing several patients with bilateral temporal cortex damage, including the patient H. M. Milner has studied two other patients with severe memory defects who also are believed to have bilateral medial temporal lobe damage. They showed many of the same phenomena as seen in H. M. One case, P. B., was a civil engineer whose left temporal lobe had been resectioned for relief of seizures. After surgery he had severe anterograde amnesia, which persisted and worsened until he died from unrelated causes 15 years later. At autopsy P. B. was found to have an atrophic right hippocampus opposite the surgically excised left hippocampus. Penfield and Milner proposed that P. B.'s right hippocampus was dead at the time of the operation, resulting in severe amnesia like H. M.'s. Other evidence for the role of the temporal lobes in memory comes from brain stimulation studies. Chapman and his associates stimulated the hippocampus bilaterally in two epileptic patients and unilaterally in 13 others and found that bilateral stimulations produced retrograde amnesia that persisted for a few hours and reached back about 2 weeks. Rasmussen and his colleagues also found that stimulation of patients undergoing surgery for temporal lobe epilepsy produced hallucinatory and interpretational responses.

Interpretations of H. M.'s Deficit

The classical characterization of H. M.'s memory impairment was based on a number of suppositions. Since he had a long-term memory store for presurgical events and could form short-term memories but not new long-term memories, his deficits were thought to be due to an inability to store or consolidate new memories. From this it followed that when his temporal lobes were removed, the structure responsible for consolidating memory was also removed. A very conspicuous structure in the temporal lobes called the hippocampus, which to that point had been thought to be involved in olfaction or emotion, was supposed to be the structure responsible for consolidating memories (see Figure 16.1). According to one version of this theory, memories are stored in the hippocampus for weeks or months and then, through the process of consolidation, they are transferred to and stored in the neocortex. It is the cortical memory store that H. M. is thought to retain and the consolidation process he is thought to have lost.

Many hundreds of experiments were subsequently performed on laboratory animals in which the hippocampus was removed or its function disrupted in order to shed light on its role in consolidating memories. Various functions of the hippocampus were uncovered, but the pattern of deficits observed in H. M. could never quite be matched in the laboratory. In retrospect, in appears there were three incorrect conclusions that derived from H. M.'s case. (1) It was assumed that the damage to the hippocampus was responsible for the anterograde amnesia. Now it appears that hippocampal damage accounts for only the spatial impairments displayed by H. M. Other areas involved in his lesion—including the amygdala, which is responsible for emotional memory, and the rhinal cortex (entorhinal cortex and perirhinal cortex), which is responsible for object-recognition memory—also contribute to his impairment. Thus, H. M.'s memory impairment is attributable to damage in at least three separate areas involved in memory (see Figure 16.1). (2) It was supposed that a single structure could be responsible for most if not all memory formation. Now it is becoming recognized that there are different classes of memory, and H. M. suffers memory impairments in only one of these classes. (3) It was supposed that short-term memories are converted into long-term memories. Now it is becoming recognized that short-term and long-term memories are independent. We will discuss each of these new views in the following sections.

Explicit and Implicit Memory

Although H. M. has a severe memory defect on many kinds of tests, he is surprisingly competent at motor learning. In one experiment Milner trained H. M. on a mirror-drawing task that required tracing a line between the double outline of a star while seeing the star and his pencil only in a mirror (Figure 16.2). This task is difficult at first even for normal subjects, but they improve with practice. H. M. had a normal learning curve, and although he did not remember having performed the task previously, he retained the skill on the following days. Subsequently, Corkin trained H. M. on a variety of manual-tracking and coordination tasks. Although his initial performances tended to be inferior to those of control subjects, he showed nearly normal improvement from session to session.

In 1981, Cohen and Corkin showed an analogous result on the Tower of Hanoi puzzle, a well-studied problem involving a number of pegs and a number of blocks of different sizes. To begin the problem, all the blocks are arranged on the "source" peg in size order, with the smallest on the top and the largest on the bottom. The task is to move these blocks one at a time onto a "goal" peg, with the largest block again at the bottom and the smallest at the top, while never placing a block onto one smaller than itself. Thus, successful solution requires the use of additional pegs in a specific order. Normal subjects require a decreasing number of moves for solution over successive trials. Despite his inability to remember particular moves and whether they advance or retard

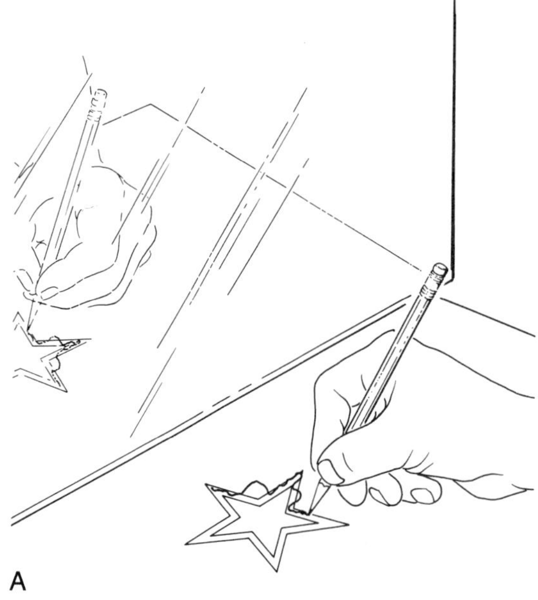

A

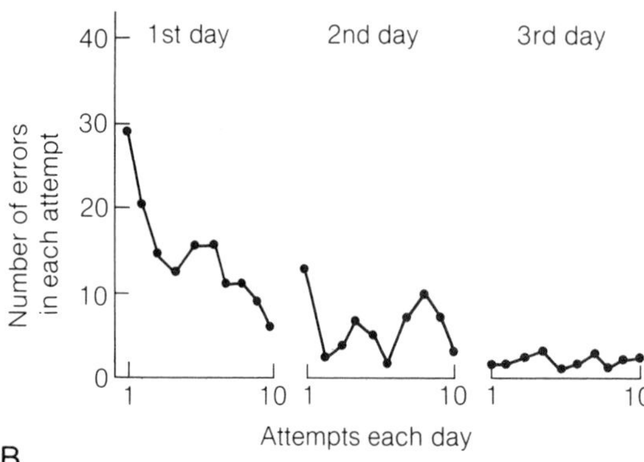

B

FIGURE 16.2. *A*. In this test the subject's task is to trace between the two outlines of the star while viewing his or her hand in a mirror. The reversing effect of the mirror makes this a difficult task initially. Crossing a line constitutes an error. *B*. H. M. Shows a clear improvement in motor tasks such as this, although he does not remember having performed them.

solution, H. M.'s performance improved systematically over days, even though his commentary during each trial sounded as though he were solving the puzzle for the first time. In short, H. M. was able to learn the procedures necessary to perform this cognitive task, despite markedly impaired memory for having ever done the task. We shall return to this dissociation in our discussion of amnesia.

The dissociation between the impairment in memory and in motor learning implies that motor skills are stored independently of the temporal lobe system. For a time motor learning was seen as a curious exception to the deficits that result from temporal lobe damage, but during the 1980s the results of a variety of lines of investigation indicated that there are many kinds of memory that survive in patients with anterograde amnesia. These kinds of memory have been grouped together and have been given a variety of names, the one we have chosen to use is implicit memory. **Implicit memory** is an unconscious, nonintentional form of memory that can be contrasted with **explicit memory,** which involves conscious recollection of previous experiences.

Some other examples of implicit memory will be helpful in understanding its features. Imagine a task in which a person is first given a list of words to read. Later they are given the beginnings of some words that they are asked to complete with the first word that comes to mind. Thus, one of the incomplete words might be TAB____. It could be completed as "table," "tablet," "tabby," "tabulation," and so forth. If one of the words on the previous list was "table," however, then "table" will be used more often than other possibilities. An important feature of this task is that amnesic subjects perform as well as normals. Thus, they indicate through their performance that they remember what was on the previous study list even though they report no conscious recollection of ever having seen the list. Implicit memory can also be demonstrated in the following way. Subjects are shown an incomplete sketch and asked what it is (Figure 16.3). If they fail to identify the sketch, they are shown another sketch that is slightly more complete. This continues until they eventually recognize the picture. When control subjects and amnesics are shown the same sketch at a later date, both groups will identify the sketch at an earlier stage than was required the first time. Thus, amnesic subjects will indicate

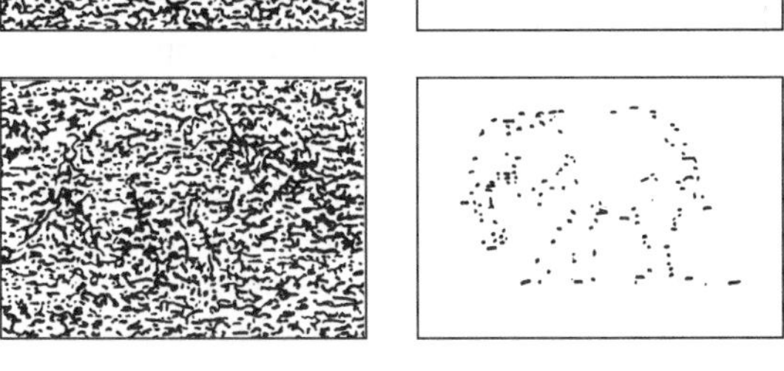

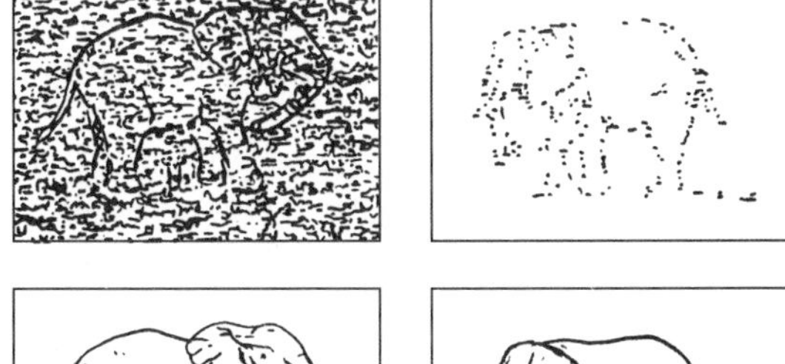

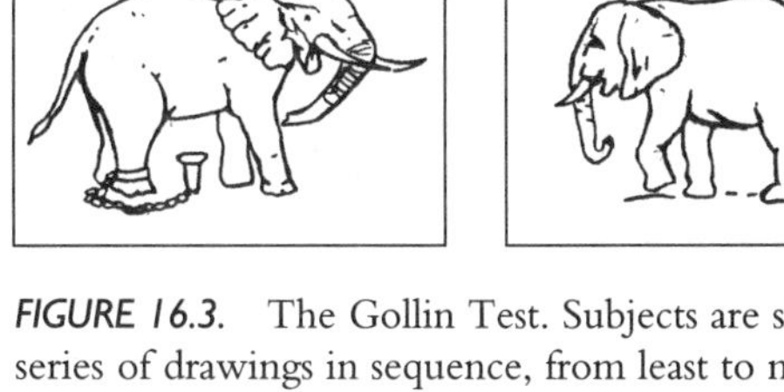

FIGURE 16.3. The Gollin Test. Subjects are shown a series of drawings in sequence, from least to most clear, and asked to identify the object. On a retention test given some time later, subjects identify the images sooner than they did on the first test. Amnesic patients also show improvement on this test (From Vokey et al., 1986.)

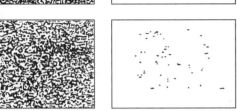

through their performance that they remember the previous experience even though they cannot recall consciously ever having been shown sketches of an elephant. Tasks of the kind described here are called **priming tasks.** That H. M., like many other amnesic patients, can perform priming tasks but has no conscious recall of having been tested in the task is taken as one kind of evidence that implicit and explicit memory are different.

The independence of implicit and explicit memory can also be demonstrated in normal subjects. If subjects are asked to think about the meaning of a word or the shape of the word, their explicit recall of the word is greatly improved by thinking about its meaning. The effect on word completion (implicit memory) is not affected by this manipulation. This is known as the **depth-of-processing effect.** If subjects are shown a word in one modality (they hear the word) and are tested for recall in another modality (they must write the word or identify it by reading), word completion is greatly reduced, whereas explicit recall is little affected. This is called a **study-test modality shift.** (A student who reads to study for an exam that must be written will recognize the wider implication of the study-test modality shift.)

The Relation of Other Kinds of Memory to Explicit-Implicit Memory

Terms for memory can be confusing because many people have proposed two-factor memory theories using their own labels (Table 16.1). Most of the terms in the left half of this table are terms for explicit memory, whereas most terms on the right are terms for implicit memory. Consider, for example, the declarative-procedural distinction that is commonly used in human memory research. Declarative refers to things that you can talk about, such as "I rode my bicycle along the river yesterday evening," whereas procedural refers to the motoric skill of bike riding. An amnesic such as H. M. could have the skill of riding a bike but be unable to recount specific instances of bike riding. The working-reference memory distinction has been widely used in animal research. Reference memory refers to knowledge of the rules of a task; for example, a rat might learn that if it runs through a maze it will find food in particular places. Working memory refers to events that

TABLE 16.1. Terms describing two kinds of memory

Explicit (conscious)	Implicit (unconscious)
Fact	Skill
Declarative	Procedural
Memory	Habit
Knowing that	Knowing how
Locale	Taxon
Cognitive mediation	Semantic
Conscious recollection	Skills
Elaboration	Integration
Memory with record	Memory without record
Autobiographical	Perceptual
Representational	Dispositional
Episodic	Semantic
Working	Reference

Note: This table illustrates different types of memory dissociations that have been made by different writers. They share the idea that memory can be subdivided into one or more processes.

Source: After Squire, 1987.

can happen on a trial; for example, a rat should remember during a trial in which arms of the maze it finds food so that it does not repeat those responses. Amnesic rats can learn to run through mazes, but they will return to places where they have received food because they do not remember having already eaten the food that was there. Of course, the inventors of some of these terms may intend them to mean something slightly different from what is suggested here, but these distinctions are not our immediate concern.

There are other kinds of learning that can also be sorted by the explicit-implicit distinction. Hull's habit learning, Skinner's operant learning, and Pavlov's classical conditioning all can be thought of as kinds of implicit learning. A rat that learns to run down an alley or press a bar and a dog that has been taught to salivate in response to the sound of a bell are both displaying memory that is known to be spared in most amnesics and also in animals with medial temporal lobe lesions. On the other hand, Krechevsky's hypothesis testing, Kohler's insights, and Tolman's purposeful behavior are all kinds of behaviors driven by what could be considered explicit memory. Again it could be imagined that an amnesic patient would have difficulty when faced with tasks demanding these skills. It should be noted that the distinctions between these kinds of theories are not clear-cut, because an animal could have both explicit and implicit memory when trained in a given way.

The Neural Basis of Explicit and Implicit Memory

Classical theories of memory supposed that there is a specific structure in the brain that houses memory more generally, but this idea is losing favor for a number of reasons. For example, it is not at all clear that there are either kinds of neurons or kinds of brain structures that are dedicated to learning. Studies of even the simplest animals or of simplified circuits, such as those in the spinal cord, have demonstrated the ubiquity of learning in neural systems. Thus, it seems reasonable to believe that every part of the nervous system is able to learn. Some areas or some neurons may be more plastic than others, but this is a separate issue.

Accepting the postulate that every part of the nervous system can learn has profound implications. It would mean that areas that process auditory information house auditory memory, areas that process visual information house visual memory, areas of the brain involved in producing movement house motor memories, and so forth. It would also mean that memory could be further subdivided with respect to the specialized regions within each of the major functional modalities. For example, for vision there would be at least partly separate memories for color, form, and motion because different areas of the brain analyze those features of the visual world. When a person views a scene, a number of memories (for example, color, form, motion) rather than a single memory would encode that scene. Additionally, since in humans the hemispheres are functionally specialized, the memory of the visual scene might be coded separately in each hemisphere.

Evidence that memories are encoded as described here comes from a number of sources. Experiments on transfer-appropriate processing demonstrate that memory performance depends on the extent to which processing operations performed during a study task match the processing operations performed during a test. If a test list contains capital letters, then priming with capital letters produces better performance than priming with lowercase letters. If a test list is given in an auditory mode, then priming with an auditory cue produces better performance than priming with a visual cue. Evidence for simultaneous but different encoding by each hemisphere has also been demonstrated by Marsolek and coworkers. In their experiment a subject is given a test list and later asked to complete three-letter stems with the first word that comes to mind. On the completion test, the stems were presented to either the left or the right hemisphere by giving a brief exposure of the three-letter stem in either visual hemifield. Priming was reduced when the case of the stem (for example, TAB____ to tab____) was changed in presentations to the right hemisphere, but changing the case of the stem in presentations to the left hemisphere did not affect priming. Thus, the encoding in each hemisphere clearly was simultaneous but different. The authors of this study suggest that the left hemisphere encodes abstract word-form representations that do not preserve specific features of the letters, whereas the right hemisphere encodes perceptually specific letter forms. This division of labor can be thought of as representing phoneme (language) as opposed to grapheme (spatial) functions of the hemispheres.

What Makes Explicit and Implicit Memory Different?

Part of the answer to this question relates to the neural areas that process explicit and implicit memories. They are different because they are housed in different neural structures with different functions. Another part of the answer relates to the way information is processed. Implicit information is encoded in very much the same way as it is perceived. Jacoby has described it as data-driven or "bottom-up" processing. Explicit memory, on the other hand, depends upon conceptually driven or "top-down" processing, in which the subject reorganizes the data. Recall of information is thus greatly influenced by the way information is processed. Since a person has a relatively passive role in encoding implicit memory, he or she will have difficulty recalling the memory spontaneously but will recall the memory more easily when primed by one of the features of the original stimulus. Since a person plays an active role in processing information explicitly, the internal cues used in processing can also be used to initiate spontaneous recall.

An analogy may help to illustrate the kinds of processes that could be involved. Imagine a sand hill; water poured onto the sand at the top runs down the hill, eroding a number of small channels. The channels will be all over the hill and so, like memory, they are not localized. If more water is poured on the hill in the same place, it will follow the same route as the first water, further deepening the channels. Since the water will always take the same route down the hill, we could say that there is a memory of the route. It could also be called an implicit memory, because the erosion is determined mainly by the water. We can do experiments with this imaginary sand hill. If we do not refresh the hill with water, the original grooves will fill in, a process analogous to forgetting. If we dig in the hill (creating a lesion) we will damage the memory but not completely destroy it. We can also do other experiments with the sand hill. Imagine that the composition of the hill varies. In a location where the sand is hard, a channel will be hard to erode, but it will endure. In softer areas the channel may form quickly and erode quickly. Thus, part of a memory will be enduring and another part less so. We can imagine digging some grooves to channel the water down a particular part of the hill. Brains probably come prepared in this way: very ready to process certain kinds of information and less prepared to process other kinds. We can imagine still further manipulations; for example, gates could be placed in the grooves to direct the flow of water. This condition would be very much like explicit memory, because the location of the erosion will be determined by an agent other than just the water.

In neurological terms we could conceive of regions of the brain as sand hills and the process of memory as the route taken by information passing through them. Sensory experience (the water) enters the brain or brain region (at the top of the hill), flows through the brain (the channels in the hill), and produces behavior (leaves the hill) at the bottom. We can see, therefore, that the memory was not stored in a place, but rather was a function of the activity of that region of the brain. This analogy demonstrates a simple way to conceive of memory as a process of neuronal connectivity rather than as a site to be found. Neural nets, which are computer networks that learn through experience, work very much like the sand hill. Information is sent through the neurons of the network repeatedly while the direction of the information is continually adjusted by modifying the synapses of the neurons that make up the network. When, after a number of trials, the information coming out of the network is correct, the network is said to have learned. Adjusting the synapses in the network is very much like channeling the water on the sand hill.

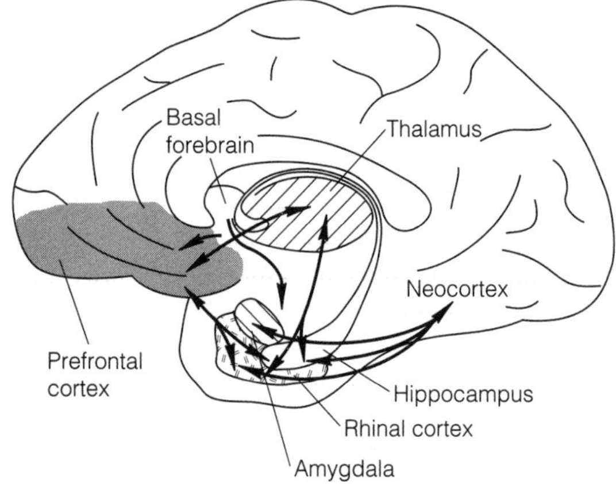

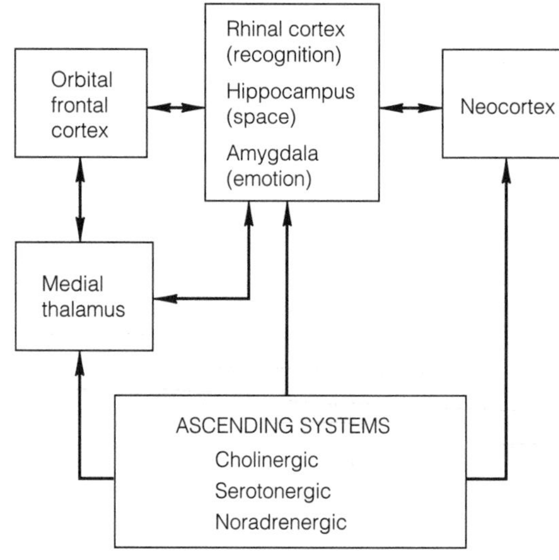

FIGURE 16.4. *A*. Anatomical areas proposed to be involved in explicit memory. *B*. Circuit diagram showing the flow of information through explicit memory circuits. Note that lesions anywhere in this circuitry can disrupt explicit memory (From Petri and Mishkin, 1994.)

A NEURAL MODEL FOR EXPLICIT MEMORIES

On the basis of animal and human studies, Petri and Mishkin have proposed models for explicit and implicit memory. Figure 16.4 illustrates the neural structures involved in explicit memory. Most of the structures are in the limbic system or closely related to it.

There are four major limbic structures: the rhinal cortex, the amygdala, the hippocampus, and the prefrontal cortex. These structures have reciprocal connections with the medial thalamus, the basal forebrain, and sensory areas of the neocortex. Experimental results, obtained mainly with monkeys and rats, suggest that the rhinal cortex is involved in object memory, the hippocampus in spatial memory, and the amygdala in emotional memory. The medial thalamus provides one set of connections between the temporal lobe structures and the frontal lobe. The basal forebrain and other structures in the brainstem are involved in maintaining appropriate levels of activity in the limbic and cortical structures so that they can process information. The limbic structures depend upon the neocortex for the information that they process. It is important to note that the patient H. M. and other amnesic patients have damage to many of these structures, and thus their anterograde amnesia is a composite of a number of separate kinds of memory disorder. We will briefly describe the role of each of these structures in memory.

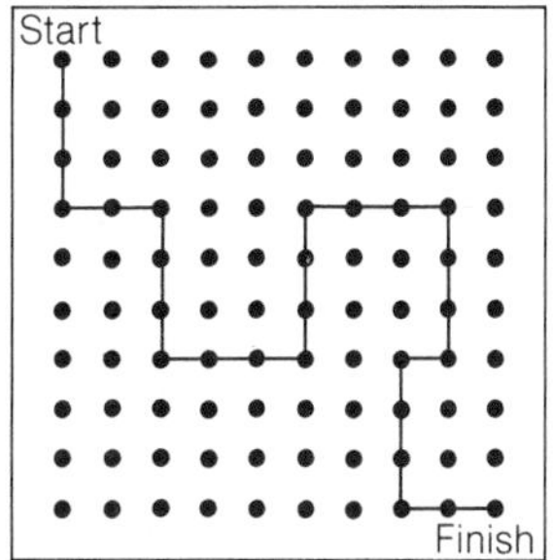

FIGURE 16.5. A visually guided stylus maze. The black circles represent metal bolt heads on a wood base. The task is to discover and remember the correct route, indicated here by the line. Deficits on this task are correlated with the amount of right hippocampus damaged. (After Milner, 1970.)

The Temporal Cortex

The temporal lobes are often the source of epilepsy. Because one treatment for epilepsy is removal of the affected temporal lobe, including both neocortical and limbic systems, there are relatively large numbers of patients who have undergone such surgery and who have been subject to neuropsychological study. The results of these studies suggest that there are significant memory impairments that are different for the left and right hemispheres. They also show that the temporal cortex makes a significant contribution to these functional impairments.

Following right temporal lobe removal, patients are impaired on face-recognition, spatial position, and maze-learning tests (Figure 16.5). Impairments in spatial position are apparent in the Corsi Block-Tapping Test, in which the subject learns to tap out a sequence on a block board, illustrated in Figure 16.6. Just as there is a memory span for digits, there is a memory span for blocks. Patients and normal control subjects are tested on a series of block sequences that are one more than their memory span. One sequence, however, repeats itself every third trial. Normal subjects learn the repeating sequence over several trials, although they are still poor at the novel sequences. Subjects with damage to the right temporal lobe do not learn the repeating sequence or do so very slowly.

Following left temporal lobe lesions, functional impairments are obtained in the recall of word lists, recall of consonant trigrams, and nonspatial associations. There are also impairments on the Hebb Recurring-Digit Test. This test is similar to the block-tapping test in that subjects are given a list of digits to repeat that exceeds their digit span. Embedded within the lists is one digit sequence that repeats. Patients with left temporal lobe lesions do not display the learning-acquisition curve illustrated in Figure 16.6C, but rather fail to learn the recurring digit sequence.

Much of our description of explicit memory disorders has centered on patients with large medial temporal lobe lesions. The structures in the medial temporal lobe, however, receive their inputs from the adjacent cortex. It might be expected, therefore, that neocortical lesions would also produce explicit memory deficits. Milner and her colleagues have doubly dissociated the effects of damage to the neocortex of the temporal lobe of each hemisphere on several memory tasks. They conclude that lesions of the right temporal lobe result in impaired memory of nonverbal material, whereas lesions of the left temporal lobe result in impaired memory of verbal material. These findings are summarized in Table 16.2, where it can be seen that removal of the right temporal lobe produces deficits on nonverbal tests, including recall of complex geometric figures; paired-associate learning of nonsense figures;

A HEBB RECURRING-DIGITS

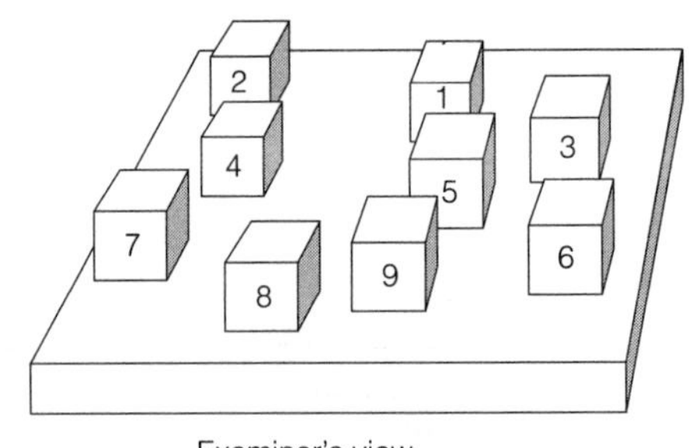

B CORSI BLOCK-TAPPING

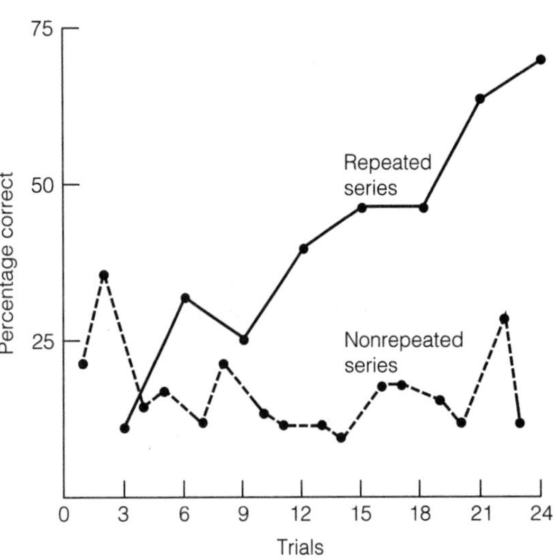

C

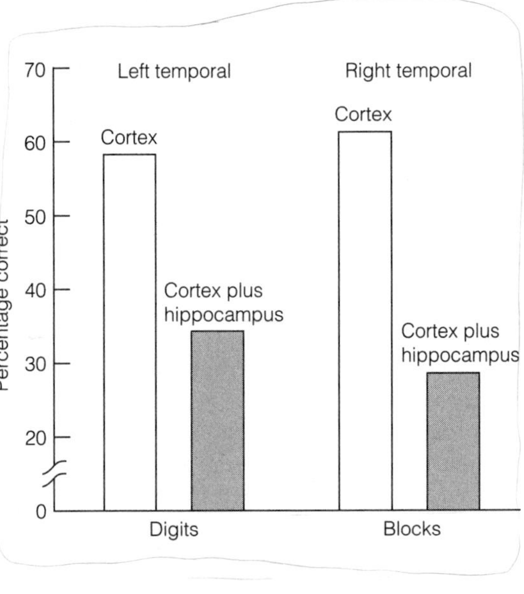

D

FIGURE 16.6. *A*. Hebb Recurring-Digits Test. The subjects are given multiple series of nine numbers, which is longer than their digit-memory span. One series repeats (R). *B*. Sketch of Crosi Block-Tapping Test. The subject must copy a sequence tapped out by the examiner on the blocks. The block's numbers are visible on the examiner's side but not on the subject's. Again, one numerical sequence repeats. *C*. Performance on repeated digits improves over trials, but there is no improvement on the nonrepeating series. *D*. Patients with medial temporal lesions on the left are impaired on the Hebb Recurring-Digits Test; subjects with medial temporal lobe damage on the right are impaired on the Corsi Block-Tapping Test.

and recognition of nonsense figures, tunes, and previously seen photographs of faces. Few deficits are seen, however, on tests of verbal memory. Removal of the left temporal lobe, on the other hand, produces deficits on verbal tests, such as the recall of previously presented stories and pairs of words and the recognition of words or numbers and recurring nonsense syllables; such removal has little effect on the nonverbal tests. These studies indicate that not only is the medial temporal lobe

TABLE 16.2. Summary of the effects of left or right temporal lobectomy on various tests of memory

	Site of lesion		
Test	Left temporal lobe	Right temporal lobe	Basic reference
Geometric recall (Rey)	—	×	Taylor, 1969
Paired-associate nonsense figures	—	×	Prisko, 1963
Recognition of nonsense figures	—	×	Kimura, 1963
Recurring nonsense figures	—	×	Kimura, 1963
Recognition of faces	—	×	Warrington and James, 1967
Recognition of unfamiliar melodies	—	×	Zatorre, 1985
Recognition of tunes	—	×	Shankweiler, 1966
Recall of stories	×	—	Milner, 1967
Paired-associate words	×	—	Milner, 1967
Recognition of words, numbers	×	—	Milner, 1967
Recurring nonsense syllables	×	—	Corsi, 1972

Note: x = significant impairment; — = normal performance.

associated with severe deficits of memory, the adjacent temporal neocortex is also associated with memory disturbance.

Cortical injuries in the parietal, posterior temporal, and possibly occipital cortex sometimes produce specific long-term memory difficulties. Examples include color amnesia, "face amnesia" (prosopagnosia), object anomia (inability to recall the names of objects), and topographical amnesia (inability to recall the location of an object in the environment). The basis for these deficits is poorly understood, and many appear to require bilateral lesions. Topographical amnesia is probably related to posterior parietal injury, but this has been poorly studied, in part because there are few patients with parietal cortex injuries who do not have significant subcortical pathology as well. The parietal cortex is not particularly epileptogenic, so there are few surgical cases.

There are a number of lines of evidence indicating that these deficits should be considered deficits in explicit memory, because tests of implicit memory demonstrate residual abilities. For example, patients with damage to area 17 report that they are unable to see. Yet when asked to point to an object they do so. Patients with temporal cortex damage, who similarly report being unable to see objects, can shape their hands and reach accurately for them. Patients with prosopagnosia, who report that they cannot recognize a face, nevertheless have a strong galvanic skin response when the name of the owner of the face is mentioned. In all these cases, the conscious recollection or explicit memory is impaired while implicit memory is retained.

Other areas of the neocortex, including the frontal cortex, are also involved in explicit memory. Tulving and coworkers, on the basis of their own experiments and the experiments of others using PET studies, have shown that the ventrolateral frontal cortex of the left hemisphere is preferentially active during memory encoding of words or series of words. Interestingly, the same regions are not involved in retrieval of this information. Their PET studies indicate that the dorsolateral frontal cortex in the right hemisphere and the posterior parietal cortex in both hemispheres are active during memory retrieval (Figure 16.7).

Memory impairments also result from diffuse damage such as occurs in herpes simplex encephalitis and Alzheimer's disease. Damasio and coworkers describe a number of cases of herpes simplex encephalitis in which there is damage to the temporal lobes comparable to that suffered by temporal lobe patients, as well as damage to the ventral medial frontal cortex. One patient,

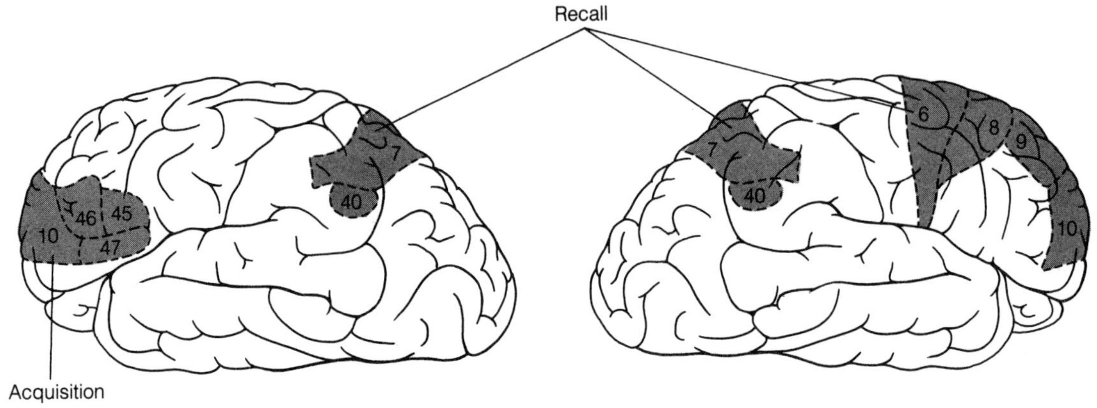

FIGURE 16.7. Areas of cortex that are active as revealed by PET during acquisition or recall of verbal information. During acquisition there is activation in the left ventrolateral prefrontal cortex (areas 10, 46, 45, 47). During recall of the same material there is activation in the right dorsolateral cortex (areas 6, 8, 9, 10) and the parietal cortex bilaterally (areas 7, 40). (From Tulving et al., 1994.)

Boswell, is described in considerable detail. Boswell is like many temporal lobe patients in that he has extensive anterograde amnesia but still has normal intelligence, language abilities, and performance on implicit memory tests. Boswell is different in that he has retrograde amnesia much more severe than that displayed by temporal lobe patients such as H. M. He is described as being entirely unable to retrieve information from any part of his life history. The medial temporal cortex damage probably accounts for his anterograde amnesia, while the additional damage in the lateral temporal cortex, the insula (a medial part of the temporal cortex within the lateral fissure; see Figure 16.1), and the medial frontal cortex is probably related to his retrograde amnesia. Damasio suggests that in Boswell and other herpes simplex encephalitis patients the insula may be especially related to retrograde amnesia. Interestingly, using a PET imaging approach, Posner and Raichle have reported that the insula is active when subjects perform a well-practiced verbal task but is not active when they perform a novel verbal task. This seems consistent with Damasio's suggestion that the insula is involved in accessing previously acquired memories.

Alzheimer's disease is a progressive disease related to the loss of cells and the development of abnormalities in association cortex. It is characterized at first by anterograde amnesia and later by retrograde amnesia. Among the first areas of the brain to show histological change is the medial temporal cortex, but as the disease progresses, other cortical areas become involved. Thus, the pattern of brain change and the pattern of memory deficit again suggests that the medial temporal cortex is related to anterograde amnesia and other temporal association and frontal cortical areas are related to retrograde amnesia. As is the case with the other amnesic patients described thus far, amnesia is displayed mainly on tests of explicit memory, but eventually implicit memory may also suffer.

The Amygdala

The amygdaloid complex is composed of a number of separate nuclei, each of which probably has specific functions, and so it is not entirely correct to consider them together as we shall do. These nuclei have been associated with emotional, olfactory, and visceral events and with arousal. There are no clear-cut studies, however, that demonstrate a relationship between these specific aspects of behavior and anatomy. Sarter and Markowitsch, in reviewing the literature on studies of animals and humans, suggest that the amygdala is involved in those memory processes associated with events that have emotional significance to the subject's life. Thus, if the amygdala makes any contribution to the amnesia of patients with medial temporal lobe lesions, it may be emotional in nature.

The Hippocampus

Although it was once thought that the amnesia displayed by hippocampal patients was due to hippocampal damage, this does not seem to be the case. Evidence comes from two sources. First, there is now an extensive literature linking the hippocampus with spatial behavior; for example, navigating to specific locations or remembering the locations of objects. Many of these studies find little evidence to indicate that the hippocampus is involved in other forms of memory. Studies in which the hippocampus has been intentionally damaged in primate models of medial temporal lobe amnesia also find spatial memory deficits (remembering the location of an object) but not other memory deficits (such as amnesia for objects). Given that medial temporal lobe patients have impairments in spatial tasks and are amnesic for spatial information, it is likely that only this impairment is related to hippocampal loss.

The Perirhinal Cortex

Recently, considerable attention has been directed to the effects of damage to the rhinal cortex (entorhinal cortex and perirhinal cortex; see Figure 16.1) in primate models of medial temporal amnesia, with surprising results. This area is the most lateral portion of the medial temporal lobe that is damaged in most medial temporal amnesics (see Figure 16.1). In a representative study, Meunier and coworkers found that when monkeys with damage to various areas in the temporal lobes were tested on visual-recognition tasks, those with perirhinal lesions were most impaired. In fact, the impairment was as severe as that associated with large medial temporal lobe lesions. These results strongly suggest that the recognition memory deficits come not from the hippocampus but from the perirhinal cortex.

Diencephalic Amnesia

Evidence of diencephalic amnesia comes from two sources: patients with focal lesions of the medial thalamus, and patients with Korsakoff's syndrome. Focal lesions of the medial thalamic area most commonly result from vascular accidents, which produce reliable memory problems, but there are few cases in which thorough behavioral and postmortem examinations have been done, so the critical lesion remains a mystery. More is known about alcohol-related diencephalic damage, although the anatomical localization remains a problem.

Long-term alcoholism, especially when accompanied by malnutrition, has long been known to produce defects of memory. In the late 1800s a Russian physician, S. S. Korsakoff, called attention to a syndrome that he found to accompany chronic alcoholism, the most obvious symptom being a severe loss of memory. He wrote:

> The disorder of memory manifests itself in an extraordinarily peculiar amnesia, in which the memory of recent events, those which just happened, is chiefly disturbed, whereas the remote past is remembered fairly well. This reveals itself primarily in that the patient constantly asks the same questions and repeats the same stories. At first, during conversation with such a patient, it is difficult to note the presence of psychic disorder; the patient gives the impression of a person in complete possession of his faculties; he reasons about everything perfectly well, draws correct deductions from given premises, makes witty remarks, plays chess or a game of cards, in a

word, comports himself as a mentally sound person. Only after a long conversation with the patient, one may note that at times he utterly confuses events and that he remembers absolutely nothing of what goes on around him: he does not remember whether he had his dinner, whether he was out of bed. On occasion the patient forgets what happened to him just an instant ago: you came in, conversed with him, and stepped out for one minute; then you come in again and the patient has absolutely no recollection that you had already been with him. Patients of this type may read the same page over and over again, sometimes for hours, because they are absolutely unable to remember what they have read. . . .With all this, the remarkable fact is that, forgetting all events which have just occurred, the patients usually remember quite accurately the past events which occurred long before the illness. What is forgotten usually proves to be everything that happened during the illness and a short time before the beginning of the illness. (Oscar-Berman, 1980, p. 410)

Korsakoff's syndrome has been studied intensively since the seminal paper of Sanders and Warrington was published in 1971, because Korsakoff patients are far more readily available than individuals with other forms of global amnesia such as H. M. Talland has described six major symptoms of the syndrome:

1. *Anterograde amnesia.* The patients are unable to form new memories. On formal memory tests they are especially bad at learning paired-associate lists.

2. *Retrograde amnesia.* The patients have an extensive impairment of remote memory that covers most of their adult life. This is easily demonstrated by their very poor recognition of famous faces from years past, faces that most normal people as well H. M. recognize accurately.

3. *Confabulation.* Patients make up stories about past events rather than admit memory loss. Because these stories are often based on past experiences, they are plausible. For example, when asked where he was last night, a man told us that he had been at the Legion with his pals. He had not, but this had been a common practice in the past and so was a plausible story.

4. *Meager content in conversation.* Korsakoff patients have little to say in spontaneous conversation, presumably in part because of their amnesia.

5. *Lack of insight.* Many patients are virtually completely unaware of their memory defect.

6. *Apathy.* Indifference and incapacity persevere in ongoing activities. The patients lose interest in things quickly and generally appear indifferent to change.

These symptoms are all observed in patients who otherwise appear quite normal. They have normal IQs, are alert and attentive, appear motivated, and generally lack other neurological signs of cerebral deficits such as abnormal EEGs.

The symptoms of Korsakoff's syndrome may appear suddenly within the space of a few days. The cause is a thiamine (vitamin B_1) deficiency resulting from prolonged intake of large quantities of alcohol. The syndrome, which is usually progressive, can be arrested by massive doses of vitamin B_1 but cannot be reversed. Prognosis is poor, with only about 20% of patients showing much recovery over a year on a B_1-enriched diet. Many patients demonstrate no recovery even after 10 to 20 years.

Although there has been some controversy over the exact effect of the vitamin deficiency on the brain, it is currently thought that there is damage in the medial thalamus and possibly in the mammillary bodies of the hypothalamus, as well as generalized cerebral atrophy. It was widely believed that the severe memory defect results from hypothalamic damage because the mammillary bodies receive hippocampal efferents through the fornix. Thus, the damage to the diencephalon was seen as a disconnection of the hippocampal circuitry, and this disconnection produced the amnesia. This seems unlikely for several reasons.

First, in many cases only the medial thalamus is degenerated and not the mammillary bodies; the reverse is not observed. Second, the major hippocampal efferents depart via the entorhinal cortex and not the fornix. (Actually, the fornical fibers do not originate in the hippocampus but in the subiculum.) In addition, there is considerable controversy over whether lesions to the fornix itself even produce amnesia. For example, Woolsey and Nelson report a case in which there was no apparent neuropsychological disturbance (that is, no obvious memory defect) from a malignant tumor that had destroyed the fornix bilaterally. Garcia-Bengochea and colleagues sectioned the fornix bilaterally as a treatment for epilepsy in 14 patients and reported that amnesia did not ensue. There have been two reports of memory loss after fornical section, but because these patients have not come to autopsy it is uncertain just where the lesion is. In summary, the bulk of the evidence suggests that damage to the mammillary bodies or the fornix is not sufficient to produce the memory loss.

There are clear differences between the memory loss experienced by diencephalic and temporal lobe patients. For example, although temporal lobe patients show normal release from proactive interference, diencephalic patients do not. Further, individuals with Korsakoff's syndrome have an extensive loss of past memories; temporal lobe patients do not. Moscovitch has suggested that Korsakoff individuals may have two problems: a diencephalic lesion and frontal lobe deterioration—the latter conclusion based on evidence from CT scans that show frontal atrophy in more than 80% of Korsakoff amnesics.

The Basal Forebrain

The basal forebrain is an area just anterior to the hypothalamus. It is the source of a number of pathways to the forebrain, among which are cholinergic fibers. The cholinergic cells project to all cortical areas and provide up to 70% of the cholinergic synapses in these areas. It was first proposed that the loss of these cholinergic cells is related to, and is responsible for, the amnesia displayed by patients with Alzheimer's disease. In animal experiments, selective lesioning of the cells using neurotoxins does result in amnesia, especially when the projection to the temporal lobe is damaged. The cholinergic cells are not thought to be involved in the storage of memory per se, but they are thought to play a role in activating cortical cells so that they function normally.

Serotonergic cells in the midbrain and noradrenergic cells in the hindbrain also project to the limbic system and cortex; these cells play a role in maintaining activation in these areas. If either of these cell groups by itself is removed in animals, no serious memory difficulty results. Profound amnesia can be produced, however, if the serotonergic cells in the midbrain and the cholinergic cells in the basal forebrain are damaged together. Vanderwolf has demonstrated that animals that receive such treatments behave as if their entire neocortex were removed, in that they no longer display any intelligent behavior. Additionally, recordings of cortical EEG show that the animals display a pattern typical of sleeping animals. Vanderwolf's experiments suggest that the cholinergic projection and the serotonergic projection are jointly responsible for maintaining waking cortical EEG activity. If one projection is removed, the other can maintain cortical activation, but if both are removed cortical activation is no longer possible. Since it is known that a number of diseases of aging are associated with loss of cholinergic and serotonergic cells, it is likely that this kind of cell loss contributes to amnesia. It is important to note that if damage is restricted to the ascending projections, there should be no degeneration of forebrain structures. Therefore, if the damage can be reversed by pharmacological treatment, it should be possible to restore memory.

IMPLICIT MEMORY

To this point most of our discussion has concerned explicit memory. It seems reasonable that if the limbic circuity is involved in explicit memory, other brain structures must be involved in implicit memory. Petri and Mishkin have suggested a brain circuit for implicit memory (Figure 16.8). The structures that are central to this circuit are the basal ganglia (the caudate nucleus and putamen). The basal ganglia receive projections from all regions of the neocortex and send projections via the globus pallidus and ventral thalamus to the premotor cortex. The basal ganglia also receive projections from cells in the substantia nigra. These projections contain the neurotransmitter dopamine, which is widely and densely distributed to the basal ganglia. Dopamine appears to be necessary for circuits in the basal ganglia to function, and so it may be indirectly involved in memory formation. It is noteworthy that the basal ganglia have traditionally been classified as motor structures because damage to them produces impairments in movement. The circuits that they form also appear to be involved in receiving sensory information from the sensory neocortex and channeling it into cortical motor areas.

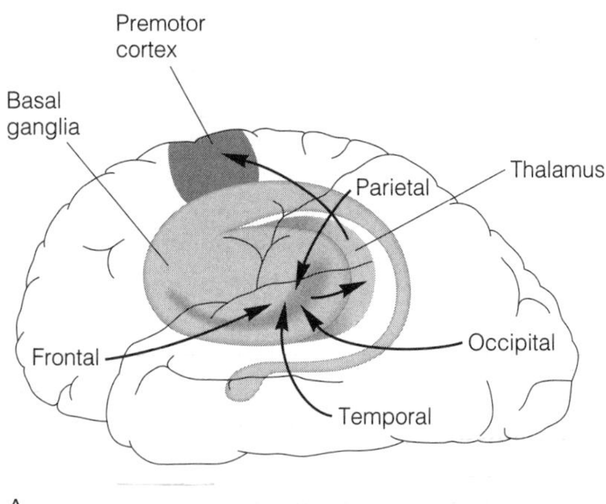

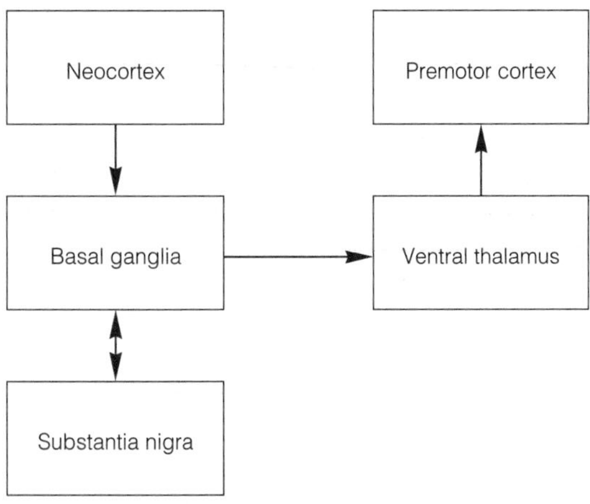

FIGURE 16.8. *A*. Neural structures proposed to be involved in implicit memory. *B*. Flow of information begins in the neocortex, flows through the basal ganglia, and ends in the premotor cortex. (From Petri and Mishkin, 1994.)

Like the model for explicit memory, the model for implicit memory has been developed from an extensive series of studies using monkeys and rats. Animals with damage in the basal ganglia circuitry should display preserved recognition memory, spatial memory, and emotional memory. On the other hand, they should be impaired at learning motor skills, at learning to make appropriate responses to cues, and at association tasks. This does seem to be the case.

In a study of patients with Huntington's chorea, Martone and her colleagues have demonstrated impairments in the mirror-drawing task, on which patients with temporal lobe lesions are unimpaired. The patients with Huntington's chorea are unimpaired on a verbal-recognition task. **Huntington's chorea** is characterized by the degeneration of cells in the basal ganglia. This suggests that the circuits identified as responsible for explicit memory in studies of monkeys and rats provide the basis for motor skills learning and implicit memory in humans. In coming to this conclusion, we should point out that the research relating explicit memory to the limbic cortex is much more extensive than that relating implicit memory to the basal ganglia.

A number of imaging studies also support the idea that structures within this circuit are involved in implicit memory. Grafton and coworkers used PET scans of regional cerebral blood flow (rCBF) in normal subjects who learned to perform a pursuit motor task. This task involves keeping a stylus in a particular location on a turning disc, which is

Huntington's - degeneration of cells in basal ganglia & damage here hurts implicit memory about the size of a record. It draws upon skills that are very like those used in mirror drawing. The researchers found that motor execution was associated with increases in rCBF in the motor cortex, basal ganglia, and cerebellum, and that acquisition of the skill was associated with a subset of these structures. These included the primary motor cortex, the supplementary motor cortex, and the pulvinar of the thalamus.

A more dramatic demonstration of the role of the motor cortex in implicit learning comes from a study by Pascual-Leone and colleagues. In this study, subjects were required to press one of four buttons, each labeled with a digit, in response to cues provided on a TV monitor; for example, when number 1 appears on the screen, push button 1 with finger 1. The measure of learning was the reaction time to push the button. The subjects received a sequence of 12 cues, which were repeated. For the control group there was no order to the sequence, but the sequence presented to the experimental group was repeated so that once they learned the pattern they could anticipate the cue provided by the monitor and so respond very quickly. The implicit memory component of this task was the improvement in reaction time that occurred with practice, whereas the explicit memory component was obtained when the subjects recognized the sequence and so generated responses without the cues. Transcranial magnetic stimulation was used to map the motor cortex area representing the limb involved in making the responses. This technique involves stimulating the motor cortex through coils placed on the skull while muscle activity is recorded simultaneously. Thus, the researchers could map the relative cortical area involved in moving the muscles in the limb at various points during learning. What they found was that the cortical maps of the muscles involved in the task became progressively larger as the task was acquired. That is, during acquisition it appeared as if the area of the cortex devoted to the limb increased in size as learning occurred. Once the subjects knew the sequence of the stimuli and thus had explicit knowledge of the task, the area of the motor cortex involved returned to baseline conditions. Thus, acquisition of implicit knowledge involved a reorganization of the motor cortex that was not required for explicit memory performance.

The motor regions of the cortex also receive projections through the thalamus from the cerebellum. Thompson has reviewed many lines of evidence that the cerebellum occupies an important position in the brain circuits involved in motor learning. He and his coworkers suggest, for example, that the cerebellum plays an important role in a form of implicit learning called classical conditioning. In their model, a puff of air is administered to the eyelid of a rabbit, paired with a stimulus such as a tone. Lesions to pathways from the cerebellum abolish the conditioned response (blink in response to the tone) but not the unconditioned response (blink in response to the air puff). They further demonstrate the importance of the cerebellum in learning by showing that the cortex is not necessary for development of the conditioned response. On the basis of experiments such as this, Thompson suggests that the cerebellum is involved in learning discrete, adaptive behavioral responses to noxious events.

SHORT-TERM MEMORY

In 1890, William James distinguished between what he called *primary* memory, which endures for a very brief time, and *secondary* memory, "the knowledge of a former state of mind after it has already once dropped from the consciousness" (James, 1890, p. 648). Not until 1958, however, were separate short-term and long-term memories specifically postulated by Broadbent, although a number of authors had hinted at this possibility.

Short-term memory, sometimes also called working memory, is the form of memory we use to hold digits, words, names, or other items in memory for a brief period of time. Baddely has described it aptly as scratch-pad memory. We pointed out earlier a misleading idea about short-term memory: that it is necessarily related to long-term memory. Repeating a list of digits may be useful for putting the list in long-term memory, but it is not the short-term memory trace that is being placed in long-term memory. It is likely, however, that items can be pulled from long-term memory and held for some use in short-term memory (for example, to solve a mathematical problem). Short-term and long-term memory are parallel mechanisms in which material is processed separately and simultaneously.

There are probably a number of kinds of short-term memory, each with different neural correlates. Baddely has suggested at least two kinds. One is a visual-spatial scratch pad on which object forms are located spatially. The second is a phonological scratch pad that holds verbal information. The function of both kinds of memory is to hold items of information "on-line" until they can be dealt with physically or mentally. Both kinds of short-term memory can be subdivided further and can take different forms in the left and right hemispheres. Baddely's two scratch pads are synonymous with the dorsal spatial visual system and the ventral object-recognition visual system, which are described below.

Warrington and her colleagues point out that short-term memory can be doubly dissociated from long-term memory with respect both to an impairment itself and to the neural structures from which deficits follow. For example, one patient, K. F., received a left posterior temporal lesion that resulted in an almost total inability to repeat verbal stimuli such as digits, letters, words, and sentences. In contrast, his long-term recall of paired-associate words or short stories was nearly normal. On the other hand, patients who display anterograde amnesia for explicit information do not show impairments in short-term memory for words and digits.

In their larger series of cases, Warrington and her colleagues found that some patients apparently have defects in short-term recall of visually presented digits or letters but have normal short-term recall of the same stimuli presented aurally. On the other hand, Luria reports patients with just the opposite difficulty: specific deficits for aurally presented but not visually presented verbal items. Additionally, there is evidence that damage to the prefrontal cortex can produce impairments in memory for the location of objects. Short-term memory deficits can result from damage to the polymodal sensory areas of the posterior parietal cortex, posterior temporal cortex, and frontal lobe. Warrington and Weiskrantz have presented several cases of specific short-term memory deficits in patients with lesions at the junction of the parietal, temporal, and occipital cortex.

If the left hemisphere mediates short-term storage of verbal material, is it possible that the right parietal lobe participates in the short-term storage of nonverbal information? Although we are not aware of any published data on this question, the idea seems reasonable. One might expect, for example, that the span on the Corsi Block-Tapping Test would be reduced in patients with right parietal lesions, and preliminary data from Milner show that this may be the case.

Historically there have been extravagant claims that the frontal lobes are responsible for the highest intellectual functions, but until quite recently there was no evidence that the frontal lobes are involved in memory. Now it is recognized that damage to the frontal cortex results in many impairments of short-term memory for tasks in which subjects must remember the temporal location of stimuli. The tasks themselves may be rather simple: given this cue, make that response after a delay. But as trials are given, both animals and people with frontal lobe lesions start to mix up the previously presented stimuli.

In 1963, Prisko devised an experiment based on previous work with experimental animals. It was a "compound-stimulus" task in which two stimuli in the same sensory modality were presented in succession, separated by a short interval. The subject's task was to report whether the second stimulus of the pair was identical to the first. On half the trials, the stimuli were the same, and on the other half they were different. Thus, the task required the subject to remember the first stimulus of a pair in order to compare it with the second, while suppressing the stimuli that had occurred on previous trials. Prisko used pairs of clicks, light flashes, tones, colors, and irregular nonsense patterns as the stimuli. The same stimuli were used repeatedly in different combinations. Patients with unilateral frontal lobe removals showed a marked impairment in matching the clicks, flashes, and colors.

In Prisko's test, the subject is required to suppress the memory of previous trials and concentrate only on the first stimulus in the pair. If this behavior is no longer possible after the frontal lesion, then, when a few stimuli constantly recur, the interfering effects of previous trials may seriously impair test performance. That is, because there is difficulty in discriminating the most recent stimulus from others that appeared earlier, the frontal lobe patient's time discriminations become rather blurred. This possibility was tested more directly in an experiment by Corsi.

In Corsi's experiment there were two tasks, one verbal and one nonverbal, and the subjects were required to decide which of two stimuli had been seen more recently. In the verbal task the subjects were asked to read pairs of words presented on a series of cards (for example, cowboy-railroad). From time to time a card appeared bearing two words with a question mark between them. The subject had to indicate which of the words he or she had read most recently. Sometimes both words had been seen before, but at other times only one had been seen. In the latter case the task became a simple test of recognition, whereas in the former case it was a test of recency memory. Patients with left temporal removals showed a mild deficit in recognition, in keeping with their difficulty with verbal memory; the frontal lobe patients performed normally. However, on the recency test, both frontal lobe groups (left and right) were impaired, although the left-side group was significantly worse.

The nonverbal task was identical with the verbal task, except that the stimuli were photographs of paintings rather than words. Patients with right temporal lobe removals showed mild deficits in recognition, consistent with their visual memory deficit, whereas those with right frontal lobe lesions performed normally. On the recency test the frontal lobe groups were impaired, but now the right-side group was significantly worse. Thus, Corsi's experiments confirm Prisko's results indicating a deficit in the memory of the temporal ordering of events. This conclusion is corroborated by Petrides' more recent experiments showing deficits in self-ordered tasks in patients with frontal lobe lesions. The data from these studies are consistent with the hypothesis that the frontal lobes play some role in the memory processes needed to separate events in time, but Prisko's data also suggest that frontal lobe patients may have another type of memory deficit related to their sensitivity to interference from exposure to new material.

This possibility was tested directly by Moscovitch and Milner. In their experiment patients were read five different lists of 12 words each and were instructed to recall each list immediately after presentation. In the first four lists the words were all drawn from the same taxonomic category, such as sports, followed by a fifth list from a different category, such as professions. Normal subjects show a decline from list 1 to 4 in the number of words recalled correctly (that is, they exhibit proactive interference), but they also exhibit an additional phenomenon on list 5: they recall as many words as they did for list 1, thus demonstrating what is referred to as release from proactive interference. Frontal lobe patients also showed strong proactive interference, as would be expected from the Prisko experiments, but surprisingly they failed to show release from proactive interference on list 5. These data imply that frontal lobe lesions produce yet another memory defect that is not observed in patients with large temporal lobe lesions.

Another memory deficit in patients with frontal lobe lesions has been demonstrated in a test of movement copying. In their study of copying of complex arm and facial movements in patients with cortical lesions, Kolb and Milner found that in addition to errors of sequence, frontal lobe patients made many errors of intrusion and omission; that is, when asked to copy a series of three discrete facial movements, frontal lobe patients left one movement out (error of omission) or added a movement seen in a previous sequence (error of intrusion). The errors of intrusion may represent another example of interference effects, but the errors of omission imply a type of short-term memory defect. Specific short-term memory deficits have been suggested previously by Moscovitch to account for the performance of frontal lobe patients on certain memory tests.

Experiments with monkeys and with humans suggest that different areas of the prefrontal cortex are involved in different types of short-term memory. Fuster has demonstrated that if monkeys are shown objects that they must remember for a short period of time until they are allowed to make a response, neurons in the frontal cortex will fire during the delay. This suggests that these neurons are actively involved in bridging the stimulus-response gap (Figure 16.9). Goldman-Rakic and her colleagues have examined this phenomenon further in two tasks, one involving memory for the location of objects and the other memory for the identity of objects. For the first task, monkeys were required to fixate on a point in the center of a screen while a light was flashed in some portion of their visual field. After a variable delay of a few seconds, they were required to shift their eyes to look at the point where the light had been. In the second task, as the monkey fixated on the center of the screen, one of two objects appeared on the screen. The monkeys were required to look to the left in response to one stimulus and to the right in response to the other. Cells that coded spatial vision were located in area

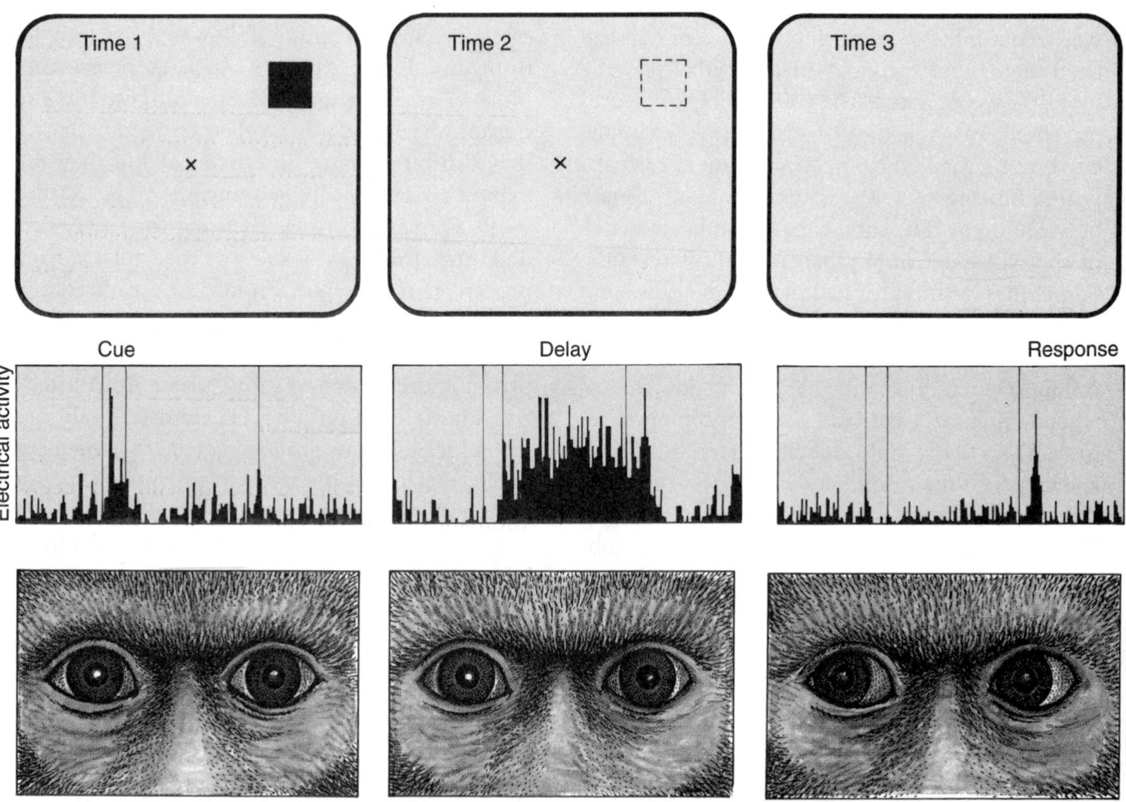

FIGURE 16.9. Single cells can code the spatial location of objects. The monkey fixes its gaze on the **x**; after the stimulus disappears it must maintain fixation for a few seconds; finally, it must look to the spatial location where the target object had been. During the delay, single cells in area 8 code the memory for the location of the object. (After Goldman-Rakic, 1992.)

8 of the dorsolateral prefrontal cortex, whereas cells that coded object recognition were located in areas 9 and 46 of the middorsolateral frontal cortex (Figure 16.10A).

Petrides and coworkers have used PET along with MRI to demonstrate similar function-anatomy relations in humans (Figure 16.10B).

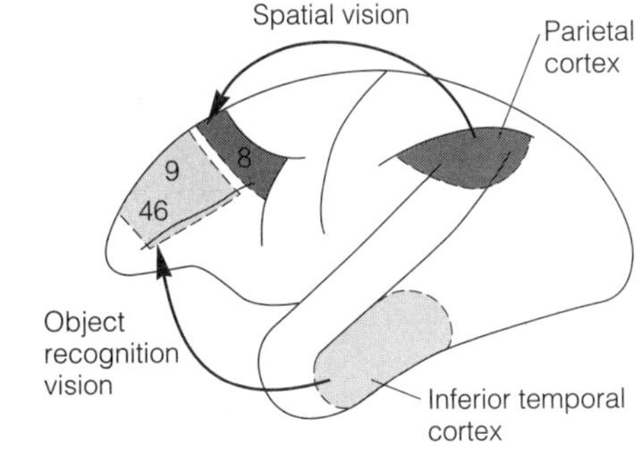

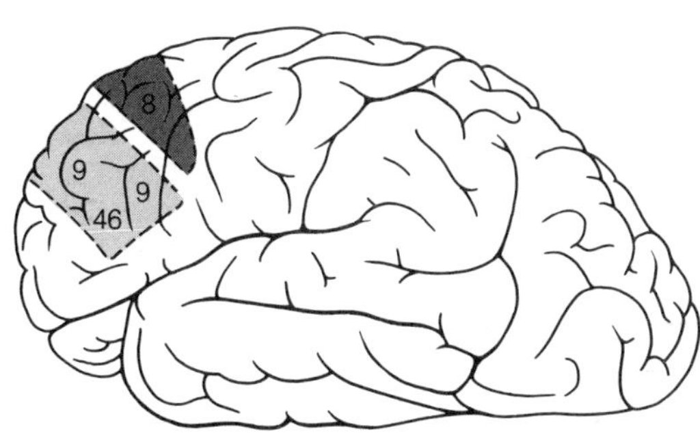

FIGURE 16.10. *A.* Frontal cortex area 8 is involved in short-term memory for the spatial location of objects. It receives projections from the parietal cortex. Frontal cortex areas 9 and 46 are involved in short-term memory for visual objects and receive information from the inferior temporal cortex. Summary based on single cell recording experiments in monkeys. (After Wilson et al., 1993.) *B.* Frontal cortex area 8 is involved in searching for an object when a stimulus is presented, and areas 9 and 46 are involved in remembering objects that are identified sequentially. Summary based on PET recording experiments in human subjects. (After Petrides et al., 1993.)

Their analogy for the spatial vision test required subjects to point to one of eight patterns on each of eight cards in response to a colored bar at the top of the card. That is, in response to a cue, the subject had to search for a specific pattern. They found increases in activity in area 8 of the left hemisphere. Their analogy for the object task required subjects to point to each of the patterns on successive cards until they had indicated each pattern sequentially. That is, they had to keep track of the objects that they had indicated already. They found increases in rCBF in the middorsolateral frontal cortex (areas 9 and 46, mainly on the right). Thus, both sets of studies indicate that different areas of the prefrontal cortex are involved in different kinds of short-term memory.

THE STRUCTURAL BASIS OF MEMORY

Hebb realized from the earlier anatomical work of Lorenté de No that neurons in the brain are interconnected with many other neurons and that each neuron receives input from many synapses on its dendrites and cell body. The resulting neuronal loops (Figure 16.11) contain neurons whose output signal may be either excitatory or inhibitory. Although the neuronal loops are usually drawn as though they were in the cortex, many of them probably run from the cortex to the thalamus or other subcortical structures, such as the hippocampus, and back to the cortex. Because each neuron is believed to both send and receive thousands of outputs and inputs, the number of possible neuronal loops is truly immense.

Hebb proposed that each psychologically important event—whether a sensation, percept, memory, thought, or emotion—can be conceived as the flow of activity in a given neuronal loop. Hebb proposed that the synapses in a particular path become functionally connected to form a **cell assembly** and assumed that if two neurons, A and B, are excited together, they become linked functionally. In Hebb's words: "When an axon of cell A is near enough to excite a cell B and repeatedly or persistently takes part in firing it, some growth process or metabolic change takes

cell assembly - if 2 cells are excited together, they become linked functionally

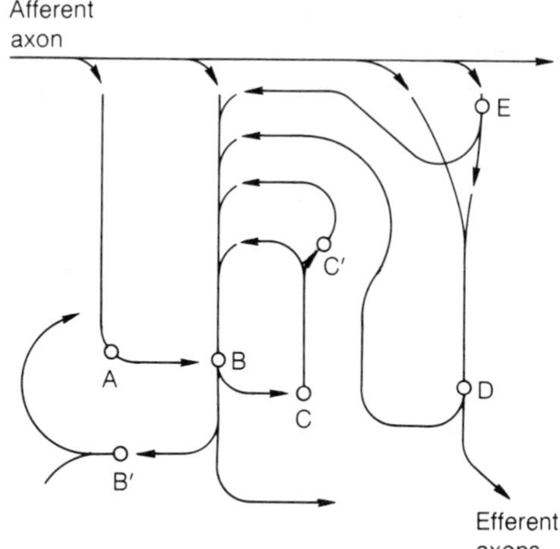

FIGURE 16.11. Simplified diagram of the interconnections of neurons to form neuronal loops (cell assemblies). The entering (afferent) axon excites four neurons, A, B, D, and E. Of these, B and D send impulses out of the system (efferent axons) to excite other systems. A-B-B′, B-C, and B-C-C′ form closed loops. (After Hebb, 1972.)

place in one or both cells such that A's efficiency, as one of the cells firing B, is increased" (Hebb, 1949, p. 62). In Hebb's view, one cell could become more capable of firing another because synaptic knobs grew or became more functional, increasing the area of contact between the afferent axon and the efferent cell body and dendrites. Finally, Hebb assumed that any cell assembly could be excited by others, which provided the basis for thought or ideation. The essence of an "idea" is that it occurs in the absence of the original environmental event to which it corresponds.

The beauty of Hebb's theory is that it attempted to explain psychological events by the physiological properties of the nervous system. Now, more than 40 years after Hebb's landmark volume, his idea that synaptic modification is the basis of memory has led to use of the term **Hebb synapse** to designate synapses that undergo change during learning.

Hebb proposed that there must be changes in the synaptic junction that make the synapse more "efficient." The nature of the synaptic change in information storage is still uncertain and leads to questions about just what changes do occur at the synapse. To find answers, we must return to the structure of the synapse. Figure 16.12 illustrates a synapse and shows the various measures of morphology that have been correlated with learning. Several lines of evidence show that alterations in each of these measures may accompany behavioral change. Thus, in an extensive series of experiments, Greenough and his colleagues have shown that when animals are trained in specific tasks or are exposed to specific environments, there are changes in the dendrites of neurons. If there is an increase in the number of dendrites of

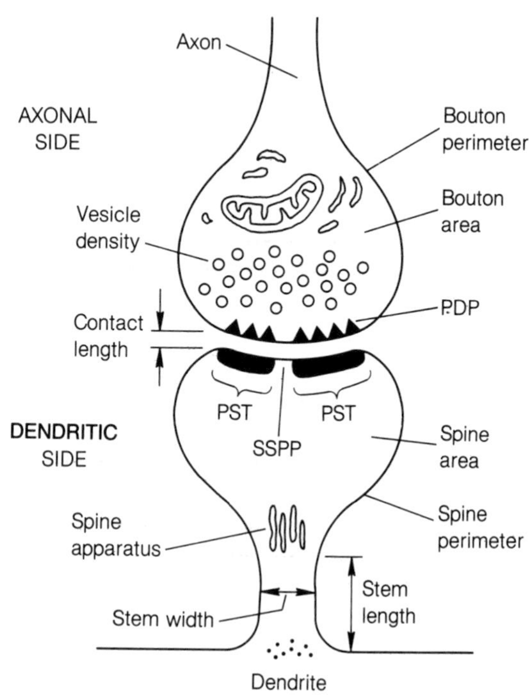

FIGURE 16.12. Measures of synaptic change that may subserve learning. PST, postsynaptic thickening; SSPP, subsynaptic plate perforation; PDP, presynaptic dense projections. (After Greenough and Chang, 1985.)

particular neurons, it follows that there might be an increase in the number of synapses on these neurons, and Greenough has shown this to be the case. In addition, he and his colleagues have shown that there are qualitative changes in the synapses. These include changes in the size of various synaptic components, in the number of vesicles, in the size of postsynaptic thickenings, and in the size of the dendritic spines.

If a morphological change is the basis of memory, then we must ask which neurons in the brain are modified by experience. It is equally unlikely that every neuron would change with each experience or that only one neuron would change with each experience. It seems reasonable to suppose that visual experiences would change neurons in the visual system, auditory experiences would alter those in the auditory system, and so on.

At least three problems arise, however. First, a sensory experience could not change every neuron in the relevant system, or all subsequent experiences would be changed. That is, cells in the primary visual cortex, for example, could not change too much, or the information sent to higher areas would be highly unstable, which would lead to very different sensory experiences and perceptions over time. We know, however, that specific visual environments do change cells in the primary visual cortex, which leaves us with a puzzle! Nonetheless, it is logical to suppose that experiences are more likely to affect higher-level sensory areas than lower-level ones. Second, if sensory experiences change sensory systems, thus permitting memories of the events, how do we remember ideas or thoughts? Third, if experiences result in widespread changes in synapses, how do we find specific memories? It would seem that if memories are widely distributed in large cell assemblies, then it would be a formidable task to locate the memories. Most of us have found ourselves totally unable to recall some answer for an examination; then we suddenly remember one small fact that appears to allow us access to the entire memory. What mechanism could account for this?

We have assumed here that memories are likely to be stored in the cortex, but they need not be. Decorticated animals can learn many behavioral tasks, and simple animals with rudimentary nervous systems can learn and show evidence of "memory." Additionally, Thompson and his coworkers have demonstrated that the cerebellum plays a role in the conditioning of certain responses. It is reasonable, therefore, to suppose that memories are stored in both cortical and subcortical structures. Furthermore, given that many memories depend upon sensory processing and that sensory processing is carried out in multiple systems, it is reasonable to think that different types of information are stored in different places in the brain.

S.: A CASE OF TOTAL RECALL

We close this chapter by noting that students may have had unenjoyable experiences with different kinds of memory when studying for and writing examinations. If a student underlines relevant passages in a text to study for a test, then that student will undoubtably do well on an examination that calls for a similar activity. Unfortunately, most examinations do not work that way because they require the quite different activity of writing a summary of the text from memory. The unpleasant experience of "I knew it but I had a mental block" can be avoided by engaging in the same operations during the study phase as will be called upon during the test phase. This usually involves top-down as opposed to bottom-up processing. We would be remiss if we were not to explain how this can be done.

S. had an extraordinary ability to form explicit memories that he could not forget. S. was a newspaper reporter who never took notes at briefings as did other reporters, and so he came to the attention of his employer. When questioned on the matter, S. repeated verbatim the transcript of the briefing. S. had not considered himself unusual, although he had wondered why other people relied so much on written notes. Nonetheless, at his employer's urging he went to see a psychologist. In this way, S. met Luria, with whom he began a

30-year study of his memory. Luria published an account of this investigation, and to this day *The Mind of a Mnemonist* is one of the most readable accounts of unusual memory.

We can document S.'s memory abilities by referring to Table 16.3. S. could look at this table for 2 or 3 min and then repeat it from memory: by columns, by rows, by diagnonals, in reverse, or in sums. Tested unexpectedly as many as 16 or more years later, S. could repeat the performance without error.

For a good part of his life S. supported himself as a mnemonist; that is, a person who exhibits his memory in performance to audiences. During the course of his work he memorized hundreds of such lists, or lists of names, letters, nonsense syllables, and so forth, and was able to recall any of these at some later date.

S.'s ability to commit things to memory hinged on three processes. He could visualize the stimuli mentally, recalling them simply by reading them from this internal image. He also made multisensory impressions of things. This ability, called **synesthesia,** involves processing any sensory event in all sensory modalities simultaneously. Thus, a word was recorded as a sound, a splash of color, an odor, and a taste, as well as an object with texture and temperature. Finally S. employed the pegboard technique used by many other mnemonists; that is, he used a number of standard images with which he associated new material. Whereas most mnemonists use this technique as their primary memory device, however, S. seemed to use it somewhat less, relying more on his internal visual images and his multisensory impressions. Here are some examples of how he saw numbers:

> Even numbers remind me of images. Take the number 1. This is a proud, well-built man; 2 is a high-spirited woman; 3 a gloomy person (shy, I don't know); 6 a man with a swollen foot; 7 a man with a mustache; 8 a very stout woman—a sack within a sack. As for the number 87, what I see is a fat woman and a man twirling his mustache. (Luria, 1968, p. 31)

> For me, 2, 4, 6, 5 are not just numbers. They have forms. 1 is a pointed number—which has nothing to do with the way it's written. It's because it's somehow firm and complete. 2 is flatter, rectangular, whitish in color, sometimes almost a gray. 3 is a pointed segment which rotates. 4 is also square and dull; it looks like 2 but has more substance to it, it's thicker. 5 is absolutely complete and takes the form of a cone or a tower—something substantial. 6, the first number after 5, has a whitish hue; 8 somehow has a naive quality, it's milky blue like lime. (Luria, 1968, p. 25)

From Luria's description of S., it seems safe to conclude that there was absolutely no limit to his ability to remember. At least Luria, in the many tests he gave S., was never able to reach such a limit. What was S.'s ability with respect to short-term memory, long-term memory, and forgetting?

Luria never really tested S. to determine whether he had a short-term memory of the sort that most of us have. That is, once given an item of information, did S. forget it a short while later? Luria's report seems to suggest that S. had no

TABLE 16.3. Example of tables memorized by S.

6	6	8	0
5	4	3	2
1	6	8	4
7	9	3	5
4	2	3	7
3	8	9	1
1	0	0	2
3	4	5	1
2	7	6	8
1	9	2	6
2	9	6	7
5	5	2	0
x	0	1	x

Note: With only 2 to 3 minutes' study of such a table, S. was able to reproduce it in reverse order, horizontally, or vertically, and to reproduce the diagonals.

short-term memory—everything was put into long-term storage. In fact, S. worried about his inability to forget and attempted to devise strategies for forgetting. He tried to write things down just as most of us do when we do not wish to carry them about as a memory, but the technique did not work:

> Writing something down means I'll know I won't have to remember it. . . . So I started doing this with small matters like phone numbers, last names, errands of one sort or another. But I got nowhere, for in my mind I continued to see what I'd written. . . . Then I tried writing all the notes on identical kinds of paper, using the same pencil each time. But it still doesn't work. (Luria, 1968, p. 70)

S. tried other strategies: burning the paper in his mind, or putting things on the blackboard and covering them up or erasing them in his mind. But none of these techniques worked, either.

Did S. forget? We have already said that his long-term memory was amazing, but from Luria's account he did not seem to forget in the same way as the rest of us. When he missed an item, it was not because it was forgotten but because it was hidden from view or hard to see. He was always able to find it. Here is how he accounted for some of the items he had missed in a list:

> I put the image of the *pencil* near a fence . . . the one down the street, you know. But what happened was that the image fused with that of the fence and I walked right on past without noticing it. The same thing happened with the word *egg*. I had put it up against a white wall and it blended in with the background. How could I possibly spot a white egg up against a white wall? (Luria, 1968, p. 36)

S.'s ability to use his imagination was not limited to memorizing things. He could raise his heart rate from 70–72 to 100 beats per minute by imagining that he was exercising and could lower it to 64–66 by imagining that he was relaxing. He could also raise and lower the temperature of his hand by imagining that it was in warm or cold water. He could deal with pain by imagining that he was no longer in his body, and he could stop his sense of time passing by imagining that the hands of a clock no longer moved. He was even able to adapt himself to darkness in a lighted room by imagining that he was in a darkened room. The incredible control he had over his autonomic system contrasts with H. M., who was reported to show no changes of galvanic skin response even when receiving mild skin shock.

Did S. pay a price for his memory abilities? Luria clearly takes the position that he did. Luria characterizes S. as a person with little aim in life and one who seemed dull and superficial. Luria suggests that S. was not able to reason, to categorize, and to see order in things, as ordinary people can do. He also had little ability to deal with metaphors; he visualized and interpreted them literally (for example, to weigh one's words) and so was puzzled by what they meant. He had difficulty understanding what was meant by simple statements and had greater difficulty understanding the sense of poetry. Thus, we can see in the behavior of S. how top-down or conscious manipulation of information aided him to form memories. The tricks of mnemonists give some insights into how explicit memories are usually formed and how this ability can be exploited to improve memory in normal people, as well as in people with memory impairments. We can also learn from S. that short-term memory helps us to assess, compare, classify, change, and otherwise manipulate information.

SUMMARY

In this chapter we suggest that there are two kinds of memory: conscious or explicit memory and unconscious or implicit memory. In addition, there are probably many forms of both types of memory distributed through neural structures.

Damage to medial temporal structures prevents the formation of new explicit memories but spares old memories and implicit memories. On the other hand, damage to structures that connect with the basal ganglia disrupts implicit memory but spares explicit memory. We also suggest that short-term memory has a structural basis different from that of long-term memory. The parietal-frontal spatial system and the inferior-temporal dorsolateral frontal system appear to be involved in short-term memory for spatial locations and objects, respectively.

REFERENCES

Amaral, D. G. Memory: Anatomical organization for candidate brain regions. In *Handbook of Physiology: The Nervous System*. Bethesda, Maryland: The American Physiological Society, 1987.

Anderson, R. Cognitive changes after amygdalectomy. *Neuropsychologia* 16:439–451, 1978.

Baddely, A. *Working Memory*. London: Oxford University Press, 1986.

Bartlett, F. C. *Remembering*. Cambridge: Cambridge University Press, 1932.

Bekhterev, V. M. Demonstration eines Gehirns mit Zerstörung der vorderen und inneren Theile der Hirnrinde beider Schlafenlappen. *Neurol. Zbl.* 19:990–991, 1900.

Broadbent, D. E. *Perception and Communication*. London: Pergamon, 1958.

Cermak, L. S., ed. *Human Memory and Amesia*. Hillsdale, N.J.: Lawrence Erlbaum Associates, 1982.

Chapman, L. F., R. D. Walter, C. H. Markham, R. W. Rand, and P. H. Crandall. Memory changes induced by stimulation of hippocampus or amygdala in epilepsy patients with implanted electrodes. *Transactions of the American Neurological Association* 92:50–56, 1967.

Corkin, S. Tactually-guided maze-learning in man: Effects on unilateral cortical excisions and bilateral hippocampal lesions. *Neuropsychologia* 3:339–351, 1965.

Corkin, S. Acquisition of motor skill after bilateral medial temporal-lobe excision. *Neuropsychologia* 6:255–265, 1968.

Corsi, P. M. "Human Memory and the Medial Temporal Region of the Brain." Ph.D. dissertation. Montreal: McGill University, 1972.

Damasio, A. R., D. Tranel, and H. Damasio. Amnesia caused by herpes simplex encephalitis, infarctions in basal forebrain, Alzheimer's disease and anoxia/ischemia. In L. Squire and G. Gainotti, eds. *Handbook of Neuropsychology,* vol 3. Amsterdam: Elsevier, 1991.

Ebbinghaus, H. *Memory*. New York: Teachers College, 1913 (originally published in 1885). Reprinted by Dover, New York, 1964.

Fisher, C. M., and R. O. Adams. Transient global amnesia. *Transactions of the American Neurological Association* 83:143, 1958.

Fuster, J. M. *The Prefrontal Cortex*. New York: Raven Press, 1989.

Gaffan, D. Monkey's recognition memory for complex pictures and the effect of fornix transection. *Quarterly Journal of Experimental Psychology* 29:505–514, 1977.

Garcia-Bengochea, F., O. de La Torre, and O. Esquivel. The section of the fornix in the surgical treatment of certain epilepsies. *Transactions of the American Neurological Association* 79:176–179, 1954.

Goldman-Rakic, P. S. Working memory and the mind. *Scientific American* 267(3):111–117, 1992.

Gollin, E. S. Developmental studies of visual recognition of incomplete objects. *Perceptual and Motor Skills* 11:289–298, 1960.

Grafton, S. T., J. C. Mazziotta, S. Presty, K. J. Friston, S. J. Frackowiak, and M. E. Phelps. Functional anatomy of human procedural learning determined with regional cerebral blood flow and PET. *The Journal of Neuroscience* 12:2542–2548, 1992.

Greenough, W. T., and F. F. Chang. Synaptic structural correlates of information storage in mammalian nervous systems. In C. W. Cotman, ed. *Synaptic Plasticity*. New York: Guilford Press, 1985.

Hebb, D. O. *Organization of Behavior*. New York: John Wiley, 1949.

Horel, J. A. The neuroanatomy of amnesia: A critique of the hippocampal memory hypothesis. *Brain* 101:403–445, 1978.

James, W. *The Principles of Psychology*. New York: Henry Holt, 1890.

Kolb, B., and B. Milner. Performance of complex arm and facial movements after focal brain lesions. *Neuropsychologia* 19:491–503, 1981.

Lashley, K. D. In search of the engram. *Symposia of the Society for Experimental Biology* 4:454–482, 1950.

Luria, A. R. *The Mind of a Mnemonist*. New York: Basic Books, 1968.

Mair, W. G. P., E. K. Warrington, and L. Weiskrantz.

Memory disorder in Korsakoff's psychosis. *Brain* 102:749–783, 1979.

Markowitsch, H. J. Transient global amnesia. *Neuroscience and Biobehavioral Reviews* 7:35–43, 1983.

Markowitsch, H. J., and M. Pritzel. The neuropathology of amnesia. *Progress in Neurobiology* 25:189–288, 1985.

Marsolek, C. J., S. M. Kosslyn, and L. R. Squire. Form-specific visual priming in the right cerebral hemisphere. *Journal of Experimental Psychology: Learning, Memory, and Cognition* 18:492–508, 1992.

Mazzucchi, A., G. Moretti, P. Caffara, and M. Parma. Neuropsychological functions in the follow-up of transient global amnesia. *Brain* 103:161–178, 1980.

Meunier, M., J. Bachevalier, M. Mishkin, and E. A. Murray. Effects of visual recognition of combined and separate ablations of the entorhinal and perirhinal cortex in rhesus monkeys. *The Journal of Neuroscience* 13:5418–5432, 1993.

Milner, B. Visually-guided maze learning in man: Effects of bilateral hippocampal, bilateral frontal, and unilateral cerebral lesions. *Neuropsychologia* 3:317–338, 1965.

Milner, B. Memory and the medial temporal regions of the brain. In K. H. Pribram and D. E. Broadbent, eds. *Biology of Memory*. New York: Academic Press, 1970.

Milner, B., S. Corkin, and H.-L. Teuber. Further analysis of the hippocampal amnesic syndrome: 14-year follow up study of H. M. *Neuropsychologia* 6:215–234, 1968.

Moscovitch, M. Multiple dissociations of function in amnesia. In L. S. Cermak, ed. *Human Memory and Amnesia*. Hillsdale, N.J.: Lawrence Erlbaum Associates, 1982.

Oscar-Berman, M. Neuropsychological consequences of long-term chronic alcoholism. *American Scientist* 68:410–419, 1980.

Pascual-Leone, A., J. Grafman, and M. Hallett. Modulation of cortical motor output maps during development of implicit and explicit knowledge. *Science* 263:1287–1289, 1994.

Penfield, W., and B. Milner. Memory deficit produced by bilateral lesions in the hippocampal zone. *Archives of Neurology and Psychiatry* 79:475–497, 1958.

Petri, H. L., and M. Mishkin. Behaviorism, cognitivism and the neuropsychology of memory. *American Scientist* 82:30–37, 1994.

Petrides, M. Deficits on conditional associative-learning tasks after frontal- and temporal-lobe lesions in man. *Neuropsychologia* 23:601–614, 1985.

Petrides, M., B. Alivisatos, A. C. Evans, and E. Meyer. Dissociation of human mid-dorsolateral from posterior dorsolateral frontal cortex in memory processing. *Proceedings of the National Academy of Sciences USA* 90:873–877, 1993.

Posner, M. I., and M. E. Raichle. *Images of Mind*. New York: Scientific American Library, 1994.

Prisko, L. "Short-Term Memory in Focal Cerebral Damage." Ph.D. dissertation. Montreal: McGill University, 1963.

Rasmussen, T., and B. Milner. Clinical and surgical studies of cerebral speech areas in man. In K. J. Zulch, O. Creutzfeldt, and G. C. Galbraith, eds. *Cerebral Localization*. Berlin and New York: Spring-Verlag, 1975.

Sanders, H. I., and E. K. Warrington. Memory for remote events in amnesic patients. *Brain* 94:661–668, 1971.

Sarter, M., and H. J. Markowitsch. The amygdala's role in human mnemonic processing. *Cortex* 21:7–24, 1985.

Schacter, D. L. Memory, amnesia, and frontal lobe dysfunction. *Psychobiology* 15:21–36, 1987.

Schacter, D. L. Implicit knowledge: New perspectives on unconscious processes. *Proceedings of the National Academy of Sciences* 89:11113–11117, 1992.

Schacter, D. L., and H. F. Crovitz. Memory function after closed head injury: A review of the quantitative research. *Cortex* 13:150–176, 1977.

Scoville, W. B., and B. Milner. Loss of recent memory after bilateral hippocampal lesions. *Journal of Neurology, Neurosurgery and Psychiatry* 20:11–21, 1957.

Squire, L. R. The neuropsychology of human memory. *Annual Review of Neuroscience* 5:241–273, 1982.

Squire, L. R. *Memory and the Brain*. New York: Oxford University Press, 1987.

Talland, G. A. *The Pathology of Memory*. New York: Academic Press, 1969.

Taylor, J. R., R. Tompkins, R. Demers, and D. Anderson. Electroconvulsive therapy and memory dysfunction. Is there evidence for prolonged defects? *Biological Psychiatry* 17:1169–1193, 1982.

Thompson, R. F. The neurobiology of learning and memory. Science 233:941–947, 1986.

Tulving, E., S. Kapur, F. I. M. Craik, M. Moscovitch, and S. Houle. Hemispheric encoding/retrieval asymmetry in episodic memory: Positron emission tomography finding. *Proceedings of the National Academy of Sciences* 91:2016–2020, 1994.

Valenstein, E., D. Bowers, M. Verfaellie, K. M. Heilman, A. Day, and R. T. Watson. Retrosplenial amnesia. *Brain* 110:1631–1646, 1987.

Vanderwolf, C. H. Cerebral activity and behavior: Control by central cholinergic and serotonergic systems. *International Review of Neurobiology* 30:255–340, 1988.

van Hoesen, G. W. The parahippocampal gyrus. New observations regarding its cortical connections in the monkey. *Trends in Neurosciences* 5:345–350, 1982.

Vokey, J. R., J. G. Baker, G. Hayman, and L. L. Jacoby. Perceptual identification of visually degraded stimuli. *Behavior Research Methods, Instruments, and Computers* 18:1–9, 1986.

von Cramen, D. Y., N. Hebel, and U. Schuri. A contribution of the anatomical basis of thalamic amnesia. *Brain* 108:993–1008, 1985.

Warrington, E., and M. James. An experimental investigation of facial recognition in patients with unilateral cerebral lesions. *Cortex* 3:317–326, 1967.

Warrington, E. K., and L. Weiskrantz. Further analysis of the prior learning effect in amnesic patients. *Neuropsychologia* 16:169–177, 1978.

Weiskrantz, L. Neuroanatomy of memory and amnesia: A case for multiple memory systems. *Human Neurobiology* 6:93–105, 1987.

Whitty, C. W. M., and O. L. Zangwill. Traumatic amnesia. In C. W. M. Whitty and O. L. Zangwill, eds. *Amnesia.* London: Butterworth, 1966.

Wilson, F. A. W., S. P. O. Scalaidhe, and P. S. Goldman-Rakic. Dissociation of object and spatial processing domains in primate prefrontal cortex. *Science* 260:1955–1958, 1993.

Woolsey, R. M., and J. S. Nelson. Asymptomatic destruction of the fornix in man. *Archives of Neurology* 32:566–568, 1975.

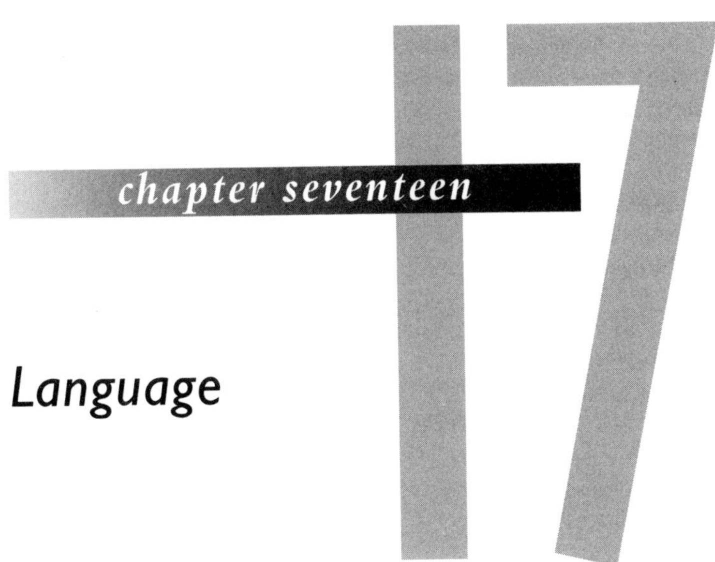

Language

Language is one of our most precious abilities, yet we usually take it for granted. We spend hours talking, listening, and reading—we even talk to ourselves. We use words to label things in our environment. As children, we learn language long before we can catch a ball or ride a bicycle. We use language to entertain ourselves in poetry, song, and humor. Indeed, much humor is based upon nuances of language and double entendres. Despite the apparent ease with which most of us use langauge, there is little doubt that it is one of our most complex cognitive and motor skills. Our nonchalance about language can dissipate quickly, however, when we find ourselves in a country where the language is unfamiliar—or if, through injury or disease, we lose our language ability. There are many ways to approach the study of language, but one place to start is to consider what language is.

WHAT IS LANGUAGE?

There is no universally accepted definition of language. Many species of animals use sound as a form of communication, but most people would agree that a cricket song and human discourse are not the same behavior. The question is where to draw the line between simple forms of communication and language. Those who emphasize the uniqueness of human language focus upon those aspects that differentiate it from other forms of communication such as birdsongs, chimpanzee gestures, or canid olfactory signals. Thus, a definition of language usually includes the use of words as referents for things or ideas and the ordering of words in different ways to alter meaning (for example, "the man's lost wallet" versus "the lost man's wallet"). Although we tend to think of words as the basis of language, linguists break down language somewhat differently (Table 17.1). Words are made from the fundamental sounds, called **phonemes,** in a language. An analysis of how phonemes are processed is called a phonological analysis. Phonemes are combined to form **morphemes,** the smallest meaningful units of words. A morpheme may be a base (*do* in *undo*), an affix (*un* in *undo* or *er* in *doer*), or an inflectional form (*ing* in *doing* or *s* in *girls*). Morphemes may be words themselves or they may be combined to form words. Once we have made words, they must be strung together following the rules of

TABLE 17.1. Components of a sound-based language

Phonemes	The individual sound units whose concatenation, in particular order, produces morphemes
Morphemes	The smallest meaningful units of a word, whose combination creates a word
Syntax	The admissible combinations of words in phrases and sentences (called grammar, in popular usage)
Lexicon	The collection of all words in a given language; each lexical entry includes all information with morphological or syntactic ramifications but does not include conceptual knowledge
Semantics	The meanings that correspond to all lexical items and all possible sentences
Prosody	The vocal intonation that can modify the literal meaning of words and sentences
Discourse	The linking of sentences such that they constitute a narrative

Source: After Damasio and Damasio, 1992.

grammar. This is known as **syntax.** Note that a key part of syntax involves the use of verbs and the appropriate choice of verb tenses. It is interesting that children develop syntax independent of formal training, a characteristic that led Chomsky to suggest that there is an innate basis for the development of human language. Finally, the stringing together of sentences to form a meaningful narrative is called **discourse.** Although our discussion has emphasized the acoustical nature of these basic parts of language, there are analogues in visual language, such as American Sign Language (ASL). A morpheme in ASL would be the smallest meaningful movement.

Although the emphasis on words and their components is the traditional way that linguists classify language, there are other ways to categorize the components of language. MacNeilage has noted that one unique characteristic of human language is its use of syllables that are made up of consonants and vowels. Nonhuman species do not produce syllables, primarily because they do not produce consonants. Thus, for MacNeilage, the unique thing about human language is that we can form the mouth to produce consonants and to combine them with vowels to produce syllables.

The emphasis on things that are unique to human language carries some pitfalls. Although no other species has language in the sense that linguists mean it, there can be little doubt that language did not appear suddenly in *Homo sapiens.* There must be some evolutionary trace of the processes and anatomical structures necessary for human language. Thus, it seems reasonable to approach the study of human language by seeking evidence of some type of behavior that could have been selected and have led ultimately to language. Finding such capacities is not an idle question of curiousity. If we can determine which capacities have been selected to allow language in humans, we will have taken a giant step toward understanding how language is represented in our brain.

ORIGINS OF SPEECH AND LANGUAGE

Origins of Language

An obvious explanation of speech is that it evolved slowly from various kinds of vocalizations. Hewes has reviewed many variants of this theory, including the "pooh-pooh" theory (speech evolved from noises associated with strong emotion), the "bow-wow" theory (speech evolved from noises first made to imitate natural sounds), the "yo-he-ho" theory (speech evolved from sounds made to resonate with natural sounds), and the "sing-song" theory (speech evolved from noises made while playing or dancing). These examples by no means exhaust the list of imaginative theories of speech origin. A major difficulty with these kinds of theories is that it is very hard to collect evidence to support them. Nevertheless, Steklis and Raleigh argue strongly for the theory that speech evolved from vocalization. They cite the following evidence. The theory is parsimonious, since it involves a direct rather than an indirect explanation; many nonhuman primates use nonemotional types of vocalizations in a rudimentary communicative style; and the evolution of new types of skilled movements would have provided a neural basis for the refined movements of the vocal system needed for speech.

There are also two other major theories that deserve consideration, if not for their explanatory power, then at least because they are supported by a substantial amount of research. One theory postulates that language in its present form is of recent origin. The other postulates that language is very old and only gradually evolved into its present form from its original gestural base. In a sense, these two theories are compatible because language may have evolved in a gestural form and then been transformed rapidly into a vocal form.

Speech as a Recently Evolved Ability

Let us consider the evidence that language (as mordern humans use it) has a relatively recent origin. Swadish developed a list of 100 basic lexical concepts that he expected to be found in every language. These included such words as "I," "two," "woman," "sun," and "green." He then calculated the rate at which these words would have changed as new dialects of language were formed. His estimates suggested a rate of change of 14% every 1000 years. When he compared the lists of words spoken in different parts of the world today, he estimated that between 10,000 and 100,000 years ago everyone spoke the same language. According to Swadish's logic, language would have had its origins at about this time because diversification would have begun almost as soon as language developed. Of course, hominids have been around for 4 million years, so how can one rule out the possibility that they were speaking much earlier than 100,000 years ago?

Lieberman has studied the properties of the vocal tract that enable modern humans to make the sounds used for language. Modern humans have a low larynx and a large throat, and these features make them unique. Modern apes and newborn humans have neither of these characteristics and cannot produce all the sounds used in human speech. On the basis of skull reconstructions, Lieberman suggests that Neanderthal man also was unable to make the sounds necessary for modern speech. Specifically, he would not have been able to produce the vowels "a," "i," and "u."

The position of the larynx in modern humans is not only important for language but also signifies a considerable change in human respiratory and feeding patterns. Figure 17.1 illustrates the location of the larynx in a human infant, in a chimpanzee, and in an adult human. Arrows indicate the flow of air during respiration and the flow of fluid during drinking. Note that the human infant can drink and breathe at the same time, since the high location of the larynx allows milk to flow around it and into the esophagus. The chimp, similarly, is able to swallow and breathe at the same time. The low larynx in the adult human, however, demands that respiration stop to prevent choking during drinking. Lieberman's theory is not without its critics. It has been argued that no animal can really breathe and swallow at the same time. Also, there is doubt that the quality of the Neanderthal skulls recovered is good enough to allow any conclusion about the position of the larnyx in Neanderthals.

If Lieberman's hypothesis about the relation between speech and the structure of the vocal tract is correct, it can be concluded that modern speech did not exist before about 100,000 years ago. Another argument for the recent development of speech is that the ability to write and the ability to speak seem to have a lot in common. Most notably, they both require very fine movements and many movement transitions. Therefore, it is possible that speech and writing appeared at about the same time. Marshack has found that the first symbols made by humans date back to about 30,000 years ago. This would be evidence that speech appeared at about this time. What seems to link these three separate lines of evidence, making the recency hypothesis plausible, is that the first appearance of modern humans,

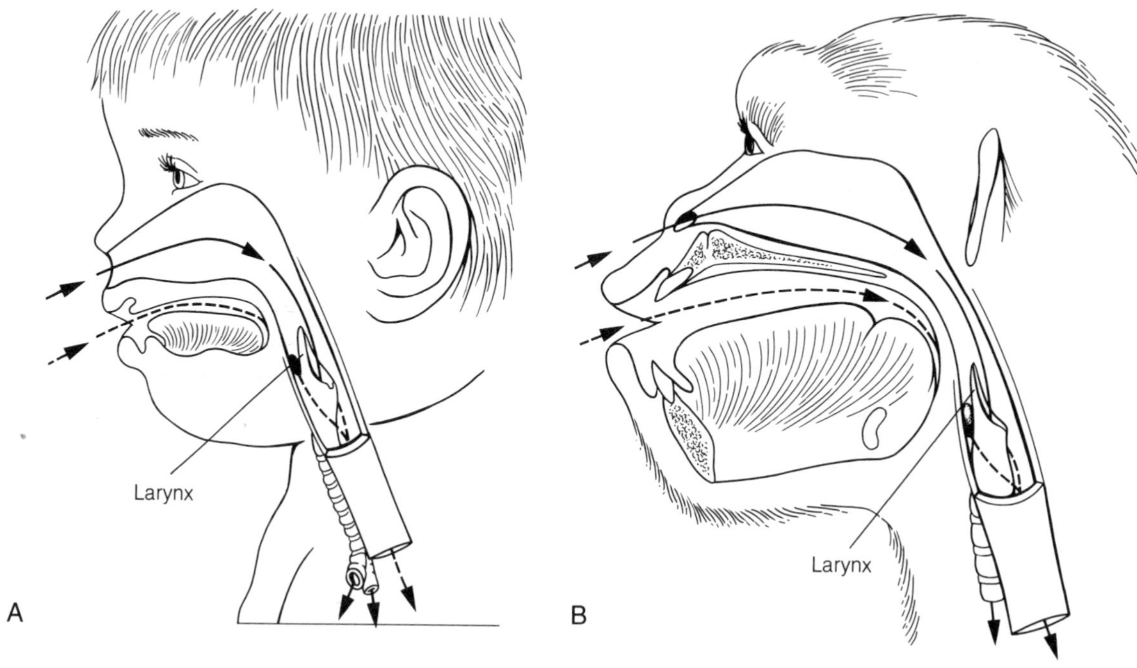

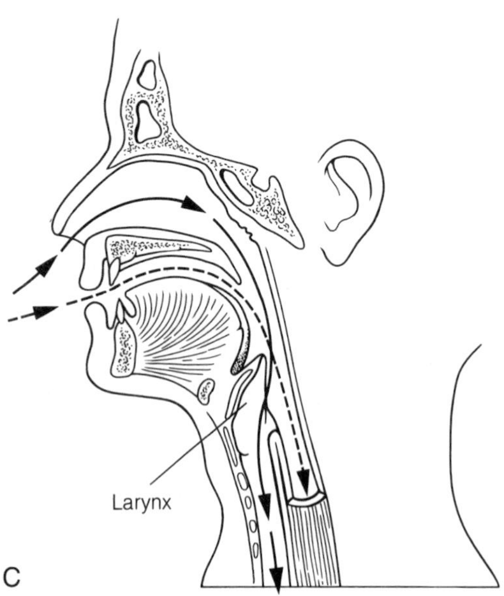

FIGURE 17.1. Cross-sectional views of the vocal tract in human baby (*A*), adult chimpanzee (*B*), and adult human (*C*). Note the high position of the larynx in the human baby and the adult chimp, which permits them to ingest food or fluids without concomitantly arresting respiration. In adult humans the low location of the larynx permits speech production but requires that respiration be arrested during swallowing. (After Laitman, 1986.)

Homo sapiens sapiens, can be dated to about 40,000 to 100,000 years ago. Possibly the evolution of modern humans was quite sudden and one of their adaptive strategies was language. In opposition to the notion of recently acquired speech, Holloway argues from paleontological evidence (for example, the size of Broca's area as revealed by endocasts) that rudimentary language was probably displayed by *Australopithecus* roughly 2.5 to 3.5 million years ago.

Although the development of the vocal tract may be crucial to human language, there also have been other changes in the mechanisms of primate vocal production. MacNeilage notes that there are three main components of the vocal production system of mammals: the respiratory, the phonatory, and the articulatory. The respiratory component is the outward flow of air under pressure. This is the source of power in the voice. The phonatory component is the process in which the vocal folds are brought together to vibrate when activated by the air flow. The articulatory component is basically what the mouth does. The mouth is usually opened once for each vocal episode, and the shape of the cavity between the lips and the vocal tract modulates the sound. The changes in the larynx described by Leiberman increase the ability of the vocal system to produce the latter two components. MacNeilage points out, however, that the key difference between humans and other mammals is the articulartory component. Consider the vocal repertoire of the chimpanzee. Jane Goodall's studies on the chimpanzees of Gombe in Tanzania indicate that our closest relatives have as many as 32 separate vocalizations (Figure 17.2). Goodall notes that the chimps seem to understand these calls much better than do humans, but she also notes that her field assistants, who were most familiar with the chimps, favored an even greater number of divisions. Despite the complexity of the chimpanzee vocalizations, they are fundamentally different from human voice sounds in that they have a limited articulatory component. In human speech, by contrast, the vocal tract alternates more or less regularly between a relatively open and a relatively closed configuration, open for vowels and

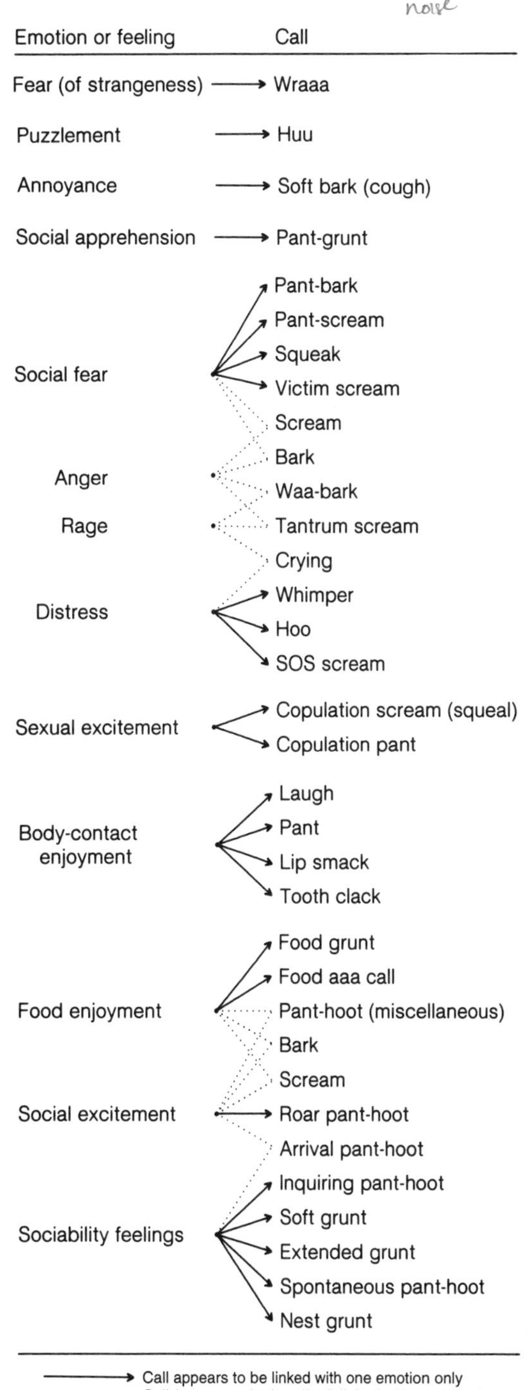

FIGURE 17.2. Chimpanzee calls and the emotion or feeling with which they are most closely associated. (From Goodall, 1986. Reprinted with permission.)

closed for consonants. Indeed, MacNeilage thinks that this characteristic of human language is basic enough to be a definitional characteristic. Thus, with the exception of a few words containing a single vowel, virtually every utterance of every one of the world's languages involves an alternation between vowels and consonants. To MacNeilage the issue is not how the vocal tract changed but how the brain changed to enable the motor control of the mouth to make syllables. This perspective on language alerts us to its importance as a motor act as well as a perceptual capacity.

Speech as a Gestural Language

Some researchers suggest that primitive gestures and other body movements gradually evolved into modern language. This theory assumes that effective hunting and farming and the maintenance of social groups required some kind of communication system and that this need was the impetus for the evolution of language. Two lines of research can be used as evidence for the gestural theory. First, gestural language and vocal language depend on similar neural systems. Second, nonhuman primates can use gestures or symbols for at least rudimentary communication. The first evidence is important because if the neural systems for gestural and vocal language were different, it would weaken the argument that one type of language evolved into the other. The second line of evidence is important because it shows that a similar, although much smaller, brain is capable of rudimentary language, thus making the evolution of an entirely new neural system for speech unnecessary.

It has long been thought that an experiment showing that gestural language and vocal language depend on the same brain structure would support the idea that gestural language evolved into vocal language. As early as 1878, Hughlings-Jackson suggested that a natural experiment, the loss of language in people using sign language, would provide the appropriate evidence, and he even observed a case that seemed to indicate that sign language was disrupted by a left hemisphere lesion, as is vocal language. A definitive review of similar cases by Kimura confirms that lesions disrupting vocal speech also disrupt signing. Of 11 patients with signing disorders following brain lesions, 9 right-handers had disorders following a left hemisphere lesion. One left-handed patient had a signing disorder following a left hemisphere lesion, and another left-handed patient had a signing disorder following a right hemisphere lesion. These proportions are identical to those found for vocal patients who become aphasic. These results strongly support the idea that at least some of the language systems that control vocal speech also control signing. Indeed, they offer little support for any alternative view (for example, that signing, being spatial in nature, is controlled by the right hemisphere).

In summary, it seems that there is a similarity between lesions that produce vocal language disturbances and those that disrupt the movements required for gestural language. But at this point one must ask if emotional sounds and facial expressions were also precursors of language or if there may have been something special about certain kinds of gestures. The evidence seems to support the idea that emotional sounds or expressions in apes cannot be conditioned for use as signs as easily as gestures can be conditioned. In addition, the neural mechanisms controlling emotional expressions in both apes and humans are different from those controlling language. Kolb and Milner have found that prefrontal lesions disrupt emotional expressions in humans independently of language.

If it is true that gestures had evolved into vocal language by the time *Homo sapiens sapiens* appeared, it is possible to make at least one testable prediction. It is very likely that the first gestures were transmitted genetically rather than culturally. These gestures should still be transmitted genetically and so should still be found in all groups of humans. A subset of this group of gestures should also be used by our close relatives, the apes. The begging gesture, hand outstretched, of chimpanzees and humans is a likely example of these gestures.

A question that can be raised with respect to

gestural theories is why there was a shift to vocalizing. There are at least two plausible explanations. First, as the individual increased the use of tools, the hands were occupied and could not be used for gesturing. Second, gesturing requires visual contact, but animals picking fruit in trees or gathering food in tall grass needed to communicate about both food and predators without being able to see one another. A relevant observation that supports the gestural proposal is that hand gestures still accompany language. Indeed, in the absence of a common language, people elaborate hand and facial gestures to communicate.

Myers has proposed a slightly different version of the gestural theory. He argues that the development of language is a logical consequence of the increasing control of facial musculature. Prosimians (lemurs) cannot produce facial expressions, rhesus monkeys and other monkeys can produce a limited range of facial expressions, and chimpanzees have a complex repertory of facial movements; but only humans have developed both the facial movements and the changes in the vocal tract necessary for speech. Myers proposes that Broca's area creates a qualitatively different type of vocal output. This idea is consistent with Kimura's notion described earlier. Kimura notes that the same movement transitions required for arm gestures are necessary for vocal speech; for example, in the transition "be-ba-be" or "de-da-de." She argues, however, that these transitions are produced by the left parietal cortex rather than by Broca's area. In her view Broca's area produces the individual syllables.

Evidence for Languagelike Processes in Apes

Although no nonhuman primates have a verbal language analogous to that of humans, there must be traces of phylogenetic development of the processes necessary for human language. Darwin argued that evolution is a matter of "descent with modification." Following this logic, language must have evolved by means of a continuum of changes in earlier states. MacNeilage has noted that the most successful theory of the evolution of human language will be the one that can characterize this process of change, with an accurate assessment of the prior steps. One approach to doing this is to attempt to determine the capacity of the nonhuman brain to acquire languagelike processes (Table 17.2).

Several people have tried to teach chimpanzees to talk, but they have been universally unsuccessful. (One reason for this failure may be the limitations in the chimpanzee vocal tract and mouth control discussed above.) These results suggest that audible communication must be bypassed in favor of visual communication. One line of experimentation, begun by the Gardners, used versions of American Sign Language; another line of

TABLE 17.2. Summary of language projects in apes

Project	Procedure	Basic reference
Washoe (chimp)	American Sign Language (ASL)	Gardner and Gardner, 1978
Sarah (chimp)	Plastic tokens to form simple "sentences" to communicate	Premack, 1983
Lana (chimp)	Keyboard communication using a language (Yerkish) based upon lexigrams	Rumbaugh, 1977
Koko (gorilla)	ASL and spoken English	Patterson, 1987
Nim (chimp)	ASL	Terrace, 1979
Kanzi (pygmy chimp)	Keyboard communication with Yerkish and spoken English	Savage-Rumbaugh et al., 1986
Chantek (orang)	Pidgin Sign Language	Miles, 1983

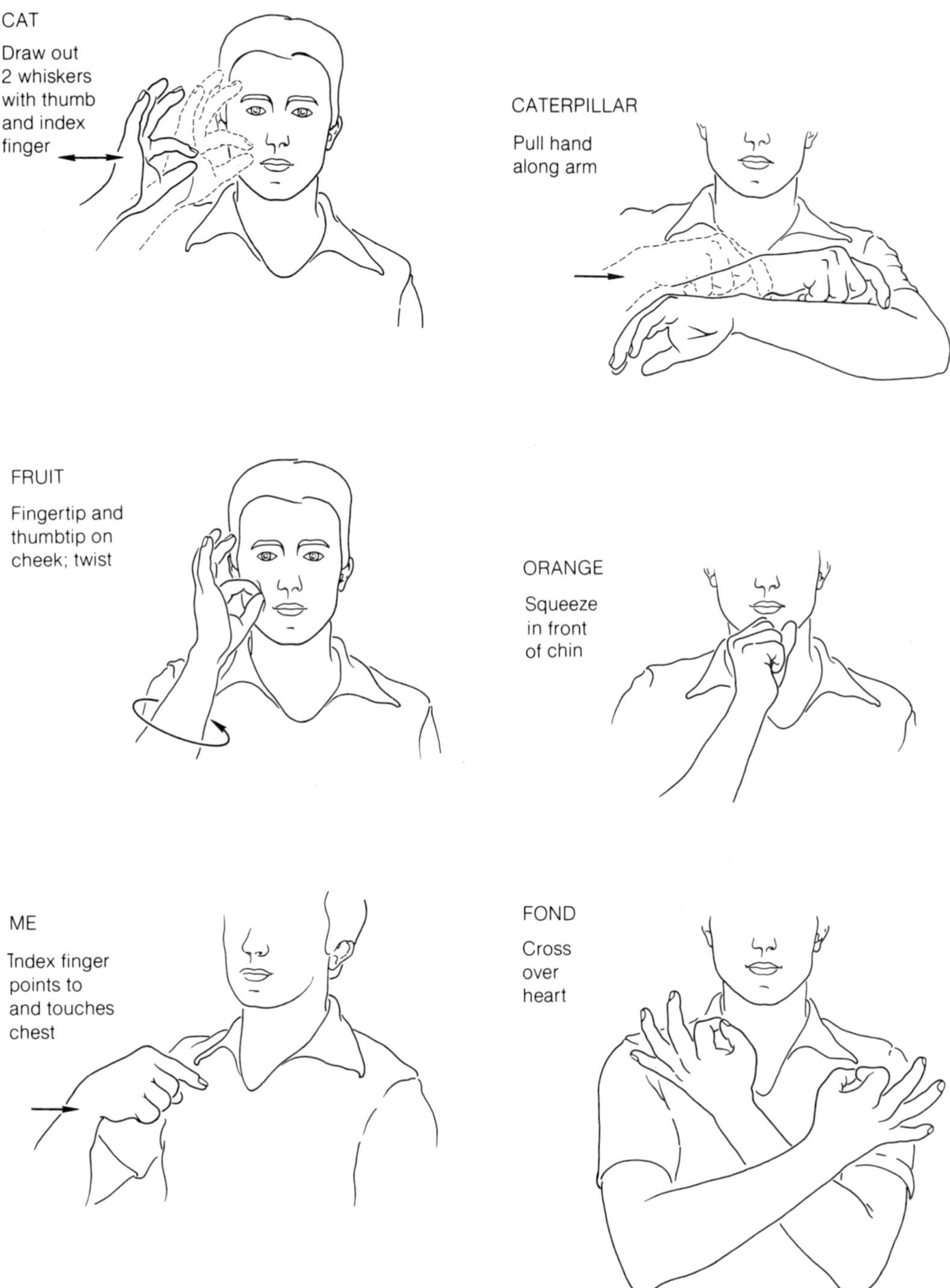
CAT
Draw out
2 whiskers
with thumb
and index
finger
CATERPILLAR
Pull hand
along arm
FRUIT
Fingertip and
thumbtip on
cheek; twist
ORANGE
Squeeze
in front
of chin
ME
Index finger
points to
and touches
chest
FOND
Cross
over
heart

FIGURE 17.3. Examples from American Sign Language. The Gardners and others taught such symbols to the chimpanzees in their studies. (After Gustason et al., 1975.)

work, initiated by Premack, focused on teaching an artificial written language.

The Gardners began by bringing Washoe, a year-old chimp, into their home. They aimed to teach Washoe ASL hand movements, or signs, that refer to various objects or actions (known as exemplars). These signing gestures, analogous to words in spoken language, involve specific movements that begin and end in a prescribed manner in relation to the signer's body (Figure 17.3). The Gardners molded Washoe's hands to form the desired shapes in the presence of the exemplar of the sign, reinforcing her for correct movements. In addition, rather than using verbal language, the Gardners used ASL to communicate with each other in Washoe's presence. Thus, Washoe was raised in an environment filled with signs. Washoe did learn to understand and to use not only nouns but also pronouns and action verbs. For example, she could sign statements such as "You go me," meaning "Come with me." Attempts to teach ASL to other species of great apes (gorilla, orangutan) have had similar results.

The sign language studies have come under very close scrutiny by critics. The principal criticism is that the apes have not been shown unequivocally to use grammatical structure, which is present even in very young human children. Furthermore, it is argued, even if there is some evidence of rudimentary grammar, apes have not been shown to understand that reordering words can give very different meanings. For example, Terrace and his colleagues analyzed more than 19,000 multisign utterances of an infant chimpanzee (Nim), as well as reanalyzing film of Washoe and other chimps. They claimed to have found no evidence of grammatical construction; most of the chimps' utterances were prompted by their teachers' prior utterances and thus could be explained by nonlinguistic processes. Indeed, the authors were struck by the absence of creativity in the apes' utterances and by their dependence on the prior utterances of their teachers. This is quite unlike the advanced multiword sequences produced by young children. In response, the Gardners have argued that Terrace used training methods that were inappropriate for a highly social animal, which chimps are.

Premack approached the study of the language abilities of chimpanzees in a different way. He taught his chimpanzee, Sarah, to read and write with variously shaped and colored pieces of plastic, each representing a word. Premack first taught Sarah that different symbols represented different nouns, just as Washoe had been taught in sign language. Thus, for example, Sarah learned that a pink square was the symbol for banana. Sarah was then taught verbs so that she could write and read such combinations as "give apple" or "wash apple." Her comprehension could be tested easily by writing messages to her (hanging up symbols) and then observing her response. This was followed by much more complicated tutoring in which Sarah mastered the interrogative ("Where is my banana?"), the negative, and finally the conditional (if, then). It is readily apparent that Sarah had learned a fairly complicated communication system analogous in some ways to simple human language.

A more recent project has demonstrated even more complex language learning ability in the chimpanzee. After carefully studying the results of the Gardners' and Premack's projects, Rumbaugh and Gill launched Project Lana, which involved teaching their chimp, Lana, to communicate by means of a keyboard programmed by a computer. The keyboard was composed of nine stimulus elements and nine primary colors, which could be combined in nearly 1800 lexigrams (Figure 17.4), to form a language now known as Yerkish.

Lana had to learn simply to type out her messages on the keyboard. She was first trained to press keys for various single incentives; the requirements then became increasingly complex as she mastered the various types of statements, such as the indicative ("Tim move into room"), the interrogative ("Tim move into room?"), the imperative ("Please Tim move into room"), and the negative ("Don't Tim move into room"). Lana was eventually capable of strings of six lexigrams.

One of the difficulties with Project Lana was that it was based upon an assumption that Lana

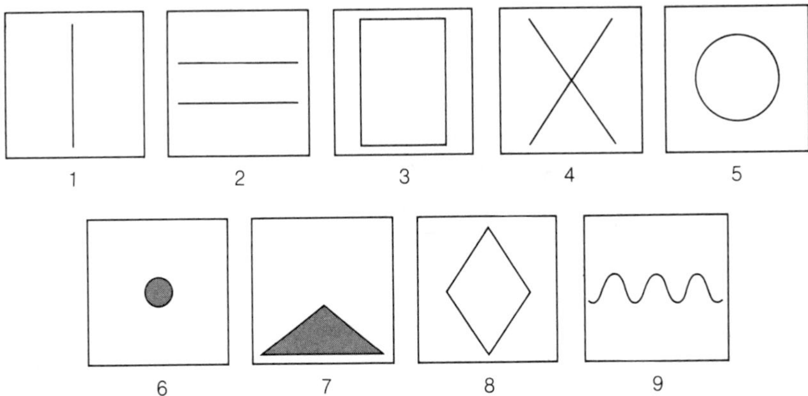

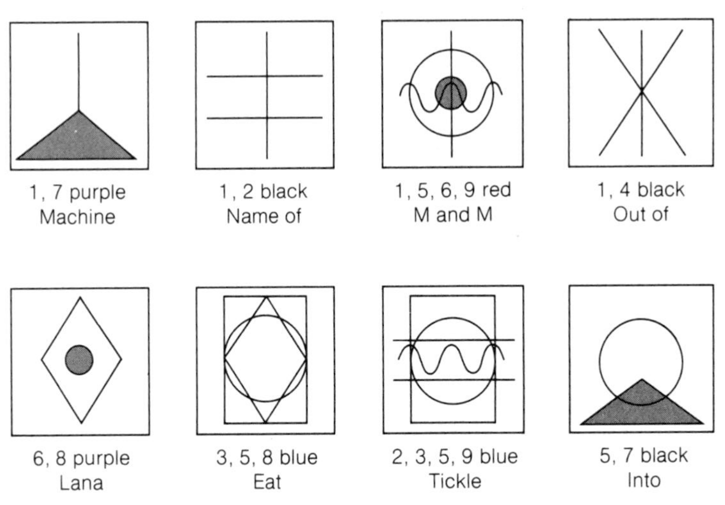

FIGURE 17.4. *A*. The nine basic design elements in Yerkish that are combined to form lexigrams. *B*. Examples of lexigrams. (From von Glaserfeld, 1977. © 1977. Reprinted with permission.)

treated the lexigrams as symbols rather than as mere paired associates for certain stimuli. Indeed, some of the harshest critics have been Rumbaugh and Gill, who were the investigators. In their most recent project, Kanzi, they have altered the format.

Savage-Rumbaugh and coworkers began teaching a wild-caught pygmy chimpanzee, Malatta, the Yerkish language used with Lana. Malatta was very slow to learn the language, probably because of her age and experience, so the workers tried using English words as well, but to no avail. Serendipitously, Malatta had a male offspring, Kanzi, that accompanied her during her language training. It turned out that even though he was not specifically trained, Kanzi learned more than his mother. Remarkably, his knowledge of English words exceeded his knowledge of the lexigrams. To facilitate his learning, his keyboard was augmented with a speech synthesizer. In the fall of 1986, when he was 6 years old, Kanzi's comprehension of multisymbol utterances was assessed. He responded correctly to 298 of 310 spoken sentences of two or more utterances. In a critical review of the literature, Wallman concludes that Kanzi's use of lexigrams represents the best evidence available to date for the referential application of learned symbols by an ape.

In summary, it is clear that nonhuman primates do not have a language in the sense that we do, nor is it likely that they can be taught human language. In addition, there is no strong evidence that they are predisposed to impose grammar onto the communication systems that they have been taught, such as ASL and Yerkish. On the other hand, it is clear that the great apes can employ at least a rudimentary manual sign language and a referential graphic language when constrained to do so. Additionally, they may have a much greater predisposition to understand language than to produce it. Anyone watching films of their performance cannot help but be impressed by their abilities. At any rate, it appears that the basic capacity for languagelike processes is there to be selected in the common ancestor of humans and apes. Thus, we are back to the question we began with: What has been selected? We consider two possibilities: (1) language as a categorizer, and (2) language as a motor act.

Language as a Categorizer

We have stressed the idea that sensory information is processed by multiple parallel hierarchical channels. Jerison has suggested that as the cortex expands and there are more channels processing parallel sensory information, it becomes increasingly difficult to integrate the information into a single reality. The brain must determine which of the many different kinds of sensory information reaching the cortex is about the same features in the external world. In a sense, it is necessary to categorize information. One could suppose that categorizing information makes it easier not only to perceive the information but also to retrieve it later when it is needed. In some ways, words are the ultimate categorizer, but the use of words to categorize must be based upon a preexisting bias to categorize sensory information. Therefore, it may be that the development of human language is actually a selection for a novel means of categorization.

The idea of language as a categorizer is consistent with the recent views of Damasio and Damasio. They suggest that the brain processes language by means of three interacting sets of structures. First, there are neural systems to categorize nonlanguage representations of sensory input. This categorization not only allows simple sensory stimuli to be combined but also provides a way of organizing events and relationships. Second, there are a smaller number of neural systems in the left cerebral hemisphere that represent phonemes, phoneme combinations, and syntactic rules for combining words. Third, there is a set of neural structures that mediate between the first two. This third system can take a concept (that is, a category) and stimulate the production of word forms about that concept; or conversely, it can take words and cause the brain to evoke the concepts. As an example, recall our case of the color-blind painter in Chapter 11. He knew the words for colors but could no longer perceive or imagine them. He had, in a sense, lost his concept of color. In contrast, other patients with left posterior temporal lesions retain their concept of color but cannot produce the word form with which it is associated. They experience color but cannot put names to color. Such patients are said to have a color anomia. It is important to note that these patients can form the words for different colors, but they simply cannot give the appropriate ones.

This three-part organization applies not only to color but also to other concepts. The idea is that as the brain classifies sensory inputs, it associates phonemic codes with the inputs in order to represent the concepts in another way. It has been suggested by Julien Jaynes and others that one of the fundamental functions of language is to allow us to talk to ourselves. In a sense, that is what Jerison has argued. Being able to use words to categorize objects and concepts *for ourselves* gives us a real advantage in understanding the world.

If we apply these ideas to the evolutionary question, we can conclude that language is a logical extension of the increase in our brain's capacity to process sensory input. We were predisposed to form language because we had fully developed systems to categorize sensory information. We can speculate that it is the third stream of sensory processing, which travels down the superior temporal sulcus and shows a large increase in the human brain, that may be crucial in this process of categorization (see Figure 11.2B). If this is the case, we might expect that temporal lobe lesions including the superior temporal sulcus would interfere with the spontaneous categorization of both verbal and nonverbal information, and this is indeed the case. It is significant that Wilson has shown temporal lobe lesions in monkeys to interfere with categorization of sensory stimuli, too, suggesting that the ability was there to be selected in our ancestors. Of course, we must also look to the cortex of the planum temporale (Wernicke's area) because it too shows a marked increase in size in the human brain and presumably plays a role in auditory categorization.

Language as a Motor Behavior

We have already considered the fact that a unique property of human language is the transition of movements of the lips and mouth to form syllables. Kimura has emphasized that left hemisphere structures associated with language are part of a system that has a fundamental role in the ordering of certain types of movements. Hence, she has shown that patients with injuries in Broca's area or in the left posterior temporal-parietal junction have deficits in the repetition of limb movements, oral movements, and syllables. This suggests to her that the left hemisphere has neural systems specialized for the selection and ordering of both speech and nonspeech movements. Therefore, it is not surprising that disorders of manual sign language occur after injury to the left hemisphere in right-handers (see our earlier discussion in this chapter).

Viewed in this light, language is an elaboration of an existing system that allows selection of nonspeech movements. This system is likely to involve the premotor cortex and its major input from the posterior parietal cortex. Broca's area can be considered an elaboration of the ventrolateral region of the premotor cortex, and the supplementary speech area can be seen as an elaboration of the dorsomedial premotor region. Thus, the development of language in humans is based upon the elaboration of the premotor cortex and associated posterior parietal regions. An important characteristic of patients with damage to Broca's area is that they have deficits in grammar. Recall that studies of chimpanzees have been criticized for the absence of evidence that word order is important to them. That is, chimpanzees do not show an understanding of syntax. We can speculate that if chimpanzees are missing the elaboration of premotor cortex seen in the human brain, then they may be handicapped in language acquisition. In fact, they may be handicapped in the ability to arrange noverbal movements in different orders to produce meaningful behavior, such as playing the piano.

It is reasonable to predict that the role of the ventral and medial premotor regions may be dissociable. MacNeilage suggests that the ventral region functions to produce syllables in response to environmental cues, whereas the medial region functions to self-generate syllables in the absence of sensory stimulation. It is interesting to note that patients with pathology in Broca's area are impaired at copying syllables presented to them, whereas patients with bilateral injury to the medial region are mute. They appear unable to generate syllables internally.

Summary

We suggest that the development of language in humans may reflect the development of two fundamental processes: (1) the elaboration of the ability to categorize sensory information and to assign phonemic tags to the categories; and (2) the ability to make the movements necessary to produce syllables that are placed in different orders. As we consider the organization of language and the disorders of language, we shall pay special attention to these two processes.

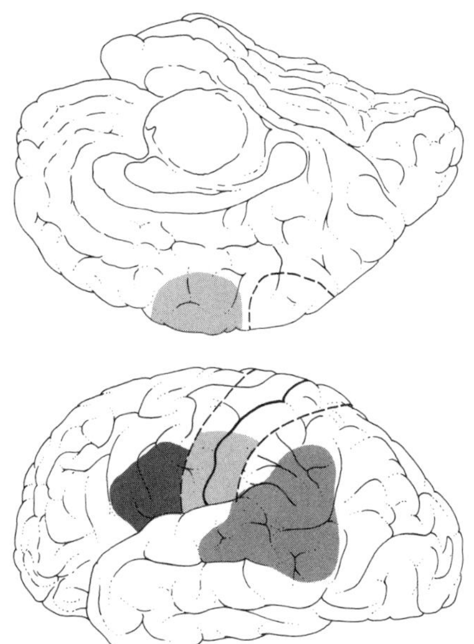

FIGURE 17.5. Summary of the regions of stimulation and surgical lesions that affect speech. Damage to the two darker areas produces chronic aphasia, damage to the lighter areas produces transient aphasia, and damage outside these areas does not produce aphasia.

LOCALIZATION OF LANGUAGE

Current ideas about the localization of language processes come from three basic lines of inquiry: (1) studies of brain stimulation in awake human patients; (2) studies of lesion patients; (3) PET and electrophysiological studies. We consider each in turn.

Speech Zones Mapped by Stimulation and Ablation

The zones of the neocortex involved in language, and particularly in speech, have been identified by careful investigations of the effects both of cortical stimulation during surgery and of surgery on behavior. Results from hundreds of patients have made it possible to construct statistically defined regions of the neocortex concerned with language processes.

The investigations undertaken by Penfield and his associates on patients undergoing surgical treatment of epilepsy were the first to identify clearly the extent of the neocortical speech zones. Subsequent work by others has confirmed Penfield's findings and has clarified and extended them by the use of more quantitative behavioral recording techniques. The major findings are as follows:

1. Stimulation of a number of cortical areas (Figure 17.5) with a low-voltage electrical current interferes with speech. These areas include the classical areas of Broca and Wernicke in the left hemisphere, as well as the sensory and motor representations of the face and the supplementary speech area in both hemispheres.

2. Penfield and Roberts conclude that stimulation produces two effects on speech:

a. Positive effects, meaning vocalization that is not speech but rather a sustained or interrupted vowel cry, such as "Oh." Vocalization can be elicited by stimulation of either the face area or the supplementary motor region of either hemisphere.

b. Negative effects, meaning the inability to vocalize or to use words properly. These include a variety of aphasialike errors: (i) Total arrest of speech or an inability to vocalize spontaneously; this occurs from stimulation throughout the shaded zones in Figure 17.5. (ii) Hesitation and slurring of speech; hesitation occurs from stimulation throughout the zones of Figure 17.5, whereas slurring occurs primarily from stimulation of the face area in either hemisphere. (iii) Distortion and repetition of words and syllables; distortion differs from slurring in that the distorted sound is an unintelligible noise rather than a word. These effects occur primarily from stimulation of the classical speech zones, although occasionally from stimulation of the face area as well. (iv) Confusion of numbers while counting; for example, a patient may jump from "six" to "nineteen" to "four" and so on. Confusion in counting results from stimulation of Broca's or Wernicke's area. (v) Inability to name despite retained ability to speak. "An example is 'That is a . . . .I know. That is a . . . .' When the current was removed, the patient named the picture correctly. Another example is, 'Oh, I know what it is. That is what you put in your shoes.' After withdrawal of the stimulating electrodes, the patient immediately said 'foot.'" (Penfield and Roberts, 1959, p. 123). Naming difficulties arise from stimulation throughout the anterior (Broca's) and posterior (Wernicke's) speech zones. (vi) Misnaming; may occur when the subject uses words related in sound such as "camel" for "comb," uses synonyms such as "cutters" for "scissors," or perseverates by using the same word twice. For example, a picture of a bird may be named correctly but the next picture, a table, is also called a bird. Misnaming, like naming difficulties, occurs during stimulation of both the anterior and the posterior speech zones.

3. Ojemann and Mateer report that during stimulation of Broca's area, patients are unable to make voluntary facial movements. Curiously, stimulation of these same points may also disrupt phonemic discrimination. These authors also describe defects in short-term memory resulting from stimulation in the posterior temporal-parietal cortex.

4. Most reports agree that the extent of the cortical language zones as marked by stimulation varies considerably among subjects, although there is little indication of what this variation may reflect. Ojemann has found that, on the whole, the language area is larger in males than in females. In view of the superior verbal skills of females, this result implies, paradoxically, that the size of the language area may be inversely related to ability. Such a hypothesis is supported by his observation that in multilinguals the poorer language is distributed over a larger area than the better one. The possibility that improved efficiency requires less neural activity is intriguing and warrants further study. One parallel result by Richard Haier is an inverse correlation between abstract reasoning and cerebral metabolic activity. One is tempted to conclude that "smart brains work better, not harder." In this regard, it would seem worthwhile to correlate the size of the speech zones with performance on a variety of verbal tests.

5. Ojemann makes two additional observations. First, he notes that stimulation at particular points has very discrete effects. Stimulation of one cortical site will alter a language function, such as naming, on every trial, and it will alter only one of several language functions tested. Second, in view of the high variability among individuals in the extent of language representations, Ojemann suggests that the biological substrate for human language meets conditions that are likely to lead to rapid evolution. That is, there is high variation in a trait that is almost certainly subject to selection by the environment.

Several important conclusions can be drawn from these results. First, the data do not support strict localizationist models of language, since stimulation of the anterior and posterior speech zones has remarkably similar effects on speech functions. Second, stimulation of the neocortex considerably beyond the classical areas of Broca and Wernicke disturbs speech functions. Third, stimulation of the speech zones affects more than just talking, since it produces deficits in voluntary motor control of facial musculature as well as in short-term memory and reading. Fourth, removal of the cortex surrounding the posterior speech zone, mapped in Figure 17.5, does not produce lasting aphasia, even though fibers connecting the visual areas to the speech regions may be disrupted. Thus, it seems clear that these connections are not essential in the coordination of these two areas. Fifth, it has proved difficult to classify the transient aphasia following surgery, because dyskinesia - disturbance of movement.

each patient appears to be unique. There is also little evidence for a distinctive type of aphasia associated specifically with damage to either the anterior or posterior speech zones. In other words, there is no evidence for pure motor or sensory aphasias as postulated by Wernicke. Sixth, chronic speech and language deficits occur only if lesions are made within the classical speech zones. Although stimulation of the face areas and supplementary motor zones arrests speech, unilateral removal of these zones has no chronic effect on speech. Recall, however, that facial area lesions do chronically impair other language functions (see Chapter 14).

One issue arising from the study of lesion patients is the relative importance of the anterior and posterior speech zones. In 1906, Marie published his celebrated paper claiming that Broca's area plays no special role in language. His conclusion was based on the study both of cases in which there appeared to be destruction of Broca's area without aphasia and of cases in which there was Broca's aphasia without damage to Broca's area. Marie undoubtedly overstated his case, but his point was well taken and led to a controversy that persists to this day. We are inclined to agree with Zangwill's suggestion that although Broca's area undoubtedly plays a significant role in the normal control of articulate speech, damage to the area does not have the severe effects on language that lesions in the posterior speech zone have. Furthermore, the severity of aphasia is far more variable following lesions to Broca's area than to Wernicke's area. Some patients with lesions in Broca's area may have only mild articulatory disorders, whereas others have severe disturbances of both expression and comprehension. Jefferson was probably correct in his suggestion that this variability reflects the extent of subcortical damage in addition to the damage to Broca's area itself.

One cortical area that is not easily studied in surgical patients is the insula (see Figure 16.1). People with strokes that involve the insula have severe aphasia and, as we shall see shortly, PET studies show that the insula is active during certain types of language processes.

Subcortical Components of Language

At the same time that Broca was describing a cortical center for speech control, Hughlings-Jackson proposed that subcortical structures are critical to language. In 1866, he wrote: "I think it will be found that the nearer the disease is to the corpus striatum, the more likely is the defect of articulation to be the striking thing, and the farther off, the more likely it is to be one of mistakes of words." Although he was the first to propose that aphasias result from subcortical damage, this proposition was not considered seriously until 1959, when Penfield and Roberts suggested that the thalamus, especially the pulvinar, functions to coordinate the activity of the cortical speech zones. In recent years, evidence from stimulation and lesion studies has supported Hughlings-Jackson's proposal, although the importance — and the precise role — of the thalamus is still under debate.

In the course of surgical treatment of **dyskinesia** (the term for any disturbance of movement), electrodes are placed in the thalamus and an electrical current is applied to define the electrode's position precisely. For example, movements evoked by stimulation would indicate placement in the motor thalamus, whereas somatosensory changes such as tingling sensations in the skin would indicate placement in the somatosensory thalamus. When the electrode is placed properly, a stronger current is applied, producing a lesion intended to relieve the dyskinesia. Careful study of language functions during these procedures, especially by Ojemann and by Cooper and their respective colleagues, has indicated that the pulvinar and the lateral-posterior, lateral-central complex of the left thalamus have a role in language not shared by other subcortical structures. Stimulation of the left ventrolateral and pulvinar nuclei of the thalamus produces speech arrest, difficulties in naming, perseveration, and reduced speed of talking. Stimulation has also been reported to produce positive effects on memory, because it improves later retrieval of words heard during the stimulation. As a result, it has been proposed that the thalamus has some role in activating or arousing the cortex.

Lesions of the ventrolateral thalamus and/or pulvinar on the left have been associated with a variety of disturbances of speech and language processes. Symptoms include postoperative dysphasia, which is usually transitory; increased verbal-response latency; decreases in voice volume; alterations in speaking rate and slurring or hesitation in speech; and impaired performance on tests of verbal IQ and memory.

Speech Zones Mapped by Regional Blood Flow

With the development of sophisticated PET procedures, cognitive psychologists have become more interested in the neural correlates of language processing. To interpret the PET cognitive studies, we must first briefly consider a popular cognitive model of language comprehension. Suppose the word "cake" is presented visually. This sensory input is hypothesized to be analyzed in several ways. First, we can analyze the surface visual characteristics of the word (for example, the shapes of the letters). We can also consider what are called the phonological aspects of the word. That is, we can consider the sound of the word and whether it rhymes with "bake." Finally, we can assess the meaning of the word, which is referred to as its semantic code. A question of considerable interest in cognitive psychology is whether these three types of analysis are done serially and thus depend upon preceding levels of analysis, or are done in parallel. This question is not trivial, because if the analyses are done serially, it means that words must be sounded mentally before they are understood. Furthermore, it means that nonwords that can be pronounced will be analyzed differently from nonwords that cannot be pronounced. That is, the nonword "twips" can be analyzed phonologically, but the nonword "tzpws" cannot be. In both cases it should be possible to show that the brain activity produced during the processing is distinctive and, since there is no semantic code in either case, it should be the case that blood flow is different again when words are processed. This division of visual language inputs into visual patterns, phonological aspects, and semantic properties can be applied to the auditory system, too. In this case, the words would be analyzed by their frequency, phonemes, and semantics. We can now turn to the PET studies.

We shall describe the experiments of Peterson and his colleagues in St. Louis in some detail, but similar experiments have been performed at Hammersmith Hospital in London by Wise and his colleagues. (See Demont et al.'s comparison of the similarities and differences in results from the two laboratories.) Peterson's group asked subjects to perform four different tasks. In the first two, words were passively presented either visually or aurally. The task was to process the word but to do nothing (a sensory task). The key difference between the tasks is that one is visual and the other is auditory. In the next task, the subject was to repeat the word (an output task). In the final one (an association task), the subject generated a use for the target word (for example, if "cake" was presented, the subject might say "eat"). The authors monitored blood flow using PET and analyzed their data using a subtraction technique. Thus, in the sensory tasks they looked for changes from baseline blood flow by taking the difference between the activity in the two states. In the output task they subtracted the sensory activity, and in the association task they subtracted the output activity. Their results (Figure 17.6) lead to several conclusions.

First, in the passive task there was increased blood flow bilaterally in the primary and secondary visual areas for the visual stimulus and in the primary and secondary auditory areas for the auditory stimulus. More dramatically, pronounceable words and nonwords activated a region in the left occipital cortex that was not activated by unpronounceable letter strings. Thus, the brain treated visual information that appeared to be language differently from how it treated nonwords. Stated another way, the brain categorized the input into either words or nonwords. Hearing pronounceable words and nonwords appeared to

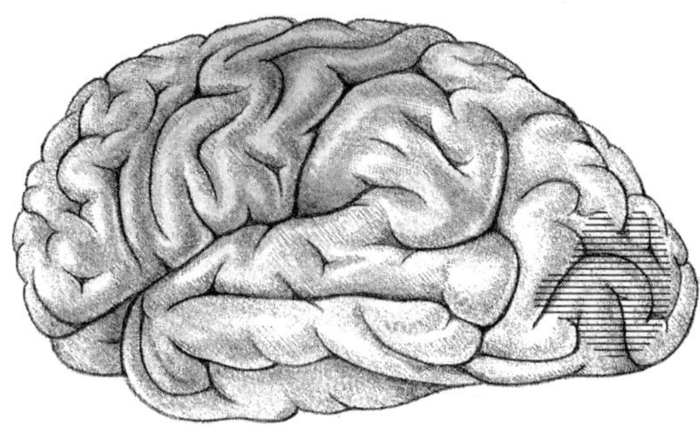

Passively viewing words

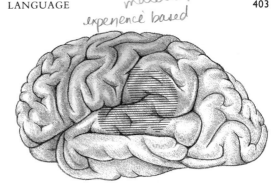

Listening to words

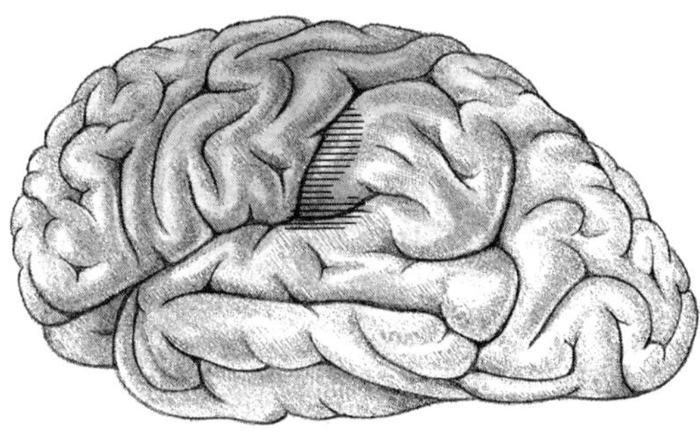

Speaking words

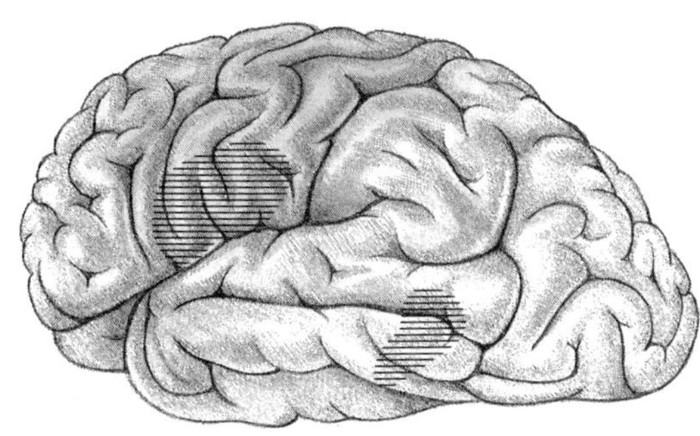

Generating verbs

FIGURE 17.6. Each of the tasks in the word-generation experiment activates a distinct set of brain areas. (After Posner and Raichle, 1994.)

activate Wernicke's area (area 22), whereas listening to simple tones and vowels did not. Again, this suggests that the brain classifies the input as word versus nonword. The recognition of language-like material must have been learned, because there is nothing inherently different about some combinations of letters. This result is important because it shows that there is a part of the brain whose activity is based upon experience-dependent changes.

Second, there was absolutely no overlap in the visual and auditory activation during the passive task, implying that the processing of the word forms in the two modalities was completely independent. This finding would seem logical, except that it seems to contradict the view of language comprehension holding that visual input is converted into a phonological code. To test whether this latter idea is true, Posner and Raichle performed an experiment in which subjects were presented with two words visually and asked to press a key to indicate if the words rhymed or not. Some of the pairs did not look alike (for example, "row" and "though"), and some looked alike but did not rhyme (for example, "lint" and "pint"), so at least theoretically the subjects had to activate phonological codes by way of the visual input. The results showed that when subjects performed this task they activated regions normally only activated by auditory presentation.

Third, during the output task there was bilateral activation of the motor and sensory face areas, as well as bilateral activation of the supplementary speech area and activation of the right cerebellum. In addition, there was activation of the insular cortex. Surprisingly, neither Broca's area nor Wernicke's area was active during the repetition task. The activation of the cerebellum presumably reflects its role in motor behavior.

Fourth, for the association task there was activation of the frontal lobe, especially the left inferior region, including Broca's area. The critical difference between this task and the word-repetition task is that the choice of answer must be selected on the basis of external input. For example, hearing the noun "cake" leads to production of the verb "eat." Recall that the frontal lobe is hypothesized to have this function (see Chapter 14).

Fifth, the association task also activated the posterior temporal cortex, the anterior cingulate cortex, and the cerebellum. The posterior temporal region activated appears to be more ventral than Wernicke's area, and Posner and Raichle suggest that it may reflect the fact that several left posterior temporal regions are involved in processing words. The anterior cingulate activation has also been observed in studies by others, but the reason for it is unclear. Posner believes the anterior cingulate cortex to be important in some aspects of attention.

Two questions arise from the PET studies: (1) Why does damage to Broca's area and the left posterior temporal area produce aphasia, in the absence of activation of these areas in the speech-repetition task? (2) What is the role of the insular cortex? These questions were addressed in another experiment by the St. Louis group. First, they gave subjects nouns and asked for a verb generation, much as before. Second, they gave subjects nouns after the subjects had been given 15 min to practice the verb-generation responses. The results showed that when subjects had an opportunity to practice their responses, so that they were no longer searching for a verb to give during the test, they no longer showed activation of the inferior frontal, anterior cingulate, and posterior temporal regions. Instead, they showed enhanced activation of the insular cortex. The researchers conclude that there are two distinct pathways involved in the generation task. One pathway, which includes the inferior frontal and posterior temporal cortex, is necessary for selecting novel responses; the other uses the insular cortex to produce "automatic" speech (Figure 17.7).

In summary, studies of this sort are confirming the role of the classical anterior and posterior speech zones in language, but they also show that other regions are involved as well. Furthermore, they suggest that the posterior speech zone may be devoted largely to the analysis of auditory input, since there was no increase in blood flow in this region for visual stimuli, and it appears that Broca's area is not simply a cortical representation

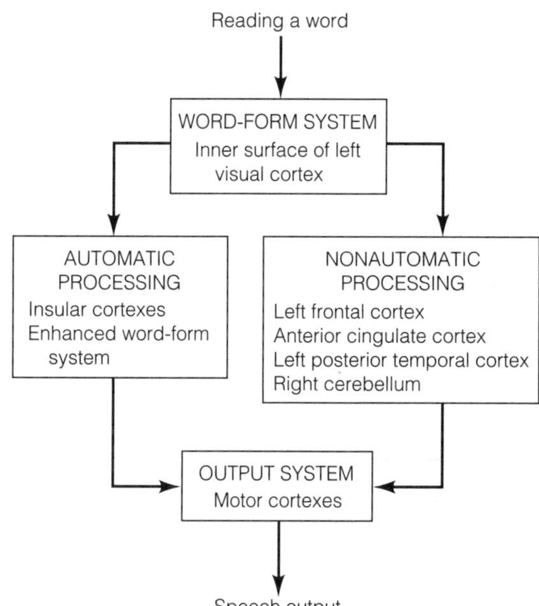

FIGURE 17.7. Posner and Raichle's two pathways for generating words. One pathway, which involves the insular areas, is used in automatic processing. The other pathway, which involves frontal and posterior temporal areas, is used in the generation of unlearned (or novel) responses.

of the movements of speech, as has been traditionally believed.

DISORDERS OF LANGUAGE

Before the neurology of language is given a theoretical description, the disorders of language must be considered, since theoretical formulations of language function must be able to account for the disorders observed. We first describe the types of deficits observed in language and then consider the classification of aphasia. Our discussion is brief, and readers are directed to recent reviews by Caplan and by Benson for more extensive discussions.

TABLE 17.3. Summary of symptoms of disorders of language

Disorders of comprehension
Poor auditory comprehension
Poor visual comprehension
Disorders of production
Poor articulation
Word-finding deficit (anomia)
Unintended words or phrases (paraphasia)
Loss of grammar and syntax
Inability to repeat aurally presented material
Low verbal fluency
Inability to write (agraphia)
Loss of tone in voice (aprosidia)

Language Deficits and Neurological Damage

Normal language depends on a complex interaction among sensory integration and symbolic association, motor skills, learned syntactic patterns, and verbal memory. **Aphasia** refers to a disorder of language apparent in speech, writing *(agaraphia)*, or reading *(alexia)* produced by injury to brain areas specialized for these functions. Thus, disturbances of language due to severe intellectual impairment, loss of sensory input (especially vision and hearing), or paralysis or incoordination of the musculature of the mouth (**anarthria**) or hand (for writing) are not considered to be aphasic disturbances. These disorders may accompany aphasia, and they complicate the study of it.

Goodglass and Kaplan have broken down language disturbances into 10 basic types, which we have subgrouped into disorders of comprehension and disorders of production and summarized in Table 17.3. We have encountered most of these language disorders already in our discussion of parietal, temporal, and frontal lobe functions. The one exception is **paraphasia,** which is the production of unintended syllables, words, or phrases during the effort to speak. Paraphasia differs from difficulties in articulation in that sounds are correctly articulated, but they are the wrong sounds; people with paraphasia either distort the intended word (for example, "pike" instead of "pipe") or produce a completely unintended word (for example, "my mother" instead of "my wife").

Classification of Aphasias

Since the time of Wernicke, people have attempted to describe identifying clusters of symptoms associated with particular brain lesions. This has proved to be a difficult task, partly because so few cases are thoroughly studied and partly because so few well-studied cases ever come to autopsy. In fact, Kimura has pointed out that the focus of attention in such studies has been upon the description of speech disorders rather than on the brain. It is rare for investigators to begin with a series of patients with similar lesions and then try to determine what the common language problem actually is. As a result, there is considerable controversy in the neurological literature over the nature and types of aphasia.

Despite disagreement over the number of types of aphasias, there are classification systems that are widely used. An example of one is given in Table 17.4. Broadly defined, aphasias are classified into three general categories: **fluent aphasias,** in which there is fluent speech but difficulties either in auditory verbal comprehension or in the repetition of words, phrases, or sentences spoken by others; **nonfluent aphasias,** in which there are

TABLE 17.4. Definition of aphasic syndromes

Syndrome	Type of speech production	Type of language errors
Fluent aphasias		
Wernicke (sensory)	Fluent speech, without articulatory disorders	Neologism and/or anomias, or paraphasias, poor comprehension; poor repetition
Transcortical (isolation syndrome)	Fluent speech, without articulatory disorders; good repetition	Verbal paraphasias and anomias; poor comprehension
Conduction	Fluent, sometimes halting speech, but without articulatory disorders	Phonemic paraphasias and neologisms; phonemic groping; poor repetition; fairly good comprehension
Anomic	Fluent speech, without articulatory disorders	Anomia and occasional paraphasias
Nonfluent aphasias		
Broca, severe	Laborious articulation	Speechlessness with recurring utterances or syndrome of phonetic disintegration; poor repetition
Broca, mild	Slight but obvious articulatory disorders	Phonemic paraphasias with anomia; agrammatism; dysprosody
Transcortical motor	Marked tendency to reduction and inertia, without articulatory disorders; good repetition	Uncompleted sentences and anomias; naming better than spontaneous speech
Global	Laborious articulation	Speechlessness with recurring utterances; poor comprehension; poor repetition
"Pure" aphasias		
Alexia without agraphia	Normal	Poor reading
Agraphia	Normal	Poor writing
Word deafness	Normal	Poor comprehension; poor repetition

Source: After Mazzocchi and Vignolo, 1979.

difficulties in articulating but relatively good auditory verbal comprehension; and *pure aphasias,* in which there are selective impairments of reading, writing, or the recognition of words. Within each of these broad categories, numerous subtypes are often distinguished, including Wernicke's aphasia, transcortical aphasia, conduction aphasia, anomic aphasia, and Broca's aphasia.

Wernicke's Aphasia. Wernicke's aphasia, or **sensory aphasia,** is the inability to comprehend words or to arrange sounds into coherent speech. Luria has proposed that this type of aphasia has three characteristics. First, to hear and make out the sounds of speech, one must be able to qualify sounds—that is, to include sounds in the system of phonemes that are the basic units of speech in a given language. An example will illustrate. In the Japanese language the sounds "l" and "r" are not distinguished; a Japanese-speaking person hearing English cannot distinguish these sounds because the necessary template is not in the brain. Thus, although this distinction is perfectly clear to English-speaking persons, it is not to native Japanese. This is precisely the problem that a person with Wernicke's aphasia has in his or her own language: the inability to isolate the significant phonemic characteristics and to classify sounds into known phonemic systems. Thus, we see in Wernicke's aphasia a deficit in the categorization of sounds. The second characteristic of Wernicke's aphasia is a defect in speech. The affected person can speak and may speak a great deal, but he or she confuses phonetic characteris-

isolation syndrome - can repeat but can't speak spontaneously (aka transcortical aphasia)
conduction aphasia - can speak but can't repeat

tics, producing what is often called **word salad.** The third characteristic is an impairment in writing. A person who cannot discern phonemic characteristics cannot be expected to write, because he or she does not know the graphemes (pictorial or written representations of a phoneme) that combine to form a word.

Transcortical Aphasia. Transcortical aphasia, sometimes called **isolation syndrome**, is a curious type of aphasia in which individuals can repeat and understand words and name objects but cannot speak spontaneously, or they cannot comprehend words although they can still repeat them. This type of aphasia is presumed to be caused by loss of the cortex outside the traditional language areas. Comprehension could be poor because words fail to arouse associations. Production of meaningful speech could be poor because even though the production of words is normal, words are not associated with other cognitive activities in the brain.

Conduction Aphasia. Conduction aphasia is a paradoxical deficit: people with this disorder can speak easily, name objects, and understand speech, but they cannot repeat words. The simplest explanation for this problem is that there is a disconnection between the "perceptual word image" in the parietal-temporal cortex and the motor systems producing the words. There has never been any clear proof, however, that cutting the connections actually causes this syndrome, and there is considerable debate over whether this aphasia really occurs in the absence of other symptoms, especially impaired short-term memory.

Anomic Aphasia. People with anomic aphasia (sometimes called **amnesic aphasia**) comprehend speech, produce meaningful speech, and can repeat speech, but they have great difficulty in finding the names of objects. For example, we saw a patient who, when shown a picture of a ship anchor, simply could not think of the name and finally said, "I know what it does. . . .You use it to anchor a ship." Although he had actually used the word as a verb he was unable to use it as a noun. Difficulties in finding nouns appear to result from damage throughout the temporal cortex. In contrast, verb-finding deficits are more likely to come from left frontal injuries. Although the distinction of nouns and verbs may seem surprising, we can see that they are different in function. Nouns are categorizers. Verbs are action words that form the core of syntactic structure. It may be reasonable, therefore, to expect them to be separated in such a way that nouns are a property of brain areas involved in recognition and classification and verbs are a property of brain areas involved in movement.

Broca's Aphasia. In Broca's aphasia, a person has difficulty in speaking, although he or she continues to understand speech. Broca's aphasia is also known as *motor, expressive,* or *nonfluent aphasia.* This aphasia features a pattern of speech in which a person speaks in a very slow, deliberate manner using very simple grammatical structure. Thus, all the forms of a verb are likely to be reduced to the infinitive or the participle. Nouns are most apt to be expressed only in the singular, and conjunctions, adjectives, adverbs, and articles are very uncommon. Only the key words necessary for communication are used.

There is still no adequate explanation for Broca's aphasia. Broca assumed that the problem was an impairment of the "motor image of the word," but it is uncertain what this supposition implies about brain function. Certainly, however, the deficit is not one of making sounds, but rather one of switching from one sound to another.

Localization of Lesions in Aphasia

One of the problems with the classification of aphasia is that patients are usually classified behaviorally, and then the lesion location is determined. Kimura and Watson classified patients in the opposite manner: they grouped subjects by lesion site, independent of the characteristics of the disorder. In their analysis, aphasic patients with anterior or posterior lesions did not differ on tests of receptive or expressive aphasia. The same patients could be distinguished in other ways, however.

anomic aphasia - cannot name nouns (but can use same words as verbs)

Broca's - understands speech, but difficulty speaking
- choppy, slow, deliberate speech (can't switch from one sound to another)

First, the anterior aphasics had a lower word fluency, which is characteristic of patients with frontal lobe injury (see Chapter 14). In addition, the anterior aphasics were severely impaired at the repetition of single speech sounds (that is, phonemes or syllables). Posterior aphasics were impaired at the reproduction of familiar phrases. Curiously, anterior aphasics performed far better on this task than on the single-syllable task. Kimura interprets this result as showing that the anterior region is involved in the generation of speech at the phonemic-syllabic level whereas the posterior zone is critical for mediating speech production at the multisyllabic level. This distinction does not fall neatly into the usual classification of aphasics, but it does suggest that people with lesions in the anterior or posterior language zones can be dissociated on the basis of their symptoms. One possible explanation for the better performance of the anterior aphasics on the familiar phrase task is that they could use the "automatic" system proposed by Posner and Raichle. Of course, this explanation would assume that their lesions did not damage significant amounts of the insula.

The important conclusion from the localization literature is that we need more studies in which patients are grouped and chosen by lesion, rather than by symptom. When patients are chosen by symptom, and the pathology is then correlated with the symptom, there is a real selection problem. Those patients with similar pathology but no symptom are excluded. The outcome is a rather biased picture.

RIGHT HEMISPHERE CONTRIBUTIONS TO LANGUAGE

Although there is little doubt that the left hemisphere of right-handed people is the predominant hemisphere in language, there is growing evidence that the right hemisphere does have language abilities. The best evidence has come from studies of split-brain patients in whom the linguistic abilities of the right hemisphere have been studied systematically using various techniques for lateralizing input to one hemisphere. These studies have shown that the right hemisphere has little or no speech but surprisingly good auditory comprehension of language, including both nouns and verbs. There also appears to be some reading but little writing ability in the right hemisphere. Thus, although the right hemisphere appears to be able to recognize words (semantic processing), it has virtually no understanding of grammatical rules and structures (syntactic processing). Complementary evidence favoring a limited role of the right hemisphere in language comes from studies of people who have had the left hemisphere removed, a procedure known as **hemispherectomy.** If the left hemisphere is lost early in development, the right hemisphere can acquire considerable language abilities (see Chapter 10 for details), although it is by no means normal. Left hemidecortication in adulthood is far more debilitating, however, and in all such cases there are severe deficits in speech. Nonetheless, these people do have surprisingly good auditory comprehension. Reading is limited, however, and writing is usually absent. In general, it appears that left hemidecorticated people have language abilities that are reminiscent of those of the right hemisphere of commissurotomy patients.

In summary, it appears that although the right hemisphere cannot speak, it is capable of considerable language comprehension, especially of auditory material. A final source of evidence comes from the effects of right hemisphere lesions on language functions. Aphasia is rare after right hemisphere lesions (this aphasia is known as **crossed aphasia**), even after right hemispherectomy, but there is growing evidence of subtle linguistic impairments associated with right hemisphere injuries. These include changes in vocabulary selection, in responses to complex statements with unusual syntactic construction, and in the comprehension of metaphors. In addition, right orbital-frontal lesions reduce verbal fluency. There is also a deficit in the comprehension of tone of voice and possibly in the production of similar emotional tone (prosody).

In reviewing the role of the right hemisphere in language, both Benson and Zaidel have con-

TABLE 17.5. Language activities of the two hemispheres

Function	Left hemisphere	Right hemisphere
Gestural language	+	+
Prosodic language		
Rhythm	++	
Inflection	+	+
Timbre	+	++
Melody		++
Semantic language		
Word recognition	+	+
Verbal meaning	++	+
Concepts	+	+
Visual meaning	+	++
Syntactic language		
Sequencing	++	
Relationships	++	
Grammar	++	

Source: Modified from Benson, 1986.

cluded that the only strictly left hemisphere function in language involves the syntactic elements of language (Table 17.5). This function includes several factors: production, timing, and sequencing of the movements required for speaking, as well as understanding the rules of grammar. The relative roles of the two hemispheres in other aspects of language comprehension still need to be clearly specified.

NEUROLOGICAL MODELS OF LANGUAGE

The early formulation of a neurological model of language by Wernicke, and its later revival by Geschwind, was based entirely upon lesion data (Figure 17.8). Although useful conceptually, it is now clear that this model cannot accommodate the available facts and speculations. Any model of language production must consider those structures that have been shown by lesion, stimulation, and PET studies to be involved in language production. As we review our discussion to date, we must consider the following facts:

1. The development of language is associated with the development of a capacity to categorize and to attach phonemic tags to the categories. The tags for these categories are primarily nouns. The capacity to categorize and attach tags appears to depend upon circuits throughout the temporal lobe, which are presumably interwoven with the basic circuitry of object recognition.

2. There are separate systems for the processing of visual and auditory language inputs. Comprehension of visual input does not require phonological coding, but visual inputs can activate phonological analyses if required.

3. The production of language requires the production of syllables and the ability to shift from one syllable to the next. The production of individual syllables is a function of the expanded premotor regions. The ability to shift from one syllable to the next probably includes circuits in the posterior parietal cortex, perhaps analogous to the circuits of the parietal cortex that control limb movements.

4. Language requires grammar. Grammar revolves around the use of verbs. In a sense, verbs can be considered phonemic tags for movements. Although rather speculative, one could propose that in the same way the temporal cortex categorizes sensory information, the frontal lobe categorizes actions in order to make selection easier. At any rate, both PET studies and lesion studies indicate that regions of the frontal lobe are involved in both syntax and verb generation.

5. Language may be relatively automatic, as in the repetition of well-learned responses or the mimicking of inputs. Different systems may be involved in the two types of language output. The insular cortex may play a critical role in producing automatic responses, whereas the premotor and posterior temporal regions are necessary for more "cognitive" processes.

6. Language requires processes of memory. The brain must store words, and we must be able to access the words. Nouns are probably stored in circuits in the posterior temporal cortex. Verbs

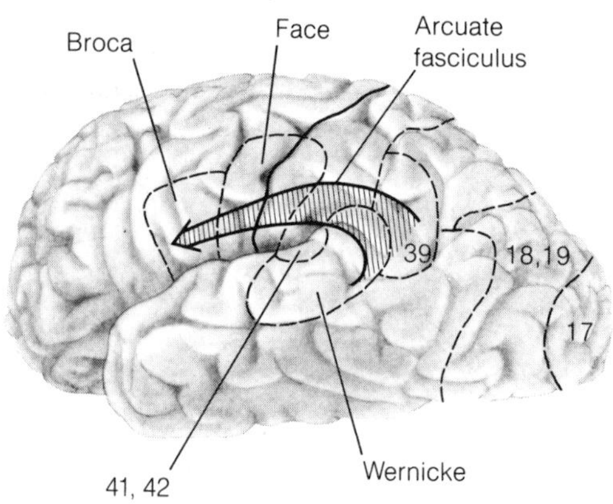

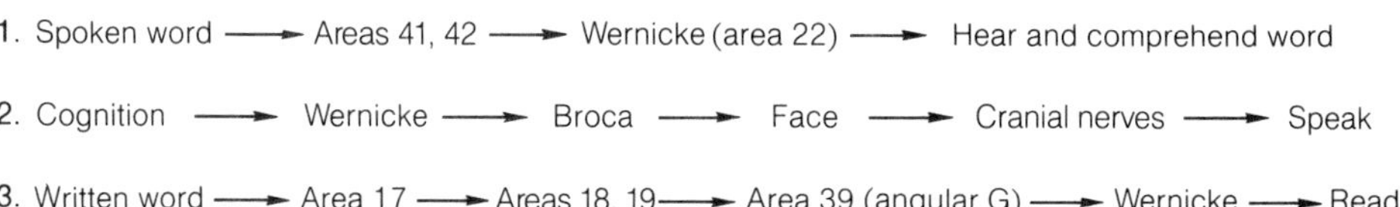

FIGURE 17.8. Geschwind's model of the neurology of language, showing the regions of the cortex involved. Items 1 through 3 illustrate how the model explains different language functions. Although the model was a useful summary when published, more recent PET data have shown it to be limited in explanatory value.

may be stored in the frontal cortex. The brain must also be able to remember words over the short term so that discourse can be understood. The fact that stimulation of the posterior regions in particular disturbs short-term memory of verbal material suggests an important role of the posterior temporal cortex in this form of memory. It seems likely that short-term representations of verbal and auditory material are stored separately.

7. Although the left hemisphere plays the most important role in language, the right hemisphere has a role in semantic processing and plays the dominant role in prosody. The only unique left hemisphere functions appear to be the production of syntax and the production and sequencing of syllables.

8. Language representation changes with experience. Words and pronounceable nonwords are processed by posterior temporal regions that are not activated by meaningless consonant strings. This distinction must be learned. Automatic and well-practiced verbal output depends upon the insular cortex, whereas novel speech generation requires the frontal and posterior temporal cortex. The size of the posterior speech zone may be affected by experience. As language ability increases, there is a reduction in the size of the posterior temporal speech area. This size reduction may be correlated with an increase in insular involvement, but this is speculation.

9. There are individual differences in the cortical representation of language. One source of the differences is sex: females appear to have a smaller posterior temporal involvement in language and possibly a larger frontal (or insular?) involvement. Even within each sex, however, there appears to be considerable intersubject variation. This variability is interesting because it provides a basis for natural selection.

As we consider these properties of the neurological bases of language, we are struck by the similarities in the general organization of language and of sensory and memory functions. First, a considerable portion of the human neocortex appears to have some role in language functions. Language is not simply a new part that was added to an existing chassis. Rather, language functions are distributed across much of the cerebrum. Second, there are multiple channels that perform language functions. These include (1) channels that process visual material and others that process auditory material, (2) channels that generate verbs (and syntax) and others that generate nouns, (3) channels that generate automatic speech and others that generate spontaneous speech, and (4) channels that control production of single phonemes and others that control production of multiple phonemes. Thus, just as we cannot point to a place in the brain that "sees" or "remembers," we cannot localize a place that "talks."

ASSESSMENT OF APHASIA

Since World War II there has been widespread interest in establishing a standard systematic procedure for assessing aphasia, both to provide standardized clinical descriptions of patients and to facilitate comparison of patient populations in neuropsychological research. In the past 25 years a number of manuals on aphasia testing have appeared. Table 17.6 summarizes the most widely used tests. Tests in the first group are considered to be test batteries, because they provide a large number of subtests designed to explore the language capabilities of the subject systematically. They typically include tests of (1) auditory and visual comprehension; (2) oral and written expression including tests of repetition, reading, naming, and fluency; and (3) conversational speech. Because these test batteries have the disadvantages of being lengthy and requiring special training to administer, some brief aphasia screening tests have been devised. The two most popular, the Halstead-Wepman Aphasia Screening Test and the token test, are often used as part of standard neuropsychological test batteries (see Chapter 26) because they are short and easy to administer and score. These tests do not replace the detailed examinations of the aphasia test batteries, but they can be used to identify language disorders. If a fine description of the linguistic deficits is desired, the more comprehensive aphasia batteries must be given.

Although models and test batteries of aphasia may be useful for evaluating and classifying the status of a patient, they are not a substitute for an experimental analysis of language disorders. In an evaluation of current interpretations of aphasic language disorders, Marshall has pointed out some of the inadequacies of batteries and has argued that the development of a psychobiology of language disorders is still needed. Whereas the test

TABLE 17.6. Summary of the major tests of aphasia

Test	Basic reference
Aphasia test batteries	
Boston Diagnostic Aphasia Test	Goodglass and Kaplan, 1972
Functional communicative profile	Sarno, 1969
Neurosensory center comprehensive examination for aphasia	Spreen and Benton, 1969
Porch Index of Communicative Ability	Porch, 1967
Minnesota Test for Differential Diagnosis of Aphasia	Schuell, 1965
Wepman-Jones Language Modalities Test for Aphasia	Wepman and Jones, 1961
Aphasia screening tests	
Halstead-Wepman Aphasia Screening Test	Halstead and Wepman, 1959
Token test	de Renzi and Vignolo, 1962

batteries attempt to classify patients into a number of groups, a psychobiological approach would concentrate on individual differences and peculiarities and from these attempt to reconstruct the processes through which the brain produces language. On the practical side, Marshall notes that only about 60% of patients will fit into a classification such as that given in Table 17.4. Others have noted a similar lack of success in classifying patients according to other methods. For example, most patients with a language impairment show a deficit in naming that can be elicited by having them look at pictures or objects. Scores on standard tests often tell little about the impairment. A number of patients might be able to name a violin, but one might know only that it is a musical instrument, another that it is a stringed instrument, and still another that it is similar to a cello and not a trumpet. Furthermore, some patients have selective naming deficits, such as being unable to name buildings, people, colors, or objects that are inside houses. Obviously, it is inappropriate to classify as simply anomic individuals who differ in this way. The differences that such patients display can reveal important insights into the neural organization of language.

ASSESSMENT OF DYSLEXIA

The assessment of reading disorders is becoming a special branch of the study of language, for several reasons. First, it is possible to be more objective in the analysis of reading than of writing and speaking. Also, there is a large pedagogical science of reading. Finally, in addition to the **acquired dyslexias** (impairments in reading that follow brain damage), **developmental dyslexias** (failure to learn to read during development) are common and require diagnosis and remediation.

Coltheart has argued that the most objective approach to the study of reading is model building. A model (which is much like an algorithm) is constructed, and then reading-disabled individuals are tested both to define the impairment and to test the utility of the model. The model-building approach differs from classical neurological approaches. Classically, dyslexia is defined in terms of whether it occurs in conjunction with other disorders, such as dysgraphia or dysphasia, and the primary intent is to correlate the impairment with the locus of brain damage. The model-building approach can be traced to Hinshelwood's analysis, first published in 1900. Hinshelwood recognized that there are different types of reading disorders: (1) the inability to name letters (letter blindness), (2) the inability to read words (word blindness), and (3) the inability to read sentences (sentence blindness). The Hinshelwood taxonomy and its subsequent elaboration have led to the current hypothesis that reading is composed of a number of independent abilities that may have an independent anatomical basis. Figure 17.9 presents some of the reading impairments that have been observed and the questions asked to help identify the type of impairment. Brief descriptions of these impairments follow:

1. *Attentional dyslexia.* When one letter is present, naming is normal. When other letters are present, naming is difficult. Even if the letter is specially colored, underlined, has an arrow pointing to it, and is pointed to by the tester, it may be named incorrectly. The same phenomenon may occur when more than one word is present.

2. *Neglect.* Persons displaying this impairment may misread the first half of a word (for example, "whether" as "smother,") or they may misread the last part of a word (for example, "strong" as "stroke"). This syndrome has received little investigation.

3. *Letter-by-letter reading.* Affected individuals read words only by spelling them out to themselves (aloud or silently). When the spelling is done silently, it can be detected by the increase in time taken to read long words. Frequently, the person can write but then has difficulty reading what was written.

4. *Deep dyslexia.* The key symptoms of this disorder are semantic errors: persons with deep dyslexia read semantically related words in place of the word they are trying to read (for instance,

ANALYZING ACQUIRED DYSLEXIA

Is naming a letter much harder when it is accompanied by other, irrelevant letters?

Yes → Attentional dyslexia

No → When words are misread, are the errors usually confined to one half of the word?

Yes → Neglect or positional dyslexia

No → Are words often read letter by letter?

Yes → Letter-by-letter reading

No → Are semantic errors made in reading aloud?

Yes → Deep dyslexia

No → Is reading aloud of nonwords very bad or impossible?

Yes → Phonological dyslexia

No → Are regular words read aloud much better than exception words?

Yes → Surface dyslexia

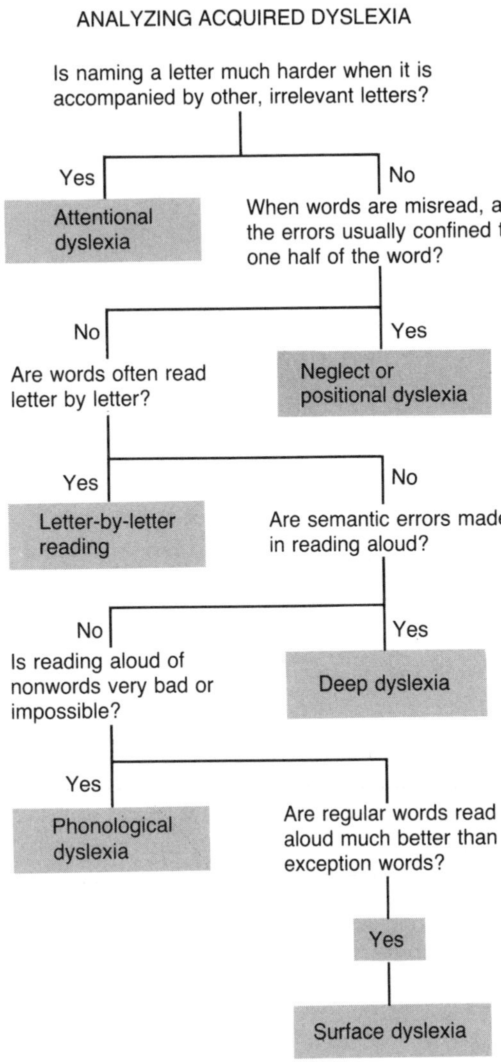

FIGURE 17.9. Flowchart for the analysis of dyslexia. (After Coltheart, 1981.)

"tulip" as "crocus" and "merry" as "Christmas"). Nouns are the easiest for them to read, followed by adjectives and then verbs. Function words present the greatest difficulty. Those who suffer from deep dyslexia also find it easier to read concrete words rather than abstract ones and are completely unable to read nonsense words. They are also generally impaired at writing and in their short-term verbal memory (digit span).

5. *Phonological dyslexia.* The one symptom of phonological dyslexia is an inability to read nonwords aloud; otherwise reading may be nearly flawless.

6. *Surface dyslexia.* The surface dyslexic cannot recognize words directly but can understand them by using letter-to-sound relations; that is, the word can be understood if it is sounded out. This reading procedure works well as long as the words are regular ones ("home," "dome"), but not if the words are irregular ("come" will be read as "comb"). Spelling is also impaired but is phonetically correct. Surface dyslexia does not occur in languages that are totally phonetic (such as Italian). Surface dyslexia is a common symptom of children who have difficulty in learning to read.

The model-building approach views reading as being composed of a number of independent skills or subsystems, one or another of which may not be functioning in an impaired reader. Marshall cleverly demonstrates this idea with the following example of two lines of poetry that can be read either for sense or for sound:

Kuh! Sie Kuh! Sie kann der . . .
Wer Du ja Wanduhr?

The sound reader will read this as "Goosey, Goosey Gander/Where do you wander?" Someone reading for the sense of the German will read it as "Cow! You Cow! Who do you think you are/You and your clock on the wall?" The central idea to be obtained from this example is that in normal readers sense and sound are computed in parallel, whereas in the dyslexic one or the other process may be absent. The deep dyslexic is unable to process for sound and so attempts to read for sense. The surface dyslexic is able to process for sound but not for sense. A model of how parallel systems may be organized and interact is illustrated in Figure 17.10. Note that there are quite separate ways of obtaining speech from print and a still different way of producing letter names.

The important features of the model-building approach are that it does not demand that function-anatomy relations be used, it can be applied

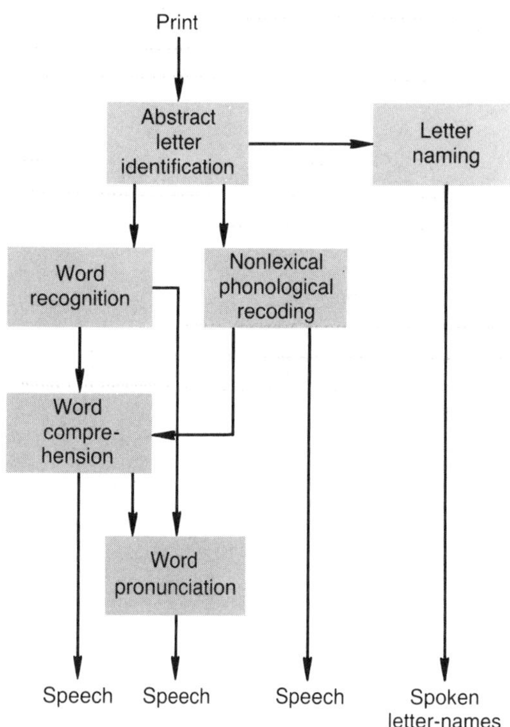

FIGURE 17.10. Examples of subsystems used in reading. Note that speech from print can follow a number of different routes and can be independent of comprehension or pronunciation. (After Coltheart, 1981.)

equally well to other disorders of speech, and it may eventually give an alternative perspective on the anatomical organization of language.

SUMMARY

Language is a unique human ability that represents an extension of the development of multiple sensory channels. It gives us a way to organize sensory inputs by assigning tags to information, which allows us to categorize objects and ultimately concepts. Language also involves the unique motor act of producing syllables. Moreover, it requires a nearly unique ability to impose grammatical rules, which dramatically increases the functional capacity of the system. Different language functions are distributed in a large region of the cortex, although there is relatively precise localization of specific functions such as the generation of verbs versus nouns or the understanding of visual versus auditory information. In this sense language is organized like other cerebral functions: in a series of parallel hierarchical channels. The evolution of language may not represent the development of a single ability but rather the parallel development of several processes, such as the ability to categorize and the ability to use gestures for communication.

REFERENCES

Benson, D. F. Aphasia and lateralization of language. *Cortex* 22:71–86, 1986.

Benson, D. F. Aphasia. In K. M. Heilman and E. Valenstein, eds., *Clinical Neuropsychology,* 3rd ed. New York: Oxford University Press, 1993.

Caplan, D. *Language: Structure, Processing, and Disorders.* Cambridge, Mass.: MIT Press, 1992.

Caplan, D., and J. C. Marshall. Generative grammar and aphasic disorders: A theory of language representation in the human brain. *Foundations of Language* 12:583–596, 1976.

Chomsky, N. On the biological basis of language capabilities. In R. W. Rieber, ed. *Neuropsychology of Language.* New York: Plenum, 1976.

Coltheart, M. Disorders of reading and their implications for models of normal reading. *Visible Language* 15:245–286, 1981.

Coltheart, M. Acquired dyslexias and normal reading. In R. N. Malatesha and H. A. Whitaker, eds. *Dyslexia: A Global Issue.* The Hague: Martinus Nijhoff, 1984.

Cooper, I. S., I. Amin, R. Chandra, and J. M. Waltz. A surgical investigation of the clinical physiology of the LP-pulvinar complex in man. *Journal of Neurological Science* 18:89–100, 1973.

Damasio, A. R., and H. Damasio. Brain and language. *Scientific American* 267(3):88–95, 1992.

Demonet, J. F., R. Wise, and R. S. J. Frackowiak. Language functions explored in normal subjects by positron emission tomography: A critical review. *Human Brain Mapping* 1:39–47, 1993.

de Renzi, E., and L. A. Vignolo. The token test: A sensitive test to detect disturbances in aphasics. *Brain* 85:665–678, 1962.

Gardner, R. A., and B. T. Gardner. Comparative psychology and language acquisition. *Annals of New York Academy of Sciences* 309:37–76, 1978.

Geschwind, N. Language and the brain. *Scientific American* 226:76–83, 1972.

Goodall, J. *The Chimpanzees of Gombe.* Cambridge, Mass.: Harvard University Press, 1986.

Goodglass, H., and E. Kaplan. *The Assessment of Aphasia and Related Disorders.* Philadelphia: Lea and Febiger, 1972.

Green, E. Psycholinguistic approaches to aphasia. *Linguistics* 53:30–50, 1969.

Gustason, G., D. Pfetzing, and E. Zawoklow. *Signing Exact English.* Silver Spring, Md.: Modern Signs Press, 1975.

Halstead, W. C., and J. M. Wepman. The Halstead-Wepman aphasia screening test. *Journal of Speech and Hearing Disorders* 14:9–15, 1959.

Hewes, G. W. Language origin theories. In D. M. Rumbaugh, ed. *Language Learning by a Chimpanzee.* New York: Academic Press, 1977.

Holloway, R. L. Human paleontological evidence relevant to language behavior. *Human Neurobiology* 2:105–114, 1983.

Jefferson, G. Localization of function in the cerebral cortex. *British Medical Bulletin* 5:333–340, 1949.

Kellogg, W., and L. Kellogg. *The Ape and the Child.* New York: McGraw-Hill, 1933.

Kimura, D. Neural mechanisms in manual signing. *Sign Language Studies* 33:291–312, 1981.

Kimura, D. *Neuromotor Mechanisms in Human Communication.* Oxford: Oxford University Press, 1993.

Kimura, D., and N. Watson. The relation between oral movement control and speech. *Brain and Language* 37:565–590, 1989.

Levelt, W. J. M. *Speaking: From Intention to Articulation.* Cambridge, Mass.: MIT Press, 1989.

Lieberman, P. *On the Origins of Language: An Introduction to the Evolution of Human Speech.* New York: Macmillan, 1975.

Luria, A. R., and J. T. Hutton. A modern assessment of basic forms of aphasia. *Brain and Language* 4:129–151, 1977.

MacNeilage, P. F. The frame/context theory of evolution of speech production. Manuscript in submission.

Marshall, J. C. Biological constraints on orthographic representation. *Philosophical Transactions of the Royal Society of London* 298:165–172, 1982.

Marshall, J. C. The description and interpretation of aphasic language disorder. *Neuropsychologia* 24:5–24, 1986.

Mateer, C. Asymmetric effects of thalamic stimulation on rate of speech. *Neuropsychologia* 16:497–499, 1978.

Miles, L. W. Apes and language: The search for communicative competence. In J. de Luce and H. T. Wilder, eds. *Language in Primates: Perspectives and Implications.* New York: Springer-Verlag, 1983.

Monrad-Krohn, H. The third element of speech; prosody and its disorders. In L. Halpern, ed. *Problems of Dynamic Neurology.* Jerusalem: Hebrew University Press, 1963.

Myers, R. E. Comparative neurology of vocalization and speech: Proof of a dichotomy. *Annals of the New York Academy of Sciences* 280:745–760, 1976.

Newcombe, F., and J. C. Marshall. On psycholinguistic classifications of the acquired dyslexias. *Bulletin of the Orton Society* 31:29–46, 1981.

Ojemann, G. A., ed. The thalamus and language. *Brain and Language* 2:1–120, 1975.

Ojemann, G. A. Models of the brain organization for higher integrative functions derived with electrical stimulation techniques. *Human Neurobiology* 1:243–250, 1982.

Ojemann, G. A., and O. D. Creutzfeldt. Language in humans and animals: Contribution of brain stimulation and recording. *Handbook of Physiology: The Nervous System,* vol. 5. Bethesda, Md.: American Physiological Society, 1987.

Ojemann, G. A., and C. Mateer. Cortical and subcortical organization of human communication: Evidence from stimulation studies. In H. D. Steklis and M. J. Raleigh, eds. *Neurobiology of Social Communication in Primates: An Evolutionary Perspective.* New York: Academic Press, 1979.

Patterson, F. G. *Koko's Story.* New York: Scholastic, 1987.

Penfield, W., and L. Roberts. *Speech and Brain Mechanisms.* Princeton, N.J.: Princeton University Press, 1959.

Petersen, S. E., and J. A. Fiez. The processing of single words studied with positron emission tomography. *Annual Review of Neuroscience* 16:509–530, 1983.

Petersen, S. E., P. T. Fox, M. I. Posner, M. Mintun, and M. E. Raichle. Positron emission tomographic studies of the processing of single words. *Journal of Cognitive Neuroscience* 1:153–170, 1988.

Porch, B. E. *Index of Communicative Ability.* Palo Alto, Calif.: Consulting Psychologists Press, 1967.

Posner, M. I., and M. E. Raichle. *Images of Mind.* New York: Scientific American Library, 1994.

Premack, D. The codes of man and beasts. *Behavioral and Brain Sciences* 6:125–167, 1983.

Raichle, M. E., J. A. Fiez, T. O. Videen, A. K. Macleod, J. V. Pardo, P. T. Fox, and S. E. Peterson. Practice-related changes in human brain functional anatomy during non-motor learning. *Cerebral Cortex,* in press.

Ricklan, M., and I. S. Cooper. Psychometric studies of verbal functions following thalamic lesions in humans. *Brain and Language* 2:45–64, 1975.

Rumbaugh, D. M., and T. V. Gill. Lana's acquisition of language skills. In D. M. Rumbaugh, ed. *Language Learning by a Chimpanzee.* New York: Academic Press, 1977.

Savage-Rumbaugh, E. S., K. McDonald, R. A. Sevcik, W. D. Hopkins, and E. Rubert. Spontaneous symbol acquisition and communicative use by pygmy chimpanzees (*Pan paniscus*). *Journal of Experimental Psychology: General* 115:211–235.

Schuell, H. *Differential Diagnosis of Aphasia with the Minnesota Test.* Minneapolis: University of Minnesota Press, 1965.

Searleman, A. A review of right hemisphere linguistic capabilities. *Psychological Bulletin* 84:503–528, 1977.

Spreen, O., and A. L. Benton. *Neurosensory Center Comprehensive Examination for Aphasia.* Victoria, Canada: University of Victoria, 1969.

Steklis, H. D., and M. J. Raleigh. Requisites for language: Interspecific and evolutionary aspects. In H. D. Steklis and M. J. Raleigh, eds. *Neurobiology of Social Communication in Primates: An Evolutionary Perspective.* New York: Academic Press, 1979.

Swadish, M. *The Origin and Diversification of Language.* J. Sherzer, ed. Chicago: Aldine-Atherton, 1971.

Terrace, H. S. *Nim.* New York: Knopf, 1979.

von Glaserfeld, E. The Yerkish language and its automatic parser. In D. M. Rumbaugh, ed. *Language Learning by a Chimpanzee.*New York: Academic Press, 1977.

Wallman, J. *Aping Language.* Cambridge: Cambridge University Press, 1992.

Wepman, J. M., and L. V. Jones. *Studies in Aphasia: An Approach to Testing.* Chicago: University of Chicago Education-Industry Service, 1961.

Whitaker, H. A. *On the Representation of Language in the Human Brain.* Edmonton, Canada: Linguistic Research, Inc., 1971.

Zaidel, E. Language in the right hemisphere. In D. F. Benson and E. Zaidel, eds. *The Dual Brain.* New York: Guilford Press, 1985.

Zangwill, O. L. Excision of Broca's area without persistent aphasia. In K. J. Zulch, O. Creutzfeldt, and G. C. Galbraith, eds. *Cerebral Localization.* Berlin and New York: Springer-Verlag, 1975.

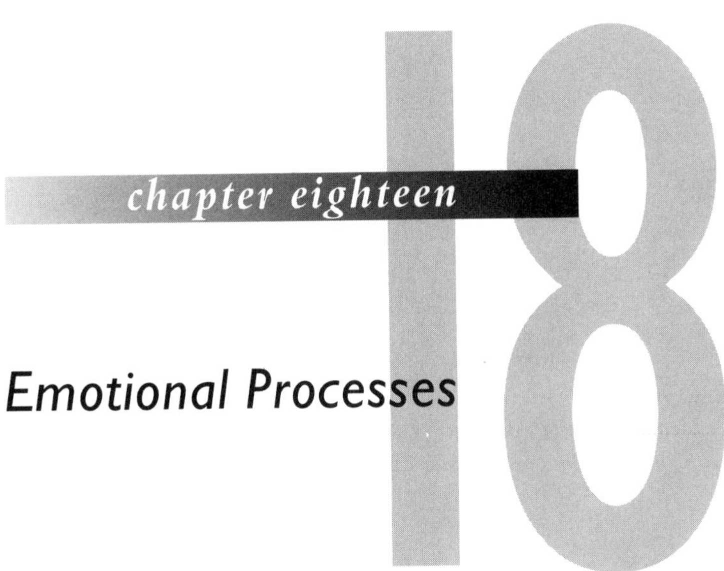

chapter eighteen

Emotional Processes

Virtually any alteration of central nervous system activity can change an individual's personality; impairments of movement, perception, language, or memory affect how a person behaves and is perceived by others. Nevertheless, the scientific study of changes in personality, emotion, and social behavior following brain injury lags far behind the study of cognitive functions, in large part because it is difficult to define, record, and evaluate these behaviors. Over the past decade a view has emerged that there is both a lateralization of control of certain emotional processes, the right hemisphere being dominant, and a localization of control to the frontal and medial temporal regions.

In this chapter we shall summarize current thinking and research on the neurological control of emotional processes in the normal and abnormal brain. We begin by reviewing the development of the neurology of emotional behavior and then consider what emotion is, what the candidate structures that play a major role in emotional behavior might be, and the recent experimental investigations of these questions.

HISTORICAL VIEWS

Interest in the biology of emotions dates back to Darwin's book, *The Expression of Emotions in Man and Animals,* published in 1872. Darwin believed that human emotional expression could only be understood in the context of the expressions of other animals because our emotional behavior is determined by our evolution. Although Darwin's book was a best-seller in its time, its influence was short-lived and it was temporarily forgotten. Psychologists began to speculate about emotions at the turn of the century, but they had little knowledge about the neural basis of emotional behavior. By the late 1920s, physiologists began to examine the relationship between autonomic, endocrine, and neurohumoral factors and inferred emotional states, with particular emphasis upon measuring indices such as heart rate, blood pressure, and skin temperature (see reviews by Dunbar and by Brady). Philip Bard made one of the first major discoveries while working in Walter Cannon's laboratory in the late 1920s.

It had been known from Franz Goltz's studies in the 1890s that decorticated dogs could show strong "rage" responses to seemingly trivial stimuli; the dogs acted as though a seriously threatening stimulus confronted them. Working with cats, Bard showed that this response depended upon the diencephalon, which includes the thalamus and hypothalamus. He found that if the diencephalon was intact, animals would show strong "emotional" responses, but if the animals were decerebrate (see Figure 8.1), leaving the diencephalon disconnected from the midbrain, they would not.

Later studies by many authors (especially Eckhard Hess in the 1940s and John Flynn in the 1960s) showed that stimulation of different regions of the hypothalamus could elicit different types of "affective responses" such as behavior associated with attack of another cat (piloerection, hissing, baring of teeth) or attack of a prey animal (crouching, whiskers and ears forward, pouncing), including eating the animal. The lesion and stimulation studies on the diencephalon were important because they led to the idea that the thalamus and hypothalamus contain the neural circuits for the expression of emotional behaviors, including both the overt behaviors and the autonomic responses such as changes in blood pressure, heart rate, and respiration. The role of the cortex was seen as being largely one of inhibiting the thalamus and hypothalamus. Conversely, the thalamus was considered to play a role in activating the cortex during autonomic arousal, which presumably would help to direct the emotion to the appropriate stimulus.

A second major idea in the history of the neurology of emotions came in 1937 when Papez proposed that the structure of the "limbic lobe" forms the anatomical basis of emotions. Papez reasoned that the limbic structures acting on the hypothalamus produce emotional states. Although for Papez the neocortex played no part in producing emotional behavior, he did believe the cortex to be necessary for transforming events produced by limbic structures into what we experience as emotions. The Papez theory had the appeal of combining behavioral phenomena having no known neurological substrates with anatomical structures having no known function.

The idea of an emotional brain gained instant broad approval because of the predominance of Freudian thinking in the 1930s. That an ancient, deep part of the central nervous system controls emotions and instincts unconsciously, with the neocortex producing consciousness, was a concept with natural appeal for a Freudian-based psychology.

A third major finding came in 1939, when Klüver and Bucy announced the rediscovery of an extraordinary behavioral syndrome that had first been noted by Brown and Schaefer in 1888. The syndrome, resulting from bilateral anterior temporal lobectomy in monkeys, included (1) tameness and a loss of fear; (2) indiscriminate dietary behavior, the monkeys being willing to eat many types of previously rejected foods; (3) greatly increased autoerotic, homosexual, and heterosexual activity, with inappropriate object choice (for example, sexual mounting of chairs); (4) hypermetamorphosis, or a tendency to attend and react to every visual stimulus; (5) a tendency to examine all objects by mouth; and (6) visual agnosia. One aspect of this extraordinary behavior was that animals that normally showed strong aversion to stimuli such as snakes or to "threat" states from humans or other animals now showed no fear of these stimuli whatsoever. Similar behavior has been seen in other species as well. For example, we once observed a cat with bilateral medial temporal lesions wander into a room housing monkeys. It showed not the slightest concern that the monkeys were screeching at it and throwing things in its general direction. Normal cats would never venture into such a room and would piloerect if they merely looked into a monkey colony.

The *Klüver-Bucy syndrome* has been observed subsequently in people with a variety of neurological diseases. For example, Marlowe and colleagues reported on a patient with Klüver-Bucy symptoms that resulted from meningoencephalitis (inflammation of the brain and the meninges):

As regards his visual functions, the patient seemed unable to recognize a wide variety of common objects. He examined each object placed before him as though seeing it for the first time, explored it repetitively and seemed unaware of its significance. As a result, he exhibited difficulty in the spontaneous employment of tools and other mechanical devices, but could initiate utilization of such objects by imitating the gestures of others, and could care for at least some daily needs in this way. Thus, when handed his razor, he would regard it in a bewildered fashion, but would accompany another patient to the bathroom and imitate all movements of his escort, even the most idiosyncratic, with precision; he could in this way succeed in shaving. Other ordinary tasks could be performed on the same imitative basis. Difficulties in recognition, it should be added, extended to people as well as to objects; he failed, for example, to recognize his parents during innumerable hospital visits. However, his ability to match simple pictures, geometric designs, letters of the alphabet and objects was demonstrably preserved when the tasks were taught nonverbally. Visual orientation was defective, the patient losing his way around the hospital when unattended, and visual distractibility was prominent; he seemed unable to distinguish between relevant and irrelevant objects and actions.

Behavioral patterns were distinctly abnormal. He exhibited a flat affect, and, although originally restless, ultimately became remarkably placid. He appeared indifferent to people or situations. He spent much time gazing at the television, but never learned to turn it on; when the set was off, he tended to watch reflections of others in the room on the glass screen. On occasion he became facetious, smiling inappropriately and mimicking the gestures and actions of others. Once initiating an imitative series, he would perseverate copying all movements made by another for extended periods of time. In addition, he commonly generated a series of idiosyncratic, stereotyped gestures employing primarily his two little fingers which he would raise and touch end-to-end in repetitive fashion.

He engaged in oral exploration of all objects within his grasp, appearing unable to gain information via tactile or visual means alone. All objects that he could lift were placed in his mouth and sucked or chewed. He was commonly observed to place his fingers in his mouth and suck them. He did not attempt to pick up objects directly with his mouth, using his hands for that purpose, but was observed to engage in much olfactory behavior. When dining he would eat with his fingers until reprimanded and a fork placed in his hand; he was thereafter able to imitate use of a fork, but failed to remaster the task of eating with utensils spontaneously. He would eat one food item on his plate completely before turning to the next, Hyperbulimia [excessive, insatiable appetite] was prominent; he ingested virtually everything within reach, including the plastic wrapper from bread, cleaning pastes, ink, dog food, and feces. Although his tastes were clearly indiscriminate, he seemed to prefer liquids or soft solids.

The patient's sexual behavior was a particular source of concern while in hospital. Although vigorously heterosexual prior to his illness, he was observed in hospital to make advances toward other male patients by stroking their legs and inviting fellatio by gesture; at times he attempted to kiss them. Although on a sexually mixed floor during a portion of his recovery, he never made advances toward women, and, in fact, his apparent reversal of sexual polarity prompted his fiancee to sever their relationship. (Marlowe, Mancall, and Thomas, 1975, pp. 55–56)

The appearance of the Klüver-Bucy syndrome apparently requires that the amygdala and inferior temporal cortex be removed bilaterally. H. M., the amnesic patient described in Chapter 16, does not exhibit the syndrome despite bilateral removal of the medial temporal structures. Furthermore, monkeys with bilateral amygdalectomies do not show the Klüver-Bucy syndrome unless the temporal cortex is also removed. Finally, there is a single case of a man with a bilateral temporal lobectomy identical to the Klüver-Bucy removal, and he showed all the Klüver-Bucy symptoms, with the exception of orality. Instead of placing novel objects in his mouth he repeatedly inspected them visually.

At about the time of Klüver and Bucy's discovery, a less dramatic, but in many ways more important, discovery was made. Jacobson studied the behavior of chimpanzees in a variety of learning tasks following frontal lobe removals. In 1935, he reported his findings on the effects of the lesions at the Second International Neurology Congress in London. He casually noted that one particularly neurotic chimp appeared more relaxed following the surgery, leading a Portuguese neurologist, Egas Moniz, to propose that similar lesions in people might relieve various behavioral problems. Thus was born psychosurgery and the frontal lobotomy! Unbelievably, not until the late 1960s was any systematic research done on the effects of frontal lobe lesions on the affective behavior of nonhuman animals. Hence, frontal lobotomies in humans were performed without an empirical basis. Experiments by several laboratories have now clearly shown that frontal lobe lesions in rats, cats, and monkeys all have severe effects on social and affective behavior.

THE NATURE OF EMOTION

Think of any significant emotional experience that has happened to you. Perhaps you have had a serious fight with a close friend or have received some unexpected, wonderful news. Such experiences cannot be described as unitary events because emotional experiences differ in multiple ways from one another and from other cognitions. Thus, an emotional experience may include all sorts of thoughts or plans about who said or did what or what will be done in the future. Further, the heart may be pounding, the throat dry, the underarms moist, the limbs trembling, or the face flushed. There may be strong emotional feelings (for example, anger, happiness) that cannot be verbalized. And there may be significant changes in facial expression, tone of voice, or body posture, and even tears of sadness or joy. Having identified (introspectively) some of the components of an emotional experience, we might then ask, "What is emotion?" As we have posed it, this question obviously is not simple.

Emotion is not a thing but an inferred state that has many components, each of which, in principle, may be quantified. Historically, theories of emotion have recognized this, and most theorists agree that the concept of emotion includes at least three principal components. First, there are physiological components that include central and autonomic system activity and the resulting changes in visceral activity, as well as neurohormonal activity. Hence, there are changes in heart rate, blood pressure, distribution of blood flow, perspiration, and the digestive system, among others, as well as the release of various hormones that may affect the brain or the autonomic system. Although a topic of some debate, it seems likely that at least some emotional states (for example, happiness versus sadness) can be differentiated by their associated physiological changes. Second, there are distinctive overt behaviors that are associated with emotional states. Examples are facial expression, tone of voice, and posture. These behaviors are especially important to others because they convey information that can be different from what we verbalize. Our perception of a person who says she is fine but is sobbing uncontrollably is different from our perception of the same person if she is smiling. Third, there are cognitive processes that are inferred from self-report. These processes include both subjective feelings such as, love or hate and other cognitions such as plans, memories, or ideas. The theoretical distinction- between the three components of an emotional experience is significant because there appears to be little correlation among the three when they are all measured in the same subjects.

It is evident that the study of the neural basis of emotion presents the psychologist with a major challenge; there is simply no uniform definition of emotion, nor is there a standardized way to quantify it. Two investigators might focus upon facial expression as a measure of emotion by filming people surreptitiously. One investigator might analyze the film by studying the asymmetry in the facial musculature of individuals during smiling and reach inferences about the role of the cerebral hemispheres in controlling smiling. The other might record the incidence of smiling in brain-damaged patients and reach conclusions about the role of different neural areas in smiling behavior. Each of these is a legitimate line of inquiry, but it is not unreasonable to ask whether either of these studies is really investigating "emotion." (We leave readers to reach their own conclusions.) Our point is that research purporting to study the neural basis of emotion must be viewed critically, with an eye to the question of how the authors are defining, and measuring, emotion.

CANDIDATE STRUCTURES IN EMOTIONAL BEHAVIOR

Multiple Systems

One of the consistent principles of neural organization is that there are multiple systems controlling virtually every behavior. Sensory information enters the cortex through multiple channels that have distinctly different roles in sensory analysis. Once in the cortex, information travels through multiple parallel systems subserving different functions. Recall that visual information follows a ventral route through the temporal lobe and a dorsal route through the parietal lobe. The former route appears to play a role in object recognition, and the latter route plays a role in spatial location. In keeping with this general principle of brain organization, it is likely that there are multiple systems, both cortical and subcortical, that contribute to the experience of an emotion. For example, there must be systems that process significant social stimuli, which are presumably species-specific, including olfactory stimuli (called pheromones), tactile stimuli (especially to sensitive body zones), visual stimuli (facial expressions), and auditory stimuli (phonemes, crying, screaming, and so forth). Although it could be argued that these stimuli are processed by the same systems that analyze other sensory inputs, there is good reason to believe that there may be at least some separate systems. Olfaction provides a good example.

Many mammals have a receptor organ, known as Jacobson's organ, that is specialized to analyze species-typical odors. When animals such as cats encounter certain odors (especially urine from other cats) they close their nostrils and appear to stare off into space with an odd "look" on their face, a behavior that is known as *flehmen* (Figure 18.1). Actually, the cats are forcing the air through the mouth and into a special duct (which allows the air access to Jacobson's organ) that is connected to the accessory olfactory system. Virtually the only odors that produce this behavior in cats are certain ones from other cats, including urine and ear wax but not feces. (Curiously, we have found that human urine is sometimes also effective.) This system is thus specialized for species-typical odors. One interesting property of this system is that it shows habituation (repeated exposure to the same urine reduces the likelihood of flehmen), and cats appear able to remember the odors of familiar cats. Thus, they do not show flehmen to their own urine or to that of cats they live with. Urine from novel cats will produce prolonged episodes of flehmen, and urine from familiar, but not coresident, cats will produce shorter episodes. Although there is little evidence of such specialized systems for other senses, there is still evidence of special processing. There are cells in the temporal lobe of monkeys that are specially tuned for species-typical calls; these cells are relatively insensitive to other sounds. Recall too that there are temporal cortical cells that are specialized for faces.

In addition to the possible specialized processing of emotionally relevant sensory information, it is possible that there are higher-level systems that process other aspects of this information. Perhaps there is a unique system for cross-modal matching of prosody and facial expression. In addition to multiple systems that may encode specific species-typical information, there may be a

FIGURE 18.1. A cat sniffs a urine-soaked cotton ball (*left*), begins the gape response of the flehmen (*middle*), and follows with the full gape response (*right*). This behavior is mediated by the accessory olfactory system, which is specialized to analyze species-typical odors.

general cortical system that is involved in identifying "affective" attributes of stimuli. An interesting experiment by Gazzaniga and Le Doux illustrates such a system. They presented split-brain subjects with visual information to one or the other visual field. The subjects' task was to describe the stimulus verbally and to give it a rating on a five-point scale from "dislike very much" to "like very much." The results were striking. As expected, only the items in the right visual field (and therefore sent to the left, speaking, hemisphere) were described accurately. In contrast, the rating was identical for stimuli in each visual field. Clearly, the pathways that process the affective significance of the stimuli are distinct from the pathways that process their objective properties. This distinction is reminiscent of the difference between knowing what a stimulus is and knowing where it is, as illustrated by blindsight (see Chapter 11). There may be a third system that processes "subjective feeling" about a stimulus independent of where or what it is. We have all had the experience of recognizing an odor or a sound, even though we cannot identify what the stimulus is. We may say that we have a "feeling" or "intuition" about the stimulus. This affective system may be important for memory and, since it probably involves the amygdala, it may account at least partly for the role of the amygdala in memory.

The analysis of multiple channels in the sensory systems has identified various properties of sensory experiences that appear to form separate processing modules. Color, orientation, motion, and depth all appear to be independent properties of visual stimuli. Applying the concept of multiple neural systems to emotion has the distinct disadvantage that we have not identified the sensory modules that appear to be processed differently. Nonetheless, it seems likely that autonomic stimuli form a distinct module, and the neural circuitry of this module is well known. The dimensions of other components remain to be determined. It seems likely, however, that there are separate modules for different aspects of overt behavior (for example, facial expression, prosody) and perhaps for cognitive processes as well.

Studies of Nonhuman Primates: Prefrontal and Paralimbic Lesions

Although it is common to hear spouses or relatives complain of personality changes in brain-damaged patients, the parameters of these changes have been poorly specified in human subjects. Even the behavioral changes in people like Phineas Gage (see Chapter 14) are described in general terms, which seldom are defined objectively. Nonetheless, the study of nonhuman subjects, particularly nonhuman primates, has made it possible to identify various brain regions that undoubtedly have a significant role in emotional processes. During the past 20 years, studies have been conducted on several species of Old World and New World monkeys with lesions of the frontal cortex, paralimbic cortex, or amygdala—the structures that now appear to be the forebrain areas most important in emotional behavior. The results of such studies show six consistent changes in emotional behavior after frontal lesions; these are summarized in Table 18.1.

First, there is an overwhelming consensus that there is a reduction in social interaction following frontal lesions, especially following orbital frontal lesions. Following such lesions, monkeys become socially withdrawn and fail even to reestablish close preoperative relationships with family members. The animals sit alone; seldom if ever engage in social grooming or contact with other monkeys; and, in a free-ranging natural environment, they become solitary, leaving the troop altogether. Anterior temporal lesions produce a milder version of this syndrome, reducing social grooming and social interaction with conspecifics. Lesions elsewhere in the cortex have no obvious effect.

Second, there is a loss of social dominance following orbital frontal lesions: monkeys that were previously dominant in a group do not maintain their dominance after their operations, although the fall may take weeks to complete. The rate of fall from dominance probably depends upon the aggressiveness of other monkeys in the group.

Third, monkeys with orbital frontal lesions show inappropriate social interaction. For example, females with such lesions may challenge and threaten unfamiliar male monkeys, whereas normal females typically exhibit gestures of submission in response to dominance gestures displayed by unfamiliar males. (Male monkeys are much larger than females.) Such monkeys may also approach any animal without hesitation, irrespective of that animal's social dominance. This behavior often results in retaliatory aggression from the dominant, intact animals. Similarly, when approached by dominant animals, monkeys with frontal lesions may simply ignore them or run away, rather than performing normal submissive gestures such as allowing mounting. Curiously, such monkeys show an increased aversion to threat by people, possibly reflecting a decrease in aggressive behavior.

Fourth, monkeys with large frontal lesions show a change in social preference. When a normal monkey is released into a large enclosure that has conspecifics behind a glass barrier, it will generally sit against the glass next to an animal sitting on the opposite side. Although normal animals prefer to sit beside intact monkeys of the opposite sex, monkeys with frontal lesions prefer to sit with other frontal monkeys of the same sex, presumably because they are less threatening.

Fifth, monkeys with frontal lesions and those with anterior temporal lesions largely lose the use of their facial expressions, posturings, and gesturings in social situations—the effects being larger after frontal than after temporal lesions. Thus, monkeys with frontal lesions show a drastic drop in the frequency and variability of facial expressions and are described as "poker-faced." The one exception is in the frequency of submissive or agitated expressions such as the "grimace" expression. This loss of facial expression is not a simple loss of muscle control of the face, because the animals do produce expressions. They just fail to produce them often. Lesions of the cingulate or visual association cortex seem to have no effect.

Finally, lesions of the frontal or anterior limbic cortex reduce spontaneous social vocalizations. Indeed, following anterior cingulate lesions, rhesus monkeys effectively make no normal vocalizations at all. Curiously, the nonvocal social behavior of these animals is normal.

TABLE 18.1. Summary of changes in social behavior of monkeys with frontal cortical lesions

1. Reduced social interaction
2. Loss of social dominance
3. Inappropriate social interaction
4. Altered social preference
5. Reduced facial expression and/or body gestures
6. Reduced vocalization

In summary, lesions of the orbital frontal cortex of monkeys produce marked changes in social behavior. In particular, such monkeys become less socially responsive and fail to produce or respond to species-typical stimuli. Damage to the paralimbic cortex produces milder effects, the animals showing a reduction in social interaction. An important point is that despite the significant changes in the sensory processing abilities of animals with visual association lesions, there appear to be very few obvious changes in their affective behavior.

The changes in emotional processes in monkeys with frontal lesions are especially intriguing because they suggest that similar changes might be found in humans with frontal lobe injuries. In particular, since monkeys fail to make appropriate vocal and gestural behaviors and fail to respond normally to those made by conspecifics, one might predict that humans with frontal lobe injuries would show similar abnormalities. Furthermore, it might be predicted that disorders such as schizophrenia, which are characterized by significant changes in social interactions, might also involve frontal dysfunction.

Studies of Nonhuman Primates: Amygdalectomy

In their original studies, Klüver and Bucy observed grossly abnormal emotional behavior after removal of the amygdala and the adjacent paralimbic cortex and temporal neocortex. Subsequent work showed that destruction of the amygdala alone produced much of the syndrome, since monkeys whose amygdalas had been removed showed a reduced aversion to biologically relevant stimuli that normal monkeys found threatening. In general, there is a loss of fear of humans and a general taming in such monkeys. Dicks and his colleagues showed that four of six animals with amygdalectomies failed to rejoin their original groups when freed and all died within a short time. The two remaining animals were younger, and they did rejoin their group but rarely initiated social activity. Studies of single unit activity in the amygdala have shown cells that respond to species-typical aversive visual stimuli, a result that is consistent with the loss of response to such stimuli after lesions.

The close anatomical connections between the orbital prefrontal cortex and the amygdala, and the emotional changes following lesions to either region, suggest that these structures belong to some neural circuit regulating emotional behavior. Disconnecting the amygdala from its visual input via the temporal lobe also produces alterations in emotional behavior, which suggests that the amygdala may form part of a system for processing socially relevant visual information.

Premorbid Emotional Processes

It is often stated that the personality of human brain-injured patients is at least partly dependent upon their premorbid, or preinjury, state. People who are depressive before their injury are more likely to be depressive afterward; people who are cheerful are more likely to remain so. There has been no systematic study of this phenomenon, but in our experience there is far more intersubject variability in the emotional behavior of brain-damaged people than there is in most tests of cognitive function. A study by Peters and Ploog on the social behavior of squirrel monkeys with frontal lesions is relevant here. Although these authors found many of the changes in social behavior previously observed by others, they also noted that some monkeys seemed less changed by their lesions. Two dominant monkeys received similar orbital frontal lesions, but whereas one completely lost his dominant position, the second remained dominant but did not exert the dominance strongly. In another social group the second monkey might have been challenged and lost this position. Differences in the premorbid behavior of the lesioned monkeys, as well as in the group structure, appear to have contributed to the change in social behavior. In contrast, when monkeys with frontal lesions are given neuropsychological learning tests such as delayed-response tests, it is typical that all animals show a much more similar behavioral change. This result is important because it is probably true of humans as well: the effects of brain damage on processes such as language and memory are more consistent than the effects on emotion. Or, stated differently, the premorbid personality of human patients with cortical injuries is likely to influence the extent of postinjury changes in emotional processes. This has been completely neglected in research to date and adds a major complication as we try to make generalizations about emotional processes.

Asymmetry and Emotion

In the 1930s, clinicians were reporting detailed observations of patients with large unilateral lesions, noting an apparent asymmetry in the effects of left and right hemisphere lesions. The best-known descriptions are those of Goldstein, who suggested that left hemisphere lesions produce "catastrophic" reactions characterized by fearfulness and depression, whereas right hemisphere lesions produce "indifference." The first systematic study of these contrasting behavioral effects was done by Gainotti in 1969, who showed that catastrophic reactions, occurred in 62% of his left hemisphere sample, compared with only 10% of his right hemisphere cases. In contrast, indifference was commoner in the right hemisphere patients, occurring in 38%, as compared with only 11% of the left hemisphere cases. Significantly, however, Gainotti reported that catastrophic reactions were associated with aphasia and indifference reactions with neglect.

Although it is tempting to assume that the emotional reactions observed in stroke patients reflect complementary functioning of the two hemispheres in emotional processes, our experience with patients undergoing cortical resections suggests that the situation is more complex. In general, right hemisphere excisions appear to increase talking, left hemisphere lesions to reduce it. (Remember that none of these patients are aphasic, nor do they exhibit persistent neglect.) These effects are especially obvious following frontal lobe lesions. The content of the speech released by right hemisphere lesions has not been carefully studied, but it is our impression that it is significantly affected by the lesion site. Patients with right frontal lesions characteristically make poor jokes and puns and tell pointless stories, often liberally embellished with profanity. Further, the right frontal lobe patient is usually intensely amused by the stories he or she is telling and will persist even if others are unmoved by them. On the other hand, lesions of the right temporal and/or posterior parietal lobe produce a totally different type of speech that is characterized by excessive concern for the individual's personal life. Such patients often go to great lengths to rationalize their personal shortcomings, and they are generally unaware that others may be bored with their talking. Many of these patients also exhibit symptoms of paranoia, often being convinced that friends or family either are not supportive or are against them. They are often excessively suspicious of neuropsychological assessments, insisting either that the assessments are unnecessary or that they would rather do them when they are "feeling better."

It is obvious that a simple left-right distinction of catastrophic reaction–indifference is far too simple; both the site and the side of the lesion are important in understanding the changes in emotional behavior. This ought not to surprise us, since the same is true of cognitive behaviors. To understand the organization of emotional processes, therefore, we must attempt to separate the components of the behaviors as we have done for the study of cognitive processes. As a first step, we shall consider the production of affective behavior separately from the interpretation of affective stimuli.

PRODUCTION OF EMOTIONAL BEHAVIOR

Mood is inferred largely from facial expression, tone of voice, and frequency of talking, and so these are sensible behaviors to study first in an analysis of emotional behavior in brain-damaged people. Another way to study emotional behavior is to assess mood and related behaviors using various rating scales—both self-administered scales and those administered by others. Finally, behavior can be studied by anesthetizing one hemisphere briefly using sodium amobarbital.

Ratings of Mood

It is not uncommon for people with cerebral strokes to appear to be depressed, especially if they are aphasic. It would seem a simple matter to measure such mood states in people using self-report inventories or psychiatric evaluations. Robinson and his colleagues reported that left frontal lesions produce depressive symptoms but right frontal lesions do not. Robinson's studies have stimulated considerable interest, and although the results have not always been replicated, the general conclusion seems to be that although left frontal lesions produce depressive symptoms soon after stroke, the symptoms decline over time and there may be little evidence of depression after a few months. Curiously, a recent study of chronic brain injuries in Vietnam War veterans has found that patients with left orbital frontal lesions have a more cavalier attitude toward interpersonal problems than do other patients. In contrast, right orbital frontal lesions made individuals more "edgy" and "anxious."

Facial Expression and Spontaneous Talking

Facial expression is one of the most salient cues to emotion in humans, and in recent years there has been a good deal of study of its production in normal people. Overall, studies of neurological patients have found a reduction in the frequency and intensity of facial expressions in people with anterior lesions relative to those with more posterior lesions. For example, in a series of studies, Kolb and his colleagues have found that whether facial expressions are measured in terms of frequency, quantitative scoring of facial-movement elements, or subjective rating by judges, both left and right frontal lobe patients show a reduction in facial expression relative to temporal lobe groups (Figure 18.2). Furthermore, this result occurs whether the expressions are spontaneous or posed. However, the side of the lesion clearly affects spontaneous talking in frontal lobe patients. Right frontal lesions appear to increase talking markedly, whereas left frontal lesions decrease it (see Figure 18.2). There can be little doubt that such changes in facial expression and talking would be perceived to produce marked changes in personality by friends and relatives of frontal lobe patients.

There is also a suggestion that large right hemisphere lesions may have greater effects on facial expression than similarly sized left hemisphere lesions. In a recent study, Blonder and colleagues videotaped interviews with patients and their spouses in their homes and found that patients with right hemisphere damage were less facially expressive than left hemisphere or control subjects. In contrast, other investigators have failed to find hemispheric differences. For example, Mammucari and colleagues showed people film clips that were intended to produce emotional responses. Using an objective scoring procedure for facial expression, these authors did not find a difference in facial expressiveness after left or right hemisphere lesions. They did, however, find that right hemisphere patients showed reduced autonomic responses (heart rate and skin conductance) relative to normal control or left hemisphere patients.

In summary, cortical lesions reduce facial expression and, at least in some circumstances, the effects appear larger from right than left side lesions.

Tone or Prosody

Spoken language carries two types of information: that derived directly from the content and that inferred from the tone of voice. There is little doubt that the former is a function of the left hemisphere, and there is reason to suspect that the latter is a function of the right. For example, when Tucker and colleagues asked patients to express particular affective states such as anger, happiness, and sadness when they read emotionally neutral sentences, patients with right hemisphere lesions produced the sentences with relatively flat affect compared to patients with left hemisphere lesions. This absence of tone in speech has been termed **aprosodia,** and it can be measured on a wide-

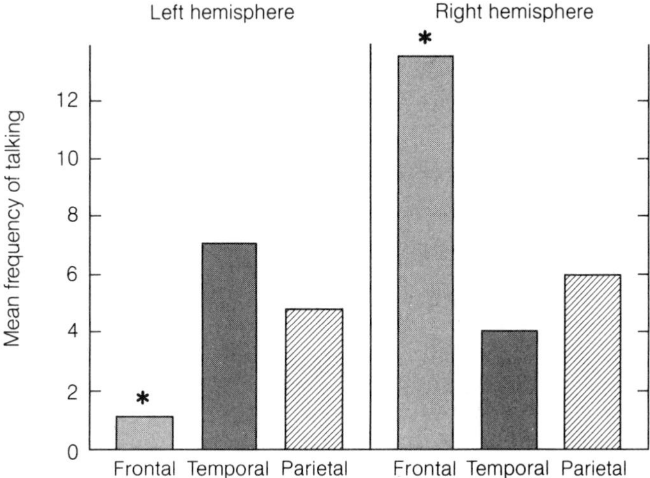

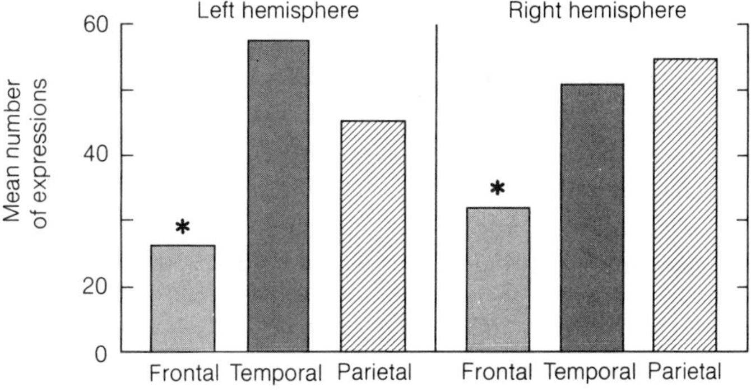

FIGURE 18.2. Relative frequencies of spontaneous talking (*A*) and facial expressions (*B*) during routine neuropsychological testing. Note that frontal lobe lesions significantly reduce the number of facial expressions. The level of spontaneous talking is significantly reduced for left frontal lesions and increased for right frontal lesions. Stars indicate a significant difference from other groups with same-side lesions. (After Kolb and Milner, 1981; Kolb and Taylor, 1981.)

band spectogram, as was done by Kent and Rosenek.

Abnormalities in tone of voice in right hemisphere patients have led Ross to propose that there may be a set of aprosodias analogous to aphasias in left hemisphere speech (Table 18.2). *Motor aprosodia,* an inability to produce affective components of language, is proposed to result from damage to Broca's area in the right hemisphere. *Sensory aprosodia,* a deficit in the interpretation of the emotional components of language, is presumed to result from damage to the region in the right hemisphere analogous to Wernicke's area. Ross's proposal may have merit and it de-

TABLE 18.2. Ross's proposed classification of aprosodias

Type	Spontaneous prosody and gesturing	Prosodic repetition	Prosodic comprehension	Comprehension of emotional gesturing
Motor	Poor	Poor	Good	Good
Sensory	Good	Poor	Poor	Poor
Global	Poor	Poor	Poor	Poor
Conduction	Good	Poor	Good	Good
Transcortical motor	Poor	Good	Good	Good
Transcortical sensory	Good	Good	Poor	Poor
Mixed transcortical	Poor	Good	Poor	Poor
Anomic (alexia with agraphia)	Good	Good	Good	Poor

serves serious consideration, but at present it is without much scientific support. Furthermore, like aphasias, which are virtually never purely of one type, aprosodias may not be as pure as Ross has suggested.

Temporal Lobe Personality

One way to quantify social or affective behavior is to have patients and their friends complete rating scales of various behavioral traits such as "anger," "sadness," and "religiosity." In their study of the behavior of temporal lobe patients, Bear and Fedio asked them and their friends to do just this, with the scales related to the traits summarized in Table 18.3. Each of these traits had previously been attributed to temporal lobe epileptics, who presumably had temporal lobe lesions producing their epileptic condition. The epileptic patients self-reported a distinctive profile of humorless sobriety, dependence, and obsessionalism; raters differentiated the temporal lobe patients on the basis of nearly every trait in Table 18.3 but rated them most strongly on the traits described as "circumstantiality," "philosophical interests," and "anger." Furthermore, right and left temporal lobe patients could be distinguished: the right temporal patients were described as more obsessional and the left temporal ones are more concerned with "personal destiny." In a 1983 study, Fedio and Martin evaluated temporal lobectomy patients on the same scale, finding that surgical removal of the epileptogenic tissue produced a decrease in the characteristic personality traits, presumably because the abnormal temporal lobe tissue that produced the seizures also interfered with normal function. Nonetheless, these patients still differed from normal control subjects: the left temporal lobectomy cases rated themselves more harshly, reported hypergraphic tendencies, and professed a reflective style of thinking that centered on themes of religiosity and personal destiny. Right temporal lobectomy patients rated themselves less adversely but claimed to have developed more feelings of anger, sadness, and aggression.

Affect under Sodium Amobarbital

From the studies detailed above, it is reasonable to expect that patients under the effects of sodium amobarbital injected into the carotid artery would exhibit changes in personality related to the site of drug injection. For example, from Gainotti's results, a depressive-catastrophic reaction could be predicted to follow injection into the speaking hemisphere and an indifference reaction to follow injection into the nonspeaking hemisphere. Study

TABLE 18.3. Summary of characteristics attributed to temporal lobe epileptics

Emotionality	Deepening of all emotions; sustained intense manic-depressive disease
Elation, euphoria	Grandiosity, exhilarated mood; diagnosis of manic-depressive disease
Sadness	Discouragement, fearfulness, self-depreciation; diagnosis of depression, suicide attempt
Anger	Increased temper, irritability
Aggression	Overt hostility, rape attacks, violent crimes, murder
Altered sexual interest	Loss of libido, hyposexualism; fetishism, transvestism, exhibitionism, hypersexual episodes
Guilt	Tendency to self-scrutiny and self-recrimination
Hypermoralism	Attention to rules with inability to distinguish significant from minor infractions, desire to punish offenders
Obsessionalism	Ritualism; orderliness; compulsive attention to detail
Circumstantiality	Loquaciousness; pedantry; being overly detailed or peripheral
Viscosity	Stickiness; tendency to repetition
Sense of personal destiny	Events given highly charged, personalized significance; divine guidance ascribed to many features of patient's life
Hypergraphia	Keeping extensive diaries, detailed notes; writing autobiography or novel
Religiosity	Holding deep religious beliefs; often idiosyncratic multiple conversions, mystical states
Philosophical interest	Nascent metaphysical or moral speculations, cosmological theories
Dependence, passivity	Cosmic helplessness, "at hands of fate"; protestations of helplessness
Humorlessness, sobriety	Overgeneralized ponderous concern; humor lacking or idiosyncratic
Paranoia	Suspicious, overinterpretative of motives and events; diagnosis of paranoid schizophrenia

Source: After Bear and Fedio, 1977.

results, however, are contradictory. The most widely cited results are those collected by Terzian and by Rossi and Rosandini. They reported that injections into the left hemisphere indeed provoked a catastrophic reaction as the drug wore off. The patient "despairs and expresses a sense of guilt, of nothingness, of indignity, and worries about his own future or that of his relatives, without referring to the language disturbances overcome and to the hemiplegia just resolved and ignored." As the drug wore off after injection into the right hemisphere, a "euphorical" reaction was reported; the patient "appears without apprehension, smiles and laughs and both with mimicry and words expresses considerable liveliness and sense of well-being." These results are provocative, but unfortunately a number of groups have been unable to confirm them. For example, in one report on 104 patients, Milner noted only rare depression, and there was no systematic asymmetry in the euphoria. Furthermore, Kolb and Milner found no asymmetry in either the frequency or the quality (for example, happy or sad) of facial expressions following injection into the left or right hemispheres.

Recently, Ross and his colleagues approached the sodium amobarbital question differently. They asked patients to recall verbally an emotional life experience that had been identified before the injection of the right hemisphere. (It is not possible to do this experiment on the speaking hemisphere.) After the injection they asked about this story. Surprisingly, most patients altered their recall of the affective, but not the factual, content of the story. For example, one patient recalled an experience of a car wreck in which he struck a tree and was thrown from the vehicle, which was "squashed like an accordion." When asked to recall his emotional state, he said that he was "scared, scared to death." After the injection, he related the same story but now said that he felt "kind of stupid." After the drug had worn off, the patient reverted to his earlier statement and denied that he had felt stupid. Analogous results were found with other patients. In general, the patients lost the basic affective memory when the right hemisphere was injected. Ross's result suggests that the right hemisphere plays a distinct role in either emotional state or emotional memory.

Psychiatric Disturbance

Although the majority of brain-damaged people do not exhibit psychotic behaviors, symptoms such as hallucinations, mania, or delusions of persecution are occasionally reported. Curiously, such symptoms are virtually always associated with right hemisphere lesions, although it may be that such symptoms are masked by aphasia after left hemisphere lesions. In any event, the cause of the psychotic symptoms in brain-damaged patients is obscure.

INTERPRETATION OF AFFECTIVE STIMULI BY NEUROLOGICAL PATIENTS

Emotional behavior might appear to be abnormal not only because a person is unable to produce the appropriate behavior but also because he or she misinterprets the social or emotional signals coming from others. The interpretation of affective stimuli by neurological patients has been studied in a number of ways, each of which is considered separately.

Judgment of Mood

Heilman and his colleagues asked patients to judge the mood of a speaker after listening to him read a sentence in which he successively feigned anger, joy, or some other emotion. Patients with right hemisphere lesions (largely temporal-parietal) were more impaired at the task than patients with analogous left hemisphere lesions. This impairment at perceiving emotional tone in language is referred to by Ross as a sensory aprosodia, and he predicts that it results from temporal-parietal lesions on the right, just as Heilman and his coworkers report. It is likely, however, that patients with right temporal lobectomies—who, it should be recalled, are impaired at musical perception—will be quite impaired at the judgment of emotional tone whether or not the analogue of Wernicke's area is removed.

Comprehension of Humor

The ability to be humorous and appreciate humor is one of our most intriguing behaviors and certainly contributes to our personality. Little is known about the neurological basis of humor competence, except for two interesting studies by Gardner and his associates. In the first they examined the comprehension and appreciation of humorous material following left or right hemisphere lesions. They asked patients to choose the funniest of four cartoons, which were either with or without captions. The results showed that all the patients were impaired at the task, but there was an asymmetry in the pattern of errors. Patients with left hemisphere lesions did well on the cartoons *without* captions, whereas patients with right hemisphere lesions did well on the cartoons *with* captions. Further, the behavior of the two patient groups differed. Those with left hemisphere lesions behaved "normally"; those with right hemisphere lesions tended to exhibit one of two extreme reactions: either they laughed at nearly every item, even when their understanding was doubtful, or, more commonly, they displayed little reaction to any item, even when their understanding seemed adequate. Thus, although both left and right hemisphere damage impaired the appreciation of humor, the right hemisphere lesions appeared to have had a more fundamental effect on the patient's behavior.

In a second study, Brownwell and colleagues assessed the appreciation of jokes by patients with right hemisphere damage. They hypothesized that the appreciation of jokes presupposes two elements: sensitivity to the surprise element entailed in the punch line of the joke, and appreciation of the coherence that results when the punch line has been integrated with the body of the joke. In other words, the surprise element must be appreciated as being related to the content of the prelude; if it is not, the humor is lost. To study the verbal humor of their patients, they presented subjects with a short story leading up to a punch line, followed by four alternative endings. One ending was a surprise that followed the story, one was a surprise that was a non sequiter with the story, and the other two contained no surprise but were statements that followed the coherence of the story. Consider the following example. "The neighborhood borrower approached Mr. Smith on Sunday afternoon and inquired: 'Say Smith, are you using your lawnmower this afternoon?' 'Yes, I am,' Smith replied warily. The neighborhood borrower then answered: 'Fine, then you won't be needing your golf clubs, I'll just borrow them.'"

In the Brownwell study the subjects did not receive the last sentence but were given four choices. (1) Correct ending: "Fine, then you won't be needing your golf clubs, I'll just borrow them." (2) Non sequitur ending: "You know, the grass is greener on the other side." (3) Neutral ending: "Do you think I could use it when you're done?" (4) Sad ending: "Gee, if only I had enough money, I could buy my own."

Patients with right hemisphere damage did poorly at this test because although they reliably chose surprise endings, they were as likely to choose a non sequitur as the correct ending. The patients recognized that a joke must end in a surprise, and they recognized which endings were surprising, but they could not establish an interpretation of the story that tied the ending coherently to the body of the joke.

Taken together, the Gardner studies imply that right hemisphere patients in particular have an atypical sense of humor, a result concordant with clinical descriptions of these patients as having inappropriate responses to jokes, stories, or conversations. There is no hint concerning where this deficit is most likely to arise, although on the basis of clinical reports, the frontal lobe would seem the obvious place to look.

Judgment of Facial Expression

There has been considerable interest over the past decade in the perception of facial expression in normal subjects, in large part because of the seminal work of Ekman and his colleagues. It is now recognized that people can discriminate between six different classes of facial expression (happy, sad, angry, surprised, afraid, and disgusted) and that this ability transcends cultural or linguistic barriers. Thus, people from New Guinea recognize the same categories of facial expression as do people from France. To study the ability of patients with cerebral lesions to appreciate different facial expressions, Kolb and Taylor did a series of experiments in which subjects were asked to match various photographs of faces on the basis of emotion inferred from the facial expression. Patients with right hemisphere lesions were especially poor at matching facial expressions, a result consistent with the inferred role of the right hemisphere in the processing of faces. Curiously, patients with left frontal lesions did poorly at the test relative to the other left hemisphere groups. In a follow-up study, Kolb and Taylor gave a similar test to a much larger sample of patients and found a significant impairment in left frontal lobe subjects, as well as in right frontal and temporal subjects (Figure 18.3). This result suggests that although the right hemisphere may be dominant for the processing of faces and facial expressions, the left hemisphere may also play a role. One possibility is that the left hemisphere assigns verbal tags to expressions, which aid in recognition.

Judgment of Emotional Situations

Like the appreciation of facial expression, the comprehension of emotional situations is central to understanding emotion in others. Cicone and associates asked patients to match a target scene,

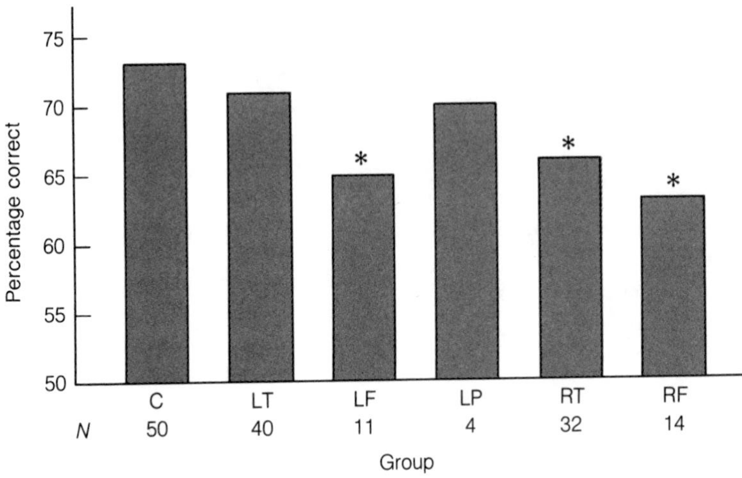

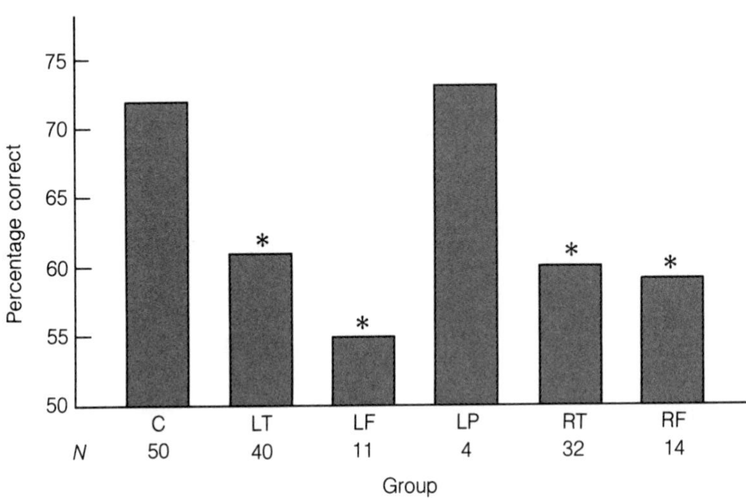

FIGURE 18.3. Performance of control subjects (C) and surgical excision patients on a test of matching facial expressions (*A*) and matching facial expressions to cartoon situations (*B*). Note that both left frontal (LF) and right frontal (RF) lobe lesions impair performance on both perceptual tests. Temporal lobe lesions have asymmetrical effects: left temporals (LT) are impaired only on the interpretative test, whereas the right temporals (RT) are impaired at both tests. Left parietals (LP) are not impaired on either test. Stars indicate significant difference from controls or other groups with same-side lesions. (After Kolb and Taylor, 1988.)

such as a man being robbed, with one of four other scenes that displayed the same emotion, although in a different situation. Thus, given a choice of a man winning a lottery, a woman shopping, a man in quicksand, and a child eating ice cream, the match to a man being robbed would be the man in quicksand, because both pictures represent frightening situations. Right hemisphere patients were more impaired than left hemisphere patients on a purely visual form of the test (drawings of scenes) and were as impaired on a verbal version (spoken or written form). These authors conclude that the difficulty in understanding emotional situations is general among right hemisphere patients but is secondary to language impairment in left hemisphere patients. This may be true, but the degree of impairment in verbal tasks is almost certainly related to the size of the lesion in the right hemisphere patients. Kolb and Taylor found that their patients with small right hemisphere excisions were not impaired at judging emotion from verbal descriptions of emotional situations, but patients with equivalent left hemisphere lesions were. For example, the patients were asked to pair the correct emotion with a propositional statement such as "This man is at a funeral"; left, but not right, hemisphere patients were less accurate than controls.

Recently, Kolb and Taylor showed subjects cartoon drawings like those illustrated in Figure 18.4 and asked them to choose one of six photographs as being appropriate for the missing face. In this situation both left and right frontal or temporal lobe patients were impaired, whereas a small group of left parietal patients performed normally. This result was unexpected and is consistent with the hypothesis that both the left and right frontal and temporal lobes are involved in judgments of emotional situations.

Much more study of the judgment of emotional situations is needed, but as a general conclusion it appears that right hemisphere lesions have a greater effect on this ability than do those on the left. This result is consistent with the inappropriate behavior seen in patients with right hemisphere lesions, especially lesions that include the frontal lobe. Nonetheless, left hemisphere lesions certainly affect the judgment of emotional situations, although not necessarily for the same reasons.

LATERALITY STUDIES

In recent years, laterality studies have turned their attention to the lateralization of affective processes. The basic approach in these studies is to present material to one hemisphere, using dichotic (or tachistoscopic) techniques, to demonstrate a difference in the performance of the two hemispheres. If one hemisphere were superior to the other at recognizing tone of voice or facial expression, for example, it could be inferred that the superior hemisphere had some dominant role in this function. We shall review these studies briefly, dividing them by whether they investigate the production of affective behavior or the perception of emotional stimuli.

Production of Affective Behavior

A series of studies by Campbell has demonstrated that facial expressions are not always symmetrical, but rather tend to occur predominantly on the left side of the face. The asymmetries may range from the hardly noticeable—such as the flicker of a smile on the left side of Mona Lisa's face (on the right of the painting, of course)—to the pronounced—such as a raised eyebrow, wink, or lopsided smile on the left side of the face. In one study, Moscovitch and Olds surreptitiously recorded the facial expressions of people in restaurants, finding a left-side preponderance of facial expression. They confirmed this observation by carefully analyzing video recordings of people recounting sad and humorous stories, again finding a left-side bias in facial expressions. Asymmetrical production of facial expression can be interpreted as showing that the right hemisphere is specialized in that function, a conclusion consistent with its presumed specialization in the per-

FIGURE 18.4. Examples of cartoon situations in which patients were asked either to produce the appropriate expression or to choose the appropriate expression from several choices for the bland face. (After Kolb and Taylor, 1988.)

ception of facial expressions. It is tempting to speculate that right hemisphere specialization in producing and interpreting facial expression is analogous to left hemisphere specialization in producing and interpreting language, but this has yet to be proved. We caution that the apparent specialization of the right hemisphere in the perception of faces could easily be interpreted as a specialization for the perception of complex visual stimuli, of which faces are an example.

Perception of Relevant Stimuli

To date, studies of perception of emotionally loaded stimuli by normal subjects have examined only the visual and auditory modalities. For both modalities, the stimulus usually is presented to one hemisphere selectively, either alone or in competition with information presented simultaneously to the opposite hemisphere. Two procedures have been used for the visual presentation. In one, faces with different expressions (for example, sad and happy) are presented tachistoscopically to the left or right visual field, and the subject is asked to identify the facial expression. The results show the left visual field to be superior at correct identification. This superiority can be interpreted as demonstrating a right hemisphere specialization for the perception of facial expression, an important aspect of nonverbal communication. The second procedure involves an ingenious technique devised by Dimond (see also a more recent study by Wittling and Roschmann). By using special contact lenses Dimond and his colleagues were able to project several types of films selectively to the left or right hemisphere. Subjects rated each film on a scale of 1 to 9 on the four emotional dimensions of humorous, pleasant, horrific, or unpleasant. Films presented to the right hemisphere were judged more unpleasant and horrific and produced greater autonomic nervous system activation (as measured by heart rate) than these same films presented to the left hemisphere of other subjects. Dimond and his colleagues concluded that the two hemispheres hold an essentially different emotional view of the world. Curiously, if the films were shown to both hemispheres simultaneously, the ratings closely resembled those of the right visual field (the left hemisphere), suggesting that left hemisphere perception is dominant. It could be predicted that a left hemisphere lesion might result in a more negative view of the films, although this has not been studied.

Studies of asymmetries in the auditory perception of emotions have generally employed a dichotic-listening technique, which generally shows a left-ear superiority for emotional material such as laughing or crying. One of the most compelling experiments was conducted by Ley and Bryden. They employed a number of short sentences spoken in happy, sad, angry, and neutral voices. These sentences were dichotically paired with neutral sentences of similar semantic content. Subjects were instructed to attend to one ear and to report the emotional tone of the target sentence and indicate its content by checking off items on a multiple-choice recognition sheet. Virtually every subject showed a left-ear advantage for identifying the emotional tone of the voice and, at the same time, a right-ear advantage for identifying the content. This result is analogous to that of Dimond and colleagues, who found that the two hemispheres deal with visual material in a different way.

SUMMARY

The research on the neural basis of emotion is subject to many criticisms, in part because of the difficulty in designing the experiments. In addition, the research can be criticized on the grounds that the sample sizes in most studies are small and the lesions are highly variable. Aphasia in left hemisphere patients makes the study of these people difficult, and some studies simply compare right hemisphere patients with controls. Nevertheless, we can conclude that lesions of the left and right hemispheres have different effects on emotional behaviors: damage to the right appears to produce larger effects, especially on interpretation. This conclusion is supported by laterality studies, but it is not universally accepted. For example, in a thoughtful review Tucker concluded that the right hemisphere has a special role in mediating negative emotions, whereas the left hemisphere is more implicated in positive emotions. It seems more parsimonious to us to view the right hemisphere as being more involved than the left in all aspects of emotional behavior however. Second, frontal lobe lesions reduce facial expression, alter spontaneous talking, and generally produce larger changes in social behavior than lesions elsewhere in the cortex. There is some asymmetry in this effect, especially in spontaneous talking. Third, temporal lobe damage is associated with a constellation of behavioral symptoms, many of which are related to damage to just the left or the right hemisphere. Finally, the occurrence in persons without known brain damage of many traits of personality or emotional behavior that are characteristic of brain-damaged groups leads us to speculate that differences in cerebral organization, whether genetically or environmentally derived, form the basis of different human personalities. For example, one could hypothesize that people who are hypercritical may have relatively smaller, or less active, temporal lobes or that people without much facial expression have smaller, or less active, frontal lobes. Since people vary widely in their performance on neuropsychological tests of cognitive behavior, it would be interesting to explore the differences in performance on measures of cognitive and emotional behavior in the *same normal subjects*.

REFERENCES

Bear, D. M., and P. Fedio. Quantitative analysis of interictal behavior in temporal lobe epilepsy. *Archives of Neurology* 34:454–467, 1977.

Bihrle, A. M., H. H. Brownell, J. A. Powelson, and H. Gardner. Comprehension of humorous and nonhumorous materials by left and right brain-damaged patients. *Brain and Cognition* 5:399–411, 1986.

Blonder, L. X., D. Bowers, and K. M. Heilman. The role of the right hemisphere on emotional communication. *Brain* 114:1115–1127, 1991.

Blumer, D. Temporal lobe epilepsy and its psychiatric significance. In D. F. Blumer and D. Benson, eds. *Psychiatric Aspects of Neurological Disease*. New York: Grune & Stratton, 1975.

Borod, J. C., E. Koff, M. Perlman Lorch, and M. Nicholas. The expression and perception of facial emotion in brain-damaged patients. *Neuropsychologia* 24:169–180, 1986.

Brady, J. V. *Emotional Behavior. Handbook of Physiology*, vol. III. Bethesda, Md.: American Physiological Society, 1960.

Brown, S., and E. A. Schaefer. An investigation into the functions of the occipital and temporal lobe of the monkey's brain. *Philosophical Transactions of the Royal Society, Part B* 179: 303–327, 1888.

Brownell, H. H., D. Michel, J. Powelson, and H. Gardner. Surprise but not coherence: Sensitivity to verbal humor in right-hemisphere patients. *Brain and Language* 18:20–27, 1983.

Bruyer, R., ed. *The Neuropsychology of Face Perception and Facial Expression*. Hillsdale, N.J.: Lawrence Erlbaum Associates, 1986.

Butter, C. M., and D. R. Snyder. Alterations in aversive and aggressive behaviors following orbital frontal lesions in rhesus monkeys. *Acta Neurobiologiae Experimentalis* 32:525–565, 1972.

Campbell, R. The lateralisation of emotion: A critical review. *International Journal of Psychology* 17:211–229, 1982.

Dimond, S. J., and L. Farrington. Emotional response to films shown to the right or left hemisphere of the brain measured by heart rate. *Acta Psychologia* 41:255–260, 1977.

Dimond, S. J., L. Farrington, and P. Johnson. Differing emotional response from right and left hemispheres. *Nature* 261:690–692, 1976.

Dunbar, H. F. *Emotions and Bodily Changes,* 4th ed. New York: Columbia University Press, 1954.

Ekman, P., W. V. Friesen, and P. Ellsworth. *Emotion in the Human Face*. New York: Pergamon, 1972.

Fedio, P., and A. Martin. Ideative-emotive behavioral characteristics of patients following left or right temporal lobectomy. *Epilepsia* 254:S117–S130, 1983.

Gainotti, G. Réactions "catastrophiques" et manifèstations d'indifférence au cours des atteintes cérébrales. *Neuropsychologia* 7:195–204, 1969.

Gainotti, G. Emotional behavior and hemispheric side of the lesion. *Cortex* 8:41–55, 1972.

Gainotti, G., and C. Caltagirone, eds. *Emotions and the Dual Brain*. Berlin: Springer-Verlag, 1989.

Gardner, H., P. K. Ling. L. Flamm, and J. Silverman. Comprehension and appreciation of humorous material following brain damage. *Brain* 98:399–412, 1975.

Gazzaniga, M., and J. E. Le Doux. *The Integrated Mind*. New York: Plenum, 1978.

Goldstein, K. *The Organism: A Holistic Approach to Biology, Derived from Pathological Data in Man*. New York: American Book, 1939.

Haggard, M. P., and A. M. Parkinson. Stimulus and task factors as determinants of ear advantages. *Quarterly Journal of Experimental Psychology* 23:168–177, 1971.

Heilman, K. M., D. Bowers, and E. Valenstein. Emotional disorders associated with neurological diseases. In K. M. Heilman and E. Valenstein, eds. *Clinical Neuropsychology,* 3rd ed. New York: Oxford University Press, 1993.

Kent, R. D., and J. C. Rosenbek. Prosodic disturbance and neurological lesion. *Brain and Language* 15:259–291, 1982.

Klüver, H., and P. C. Bucy. Preliminary analysis of the temporal lobes in monkeys. *Archives of Neurology and Psychiatry* 42:979–1000, 1939.

Kolb, B., and B. Milner. Observations on spontaneous facial expression after focal cerebral excisions and after intracarotid injection of sodium Amytal. *Neuropsychologia* 19:505–514, 1981.

Kolb, B., and L. Taylor. Affective behavior in patients with localized cortical excisions: Role of lesion site and side. *Science* 214:89–91, 1981.

Kolb, B., and L. Taylor. Facial expression and the neocortex. *Society for Neuroscience Abstracts* 14:219, 1988.

Le Doux, J. E. Cognition and emotion. In M. S. Gazzaniga, ed. *Handbook of Cognitive Neuroscience*. New York: Plenum, 1984.

Ley, R. G., and M. P. Bryden. Hemispheric differences in processing emotions and faces. *Brain and Language* 7: 127–138, 1979.

Ley, R. G., and M. P. Bryden. A dissociation of right and left hemispheric effects for recognizing emotional tone and verbal content. *Brain and Cognition* 1:3–9, 1982.

Marlowe, W. B., E. L. Mancall, and J. J. Thomas. Complete Klüver-Bucy syndrome in man. *Cortex* 11:53–59, 1975.

Milner, B. Brain mechanisms suggested by studies of the temporal lobes. In C. H. Millikan and F. L. Darley, eds. *Brain Mechanisms Underlying Speech and Language*. New York: Grune & Stratton, 1967.

Moscovitch, M., and J. Olds. Asymmetries in spontaneous facial expressions and their possible relation to hemispheric specialization. *Neuropsychologia* 20:71–82, 1982.

Myers, R. E. Role of the prefrontal and anterior temporal cortex in social behavior and affect in monkeys. *Acta Neurobiologiae Experimentalis* 32:567–579, 1972.

Myers, R. E., C. Swett, and M. Miller. Loss of social group affinities following prefrontal lesions in free-ranging macaques. *Brain Research* 64:257–269, 1973.

Papez, J. W. A proposed mechanism of emotion. *Archives of Neurology and Psychiatry* 38:725–744, 1937.

Peters, M., and D. Ploog. Frontal lobe lesions and social behavior in the squirrel monkey (*Saimiri*): A pilot study. *Acta Biologica Medica* (Germany) 35:1317–1326, 1976.

Raleigh, M. J., and H. D. Steklis. Effects of orbitofrontal and temporal neocortical lesions on the affiliative behavior of vervet monkeys (*Ceropithecus aethiops sabaeus*). *Experimental Neurology* 73:378–389, 1981.

Robinson, R. G., K. Kubos, L. B. Starr, K. Rao, and T. R. Price. Mood disorders in stroke patients. *Brain* 107:81–93, 1984.

Ross, E. D. The aprosodias: Functional-anatomical organization of the affective components of language in the right hemisphere. *Archives of Neurology* 38:561–569, 1981.

Ross, E. D., R. W. Homan, and R. Buck. Differential hemispheric lateralization of primary and social emotions. *Neuropsychiatry, Neuropsychology, and Behavioral Biology*. In press.

Ross, E. D., and A. J. Rush. Diagnosis and neuroanatomical correlates of depression in brain-damaged patients. *Archives of General Psychiatry* 38:1344–1354, 1981.

Sachdev, H. S., and S. G. Waxman. Frequency of hypergraphia in temporal lobe epilepsy: An index of interictal behaviour syndrome. *Journal of Neurology, Neurosurgery, and Psychiatry* 44:358–360, 1981.

Suomi, S. J., H. F. Harlow, and J. K. Lewis. Effect of bilateral frontal lobectomy on social preferences of rhesus monkeys. *Journal of Comparative and Physiological Psychology* 70:448–453, 1970.

Terzian, H. Behavioral and EEG effects of intracarotid sodium Amytal injection. *Acta Neurochirurgica* 12:230–239, 1964.

Thorne, B. M. Brain lesions and affective behavior in primates. A selected review. *Journal of General Psychology* 86:153–162, 1972.

Tompkins, C. A., and C. A. Mateer. Right hemisphere appreciation of intonational and linguistic indications of affect. *Brain and Language* 24:185–203, 1985.

Tucker, D. M. Lateral brain function, emotion, and conceptualization. *Psychological Bulletin* 89:19–46, 1981.

Tucker, D. M., R. T. Watson, and K. M. Heilman. Discrimination and evocation of affectively intoned speech in patients with right parietal disease. *Neurology* 27: 947–950, 1977.

Wittling, W., and R. Roschmann. Emotion-related hemisphere asymmetry: Subjective emotional responses to laterally presented films. *Cortex* 29:431–438, 1993.

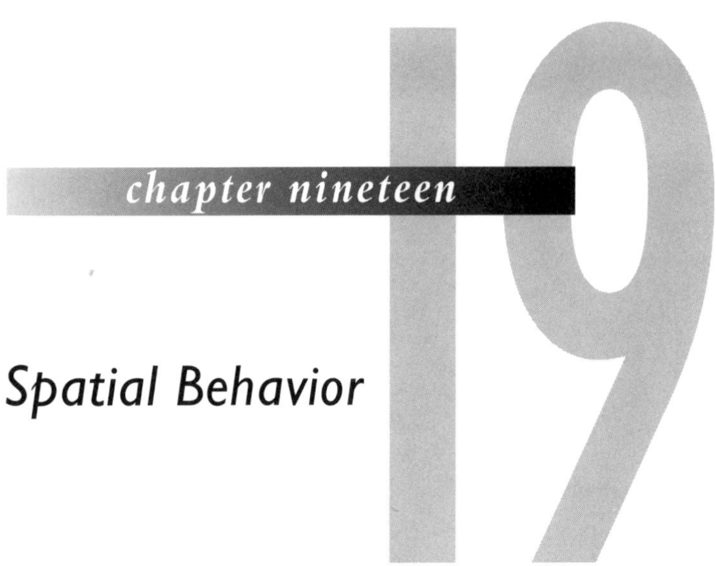

Spatial Behavior

There is the well-known story of the rambler who, making his way to Down, became lost. Meeting a farmer, he asks if the farmer knows where Down is.

"Yes, it's over yonder," says the farmer.

"And how do I get there?" asks the rambler.

"You can't get there from here," says the farmer.

An attempt to give a comprehensive account of the concept of space may leave us in much the same position as the rambler. Our body occupies space, it moves through space, and it interacts with things in space; our brain rotates and manipulates representations of space mentally. Other objects also occupy space and maintain relations in space with one another and with us. Philosophers have asked whether objects exist without space, or conversely, whether space exists without objects. They also ask whether space is a feature of the universe or merely a creation of our brain. How do the concepts of space develop as humans grow from infancy? The representations of space of small animals (for example, dogs, cats, and children) must be very different from that of airline pilots. What further complicates the issue is that many of the elements that can be subsumed under the concept "space" fit equally well into other domains, such as sensory abilities, memory or attention processes, or motor behaviors. It is no doubt this diversity that led Ratcliff to comment at the end of a 1982 review, "This has been a selective and highly speculative review and its conclusions are certainly incomplete and quite probably wrong" (p. 325). In this chapter we will suggest that there are a number of spatial systems, each with a separate neural structure and each with a separate function.

BACKGROUND

In modern accounts of cerebral organization, it is assumed that spatial processing is a special function of the right hemisphere. John Hughlings-Jackson was the first to propose that the right hemisphere might have some special perceptual function to complement the language functions of the left hemisphere. In his famous 1874 paper, "On the Nature of the Duality of the Brain," he predicted that a person with damage restricted to the posterior part of the right hemisphere would have a distinctive syndrome:

> The patient would have difficulty in recognizing things; he would have difficulty in relating what had occurred, not from lack of words, but from a prior inability to revive images of persons, objects and places, of which the words are symbols. . . . He could not put before himself ideal images of places one after another; could not re-see where he had been, and could not therefore tell of it in words. (Taylor, 1932, p. 144)

Hughlings-Jackson was proposing a spatial-perceptual function for the right hemisphere, although he admitted that the evidence for his position was not strong, remarking that "as will be seen, my facts are very few" (Taylor, 1932, p. 145). A series of papers by a number of investigators between 1876 and 1905 described various cases with spatial-perceptual difficulties, confirming Hughlings-Jackson's view that such disorders exist. Although most of these cases appeared to have bilateral damage, rather than right posterior damage, the view nonetheless persisted.

World War I led to further advances in the understanding of spatial disturbances accompanying brain injury, but the possibility of an association between spatial deficits and right hemisphere damage was largely ignored. By 1950, a large number of spatial deficits had been described (Table 19.1), but the main point that had escaped notice was the asymmetrical representation of spatial function in the two hemispheres, perhaps because most of the published reports were single case studies, which could be easily discounted. It was the systematic studies of Zangwill and of Hécaen and their coworkers in the 1950s that forced a reexamination of the role of the right hemisphere in spatial performance. There now is little doubt that the right hemisphere has a selective role in spatial behavior, but as documented by Mehta and coworkers, disorders of spatial processing are also observed in people with damage to the left hemisphere or with bilateral damage.

TABLE 19.1. Summary of types of spatial deficits described in the clinical literature

Behavior	Basic reference
Impaired eye movements to points in space	Balint, 1909; Tyler, 1968
Poor localization of visual, auditory, or tactile stimuli in space	Head, 1920; Shankweiler, 1951; Holmes, 1919
Misreaching for objects	Brain, 1941
Neglect for left hemispace	Brain, 1941; Oxbury et al., 1974
Right-left confusion	Benton, 1959
Constructional apraxia	Benton, 1979
Amnesia for routes and locations	Paterson and Zangwill, 1944
Impaired performance on mazes	Corkin, 1965; Milner, 1965
Defective locomotion in space	Semmes et al., 1963
Poor drawing	McFie and Zangwill, 1960
Impaired performance at tests of mental spatial transformations (geometry, mazes, mental rotation)	de Renzi, 1982
Inability to determine visual or tactile line orientation	Benton et al., 1978; de Renzi et al., 1971
Defective shape discrimination	de Renzi and Scotti, 1969

THE ORGANIZATION OF SPATIAL BEHAVIOR

Space can be conceptualized as a number of subspaces (Figure 19.1). There is the surface of the body on which things can be localized, grasping space surrounding the body, and distal space that the body moves into or out of. Space can also be conceived as having a time dimension of past and future as well as an internal or brain representation. Upon or within all these subspaces are real or imagined objects. The challenge in the study of spatial behavior is to discover how the kinds and properties of space are represented.

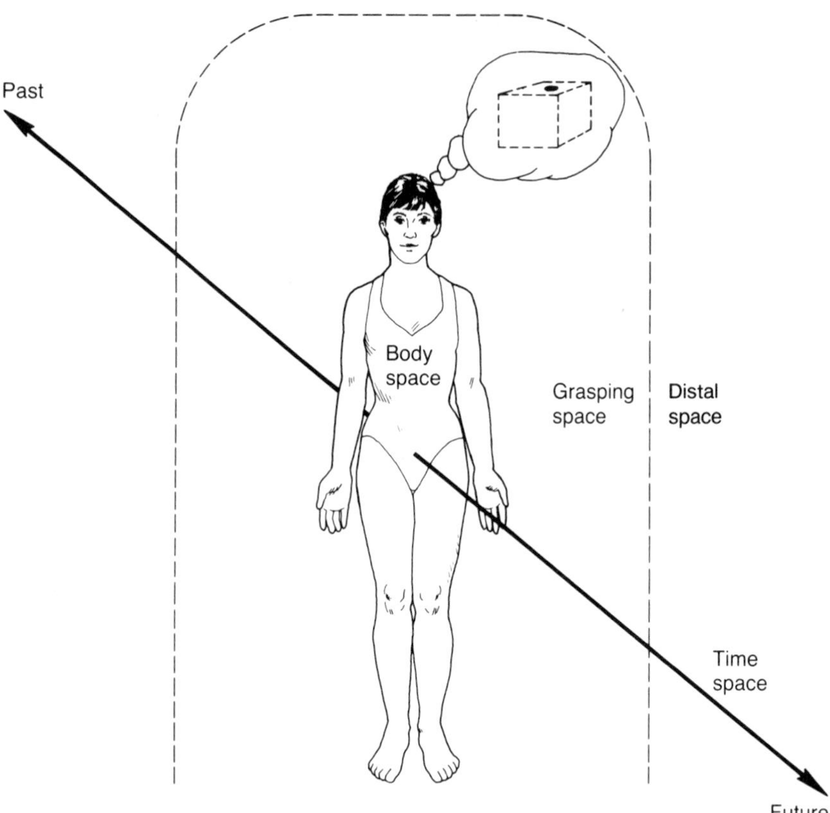

FIGURE 19.1. A conceptual model of the compartments of space. Grasping space is the zone in which objects can be grasped in a hand. Distal space refers to space that is located away from grasping space. Time space is mainly conceptual and refers to present, past, and future. Mental image (the box in the imagined space) is the brain's concept of space.

Position, Cue, and Place Responses

One way of classifying spatial activities is in terms of the sensory-motor responses that people and animals make. O'Keefe and Nadel have divided these behaviors into three types: position, cue, and place responses. These classifications were designed to describe movements of the entire body through space, but there is no impediment to using them to describe movements of a body part, such as a hand reaching for an object.

Position responses are movements made with the body used as a reference; for example, turning to the left or right or moving a limb or body part. No external cue is required. Examples of common responses include always turning left when entering a given door; automatically putting objects such as keys on a hook or a table; and characteristic expressions, gestures, and utterances. Once the movements are acquired, they are performed almost automatically and without conscious monitoring. Position responses are referred to as *egocentric* in the sense that they are made with respect to a person's own body. **Cue responses** are movements guided by a cue; for example, walking toward or away from an object, following an odor or sound, or reaching to pick up a visible object. Changes in **stimulus gradient** (the sound gets louder when approached) are sufficient to direct the movement. Salmon that select appropriate rivers and swim to their spawning grounds are thought to do so using olfactory cue responses. Moths that fly to light are thought to be making visual cue responses. Cue responses are referred to as *allocentric,* since control of movement is exerted by an external object. **Place responses** take a person to a particular location or object, which may even be hidden from view. The relational properties of the surrounding cues, no one of which is necessary, guide the movement. The cues must be far enough away that they change relationship with one another (from the point of view of the traveler) slowly enough that the viewer can use them to orient himself or herself. An example is the response of a person who parks a car in an empty parking lot, then returns to find the parking lot full and the car hidden. The person might nevertheless walk directly to the car by remembering where it was in relation to the size of the lot and surrounding buildings.

These different strategies are used routinely in everyday life, and they may be used concurrently or sequentially. Some kinds of position and cue responses can be performed by animals with no cortex, but place responses require an intact cortex.

Researchers design tasks that force the use of one strategy or another so that it can be studied in isolation. Figure 19.2 illustrates a number of tasks used to study the spatial navigation strategies of the rat. Figure 19.2D illustrates a typical research room with a rich array of visual cues including cupboards, pictures, windows, and so forth. In the center of the room is a swimming pool in which a rat's spatial abilities can be tested. The rat's task is to escape from the water onto a platform, which can be visible (cue response) or hidden (place response). For the place response the rat will use room cues to locate the platform. (Rats are excellent swimmers and because of their small size, which leaves them at risk of losing normal body temperature if they stay in water for long, are highly motivated to escape from water.) The various mazes illustrated in Figures 19.2A, 19.2B, and 19.2C can be placed where the swimming pool is located.

Earlier in this century it was thought that animals such as rats learned mazes by making position responses. Tolman, however, suggested that rats and humans create spatial maps of their environment and solve maze tasks using place responses. Recent work with mazes has demonstrated that rats can learn a place response in a single trial (as quickly as humans) and remember it for days. Sherry has demonstrated that food-storing birds can remember thousands of locations where they have previously stored food. Further testament to the power of place response comes from an everyday experience of students. We can often remember where in a book we read a passage even though our retention of the content of the passage may be negligible.

Similar tests have been tailored for humans and primates. In the Acredolo Test, children are brought into a small, nondistinctive room that has a door at one end, a window at the other end, and a table along one wall. They are walked to a corner of the table and blindfolded. While blindfolded, they are walked in a circuitous route back to the door or to the window, the blindfold is removed, and they are asked to return to the point at which they had been blindfolded. Unknown to the children, sometimes the table has been moved. If a child uses a place response, he or she returns to the correct place, even though the table has been moved from that location. If a child uses a cue response, she or he walks directly to the table. If a child uses a position response, he or she turns in the direction he or she had originally turned when first entering the room.

Two general types of test are used for primates. In a well-known experiment by Menzel, food was hidden in a number of places in a field as chimpanzees watched. Sometime later, when they were allowed to look for it, they found it quickly and accurately, taking the shortest route. The most widely used tests are performed in the Wisconsin General Test Apparatus (WGTA). The primate sits in a cage and a screen is raised in

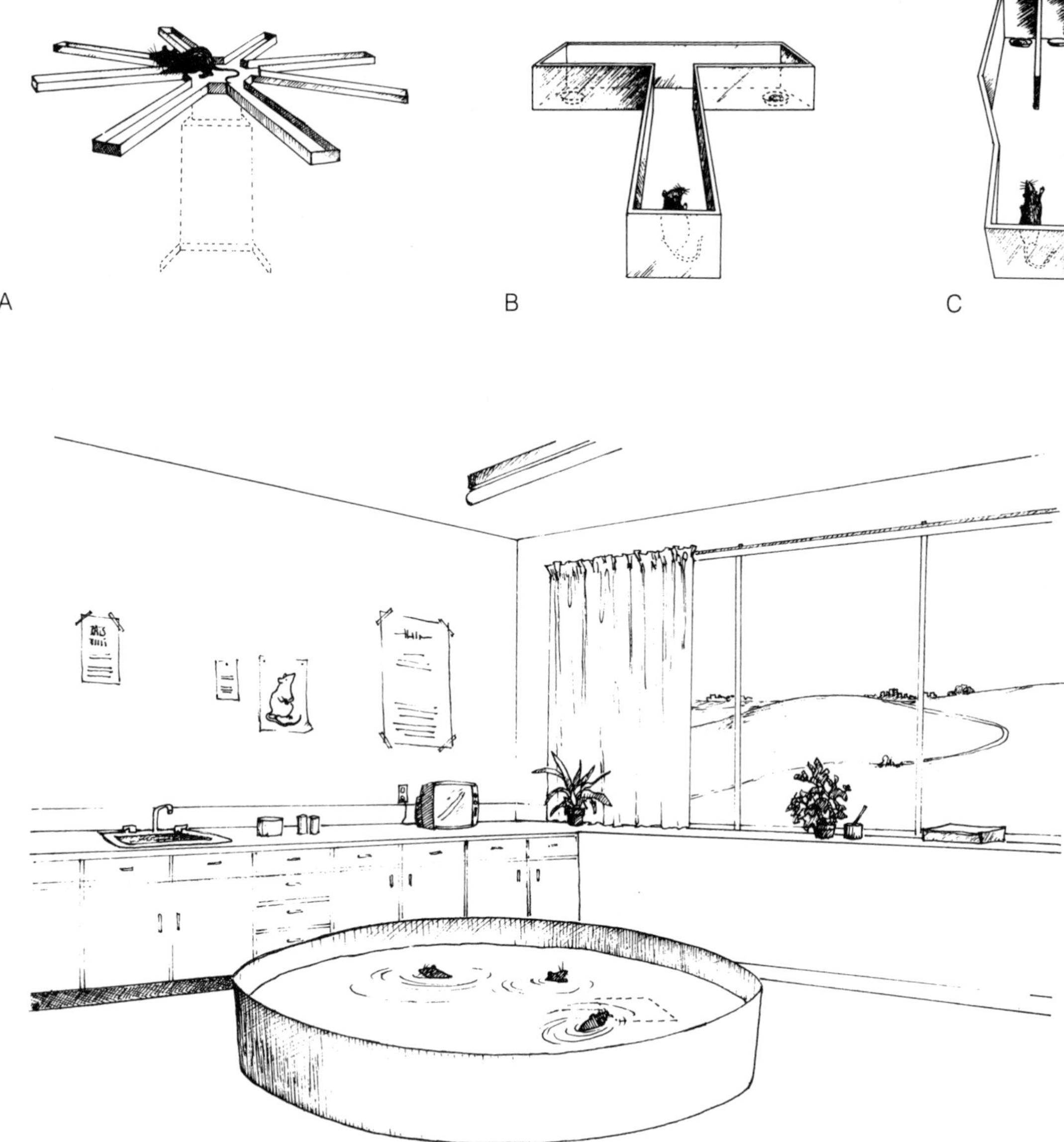

FIGURE 19.2. Tasks used to study spatial behavior in rodents. *A.* Olton Radial-Arm Maze. The radial-arm maze was designed as a test of foraging behavior in animals. The rat must learn which alleys contain food and which alleys have been visited on a given day. *B.* T-maze. *C.* Grice Box. This is a test of left-right differentiation. The food is placed in one alley until the animal has learned its location, then the position of the food is reversed to the other alley. *D.* Morris Water Task. The swimming pool task requires the animal to learn the location of a submerged, hidden platform. The only cue to the position of the platform is its spatial relation to cues about the room. All of the mazes are usually used in open rooms in which the animals can use the many surrounding cues as aids to orientation.

front of the cage, allowing the animal to see a table on which objects are located. Usually, a peanut is hidden under one object. The correct object may be always the one on the animal's right (position task), always the only novel object (cue task), or always the object that is found in the same location on two consecutive trials (place task) (Figure 19.3).

Spatial tasks can be done at home with pets. If you have a dog, walk through the house with it while you hide treats. You will notice that when it searches for them later it will generate novel and accurate routes. You could have a number of identical cups, each of which is located in a particular place. If you leave food only in some of them, your pet will quickly learn to visit only the baited cups. Alternatively, the appearance of the cups could differ and the cups could move on each test. Now the animal will not be able to use environmental cues to find food (place task) but will have to attend to the features of the cup (cue task).

The Evolution and Development of Spatial Behavior

In the course of evolution, animals first navigated with whole-body movements, then with coordinated limb movements; finally, they became capable of making discrete limb movements. Was there a parallel evolution of spatial navigation strategies? It is thought that position responses and cue responses evolved quite early, whereas place responses evolved and became more versatile as the neocortex developed. As discrete limb movements developed, the guidance strategies became

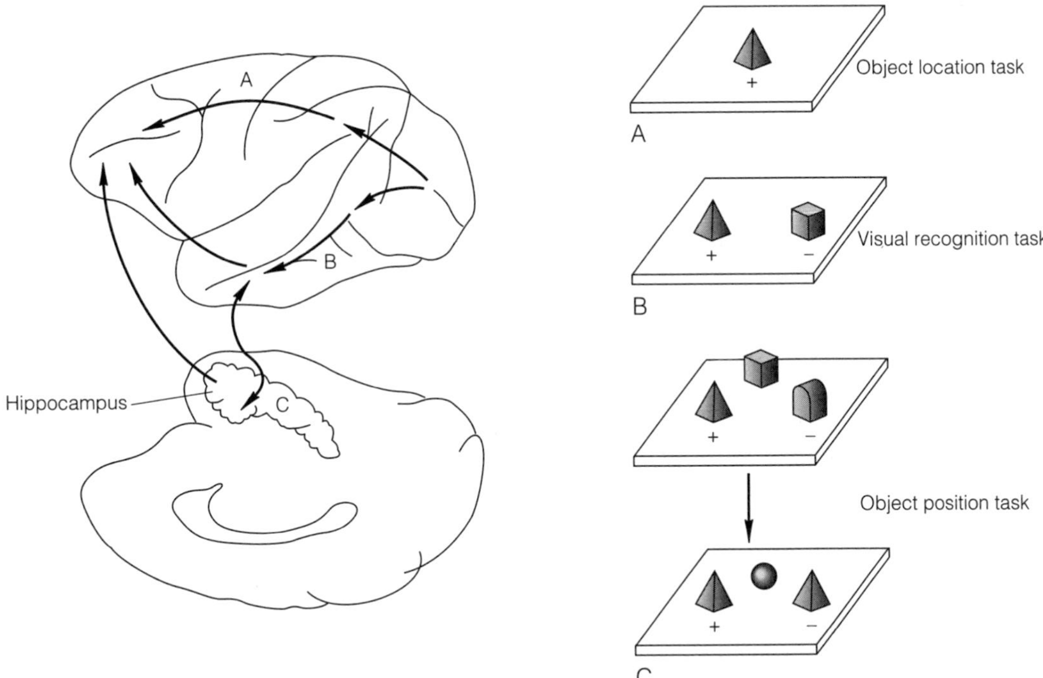

FIGURE 19.3. Spatial systems. *A.* The dorsal system represents the location of objects within a global framework. *B.* The ventral system represents the identity of objects. *C.* The hippocampus identifies the location of an object. Both the dorsal and ventral systems are connected to the hippocampus.

elaborated, not just for guiding locomotion but also for directing the limb movements. Developmentally, there is evidence that strategies develop in this order: position response, cue response, place response. Studies on baby rats show that they are capable of cue responses before 22 days of age (the age of weaning) and can make place responses only after this age. Acredolo, using the room-and-table test described above, has reported that 3-year-old children tend to use position response, turning in the direction previously turned; older children use a cue response and go to the table; and the oldest children, 7-year-olds, use a place response and go to the correct location in the room. This development of spatial navigation strategies has an analogue in Piaget's developmental stages: egocentric (position), concrete (cue), and formal (place), which develop roughly over the same age range.

Sensory Control of Spatial Behavior

Body and vestibular cues (for balance) are generally not very useful for guiding us around the world. But they are very useful for indicating body posture and movement of body parts and for providing a body-centered framework (position responses). Olfaction and audition also have properties that seem to limit their use in navigation. Both are excellent stimuli for cue responses (for example, a salmon swimming up a river to spawn) but superficially it appears that they are less likely to be used for place responses. For both senses, however, the stimuli that they represent (as smoke represents a fire) are likely to be out of visual range and so, using only the stimulus, an animal can form a representation of the target object (out of sight but in mind). For example, a dog tracking a person using odor probably knows that it is tracking a person and not a rabbit. This process may contribute to spatial comprehension as well as to the mental representation of objects.

In humans, visual cues are usually used for place responses. A boatman traveling by night from the mouth of the Seal River across Hudson's Bay to Churchill, Ontario, can reach port simply by keeping the North Star to the left and 45° to the rear. According to Pick and Rieser, Pulawat Islanders can travel thousands of miles in open boats using a conceptual navigation strategy. A hypothetical island is placed over the horizon off to the side of the route between their starting point and destination. They then mark off their journey using the relations between this point, themselves, stars, and other cues. That humans and many other animals use visual information to make complex navigation decisions with such ease almost compels us to expect that vision has a special role in spatial navigation.

Real Space and Cognitive Space

It is usual in the experimental literature to postulate that space has the features that it appears to have. Consequently, it is referred to as **Euclidian space,** but we could just as well refer to it as **real space.** There also must be an internal representation of space. We can draw a mental map of a route from one point to another or imagine looking at an object from the side opposite our actual vantage point. This representation can be referred to as **cognitive space.** We should not expect cognitive space to have the rich detail of real space, both because such detail would be impossible to store and because we have ready access to the details of places simply by going to them. Cognitive representations of space depend on experience and they become more elaborate with experience. This is why children cannot form complex cognitive representations, especially of distal space. But even adult representations are not necessarily accurate. One of us recalls returning to the farm where he grew up only to find that the big farmhouse had shrunk to a cottage and the huge lawns that he had had to mow were little more than small patches of grass. The other of us had a representation of the eastern part of North America as a series of cities from Chicago to Montreal, separated by short distances. The territory west of Chicago, however, was vast, and cities were far apart. This cartography led him to attempt to drive from Ontario to Nova Scotia in an afternoon (for those not familiar with the trip, it takes 3 days).

One of the properties of cognitive space is mental rotation. Mental rotation is the ability to adopt novel perspectives, to imagine the other side of things, to see ourselves, and so on. **Factor analysis** (a mathematical procedure for finding what is common within a heterogeneous group of elements) of spatial abilities suggests that they can be subdivided into two categories: visualization and orientation. **Visualization** is the ability to manipulate or rotate two- and three-dimensional stimulus objects that are presented pictorially. **Orientation** is the ability to remain unconfused by the changing orientation in which a spatial configuration may be presented. The neural mechanisms that represent cognitive space do place constraints on how real space is represented. For example, horizontal and vertical lines separated by 90° are readily differentiated, whereas oblique lines separated by the same angle are not. In fact, some animals and some patients with brain damage may be unable to differentiate oblique lines at all.

Some researchers have suggested that cognitive space is organized analogously to real space and that animals and people have "cognitive maps" representing the world. O'Keefe and Nadel have argued that the hippocampus is the neural substrate for cognitive maps. Thus, the hippocampus allows us to find our way about in the real world. They further suggest that the hippocampus helps us to find our way around in our own brain. That is, for language, words of one kind are in one location and words of another kind are in another, and the hippocampus is used for finding them. If we need the name of a bird we search in restricted parts of neural space for birds names, pushing incorrect bird names and even the names of other flying creatures out of the way as we go. The idea that we have a structure dedicated to finding things in our brain provides an explanation for curious slips of the tongue, such as when we are thinking of the name of one person but accidentally and inappropriately blurt out the name of another. It might also account for the curious symptoms of deep dyslexics; when given a word like "bird" to read, they may say "butterfly." Possibly these errors indicate that the finding system has made a mistake.

We may also store other kinds of information in coordinate systems. People find graphs and figures to be good ways of representing large amounts of information. Look at the map of the world in Figure 19.4. The shadings represent distributions of brain size of people around the world. The map summarizes an enormous number of calculations in a simple way and at the same time shows us that there is a very good relationship between brain size and climate. (The explanation seems to be that round heads conserve heat and narrow heads dissipate it. Incidentally, round heads also have a larger internal volume than narrow heads.)

NEURAL REPRESENTATION OF SPACE

Some theories of spatial behavior find it useful to divide space into focal space (a part of space that we are looking directly at so that the image is detected by the fovia of the retina) and global space (the space that lies around the foviated space and which is detected with the surrounding retinal receptors). The part of space that is foviated is clear and its details are seen, whereas the area around it will have a fuzzy appearance and its details will not be noticed. Despite its fuzzy appearance, things can be seen in the fuzzy global space, and what is seen in that space provides the context for focal space. For example, our body makes up a major portion of our global space. Even when we look at a distant object, we retain an awareness of our body, and if we move a hand or a foot, we notice the motion. If another object moves in our global space—whether it be a bird flying above us or a bee coming from the side—we notice the movement. We can view the world at a glance, so to speak, without noticing any of its details. Many of the movements that we make within grasping space also occur within this global

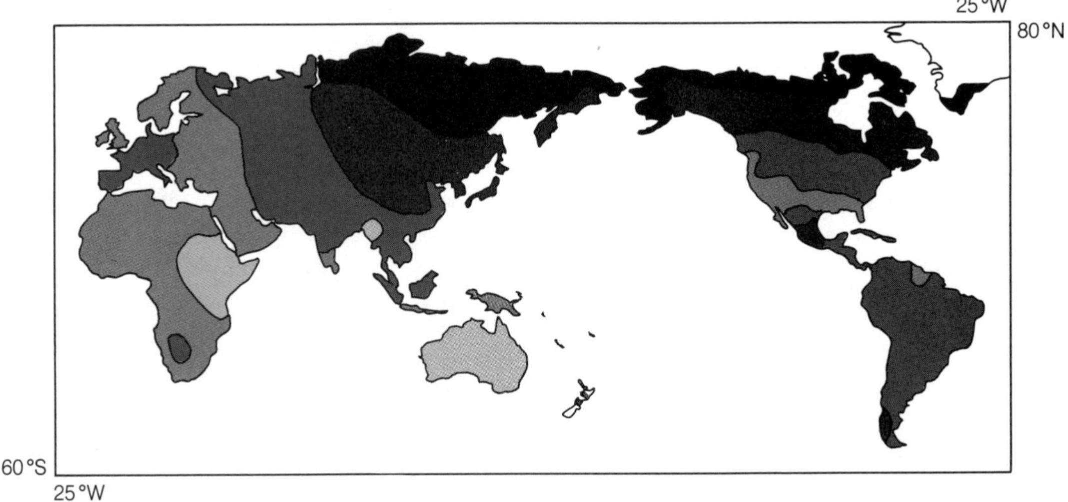

FIGURE 19.4. Map of cranial capacity of people originating in different parts of the world. Darker shading indicates larger cranial capacity. Maps like this can represent an enormous amount of information spatially. (After K. L. Beales et al., 1984.)

space. For example, when we lift a hand to reach, we see only the fuzzy outlines of the hand for most of the reach. Even when the fingers stop to pick up an object, they retain a fuzzy appearance. Global space probably includes a sense of time. Without considering any of the details of the past or thinking about events in the future, we are nevertheless aware of those dimensions.

Focal space, by contrast, is the space that we foviate. Objects in this space are clear, have color, and can be identified by their patterns and form. Global space appears to provide a framework within which we monitor our own movements and the movements of other objects. Focal space is a subportion of global space and represents the identity of objects, rather than their movements and location.

Spatial movements may be differentially related to global and focal space. When we move through space, we use global space as a frame of reference. If something "catches our eye" (such as a distant object that moves suddenly), we reset our global spatial frame by making an orienting movement. We first move our eyes, then our head, and if we reach for the object, our hand. Although these movements appear to take place sequentially, recordings of muscle activity show that they are initiated at the same moment and are thus a unified **orienting reaction.** By contrast, the movements that we make with respect to focal space are different—the head and body remain still while the eyes make small saccades to scan the object. (You can judge the differences in the effects of these movements for yourself. Try reading the text of a page using head movements. On the other hand, try tracking the movement of an object using only saccades.)

Keeping these two kinds of space in mind, try the following mental experiment. Imagine that you have no ability to see focal space while global space remains intact. Perhaps you will see yourself as having an awareness of your surroundings while, at the same time, having no ability to identify things when you look at them carefully. Alternatively, if your ability to see focal space is intact but your ability to see global space is not, you would only see the things that you looked at directly, and you would be unable to take context into account or shift attention to such things as the novel appearance of novel objects. As the following sections will describe, these are the kinds of impairments that are observed in humans with brain damage and in animal preparations used to investigate the neural basis of spatial behavior.

In a series of experiments carried out over the past 20 years, Mishkin and his coworkers have suggested that there are at least two neural systems that process the information involved in representing objects in visual space: the posterior parietal cortex and the temporal cortex. Both receive information over pathways that begin in the visual cortex. A dorsal pathway projects to the posterior parietal cortex. A ventral pathway projects to the inferior temporal cortex. These pathways and their targets are shown in Figure 19.3. Both the posterior parietal cortex and the inferior temporal cortex send projections to the frontal cortex, where they instruct movements, including eye movements, reaching, and locomotion.

A number of theories associate global and focal vision with these two neural systems. Previc has suggested that the lower visual fields are more responsible for global vision (when you are walking and looking at the ground ahead, you simultaneously monitor the surrounding world and especially the part of the world directly around you) and the upper visual fields are more important for focal vision (the precise location to which you are looking). It is thought that the magnocellular cells of the visual system—which are sensitive to movement and form and which project through visual area V5 to area 7a (PG) of the parietal cortex and then to the frontal eye fields of the dorsolateral frontal cortex (area 8)—are responsible for executing actions within global space. These actions include the orienting reaction that aligns the eyes, head, and eventually the hand to the object. On the other hand, the parvocellular system—which is sensitive to form and color and which projects through visual areas V3 and V4 to the inferior temporal cortex and from there to the midlateral frontal cortex (areas 9 and 46)—is responsible for executing actions in focal space.

It might seem peculiar that the location of an object and its identity are separated neurally. How then do we know that "the pen is on the far left corner of the desk"? The separation of the pathways may be functional. There is no necessary relation between objects and space: one location in space could be occupied by different objects at different times, and any object could occupy many different spaces at different times. There also may be occasions when spatial location is important but the identity of the object occupying it is not, and vice versa. By analogy, a large map (representing visual space) and a box of model cars (representing objects) can provide a simple illustration of how the system works. Both map and cars exist quite independently, but when a car is placed on the map, the two make a meaningful spatial representation: Harry's taxi is at the corner of 4th and Main. Although it is not known precisely what role the parietal lobe and temporal lobe systems play in spatial behavior, and even less is known about how they interact, the following sections will summarize some evidence suggesting that the parietal and temporal lobes and their projections to the frontal cortex are involved in spatial behavior.

THE TEMPORAL LOBES

The hippocampus is most intimately connected with the olfactory system, and for this reason it is also considered part of the **rhinencephalon** (smell-brain). It is surprising to find, therefore, that it has variously been associated with space. The hippocampus is one of a number of interrelated structures that together compose the hippocampal formation. The hippocampal formation has extensive reciprocal connections with the temporal lobes at its most posterior end and extensive connections to a number of subcortical structures—including the septum, mammillary bodies, basal forebrain, and thalamus—at its most anterior end (Figure 19.5).

The idea that the hippocampus plays a role in spatial behavior originated with a report on the activity of eight cells by O'Keefe and Dostrovsky in 1971. These cells fired when rats were placed on certain locations on a testing platform facing in

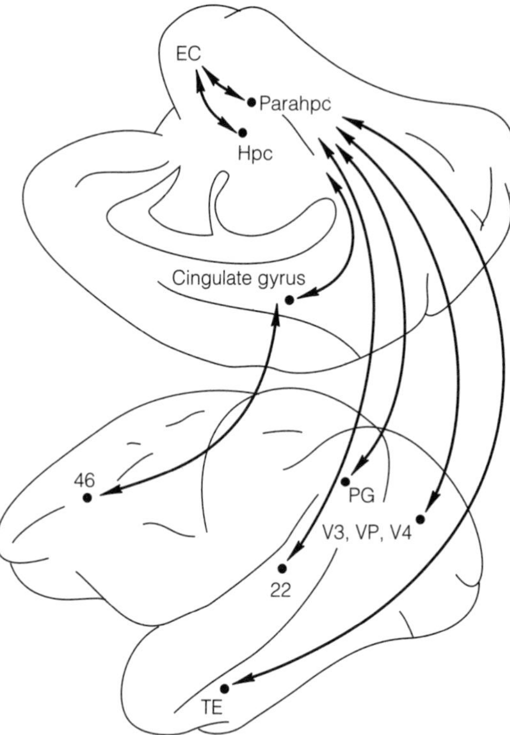

FIGURE 19.5. The afferent and efferent connections between the cortex and the hippocampus via the entorhinal cortex.

a certain direction. In the case of the cell illustrated in Figure 19.6, the rat had to be both restrained and pointing in an appropriate direction. On the basis of the activity of these cells, the authors proposed that the hippocampus is a map that represents features of the world and can anticipate spatial relationships that are a consequence of its movements.

As speculative as this initial proposal might seem to be, it has been substantiated by further studies of the activity of single hippocampal cells and the effects of damage to the hippocampus, as well as by comparisons of hippocampal size in different species. The single cell recording studies demonstrate that within a short time of a rat being placed in a novel environment, single cells begin to discharge when the animal is in certain places in that environment. For some cells it does not seem to matter whether the rat walks there itself or is carried there by the experimenter. Other cells encode the rat's location as well as the direction and speed that it is moving. If the cues in the environment are changed, then the cells will modify their activity to represent the new environment.

Damage to the hippocampus disrupts the ability of an animal to navigate through its environment. In their book, *The Hippocampus as a Cognitive Map,* O'Keefe and Nadel reviewed an extensive literature on maze learning by animals and concluded that most of the impairments displayed by the animals could be accounted for in terms of loss of a cognitive map. A few findings from swimming pool experiments will demonstrate the basic result. A rat is placed in the swimming pool and somewhere in the pool, hidden just below the surface of the water, is a platform onto which it can escape (see Figure 19.2). On the first trial, after being placed at a start location, it swims al-

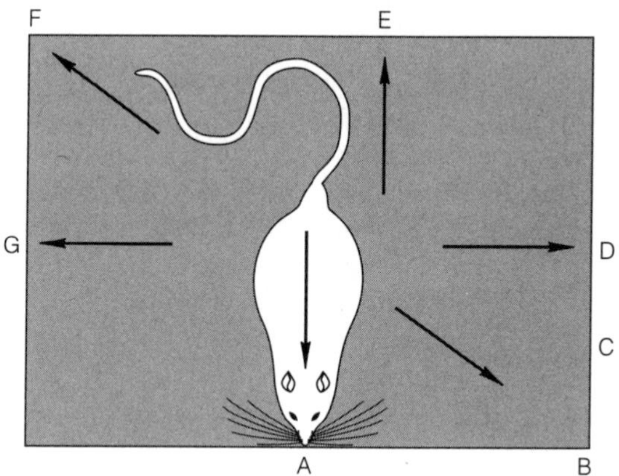

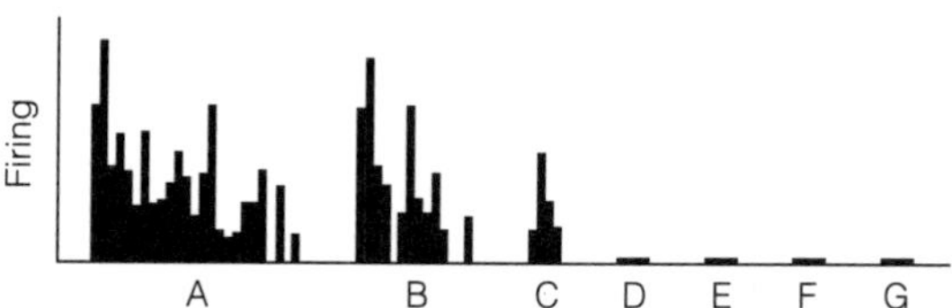

FIGURE 19.6. Response of a specific cell in the hippocampus to the orientation of a rat. The cell fires strongly when the rat is held pointing in direction A and less strongly when pointing in other directions. (After O'Keefe and Dostrovsky, 1971.)

most randomly around the pool until it accidentally bumps into the platform. The rat is then given another trial beginning at another point within the pool, and this time it finds the platform a little more quickly. Within a dozen trials or so, the rat swims directly to the platform from any starting location. Since the platform is not visible, the only way that the rat can find it is to know that it is in a specific location with respect to cues in the surrounding room. Thus, the rat must represent the location of the platform in relation to the room cues in some way. If the hippocampus or the pathways leading into it or out of it are damaged, the rat is severely impaired in locating the platform. This is not a general learning impairment. If a visible platform is placed in the pool, the rat quickly learns to swim directly to it. If the platform is again hidden, the rat is again impaired. That the rat is impaired in solving a place task indicates that the hippocampus must play a role in guiding the animal's swim to the platform using surrounding room cues.

The third kind of evidence supporting a role for the hippocampus in space comes from studies of birds. Many birds will take food items, like sunflower seeds, and hide them for later consumption. Some birds can hide many hundreds of items and find them later. To evaluate whether the hippocampus plays a role in this activity, Sherry and coworkers have measured hippocampal size in bird species that are closely related but in which one is a food cacher and the other is not. The hippocampal formation is larger in birds that are food cachers than in birds that do not cache food.

The finding that the hippocampus is related to spatial behavior has been extended to monkeys. Angeli and coworkers report that monkeys with selective hippocampal removals are impaired if required to choose among more than two different locations (see Figure 19.3). If they are required to remember the identity of objects, they have no difficulty.

Although the data we have presented to this point do support the idea that the hippocampus serves as a cognitive map through which spatial problems can be solved, there is a problem. If a rat is trained on a place task before surgery, or if it is tested for a long time after surgery, it is possible to demonstrate that it can learn a place task. By definition, this means that it must still have a spatial map that is not in the hippocampus. Similarly, patients with anterograde topographical amnesia have a map for places experienced before their amnesia, so they too must have a surviving map. It is not known whether this other map is the only map, and it is not known where it is located. It is very likely that it is located in the cortex, however.

Spatial Disorientation in Humans

There are many clinical reports of patients with a gross disability in finding their way about, even in environments with which they were familiar before the onset of their disease. The term used to describe this condition is **topographical amnesia.** Many of these reports are difficult to interpret because the patients also experienced other spatial deficits such as left-right confusion, contralateral neglect, deficits of sensory-spatial analysis, and visual-field defects. The first report of a topographical memory disorder was that of Hughlings-Jackson's (1876) patient with a glioma in her right temporal lobe. This patient had difficulty finding her way in a park near her home. In 1890, Foerster provided a more extensive report. His patient was a 44-year-old postal clerk who developed a right hemianopia, followed a few days later by a left hemianopia, leaving him with a small area of central vision. The patient's most striking disability was in remembering where objects were located and building up a picture of a route. When blindfolded, he was unable to learn to point to furniture in his room or to remember the location of a toilet a few steps from his room. His amnesia was retrograde. He could not describe or draw the spatial arrangement of his office or home or of well-known places in the city. He also could not draw maps of areas of the world or the city, yet he could express some geographical ideas verbally.

De Renzi summarizes a case studied thoroughly by Meyer at the turn of the century that is considered a landmark description of topographical disorientation:

> Whenever he left his room in the hospital, he had trouble in finding the way back, because at any chosen point of the route he did not know whether to go right, left, downstairs or upstairs (on one occasion, he walked from the main floor down to the basement, instead of going up to the first floor, where his bed was located). When he eventually arrived in front of his own room, he did not recognize it unless he chanced to see some distinguishing feature, such as the black beard of his roommate, or a particular object on the bedside table. . . .
>
> When taken to sections of the city he knew before his illness and required to lead the way, he tried hard to find familiar landmarks, such as a signboard, the name of a street, the tramcar numbers, etc., but this information, though effectively indicating to him he was near his home, failed to provide clues for choosing the right direction. . . .
>
> Required to provide verbal information concerning routes or places well known before the disease, he performed fairly well as long as he could rely on purely verbal knowledge. Thus he was able to give the names of the intermediate stations on the railway line he used daily, or the location of the main building of the city. Yet, he met with considerable difficulty when the way had to be retraced from spatial memory; for instance, when required to tell how he would walk between two sites chosen at random in the city, he could only say the initial street and then he became confused. . . .
>
> He grossly mislocated cities and states on a map of his country as well as of Europe, a task with which he was familiar, since he had been a postoffice clerk. (de Renzi, 1982, p. 213)

Subsequent studies have described a number of variations in the symptoms of topographical disorientation. Some patients are unable to name buildings or landmarks that had been familiar. Others retain this ability. Some patients can describe routes and draw maps but are disoriented because they cannot identify familiar buildings or landmarks. Other patients can navigate routes but cannot describe or draw maps of them. Some patients can navigate in familiar places but become disoriented in new places, and others can eventually learn to navigate in new places by painstakingly memorizing buildings and landmarks and the routes that they should choose between them.

It would be helpful to be able to sort out these complex clusters of symptoms by identifying subcomponents with different anatomical loci. Paterson and Zangwill have suggested that topographical disorders can be subdivided into two different impairments: topographical agnosia and topographical amnesia. **Topographical agnosia** is defined as a failure to identify the individual features of places or buildings while retaining the ability to identify and recognize classes of objects such as hills, buildings, or churches. Topographical amnesia refers to an inability to remember topographical relationships between landmarks that can be identified individually. But we should also distinguish between the anterograde and the retrograde features of the disorder. People who retain the ability to orient in environments that were familiar before their injury but who cannot orient in novel environments are obviously different from patients who lose all topographical ability. Finally, it is necessary to identify patients who have true topographical disorders but compensate by using other strategies.

At present, the most useful anatomical distinction that can be used to subdivide topographical disorders is that between the contributions of the temporal and posterior cortex. As we argued earlier, identifying the spatial locations of objects requires knowledge of both the object and its location. Since these two features of spatial analysis are performed by different cortical systems, the information must be brought together. The structure thought to be involved in encoding the relationship is the hippocampus. If this supposition is correct, patients with only hippocampal damage should show symptoms of topographical disorientation. According to Smith and her colleagues, the well-studied patient H. M. does show a complete inability to navigate in novel environments or even to learn to navigate in them. He can, however, find his way in environments with which he was familiar before his surgery. For a time it was thought that H. M.'s severe memory problems occurred because he had combined lesions of the amygdala and hippocampus. Now the studies on animals suggest that most of H. M.'s anterograde memory impairments are attributable to perirhinal cortex damage. The studies with animals also suggest that his spatial impairments may be attributed to hippocampal damage. A growing body of anatomical evidence shows that the major connections of the hippocampus are with the neocortex via the temporal lobe. It is very likely, therefore, that patients with temporal lobe damage will show spatial disorders. We have pointed out that most patients described as having topographical disorders do have posterior neocortical damage.

A Word of Caution

Despite the substantial body of evidence suggesting that the hippocampus, through its connections with the temporal lobe, plays some role in spatial behavior, there is some evidence that is partially inconsistent. Zola-Morgan and coworkers have described the case of R. B., who displayed a general anterograde amnesia. He was a male postal worker who, at 52 years of age, had an ischemic episode secondary to a coronary bypass operation. During the next 5 years until his death, R. B. exhibited a marked anterograde amnesia. Upon his death a postmortem examination revealed a bilateral loss of all cells in CA1, a restricted portion of the hippocampus. R. B.'s case seems to suggest that a general anterograde amnesia can follow hippocampal damage, and this would be inconsistent with the idea the hippocampus is selectively involved in spatial behavior. It is possible that R. B. had other damage that was missed at autopsy or was not possible to detect. Until further evidence is obtained on this point, or until other similar cases are obtained, R. B. should serve as a caution against attributing only spatial behavior to the hippocampus.

A second line of evidence also suggests that the hippocampus may not be selectively involved in spatial behavior. Vanderwolf and his coworkers have found that a rhythmical EEG waveform in the hippocampus, the theta rhythm, is associated with locomotion. They also found that faster bursts of EEG waves will occur in the hippocampus when animals sniff certain odors, especially the odors of predatory animals. They interpret this evidence to suggest that the hippocampus is a "smell-brain" and plays some role in organizing behavior in response to olfactory cues. Their results do not rule out a role for the hippocampus in spatial behavior, but they do suggest that space is not an exclusive function of the hippocampus.

THE PARIETAL LOBES

Disorders of visual-spatial exploration were described by Badal in 1889, but it was Balint and later Holmes who first analyzed defective visual exploration in detail. There now appear to be about eight different defects of visual exploration, which usually result from bilateral lesions of the posterior cortex and do not occur all at once (Table 19.2). Perhaps the most dramatic symptoms are those first described by Balint.

Balint's patient had bilateral damage to the occipital and parietal cortex that included parts of the dorsal temporal lobes. The patient also had a zone of unilateral damage to the dorsal parietal and motor cortex (Figure 19.7). He came to Balint's attention after suffering a stroke, and his condition remained unchanged for 6 years. The

TABLE 19.2. Deficits in visual-spatial exploration

Displaced visual attention
Inability to perceive more than one stimulus
Defective visual control of movement (optic ataxia)
Inability to follow a moving target
Defective accommodation and convergence
Inability in maintaining fixation
Inability to voluntarily direct gaze to targets (gaze apraxia)
Abnormal visual search

patient had complete visual fields; was reported to be capable of eye movements; and recognized and named colors, objects, and pictures. When stimuli were presented, he directed his gaze 35° to 40° to the right and saw only what was in that direction. Only after prompting would he look to the left and notice objects there. Once his attention was directed to an object, he noticed nothing else. This was true for objects of all sizes, from a pin to a human figure. The patient would not look over a picture or scene. The impairment resulted in a reading defect because he focused on a single letter and only with difficulty would work backward through a word to decode it. The patient was impaired in reaching. If requested to grasp an object or point to a target, he groped and hit the target only by chance. Misreaching extended even to lighting a cigar, which he attempted to light in the middle. The patient was also unable to estimate distance and could not tell which of two objects was closer.

There are some differences in symptoms in Holmes's patients, who had penetrating missile wounds of the brain. Most notably, these patients were impaired in a number of aspects of eye movement. They had difficulty in looking at a stimulus whether it was presented visually or verbally, in maintaining visual fixation, in following a moving target, in converging to an approaching object, and in blinking in response to a visual threat. These patients also failed to appreciate the spatial features of a stimulus at which they were looking and that they could recognize. They had trouble localizing objects in space, estimating distance, discriminating length and size, and evaluating depth and thickness. As a result, they ran into objects when walking and had difficulty in reading and in counting scattered objects. The patients also sometimes failed to notice objects placed before them and, like Balint's patient, did not notice anything else once their attention had been attracted by a stimulus.

Since these early reports, there have been many accounts of patients with similar symptoms. Symptoms vary, however, depending upon how an injury was acquired, whether it was bilateral, and where it was located. Figure 19.8 illustrates misjudgment by a patient studied by Allison and his colleagues who had bilateral posterior cortical lesions resulting in small lower temporal-quadrant field defects, accompanied by dramatic deficits in the visual control of reaching and other movements (so-called optic ataxia) and by deficits in eye movements:

> A manifestation of visual disorientation noted by the nursing staff five months after operation was when he attempted to light a cigarette. He took it out of the packet and put it in his mouth, then clumsily took a match out of the matchbox and lit it, afterwards directing the flame towards his lower lip, missing the cigarette. . . . He could not pour fluid from a bottle into a glass but spilled it on the tablecloth. He was unable to shake hands without first groping for the preferred hand.

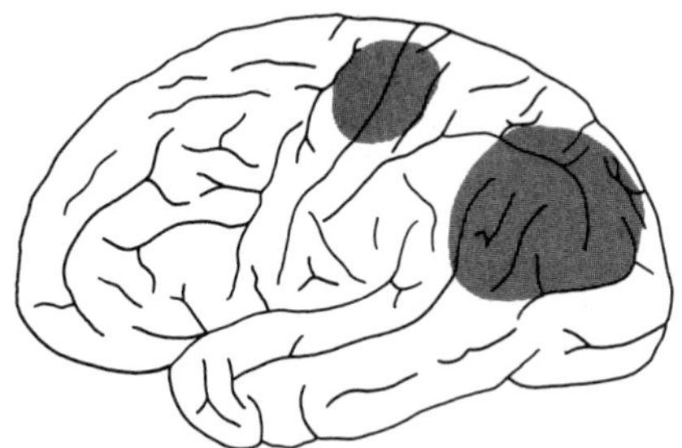

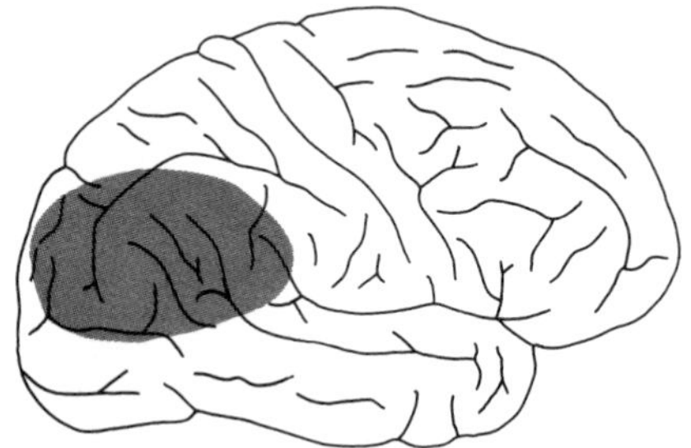

FIGURE 19.7. Balint's drawing of the areas of softening in his patient's brain. (After de Renzi, 1982.)

FIGURE 19.8. A patient with Balint's syndrome demonstrates a visual-spatial deficit in his attempt to pour fluid into a glass. (After Allison et al., 1969.)

> It could be demonstrated that visual memory was intact and did not contribute to his errors. When an object (e.g., a matchbox) was held up either above his head, to the right or to the left and he was asked to note its position, close his eyes for a moment and then point in the general direction in which he had seen the object, he did this correctly. Therefore, it appeared that his ability to remember the position of an object in space was not impaired. (Allison et al., 1969, pp. 324–326)

To differentiate the many deficits that such patients suffer, various investigations have centered on two aspects of visual function: *visual localization* and *depth perception*. Consider the following representative studies. To demonstrate a disorder of spatial localization independent of a disorder of reaching or pointing, Hannay and coworkers projected one or two dots on a screen for 300 msec. Two seconds later an array of numbers, each of which identified a point where a dot may have been, was projected, and the task was to indicate the position of the dot. Patients with right hemisphere lesions were impaired at this task in comparison with those with left hemisphere lesions and normal controls. This deficit is not simply a manifestation of neglect, since errors were equally distributed in the left and right visual fields. It is apparent that an inability to localize points in space would make it difficult indeed to direct movements, resulting in an apparent spatial deficit.

An important cue to the spatial location of objects is depth. To discover its importance, try to catch a ball with one eye closed. The discovery of a profound impairment in depth perception has been claimed dating back to Balint, but a significant problem of interpretation arises when the inference of impaired depth perception is based on misreaching, since misreaching might result from many different deficits. Nonetheless, there is now good evidence that depth perception can be markedly abnormal in the presence of good acuity. A study by Carmon and Bechtoldt provides a compelling example. Their patients were presented with random dot stereograms developed previously by Julesz to study the cues necessary to perceive depth. Subjects look into eyepieces and are shown an apparently random array of dots. When viewed with one eye alone, the array has no contour or depth, the pattern looking rather like a complex crossword puzzle with black and white boxes. When each eye views a stereogram independently, however, a striking figure-ground contour suddenly appears because of slight disparities between the stereograms shown to the two eyes. Most normal subjects and patients with left hemisphere damage easily perceive the contours, but patients with right hemisphere damage are very poor at this test, illustrating a defect in depth perception. This result has been replicated by others, supporting the idea that the mechanism involved in at least some aspect of depth perception is more strongly represented in the right hemisphere.

Many of the deficits displayed by these patients appear to be related to parietal cortex damage. Given Mishkin's studies outlined earlier in this chapter, the parietal spatial system, which projects to the frontal cortex, may be involved. Its function is to provide a coordinate system of visual space and to locate objects in this space. In the absence of this system, a patient will still see an object but will not be able to direct eye or hand movements to it accurately. Furthermore, various investigators have identified neurons in the posterior parietal cortex of monkeys that respond to stimuli within grasping space. It is likely that these cells can project to the motor system to guide the limbs during voluntary movements toward targets in various spatial locations. Finally, there are neurons that appear to have a role in directing head and eye movements toward stimuli in grasping space, which again provides evidence that the parietal cortex has a special role in directing movements to visual targets.

THE FRONTAL CORTEX

A number of studies indicate that the frontal cortex is important for spatial discriminations. The most dramatic demonstration comes from experiments by Nakamura and his coworkers. They spared all the visual areas of the posterior cortex while removing all the cortex anterior to it in monkeys. The monkeys failed to show any signs of vision, but recordings of single cell activity in the visual areas revealed that the cells were functioning normally. Thus, removal of the frontal cortex renders animals chronically blind even though the visual system is functioning. A number of studies have demonstrated that more selective impairments follow more restricted lesions in the visual cortex. Haaxma and Kuypers have demonstrated that if the finger area of the motor cortex is disconnected from the visual centers, a monkey can no longer pick up food using the pincer grasp.

It is difficult to distinguish impairments in the detection of objects from impairments in memory. Some features of object-detection impairments, however, do suggest a memory impairment. Goldman-Rakic has reported a series of studies using rhesus monkeys that had small lesions placed in the frontal cortex, along the principal sulcus. The monkeys were trained to fixate on a spot of light in the center of a TV monitor. A dot of light was flashed briefly in their visual field. The monkeys were required to wait for the fixation spot to disappear before directing their gaze to the visual target. With unilateral lesions, the monkeys could not direct their gaze to the target even with short delays. If there was no delay, they could make the response. By varying the location of the lesion, it was possible to produce selective deficits in different parts of the visual field. These experiments demonstrate that the principal sulcus contains a mechanism for guiding responses on the basis of stored information in the absence of external cues. They also demonstrate that the memory for the location of objects may be mapped in visuospatial coordinates. There is a parallel to these eye-movement results in experiments that require monkeys to reach to a target. If a monkey with lesions to the principal sulcus is given a delayed-response task in which location of the object is the relevant task variable, impairments are obtained after short delays. Other discrimination tasks that do not require memory for spatial location are not impaired by these lesions.

Passingham has also reported memory impairments in a less artificial task in rhesus monkeys with principal sulcus lesions. In his experiment the monkeys were trained to retrieve peanuts from behind 25 different doors in the shortest number of trials, without returning to a door a second time. This task tested the monkey's spatial memory for doors it had opened. The monkeys with lesions were severely impaired at this task. A somewhat analogous deficit has been reported by Petrides and Milner in people with frontal lobe damage. Patients were presented with a set of pages containing the same array of visual stimuli, but the position of the stimuli varied from page to page. They were required to point to one of the stimuli on each page but were asked not to point to the same place twice. Thus, the patients had to remember the selections they had made previously. The frontal lobe patients displayed impairments at this task.

As we discussed earlier, the frontal cortex has important connections with the basal ganglia, and so it might be expected that spatial memory impairments of a similar kind could follow basal ganglia lesions. Ingle and Hoff have reported an interesting finding with frogs, indicating that just such an impairment can be obtained. A visible barrier was placed beside a frog and then removed. After a delay, a large dark object loomed toward the frog, causing it to leap away. Normal frogs avoided leaping into the barrier's previous location or leaped in such a way that they landed behind it, indicating that they remembered where it had been. Frogs with basal ganglia lesions behaved as if they failed to remember the barrier's previous location, although they avoided it quite well when it was present.

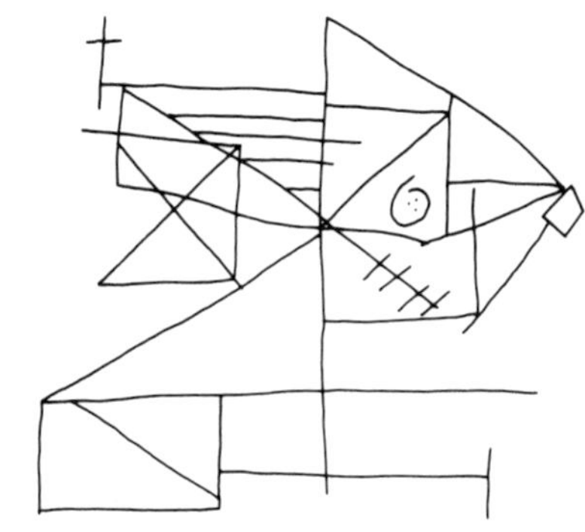

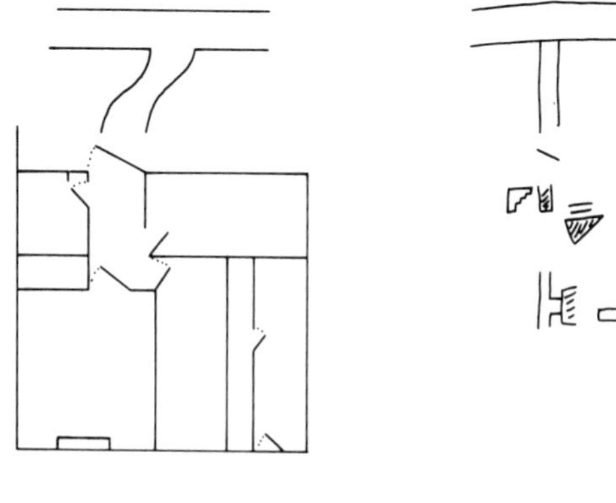

FIGURE 19.9. *A.* A copy of the Rey figure drawn by a patient with a right parietofrontal missile wound. (After Ratcliff, 1982.) *B.* Drawing of the floor plan of the house of a patient with a right parietofrontal tumor: by a psychologist (*left*) and by the patient (*right*). (After McFie et al., 1950.)

CONTRALATERAL NEGLECT AND THE SPECIAL ROLE OF THE RIGHT HEMISPHERE

It is often noted that right hemisphere damage results in more frequent and more obvious spatial deficits than left hemisphere damage (Figure 19.9). This view is supported by (1) neuropsychological studies of normal populations, (2) the phenomenon of contralateral neglect that follows right hemisphere damage in humans, and (3) studies of human patients who have undergone elective surgery involving unilateral hippocampal removal. We will discuss only the last two phenomena here, because the first was discussed in the chapters on cerebral asymmetry (see Chapters 9 and 10).

Perhaps one of the most interesting and puzzling findings in the clinical literature is the profound contralateral neglect that is reported to follow some instances of right parietal cortex damage. We discussed the symptoms and stages of recovery in detail in the chapter dealing with the parietal cortex (see Chapter 12). Here is a brief recap. Following right parietal cortex lesions, patients ignore the contralateral half of the world and of their body in all sensory modalities. They behave as if nothing in the contralateral half of their world exists. When asked to draw a picture, bisect a line, or read, they perform as if the left half of the object, line, or word does not exist. There are a number of puzzling features to the phenomenon. First, it is not simply the case that each hemisphere constructs a representation of the contralateral field. Comparable left hemisphere damage does not produce a comparable effect. Also, if the right hemisphere does play a special role in spatial abilities, one would expect spatial deficits to be bilateral, and that is obviously not the case. De Renzi has reviewed the many explanations that attempt to account for this finding, including hypotheses that relate to attention, eye movements, and hemispheric competition. His most compelling explanation is that the right hemisphere is somehow involved in constructing central representations of space.

Results supporting this view come from two clever studies by Bisiach and his associates. Patients were asked to give a verbal description of a place that was previously ascertained to be familiar to them—the cathedral square in Milan. The subjects were first requested to imagine themselves facing the front of the cathedral from the opposite side of the square and to describe the scene. Then they were asked to imagine the vantage point to be the central entrance of the cathedral, facing their former position. Patients with contralateral neglect failed to describe details of the left side of the square regardless of their vantage point. In other words, when they switched from the first vantage point to the second, they described the side of the square they had previously neglected. This neglect is clearly not one of memory, nor is it attributable to field defects or other primary sensory loss. Neglect in this test is probably due to a loss of a cerebral representation or image of a part of the external world, the lost part varying with the frame of reference of the observer of the image.

In a second experiment, Bisiach's patients were given two tasks. In both they were required to view objects and to judge whether their two sides were the same or different from the central portion. In a static viewing condition, they were allowed to see the entire design for 2 sec. As expected, the patients ignored the left side of the designs. In the second viewing condition, the design was passed behind a slit in front of the patient over a 2-sec period. The subject was able to see the entire design in the same viewing location as it passed by. Again, the patients made errors that were attributable to left-side neglect. Since the characteristics of neglect described in these two experiments cannot be easily attributed to perceptual errors or biases, it seems more likely that they stem from processes of reconstructing central representations of the world.

Neglect may also follow left hemisphere damage. Caramazza and Hillis report that a patient, N. G., who had a large left hemisphere stroke, showed contralateral neglect for the right side of objects and words either when they were read or when they were spelled. The reading and spelling errors on the right half of words occurred regardless of their length. Caramazza and Hillis suggest that N. G.'s deficit stems from a deficit in processing internal representations of words.

Smith and Milner's studies of patients who had received elective surgery to remove the hippocampus as a treatment for epilepsy show a selective involvement of the right hippocampus in spatial memory. In the task the researchers used, 16 small toys were employed as stimulus objects and were spread out over a table. The subject was told that this was a test of ability to estimate prices and that an estimate of the average price of a real object represented by the toy would be required. The subject was told to point at the toy, name it, and think of a price. After 10 sec the price was asked for; the subject then moved on to the next toy. Then the subject moved away from the table and was asked to recall the objects that had been seen. Following the test of object recall, a sheet of brown paper, the same size as the original table, was placed before the subject and he or she was asked to place the toys in their original locations. The recall tests were then repeated 24 hours later. The object array is illustrated in Figure 19.10A. Scores were given for the recall of the objects' names; in addition, the researchers measured the displacement distances between the object's original location and the patient's immediate placement, and between the original location and the patient's delayed placement. On the measure of name recall, both patients with right hippocampus damage and those with left hippocampus damage were moderately impaired, with the left hippocampal patients having lower scores than the right hippocampal patients. The results for the spatial component of the experiment are shown in Figure 19.10B. Scores for the left temporal and

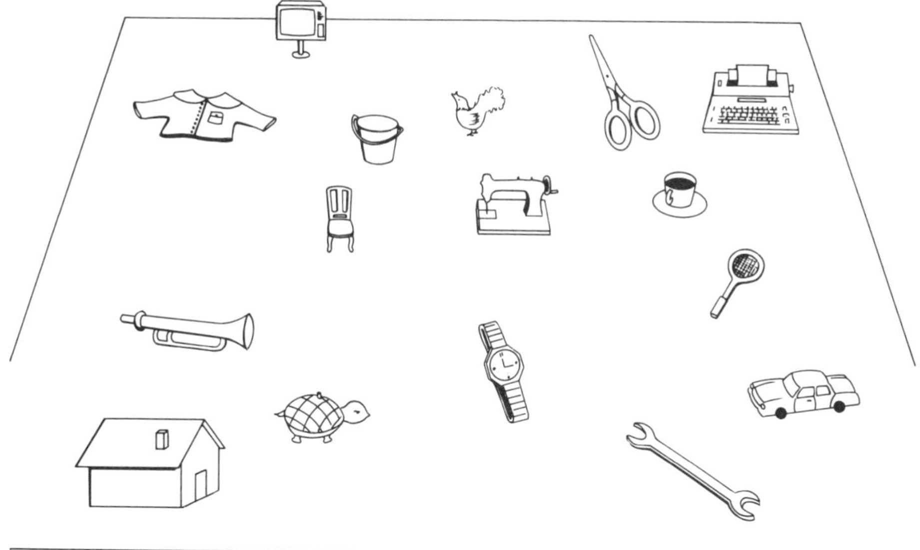

A

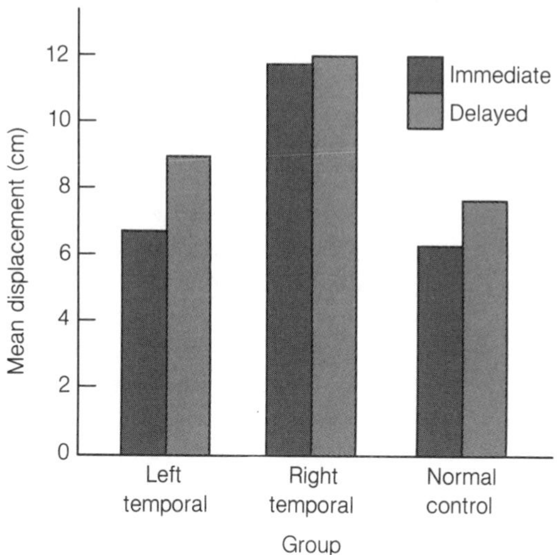

B

FIGURE 19.10. *A*. Test of spatial memory for objects with the typical arrangement of the toys on the 16 fixed locations. Subjects are required to point to the objects and estimate their individual prices. The objects are then removed and the subjects are required to reposition them. *B*. Graph of the performance by left temporal and right temporal patients and by controls on the recall of absolute location. (After Smith and Milner, 1981.)

control groups were comparable, but scores for the right hippocampal group were extremely poor on both immediate and delayed recall tests.

INDIVIDUAL DIFFERENCES

Sex Differences

There is agreement that there are differences in spatial abilities between the sexes. Adult males usually perform better on spatial tests than adult females. The male advantage in spatial ability is generally contrasted with a female advantage in language skills, fine-motor movements, and perceptual speed. The female advantage is conceded to be quite small in statistical terms, about 0.2 standard deviation, but the male advantage is thought to be large, about 0.5 standard deviation. Spatial abilities first came to the attention of researchers in the early part of this century in studies designed to predict mechanical aptitude. As interest in spatial abilities developed, studies eventually began to include mixed age and sex groups, from which the generalization that adult males perform better than adult females gradually emerged. When Maccoby and Jacklin reviewed this literature in 1974, the idea that this sex difference emerges in adolescence and is due to environmental influences became a dominant view. Subsequently, many studies have demonstrated sex differences in much younger children. Part of the difficulty in resolving age and sex differences in spatial abilities relates to the large number of tests that have been used and the diversity of the populations tested. In a review, however, Newcombe has interpreted the evidence as suggesting that small sex differences are present in childhood and increase slightly with age.

Females and males apparently differ in their abilities on such skills as chess, mathematics, music, and art. Mathematical aptitude has received the closest scrutiny. A large number of studies have shown that males outperform females on tests of quantitative ability. Studies in the United States, including the Scholastic Aptitude Test and the Johns Hopkins University mathematical talent search, suggest that these differences become apparent in adolescence and become more evident at the high end of the performance scale. Among top scorers on the college board's aptitude tests, males outnumber females by about 17 to 1. By this point there are only a small number of individuals in the sample. It has been suggested that if males have a slight advantage over females in spatial abilities, this will lead them to be somewhat more successful in occupations demanding spatial skill.

Our primary interest is in explaining brain function, and this is why sex-related differences in spatial ability are of interest. Just the same, here are some cautions. First, findings of sex difference do not mean that the cognitive abilities of the sexes are vastly different. Females and males use the same cognitive processes effectively. Second, the range of abilities within female and male groups is larger than that between sex groups. Consequently, females and males will be found at all levels of the ability scale. Third, if females are given practice on spatial tasks, their performance improves toward male levels. Thus, there is no reason to believe that occupational success will be primarily a result of differences in spatial ability. Fourth, under most test conditions and for most test groups, environmental influences cannot be factored out easily. Boys are much more likely than girls to be allowed to explore their spatial environment without restriction. After a period of years, this differential experience could produce small advantages. Finally, even in occupations such as engineering and architecture, which are traditionally thought to be heavily dependent on spatial factors, women can be as successful as men. Russia is usually given as an example of a country in which there are more women in these occupations than men.

Nevertheless, the existence of gender differences, however small, are of real interest to students of brain function. On the practical side, they must be considered when tests of brain function are developed, normed, and administered. They must also be considered a relevant factor in interpreting the consequences of brain damage. More important, they provide a key to understanding brain organization and function. There are a limited number of explanations for the differences between individuals (ignoring environmental influences), and isolation of the relevant factors is a real possibility. The differences may be genetic, in which case they are sex-linked and are probably determined by a recessive gene on the X chromosome. Alternatively, they may be hormonally produced and emerge as a result of the action of hormones on neural organization and function.

Genetic Contributions

The usual explanation of a genetic basis for spatial ability goes something like this. During the formative period of the evolution of modern humans, a differentiation of roles in food gathering was adaptive. A primary occupation of males was hunting, which required an ability to find one's way about in space. Hunting also required the ability to throw spears and aim arrows, both of which are putative spatial skills. Males endowed with these abilities would be more successful than those who were not and consequently would be selected. It is quite irrelevant that those skills are no longer needed today; males will tend to get them anyway.

McGee has reviewed a large body of literature suggesting that spatial skills are heritable. A number of studies have suggested that spatial abilities may be enhanced by an X-linked, recessive gene. Traits that are thought to be carried by a single gene on the X chromosome are said to be sex-linked. If the gene is recessive, more males than females will be affected. Under this arrangement, according to the usual estimates, about 50% of males and about 25% of females will carry the gene and have enhanced spatial abilities. Thus, about one-fourth of females will score above the male median on tests of spatial abilities, a finding obtained in most studies. The recessive-gene hypothesis has been put to a number of tests, but it has not emerged unscathed. According to the hypothesis, certain correlations should emerge in the offspring of different families, but these correlations have not been obtained. A more difficult problem concerns the tests used to obtain scores for correlations. Studies using different tests have obtained different correlations, raising the possibility that there may be different kinds of spatial abilities. The results suggest either that alternative inheritance models should be considered or sex-related differences have other explanations.

Hormonal Influences

Three lines of evidence suggest that hormones influence sex differences in spatial abilities: (1) developmental studies, (2) studies of persons with chromosomal-hormonal abnormalities, and (3) studies investigating the relationship between androgenicity and spatial abilities.

We noted earlier that sex differences are found more reliably in adults than in prepubescent children. This suggests that sex-related cognitive differences may be attributable to the hormonal changes that occur during puberty. That some differences are obtained earlier could also be accounted for by sex-related hormonal influences that occur prenatally or in the early postnatal period. This hypothesis seems to be supported by studies of patients with **Turner's syndrome.** Females with Turner's syndrome have a single X chromosome rather than the normal XX pair. Their intelligence and verbal abilities are normal and are distributed throughout the population range, but their spatial abilities are impaired. They get extremely low scores on tests of mental rotation, the block design test of the Wechsler Adult Scale, the spatial subtest of the Primary Mental Abilities Test, the Road-and-Map Test of Direction Sense, and tests of imaginary movements and direct rotation. The results are counterintuitive and are at variance with the recessive-gene hypothesis, which would predict that females with a single X chromosome ought to be similar to males, who also have one X chromosome. Since females with Turner's syndrome produce no gonadal hormones, the suggestion is that gonadal hormones influence spatial abilities. Studies examining this hypothesis now propose that the levels of androgens (masculinizing hormones) or the balance between estrogen and androgens might determine spatial abilities. Some workers have even argued that the more androgens females receive, the better their spatial abilities. For males, who are already receiving a high level of androgens, more might be too much, and spatial and other abilities might be impaired. Consequently, females receiving large amounts of androgen and males receiving moderate amounts would be expected to have enhanced spatial skills. The mechanisms that hormones are thought to influence in modulating spatial abilities are in the brain. Presumably, they are the same neural systems, discussed above, that are responsible for spatial abilities in general. How these mechanisms work is not known. Early in life, hormones may influence neural connections, neural growth, and cell death, thus sculpting quite a different spatial-neural system for individuals with enhanced spatial abilities. On the other hand, hormones can selectively modulate neural function in these systems via still unknown mechanisms.

Handedness

It is often proposed that left-handedness might confer a special spatial advantage. Some well-known artists such as da Vinci and Michelangelo were left-handed, left-handedness is common in tennis players and baseball pitchers, and there are some reports that left-handers are disproportionately represented in faculties of engineering and architecture.

In an extensive study on cognitive abilities and brain organization, Harshman and colleagues have reported results suggesting that relations to handedness may be complex. Harshman's group administered a large battery of tests to three large populations. In some of the populations, a sex-by-handedness interaction was obtained. Overall, males performed better on spatial tests than females, as was expected. In some of the populations, left-handedness in males was associated with lower spatial scores, but it was associated with higher spatial scores in females. In an attempt to find out why this effect occurred only in certain populations, Harshman's group examined the effects of other variables and uncovered a three-way interaction of sex, handedness, and reasoning ability. Among what he defined as a high-reasoning group, left-handed males had lower spatial scores and left-handed females had higher spatial scores than right-handed comparison groups. Among low-reasoning groups the relationship was reserved: left-handed males had high spatial scores and left-handed females had low spatial scores in relation to their comparison groups. In a retrospective analysis of previous studies, Harshman and his coworkers suggest that contradictory results obtained in previous work could be accounted for by differences in the groups sampled. That is, if a sample group was a university population, high spatial scores might be expected from left-handed females and low spatial scores from left-handed males. If a sample population was more heterogeneous, the opposite pattern of results might be obtained.

Neuropsychological Spatial Tests

A surprising number of tests have been used to measure spatial abilities. Our problem in understanding them can be simplified by considering factor-analysis results of the kinds reported by McGee. Factor analysis is a mathematical procedure used to find what is common within a heterogeneous group of elements. When the procedure has been applied to spatial tests, two separate spatial factors, or abilities, have been identified: visualization and orientation. Examples of the kinds of tests that are used to measure each spatial ability are illustrated in Figure 19.11.

Visualization tests evaluate the ability to manipulate, rotate, twist, or invert two- or three-dimensional stimulus objects mentally. The underlying ability seems to involve a process of recognition, retention, and recall of a configuration in which there is movement among the internal parts of the configuration, such as an object manipulated in three-dimensional space or the folding and unfolding of flat patterns (Figure 19.11A). McGee has suggested that visualization is important to two areas of mental functioning: imagery and mathematical ability, especially for the understanding of geometry and algebra.

Orientation tests evaluate comprehension of the arrangement of elements within a visual stimulus pattern and the aptitude to remain uncon-

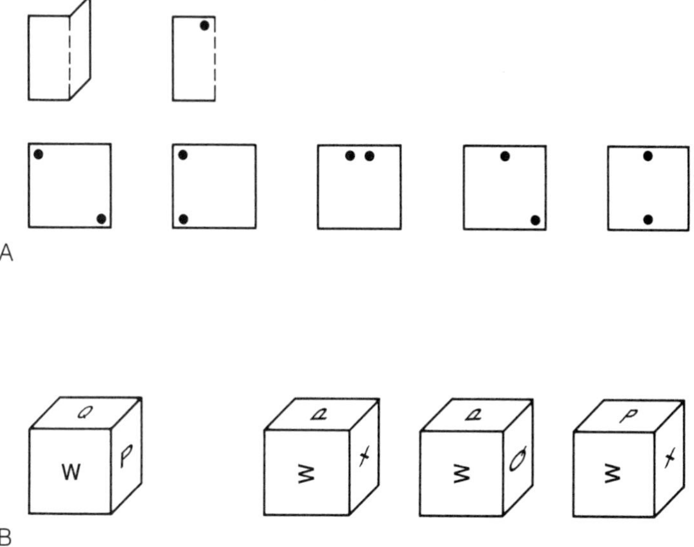

FIGURE 19.11. Sample test items similar to those used to measure visualization and orientation spatial abilities. *A.* Visualization. Imagine folding and unfolding a piece of paper. After being folded, a hole is punched through all of the thicknesses. Which figure is correct when the paper is unfolded? *B.* Orientation. Compare the three cubes on the right with the one on the left. No letter appears on more than one face of a given cube. Which of the three cubes on the right could be a different view of the cube on the left? (After Halpern, 1986.)

fused by the changing orientation in which a spatial configuration may be presented (Figure 19.11B). McGee suggests that orientation ability is related to field independence—the ability to orient an object accurately while ignoring the background that encloses it.

If spatial abilities are in fact limited to two factors, a number of specific predictions can be made about the effects of brain damage on performance in spatial tests. All spatial tests containing unfamiliar test items should be impaired by posterior parietal and frontal eye-field damage, because this cortical system sets up the spatial coordinates within which objects are located. Inferior temporal damage or hippocampal damage should disrupt performance only on orientation tests, since these tests require both object identification and a spatial-coordinate system.

SUMMARY

There are a number of kinds of spatial abilities. We orient using our body as a reference, we move toward or away from cues, and we use the relational properties of a number of objects to guide our movements. This last ability is dependent upon the cortex, especially the hippocampus. In humans the right hemisphere appears to be especially involved in spatial behavior. Additionally, patients with right hemisphere damage can display a syndrome of contralateral neglect in which they fail to recognize things that are contralateral to their lesion, including their own body. A number of lines of evidence suggest that sex and handedness influence spatial abilities in humans. Thus, the sex hormones and cortical organization can influence spatial behavior.

REFERENCES

Acredolo, L. P. Frames of reference used by children for orientation in unfamiliar spaces. In G. Moore and R. Gooledge, eds. *Environmental Knowing*. Stroudsberg, Pa.: Dowden, Hutchinson, and Ross, 1976.

Allison, R. S., L. J. Hurwitz, J. G. White, and T. J. Wilmot. A follow-up study of a patient with Balint's syndrome. *Neuropsychologia* 7:319–333, 1969.

Angeli, S. J., E. A. Murray, and M. Mishkin. Hippocampectomized monkeys can remember one place but not two. *Neuropsychologia* 31:1021–1030, 1993.

Archibald, Y. M. Time as a variable in the performance of hemisphere-damaged patients on the Elithorn Perceptual Maze Test. *Cortex* 14:22–31, 1978.

Balint, R. Seelenlähmung des Schauens, optische Ataxie, räumlielie Störung der Aufmerksamkeit, Mschr. *Psychiatry and Neurology* 25:51–81, 1909.

Beales, K. L., C. L. Smith, and S. M. Dodd. Brain size, cranial morphology, climate, and time machines. *Current Anthropology* 25:301–330, 1984.

Benton, A. L. *Right-Left Discrimination and Finger Localization*. New York: Hoeber-Harper, 1959.

Benton, A. L. Disorders of spatial orientation. In P. J. Vinkey and G. W. Bruyn, eds. *Handbook of Clinical Neurology*, vol. 3. Amsterdam: Elsevier North-Holland, 1969.

Benton, A. L. Visuoperceptive, visuospatial, and visuoconstructive disorders. In K. M. Heilman and E. Valenstein, eds. *Clinical Neuropsychology*. New York: Oxford University Press, 1979.

Benton, A. L. Spatial thinking in neurological patients: Historical aspects. In M. Potegal, ed. *Spatial Abilities: Development and Physiological Foundations*. New York: Academic Press, 1982.

Benton, A. L., A. Elithorn, M. L. Fogel, and M. Kerr. A perceptual maze test sensitive to brain damage. *Journal of Neurology, Neurosurgery, and Psychiatry* 26:540–544, 1963.

Benton, A. L., K. deS. Hamsher, N. R. Varney, and O. Spreen. *Contributions to Neuropsychological Assessment*. New York: Oxford University Press, 1983.

Benton, A. L., and H. Hécaen. Stereoscopic vision in patients with unilateral cerebral damage. *Neurology* 20:1084–1088, 1970.

Benton, A. L., N. R. Varney, and K. deS. Hamsher. Visuospatial judgment: A clinical test. *Archives of Neurology* 35:364–367, 1978.

Bisiach, E., E. Capitani, C. Luzzatti, and D. Perani. Brain and conscious representation of outside reality. *Neuropsychologia* 19:543–552, 1981.

Bisiach, E., and C. Luzzatti. Unilateral neglect of representational space. *Cortex* 14:129–133, 1978.

Brain, W. R. Visual disorientation with special reference to lesions of the right cerebral hemisphere. *Brain* 64:244–272, 1941.

Caramazza, A., and Hillis, A. E. Spatial representation of words in the brain implied by studies of a unilateral neglect patient. *Nature* 346:267–269, 1990.

Carmon, A., and H. P. Bechtoldt. Dominance of the right cerebral hemisphere for stereopsis. *Neuropsychologia* 7:29–39, 1969.

Corballis, M. C. Mental rotation: Anatomy of a paradigm. In M. Potegal, ed. *Spatial Abilities: Development and Physiological Foundations*. New York: Academic Press, 1982.

Corkin, S. Tactually-guided maze-learning in man: Effects of unilateral cortical excisions and bilateral hippocampal lesions. *Neuropsychologia* 3:339–351, 1965.

Corkin, S. The role of different cerebral structures in somaesthetic perception. In E. C. Carterette and M. P. Friedman, eds. *Handbook of Perception*, vol. 6. New York: Academic Press, 1978.

Cowie, R. J., J. R. Krebs, and D. F. Sherry. Food storing by marsh tits. *Animal Behavior* 29:1252–1259, 1981.

de Renzi, E. *Disorders of Space Exploration and Cognition*. New York: John Wiley, 1982.

Goldman-Rakic, P. S. Circuitry of primate prefrontal cortex and regulation of behavior by representational memory. In V. B. Mountcastle, F. Plum, and S. R. Geiger, eds. *Handbook of Physiology*, vol. 5. Bethesda, Md.: American Physiological Society, 1987.

Grusser, O. J. The multimodal structure of the extrapersonal space. In A. Hein and M. Jeannerod, eds. *Spatially Oriented Behavior*. New York: Springer-Verlag, 1987.

Haaxma, R., and H. G. J. M. Kuypers. Intrahemispheric cortical connections and visual guidance of hand and finger movements in the rhesus monkey. *Brain* 98:239–260, 1975.

Halpern, D. F. *Sex Differences in Cognitive Abilities*. Hillsdale, N.J.: Lawrence Erlbaum, 1986.

Hannay, H. J., N. R. Varney, and A. L. Benton. Visual localization in patients with unilateral brain disease. *Journal of Neurology, Neurosurgery and Psychiatry* 39:307–313, 1976.

Hashman, R. A., E. Hampson, and S. A. Berenbaum. Individual differences in cognitive abilities and brain organization. Part I: Sex and handedness differences in ability. *Canadian Journal of Psychology* 37:144–192, 1983.

Head, H. *Studies in Neurology*. London: Oxford University Press, 1920.

Hécaen, H., J. de Ajuriaguerra, and J. Massonet. Les troubles visuoconstructifs par lésions parieto-occipitales droites. Role des perturbations vestibulaires. *Encephále* 1:122–179, 1951.

Hécaen, H., C. Tzortzis, and M. C. Masure. Troubles de l'orientation spatiale dans une pereuve de recherce d'itineraire lors des lésions corticales unilaterales. *Perception* 1:325–330, 1972.

Hécaen, H., C. Tzortzis, and P. Rondot. Loss of topographical memory with learning deficits. *Cortex* 16:525–542, 1980.

Holmes, G. Disturbances of visual space perception. *British Medical Journal* 2:230–233, 1919.

Holmes, G., and G. Horax. Disturbances of spatial orientation and visual attention, with loss of stereoscopic vision. *Archives of Neurology and Psychiatry* 1:385–407, 1919.

Ingle, D., and K. S. Hoff. Neural mechanisms of short-term memory in frogs. *Society for Neuroscience Abstracts* 14:692, 1988.

Jackson, J. H. On the nature of duality of the brain. *Brain* 38:80–103, 1915.

Klingon, G. H., and D. C. Bontecou. Localization in auditory space. *Neurology* 16:879–886, 1966.

Levy, J. Possible basis for the evolution of lateral specialization of the human brain. *Nature* 224:614–615, 1969.

Maccoby, E. E., and C. N. Jacklin. *The Psychology of Sex Differences*. Stanford, Calif.: Stanford University Press, 1974.

McFie, J., M. F. Piercy, and O. L. Zangwill. Visual-spatial agnosia associated with lesions of the right cerebral hemisphere. *Brain* 73:167–190, 1950.

McFie, J., and O. L. Zangwill. Visual-constructive disabilities associated with lesions of the left hemisphere. *Brain* 83:243–260, 1960.

McGee, M. G. Human spatial abilities: Psychometric studies and environmental, genetic, hormonal, and neurological influences. *Psychological Bulletin* 86:889–918, 1979.

Mehta, Z., F. Newcombe, and H. Damasio. A left hemisphere contribution to visuospatial processing. *Cortex* 23:447–461, 1987.

Menzel, E. W. Chimpanzee spatial memory organization. *Science* 192:943–945, 1973.

Milner, B. Visually-guided maze learning in man: Effects of bilateral hippocampal, bilateral frontal, and unilateral cerebral lesions. *Neuropsychologia* 3:317–338, 1965.

Milner, B. Interhemispheric differences in the localization of psychological processes in man. *British Medical Bulletin* 27:272–277, 1971.

Milner, B., S. Corkin, and H.-L. Teuber. Further analysis of the hippocampal amnesic syndrome: 14-year follow-up study of H. M. *Neuropsychologia* 6:215–234, 1968.

Morris, R. G. M., P. Garrud, J. Rawlings, and J. O'Keefe. Place navigation impaired in rats with hippocampal lesions. *Nature* 297:681–683, 1982.

Nakamura, R. K., S. J. Schein, and R. Desimone. Visual responses from cells in striate cortex of monkeys rendered chronically "blind" by lesions of nonvisual cortex. *Experimental Brain Research* 63:185–190, 1986.

Newcombe, N. Sex-related differences in spatial ability: Problems and gaps in current approaches. In M. Potegal, ed. *Spatial Abilities: Development and Physiological Foundations*. New York: Academic Press, 1982.

O'Keefe, J., and J. Dostrovsky. The hippocampus as a spatial map. Preliminary evidence from unit activity in the freely-moving rat. *Brain Research* 34:171–175, 1971.

O'Keefe, J., and L. Nadel. *The Hippocampus as a Cognitive Map*. New York: Clarendon Press, 1978.

Olton, D. S. The function of septo-hippocampal connections in spatially organized behaviour. In *Functions of the Septo-Hippocampal System, Ciba Foundation Symposium 58*. New York: Elsevier North-Holland, 1978.

Oxbury, J. M., D. C. Campbell, and S. M. Oxbury. Unilateral spatial neglect and impairments of spatial analysis and visual perception. *Brain* 97:551–564, 1974.

Parkinson, J. K., E. A. Murray, and M. Mishkin. A selective mnemonic role for the hippocampus in monkeys: Memory for the location of objects. *The Journal of Neuroscience* 8:4159–4167, 1988.

Passingham, R. E. Memory of monkeys *(Maccaca mulatta)* with lesions in prefrontal cortex. *Behavioral Neuroscience* 99:3–21, 1985.

Paterson, A., and O. L. Zangwill. Disorders of visual space perception associated with lesions of the right cerebral hemisphere. *Brain* 67:331–358, 1944.

Petrides, M., and S. K. Iversen. Restricted posterior parietal lesions in the rhesus monkey and performance on visuospatial tasks. *Brain Research* 161:63–77, 1979.

Petrides, M., and B. Milner. Deficits on subject-ordered tasks after frontal- and temporal-lobe lesions in man. *Neuropsychologia* 20:249–292, 1982.

Pick, H. L., and J. J. Rieser. Children's cognitive mapping. In M. Potegal, ed. *Spatial Abilities: Development and Physiological Foundations*. New York: Academic Press, 1982.

Posner, M. I., and M. E. Raichle. *Images of Mind*. New York: Scientific American Library, 1994.

Potegal, M., ed. *Spatial Abilities: Development and Physiological Foundations*. New York: Academic Press, 1982.

Ratcliff, G. Spatial thought, mental rotation and the right cerebral hemisphere. *Neuropsychologia* 17:49–54, 1979.

Ratcliff, G. Disturbances of spatial orientation associated with cerebal lesions. In M. Potegal, ed. *Spatial Abilities:*

Development and Physiological Foundations. New York: Academic Press, 1982.

Ratcliff, G., and G. A. B. Davies-Jones. Defective visual localization in focal brain wounds. *Brain* 95:49–60, 1972.

Ratcliff, G., and F. Newcombe. Spatial orientation in man: Effects of left, right, and bilateral posterior cerebral lesions. *Journal of Neurology, Neurosurgery, and Psychiatry* 36:448–454, 1973.

Ratcliff, G., R. M. Ridley, and G. Ettlinger. Spatial disorientation in the monkey. *Cortex* 13:62–65, 1977.

Semmes, J. A non-tactual factor in astereognosis. *Neuropsychologia* 3:295–315, 1965.

Shankweiler, D. Performance of brain damaged patients on two tests of sound localization. *Journal of Comparative and Physiological Psychology* 54:375–381, 1951.

Sherry, D. F. Food storage by birds and mammals. *Advances in the Study of Behavior* 15:153–188, 1985.

Sherry, D. F., A. L. Vaccaromp, K. Buckenham, and R. S. Herz. The hippocampal complex of food-storing birds. *Brain Behavior and Evolution* 34:308–317, 1989.

Smith, M. L., and B. Milner. The role of the right hippocampus in the recall of spatial location. *Neuropsychologia* 19:781–793, 1981.

Taylor, J. *The Selected Writings of John Hughlings-Jackson.* London: Hodder, 1932.

Thompson, R. Hippocampal and cortical function in a maze devoid of left and right turns. *Physiology and Behavior* 23:601–603, 1979.

Tolman, E. C. Cognitive maps in rats and men. *Psychological Review* 55:189–208, 1948.

Tyler, H. R. Abnormalities of perception and defective eye movements (Balint's syndrome). *Cortex* 4:154–171, 1968.

Ungerleider, L. G., and M. Mishkin. Two cortical visual systems. In D. Ingle, M. A. Goodale, and R. J. W. Mansfield, eds. *Analysis of Visual Behavior.* Cambridge, Mass.: MIT Press, 1982.

Vanderwolf, C. H. Hippocampal activity, olfaction, and sniffing: An olfactory input to the dentate gyrus. *Brain Research* 593:197–208, 1992.

Whishaw, I. Q. The decorticate rat. In B. Kolb and R. Tees, eds. *The Cortex of the Rat.* Cambridge, Mass.: MIT Press, 1989.

Zangwill, O. L. *Cerebral Dominance and Its Relation to Psychological Function.* Edinburgh: Oliver & Boyd, 1960.

Zola-Morgan, S., L. Squire and D. G. Amaral. Human amnesia and the medial temporal region: Enduring memory impairment following a bilateral lesion limited to field CA1 of the hippocampus. *The Journal of Neuroscience* 6:2950–2967, 1986.

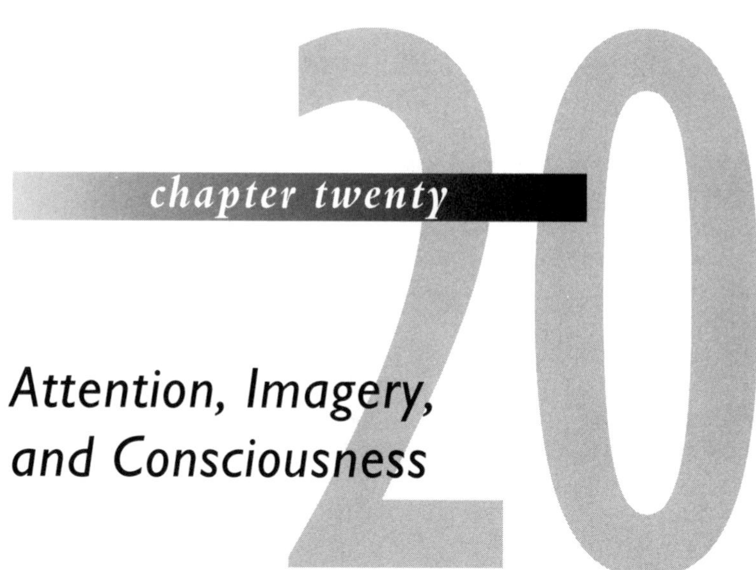

chapter twenty

Attention, Imagery, and Consciousness

Hebb and others have argued that the central question in neuropsychology is the relationship between the mind and the brain. The question is easy to state, yet it is not so easy to grasp what it is we need to explain. One thing that needs explanation is how we select information to act upon. Another is how we select behaviors. Animals like simple worms have a limited sensory capacity and an equally limited repertoire of behaviors. Animals like dogs have a much more sophisticated sensory capacity and a corresponding increase in behavioral options. Primates, including humans, have gone even further. Thus, we can see that as sensory and motor capacities increase, so does the problem of selection. Furthermore, as the brain expands, memory increases, providing yet another variable in both stimulus interpretation and response selection. Finally, as the number of sensory channels increases, there is a need to correlate the different inputs to produce a single "reality."

One way to consider these evolutionary changes is to posit that as the brain expands to increase sensory-motor capacity, so does some other process (or processes) that is involved in sensory and motor selection. One proposed process is known as **attention.** The concept implies that somehow we focus a "mental spotlight" on certain sensory inputs, motor programs, memories, or internal representations. This spotlight might be unconscious, in that we are not aware of the process, or it might be conscious, such as when we scan our memory for someone's name. The development of language would seem to increase the likelihood of conscious attention, but it is unlikely that all conscious processing is verbal. One can speculate, for example, that the "Eureka" insight of Archimedes involved conscious processing that was more than just verbal. The point is that as sensory-motor capacities expand, so too do the processes of attention and consciousness. The clear implication is that consciousness is not a dichotomous phenomenon; there is a gradual evolutionary increase in consciousness that is correlated with the ability to organize sensory and motor capacities. The most evolved organizer is language, which implies an increased capacity for the processes of attention.

We have encountered problems of attention and conscious awareness earlier in this book. Recall, for example, the concepts of blindsight and blindtouch discussed in Chapter 11. Patients can describe the location of sensory information for which they have no conscious awareness. Similarly, amnesic patients can show evidence of procedural memory even when they have no conscious recollection of having even been in a room before, let alone having learned a task. And people with right posterior parietal-temporal lesions show hemispatial neglect: they behave as though the left side of the world were not present. That this is not an input problem was illustrated beautifully in the experiments showing that patients have a cognitive hemispatial neglect, too. Thus, when asked to imagine a familiar scene from a particular perspective, patients neglected the left side, but when asked to imagine the same scene from a perspective 180° removed, they described the previously neglected portions and now neglected the previously described regions.

The concept of attention has had an uneven history in psychology. At the turn of the century, it was a popular topic of study. In 1908 Tichener confidently asserted that "the doctrine of attention is the nerve of the whole psychological system, and that as men judge it, so shall they be judged before the general tribunal of psychology" (p. 173). The development of behaviorism and Gestalt psychology in the 1920s specifically denied the necessity of studying processes like attention, and the "general tribunal of psychology" rejected such concepts. For example, the behaviorist view held that a full account of behavior is possible in strictly physiological terms, with no reference to cognitive concepts such as attention or even consciousness. The emergence of cognitive science has led to a reevaluation of this perspective. Investigators in both cognitive science and neuroscience have returned to the position first espoused by William James: "Everyone knows what attention is. It is the taking possession by the mind, in clear and vivid form, of one out of what seems several simultaneously possible objects or trains of thought." The development of renewed interest in such concepts as attention has led to the establishment of distinct subcultures among students of attention. Perhaps the biggest division is between investigators interested in the automatic processes involved in attention and those interested in the conscious selection of sensory information. There has been less interest in the question of motor attention, which could be defined as the process of selecting behaviors. In addition, some researchers are interested in imagination (or imagery) and the role it plays in behavioral selection.

AUTOMATIC VERSUS ATTENTIVE PROCESSING

One of the areas of agreement in cognitive psychology is that certain behaviors can be performed with little, if any, attention whereas others are highly sensitive to the allocation of attention. Posner and Snyder define automatic processes as behavior occurring without intention, involuntarily, without conscious awareness, and without producing interference with ongoing activities. Automatic processing may be an innate property of the way in which sensory information is processed, or it can be produced by extended training. We note, parenthetically, that there may be more than one form of automaticity. Treisman uses the term automaticity to refer to the effortless extraction of features of perception, whereas Anderson excludes this category and restricts his consideration to automatic behaviors that accrue with practice of a particular skill. Reviews by Logan and by Bargh suggest that even finer distinctions can be made.

Operations that are not automatic have been referred to by various terms, including controlled, effortful, attentive, and conscious. It is argued that these operations differ fundamentally from automatic processing. One way to look at the difference is to consider the automatic processes as bottom-up processing and the attentive processes as top-down processing. Bottom-up processing is data-driven; that is, it relies almost exclusively on the stimulus information being presented in the environment. In contrast, top-down processing is conceptually driven. It relies on the use of information already in memory, including whatever expectation there might be regarding the task at hand. Viewed in this way, it is reasonable to presume that automatic and attentive processing will involve at least some different cortical circuits. One hypothesis is that whatever unique cortical circuits are recruited in attentive processing must reflect processes of consciousness.

One way to examine the difference between automatic and attentive processing is reflected in the experiments of Anne Treisman and her colleagues. Consider the following experiment. Subjects are presented with arrays of stimuli such as those shown in Figure 20.1. The task is to identify the target that is different from all the others. There is a dramatic difference in the response time depending upon the nature of the stimulus. When the task requires the subject to find a target distinguished by the fact that it lacks a feature present in the other items, the time taken to find the target varies directly with the number of distractors. Evidently, the items in the display are subjected to a serial search. When the task requires the identification of a target with an extra line, however, the search time is independent of the number of distractors. Apparently, the target visually "pops out" of the display.

The result of Treisman's experiment is not intuitive. After all, each case involves the same discrimination between the same two stimuli. Thus, certain aspects of visual processing seem to be accomplished automatically without attention being specifically focused on any particular aspect of the visual field (the popout). In contrast, other aspects of visual processing seem to depend upon focused attention and are done serially, as if a mental spotlight were being moved from one location to another. The former type of analysis has been called a **feature search;** the general idea is that a specific visual feature, such as a vertical line, is sufficient to locate the target. The latter process has been called a **conjunction search,** because only a

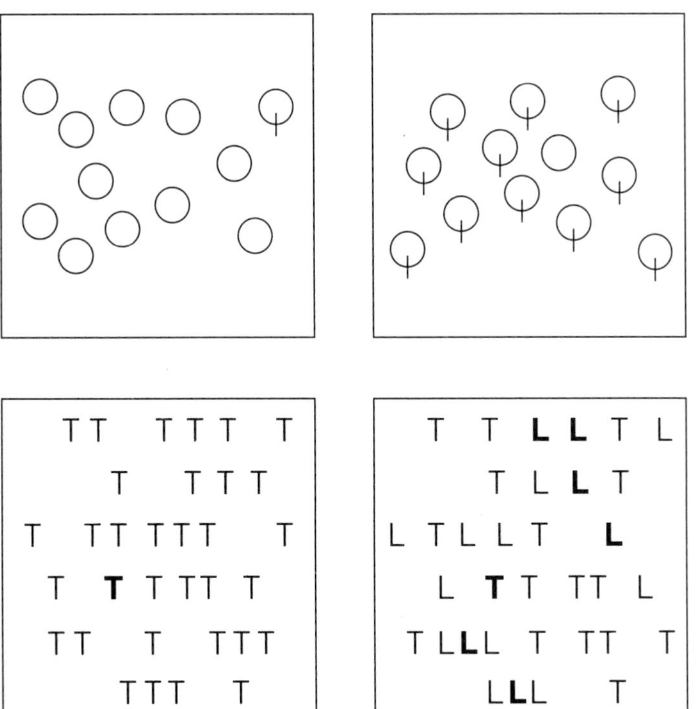

FIGURE 20.1. Examples of visual processing tasks. In the top left example, the ⚲ "pops out," but on the right the ○ must be serially searched. In the bottom left example, the **T** pops out, but on the right it must be serially searched.

search of combinations of features, such as circles and lines, will lead to the target. This is illustrated clearly in the lower panels of Figure 20.1 where it is a conjunction of shading and form that will identify the target.

In principle, it should be possible to develop feature processing with practice. Treisman and her colleagues have studied this possibility intensively, but they conclude that although practice can speed up feature processing, it remains dependent upon specific associations between features and upon serial processing. Feature processing appears to be an innate property of the visual system.

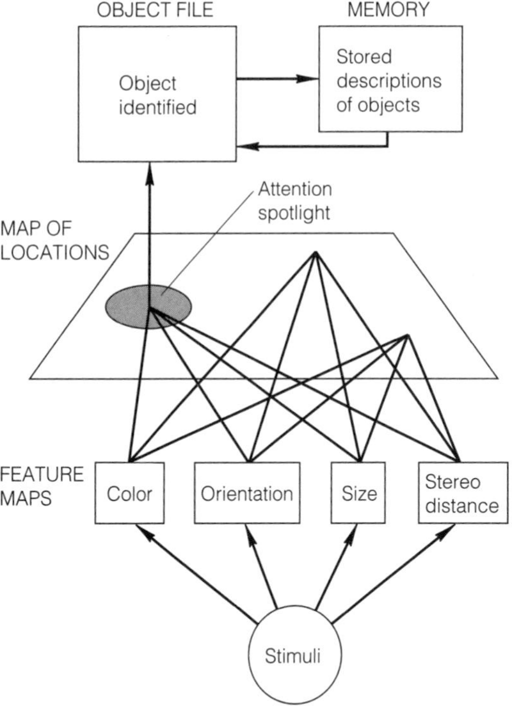

FIGURE 20.2. Treisman's model of visual searching. She proposes that early vision encodes some simple and useful properties of a scene in a number of feature maps, which may preserve the spatial relations of the visual world but do not themselves make spatial information available to subsequent processing stages. Instead, focused attention selects and integrates the features present at particular locations. At later stages, the integrated information serves to create and update files on perceptual objects. In turn, the file contents are compared with descriptions stored in a recognition network. (After Treisman, 1985.)

Treisman has explained her results with the perceptual model illustrated in Figure 20.2. A stimulus is registered in area V1 and is broken down into separate features (see Chapter 11 for more details). This information is then serially processed in parallel pathways (for example, to V3, V4, V5). One feature of the later processing is that at some point different features of the object are integrated or conjoined. Since no visual area specifically does this job, it is necessary to process bits of the visual world serially, presumably by using some sort of reentry process (see Chapter 8). Thus, the idea is that attention is directed to each location in turn and that features present in the same "fixation" of attention are combined to form a single object. Posner and Raichle suggest that, in a sense, the attentional process provides the "glue" that integrates features into a unitary object. Once the features have been put together, the object can be perceived and held in memory as a unit.

One implication of Treisman's model is that the spotlight focuses sharply on certain aspects of the sensory world, but this seems unlikely. Rather, it seems more reasonable that there is a sharp image at the center of the spot of attention, with a gradual degradation of attention around the central spot (Figure 20.3).

A clear prediction from Treisman's theory is that neurons in the visual areas outside V1, and probably outside V2, should respond differentially depending upon whether attention is focused on the corresponding receptive field or not. In the next section, we consider evidence that this is indeed the case.

NEUROPHYSIOLOGICAL EVIDENCE OF ATTENTION

Any experiment purporting to demonstrate that the responses of neurons are determined by the focus of attention must meet one important crite-

FIGURE 20.3. Illustration of the fuzzy edges of the attentional spotlight in searching for a face in a crowd. At the focus of attention, the face is analyzed in detail. As we move away from the central focus, the detail is degraded.

rion. The *same stimulus* must activate a neuron at one time and not at another. This condition rules out the possibility that the changes in neural activity are somehow related to the actual features of the stimulus. Consider the following experiment. Moran and Desimone trained monkeys on a modified version of the matching-to-sample task (see Figure 14.8). The monkey's task was to hold a bar while it gazed at a fixation point on a screen. A sample stimulus (for instance, a vertical red bar) appeared briefly at one location in the receptive field, followed about 500 msec later by another stimulus at the same location. When the test stimulus was identical to the sample, the animal was rewarded if it released the bar immediately. Each animal was trained to attend to stimuli presented in one particular part of the visual field and to ignore them in any other. In this way, the same visual stimulus could be presented to different regions of the neurons' receptive field, but the importance of the information varied with its location.

As the animals performed the task, the researchers recorded the firing of cells in area V4. Cells in V4 are color and form sensitive, so different neurons responded to different conjunctions of features. Thus, a given cell might respond to one stimulus (for example, a horizontal green bar) and not to another (for example, a vertical red bar). These stimuli were presented either in the correct location or in an incorrect location for predicting reward. The critical result is the behavior of the neuron in response to the effective stimulus. When the effective stimulus was presented in the correct location, the cell was highly active. However, when the *same stimulus* was presented in an incorrect location, the cell was not responsive. Hence, it appears that when attention was focused upon a place in the visual world, the cell responded only to appropriate stimuli in that place. Ineffective stimuli remained so regardless of where they were in the visual field. Moran and Desimone considered the possibility that visual areas activated earlier (V1) or later (TE) in visual processing might also show attentional effects. Cells in V1 did not show attentional effects, whereas cells in TE did. The failure to find attentional effects in V1 is important for Treisman's theory because it implies that V1 acts to encode simple properties of a scene, whereas areas activated later in visual processing have different functions.

Moran and Desimone's results were also theoretically important to the general issue of space. The cells showing constraints in spatial attention were in V4 and TE, which are both part of the object-recognition stream. Thus, neurons in this system are coding spatial location. This is not consistent with the notion that the dorsal visual stream is for spatial information and the ventral stream is for object recognition. Rather, it is consistent with the idea of Goodale and Milner that both the dorsal and ventral streams of visual processing play a role in perceiving space, but the role is different. Note that the animal did not have to make a movement in space. If it did, we would predict that cells in the posterior parietal cortex would be sensitive to attentional demands. In fact, Mountcastle and his colleagues have reported just such results. These cells are active when animals reach to obtain an object, such as food, but are not active when the same movements are made for other reasons. Notice that these cells are not responding to the features of the stimuli but rather to the movements needed to get to it. Thus, there appear to be two types of visual attention, one related to the selection of stimuli and the other to the selection and direction of movements.

Attention can affect neurons in other ways as well. Kahneman has noted that perceptual systems do not always work at peak efficiency. One explanation for this observation is that we can only process so much information at once, and if we are overloaded there is a "bottleneck" in processing. Kahneman prefers a different explanation. He proposes that there is a limit on the capacity to perform mental activity and that this limited capacity must be allocated among concurrent activities. Thus, for Kahneman, one aspect of attention is the amount of effort that is directed toward a particular task. If a task is routine (such as driving on a road without much traffic), little attentional capacity is used and the driver can carry on a conversation. When the driver is turning across traffic at a busy intersection, however, more mental capacity must be shifted to the task and the conversation is briefly interrupted. Some process must be active to shift attention to different tasks in response to changes in task demands.

Spitzer, Desimone, and Moran wondered if cells in V4 might vary their firing characteristics depending upon the amount of effort needed to solve a particular visual problem. They trained monkeys much as they did in their earlier experiment, except that they varied the difficulty of the task. This was done by taking advantage of the fact that cells respond to a range of stimuli. Thus, a given cell responds optimally to a given orientation and color (Figure 20.4A). This tuning is not precise, however, and the cell will respond to orientations and colors that approximate the preferred one. In the Spitzer experiment, the authors reasoned that it should be easy for a cell to discriminate between a stimulus within its preferred orientation or color and a stimulus outside this orientation or color. For example, an easy discrimination would be one in which the test stimulus is orthogonal (oriented at 90°) to the sample (Figure 20.4B). In contrast, a difficult discrimination would be one in which both stimuli are within the range of a cell's preferred orientations —say, if the difference in orientation were only 22.5°, which is within the acceptable range for most cells. The performance by the animals con-

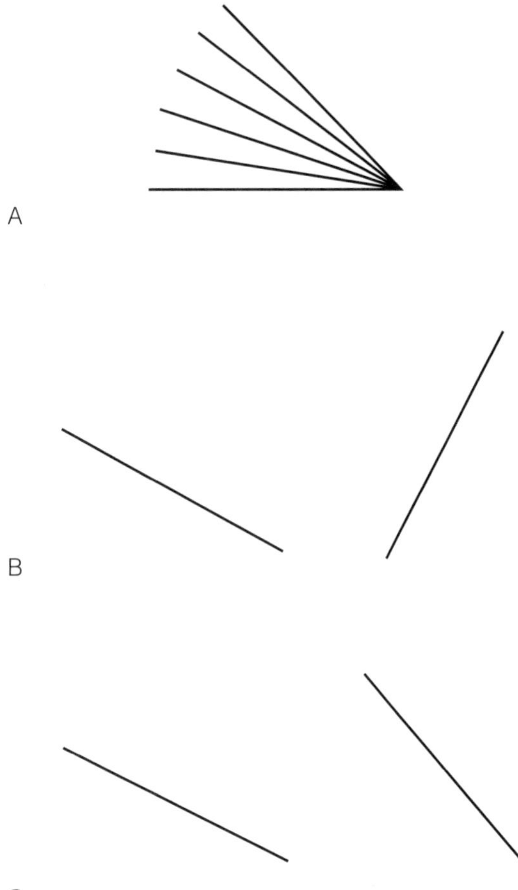

FIGURE 20.4. *A*. Range of line orientations to which a given cell will respond. *B*. An example of an easy discrimination. The left line is within the orientation preference of the cell, but the right line is outside this range. *C*. An example of a difficult discrimination. The two lines are both within the range of orientations to which a cell will normally respond.

firmed that the finer discrimination was more difficult; they made 93% versus 73% correct responses in the easy and difficult conditions, respectively. It is the change in response characteristics of the V4 cells that is intriguing. First, in the difficult condition the cells increased their firing rate by an average of about 20%. Second, the tuning characteristics of the cells changed. Thus, whereas the cells tolerated an orientation difference of about 81° in the easy condition, the same cells now became more selective about which stimuli they would respond to, the orientation range being reduced to 53°. Thus, it appears that the more difficult task required increased attention to the differences between the stimuli, and this was reflected in a change in the stimulus selectivity of neurons in V4. Stated differently, both the behavioral and the electrophysiological results indicate that increasing the amount of effort needed to perform a perceptual task can affect how information is processed in the visual system. These results contrast with those of an earlier experiment by Spitzer, Desimone, and Moran in which the spatial location was critical. In that experiment, spatial attention caused the suppression of responses to unattended stimuli, whereas in the second experiment, increased effort appeared to enhance responses and sharpen selectivity for attended stimuli.

Of course, it is not known *how* this attentional effect can alter the cell's activity. One possibility is that a signal from the pulvinar of the thalamus plays some role. Cells in the pulvinar also respond to visual stimuli in a way that implies some type of selection process. Petersen and his colleagues found that neurons in the pulvinar respond more vigorously to stimuli that are targets of behavior than they do to the same stimuli that are not targets of behavior. Since the pulvinar complex projects to the posterior parietal cortex, temporal cortex, and prefrontal cortex, it may play some role in directing Treisman's "spotlight" to different parts of space. If this is true, then one would predict that interfering with the activity in the pulvinar would disrupt spatial attention. In fact, Petersen and his colleagues have shown that monkeys with chemical blockage of the pulvinar show difficulty in tasks requiring covert orienting. They trained monkeys to fixate on a dot, and when the animal detected a stimulus elsewhere it was to release a bar to obtain reward. In cases where an irrelevant visual stimulus was shown in the same visual field prior to the probe stimulus presentation, the monkeys responded more quickly. It was as though the irrelevant stimulus "primed" the brain to expect another stimulus in the same region. In contrast, when the irrelevant stimulus was presented to the opposite visual field (and therefore acted as a signal in the wrong direction), the monkeys' reaction time slowed. These results are identical to those described for a similar task in our discussion of parietal lobe patients (see Chapter 12). Petersen slowed normal neuronal activity in the pulvinar by injecting muscimol, which increases inhibition, and the animals performed as if they did not respond to the irrelevant cue. That is, when the valid cue was presented they were slower than control, but when an invalid cue was presented they were faster than control. The pulvinar receives visual input from the colliculus, which is known to play a role in orienting to visual information, so it may be a collicular-pulvinar spotlight that is at work. Of course, we are still left with the problem of how the collicular-pulvinar spotlight is turned on. At present, we must be satisfied with the observation that knowledge of the task demands can somehow alter the activity of neurons in the visual system. This is the essence of a top-down process.

We often search for particular objects or perhaps for a familiar face in a crowd. This type of visual search has several task demands. First, we must compare what we perceive as we scan with some kind of memory representation of the search object. Second, we must have some way to select an object from among others in the world. A study by Chelazzi and colleagues addressed these processes by recording neurons in area TE of monkeys during a visual-search task. The animals were presented with an initial cue followed by an array of two to five test items. The monkey was required to make an eye movement to the item in the test array that matched the cue (Figure 20.5). The stimuli used for any cell were chosen such

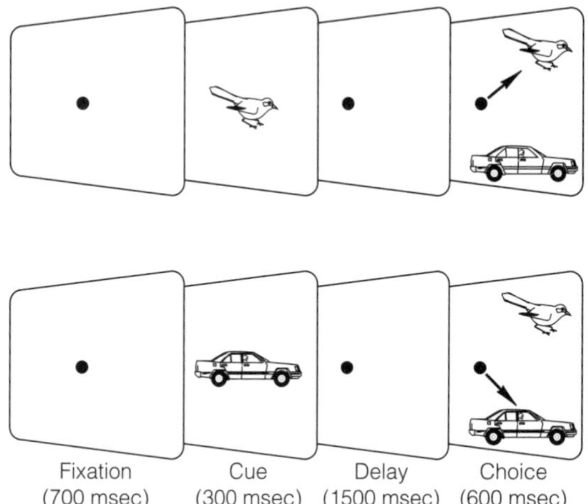

FIGURE 20.5. Visual search task for the rhesus monkey. The monkey is required to remember the cue stimulus during the delay interval and then make an eye movement to the matching item in the test array. (After Chelazzi, Miller, Duncan, and Desimone, 1993.)

that one stimulus was effective in driving the cell but the other stimuli in the array were not. Thus, the monkey could be presented with a cue that drove the cell or one to which the cell was unresponsive. The critical result was in the test phase. If a monkey was presented with an ineffective cue stimulus and then with an array of stimuli including the effective cue, the cell behaved in a curious manner. It initially responded, reflecting the presence of its preferred stimulus, but it then suppressed its response, *even though the stimulus was still present in the receptive field*. In other words, the cell appeared to notice the stimulus, but since it was not to be attended to, it shut off. It is likely that the cell itself doesn't "choose" to shut off but rather that this behavior is a result of inhibition from cells responsive to the correct target. Such behavior could result if there were a memory trace of the activity of the cells that were responsive to the target, so that when they were presented with the same target again, their response was enhanced. A similar logic could be applied to cells looking for a face in a crowd. There must be some type of memory trace of the appropriate face that enhances the activity of the TE neurons that encounter the face. Other cells responding to other faces are inhibited, and the eyes are directed to the appropriate target. Of course, TE does not actually move the eyes. This is accomplished by cells in the frontal eye fields. A reasonable prediction is that neurons in the frontal eye fields also should be suppressed if they would move the eyes to the incorrect target. Schall and Hanes have recently shown this to be the case.

PET STUDIES OF ATTENTION

One place to start in our search for neural correlates of attention in normal humans is with a task similar to those used for Posner's parietal patients or Petersen's pulvinar monkeys. Corbetta and colleagues designed the experiment illustrated in Figure 20.6A. A row of boxes ran across a screen viewed by subjects who fixated on another box located just above the row. The task required subjects to maintain fixation on the upper box and to do one of two things: (1) to shift attention as a light moved from box to box across the row, or (2) to maintain fixation on the central box and to ignore the movement of the light. Thus, as in the Moran and Desimone study of monkeys, the stimuli presented were identical but the attentional requirements were different. The results were clear. Relative to the fixed attention task, attending to the moving light increased activation in the posterior parietal cortex (Figure 20.6B). Furthermore, if the moving light was presented to the left visual field, only the right parietal cortex was activated; whereas if the moving light was presented to the right visual field, both the left and right parietal cortexes were activated. In other words, the right parietal cortex was active when the stimulus was either in the left or right visual field, but the left parietal cortex was active only when the stimulus was in the contralateral (right) visual field. In addition, there were two distinct foci of activation in the right parietal lobe, one corresponding to the left visual field and one to the right. These findings may explain why pa-

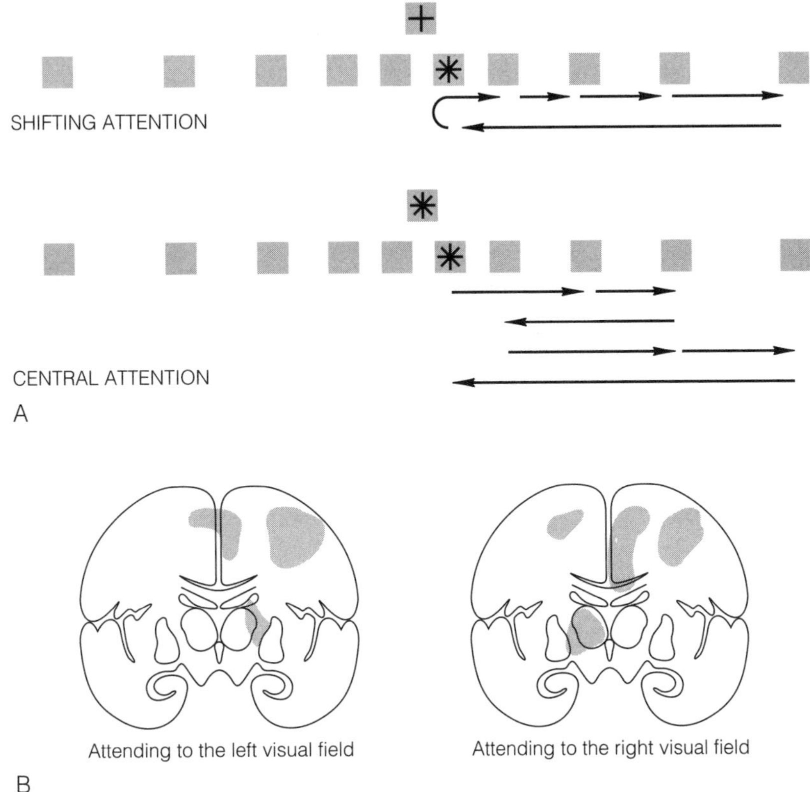

FIGURE 20.6. Model of the shifting attention experiment of Corbetta et al. *A*. In the top condition (shifting attention), the subject must fixate on the cross hair and covertly shift attention to follow the light from box to box in the pattern shown by the arrows. In the bottom condition (central attention), the subject must fixate on the central light and ignore the moving light in the boxes. *B*. A summary of PET scans for the shifting attention task reveals that compared to the central attention task, there is increased activation of the parietal cortex. The left parietal lobe is activated only when the stimulus is in the left visual field, whereas the right parietal lobe is activated when the stimulus is in either visual field. Note also that the activation is more extensive in the right parietal lobe. (After Corbetta, Miezin, Shulman, and Petersen, 1993.)

tients with right posterior parietal-temporal lesions show greater neglect than patients with left hemisphere lesions. In the absence of the left parietal cortex, there is still a representation of the right visual field, which is in the right parietal cortex. In the absence of the right parietal cortex, there is no representation of the left visual field in the parietal cortex, and the region is neglected.

An intriguing aspect of this study is that there was no activation in V4, as one might predict from the electrophysiological studies of monkeys. One explanation is that the task did not require an integration of different stimulus properties but simply a record of where something was. This possibility was confirmed in a parallel study by the same authors. In this case the researchers presented the subjects with a screen with a small white spot in the center. A stimulus was presented for 400 msec, followed by a second stimulus 200 msec later. Each stimulus was a spatially random distribution of 30 elements, all of which were of identical shape and color and were moving horizontally as a coherent sheet to the left or right (Figure 20.7). The shape, color, and/or speed of movement might be changed in the second stimulus. The subject had two different tasks. In one, which the authors called the "selective attention" task, the subjects were to report if the two sets of stimuli differed for a specific stimulus feature (for example, color). In the other, called the "divided attention" task, the subjects were instructed to indicate if a change occurred in *any* feature. The fundamental difference between the two tasks is that the selective task requires the adoption of a specific mental set for a specific feature, whereas the divided task does not. The authors posited that the selective task would require more focused attention and the divided task would require more memory. Therefore, they predicted a different pattern of cortical activation in the two tasks. PET measurements showed that the selective attention task activated specific visual regions, the region varying with the feature detected. Thus, attention to color activated a region probably corresponding to V4, whereas attention to shape activated areas corresponding to V3 and TE. The selective task also activated the insula, the posterior thalamus (probably pulvinar), the superior colliculus, and the orbital frontal cortex. In contrast, the divided attention task activated a mutually exclusive set of areas. Thus, although there was no activation of visual areas beyond the activation upon passive presentation of the stimuli, there was activation of the anterior cingulate and dorsolateral prefrontal cortex. The important point is that the stimuli were identical in the two conditions even though the task was different. The selective attention task led to increased activation of visual areas that presumably were recruited to solve the task.

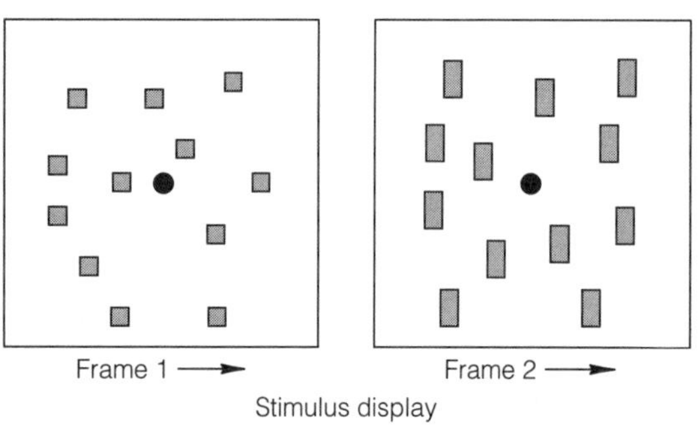

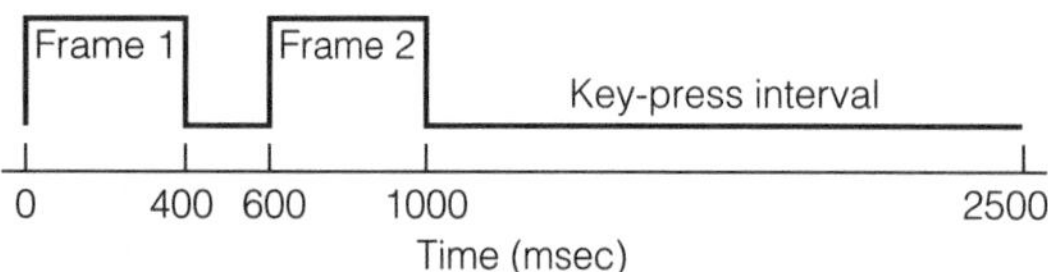

FIGURE 20.7. Stimulus display in the study by Corbetta et al. The task is to determine if there was a change in a particular feature (such as color, shape, speed of movement), which was the selective attention task, or a change in any feature, which was the divided attention task. (After Corbetta, Miezin, Dobmeyer, Shulman, and Petersen, 1991.)

Taken together, the results of the Corbetta studies show that different cortical areas are activated in different attentional tasks. The parietal cortex is activated for attention to location, and the occipital-temporal cortex is activated for attention to features such as color and form. Näätänen has summarized analogous, although somewhat more complex, results from ERP studies. The PET and ERP data are thus concordant with the single unit studies in monkeys and lead to the conclusion that different regions of the posterior cortex are involved in different aspects of selective attention. We will return to these different aspects shortly.

NETWORKS OF ATTENTION

Let us recap what we have learned. First, the electrophysiological evidence from monkeys shows three different types of attentional mechanisms: one in the parietal cortex that enhances spatial attention; one in the visual and posterior temporal cortex that selects object features; and one in the inferior temporal region that selects objects themselves. In addition, there are cells in the frontal eye fields that select movements. Second, PET studies show parallel results in human subjects. Third, many studies have shown that regions of the frontal lobe are also activated during response selection. In particular, there is activation of the anterior cingulate cortex in divided attention tasks (see the previous section), as well as in tasks requiring response selection (see Chapter 14) or verb generation (see Chapter 17). In addition, there is activation of the premotor and prefrontal regions in specific tasks. Recall that the divided attention task just discussed activated the dorsolateral prefrontal cortex. Similarly, in PET studies performed during verb-generation tasks (see Chapter 17), it was found that verb generation activates the inferior frontal cortex. Our task is to put these observations together.

Posner has proposed that when we search for objects in the world, our focus of attention shifts from one location to another. To do this, attention must disengage from the current object of interest, move to a new object, and engage it. In an environment that is visually cluttered, another system that inhibits or filters out irrelevant information may be required. The posterior parietal system may function to disengage, move, or engage attention. Indeed, damage to the posterior parietal cortex impairs performance on any task that requires this ability (see Chapter 12). In contrast, the focusing of attention on features of the object engaged may be a function of the posterior temporal regions. Damage to these regions produces agnosias, which must reflect, in part, a deficit in attending to specific features of stimuli. In a sense, we are suggesting two spotlights; the first highlights a place in the world to analyze, and the second selects specific features for analysis.

Posner and Petersen have proposed that there is a second type of attentional system. This one is based in the frontal lobe and is closely related to the short-term memory functions of the frontal lobe. Posner and Petersen cite four lines of evidence for an anterior attentional system:

1. Various frontal lobe sites, especially the anterior cingulate, are active in a variety of tasks, both those involving perceptual demands and those involving response selection. Consider the divided attention task described earlier. The subject must detect a feature and then respond. This requires a working memory of what the features are and a recognition that one of the features has been detected. Posner and Raichle emphasize the importance of feature detection in response selection. Frontal lobe patients are notorious for doing one thing and saying another, as though they do not detect the incongruity.

2. The involvement of frontal lobe structures is proportional to the attentional effort. Thus, as the number of targets in a target-monitoring task increases, the involvement of frontal lobe regions increases.

3. The frontal lobe involvement in response selection is inversely related to practice. For example, in Chapter 17 we considered a verb-generation task in which subjects had to generate an action word in response to a noun (for instance, "cake-eat"). If subjects practiced on specific nouns before the test, the insular cortex was active but the frontal areas were not.

4. Evidence from studies in both human patients and laboratory animals confirm that the frontal lobe has an important role in working memory for both sensory events and movements.

Posner and Petersen call their frontal lobe attentional system an "executive attentional system" and make the bold proposal that the contents of consciousness consist of the information being operated on by this executive system. In their view, the frontal lobe is in charge of programming mental operations. Thus, it must play a major role in the activation of the selective attention systems of the posterior cortex.

The direct evidence in favor of the Posner and Petersen model is not overwhelming, but their proposal does provide an interesting way to think about the brain systems involved in consciousness. One feature of cortical evolution is that as each new sensory channel was added, there was a corresponding development of the frontal lobe. It may very well be that this increase is necessary for the brain to operate on the sensory world and make sense of it. In the absence of frontal lobe structures, or in the event of dysfunction (such as schizophrenia), behavior would become muddled because conscious awareness of what the overwhelming sensory inputs mean and how they relate one to another would be lacking.

One feature of attention that we have not yet considered in this framework is the conscious selection of movements. We consider this next.

IMAGES

When freestyle ski jumpers stand at the starting position, they spend some time going through contortions, moving their feet and their arms. They seem to be rehearsing the upcoming jump. Divers, in contrast, stand very still and then jump. Since they are going to make similar movements, and their style is evaluated from the time they arrive on the diving board, they presumably must rehearse without making movements. What is it that goes on in the brains of these representative athletes? They describe their activities as preparing, focusing, and rehearsing. Are they examining the layout of the jump or dive visually? Are they practicing the movements? Are they comparing the movements that they are going to make with the conditions of the moment? An early theory of what occurs during this preparation is that people, in their heads, adjust sensory and motor events so that the right outcome will occur. Although people may report that this is exactly what they are doing, psychologists invariably argue that there is no little person in their heads to do such adjusting.

To escape the problem of the "little person in the head" various proposals have been advanced and abandoned over the past 200 years. The **theory of afference** suggested that sensations, presumably arising from the environment and the act of moving, guide behavior. The source of this notion was the idea that the brain is a passive recipient of impulses and is not capable of generating spontaneous activity. The **theory of efference,** which replaced the afference theory, suggested that the sensations of movement arise from the perception of the nervous system's activity in generating a movement. The problem with both of these theories is the difficulty they had in explaining how errors of movement are corrected. The problem can be seen more clearly in the strength of the theory that replaced them, the **theory of reafference** (**theory of corollary discharge**). According to this theory, when a movement is initiated, it leaves a trace or record of what the intended movement should be. As the movement is performed, it generates a second record that can be compared with the first. If the movement is not performed correctly, the error can be detected by comparing the two records and then making an adjustment on the next attempt.

The theory of reafference was generated separately by Roger Sperry and E. von Holst. Sperry rotated the eyes of frogs so that the perceived location of an object was in a direction opposite to its true location. The rotation caused the frogs to move in a direction opposite to the real location of the object. Von Holst asked how an animal could disentangle its own movement from the movements of objects around it; that is, how does one distinguish self-movement from object movement? Both Sperry's experiments and von Holst's questions led to the conclusion that to move successfully, an animal must generate a record of its movement and use this record as a reference to locate or plot the movements of other objects.

The idea that an animal generates a record of its movements, separate from the activity that generates the movement or the sensory information generated by the movement, suggests that there is a central process or representation that contains schemas of movements. The function of sensations produced by movements is to update and correct the central representation. A simple experiment will illustrate this point. If goggles containing prisms that displace objects 15° to the right are worn by subjects, they will misreach the first few times they try to grasp an object. After a number of trials, they correct the movement. When they remove the goggles, they misreach in the opposite direction and again correct the reach after a number of tries. People can correct for massive distortions produced by goggles, including left-right reversals and dorsal-ventral reversals. The important point is that even though sensory information is grossly misleading, the system that represents and instructs movements is very good at compensating for the sensory distortions. A still more dramatic example of the reconstructive powers of the brain systems that generate representations is given by Rock and Harris. They created a situation in which subjects manipulated an oblong object while what they thought they saw being manipulated was a round object. After a number of trials, the subjects reported, upon touching the oblong object without looking at it, that it was round. The now false tactile representation was derived from visual information.

There have been a number of attempts to characterize the properties of central representations or images. That is, what do they look like? Experiments designed to answer this question examine whether the formation and topography of representations, and changes in them, match similar features of the real world. For example, a person asked to take one die of a pair of dice and rotate it so that the numbers that are visible match those of its mate will manipulate it several times until the two are matched. The manipulation involves a number of movements and takes a certain amount of time. When asked to perform the same task mentally, the person appears to require the same number of mental movements and to take about the same amount of time. Similarly, if people are asked to imagine walking a certain distance, they take about the same amount of time and make the same number of steps as they would to walk the same distance in reality. Experiments such as these suggest that images have very much the same features as real movements.

One criticism that can be made of equating the real dimensions of movements with those of representations on the basis of the experiments described above is that subjects have some knowledge of the tasks and so can generate appropriate parallels. This criticism does not seem to be entirely valid, because when subjects are given tasks that contain answers they do not know in advance, similar results are obtained. For example, when people reach for an object that is close by or for one that is farther away, they take the same length of time. When they write their name in small script and in large script, the times are again equivalent. A priori, most subjects do not know this and, if asked, will say that the times required for the tasks are different. Nevertheless, when people are asked to imagine reaching different distances or writing their name in letters of different sizes, the times that they report for the tasks are similar to the times actually required to perform those tasks. This result strengthens the idea that such features as the time and topography of movement images parallel those of actual movements.

The Neural Basis of Images

Where are images located? There are three possibilities: (1) The very same structures that produce movements could produce images. (2) Only a portion of the structures that produce movements could produce images. (3) There are completely independent areas of the brain that produce movements and produce images. Surprisingly, whereas it once might have been thought that the third possibility was most likely, at present most of the debate surrounding these three possibilities considers only the first two as serious options.

Roland performed one of the first experiments in which imagined movements and real movements were compared while regional cerebral blood flow (rCBF) was monitored. When subjects imagined a series of finger movements, the premotor cortex was active. When they performed the movements, both the premotor cortex and the motor cortex were active. This experiment demonstrated that imagined and real movements are represented in the premotor cortex. It also favored the second possibility: that only a portion of an area involved in making a movement is involved in forming images of that movement. Similar results favoring this position come from case studies of patients with visual system lesions, including one study of a patient who could recognize visual patterns but could not form visual images of them. Other favorable results, as described by Moscovitch and coworkers, are of patients who have severe trouble identifying real objects but have preserved visual imagery. These case studies suggest that earlier cortical visual levels (for example, areas V1–V5) are involved in perception, while only later visual levels are involved in forming images.

Roland and Gulyás have presented further evidence that it is the higher-level cortexes that are involved in both memory and images. They have presented auditory, motor, and a variety of visual tasks to subjects and measured rCBF. In all their experiments, the areas activated were in the association cortexes of the temporal, parietal, and frontal cortex. Lower-level sensory areas were not activated, nor were primary motor areas. Roland and Gulyás favor the idea that the higher-level areas form a distributed system whose function is also to represent memory. These memories do not contain the dimensions of time and space, but the simultaneous activation of a number of regions could generate these properties. For Roland and Gulyás, images are activated memories.

There is also evidence against this view. There are three kinds of evidence from studies of the visual system that favor the idea that the same structures involved in perception are involved in forming images in the absence of visual stimulation. This position does not disagree that higher visual areas are involved in imagery but argues that lower areas of the visual system are also involved. Thus, during normal viewing, visual stimulation successively excites lower visual areas and then higher visual areas; whereas during imagining, higher visual areas activate lower visual areas through reentrant fibers so that the same sets of neurons are activated in both perception and imaging. First, Farah and coworkers describe the patient M. G. S., before and after the occipital cortex was unilaterally removed as a treatment for epilepsy. She was asked to imagine walking toward an object, such as a mouse or a dog, or to imagine an approaching car. The patient was to indicate when the object completely filled the visual field (this would occur when the person was closer to the mouse than to the dog). Prior to surgery, the response of the patient was similar to that of control subjects, but after surgery the visual angle was reduced significantly relative both to the normal subjects and to her preoperative results (the objects now filled her visual field when she was farther away from them, presumably because her visual field was smaller). This finding is consistent with the idea that images have a topographical organization in the visual areas and that the area available to contain an image is reduced after loss of the primary visual cortex. Second, there are a number of rCBF studies that find activation in primary visual areas during imagining. Third, an additional kind of evidence that could be taken to support the commonality of structures involved in perception and imagining comes from studies of eye movements. During viewing, the eyes make saccades in a typical way to catch key elements of the stimulus. Norton and Stark have reported that the same kinds of eye movements occur when looking at an object and during later imagining of the same object.

At present, research cannot distinguish between the position that only higher-level structures are involved in imagining and the position that the same set of structures involved in viewing are also involved in imagining. The disagreement between studies using rCBF may be related to differences in the kinds of tasks presented to the subjects, differences in the methods used to subtract baseline blood-flow activity in control conditions and test conditions, or even differences in subject populations. With respect to the last point, we were surprised to learn from a colleague, who is internationally known for his work in visual perception, that he has no idea what visual imagery is because he is unable to experience it. We both asserted, to his surprise, that we had no difficulty forming visual images. An additional problem with studies comparing perception and imaging relates to quantifying what it is that is seen. When two viewers look at a scene, they can come to reasonable agreement about what they are seeing. When they compare their mental images of the same scene, they have no reliable way to confirm that they are imagining the same thing.

Kinds of Images

Is there more than one type of image? If we return to our ski jumpers, we can see that there are at least two different ways that they can imagine their jump. They can use a process that has been referred to as **internal imagery.** This is a first-person process in which they imagine that it is themselves making the movement. Alternatively, they can use what is called **external imagery,** in which they see some person, perhaps themselves or perhaps someone else, making the jump. In the first case, the imagery that they have is of the movements that they themselves will make; the anticipatory movements that they make during the imagery presumably reflect the movements that they will make when they jump. This is somewhat like practicing a golf swing before hitting the ball, without actually making the swing. In the second case, they are imagining themselves or some other person. They see that person, they see the jump, and they see the surrounding area. Furthermore, the view that they have can change at will. It is as though they are actually watching some other person jump or are watching a jump on television.

The properties of the two kinds of images are quite different, although both are images of movement and both can represent the upcoming jump. Jeannerod refers to the first kind of imagery as motor imagery; it is the self in action. The second kind of imagery is really the imagery of objects: a jumper, a jump, the surrounding area. To gain an idea of how the two differ, consider the following example. A coach demonstrates a basketball shot to a player. The player watches and forms an image of the movements that the coach has made. The player then tries the shot. As the player does so, the coach (mentally, and perhaps with a little muscle tensing and grimacing) makes the same shot along with the player. If the player succeeds the coach gives a little cheer, and if the player misses the coach groans and they begin again. The two kinds of imagery differ in another way. When the player imagines the coach's movements, the image is created without muscle tension, effort, or exertion. When the coach imagines the player's shot, the image includes tension, effort, and exertion, as if the coach were actually taking the shot.

Images of the movements used in sports are relatively simple. They are movements that the participant has practiced and viewed hundreds of times. People form other images as well, images that are more complex and that can be unique in some way. Consider the following example. You need a book on bats. You look up the catalogue number on your computer and then set off to the library to get the book. On the way to the library you meet a friend who wants to know where you are going. You explain. You both talk about bats, and then you continue on your way. When you get to the library, you find that you have forgotten the catalogue number. You look it up. When you get to the stacks you find that the book is not there. The librarian tells you that the book is checked out and it is impossible to get it back. In this example, you have an image of a goal but no image of the movements you must make or the terrain you must traverse to reach the goal and certainly no image of where the book might be located. A goal image is very flexible in that it allows the incorporation of a variety of actions and subgoals. Other images that we have include thoughts, which are usually verbal images. That is, we talk to ourselves and hear the sounds of words, but we do not make sounds or movements. We also hum tunes and sing little songs to ourselves.

If we consider all the different kinds of images that we can form, it becomes clear that they closely parallel the things that we do. If we postulate that the images are formed by the same brain areas that produce actions, then each kind of image maps onto its own brain area. Thus, verbal images or thinking to oneself will use language phonemic circuitry in the left hemisphere, whereas images of music or spatial events will use right hemisphere structures that normally subserve those events. A dramatic example of the interplay between image and movement comes from an experiment by Di Pellegrino and his co-workers. They observed that neurons in the premotor cortex of a monkey would fire when it picked up a piece of food with its fingers. The same neurons fired when the experimenter made the same movements. These neurons did not fire when the monkeys or experimenters made other movements.

The portions of the brain involved in internal versus external imagery are not known, but it seems unlikely that the same brain regions produce the two kinds of images. Internal imagery of movements may use the object-location system (dorsal stream or parietal-frontal cortex system), and external imagery of movements in relation to objects may use the object-recognition system (inferior temporal-frontal cortex system). Images are probably also closely related to memories, as Roland suggests, in that they are in some ways active memories. Thus, each brain system is responsible for a triumverate of functions: action, memory, and imagining.

Apraxia

How we view the relationship among perceptions, actions, and images has some consequences for how we interpret various symptoms of brain damage. For example, if the same neural structures represent perception and images, then damage to those structures will have equivalent effects on perception and images. If the same structures are involved in movements and their images, then brain damage will have equivalent effects on actions and their images. If, on the other hand, images are formed in only a portion of the circuitry or in some other location, then damage to the structures involved in images will have different effects from damage to structures involved in perceptions or actions. Traditional attempts to categorize the effects of brain damage on movements have been based on the view that perceptions, memories, and images are distinct.

Stendhal coined the term **apraxia** in 1871, but the symptoms had first been described some 5 years earlier by Hughlings-Jackson. He noted that some aphasic patients were totally unable to perform voluntary movements, such as protruding the tongue, even though there was no evidence of weakness in the muscles involved and the tongue could be protruded as part of licking the lips after drinking. Although this symptom was subsequently noted by several authors, it was Liepmann who began the first detailed analysis of apraxic symptoms. In 1900 he reported the case of an aphasic man who was unable to carry out hand movements when asked to do so. Curiously, he could follow directions if the required movement was a whole-body movement, such as sitting down, and he could make *spontaneous* hand movements.

Liepmann's patient was an imperial councilor, 48 years of age, hospitalized on a psychiatry service for "dementia." He displayed a motor aphasia, but he also manipulated objects in a peculiar fashion and the difficulty he had was limited to his right arm. This arm was not paralyzed, its muscular power was preserved, and it performed most of the movements required of daily life. In contrast, when the patient was asked to perform with his right hand such gestures as pointing to his nose, making a fist, or showing how to use a harmonica or a brush, he failed completely. Even though he made movements indicating that he understood the instructions, he could not make the appropriate movements. If the right arm was held by the observer, all the movements were carried out by the left arm. When the gesture required the coordinated use of both hands, the right hand prohibited the execution of the gesture, even while the left hand was responding correctly. For example, when the patient attempted to pour water into a glass, the left hand took the pitcher in order to pour while the right hand was bringing the glass to the mouth.

Since neither the comprehension of the instructions nor the motor execution itself was defective, the difficulty that produced the apraxia had to be located at another level. Liepmann placed it between the sensory memories (which understood instructions) and the motor memories (which allowed the patient to transform the instructions into an action). Liepmann offered the hypothesis that the disconnection must have involved not only the association pathways in the interior of the left hemisphere but also the corpus callosum connecting the two hemispheres. The death of the imperial councilor allowed the hypothesis to be verified.

In the ensuing years, Liepmann studied many patients with this unusual movement problem, and in 1920 he proposed his now classic theory of apraxia, of which two important points are that (1) apraxia results from lesions of the left hemisphere or of the corpus callosum; and (2) there are several different types of apraxia, each most likely resulting from damage to a specific locus in the left hemisphere.

Strictly defined, *apraxia* means no action (the Greek *praxis* means action). The term apraxia, however, is hardly ever used in this strict sense; today it is used to describe all sorts of missing or inappropriate actions that cannot be clearly attributed to paralysis, paresis, or other more primary motor deficits on the one hand, or to lack of comprehension or motivation on the other. The modern concepts have their origins in Dejerine's reinterpretation of Liepmann. Because movements can be conceived as consisting of a goal, a series of subgoals, and a series of movements, there should also be different kinds of apraxia that are related to impairments in subcomponent of the actions. Consider the following patient:

> A woman with a biparietal lesion had worked for years as a fish-filleter. With the development of her symptoms, she began to experience difficulty in carrying on with her job. She did not seem to know what to do with her knife. She would stick the point in the head of a fish, start the first stroke and then come to a stop. In her own mind she knew how to fillet fish, but yet she could not execute the maneuver. The foreman accused her of being drunk and sent her home for mutilating fish.
>
> This same patient also showed another unusual phenomenon which might possibly be apraxic in nature. She could never finish an undertaking. She would begin a job, drop it, start another, abandon that one, and within a short while would have four or five uncompleted tasks on her hands. This would cause her to do such inappropriate actions as putting the sugar bowl in the refrigerator, and the coffee pot inside the oven. (Critchley, 1966, pp. 158–159)

If the fish-filleter could not conceive of the goal of filleting fish, she would perform the actions of filleting but they would be somewhat haphazard (as was the case). She would be classified as having **ideational apraxia.** (Remember the example of going to the library for a book on bats—ideational apraxia would prevent formation of this goal.) On the other hand, the fish-filleter might be able to form the goal of filleting a fish but not be able to form the subgoals of making the appropriate steps of filleting. In this case, she would be classified as having **ideomotor apraxia.** (In the library example, one might set off for the library but never arrive there because of an inability to make appropriate adjustments along the way.) Finally, if the fish-filleter could form the goal and know the movement sequence but not execute the movement, she would be classified as having **motor apraxia.** (In the library example, one could not get the catalogue number of the book because the fingers would not produce the movements to operate the keys of the computer, and possibly one would not be able to execute the walking movements.)

The classification of apraxia in this way is both a strength and a weakness. The classification appears to allow some obvious distinctions between knowing what to do and being able to do it, which is diagnostically useful. But it is also hard to make this distinction. For example, in the case of the fish-filleter, which kind of apraxia does she really have? When she stabs at the fish, is her problem not knowing what she wants to do or not knowing how to do it?

The several standard clinical tests often used to assess apraxia have similar weaknesses. For example, a patient might be asked to demonstrate the use of a particular object in its absence; to comb the hair or to hammer a nail. An apraxic person's response might be to do nothing or to use a part of the body as if it were the implement—to stroke a finger through the hair as if it were a comb or to hit the table with a fist as though it were a hammer. A normal person would pretend to be holding the comb or hammer. Another test of apraxia might be to ask a person to perform such symbolic movements as saluting or waving good-bye; the person might remain still or respond by making an unrecognizable movement. Although these tests are useful for on-the-spot assessments of apraxia, they do not permit objective quantification or more penetrating analysis. Clinical description presents a further difficulty, in that classifications of apraxia tend to be somewhat arbitrary. Also, new types of apraxia tend to proliferate not because actual new symptoms are discovered but because new questions are put to the patients or new ways of assessing the responses are developed. Finally, slight variations in lesion location might be used as justification that one apraxia differs from another.

Asymmetry of Movement Control

One of the most important proposals in Liepmann's theory of apraxia was that the left hemisphere plays a special role not shared by the right hemisphere in the control of movement. Another line of evidence supporting Liepmann's left hemisphere proposal comes from a study by Milner and her colleagues. They taught patients a complex series of arm movements prior to intracarotid sodium amobarbital injections. After the injections the patients were required to perform the movements. Only injections into the speaking hemisphere disrupted the movements, even though the movements were to be performed with the ipsilateral limb (controlled by the contralateral motor cortex that had not received an injection). Thus, the results of sodium amobarbital testing support the results of lesion studies in confirming a special role for the left hemisphere in the control of movement.

Given the left hemisphere's special control of many types of movement, one might ask whether the right hemisphere might not also control certain types of movements. In fact, there is a group of movements that can be selectively disrupted by right hemisphere lesions. These movements are used in tests in which a variety of components must be assembled to form an object. Examples of such tasks include (1) assembling pieces of a jigsaw puzzle to form a picture, (2) drawing a clock face or map, (3) copying a design composed of sticks of various lengths, (4) building bridges and towers with blocks, and (5) copying designs made up of differently colored blocks. Deficits on such tests are sometimes called constructional apraxias.

What is special about these constructional tasks? They all require that objects be ordered in extrapersonal space. Dealing with the spatial relations of objects is believed to be a function of the right hemisphere, especially of the right parietal cortex. Although left parietal lesions can also produce some similar deficits, these deficits may have a different cause: left hemisphere deficits may result from the person's inability to adjust the parts of his or her own body, rather than from the inability to adjust the position of an external object. This theoretically interesting proposition has yet to be clearly tested experimentally.

Neuroanatomical Basis of Apraxia

Classical neurological theory about the basis of apraxia is derived from a model originally proposed by Liepmann and subsequently popularized by Geschwind. Briefly, Liepmann proposed that the left parietal cortex (specifically around area 40) is the critical region for control of complex movement. This control would be mediated via the left frontal lobe and area 4 for the right side of the body. Disruption anywhere along this route in the left hemisphere would produce apraxia of the right limbs. Control over the limbs of the left side was proposed to be mediated through a series of cortico-cortical connections running from the left parietal cortex to the left frontal cortex and finally to the right frontal cortex via the corpus callosum. This model is often cited in psychology and neurology texts, but it has several serious shortcomings.

First, since there are clearly separable motor systems, each with unique anatomical input, models and studies of apraxia should consider different types of movements separately. The Liepmann-Geschwind model does not consider different movement types separately, nor have most studies of apraxic behaviors. It is possible that subtypes of apraxia can be distinguished on the basis of the system(s) disrupted. For example, Kolb and Milner compared the performance of patients with unilateral cortical excisions in copying both arm- and facial-movement sequences and did indeed find evidence of differential input of the frontal and the parietal cortex to the control of movement. Whereas left parietal lobe lesions significantly disrupted the copying of arm-movement sequences, these lesions had no significant effect on the copying of facial-movement sequences. In contrast, left frontal lobe lesions had relatively little effect on the copying of arm-movement sequences but produced larger impairment in the copying of facial-movement sequences. Similar results have also been obtained by Kimura in her study of stroke patients. An important additional finding by Kimura, however, was that the complexity of the movement is important. She found that patients with either left anterior or left posterior lesions performed more poorly than those with equivalent right hemisphere damage at tasks requiring the reproduction of a series of multiple oral or manual sequences. On a test requiring the reproduction of single facial movements, however, the only group significantly impaired was the left anterior group, whereas on single hand postures the only group impaired was the left posterior group.

Although it is widely assumed that the posterior parietal and prefrontal cortexes are the primary cortical regions involved in apraxia, patients with circumscribed cortical excisions do not typically demonstrate chronic abnormalities on standard clinical tests of apraxia. Compared with stroke patients, these patients have relatively minor impairments on tests of movement copying; even massive removals of the left hemisphere produce rather small movement-copying deficits when compared with the performance of persons with naturally occurring lesions. The implications of these results are important: the direct contributions to praxis of the prefrontal and the parietal cortex (and the connections between them) must be less than is generally implied from clinical-anatomical studies. The Liepmann-Geschwind model does not recognize the likely role of the basal ganglia and the thalamus in apractic syndromes. These regions provide major access routes for the cortex to influence motor output. The fact that cortical excisions have far lesser effects on praxis than do strokes, which presumably affect the basal ganglia and/or the thalamus as well as the cortex, implies that damage to subcortical structures may be essential in producing severe clinical apraxia.

Since the limbs and face, but not the hands, are connected via the corpus callosum, it should be determined whether or not the extent of bilateral apraxia is similar in tests of hand, finger, face, and limb movements. Although the importance of transcallosal connections has been noted in accounts of apractic syndromes, emphasis usually has been placed on the inability of the hand ipsilateral to the speaking hemisphere to perform movements in response to verbal commands. Few attempts have been made to describe carefully the abilities of the limbs, fingers, and face to perform particular movements. In one attempt to consider this problem, Milner and Kolb studied the ability of four patients, in whom the corpus callosum had been severed as a treatment for epilepsy, to copy meaningless sequences of arm or facial movements with either the left or the right hand. The data showed that the subjects were very badly impaired at copying these movements, even when compared with patients with left parietal lesions. Perhaps most surprisingly, in the arm movements the patients were equally impaired with either hand, a result that would not have been predicted from previous clinical-anatomical studies, and certainly not by the Liepmann-Geschwind model.

In summary, although the Liepmann model of the neuroanatomical basis of apraxia is useful, the central problem in classification of motor disorders still relates to the question of the separability of perceptions, representations, and actions. If each of these components of behavior has a separate representation, then it should be possible to see in the abnormalities of behavior the loss or sparing of one or the other function. If, on the other hand, perceptions, representations, and actions have a complete or partial commonality in their neural representation, then damage to a neural system will degrade all three components to much the same extent.

CONSCIOUSNESS

Consciousnes is usually defined in terms of what people think it is and what they think it is not. Hebb describes consciousness as equivalent to complex thought processes. Eccles refers to it as the process of knowing that one knows. These are reasonably representative definitions. Consciousness is thought not to be a unitary process. A human at different ages of life is not thought to be equally conscious at each age; young children and demented adults are usually not considered to experience the same type of consciousness as healthy adults. Indeed, part of the process of maturation is becoming conscious. Across the span of a day, consciousness in individuals varies as they pass through various states of sleep and waking. Humans are thought to have greater consciousness than other animals. Other animals are thought to vary in their degree of consciousness, too, with rather simple animals, such as ants, experiencing little consciousness and more complex animals, such as cats and dogs, displaying a great deal more consciousness. Brain damage can reduce or distort consciousness but does not eliminate it unless it produces coma and death. Interestingly, the first experimenters to analyze the function of the isolated spinal cord or of isolated nerve-muscle preparations referred to the conditions in which they could elicit movements as ministates of consciousness. It is unlikely that most modern experimenters would go that far.

Most definitions of consciousness exclude the conditions of simply being responsive to sensory stimulation or simply being able to produce movement. Thus, animals whose behavior is simply reflexive are not conscious. Similarly, the isolated spinal cord, although a repository for many reflexes, is not conscious. Machines that are responsive to sensory events and are capable of complex movements are not conscious. Many of the functions of normal humans, such as the beating of the heart, are not conscious processes. Similarly, many processes of the nervous system, including simple sensory processes and motor actions, are not conscious. Thus, consciousness involves processes that are different from all of these.

Consciousness is not defined as a single process. The implication of such terms as "levels of consciousness" or "degrees of consciousness" is that consciousness is composed of a number of processes. Similarly, Hebb's definition of consciousness as "complex thought processes" incorporates the notion of a number of relatively separate functions that together form consciousness. Jerison's view that the human brain achieved its current form not simply through growth but by the addition of new areas and connections is consistent with the view of consciousness as being built piece by piece through the addition of new processes. The idea that consciousness is a property of a single system or brain area receives no support from clinical studies of people who have suffered brain damage or cortical excisions. Brain damage can change, reduce, or limit consciousness, but there are no reports that individuals who have lost a certain restricted portion of the brain have lost their consciousness. For example, people who have a visual scotoma may no longer be conscious of what is in a portion of their visual field, but they still have visual consciousness. People who have lost all of their occipital cortex may no longer be conscious of visual events, but they are still conscious of the world through their other senses.

Francis Crick, a well-known geneticist, has written that the problem of consciousness does not receive its fair share of scientific attention. If consciousness is produced through the function of many independent systems, then it is not likely that an experimental assault on the problem of consciousness will be very productive. Rather, only the humdrum labor to determine how various systems work will lead to an understanding of consciousness. Indeed, it can be argued that consciousness is not an entirely mysterious process. There is a growing understanding of many of the systems of the brain, and this understanding reveals quite a lot about consciousness.

Some people have argued that certain processes are much more important for consciousness than others. It is often argued that language is essential to consciousness. Yet people who suffer from aphasia and who cannot articulate or understand words give every sign of consciousness and communicate feelings and needs in other ways. People who are mute and who have never learned to speak can care for themselves, can work, can interact with others, and are considered conscious by others. Some writers have suggested that the left hemisphere is essential for consciousness because it is the structural basis of language. Yet patients who have lost the left hemisphere are not described as having lost consciousness. Neither are patients who have lost the right hemisphere. Thus, neither the left nor the right hemisphere of itself is essential for consciousness. A number of writers have postulated that the hippocampus is the essential structure for consciousness because of its importance in the formation of memories. The patient H. M., who has had the medial temporal cortex surgically removed bilaterally and has dense anterograde amnesia, describes himself as being continually in a state of waking from a dream, but he is nonetheless quite conscious and can carry on intelligent conversations. Thus, neither the hippocampus nor the medial temporal lobe structures involved in memory are essential for consciousness.

The reason that no one structure or function can be equated with consciousness is that consciousness is a composite or a product of all cortical areas and their connections. Understanding the functions of various brain systems thus leads to an understanding of consciousness. Some of the important elements of brain function that lead to normal consciousness include (1) the property of spontaneity of brain activity, (2) a system that allows action in space, (3) a system that allows action in relation to objects, (4) a system that supports language, and (5) the division of function between the two hemispheres. Some of these elements are features of all nervous systems, whereas others are more characteristic of humans than of other animals.

The nervous system is always spontaneously active and is never quiescent. Even sleep is an active process that is produced by the action of certain brainstem nuclei. The activity of the brain is influenced, of course, by sensory events, but sensory events are not necessary for maintaining the brain's activity. In other words, the brain is not like a sailing ship, propelled by the wind at one time and becalmed at another. Rather, it is like a motorboat, which is active and is doing something whether or not the wind is blowing. All nervous systems appear to have this property, and it is this property that allows these systems to be receptive in anticipation of sensory events.

The nervous system is designed to move the body through space. All animals that move have nervous systems that, to some extent, subserve this function. In humans and most other animals with well-developed brains, there is also an ability to correct for sensory and motor errors. As we discussed earlier in this chapter, to correct for errors, the brain uses the process of reafference, through which it lays down a trace of the intended action and then compares the intended and actual movement. The process of reafference allows the nervous system to ask itself, "Is what I have done what I intended to do?" This property must be an important feature that allows the nervous system to be "self-conscious" as Eccles defines consciousness. The nervous system of larger-brained animals also produces movement in relation to objects. To do so, it must also use the process of reafference. Consider the following problem. A person is walking through a garden in which there are a variety of trees and plants (Figure 20.8A). She imagines that one tree would look especially good at the corner of her house, and she begins to think of buying such a tree. This is an everyday event, but there is a problem in the way we have constructed the situation. In reality,

FIGURE 20.8. *A*. When we look at the world, we place objects that we see there outside ourselves. When we think of one of those objects, we place it within ourselves. *B*. The real state of affairs is that both the objects we see and the objects we imagine are products of our brain. How do we separate them, then?

the garden and all of its trees are creations of the nervous system (Figure 20.8B). How does a person distinguish the tree images elicited by real trees from the images of trees that she imagines? There must be something in the properties of seen trees and imagined trees, perhaps something about the difference in their details, that allows them to be distinguished. The process of distinguishing real trees from imagined ones is like the process of reafference in the system for movement in space, in that it allows the nervous system to disentangle imagined from seen objects. The problems that arise when the nervous system loses this ability are illustrated by the hallucinations experienced by people who are subjected to sensory deprivation or people who suffer from schizophrenia.

In humans, the complex thought processes of which the nervous system is capable are increased by the ability to classify movements and objects with linguistic tags. They are further enhanced by the division of function of the two hemispheres. It is these factors that allow humans to be more conscious than other animals. Since there is growing evidence that the various systems of the brain can interact and "look at what the others are doing," it is becoming increasingly possible to imagine how complex thought processes can be equated with consciousness and how "self-consciousness" is possible.

SUMMARY

We still do not know exactly what attention, images, and consciousness are. It is now possible, however, to create theories and to suggest that they are functions of one or another brain region. It is also possible to create theories of how brain processes produce these phenomena. The important point of this chapter is that these processes are not epiphenomena, or properties that emerge simply because the brain is complex. They are properties of the nervous system that allow it to achieve complex actions. The process of attention allows the nervous system to focus on aspects of the world and also on aspects of the brain itself. The process of imagining allows the nervous system to represent places and objects so that it can reach those places and obtain those objects. The process of consciousness is essential for distinguishing real movements from mental movements, real objects from mental objects, and ongoing events from memories. It is therefore essential to the construction of what we believe is reality.

REFERENCES

Anderson, J. R. Automaticity and the ACT theory. *American Journal of Psychology* 103:165–180, 1992.

Bragh, J. A. The ecology of automaticity: Toward establishing the conditions needed to produce automatic processing effects. *American Journal of Psychology* 105:181–200, 1992.

Brinkman, J., and H. G. J. M. Kuypers. Cerebral control of contralateral and ipsilateral arm, hand and finger movements in the split-brain rhesus monkey. *Brain* 96:653–674, 1973.

Carmon, A. Sequenced motor performance in patients with unilateral cerebral lesions. *Neuropsychologia* 9:445–449, 1971.

Carr, T. H. Automaticity and cognitive anatomy: Is word recognition automatic? *American Journal of Psychology* 105:201–238, 1992.

Chelazzi, L., E. K. Miller, J. Duncan, and R. Desimone. A neural basis for visual search in inferior temporal cortex. *Nature* 363:345–347, 1993.

Corbetta, M., F. M. Miezin, S. Dobmeyer, G. L. Shulman, and S. E. Petersen. Selective and divided attention during visual discrimination of shape, color, and speed: Functional anatomy by positron emission tomography. *Journal of Neuroscience* 11:2383–2402, 1991.

Corbetta, M., F. M. Miezin, G. L. Shulman, and S. E. Petersen. A PET study of visuospatial attention. *Journal of Neuroscience* 13:1202–1226, 1993.

Crick, F., and C. Koch. The problem of consciousness. *Scientific American* 267:152–159, 1992.

de Renzi, E., A. Pieczuro, and L. A. Vignolo. Oral apraxia and aphasia. *Cortex* 2:50–73, 1966.

de Renzi, E., A. Pieczuro, and L. A. Vignolo. Ideational apraxia: A quantitative study. *Neuropsychologia* 6:41–52, 1968.

Di Pellegrino, G., G. Fadiga, L. Fogassi, V. Gallese, and G. Rizzolatti. Understanding motor events: A neurophysiological study. *Experimental Brain Research* 91: 176–180, 1992.

Eccles, J. C. *The Human Psyche.* New York: Springer-Verlag, 1980.

Farah, M. J. *Visual Agnosia.* Cambridge, Mass.: MIT Press, 1990.

Geschwind, N. The apraxias: Neural mechanisms of disorders of learned movement. *American Scientist* 63:188–195, 1975.

Haaxma, R., and H. G. J. M. Kuypers. Intrahemispheric cortical connections and visual guidance of hand and finger movements in the rhesus monkey. *Brain* 98:239–260, 1975.

Hebb, D. O. *Essay on Mind.* Hillsdale, N.J.: Lawrence Earlbaum Associates, 1980.

Heilman, D. M., H. D. Schwartz, and N. Geschwind. Defective motor learning in ideomotor apraxia. *Neurology* 25:1018–1020, 1975.

Jeannerod, M. *The Brain Machine.* Cambridge, Mass.: Harvard University Press, 1985.

Jeannerod, M. The representing brain: Neural correlates of motor intention and imagery. *Behavioral and Brain Sciences* 17:187–245, 1994.

Jenkins, I. H., D. J. Brooks, P. D. Nixon, R. S. J. Frackowiak, and R. E. Passingham. Motor sequence learning: A study with positron emission tomography. *Journal of Neuroscience* 14:3775–3790, 1994.

Kahneman, D. *Attention and Effort.* Englewood Cliffs, N. J.: Prentice-Hall, 1973.

Kimura, D. *Neuromotor Mechanisms in the Evolution of Human Communication.* New York: Oxford University Press, 1993.

Kimura, D. The neural basis of language and gesture. In H. Avakina-Whitaker and H. A. Whitaker, eds. *Studies in Neurolinguistics.* New York: Academic, 1976.

Kimura, D. Acquisition of a motor skill after left-hemisphere damage. *Brain* 100:527–542, 1977.

Kimura, D. Left-hemisphere control of oral and brachial movements and their relation to communication. *Philosophical Transactions of the Royal Society of London* B298:135–149, 1982.

Kimura, D., and Y. Archibald. Motor functions of the left hemisphere. *Brain* 97:337–350, 1974.

Kolb, B., and B. Milner. Performance of complex arm and facial movements after focal brain lesions. *Neuropsychologia* 19:491–503, 1981.

Liepmann, H. *Die linke Hemisphare und das Handeln. Drei Aufsatze aus dem Apraxiegebiet.* Berlin: Springer, 1908.

Logan, G. D. Attention and preattention in theories of automaticity. *American Journal of Psychology* 105:317–340, 1992.

Luck, S. J. Cognitive and neural mechanisms of visual search. *Current Opinion in Biology* 4:183–188, 1994.

Mateer, C., and D. Kimura. Impairment of nonverbal or oral movements in apraxia. *Brain and Language* 4:262–276, 1977.

Milner, B. Hemispheric asymmetry in the control of gesture sequences. *Proceedings of XXI International Congress of Psychology.* Paris, 1976, p. 149.

Milner, B., and B. Kolb. Performance of complex arm movements and facial-movement sequences after cerebral comissurotomy. *Neuropsychologia* 23:791–799, 1985.

Moran, J., and R. Desimone. Selective attention gates visual processing in the extrastriate cortex. *Science* 229:782–784, 1985.

Moscovitch, M. Do PETS have long or short ears? Mental imagery and neuroimaging. *Trends in Neurosciences* 17:292–294, 1994.

Näätänen, T. *Attention and Brain Function.* Hillsdale, N.J.: Erlbaum, 1992.

Norton, D., and L. Stark. Eye movements and visual perception. In R. Held and W. Richards, eds. *Perception: Mechanisms and Models. Readings from Scientific American.* San Francisco: W. H. Freeman, 1972.

Olshausen, B. A., C. H. Anderson, and D. C. van Essen. A neurobiological model of visual attention and invariant pattern recognition based on dynamic routing of information. *Journal of Neuroscience* 13:4700–4719, 1993.

Petersen, S. E., D. L. Robinson, and J. D. Morris. Contributions of the pulvinar to visual spatial orientation. *Neuropsychologia* 25:97–106, 1987.

Poeck, K., and M. Kerschensteiner. Analysis of the sequential motor events in oral apraxia. In K. J. Zulch, O. Creutzfeldt, and B. C. Galbraith, eds. *Cerebral Localization.* Berlin: Springer-Verlag, 1975.

Posner, M. I., and S. E. Petersen. The attention system of the brain. *Annual Review of Neuroscience* 13:25–42, 1990.

Posner, M. I., and M. E. Raichle. *Images of Mind.* New York: Scientific American Library, 1993.

Posner, M. I., and C. R. R. Synder. Facilitation and inhibition in the processing of signals. In P. M. A. Rabbitt and S. Dornic, eds. *Attention and Performance V.* New York: Academic, 1975.

Rock, I., and C. Harris. Vision and touch. In R. Held and W. Richards, eds. *Perception: Mechanisms and Models. Readings from Scientific American.* San Francisco: W. H. Freeman, 1972.

Roland, P. E. *Brain Activation.* New York: John Wiley, 1993.

Roland, P. E., and B. Gulyás. Visual imagery and visual representation. *Trends in Neuroscience* 17:281–287, 1994.

Roy, E. A., ed. *Neuropsychological Studies of Apraxia and Related Disorders*. New York: North-Holland, 1985.

Schall, J. D., and D. P. Hanes. Neural basis of saccade target selection in frontal eye field during visual search. *Nature* 366:467–469, 1993.

Schneider, W., M. Pimm-Smith, and M. Worden. Neurobiology of attention and automaticity. *Current Opinion in Neurobiology* 4:177–182, 1994.

Spitzer, H., R. Desimone, and J. Moran. Increased attention enhances both behavioral and neuronal performance. *Science* 240:338–340, 1988.

Treisman, A. Features and objects in visual processing. *Scientific American* 254(11):114–124, 1986.

Treisman, A., and S. Gormican. Feature analysis in early vision. *Psychological Review* 95:15–30, 1988.

Wyke, M. Effect of brain lesions on the rapidity of arm movement. *Neurology* 17:1113–1120, 1967.

Wyke, M. The effect of brain lesions in the performance of an arm-hand precision task. *Neuropsychologia* 6:125–134, 1968.

part four

IV

Issues and Abnormalities

The first three parts of the book have emphasized what we know about how the brain works. Part Four examines issues related to the abnormal functioning of the brain. We begin by considering brain development, both normal and abnormal, before considering various types of neurological and psychiatric disorders. We discuss learning disabilities separately, because this topic does not fit comfortably with the clinical disorders. Finally, we review the nature of neuropsychological assessment.

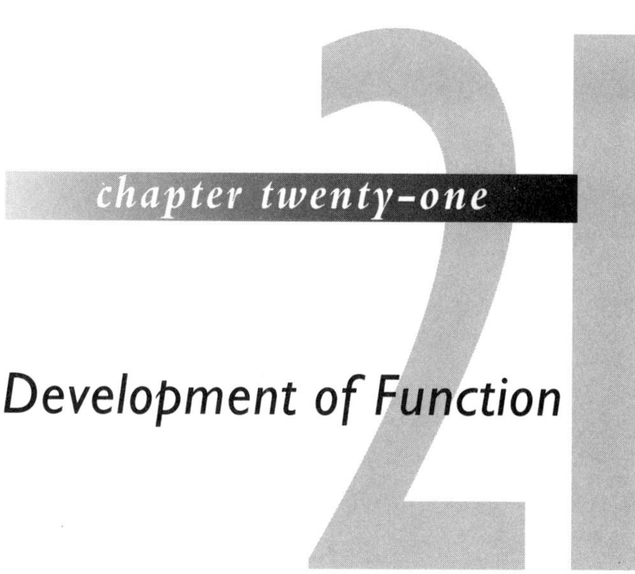

Development of Function

Some people are attracted to the study of developmental neuropsychology because they believe that children are neurologically simpler than adults and therefore easier to study. Others believe that analysis of the behavior and development of children will give important clues about the relative contributions of heredity and environment to the development of particular behaviors. Still others are impelled by practical necessity: they must develop programs for children who have special problems in school. The growth of developmental neuropsychology as a field of inquiry has raised interesting questions. Why does the brain, early in life, appear to be so flexible in compensating for injury and for variations in the environment? Is there an optimal environment in which development should occur? Is there an optimal method of instruction that should be used in education? The objective of developmental neuropsychology is to understand nervous system function in early life and to see whether such an understanding can provide answers to such questions.

Behavioral changes related to neural function can be examined in three ways. The first is to look at nervous system maturation and correlate it with the development of specific behaviors. Ordinarily, the development of both the nervous system and behavior is orderly and is similar in sequence from person to person, suggesting that correlations can be made easily (Figure 21.1). The second approach, the converse, is to look at behavior and then make inferences about neural maturation. This procedure has not been widely used; hypotheses about brain function are hard to verify because the human nervous system cannot be manipulated during development. The improvement of imaging procedures will overcome this difficulty because imaging of the brain at different ages will permit correlations to be made between neural function and behavior. The third approach is to relate brain malfunction or damage to behavioral disorders or cognitive deficits. This approach has drawbacks when applied to developmental problems. The infant brain is not like the adult brain because, first, the immature brain is incapable of certain adult functions and, second, there is no one immature brain. That is, the brain develops in such a way that principles applicable at one age are inapplicable at another age. This discontinuity may be one reason that estimates of intelligence obtained from very young children correlate poorly with their adult intelligence. Also, developing brains are plastic.

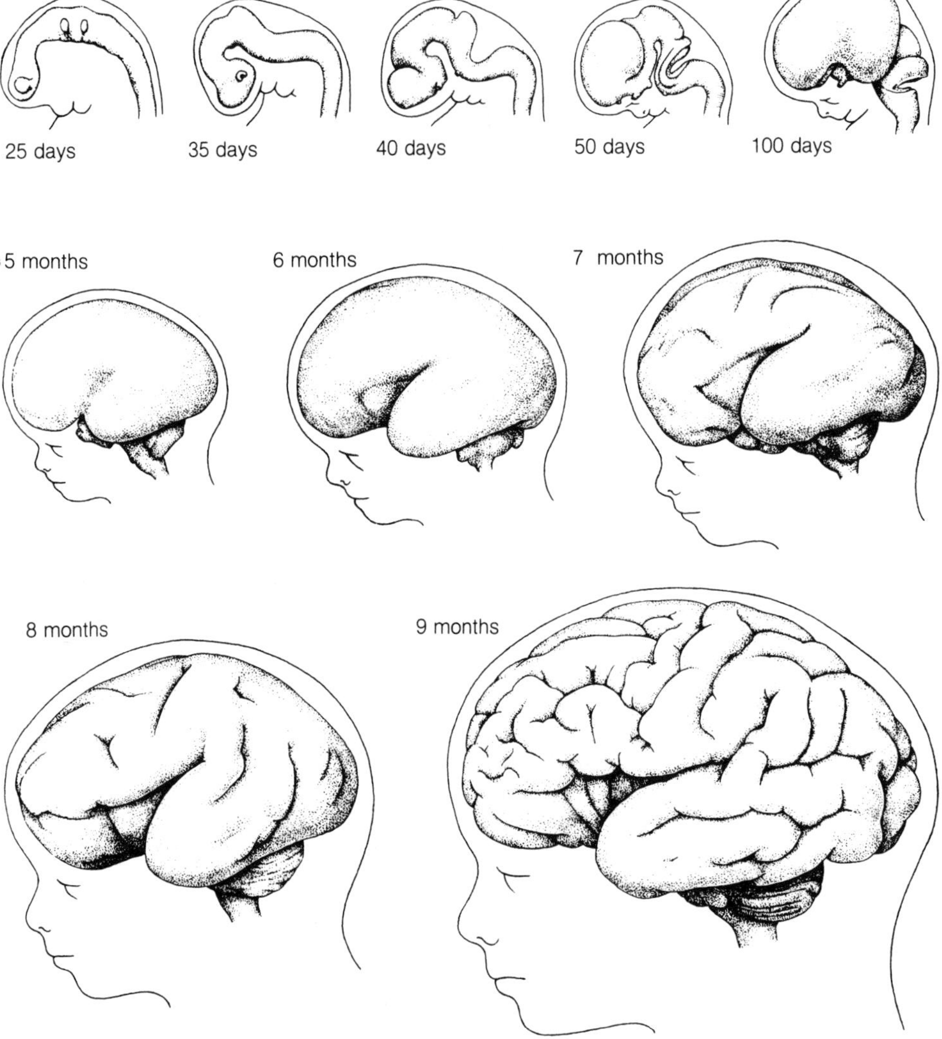

FIGURE 21.1. Prenatal development of the human brain showing a series of embryonic and fetal stages. (Adapted from W. M. Cowan. The development of the brain. *Scientific American* 241:112–133, 1979.)

Brain damage occurring in infancy may go unnoticed because an undamaged portion of the brain adopts the function of the damaged part. In the following sections, we will consider some findings derived using these different approaches.

A NEURAL PERSPECTIVE ON DEVELOPMENT

Cellular Basis of Brain Development

The process of brain growth and differentiation consists of a series of changes that occur in a relatively fixed sequence. These include (1) the migration of cells, (2) the formation and growth of axons, (3) the formation of dendrites, (4) the formation of synaptic connections, and (5) myelination. This program of development has two extraordinary features. First, subcomponents of the nervous system are formed from cells whose destination and function are largely predetermined before they migrate from the wall of the ventricles. Second, development is marked by an initial abundance of cells, branches, and connections, with an important part of subsequent maturation consisting of cell death or pruning back of the initial surfeit.

Because of deficits in the genetic program, intrauterine trauma, the influence of toxic agents, or other factors, peculiarities or errors in development can occur that may contribute to obvious and severe deformities, such as those listed in Table 21.1. Less pronounced deficits may become manifest in such problems as learning disabilities or may appear only as subtle changes in behavior. In the following sections, we will describe the normal biological processes of development, as well as abnormalities that occur when a process is not completed properly

Cell Migration

Nerve cells form by division in the inner, or ventricular, lining of the brain. Here each cell gives rise to two daughter cells that either migrate or undergo further division. The division of germinal cells may be complete by the middle of gestation, whereas the migration of cells to various regions may continue for a number of months, even postnatally. The precise timing of the development and migration of cells to different cytoarchitectonic regions varies by area. At the same time, adjacent germinal areas on the ventricular wall may produce cells destined for quite distinct layers in different cortical areas. By the fifth embryonic month, cortical layers V and VI are visible, and subsequent layers develop and continue to mature up to about 8 months after birth. The mechanisms that control migration and determine the destination of migrating cells are not well understood. It is known that specialized filaments provide a pathway for the migrating cells to follow.

Once a group of cells has arrived at the surface of the brain, differentiation (the formation of axons, dendrites, and so on) begins. Subsequently,

TABLE 21.1. Types of abnormal development

Type	Symptom
Anencephaly	Absence of cerebral hemispheres, diencephalon, and midbrain
Holoprosencephaly	Cortex forms as a single undifferentiated hemisphere
Lissencephaly	Brain fails to form sulci and gyri and corresponds to a 12-week embryo
Micropolygyria	Gyri are more numerous, smaller, and more poorly developed than normal
Macrogyria	Gyri are broader and less numerous than normal
Microencephaly	Development of the brain is rudimentary and the person has low-grade intelligence
Porencephaly	Symmetrical cavities in the cortex, where cortex and white matter should be
Heterotopia	Displaced islands of gray matter appear in the ventricular walls or white matter, caused by aborted cell migration
Agenesis of the corpus callosum	Complete or partial absence of the corpus callosum
Cerebellar agenesis	Portions of the cerebellum, basal ganglia, or spinal cord are absent or malformed

a new group of cells migrates from the inner lining through the layers already present to form a new outer layer. Thus, a structure such as the cortex matures from its inner to its outer surface.

Migration can stop prematurely, leaving a group of cells that should appear as an outer layer scattered instead among inner layers of cells. Caviness and Sidman have made a major study of disturbed cell migration in the cortex of a genetic mutant mouse called the reeler mouse. In this animal, the cells generated first lie near the surface and those generated last lie deepest, creating a cortex that is inverted from that of a normal mouse. Despite their aberrant position, the cells receive and give off appropriate connections, but the mice have an abnormal, reeling movement. Failed or incomplete cell migration in humans has also been described.

Axonal Growth

Axons begin sprouting from neurons as they migrate to their targets. Sprouting axons grow in a given direction either because the cell body is oriented in a particular way or because of other, unknown factors. The growing end of the axon, called the growth cone, was first recognized and described by Ramón y Cajal in the 1890s. He wrote:

> I had the good fortune to behold for the first time that fantastic ending of the growing axon. In my sections of the three-day chick embryo, this ending appeared as a concentration of protoplasm of conical form, endowed with ameboid movements. It could be compared with a living battering ram, soft and flexible, which advances, pushing aside mechanically the obstacles which it finds in its way, until it reaches the area of its peripheral distribution. This curious terminal club, I christened the growth cone. (Ramón y Cajal, 1937)

The axon grows at a rate of 7 to 170 μm per hour. Axon branching occurs at the growth cone. It is possible that the growth cone forms synapses and retains the capacity to renew growth, and this capacity may underlie the formation of new synapses during the course of learning.

A major unknown in developmental neurobiology is the forces that initiate and guide axonal growth. Axons have specific targets that they must reach if the neuron is to survive and become functional. Some axons grow because they are towed from their cell bodies by a structure that is growing away from the region, such as when the muscles grow away from the spinal cord early in development. Other axons traverse enormous distances and overcome such obstacles as being moved to another location, having their cell bodies rotated, or having their targets moved. Axons can follow an electrical or chemical gradient or a particular physical substrate, or they can send out many branches or shoots, and when one reaches an appropriate target, the others follow. It is also possible that several such mechanisms operate simultaneously or sequentially.

The formation of appropriate neural pathways can be disrupted in any of a number of ways. Axons may be unable to reach their target if their way is blocked, as can happen following scarring from head trauma during the early months of life. The development of axons can also be disrupted by anoxia, ingestion of toxic materials, malnutrition, or some other disturbance. Several reports of anomalous fiber systems in mutant strains of mice also suggest that abnormalities can have a genetic basis. There have been mouse strains in which the corpus callosum is of abnormal size or is absent and mouse strains in which the fiber pathways in the hippocampal system are abnormal. In a number of albino animal species, and possibly also in human albinos, the ipsilateral optic pathway is reduced in size and area of distribution. Since the brain processes information sequentially, similar disruption of transcortical or interhemispheric connections during development could be related to the cognitive difficulties that some humans experience.

Axonal development can also be disrupted if the axons' target is damaged, in which case the axonal system may degenerate or may occupy an inappropriate target. Should the latter event occur, the behavior supported by the invaded area may also be disrupted. In a well-documented study of abnormal fiber growth, Schneider has shown that if the optic tectum in the hamster is removed on one side at birth, the fibers that should normally project to it project instead to the opposite side. This aberrant pathway is functional, but in a curious way. If a visual stimulus is presented to the eye contralateral to the damaged tectum, the hamster turns in the direction opposite to that of the stimulus. The message has traveled from the eye to the tectum that would ordinarily receive input from the opposite side of the world. The abnormalities of posture and movement seen in some sorts of **athetosis** (slow involuntary movement) and **dystonia** (imbalances in muscle tone) in children may occur because fiber systems supporting posture and movement invade the wrong target.

Axons appear to be capable of overcoming obstacles to reach their targets. For example, if the spinal cord is partially sectioned, pyramidal tract axons that should pass through the damaged portion of the cord may cross over to the undamaged side of the cord and then complete their journey to the appropriate target by recrossing the cord. Axons may also fill in for other axons. If the pyramidal cells of one hemisphere of the cortex are destroyed early in life, the axons of pyramidal cells from the other hemisphere will occupy the targets of the missing cells. These examples show that there are many ways that a developing brain can adjust its growth to achieve normal connections if its normal development is hindered.

Dendritic Growth

Dendrite growth usually starts after the cell reaches its final position in the cortex, and it proceeds at a relatively slow rate. The growth of dendrites parallels that of axons, growth and division also occurring at a growth cone. Generally, the growth of dendrites is timed to intercept the axons that are to innervate them. Although dendritic development begins prenatally in humans, it continues for a long time postnatally. Before birth there are few spines on dendrites, but after birth the spines begin to develop and cover the maturing dendrites densely. During development, cells go through stages in which they have an overabundance of branches and spines. They subsequently lose the dendrites, in a process sometimes referred to as *pruning,* and spines, in a process referred to as *shedding*. The remaining branches may undergo extensive growth and branching (Figure 21.2).

In studies of dendrite abnormalities, it is difficult to determine whether a disorder is specifically dendritic or is secondary to inappropriate cell location, abnormal innervation, ingestion of a neurotoxin, or some other cause. Reduced afferent innervation is known to lead to a reduction in the number of dendritic spines. Studies of the cerebral cortex in various types of mental retardation indicate a number of dendritic abnormalities. Dendrites may be thinner, with fewer than the normal numbers of spines; the dendrites may be short stalks with small spines; or there simply may be a reduction in spine number. What causes these changes is not known, but the histology gives the general impression that they are a carryover from the embryonic condition.

Synaptic Formation

It was thought that synaptic formation might be orderly and might parallel the various developmental patterns of cell migration and maturation. Surprisingly, Rakic and his coworkers have found that synaptic formation occurs concurrently in all cortical layers and in all cortical areas. Synapses in the rhesus monkey were found to start developing in the last 2 months before birth and to continue for several months after birth. Thereafter, there was a rapid decline during the second part of the first year of life and a slower decline during the rest of life. In humans, synaptic density is thought to increase until about 2 years of age, after which about 50% of synapses are lost by age 16.

It is clear from many studies that a given brain region sends axons to a limited number of other regions and that synapses are made only in a specific part of certain cells in that region. The locations of synapses are determined by genetic in-

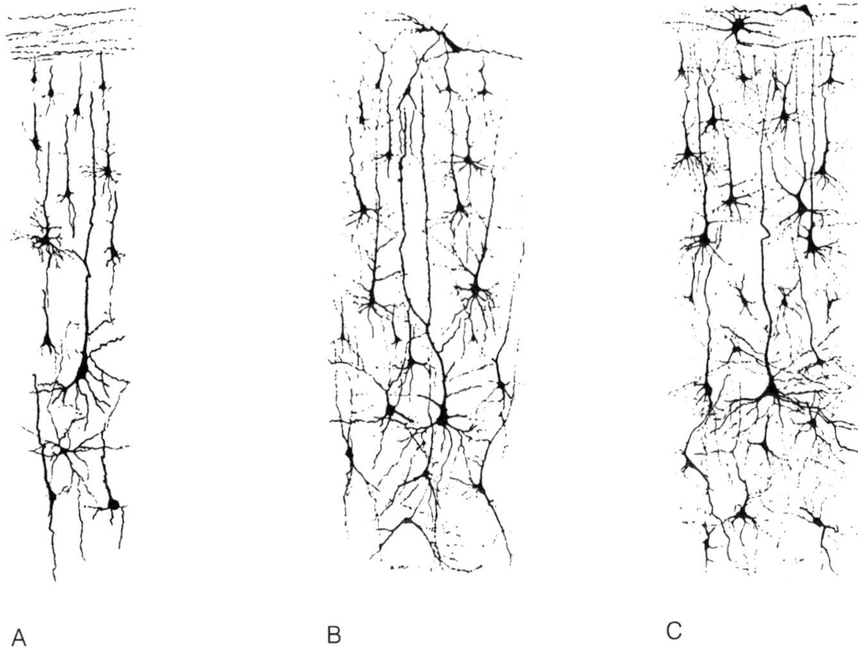
A
B
C

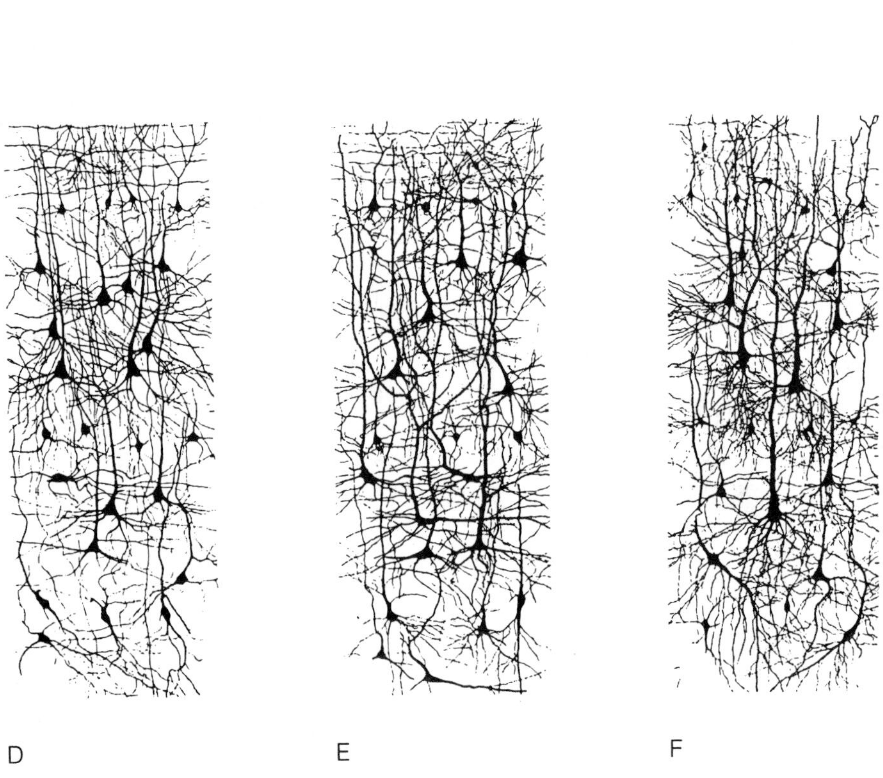
D
E
F

struction, by the orientation of the cell when the axons arrive, by the timing of axon arrival (axons apparently compete for available space), and by the use the axons are given once a connection is made. In addition, the pharmacology of the synapse is flexible. For example, it has been found that individual neurons can become either norepinephrinergic or cholinergic depending on their environment. Malfunctions in any of these features of synaptic formation may cause abnormal brain development.

Myelination

Myelination is the process by which the support cells of the nervous system begin to surround axons and provide them with insulation. Although nerves can become functional before myelination, it is assumed that they reach adult functional levels as myelination is completed. Thus, myelination provides an index of the maturity of structures from which and to which axons project.

If myelination is used as an index of maturation, then the work of Flechsig on anatomical development indicates that the neocortex begins a sequential development at a relatively early age. The primary sensory areas and motor areas show some myelination just before term. The secondary cortical areas become myelinated within the next 4 postnatal months, and by the fourth month the remaining areas of the cortex are becoming myelinated. Although myelination begins during the early postnatal period, it continues to increase beyond 15 years of age and may increase in density as late as age 60. Any disruption in this ongoing process can cause neural, and hence behavioral, abnormalities.

Postnatal Brain Development

After birth, the brain does not grow uniformly but rather tends to increase its mass during irregular periods commonly called *growth spurts*. In his analysis of brain–body weight ratios, Epstein found consistent spurts in brain growth at 3–10 months to 1.5 years and at 2–4, 6–8, 10–12, and 14–16 years. The increment during the first spurt was about 30% by weight, and increments during subsequent spurts were about 5% to 10% by weight. Paradoxically, the increases take place concurrently with losses of neurons, dendrites, and synapses and are probably due to an increase in growth of the cell processes that remain. It might be thought that cognitive changes accompany the periods of brain growth, and that is the case. Significantly, the first four brain-growth stages coincide with the classically given ages of onset of the four main stages of intellectual development described by Piaget.

ENVIRONMENTAL INFLUENCES ON DEVELOPMENT

The environment in which development occurs can profoundly influence behavior. Singh and Zingg report that children raised by wolves behave like wolves and are difficult to socialize. On

FIGURE 21.2. Postnatal development of human cerebral cortex around Broca's area taken from camera-lucidia drawing of Golgi-Cox preparations. *A*. Newborn: Sucking, rooting, swallowing, infantile grasping, blinks to light. *B*. One month: Extends and turns neck when prone, looks at mother, follows objects, smiles when played with. *C*. Three months: Infantile grasp and sucking modified at will, looks at moving objects, watches hands. *D*. Six months: Grasps objects with both hands, supports weight on hands when prone, stands briefly, laughs, primitive "ga-goo" sounds, smiles at self in mirror. *E*. Fifteen months: Smiles at self in mirror, grasps objects between thumb and forefinger (pincer grasp), walks, understands and says words. *F*. Twenty-four months: Walks up and down stairs, partial self-dressing, uses simple sentences, points to body parts, says no ("terrible twos"). (After E. Lenneberg, *Biological Foundations of Language*. New York: John Wiley, 1967.)

the other hand, Skeels reports that children removed from substandard orphanages (and placed in a mental institution) developed normal intelligence by adulthood, whereas those who were not removed remained retarded. The children in the mental institution apparently received attention from the patients; such attention was not given to those who remained in the orphanages. These reports are confirmed by Harlow in formal studies of the effects of early deprivation on the maturation of monkeys, which show maladaptive adult behavior when deprived in infancy.

How do the conditions of early environment affect nervous system development? There are several possibilities, each of which has received some support in recent experimental work. (1) The nervous system develops independently of environment but requires stimulation for maintained function. (2) The nervous system develops independently in part, but requires stimulation for continued maturation beyond some point. Inappropriate stimulation may change the system's properties. (3) The properties of the nervous system are not innate but develop only with appropriate stimulation. Experimental work using the visual system as a model has provided support for each of these possibilities. In all cases, the importance of stimulation is emphasized. The term **functional validation** is used to express the idea that to become fully functional a neural system requires stimulation at some point.

Environmental Influences on Brain Size

The simplest measure of the effects of environment on the nervous system is brain size. Environmental influences on animal brain size have been investigated; domestic animals have certain cortical areas that are as much as 10% to 20% smaller than those of animals of the same species and strain raised in the wild. These differences are apparently related to factors that occur early in life, since animals born in the wild and later domesticated have brains the same size as animals raised in the wild. The part of the brain that seems to be most affected by a domestic upbringing is the occipital cortex, which is reduced in size by as much as 35% in some animals. This reduction may be related to smaller eye and retina size.

Exposure to an enriched environment increases brain size, most noticeably of the neocortex, with the greatest increase occurring in the occipital neocortex. Related to increased size are increases in the density of glial cells, in the number of higher-order dendritic spines on neurons, in the number of synaptic spines, and in the size of synapses. These changes are most pronounced if enriched experience is given in early life; similar, less pronounced effects can be obtained with more prolonged exposure given in later life. In addition to these anatomical changes, enriched animals can perform better than their impoverished counterparts on a number of tests of learning and memory.

Environmental Influences on Function: Examples from the Visual System

Disturbances of the optics of the eye (for example, cataracts and astigmatism) during early life cause long-lasting impairments of vision even after the optical defects are corrected. Adults who have had cataracts removed to restore light entry to the retina have difficulty learning the identity of objects through vision. (Similarly, people who have grown up deaf and have had their hearing restored with cochlea implants have trouble making sense of sounds and prefer not to use the implants.) These visual impairments, called amblyopia—dimness of vision without obvious impairment of the eye—are presumed to be caused by changes in the central nervous system. Behavioral studies have shown that amblyopia can be produced in animals; its cause has been analyzed extensively in studies using cats and monkeys. This area of research now provides some of the most penetrating insights into the factors affecting development and deserves careful study.

Hubel and Wiesel and others have described the response patterns of normal cells in area 17 of the visual cortex. They recorded the activity of cells in anesthetized animals while visual stimuli were presented on a screen placed in the animal's visual field. The cells respond to a number of the properties of a visual stimulus, including its orientation and direction; they also respond according to which eye is presented with the stimulus and are affected by binocular disparity (the different view each eye has of the stimulus). Using a profile of the activity of cells in a normal cat's area 17, Hubel and Wiesel investigated the function of area 17 in kittens whose eyes had not yet opened. In 8-day-old kittens, they found that although the cells are sluggish and become fatigued quickly, they show the same properties as the adult cat's cells to the first presentation of visual stimulation. The results of this and similar studies suggest that the visual system has normal response capacity at birth. What, then, of the environment's contribution?

To assess the contributions of the environment, two conditions of visual deprivation have been used: **binocular deprivation** and **monocular deprivation.** In the first, animals are deprived by being reared in the dark or by having their eyelids sutured before they open. This deprivation produces no change in the retina and only mild changes in the lateral geniculate nucleus—the major relay of the visual cortex. By contrast, cells in the visual cortex undergo disturbances of protein synthesis and have fewer and shorter dendrites, fewer spines, and 70% fewer synapses than normal. Analysis of the properties of these cells shows that after a number of months of early deprivation there are severe abnormalities, which disappear to some extent with normal visual experience. Deprivation in later life does not produce the same initial period of abnormality. Thus, visual stimulation in early life is important for continued development of visual cells, but the visual system retains some ability to compensate.

The second condition, monocular deprivation, surprisingly has a more severe effect than binocular deprivation. If one eyelid is sutured during early life, the eye appears to be essentially blind for a period of weeks after opening, although its function does improve somewhat with time. Cell recording studies show that either stimulation in the deprived eye cannot activate cells in the cortex or, in those few cases in which it can, the cells are highly abnormal. The experiments also show that the earlier deprivation occurs, the shorter the deprivation period required and the more severe the effects. These results confirm that deprivation can retard development and that early deprivation is the most influential. The experiments also suggest that factors other than deprivation alone must be operative to produce the severe effects found.

Apparently competition also contributes to the severity of deficits in the deprived eye. Kratz and coworkers found that if the normal eye of an animal was removed after the other eye had been deprived for 5 months, the deprived eye gave comparatively normal responses in 31% of the cells, compared with only 6% when the normal eye was present. This finding is confirmed by a number of more indirect experiments. These results imply that the deprived portion of the visual system has the capacity to function but is inhibited from doing so by the good portion of the visual system. If inhibition of function is removed, the deprived portion of the visual system begins to function.

Can the visual system be changed by manipulation less drastic than complete sensory deprivation? Hirsch and Spinelli fitted kittens with lenses that brought a set of horizontal stripes into focus on one retina and a set of vertical stripes into focus on the other. After later removal of the lenses, they found that cells responded only to a stimulus oriented close to the horizontal when viewed with the eye that had seen horizontal stripes during the exposure period, and only to a stimulus oriented close to the vertical when viewed with the eye that had seen vertical stripes. These findings have been confirmed for kittens raised in an environment of stripes or spots or in one organized to be devoid of movement. In fact, work by Blakemore and Mitchell indicates that 1 hour of exposure on day 28 after birth is sufficient to bias a cortical unit to respond to a particular pattern.

In summary, this work suggests that the visual system is genetically programmed to make normal connections and normal responses, but it can lose much of this capacity if it is not exercised during the early months of life. When part of the system is deprived, in addition to the loss of capacity caused by the deprivation, that part of the system is inhibited by the remaining functional areas, and the defect is potentiated. Removal of inhibition can permit some degree of recovery. Finally, if the environment is so arranged that the system is exposed to stimuli of one type, the cells in the system are biased to respond to stimuli of that type.

BRAIN INJURY AND DEVELOPMENT

Although it was known in 1861 that damage to the left frontal cortex could abolish speech, by 1868 Cotard had observed that children with left frontal lesions developed normal adult language functions. This was the origin of the idea that brain injury has milder and more short-lived effects if it is sustained in childhood. In the 1930s, Margaret Kennard compared the effects of unilateral motor cortex lesions on infant and adult monkeys. The impairments in the infant monkeys seemed milder than those in the adults. The generalization that sparing of function follows infant lesions became known as the Kennard principle. For a time the idea received wide acceptance, but then gradually it became evident that earlier may not always be better and may sometimes be worse. Which effect is obtained depends on the behavior, the extent of brain damage, and the age of injury. With respect to cognitive function in humans, it is clear that speech survives early brain damage, but some elements of syntax and some nonlanguage functions may not survive, and general intellectual ability may decline.

Effects of Age

Age is an important variable when considering the effects of early lesions. Studies suggest that there are three critical age divisions: before 1 year of age, between 1 and 5 years, and over 5 years. Lesions incurred before the age of 1 tend to produce disproportionately greater impairments than those incurred later. Lesions incurred between 1 and 5 years of age do allow reorganization of brain function, including sparing of language functions. Lesions incurred later than age 5 permit little or no sparing of function. For example, in a comparison of the effects of lesions incurred before and after age 1, Riva and Cazzaniga found that earlier lesions reduced IQ more than the later lesions.

Effect of Brain Damage on Language

Language deficits resulting from cerebral injury in childhood are usually short-lived and recovery is nearly complete. Furthermore, transient language disorders following right hemisphere damage are more common in children than in adults, the incidence being about 8% and 2%, respectively (Table 21.2). The Basser study, which gave a

TABLE 21.2. Summary of studies of aphasia resulting from unilateral lesions

Study	Age range of subjects	Number of cases	Percentage with right hemisphere lesions
Childhood lesions			
Guttman, 1942	2–14	15	7
Alajouanine and Lhermitte, 1965	6–15	32	0
McCarthy, 1963	After language acquisition	114	4
Basser, 1962	Before 5	20	35
Hécaen, 1976	$3\frac{1}{2}$–15	17	11
TOTAL	2–15	198	8
Adult lesions			
Russell and Espir, 1961	—	205	3
Hécaen, 1976	—	232	0.43
TOTAL	—	437	1.6

Source: Adapted from Krashen, 1973, and Hécaen, 1976.

value of 35% with aphasia, is thought to be inaccurate, since many of the subjects may have had bilateral lesions.

Alajouanine and Lhermitte studied 32 cases of childhood aphasia, finding writing deficits in all and reading deficits in about half of the children, in addition to difficulty in speaking. Six months after the injury, they observed total recovery of spontaneous language in about one-third, although significant improvement was noted in all the others. When reexamined 1 year or more after the injury, 24 of the 32 children had normal or almost normal language, although 14 still had some degree of dysgraphia; 22 of the children were eventually able to return to school.

Similarly, Hécaen followed postinjury recovery of aphasia and related symptoms in 15 children with left hemisphere unilateral lesions, as summarized in Table 21.3. Besides disorders of speech, nearly all the children had disorders of writing and calculation. Of these 15 children, 5 showed complete recovery within 6 weeks to 2 years. Most of the remaining children showed considerable improvement, the only remaining deficit often being a mild difficulty in writing, a finding similar to that of Alajouanine and Lhermitte.

Woods and Teuber studied about 50 patients with prenatal or early postnatal brain damage to either the left or the right hemisphere. Using normal siblings as controls, they came to the following conclusions:

1. Language survives after early left hemisphere injury.

2. Much of this survival seems attributable to occupancy of a potential language zone in the right hemisphere.

3. This shift of language location is not without a price, because some kinds of visuospatial orientation are impaired.

4. Early lesions of the right hemisphere produce deficits similar to those produced by such lesions in adulthood.

In other words, if a child sustains a lesion of the left hemisphere that produces right hemiplegia, language functions are remarkably more intact than after a comparable lesion in an adult, presumably because some or all of the language abilities have moved to the right hemisphere. Presumably, language crowds into the right

TABLE 21.3. Frequency of different symptoms in 15 cases caused by left hemisphere lesions in childhood

Symptom	Number of cases	Percentage	Evolution of symptoms
Mutism	9	60	From 5 days to 30 months
Articulatory disorders	12	80	Persistent in 4 cases
Auditory verbal comprehension disorders	6	40	Persistent in 1 case
Naming disorders	7	46	Persistent in 3 cases
Paraphasia	1	7	Disappearance
Reading disorders	9	60	Persistent in 3 cases
Writing disorders	13	86	Persistent in 7 cases
Facial apraxia	2	—	Transient
Acalculia	11	—	(Not reported)

Source: Adapted from Hécaen, 1976.

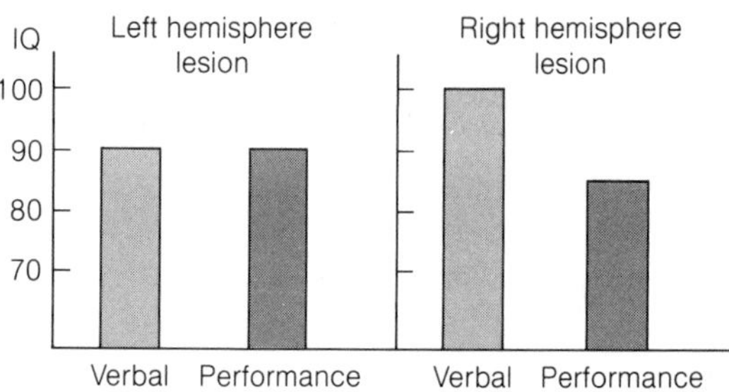

FIGURE 21.3. IQs on subtests of the Wechsler Intelligence Test for Adults. These adults, while infants, had suffered a lesion of the left or the right hemisphere, as determined by the occurrence of hemiparesis. Note that both verbal and performance scores are depressed by left hemisphere lesions, whereas only performance scores are depressed by right hemisphere lesions. The results suggest that if language moves to the right hemisphere, that hemisphere's functions are sacrificed to accommodate this shift. The results also suggest that right hemisphere functions do not shift sufficiently to interfere with language. (After Teuber, 1975.)

hemisphere at the expense of visuospatial functions. On the other hand, a lesion of the right hemisphere, which produces left hemiplegia, does not produce impairments in language ability.

A summary of this pattern of results, obtained from verbal and performance scores of the Wechsler Intelligence Test, is shown in Figure 21.3. Left hemisphere lesions depress both verbal and performance scores. Right hemisphere lesions depress only performance scores. In a subsequent study, Woods examined the effects of lesions incurred earlier than age 1. The main finding was that right hemisphere lesions impaired both verbal and performance IQ. Riva and Cazzaniga confirm these results and also note that lesions occurring before 1 year of age produce more severe overall impairments than those occurring after age 1.

It is worth noting that not all aspects of language function are spared after early lesions. Woods has found that on a speech-shadowing task, which requires a person to repeat passages of speech as they are read, adult right and left hemisphere lesions produce equal impairments. Virtually identical impairments follow early childhood lesions, even though speech is significantly spared by the early left hemisphere lesions.

Reorganization of Language

The evidence that early brain damage spares language and that sparing may occur because the control of language is transferred to the opposite hemisphere raises three questions. What actual language functions are transferred? What type of brain damage causes them to be transferred? What is the age range during which transfer can take place? The first two questions have been addressed experimentally by Rasmussen and Milner, but the third is not yet answered completely.

Using the carotid sodium amobarbital and dichotic-listening tests, Rasmussen and Milner localized language in a large number of patients who had received left hemisphere injury early in life but had returned to the hospital later in life because of complications. They found that the patients divided into three groups, as shown in Table 21.4. In the first group speech was in the left hemisphere, in the second group speech was represented bilaterally, and in the third group speech was in the right hemisphere. The patients who had speech in the left hemisphere were found to have damage that did not invade the anterior speech zone (Broca's area) or the posterior speech zone (Wernicke's area). Examples of brain dam-

TABLE 21.4. Changes in hemispheric speech representation following early brain damage

		Percentage with speech representation		
	Handedness	Left	Bilateral	Right
No early damage	Right	96	0	4
	Left or mixed	70	15	15
Early damage	Right	81	7	12
	Left or mixed	28	19	53

Source: Adapted from Rasmussen and Milner, 1975, pp. 248–249.

age that did not produce a shift in language lateralization are shown in Figure 21.4A. Both exemplar lesions are large, yet the dichotic-listening test showed a right-ear advantage. In the sodium amobarbital tests the patients were mute on both naming tasks (giving the names of objects; for example, "What is?"—experimenter holds up object) and repetition tasks (for example, "Name the days of the week in order") after left hemisphere injection. The light shading in the left-hand portion of Figure 21.4A shows the locations of the anterior and posterior speech zones.

An example of a lesion that produced a complete shift of language to the right hemisphere is illustrated in Figure 21.4B. This patient showed a left-ear advantage on the dichotic-listening test and was mute for naming and repetition after right hemisphere sodium amobarbital injection. Note that the lesion invaded both the anterior and posterior speech zones, which was typical for patients who developed right hemisphere speech after early left hemisphere lesions.

Examples of the lesions in patients who had bilateral speech are shown in Figures 21.4C and 21.4D. The patient whose lesion is shown in Figure 21.4C had a large left frontal lobe lesion at 6 years of age that included the anterior language zone. At age 18 the patient was right-handed and had a right-ear advantage for digits and a left-ear advantage for melodies. On the sodium amobarbital tests, a left hemisphere injection produced a disturbance in series repetition (counting, reciting the days of the week forward or backward, or oral spelling), but naming was less disturbed. A right hemisphere injection produced a disturbance in both series repetition and naming. Since it is assumed that the right-ear advantage for digits is an indication of left hemisphere speech and that the absence of series repetition after left hemisphere sodium amobarbital injection is an indication of intact speech in the left posterior speech zone, it can be concluded that the lesion did not cause a complete shift of speech from the posterior left speech zone. Since naming was disturbed after a right hemisphere injection of sodium amobarbital, it is assumed that the left hemisphere speech

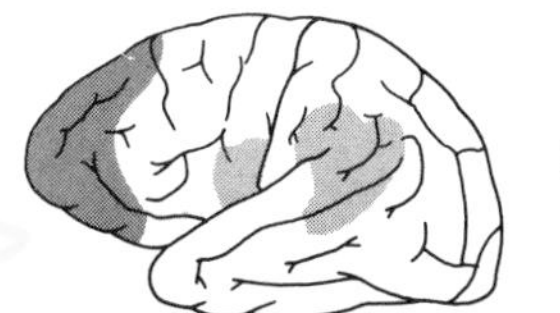
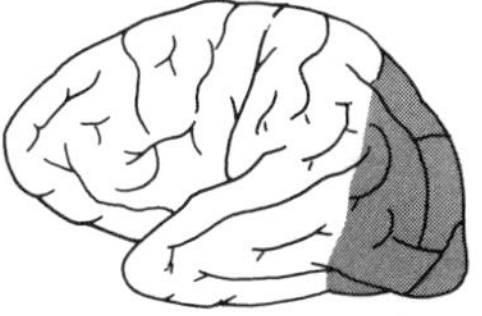

A No shift in language

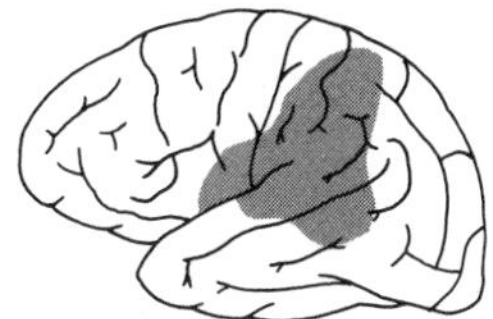

B Complete shift of language

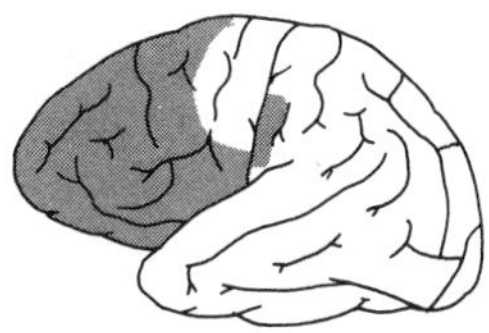

C Shift of anterior speech functions

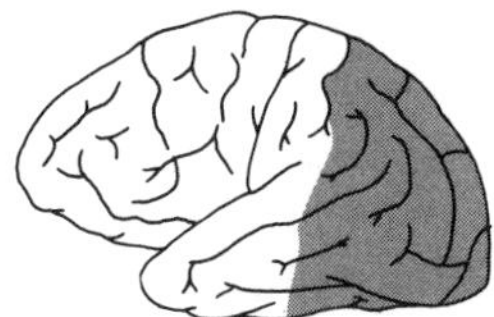

D Shift of posterior speech functions

FIGURE 21.4. Relations between early brain damage and hemisphere changes in language organization. *A.* Anterior and posterior lesions after which language remained in the left hemisphere. The lightly shaded portion of the figure on the left shows the location of language zones. *B.* An anterior-posterior lesion that causes all language to move to the right hemisphere. *C.* An anterior lesion that causes the anterior speech zone to shift to the right hemisphere. *D.* A posterior lesion that causes the posterior zone to shift to the right hemisphere. (After Rasmussen and Milner, 1977.)

functions of the anterior zone had shifted to the right hemisphere.

The patient whose lesion is shown in Figure 21.4D had a large posterior lesion that was incurred at 2½ years of age. Testing at age 16 showed that she was left-handed and had a left-ear advantage for both digits and melodies. Sodium amobarbital tests showed that naming was disturbed by both left and right hemisphere injections, whereas series repetition was done well after the left but not the right hemisphere was injected. In this case it is thought that the large posterior lesion incurred early in life had caused speech functions of the posterior zone to shift to the right, while the anterior speech zone still retained some speech function.

The results that we have described to this point, particularly those of Rasmussen and Milner, show that speech has a strong affinity for the left hemisphere and will not abandon it unless an entire center is destroyed, and even then it might shift only partly to the other hemisphere. This affinity is thought to be based on the special innate anatomical organization of the left hemisphere. In the examination of their series of patients with early left hemisphere lesions, Rasmussen and Milner also noted that childhood injuries to the left hemisphere occurring after 5 years of age rarely changed speech patterns. They argued that recovery occurring after about age 6 is not due to transfer to the other hemisphere but to intrahemispheric reorganization, possibly with intact surrounding zones acquiring some control over speech. Further evidence comes from the study of Woods and Teuber. As illustrated in Figure 21.3, left but not right hemisphere lesions cause a decline in both verbal and performance IQ scores, a result that argues against the idea that the right hemisphere has equal potential for language.

Given that the evidence supports the left-for-speech hypothesis, there is reason to believe that functional validation must still occur; that is, practice with language is necessary to establish left hemisphere preeminence. Woods has reported that if left hemisphere lesions occur before the first birthday, both verbal and performance IQ are severely depressed. If left hemisphere lesions occur after 1 year of age, neither verbal or performance IQ is affected. Right hemisphere lesions at any age lower only performance IQ. It seems likely that the effects of the lesions before age 1 might be due to a disruption of verbal functions that had been insufficiently validated or perhaps disrupted by the invasion of performance functions. We must note, however, that this suggestion is speculative, that IQ is at best an imprecise measure of language, and that a more systematic study of these patients using linguistic tests is called for.

Absence of Language after Bilateral Lesions

Bilateral cortical lesions in children are rare. Nevertheless, there are a number of reports suggesting that if bilateral lesions do occur, the plasticity required for the acquisition or reacquisition of language following injury is not present. Vargha-Khadem and coworkers report such a case. A. C. was born after a normal pregnancy, but delivery was difficult and forceps were used. The following day he began to have epileptic seizures. He was treated with anticonvulsants and was seizure-free after a couple weeks of treatment. When he began to walk, he had left hemiparesis that affected the left limbs. He was very delayed in speech development and thereafter developed only primitive speech. He was eventually able to make only a few two-word utterances, and his rare attempts to make sentences could not be understood. He could follow instructions, suggesting a relatively preserved comprehension. Nevertheless, he did poorly on the token test, which evaluates the ability to follow a number of sequentially presented instructions, and he performed very poorly on most other tests of language ability. His performance on nonverbal portions of IQ tests suggested that he had at least normal intelligence. A CT scan performed at age 6½ indicated that he had a lesion largely restricted to Broca's area in the left hemisphere and another lesion restricted to the middle portion of the sensorimotor cortex on the right side. Thus, even though A. C. had a spared Broca's area on the right and spared posterior speech zones on both the left and the right, he failed to acquire language, as might be expected had he received only a unilateral left hemisphere lesion. The reason A. C. failed to show plasticity is not known, but this case history strongly suggests that for some reason plasticity depends upon at least one intact hemisphere.

EXPERIMENTAL APPROACHES TO EARLY RECOVERY

It is becoming increasingly clear that the mechanisms mediating recovery of function from injury sustained in infancy are behaviorally and anatomically quite different from the mechanisms that mediate recovery after lesions sustained in adulthood. This is due in part to anatomical changes that follow damage to an infant brain that are different from those that follow damage to an adult brain. It is also due to compensatory strategies that can be accessed by infant but not adult brains. Nevertheless, there is a limit to the recovery and compensation that can occur after infant lesions, and for some behaviors there may be no recovery at all.

Brain Size and Morphological Changes

A dramatic consequence of brain damage in infancy is that it causes the brain to be smaller in adulthood. Furthermore, the earlier the lesion occurs, the greater the effect on brain size. For example, as shown in Figure 21.5, the brains of rats with neonatal lesions were reduced in size by as much as 25%, whereas the brains of rats that were operated on as adults shrank by less than 12%. This size reduction, which in humans would be the equivalent of about 200 g, was not due to a larger lesion but was produced by shrinkage of the entire neocortex. No systematic analysis of this phenomenon has been made in monkeys or humans, but it is likely that the same result does occur in humans (Figure 21.6). To examine why such shrinkage might occur, Kolb and his coworkers examined the structure of cells in the neocortex. With very early lesions given to rats at the day of birth, the cells showed reduced complexity compared to adult cells. If the lesions were performed at 10 days of age, the cells were more complex than adult cells. To explain this phenomenon, Kolb suggests that the effect is analogous to the effect that occurs when plants are pruned: if they are pruned too early, growth is stunted; whereas if they are pruned after growth is initiated, growth is enhanced. Presumably, the early lesions have their effects through their influences on trophic factors or other mechanisms regulating brain growth.

Kolb and coworkers have adapted the neuropsychological procedures developed for humans and applied them to investigations of animals with early brain lesions. Rats that had received neonatal or adult frontal cortex damage were examined using a test battery that evaluated many different aspects of the animals' learned and unlearned behavior. It was found that learned behaviors (for example, spatial reversals) were spared by the neonatal lesions, but species-typical behaviors (for example, nest building, food hoarding) were abolished. The researchers interpreted the results to mean that what rats are preprogrammed to do cannot survive lesions at any age, whereas behavior that is heavily dependent on learning is somehow spared by the early lesions. Humans who have received frontal lobe injury in infancy show inappropriate (species typical) social behavior, whereas cognitive functions are relatively more intact. (See the case of J. P. below.)

Effects of Early Brain Lesions on Explicit and Implicit Learning

Bachevalier and Mishkin have examined the development of visual implicit and explicit learning in monkeys. Implicit memory was tested in a visual-discrimination task. For the test, the monkeys are presented with pairs of objects, one of which has food hidden beneath it. There are a total of 20 pairs of objects, and each pair is presented each day. Monkeys that are 3 months old learn to select the baited pairs almost as quickly as animals that are 3 years old. Explicit

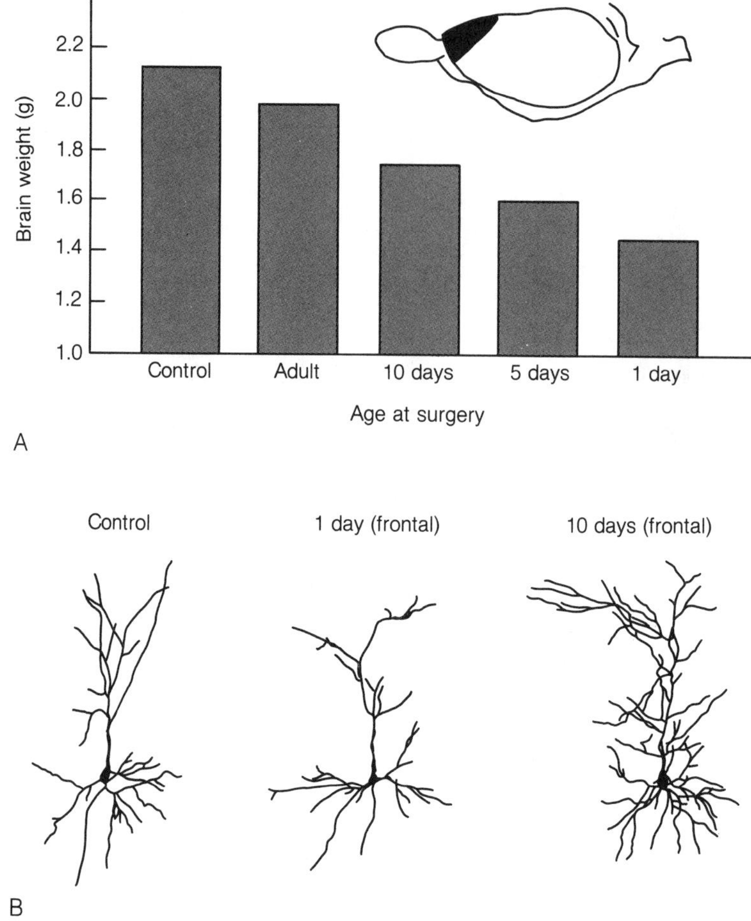

FIGURE 21.5. Effects of neonatal lesions on brain weight and cell structure. *A.* Brain weights of control rats and rats that received frontal lesions (see insert) as adults or at 1, 5, and 10 days of age. *B.* Drawings of cortical pyramidal cells from the parietal cortex. Note the very low brain weights and poorly developed dendritic arbor on the cells following the 1-day lesions. (After Kolb and Whishaw, 1989.)

memory is tested with an object-recognition task, the delayed nonmatching to sample (DNMS) task. The monkey is presented with an object under which is hidden food. After a delay, that object and a second object are presented, and the monkey will find food under the second object. Monkeys receive repeated trials with new objects until their performance is error-free. Task difficulty is increased by increasing the delay between presentation of the single object and the object pairs. Monkeys at 3 months of age are impaired relative to adults on this task and are unable to achieve adult performance levels until they are more than 1 year old. The superiority in implicit versus explicit learning on visual-recognition tasks has also been obtained in human children by Overman and his coworkers.

Bachevalier and Mishkin have also examined the effects of neonatal visual system lesions on the performance of a DNMS task. In adult monkeys,

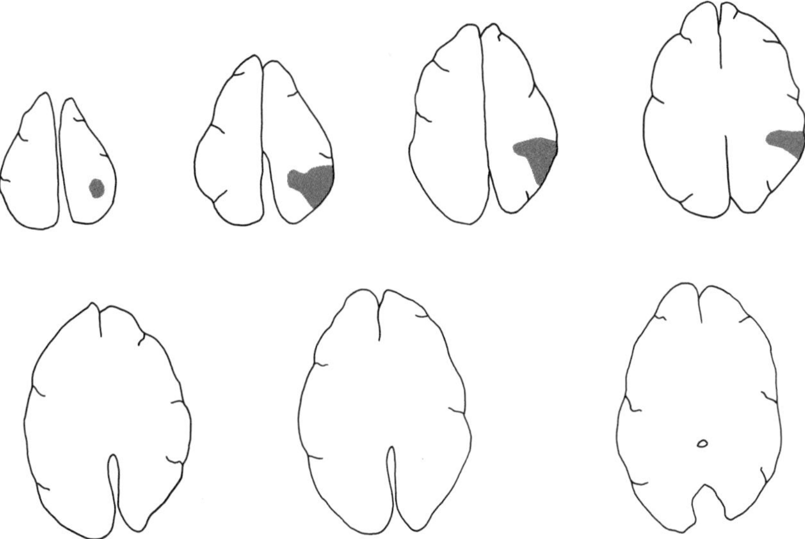

FIGURE 21.6. Summary of the CT scan from S., who had a birth-related injury to the right posterior cortex. Note that the right hemisphere is smaller at every plane. (After Kolb and Whishaw, 1989.)

lesions of the medial temporal cortex and of more laterally placed neocortex (area TE) severely impairs performance on the task, especially with the longer delays. They removed these areas in monkeys that were 1 to 2 weeks old and then tested them on a DNMS task beginning at 10 months of age. The monkeys with medial temporal lesions were nearly as impaired as monkeys that received adult lesions, whereas the monkeys with TE lesions in infancy showed considerable sparing relative to monkeys that received adult lesions (Figure 21.7). The researchers interpret these results to mean that if TE is damaged in infancy, other

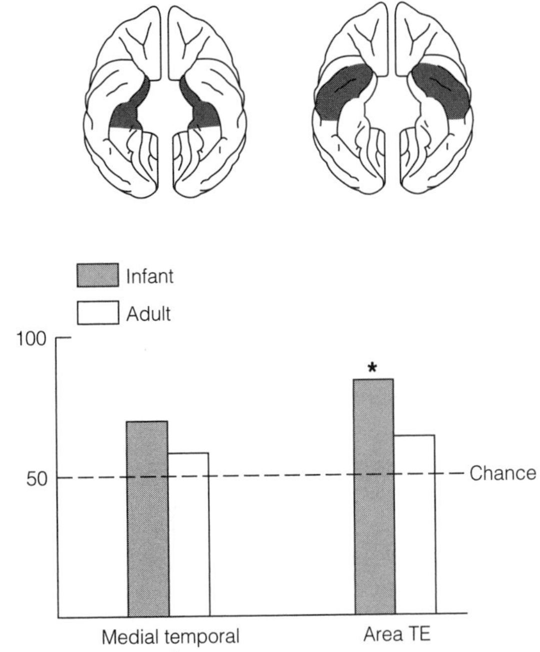

FIGURE 21.7. Performance of monkeys on DNMS task after infant or adult lesions of the medial temporal cortex or TE. The early lesions to TE produced sparing relative to adult lesions, whereas early lesions to the medial temporal cortex did not produce significant sparing. Above the graph, in a ventral view of the brain, medial temporal lobe (*left*) and TE (*right*) removals are shaded (front is up). (After Bachevalier and Mishkin, 1994.)

areas of the brain can reorganize to pass on visual information to the medial temporal lobe. In support of this interpretation, they find that early in infancy, another area of the temporal cortex, TEO, has connections to the medial temporal area that regress with maturation. If TEO is damaged, however, the connections between TEO and the medial temporal areas remain. Thus, they suggest that this anatomical modification underlies the spared DNMS performance obtained following neonatal TEO lesions.

Effects of Early Lesions on Short-Term Memory

The dorsolateral cortex receives projections from the parvocellular subdivision of the dorsomedial nucleus of the thalamus (Figure 21.8). In fact, the distribution of this projection defines this cortical zone. Many studies of the function of this area show that if it is damaged in adult monkeys, rats, or other animals, they show impairments of spatial delayed responses or spatial delayed alternation. In these tasks, the animal must choose between two spatially located objects, and each trial is separated by a delay. For example, a monkey must remember that a peanut is located in one of two cups, but each trial is separated by a short delay during which it cannot see the cup. Generally, lesioned animals do not perform above chance on this task, and the deficit is not attributable to interference with performance by sensory or motor difficulties, surgical shock, or lack of opportunity to learn. That is, even though they seem to "know" what to do, they make errors. On a host of other tasks, such as visual discriminations, these monkeys show no deficits. Histological analysis shows that the projecting fibers from the dorso-

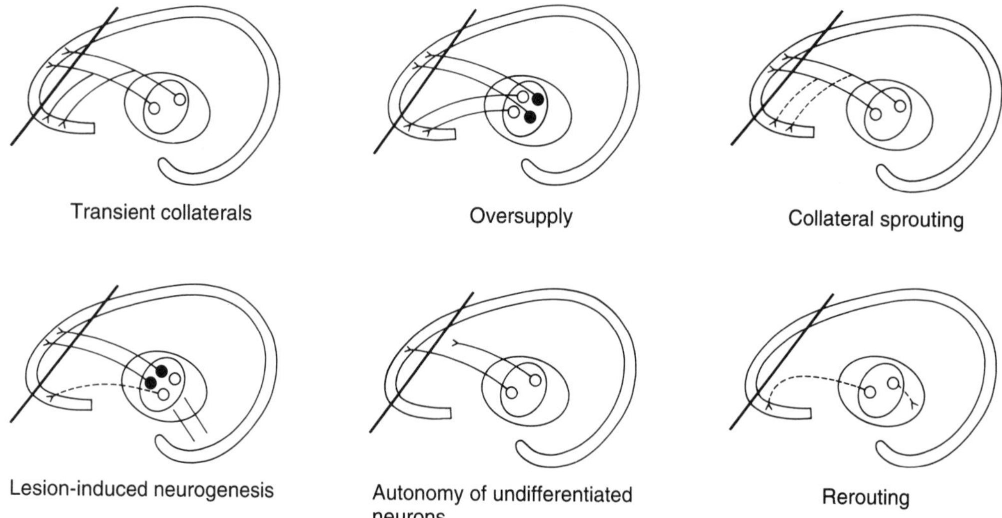

FIGURE 21.8. Explanations of the preservation of neurons in the dorsomedial nucleus of the thalamus after surgical resection of the dorsolateral frontal cortex (black line) in the monkey prior to birth. Black circles indicate degenerated neurons; open circles, preserved neurons. All the models stress that when a target area is removed, existing collaterals or new collaterals to another area sustain the cells that normally project to that target. (From Goldman and Galkin, 1978. Reprinted with permission.)

medial nucleus die after lesioning, and the cell bodies of these fibers degenerate.

Akert and colleagues and subsequently others removed the dorsolateral cortex of monkeys within the first 2 months of life and studied the monkeys on spatial reversals over the next year of life. During this time the monkeys showed no impairment when compared with age-matched control animals. Nevertheless, degeneration of cells in the thalamus was found. These early studies seemed to suggest that other brain structures could assume this function. However, this simple interpretation was complicated by Goldman's finding that if the monkeys were tested for as long as 2 years, they gradually developed the adult deficit or, as it has been phrased, they "grew into" the deficit.

Goldman and Galkin also studied the behavior and anatomy of monkeys that had been removed from the womb before term, subjected to surgery, and then replaced. These animals showed no deficits as infants or when mature and also showed no cellular degeneration in the dorsomedial thalamus. Earlier, Kolb and Nonneman had obtained identical results with the rat, which does not require preterm surgery because it is more immature at birth than the monkey. These studies imply that if cortical damage occurs early enough in life, the brain is able to reorganize in some way to achieve complete compensation. One type of evidence for such reorganization is that the monkeys have gyri and sulci not observed in normal monkeys. Other evidence is that cells of the dorsomedial nucleus remain intact, leading to the hypothesis that the new connections they make most likely sustain behavior. Goldman and Galkin have suggested a number of types of reorganization that might account for the survival of these cells (see Figure 21.8).

Effects of Early Lesions on Social Behavior

As noted earlier, studies with rats suggest that neonatal frontal cortex lesions have an especially severe effect on social behavior. Most studies of the effects of early lesions in primates and humans have not examined social behavior. Those that have, however, attest to the deleterious consequences of early cortical injury. In studies using monkeys, Bachevalier has reported that early damage to the temporal lobes in infancy changes the behavior of the animals so that they appear autistic when adult. That is, they shun social contact with other monkeys, display stereotyped behavior, display excessive self-directed behavior, and show a lack of facial expression. If the temporal lobe lesions are restricted to the amygdala and entorhinal cortex, the autistic behavior is present but is not as severe. If the lesion is restricted to the parahippocampal gyrus and hippocampus, the autistic behavior emerges only in adulthood. Monkeys that receive damage to TE neonatally are not autistic but hyperactive. Their behavior is annoying to adult monkeys, who do not like to interact with them. Bachevalier suggests that the behavioral patterns displayed by the monkeys may serve as a model to explain autism in human children.

After frontal cortex damage in infancy, humans seem to show the same sparing of learned behaviors despite the loss of what could be called human-typical behaviors. The case history of Ackerly's patient J. P. illustrates this point. At the age of 20, J. P. was referred for psychiatric examination because of his repeated difficulties with the law. A pneumoencephalogram plus follow-up exploratory surgery showed that J. P. had what seemed to be a congenital absence of both frontal lobes.

J. P.'s behavior had always been peculiar. In his preschool years he was noted for his wandering, which carried him miles from home, and for his Chesterfielding, or valetlike manners. He had school difficulties from the beginning. On one occasion his first-grade teacher had just written a letter to his parents complimenting them on having such a well-mannered child, when she looked up and found him exposing himself and masturbating before the class. He got by in school because of his language abilities, but he failed the third and fourth grades and did not finish high school, even after being sent to a variety of special schools. Throughout his life he was known for his wanderings and his love of taking cars and driving them hundreds of miles from home using the navigational criterion of "I steer by the compass and never make turns." In later life he was tested by Ralph Reitan, Brenda Milner, and others. His IQ was strictly average, but he failed all tests of frontal lobe function, including the category test and the Wisconsin Card-Sorting Test. Halstead, after testing J. P., thought he resembled a computer, so stereotyped were his responses. Everyone who met J. P. was struck by how dissociated he seemed from the world. He had no friends and had made no sexual contacts or other social attachments. He once took a girl out to dinner, but ran off with her purse when she went to the washroom. In school he was hated by all the boys. He was once described as a "stranger in the world without knowing it." Ackerly summarized his impressions of J. P. in the following way:

> What seemed to command our attention and sympathy was his "aloneness"—detachment not from the immediate physical environment of things and people, but from anything beyond that—anything that gave meaning to life, love, friendship, comradeship. He is indeed a veritable stranger in this world with no other world to flee to for comfort. (Ackerly, 1964)

Throughout his life, J. P. was never able to hold a job for more than a few weeks. Ackerly seems to have pinpointed the dichotomy of J. P.'s existence by describing him as a case not of mental deficiency but of social deficiency.

Evidence of social deficiency following neonatal frontal lesions appear to be confirmed by a report by Price and coworkers. They describe two individuals who had suffered bilateral frontal lobe damage early in life. Frontal lobe damage and dysfunction were confirmed using MRI scans and neuropsychological tests. They found that the lives of these individuals were characterized by lack of insight, foresight, social judgment, empathy, and complex reasoning. Both lived lives in which their behavior was characterized by social deviance. (The areas in the frontal cortex associated with moral behavior are not identified in these studies.) Interestingly, Posner and Raichle found in PET studies that the anterior cingulate cortex is active in response to painful stimuli and also in conflict situations; that is, situations in which one response must be inhibited to allow another to occur. Thus, they propose that these medial frontal cortical areas may be involved in inhibiting inappropriate behaviors so that appropriate, but less obvious, behaviors can be selected.

SUMMARY

The pattern of nervous system development is specified genetically, from the very earliest stages of development. Nevertheless, neural development is marked by an initial superabundance of cellular elements and connections, the loss of which appears to be related to behavioral maturation. It is becoming increasingly clear that damage to the developing nervous system can produce behavioral changes that are different from those that follow adult lesions. During infancy there may also be periods of differential sensitivity. In humans, the most striking result is that language is spared following left hemisphere lesions. Still, age-related effects do occur. Damage before age 1 is associated with sparing of language function but also is accompanied by widespread deficits in other abilities. Damage after 1 year of age but before age 5 is more selectively associated with the sparing of language. After 5 years of age, even sparing of language does not occur. Processes that mediate these changes can be studied effectively using animal models. Animal studies have revealed a number of paradigms in which the neural consequences of early damage are different from those of adult damage. In some cases early lesions result in widespread cortical shrinkage, whereas in other cases certain populations of cells are spared following infant, but not adult, damage.

REFERENCES

Ackerly, S. S. A case of paranatal bilateral frontal lobe defect observed for thirty years. In J. M. Warren and K. Akert, eds. *The Frontal Granular Cortex and Behavior.* New York: McGraw-Hill, 1964.

Akert, K., O. S. Orth, H. Harlow, and K. A. Schultz. Learned behavior of rhesus monkeys following neonatal bilateral prefrontal lobotomy. *Science* 132:1944–1945, 1960.

Alajouanine, T., and F. Lhermitte. Acquired aphasia in children. *Brain* 88:653–662, 1965.

Basser, L. Hemiplegia of early onset and the faculty of speech with special reference to the effects of hemispherectomy. *Brain* 85:427–460, 1962.

Bachevalier, J., and M. Mishkin. An early and a late developing system for learning and retention in infant monkeys. *Behavioural Neuroscience* 98:770–778, 1984.

Bachevalier, J., and M. Mishkin. Effects of selective neonatal temporal lobe lesions on visual recognition memory in rhesus monkeys. *The Journal of Neuroscience* 14:2128–2139, 1994.

Blakemore, C., and D. E. Mitchell. Environmental modification of the visual cortex and the neural basis of learning and memory. *Nature* 241:467–468, 1973.

Caviness, V. S., Jr., and R. L. Sidman. Time of origin of corresponding cell classes in the cerebral cortex of normal and reeler mutant mice: An autoradiographic analysis. *Journal of Comparative Neurology* 148:141–152, 1973.

Epstein, H. T. Growth spurts during brain development: Implications for educational policy and practice. In J. S. Chard and A. F. Mirsky, eds. *Education and the Brain.* Chicago: University of Chicago Press, 1978.

Flechsig, P. *Anatomie des menschlichen Gehirns und Rückenmarks.* Leipzig: Georg Thieme, 1920.

Goldman, P. S. Functional development of the prefrontal cortex in early life and the problem of neuronal plasticity. *Experimental Neurology* 32:366–387, 1971.

Goldman, P. S., and T. W. Galkin. Prenatal removal of frontal association cortex in the fetal rhesus monkey: Anatomical and functional consequences in postnatal life. *Brain Research* 152:451–485, 1978.

Guttman, E. Aphasia in children. *Brain* 65:205–219, 1942.

Harlow, H. F. *Learning to Love.* San Francisco: The Albion Publishing Co., 1971.

Hécaen, H. Acquired aphasia in children and the ontogenesis of hemispheric functional specialization. *Brain and Language* 3:114–134, 1976.

Hirsch, H. V. B., and D. N. Spinelli. Modification of the distribution of receptive field orientation in cats by selective visual exposure during development. *Experimental Brain Research* 13:509–527, 1971.

Hubel, D. H., and T. N. Wiesel. Receptive fields of cells in striate cortex of very young, visually inexperienced kittens. *Journal of Neurophysiology* 26:994–1002, 1963.

Kolb, B., and A. J. Nonneman. Sparing of function in rats with early prefrontal cortex lesions. *Brain Research* 151:135, 1978.

Kolb, B., and I. Q. Whishaw. Neonatal frontal lesions in the rat: Sparing of learned but not species typical behavior in the presence of reduced brain weight and cortical thickness. *Journal of Comparative and Physiological Psychology* 95:863–879, 1981.

Kolb, B., and I. Q. Whishaw. Plasticity in the neocortex: Mechanisms underlying recovery from early brain damage. *Progress in Neurobiology* 32:235–276, 1989.

Kornhuber, H. H., D. Bechinger, H. Jung, and E. Sauer. A quantitative relationship between the extent of localized cerebral lesions and the intellectual and behavioural deficiency in children. *European Archives of Psychiatry and Neurological Sciences* 235:129–133, 1985.

Kratz, K. E., P. D. Spear, and D. C. Smith. Postcritical-period reversal of effects of monocular deprivation on striate cells in the cat. *Journal of Neurophysiology* 39:501–511, 1976.

Lomas, J., and A. Kertesz. Patterns of spontaneous recovery in aphasic groups: A study of adult stroke patients. *Brain and Language* 5:388–401, 1978.

Milner, B. Psychological aspects of focal epilepsy and its neurological management. *Advances in Neurology* 8:299–321, 1975.

Overman, W. H., J. Bachevalier, F. Sewell, and J. Drew. A comparison of children's performance on two recognition memory tasks: Delayed nonmatch-to-sample versus visual paired-comparison. *Developmental Psychobiology* 26:345–357, 1993.

Piaget, J. *Biology and Knowledge.* Chicago: University of Chicago Press, 1971.

Posner, M. I., and M. E. Raichle. *Images of Mind.* New York: W. H. Freeman, 1994.

Price, B. H., K. R. Daffner, R. M. Stowe, and M. M. Mesulam. The comportmental learning disabilities of early frontal lobe damage. *Brain* 113:1383–1393, 1990.

Rakic, P., J.-P. Bourgeois, M. F. Eckenhoff, N. Zecevic, and P. S. Goldman-Rakic. Concurrent overproduction of synapses in diverse regions of the primate cerebral cortex. *Science* 232:232–235, 1986.

Ramón y Cajal, S. *Recollections of My Life.* Memoirs of the American Philosophical Society (vol. 8), 1937.

Rasmussen, T., and B. Milner. Clinical and surgical studies of the cerebral speech areas in man. In K. J. Zulch, O. Creutzfeldt, and G. C. Galbraith, eds. *Cerebral Localization.* Berlin and New York: Springer-Verlag, 1975.

Rasmussen, T., and B. Milner. The role of early left-brain injury in determining lateralization of cerebral speech functions. *Annals of the New York Academy of Sciences* 299:355–369, 1977.

Riva, D., and L. Cazzaniga. Late effects of unilateral brain lesions sustained before and after age one. *Neuropsychologia* 24:423–428, 1986.

Russell, R., and M. Espir. *Traumatic Aphasia.* Oxford: Oxford University Press, 1961.

Schneider, G. E. Early lesions of superior colliculus: Factors affecting the formation of abnormal retinal projections. *Brain Behavior and Evolution* 8:73–109, 1973.

Sidman, R. L. Development of interneuronal connections in brains of mutant mice. In F. P. Carlson, ed. *Physiological and Biochemical Aspects of Nervous Integration.* Englewood Cliffs, N.J.: Prentice-Hall, 1968.

Singh, J. A. L., and R. M. Zingg. *Wolf Children and Feral Man.* New York: Harper, 1940.

Skeels, H. M. Adult status of children with contrasting early life experiences. *Monographs of the Society for Research in Child Development* 31:1–65, 1966.

Teuber, H.-L. Recovery of function after brain injury in man. In *Outcomes of Severe Damage to the Nervous System, Ciba Foundation Symposium 34.* Amsterdam: Elsevier-North Holland, 1975.

Vargha-Khadem, F., and G. V. Watters. Development of speech and language following bilateral frontal lesions. *Brain and Language* 25:167–183, 1985.

Wechsler, A. F. Crossed aphasia in an illiterate dextral. *Brain and Language* 3:164–172, 1976.

Woods, B. T. The restricted effects of right-hemisphere lesions after age one; Wechsler test data. *Neuropsychologia* 18:65–70, 1980.

Woods, B. T. Impaired speech shadowing after early lesions of either hemisphere. *Neuropsychologia* 25:519–525, 1987.

Woods, B. T., and H.-L. Teuber. Early onset of complementary specialization of cerebral hemispheres in man. *Transactions of the American Neurological Association* 98:113–117, 1973.

chapter twenty-two

Learning Disabilities

Once upon a time, the animals decided they must do something heroic the meet the problems of a "new world." So they organized a school. They adopted an activity curriculum consisting of running, climbing, swimming, and flying. To make it easier to administer the curriculum, all the animals took all the subjects. The duck was excellent in swimming, in fact better than his instructor. But he made only passing grades in flying and was very poor in running. Eventually his web feet were badly worn from running and he became only average in swimming. But average was quite acceptable, so nobody worried about that—except the duck. The rabbit started at the top of his class in running but had a nervous breakdown because of so much make-up work in swimming. The squirrel was excellent in climbing, but he developed frustrations in flying class because his teacher made him start from the ground up instead of from the treetop down. He developed charley horses from overexertion and got a C in climbing and a D in running. The eagle was a problem child and was severely disciplined. In climbing classes he beat all the others to the top of the tree but insisted on using his own way to get there. At the end of the year, an abnormal eel that could swim exceedingly well, and could also run, climb, and fly a little, had the highest marks and was class valedictorian. The prairie dog stayed out of school and fought the tax levy because the administration would not add digging and burrowing to the curriculum. The prairie dog's parents apprenticed their child to a badger and later joined the groundhogs and gophers to start a free school. (Author unknown, but told by Sam Rabinovich.)

This fable expresses one view of the challenge for neuropsychology in education. Are learning problems a manifestation of disabilities or of individual variations? Large numbers of children enter schools in which they are required to master a core curriculum. Some of them are completely unable to meet any demands of the school system they enter, some learn but only with great difficulty, some have to repeat one or more grades, some graduate but fail to master certain subject areas, and some even graduate without mastering basic knowledge in any area. For those who fail, the educational experience often leaves emotional and attitudinal scars that are carried throughout life. Of course, the difficulties that individuals encounter in school can have any of a number of causes. A child may be disturbed by an unhappy home life, be bored by school, dislike school, dislike a teacher, have no aptitude for school, have low "intelligence," or have a physical handicap, including brain damage. Some school systems may be equipped to assess these kinds of problems and deal with them objectively. Most have no resources for either assessment or remediation. Whether or not a school system is equipped to deal with the learning problems of an individual, neuropsychology now receives enough publicity that the question of whether a child has brain damage or a cognitive problem that precludes effective learning will probably arise.

HISTORICAL BACKGROUND

Learning disability is an umbrella term that is used to refer to a wide variety of school-related problems. Formal definitions of learning disabilities include assumptions that the individual has adequate intelligence, opportunity to learn, instruction, and home environment, yet still does not succeed. These features are illustrated by the definition of dyslexia devised by the World Federation of Neurology: "A disorder manifested by difficulty in learning to read despite conventional instruction, adequate intelligence, and sociocultural opportunity. It is dependent upon fundamental cognitive disabilities which are frequently of constitutional origin." Every phrase of this and similar definitions has been disputed. For example, why should it be called a disorder? What is meant by conventional instruction? What is meant by adequate intelligence? And so on. To appreciate the difficulties with definitions, it is helpful to know some of the history of ideas about learning disabilities.

Aphasiological Origins

The early study of learning disabilities was concerned with **dyslexia,** an inability to read properly. Critchley points out that the term emerged within an "aphasiological context," so that it was thought of as being due to brain damage that occurred in language areas at an early age. Kussmaul is thought to have been the first person, in 1877, to isolate "word blindness," or an inability to read that was caused by brain damage and that persisted in the presence of intact sight and speech. In 1892 Dejerine placed the responsible lesion in the posterior portions of the left hemisphere. The word "dyslexia" was coined by Berlin in 1887. When James Hinshelwood (1895), a Glasgow eye surgeon, and Pringle Morgan (1896), a Seaford general practitioner, first observed students who could not learn to read, they assumed that their reading failed to develop because their prerequisite brain areas were absent or abnormal. It seemed logical to conclude that **developmental dyslexia** (congenital dyslexia) is similar in form to **acquired dyslexia** (dyslexia due to brain damage after reading has been achieved). Developmental deficits in other spheres, such as math, also would be due to some underlying brain problem.

Strephosymbolia

In the 1920s and 1930s Samuel T. Orton proposed that dyslexia is due to delayed function, not anatomical absence. Orton, the director of a medical clinic in Iowa, noted that dyslexia was correlated with left-handedness and tendencies toward letter and word reversals or inversions when learning to read or write. He termed such dyslexia **strephosymbolia** (from the Greek, meaning twisted symbols). Orton thought that the nondominant hemisphere, which he postulated had a reversed image of things, was excessively dominant or not sufficiently controlled. He also suggested that if the instructor was clever or persevered, education could establish normal dominance and thus normal reading.

Environment

When sociologists and educational psychologists became interested in learning disabilities, they thought that environmental explanations, rather than neurological ones, could account for dyslexia. This was perhaps motivated by the belief, or hope, that environmental causes could be reversed more easily than neurological ones.

TABLE 22.1. "Do-it-yourself terminology generator"

Secondary	Nervous	Deficit
Minimal	Brain	Dysfunction
Mild	Cerebral	Damage
Minor	Neurological	Disorder
Chronic	Neurologic	Desynchronization
Diffuse	CNS	Handicap
Specific	Language	Disability
Primary	Reading	Retardation
Developmental	Perceptual	Deficiency
Disorganized	Impulsive	Impairment
Organic	Visual-motor	Pathology
Clumsy	Behavior	Syndrome
Functional	Psychoneurologic	Complex

Directions: Select any word from first column, add any word from second and third columns. If you don't like the result, try again. It will mean about the same thing.

Source: From Fry, 1968. Reprinted with permission of Edward Fry and the International Reading Association.

Learning Disabilities

The term "learning disability" had its origins in an address given in 1963 by Samuel A. Kirk. Kirk argued for better descriptions of children's school problems, but he excluded children with sensory handicaps and mental retardation from the children he called learning-disabled. His definition and address were influential because members of his audience got together and formed the Association for Children with Learning Disabilities, and this society in turn popularized the label.

The search for causes has resulted in a proliferation of terms that ostensibly attempt to dissociate the learning-disabled from the retarded and brain-damaged. Fry published a "Do-It-Yourself Terminology Generator," shown in Table 22.1, to emphasize the proliferation of terms in the field and the inaccuracies in description. From this list about 2000 terms can be constructed.

THE INCIDENCE OF LEARNING DISABILITIES

Gaddes tried to determine the proportion of children with learning disabilities as reported in various prevalence studies from both North America and Europe. He found that most estimates of the need for special training for learning disabilities range from 10% to 15% of the school-age population, although only about 2% actually receive special education.

A problem in collecting prevalence estimates is that a learning disability is an emerging problem. When children enter the first grade, few are as yet learning-disabled. One method of defining a learning disability is to use a 2-year cutoff criterion; that is, if an individual is 2 years behind as determined by a standard test, then that individual is learning-disabled. When this criterion is used, less than 1% of 6-year-olds are disabled, 2% of 7-year-olds are disabled, and so on, until at age 19, 25% would be disabled. This emerging incidence occurs because the learning-disabled are falling behind at a rate that is proportional to their degree of impairment. Even these kinds of calculations may be difficult to apply in certain regions. For example, the Wide Range Achievement Test (WRAT) is often used to determine grade-equivalent performance, but not all school populations should be expected to display equivalent performance. Teachers could be asked how many children in their classes are receiving special help. Unfortunately, many schools cannot provide such information because they have no resources for special education.

TYPES OF LEARNING DISABILITIES

The classification and incidence of learning disabilities reflect the emphasis placed on appropriate conduct and certain academic specialties in school systems. Good behavior, reading, arithmetic, and spelling are emphasized, and learning-disability classification reflects this emphasis. Although art, music, and physical education are taught in most schools, referrals for failure in these areas are uncommon. If art, rather than reading, were the core subject in the early years of school, we suspect that current catalogues of types of disabilities would be different. Nevertheless, as Semrud-Clikeman and Hynd note in their review, there are disabilities that are related to social skills, spatial orientation, mathematics, and other nonverbal behaviors.

In summarizing syndromes presented to a clinic specializing in learning disabilities over a 2-year period, Denckla reports that of 484 children aged 6 to 16 years, 76% were classified as primarily dyslexic, with or without some associated problems, and 18% were classified as hyperactive. Thus, reading and behavior problems were the most common reasons for referral. The *Diagnostic and Statistical Manual of Mental Disorders* (DSM-III-R), providers a number of classifications of disorders arising in childhood. Excluding mental retardation and mental disorders, the DSM-III describes disorders in reading, arithmetic, and motor activity, along with some mixed classifications. The U.S. Department of Health, Education, and Welfare identifies 10 characteristics most often cited by various authors as being associated with a learning disability: (1) hyperactivity; (2) perceptual-motor impairments; (3) emotional lability; (4) general coordination deficits; (5) disorders of attention (short attention span, distractibility, perseveration); (6) impulsivity; (7) disorders of memory and thinking; (8) specific learning disabilities, including especially those of reading (dyslexia), arithmetic, writing, and spelling; (9) disorders of speech and hearing; and (10) equivocal neurological signs and irregular EEG. Of course, not all learning-disabled children exhibit all the symptoms. Critchley points out that for every learning-disabled child with coordination problems, there is a child with better than normal coordination. Some authors categorize the learning disabilities into four symptom complexes, which are not mutually exclusive: (1) dyslexia-dysphasia, (2) motor-perceptual, (3) language delay, and (4) hyperactivity.

VERBAL DISABILITIES

Reading requires letter identification skills, phonological skills (converting letters into sounds using certain rules), grapheme skills (the visual gestalt of a word is used to access a previously learned sound), sequencing skills in which a number of sounds are analyzed and combined in sequence, and short-term memory skills to retain pieces of information as they are sequentially extracted from written material. Acquired information is also important. Knowledge of words in the form of a **lexicon** (a dictionarylike store of words in the brain)—containing their meanings, knowledge of the way in which they can be combined, and information about the ideas with which they can be associated—is related to reading. Thus, reading is a multiprocess and multistage behavior. As such, it is possible, in theory if not in fact, for it to be disrupted in many different ways.

Reading can be accomplished in one of two ways. Consider the following example. Imagine that you are reading a novel about a man named Fzylx from Worcester. Let us assume that you have never encountered either the man's name or his hometown before. When you read the names, you presumably attempt to pronounce the various letters to arrive at a satisfactory pronunciation of the words. Suppose that the next day you overhear two people discussing a novel about a man named Felix from Wooster. At first, you might be struck by the similarity between the plot of your book and theirs, until you realize that they are actually talking about Fzylx from Worcester! What has happened? When you read Fzylx and Worcester, you encountered two common problems in reading English. First, you had to read a name that is not English and so you had no rules by which to read it. You may feel comfortable with your pronunciation, since it allows you to read the name. Second, you encountered an irregular word; that is, a word that is not pronounced the way it is spelled. The only way to pronounce this type of word correctly is to memorize it. This type of reading is called **graphemic reading** (sometimes called lexical reading). It can be used for regular words as well, but it must be used for irregular words or words that are not found in English. It is also the way Arabic numerals (such as 4) and international symbolic road and direction signs must be read. The other way to read is to do what you tried to do with Fzylx and Worcester. You simply convert a letter or group of letters into sounds (phonemes) that will provide the clue to the meaning of the words. Stated differently, the sounds that you get by analyzing letter groups will lead you to the correct pronunciation, and you will be able to access your memory, or lexicon, for the meaning and connection of the word. This is known as **phonological reading.**

Bradley and Bryant have suggested that the phonological procedure is used by beginning readers, but that as reading skill is attained the graphemic procedure becomes more important. They suggest that the transition occurs between 6 and 10 years of age. Thus, normal reading initially involves phonological skills and later becomes dependent on grapheme skills. This may be why many people have difficulty finding typographical errors when they proofread. Rather than reading phonologically, they read graphemically and, with practice at graphemic reading, only part of the word need be read before attention is shifted to the next word. If the spelling error is not within the portion of the word actually read, it will not be noticed. As we shall see shortly, it has been suggested that phonological reading may be a function of the left hemisphere and grapheme reading a function of the right.

Given that there are two reading processes, we should find at least two different kinds of impairments, which could occur at different ages. A child who is incompetent in the phonological procedure will have difficulty in the early stages of reading. A child who is competent in the phonological procedure but incompetent in the grapheme procedure will have difficulty later on. Frith has demonstrated just such types of age-related disabilities among poor readers. It may also follow that a child who is impaired at the first type also will be hampered in making the transition to the second type. We should note here that by no means would these types of impairments exhaust the class of poor readers. People with a poor short-term auditory memory may not derive the sense of written material correctly because they forget the meaning of phrases as they proceed. This type of disability may be particularly obvious at older ages, once reading material becomes more complex. People with poor long-term memory may not understand the sense of words despite good decoding skills, simply because they do not have much information about the meaning of the words. This type of individual would be like English-speaking people who are reading Italian. They would be able to read the words because they know phonetic rules, but they would not understand what they have read because they would not know what the words meant. In fact, people who are demented are often just like this. They can read but they understand nothing.

There are three approaches to analyzing the problem of the dyslexic individual. The first is to identify the reading problem without regard to its underlying causes. Such an approach may also give some information about underlying causes, but this is by no means certain. The second approach is to describe and analyze the dyslexic in a variety of different ways, cataloguing various symptoms, in order to come to conclusions about underlying causes. The third approach is to use neuropsychological assessment procedures, derived from research on adult brain-damaged patients, to evaluate brain and cognitive function in the disabled reader and relate that information to the reading disorder. All three approaches have generated interesting insights into the dyslexic individual, although it would also be correct to say that the amount and complexity of the information they have generated is astonishing.

Malatesha and Cougan have reviewed studies that provide various subclassifications of dyslexia. They found that 7 studies describe two subtypes, 21 studies describe three subtypes, and 3 studies describe four subtypes. To add to this complexity, most subtypes in most of the different studies are derived in quite different ways, using different assessment techniques and classification criteria. Some studies emphasize visual and auditory processing differences, some emphasize hemisphere specialization, some emphasize memory differences, and some emphasize deficits in certain aspects of reading, whereas others are based on postulated types of brain damage or dysfunction. It appears to us that the problem of classification and subclassification will remain complex. As we shall see, there is a great deal of variation in test performance even in individuals who are reported to have the same type of learning disability. It would seem, therefore, that assessment providing a number of different evaluation criteria combined with counseling directed toward the special problems of each individual will remain the most effective approach to both research and remediation of people with verbal disabilities.

The reading tests described to this point depend on the fact that some education in reading has taken place. Bradley and Bryant have developed an interesting approach that is initially reading-independent. They tested children's ability in sound categorization before they started to read. The tests involve giving the child three or four words and asking him or her to pick out the word that does not share a phoneme in common with the others. For example, in the series "hill, pig, pin," "hill" would be the correct choice; in the series "cot, pot, hat," "hat" would be the correct choice, and in the series "pin, bun, gun," "pin" would be the correct choice. Bradley and Bryant found that when the same children were older and had started to learn to read, those who were initially poor at sound categorization were those who became backward in reading and spelling. They argue that the initial insensitivity to rhyme and alliteration causes subsequent reading impairment, because if the children who were initially impaired were given special training on rhyme and alliteration, their reading was far less impaired after training in reading began. According to Bradley and Bryant, at least one cause of reading deficiency is a basic deficiency in phonological awareness.

It is possible that children who are at risk for learning disabilities could be detected still earlier. Frith has suggested that the babbling of babies may give clues about those who are at risk. Tees and his coworkers have reported that young infants can detect differences between all known speech sounds, but as they acquire language their detection abilities become restricted to only those sounds used in their own language, which they are exposed to daily. Impairments in refining detection abilities could lead to language difficulties.

Tallal and her coworkers have examined the sensory detection abilities of children with learning disabilities and found that they are impaired in detecting sensory events that occur in rapid succession. If two sensory stimuli, such as two tones, are presented in succession very quickly, they will be heard as one tone. If the interval between the tones is gradually increased, a point will be reached at which they are heard as two tones. For most individuals a separation of *tens of milliseconds,* or about 10 to 40 msec, is required before the two tones are discriminated. For individuals with language impairments, a much greater separation is needed (Figure 22.1). The impairment in separating the individual stimuli occurs in all sensory modalities and in producing movements. Thus, language-impaired individuals require longer intervals to detect two separate lights or two separate tactile stimuli and are impaired in producing rapid movements. The relevance of this finding to language impairments is that stop consonants ("ba," "da," "ga," "pa," and "ta") contain a transition period in which the sounds (called formants) change very rapidly, usually within 40 msec. When stop consonants are used as stimuli, language-impaired individuals have difficulty detecting them, whereas they have no

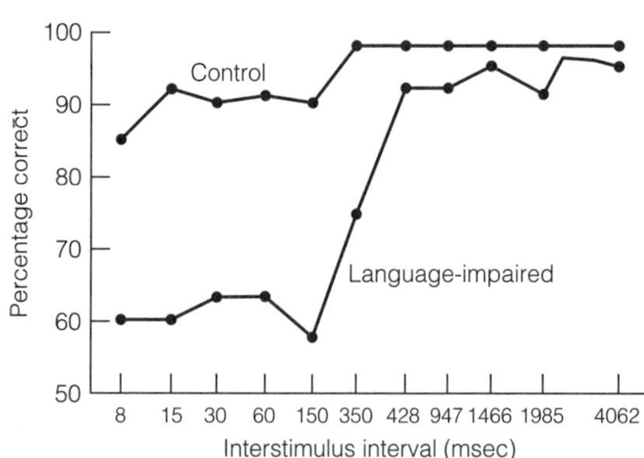

FIGURE 22.1. Percentage of time that control and language-impaired individuals discriminate two tones of different interstimulus intervals. Note that the controls can discriminate tones with intervals as short as 10 msec, whereas the language-impaired individuals require much longer intervals. (After Tallal, 1993.)

difficulty detecting vowels. They also have no difficulty in detecting stop consonants if the transition period is increased. When this difficulty is detected in infants, it is predictive of later language impairment.

On the basis of studies of patients with brain lesions and PET studies, Tallal and coworkers suggest that the left hemisphere is specialized for making these rapid sensory discriminations and movements. Thus, it has the prerequisite capacity to become dominant for language. It follows that impairments of the left hemisphere will impair discrimination abilities that are important for both the acquisition and production of language. These results have implications for remediation. Merzenich and coworkers have suggested on the basis of animal studies that it is possible to improve discrimination of rapidly presented stimuli with specific training. Thus, they suggest that remediation of language-related disorders should focus on training in discrimination rather than on more generalized training in language-related skills.

Analysis of Correlated Deficits

It might be hoped that reading deficits would display themselves in a straightforward manner. This seems not to be the case, however, since it has long been known that dyslexic individuals have a wide variety of different symptoms that occur in clusters and that vary considerably between individuals. We cannot discuss each of the many particular symptoms here, but they include deficits in attention, eye movement, development, memory, coordination, spatial abilities, movement sequencing, map reading, and visuospatial processing. These symptoms should not be thought of as necessarily uninformative, unrelated, or irrelevant. Dyslexia may be associated with many kinds of symptoms because language has a superordinate role in the control of behavior, because there is a close relationship between the control of language and the control of movement, and because the development of dyslexia itself may produce secondary symptoms. Just the same, attempts have been made to see if the various symptoms are causally related to dyslexia. Rutter suggests that clumsiness and incoordination; difficulties in the perception of spatial relations; directional confusion; right-left confusion; disordered temporal orientation; difficulties in naming colors and recognizing the meaning of pictures; inadequate, inconsistent, or mixed cerebral dominance; bizarre spelling; and a family history of reading difficulties do seem related to dyslexia, but it is not clear that the relationship is causal. On the other hand, he concludes that low intelligence and mixed-handedness are definitely not important as causal factors. Vellutino has asked which specific capacities of visual perception and visual memory, intersensory integration, temporal order and recall, and verbal processing are of central importance to reading. On the basis of a review of the available research and logical argument, he finds that only a deficit in verbal processing is causally related to dyslexia. He suggests that many of the other deficits occur because tests require verbal processing for their solution. When the verbal component of the test is removed, there is improvement or even normal performance.

Neuropsychological Evaluation

The neuropsychological approach to the assessment of dyslexia generally includes the following assumptions: (1) A disability may exist in only one or a few spheres of endeavor. (2) A specific skill or lack of that skill can be detected using a neuropsychological testing procedure. (3) If one method or strategy of instruction is unsuccessful, another might be more successful. (4) It should be possible to develop a strategy for remediation of a learning disability from that neuropsychological test results. Although none of these assumptions has yet received anything like adequate scientific support, at least one reason that neuropsychology is becoming a popular approach is that the assumptions do hold out hope for helping learning-disabled children. Even if neuropsychology offers no help in remediation, however, it may still be useful for purposes of counseling. The case of Ms. P. illustrates this point.

Ms. P., a 19-year-old woman, was referred to us by a friend. She was working as a nurse's aide and had found her work so enjoyable that she was considering entering a nursing program. She had not completed high school and generally had a poor academic record. She came to us for guidance as to whether or not she could handle the nursing program. In discussing her academic record, we learned that Ms. P. had particular difficulty with language skills, and her reading was so poor that she was unable to pass the written exam for a driver's license. In view of Ms. P.'s interest in further education in nursing, we decided to administer reading tests plus a complete neuropsychological battery. The results showed an overall IQ of 85 on the Wechsler Adult Scale, but there was a 32-point spread between her verbal IQ of 74 and her performance IQ of 106. Her performance on specific tests of left hemisphere function confirmed this hypothesis, because her verbal memory, verbal fluency, spelling, reading, and arithmetic skills were extremely poor. On the other hand, her spatial skills were good, as were her nonverbal memory and her performance on tests such as the Wisconsin Card-Sorting Test and the Semmes Body-Placing Test. In short, her language skills were those of a 6-year-old although she had attended school for 11 years. This verbal ability contrasted with her other abilities, which were normal for a person of her age.

In view of the test results, we explained to Ms. P. our belief that it was unlikely that she could handle a nursing program, because of her deficient language skills. We also believed that she was unlikely to develop these skills, especially since—as we inadvertently discovered—none of her five brothers and sisters could read, either. We explained to Ms. P. that she was by no means retarded, but that just as some people had poor musical ability, she had poor verbal ability. (We were able to arrange an aural administration of the driver's test, which she passed.) Finally, we explained Ms. P.'s problem to her husband, a well-educated man with a master's degree. In the short time they had been married, he had become totally frustrated with her inability to balance the bank account, read recipes, and so forth, and he was beginning to believe that his wife was either "crazy or retarded." They now had an understanding of their problem, which we hoped would help them work out domestic routines to minimize its impact. We learned later though, that the marriage did not last.

Neuropsychological assessment should offer insight into the abilities of any particular learning-disabled child because it assesses performance on a wide range of tests that are sensitive to all areas of brain function. Usually children are not dyslexic or dyscalculic alone but have a number of associated symptoms. Teachers and parents are usually unaware of the associated deficits, and an explanation of the deficits often makes it easier for them to understand the learning-disabled child. Neuropsychological tests should be able to distinguish between children who have central reading impairments and those who have problems with emotional or environmental causes. Individual test results should also give some indication of potentially successful strategies for special instruction. Details about the application of various neuropsychological assessment procedures can be obtained from reviews such as those by Denckla, Gaddes, and Rourke.

There have been many studies on the IQ test results of learning-disabled children. These analyses attempt to relate learning impairments with performance on the subtests of the Wechsler Intelligence Scale for Children. Rugel has summarized the results from studies that included a total of 1521 reading-disabled children and 554 control children. We have produced a graphic representation of these results in Figure 22.2. The dyslexic group displays low subscale scores on four tests: arithmetic, coding, information, and digit span. This profile, typical in many studies, is referred to as the ACID profile. Dyslexic children typically have a mean full-scale IQ that averages about 7 points lower than that of control children, but their mean IQ is roughly 100. Whishaw and Kolb have found that children over the age of 8 show the ACID profile, whereas those younger than 8 may not show a deficit in the information or arithmetic subscales. This suggests that these deficits in older children and adults are secondary to the underlying impairment that produces dyslexia. Although the deficits in digit span and coding are

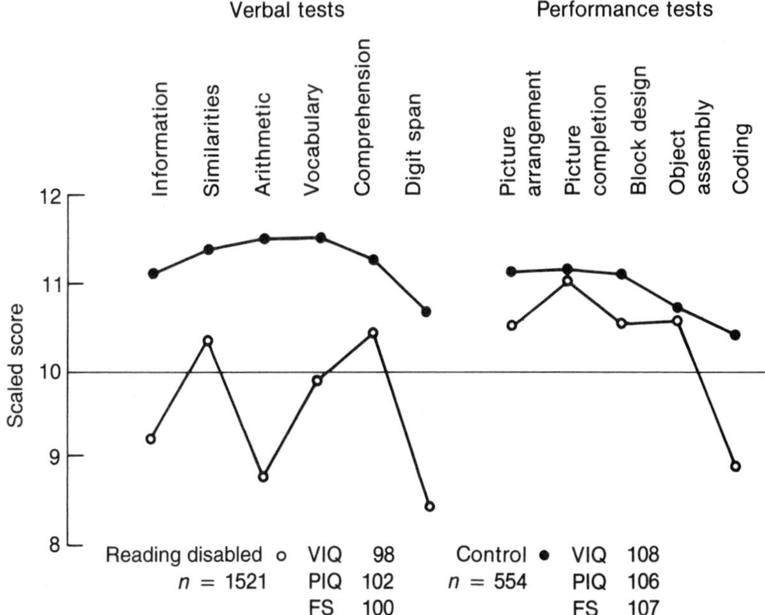

FIGURE 22.2. Intelligence test profiles of developmentally dyslexic and control subjects. Note the low scores on arithmetic, coding, information, and digitspan, referred to as the ACID profile. (VIQ, verbal IQ; PIQ, performance IQ; FS, full-scale IQ) (From Rugel, 1974; after Whishaw and Kolb, 1984.)

common, there is no agreement that they are necessarily related to a disability in reading.

Many researchers have commented that there are large differences between verbal IQ and performance IQ in dyslexic individuals, and it has been suggested that two types of dyslexics can be identified on the basis of these scores. In addition, Denckla has pointed to the scatter of the IQ subscores. Nevertheless, for an experienced counselor, the pattern displayed by any individual may be meaningful.

In comparing a dyslexic group to the control group on other tests of our composite test battery, it was found that the tests did discriminate between the two groups, but their effectiveness depended in part on the individual's age. This age-dependent effect was particularly clear in three tests. In the test of left-right differentiation (Figure 22.3) neither control nor dyslexic children could score above chance if they were younger than 8 years old. After the age of 8, the control children performed well whereas the dyslexic children continued to perform at chance. A different kind of emerging difference was found on tests of word fluency (for example, "Give as many words beginning with the letter 'S' as you can"), in which the differences between dyslexic and control groups did not occur in children younger than 8 years but became increasingly large in older age groups. This result seems to suggest that the control group showed improved fluency performance whereas the dyslexic group remained almost static. A third pattern was obtained on the Semmes Body-Placing Test. Here, significant group differences emerged only in adults, and then they seemed to depend on the fact that adult control subjects displayed virtually perfect performance on the tests. The results of these various tests suggest to us that although the tests can be applied to children with some success, a great deal

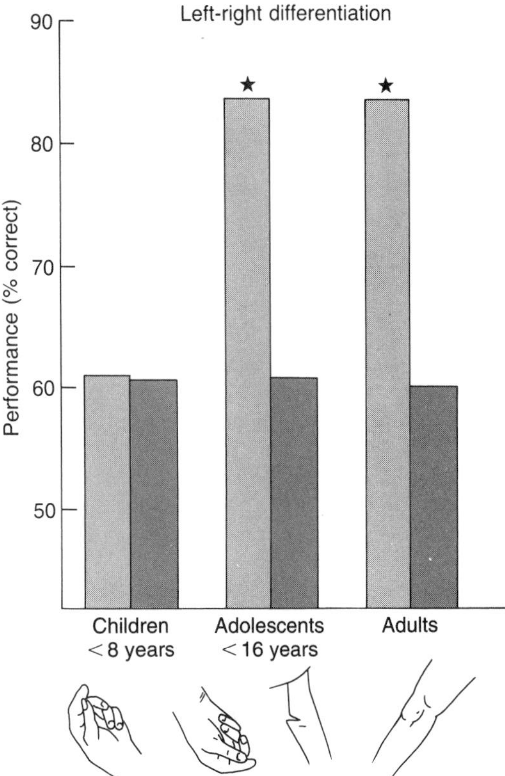

FIGURE 22.3. Performance on the left-right discrimination test by control subjects (light bars) and dyslexic subjects (dark bars). Stars signify significant group differences. (After Whishaw and Kolb, 1984.)

of caution in interpretation is required for the younger children, and retesting at different ages is worthwhile.

NONVERBAL DISABILITIES

Nonverbal learning disabilities are characteristic of children who have difficulty in comprehending aspects of their environment, in pretending and anticipating, and in interpreting the facial and emotional gestures of others. Whereas children with nonverbal disabilities have little difficulty with the superficial aspects of speaking and reading, they do have difficulty with the deeper meanings of language. Such children are often immature and have difficulty making the judgments needed to succeed in life. They may also have difficulty developing social relations, learning to read maps, following directions, performing mathematical tasks, and interpreting the emotions of others. Whereas children who have difficulty with language are often thought to have left hemisphere dysfunctions, children with nonverbal disabilities are thought to have right hemisphere dysfunctions.

Included among the nonverbal disabilities are certain forms of **autism,** a condition characterized by extreme social withdrawal. A less severe condition of withdrawal is referred to as *Asperger's syndrome.* These children are not only withdrawn but are also characterized by early speech, good grammar, narrow repetitive play, poor peer relations, and a need for routine and sameness.

Included among the nonverbal disability symptoms are conditions in which children excel in some aspect of behavior, such as reading, calculations, music, or art. *Hyperlexia* is a term for unusual reading ability in otherwise cognitively impaired individuals. Hyperlexia is marked by a precocious development of reading abilities between the ages of 3 and 5 years. Very often the children teach themselves to read. Their precocious reading ability is often accompanied by exceptional memory abilities, such as remembering words, TV shows, names of streets, the weather, birthdays, and so forth. Reading may not be completely fluid, since there are often articulatory defects and prosodic abnormalities involving intonation and rate of speech. Generally, comprehension of what is read is impaired, and the children show emotional withdrawal, occasional echolalaia, and autistic symptoms. As Cobrinik has demonstrated, tests of intelligence often show IQs below 50, with sparing on only a few subtests, usually digit span and occasionally block design and similarities.

The causes of hyperlexia and its associated cognitive abnormalities, or of other precocious abilities displayed by otherwise cognitively impaired individuals, are not known. It has been suggested that these children have islands of a normally functioning brain in an otherwise impaired brain, that through some developmental abnormality they are overdeveloped in some brain areas and underdeveloped in others, or that they are using otherwise adequate brains in a functionally unusual manner.

Related to hyperlexia is the **savant syndrome,** and hyperlexics may be special cases of savants. The savant syndrome or idiot savant syndrome was first described by Down in 1887 and has recently been reviewed by Treffert. Since Down's description, there have been several hundred cases reported in the literature. They are remarkably similar in that they have a narrow range of special abilities and the triad of symptoms of retardation, blindness, and musical genius is common. The term idiot savant was coined by combining the once acceptable classification of mental retardation—idiot—with savant, or knowledgeable person. The term has endured despite its now pejorative connotation. Savants are marked by mental handicaps resulting from a developmental disability or mental illness combined with a talent that stands in contrast to their other abilities (talented savants) or in contrast to the abilities of the general population (prodigious savants). The syndrome is estimated to occur in males about six times more frequently than in females. The special skill can appear quite suddenly and disappear equally quickly. Skills that are often displayed by savants include calendar calculations (some can tell the day of a person's birthday over 1000-year periods); mathematical ability; musical ability, including the ability to play new pieces of music after hearing them once; sculpting; drawing; and peculiar feats of memory, including memory of the weather for every day of the person's life, retention of the names and dates of all visits received, and the date of every burial and the names of those in attendance in a parish over a 35-year time span.

At present there are no adequate theories to explain the special abilities or to explain the impairments that are manifest by autistic individuals. Available evidence, reviewed by Bauman and Kempor, suggests that there are brain abnormalities that can be quite variable from one individual to another but which might corrrelate with the degree of impairment displayed by an individual. Abnormalities seem to be especially marked in the temporal lobes and in the cerebellum. It seems possible that impairments in explicit memories (memories for daily events) are related to temporal lobe abnormalities, where impairments in implicit memory (skills and conditioned responses) are related to cerebellum abnormalities. In light of these reports concerning the involvement of these brain areas in autism, it is interesting to speculate that individuals with special skill in the implicit memory domain have intact temporal lobe structures but abnormal cerebellar structures. The desire for sameness and the avoidance of novelty may also be related to cerebellar abnormality. According to some views of cerebellar function, it is involved in conditioned responses. One feature of conditional learning is habituation, or learning to ignore irrelevant or repeated stimuli. In the absence of an ability to habituate to ongoing events, an individual may find them especially noxious and so avoid them in favor of maintaining sameness. In this respect it is interesting that autistic individuals have reported that the sound of traffic, to which most people quickly habituate, remains for them frighteningly loud.

HYPERACTIVITY

The **hyperactive child syndrome** is distinguished from other types of learning disabilities in that the child is a behavioral problem in school and all aspects of school performance are usually disrupted. Hyperactive children may have specific learning disabilities in addition to hyperactivity, and these may contribute to hyperactivity. A number of diagnostic labels have been given to this disorder, including minimal brain dysfunction, hyperkinetic child syndrome, and hyperkinetic impulsive disorder. The DSM-III-R gives the following characteristics of the disorder:

1. Excessive general hyperactivity or motor restlessness for the child's age. In preschool and early school years, there may be incessant haphazard, impulsive running, climbing, or crawling. During middle childhood or ado-

lescence, marked inability to sit still, up and down activity, and fidgeting are characteristic. The activity differs from the norms for the age both in quality and quantity.

2. Difficulty in sustaining attention, such as inability to complete tasks initiated or a disorganized approach to tasks. The child frequently "forgets" demands made or tasks assigned and shows poor attention in unstructured situations or when demands are made for independent, unsupervised performance.

3. Impulsive behavior.

4. Duration of at least one year.

It is thought that in infancy hyperactive children are characterized by poor and irregular sleep, colic, and feeding problems. They are not cuddly and do not like to be held still for long. Later they are described as learning to run rather than to walk and as being driven to handle and play with everything. By the time they reach kindergarten, they are demanding, do not listen, and do not play well with other children. Other people, outside the home, may begin to reject the child because of his or her behavior. By the time the child enters school, his or her activity, low tolerance for frustration, poor concentration, and poor self-esteem lead to a referral for assessment. By adolescence, the individual is a school failure, and 25% to 50% of hyperactive children may begin to encounter problems with the law. Their behavior remains restless, they withdraw from school, and they fail to develop social relations and maintain steady employment.

The hyperactive syndrome is described by Weiss and Hechtman as the commonest behavioral disturbance among children. Estimates of its incidence vary because of problems with definition and differences in tolerance shown by different societies. Estimates of the ratio of boys to girls are as high as 5 : 1 to 9 : 1. In the Isle of Wight study made by Rutter, an incidence of 1 in 1000 was reported, but in North America, where the tolerance for hyperactive behavior seems lower, estimates of incidence are as high as 6 in 100. It does seem that parents' and teachers' estimates of what comprises normal behavior may be unrealistic, for Weiss and Hechtman note that in surveys of parents and teachers, as many as 50% of children are reported as hyperactive.

The suggested causes of hyperactivity include brain damage, encephalitis, genetics, dopamine decreases, food allergies, high lead concentrations, and various home and school environments. It is unlikely that there is a single cause, and so comprehensive, multidisciplinary assessment is recommended. Therapy includes counseling for the child and parents and careful structuring of the home and school environments. Beginning in the 1960s and continuing to the present, treatment with amphetaminelike stimulant drugs such as Ritalin has been popular. The effectiveness of Ritalin or other drug treatment as a long-term solution is doubtful. When Ritalin is effective, it may be because, as a stimulant, it allows the individual to concentrate on the task at hand. The drug may also have a general sedating effect on children.

CEREBRAL PALSY

Cerebral palsy is a disorder primarily of motor function caused by brain trauma during fetal development or birth. Any simple definition is difficult, however, because (1) the motor symptoms take many forms, (2) there can be many different accompanying cognitive impairments, and (3) the disorder has diverse causes. As such, cerebral palsy cannot be called a disease, a syndrome, or even a condition; depending on the nature of the brain damage, it will take a different form in each individual. Because brain damage is involved, it is not curable, but it often is amenable to therapy and training. The term "cerebral palsy" is most useful in an administrative sense, for it covers individuals who are handicapped in many different ways by motor disorders due to nonprogressive brain abnormalities. A more detailed discussion of the problems of definition, form, incidence, and treatment has been presented by Cruickshank.

Cerebral palsy was first described in the medical literature in 1853 by the London physician William Little. He recognized that the motor abnormalities of some babies are related to abnormal parturition, difficult labor, premature birth, and asphyxia. He also recognized the permanence of the disabilities and their associated intellectual impairments; changes in personality, such as irritability and temper tantrums; and epilepsy. More important, he pointed out that the problems could be severely aggravated by subsequent improper training and education.

The incidence of cerebral palsy is not known precisely, because many cases are not reported, but it is estimated at about 6 per 1000 births. The numbers of males and females afflicted are about equal. Estimates of the degree of impairment suggest that about 10% of afflicted persons require no special services, 65% need services on an ambulatory basis, and about 25% need special schooling or custodial care. With respect to type of cerebral palsy by motor symptoms, about 50% of persons with the disorder are spastic, about 25% are athetoid, about 10% are afflicted with rigidity, and about 10% are ataxic. As noted earlier, cerebral palsy has many causes, the most frequent of which are listed in Table 22.2. Nearly 50% of all cases are due to birth injury or injury suffered during development, 9% are secondary to convulsions, and 8% are due to prematurity. Smaller numbers result from other diverse causes. Incidence is also related to the mother's ability to carry a baby to term and to factors such as her body size, health habits, and weight gain during pregnancy.

TABLE 22.2. Potential causes of cerebral palsy

Hereditary
- Static—familial athetosis, familial paraplegia, familial tremor
- Progressive—demyelinating diseases of viral or undetermined origin (chromosomal breakages are rare in cerebral palsy, as are disorders of metabolism)

Congenital (acquired in utero)
- Infectious rubella, toxoplasmosis, cytomegalic inclusions, herpes simplex, and other viral or infectious agents
- Maternal anoxia, carbon monoxide poisoning, strangulation, anemia, hypotension associated with spinal anesthesia, placental infarcts, placenta abruptio
- Prenatal cerebral hemorrhage, maternal toxemia, direct trauma, maternal bleeding, diathesis
- Prenatal anoxia, twisting or kinking of the cord

Miscellaneous toxins, drugs

Perinatal (obstetrical)
- Mechanical anoxia—respiratory obstruction, narcotism due to oversedation with drugs, placenta previa or abruptio, hypotension associated with spinal anesthesia, breech delivery with delay of the after-coming head
- Trauma—hemorrhage associated with dystocia, disproportions and malpositions of labor, sudden pressure changes, precipitate delivery, caesarean delivery
- Complications of birth—"small for date" babies, prematurity, immaturity, dysmaturity, postmaturity, hyperbilirubinemia and isoimmunization factors (kernicterus due to Rh factor, ABO incompatability), hemolytic disorders, "respiratory distress" disorders, syphilis, meningitis, and other infections, drug addiction reactions, hypoglycemic reactions, hypocalcemic reactions

Postnatal-Infancy
- Trauma (subdural hematoma, skull fracture, cerebral contusion)
- Infections (meningitis, encephalitis, brain abscess)
- Vascular accidents (congenital cerebral aneurism, thrombosis, embolism, hypertensive encephalopathy, sudden pressure changes)
- Toxins (lead, arsenic, coal tar derivatives)
- Anoxia (carbon monoxide poisoning, strangulation, high-altitude and deep-pressure anoxia, hypoglycemia)
- Neoplastic and late neurodevelopmental defects (tumor, cyst, progressive hydrocephalus).

Source: From E. Denhoff, Medical aspects. In W. M. Cruickshank, ed. Cerebral Palsy. *Syracuse, N.Y.: Syracuse University Press, 1976, p. 33. Reprinted with permission.*

Denhoff has described the medical features of the movement disorders and the part of the body involved—that is, spastic, ataxic, choreiform, and so forth. In addition to these characteristics, the degree of the impairment (mild, moderate, or severe) with a description of muscle tone (hypertonic, hypotonic) and other associated dysfunctions may also be specified. Lesions involving the corticospinal tracts, basal ganglia, brainstem, and cerebellum are presumed to be responsible for the disorders. Yet clear-cut relations between lesion and clinical findings are difficult to make. A conservative classical interpretation would associate corticospinal damage with spasticity, basal ganglia damage with dyskinesia, and cerebellum damage with ataxia. Simply because many of these brain systems traverse the entire brain and make many connections throughout it, localization is difficult.

HYDROCEPHALUS

Hydrocephalus is characterized by an increase in the volume of the cerebrospinal fluid (CSF). This can occur in two ways. First, enlarged ventricles can be a secondary result of shrinkage or atrophy of surrounding brain tissue. This is more likely to occur in adults. The second, more typical cause of hydrocephalus is obstruction of the flow of CSF, resulting in a buildup of pressure in one or more ventricles that eventually causes their expansion. This type is more typical in infants. It is not certain that a simple overproduction of CSF is ever a cause of hydrocephalus.

Figure 22.4 is a drawing made from a cast of the lateral ventricles. Normally the ventricles are filled with CSF. In all, there is only about 130 cm^3 of CSF in an adult, and about one-third of this is in the spinal cord's great lumbar cistern. CSF is made by the choroid plexus in the ventricles, most of it in the lateral ventricles. From there it flows through the interventricular foramina (windows) of Monro into the third ventricle, through the cerebral aqueduct, and then into the fourth ventricle. It finally escapes through three little holes in the roof of the fourth ventricle. These are the two laterally located foramina of Luschka and the medial foramina of Magendia. (The mnemonic is: lateral, Luschka; medial, Magendie). The fluid then enters the subarachnoid space—the space

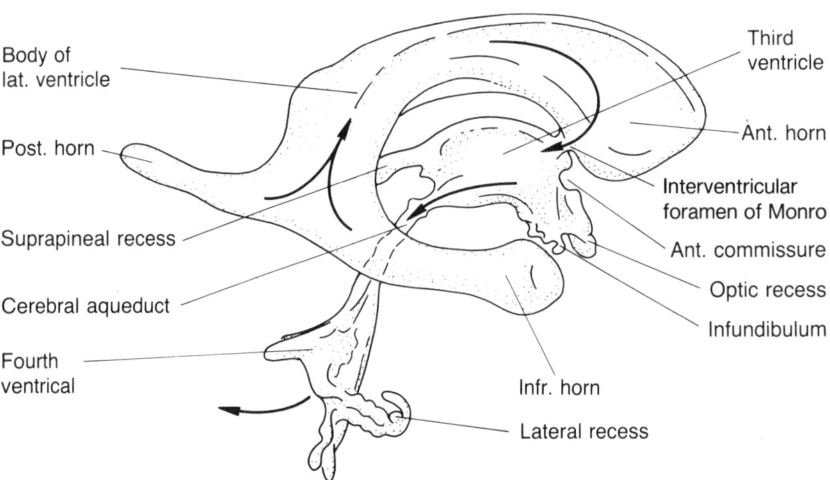

FIGURE 22.4. Drawing of a cast of the ventricular system of the brain as seen from the side. The arrows show the direction of flow of cerebrospinal fluid. A blockage of the flow in the narrower portions of the ventricles (for example, the cerebral aqueduct) can cause the symptoms of hydrocephalus. (After Everett, 1965.)

beneath the arachnoid covering of the brain and spinal cord. It is absorbed into the veins and carried away by the bloodstream.

The circulation in the ventricles can be blocked at either of the interventricular foramina, causing an increase in pressure followed by expansion of either lateral ventricle. It can also be blocked at the level of the cerebral aqueduct (causing hydrocephalus of the first three ventricles) or by closure of the foramina in the roof of the fourth ventricle (producing hydrocephalus of the entire ventricular system). If CSF flow is suddenly obstructed, there is a rapid rise in intracranial pressure, ventricular dilation, and finally coma. If CSF pathways are gradually obstructed, as by a tumor, increase in pressure and dilation is less rapid and symptoms may include the gradual appearance of visual disturbances, palsies, dementia, and so on.

Infant hydrocephalus is characterized by a conspicuous enlargement of the head. It usually occurs during the first few months of life. As many as 27 of 100,000 newborn babies may suffer from hydrocephalus. In about 14% of cases there is a malformation that impedes CSF circulation; inflammation or trauma produces most other cases. About 4% of cases are due to tumors. As the ventricles distend, they push the cerebral hemispheres into a balloon shape. Because the skull bones of an infant are not yet fused, continued pressure causes the expansion of the head in all directions. If expansion damages the cortex, intelligence may be impaired and dementia may result. If the cortex is undamaged, intelligence may be unimpaired even after the cortex is stretched into a sheet of tissue less than a centimeter thick. If untreated, hydrocephalus often causes death or severe mental or motor disabilities. It can now be treated with some success by inserting a valve and tube into one lateral ventricle that passes into a jugular vein to drain into the cardiac atrium. Lorber reports that individuals with extreme hydrocephalus and extensive cortical loss develop normally and have normal abilities as adults. We question this conclusion. Perhaps in these cases the cortex is quite thin and has been unfolded and spread out by fluid pressure while still maintaining its integrity and connections. If people were able to develop normally without a cortex, most of the conclusions of this text and neuropsychology in general would be in question. It is certainly the case that cortical removals in animals, no matter when they are made or how they are made, produce severe behavioral impairments.

CAUSES OF LEARNING DISABILITIES

Four major factors are most often cited as possible cases of learning disabilities: (1) structural damage, (2) abnormal cerebral lateralization, (3) maturational lag, and (4) environmental deprivation.

Structural Damage

Since the symptoms of brain damage in adulthood resemble childhood learning disabilities (for example, dyslexia), the cause of learning disabilities may be similar structural damage, perhaps resulting from birth trauma, encephalitis, anoxia, early childhood accidents, and so forth. Although no doubt a cause for a small minority of children, structural damage is not likely to be the cause in most children, since many neurological symptoms associated with brain damage in adults are not typically observed in children. For example, children with developmental dyslexia do not have hemianopsias or scotomas, symptoms that would certainly occur in a large percentage of brain-damaged adults with dyslexia. Further, EEG and CT scan studies have not demonstrated structural damage: abnormal EEGs similar to those correlated with known brain damage are not consistently correlated with learning disabilities.

It is not necessary to have direct brain damage to have neurological deficits. Thus, it has been proposed that learning disabilities may result from malfunction of some portion of the cerebral cortex rather than from direct damage. One view of the brain dysfunction hypothesis holds that the dysfunction results from defective arousal mechanisms. Douglas and her colleagues have found that learning-disabled children have difficulty on continuous-performance tests requiring them to react to particular stimuli while ignoring others. Similarly, reaction-time studies show the children to have slower mean reaction times to signals. On tests of visual searching—in which the child is asked to search among several alternatives to find a picture identical to a standard picture—the learning-disabled children choose impulsively and quickly, making many more errors than normal children, who perform more slowly. Thus, learning disabilities should improve with drugs that increase cerebral activation, and both amphetamine and caffeine, cerebral stimulants, do improve performance. An alternative dysfunction theory proposes that brain malfunction results from abnormal metabolism, due either to diet or to abnormal metabolic processes. Analyzing specimens of hair from normal and learning-disabled children, Pihl and Parkes found significant differences between the groups in the levels of sodium, cadmium, cobalt, lead, manganese, chromium, and lithium. When levels of these elements were measured in the hair, it was possible to identify 98% of all the children diagnosed as learning-disabled from a second sample of children. Although Pihl and Parkes could not identify the cause of the abnormal levels of trace elements, their success in diagnosing learning-disabled children leads us to consider biochemical factors seriously as causal factors in learning disabilities.

The Geschwind-Galaburda hypothesis provides a different view of how developmental brain changes can occur. The beginning of this hypothesis lay in Geschwind's observation that the planum temporale (an area thought to represent speech in the left hemisphere) is asymmetrical, being larger on the left and smaller on the right in most right-handers. This asymmetry is proposed to represent the underlying neural asymmetry that gives rise the left hemisphere's dominant role in language. Since males are thought to show greater deviance from this asymmetrical pattern, the possibility that testosterone plays a role is suggested. During embryonic development, the male fetal gonads produce high levels of testosterone, comparable to the levels of adult males. Levels fall just before birth, rise and fall again just after birth, and rise yet again at puberty. It is proposed that the embryonic surges of testosterone delays the development of the left hemisphere, allowing the right hemisphere both space and time for greater development. Thus, males in general have some comparatively better developed areas in the right hemisphere, which would presumably endow them with excellent spatial skills. If the testosterone-induced asymmetry produces some particularly large right hemisphere areas, this could result in special abilities, such as precocious mathematical reasoning ability. It is proposed that testosterone also produces some casualties manifest by brain changes and learning disabilities. An additional aspect of the hypothesis is that, among both males in general and males with exceptional abilities, there is a high incidence of autoimmune disorders (migraines, allergies, asthma, thyroid disorders, ulcerative colitis, and so forth). The hypothesis is that testosterone also affects the development of the immune system, with the consequence that there is increased susceptibility to autoimmune disorders.

The appeal of the Geschwind-Galaburda hypothesis is that it can account for the general observation that females tend to do better at language-related tasks than males and males tend to do better at spatial tasks than females. It can also account for the high incidence both of precocity and of learning disabilities among males. The proposed shift in cerebral dominance can also provide an explanation for the high incidence of left-handedness among the precocious and among the learning-disabled. Finally, since the effects of testosterone on the brain in some ways will be paralleled by its effects on the immune system, the hypothesis accounts for the high incidence of autoimmune disease in the precocious and learning-disabled male populations. In addition, the theory can allow for deviations in hormonal functions to produce increased incidences of learning disabilities, precociousness, left-handedness, and autoimmune disorders in females. An additional appeal is that the hypothesis is testable and allows for the development of animal models. Unfortunately, the bulk of the evidence to date does not support the theory.

The first examination of the brain of an individual with a reading disability was made by

Drake, who examined the brain of a 12-year-old boy who died of cerebral hemorrhage. In school he had been impaired in arithmetic, writing, and reading, but he had normal intelligence. Autopsy showed that there were atypical gyral patterns in the parietal lobes, an atrophied corpus callosum, and neurons in the underlying white matter that should have migrated to the cortex. Galaburda's group then examined the brain of a 20-year-old male who had had a reading disability despite average intelligence. Visual inspection of the brain showed it to be normal, but microscopic examination showed several abnormalities. Polymicrogyria (numerous small convolutions) and other architectonic abnormalities were found in the left frontal and parietal cortex. The locations of abnormal brain regions are shown in Figure 22.5. Subcortical abnormalities occurred in the medial geniculate nucleus and the lateral posterior nucleus of the thalamus of the same individual. Since the original report, this group has reported similar findings in additional cases.

Galaburda and coworkers have made a detailed examination of the planum temporale and reported that the normal pattern of left larger than right was not present in children with learning disabilities. A reexamination of the original data has shown, however, that when there was no asymmetry in the planum temporale it was not because the areas on both sides were small but because both sides were large. When the asymmetry was reversed, the size of the areas was also completely reversed. Simply slowing down the development of the left hemisphere would be unlikely to account for this result. Thus, a new hypothesis was favored. It was suggested that in early development both sides are equal and large, but as development progresses one or the other side can be reduced in size through the loss of neurons. Presumably, testosterone would play a deciding role in how this development was to proceed. This new mechanism, however, does not provide the same attractive explanation for the anomalous cell growth observed in the learning-disabled brains.

There have now been a number of studies directed toward finding abnormalities and asymmetries in the area of the planum temporale. These include studies using CT scans and studies using MRI. The latter technique is increasingly favored because it can provide excellent resolution. In reviewing many of these studies, Hynd and Semrud-Clikeman question their adequacy and enumerate the difficulties of testing hypotheses using anatomical approaches. One difficulty is that if strict criteria of learning disabilities are adhered to (for dyslexia, for example, average IQ, evidence of a selective reading impairment, absence of other abnormalities, and so forth), then the results of many studies are compromised. Such ideally defined individuals are not easy to find. Another difficulty relates to the adequacy of control groups. The control group should be selected in such a way that the incidence of any supposed abnormality can be determined. Ideal control groups should include age-matched peers and family members. An additional and emerging problem is that as the quality of imaging improves, the problem of knowing what to measure and correlate with learning disabilities becomes more complex.

At least three general conclusions can be drawn from studies examining brain patterns in individuals with learning disabilities. First, there is substantial evidence for brain abnormalities in individuals with learning disabilities. Second, not all individuals with learning disabilities display brain abnormalities, or the same abnormalities. Third, some individuals in the control groups, although not learning-disabled, display some abnormalities that are found in those with learning disabilities. The studies do not consistently support the Geschwind-Galaburda hypothesis, however. The subjects of many studies do not seem to have an increase in autoimmune disorders, brain abnormalities are often bilateral rather than unilateral, and in some studies the learning-disabled individuals show exaggerated asymmetry in the planum temporale. One of the more recent studies highlights the complexities of measuring the planum temporale. Leonard and coworkers report that the planum temporale consists of two parts, the more or less horizontal portion called the temporal portion and the more or less vertical portion called

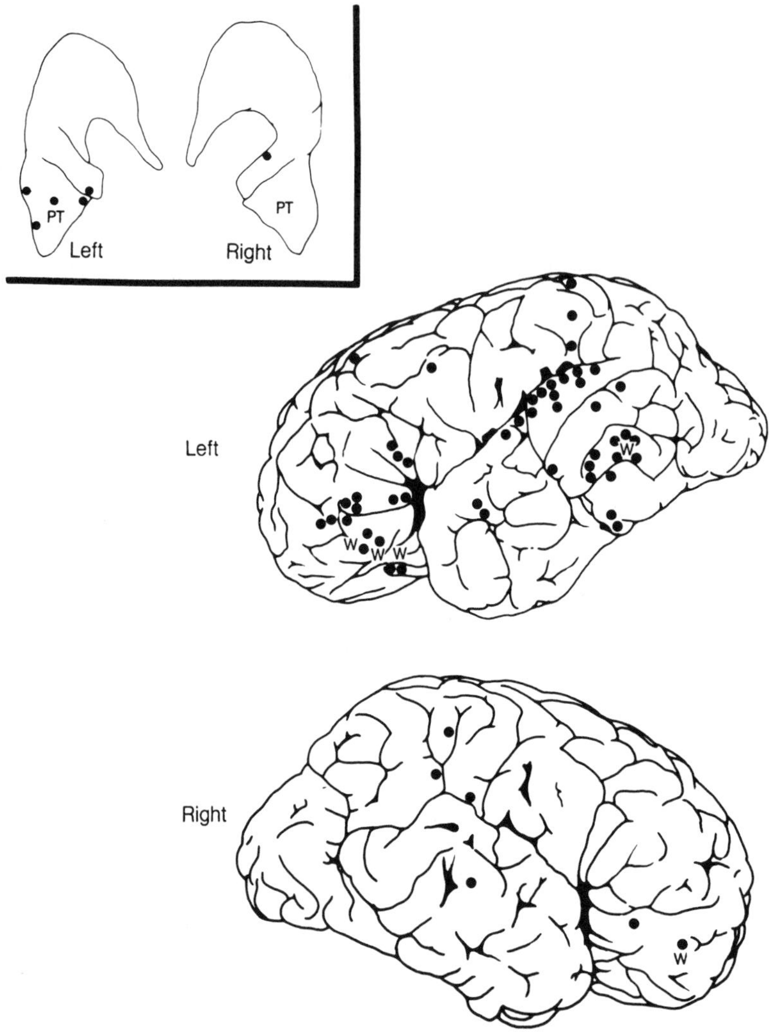

FIGURE 22.5. Drawings of the two hemispheres showing with closed circles the locations of areas of cell abnormalities in the brain of an individual who was diagnosed as reading-disabled. The inset shows a horizontal section of the planum temporale (PT) to illustrate its symmetrical pattern. The dots on the sections show areas of cortical anomalies and indicate that the involvement is asymmetrical. (W, brain warts.) (From N. Geschwind and A. M. Galaburda, *Cerebral Lateralization*. Cambridge, Mass.: MIT Press, 1985.)

the parietal portion. When the entire length of the planum is measured, it is symmetrical, with the temporal bank asymmetrical in the left hemisphere and the parietal bank asymmetrical in the right hemisphere in both learning-disabled and control individuals. The learning-disabled individual has an exaggerated asymmetry in the right hemisphere characterized by a shift of planar tissue from the temporal to the parietal bank. Additionally, this study found that the planum temporale has a number of patterns, as do its gyri. Even in this study, however, there are difficulties with control groups; both unrelated control subjects and related control subjects had much higher IQ scores than the learning-impaired group.

Perhaps one lesson that is beginning to emerge from brain analysis of learning-disabled individuals is that cortical features and abnormalities can take many forms, as can the deficits of those who have difficulty learning in a school setting. Thus, what is required before theories can be tested adequately is a better understanding of the topographic features of normal brains and of the range of abnormalities that can be present in brains, as well as more detailed correlations of individual learning profiles with brain profiles.

Abnormal Cerebral Lateralization

A variety of theories rest on Orton's premise that learning disabilities result from reduced or abnormal functional cerebral lateralization. This premise is based on the assumption that, since language is lateralized in the left hemisphere of most adults, such lateralization must be advantageous, and its absence would be deleterious to the acquisition of language skills. In the past 20 years, dozens of studies have examined dichotic and visual-field asymmetries, but the data are far from unequivocal. Satz concludes:

> One might ask what light the preceding review of laterality studies sheds, if any, on the problem of cerebral dominance and reading disability. The answer should be—not much. The reason for this somewhat discouraging view lies in the numerous methodological and conceptual problems that continue to plague research efforts in this area. (Satz, 1976, p. 288)

Witelson argues that there may be an association between developmental dyslexia and two neurological abnormalities: a lack of right hemisphere specialization for spatial processing, and a dysfunction in left hemisphere processing of linguistic functions. That is, spatial functions, being located in both hemispheres, result in an interference with the left hemisphere's processing of linguistic functions. The person approaches linguistic functions in a visual-holistic manner rather than a phonetic-analytic manner, which would be expected to produce deficits in language but superiority in spatial skills. Kinsbourne and Hiscock have been outspoken critics of this theory. Their criticism centers on the assumption that reduced lateralization of language should be detrimental to language development and school performance. Anomalous language lateralization in left-handers is not consistently correlated with cognitive deficit, nor is left-handedness consistently correlated with learning disability.

Maturational Lag

The maturational-lag hypothesis postulates that the cognitive functions involved in language, reading, and other complex behaviors are organized hierarchically and that the levels of the hierarchy develop sequentially during ontogeny. Should one level of the hierarchy be slow to develop, the entire hierarchy is retarded in development, since higher functions depend on the integrity of lower ones. The delayed maturation of cortical functions could result from a variety of factors. Two examples are delayed myelinization of a particular region and slow development of cortical connections. Although some studies suggest that various functions in learning-disabled children are slow in maturing, the type of study needed here is a careful longitudinal analysis of children tested on a large number of perceptual, motor, and cognitive skills for a period of 10 to 15 years. When learning-disabled children have been reexamined in adulthood, they have been found to still have their characteristic impairments. For example, Frauenheim studied 40 adults who were diagnosed as dyslexic in childhood and found that on test performance and on self-report evaluations, they were essentially unchanged from the time of diagnosis. This result does not support the maturational-lag hypothesis.

Environmental Deprivation

The work of Rosensweig and colleagues has shown that environmental factors can alter the neocortical development of rats. Rats raised in enriched environments have a thicker cortex with increased numbers of dendritic spines. This implies, then, that the environment in which children are raised may affect behavior indirectly by altering brain development. The notion has appeal and has led to the development of programs such as Operation Headstart. Additionally, Money has argued that institutional confinement, neglect, and child abuse can retard intellectual development and even physical growth. Accordingly, he states that environmental deprivation should rank high on the list of causes of learning disabilities.

A subtle variant of the deprivation hypothesis is called the **birthdate effect.** One perspective on this hypothesis comes from Barnsley's studies of birthdays of North American hockey players. In senior hockey leagues, there is a negative relationship between birth month and number of players. More than 30% of players have birth dates in the first quarter of the year (16% in January) while less than 15% have birth dates in the last quarter of the year (5% in December). Furthermore, a disproportionate number of the superstars have first-quarter birthdays. This birth discrepancy is not present in beginning leagues but emerges progressively as players are promoted through the leagues. The explanation appears to be straightforward. Players enter the most junior league according to age—children must be 8 years old between January 1 and December 31 of the year they enter Mite hockey. Equal numbers of children born in each month enter. But children born in December enter hockey almost a year earlier than children born in January, who in effect have had to wait a year. The younger, smaller children are at a developmental disadvantage from the outset. They receive less playing time and reinforcement and are more likely to drop out.

Research on the effects of relative age on educational achievement produces similar results. Beattie has reported that children entering school at a younger age achieve significantly less than their older classmates. Diamond and Maddux have found that children entering first grade at an early age were more likely than their older classmates to be classified as learning-disabled later on in their school career. Furthermore, Maddux and coworkers have found that among children who are classified as gifted, a larger population entered school late than entered school early. This effect may last into later grades and even into university. The rather simple birthdate effect stands in sharp contrast to the brain hypotheses and should be cause for sober reflection by neuropsychologists who are making a diagnosis.

Do Learning Disabilities Have a Genetic Basis?

Any consideration of the possibility that learning disorders have a genetic basis must recognize some of the obstacles to the demonstration of such a hypothesis. First, learning disabilities may have many environmental causes. Second, learning disabilities take many forms. At present, criteria for categorizing types of learning disabilities are poorly developed. Third, the incidence of learning disabilities is related to the quality of schooling. The average length of schooling and the demands made by schools on students have undergone rapid change in the past two generations. Thus, it is difficult to compare the reading abilities of children with those of their parents. Fourth, learning-disabled individuals are typically of average intelligence, as are their parents (that is, full-scale IQs around 100), and people with strictly average IQs generally find school difficult. Fifth, the ability to read is itself probably inherited, making it difficult to sort out the contribution made by inherited reading skill from that made by a supposed inherited causal factor underlying a disability.

Despite the difficulties, the possibility of genetic causes has been raised repeatedly. As early as 1905, Thomas noted that familial nature of "word blindness," and since then many authors have made reference to the high incidence of learning disabilities within certain families. Two other types of evidence also support the genetic hypothesis. For dyslexia, the ratio of about four males to one female is commonly reported (see

Critchley for a summary of studies between 1927 and 1968). If only environmental factors were responsible, a more equal sex ratio would be expected. Studies of twins also find a higher incidence of dyslexia in identical than in fraternal twins. Despite the familial nature of learning disabilities, however, attempts by Defries and Decker and others have not been successful in relating this incidence to any genetic model.

ADULT OUTCOME OF LEARNING DISABILITIES

There are a variety of views about the outcome of children with learning disabilities. The most optimistic outcome study is reported by Critchley, in which 20 dyslexic boys attended a private school and received special instruction according to the Orton-Gillingham-Stillman method. The eventual occupations held by these individuals were two medical doctors, two college professors, one lawyer, two research scientists, six owners or managers of businesses, one school principal, three teachers, one actor, one factory foreman, and one skilled laborer. There are some reports in the popular press of similar, though perhaps not so absolute, success of various private schools for learning-disabled individuals. The majority of these studies do not report such optimistic outcomes, and the most thorough of them gives frankly pessimistic results about academic outcome. Spreen has examined the progress of 203 learning-disabled individuals over a long period. The sample included a group diagnosed as learning-disabled with no neurological impairments, a group diagnosed as minimally brain-damaged, and a group that had definite brain damage. The learning-disabled groups were compared with 52 control individuals. The following conclusions derive from assessments, personal interviews, parental interviews, and other observations made of these groups:

1. Typically, the control group fared better than the learning-disabled group, which fared better than the minimally brain-damaged group, which fared better than the brain-damaged group in all areas of assessment. Spreen argues that this result has important implications, because educators may not think that the presence or absence of neurological impairments is relevant to the outcome of school programs. It was also found that all three handicapped groups were inferior to the control group in all areas of study including art and physical education. They also had a poorer attitude toward school.

2. Individuals in all but the control group suffered through a miserable and usually short school career and then suffered a miserable social life full of disappointments and failures. They also had a relatively poor chance for advanced training and skilled employment. They did not, however, have a higher incidence of juvenile delinquency or psychiatric problems.

3. Interviews with subjects and their parents gave similar factual information about their situations. Parents, however, tended to report more serious effects on the well-being, happiness, and social interaction of their children than were reported by the children. The children also had less clear memories of their childhood than the control children. As the subjects aged, they developed firmer plans for their future and made better occupational adjustments, but they also gave increasingly poor impressions of their school experiences. The eventual social adjustments in females were poorer than they were in males.

Although learning-disabled individuals eventually managed to make personal adjustments and find jobs, their dislike of and dissatisfaction with school remained. The major evidence from this and other follow-up studies also suggests that the effects of remedial educational programs were not particularly significant. Reports of extravagant success seem to derive largely from private schools that select only high-IQ students from relatively affluent homes.

Weiss and Hechtman have reported that the prognosis for hyperactive children is relatively poor. Their life-style continues to be impulsive and it is often marked by geographical moves, accidents, problems with the law, and so forth. In later life, their major problems may be with poor self-esteem and social skills, but they are not regarded as hyperactive by their employers, and they do not become mentally disturbed or adult criminals.

We should end this section, perhaps, with some suggestions. Impairments should be adequately assessed to evaluate the cognitive deficits that are likely to be particular to each child. Once problem areas have been identified, specialized teaching programs can be devised to circumvent handicaps. There may be little point in trying to teach children those things that it seems clear they are not going to learn. It may be that education should be directed more explicitly to the acquisition of skills that can be used to gain employment. Counseling should be an important part of the educational process both for the learning-disabled individual and for parents. Counseling should be directed not only toward helping them overcome their own negative attitudes toward the educational system but also toward helping them come to understanding their own unique handicaps, including some strategies that they can use to circumvent some of those handicaps.

REFERENCES

Barnsley, R. H., A. H. Thompson, and P. E. Barnsley. Hockey success and birthdate: The relative age effect. *Canadian Association of Health, Physical Education, and Recreation.* 23–27, Nov.-Dec. 1985.

Bauman, M. L., and T. L. Kempor. *The Neurobiology of Autism.* Baltimore: The Johns Hopkins University Press, 1994.

Benton, A. *Right-Left Discrimination and Finger Localization.* New York: Hoeber-Harper, 1959.

Bradley, L., and P. E. Bryant. Categorizing sounds and learning to read: A causal connection. *Nature* 301:419–421, 1983.

Cobrinik, L. Unusual reading ability in severely disturbed children. *Journal of Autism and Childhood Schizophrenia* 4:163–175, 1974.

Critchley, M. *Developmental Dyslexia.* Springfield, Ill.: Charles C. Thomas, 1964.

Cruickshank, W. M. *Cerebral Palsy.* Syracuse, N.Y.: Syracuse University Press, 1976.

Defries, J. C., and S. N. Decker. Genetic aspects of reading disability: A family study. In R. N. Malatesha and P. G. Aaron, eds. *Reading Disorders: Varieties and Treatments.* New York: Academic, 1982.

Denckla, M. B. Critical review of "electroencephalographic and neurophysiological studies in dyslexia." In A. L. Benton and D. Pearl, eds. *Dyslexia: An Appraisal of Current Knowledge.* New York: Oxford University Press, 1978.

Denhoff, E. Medical aspects. In W. M. Cruickshank, ed. *Cerebral Palsy.* Syracuse, N.Y.: Syracuse University Press, 1976.

Diamond, G. H. The birthdate effect: A maturational effect? *Journal of Learning Disabilities* 16:161–164, 1983.

Douglas, V. I. Perceptual and cognitive factors as determinants of learning disabilities: A review chapter with special emphasis on attentional factors. In R. M. Knights and D. J. Bakker, eds. *The Neuropsychology of Learning Disorders.* Baltimore: University Park Press, 1976.

Drake, W. Clinical and pathological findings in a child with a developmental learning disability. *Journal of Learning Disabilities* 1:468–475, 1968.

Frank, J., and H. H. Levinson. Dysmetric dyslexia and dyspraxia. *Academic Therapy* 11:133–143, 1976.

Frauenheim, J. G. Academic achievement characteristics of adult males who were diagnosed as dyslexic in childhood. *Journal of Learning Disabilities* 11:476–483, 1978.

Frith, U. Experimental approaches to developmental dyslexia. *Psychological Research* 43:97–109, 1981.

Fry, E. A do-it-yourself terminology generator. *Journal of Reading* 11:428–430, 1968.

Gaddes, W. H. *Learning Disabilities and Brain Function.* New York: Springer-Verlag, 1980.

Galaburda, A. M., J. Corsiglia, G. D. Rosen, and G. F. Sherman. Planum temporale asymmetry, reappraisal since Geschwind and Levitsky. *Neuropsychologia* 25:853–868, 1987.

Geschwind, N., and A. M. Galaburda. *Cerebral Lateralization.* Cambridge, Mass.: MIT Press, 1985.

Gould, S. J. *The Mismeasure of Man.* New York: Norton, 1981.

Huelsman, C. B. The WISC syndrome for disabled readers. *Perceptual and Motor Skills* 30:535–550, 1970.

Hynd, G. W., and M. Semrud-Clikeman. Dyslexia and brain morphology. *Psychological Bulletin* 106:447–482, 1989.

Johnson, D. J., and H. R. Myklebust. *Learning Disabilities.* New York: Grune & Stratton, 1967.

Jorm, A. F. The cognitive and neurological basis of developmental dyslexia: A theoretical framework and review. *Cognition* 7:19–33, 1979.

Kinsbourne, M., and M. Hiscock. Does cerebral dominance develop? In S. J. Segalowitz and F. A. Gruber, eds. *Language Development and Neurological Theory*. New York: Academic, 1977.

Langmore, S. E., and G. J. Canter. Written spelling deficit of Broca's aphasics. *Brain and Language* 18:293–314, 1983.

Leonard, C. M., et al. Anomalous cerebral structure in dyslexia revealed with magnetic resonance imaging. *Archives of Neurology* 50:461–469, 1993.

Levinson, H. N. *Dyslexia*. New York: Springer-Verlag, 1980.

Little, W. J. *Deformities of the Human Frame*. London: Longmans, 1853.

Lorber, J. The results of early treatment of extreme hydrocephalus. *Developmental Medicine and Child Neurology Supplement* 16:21–29, 1968.

Lovegrove, W. J., M. Heddle, and W. Slaghuis. Reading disability: Spatial frequency specific deficits in visual information store. *Neuropsychologia* 18:111–115, 1980.

Lyle, J. G., and J. D. Goyen. Performance of retarded readers on the WISC and educational tests. *Journal of Abnormal Psychology* 74:105–112, 1969.

Lyle, J. G., and J. D. Goyen. Effect of speed of exposure and difficulty of discrimination on visual recognition of retarded readers. *Journal of Abnormal Psychology* 84:673–676, 1975.

Maccario, M., S. J. Hefferen, S. J. Keblusek, and K. A. Lipinski. Developmental dysphasia and electroencephalographic abnormalities. *Developmental Medicine and Child Neurology* 24:141–155, 1982.

Maddux, C. D. First-grade entry age in a sample of children labeled learning disabled. *Learning Disability Quarterly* 3:79–83, 1980.

Maddux, C. D., D. Stacy, and M. Scott. School entry age in a group of gifted children. *Gifted Child Quarterly* 25:180–184, 1981.

Malatesha, R. N., and D. R. Dougan. Clinical subtypes of developmental dyslexia: Resolution to an irresolute problem. In R. N. Malatesha and P. G. Aaron, eds. *Reading Disorders*. New York: Academic, 1982.

Merzenich, M. M., C. Schreiner, W. Jenkins, and X. Wang. Neural mechanisms underlying temporal integration, segmentation, and input sequence representation: Some implications for the origin of learning disabilities. In P. Tallal, A. M. Galaburda, R. R. Llinás, and C. von Euler, eds. *Temporal Information Processing in the Nervous System*. New York: The New York Academy of Sciences, 1993.

Money, J. Child abuse: Growth failure. IQ deficit, and learning disability. *Journal of Learning Disabilities* 15:579–582, 1982.

Orton, S. T. *Reading, Writing and Speech Problems in Children*. New York: Norton, 1937.

Pavlidis, G. Th. Do eye movements hold the key to dyslexia? *Neuropsychologia* 19:57–64, 1981.

Pihl, R. O., and M. Parkes. Hair element content in learning disabled children. *Science* 198:204–206, 1977.

Reed, J. C. Reading achievement as related to differences between WISC verbal and performance I. Q.'s. *Child Development* 38:835–840, 1967.

Rosensweig, M. R., D. Krech, E. L. Bennett, and M. C. Diamond. Effects of environmental complexity and training on brain chemistry and anatomy: A replication and extension. *Journal of Comparative and Physiological Psychology* 55:427–429, 1962.

Rourke, B. P. Neuropsychological assessment of children with learning disabilities. In S. B. Filskov and T. J. Boll, eds. *Handbook of Clinical Neuropsychology*. New York: Wiley, 1981.

Rugel, R. P. WISC subtest scores of disabled readers: A review with respect to Bannatyne's categorization. *Journal of Learning Disability* 17:48–55, 1974.

Rutter, M., and W. Yule. The concept of specific reading retardation. *Journal of Child Psychology and Psychiatry* 16:181–197, 1975.

Satz, P. Cerebral dominance and reading disability: An old problem revisited. In R. M. Knights and D. J. Bakker, eds. *The Neuropsychology of Learning Disorders*. Baltimore: University Park Press, 1976.

Semrud-Clikeman, M., and G. W. Hynd. Right hemispheric dysfunction in nonverbal learning disabilities: Social, academic, and adaptive functioning in adults and children. *Psychological Bulletin* 107:196–209, 1990.

Spreen, O. *Learning Disabled Children Growing Up*. New York: Oxford University Press, 1988.

Tallal, P., S. Miller, and R. H. Fitch. Neurobiological basis of speech: A case for the preeeminence of temporal processing. In P. Tallal, A. M. Galaburda, R. R. Llinás, and C. von Euler, eds. *Temporal Information Processing in the Nervous System*. New York: The New York Academy of Sciences, 1993.

Treffert, D. A. The idiot savant: A review of the syndrome. *American Journal of Psychiatry* 145:563–572, 1988.

U.S. Department of Health, Education and Welfare. Minimal brain dysfunction in children. *National Institute of Neurological Diseases Monograph* 3:1–18, 1966.

Vellutino, F. R. Toward an understanding of dyslexia: Psychological factors in specific reading disability. In A. L. Benton and D. Pearl, eds. *Dyslexia: An Appraisal of Current Knowledge*. New York: Oxford University Press, 1978.

Weiss, G., and L. Hechtman. The hyperactive child syndrome. *Science* 205:1348, 1979.

Whishaw, I. Q., and B. Kolb. Neuropsychological assessment of children and adults with developmental dyslexia. In R. N. Malatesha and H. A. Whitaker, eds. *Dyslexia: A Global Issue*. The Hague: Martinus Nijhoff, 1984.

Witelson, S. F. Early hemisphere specialization and interhemispheric plasticity, an empirical and theoretical review. In S. J. Segalowitz and F. A. Gruber, eds. *Language Development and Neurological Theory*. New York: Academic, 1977.

Zaidel, E. The split and half brains as models of congenital language disability. In C. L. Ludlow and M. E. Doran-Quine, eds. *The Neuropsychological Basis of Language Disorders in Children*. Bethesda, Md.: National Institute of Neurological and Communicative Disorders and Stroke, 1978.

Zangwill, O. L., and C. Blakemore. Dyslexia: Reversal of eye-movements during reading. *Neuropsychologia* 10: 371–373, 1972.

chapter twenty-three

23

Recovery of Function

> On the afternoon of June 16, 1783, Dr. Samuel Johnson, the famed English lexicographer, sat for his portrait in the studio of Miss Frances Reynolds, the sadly untalented sister of Sir Joshua Reynolds. Despite his 73 years and marked obesity, Johnson afterwards walked the considerable distance from the studio to his home. He went to sleep at his usual hour in the evening and awoke according to his account around 3 A.M. on June 17. To his surprise and horror, he found that he could not speak. He immediately tested his mental faculties by successfully composing a prayer in Latin verse. Next he tried to loosen his powers of speech by drinking some wine, violating his recently acquired habits of temperance. The wine only put him back to sleep. Upon reawakening after sunrise, Johnson still could not speak. He found, however, that he could understand others and that he could write. His penmanship and composition were somewhat defective. . . . Johnson proceeded to summon his physicians, Drs. Brocklesby and Heberden, who came and examined him. They prescribed blisters on each side of the throat up to the ear, one on the head, and one on the back, along with salts of hartshorn (ammonium carbonate). Heberden, who was one of London's leading doctors, predicted a speedy recovery. His confidence proved quite justified: the therapeutic regimen was so efficacious that Johnson's speech began returning within a day or two. Recovery proceeded smoothly over the next month, and even the mild disorders in writing lessened. Johnson finally was left with a slight but stable dysarthria until he succumbed to other causes later in the next year. (Rosner, 1974, p. 1)

The case of Dr. Johnson has been described and discussed a number of times because he was an interesting person and because his transitory illness is not fully explained. (The reader might try a diagnosis and then compare the result with that published by Critchley.) His aphasia provides an example of almost complete loss of a specific function (speech) and seemingly rapid and almost complete recovery. The story also contains a testimony to the knowledge and insight of his doctors, because their prediction of the outcome was correct. There are, however, many questions the critical reader may wish to ask. How much weight should self-testimony be accorded? Did Johnson in fact have a stroke or any other brain disorder? It is reasonable to believe that he might discover, when alone in the middle of the night, that he could not speak, because he was known to have the habit of talking to himself. But, since he was an eccentric, we might also wonder if the stroke was faked for some purpose. If his disorder was real, what was it and where was it? Some neurologists have thought that the lesion was very small or was only a transitory blood clot. Others, such as Critchley, have speculated that because he could not speak but could think, compose Latin verse, and write, he might have had the function of speech in both hemispheres. This idea would be incorrect if Murray's hypothesis were accepted: that Johnson had Tourette's syndrome, which is thought to involve a dysfunction of the right hemisphere.

Luria describes a case with more severe loss of function and less complete recovery in his book *The Man with a Shattered World.* A soldier, Lyova Saletsky, received a fractured skull and accompanying brain damage from a bullet wound in the battle of Smolensk. The damage was centered in the posterior left hemisphere intersections of the occipital, temporal, and parietal cortex. Luria first saw Saletsky 3 months after the injury and then at 3-week intervals for the next 26 years. During this time, Saletsky painfully and slowly relearned the art of reading and writing. In doing so, he compiled a diary, in which he gives a moving account of his initial deficits, recovery, and residual problems. The following excerpt is an example of what Saletsky had to say about his condition:

> I remember nothing, absolutely nothing! Just separate bits of information that I sense have to do with one field or another. But that's all! I have no real knowledge of any subject. My past has just been wiped out!
>
> Before my injury I understood everything people said and had no trouble learning any of the sciences. Afterwards I forgot everything I learned about science. All my education was gone.
>
> I know that I went to elementary school, graduated with honors from the middle school, completed three years of courses at the Tula Polytechnic Institute, did advanced work in chemistry, and before the war, finished all these requirements ahead of time. I remember that I was on the western front, was wounded in the head in 1943 when we tried to break through the Germans' defense in Smolensk, and that I've never been able to put my life together again. But I can't remember what I did or studied, the sciences I learned, subjects I took. I've forgotten everything. Although I studied German for six years, I can't remember a word of it, can't even recognize a single letter. I also remember that I studied English for three straight years at the Institute. But I don't know a word of that either now. I've forgotten these languages so completely I might just as well never have learned them. Words like *trigonometry, solid geometry, chemistry, algebra,* etc., come to mind, but I have no idea what they mean. (Luria, 1972, pp. 140–142)

Many people show less resilience than Saletsky. Here are two examples of patients we have known. H. P. was an extremely intelligent teacher who, after a left hemisphere stroke that occurred in middle age, suffered from what might best be described as Broca's aphasia. Despite showing almost daily signs of excellent recovery and frequent excellent good humor and insight, he committed suicide within months of his stroke. Knowing H. P., we cannot help but feel that this was his reasoned solution to an infirmity he could not accept. Nevertheless, feelings of depression are common after brain damage, and his act may have been pathological rather than reasoned and free. D. S. was an equally intelligent middle-aged man who worked in the theater industry but whose real pleasure was his hobby of carpentry. After a right hemisphere stroke, he no longer showed an interest in theater, cinema, or even watching TV, and he no longer displayed any interest or skill in carpentry. He remained in a passive and dependent condition and gave no indication of trying to improve his lot.

There are cases in which recovery does not occur, as illustrated by the Quinlan's story of their daughter, Karen Ann. Twenty-one years after her birth, Karen Ann was returned to the same hospital where she was born, St. Clare's, in a deep coma. After attending a birthday party the night of 14 April 1975 and consuming a few gin and tonics, she slipped into unconsciousness. No one ever determined exactly why. She had been on a crash diet to slim down to a size 7 bikini and had not eaten all day. It was later found that she also had taken a small "therapeutic" amount of a mild tranquilizer, and aspirin. Whatever the cause, Karen Ann fell quickly into a coma and for a period of time—no one ever knew exactly how long—she stopped breathing. The resulting oxygen starvation caused brain damage. In the hospital, Karen Ann was fed by tubes inserted in her nostrils, and her breathing was supported by a respirator. Her weight dropped from 120 to 70 pounds. Her body gradually contracted to the fetal position and became rigid. By the end of July, Karen Ann's family, on the advice of their physicians, Morse and Javed, gave their permission to remove the respirator that was assumed to be keeping their daughter alive. However, the attorney for the hospital, Theodore Einhorn, informed the Quinlans that because Karen Ann was over 21 they were not her legal guardians and would have to be appointed by a judge as legal guardians before their request would be followed. The subsequent legal cases, in which the family was represented by Paul Armstrong, a Legal Aid Society attorney, attracted international interest. The central issue of the case was whether Joseph Quinlan could be named her legal guardian for the purpose of authorizing the discontinuance of all extraordinary means of sustaining her life, since no recovery was expected and medical science could not help her. The case was lost in the initial trial but was eventually won before the Supreme Court of New Jersey. This was a landmark decision because it was the first right-to-die ruling ever made in legal history. Karen Ann was subsequently removed from the respirator and moved to a nursing home. There she remained unchanged until she died more than 10 years later.

INCIDENCE OF BRAIN DAMAGE AND PROSPECTS FOR RECOVERY

Strokes account for almost half of the hospitalizations for neurological disability and about 10% of all deaths. In addition, there are thousands of cases of head injury admitted to hospitals each year, and of these three-quarters will show evidence of brain damage. Of the people who become permanently disabled each year, most are neurological cases.

Figure 23.1 summarizes the consequences to 1285 patients of a closed-head injury that was of sufficient severity to produce 6 hours of coma, during which no eye opening occurred, no recognizable words were uttered, and no commands were followed. There is enormous variation in the prospects for recovery. More than 40% of the patients die, but among those who survive the majority make a reasonably good recovery. Among those in the good recovery group, less than 50% can return to work, and many of these may not regain complete job competency. As

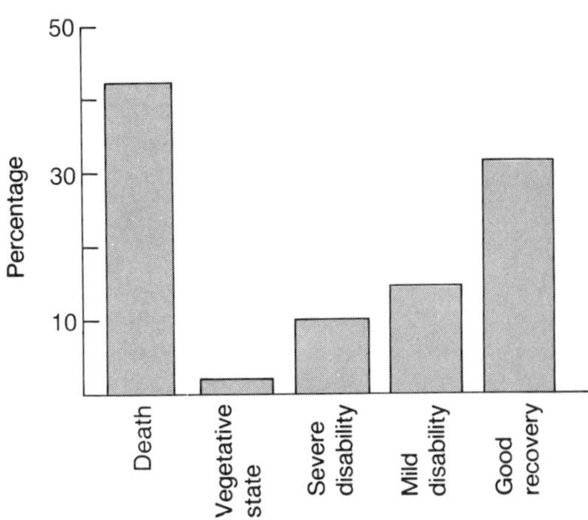

FIGURE 23.1. Recovery prospects from a closed-head injury that produces 6 hours of coma. (After Levin, Benton, and Grossman, 1982.)

Finger and Stein point out, many people expect that recovery will not occur, and so they do not encourage rehabilitation. Others may be overly optimistic. In the following sections, we describe the processes of recovery and the cellular changes that take place after brain damage.

EXAMPLES OF THE PROCESS OF FUNCTIONAL RECOVERY

Recovery is seldom sudden. Examination of the stages of recovery and their associated behaviors often reveals a slow reemergence of restored functions. In Hughlings-Jackson's terms, the lesion or trauma produces a complete de-volution of the behavior, followed by re-evolution. Teitelbaum and his coworkers have pointed out that recovery often parallels the sequential development of the behavior in infants.

Recovery from Spinal Cord Section

Kuhn describes considerable variability in the extent to which spinal reflexes recover after cord section. Some people show virtually no recovery, and their muscles atrophy; others recover sufficiently that their legs will support their weight, and they show no muscle atrophy. For those who show pronounced recovery of spinal reflexes, Kuhn describes four major stages or steps in the process of recovery. Estimates about the extent of recovery can be made from the rapidity with which a patient enters each stage:

1. *Spinal shock.* Spinal shock is a state of profound depression of all reflexes below the level of section. Shock varies in severity from person to person and also varies in duration, lasting from 1 to 6 weeks. Some reflexes, such as penile erection in males, may not be depressed at all. For some few individuals, there is no evidence of recovery beyond this stage.

2. *Minimal reflex activity.* In this stage, slight flexion or extension of the foot, some toe twitches, and extension of the large toe occur. Anal and bladder reflexes for waste secretion may also be present.

3. *Flexor activity.* The first major reflexes to return are flexor reflexes, consisting of such movements as dorsiflexion of the big toe and fanning of the toes, dorsiflexion of the foot, and flexion of the leg and thigh. Tactile stimuli are most effective in eliciting limb flexion, unpleasant stimuli are particularly effective, and the zones with the lowest thresholds are the foot area and the genital area.

4. *Extensor activity.* Extensor movements generally become apparent as early as 6 months after injury and continue to develop for years. They consist of extension and stiffening of one or both legs; in some patients there is only a slight tightening of limbs, whereas in others the limbs assume pillarlike rigidity. In some people in the latter group, this activity is sufficient to permit prolonged standing in warm water without support.

Although recovery from spinal cord section can be quite extensive, patients can make no voluntary movements and receive no sensation from below the area of the lesion.

Recovery from Brainstem Damage

In 1951, Anand and Brobeck observed that lesions of the lateral hypothalamus of rats and cats produced **aphagia** (the inability to eat or chew), which ultimately led to death. The animals were also somnolent and failed to respond to sensory stimulation. Teitelbaum and Stellar reported 3 years later that if the animals were fed artificially for a period of time, they recovered the ability to eat. Feeding behavior recovered in an orderly sequence: first the animals ate only small amounts of wet food, later they began to eat dry food, and eventually they maintained themselves on dry food and water. Golani and his coworkers found that animals recover movements along several relatively independent dimensions that appear successively (Figure 23.2). During recovery, the animal develops antigravity support, which allows it to stand and support its weight. Then it devel-

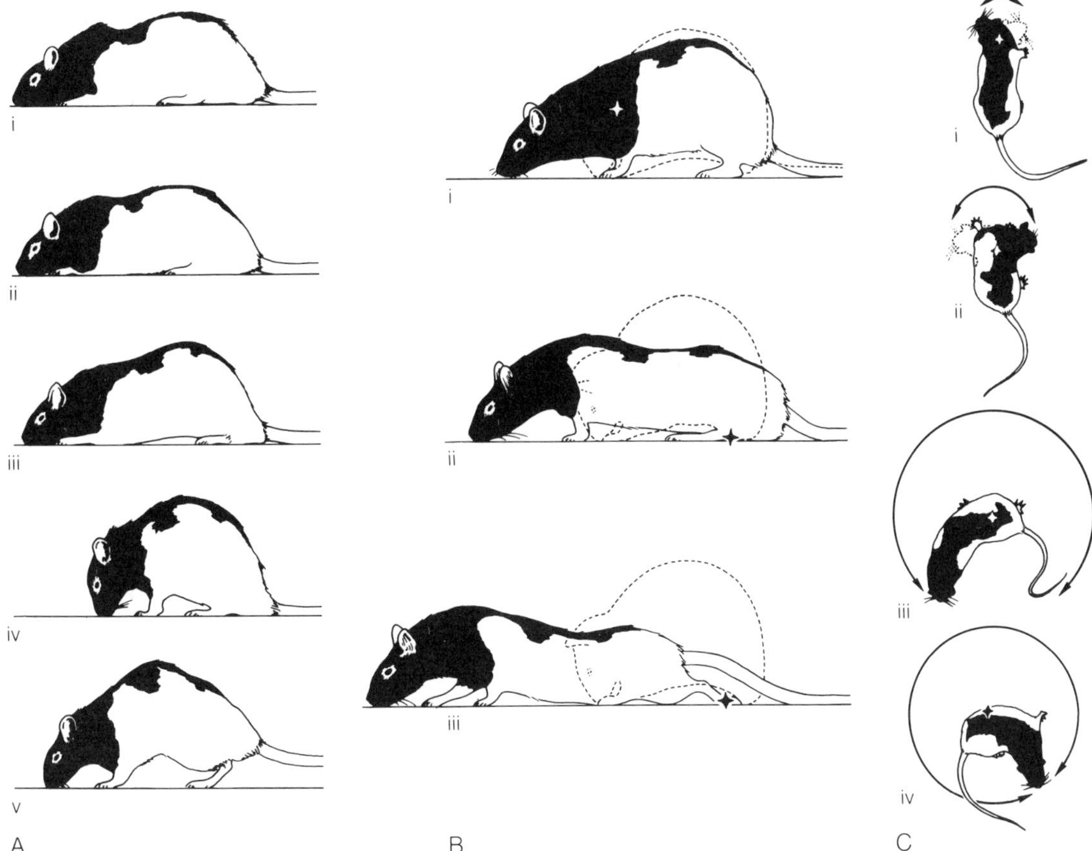

FIGURE 23.2. Recovery of (*A*) posture, (*B*) forward scanning, and (*C*) turning in a rat that had been given large posterior lateral hypothalamic lesions. Broken-line and solid-line drawings indicate the extreme positions that the rat assumes during each phase. Recovery occurs over time, in the sequence indicated by the Roman numerals. In each sequence, recovery begins with the head and proceeds caudally. (After I. Golani, D. L. Wolgin, and P. Teitelbaum. A proposed natural geometry of recovery from akinesia in the lateral hypothalamic rat. *Brain Research* 164:237–267, 1979. Reprinted with permission.)

ops longitudinal movements that allow it to extend forward. Finally, the animal can move its head in a forward and lateral direction; this movement increases in amplitude over days, until the animal can turn completely around as well as walk forward. Interestingly, each time the animal initiates walking, it does so with the sequence of movements illustrated during recovery. These authors argue that the isolation of relatively independent dimensions of movement during recovery suggests the existence of corresponding neural systems. The development of behavior in infant rats follows a similar sequence to that seen during recovery.

The hypothalamic lesions damage many ascending and descending fiber systems between the brainstem and forebrain (including dopaminergic, norepinephrinergic, cholinergic, and serotonergic nonspecific systems; ascending somatosensory fibers; and descending motor tracts).

Thus, the animal model is an analogue for coma produced by brainstem damage. If we consider only what happens when dopamine-containing fibers are cut, we can observe some of the mechanisms by which a system that had been extensively damaged can recover. The many changes that are postulated to underlie this recovery are illustrated in Figure 23.3. They include (1) increased firing in the remaining dopamine cells; (2) sprouting of the remaining dopamine cells so that they can fill in for cells that have been destroyed; (3) an increase in the number of dopamine receptors, permitting a more potent action of the remaining dopamine; (4) a decrease in the activity of cells that are normally antagonistic to dopamine; and (5) an increased release of dopamine from the remaining terminals. The range of changes that occur after the lesions is quite surprising in that animals can recover almost normal behavior if as little as 10% of the dopamine system is left intact. Presumably, similar processes are taking place in many other systems, and these changes allow the recovery that is observed to follow brainstem damage.

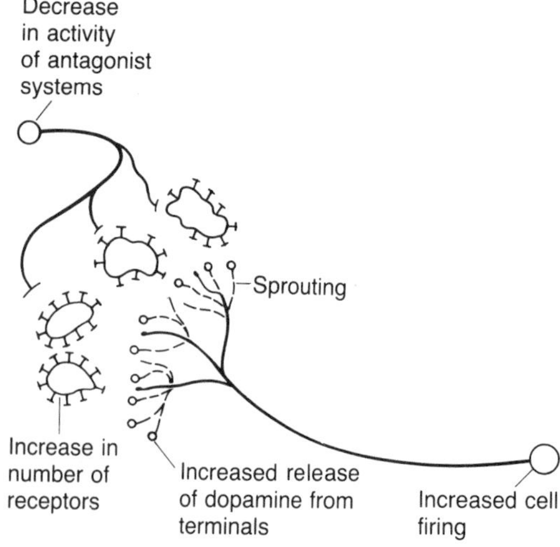

FIGURE 23.3. Hypothetical changes in dopamine and allied systems that might underlie behavior recovery that takes place after the system has been damaged.

Recovery from Motor Cortex Damage

Twitchell has described recovery from hemiplegia produced by thrombosis, embolism, or stroke of the middle cerebral artery in humans. The recovery sequence closely parallels the development of reaching and the grasp response described by Twitchell in infants. Immediately following damage, hemiplegia (inability to move the contralateral limbs) occurred, marked by complete flaccidity of the muscles and loss of all reflexes and voluntary movements. Recovery occurred over a period of days or weeks and followed a relatively orderly sequence. Some patients recovered relatively normal use of their limbs; for others, recovery was arrested at one stage or another. Complete recovery of use of the arms, when it occurred, appeared between 23 and 40 days after the lesion. Recovery occurred in the following sequence: (1) return of reflexes; (2) development of rigidity; (3) grasping that was facilitated by, or occurred as part of, other movements; and (4) development of voluntary grasping (this involved recovery of movement in the sequence of shoulder, elbow, wrist, and hand, first in the flexor musculature, then in the extensor musculature). Voluntary grasping continued to improve until independent movements of the fingers were well developed. About 30% of patients reached the last stage of recovery; the others showed arrested recovery at one of the preceding stages.

Recovery from Aphasia

Kertesz has reviewed the prospects of recovery from aphasia with examples of his own case histories. Figure 23.4 is a graph showing the recovery of an example patient from each of his subgroups. All the patients received the Western Aphasia Battery, which assesses spontaneous speech content, fluency, comprehension, repetition, and so forth, from which an aphasia quotient was derived. Kertesz makes the following generalizations: (1) Posttrauma (head-injury) patients showed the most rapid, and often almost complete, recovery, whereas recovery in stroke patients was less pronounced and in some groups

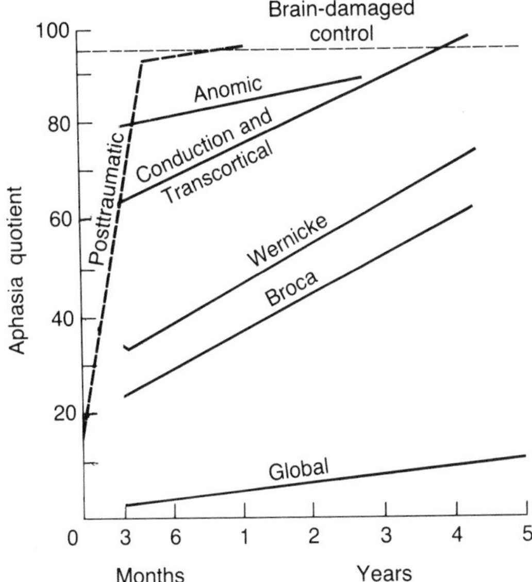

FIGURE 23.4. Initial deficits and recovery in stroke patients with different language disorders (solid lines) and in a posttrauma patient (heavy dashed line). Each line is a representative patient. (After Kertez, 1979.)

was almost absent. (2) Initial deficits in anomic patients were the least severe and in global aphasics were the most severe, with intermediate severity occurring for other groups. The actual rate of recovery, given initial impairments, was often quite similar in all groups. (3) There was a tendency, when recovery occurred, for the patient to progress to one of the other stages, but recovery usually stopped with anomic aphasia. (4) Most recovery occurred in the first 3 months (illustrated only for the posttrauma patient in Figure 23.4), with some recovery occurring in the next 6 months and less recovery occurring in the following 6 months. Thereafter, little or no recovery occurred. (5) There was some evidence that younger patients showed better recovery, and the effects of intelligence, occupation, and sex in these patients were slight if present. (6) The language components that were the most resistant to brain damage were naming, oral imitation, comprehension of nouns, and yes-no responses, functions that may be partly mediated by the right hemisphere.

Recovery from Amnesia

There are many reports of the loss of memory and its subsequent recovery following brain lesions or concussions. There is some difference of opinion about the sequence of events during recovery. Barbizet reports a case that illustrates one point of view, or possibly one type of recovery syndrome. A 40-year-old man suffered a head trauma and was in a coma for 7 weeks. Five months after the trauma, he was completely amnesic for the 2 preceding years and had gross memory disturbances for events back to early childhood. Eight months after trauma, the period of complete amnesia had shrunk to 1 year, and the period of partial amnesia extended back to the age of 4. Sixteen months after trauma, his amnesia was limited to the 2-week period before trauma. Thus, his recovery represented a progressive shrinkage of the amnesia, from past to present.

Whitty and Zangwill report a somewhat different pattern of recovery following less severe head injury. They report that, as a rule, retrograde amnesias are very short, usually of a few seconds' duration. If they are longer, the shrinkage of amnesia may not be strictly chronological. Sometimes more recent events are recalled first and then serve as a magnet for piecing together a continuous memory.

The parallel between the recovery of memory and the recovery from aphagia, paralysis, and so forth, suggests that recovery from all types of brain trauma involves some common processes. Descriptions of recovery as a sequential development have obvious practical and theoretical utility. From a practical perspective, good sequential descriptions allow any patient to be monitored for rate and degree of recovery. If recovery is arrested before completion, residual abilities can be understood within the context of the recovery stage reached. Theoretically, stages of recovery provide insights into the brain's organization and background information for enhancing recovery or for overcoming residual deficits.

CELLULAR EVENTS ASSOCIATED WITH BRAIN DAMAGE

Brain damage produces a number of short-, intermediate-, and long-term changes in brain tissue, in addition to the actual loss of tissue caused by the initial insult. Precisely what changes occur will depend on the type of brain damage, and so, for simplicity, the following descriptions derive from the changes that follow brain lesions. Terms associated with these processes are defined in Table 23.1.

Changes at the Site of Damage

A lesion made either by a puncture wound or by ablation leaves a vacuole or cavity of variable size. Due to degeneration of surrounding tissue, accumulation of fluid, and shrinkage of surrounding tissue, the cavity may expand for about a week and then begin to contract. With time, it may disappear completely and thus not be visible on CT scans. The shrinkage of the cavity can cause distortions of surrounding tissue such that the ventricles expand to compensate for the loss in tissue volume. When ventricular expansion is visible on CT scans, it provides a clue that damage has been incurred. Within about an hour after damage, dead tissue surrounds the cavity and, surrounding this area of **necrosis** is an area of tissue consisting of injured, dead, and normal cells. Within 24 hours, phagocytes (astrocytes and microglia) infiltrate the area to remove debris. By 3 to 7 days, new capillaries proliferate in the area. These processes may continue for several months until the debris is removed and only the glial cells remain. Inspection of stained tissue may show many small, dark glial cells filling the area, a process called **gliosis,** and among these cells the astrocytes form a scar in the area. The scar may hamper or block any functional regeneration of remaining neural cells.

TABLE 23.1. Degenerative events following brain damage

Term	Definition
Anterograde degeneration	Also called orthograde or Wallerian degeneration. The certain degeneration of an axon after it has been cut from the cell body.
Astrocyte activity	Astrocytes invade areas of damage to remove debris and seal or scar the area through attachments made by their many processes.
Calcification	Large deposits of calcium accumulate at some locations where neural degeneration takes place. Deposits can be seen on brain scans.
Chromatolysis	Literally, color dissolution. After injury, fatigue, or exhaustion, cell Nissl substance breaks down. Loss of Nissl substance and affinity for stain makes the cell colorless to microscopic examination.
Gliosis	Replacement of cell bodies by glial cells in areas undergoing degeneration.
Necrosis	Localized death of individual cells or groups of cells.
Phagocytosis	Removal of dead cells by mitochondria and astrocytes.
Retrograde degeneration	The death of the remaining axon, cell body, and dendrites after the axon is cut. The process may be reversible before it is complete.
Terminal degeneration	The shrinkage and degeneration of terminals after the axon is cut from the cell body.
Transneuronal degeneration	The death of neurons that innervate or are innervated by a damaged or destroyed neuron.

Changes Distal to the Site of Damage

Damage in one area not only kills local cells but also can cut the fibers of cells located at a distance and produce changes in cells that previously innervated the region or were innervated by it. These changes may involve the breakdown or death of the tissue, a process called **degeneration** (Figure 23.5).

When a nerve is severed, the portion distal to the cut always degenerates. This fact was first noted by Waller in the early 1850s and is so certain that it is thought to constitute the only law of neuroanatomy. Such degeneration is called **Wallerian** or **anterograde degeneration.** The process of Wallerian degeneration in the central nervous system is different in part from what occurs in the peripheral nervous system. Centrally, the axons degenerate, as does the myelin that wraps around them, and normally there is little or no regeneration. In the peripheral nervous system, the Schwann cells that form the myelin do not all die, and they subsequently multiply and form a bridge that regenerating fibers can cross to reinnervate their target. Reinnervation may not occur in the central nervous system because the oligodendrites that form its myelin do not proliferate and also because scarring may block regrowth. The synaptic terminals of cut axons also change, becoming dense and small. The degeneration of the synaptic endings is called **terminal degeneration.**

The proximal portions of the axon and the cell body may not always degenerate, but if they do, the process is called **retrograde degeneration.** In the cell body the Nissl substance disappears, the nucleus is displaced to the periphery of the cell, and the cell may swell to double its normal size. In some neurons (for example, motor neurons) retrograde degeneration is reversible, whereas in others (for example, thalamic neurons) it is not. In the former case the cells return to normal size, but in the latter they shrink and are removed by phagocytosis.

Cells that innervate or are innervated by a degenerating neuron may also die, a process called **transneuronal degeneration.** This process was first observed in the visual system. When the optic nerve is cut, cells of the lateral geniculate body degenerate completely. It is thought that the cells degenerate either because they require an optimal level of stimulation from the optic nerve to survive or because some necessary trophic substance is supplied by its synaptic endings. Transneuronal degeneration can occur across more than one synapse; for example, cells in the visual cortex may also begin to die after the lateral geniculate body degenerates. Transneuronal degeneration can also occur in the opposite direction, in the cells of innervation. The former process is referred

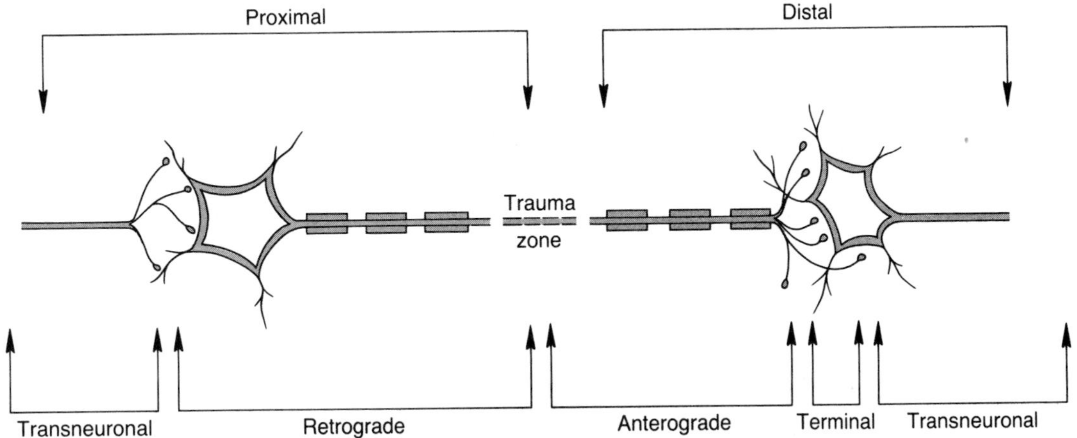

FIGURE 23.5. The spatial terminology for cell and fiber degeneration. (After Beresford, 1965.)

to as anterograde and the latter as retrograde transneuronal degeneration. Transneuronal degeneration can also be associated with accumulating deposits of calcium, a process called **calcification.** In response to neocortex damage, for example, calcification may occur in degenerating thalamic neurons (also a site of retrograde degeneration) and in the basal ganglia (a possible site of secondary transneuron degeneration). These deposits can be so pronounced that they are seen easily in histological material or with CT scans. The reasons for calcification and the way that it occurs are not known, but its presence in CT scans can be taken as an indication of certain kinds of cortical or subcortical damage.

The fact that degenerative changes occur in so many places and in so many ways makes it impossible to state that even the most refined lesion can be localized. For example, a small ablation may appear to be localized, but retrograde degeneration and calcification will occur in many connecting brain regions. Clearly, brain damage cannot be strictly localized. Additionally, many of these degenerative changes are known to continue for years. Evidence is now beginning to emerge that brain injury sustained in youth can even speed degenerative changes associated with aging.

PHYSIOLOGICAL EVENTS ASSOCIATED WITH BRAIN DAMAGE

It is now recognized that there is not one physiological event that can be unequivocally related to the depression of function that follows brain damage or to subsequent recovery when it occurs. Changes include shock in areas remote to the damage, edema or swelling of traumatized tissue, reductions in blood flow, changes in neurotransmitter release, reductions in glucose use, and autoneurotoxicity.

Shock

In 1911, von Monakow formulated the concept that he called **diaschisis** (from the Greek, meaning to split in two or to split apart): after a brain injury, not only is neural tissue and its function lost, but also several neural areas related to the damaged area are depressed and their function is consequently absent for a period of time. In von Monakow's words:

> What characterizes all kinds of shock is a temporary cessation of function which affects a wide expanse of physiologically built up functions, and a restitution which goes on in well defined phases, sometimes shorter, sometimes longer, sometimes even retrospectively in the shape of fragments of functions in retrograde amnesias. The diaschisis proper has its point of attack beyond the limits of anatomically disturbed tissue in those parts of the grey substance which are connected with the focus by fibers. (von Monakow, 1911, p. 241)

Marshall Hall recognized in 1841 that damage to the spinal cord results in a temporary loss of spinal reflexes, a phenomenon that became known as spinal shock. In the early 1900s, Sherrington demonstrated that the shock is caused by depriving the spinal cord of its connections from the brain. Cutting the cord or transecting it with the local anesthetic procaine produced shock, but recutting it after reflexes had recovered did not reinstate shock. Shock also has a shorter duration if only some of the input to the spinal cord is interrupted or if it is interrupted in a number of stages.

To explain shock, it is hypothesized that spinal cells have an optimal resting excitation that is maintained in part by the release of neural transmitter substances from descending fibers. Grillner has found that, when this tonic influence is lost, pharmacological agents that stimulated spinal cord norepinephrine receptors could arrest spinal shock. The understanding of spinal shock has played an important role in the therapy of people who have received spinal injury. Before World War I it was believed that reflexes were permanently abolished. In 1917, Head and Riddoch showed that if infections were controlled, patients could be maintained indefinitely and that reflexes began to return within 2 to 3 weeks. By analogy, the principle of spinal shock can be generalized to other parts of the brain with the assumption that cells everywhere will show temporary depression when their input is removed.

Edema

Edema (from the Greek for swelling), or swelling of tissue following trauma, occurs in the area surrounding the lesion but may affect distant areas through pressure and other mechanisms. In general, interstitial (between-cell) tissue is like a collapsed balloon with respect to fluid, and in the brain it contains less fluid than other tissue. Due to increased capillary pressure, changes in the constituency of capillary fluid, or increased porosity of the capillaries, fluid flows into or accumulates in the interstitial space, causing it to balloon. The ensuing pressure probably depresses neuronal function. Edema can be lessened by cortisone. Some posttrauma deficits may be caused by edema. The drop in IQ that occurs after cortical surgery for the treatment of epilepsy, as reported by Milner, is shown in Figure 23.6. Immediately after surgery, IQ, irrespective of the lesion location (temporal, frontal, parietal), drops and then returns to preoperative levels within a year. The initial drop may be due in part to edema, because it is lessened by treatment with cortisone.

Blood Flow

The amount or rate of blood flow through the arteries of the brain can be used as a measure of its metabolic activity. It is thought that blood flow is controlled by carbon dioxide that is released by tissue metabolic activity; accordingly, if activity is high, carbon dioxide release will be high, which in turn will increase blood flow. Blood flow can be measured by placing special detectors on the

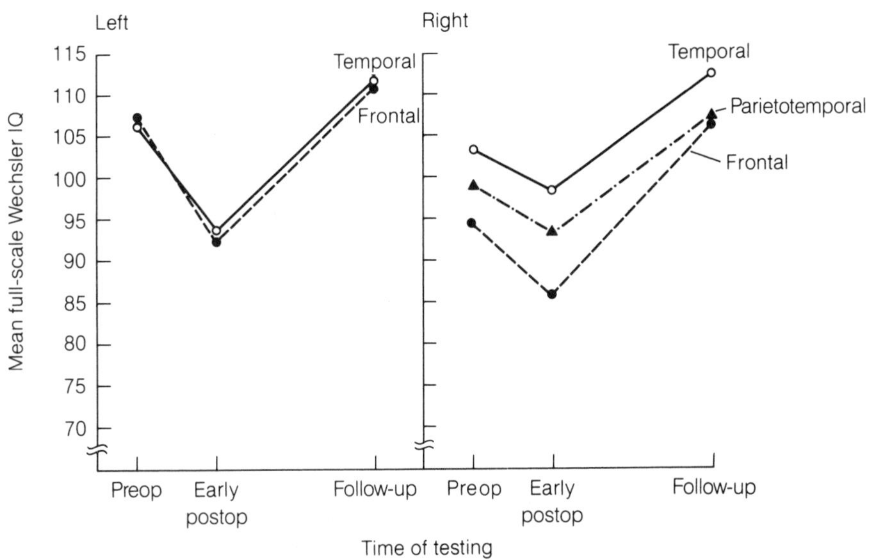

FIGURE 23.6. Mean preoperative, early postoperative, and long-term follow-up Wechsler IQ rating for 51 patients (38 male, 13 female) classed according to side and site of the cortical excisions carried out to relieve epilepsy. Number of cases: left temporal, 19; left frontal, 6; right temporal, 13; right frontal, 6; right parietotemporal, 7. (From B. Milner. Psychological aspects of focal epilepsy and its neurosurgical management. In D. Purpura, J. P. Penry, and R. D. Walker, eds. *Advances in Neurology,* vol. 8. New York: Raven Press. Copyright © 1975. Reprinted with permission.)

skull that measure the flow of a radioactive inert gas that has been injected into the carotid artery. The more blood that flows, the higher the radioactivity count. Using this technique with brain-damaged patients shows an immediate reduction in blood flow after injury that may last for as long as a month after injury. It is thought that when tissue is damaged, its metabolic activity drops, causing a decrease in the release of carbon dioxide and a concomitant reduction in blood flow.

Neurotransmitter Release

The levels of many brain neurotransmitters are known to change after brain damage, but these neurotransmitters have not been examined exhaustively nor have their changes been correlated with behavioral changes. Here we will give only one example of the types of correlations that are being attempted. In an animal model of human stroke, Robinson and his coworkers have cut the middle cerebral artery on one side of the rat brain and measured brain catecholamines (norepinephrine and dopamine) in various locations. They found reduced levels of these transmitters in many brain areas 5 days later, with recovery, and even overcompensation, occurring 3 weeks later. Robinson proposes that both the physical and the behavioral apathy that follows strokes may be caused in part by the decline in transmitter function.

Glucose Uptake

The Sokoloff technique of deoxyglucose labeling has been used by Pappius to evaluate changes in the brain after trauma. The technique involves injecting ^{14}C-labeled deoxyglucose into the circulatory system. The deoxyglucose has many of the same biochemical properties as glucose; it is mistaken for glucose by energy-requiring active brain cells and so crosses the blood-brain barrier to enter brain cells as an energy source. Unlike glucose, its metabolism is relatively incomplete, and because it is unable to pass back out of the cells, it accumulates in them for a period of time. If the brain is removed and cut about an hour after injection and placed on a film negative, the film will receive the most intense exposure from the ^{14}C in areas that had high glucose utilization. Pappius, recognizing that brain metabolism and function are closely coupled, damaged the neocortex of rats and then measured glucose uptake over a number of days. In the neocortex ipsilateral to the lesion, glucose utilization fell by more than 60% 3 days after the injury and did not return to normal until 5 days after it. Metabolism also fell by nearly 25% in the undamaged hemisphere. Pappius was able to show that the decline in metabolic activity was not due entirely to edema and so must be caused by some still unknown process. These results provide another explanation for the behavioral depression that follows brain damage.

Autoneurotoxicity

It has been known for a long time that brain damage, strokes, or ischemic attacks (arterial constriction) that cut off blood flow to parts of the brain also produce damage in those parts of the brain. Recent studies show that tissue death is not immediate but delayed, sometimes for hours or days, and that some parts of the brain (for example, the CA1 cells of the hippocampus) are particularly sensitive to oxygen deprivation. These observations suggested that something other than oxygen loss might produce the damage. One causative agent for this delayed cell death has now been identified. It is thought that the excitatory neurotransmitter glutamate is released by oxygen deprivation and then overexcites cells, causing them to die. In a sense, the cells release a neurotoxin that kills them. This idea has been supported experimentally by results indicating that substances that excite glutamate receptors are potent neurotoxins. The identificaton of a causative agent in cell death, combined with the fact that cell death is not immediate, suggests that there is a window of opportunity for preventing cell death. This may be done in one of two ways: by blocking the release of glutamate or by blocking glutamate receptors. Very vigorous experimental research is now flourishing to achieve one of these two objectives in a clinically acceptable way.

RECOVERY IN THE CORTEX

One of the earliest theories of recovery of function was formulated by Munk in 1881. He suggested that regions of the brain that were not otherwise occupied could assume functions previously mediated by the injured area. The area substituting for the damaged one ordinarily would not have become involved in mediating the function in question. There is little evidence, however, that any portions of the brain are standing by unused until required.

Lashley believed that recovery of function not only was to be expected but was relatively easy to explain, because the brain works on the principles of mass action (the entire cortex participates in each function) and equipotentially (each area of the cortex is equally able to assume control of any given behavior). The following experiment illustrates the type of evidence that Lashley used to support his position. He electrically stimulated the precentral gyrus of rhesus monkeys on four separate occasions over a period of 18 days. On each test he obtained relatively constant responses from each site stimulated, and on different tests he found that arm and leg areas, for example, remained relatively fixed. However, within any one area, stimulation of the same point on different tests resulted in widely different movements, and at different times the same movement was obtained from separate and shifting areas. These results suggested to Lashley that "within the segmental areas the various parts of the cortex may be equipotential for the production of all of the movements within that area" (Lashley, 1929, p. 154).

Glees and Cole reported a result that supports this hypothesis. They identified the thumb area of the monkey neocortex with electrical stimulation, removed the area, and then remapped the surrounding tissue after a period of recovery. During recovery, the animals began to use the thumb, and when the cortex was remapped, the areas surrounding the lesion were found to produce thumb movements. Thus Glees and Cole suggested that rehabilitation could result in restoration of a lost cortical area.

More recent work has confirmed that the brain retains plasticity into adulthood, but it also shows that it is not as plastic as is suggested by the results of Glees and Cole. Nudo and his coworkers mapped the motor cortex of monkeys to identify the hand and digit areas of the motor cortex. When they removed a portion of the digit area, they found that the monkeys showed reduced use of the contralateral hand (Figure 23.7). When they remapped the motor cortex, they found that they were unable to produce movements of the lower portion of the limb, wrist, and digits. That is, the hand area was gone from the cortical map, and only a stump of the upper arm remained. They subjected additional animals to the same procedure, except that following surgery they provided therapy for the affected limb, which consisted of substantial forced use. The good limb was bound so that the monkey was forced to use the affected limb. When they examined the motor map of these monkeys again, the hand and digit area was present, but the area that subserved the digits—which had had its cortical representation removed—was not restored. Nevertheless, even though the representation for the affected digits was not restored, therapy did allow some recovery of the use of those digits. Presumably, the movements made by the digits that had lost their cortical representation were mediated by the representations of the remaining digits.

The significant feature of the Nudo experiments is the importance of therapy. Therapy is necessary to maintain the functions of the undamaged cortex and the movements it represents. Therapy can also enable compensation for the affected body parts. Additionally, the results indicate that Glees and Cole were wrong in suggesting that the remaining cortex could represent a portion of the body that had lost its cortical representation, but right in demonstrating that therapy could produce some recovery.

The form of plasticity described by Nudo and coworkers may explain the recovery in the following case reported by Bucy and coworkers. They studied a man with a pyramidal tract sectioned in the lower brainstem as a treatment for involuntary movements. During the first 24 hours

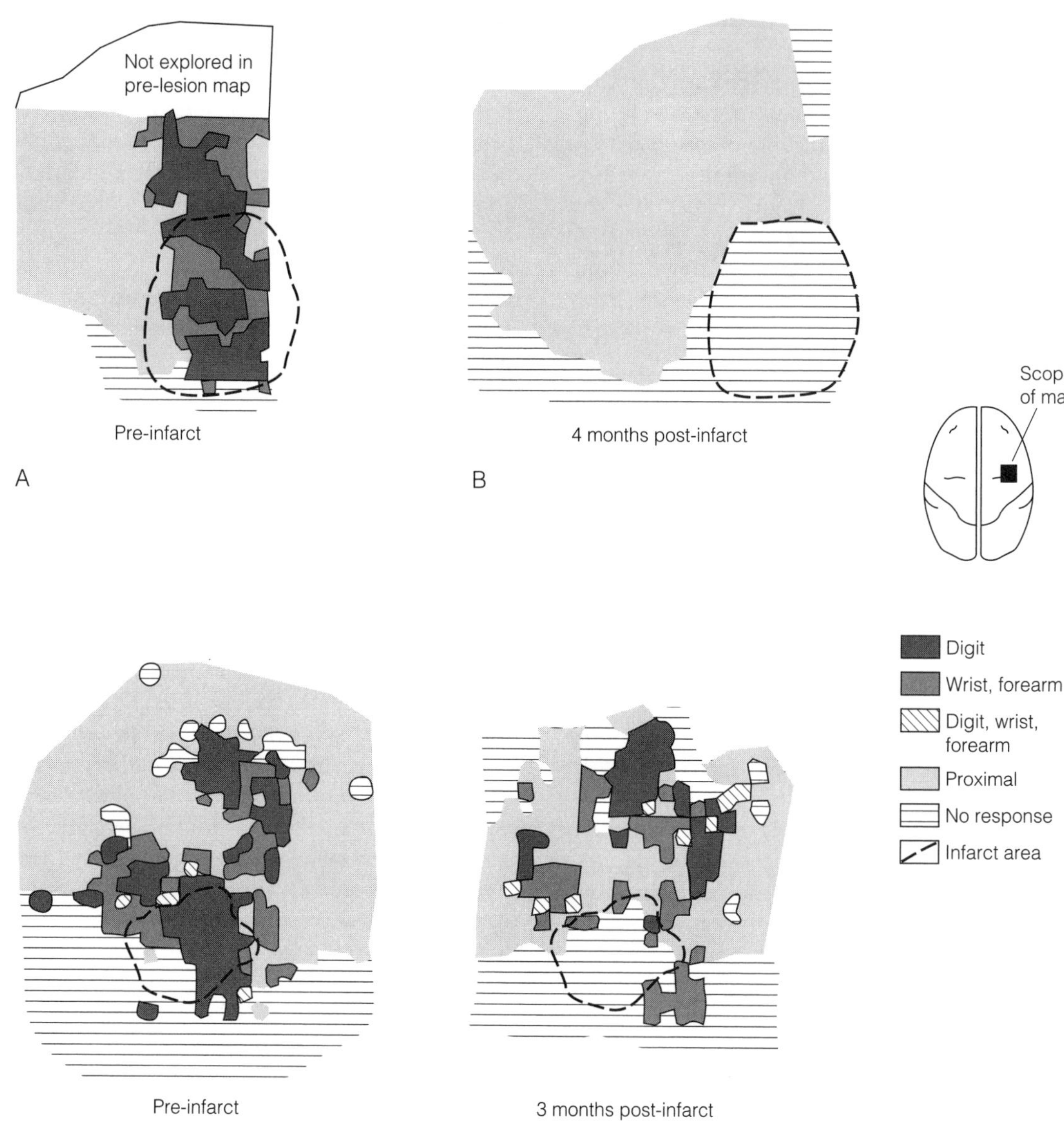

FIGURE 23.7. Influence of experience on the cortical representation of the forelimb in the motor cortex of a monkey after brain damage. *A* and *C*. Weak electrical stimulation shows the areas of the cortex that produce digit, wrist and forearm (proximal) movements in two monkeys prior to an infarct (a small lesion made with a larger electrical current through a wire electrode). The area that will receive the infarct is indicated by the dashed lines. *B*. In the monkey that was not forced to use its affected limb, the digit and wrist areas have no cortical representation as only upper limb movements are obtained with electrical stimulation. *D*. In a monkey that was forced to use the affected limb because the good limb was bound, wrist and digit movements retain their cortical representation. (After R. J. Nudo, and R. Grenda. *Society for Neuroscience Abstracts,* vol. 18. 1992, with permission.)

after surgery, he had complete flaccid hemiplegia, followed by a slight return of voluntary movement in his extremities. By the 10th day he could stand alone and walk with assistance. By the 24th day he could walk unaided. Within 7 months, maximum recovery seemed to have been reached, and he could move his feet, hands, fingers, and toes with only slight impairment. At autopsy, $2\frac{1}{2}$ years later, about 17% of his pyramidal tract fibers were found to be intact. The recovery of his ability to move his toes and fingers seems attributable to that remaining 17%, which did the job previously done by the entire tract. We might predict that if the man were discouraged from using the afflicted limbs, his recovery would have been lessened.

MECHANISMS UNDERLYING RECOVERY

Several neural mechanisms have been suggested as important in mediating such recovery, including (1) regeneration, (2) sprouting, (3) denervation supersensitivity, and (4) disinhibition or release of potential compensatory zones from inhibition. Associated with these mechanisms are several possible ways to facilitate the process of recovery. In attempts to account for recovery, a number of terms have become popular; some of the most common are defined in Table 23.2.

Regeneration

Regeneration is the process by which neurons damaged by trauma regrow connections to the area they previously innervated. Regeneration is a well-known and common occurrence in the peripheral nervous system, where both sensory and motor neurons send forth new fibers to reinnervate their previous targets (Figure 23.8). It is believed that Schwann cells, the cells that provide myelin on peripheral fibers, multiply and provide a tube or tunnel that guides the regenerating fibers to their appropriate destination.

There are potentially a number of ways to improve regeneration in the central nervous system. Two approaches have been developed to help regeneration fibers bridge areas of scarring. One is to build artificial tubes or bridges across the area of scarring; the second is to place relatively undifferentiated neural tissue in the lesion to provide a medium through which regenerating fibers can grow. There are also ways to promote fiber growth. One is the use of trophic or growth factors, such as a substance called **nerve growth factor** (**NGF**), a high-molecular-weight protein that is either produced or taken up from glia by nerve terminals and then transported to the cell body to play some role in maintaining normal cell growth or health. Another approach is based on the idea that there are molecules in the developed nervous system that inhibit new axonal growth after the brain is mature. After brain damage, if these molecules themselves could be inhibited temporarily, then regrowth could occur.

Sprouting

Sprouting is the growth of nerve fibers to innervate new targets, particularly if they have been vacated by other terminals. Studies on the effect of sectioning some of the afferent fibers to muscles have suggested that the remaining fibers sprout branches that occupy the sites left vacant by the lesioned axons. Similar sprouting takes place in the brain after lesions (see Figure 23.8). For example, Lynch and his coworkers and others have examined the rate at which sprouting occurs and have addressed the question of whether the newly formed connections are functional. Using the rat's hippocampus as their model, they cut one of the inputs to the granule cells of the hippocampus. Then they addressed the question of function by recording evoked potentials from the denervated area. In addition, they examined the anatomical basis of regrowth by staining the hippocampus with chemicals that highlight the synaptic terminals of interest, so that synaptic distribution could be assessed with the electron microscope. Their results showed that the remaining fibers send sprouts to reinnervate vacated portions of the granule cells, fibers from adjacent portions of the cell sprout and reinnervate the unoccupied area, and even fibers not connected with the cells grow and occupy a deserted space. The process of

TABLE 23.2. Compensatory mechanisms that may follow brain damage

Term	Definition
Behavioral compensation	Use of a new or different behavioral strategy to compensate for a behavior lost due to brain damage; e.g., notetaking to compensate for loss of memory
Collateral sprouting	The growth of collaterals of axons to replace lost axons or to innervate targets that have lost other afferents
Denervation supersensitivity	The proliferation of receptors on a nerve or muscle when innervation is interrupted that results in an increase in response when residual afferents are stimulated or when chemical agonists are applied
Disinhibition	Removal of inhibitory actions of a system, usually by destroying it or blocking its action pharmacologically
Nerve growth factor	A protein that may be secreted by glial cells that promotes growth in damaged neurons and facilitates regeneration and reinnervation by cut axons
Regeneration	Process by which damaged neurons, axons, or terminals regrow and establish their previous connections
Rerouting	Process by which axons or their collaterals seek out new targets when their normal destination has been removed
Silent synapse	A hypothetical synapse that is thought to be present but whose function is not behaviorally evident until the function of some other part of the system is disrupted
Sparing	A process that allows certain behaviors or aspects of behavior to survive brain damage
Sprouting	Growth of nerve fibers to innervate new targets, particularly if they have been vacated by other terminals
Substitution	The idea that an unoccupied or underused area of the brain will assume functions of a damaged area (not in vogue today)
Transient collaterals	Collaterals that at some time during development innervated targets that they subsequently abandoned as development proceeded
Vicaration	A version of substitution theory suggesting that the functions of damaged areas can be assumed by adjacent areas (the term is unlikely to catch on)

sprouting appears to be quite rapid and may be complete in 7 to 10 days. Evoked potentials indicate that the new connections are electrophysiologically functional. A number of studies suggest that sprouted fibers do mediate behavioral recovery.

Denervation Supersensitivity

The idea of **denervation supersensitivity** arose from the work of Cannon and Rosenblueth in 1949. They found that when the afferent fibers to a muscle were cut, the muscle became hyperresponsive to the application of its neurotransmitter. Hypersensitivity is presumed to occur because receptors proliferate on the muscle cell in areas where they were not previously located. As a result, a given amount of drug produces a greater effect because there are more receptors available to be stimulated. Similar receptor proliferation is thought to occur in the brain. Denervation su-

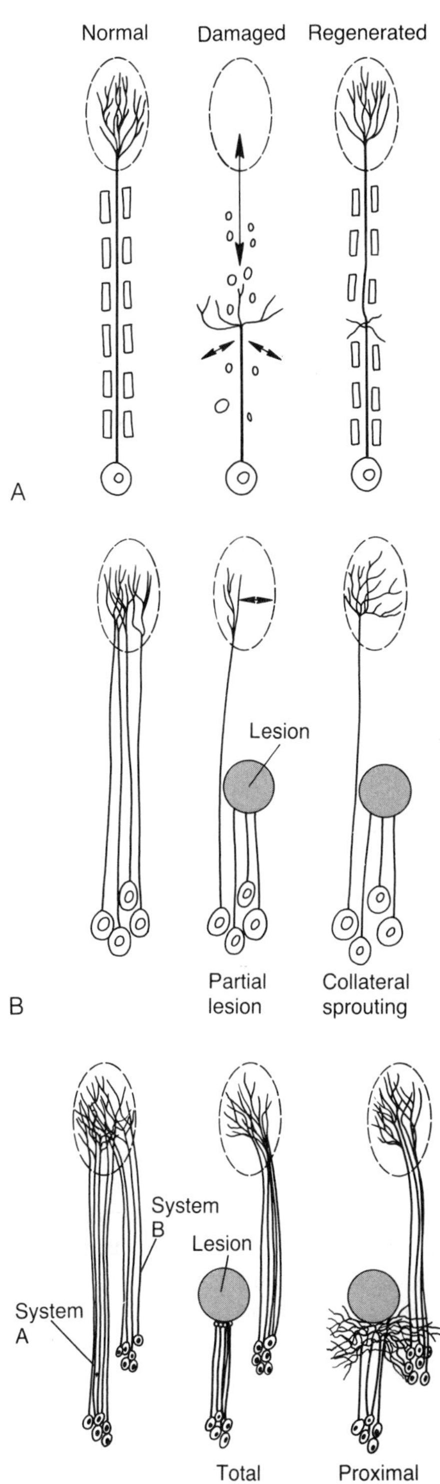

FIGURE 23.8. Three models of axonal sprouting by which lesioned central axons might reestablish functional connections. *A.* True regeneration of severed axons involving regrowth of the axon back to its target site. Present in the human peripheral nervous system, in invertebrates, and in the central nervous system of rats under favorable conditions. *B.* Collateral sprouting in intact neurons. Known to occur and to be functional in the brain catecholamine and serotonin fibers. *C.* Reinnervation of systems that have been disconnected, as yet a hypothetical explanation of recovery. (After Bjorklund, 1979.)

persensitivity is a mechanism with some adaptive or compensatory value because it allows remaining portions of a system to increase the system's effective action.

Disinhibition of Potential Compensatory Zones

In 1971, Wall and Egger mapped the thalamic and neocortical regions in which stimulation of a rat's forelimb or hind limb resulted in an evoked potential. After cutting the pathway from the lower spinal cord to the brain to sever the connections with the hind limb, they again stimulated the forelimb or hind limb. As expected, there was no response in the hind-limb regions, but the forelimb region was normal. After 3 days, however, there was a remarkable change. The region that had previously exihibited evoked potentials upon stimulation of the hind limb now showed these potentials upon stimulation of the forelimb. The response looked normal, as if this region had always been wired up to the forelimb. Why?

Most available evidence indicates that there must be preexisting **silent synapses.** It seems likely, therefore, that fibers from the forelimb were always connected to the hind limb area but were kept under some form of inhibition and thus were not functional. Once fibers from the hind limb area were severed, the competing input was lost and the area became functionally a forelimb area. These findings seem to indicate that the area that could potentially become involved in a response is larger than the mapping studies usually suggest. The results also suggest that the areas may not become involved in a response unless competing or inhibitory systems are abolished; that is, unless disinhibition occurs. Finally, the results imply that there is considerable overlap in innervation in various parts of the brain but that specificity is maintained through inhibition. Removal of inhibition allows some takeover by the previously inhibited area.

CHRONIC EFFECTS OF BRAIN DAMAGE IN ADULTS

The use of such words as "plasticity" and the emphasis placed on recovery of function in a great deal of basic research might give the impression that the brain has an unlimited potential for recovery and reorganization after injury. Although there is a paucity of information about long-term recovery, on the basis of the available evidence the following generalizations can be made: (1) Recovery is likely in complex behaviors that are composed of many components, through processes that are referred to as **behavioral compensation.** (2) Recovery is most pronounced with incomplete lesions, such as those that commonly occur after trauma from concussions or penetrating head wounds. (3) Recovery of specific functions controlled by localized brain areas is unlikely if all of the area is removed.

Behavioral Compensation

The ability to be employed and self-supporting clearly depends on many behavioral abilities and configurations of those abilities. Brain damage may affect some of those behaviors more than others, but there are numerous possibilities for compensation. Studies by Dresser and his coworkers show that when gainful employment is used as a measure of recovery, as was done for veterans injured in the Korean War, recovery was pronounced: approximately 80% were employed. This measure gives the highest rate of recovery of any we have found in the literature and strongly suggests that some factor such as behavioral compensation is operating. This is not to minimize the seriousness of the problem that 20% were not employed. Nor does it speak to the quality of employment. Oddy and Humphrey suggest that work is not a sensitive index of recovery. Forty-eight of their 54 patients with closed-head injuries were back at work within 2 years, but many were restricted in their work activity and believed that they had not regained their full working capacity. Other aspects of life also suffered, as they had not resumed all leisure activities and social contacts. Interestingly, of all aspects of social relations, relationships with siblings suffered most. Oddy and Humphrey emphasize that therapy should be directed not only toward return to work but also toward leisure activities and social relations.

One way to examine the chronic effects of brain damage and how individuals cope is to study self-reports of people who have been brain-damaged. Generally, very little attention is given to these reports, but they provide a valuable insight into questions of recovery. Fredrick Linge, a clinical psychologist we know, has described the changes he underwent after suffering brain damage in an automobile accident. He was in a coma for the first week after the accident and was not expected to achieve significant recovery. Nevertheless, he was able to return to a relatively demanding clinical practice about a year after his accident. But he was changed by the brain damage and had to make changes in his life-style and work routine to cope. He describes his adjustments in the following way:

> In learning to live with my brain damage, I have found through trial and error that certain things help greatly and others hinder my coping. In order to learn and retain information best, I try to eliminate as many distractions as possible and concentrate all my mental energy on the task at hand. A structured, routine, well-organized and serene atmosphere at home, and, as far as possible, at work, is vital to me. In the past I enjoyed a rather chaotic life style, but I now find that I want "a place for everything and everything

in its place." When remembering is difficult, order and habit make the minutiae of daily living much easier.

I cannot cope with anger as well as I was able to do before my accident. Rage, related to my losses, does not lie just under the surface waiting to explode as it did earlier in my recovery. Yet, like any other person living in the real world, situations arise which make me justifiably angry. Before my accident, it took a lot to make me angry, and I am still, today, slow to anger. The difference is that now, once I become angry, I find it impossible to "put the brakes on" and I attribute this directly to my brain damage. It is extremely frightening to me to find myself in this state, and I still have not worked out a truly satisfactory solution, except insofar as I try to avoid anger-provoking situations or try to deal with them before they become too provoking.

My one-track mind seems to help me to take each day as it comes without excessive worry and to enjoy the simple things of life in a way that I never did before. As well, I seem to be a more effective therapist, since I stick to the basic issues at hand and have more empathy with others than I did previously. (Linge, 1980, pp. 6–7)

The self-report by Linge shows that studies on recovery cannot be limited to measures such as reemployment or even renewed social contacts. These measures, in many cases, may indicate that recovery is complete, but they do not detail how the individual has changed, and has changed other aspects of the world, in order to cope. It is noteworthy that Linge was a professional psychologist who lived in a social milieu in which people were willing to help him reestablish himself. Many people who do not have a similar position will have a much more difficult time recovering. Linge makes our point well by stating that the brain-damaged person must change not only the external environment but the internal environment as well.

Recovery from Traumatic Lesions

Teuber has described the deficits of war veterans on tests given 1 week after injury and 20 years later. These patients are excellent candidates for study because they received standard tests after induction into the army and were relatively young at the time of injury, the immediate aftermath of the injury is documented, and the kind and extent of recovery can be documented through prolonged follow-up by veterans' services. A summary of Teuber's results is given in Figure 23.9. They reveal that 4% of the veterans showed some recovery from motor defects, 36% showed some recovery from somatosensory defects, 43% showed some recovery from visual defects, and 24% showed some recovery from initial dysphasia. These findings are probably quite reliable if we can generalize from the visual-field tests; according to Teuber, the Harms procedure of determining field defects allows for an extremely accurate assessment and is highly reliable in the hands of different testers at different times. Two comments can be made about Teuber's analysis. First, it must be noted that more than half the patient population showed no recovery at all, and the failure of more than 75% of patients to show recovery from dysphasia is not encouraging. The latter figure is supported by Luria's report that 66% of his dysphasic patients showed no recovery. Second, the analysis is not quantitative and there is no estimate of the degree of recovery. A study of a larger population of veterans, those from the Vietnam War, has been made by Mohr and his coworkers. In general, their results are consistent with those of Teuber in that a great deal of recovery of function is to be expected from penetrating brain injury. In fact, Mohr reports more extensive recovery from aphasia (34%) than does Teuber and also reports that the recovery continued for years after injury. An addendum to these studies can be made. Zihl and Cramon report that practice in localizing lights led to an increase in visual field in partially blind patients, an increase that would not have occurred without the practice. It is not known what effect specific

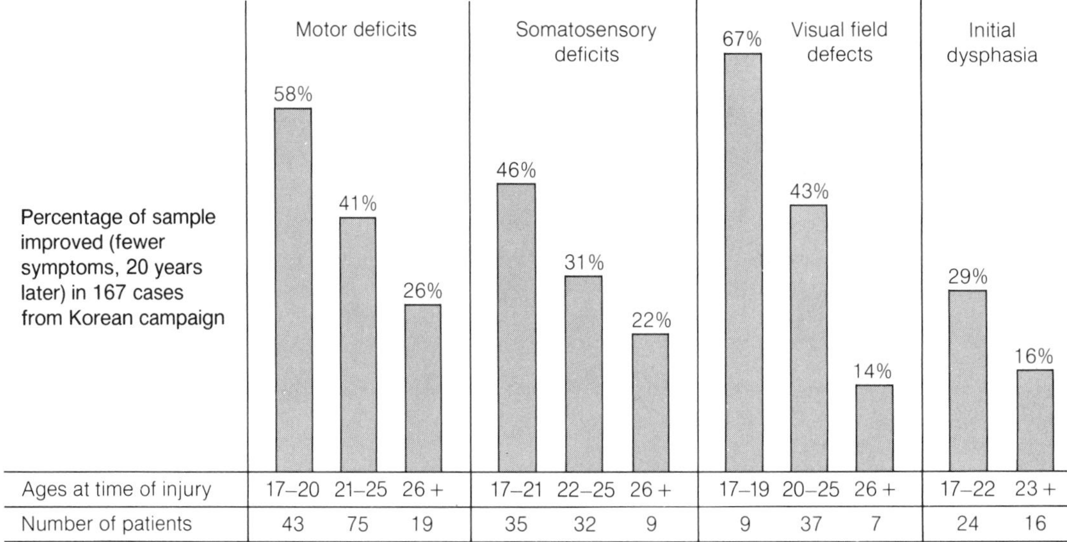

FIGURE 23.9. Estimated improvement from initial examination (within no more than 1 week of injury) and follow-up examination (20 years later) for some body regions (extremities, sides of face) for which symptoms were recorded (reflex changes, paralysis, weakness) in the motor system; for noted sensory losses in the somatosensory system; for the visual field (diminution in number of quadrants known to be affected); and in symptoms interpreted as dysphasia. Note the advantage of groups of lower age at the time of wounding. (After Teuber, 1975.)

therapy might have had on the patients reported in the veteran studies.

Recovery from Surgical Lesions

Tests have been given to patients within days of surgery and as long as 20 years after surgery. Unfortunately, recovery seems to have occurred so infrequently that the breakdown of data at different test-retest intervals is not reported. Table 23.3 summarizes the results from some studies in which tests were given a few days before surgery, within 20 days after surgery, and 1 to 20 years after surgery. The results show that after dorsolateral frontal lesions there was no recovery in card sorting, after right temporal lesions there was no recovery in recall of the Rey figure, and after parietal lesions there was no recovery in finger-position sense or arm-movement copying. The finding of no recovery is also reported in some other studies. Jones-Gottman and Milner tested patient groups within 2 weeks of surgery and 1 or more years later on spontaneous drawing tasks. The subjects were told to invent as many unnameable drawings as they could within 5 min. Although all patient groups showed some reduction in performance relative to control groups, patients with right frontal lesions were the most impaired, and there were no differences in performance between patients tested shortly after surgery and those tested more than a year after it. There also seems to be little or no recovery in memory after bilateral medial temporal lobe removal. In a 14-year follow-up, Milner, Corkin, and Teuber report that the amnesic patient H. M. had a presurgical IQ of 104, a 2-year follow-up IQ of 112, and a 9-year follow-up IQ of 118. Yet despite this improvement in intelligence score, his anterograde amnesia remained essentially unchanged.

TABLE 23.3. Presurgical, postsurgical, and follow-up performance on neuropsychological tests by patients with cortical lesions

Test	Lesion	Preop	Postop	Follow-up	Control	Reference
Card-sorting categories	Frontal	3.3	1.4	1.3	4.6	Milner, 1963
Card-sorting errors	Frontal	54.9	73.2	78.2	37.7	Milner, 1963
Rey-figure copy score	Right temporal	31.2	30.6	29.8	34.9	Taylor, 1969
Rey-figure recall score	Right temporal	15.4	15.3	13.8	24.2	Taylor, 1969
Finger-position sense	Central					
Incidence of deficit (%)						
Ipsilateral		24	14	6	—	Taylor, 1969
Contralateral		36	43	65	—	
Arm-movement copying	Left parietal		73	75.8	90.2	Kolb and Milner, 1981

In some studies of patients with atrophic lesions, a degree of recovery has been noted on some tests. Milner reported in 1975 that patients with left temporal lesions had preoperative memory scores of 12, early postoperative scores of 4.4, and 5- to 20-year follow-up scores of 8. This improvement is significant. There are a number of possible explanations for why recovery should have occurred on this test. First, the score is a composite of logical memory (recall of stories) and paired-associate learning. It is not clear which component of the test showed recovery. Blakemore and Falconer studied paired-associate learning in 86 temporal lobectomy patients for up to 10 years after surgery. They found that the deficit lasted for 2 to 3 years, but thereafter there was progressive recovery, provided the patients were young. Hence recovery could have been due to improvement in one facet of the task. Second, Jones has shown that if left temporal lobe patients are taught to use imagery (for example, for the associate word pair "bouquet-elephant" they imagine an elephant with a bouquet of flowers in its trunk), they show substantial improvement in memory. Hence recovery may have been due to the development of alternative memory strategies. Third, the temporal cortex must have rather special properties to allow rapid memory storage. Those properties probably also make it especially prone to epilepsy. It is possible that if any of the area remains, it retains a special capacity for plasticity that is not as evident in other brain areas. Although recovery occurs on the paired-associate test, it is not clear that it is due to recovery of verbal memory per se.

In summary, we think that the results from some of the studies reported here are very important to the question of recovery of function. The results imply that if the test is specific for certain brain areas and if the lesions remove the entire area, recovery will not occur. What makes this position particularly persuasive is that the surgical patients had tumors or epilepsy at the site of the lesions, which could have encouraged the function to move elsewhere. Yet there is little or no evidence in the test results to suggest that any such transfer took place.

VARIABLES AFFECTING RECOVERY

There are many variables in addition to lesion size that affect the rate of recovery from brain damage. These are not discussed fully in many papers because measurements are so difficult to make; because patient groups are often small to begin with, which precludes fractionation; or simply because a particular researcher may not think they are important. These variables include age, sex, handedness, intelligence, and personality. Overall, it is thought that recovery from brain damage will be best if the patient is a young, intelligent, optimistic, left-handed female.

Youth is one of the easier variables to measure. Teuber and coworkers have found that on a number of tests, recovery by soldiers from natural lesions is greater in the 17 to 20 age group than in the 21 to 25 age group, which in turn is greater than in the age group 26 and over (see Figure 23.9). Milner reports that patients over 40 who have removals near the posterior temporal speech zone in the left hemisphere show less recovery than younger patients. It is noteworthy that age does not always appear as a significant factor in studies of recovery, as reported by Kertesz. Age is also a contributing factor to many kinds of brain damage; that is, strokes and other kinds of brain abnormality are common in older people, and these are just the people who may be showing declines in motor and cognitive function due to the normal processes of aging. Thus, recovery may tend to be obscured by aging.

Handedness and sex, both for much the same reason, may influence the outcome of brain damage. Recall that a number of theories argue that female and male brains differ in both anatomy and functional organization, with less lateralization in the female. Likewise, familial left-handers are thought to be less lateralized in function than right-handers. For both groups, it is thought that damage in a particular location can be ameliorated to some extent by the remaining functional portions of the system that are located in the undamaged hemisphere. There is an inherent logical weakness in this view, however: if part of a functional area is located elsewhere and remains undamaged, then the lesions are not really complete and behavioral comparisons of recovery will be confounded. A similar confounding may well be applicable to considerations of the factor of intelligence. Although the ultimate recovery of a very intelligent individual may be excellent in relation to the recovery of others, the actual residual deficit may be equal simply because the very intelligent person would normally function at a higher level. The factor of personality is still more difficult to evaluate. It is widely thought that optimistic, extroverted, and easygoing people have a better prognosis; yet personality is notoriously difficult to measure, and brain damage may change personality.

THERAPEUTIC APPROACHES TO BRAIN DAMAGE

There are three major experimental therapeutic approaches to brain damage: (1) Rehabilitation procedures consist of a variety of behavioral and psychological therapies. (2) Pharmacological therapies can be used to promote recovery in the immediate postsurgery period. (3) Transplantation techniques can be used to restore normal brain functioning. Rehabilitation procedures are widely used, with mixed results; pharmacological and transplantation techniques are in the stage of animal experiments.

Rehabilitation

The goal of rehabilitation is to return a patient to a level of function that approximates that person's previous level of normal function. From a practical point of view, knowing what goes on in the brain is not essential for this endeavor. It is more important to know what procedures may be useful to restore function. Bach-y-Rita has reviewed some of the key factors that relate to this objective:

1. Stimulation in the early postoperative stage is thought to be useful. This can include talking to people even though they are in a coma, interacting with them, and playing music with an upbeat rhythm.

2. If the use of a body part is impaired, forced use is helpful. One example is tying a patient's good arm to force the use of the impaired arm.

3. Practice should be extensive and far in excess of what would be required for an unimpaired individual. This is because increments of improvement may be small and substitution behaviors (behaviors different from those normally used) may have to be developed to accomplish a given amount of improvement.

4. Tasks for which training is given should be relevant to real life and should include tasks needed for daily living. In some hospitals, nurses feed and care for patients in other ways, and the

patients are taken in wheelchairs to physiotherapy. Much of the therapy that they require could be done at the bedside.

5. Nonprofessionals, particularly family members, should be included in therapy. Therapy and training are usually labor-intensive and time-consuming, making costs prohibitive if only professionals are used.

6. Motivation should be considered an important component of therapy; long work periods, sometimes accompanied by only small gains, can be frustrating.

7. Training should be continued even after plateaus are reached. Very often therapy ceases once progress in recovery slows. Continued work, however, even if it produces only small improvements, may eventually mean the difference between dependency and self-sufficiency.

8. Finally, tasks should be broken down into simpler components because the patient's attention span or motor abilities may be limited at first.

Therapy for brain damage often requires innovation and the development of techniques that are relevant to individual patients. We were once asked to recommend a therapy for a depressed motorcycle racer who had suffered extensive brain damage after crashing a hang glider. We half-seriously suggested a tricyle, which his caregivers then had constructed for him. His attitude improved dramatically, and he was soon racing the tricycle around the hospital grounds and taking trips to town. The exercise and attitude change helped him tackle other tasks to further his recovery. Substitution systems may be useful for some patients. For example, visual information can be recorded from a video camera and presented in a tactile form on the skin as a partial substitute for vision. Various machines, especially computers, can be used to perform specific tasks. A number of programs have provided trained animals to perform certain routine tasks. Biofeedback techniques are useful for the reeducation of certain motor skills.

Pharmacological Therapies

There has been a long-standing interest in the use of pharmacological therapies for ameliorating the effects of brain damage. The extensive research has been reviewed by Feeny and Sutton. Much of the impetus for the research comes from observations that amphetamine treatment can restore certain functions in brain-damaged animals. The results suggest that the rate of recovery can be increased if pharmacological treatments and experience are combined shortly after brain damage. A vigorous search is being conducted for the mechanisms underlying the therapeutic effects. This research consists of studying the underlying transmitter systems that may be involved in recovery and the neurotrophic factors that might promote recovery.

Brain Tissue Transplants

The idea of transplanting neural tissue in mammals and the techniques for doing so go back to the first decade of this century. Yet until a few years ago, the possibility that neural transplantation had any practical application was viewed as rather remote. This view has now radically changed. A model procedure for tissue transplantation is illustrated in Figure 23.10. Fetal tissue, containing undeveloped embryonic cells, is dissected from a fetal brain. The tissue is transferred to a dish containing saline solution and treated in a test tube to disocciate the fetal brain cells from glia, blood vessels, and other tissue. It is then transferred to a syringe and injected into an appropriate location in the brain of a recipient animal. All aspects of the procedure can be varied in different ways. Tissue may come from different brain sites, donors of different ages, or different donor species. In the future, the separation procedures may include techniques that extract only the cells of interest or that involve the cloning of cells for transplant. The injection procedures may eventually involve injections of other substances (such as nerve growth factor) that enhance incorporation of the graft into the host brain.

The brain appears to be sheltered from the normal rejection processes that hamper transplant

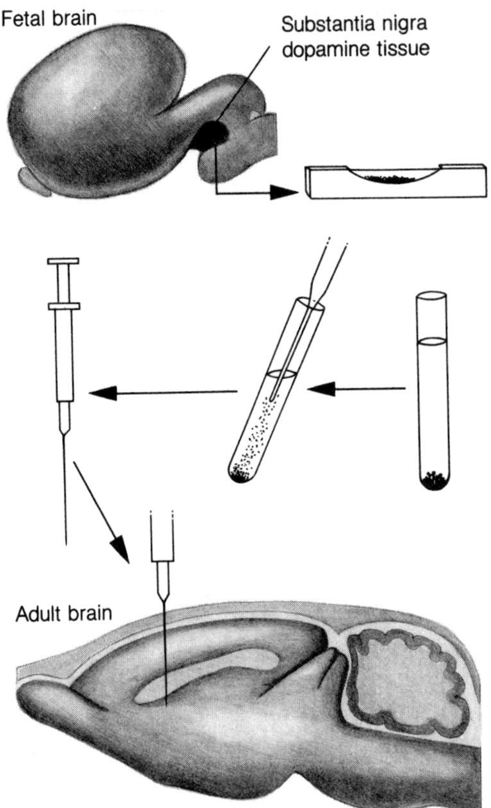

FIGURE 23.10. Principal steps in the brain tissue grafting procedure, as described in the text. (After A. Bjorklund, U. Stenevi, R. H. Schmidt, S. B. Dunnett, and F. H. Gage. Introduction and general methods of preparation. *Acta Physiologica Scandinavica* 522:1–8, 1983.)

success in the rest of the body. As a result, successful grafts can be made not only between different sites in the body but also between individuals and across species. Fetal grafts survive best, and the grafts must receive a blood supply quickly. Successful transplants show a high degree of normal differentiation and organization. They also make connections with the host tissue. A particularly positive feature of the grafts is that when they are placed almost anywhere, they send axons to make appropriate connections. Thus, the graft works when placed in the zone of damage, in the ventricle, or at other sites convenient for the technological manipulations of the experimenter. The embryonic cells seem to have a homing instinct and a passport no longer available to adult cells and so travel through the nervous system at will. But a word of caution! The transplants may go not only to their appropriate locations but also to inappropriate ones.

The application of the technology of brain grafts is obvious. After brain damage, degenerating tissue would be simply replaced. An almost immediate application is to Parkinson's disease, which seems to be caused by the loss of a specific group of cells. In Parkinson's, cells of the substantia nigra degenerate and the brain is thus depleted of the transmitter substance dopamine, which the cells supply to their terminals. The loss of dopamine produces the constellation of symptoms that constitute the disease. Figure 23.11A is a box diagram of the presumed role of dopamine as a behavioral modulator in the normal brain. Figure 23.11B shows the Parkinsonian condition. A putative remedy for the disease is to place a brain graft of embryonic cells into the brain (Figure 23.11C).

Can it work? A substantial literature shows that some symptoms of dopamine loss can be overcome with brain transplants in rats and monkeys. The application of this technology to humans is already in the experimental stage; more than 100 patients have received transplants. Some of the research groups making the implants have not been involved in the experimental animal tests, and some have not done adequate preoperative or postoperative evaluations of the patients. The results from most reports are not encouraging. Relief from symptoms is minor or only short-lived. The difficulties with the transplants in humans may be that they do not grow sufficiently in the large human brain, they are not adequately incorporated into brain circuitry, and they are subject to the same disease process that is causing the original loss of dopamine cells.

The most positive report is that by Widner and coworkers from transplants made into the basal

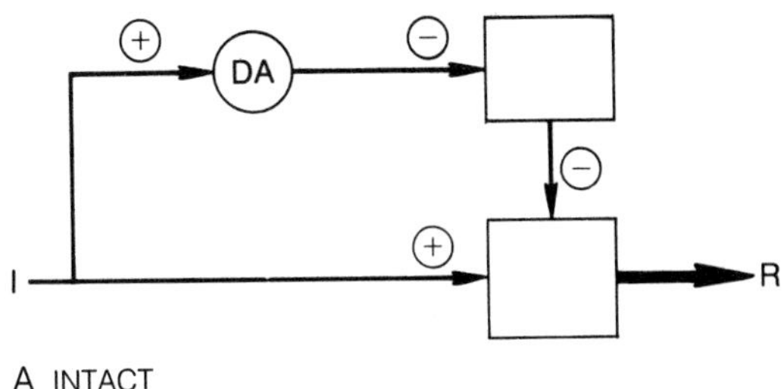

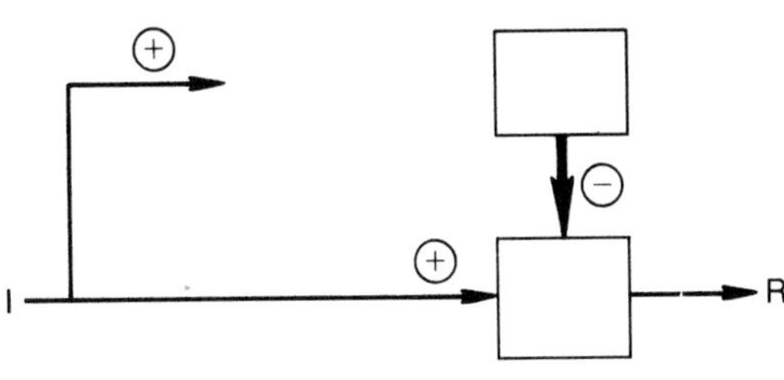

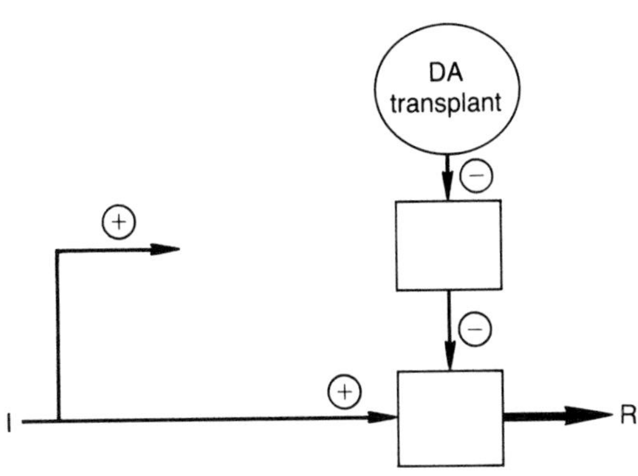

FIGURE 23.11. Proposed mode of action of the dopamine (DA)-producing brain grafts in the promotion of behavioral recovery. *A.* The behavioral response (R) evoked by an activating sensory input (I) is modulated through an inhibitory control mechanism of which the dopamine pool forms an important part. *B.* The response can no longer occur in the absence of dopamine. *C.* The sensory response pathway is reopened by the dopamine transplant.

ganglia of two patients (a 42-year-old man and a 30-year-old woman) who developed Parkinson's symptoms due to drug use. They had taken a synthetic morphine that unfortunately contained the substance MPTP. This compound is converted by the liver into a second compound that is toxic to substantia nigra dopamine cells. Because they developed parkinsonism at a relatively young age, these patients were not subject to any progressive disease. As a result of the grafts, they became more independent in their motor function, and the drug treatments that they had been receiving were reduced. Although the patients were clearly still impaired and the transplants were not a cure for their condition, the improvements in motor ability to the point that they could initiate voluntary movements must be considered very significant.

Future Approaches

Although it was believed that once the brain forms there is no possibility that new cells can form, this turns out not to be the case. Reynolds and Weiss have reported that there are stem cells in a portion of tissue adjacent to the lateral ventricles that retain the ability to divide and form neurons. Normally, they continue to divide (presumably throughout life), producing one cell that will subsequently divide again and one daughter cell that dies. These cells can be cultured in dishes to form neurospheres, or little balls of cells, that can subsequently differentiate into neurons or glial cells. Potentially, these cells could be treated with growth factors to form special lines of cells (for example, dopamine cells) that then could be used for brain grafts. Alternatively, these cells could be encouraged to grow, again using growth factors, to restore lost cells in the brain of someone who has suffered brain damage. Admittedly, these procedures, if they prove to be feasible, lie in the future, but they are achievable.

SUMMARY

Brain damage is a major cause of loss of function. Generally, traumatic injury that spares portions of functional areas is followed by greater recovery than injury that results in loss of an entire functional area. The processes of recovery can last for years, with recovery often restored in the same sequence in which behavior developed in infancy. Vigorous and sustained therapeutic measures not only will prevent regression in the face of a handicap but also will substantially enhance recovery over what might normally be expected. There are many interesting and potentially useful ways to restore tissue once it is lost or damaged, but few of these measures are sufficiently developed to be used clinically. Consequently, behavioral therapy remains the single most useful treatment, and compensation is its single most beneficial result.

REFERENCES

Anand, B. K., and J. R. Brobeck. Hypothalamic control of food intake. *Yale Journal of Biology and Medicine* 24:123–140, 1951.

Bach-y-Rita, P., ed. *Recovery of Function: Theoretical Considerations for Brain Injury Rehabilitation.* Bern, Switzerland: Hyuber Publishers, 1980.

Barbizet, J. *Human Memory and Its Pathology.* San Francisco: W. H. Freeman, 1970.

Barnes, C. D., R. T. Joynt, and B. A. Schottelius. Motor neuron resting potentials in spinal shock. *American Journal of Physiology* 203:1113–1116, 1962.

Basso, A., E. Capitani, and E. Zanobio. Pattern of recovery of oral and written expression and comprehension in aphasic patients. *Behavioral Brain Research* 6:115–128, 1982.

Blakemore, C. B., and M. A. Falconer. Long-term effects of anterior temporal lobectomy on certain cognitive functions. *Journal of Neurology, Neurosurgery, and Psychiatry* 30:364–367, 1967.

Bucy, P. C., J. E. Keplinger, and E. B. Siqueira. Destruction of the "pyramidal tract" in man. *Journal of Neurosurgery* 21:385–398, 1964.

Cannon, W. B., and A. Rosenblueth. *The Supersensitivity of Denervated Structures.* New York: Macmillan, 1949.

Critchely, M. Dr. Samuel Johnson's aphasia. *Medical History* 6:27–44, 1962.

Dresser, A. C., A. M. Meirowsky, G. H. Weiss, M. L. McNeel, A. G. Simon, and W. F. Caveness. Gainful employment following head injury. *Archives of Neurology* 29:111–116, 1973.

Feeney, D. M., and R. L. Sutton. Pharmacotherapy for recovery of function after brain injury. *CRC Critical Reviews in Neurobiology* 3:135–197, 1987.

Finger, S., and D. G. Stein. *Brain Damage and Recovery.* New York: Academic, 1982.

Geschwind, N. Late changes in the nervous system: An overview. In D. G. Stein, J. J. Rosen, and N. Butters, eds. *Plasticity and Recovery of Function in the Central Nervous System.* New York: Academic, 1974.

Glees, P., and J. Cole. Recovery of skilled motor function after small repeated lesions of motor cortex in macaque. *Journal of Neurophysiology* 13:137–148, 1950.

Golani, I., D. L. Wolgin, and P. Teitelbaum. A proposed natural geometry of recovery from akinesia in the lateral hypothalamic rat. *Brain Research* 164:237–267, 1979.

Grillner, S. Locomotion in the spinal cat. In R. B. Stein, K. G. Pearson, R. S. Smith, and J. B. Redford, eds. *Control of Posture and Locomotion.* New York: Plenum, 1973.

Hall, M. *On the Diseases and Derangements of the Nervous System.* London: Bailliere, 1841.

Head, H., and G. Riddoch. The automatic bladder, excessive sweating and some other reflex conditions in gross injuries of the spinal cord. *Brain* 15:188–263, 1917.

Hughlings-Jackson, J. *Selected Writings of John Hughlings-Jackson.* J. Taylor, ed. London: Hodder, 1932.

Jones, M. K. Imagery as a mnemonic aid after left temporal lobectomy: Contrast between material-specific and generalized memory disorder. *Neuropsychologia* 12:21–30, 1974.

Jones-Gottman, M., and B. Milner. Design fluency: The invention of nonsense drawings after focal cortical lesions. *Neuropsychologia* 15:653–674, 1977.

Kertesz, A. *Aphasia and Associated Disorders.* New York: Grune & Stratton, 1979.

Kolb, B., and B. Milner. Performance of complex arm and facial movements after focal brain lesions. *Neuropsychologia* 19:491–503, 1981.

Kuhn, R. A. Functional capacity of the isolated human spinal cord. *Brain* 73:1–51, 1950.

Lashley, K. S. Temporal variation in the function of the gyrus precentralis in primates. *American Journal of Physiology* 65:585–602, 1923.

Levin, H. S., A. L. Benton, and R. G. Grossman. *Neurobehavioral Consequences of Closed Head Injury.* New York: Oxford, 1982.

Linge, F. What does it feel like to be brain-damaged? *Canada's Mental Health* 28:4–7, 1980.

Luria, A. R. *The Man with a Shattered World.* Lynn Solotoroff. New York: Basic Books, Jonathan Cape, Ltd., 1972.

Lynch, G. S., S. Deadwyler, and C. W. Cotman. Post lesion axonal growth produces permanent functional connections. *Science* 180:1364–1366, 1973.

Lynch, G., G. Rose, C. Gall, and C. W. Cotman. In M. Statini, ed. *Golgi Centennial Symposium Proceedings.* New York: Raven Press, 1975.

Milner, B. Effect of different brain lesions on card sorting. *Archives of Neurology* 9:90–100, 1963.

Milner, B. Psychological aspects of focal epilepsy and its neurosurgical management. *Advances in Neurology* 8:299–321, 1975.

Milner, B., S. Corkin, and H.-L. Teuber. Further analysis of the hippocampal amnesic syndrome: 14-year follow-up study of H. M. *Neuropsychologia* 6:215–234, 1968.

Mohr, J. P., G. H. Weiss, W. F. Caveness, J. D. Dillon, J. P. Kistler, A. M. Meirowsky, and B. L. Rish. Language and motor disorders after penetrating head injury in Viet Nam. *Neurology* 30:1273–1279, 1980.

Munk, H. *Uber die Funktionen der Grosshirnrinde. Gesammelte Mitteilungen aus den Jahren.* 1877–1880. Berlin: August Hershwald, 1881.

Murray, T. J. Dr. Samuel Johnson's abnormal movements. In A. J. Friedhoff and T. N. Chase, eds. *Advances in Neurology,* vol. 35. New York: Raven Press, 1982.

Oddy, M., and M. Humphrey. Social recovery during the year following severe head injury. *Journal of Neurology, Neurosurgery, and Psychiatry* 43:798–802, 1980.

Quinlan, J., and J. Quinlan. *Karen Ann: The Quinlans Tell Their Story.* Toronto: Doubleday, 1977.

Reynolds, B. A., and S. Weiss. Generation of neurons and astrocytes from isolated cells of the adult mammalian central nervous system. *Science* 255:1613–1808, 1992.

Robinson, R. G., F. E. Bloom, and E. L. F. Battenberg. A fluorescent histochemical study of changes in noradrenergic neurons following experimental cerebral infarction in the rat. *Brain Research* 132:259–272, 1977.

Rosner, B. B. Recovery of function and localization of function in historical perspective. In D. G. Stein, J. J. Rosen, and N. Butters, eds. *Plasticity and Recovery of Function in the Central Nervous System.* New York: Academic, 1974.

Sherrington, C. S. *The Integrative Action of the Nervous System,* 2nd ed. New Haven: Yale University Press, 1947.

Sokoloff, L. The deoxyglucose method: Theory and practice. *European Neurology* 20:137–145, 1981.

Taylor, L. B. Localization of cerebral lesions by psychological testing. *Clinical Neurosurgery* 16:269–287, 1969.

Taylor, L. B. Psychological assessment of neurosurgical patients. In T. Rasmussen and R. Marino, eds. *Functional Neurosurgery.* New York: Raven Press, 1979.

Teitelbaum, P., and A. N. Epstein. The lateral hypothalamic syndrome: Recovery of feeding and drinking after lateral hypothalamic lesions. *Psychological Review* 69:74–90, 1962.

Teuber, H.-L. Recovery of function after brain injury in man. In *Outcome of Severe Damage to the Nervous System, Ciba Foundation Symposium 34.* Amsterdam: Elsevier North-Holland, 1975.

Twitchell, T. E. The restoration of motor function following hemiplegia in man. *Brain* 74:443–480, 1951.

Twitchell, T. E. The automatic grasping response of infants. *Neuropsychologia* 3:247–259, 1965.

von Monakow, C. V. *Lokalization der Hirnfunktionen. Journal für Psychologie and Neurologie* 17:185–200, 1911. Reprinted in G. von Bonin. *The Cerebral Cortex.* Springfield, Ill.: Charles C. Thomas, 1960.

Wall, P. D., and M. D. Egger. Formation of new connections in adult rat brains after partial deafferentation. *Nature* 232:542–545, 1971.

Waller, A. V. Experiments on the section of the glossopharyngeal and hypoglossal nerves of the frog, and observations of the alterations produced thereby in the structure of their primitive fibers. *Philosophical Transactions* 140:423–429, 1850.

Whitty, C. W. M., and O. L. Zangwill. Traumatic amnesia. In C. W. M. Whitty and O. L. Zangwill, eds. *Amnesia.* London: Butterworths, 1966.

Widner, H., et al. Bilateral, fetal, mesencaphalic grafting in two patients with parkinsonism induced by 1-methyl-4-phenyl-1,2,3,6-tetrahydropridine (MPTP). *The New England Journal of Medicine* 327:1556–1563, 1992.

Neurological Disorders

People suspected of having some disorder of the nervous system are usually examined by a **neurologist,** a physician specializing in the treatment of such disorders. The neurological examination is guided by the principle that every function is abnormal until it is examined and found to be normal. The neurologist first takes a history from the patient and makes a general assessment of the patient's personality, facial appearance, and body structure. The neurologist then thoroughly examines the skin and mucous membranes, the orifices, and the sensory systems; tests motor functions; listens to the heart, abdomen, head, and blood vessels; and examines every organ system. If an apparent deviation is found, it is evaluated with respect to the way and degree to which the affected body part differs from the same body part on the opposite side, that body part of family members, and the theoretical norm for a person of like age and sex. The neurologist may recommend additional tests (for example, EEG, brain scans, and so forth) as indicated by the person's history or the initial neurological exam. At the end of an examination the neurologist writes a case summary.

THE NEUROLOGICAL EXAM

The Patient's History

The neurologist's first step is to ask the patient about the problem. Information is collected about the person's background, with emphasis placed on previous disease, accidents, and the occurrence of symptoms such as headache, loss of consciousness, and sleep disturbances. Family background is significant because many diseases, such as epilepsy, have a high familial incidence.

While the history is being taken, the physician observes other aspects of the patient's behavior. For example, mental status is assessed, facial features are examined for abnormalities or asymmetries, speech is assessed for abnormalities, and posture is observed. The patient's state of awareness is described with adjectives such as *alert, drowsy, stuporous, confused,* and so forth. Facial features and behavior reveal whether the person is agitated, anxious, depressed, apathetic, or restless. Some of the simpler aspects of memory may also be tested by presenting digits and asking for their recall. Delusions and hallucinations are noted when present. The neurologist may also determine whether the person is left- or right-handed and the history of handedness in the family, since this can provide clues about which hemisphere controls speech. A number of simple tests for speech may be given, such as asking the meaning of words, having rhymes or words repeated (for example, "la-la," "ta-ta"), having objects named, and having the patient read and write.

The Physical Examination

The neurologist uses a number of instruments in the course of the physical examination. These include (1) a measuring tape to measure head and body size, the size of skin lesions, and so on; (2) a stethoscope to listen to the sounds of the heart and blood vessels and an otoscope to examine the auditory canal and drum; (3) a flashlight to elicit pupillary reflexes; (4) tongue blades to elicit the gag reflex and abdominal and plantar reflexes; (5) a vial of coffee to assess smell and vials of salt and sugar to assess taste; (6) a 256-Hz tuning fork to test vibratory sensation and hearing; (7) a cotton wisp to elicit the corneal reflex and to test sensitivity to light touch, plastic tubes to test temperature sensations, and pins to test pain sensation; (8) a hammer to elicit muscle stretch reflexes, such as knee jerk; (9) some coins and keys to test stereognosis (the recognition of objects through touch); and (10) a blood-pressure cuff to take blood pressure.

One of the most important parts of the neurological exam is the study of the head. Its general features such as size and shape are assessed, and a detailed examination is made of sensory and motor functions. The head is innervated by 12 sets of cranial nerves, many of which have both sensory and motor functions. The study of the head may reveal cranial nerve malfunctions, providing important clues about the location and nature of nervous system damage.

The motor system is examined to assess muscle bulk, tone, and power; to test for the occurrence of involuntary muscle movements, such as shaking and tremors; and to assess the status of reflexes. In addition, coordination is examined by having a patient do such tasks as walking heel to toe in a straight line, touching the neurologist's finger and his or her own nose repeatedly, making rapid alternating movements of the fingers, tapping the foot as rapidly as possible, and so on. Generally, all the muscles of the body are tested in head-to-foot order, and the status of each is recorded on a standard chart.

A complete sensory examination includes an investigation of sensitivity to painful stimulation, touch, and temperature, as well as an analysis of vibration sense, joint-position sense, two-point discrimination, tactile localization, stereognosis, and graphesthesia (the ability to identify numbers or letters traced on the skin with a blunt object). These sensory tests allow the functions of individual sensory systems to be assessed and also give information about the location of possible dysfunctions.

NEUROLOGICAL DISORDERS

The normal functioning of the central nervous system can be affected by a number of disorders, the most common of which are headaches, tumors, vascular problems, infections, epilepsy, trauma from head injury, demyelinating diseases, and metabolic and nutritional diseases. The following is a brief overview of these disorders.

Vascular Disorders

A neuron or glial cell can be damaged by any process that interferes with its energy metabolism, including a reduction in oxygen or glucose; an introduction of some poison or toxic substance; or, more importantly, an interruption in blood supply. Vascular disease can produce serious—even total—reduction in the flow of both oxygen and glucose, resulting in a critical interference with cellular metabolism. If such interference lasts longer than 10 min, all cells in the affected region die. Cerebral vascular diseases are among the most common causes of death and chronic disability in the Western world.

A common term used in the discussion of cerebral vascular disorder is **stroke,** also known as

cerebral vascular accident. A stroke is the sudden appearance of neurological symptoms as a result of severe interruption of blood flow. Stroke can result from a wide variety of vascular diseases, but not all vascular disorders produce stroke. The onset of dysfunction can be insidious, spanning months or even years. Stroke often produces an **infarct,** an area of dead or dying tissue resulting from an obstruction of the blood vessels normally supplying the area. Most disease of the cerebral vascular system affects the arterial system; disease of venous drainage is uncommon in the central nervous system.

If small blood vessels, such as capillaries, are interrupted, the effects are more limited than the often devastating consequences of damage to large vessels (Figure 24.1). If a stroke or other cerebral vascular disorder occurs in one restricted portion of a vessel of unusual weakness, the prognosis can be rather good, because vessels in the surrounding areas can often supply blood to at least some of the deprived area. On the other hand, if a stroke affects a region surrounded by weak or diseased vessels, the effects can be much more serious, because there is no possibility of compensation. In addition, the surrounding weak zones themselves may be at increased risk of stroke. In the long run, a small vascular lesion in a healthy brain will have a good prognosis for substantial recovery of function. In the event of preexisting vascular lesions,

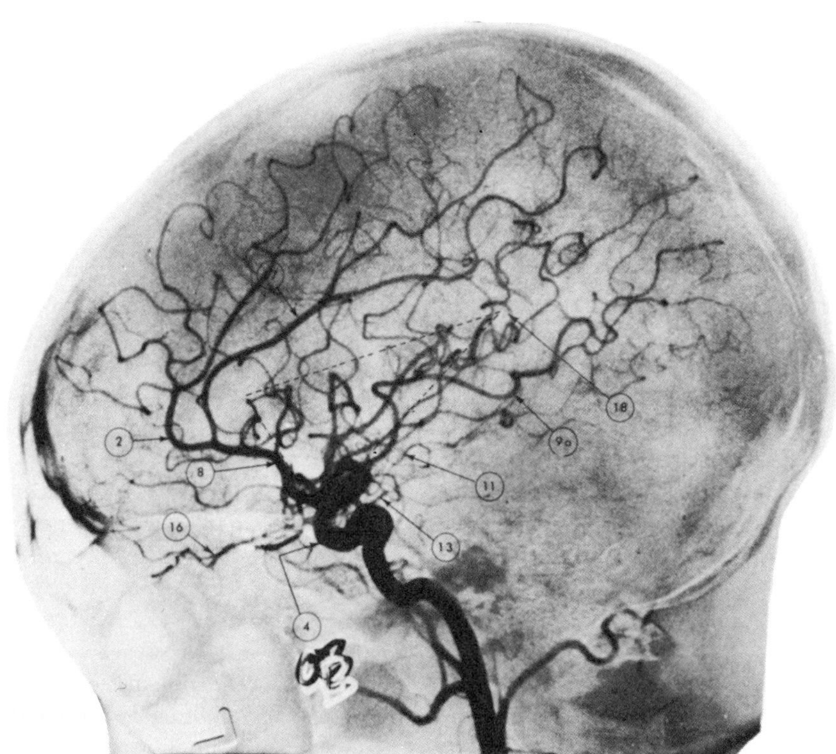

FIGURE 24.1. A normal carotid angiogram showing the large blood vessels. The face is pointed down to the left. Number key: 2, callosomarginal artery; 4, internal carotid artery; 8, anterior cerebral artery; 9a, middle cerebral artery; 11, anterior choroidal artery; 13, posterior communicating artery; 16, ophthalmic artery; 18, approximate end of the Sylvian (lateral) fissure. (From S. J. DeArmond et al., 1976. Copyright © 1976 by Oxford University Press, Inc. Reprinted with permission.)

the effects of the second lesions may be extremely variable. The lesions can be cumulative and obliterate a functional zone of brain tissue, producing serious consequences. As with other lesions, the behavioral symptoms following vascular lesions depends on the location of damage.

An **anastomosis** is a connection between parallel blood vessels that allows them to mingle their blood flows. The presence of an anastomosis in the brain allows cerebral blood supply to take more than one route to a given region. If one vessel is blocked, a given region might be spared an infarct because the blood has an alternative route to the affected zone. The presence of anastomoses is highly idiosyncratic among individuals, making it very difficult to predict the extent of damage resulting from a stroke to a given vessel. The difficulty is exacerbated by substantial variation in the exact route of even major blood vessels in the brain.

Types of Vascular Disorders

Of the numerous vascular disorders that affect the central nervous system, the most common are ischemia, migraine stroke, cerebral hemorrhage, angiomas, and arteriovenous aneurysms.

Cerebral Ischemia. Ischemia includes a group of disorders in which the symptoms are caused by an insufficient supply of blood to the brain. The ischemia may occur suddenly (in which case the term stroke is often used) or it may appear gradually. Decreases in blood flow can have any of three causes:

1. **Thrombosis:** a plug or clot in a blood vessel that has coagulated and remained at the point of its formation.

2. **Embolism:** a clot or other plug brought through the blood from a larger vessel and forced into a smaller one, where it obstructs circulation. An embolism can be a blood clot, a bubble of air, a deposit of oil or fat, or a small mass of cells detached from a tumor. Curiously, embolisms most often affect the middle cerebral artery of the left side of the brain.

3. Reduction of blood flow such that not enough oxygen and glucose are supplied. This reduction in blood flow can result from a variety of factors that produce narrowing of the vessel. The most common example of such narrowing is **cerebral arteriosclerosis,** a condition marked by thickening and hardening of the arteries. Other causes of narrowing include inflammation of the vessels *(vasculitis)* or spasm of the vessels.

Aside from embolism, which occurs suddenly, **encephalomalacia** (literally "softening of the brain") usually develops gradually, taking hours or sometimes days. When the disease is episodic, it may be termed **cerebral vascular insufficiency** or **transient ischemia,** indicating the variable nature of the disorder. The onset of transient attacks is often abrupt, frequently occurring as fleeting sensations of giddiness or impaired consciousness.

Migraine Stroke. People with classic **migraine** experience a transient ischemic attack with a variety of neurological symptoms, including impaired sensory function (especially vision), numbness of the skin (especially in the arms), difficulties in moving, and aphasia. The precise symptoms depend on the vessels involved; however, the posterior cerebral artery is most commonly affected. Although relatively rare, it has been known since the late 1800s that migraine attacks may lead to infarcts and permanent neurological deficits. **Migraine strokes** are believed to account for a significant proportion of strokes in young people (under 40 years of age), especially women. The cause of these strokes is probably some form of vasospasm, but the underlying cause of vasospasm remains a mystery.

Cerebral Hemorrhage. **Cerebral hemorrhage** is a massive bleeding into the substance of the brain. The most frequent cause is high blood pressure (*hypertension*). Other causes include congenital defects in cerebral arteries, blood disorders such as leukemia, and toxic chemicals. The onset of cerebral hemorrhage is abrupt and may quickly prove fatal. It usually occurs during waking hours, presumably because the person is more active and thus has higher blood pressure. Prognosis is poor in cerebral hemorrhage, especially if the patient is unconscious for more than 48 hours.

Angiomas and Aneurysms. **Angiomas** are congenital collections of abnormal vessels, including capillary, venous, or **arteriovenous (A-V) malformations,** that result in abnormal blood flow. Angiomas are composed of a mass of enlarged and tortuous cortical vessels that are supplied by one or more large arteries and are drained by one or more large veins, most often in the field of the middle cerebral artery. By causing abnormal blood flow, angiomas may lead to stroke, because they are inherently weak, or to an inadequate distribution of blood in the regions surrounding the vessels. In some cases arterial blood may flow directly into veins after only briefly, or sometimes not at all, servicing the surrounding brain tissue.

Aneurysms are vascular dilations resulting from localized defects in the elasticity of the vessel. These can be visualized as balloonlike expansions of vessels, which are usually weak and prone to rupture. Although aneurysms are usually due to congenital defects, they may also develop from hypertension, arteriosclerosis, embolisms, or infections. Symptoms of aneurysm especially include severe headache, which may be present for years because of pressure on the dura from the aneurysm.

Treatment of Vascular Disorders

Most vascular disorders have no specific treatment, although the most common remedies include drug therapy and surgery. Supportive therapies include such drugs as anticoagulants to dissolve clots or prevent clotting, vasodilators to dilate the vessels, drugs to reduce blood pressure, and salty solutions or steroids to reduce cerebral edema (swelling). Surgical techniques have been greatly improved in recent years but are practical only for some disorders. For example, the only certain cure for aneurysm is total removal, which is usually not feasible. Aneurysms are sometimes painted with various plastic substances, but the efficacy of this treatment is disputed. In the case of cerebral hemorrhage, it may be necessary to perform surgery to relieve the pressure of the blood from the ruptured vessel on the rest of the brain.

TRAUMATIC HEAD INJURIES

Brain injury is an all-too-common result of automobile and industrial accidents; **cerebral trauma** is the most common form of brain damage in people under the age of 40. Because there has been no agreement on what constitutes an injury sufficient to affect the brain, it has proved difficult to obtain reliable estimates of the frequency of closed-head injuries. Nonetheless, with the development of sophisticated neuroradiological procedures such as MRI and PET, it is becoming evident that brain injury from head trauma is a major public health problem in industrialized countries. In one telephone survey in Sweden, cerebral concussion producing at least brief unconsciousness was reported by 5% of those interviewed. In addition, it is estimated that an equal number of people are likely to have a concussion without obvious unconsciousness, although they would have been confused about the events surrounding the blow to the head. Overall, it appears that the frequency of closed-head injuries in industrialized countries ranges from about 300 to 450 per 100,000 population per year. Projected over one's life span, the chances of such an injury are high indeed. Thus, it has been estimated that a child's chance of having significant closed-head injury before he or she is old enough to drive is 1 in 30! The two most important factors in the incidence of closed-head injury are age and sex. Children and elderly people are more likely to suffer injuries from falls than are others, and males between 15 and 30 are very likely to have brain injuries, especially from automobile and motorcycle accidents (Figure 24.2), a statistic that is reflected in automobile insurance rates.

Cerebral trauma can affect brain function in a

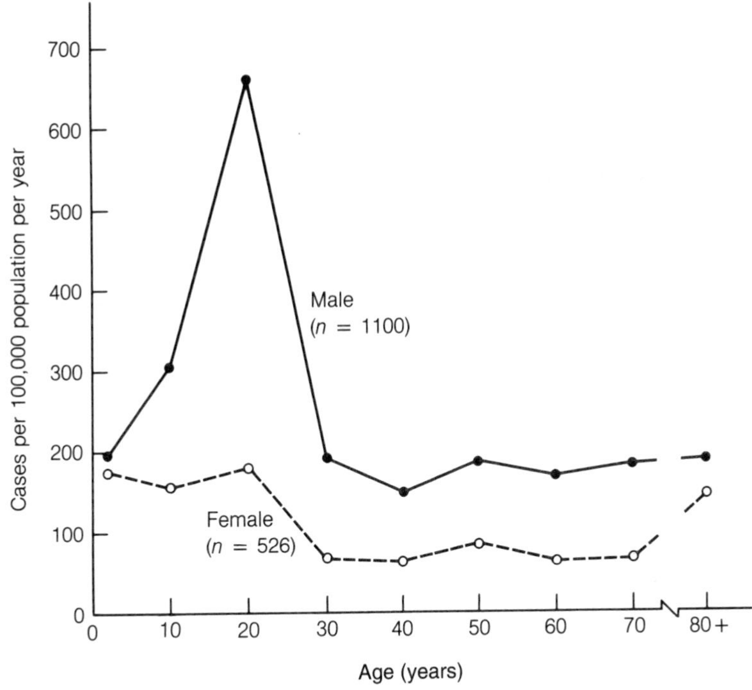

FIGURE 24.2. Incidence rates of head trauma in Olmsted County, Minnesota, 1965–1974. (After Annegers et al., 1980.)

number of ways: (1) Trauma, such as a gunshot wound, can result in direct damage to neurons and support cells in the brain. (2) Trauma can disrupt blood supply, resulting in ischemia and, if the interruption is prolonged, infarction. (3) Trauma can cause bleeding within the skull, leading to increased intracranial pressure and subsequent additional damage. (4) Like most tissues in the body, the brain swells when traumatized, leading to increased intracranial pressure and the possibility of brain damage. (5) Compound fracture of the skull opens the brain to infection. (6) Head trauma can produce scarring of brain tissue; the scarred tissue becomes a focus for later epileptic seizures. Indeed, the sudden appearance of epileptic seizures in adulthood often can be traced to head injury (particularly from automobile accidents) in preceding months or years.

Open-Head Injuries

Open-head injuries include traumatic brain injuries in which the skull is penetrated, as in gunshot or missile wounds, or in which fragments of bone penetrate the brain substance. Open-head injuries show striking differences from closed-head injuries. Many people who have open-head injuries do not lose consciousness, and such injuries tend to produce distinctive symptoms that may undergo rapid and spontaneous recovery. Neurological signs may be highly specific, and the effects of the injuries often closely resemble those of surgical excision of a small area of cortex.

The specificity of neurological symptoms following open-head injuries makes such patients especially good research subjects. Three thorough investigations of World War II veterans with open-head injuries have been published—by Newcombe, by Luria, and by Teuber and his associates.

Closed-Head Injuries

These injuries result from a blow to the head, which subjects the brain to a variety of mechanical forces. First, there is damage at the site of the blow, called a *coup*. The brain is compacted by molding of the bone inward, even if the skull is not fractured. Second, this pressure on the brain at the time of the coup may force the brain against the opposite side of the skull, producing an additional bruise (contusion) known as a *countercoup* (Figure 24.3). Third, the movement of the brain may cause a twisting or shearing of nerve fibers, producing microscopic lesions. These may occur throughout the brain but are most common in the frontal and temporal lobes. In addition, the twisting and shearing may produce damage to the major fiber tracts of the brain, especially those crossing the midline, such as the corpus callosum and anterior commissure. As a result, connection between the two sides of the brain may be disrupted, leading to a disconnection syndrome. Fourth, the bruises and strains caused by the impact may produce bleeding (hemorrhage). Because the blood is trapped within the skull, it acts as a growing mass (hematoma), which exerts pressure on surrounding structures. Finally, as with blows to other parts of the body, blows to the brain produce *edema,* which is a collection of fluid in and around damaged tissue; edema is another source of pressure on the brain tissue.

Closed-head injuries are commonly accompanied by a loss of consciousness resulting from strain on fibers in the brainstem reticular formation. These fibers often sustain permanent damage, even in cases of simple concussion. According to Lezak, the duration of loss of consciousness —or length of coma—can serve as a measure of the severity of damage, because it correlates directly with mortality, intellectual impairment, deficits in social skills. The longer lasting the

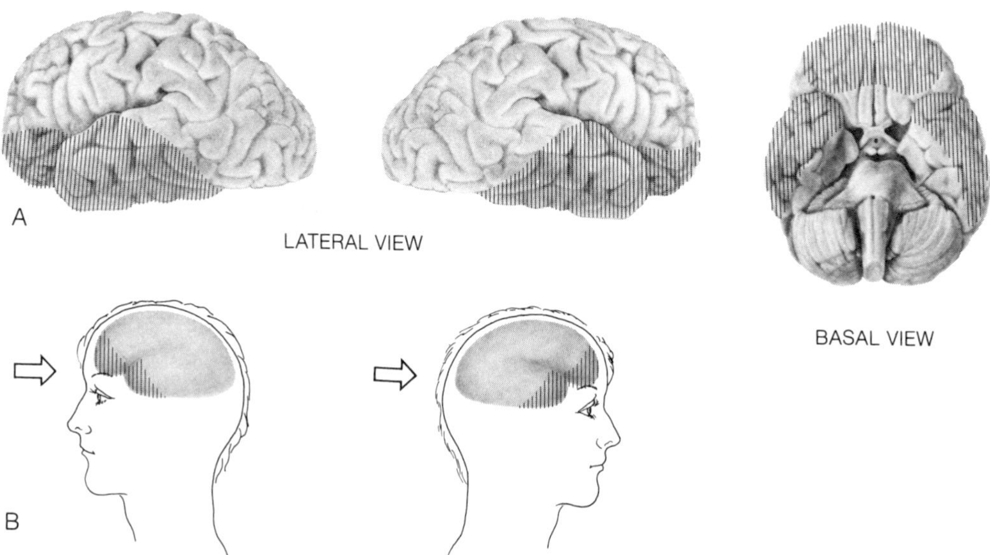

FIGURE 24.3. *A*. Regions (shaded) of the cerebral hemispheres most often damaged in cerebral contusion. *B*. Demonstration of how a blow (arrow) to the forehead or occiput can produce a cerebral contusion of the frontal and temporal lobes. *Left:* The blow directly damages the brain. *Right:* The blow causes the brain to be compressed forward, producing a countercoup injury. (Illustrations after Courville, 1945.)

coma, the greater the possibility of serious impairment and death.

Closed-head injuries resulting from traffic accidents are particularly severe because the head is moving when the blow is struck, thereby increasing the velocity of the impact and multiplying the number and severity of small lesions throughout the brain. CT scans of accident victims suffering prolonged coma show diffuse brain injury and enlarged ventricles—signs associated with poor outcomes.

Two kinds of behavioral effects result from closed-head injuries: discrete impairment of those functions mediated by the cortex at the site of the coup or the countercoup lesion, and more generalized impairments from widespread damage throughout the brain. Discrete impairment is most commonly associated with damage to the frontal and temporal lobes, those areas most susceptible to closed-head injuries (see Figure 24.3). More general impairment, resulting from minute lesions and lacerations scattered throughout the brain, is characterized by a loss of complex cognitive functions, including reductions in mental speed, ability to concentrate, and overall cognitive efficiency. These difficulties are usually reflected in patients' complaints of inability to concentrate or to do things as well as they could before the accident, even though the intelligence rating may still be well above average. Indeed, in our experience, bright people are the most affected by closed-head injuries because they are acutely aware of a loss of cognitive skill that prevents them from returning to their previous competence level.

Closed-head injuries that damage the frontal and temporal lobes also tend to have significant effects on people's personality and social adjustment. According to Lezak, relatively few victims of traffic accidents who have sustained severe head injuries ever resume their studies or return to gainful employment, or if they do reenter the work force, they do so at a lower level than before their accidents.

Often, the chronic effects of closed-head injuries are not associated with any neurological signs and patients may be referred for psychiatric evaluation. Psychological assessments are especially useful in these cases, because seriously handicapping cognitive deficits may become apparent in the course of a thorough assessment.

The pathological effects of closed-head injury are summarized in Table 24.1. In addition, there are numerous secondary effects, of which the most important may be ischemia, edema, and damage to white matter, especially the corpus callosum. We have seen that certain regions of the brain such as the hippocampus are especially sensitive to ischemia, so it would not be surprising to see medial temporal lobe degeneration after head trauma. Edema is common from trauma anywhere in the body, but it is particularly problematic inside the skull because it leads to increased cranial pressure, which itself can damage the brain. Postmortem examination of brains from patients with severe closed-head injuries show dilation of the ventricles and a diffuse loss of myelin.

TABLE 24.1. Primary and secondary brain injury after closed-head trauma

Primary (immediate on impact) brain injury
- Macroscopic lesions
  - Contusions underlying the site of impact (coup)
  - Countercoup contusion frequently in the undersurfaces of the frontal lobes and the tips of the temporal lobes
  - Laceration of the brain from depressed skull fracture
- Microscopic lesions
  - Widespread shearing or stretching of nerve fibers

Secondary mechanisms of brain injury
- Intracranial hemorrhage
- Edema in white matter adjacent to focal mass lesions
- Diffuse brain swelling—hyperemia
- Ischemic brain damage
- Raised intracranial pressure
- Brain shift and herniation

Secondary insult from extracerebral events
- Effects of multiple/systemic injury
  - Hypoxia
  - Fat embolism

Delayed effects
- Degeneration of white matter
- Disturbed flow of cerebrospinal fluid—hydrocephalus

Source: After Levin et al., 1982.

Oppenheimer studied the brains of patients who sustained "mild concussion" and concluded that permanent damage in the form of microscopic lesions can be inflicted on the brain from what usually are regarded as trivial head injuries. Although some of these lesions may be visible in CT scans (on the order of 5% of cases with mild head injuries), recent studies with MRI suggest that the majority of cases with mild head injury may have lesions. For example, Wilberger and his colleagues reported that in a series of 24 patients without any evident lesion on repeated CT scans, all demonstrated lesions on MRI scans. Similarly, a parallel study by Levin and his colleagues reported that of 16 consecutive admissions with "minor or moderate" closed-head injury, 1 had an abnormal CT scan and 14 had abnormal MRI scans. In summary, the conclusion appears inescapable that even mild head trauma may be associated with some pathology.

People who sustain head injuries are more likely to sustain subsequent head injuries, and there is a strong suggestion in the literature that the effects of even very mild head injuries may be cumulative. Boxers provide an excellent example because it is well established that they sustain significant brain injuries leading to a condition called *traumatic encephalopathy* (known more commonly as the punch-drunk syndrome) even though the periods of unconsciousness experienced by indi-

TABLE 24.2. The Glasgow Coma Scale

Response	Points	Index of wakefulness
		Eye opening (E)
None	1	Not attributable to ocular swelling
To pain	2	Pain stimulus is applied to chest or limbs
To speech	3	Nonspecific response to speech or shout; does not imply the patient obeys command to open eyes
Spontaneous	4	Eyes are open, but this does not imply intact awareness
		Motor response (M)
No response	1	Flaccid
Extension	2	"Decerebrate;" adduction, internal rotation of shoulder, and pronation of the forearm
Abnormal flexion	3	"Decorticate," abnormal flexion, adduction of the shoulder
Withdrawal	4	Normal flexor response; withdraws from pain stimulus with abduction of the shoulder
Localizes pain	5	Pain stimulus applied to supraocular region or fingertip causes limb to move to attempt to avoid it
Obeys commands	6	Follows simple commands
		Verbal response (V)
No response	1	(Self-explanatory)
Incomprehensible	2	Moaning and groaning, but no recognizable words
Inappropriate	3	Intelligible speech (e.g., shouting or swearing), but no sustained or coherent conversation
Confused	4	Patient responds to questions in a conversational manner, but the responses indicate varying degrees of disorientation and confusion
Oriented	5	Normal orientation to time, place, and person

Note: The summed Glasgow Coma Scale is equal to E + M + V (3–15 points).
Source: After B. Teasdale and B. Jennett, 1974.

vidual boxers may have been few and of short duration.

BEHAVIORAL ASSESSMENT OF THE SEVERITY OF BRAIN INJURY

Assessment of Closed-Head Injury

Although neuroradiological measures can provide objective indicators of neural status after closed-head injury, behavior is the most important measure of the integrity of the nervous system. In the immediate postinjury period there are two common measures of behavior: coma and amnesia. In fact, before the development of CT and MRI scans, the depth and duration of coma were the most useful indicators of brain injury. Since clinical judgment of the depth of coma was largely subjective and unreliable the Glasgow Coma Scale (Table 24.2) was designed to provide an objective indicator of the degree of unconsciousness. In this scale, three indices of wakefulness are evaluated: eye opening, motor response, and verbal response. By giving the Glasgow Scale serially, it has proved possible to identify the recovery from unconsciousness objectively. A score of 8 or less is often used as a criterion for severe closed-head injury, and a score of 9 to 12 is the criterion for moderate injury. One difficulty with the scale as a measure of the severity of brain injury is that up to 50% of hospital admissions have scores of 13 to 15, thus indicating no coma, but these patients may have significant sequelae of the head injury.

Posttraumatic amnesia (PTA) is an alternative measure of severity of injury; it was first suggested by Russell in the 1930s. The definition of PTA varies because it may include the period of coma or be restricted to the period of anterograde amnesia. In any event, there is good evidence that the duration of PTA is correlated (imperfectly) with later memory disturbance, as illustrated in Figure 24.4B. A commonly used scale is as follows: PTA $<$ 10 min = very mild injury; PTA 10–60 min = mild injury; PTA 1–24 hours = moderate injury; PTA 1–7 days = severe injury; PTA $>$ 7 days = very severe injury. However,

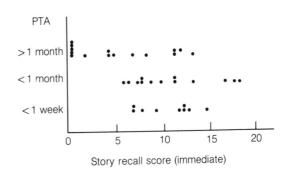

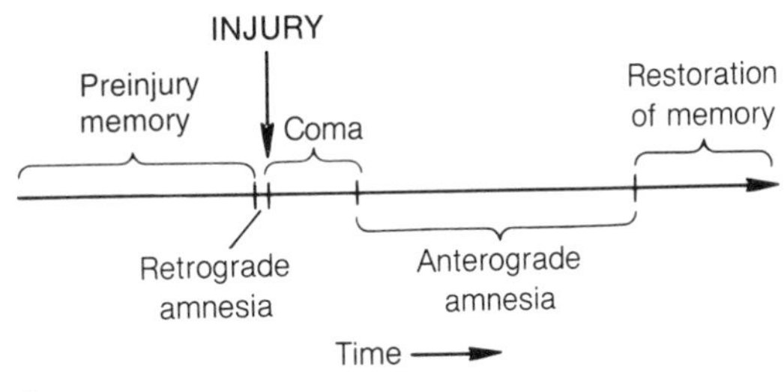

A

PTA
$>$1 month
$<$1 month
$<$1 week
0 5 10 15 20
Story recall score (immediate)

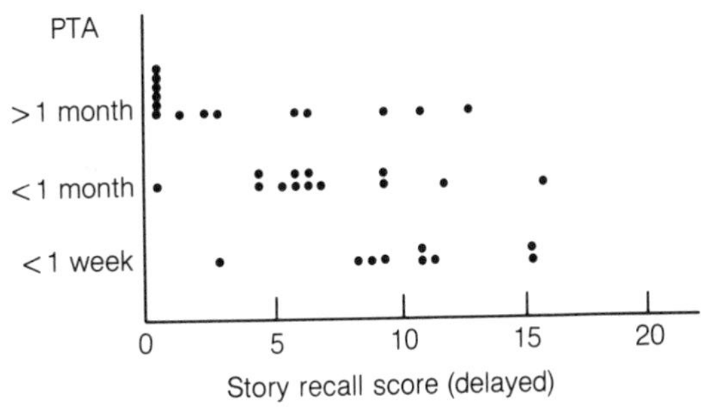

B

FIGURE 24.4. *A*. Schematic sequence of acute alterations in memory after closed-head injury. The period of coma and anterograde amnesia are often called the period of posttraumatic amnesia (PTA), although PTA may sometimes be equivalent to the anterograde amnesia. (After Levin et al., 1982.) *B*. Histograms showing the distribution of individual scores of story recall by patients in three groups distinguished by the period of PTA. Scores represent recall of the second of two stories. (After Newcombe, 1987.)

one problem with using PTA is that there is no consistent method of measuring it in different studies. Thus, it is evaluated by retrospective questioning, by measures of disorientation, or by neuropsychological assessment, each of which yields a different estimate of severity of injury. Two useful procedures have been proposed recently, one in the United States by Levin and his colleagues and another in England by Fortuny and colleagues, and if they become widely used it should be easier to compare patients in different studies.

Recovery from Closed-Head Injury

Although it is often stated that recovery from head trauma may continue for 2 to 3 years, there is little doubt that the bulk of the cognitive recovery occurs in the first 6 to 9 months. In general, recovery of memory functions appears to be somewhat slower than recovery of general intelligence, and the final level of memory performance is lower than for other cognitive functions. Levin and his colleagues have suggested that people with brainstem damage, as inferred from oculomotor disturbance, have a poorer cognitive outcome, and this is probably true of people with initial dysphasias or hemiparesis as well. Although the prognosis for significant recovery of cognitive functions is good, there is less optimism about the recovery of social interactions or personality, which often show significant change. Numerous studies support the conclusion that the quality of life—in terms of social life, perceived stress levels, and leisure activities— is significantly poorer following closed-head injury and that this condition is chronic. For example, Klonoff and her colleagues administered various self-report inventories to patients 2 to 4 years after their injuries. More than 50% of the cases reported physical problems including limb weakness and pain and stiffness, which indicates that people often have multiple problems in addition to the brain injury. More important, patients complained about their social contacts and leisure activities. Furthermore, relatives of patients report great strain, which appears to increase over time. A study by Brooks and colleagues found that the relatives (spouses and parents) of 74% of patients complained of personality change 5 years after injury, and more than 50% complained of mood changes, temper, irritability, and threats of violence. Unfortunately, there have been few attempts to develop tools to measure changes in psychosocial adjustment in brain-injured people, so we must rely largely on descriptions and self-reports, which provide little insight into the causes of these problems.

EPILEPSY

Epilepsy is a condition characterized by recurrent electrographic seizures of various types that are associated with a disturbance of consciousness. Although epileptic episodes have been termed convulsions, seizures, fits, and attacks, none of these terms is entirely satisfactory, since the episodes can vary greatly. Epileptic seizures are very common; 1 person in 20 will experience at least one seizure during his or her lifetime. The prevalence of multiple seizures is much lower, about 1 in 200.

Sometimes epileptic seizures are classifiable as **symptomatic seizures;** that is, they can be identified with a specific cause, such as infection, trauma, tumor, vascular malformation, toxic chemicals, very high fever, or other neurological disorders. But other seizure disorders, called **idiopathic seizures,** appear to arise spontaneously and in the absence of other diseases of the central nervous system. The cause of the abnormal electrical discharge by the cell is poorly understood, although it is likely that it stems from some type of abnormality of the neuronal membrane.

Although it has long been known that epilepsy runs in families, it is unlikely that there is a single gene responsible for the seizures, because the incidence is lower than would be predicted from genetic models. It is more likely that certain genotypes have a predisposition to seizure problems given certain environmental circumstances.

Symptoms and Diagnosis

The most remarkable clinical feature of epileptic disorders is the widely varying intervals between attacks—which can be minutes, hours, weeks, or even years. Thus, it is almost impossible to describe a basic set of symptoms to be expected in all, or even most, people with the disease. Three symptoms, however, are found in many types of epilepsy. (1) An aura, or warning, of impending seizure. This may take the form of sensations such as odors or noises, or it may simply be a "feeling" that the seizure is going to occur. (2) Loss of consciousness. This may take the form of complete collapse or simply staring off into space. There is often amnesia, the victim forgetting the seizure itself and the period of lost consciousness. (3) Movements. It is common for seizures to have a motor component, although the characteristics vary considerably. In some cases there are shaking movements; in others, there are automatic movements such as rubbing the hands or chewing.

The diagnosis of epilepsy is usually confirmed by EEG. In some epileptics, however, seizures are difficult to demonstrate except under special circumstances (for example, an EEG recorded during sleep), and not all persons with an abnormal EEG actually have seizures. In fact, some estimates suggest that 4 people in 20 actually have abnormal EEG patterns! Recently, PET has provided a more reliable measure of functional abnormalities.

Types of Epilepsy

Several classification schemes for epilepsy have been published. Table 24.3 summarizes the ones in common use.

TABLE 24.3. Classification of epilepsy

- Partial seizures (focal)
  - Simple partial seizures
    - Motor (Jacksonian)
    - Sensory (Jacksonian)
    - Autonomic
  - Complex partial seizures (temporal lobe, psychomotor)
    - Absences
    - Complex hallucinations
    - Affective symptoms
    - Automatism
  - Partial seizures secondarily generalized
- Generalized seizures
  - Bilaterally symmetrical without local onset
    - Absence attacks (petit mal)
    - Tonic-clonic (grand mal)
    - Bilateral myoclonic
    - Drop attacks (akinetic)
- Unclassified seizures
  - Because of incomplete data, includes many persons with apparently generalized seizures

Focal seizures are those that begin locally and then spread. In **Jacksonian seizures,** for example, the attack begins with jerks of single parts of the body, such as a finger, a toe, or the mouth, and then spreads. If the attack begins with a finger, the jerks might spread to other fingers, then the hand, the arm, and so on, producing the so-called Jacksonian march. Jackson predicted in 1870 that such seizures probably originate from the point (focus) in the neocortex representing that region. He was later proved correct.

Complex partial seizures originate most commonly in the temporal lobe and somewhat less frequently in the frontal lobe. Complex partial seizures are characterized by three common manifestations: (1) subjective feelings, such as forced, repetitive thoughts, alterations in mood, feelings of déjà vu, or hallucinations; (2) **automatisms,** which are repetitive stereotyped movements such as lip smacking or chewing or acts such as undoing buttons; and (3) postural changes, in which afflicted persons sometimes assume catatonic, or frozen, postures.

Generalized seizures are bilaterally symmetrical without local onset. The **grand mal attack** is characterized by loss of consciousness and stereotyped motor activity. Typically, patients go through three stages: (1) a tonic stage, in which the body stiffens and breathing stops; (2) a clonic stage, in which there is rhythmic shaking; and (3) a postseizure (also known as postictal) depression, in which the patient is confused. About 50% of these seizures are preceded by an aura.

In the **petit mal attack,** there is a loss of awareness during which there is no motor activity except for blinking, turning the head, or rolling the eyes. These attacks are of brief duration, seldom exceeding about 10 sec. The EEG record of a petit mal seizure has a typical pattern known as the 3/sec spike and wave.

Akinetic seizures are ordinarily seen only in children. Usually the child collapses suddenly and without warning. These seizures are often of very short duration, and the child may get up after only a few seconds with no postictal depression. The falls that these children have can be dangerous, and it is not uncommon for the children to wear football helmets until the seizures can be controlled by medication.

Myoclonic spasms are massive seizures that basically consist of a sudden flexion or extension of the body and often begin with a cry.

As mentioned earlier, seizures are not continual in any epileptic patients, even though the EEG may be chronically abnormal. Table 24.4 summarizes the great variety of circumstances that appear to be able to precipitate seizures. Although one is struck by the range of such factors, a consistent feature is that the brain is most epileptogenic when it is relatively inactive and the patient is sitting still.

TABLE 24.4. Factors that may precipitate seizures in susceptible individuals

Hyperventilation
Sleep
Sleep deprivation
Sensory stimuli
Flashing lights
Reading, speaking, coughing
Laughing
Sounds: music, bells
Trauma
Hormonal changes
Menses
Puberty
Adrenal steroids
Adrenocorticotrophic hormone (ACTH)
Fever
Emotional stress
Drugs
Phenothiazines
Analeptics
Tricyclic antidepressants
Alcohol
Excessive anticonvulsants

Source: After Pincus and Tucker, 1974.

Treatment of Epilepsy

The treatment of choice for epilepsy is an anticonvulsant drug such as diphenylhydantoin (DPH, Dilantin), phenobarbital, and several others. Although the mechanism by which these drugs act is uncertain, they presumably inhibit the discharge of abnormal neurons by stabilizing the neuronal membrane. If medication fails to alleviate the seizure problem satisfactorily, surgery can be performed to remove the focus of abnormal functioning in patients with focal seizures.

The surgical treatment of epilepsy dates back to the late 1800s, when W. Horsley and others removed the cortex in an attempt to alleviate seizures. The modern technique of surgery for epilepsy was pioneered by Otfrid Foerster in the 1920s in Germany. Wilder Penfield, stimulated by his studies with Foerster, began a prolonged scientific study of the surgical treatment of epilepsy in 1928, when he founded the Montreal Neurological Institute for that purpose. Penfield was soon joined by Herbert Jasper, who introduced EEG to the operating room, and by D. O. Hebb and Brenda Milner, who introduced the neuropsychological assessment of Penfield's surgical patients. These four researchers and their colleagues developed a technique for cortical removal of the epileptogenic tissue from victims of focal epilepsy, which has been a remarkably successful treatment for this form of epilepsy. Their team approach provides a model of the integration of basic and applied disciplines to develop an effective treatment for a neurological disorder.

TUMORS

A **tumor** (or neoplasm) is a mass of new tissue that persists and grows independently of its surrounding structures and has no physiological use. Brain tumors grow from glia or other support cells rather than from neurons. The rate at which tumors grow varies widely, depending on the type of cell that gives rise to the tumor. Tumors account for a relatively high proportion of neurological disease, and next to the uterus, the brain is the most common site for tumors. It is possible to distinguish between benign tumors (those not likely to recur after removal) and malignant tumors (those that are likely to recur after removal and that often progress, becoming a threat to life). Although the distinction between benign and malignant tumors is well-founded, the benign tumor may be as serious as the malignant one, since many benign tumors in the brain are inaccessible to the surgeon without risk to life. The brain is affected by many types of tumors, and no region of the brain is immune to tumor formation.

Tumors can affect behavior in a number of ways. A tumor may develop as a distinct entity in the brain, a so-called encapsulated tumor, and put pressure on the rest of the brain (Figure 24.5). Encapsulated tumors are also sometimes cystic, which means that they produce a fluid-filled cavity in the brain, usually lined with the tumor cells. Since the skull is of fixed size, any increase in its contents compresses the brain, resulting in dysfunctions. Other tumors, so-called infiltrating tumors, are not clearly marked off from the surrounding tissue; they may either destroy normal cells and occupy their place or surround existing cells (both neurons and glia) and interfere with their normal functioning (Figure 24.6).

Symptoms and Diagnosis of Brain Tumors

The recognition of a brain tumor may be divided into three phases: (1) the suspicion that a tumor may be present, (2) the diagnostic confirmation of the tumor, and (3) the precise location of the tumor within the nervous system.

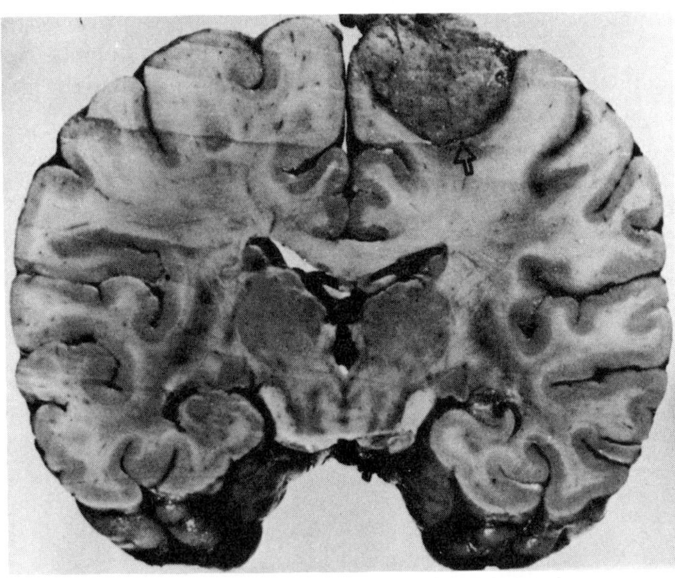

FIGURE 24.5. Frontal section showing a meningioma (arrow) arising in the dura and compressing the right cerebral hemisphere. Notice that the tumor has not infiltrated the brain. (From S. I. Zacks, 1971. Copyright © 1971 by Harper & Row. Reprinted with permission.)

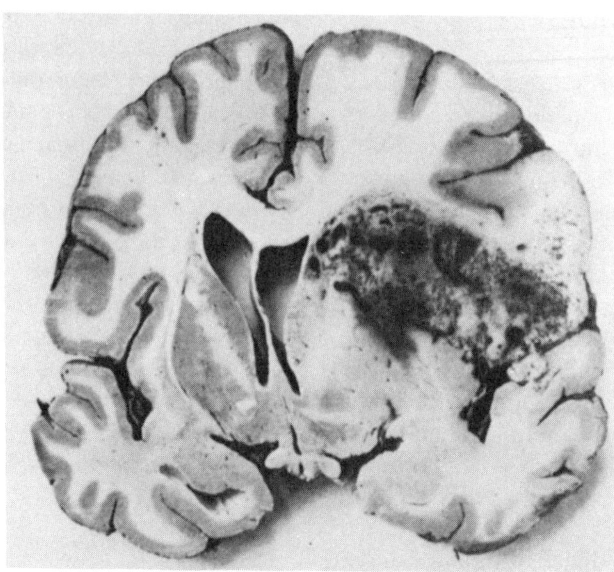

FIGURE 24.6. Frontal section showing a glioblastoma in the right cerebral hemisphere. Note the displacement of the ventricular system and the invasion of brain tissue (dark area). (From R. Bannister, 1978. Copyright © 1978 by Oxford University Press, Inc. Reprinted with permission.)

The generalized symptoms of brain tumors, which result from increased intracranial pressure, include headache; vomiting; swelling of the optic disk (papilledema); slowing of the heart rate (bradycardia); mental dullness; double vision (diplopia); and, finally, convulsions. It would be rare indeed for a patient to exhibit all these symptoms. Other signs and symptoms depend on the exact location of the tumor. Thus, a tumor in the speech zones would be more likely to disrupt speech than would a tumor in the visual cortex.

Types of Brain Tumors

There are three major types of brain tumors, distinguished on the basis of where they originate: gliomas, meningiomas, and metastatic tumors.

Gliomas. **Glioma** is a general term for those brain tumors that arise from glial cells and infiltrate the brain substance. Roughly 45% of all brain tumors are gliomas. Gliomas, ranging from the relatively benign to the highly malignant, vary considerably in their response to treatment. Because the detailed description of types of gliomas is more important to the neurologist and neurosurgeon than to the neuropsychologist, we shall briefly describe only the most frequently occurring types of gliomas; astrocytomas, glioblastomas, and medulloblastomas.

Astrocytomas result from the growth of astrocytes and are usually slow-growing. Astrocytomas account for about 40% of gliomas, being most common in adults over 30 years of age. Because they are not very malignant, and because of their slow growth rate, they are relatively safe once treated. Thus, the prognosis for patients with this type of tumor is relatively good, with postoperative survivals occasionally exceeding 20 years.

Glioblastomas are highly malignant, rapidly growing tumors most common in adults, especially men, over 35 years of age (see Figure 24.6). Glioblastomas account for 30% of gliomas.

They may result from the sudden growth of *spongioblasts,* cells that are ordinarily formed only during development of the brain, although some texts suggest that astrocytes cannot be ruled out as the source of glioblastomas. The tumor may be made up of a variety of cell types (glioblastoma multiforme) or of a single cell type (glioblastoma unipolare). Because these tumors grow so rapidly, a patient's life expectancy is usually short, seldom extending beyond 1 year after surgery.

Medulloblastomas are highly malignant and are found almost exclusively in the cerebellum of children. Medulloblastomas account for about 11% of all gliomas. The tumor results from the growth of germinal cells that infiltrate the cerebellum or underlying brainstem. The prognosis for children with these tumors is poor; the postoperative survival period ranges from 1.5 to 2 years.

Meningiomas. **Meningiomas** are growths attached to the meninges, or protective outer layer of the brain (see Figure 24.5). They grow entirely outside the brain, are well encapsulated, and are the most benign of all brain tumors. Although meningiomas do not invade the brain, they are often multiple and disturb brain function by putting pressure on the brain, often producing seizures as a symptom. Although most meningiomas lie over the hemispheres, some occur between them. The latter location makes removal more complicated. It is not uncommon for these tumors to erode the overlying bone of the skull. If meningiomas are removed completely, they tend not to recur.

Metastatic Tumors. **Metastasis** is the transfer of disease from one organ or part to another not directly connected with it. Thus, a **metastatic tumor** in the brain is one that has become established by a transfer of tumor cells from some other region of the body, most often a lung or a breast. Indeed, it is not uncommon for the first indication of lung cancer to be evidence of a brain tumor. Metastases to the brain are usually multiple, making treatment complicated and prognosis poor.

Other Tumors. We have considered only the major types of primary brain tumors; there are, however, many more less common types. One of these, the *pituitary adenoma,* is a tumor of the pituitary region. Although the pituitary is not really part of the brain, tumors there produce pressure on the brain, and because of the close relation between the hypothalamus and the pituitary, such tumors can produce significant functional abnormalities in the hypothalamus.

Treatment of Brain Tumors

The most obvious treatment of brain tumors is surgery, which is the only way to make a definite histological diagnosis. If feasible, tumors are removed, but, as with tumors elsewhere in the body, success depends on early diagnosis. Radiation therapy is useful for treating certain types of tumors, such as glioblastomas and medulloblastomas, as well as for some metastatic tumors. Chemotherapy has not yet been very successful in the treatment of brain tumors, partly because of the difficulty in getting drugs to pass the blood-brain barrier and distribute in the tumor.

HEADACHES

Headache is so common among the general population that rare indeed is the person who has never suffered one. Headache may constitute a neurological disorder in itself, as in migraine; it may be secondary to neurological disease such as tumor or infection; or it may result for psychological factors, especially stress, as in tension headaches. The pain-sensitive structures within the skull that can be responsible for a headache include the dura; the large arteries of the brain; the venous sinuses; and the branches of the 5th, 9th, and 10th cranial nerves and the 1st and 3rd cervical nerves. Pain can be elicited from these structures by pressure, displacement, or inflammation.

Types of Headaches

Migraine. **Migraine** (derived from the Greek *hemi* and *kranion,* meaning half of skull) is perhaps the most common neurological disorder, afflicting some 5% to 20% of the population at some time in their lives. The World Federation of Neurology defines migraine as a "familial disorder characterized by recurrent attacks of headache widely variable in intensity, frequency and duration. Attacks are commonly unilateral and are usually associated with anorexia, nausea and vomiting. In some cases they are preceded by, or associated with, neurological and mood disturbances." There are several types of migraine including classic migraine, common migraine, cluster headache, and hemiplegic and opthalmoplegic migraine. *Classic migraine* is probably the most interesting form, occurring in about 12% of migraine sufferers, since it includes an aura, which usually lasts for 20 to 40 min. Karl Lashley, perhaps the first neuropsychologist, suffered from classic migraine and carefully described his visual aura (Figure 24.7), which turned out to be common to many migraine sufferers. The aura is presumed to occur because constriction of one or more cerebral arteries has produced ischemia of the occipital cortex. PET studies have shown that during the aura there is a reduction in blood flow in the posterior cortex, and this reduction spreads anteriorly at the rate of about 2 mm/min without respecting major vascular distributions. This rate and the distribution of spread are similar to a phenomenon known as spreading depression. A puzzle surrounds the question of why the reduced blood flow moves independently of the major vessels, an observation suggesting that the vascular changes are secondary to changes in neural function. The actual headache begins as the vasoconstriction reverses (ending the neurological disturbance) and vasodilation occurs. The headache is manifested as an intense pain localized in one side of the head, although it often spreads on the affected side and sometimes to the opposite side as well. A severe headache can be accompanied by nausea and vomiting, and it may last for hours or even days. A significant number of people with classic migraine never suffer the headache but only experience the aura.

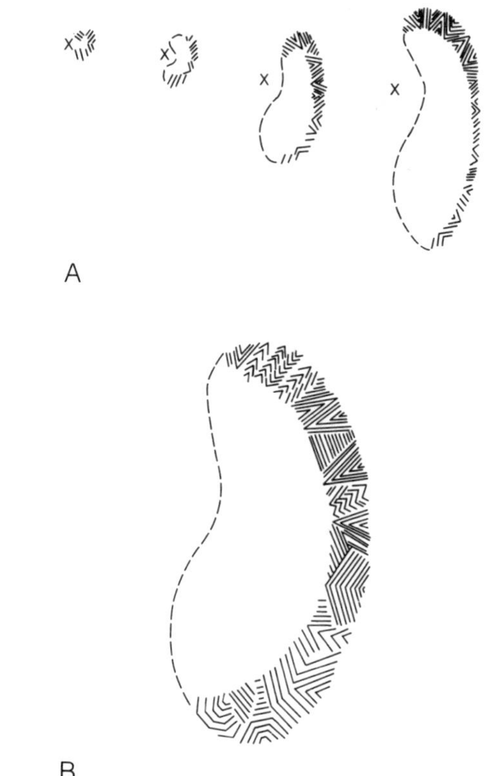

FIGURE 24.7. *A*. Successive maps of a scintillating scotoma (blind spot), showing the characteristic increase in the size of the scotoma and the location of the so-called fortification figures. The x in each case indicates the fixation point. The scotoma typically takes about 10 min to fill the visual field. *B*. A sketch showing the fortification figures in detail. (After Lashley, 1941.)

Common migraine is the most frequent type of migraine, occurring in more than 80% of migraine sufferers. There is no clear aura as in classic migraine, but there may be a gastrointestinal or other "signal" that an attack is pending. *Cluster headache* is a unilateral pain in the head or face that rarely lasts longer than 2 hours but recurs repeatedly for a period of weeks or even months before disappearing, sometimes for long periods, before returning. The final two types of migraine, *hemiplegic migraine* and *opthalmoplegic migraine,* are relatively rare and involve loss of movement of the limbs or eyes, respectively.

The frequency of migraine attacks varies from

as often as once per week to as seldom as once in a lifetime. In cases where migraine is frequent, the occurrence generally decreases with age and usually ceases in middle age. Migraine was generally believed to be rare prior to adolescence, but in recent years it has been recognized to afflict children as well, although the actual incidence in this population is uncertain.

A large number of environmental factors appear to trigger migraine attacks, including anxiety; the termination of anxiety (relaxation); fatigue; bright light; and, in many persons, specific allergies, particularly to foods and wines.

Headache Associated with Neurological Disease. Headache, a common symptom of many nervous system disorders, usually results from distortion of the pain-sensitive structures. Common disorders producing headache include tumor, head trauma, infection, vascular malformations, and severe hypertension (high blood pressure). The characteristics and location of these headaches vary according to the actual disorder. For example, headache from brain tumor is almost always located on the same side of the head as the tumor, particularly in the early stages of the tumor. However, headaches related to brain tumor have no characteristic severity, for they vary from mild to excruciating. Likewise, hypertension headache, although it is nearly always located in the occipital region, is highly variable in severity.

Muscle-Contraction Headache. *Muscle-contraction headaches* are the most common form of headache, also being known as tension or nervous headaches. These headaches result from sustained contraction of the muscles of the scalp and neck caused by constant stress and tension, especially if poor posture is maintained for any time. Patients describe their symptoms as steady, nonpulsing, tight, squeezing, pressing, or crawling sensations or as the feeling of having the head in a vise. The headaches may be accompanied by anxiety, dizziness, and bright spots in front of the eyes. In some people, caffeine may exacerbate the headaches, presumably because anxiety is increased.

Nonmigrainous Vascular Headaches. A wide variety of diseases and conditions induce headache that is associated with dilation of the cranial arteries. The most common causes are fever, anoxia (lack of oxygen), anemia, high altitude, physical effort, hypoglycemia (low blood sugar), foods, and chemical agents. In addition, headache may result from congestion and edema of the nasal membranes, often termed vasomotor rhinitis, which is assumed to represent a localized vascular reaction to stress.

Treatment of Headaches

Migraine is treated by specific drugs at the time of an attack and by preventive measures between attacks. In an acute attack, **ergotamine** compounds, often given in conjunction with caffeine, are useful in alleviating the headache, probably because they produce constriction of the cerebral arteries, thus reducing dilation, which is the source of the pain. In addition, most migraine sufferers find that the headache is reduced in a totally dark room.

The most obvious treatment for headache arising from neurological disease is to treat the disease itself. Tension headaches can be relieved by muscle-relaxant drugs, minor tranquilizers, application of heat to the affected muscles, and improvement of posture. They can also be prevented by avoiding the life situations that give rise to stress.

INFECTIONS

Infection is the invasion of the body by disease-producing (pathogenic) microorganisms and the reaction of the tissues to their presence and to the toxins they generated. Because the central nervous system can be invaded by a wide variety of infectious agents—including viruses, bacteria, fungi, and metazoan parasites—the diagnosis and treatment of infection are important components of clinical neurology. Although infections of the nervous system usually spread from infection elsewhere in the body—especially the ears, nose, and throat—they also may be introduced directly into the brain as a result of head trauma, skull fractures, or surgery. Infections of the nervous system are particularly serious because the affected neurons and glia usually die, resulting in lesions.

There are a number of processes by which infections kill neural cells. First, infections may interfere with the blood supply to neurons, thus producing thrombosis, hemorrhage of capillaries, or even the complete choking off of blood vessels. Second, there may be a disturbance of glucose or oxygen metabolism in the brain cells that is serious enough to kill them. Third, the infection may alter the characteristics of the neural cell membranes, thus changing the electrical properties of the neurons; alternatively, it may interfere with the basic enzymatic processes of the cell, producing any number of abnormal conditions. Fourth, a by-product of the body's defense against infection is *pus*—a fluid composed basically of white blood cells, their by-products, and those of the infectious microorganisms—and a thin fluid called liquor puris. Pus impairs neuronal functioning in at least two ways: it significantly alters the extracellular fluids surrounding a neuron, thus altering neuronal function; and, because pus occupies space, its production increases pressure on the brain, disturbing normal functioning. Fifth, and finally, infection often causes edema, which compresses the brain, again resulting in dysfunction.

Symptoms and Diagnosis of Infection

Many infections of the nervous system are secondary to infections elsewhere in the body and are accompanied by symptoms associated with those other infections, including lowered blood pressure and other changes in blood circulation, fever, general malaise, headache, and delirium. In addition, symptoms of cerebral infections include both generalized symptoms of increased intracranial pressure—such as headache, vertigo, nausea, convulsions, and mental confusion—and focalized symptoms of disturbance of specific brain functions.

Diagnostic tests for infection include CSF studies in addition to conventional methods of infection identification, such as smear and culture studies. CT scans and other brain scans may also be used to diagnose and locate some infectious disorders.

Types of Infections

Unfortunately, there is a good deal of semantic disagreement about the terminology of infections. We shall use the term **encephalitis** to refer to inflammation of the central nervous system caused by infection and the term **encephalopathy** for chemical, physical, allergic, or toxic inflammations. Note that, strictly speaking, encephalitis and encephalopathy do not refer to specific diseases, but rather to the effects of the disease processes.

Four types of infection can affect the central nervous system: viral, bacterial, mycotic (fungal), and parasitic infestations.

Viral Infections. A *virus* is an encapsulated aggregate of *nucleic acid* that may be made up of either DNA or RNA. Some viruses, such as those causing poliomyelitis and rabies, are called **neurotropic viruses,** because they have a special affinity for cells of the central nervous system. These are different from **pantropic viruses** (such as those that cause mumps and herpes simplex), which attack other body tissues in addition to the central nervous system. Most viral infections of the nervous system produce nonspecific lesions affecting widespread regions of the brain, such as occur in St. Louis encephalitis, rabies, and poliomyelitis.

Bacterial Infections. *Bacterium* is a loose generic name for any microorganism (typically one-celled) that has no chlorophyll and multiplies by simple division. Bacterial infections of the central nervous system result from an infestation of these organisms, usually via the bloodstream. The most common disorders resulting from bacterial infection are meningitis and brain abscess. In **meningitis,** the meninges are infected by any of a variety of bacteria. **Brain abscesses** are also produced by a variety of bacteria, secondary to infection elsewhere in the body. Abscesses begin as a small focus of purulent (pus-producing) bacteria that cause necrosis (death) of cells in the affected region. As the organisms multiply and destroy more brain cells, the abscess behaves as an expanding mass, often hollow in the center; as it expands, it produces increasing intracranial pressure.

Mycotic Infections. Invasion of the nervous system by a fungus is known as a **mycotic infection.** A fungus is any member of a large group of lower plants that lack chlorophyll and subsist on living or dead organic matter; the fungi include yeasts, molds, and mushrooms. Ordinarily the central nervous system is highly resistant to mycotic infections, but fungi may invade a brain whose resistance has been reduced by various diseases such as tuberculosis or malignant tumors.

Parasitic Infestations. A *parasite* is an organism that lives on or within another living organism (the host) at the host's expense. Several kinds of parasites invade the central nervous system and produce significant diseases, the most important of which are amebiasis and malaria. *Amebiasis* (also known as amebic dysentery), caused by an infestation of the protozoan amoeba *(Entamoeba histolytica),* results in encephalitis and brain abscesses. *Malaria* is caused by protozoa of the genus *Plasmodium,* which are transmitted by the bites of infected mosquitoes. Cerebral malaria occurs when the plasmodia infect the capillaries of the brain, producing local hemorrhages and the subsequent degeneration of neurons.

Treatment of Infections

Treatment varies with the type of infection. Viral infections are extremely difficult to treat, for there are no specific antidotes, and the only option is to let the diseases run their course. Sedatives are sometimes administered to make the patient more comfortable. The important exception to this is the treatment of rabies. Once it is ascertained that a person has had contact with a rabid animal, antirabies vaccine is administered over a period of 2 to 4 weeks to produce an immunity before the disease actually develops. Once the disease does develop, rabies is fatal.

Bacterial cerebral infections have become less common with the introduction of antibiotic drugs, the usual treatment for these infections. In some cases it may be necessary to drain abscesses to relieve intracranial pressure, or to do spinal taps to remove CSF and reduce pressure where there is edema or a buildup of pus.

Neither mycotic nor parasitic infections can be treated satisfactorily, although antibiotics are often used to treat associated disorders.

DISORDERS OF MOTOR NEURONS AND THE SPINAL CORD

The following sections describe a number of movement disorders produced by damage to the spinal cord and cortical projections to the spinal cord. These include myasthenia gravis, a disorder of the muscle receptors; poliomyelitis, a disorder of the motor neuron cell bodies; multiple sclerosis, a disorder of myelinated motor fibers; paraplegia and Brown-Sequard's syndrome, which are caused by complete transection or hemitransection of the spinal cord, respectively; and hemiplegia, which is caused by cortical damage. Table 24.5 provides some common terms for movement disorders.

Myasthenia Gravis

Myasthenia gravis (severe muscle weakness) is characterized by muscular fatigue after muscles have been exercised a few times. It may be apparent after a short period of exercise or work, toward the end of a long conversation, or sometimes even after a few repetitions of a movement. Recovery follows a period of rest. Its rapid onset after exercise distinguishes it from other disorders such as depression or general fatigue. Examination of the muscles shows that there is no obvious muscle pathology. While myasthenia can occur in people of any age, it is most common in the third decade of life, and women are more often

TABLE 24.5. Some commonly used terms for movement disorders

Apraxia. Inability to carry out purposeful movements or movements on command in the absence of paralysis or other motor or sensory impairments. Usually follows damage to neocortex.

Ataxia. Failure of muscular coordination or an irregularity of muscular action. Commonly follows cerebellar damage.

Athetosis. A condition in which ceaseless slow, sinuous writhing movements occur, especially in the hands. Due to abnormal function of the extrapyramidal system.

Catalepsy. A condition marked by muscular rigidity in which voluntary movements are reduced or absent but posture is maintained. It is a feature of Parkinson's disease due to dopamine loss.

Cataplexy. Complete loss of movement and posture during which muscle tone is absent but consciousness is spared.

Chorea. Literally means dance but refers to the ceaseless occurrence of a wide variety of jerky movements that appear to be well coordinated but are performed involuntarily.

Hemiplegia. Complete or partial paralysis to one half of the body. Usually follows damage to the contralateral motor cortex.

Palsy. Means a paralysis of movement and usually refers to persisting movement disorders due to brain damage acquired perinatally.

Paralysis. Complete loss of movement or sensation (but more commonly movement) in a part of the body. Usually permanent after damage to motor neurons; temporary after damage to motor cortex (area 4).

Paraplegia. Paralysis or paresis of the lower torso and legs, as can occur following spinal cord damage.

Spasticity. An increase in the tone of certain muscle groups involved in maintaining posture against the force of gravity. If the limb is moved against the rigidity, resistance will initially increase, but then tone will suddenly melt (clasp-knife reflex). Spasticity is thought to be produced by damage to the extrapyramidal motor fibers.

Tardive dyskinesia. The occurrence of slow, persistent movements, particularly of the mouth and tongue. Usually follows long-term treatment with antipsychotic drugs.

affected. All the muscles of the body may be affected, but those supplied by the cranial nerves are usually involved first. In this case, the initial symptoms are diplopia (double vision), ptosis (drooping of the eyelid), weakness of voice, and difficulty in chewing and swallowing or holding up the head. In some people, only the limbs are involved. Usually the symptoms are most apparent at the end of the day and are relieved after sleep. The severity of the disease varies from a mild unilateral ptosis in some people to an incapacitating generalized weakness with a threat of loss of life coming from respiratory paralysis in others.

Muscular weakness is caused by a failure of normal neuromuscular transmission. It has long been known that drug treatment to prevent the destruction of acetylcholine (ACh), allowing it to remain in the area of the neuromuscular junction for a longer period, will partially reverse symptoms. The breakdown of ACh in the synaptic space requires the enzyme acetylcholinesterase (AChE). The action of AChE can be blocked by drugs such as physostigmine (eserine), which permits the accumulation of ACh. If, on the other hand, the neuromuscular junction is partially blocked with drugs such as curare, neuromuscular weakness is enhanced. There are at least three possible explanations of myasthenia in terms of transmitter function. The terminal may release an insufficient supply of ACh, the postsynaptic receptors may be reduced in number or may function ineffectively, or there may be an excessive supply of AChE in the vicinity of the terminal. Research since 1980 suggests that the problem is with the receptor.

In 1970, Changeux and colleagues, a group of chemists studying snake venom, isolated the toxin α-bungarotoxin, which causes paralysis by binding irreversibly with the motor end plate. Their discovery led to the chemistry that made possible the isolation of the nicotinic receptor for acetylcholine (AChR). When the receptors were bound with α-bungarotoxin, they could be separated from the muscle. In 1973, Patrick and Lindstrom in the United States injected the receptor, isolated from the electric eel *Torpedo* (the electric organ of the animal is a rich source of receptors), into rabbits to induce the formation of antibodies to the receptor. It was intended that these antibodies could be labeled in turn and used to locate the receptors. When the antibodies formed, however, the rabbits became "myasthenic," with symptoms similar to those shown by humans. Their weakness was reversed by physostigmine and enhanced by curare. The explanation for their myasthenia was that antibodies formed to attack the foreign receptors also attacked the rabbits' own receptors, which appeared identical. This finding suggests that the disease in humans might be an **autoimmune disease;** that is, humans form antibodies to their own AChR. Subsequently, antibodies to human AChR have been found in a majority of myasthenic patients' serum. Furthermore, drainage of the lymph fluid, which contains antibodies, improved symptoms; the symptoms returned when the lymph fluid was replaced. Finally, Albuquerque and coworkers demonstrated in 1976 that the receptor responsiveness in myasthenic muscle is reduced, and Fambrough and colleagues showed that there is a reduction in the number of receptors in the myasthenic muscle.

It is not known how the production of antibodies starts, and it is not completely clear how the antibodies deactivate the receptors. It is also unclear why circulating antibodies are absent in some patients and why all the muscles of the body are not equally affected. Treatment now has two objectives. First, AChE therapy is used to relieve symptoms. Second, for prolonged relief, attempts are made to arrest the disease with *thymectomy* (surgical removal of the thymus to reduce antibody formation) and with immunosuppressive drug treatment. As a result of treatment, mortality is currently very low.

Poliomyelitis

Poliomyelitis is an acute infectious disease caused by a virus that has a special affinity for the motor neurons of the spinal cord and sometimes also for the motor neurons of the cranial nerves. In extreme infections, it causes paralysis and wasting of the muscles. If it attacks the motor neurons of the respiratory centers, death can result from asphyxia. Not all people who are infected by the virus show symptoms of the disease, but they nevertheless can pass on the disease to others. Infections in individuals can be accelerated by exercise, exertion, or minor surgical operations. Even exercise of a limb may hasten the viral attack on the motor neurons that innervate that limb. The disease usually occurred sporadically and sometimes epidemically in North America until, the Salk and Sabin vaccines were developed in the 1950s and 1960s. Since then, the disease has been well controlled. There are cases reported every year, however, and the incidence of the illness in developing tropical countries is still a concern. Many of those infected by the virus after vaccination against it show no symptoms; others show signs of a mild infection; and still others have fever, headache, malaise, and so forth, but only a minority develop paralysis. Paralysis usually reaches its maximum within the first 24 hours, and improvement occurs after about a week. Of the muscles that are paralyzed, only a portion remain permanently paralyzed, so that after an attack considerable recovery of movement is possible. The process of recovery often lasts for more than a year. It is not known why the virus has a special affinity for motor neurons.

Multiple Sclerosis

Multiple sclerosis (MS) (*sclerosis* is from the Greek meaning hardness) is a disease characterized by the loss of myelin largely in motor tracts but also in sensory tracts. The loss of myelin is not uniform but occurs in patches. In many cases the early signs of the disease are followed by improvement, so that remissions and relapses are a striking feature of the disease. The course of the disease may run from a few years to as long as 50 years. The eventual condition may be one in which the affected person is confined to bed with the classic feature of ataxic paraplegia.

The first pathological accounts of the disease were given in the early part of the 19th century. The signs of the disease consist of small circumscribed lesions in which the myelin sheath and sometimes the axons are destroyed. Eventually a *sclerotic plague* may form in these areas. The cause of MS is still not known. It has been thought that it is due to an infection, a virus, environmental factors, or an immune response of the central nervous system. It often occurs a number of times in the same families, but there is no clear evidence that it is inherited or that it is transmitted from one individual to another. MS is most prevalent in northern Europe and somewhat less common in North America. It is rare in Japan and in more southerly or tropical countries. In regions in which it occurs, its incidence of 50 per 100,000 still makes it one of the most common structural diseases of the nervous system. Only Parkinson's disease is equally common. It occurs in a female-to-male ratio of about 3 to 2, and progress of the disease is often more rapid in females than in males.

The onset of MS is usually rapid; symptoms are fully apparent within a day or two. In half of affected persons, the first symptoms are weakness or loss of control over the limbs; in 30% the symptoms are blindness or other disorders of vision in one or both eyes; and in 20% the symptoms are sensory: tremors, epilepsy, or vertigo. The motor symptoms usually consist of a loss of power in the lower limbs or arms. Muscular wasting is rare because the disease is patchy and because muscles receive multiple innervation from many motor neurons. The first symptoms usually appear in adulthood, and after remission symptoms may not occur again for years. In cases in which the disease is fatal, the average age of death is between 65 and 84 years. There are no specific treatments for MS other than to treat the symptoms and encourage the affected persons to continue working and leading an active life as long as possible. Some people with MS are described as displaying an optimistic euphoria, possibly because the disease has attacked diencephalic structures; this optimism is thought to be helpful in their management. Affected persons, however, may also occasionally show symptoms of apathy and depression.

Paraplegia

Paraplegia (from the Greek *para,* beyond, and *plegia,* stroke) is a condition in which both lower limbs are paralyzed (*quadriplegia* is the paralysis of all four extremities). It is a direct consequence of a complete transection of the spinal cord. Immediately after a complete section, the cord distal to the section is devoid of all activity, and all movement sensation and reflexes are absent. Due to loss of reflex activity, thermoregulatory control is absent (leaving the skin cool and dry without sweating), as is bladder control (requiring drainage of the bladder to prevent urinary retention). This condition, called spinal shock, lasts from 4 days to about 6 weeks. Gradually, there is a return of some spinal reflexes until a stabilized condition is reached after a year or so. No sensations, voluntary movements, or thermoregulatory control ever reappears below the lesion. Even though no sensation is felt, certain reflexes can be elicited. A pinprick, for example, may elicit a withdrawal reflex such as the *triple response,* which consists of flexion of the hip, knee, and ankle. Later, extensor activity may become sufficiently strong that weight can be supported briefly, but spinal circuits are too dependent on brain facilitation to permit prolonged standing in its absence. After a year or two, a paraplegic person may be in one of a number of conditions: (1) *Paraplegia in extension,* in which tone predominates in extensor muscles, resulting in a predominantly extensor, or rigidly straight, posture. In this condition (about two-thirds of all paraplegics) the withdrawal reflex is difficult to produce. (2) *Paraplegia in flexion,* in which flexor spasms predominate and major flexor activities can occur, including the flexor withdrawal reflexes and excretory and sexual reflexes. (3) *Flaccid paralysis,* in which no tone is present, occurs in fewer than 20% of paraplegics.

Brown-Sequard Syndrome

Brown-Sequard syndrome refers to the consequences of a unilateral section through the spinal cord. Since some of the ascending and descending pathways are uncrossed and some are crossed, symptoms occur on both sides of the body below the cut. Contralateral to the side of section, a loss of pain and temperature sensation occurs, since these pathways cross at the point where they enter the cord. Sensations of fine touch and pressure are preserved, since their pathways do not cross until they reach the caudal medulla. Ipsilateral to the section there is a loss of fine touch and pressure but not of pain and temperature sensation; sensation and voluntary movements of distal musculature are lost. According to Nathan and Smith, walking recovers well within 2 to 3 days because control of this movement is bilateral.

Hemiplegia

The characteristics of **hemiplegia** are loss of voluntary movements on one side of the body, changes in postural tone, and changes in the status of various reflexes. Hemiplegia results from cortical damage that occurs contralateral to the motor symptoms. Once referred to as a pyramidal, as opposed to an extrapyramidal, disorder, it is now recognized that the complete range of symptoms is not produced by pyramidal tract damage only and thus must result from damage to the cortex and its corticospinal fibers and from associated damage in the basal ganglia. In infancy, damage may result from birth injury, epilepsy, or fever. Infant hemiplegia is usually discussed under the umbrella of cerebral palsy. In young adults, hemiplegia is usually caused by rupture of a congenital aneurysm, an embolism, a tumor, or a head injury. The largest group to suffer from hemiplegia is the middle-aged to elderly, and their hemiplegia is usually due to hemorrhage occurring as a consequence of high blood pressure and a degenerative condition of the blood vessels.

The most common site of a vascular disease producing a hemiplegia is in the middle cerebral artery, which supplies the greater part of the main motor area and basal ganglia (Figure 24.8). Damage to the motor cortex first produces a loss of all voluntary movement on the contralateral side of the body and a paralysis of movement in which muscles are in an almost flaccid state and reflexes are absent. The course and rate of recovery in individuals are quite variable, as has been described by Twitchell. Within a period of days to weeks, the muscles become spastic until they become hypertonic. At the same time, there is an increase in tendon reflexes (stretch reflexes such as the knee-jerk reflex) until they are more responsive than normal *(hyperreflexia)*. The spasticity is most pronounced in the antigravity muscles. (The antigravity muscles are also called *physiological extensors* even though the action of some of them is to produce flexion; for example, flexors hold the arm up against gravity, and flexion, or curling

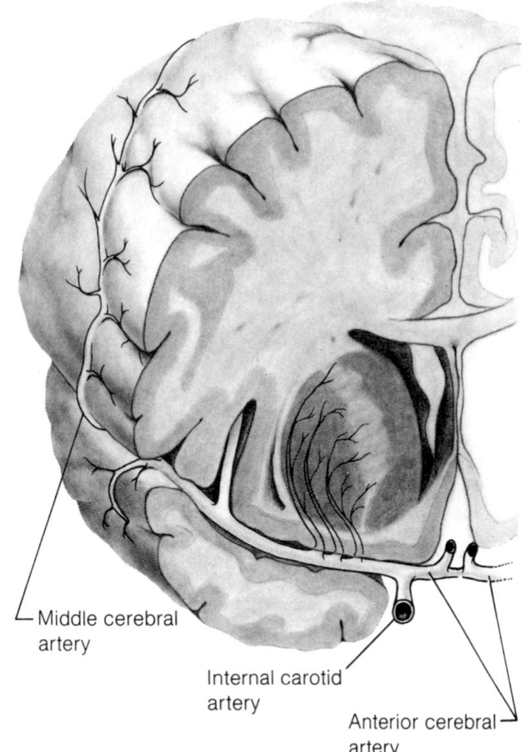

FIGURE 24.8. Irrigation of the deep structures of the brain by the same arteries as irrigate the surface structures. Thus, interruption of the blood supply can produce both cortical and subcortical damage, as is characteristic of hemiplegia. (After Raichle et al., 1978.)

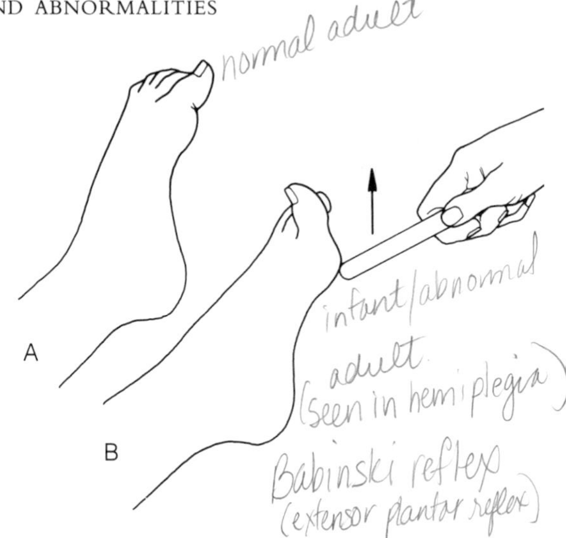

FIGURE 24.9. The Babinski sign. *A*. The normal adult response to stimulation of the lateral planar surface of the left foot. *B*. The normal infant and abnormal adult response. (After Gardner, 1968.)

down, of the toes helps maintain standing against gravity.) Once spasticity develops, it affects posture in a definite, recognizable pattern. The arm is abducted and flexed at the elbow, with the fingers tightly curled into the palm (an exaggeration of the posture of the abducted arm typical of a person running or sitting). The extension of the leg is exaggerated, giving it a pillarlike character that also permits it to be used for walking. Inability to move the joints independently, however, requires that the leg be moved as a whole: steps with the affected leg are initiated by raising the pelvis on that side and bringing the leg through with circumduction from the hip, keeping the knee extended. Spasticity is dependent on posture. When a person takes a quadrupedal position, the arms become spastic in an extended position. Thus, the spasticity is still serving the function of antigravity support; spasticity is not a property of independent muscles, but occurs in groups of muscles in a purposeful way.

The spasticity of hemiplegia has a number of characteristics that distinguish it from the rigidity of extrapyramidal disorders such as Parkinson's disease. It is unidirectional as a result of being greater in antigravity muscles. The resistance of the spastic muscle to passive movement is greater with rapid than with slow movements. Tendon reflexes are hyperactive. Finally, the limbs show a clasp-knife response after initially resisting forced movement. For example, when an attempt is made to extend the forearm, resistance to the forced movement gradually increases and then quite suddenly melts away (the name comes from the sudden snap of the blade of a jackknife when it is closed; the blade is stiff during the first half of the closure and then suddenly snaps shut).

The damage that produces hemiplegia also results in changes in a number of reflexes that are diagnostically important. Scratching the sole of the foot of a normal person with a dull object produces a downward flexion of all toes. In hemiplegia there is an upward flexion, especially of the big toe, and outward fanning of the toes (Figure 24.9). This response is caused by activation of physiological flexors and is often accompanied by flexion of the leg at the knee and hip. The response is called the *Babinski sign* or *extensor plantar response*. This sign is one of a family of flexion responses that occur after motor cortex or pyramidal tract damage. Two other reflexes are absent in hemiplegia. In normal people, stroking the abdominal muscles causes their retraction (the *abdominal reflex*), and in males stroking the inner thigh causes retraction of the testicles *(cremasteric reflex);* these reflexes are also absent.

Since the neocortex is the source of the pyramidal tract, which projects to the spinal cord through the pyramids, as well as the source of motor fibers that project to other brain areas involved in movement, one could ask: What contribution do each of the different motor projections make to the motor disturbances of hemiplegia? Damage to the pyramidal tract produces loss of fine movements of the limbs, loss of strength, and loss of movement speed. It also produces loss of reflexes; the Babinski sign is present, and abdominal and cremasteric reflexes are absent. Damage to the basal ganglia is thus responsible for the spasticity and the exaggerated stretch reflexes. The distinction between the contributions of the two efferent systems allows the damage to be localized to some extent by the degree to which one or the other group of symptoms is present.

Hemiplegia also involves abnormalities in muscles other than those in the limbs. There is difficulty in deviating the eyes and rotating the head opposite to the side of the lesion, weakness of voluntary movements of the lower face (such as in retracting the lips and pursing them), and weakness in the jaw and the tongue on the opposite side. Emotional expressions, however (smiling, crying), are usually not affected. Because muscles of the head are under greater bilateral control than those of the limbs, most affected head movements show relatively rapid recovery.

There is a great deal of variation in the recovery that occurs after hemiplegia, but treatment may have one or a combination of objectives. The person may be trained to use the unaffected side, to use the affected side as much as spasticity and residual abilities allow, or to make movements that lessen spasticity so that voluntary movements can be performed as much as possible. The last therapeutic procedure is described in detail by Bobath. It is based on the fact that the strength of spasticity is related to posture. Bending over lessens spasticity, so if the arm is extended and the head is turned toward the arm, flexion spasticity is lessened. Use of such alternative movements may be effective enough to allow an affected limb to be used.

DISORDERS OF SLEEP

The need for sleep varies considerably among individuals and for the same individual at different stages of life. We have all been told that we need 8 hours sleep each night for good health. In fact, there are both long and short sleepers. It has been found that some people can stay healthy on as little as an hour of sleep per day, whereas others may need to sleep as much as 10 to 12 hours. Webb studied long sleepers (longer than 9.5 hours per day) and short sleepers (fewer than 4.4 hours per day) and found little difference in their overall health. The proper amount of sleep does seem to be an individual affair. Short sleepers may not be able to sleep any longer, and long sleepers may not function efficiently if they don't get enough sleep. The definition of what constitutes adequate sleep must be made within the context of an individual's past sleep history.

Sleep was thought to be a passive act that resulted when sensory stimulation was low. The work of Bremer seemed to support this view. In 1935, he transected the brain between colliculi in cats (called the *cerveau isolé* preparation) and observed that large-amplitude slow waves characteristic of sleep were a permanent feature of the cat's EEG. If the transection was made lower down (the *encéphale isolé* preparation), the cat showed normal sleep and waking EEG cycles. Bremer believed that the differences between these two preparations was that the cranial nerves provided stimulation in the latter preparation, whereas in the former they were separated from the forebrain and could not do so. Bremer's idea was referred to as the *passive hypothesis of sleep*. Experiments that deprived humans of sensory stimulation, however, showed that deprivation did not induce or prolong sleep. Perhaps the single most influential experiment performed to oppose the passive view was done by Moruzzi and Magoun in 1949. They implanted stimulating electrodes into the brainstem of cats and recording electrodes into the neocortex. When the brainstem was stimulated, the slow waves of the cortex were replaced by a pattern of low-voltage fast activity characteristic of a waking cat. The fast activity outlasted the period of stimulation by a considerable duration. The consequence of Moruzzi and Magoun's experiment was that the dominant theory of sleep became what is known as the *active hypothesis of sleep*. Stated simply, sleep is produced by changes in the activity in sleep-waking structures located between Bremer's two cuts.

Sleep comprises at least two states that periodically alternate during a complete sleep session. Studies by Dement and Kleitman and by others, in which sleeping people are awakened, have shown that one state is a time during which vivid dreaming invariably occurs. This state is called **dream sleep (D-sleep)**, and the other is called **slow-wave sleep (S-sleep)**. Dream sleep is characterized by a wakinglike EEG, during which rapid eye movements (REM) and twitches of the fingers, toes, and other body parts occur in short bursts. Slow-wave sleep is characterized by a slow-wave EEG of various degrees. Large movements such as tossing and turning occur. Slow-wave sleep is generally divided into four stages: stage 1 has the least amount of slow-wave activity and stage 4 has the most, with stages 2 and 3 falling between the two. S-sleep and D-sleep occur in a typical alternating pattern, as illustrated in Figure 24.10. When sleep begins, stages 1 through 4 of S-sleep appear in succession and then give way to D-sleep. After a period of D-sleep, S-sleep again occurs, and so on throughout the night. As a night's sleep progresses, however, stage-4 sleep becomes less frequent and the periods of D-sleep tend to last longer.

A biological explanation of sleep is that it is an adaptive process to conserve energy at night (a time during which food gathering would be difficult). A problem with sleeping all night, however, is that the process of evolution has also placed a premium on rhythms of locomotor activity (thought to occur every 2 hours or so, during which food-gathering and other survival activities would occur). These activity cycles would be incompatible with a full night's sleep. To cope with the dual demands of conserving energy and maintaining activity cycles, an innovative adaption occurred. Periodically, when a waking cycle should occur, immobility is maintained by inhibiting the musculature selectively, while only the brain enters the active cycle. So, we dream rather than going in search of food.

The notion of active inhibition is supported by two kinds of evidence. Pompeiano has recorded electrical activity from the brainstem, spinal cord, motor neurons, and musculature during sleep. During dream sleep there is an increase in the activity of certain brainstem and spinal cord pathways, while motor neuron and muscle activity are almost completely suppressed. Presumably, some central structure (located just below the cerebellum) is actively suppressing movement. Thus we are paralyzed during dream sleep. When this area is damaged in cats, they start moving around as they enter dream sleep, as if acting out a dream.

Disorders of sleep are generally classified into two major groups: (1) **narcolepsy,** which is characterized by excessive sleep or brief inappropriate episodes of sleep, often associated with

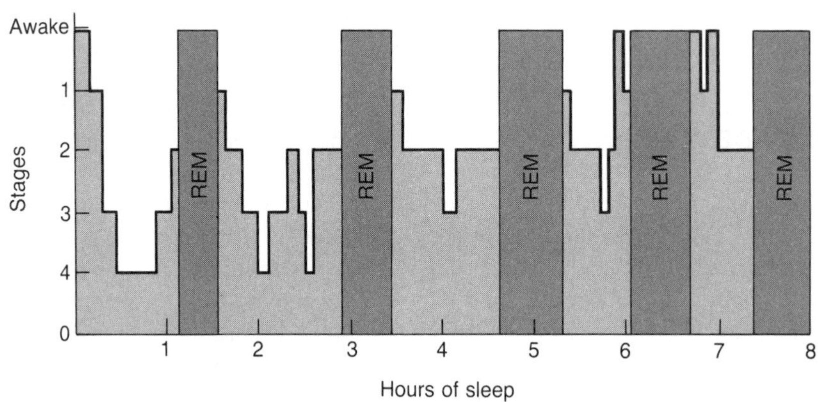

FIGURE 24.10. Course of events during a typical night's sleep for one individual. Stages represent those defined by EEG recordings. The light gray areas represent S-sleep (slow-wave sleep); the dark areas represent D-sleep (dream sleep). Note: Stage-4 S-sleep typically occurs early in the evening; D-sleep increases in duration as the night's sleep progresses. (After Hartmann, 1967.)

other symptoms; and (2) **insomnia,** which is characterized by an inadequate amount of sleep, an inability to fall asleep, or frequent inconvenient arousals from sleep. Both disorders can have a variety of causes, including brain damage, viral infections, and drug abuse. These disorders may also occur, however, in the absence of obvious precipitating factors. In addition to these two disorders, there are many other behaviors that occur during sleep that are disturbing to the afflicted individual. These include night terrors, sleepwalking, grinding of the teeth, and *myoclonic jerks* (sudden vigorous movements), but these are usually transitory, infrequent, or not sufficiently disruptive to be called sleep disorders, per se.

Narcolepsy

Narcolepsy is defined as an inappropriate attack of sleep. The affected individual has an overwhelming impulse to fall asleep or simply collapses into sleep at inconvenient times. The attacks may be infrequent or occur many times a day. The disorder is surprisingly common: estimates suggest that as much as 0.02% of the population may suffer from these attacks. Males and females seem equally affected. Although there is a high incidence of narcolepsy in the families of afflicted individuals, no genetic causality has been demonstrated. Symptoms usually appear when people are between the ages of 10 and 20, and once sleep attacks develop they continue throughout life. Amphetaminelike stimulants and tricyclic antidepressants have been found useful in treatment.

Narcolepsy actually comprises a number of disorders: (1) sleep attacks, (2) cataplexy, (3) sleep paralysis, and (4) hypnagogic or hypnopompic hallucinations. All the symptoms do not necessarily occur at once or in the same individual, but they do occur together often enough to be considered interrelated.

Sleep Attacks. Sleep attacks are brief, often irresistible episodes of sleep that last about 15 min and can occur at any time. Their onset is sometimes recognizable, but they can also occur without warning. The episodes are most apt to occur during times of boredom or after meals, but they can also occur during such activities as sexual intercourse, scuba diving, or baseball games. After a brief sleep attack the individual may awaken completely alert and be resistant to a second attack for a number of hours. Sleep attacks are probably an attack of slow-wave sleep (like an irrestible desire to nap).

Cataplexy. *Cataplexy* (from the Greek *cata,* down, and *plexy,* strike) is a complete loss of muscle tone or a sudden paralysis that results in "buckling" of the knees or complete collapse. The attack may be so sudden that the fall results in injury, particularly because the collapse involves a loss of muscle tone and loss of the reflexes necessary to break the fall. During the attack the person remains conscious, and if the eyelids are open or are opened, the patient can recall visual events that occur during the attack. In contrast to sleep attacks, cataplexic attacks usually appear at times of emotional excitement, such as when a person is laughing or angry. If emotions are held under tight control, the attacks can be prevented. Cataplexy is probably an attack of dream sleep.

Sleep Paralysis. *Sleep paralysis* is an episode of paralysis that occurs at the transition periods between wakefulness and sleep. The period of paralysis is usually brief but can last as long as 20 min. Sleep paralysis has been experienced by half of all people, if classroom surveys are an indication of its frequency. In contrast to cataplexy, the paralyzed individual can be aroused easily by touching or name-calling, and if the person is experienced with the attacks, he or she can terminate them by using a strategy such as grunting. What appears to happen in sleep paralysis is that the person wakes up but is still in the state of paralysis associated with dream sleep.

Hypnagogic and Hypnopompic Hallucinations. *Hypnagogic* (from the Greek *hypo,* sleep, and *gogic,* enter into) *hallucinations* are episodes of auditory, visual, or tactile hallucination that occur during sleep paralysis as the individual is falling asleep. *Hypnopompic (pompic,* leading away) ***hallucinations*** are similar experiences that occur during paralysis as the individual is awakening. The hallucinations are similar experiences that occur during paralysis as the individual is awakening. The hallucinations are generally frightening: the person may feel that a monster or something equally terrifying is lurking nearby. The same kinds of hallucinations can occur during episodes of cataplexy. A curious feature of the hallucinations is that the person is conscious and often aware of things that are actually happening, so that the hallucinations are even more bizarre, because they can become intermixed with real events. These hallucinations may actually be dreams that occur while an individual is still conscious.

Rechtschaffen and Dement have described evidence to support the idea that the various symptoms of narcolepsy are actually attacks of normal sleep states. Recall that dream sleep is characterized by muscular paralysis and vivid dreams. In narcolepsy, cataplexy is the equivalent of paralysis, and hypnagogic hallucinations are the eqivalent of dreams. Two types of evidence support Rechtschaffen and Dement's view. First, during an attack of cataplexy or sleep paralysis, individuals experience hallucinations that have a dreamlike character, even though they are conscious. Second, EEG recordings taken from narcoleptics have shown that they enter D-sleep almost immediately, rather than first going through an hour or so of S-sleep. People who suffer from narcolepsy display the typical symptoms at different times and in different combinations, but the usual pattern is that the sleep attacks appear first (usually without other symptoms). Cataplexy, which may be a sudden onset of D-sleep, will develop in about 70% of patients. Sleep paralysis with hallucinations occur in about 30% of patients. Sleep paralysis may involve entering a D-sleep stage before losing consciousness or regaining consciousness during a D-sleep stage.

Obviously, one of the problems with describing narcolepsy is that it is difficult to distinguish it from genuine fatigue. Narcolepsy should not be confused with napping, which is common and also somewhat irresistible for some people.

Insomnia

Studies of people who claim that they do not sleep, do not sleep well, or wake up frequently from sleep show that their insomnia can have many causes. Rechtschaffen and Monroe recorded EEGs from poor sleepers before and during sleep and found that they exaggerated the length of time it took them to get to sleep. But poor sleepers did have decreased dream sleep, make more body movements, and go through more changes in sleep stages than did normal individuals. When awakened from slow-wave sleep, they also claimed that they were not sleeping. The investigators concluded that even though these poor sleepers did sleep by EEG criteria, they did not seem to benefit completely from the restorative properties of sleep. Surveys suggest that as many as 14% of people claim to suffer from insomnia, but the causes are diverse and include general factors such as anxiety, depression, fear of sleeping, environmental disturbances, and travel into new time zones (jet lag). Some factors in insomnia seem directly related to the sleep situation. These include (1) nightmares, (2) sleep apnea, (3) restless-legs syndrome, (4) myoclonus, (5) drug-induced insomnia, and (6) insomnia due to brain damage.

Nightmares are intense, frightening dreams that lead to waking. They are more common than night terrors *(parvor nocturnus). Night terrors* are attempts to fight or flee accompanied by panic and such utterances as bloodcurdling screams. Nightmares occur during dream sleep, but night terrors occur during stage-4 S-sleep. Night terrors are usually brief (1 or 2 min), and the person usually cannot remember the episode. Both kinds of events are more common in children than in adults, perhaps because adults are more experienced with disturbing dreams and so are not easily awakened. Both types of events can be sufficiently disturbing to disrupt sleep and lead to insomnia.

Sleep apnea (from the Greek for not breathing) is a cessation of respiration that occurs periodically, lasting about 10 sec or more, and occurs only during sleep. There are two types of sleep apnea. **Obstructive sleep apnea** occurs mainly during dream sleep and seems to be caused by a collapse of the oropharynx during the paralysis of dream sleep. Patients with this problem invariably have a history of loud snoring—sounds produced as a consequence of the difficult breathing through the constricted air passage. The obstruction can be reduced through surgical intervention. **Central sleep apnea** stems from a central nervous system disorder. It occurs primarily in males and is characterized by a failure of the diaphragm and accessory muscles to move. Apnea periods may last for up to 3 min. All-night recording sessions are needed to detect both types of sleep apnea. Both types interrupt sleep, for the individual is awakened partly or fully by the oxygen deprivation. Although people may be unaware of their apnea, they complain of chronic daytime fatigue.

Most drugs, whether stimulants or sedatives, eventually lead to insomnia. Hypnotics and sedatives may promote sleep at first, but habituation occurs. These drugs also deprive the user of dream sleep. Stimulants directly reduce sleep, but they may have their greatest effect on slow-wave sleep. Drug withdrawal is usually an effective treatment.

Brain-damage-induced insomnia is relatively rare, but there are descriptions of patients who showed reduced sleep or no sleep following brain damage. Certain viral infections, such as in the condition of *encephalitis lethargica* (sleep produced by brain infection) of the 1920s, described by von Economo, can lead to insomnia that is so long-lasting it can prove fatal. One treatment given for this type of insomnia was to anesthetize the patients for 8 to 10 days, with brief respites for feeding, until recovery occurred. It is likely that the virus of encephalitis attacks brain centers responsible for sleep induction. Nauta has described a rat analogue of this condition: he observed that rats with large anterior hypothalamic lesions became excessively active and insomniac until they died.

SUMMARY

This chapter has reviewed a number of nervous system disorders that typically would be diagnosed by a neurologist. They include closed- and open-head injuries, infections, migraines, tumors, motor disorders, and sleep disorders. Despite their diversity, these disorders are relatively common and lead to disruptions of normal living. They may also require neuropsychological analysis to evaluate behavioral abilities and to aid with counseling and therapy.

REFERENCES

Albuquerque, E. X., J. E. Rash, R. F. Myer, and J. R. Satterfield. An electrophysiological and morphological study of the neuromuscular junction in patients with myasthenia gravis. *Experimental Neurology* 51:536–563, 1976.

Annegers, J. F., J. D. Grabow, R. V. Groover, E. R. Laws, L. R. Elveback, and L. T. Kurland. Seizures after head trauma: A population study. *Neurology* 30:683–689, 1980.

Bakal, D. A. Headache: A biopsychological perspective. *Psychological Bulletin* 82:369–382, 1975.

Bannister, R. *Brain's Clinical Neurology,* 5th ed. New York: Oxford University Press, 1978.

Bobath, B. *Adult Hemiplegia: Evaluation and Treatment.* London: Heinemann Medical Books, 1970.

Bond, M. R. Neurobehavioral sequelae of closed head injury. In I. Grant and K. M. Adams, eds. *Neuropsychological Assessment of Neuropsychiatric Disorders.* New York: Oxford University Press, 1986.

Brooks, N., L. Campsie, C. Symington, A. Beattie, and W. McKinlay. The five year outcome of severe blunt head injury: A relative's view. *Journal of Neurology, Neurosurgery, and Psychiatry* 49:764–770, 1986.

Changeux, J.-P., M. Kasai, and C.-Y. Lee. The use of a snake venom toxin to characterize the cholinergic receptor protein. *Proceedings of the National Academy of Sciences* 67:1241–1247, 1970.

Courville, C. B. *Pathology of the Nervous System,* 2nd ed. MountainView, Calif.: Pacific Press, 1945.

Dement, W., and N. Kleitman. Cyclic variations in EEG during sleep and their relation to eye movements, body motility and dreaming.

Fortuny, L. A., M. Briggs, F. Newcombe, G. Radcliffe, and C. Thomas. Measurement of the duration of post-traumatic amnesia. *Journal of Neurology, Neurosurgery, and Psychiatry* 43:377–379, 1980.

Gardner, H. *Fundamentals of Neurology*. Philadelphia: Saunders, 1968.

Hartmann, E. *The Biology of Dreaming*. Springfield, Ill.: Charles C. Thomas, 1967.

Klonoff, P. S., W. G. Snow, and L. D. Costa. Quality of life in patients 2 to 4 years after closed head injury. *Neurosurgery* 19:735–743, 1986.

Lashley, K. S. Patterns of cerebral integration indicated by the scotomas of migraine. *Archives of Neurology and Psychiatry* 46:331–339, 1941.

Levin, H. S., A. L. Benton, and R. G. Grossman. *Neurobehavioral Consequences of Closed Head Injury*. New York: Oxford University Press, 1982.

Levin, H. S., H. E. Gary, W. M. High, S. Mattis, R. M. Ruff, H. M. Eisenberg, L. F. Marshall, and K. Tabaddor. Minor head injury and the postconcussional syndrome: Methodological issues in outcome studies. In H. S. Levin, J. Grafman, and H. M. Eisenberg, eds. *Neurobehavioral Recovery from Head Injury*. New York: Oxford University Press, 1987.

Lezak, M. D. *Neuropsychological Assessment,* 2nd ed. New York: Oxford University Press, 1983.

Luria, A. R. *The Working Brain*. New York: Penguin Books, 1973.

McNeil, E. B. *The Psychoses*. Englewood Cliffs, N.J.: Prentice-Hall, 1970.

Marinkovic, S. V., M. M. Milisavljevic, V. Lolic-Draganic, and M. S. Kovacevic. Distribution of the occipital branches of the posterior cerebral artery: Correlation with occipital lobe infarcts. *Stroke* 18:728–732, 1987.

Moruzzi, G., and H. W. Magoun. Brainstem reticular formation and activation of the EEG. *Electroencephalography and Clinical Neurophysiology* 1:455–473, 1949.

Nathan, P., and M. Smith. Effects of two unilateral cordotomies on the mobility of the lower limbs. *Brain* 96:471–494, 1973.

Nauta, W. J. H. Hypothalamic regulation of sleep in rats: An experimental study. *Journal of Neurophysiology* 9:285–316, 1946.

Newcombe, F. *Missile Wounds of the Brain*. London: Oxford University Press, 1969.

Newcombe, F. Psychometric and behavioral evidence: Scope, limitations, and ecological validity. In H. S. Levin, J. Grafman, and H. M. Eisenberg, eds. *Neurobehavioral Recovery from Head Injury*. New York: Oxford University Press, 1987.

Oppenheimer, D. R. Microscopic lesions in the brain following head injury. *Journal of Neurology, Neurosurgery, and Psychiatry* 31:299–306, 1968.

Patrick, J., and J. Lindstrom. Autoimmune response to acetylcholine receptor. *Science* 180:871–872, 1973.

Pincus, J. H., and G. J. Tucker. *Behavioral Neurology*. New York: Oxford University Press, 1974.

Pompeiano, O. Mechanisms of sensorimotor integration during sleep. In E. Stellar and L. Sprague, eds. *Progress in Physiological Psychology,* vol. 3. New York: Academic, 1970.

Raichle, M. E., C. D. de Vivo, and J. Hanaway. Disorders of cerebral circulation. In S. G. Eliasson, A. L. Prensky, and W. B. Hardin, eds. *Neurological Pathophysiology,* 2nd ed. New York: Oxford University Press, 1978.

Rasmussen, T. Cortical resection in the treatment of focal epilepsy. *Advances in Neurology* 8:139–154, 1975.

Rechtschaffen, A., and W. Dement. Studies on the relation of narcolepsy, cataplexy, and sleep with low voltage random EEG activity. *Research Publications: Association for Research in Neurons and Mental Disease* 45:488–498, 1967.

Rechtschaffen, A., and L. J. Monroe. Laboratory studies of insomnia. In A. Kales, ed. *Sleep: Physiology and Pathology*. Philadelphia: Lippincott, 1969.

Teasdale, G., and B. Jennett. The Glasgow coma scale. *Lancet* 2:81–84, 1974.

Terry, R. D., and P. Davies. Dementia of the Alzheimer type. *Annual Review of Neuroscience* 3:77–95, 1980.

Teuber, H.-L., W. S. Battersby, and M. B. Bender. *Visual Field Defects after Penetrating Wounds of the Brain*. Cambridge, Mass.: Harvard University Press, 1960.

Twitchell, T. E. The restoration of motor function following hemiplegia in man. *Brain* 74:443–480, 1951.

Webb, W. B. *Sleep the Gentle Tyrant*. Englewood Cliffs, N.J.: Prentice-Hall, 1975.

Wilberger, J. E., Z. Deeb, and W. Rothfus. Magnetic resonance imaging in cases of severe head injury. *Neurosurgery* 20:571–576, 1987.

Zacks, S. I. *Atlas of Neuropathology*. New York: Harper & Row, 1971.

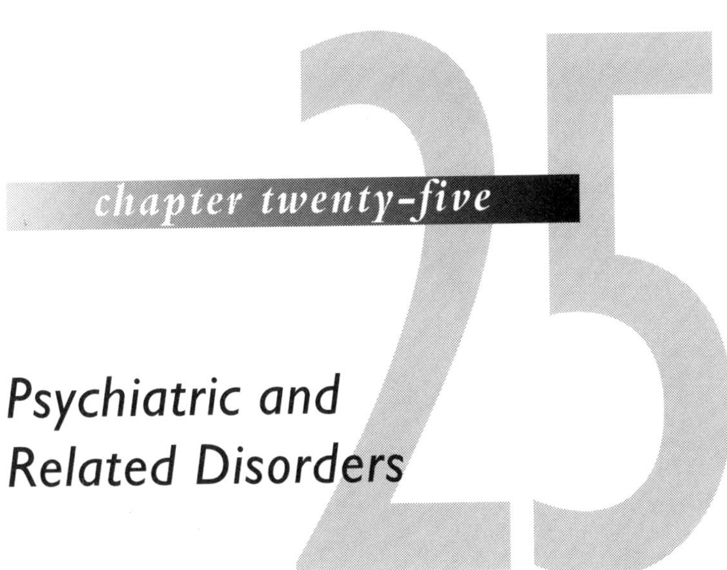

chapter twenty-five

Psychiatric and Related Disorders

Throughout the centuries, there has been a contrast between psychological and biological views of mental disorders. Religion and poetry have seen madness as an affliction of the spirit, and many famous plays and other writings have forms of madness as central features (for example, Shakespeare's *MacBeth* and *Othello;* Dostoyesky's *The Idiot*). In contrast, medicine has explained madness as a disorder of various humors and organs, although in most cases without much evidence or success. In the past two decades, it has become clear that certain forms of mental, or psychiatric, disorders have biochemical, anatomical, and genetic bases. It also has become clear that the distinction between traditional psychiatric illness, such as schizophrenia, and motor disorders, such as Parkinson's disease, is not as clear-cut as it once seemed. This chapter will focus on disorders that are characterized by dramatic abnormalities in cognitive functioning, in the absence of obvious lesions to the brain. We begin with the two major types of psychiatric disorders (schizophrenia and affective disorders) and then consider motor disorders including Huntington's chorea, Tourette's syndrome, and Parkinson's disease. We then consider dementias related to aging and conclude with a discussion of psychosurgery.

SCHIZOPHRENIA

Consider the following case history:

> When Mrs. T. was 16 years old, she began to experience her first symptom of schizophrenia: a profound feeling that people were staring at her. These bouts of self-consciousness soon forced her to end her public piano performances. Her self-consciousness led to withdrawal, then to fearful delusions that others were speaking of her and finally to suspicions that they were plotting to harm her. At first Mrs. T.'s illness was intermittent, and the return of her intelligence, warmth and ambition between episodes allowed her to complete several years of college, to marry and to rear three children. She had to enter a hospital for the first time at 28, after the birth of her third child, when she began to hallucinate.
>
> Now, at 45, Mrs. T is never entirely well. She has seen dinosaurs on the street and live animals in her refrigerator. While hallucinating, she speaks and writes in an incoherent, but almost poetic, way. At other times, she is more lucid, but even then her voices some-

times lead her to do dangerous things, such as driving very fast down the highway in the middle of the night, dressed only in a nightgown. . . . At other times and without any apparent stimulus, Mrs. T has bizarre visual hallucinations. For example, she saw cherubs in the grocery store. These experiences leave her preoccupied, confused and frightened, unable to perform such everyday tasks as cooking or playing the piano. (Gershon and Rieder, 1992, p. 127)

Schizophrenia is an extraordinary disorder. There have been various attempts to define the symptoms, but it has always been easier to identify schizophrenic behavior than to define what schizophrenia is. Perhaps the one universally accepted criterion for diagnosing schizophrenia is the elimination of the presence of other neurological disturbance or affective disorder. This is a definition by default. Some authors have emphasized the presence of bizarre hallucinations and disturbances of thought, much as seen in Mrs. T. The important point is that the symptoms of schizophrenia are heterogeneous, which suggests that the biological correlates will also be heterogeneous.

Kraepelin first proposed in 1913 that schizophrenia was characterized by a progressively deteriorating course with a dismal final outcome. This was the dominant opinion through most of this century, but a consensus is emerging that this view is probably incorrect. Most patients appear to stay at a fairly stable level after the first few years of the disease, with little evidence of a decline in neuropsychological functioning. The symptoms come and go, much as in Mrs. T.'s case, but the severity is relatively constant after the first few years.

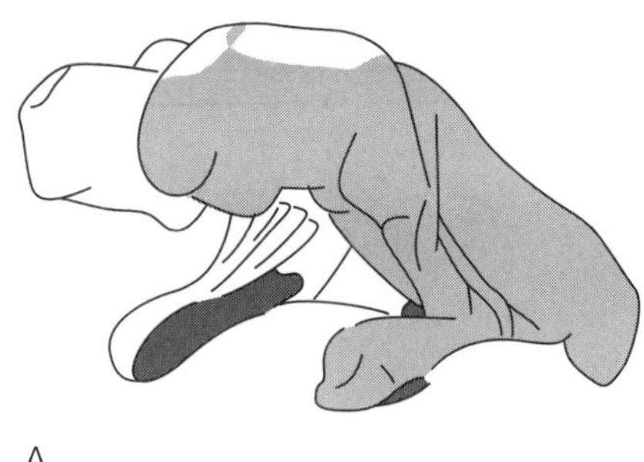

FIGURE 25.1. Structural changes in the hippocampus and ventricles of the brain of a schizophrenic patient (*A*) as contrasted with a normal volunteer (*B*). Made from a three-dimensional MRI. (After Gershon and Rieder, 1992.)

Structural Abnormalities in Schizophrenic Brains

Numerous studies have looked at the gross morphology of the brains of schizophrenics, both in autopsied tissue and in MRI and CT scans. Although the results are variable, most researchers agree that schizophrenics have brains that weigh less than normal and in which the ventricles are enlarged (Figure 25.1). There have also been suggestions that schizophrenics have smaller frontal lobes, or at least a reduction in the number of neurons in the prefrontal cortex, and thinner parahippocampal gyri. One of the most interesting findings is that of Kovelman and Scheibel, who discovered pronounced abnormalities in the orientation of cells in the hippocampi of deceased schizophrenics. Rather than the consistent parallel orientation characteristic of normal brains, the brains of schizophrenics had a more haphazard organization (Figure 25.2). There are two important aspects of this result. First, whereas the brains of schizophrenic patients showed this pathology, it was not found in other pathologies involving the hippocampus, including chronic alcoholism, Alzheimer's disease, temporal lobe epilepsy, and Huntington's chorea. Second, it seems unlikely that disorientation of the hippocampal neurons can develop at any time except during embryogenesis. This is consistent with the long-held view that schizophrenia is a developmental disorder.

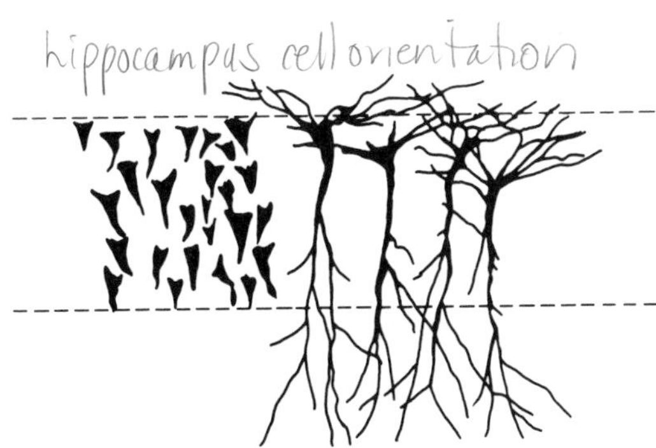

A ORGANIZED (NORMAL)

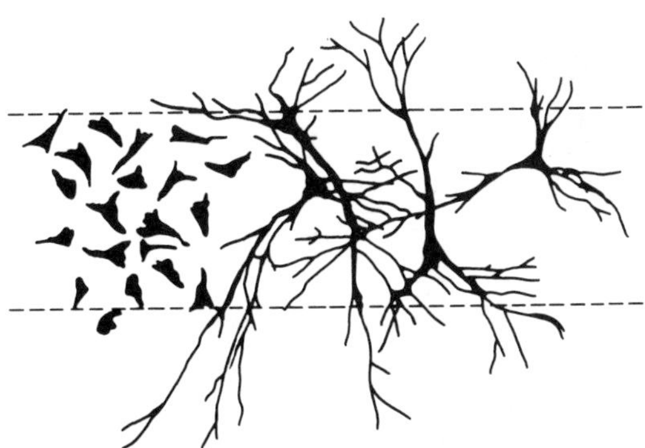

B DISORGANIZED (SCHIZOPHRENIC)

FIGURE 25.2. Examples of pyramidal cell orientation from the hippocampus of (*A*) normal (organized) and (*B*) schizophrenic (disorganized) brains. (After Kovelman and Scheibel, 1984.)

Recently, investigators have begun to use PET to study the activation of the brains of schizophrenics during tasks such as the Wisconsin Card-Sorting Test (see Figure 14.7). For example, experiments by Weinberger and his colleagues have shown that whereas normal control subjects exhibit significant activation of the prefrontal cortex during card-sorting performance, patients with schizophrenia do not. In one intriguing study, Berman and colleagues showed that in identical twins who were discordant for schizophrenia (that is, only one was schizophrenic), there were no PET differences between the twins during resting or control conditions, but during card sorting every schizophrenic twin was hypofrontal compared to the well twin. This result is consistent with the hypothesis that the prefrontal cortex of schizophrenic patients is abnormal in both structure and function.

One of the important features of the prefrontal cortex is its dopaminergic input from the tegmental area. Interference with dopamineric function is known to disturb performance of cognitive tasks in laboratory animals, so it is reasonable to infer that an abnormality in dopamine activity in the frontal lobe could be responsible for at least some symptoms of schizophrenia. Perhaps the strongest evidence favoring a role for dopamine in schizophrenia comes from studies of the action of antipsychotic drugs (also called neuroleptic drugs). These drugs are known to act on the dopamine synapse, and dopamine agonists (such as cocaine, amphetamine, and L-dopa), which enhance the action of dopamine, can induce psychotic symptoms that are almost indistinguishable from classic paranoid schizophrenia. Moreover, if a schizophrenic takes amphetamine, the schizophrenic symptoms are heightened.

Since there is no evidence of cell loss, as in Parkinson's or Alzheimer's diseases, we must ask what type of abnormality in the dopamine system is responsible for schizophrenic symptoms. There are five possibilites: (1) too much dopamine is released by the dopaminergic neurons; (2) too little dopamine is released and the receptors are hypersensitive, a condition known as denervation supersensitivity; (3) dopaminergic receptors are hypersensitive to the normal amount of dopamine released; (4) some other system, which is antagonistic to dopamine, is underactive; or (5) there is a malfunction of a feedback pathway that controls some component of the dopamine system. Carlsson and Carlsson have proposed that schizophrenia is characterized by an imbalance between dopamine neurons and glutamate neurons in the cortex. This could result from a reduction in the number of glutamate neurons, which would be consistent with the apparent frontal atrophy in schizophrenic patients.

Two Types of Schizophrenia?

The limitations on the effectiveness of neuroleptic drugs in treating schizophrenia, and the evidence of structural abnormalities in the schizophrenic brain, led Crow to propose that there may be two distinct pathological syndromes in schizophrenia. The first (type I, equivalent to acute schizophrenia) is characterized by positive symptoms including delusions, hallucinations, and thought disorder. The second (type II, equivalent to chronic schizophrenia) is characterized by negative symptoms including flattened affect and poverty of speech. Crow proposed that type I would be associated with dopaminergic abnormality and would be more responsive to neuroleptic medication, whereas type II would be related to structural changes in the brain. Since chronic amphetamine use has long been known to produce positive schizophrenic symptoms, Crow's hypothesis would explain why amphetamine could produce psychosis in the absence of the structural abnormalities found in many schizophrenic brains.

Crow's hypothesis led to considerable interest, but attempts to validate it have met with limited success. It is difficult to classify patients reliably into one group or the other, and this presents serious difficulties for testing the theory. A consensus is developing that while Crow has made an important contribution in calling attention to the heterogeneous nature of schizophrenia, the disorder is too complex for a dichotomous scheme; it is more likely that there are multiple types of schizophrenia.

Neuropsychological Performance

Heaton and Crowley reviewed 132 studies published between 1960 and 1978 that considered the accuracy of neuropsychological tests in discriminating patients with various psychiatric diagnoses from patients with known brain damage. Overall, Heaton and Crowley conclude that, with the exception of chronic schizophrenia, the majority (75%) of psychiatric patients could be classified correctly. Hence, there appears to be a consensus that schizophrenics do poorly on neuropsychological tests. The crucial question, however, is *how* they do poorly.

Although the nature of the neuropsychological impairment in schizophrenia has been controversial, overall it appears that schizophrenics do perform poorly on neuropsychological measures and may have a reliable pattern of test results: they perform poorly on tests of long-term verbal and nonverbal memory, as well as on tests sensitive to left or right frontal lobe function. Performance on tests of visual discrimination, spatial orientation, and short-term verbal and nonverbal memory appears to be less affected. These results are concordant with the view that schizophrenia primarily affects frontal and temporal lobe structures. (We must caution, however, that people who have been chronically institutionalized as schizophrenics may not perform normally on *any* test, rendering the assessment of them futile.)

AFFECTIVE DISORDERS

The term "affect" refers to feeling state, or mood. Affective disorders are those in which there is a disturbance of mood. Although there may be many types of affective disorders, there are two major disorders that represent the extremes in mood. Depression refers to severe dejection; mania signifies an extremely elated feeling. Most people have experienced some form of mild depression and can understand what the feelings must be like in extreme form. Mania is more difficult to imagine and is illustrated by the following case.

Josh Logan had his first manic attack when he was directing the Broadway production of *Charlie's Aunt*. It was an exciting time, as the play was a smash hit:

> *Charlie's Aunt* continued to be my entree everywhere. My checks were accepted easily. I handed tickets out like handbills—to a shoe salesman, a stenographer. . . . I sent flowers by the carloads and I began investing in plays, which merely increased the script load and seekers of advice. I had a self assurance that was incredible even to me, and I seemed able to convince anybody of anything. It was as though I was speaking someone else's lines. I'd say to a girl in a store, "You're coming to bed with me tonight at 8:00—here's my card." And she came. My wishes were granted almost too easily. Life was a fantasy of utter freedom.

Of course, there was some justification for the elation, but it quickly progressed beyond mere joy. As the attack develops, judgment deteriorates and the person is unwilling to accept the idea that he or she is behaving abnormally:

> There was no way I could make him [a psychiatrist] understand that this high whizzing feeling I had now delighted me. It was true that when people crossed me I turned nasty, but as long as I got my way I considered myself the nicest guy in the world. I was full of extra warmth for taxi drivers, waitresses, clerks, anyone who was helpful—and I kept talking nice, no matter how nervous my behavior made them. I was forever offering everyone free dinners or seats to *Charlie's Aunt*. If this sense of freedom and expansiveness was manic, then manic was what I'd been hoping for all my life (Logan, 1973, p. 30)

Insight into the neurobiological basis of depression came from the observation that patients given reserpine for high blood pressure often became severly depressed. Reserpine depletes monoamines, which include norepinephrine, dopamine, and serotonin. This led to the idea that monamines might be reduced in depression and enhanced in mania. Research in the past few years has complicated the picture, because it is now clear that there are many different receptors for each monamine and that specific monoamine receptors may be disrupted in depression. Furthermore, depression turns out to involve hormonal systems (Figure 25.3). Both norepinephrine and serotonin modulate the secretion of hormones by the hypothalamic-adrenal system. The best-established abnormality in the hypothalamic-adrenal system is an oversecretion of the hormone hydrocortisone (cortisol). Cortisol, which is secreted by the adrenal glands, is associated with stress. When stressed, the hypothalamus secretes corticotropin-releasing hormone, which stimulates the pituitary to produce adrenocorticotropin (ACTH). The ACTH circulates through the blood and stimulates the adrenal gland to produce cortisol. The hypothalamic neurons that begin this cascade are regulated by norepinephrine neurons in the locus coeruleus. Since antidepressent drugs effect norepinephrine, these drugs must also influence the regulation of the stress system. The possibility that the body's stress reaction is abnormal in depression has important implications, because stress-related hormones and transmitters have a widespread influence on cerebral functioning.

The recent development of antidepressants such as Prozac that have specific actions on serotonin has led to the conclusion that an abnormality in serotonergic activity must also be a component of depression. Since serotonin is a vasodilator, its absence would be predicted to reduce blood flow because of relative vasoconstriction. In fact, it does: both blood-flow and PET studies have shown a bilateral reduction of cerebral activity in depressed persons. Diffuse reduction of cerebral activity might be expected to produce a variety of neuropsychological symptoms related to poor cerebral processing through-

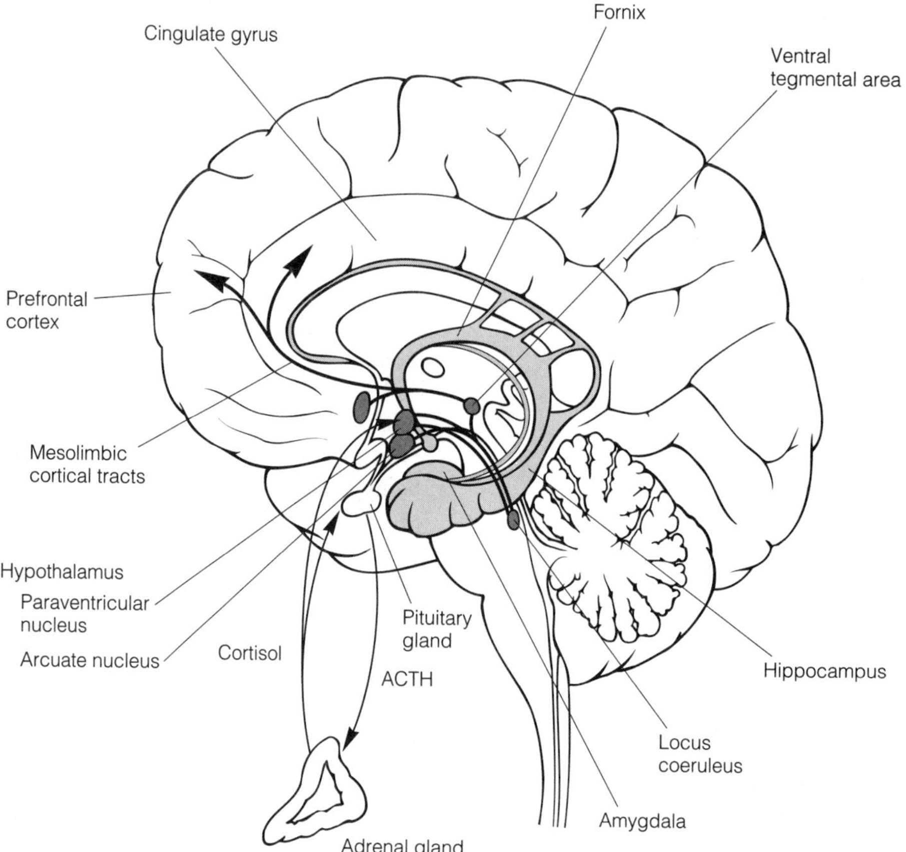

FIGURE 25.3. Medial view of the right hemisphere illustrating the brain stress system. It includes neurons containing norepinephrine, which have their cell bodies in the locus coreuleus; neurons containing corticotrophin-releasing hormone, which are in the hypothalamus; and neurons containing dopamine, which have their cell bodies in the ventral tegmentum. When activated, the system affects mood and thought and, indirectly, the secretion of cortisol by the adrenal glands. Deactivation normally begins when cortisol binds to hypothalamic receptors. In depression, this shutdown fails, producing chronic activation.

out the cortex. The extent of the deficit would be revealed by the difficulty of the test, rather than by the specific function assessed.

Since serotonin is thought to play a key role in the sleep-waking cycle, it might be expected that EEG studies would reveal cortical abnormalities in this cycle. Kupfer and Thase have found that slow-wave sleep is abnormal and that the onset of paradoxical sleep (REM sleep, or dreaming) is more rapid in depressed people. The researchers believe this measure to be a sensitive clinical test for depression. Further, they believe that the prognosis for the effectiveness of any particular antidepressant agent is likely to appear in the EEG before it does so clinically. Finally, it might be predicted that some depressed people would exhibit only regional reduction in cortical activity because of some local disruption of neurotransmitter levels, and thus there might be different types of depressions characterized by different patterns of cerebral dysfunction.

MOTOR DISORDERS

There is a group of diseases having clinical symptoms marked by abnormalities in movement and posture that are referrable to dysfunctions of the basal ganglia. Although the most obvious symptom of these diseases is the motor affliction, they all produce cognitive changes as well, which become especially marked as the diseases progress. Indeed, many patients with these diseases develop symptoms similar to those of schizophrenia. Clinically, two groups of symptoms are distinguished: (1) a loss of movement, which is referred to as a hypokinetic-rigid syndrome (for example, Parkinson's disease); and (2) an increase in motor activity, which is known as a hyperkinetic-dystonic syndrome (for example Huntington's chorea).

Huntington's Chorea

Huntington's chorea (*chorea* is from the Greek for dance) is a genetic disorder that results in intellectual deterioration and abnormal movements as the person afflicted reaches certain ages. George Huntington was 8 years old when he first saw people with "that disorder," as it was then called. He was driving with his father in his native New York when they came upon two women who were tall, thin, and twisting and grimacing. No doubt the disorder was familiar to his father and grandfather, who were both physicians. Nevertheless, the sight of these women left such a profound impression on him that he studied the disease when he later became a physician. In 1872, when he was 22, he wrote the first complete description of the disease. The history of the disease and its origin in the United States has been told by Vessie, who traced it to the village of Bures in England in 1630. At that time whole families in Bures and its vicinity were branded and tried as witches. Some family members, who had or carried the disease, sailed to America among the 700 passengers of the John Winthrop fleet in 1630. In 1653, Ellin Wilkie (name fictitious), who had arrived with Winthrop, apparently had the disorder, for she was tried and hanged for witchcraft. Her granddaughter was later tried and pardoned in 1692. Part of the early history of establishing the genetic basis for the disease involved tracing the family background of afflicted individuals whose ancestors had arrived among the Winthrop passengers and who had moved to other areas of the country. In other countries that were colonized by Europeans, similar family histories have been constructed that trace the disease back to one or a few immigrants. Huntington's chorea is relatively rare, with death rates of 1.6 per million population per year. It is most common among white Europeans and their descendants; it is very rare in other racial groups such as Asians and Africans. The number of people who will develop the disease is now thought to be on the decline because of advances in genetic counseling.

Huntington's chorea, or hereditary chorea, is a progressive degenerative disease. The first symptom is usually a reduction of activity and restriction of interest. The first restless and involuntary movements may be attributed to hysteria or some other disorder. The first movements usually appear within a year of the onset of the psychiatric symptoms. The involuntary movements are initially slight and consist of little more than continual fidgeting, but they slowly increase until they are almost incessant. The movements never involve single muscles but include whole limbs or parts of a limb. They are also irregular and follow no set pattern. A reliable sign of the disease is that a sustained muscular contraction is not possible: when an object is held, the grip fluctuates; also, the tongue cannot be held protruded. Eventually, the movements become uncontrollable and affect the head, face, trunk, and limbs—impeding speech, swallowing, walking, writing, and other voluntary movements. Sometimes individuals attempt to mask the abnormal movements with purposeful ones. There are emotional and personality changes, impairments of recent memory, defective ability to manipulate acquired knowledge, and slowing of information processing. Apraxia, aphasia, and agnosias, which result from certain cortical diseases such as Alzheimer's disease do not develop, however. The emotional changes include anxiety, depression, mania, and schizophrenialike psychoses. Suicide is not uncommon in younger patients.

The first symptoms of the disorder usually occur in people 30 to 50 years of age. About 5% of cases, sometimes called "juvenile chorea," begin before age 20. In contrast with adult cases, juvenile cases may exhibit muscle rigidity and slow movements, somewhat similar to those in Parkinson's disease, and they may also have muscle spasms, tremor, disturbances of eye movement, and epilepsy. Adult patients live an average of 12 years after disease onset, but the progress of the disease is far more rapid in the juvenile cases.

Huntington's chorea is transmitted genetically as an autosomal dominant with complete penetrance, meaning that half the offspring of an affected individual will develop the disease. The approximate location of the gene is now known, and a marker can be used before symptoms appear to determine whether a family member (even in utero) will develop the disease. Using recombinant DNA procedures and a population in Venezuela, Gusella and colleagues have narrowed the locus of the gene to a portion of the short arm of chromosome 4 and have detected a marker linked with this gene.

At autopsy, the brains of people with Huntington's chorea show shrinkage and thinning of the cerebral cortex. The basal ganglia are also grossly atrophied and show a marked loss of intrinsic neurons. One dominant explanation of the disease is that there is an imbalance among the various neurotransmitter systems of the basal ganglia. A simplified model of the transmitter systems involved is shown in Figure 25.4. They include (1) a glutamate projection from the cortex to the basal ganglia, (2) a γ-aminobutyric acid (GABA) projection from the basal ganglia to the substantia nigra, (3) a dopamine (DA) projection from the substantia nigra to the basal ganglia, and (4) acetylcholine (ACh) neurons in the basal ganglia. It is postulated that the intrinsic neurons of the basal ganglia (GABA and ACh neurons) die during the course of the disease, leaving a largely intact nigrostriatal DA pathway. As a result of the decrease in inhibition of the DA cells by the GABA pathway, there is an increase in DA release in the basal ganglia. The hyperactivity of the dopamine system is thought to produce the characteristic abnormal movements. Exactly how the movements are produced is not clear, but if the basal ganglia have a modulatory effect on the corticobublar and corticospinal systems, then the release of these two systems from modulation could produce the typical abnormal movements. Support for the idea that there is an increase in dopamine activity comes from two sources. First, biochemical analysis of the brain tissue of Huntington patients at autopsy shows a significant increase in dopamine levels. Second, drugs that tend to ameliorate chorea, such as major tranquilizers, are those that block dopamine, whereas those that aggravate chorea, such as amphetamines, are dopamine agonists.

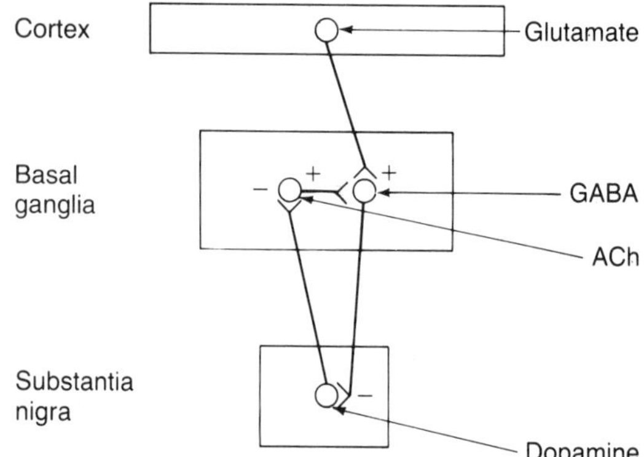

FIGURE 25.4. Model of transmitter systems involved in Huntington's chorea. It is thought that ACh and GABA neurons in the basal ganglia die, and as a result dopamine cells are released from GABA inhibition and become hyperactive, thus producing abnormal movements. The death of GABA cells may be caused by excessive activity of the glutamate pathway.

Extensive neurpsychological studies by Fedio and colleagues and by Wexler have shown that Huntington patients are impaired at a broad range of memory tests, as well as at visual, auditory, and tactile perceptual tests. In addition, such patients are especially poor at performing various frontal lobe tests (for example, Chicago Word-Fluency Test, stylus-maze test). People who have at least one parent with the disease, and thus can be considered at risk, appear to perform poorly only on the frontal lobe tests, suggesting that these tests might be useful as predictors of the disease. The effectiveness of these tests as predictors will be seen in the coming years as the subjects from these studies do, or do not, begin to display other symptoms. There is a large-scale study currently being conducted in Canada in which people at risk are having genetic tests (which can now identify those individuals who will develop Huntington's symptoms) as well as neuropsychological assessments. Notwithstanding the moral challenges of such a study, it is likely to provide valuable clues about the neuropsychological changes that are (or are not) present in the early stages of Huntington's chorea.

Gilles de la Tourette's Syndrome

Tourette's syndrome (**TS**) was described by Gilles de la Tourette in a two-part paper published in 1885. In most important ways this paper is still a remarkably good description of the disorder. Until Gilles de la Tourette's review, this syndrome was seen either as an undifferentiated chorea or as a symptom of hysteria, and it went by a variety of names depending on where it had been observed. The symptoms tend to evolve and to become more elaborate with age. Gilles de la Tourette described three stages of the syndrome. In the first stage, only multiple tics (twitches of the face, limbs, or the whole body) occur. In the second stage, inarticulate cries are added to the multiple tics. In the third stage, the emission of articulate words with **echolalia** (repeating what others have said, and also repeating actions) and *coprolalia* (*copro* from the Greek for dung, but now meaning obscene or lewd, and *lalia,* meaning speech) are added to the multiple tics and inarticulate cries. The following is a case history reported by Gilles de la Tourette that illustrates most of the major features of the syndrome:

Miss X, fifteen years old, spent several months at the Longchamps hydrotherapy institution at Bordeaux during the winter of 1883, where she was treated for convulsive attacks of chorea and ejaculations of loud vulgar and obscene words. Miss X. was very intelligent, she learned the lessons given her by her teacher with the greatest ease, and she played the piano well. She was tall and largely built. She was not well disciplined.

Her mother had never had a neurological disease. Her father had a convulsive, though not painful, facial tic. She had a strange, almost crazy, aunt, who lived alone. She had fits of hysteria, morbid hunger, and sometimes long periods of melancholy in which she refused to talk to anyone.

When nine, Miss X. began having violent and irregular choreiform tics of the face, arms, and legs. At the same time she occasionally uttered a few vulgar words. After a few months the attacks disappeared. A year later they came back again. The tics first reappeared in the shoulders, then in the arms, and then in the face, where they were accompanied by loud guttural sounds. These indistinct sounds became very clearly articulated when she was thirteen. At that time her most frequent words were "get away, go away, imbecile." A little later her words became more frequent and much clearer, and were rough and lewd. She remained that way until the present.

Miss X. belonged to an upper-class family. Her education was excellent. She never left her mother, who surrounded her in continuous, tender loving care. One had to wonder how and where she picked up the words she continually uttered: e.g., "In God's name, fuck, shit, etc." When she is in her calm normal state such words never pass her lips.

Whenever Miss X. was in the presence of someone she was afraid of, or who intimidated her, she was able to suffocate the sounds by a sheer effort of will. By clenching her teeth convulsively she could prevent the words from being understood. All one heard

> then was a kind of vague growling. As soon as she was alone the usual words poured out in added abundance.
>
> The words were always pronounced with a series of convulsive tics of the face, the shoulders, the trunk. Often, convulsive attacks happened without any word being spoken. At other times the words could be smothered and rendered incomprehensible by an intense effort of will. During sleep, spasmodic movements and involuntary words ceased altogether. (Gilles de la Tourette, 1885, pp. 41–42; translated by Lorna Whishaw)

Gilles de la Tourette recognized that individuals with the syndrome could be intelligent and productive and that they were not neurotic or psychotic. He also noted that the syndrome, or parts of it, ran in families and thus seemed hereditary. Gilles de la Tourette pointed out that there was no treatment (although the symptoms lessened or disappeared during fevers), so that the symptoms were likely to be with the person for life. Recently, there has been renewed interest in TS largely through the work of the Tourette Society in North America. Many TS patients have been misdiagnosed as troublemakers, hysterics, schizophrenics, and so forth, no doubt because they seemed intelligent yet displayed bizarre behavior. This is now changing, and there is great interest in trying to understand the cause of the disorder in terms of brain function.

The incidence of TS is less than 1 in 100,000, but the incidence can vary with the degree of professional knowledge about the disorder. In our area, which has a population base of about 100,000, a child psychiatrist interested in the disorder has diagnosed more than 10 cases. Thus, the actual incidence may be somewhat higher than the estimated incidence. From work by Shapiro and Shapiro, the following features of TS are known. TS occurs in all racial groups, and the male-to-female ratio is about 3 to 1. It seems to be hereditary, because between 30% and 40% of TS individuals have a family member who either has the disorder or displays various types of tics. It also seems more common for females to transmit the disorder. Nevertheless, the genetic basis of TS is not known, and it has been suggested that there are hereditary and nonhereditary groups of TS individuals. The average age of onset ranges between 2 and 15 years, with a median of 7 years, and by 11 years symptoms have appeared in 97% of cases. The most frequent symptoms are tics involving the eye, head, or face (97%), upper limbs (81%), and lower limbs and body (55%). Complex movements including touching, hitting, and jumping occur in between 30% and 40% of cases. Coprolalia may develop in up to 60% of cases and then disappear in a third of these. As noted above, TS is not associated with neuroses, psychoses, or other disorders. EEG activity is often normal, although some patients may display abnormalities. Evoked-potential studies show that the premovement potentials associated with willed, voluntary movements do not occur with the tics in TS patients, which confirms that these movements are involuntary.

It is thought that TS has a subcortical origin, possibly in the basal ganglia. This idea is supported in part by studies that have found Tourette-like symptoms in patients with other basal ganglia disorders that have been induced by other diseases or by long-continued use of major tranquilizers. There have been very few autopsy examinations of the brains of TS patients, and of those that have been done there is one report of an excessive number of small cells in the basal ganglia and reports that the cells there are normal. A major piece of evidence that implicates the basal ganglia comes from effective drug therapy. To date, the most consistent improvements are obtained with antidopaminergic agents such as haloperidol; thus it is thought that there may be some abnormality in the dopamine system in the basal ganglia. Clonidine, a norepinephrine receptor agonist, also is reported to be effective in some cases.

A number of neuropsychological studies have been done, and these studies suggest that there are abnormalities in some cognitive functions usually supported by the right hemisphere. Sutherland and his colleagues gave a composite test battery to a large sample of children and adults with

Tourette's syndrome and found that the patients were especially bad at drawing and remembering complex geometric figures, although they also performed poorly on the Chicago Word-Fluency Test, which is especially sensitive to orbital frontal dysfunction. The poor performance of these patients on the Rey Complex-Figure Test was particularly striking, since even patients with superior verbal IQs performed very poorly when compared with control children or schizophrenic patients (Figure 25.5). These results, as well as similar findings by Shapiro, suggest that Tourette patients may have a right frontotemporal dysfunction, but owing to the limited number of studies published to date, this conclusion must be considered tentative.

Parkinson's Disease

The individual symptoms of **Parkinson's disease** have been described by physicians from the time of Galen, but their occurrence as a syndrome was not recognized until 1817. In that year James Parkinson, a London physician, published an essay in which he argued that several different motor symptoms could be considered together as a group forming a distinctive condition. His observations are interesting not only because his conclusion was correct, but also because he made his observations in part at a distance by watching the movements of victims of Parkinson's disease in the streets of London. Parkinson's disease has been called the *shaking palsy* or its Latin equivalent, *paralysis agitans,* but it received its more common designation from Jean Charcot, who suggested that the disease be renamed to honor James Parkinson's recognition of its essential nature.

Parkinson's disease is fairly common; estimates of its incidence vary from 0.1% to 1.0% of the population, and the incidence rises sharply in old age. It is also of interest for a number of other reasons. First, the disease seems to be related to the degeneration of the **substantia nigra** and to the loss of the neurotransmitter dopamine, which is produced by cells of this nucleus. The disease, therefore, provides an important insight into the role of this brainstem nucleus and its neurotransmitter in the control of movement. Second, because a variety of pharmacological treatments for Parkinson's disease relieve different features of its symptoms to some extent, the disease provides a model for understanding pharmacological treatments of motor disorders more generally. Third, although Parkinson's is described as a disease entity, the symptoms vary enormously among people, thus illustrating the complexity with which the components of movement are organized to produce fluid motion. Fourth, because many of the symptoms of Parkinson's disease strikingly resemble changes in motor activity that occur as a consequence of aging, the disease provides indirect insight into the more general problems of neural changes in aging.

There are four major symptoms of Parkinson's disease: tremor, rigidity, akinesia, and disturbances of posture, each of which may be manifest in different body parts in different combinations. Since some of the symptoms involve the appearance of abnormal behaviors and others the loss of normal behaviors, we shall discuss the symptoms in these two major categories: positive and negative. Positive symptoms are behaviors not seen in normal people or seen only so rarely, and then in such special circumstances, that they can be considered abnormal. Negative symptoms are marked not by any particular behavior but rather by the absence of a behavior or by the inability to engage in an activity.

Positive Parkinson's Symptoms. Since positive symptoms are common in Parkinson's disease, they are thought to be held in check, or inhibited, in normal people but released from inhibition in the process of the disease. The most common positive symptoms are the following:

1. Tremor at rest. Tremor consists of alternating movements of the limbs when they are at rest; these movements stop during voluntary movements or during sleep. The tremors of the hands often have a "pill-rolling" quality, as if a pill were being rolled between the thumb and forefinger.

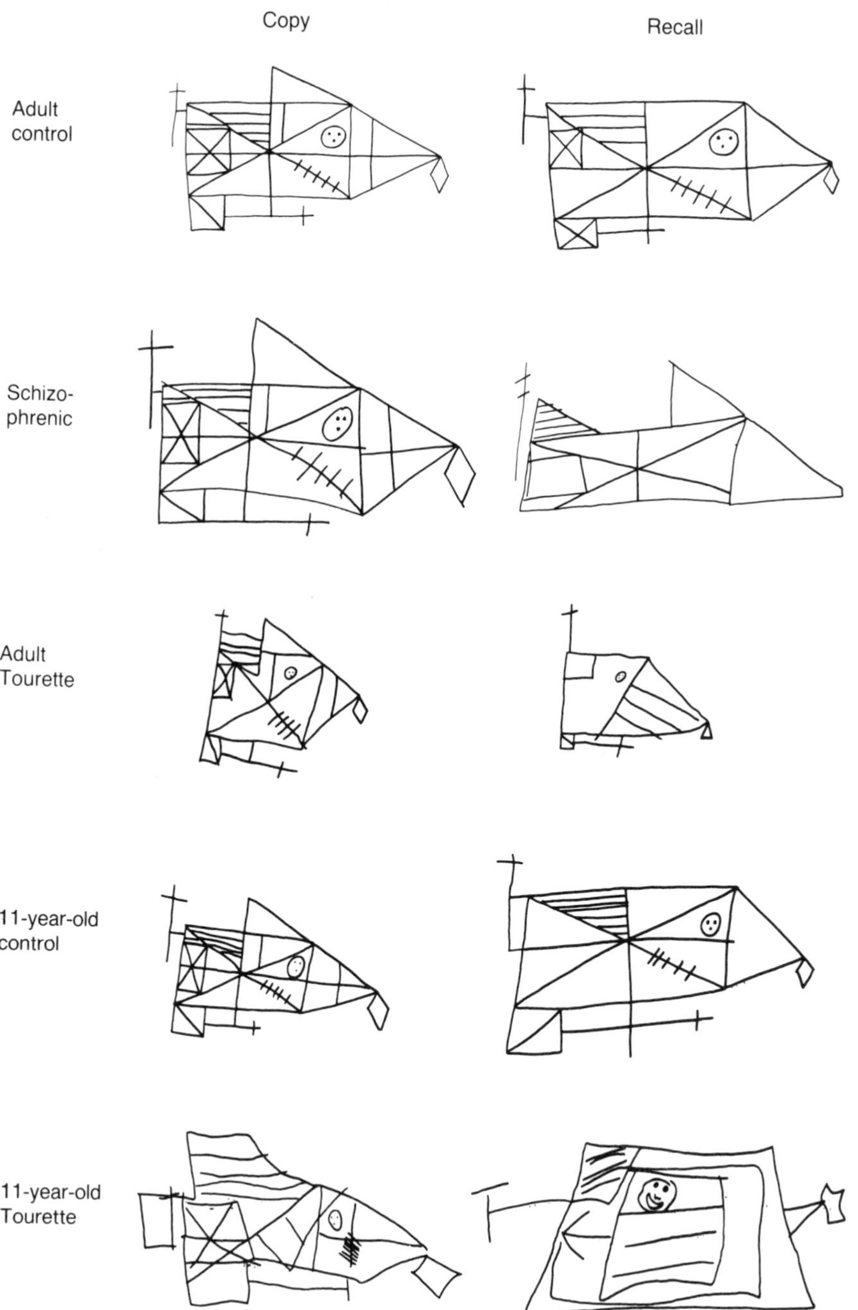

FIGURE 25.5. Representative performance by a normal adult control, a schizophrenic, an adult Tourette patient, a normal child, and a child Tourette patient on the Rey Complex-Figure Test: copying and recall. The Tourette patients are impaired at both the copying and the recall; the schizophrenic patient is impaired only at the recall. (After Sutherland et al., 1982.)

2. Muscular rigidity. Muscular rigidity consists of increased muscle tone simultaneously in both extensor and flexor muscles. It is particularly evident when the limbs are moved passively at a joint; movement is resisted, but with sufficient force the muscles yield, for a short distance, then resist movement again. Thus, complete passive flexion or extension of a joint occurs in a series of steps, giving rise to the term cogwheel rigidity. The rigidity may be severe enough to make all movements difficult. One man less severely afflicted by rigidity was moved to comment to us, "The slowness of movement is conscious but not willed. That is, I form a plan in my mind; for instance, I wish to uncork that bottle. Then I deliberately invoke the effort that sets the muscles in motion. I'm aware of the slowness of the process; I'm unable to increase [its speed], but I always get the bottle open."

3. Involuntary movements. These may consist of continual changes in posture, sometimes to relieve tremor and sometimes to relieve stiffness, but often for no apparent reason. These small movements or changes in posture, sometimes referred to as **akathesia** or "cruel restlessness," may be concurrent with general inactivity. Other involuntary movements are distortions of posture, such as occur during *oculogyric crisis* (involuntary turns of the head and eyes to one side), which last for periods of minutes to hours.

Since the positive symptoms are "actions," they are caused by the activity of some brain area. Before drug therapy became more common, one of the treatments used to stop the positive symptoms was to localize the source of the symptom and make a lesion there. For example, tremor was treated by lesions made in the ventral lateral thalamus. This treatment was abandoned because improvement was only temporary. Recently, improvements in how the lesions are made and in their accurate placement has led to a resurgence in this therapy. Additionally, it has been found that the best results are obtained with lesions to the internal portion of the globus pallidus (which eventually projects to the ventral lateral thalamus).

Negative Parkinson's Symptoms. J. P. Martin divided patients severely affected with Parkinson's disease into five groups, after detailed analysis of negative symptoms:

1. Disorders of posture. There are disorders of fixation and of equilibrium. A *disorder of fixation* consists of an inability to maintain, or difficulty in maintaining, a part of the body (head, limbs, and so forth) in its normal position in relation to other parts. Thus, a person's head may droop forward, or a standing person may gradually bend farther forward until he or she ends up on the knees. *Disorders of equilibrium* consist of difficulties in standing or even sitting when unsupported. In less severe cases, individuals may have difficulty standing on one leg, or, if pushed lightly on the shoulders, they may fall passively without taking corrective steps or attempting to catch themselves.

2. Disorders of righting. These disorders consist of difficulty in achieving a standing position from a supine position.

3. Disorders of locomotion. Normal locomotion requires support of the body against gravity, stepping, balancing while the weight of the body is transferred from one limb to another, and pushing forward. Parkinson patients have difficulty initiating stepping, and when they do, they shuffle with short footsteps on a fairly wide base of support because they have trouble maintaining equilibrium when shifting weight from one limb to the other. Often, Parkinson patients who have begun to walk demonstrate **festination:** they take faster and faster steps and end up running forward.

4. Disturbances of speech. These disturbances consist mainly of difficulties in the physical production of sound and in changing tone of voice. In fact, one of the symptoms most noticeable to relatives is the almost complete absence of tone in the speaker's voice.

5. Akinesia. Akinesia refers to a poverty or slowness of movement, which may also manifest itself in a blankness of facial expression or a lack of

blinking, swinging of the arms when walking, spontaneous speech, or normal movements of fidgeting. It is also reflected in difficulty making repetitive movements, such as tapping, even in the absence of rigidity. People who sit motionless for hours show akinesia in its most striking manifestation.

The symptoms of Parkinson's disease begin insidiously, often with a tremor in one hand and with slight stiffness in the distal portions of the limbs. Movements may then slow, the face becoming masklike with loss of eye blinking and poverty of emotional expression. Thereafter the body may become stooped, while the gait becomes a shuffle with the arms hanging motionless at the sides. Speech may become slow and monotonous, and difficulty in swallowing saliva may make drooling a problem. Although the disease is progressive, the rate at which the symptoms worsen is variable, and only rarely is progression so rapid that a person becomes disabled within 5 years; usually 10 to 20 years elapse before symptoms cause incapacity. One of the most curious aspects of Parkinson's disease is its on-again/off-again quality: symptoms may appear suddenly and disappear just as suddenly. Partial remission of Parkinson's disease may also occur in response to interesting or stimulating situations. Sacks recounts an incident in which a Parkinson patient leaped from his wheelchair at the seaside and rushed into the breakers to save a drowning man, only to fall back into his chair immediately afterward and become inactive again. Although remission of some symptoms in activating situations is common, remission is not usually as dramatic as in this case.

Causes of Parkinsonism. There are three major types of Parkinson's disease: idiopathic, postencephalitic, and drug-induced. Parkinson's disease may also result from arteriosclerosis, follow poisoning by carbon monoxide or manganese intoxication, or result from syphilis or the development of tumors. As suggested by its name, the *idiopathic* cause of Parkinson's disease is not known. Its origin may be familial or it may be part of the aging process, but it is also widely thought that it might have a viral origin. It most often occurs in people who are over 50 years of age. The *postencephalitic* form originated in the sleeping sickness (*encephalitis lethargica*) that appeared in the winter of 1916–1917 and vanished by 1927. Although the array of symptoms was bewilderingly varied, such that hardly any two patients seemed alike, Constantin von Economo demonstrated a unique pattern of brain damage associated with a viral infection in the brains of patients who had died from the disease. A third of those affected died in the acute stages of the sleeping sickness, in states of either coma or sleeplessness. Although many people seemed to recover completely from the sickness, most subsequently developed neurological or psychiatric disorders and parkinsonism. The latency between the initial and subsequent occurrences of the disease has never been adequately explained. Specific searches for viral particles or virus-specific products in Parkinson patients have revealed no evidence of viral cause. The third major cause of Parkinson's disease is more recent and is associated with ingestion of various drugs, particulary major tranquilizers that include reserpine and several phenothiazine and butyrophenone derivatives. The symptoms are usually reversible, but they are difficult to distinguish from those of the genuine disorder.

Recently, it has been found that external agents can cause Parkinson's symptoms quite rapidly. Langston and coworkers have reported that a contaminant of synthetic heroin, MPTP, is converted into MPP^+, which is extremely toxic to dopamine cells. A number of young drug users were found to display a complete Parkinsonian syndrome shortly after using contaminated drugs. This finding has suggested that other substances might cause similar effects. Demographic studies of patient admission in the cities of Vancouver and Helsinki show an increase in the incidence of patients getting the disease at ages younger than 40. This has raised the suggestion that water and air might contain environmental toxins that work in a fashion similar to MPTP.

Although Parkinson patients can be separated into clinical groups on the basis of cause of the disease, it is nevertheless likely that the mechanisms producing the symptoms have a common origin. Either the substantia nigra is damaged, as occurs in idiopathic and postencephalitic cases, or the activity of its cells is blocked or cells are killed, as occurs in drug-induced parkinsonism. The cells of the substantia nigra contain a dark pigment (hence its name); in Parkinson's disease this area is depigmented by degeneration of the melatonin-containing neurons of the area. Why the relatively selective degeneration occurs is not known, but it is possible that in viral cases the virus disturbs the metabolic pathways related to the formation of the pigment. The cells of the substantia nigra are the point of origin of fibers that go to the frontal cortex and basal ganglia and to the spinal cord. The neurotransmitter at the synapses of these projections is dopamine. It has been demonstrated by bioassay of the brains of deceased Parkinson patients, and by analysis of the major metabolite of dopamine—homovanallic acid, which is excreted in the urine—that the amount of dopamine in the brain is reduced by more than 90% and is often reduced to undetectable amounts. Thus, the cause of Parkinson's disease has been identified with some certainty as a lack of dopamine or, in drug-induced cases, as a lack of dopamine action. Dopamine depletion may not account for the whole problem in some people, however, since decreases of norepinephrine have been recorded, and there have been a number of reports that cells in some of the nuclei in the basal ganglia may degenerate as well.

Treatment of Parkinson's Disease. There is no known cure for Parkinson's disease, and none will be in sight until the factors that produce the progressive deterioration of the substantia nigra are known. Thus, treatment is symptomatic and directed toward support and comfort. The major symptoms of parkinsonism are influenced by psychological factors, a person's outcome being affected by how well he or she can cope with the disability. As a result, individuals should be counseled early regarding the meaning of symptoms, the nature of the disease, and the potential for most of them to lead long and productive lives. Physical therapy should consist of simple measures such as heat and massage to alleviate painful muscle cramps and training and exercise to cope with the debilitating changes in movement.

The drug treatments for Parkinson's disease are of considerable theoretical as well as practical interest. In recent years, understanding of the structure and function of synapses has been greatly advanced. Parkinson's disease provides an excellent model for understanding brain function with respect to synaptic action, because a specific constellation of symptoms has been linked with changes in a known neurotransmitter. Pharmacological treatment has two main objectives: first, increase the activity in whatever dopamine synapses remain; second, suppress the activity in structures that show heightened activity in the absence of adequate dopamine action. Drugs such as L-dopa, which is converted into dopamine in the brain; amantadine; amphetamine; monoamine oxidase inhibitors; and tricyclic antidepressants are used to enhance effective dopamine transmission. Naturally occurring anticholinergic drugs, such as atropine and scopolamine, and synthetic anticholinergics, such as benztropine (Cogentin), and trihexyphenidyl (Artane), are used to block the cholinergic systems of the brain that seem to show heightened activity in the absence of adequate dopamine activity.

Psychological Aspects of Parkinson's Disease. Although Parkinson patients are often described as manifesting many features of depression, they are also widely thought to show no psychological changes that parallel their motor disabilities. This latter view may be incorrect. On the basis of clinical observations, Sacks suggests that there are cognitive changes parallel to those reflected in motor activity. He emphasizes festination and resistance as positive symptoms of cognitive activity. As mentioned earlier, festination is manifested as an acceleration of walking, but it is also seen as a rushing of speech and even of thought. Resistance, however, has the opposite effect: as soon as speech or thought is attempted, it may be blocked by resistance. Thus, the two positive effects are in a sense opposites, and Parkinson patients might find themselves embattled, with festination counteracting resistance. Sacks has also emphasized that there are negative effects of the disease on cognitive function. There is an impoverishment of feeling, libido, motive, and attention; people may sit for hours, apparently lacking the will to enter or continue any course of activity.

Neuropsychological studies have confirmed that Parkinson's disease would seem to be associated with cognitive changes, particularly those changes normally found in patients with frontal lobe or basal ganglia lesions. This association is not so surprising, because there are close relations between the functions of the basal ganglia and the frontal cortex, and because there are dopamine projections into the frontal cortex that might be expected to degenerate in the same way that those of the basal ganglia degenerate. Having also tested patients before and after L-dopa treatment, Bowen reports that test performance is not noticeably improved by drug therapy.

It has been known for some time that Parkinson patients who are clearly demented at death show structural cortical changes similar to those of Alzheimer's disease, but it has been suggested more recently that Alzheimer-like neocortical abnormalities may be a characteristic of all Parkinson patients. For example, Hakim and Mathieson found that of 34 Parkinson patients' brains they examined, only 1 did not have clear evidence of Alzheimer-like abnormalities. Further, only 19 were claimed to have shown any clinical evidence of dementia, although no psychological tests were done on their sample.

Neuropsychological investigations of other populations have confirmed the possibility of a general cognitive deterioration in Parkinson patients. For example, in their extensive study, Pirozzolo and coworkers found Parkinson patients to be significantly impaired—relative to age-matched controls—on several subtests of the Wechsler Adult Intelligence Scale (WAIS) (information, digit span, digit symbol, and block design) and on measures of verbal memory (logical stories and paired associates). In addition, Parkinson patients are impaired on the Wisconsin Card-Sorting Test. There is no evidence of aphasia, agnosia, or apraxia in Parkinson patients, however.

In addition to symptoms of generalized dementia in Parkinson patients, there is evidence of an independent deficit in visuospatial abilities. For example, Boller and his colleagues have found Parkinson patients to be impaired on a wide array of visuospatial tests, independent of intellectual impairment.

Finally, like schizophrenia, the symptoms of Parkinson's disease are heterogeneous, and no two patients are identical in symptomatology. It has been estimated that there may be as many as 40 different types of Parkinson's disease, the variety presumably depending upon the pattern of pathology in individual cases.

ALZHEIMER'S DISEASE

That people can become depressed, suffer from lapses in memory, and become senile and demented in old age is well known. Furthermore, beginning with the earliest writings, references to "fatuity" and "dotage" appear regularly in the literature associated with aging. Historically, social attitudes toward aging and age-related changes have been quite variable, with some societies respecting people of old age and looking to them for guidance and wisdom and other societies displaying disinterest or even contempt for the aged. Explanations for age-related changes have been equally variable, with occasional writers suggesting that some of the debilitating age-related changes represent the process of disease and others suggesting that they are a routine part of the aging process. An additional important factor in influencing views toward aging has been the structure of societies. Attitudes vary between societies that are well established and those in flux, and between societies with disproportionately young and disproportionately old populations.

Population structures like those now developing in North America and Europe have never been experienced before. Since 1900, the percentage of older people has been steadily increasing. In 1900, about 4% of the population had attained 65 years of age. By 1980, about 10% of the population was over 65. It is fully expected that this trend will continue in developed nations and begin to emerge in developing nations. With the rise in the number of older people, there are parallel increases in the numbers of people with cognitive impairments related to an aging brain. This becomes a significant social and medical problem, because of the stress imposed on families and medical support systems.

Obviously, not every person who becomes old also becomes depressed, forgetful, or demented. Some people live to very old age and enjoy active, healthy, productive lives. Other people may show symptoms of senility at what would be considered a young age. Prevalence studies have found that in the population of people 65 and older, the incidence of severe dementia is between 1% and 6% and the incidence of mild dementia is between 3% and 20%. This range is wide and the values are imprecise because it is difficult to obtain reliable estimates. Attitudes toward aging, methods of reporting conditions in the aged, whether a family looks after a disabled person or sends him or her to an institution, and the criteria used by researchers all influence the data obtained from prevalence studies. The prevalence of dementia also varies with aging, with older age groups having higher incidences. Between ages 65 and 70, approximately 3% to 5% may be demented. This value rises to about 5% to 7% between ages 70 and 75, 7% to 9% between ages 75 and 80, and about 25% by age 85 and over. Interestingly, people living into their 90s or 100s have a reduced incidence of dementia, presumably because the demented subgroups have died at an earlier age. Although the incidence of dementia increases in populations 65 and older, cases do occur even among people 30 to 40 years old. At present there is relativey little known about prevalence based on other characteristics, including sex, social class, and country of domicile.

There are many causes of the dementia of old age, and some of the more prevalent are listed in Table 25.1. It is estimated, however, that more than 65% of the people suffering from various degrees of dementia have Alzheimer's disease.

TABLE 25.1. A short list of possible causes of dementia

Alzheimer's disease
Down's syndrome
Multiinfarct dementia
Toxic substances (drugs, alcohol)
Metabolic deficiency (e.g., vitamin B_{12})
Endocrine (e.g., hypothyroidism)
Infectious (e.g., neurosyphilis)
Inflammatory (e.g., vasculitis)
Posttrauma and postanoxia
Genetic (e.g., Huntington's chorea)
Degenerative (e.g., Parkinson's disease)
Cerebral tumors
Subdural hematoma
Hydrocephalus

Source: After van Crevel, 1986.

Alzheimer's disease is becoming more prevalent than Parkinson's disease. It has been estimated that about half a million people were afflicted with Parkinson's disease and half a million with Alzheimer's disease in the United States in 1976. By the 1980s the number of dementia cases had grown to more than 1 million, and by 1985 one estimate had put the number between 1.5 and 2 million people. In comparison, about one-quarter million had multiple sclerosis, 10,000 had Huntington's chorea, and 5000 had amyotrophic lateral sclerosis (Lou Gehrig's disease). A still more instructive aspect of these numbers is the care required for the dementia patients. About half are under institutional care, where they make up more than 60% of the population of nursing homes and various chronic care hospitals.

Definition of Alzheimer's Disease

By the 1800s, it was recognized that there are age-related changes in the brain. It was noted that the cortex of the brain undergoes ventricular dilation and atrophy, and the association between atrophy and senile dementia was noted by a number of people. The modern definition of **Alzheimer's disease** stems from a case study published by the German physician Alois Alzheimer in 1906. The patient was a 51-year-old woman for whom Alzheimer described a set of clinical and neuropathological findings. This description of symptoms and pathology became known as Alzheimer's disease.

The clinical definition of Alzheimer's disease according to the DSM-III includes the following three criteria: (1) dementia; (2) insidious onset with uniformly progressive deteriorating course; and (3) exclusion of all other specific causes of dementia by the history, physical examination, laboratory tests, psychometric tests, and other special studies. The definition takes into account that there can be other forms of dementia and that these can have different causes and courses.

Anatomical Correlates

Increased attention to Alzheimer's disease is leading to the identification of an enormous number of associated brain changes. The notion that the disease is primarily related to the loss of acetylcholine neurons that project from the basal forebrain (just anterior to the hypothalamus) to the neocortex, and is secondarily the cause of the anatomical changes in the brain, has gained recent currency. As the following descriptions will show, this is a simplistic view. There are widespread changes in the neocortex and limbic cortex and associated changes in a number of neurotransmitter systems, none of which alone can be correlated simply with the clinical symptoms. Interestingly, most of the brainstem, cerebellum, and spinal cord are relatively spared:

1. Neuritic plaques. Neuritic plaques, also known as senile plaques, are found chiefly in the cerebral cortex. Increased concentration of these plaques in the cortex has been correlated with the magnitude of cognitive deterioration. The plaques consist of a central core of homogeneous protein material known as *amyloid,* surrounded by degenerative cellular fragments. These include axonal and dendritic processes and other components of cells. These plaques are generally considered to be nonspecific phenomena in that they can be found in non-Alzheimer's patients, in dementias caused by other known events, and in patients with Down's syndrome.

2. Paired helical filaments. Paired helical filaments are also known as neurofibrillary tangles and are found in both the cerebral cortex and the hippocampus, with the posterior half of the hippocampus more severely affected than the anterior half. Light-microscope examination has shown that the filaments have a double helical configuration. They have been described mainly in human tissue and have also been observed in patients with Down's syndrome, patients with Parkinson's disease, and patients with other forms of dementias.

3. Granulovacuolar bodies. Granulovacuolar bodies consist of an outer membrane with a small dense granule in its center. These bodies are more common in Alzheimer's patients than in the general aged population.

4. Neocortical changes. The changes in the neocortex are not uniform. Although the cortex becomes shrunken or atrophied, losing as much as one-third of its volume as the disease progresses, some areas are relatively spared. Figure 25.6 shows lateral and medial views of the human brain; stippling indicates the areas of degeneration. The darker the stippling, the more severe the degeneration. As is clearly shown in this illustration, the primary sensory and motor areas of the cortex, especially the visual cortex and the sensorimotor cortex, are spared. The frontal lobes are less affected than the posterior cortex, but the areas of most extensive change are the posterior parietal areas, inferior temporal cortex, and limbic cortex.

5. Limbic cortex changes. The limbic system undergoes the most severe degenerative changes in Alzheimer's disease, and of the limbic structures the entorhinal cortex is affected earliest and most severely. A number of sources agree that the entorhinal cortex shows the clearest evidence of cell loss. This has important implications for understanding some of the symptoms of the disease. The entorhinal cortex is the major relay through which information from the neocortex gets to the hippocampus and related structures and then is sent back to the neocortex. Damage to the entor-

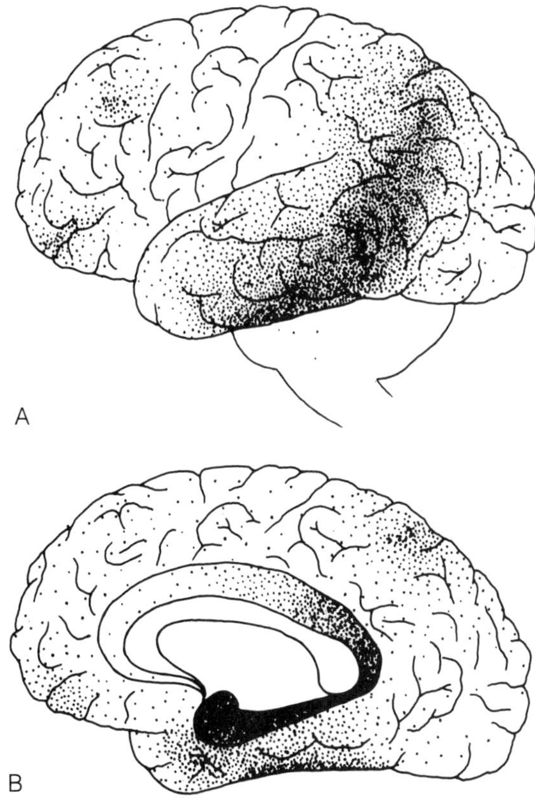

FIGURE 25.6. Schematic representation of the distribution and severity of degeneration on (*A*) lateral and (*B*) medial aspects of the brain in an average Alzheimer case. The darker the area, the more pronounced the degeneration. White areas are spared, with only basic change discernible. (After Brun, 1983.)

hinal cortex is associated with memory loss. Since memory loss is an early and enduring symptom of the disease, it is most likely caused by the degenerative changes that take place in this area of the cortex.

6. Cell changes. Although many studies describe loss of cells in the cortex of Alzheimer's patients, there is dispute. There seems to be a substantial reduction in large cells, but these cells may shrink rather than disappear. The more widespread cause of cortical atrophy, however, appears to be loss of dendritic arborization. Figure 25.7 illustrates cells drawn by Scheibel showing a normal adult pattern and early, advanced, and terminal patterns of pyramidal cells obtained from patients who had Alzheimer's disease. The earliest change appears to be a loss of dendritic spines, followed by a loss of small dendrites and then a loss of larger dendrites. In advanced stages, the triangular pattern of the cell gives way to a pear shape, and irregular swellings appear on the dendritic shaft. According to Scheibel, this pattern of changes appears to reverse the maturational pattern of the cells. The cause of these changes is not known. It is worth noting, however, that the changes are not simply typical of aging. Flood and Coleman have demonstrated that normal old people show increases in dendritic arborization between middle age (50s) and the 70s (see Figure 25.7). It is only in very old age that there is a pattern of degeneration that begins to look like Alzheimer's disease.

7. Neurotransmitter changes. A great deal of publicity has been given to findings that acetylcholine levels are reduced in Alzheimer's disease, and this has led to the idea that changes in this transmitter are causal in the memory declines shown by patients. Two points are relevant here, however. First, there are marked reductions in many transmitter systems. Second, the reductions in any one system are uneven from patient to patient. There are problems in estimating transmitter system levels through the course of the disease. The brain is not accessible for samples, so estimates are usually taken from urine or blood samples and these measures are usually by-products of neurotransmitter metabolism. The other source of tissue is that obtained at autopsy, and so such samples represent terminal levels of biochemical activity. There are a number of published studies on transmitter levels. The most representative of these, from Carlsson, shows reductions of about 50% in dopamine, 25% in norepinephrine, 50% in acetylcholine, and about 50% in serotonin. The most interesting feature of the changes is not the absolute decreases in any individual patient but the pattern of decreases. Although age-matched

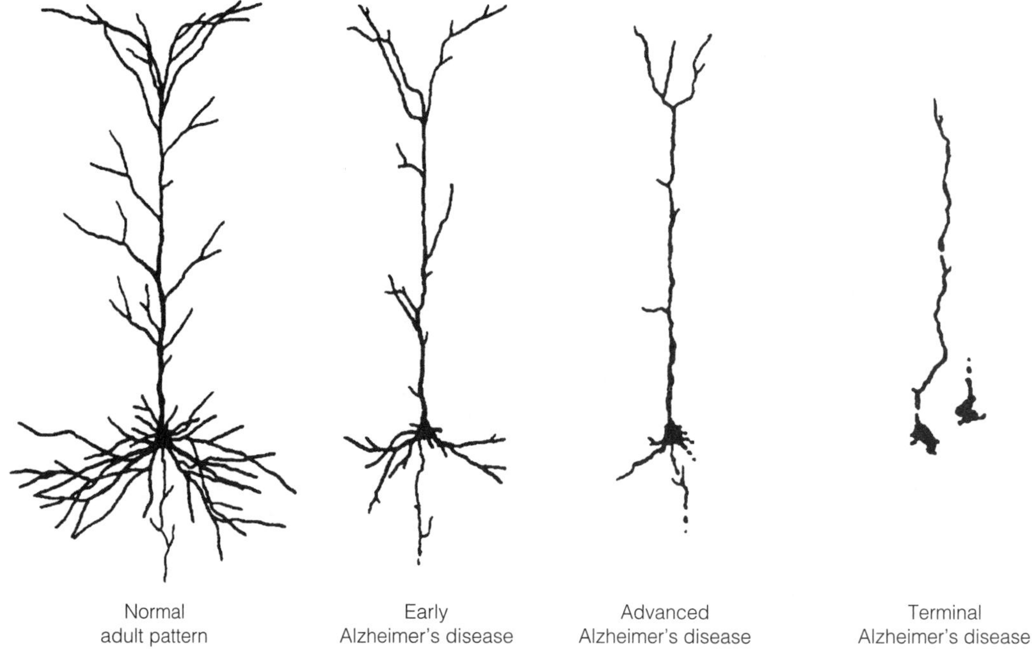
Normal
adult pattern
Early
Alzheimer's disease
Advanced
Alzheimer's disease
Terminal
Alzheimer's disease
A

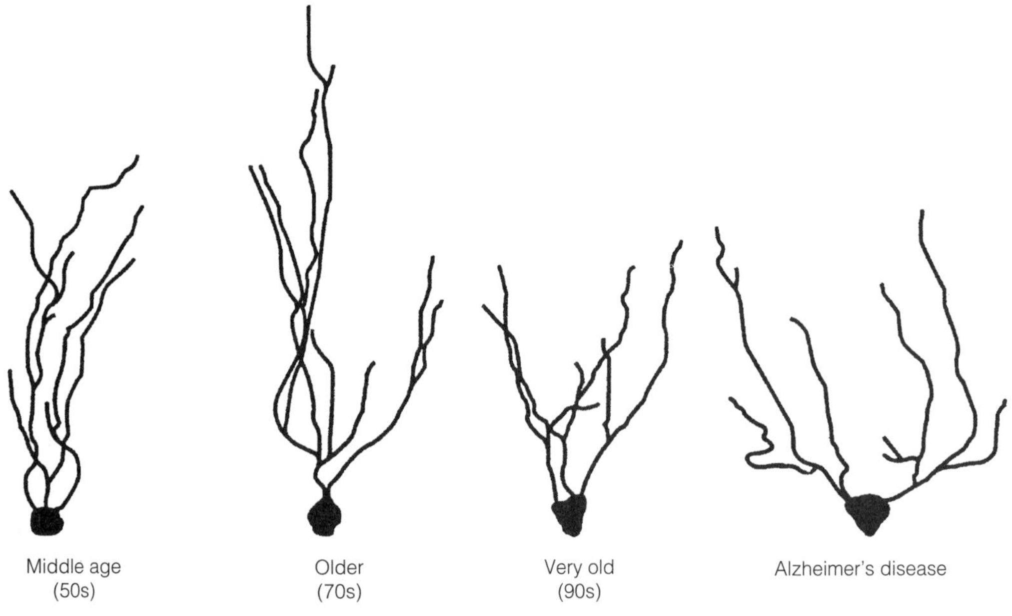
Middle age
(50s)
Older
(70s)
Very old
(90s)
Alzheimer's disease
B

FIGURE 25.7. *A.* Sequence of changes in a cortical pyramidal cell during development of Alzheimer's dementia (from left to right): normal adult pattern; early stages of disease marked by patchy spine loss and thinning out of the dendritic tree, especially horizontally oriented branches; advanced stage with almost complete loss of basilar dendrites; and terminal stage. (Drawn from Golgi-stained sections of human prefrontal cortex; after Scheibel, 1983.) *B.* Comparison of dendritic length of hippocampal neurons drawn from brain specimens of healthy humans in their 50s, 70s, and 90s and from a patient with Alzheimer's disease. The average length of dendrites increases from middle age into old age, decreasing only in late old age. Dendrites in brains with Alzheimer's disease do not show the age-related growth. (After Selkoe, 1992.)

controls also show reductions in transmitter levels, when the pattern of reductions in all three transmitter substances is plotted, the Alzheimer patients distinguish themselves from the control groups by showing greater reductions in two or more transmitters. The observation of combined neurotransmitter reductions, especially of acetylcholine and serotonin, may be extremely relevant to cognitive declines. Using the rat, Vanderwolf and his coworkers have demonstrated that one of the two activated EEG patterns of the neocortex requires acetylcholine; the other requires serotonin. If both are absent, rats display chronic sleeplike EEG activity even though they walk around. If they are asked to perform in learning tests, they show a complete absence of learning and memory, behaving essentially as if they had no neocortex at all. If Alzheimer's patients undergo the same EEG changes and end up with a "sleeping" neocortex, this might explain their severe cognitive impairments.

Putative Causes of Alzheimer's Disease

At present the cause of Alzheimer's disease is unknown. Consequently, research is being directed toward a large number of potential causes. We should note here, though, that most of the research is quite new. Only a few years ago there was very little research on aging and there were no funding agencies directing their interests toward diseases that complicate the aging process. That is gradually changing, and a large number of research projects now focus on aging in general and Alzheimer's disease in particular. These new research fronts are directed toward the following putative causes:

1. Genetics. There is an increased frequency of Alzheimer's disease in families that have had a member with Alzheimer's disease. The risk is 3.8% if a sibling has had the disease and 10% if a parent has had the disease. Researchers are also interested in the relationships between Down's syndrome and Alzheimer's disease because the neural changes that lead to dementia in Down's syndrome are very similar to those found in Alzheimer's disease. There is also increased risk of Alzheimer's disease in families that have had a member with Down's syndrome. Consequently, it is thought that a gene or a group of genes, possibly close to the Down's syndrome gene, could be identified as promoting or causing Alzheimer's disease.

2. Trace metals. Early studies with animals have identified neurofibrillary degeneration, similar to that in Alzheimer's disease, after the animals were given aluminum salts. Research that followed up this hint found increases of 10 to 30 times the normal concentration of aluminum in Alzheimer patients' brains. At present it is not known why aluminum accumulates or whether taking action to reduce accumulation could be helpful.

3. Immune reactions. Some researchers think that in old age the immune system loses its ability to recognize the individual's own body. As a result, it develops antibrain antibodies that then cause neuronal degeneration.

4. Slow viruses. The existence of slow viruses was suggested by studies on a Papua New Guinea tribe that ate the brains of deceased members. Years later, individuals would become ataxic with

a disease called *kurul,* die, and apparently pass on a virus—which in turn took years to produce symptoms—to others. Likewise, a disease called **Creutzfeldt-Jakob's disease** also appears to be caused by slow viruses and can be passed on to other humans and animals. In both diseases, the brain changes have some similarity to those of Alzheimer's disease. It has been suggested that material from human patients has caused Alzheimer's in chimpanzees. Attempts to replicate the experiment, to locate viruses, or to identify their source have been unsuccessful so far.

5. Blood flow. Originally, most Alzheimer's disease was attributed to poor circulation. More recent studies have confirmed that there is a profound reduction in the amount of blood delivered to the brain and the amount of glucose extracted from the blood. This has become readily apparent from PET studies. In normal people, blood flow to the brain declines by more than 20% between the ages of 30 and 60, but the brain compensates by more efficient oxygen uptake. In Alzheimer's, there is an enhanced decline but no compensatory mechanisms. The greatest decreases in blood flow are found in those areas of the brain in which the most degenerative change is seen. What is not known is whether the declines in blood flow and glucose use are causal or secondary to degenerative brain changes. At least one pharmacological attempt to treat Alzheimer's involves stimulating brain blood flow.

6. Abnormal proteins. The three main pathological changes associated with Alzheimer's disease—plaques, neurofibrillary tangles, and granulovacuolar bodies—reflect an accumulation of protein that is not seen in normal brains. This has led to the suggestion that unusual proteins are being produced and are accumulating, thus disrupting normal protein production and use. It has been proposed that the increased protein accumulation in the brain of an Alzheimer patient may reflect the brain's attempt to repair itself. During development, the brain makes various proteins that play an important role in cell growth. When the entorhinal cortex of laboratory animals is damaged unilaterally, the intact side reinitiates the protein manufacture of youth, leading to the sprouting of new connections. Thus, it is thought that the loss of neurons in the entorhinal cortex of the Alzheimer patient may initiate similar processes that go awry.

Clinical Symptoms and Progress

The most insidious feature of Alzheimer's disease is its slow onset and steady progress, which gradually rob a patient first of recent memory, then of more remote memory, and finally of the abilities to recognize family members and to function independently. A detailed description of the stages of the disease and clinical symptoms has been given by Reisberg and is reproduced in Table 25.2. As Reisberg points out, the disease progress is gradual, and patients spend several months to several years in each of the stages. Reisberg also describes levels of impairments in five measures of cognitive function (concentration, recent and past memory, orientation, social functioning, and self-care) that are descriptive parallels of the stages shown in Table 25.2.

Studies on the prognosis of the disease suggest that patients rated as being in the forgetfulness stage may remain there and show no further deterioration. Therefore, the symptom of forgetfulness has doubtful prognostic value. For patients classified in the later stages on the scale, 2-year follow-ups generally find further deterioration. Thus, rating in the later stages clearly has prognostic value. In the final stages of the disease, patients become susceptible to other disorders, infections, or pneumonia.

Neuropsychological Assessment

The diagnosis of Alzheimer's disease is necessarily postmortem, but recent adaptations of MRI scanning suggest that plaques and tangles can be detected in living patients. In view of the distinctive pattern of anatomical changes in the disease, one might expect a distinctive pattern of cognitive changes. Finding such a pattern would be important, because the symptoms displayed by Alzheimer's patients are often confused with those seen in other disorders, such as depression or a

TABLE 25.2. Scale of behavioral change in Alzheimer's disease

Degree of cognitive decline	Symptoms
None	No subjective complaints of memory deficit. No memory deficit evident on clinical interveiw.
Very mild	Complaints of memory deficit, most often in the following areas: (1) forgetting where one has placed familiar objects: (2) forgetting names one formerly knew well. No objective evidence of memory deficit on clinical interview. No objective deficits in employment or social situations. Appropriate concern with respect to symptomatology.
Mild	Earliest clear-cut deficits. Manifestations in more than one of the following areas: (1) patient may have gotten lost when traveling to an unfamiliar location; (2) coworkers become aware of patient's relatively poor performance; (3) patient may read a passage or a book and retain relatively little material; (4) patient may demonstrate decreased facility in remembering names upon introduction to new people; (5) patient may have lost or misplaced an object of value; (6) concentration deficit may be evident on clinical testing. Objective evidence of memory deficit obtained only with formal tests. Decreased performance in demanding employment and social settings. Denial begins to occur, and mild to moderate anxiety is displayed.
Moderate	Clear-cut deficit on clinical interview in (1) decreased knowledge of current and recent events; (2) memory of personal history; (3) concentration deficit on serial subtractions; (4) decreased ability to travel, handle finances, etc. Inability to perform complex tasks. Denial is dominant defense mechanism. Flattening of affect and withdrawal from challenging situations.
Moderately severe	Cannot function without some assistance. Unable to recall a major relevant aspect of current life: e.g., address or telephone number, names of close family members, name of schools from which they graduated. Frequent disorientation to date, day, season, and place. An educated person may have difficulty counting backward by 4s from 40 and 2s from 20.
Severe	May occasionally forget the name of spouse. Will be largely unaware of all recent events and experiences in their lives. Retain some knowledge of their past lives, but this is sketchy. May have difficulty counting back or forward to and from 10. Will require some assistance with activities of daily living; e.g., may become incontinent, will require travel assistance but occasionally will display ability to travel to familiar locations. Diurnal rhythm often disturbed. Can recall their own name and distinguish familiar from unfamiliar persons in their environment. Personality and emotional changes occur. These may include delusional behavior, obsessive symptoms, anxiety, or loss of purposeful behavior.
Very severe	All verbal abilities are lost. Often there is no speech at all—only grunting; incontinent of urine; requires assistance in toileting and feeding. Loses basic psychomotor skill; e.g., ability to walk. The brain appears no longer to be able to tell the body what to do.

Source: After Reisburg, 1983.

series of small strokes. In view of the distinctly different approaches to managing depressed and Alzheimer patients, differential diagnosis would be very useful. Fuld has used IQ subtest scales from the WAIS to distinguish the impairment patterns of Alzheimer's disease from those produced by cerebrovascular disease. Alzheimer patients are marked by the striking deficits they show on digit symbol and block design, with successively milder impairments on object assembly, similarities and digit span, and information and vocabulary. Other Alzheimer's-sensitive tests include backward digits, telling the time on clocks without numbers, and object naming. Additionally, Alzheimer patients can be expected to have deficits on tests of both left and right hemisphere function, and the impairments will not be marked by sudden onset.

In an examination of the encoding of memory, Becker and coworkers have reported that Alzheimer patients encode less than control subjects during learning, although they forget what they have learned at the same rate as control subjects. Martin and coworkers have confirmed this specific encoding deficit. In study of reading patterns, Cummings and coworkers have found that reading aloud remains relatively preserved, but memory for what is read is severely impaired. In an investigation of naming impairments, Huff and coworkers have observed that Alzheimer patients have difficulties in producing the names of objects and in distinguishing among objects within a category. They conclude that the anomia deficit is characterized by a loss of information about specific objects and their names, rather than by a simple difficulty in retrieving information. Murdoch and coworkers have examined the language impairments connected with Alzheimer's and compared them with impairments in other disorders. They note that the language impairments are most obvious on tasks requiring cognitive processing. Finally, others, such as Wilson and coworkers, have undertaken studies to compare different cognitive functions. They note, for example, that the pattern of deficits on language tasks is much more severe than on facial-recognition tasks, presumably because the language tasks require more demanding cognitive processing. These lines of inquiry will probably become more fruitful as brain metabolism studies are combined with specific forms of cognitive analysis.

PSYCHOSURGERY

The use of surgery to treat psychiatric disorders is a contentious issue, especially in the United States. We do not wish to enter the debate but rather will describe psychosurgery and its uses. For an excellent discussion of the psychosurgery issue, we recommend the 1980 text by Valenstein, *The Psychosurgery Debate.*

What Is Psychosurgery?

Valenstein defines **psychosurgery** as the destruction of some region in the brain to alleviate severe and otherwise intractable psychiatric disorders. To distinguish current psychosurgical techniques from earlier and cruder lobotomy operations, the term *psychiatric surgery* has been suggested as a substitute, although the term refers to the same procedures. Brain surgery intended to repair damage to alleviate symptoms resulting from known neurological disease is not considered psychosurgery, even if the patient has severe behavioral and emotional symptoms. Brain surgery to alleviate intractable pain is normally considered to be psychosurgery because the operations are performed on normal brain tissue and because serious emotional disturbances often accompany chronic pain.

The belief that mental aberrations are related to disturbances of brain function goes back to primitive times. The practice of opening the skull (trepanning) for magical-medical purposes was apparently performed extensively dating back at least to about 2000 B.C. Modern psychosurgery is usually traced to the Portuguese neurologist Egas Moniz, who started the prefrontal procedures in 1935. On the basis of studies of a small sample of monkeys and chimpanzees by Jacobsen, Moniz reasoned that destruction of the frontal lobe of psychiatrically ill people might be beneficial. Although he initially used alcohol injected into the frontal lobes to induce a frontal lesion, he soon switched to a technique in which nerve fibers were cut with a special knife called a *leukotome* (from the Greek *leuko,* meaning white nerve fibers: *tome,* meaning a cutting instrument). The procedure involved drilling holes over the white matter to sever the frontal connections. Later modifications in the procedure were made in the United States by Freeman and Watts, including the Freeman-Watts procedure of drilling holes in the temples and the lateral transorbital procedure of Freeman in which the leukotome was inserted through the bony orbit above the eyeball. It is impossible to estimate accurately how many psychosurgical procedures were performed worldwide, although Valenstein thinks that the best estimate for the United States is about 35,000 between 1936 and 1978.

The introduction of antipsychotic drugs in the mid-1950s led to a sharp reduction in the number of psychosurgical operations, but there still were a significant number of psychiatric patients who were not helped by the drugs. Thus, there has been a continuing interest in surgical intervention to change behavior, but since the 1960s there has been a change in the psychosurgical procedures employed, in part because of advances in the neurosciences. There are currently about 13 different targets of psychosurgical operations, which are summarized in Figure 25.8. These procedures generally produce smaller lesions than the original lobotomy-type procedures.

Who Receives Psychosurgery?

According to Valenstein, there is general agreement among psychiatrists and neurosurgeons who recommend or practice psychosurgery about who are the most appropriate patients for these operations. The major group of patients are described as "suffering from very intense and persistent emotional responses." This group includes patients suffering from depression, obsessive-compulsive disorders, anxiety, and phobias. Further, psychosurgery is performed for another group of patients to alleviate pain symptoms, the pain usually being described as "intense, persistent, crippling, and intractable." Typically, prior to pychosurgery, all these disturbances are claimed to be of long duration and resistant to other treatments such as drugs, ECT, and psychotherapy.

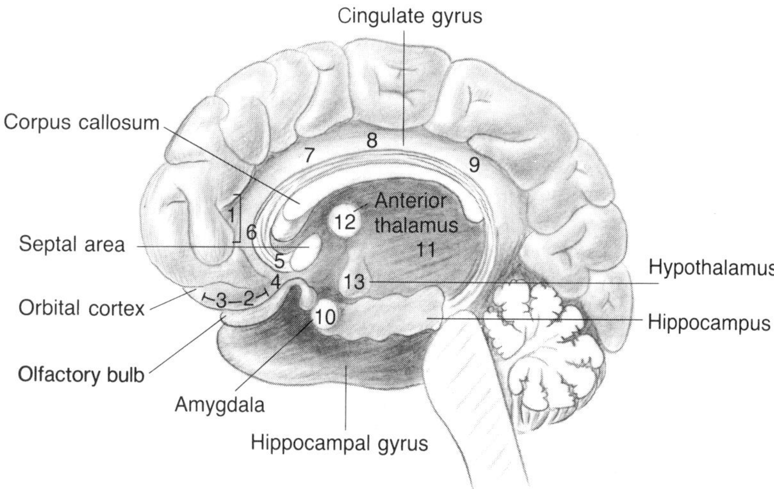

FIGURE 25.8. Approximate targets of psychosurgical operations currently in use. *Frontal lobe procedures:* (1) bimedial leukotomy; (2) yttrium lesions in subcortical white matter; (3) orbital undercutting; (4) bifrontal stereotaxic subcaudate tractotomy; (5) anterior capsulotomy (destruction of fibers of internal capsule); (6) mesoloviotomy (similar to rostral cingulotomy, but lesion invades the genu—"knee"—of the corpus callosum). *Cingulotomies:* (7) anterior cingulotomy; (8) midcingulotomy; (9) posterior cingulotomy. *Amygdalectomy:* (10) amygdalectomy or amygdalotomy. *Thalamotomies:* (11) thalamotomy of the dorsomedial, centromedian, or parafascicular nuclei; (12) anterior thalamotomy. *Hypothalamotomy:* (13) section of the posterior, ventromedial, or lateral hypothalamus. (After Valentstein, 1980.)

It is difficult to estimate the amount of psychosurgery currently performed. Valenstein estimates that 141 neurosurgeons in the United States performed approximately 400 operations per year between 1971 and 1973, a figure that has declined steadily since then. In England, approximately 200 to 250 psychosurgical procedures per year were performed between 1970 and 1977—a figure about twice as high as in the United States. Less psychosurgery seems to be performed in Canada, however, the rate being about half that in the United States.

The psychosurgery issue has broader implications. These have been spelled out in detail by Valenstein and are worth considering because they apply to many treatment strategies involving mental and psychiatric health. Central among the important questions is when it is permissible to institute or experiment with a new treatment. Psychosurgical treatment was begun and promoted without adequate background animal research. Treatment and patient selection were not subject to screening by an ethical committee. Follow-up studies, when done, were usually superficial and lacked scientific rigor. Nevertheless, in the view of the treatment-founding experimenters, competitive therapies and the general prognosis for patients were sufficiently dismal to warrent the use of psychosurgery. This dilemma is still with us, but now it also applies to the chronic administration of drugs and trophic factors, the use of electroconvulsive shock therapy, and the developing use of brain grafts for the treatment of degenerative brain disorders.

SUMMARY

Historically, psychiatry and neurology were the same field, and it is only recently that two separate specialties have emerged. It is clear, however, that for many patients the distinction is arbitrary. Diseases of the brain can produce profound psychological disturbances, even in such traditionally neurological disorders as Parkinson's disease. One characteristic of these disorders is that they often involve an imbalance of neurotransmitter systems, especially the catecholamines and acetylcholine. A second characteristic is that many involve frontal lobe dysfunction, which presumably leads to profound changes in affective behavior, or temporal lobe dysfunction, which is manifested in memory problems. Finally, none of the disorders has a focal abnormality, but rather a more generalized dysfunction. Even Parkinson's disease, with a discrete loss of cells in the substantia nigra, involves a widespread neurological disruption. It is clear that the treatment of these disorders provides a major challenge for research over the coming years.

REFERENCES

Becker, J. T., F. Boller, J. Saxton, and K. L. McGonigle-Gibson. Normal rates of forgetting of verbal and nonverbal material in Alzheimer's disease. *Cortex* 23:59–72, 1987.

Benes, F. M., J. Davidson, and E. D. Bird. Quantitative cytoarchitectural studies of the cerebral cortex of schizophrenics. *Archives of General Psychiatry* 43:31–35, 1986.

Berman, K. F., and D. R. Weinberger. Regional cerebral blood flow in monozygotic twins concordant and discordant for schizophrenia. *Archives of General Psychiatry* 49:927–934, 1992.

Boller, F., D. Passafiume, M. C. Keefe, K. Rogers, L. Morrow, and Y. Kim. Visuospatial impairment in Parkinson's disease: Role of perceptual and motor factors. *Archives of Neurology* 41:485–490, 1984.

Bowen, F. P. Behavioral alterations in patients with Parkinson's disease. In M. D. Yahr, ed. *The Basal Ganglia.* New York: Raven Press, 1976.

Bowen, F. P., M. M. Hoehn, and M. D. Yahr. Parkinsonism: Alterations in spatial orientation as determined by a route walking test. *Neuropsychologia* 10:335–361, 1972

Bowles, N. L., L. K. Obler, and M. L. Albert. Naming errors in healthy aging and dementia of the Alzheimer type. *Cortex* 23:519–524, 1987.

Brooks, N., L. Campsie, C. Symington, A. Beattie, and W. McKinlay. The five year outcome of severe blunt head injury: A relative's view. *Journal of Neurology, Neurosurgery, and Psychiatry* 49:764–770, 1986.

Brown, R., N. Colter, J. A. Corsellis, T. J. Crow, C. D. Frith, R. Jagoe, and E. C. Johnstone. Postmortem evidence of structural brain changes in schizophrenia. *Archives of General Psychiatry* 43:35–42, 1986.

Brun, A. An overview of light and electron microscopic changes. In B. Reisberg, ed. *Alzheimer's Disease.* New York: The Free Press, 1983.

Carlsson, M., and A. Carlsson. Interactions between gluatamatergic and monoaminergic systems within the basal ganglia: Implications for schizophrenia and Parkinson's disease. *Trends in Neurosciences* 13:272–276, 1990.

Carroll, B. J., G. C. Curtis, and J. Mendels. Neuroendocrine regulation in depression. II. Discrimination of depressed from non-depressed patients. *Archives of General Psychiatry* 33:1051–1058, 1976.

Chase, T. N., N. S. Wexler, and A. Barbeau, eds. *Hungington's Disease. Advances in Neurology,* vol. 23. New York: Raven Press, 1979.

Coleman, P. D., and D. G. Flood. Neuron numbers and dendritic extent in normal aging and Alzheimer's disease. *Neurobiology of Aging* 8:521–545, 1987.

Corkin, S. A prospective study of cingulotomy. In E. Valenstein, ed. *The Psychosurgery Debate.* San Francisco: W. H. Freeman, 1980.

Crow, T. J. Neurohumoral and structural changes in schizophrenia: Two dimensions of pathology. *Progress in Brain Research* 55:407–417, 1982.

Crow, T. J., and E. C. Johnstone. Schizophrenia: Nature of the disease process and its biological correlates. In F. Plum, ed. *Handbook of Physiology,* vol. 5. Bethesda, Md.: American Physiological Society, 1987.

Cummings, J. L., J. P. Houlihan, and M. A. Hill. The pattern of reading deterioration in dementia of the Alzheimer type: Observations and implications. *Brain and Language* 29:315–323, 1986.

Fedio, P., C. S. Cox, A. Neophytides, G. Canal-Frederick, and T. N. Chase. Neuropsychological profile of Huntington's disease: Patients and those at risk. *Advances in Neurology* 23:239–256, 1979.

Friedhoff, A. J., and T. N. Chase, eds. *Gilles de la Tourette Syndrome. Advances in Neurology,* vol. 35. New York: Raven Press, 1982.

Fuld, P. A. Psychometric differentiation of the dementias: An overview. In B. Reisberg, ed. *Alzheimer's Disease.* New York: The Free Press, 1983.

Gershon, E. S., and R. O. Rieder. Major disorders of mind and brain. *Scientific American* 267(3):126–133, 1992.

Gilles de la Tourette, G. Etude sur un affection, nerveuse charactérisée par l'incoordination motrice accompanagnée d'écholalie et de copralalie (Jumping, Latah, Myriachit). *Archives of Neurology* 9:19–42, 158–200, 1885.

Grady, C. L., J. B. Haxby, B. Horowitz, G. Berg, and S. I. Rapoport. Neuropsychological and cerebral metabolic function in early vs. late onset dementia of the Alzheimer type. *Neuropsychologia* 25:807–815, 1987.

Grant, I. and K. M. Adams, eds. *Neuropsychological Assessment of Neuropsychiatric Disorders.* New York: Oxford University Press, 1986.

Gusella, J. F., N. S. Wexler, P. M. Conneally, S. L. Naylor, M. A. Anderson, R. E. Tanzi, P. C. Watkins, K. Ottina, M. R. Wallace, A. Y. Sakaguchi, A. G. Young, I. Shoulson, E. Bonilla, and J. B. Martin. A polymorphic DNA marker genetically linked to Huntington's disease. *Nature* 306: 234–238, 1983.

Hakim, A. M., and G. Mathieson. Dementia in Parkinson's disease: A neuropathologic study. *Neurology* 29:1209–1214, 1979.

Healy, D. Rhythm and blues. Neurochemical, neuropharmacological and neuropsychological implications of a hypothesis of circadian rhythm dysfunction in the affective disorders. *Psychopharmacology* 93:271–285, 1987.

Heaton, R. K., L. E. Badde, and K. L. Johnson. Neuropsychological test results associated with psychiatric disorders in adults. *Psychological Bulletin* 85:141–162, 1978.

Heaton, R. K., and T. J. Crowley. Effects of psychiatric disorders and their somatic treatments on neuropsychological test results. In S. B. Gilskov and G. J. Boll, eds. *Handbook of Clinical Neuropsychology.* New York: John Wiley, 1981.

Hornykiewicz, O. Parkinson's Disease. In T. J. Crow, ed. *Disorders of Neurohumoural Transmission.* New York: Academic, 1982.

Huff, F. J., S. Corkin, and J. H. Growdon. Semantic impairment and anomia in Alzheimer's disease. *Brain and Language* 28:235–249, 1986.

Huntington, D. On chorea. *Medical Surgical Reporter* 26:317–321, 1872.

Incagnoli, T., and R. Kane. Neuropsychological functioning in Tourette's syndrome. *Advances in Neurology* 35:305–310, 1982.

Joschko, M., and B. Rourke. Neuropsychological dimensions of Tourette's syndrome: Test-retest stability and implications for intervention. *Advances in Neurology* 35:297–304, 1982.

Kolb, B., and I. Q. Whishaw. Performance of schizophrenic patients on tests sensitive to left or right frontal, temporal, or parietal function in neurological patients. *Journal of Nervous and Mental Disease* 171:435–443, 1983.

Kovelman, J. A., and A. B. Scheibel. A neurohistologic correlate of schizophrenia. *Biological Psychiatry* 19: 1601–1621, 1984.

Kupfer, D. J., and M. E. Thase. The use of the sleep laboratory in the diagnosis of affective disorders. *Psychiatric Clinics of North America* 6:3–25, 1983.

Langston, J. W., P. Ballard, J. W. Tegrud, and I. Irwin. Chronic parkinsonism in humans due to a product of meperidine-analog synthesis. *Science* 219:979–980, 1983.

Logan, J. Address to the American Medical Association, 1973. In R. R. Fieve, ed. *Mood Swing*. New York: Bantam Books, 1976.

Loring, D. W., and J. W. Largen. Neuropsychological patterns of presenile and senile dementia of the Alzheimer type. *Neuropsychologia* 23:351–357, 1985.

Martin, A., P. Brouwers, C. Cox, and P. Fedio. On the nature of the verbal memory deficit in Alzheimer's disease. *Brain and Language* 25:323–341, 1985.

Martin, A., C. Cox, P. Brouwers, and P. Fedio. A note on different patterns of impaired and preserved cognitive abilities and their relation to episodic memory deficits in Alzheimer's patients. *Brain and Language* 25:181–198, 1985.

Martin, J. P. *The Basal Ganglia and Posture*. London: Ritman Medical Publishing, 1967.

McHugh, P. R., and M. F. Folstein. Psychiatric syndromes of Huntington's chorea. In. D. F. Benson and D. Blumer, eds. *Psychiatric Aspects of Neurological Disease*. New York: Grune & Stratton, 1975.

Mathew, R. J., J. S. Meyer, D. J. Francis, K. M. Semchuk, K. Mortel, and J. L. Claghorn. Cerebral blood flow in depression. *American Journal of Psychiatry* 137:1449–1450, 1980.

Murdoch, B. E., H. J. Chenery, V. Wilks, and R. S. Boyle. Language disorders in dementia of the Alzheimer type. *Brain and Language* 31:122–137, 1987.

Parkinson, J. Essay on the shaking palsy. Reprinted in M. Critchley, eds. *James Parkinson*. London: Macmillan, 1955.

Pirozzolo, F. J., E. C. Hansch, J. A. Mortimer, D. D. Webster, and M. A. Kuskowski. Dementia in Parkinson's disease: A neuropsychological analysis. *Brain and Cognition* 1:71–83, 1982.

Randolph, C., T. E. Goldberg, and D. Weinberger. The neuropsychlogy of schizophrenia. In K. M. Heilman and E. Valenstein, eds. *Clinical Neuropsychology,* 3rd ed. New York: Oxford, 1993.

Reisberg, B., ed., *Alzheimer's Disease*. New York: The Free Press, 1983.

Reisberg, B. Clinical presentation, diagnosis, and symptomatology of age-associated cognitive decline and Alzheimer's disease. In B. Reisberg, ed. *Alzheimer's Disease*. New York: The Free Press, 1983.

Ross, E. D., and A. J. Rush. Diagnosis and neuroanatomical correlates of depression in brain-damaged patients. *Archives of General Psychiatry* 38:1344–1354, 1981.

Scheibel, A. B. Dendritic changes. In B. Reisberg, ed. *Alzheimer's Disease*. New York: The Free Press, 1983.

Selkoe, D. J. Aging brain, aging mind. *Scientific American* 267(3):135–142, 1992.

Shapiro, E., E. K. Shapiro, and J. Clarkin. Clinical psychological testing in Tourette's syndrome. *Journal of Personality Assessment* 38:464–478, 1974.

Spinnler, H., and S. Della Sala. The role of clinical neuropsychology in the neurological diagnosis of Alzheimer's disease. *Journal of Neurology* 235:258–271, 1988.

Sutherland, R. J., B. Kolb, W. M. Schoel, I. Q. Whishaw, and D. Davies. Neuropsychological assessment of children and adults with Tourette's syndrome: A comparison with learning disabilities and schizophrenia. *Advances in Neurology* 35:311–322, 1982

Swaab, D. F., E. Fliers, M. Mirmiran, W. A. van Gool, and F. van Haaren. Aging of the brain and Alzheimer's disease. *Progress in Brain Research* 70:299–311, 1986.

Valenstein, E. S., ed. *The Psychosurgery Debate*. San Francisco: W. H. Freeman, 1980.

Valenstein, E. S. *Great and Desperate Cures*. New York: Basic Books, 1986.

van Crevel, H. Clinical approach to dementia. *Progress in Brain Research* 70:3–13, 1986.

Vanderwolf, C. H. Near-total loss of "learning" and "memory" as a result of combined cholinergic and serotonergic blockade in the rat. *Behavioral Brain Research* 23:43–57, 1987.

Vessie, P. R. On the transmission of Huntington's chorea for 300 years: The Bures family group. *Journal of Nervous and Mental Disorders* 76:533–565, 1932.

Weinberger, D. R., K. F. Berman, R. L. Suddath, and E. F. Torrey. Evidence for dysfunction of a prefrontal-limbic network in schizophrenia: An MRI and regional cerebral blood flow study of discordant monozygotic twins. *American Journal of Psychiatry* 149:890–897, 1992.

Wexler, N. S. Perceptual-motor, cognitive, and emotional characteristics of persons at risk for Huntington's disease. *Advances in Neurology* 23:257–272, 1979.

chapter twenty-six

26 Neuropsychological Assessment

The original goal of neuropsychological assessment was the identification of people suffering from organic versus functional disorders. The underlying assumption was that some sort of functional deficit would be common to all forms of cerebral dysfunction. It is a small step from that assumption to the idea that it would be possible to construct a single test for brain damage and that there is a cutoff point that separates the brain-damaged from the non-brain-damaged. By the 1960s, knowledge about cerebral function and dysfunction was growing exponentially, and it became apparent that commonly used tests of organicity, such as the Bender Gestalt Test and the Memory for Designs Test, simply could not determine the functional integrity of something as complex as the human brain. Nonetheless, the basic idea that there ought to be a cutoff between normal and abnormal remained a central tenet as neuropsychologists began to develop batteries of tests to replace the single-measure tests. The premier example is the Halstead-Reitan Neuropsychological Test Battery.

Essentially, this battery is a series of tests originally devised by Halstead in the late 1940s. It began as a battery of seven tests selected for their ability to discriminate between patients with frontal lobe lesions and other patient groups or normal controls. To ascertain the presence of brain damage, a summary value known as an impairment index is obtained. Implicit in the idea of an impairment index is the assumption that the combination of scores from an aggregation of apparently unrelated tests can distinguish a damaged from a normal brain. There are difficulties with this assumption. First, cerebral organization varies with such factors as sex, handedness, age, education, and experience. Second, test problems can be solved using different strategies and thus can involve different cortical regions. Third, symptoms of cortical injury can be highly specific—recall the case of the color-blind painter in Chapter 11. Finally, since many tests require problem solving of various kinds, we might expect task performance to vary with intelligence. All these factors make the use of cutoff scores difficult to justify.

An alternative to the test battery and cutoff-score approach to neuropsychological assessment developed directly from the establishment, in the 1950s and 1960s, of neuropsychological research groups, most notably in Oxford, Cambridge, Moscow, Montreal, Boston, and Iowa City. These groups began to develop tests to measure specific cognitive functions. In contrast to the approach of Halstead, which was to find tests that discriminated brain-damaged from control subjects, the new tests were theoretically based with a specific interest in measuring cerebral functions. The development of these tests in the 1950s through the 1970s led to the creation of composite test batteries. These batteries are characterized by the absence of cutoff scores and the reliance on qualitative measures and patterns of test performance. By the early 1980s, neuropsychology was no longer confined to a few elite laboratories, and the new field of clinical neuropsychology developed in clinics and hospitals. One effect of this growth is that there has been a diversification of methods used by individual neuropsychologists, the choice of tests varying with the disorder being investigated. Indeed, there are now two texts dedicated to a summary of the various tests available (see Lezak; Spreen and Strauss). It is not our goal to review all this material. Rather, we shall describe the rationale behind assessment, consider the usefulness of current test batteries, and provide some examples of assessments.

CHOOSING NEUROPSYCHOLOGICAL TESTS

In the 1990s, neuropsychologists have an impressive array of tests to choose from. At one end of the spectrum are standardized test batteries with fixed criteria for organicity that have the advantage of straightforward administration, scoring, and interpretation. There is little need to understand the theoretical bases of the tests or the nuances of cerebral organization. Examples of such tests are the Halstead-Reitan Battery (Table 26.1) and the Luria-Nebraska Battery (see Golden). At the other end of the spectrum are individualized test batteries that require a particular kind of theoretical knowledge to administer and interpret. These assessments are more qualitative than quantitative. The testing of each patient is tailored to the etiology and by the qualitative nature of the performance on each test. An example of this type of battery is Luria's test (Table 26.2). There is a middle ground, too. This is represented by composite batteries of tests in which each test is given in a formalized way and may

TABLE 26.1. Summary of the tests in the Halstead-Reitan battery

Test	Description
WAIS-R	Wechsler Adult Intelligence Scale-Revised
Category	Test of the abstracting ability in which stimuli must be grouped by abstract principles
Critical flicker fusion	Measure of rate at which a flashing light is perceived as a single light
Tactile performance	Tactile placing of wooden blocks into holes of similar shape
Rhythm	Discrimination between like and unlike pairs of musical beats
Speech-sounds perception	Auditory acuity test
Finger oscillation	Measure of finger-tapping speed
Time sense	Measures of reaction time and ability to estimate elapsed time
Trail marking	Drawing of lines to connect consecutive numbers or letters
Aphasia screening	Wepman Aphasia Screening Test
MMPI	Minnesota Multiphasic Personality Inventory

Note: These tests form a commonly used version of the battery. Not all tests are used by all testers.

TABLE 26.2. Interpretative guideline for Luria's test of objects and pictures

Behavior	Lesion
Perception of objects and pictures	
The patient perceives only one sign—the most conspicuous or prominent—but fails to correlate it with the other signs or to integrate the necessary group of signs; he draws premature conclusions regarding the meaning of the pictures, guessing at it from a single fragment that he has perceived. E.g., he may identify the pair of spectacles . . . as "a bicycle" because he cannot synthesize two circles and a series of lines into the required image. In less marked cases these difficulties are only brought to light during the examination of the most complex visual structures. The patient hardly ever expresses confident opinions regarding the meaning of pictures; he is constantly in doubt or he complains of his poor eyesight.	Lesions in occipitoparietal divisions of the cortex *Optic agnosia*
The patient can perceive a picture and evaluate it properly, but he can only perceive one picture or one element at a time.	*Simultaneous agnosia*
The patient loses sight of the whole picture if he examines its details. His examination of the objects is accompanied by ataxia of gaze.	
The patient looks at the picture passively; he does not change the direction of his gaze and he does not seem to attempt to "seek out" the identifying signs; usually he reaches a confident conclusion about what the picture represents; he shows no doubt and there is no attempt at correction.	Lesion of the frontal lobes
The patient evaluates the picture in the position it is shown to him; he does not turn it over and he makes no attempt to invert it mentally. Complex visual stimuli give him the impression of chaos. . . . He may also persevere in the same perception; i.e., the different pictures begin to be interpreted in the same way.	
The patient neglects the left side.	Lesion of the right hemisphere

Source: From Christensen, 1975, pp. 72–73.

have comparison norms, but the qualitative performance on tests and the pattern of test results are considered. An example of this type of battery is the Boston Process Approach (Table 26.3). Other examples are described by Benton and colleagues; Lezak; McKenna and Warrington; Milberg and colleagues; Newcombe; Smith; and Taylor.

There has been considerable controversy in the literature over the relative merits of various test batteries, and it is unlikely that there will be any consensus in the near future. The debate has been hottest over the usefulness of the formal test batteries, which have been subject to serious criticisms (see Lezak for an extensive review). The real issue, however, revolves around the question of why the tests are being performed and what the information will be used for. In the 1950s, there were few diagnostic techniques that could provide information on the presence or localization of cerebral injury. Behavior, therefore, was the most sensitive measure of cerebral functioning. In the 1990s, the technology of MRI, PET, and magnetic and electrical recording procedures makes many of the neuropsychological assessment tests unnecessary. There are still important reasons for assessments, but many of these reasons are specialized for particular patient populations and require specific types of functional tests. The informal composite batteries seem like the most practical way to approach these assessments. One constraint on the choice of these tests, however, is the training of neuropsychologists. The use of

TABLE 26.3. A representative sample of the tests used in the Boston Process Approach to neuropsychological assessment

Intellectual and conceptual functions
- WAIS-R
- Raven's Standard Progressive Matrices
- Shipley Institute of Living Scale
- Wisconsin Card-Sorting Test
- Proverbs test

Memory functions
- WMS
- Rey Auditory Verbal Learning Test
- Rey Complex Figure
- Benton Visual-Recognition Test
- Consonant trigrams test
- Cowboy Story-Reading Memory Test
- Corsi Block-Tapping Test

Language functions
- Narrative writing sample
- Tests of verbal fluency

Visuoperceptual functions
- Cow-and-circle experimental test
- Automobile puzzle
- Parietal lobe battery
- Hooper Visual Organization Test

Academic skills
- WRAT

Self-control and motor functions
- Porteus Maze Test
- Stroop Color-Word Interference Test
- Luria Three-Step Motor Program
- Finger tapping

tests that are theoretically based requires an understanding of the theory of cerebral organization. It is not possible to take weekend workshops and emerge qualified to use such tests.

Factors Affecting Test Choice

Throughout this book, we have seen that circumscribed lesions in different cortical regions can produce discrete behavioral changes. Thus, it would seem reasonable to work backward from this knowledge to localize unknown brain damage. That is, given a particular behavioral change, one should be able to predict the site or sites of the disturbance most likely to be causing the change. There are problems in working backward in such a manner, however. Research patients are often chosen for specific reasons. For example, whereas patients with rapidly expanding tumors would not be chosen for research because their results are so difficult to interpret, neurosurgical patients are ideal research subjects because the extent of their damage is known. Therefore, differences in the etiology of the neurological disorder might be expected to make assessment difficult. Indeed, it seems likely that people with diffuse dysfunction, such as in head trauma, would perform very differently from people with surgical removals.

Even after we have chosen tests that are appropriate for the etiology in question, we have significant issues to resolve. First, there is a question about the sensitivity of the tests. If a large region of the brain is dysfunctioning, the assessment test need not be particularly sensitive to demonstrate the dysfunction. If the lesion is small, on the other hand, the behavioral effect may be rather specific (as we have seen). For example, a lesion in the right somatosensory representation of the face may produce very subtle sensory changes, and unless specific tests of nonverbal fluency are used (see Chapter 15), the cognitive changes may go unnoticed, even with dozens of tests. A related problem is that various factors may interact with brain pathology to make interpretation of test results difficult. Tests are seldom developed for subjects who are older than 60 or who are culturally disadvantaged. Therefore, test scores cannot be interpreted with strict cutoff criteria—that is, performance below a particular level cannot always be taken as indicating brain damage. Further, intelligence alters the investigators' expectations of performance on tests: someone with an IQ of 130 may be relatively impaired on a test of verbal memory but may appear normal compared to someone with an IQ of 90. Thus, unlike standard psychometric assessment, neuropsychological assessment must be flexible. This makes interpretation difficult and requires extensive training in fundamental neuropsychology and neurology as well as in neuropsychological assessment. Finally, we have seen in several earlier discussions that there are significant differences in test performance that are related to factors such as sex and handedness. In addition, test performance is often biased by demographics. For example, in one three-city study of the effects of head trauma, it was found that normal subjects in one city performed as poorly as brain-damaged subjects in another. There were significant demographic differences that influenced the test performance and thus had to be considered in the interpretation of the results.

Goals of Neuropsychological Assessment

The goal of assessment in general clinical psychology is the diagnosis of the disorder for the purpose of changing behavior. For example, intelligence and achievement tests may be given to schoolchildren to try to identify particular problem areas as an aid in teaching. Similarly, personality tests are used with an eye toward defining and curing a behavioral disorder.

The goals of clinical neuropsychology are different in some respects. First, the assessment aims to diagnose the presence of cortical damage or dysfunction and to localize it where possible. In doing so, there is an attempt to provide an accurate and unbiased estimate of a person's cognitive capacity. Second, assessment is used to facilitate patient care and rehabilitation. Serial assessments can provide information about the rate of recovery and the potential for resuming a previous lifestyle. Third, neuropsychological assessment can identify the presence of mild disturbances in cases in which other diagnostic studies have produced equivocal results. Examples might be the effects of head trauma or the early symptoms of a degenerative disease. Fourth, a related goal is to identify unusual brain organization that may occur in lefthanders or in people with childhood brain injury. This information is particularly valuable to the surgeon, who would not wish to remove primary speech zones inadvertently during surgery, and such information is likely to be obtained only from behavioral measures. In such disorders as focal epilepsy, the primary evidence corroborating abnormal EEG may be behavioral, because radiological procedures often fail to pinpoint the abnormal brain tissue giving rise to the seizures. In addition, because some recovery of function may be expected following brain injury, this recovery must be documented not only with rehabilitation in mind but also to determine the effectiveness of any medical treatment, particularly for neoplasms or vascular abnormalities. Further, the patient and the family must understand the patient's possible residual deficits so that realistic life goals and rehabilitation programs can be planned.

Intelligence Testing in Neuropsychological Assessment

Most neuropsychological assessments begin with a measure of general intelligence, most often the Wechsler Adult Intelligence Scale-Revised (WAIS-R). The Wechsler scales have proved invaluable in determining a base level of cognitive functioning. These scales provide the distinct advantage of producing separate scores for verbal and performance subtests, as well as an overall IQ.

The verbal scale consists of six subtests: (1) information: questions such as "Where is Egypt?" "Who wrote *Hamlet*?"; (2) comprehension: questions requiring some reflection before answering, such as "Why are child-labor laws needed?"; (3) arithmetic: questions such as "How many hours will it take a man to walk 24 miles at the rate of 3 miles an hour?"; (4) similarities: questions such as "In what way are these two pairs of items alike—an orange and a banana, an egg and a seed?" (5) digit span: tests the number of digits that can be repeated in correct sequence, forward and backward; (6) vocabulary: asks the meaning of words ranging from easy (for example, "winter") to difficult (for example, "travesty").

The performance scale consists of five subtests: (1) digit symbol: nine symbols (such as a +) are paired with the digits 1–9 in a key above the response sheet. The task is to pencil in as many of the symbols corresponding to each of 90 digits as possible in 90 sec. This requires rapid eye movement and short-term visual store. (2) Picture completion: the subject indicates what is missing in each of a series of pictures. (3) Block design: red and white blocks must be used to form a design presented on a card. (4) Picture arrangement: several cards with cartoonlike drawings are presented in mixed-up order, and the subject is required to order them so that they tell a coherent story. (5) Object assembly: pieces of simple jigsaw puzzles are given to the subject, who must assemble them as quickly as possible.

Although the distinction between the verbal and performance subtests is serendipitous, the subtests have proved useful as a rough measure of left and right hemisphere function, respectively. The IQs obtained on the verbal and performance sections both have a mean of 100 and a standard deviation of 15. A difference of more than 10 points between the verbal and performance scores is usually taken to be a clinically significant difference, although statistically this interpretation is somewhat liberal. A number of studies have shown that well-defined left hemisphere lesions produce a relatively low verbal IQ, whereas well-defined right hemisphere lesions produce a relatively low performance IQ. Diffuse damage, on the other hand, tends to produce a low performance IQ, leading to the erroneous belief that the verbal-performance IQ difference is not diagnostically useful. Although a reduced performance IQ is not definitive, it is rare to obtain a relatively low verbal IQ, and its appearance should not be ignored.

A recent evaluation of the WAIS subscales and IQ values was performed by Warrington and her colleagues, who did a retrospective study of 656 unselected patients with unilateral brain damage. Table 26.4 summarizes their results, showing that lesions of the left hemisphere depressed verbal IQs, whereas lesions of the right hemisphere depressed performance IQs, the exception in both cases being that of occipital lesions. However, the verbal-performance discrepancy score was less than 10 in 53% of left hemisphere cases and in 43% of right hemisphere cases. A small number of cases had discrepancy scores greater than 10 in the opposite direction: 6% with left hemisphere lesions and 3% with right hemisphere lesions. (It is curious that the patients with left parietal or temporal-parietal lesions did not show a large IQ drop, considering that one would expect them to be dysphasic. Since language skills were not mentioned in the Warrington study, it is possible that her analysis excluded aphasic subjects. In our experience, dysphasic patients have very depressed verbal IQs, as would be expected.)

Warrington also analyzed seven subtests on the WAIS, including arithmetic, similarities, digit span, vocabulary, picture completion, block design, and picture arrangement. Overall, the four verbal tests were performed significantly more poorly by left hemisphere frontal, temporal, and parietal patients. There were no differences be-

TABLE 26.4. Mean WAIS verbal and performance IQs for different patient groups

	Left hemisphere lesion			Right hemisphere lesion		
Group	*n*	VIQ	PIQ	*n*	VIQ	PIQ
Frontal	40	94.2	99.8	38	107.01	101.3
Temporal	58	97.0	102.1	50	108.0	98.5
Parietal	49	98.0	100.9	33	108.2	87.9
Occipital	16	109.8	95.6	5	104.4	108.8
Frontal-temporal	47	93.6	97.4	27	105.0	98.0
Frontal-parietal	48	96.1	103.2	34	105.9	97.7
Temporal-parietal	48	85.3	97.5	31	109.5	92.8
Parietal-occipital	24	86.7	88.9	22	102.3	81.0
Frontal-temporal-parietal	17	87.0	97.4	19	105.1	89.8
Frontal-temporal-parietal-occipital	23	98.0	107.0	19	111.1	96.8

Source: After Warrington et al., 1986.

tween these left hemisphere groups on these tests, however. The performance tests were less predictive of lesion side, since only the right parietal patients were significantly poorer on block design and picture arrangement.

One difficulty with postinjury intelligence testing is that there must be a premorbid estimate of intellectual level. A relatively low IQ cannot be asscribed to a brain injury unless there is some idea of what the IQ was before the injury. This estimate is usually informal and based upon the person's education, occupation, and socioeconomic background. Wilson and colleagues describe a statistical procedure for estimating premorbid IQ.

CASE HISTORIES

Having surveyed the basic principles of neuropsychological theory and assessment, we now provide examples of the application of the tests and theory to clinical problems. In this section we describe the test results and case histories of six patients. These case histories illustrate the use of neuropsychological tests in neuropsychological assessment. Because of our affiliation with the Montreal Neurological Institute, our composite assessment battery is based upon the tests derived from the study of neurosurgical patients by Brenda Milner, Laughlin Taylor, and their colleagues. Most of the tests have been discussed elsewhere in the text, especially in Chapters 12, 13, and 14 in our description of neuropsychological tests of parietal, temporal and frontal lobe function. Cases 1 and 2 are borrowed from Laughlin Taylor.

Case 1

This 33-year-old man had a history of seizures beginning 4 years before his admission to the hospital. His neurological examination upon admission was negative, but he was having increasingly frequent seizures, which were characterized by his head and eyes turning to the right, a pattern that suggests supplementary motor cortex involvement. Radiological and EEG studies suggested a left frontal lobe lesion (Figure 26.1A), which was confirmed at surgery when a poorly differentiated astrocytoma was removed. The only difficulty the patient experienced before surgery was in doing the Wisconsin Card-Sorting Test, where numerous perseverative errors were made and only one category was sorted correctly. Two weeks after surgery, all the intelligence ratings, memory quotients, and delayed verbal-recall scores decreased, but these scores remained in essentially the same ratio to one another. Other tests were unchanged, the only significantly low score again being on the sorting test. If this patient was like other patients with similar lesions, it is likely that on follow-up a year after surgery his intelligence ratings and memory scores would have returned to the preoperative level, although his card sorting would be unlikely to show any improvement.

Case 2

This 26-year-old man had a history of 8 years of seizures dating back to an episode of meningitis in which he was thought to have an intracerebral abscess. Subsequently, he developed seizures beginning in the left side of his face and hand, and he was referred as a candidate for surgery because his seizures were uncontrolled by medication. Before surgery, the patient scored within normal limits on tests of intelligence and general memory, although he did have difficulty with delayed recall of verbal material. He had slight defects of finger-position sense on the left hand, which together with some weakness in the left arm and leg pointed to damage in the right central area. In addition, he had difficulty copying and recalling the Rey Complex Figure and was unable to perform the Wisconsin Card-Sorting Test, which suggested that his lesion might extend into the frontal and temporal areas as well.

The right face area and a region extending into the right frontal lobe were removed at surgery (see Figure 26.1B). After this removal, there remained some residual epileptiform abnormality in both the frontal lobe and the superior temporal gyrus. Postoperative testing showed improvement in both verbal IQ and long-term verbal

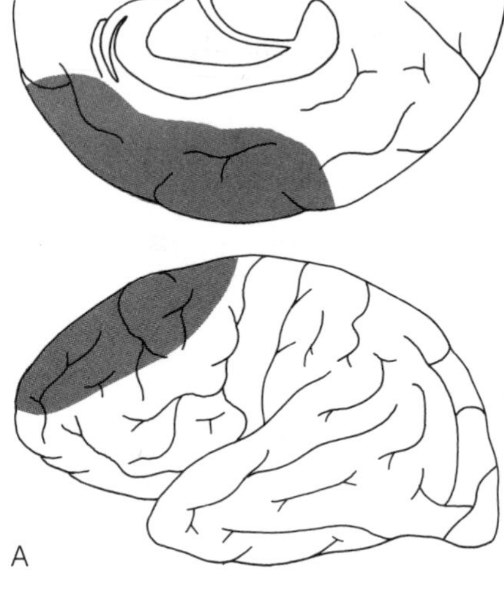

Case 1	Preop		Postop	
Full-scale IQ	115		102	
Verbal IQ	111		103	
Performance IQ	117		99	
Memory quotient	118		108	
Verbal recall	20		14	
Nonverbal recall	10.5		10	
Card sorting	1 cat.[a]		1 cat.[a]	
Finger-position sense	Left	Right	Left	Right
	60/60	60/60	60/60	60/60
Drawings: Copy	36/36		35/36	
Recall	21/36		24/36	

[a] *Significantly low score.*

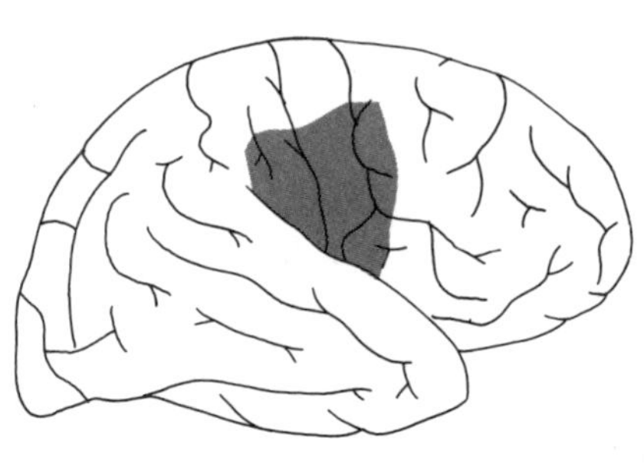

Case 2	Preop		Postop	
Full-scale IQ	97		97	
Verbal IQ	100		106	
Performance IQ	94		88[a]	
Memory quotient	94		92	
Verbal recall	13.5		14.0	
Nonverbal recall	3.5[a]		7.0	
Card sorting	0 cat.[a]		1 cat.[a]	
Finger-position sense	Left	Right	Left	Right
	55/60[a]	59/60	54/60[a]	60/60
Drawings: Copy	28/36[a]		26.5/36[a]	
Recall	4/36[a]		9.5/36[a]	

[a] *Significantly low score.*

FIGURE 26.1. Psychological test results before and after operation in two cases.

memory, but the patient had persistent difficulties on the card-sorting test, with finger-position sense on the left hand, and on the copy and recall of the Rey Complex Figure. There was also a decline in performance IQ. The difficulty with finger position would be expected in a case like this, but the continuing difficulties with card sorting and the Rey Complex Figure imply that there are still dysfunctioning areas in his right hemisphere, as reflected by residual spiking in the frontal and temporal regions.

Case 3

This 28-year-old right-handed woman had undergone emergency surgery following the bursting of an aneurysm in the right temporal lobe. Surgical reports indicated that portions of the right temporal and parietal cortex were damaged, and she had a left quadrantic hemianopsia, indicating that the lesion extended posteriorly into the visual cortex. She was referred to us 2 years after the accident, at which time she was in good health and attending a university, but she was having social problems as well as difficulty with mathematics. The results of her neuropsychological assessment are summarized in Table 26.5, where it can be seen that she experienced several deficits consistent with right posterior damage. Her performance IQ was 10 points lower than her verbal IQ, she had difficulty obtaining closure on

TABLE 26.5. Examples of neuropsychological assessments of neurological patients

		Case 3	Case 4	Case 5	Case 6
Test	Normal control	Right temporal aneurysm	Left temporal epilepsy	Left hemisphere stroke	Traffic accident
Speech lateralization, dichotic					
Words					
Left ear	25	18	2[a]	F	16
Right ear	46	50	15	F	25
Handedness	R	R	R	R	R
General intelligence					
Full-scale IQ	107	113	104	F	115
Verbal IQ	109	117	95[a]	F	127
Performance IQ	105	107[a]	111	108	96[a]
Visuoperceptual					
Mooney Faces (abbreviated)	18/19	12/19[a]	16/19	16/19	17/19
Rey Complex Figures—copy	32/36	24/36[a]	31/36	30/36	34/36
Memory					
Wechsler Memory quotient	107	115	87[a]	F	100[a]
Rey Complex Figures—recall	22/36	11/36[a]	18/36[a]	17/36[a]	13/36[a]
Delayed recall of stories and paired-associates	13	17	7[a]	—	23
Delayed recall of drawings	12	6[a]	10	9	2[a]
Spatial					
Right-left differentiation	52/60	48/60	43/60	51/60	35/60[a]
Semmes Body Placing	32/35	30/35	30/35	—	35/35
Language					
Reading	12	12	7[a]	F	20
Object naming	23/36	20/26	14/26[a]	F	—
Frontal lobe					
Wisconsin Card Sorting	6.0 cat.	5.8 cat.	4.0 cat.	3.0 cat.	2.4 cat.[a]
Chicago Word Fluency	62	50	38	F	52
Motor function					
Complex arm	92%	94%	89%	72%[a]	82%[a]
Face	88%	90%	89%	20%[a]	30%[a]

[a] Abnormally poor score.
F = could not be assessed because of dysphasia.

the Mooney Faces Test, and her recall of visual material was well below the level expected for a woman of her age and intelligence. In contrast, she performed within expected limits on tests of left hemisphere and frontal lobe function.

Case 4

A 22-year-old woman was referred to us by a clinical psychologist to assess the possibility of organic dysfunction. On several occasions, she had engaged in bizarre behaviors such as undressing in public and urinating on other people, and on one occasion she had attacked her roommate. Following these episodes she was confused and amnesic about her behavior during the attack, as well as about the period just prior to the outburst. Her neuropsychological test results indicated that her left temporal lobe was abnormal, because her verbal memory, reading, and object-naming were impaired, and she had a very low recall of dichotic words (see Table 26.5). Our diagnosis of temporal lobe epilepsy with a left-side focus was partially confirmed by a neurologist when EEG studies showed left hemisphere abnormality. As often occurs in epilepsy, a CT scan failed to reveal any unusual features, and there is nothing in the woman's history to account for the epilepsy. The seizures are completely controlled with Dilantin, but her neuropsychological deficits remain.

Case 5

This 60-year-old woman suffered a stroke that, from her CT scan, appeared to be localized in the face area and Broca's area on the left. She was referred to us a year after the stroke because of her poor progress in regaining her speech through speech therapy. In view of her marked dysphasia, we first administered a token test. Although this woman appeared to understand many of the things spoken to her, she was severely dysphasic and therefore obtained a very poor score on the token test. In view of this result, we gave her only a modified battery, designed to answer the referral question of what could be expected if she were to continue speech therapy. Her test results, which are summarized in Table 26.5, showed that she was of average intelligence when measured with a nonverbal test, and she performed normally on all nonverbal tests of memory and perception that we administered. In contrast, she had real difficulty in copying movements, even though she had no hemiparesis. Indeed, she was totally unable to copy sequences of facial movements, although she could manage individual facial movements with some difficulty. These results led us to conclude that this woman was aphasic and had a facial apraxia, leading us to be pessimistic about her chances for further recovery of speech functions.

Case 6

This is the case of a 37-year-old man who had been in a traffic accident some 15 years earlier. He was in a coma for 6 weeks and suffered secondary injury from brain infection. At the time of his accident, he was a student in a graduate program in journalism, having previously obtained a B.A. with honors in English literature. When we first met him, he had severe motor problems, needing canes to walk, and was both apraxic and ataxic. He had great difficulty in pronouncing words, especially when hurried or stressed, but careful language testing on the token test revealed no aphasic symptoms; his language problems were entirely anarthric. Since the time of his accident this man had lived at home with his parents and had not learned the social skills necessary to cope with his handicap. In short, he was being treated as though he were retarded and was being completely looked after by his family. Indeed, the patient himself believed he was retarded and was very reluctant to attempt rehabilitation programs. At the urging of his family, we gave him a thorough assessment to evaluate his potential. His results were surprising, even to us. As summarized in Table 26.5, his IQ was superior (WAIS verbal IQ 127), and although he had deficits on some tests, especially those involving motor skills, his performance on most tests was average or above average. Despite his obvious motor handicaps, this man clearly was not retarded. One significant cognitive loss, however, was his nonverbal memory, which was very poor. Armed with our test results, we were able to show him—and his family—that he could look after himself and should seek occupational therapy through a government agency for the handicapped.

CONCLUSIONS

Neurology has changed significantly in the past 20 years. First came the CT scan, which allowed entrance to the brain without invading the body. Then the technology born from the CT scan arrived, including MRI, fMRI, PET, SPECT, and MEG. These scanning devices have had a significant impact on the field of clinical neuropsychology. Whereas neuropsychological assessment promised a way to localize focal cerebral injury, it now has been largely replaced in this function by

MRI. This is not to imply that clinical neuropsychology is in decline. The most sensitive measure of cerebral integrity is behavior, and behavioral analysis consistently finds dysfunction that is not seen in MRI, especially in cases of closed-head injury and epilepsy. Thus, the role of neuropsychology is changing as it attempts to find explanations for behavioral loss and dysfunction in more complex disorders. In addition, as the population ages, there will be an increasing need to determine people's cognitive capacities to ensure appropriate placements. Finally, the silent epidemic of closed-head injuries in the Western world is unlikely to abate, and all of these patients must be assessed to determine loss and recovery of function as well as appropriate rehabilitative therapies. Clinical neuropsychology will also play a leading role in the development of programs for cognitive rehabilitation. The evolution of clinical neuropsychology in these settings will require a continued development of assessment tools that are appropriate to the tasks at hand.

REFERENCES

Benton, A. L. Neuropsychological assessment. *Annual Review of Psychology* 45:1–23, 1994.

Benton, A. L., D. de S. Hamsher, N. R. Varney, and O. Spreen. *Contributions to Neuropsychological Assessment: A Clinical Manual.* New York: Oxford University Press, 1983.

Christensen, A.-L. *Luria's Neuropsychological Investigation.* New York: Spectrum Publications, 1975.

Damasio, H., and A. R. Damasio. *Lesion Analysis in Neuropsychology.* New York: Oxford University Press, 1989.

Golden, C. J. A standardized version of Luria's neuropsychological tests. In S. Filskov and T. J. Boll, eds. *Handbook of Clinical Neuropsychology.* New York: Wiley-Interscience, 1981.

Kimura, D., and J. McGlone. *Neuropsychology Test Procedures.* Manual used at the University Hospital, London, Ontario, Canada, 1983.

Levin, H. S., and A. L. Benton. Neuropsychologic assessment. In A. B. Baker and R. J. Joynt, eds. *Clinical Neurology,* vol. 1. New York: Harper & Row, 1986.

Lezak, M. D. *Neuropsychological Assessment,* 3rd ed. New York: Oxford University Press, 1995.

McFie, J. *Assessment of Organic Intellectual Impairment.* New York: John Wiley, 1975.

McKenna, P., and E. K. Warrington. The analytical approach to neuropsychological assessment. In I. Grant and K. M. Adams, eds. *Assessment of Neuropsychiatric Disorders.* New York: Oxford University Press, 1986.

Milberg, W. P., N. Hebben, and E. Kaplan. The Boston process approach to neuropsychological assessment. In I. Grant and K. M. Adams, eds. *Assessment of Neuropsychiatric Disorders.* New York: Oxford University Press, 1986.

Newcombe, F. *Missile Wounds of the Brain.* London: Oxford University Press, 1969.

Owen, A. M., A. C. Roberts, C. E. Polkey, B. J. Sahakian, and T. W. Robbins. Extra-dimensional versus intradimensional set shifting performance following frontal lobe excisions, temporal lobe excisions or amygdalo-hippocampectomy in man. *Neuropsychologia* 29:993–1006.

Reitan, R. M., and L. A. Davison. *Clinical Neuropsychology: Current Status and Application.* New York: John Wiley, 1974.

Smith, A. Principles underlying human brain functions in neuropsychological sequelae of different neuropathological processes. In S. B. Filskov and T. J. Boll, eds. *Handbook of Clinical Neuropsychology.* New York: Wiley-Interscience, 1981.

Sohlberg, M. M., and C. A. Mateer. *Introduction to Cognitive Rehabilitation.* New York: Guilford Press, 1989.

Spiers, P. A. Have they come to praise Luria or to bury him: The Luria-Nebraska controversy. *Journal of Consulting and Clinical Psychology* 49:331–341, 1981.

Spreen, O., and E. Strauss. *A Compendium of Neuropsychological Tests.* New York: Oxford University Press, 1991.

Taylor, L. B. Psychological assessment of neurosurgical patients. In T. Rasmussen and R. Marino, eds. *Functional Neurosurgery.* New York: Raven Press, 1979.

Walsh, K. W. *Understanding Brain Damage,* 2nd ed. London: Churchill Livingstone, 1991.

Warrington, E. K., M. James, and C. Maciejewski. The WAIS as a lateralizing and localizing diagnostic instrument: A study of 656 patients with unilateral cerebral excisions. *Neuropsychologia* 24:223–239, 1986.

Wilson, R. S., G. Rosenbaum, and G. Brown. The problem of premorbid intelligence in neuropsychological assessment. *Journal of Clinical Neuropsychology* 1:49–56, 1979.

Glossary

ablation. Intentional destruction or removal of portions of the brain or spinal cord; brain lesion.
absence attack. Temporary loss of consciousness in some forms of epilepsy.
acalculia. Inability to perform mathematical operations.
accessory cells. Cells that originate from germinal cells (spongioblasts) and contribute to the support, nourishment, conduction, and repair of neurons; occasionally the origins of tumors. Accessory cells are the astrocytes; oligodendrocytes; and ependymal, microglial, and Schwann cells.
achromatopsia. Inability to distinguish different hues despite normally pigmented cells in the retina. Sometimes called *cortical color blindness.*
acopia. Inability to copy a geometric design.
acquired dyslexia. Inability to read that is caused by brain damage in an individual who previously knew how to read; as distinguished from developmental dyslexia, which is a failure to learn to read.
action potential. Brief electrical impulse by which information is conducted along an axon, which results from brief changes in the membrane's permeability to potassium and sodium ions.
adenosine triphosphate (ATP). Molecule important to cellular energy metabolism. The conversion of ATP to ADP (adenosine diphosphate) liberates energy. ATP can also be converted to cyclic AMP (adenosine monophosphate), which serves as an intermediate messenger in the production of postsynaptic potentials by some neurotransmitters and in the mediation of the effects of polypeptide hormones.
afference theory. Theory that all behavior is driven by sensory events; as opposed to efference theory.
afferent. Conducting toward the central nervous system or toward its higher centers.
afferent paresis. Loss of kinesthetic feedback resulting from lesions to the postcentral gyrus (areas 1, 2, 3), producing clumsy movements.
afterdischarge. Abnormal discharges from neurons that occur following an epileptic seizure or brain stimulation.
agenesis of the corpus callosum. Condition in which the corpus callosum fails to develop.
agnosia. Partial or complete inability to recognize sensory stimuli, unexplainable by a defect in elementary sensation or by a reduced level of alertness.
agraphia. Decline or loss of the ability to write.
akathesia. Condition of motor restlessness, ranging from a feeling of inner disquiet to an inability to sit or lie quietly.
akinesia. Absence or poverty of movement.
akinetic seizures. Seizures producing temporary paralysis of muscles, characterized by a sudden collapse without warning; most common in children.
alexia. Inability to read.
allesthesia. Sensation of touch experienced at a point remote from the place touched.
allospatial. Spatial relations between objects, independent of the perspective of the observer.
alpha rhythm. Regular (approximately 10-Hz) wave pattern in the EEG, found in most people when they are relaxed with eyes closed.
Alzheimer's disease. Degenerative brain disorder that first appears as a progressive memory loss and later develops into a generalized dementia. The origin of the disease is unknown, but cholinergic cells in the basal forebrain and cells in the entorhinal cortex appear to degenerate first.
amativeness. Inclination to love; localized by the phrenologists in the nape of the neck.
amblyopia. Dimness of vision without obvious impairment of the eye itself.

amines. Class of compounds, including neurotransmitters, which have a component that is formed from ammonia by replacement of one or more hydrogen atoms and that thus has an NH attached.

amino acids. Class of biologically active compounds containing an NH_2 chemical group.

Ammon's horn. Part of the hippocampus.

amnesia. Partial or total loss of memory.

amnesic aphasia. Aphasic syndrome characterized by the inability to name objects and the production of unintended syllables, words, or phrases during speaking.

amusia. Inability to produce (motor) or to comprehend (sensory) musical sounds.

amygdala. Set of nuclei in the base of the temporal lobe; part of the limbic system.

anarthria. Incoordination of the musculature of the mouth, resulting in speechlessness.

anastomosis. Connection between parallel blood vessels that allows them to communicate their blood flows.

aneurysm. Vascular dilation resulting from a localized defect in vascular elasticity; a sac is formed by the dilation of the walls of an artery or a vein and is filled with blood.

angiography. Radiographic imaging of blood vessels filled with a contrast medium.

angioma. Collections of abnormal blood vessels, including capillary, venous, and arteriovenous malformations, resulting in abnormal blood flow.

angular gyrus. Gyrus in the parietal lobe corresponding roughly to Brodmann's area 39; important in language functions.

anomia. Difficulty in finding words, especially those naming objects.

anomic aphasia. Inability to name objects.

anopia. Loss of vision.

anosmia. Absence of the sense of smell.

anosodiaphoria. Indifference to illness.

anosognosia. Loss of ability to recognize or to acknowledge an illness or bodily defect; usually associated with right parietal lesions.

anterior cerebral artery. Artery originating from the carotid artery that services the orbital frontal and dorsolateral frontal regions, the anterior cingulate cortex, corpus callosum, and striatum.

anterior commissure. Fiber tract that joins the temporal lobes.

anterograde amnesia. Inability to remember events subsequent to some disturbance of the brain such as head injury, electroconvulsive shock, or certain degenerative diseases.

anterograde degeneration. Degeneration of the parts of a nerve cell that lie distal to damage to the cell, with the cell body used as reference; for example, when an axon is cut, anterograde degeneration occurs in the section from the cut to the synaptic terminals. Also called *Wallerian degeneration.*

anterograde transport. Transport by a neuron, usually along axons, of substances in a direction that is away from the cell body.

aphagia. Inability to eat or chew.

aphasia. Defect or loss of power of expression by speech, writing, or signs, or of comprehending spoken or written language due to injury or disease of the brain.

apperceptive agnosia. Broad category of visual agnosia in which elementary sensory functions appear to be relatively intact but a perceptual deficit that prevents recognition of an object is present.

apraxia. Inability to make voluntary movements, in the absence of paralysis or other motor or sensory impairment, especially an inability to make proper use of an object.

aprosodia. Condition in which there is a loss of production or comprehension of the meaning of different tones of voice.

arachnoid. Thin sheet of delicate collagenous connective tissue that follows the contours of the brain.

archicortex. Portion of the cerebral cortex that develops in association with the olfactory cortex and is phylogenetically older than the neopallium and lacks its layered structure. Also called *archipallium, allocortex,* or *olfactory cortex.* Corresponds to the dentate gyrus and hippocampal gyrus in mature mammals.

arcuate fasciculus. Long bundle of fibers joining Wernicke's and Broca's areas.

Argyll-Robertson pupil. Constriction of the pupil of the eye to accommodation, but not to light; used to diagnose damage to the midbrain relays of the third cranial nerve (oculomotor).

arteriovenous (A-V) malformation. Abnormality of both the arterial and venous blood flow, which often appears as a mass of vessels that are intertwined and lie on the surface of the cortex.

asomatognosia. Loss of knowledge or sensory awareness of one's own body and bodily condition; may occur on one or both sides of the body; most commonly results from damage to the right parietal lobe.

aspiny neurons. Class of inhibitory neurons that do not have dendritic spines.

association cortex. All cortex that is not specialized motor or sensory cortex (the term survives from an earlier belief that inputs from the different senses meet and become associated). *See also* **prefrontal cortex** and **tertiary projection area.**

associative agnosia. Form of agnosia in which there is an object identification deficit in the context of a preserved ability to copy or match stimuli presented in the affected modality.

astereognosis. Inability, with no defect of elementary

tactile sensation, to recognize familiar objects by touch.

astrocyte. Type of glial cell. *See also* **accessory cells.**

astrocytoma. Slow-growing brain tumor resulting from the growth of astrocytes.

asymbolia. Inability to employ a conventional sign to stand for another object or event.

asymbolia for pain. Inability to understand the meaning of pain.

ataxia. Failure of muscular coordination; any of various irregularities of muscular action.

athetosis. Motor disorder marked by involuntary movements or slow writhing movements, especially in the hands.

attention. Hypothetical process that either allows a selective awareness of a part or aspect of the sensory environment or allows selective responsiveness to one class of stimuli.

attentional dyslexia. Disorder in which naming a letter is more difficult when it is accompanied by a second letter.

auditory agnosia. Impaired capacity to identify nonverbal acoustic stimuli.

aura. Subjective sensation, perceptual experience, or motor phenomenon that precedes and marks the onset of an epileptic seizure or migraine.

autism. Condition in which a person is dominated by self-centered thoughts or behaviors that are not subject to change by external stimulation. In children, the condition is often called *infantile autism* and is characterized by a failure to relate normally to people or external stimulation. These children generally have severe language disorders and exhibit repetitive behaviors such as rocking.

autoimmune disease. Immune reaction that is directed against one's own body.

automatic behaviors. Stereotyped units of behavior linked in a fixed sequence; for example, grooming and chewing. Also called *reflexive, consummatory,* or *respondent behaviors,* and *automatisms.*

automatic movements. Spontaneous or involuntary movements.

automatisms. Performance of nonreflex acts without conscious volition. Also called *automatic behavior.*

autoradiography. Process by which radiolabeled substances are injected into the bloodstream, incorporated into cells, and transported along the cells' processes. When the tissue is exposed to a photographic film, it "takes its own picture" and reveals the route taken by the radiolabeled substance.

autotopagnosia. Inability to localize and name the parts of one's own body; for example, finger agnosia.

average evoked potential (AEP). Computerized average of a number of evoked potentials from sensory input.

axon. Thin neuronal process that transmits action potentials away from the cell body to other neurons (or to muscles or glands).

axon hillock. Site of origin of a nerve impulse.

Balint's syndrome. Agnosic syndrome that results from large bilateral parietal lesions and is composed of three deficits: (1) paralysis of eye fixation with inability to look voluntarily into the peripheral visual field, (2) optic ataxia, and (3) disturbance of visual attention such that there is neglect of the peripheral field.

basal ganglia. Group of large nuclei in the forebrain, including the caudate nucleus, putamen, globus pallidus, claustrum, and amygdala.

behavioral compensation. Mechanism of recovery from brain injury in which behavior is modified in order to compensate for lost functions; neither the recovered behavior nor the area that mediates recovery are the same as those that are lost.

Bell-Magendie law. Law, named after its cofounders, stating that the dorsal roots of the spinal cord are sensory and the ventral roots of the spinal cord are motor.

beta rhythm. Irregular EEG activity of 13 to 30 Hz, generally associated with an alert state.

bilateral. Occurring on or applying to both sides of the body.

binding problem. Theoretical problem with the integration of sensory information. Because a single sensory event is analyzed by multiple parallel channels that do not converge on a single region, there is said to be a problem in binding together the segregated analyses into a single sensory experience.

binocular deprivation. Removal of visual stimulation from both eyes by raising an animal in the dark, bandaging the eyes, or some similar technique.

biochemical techniques. Techniques that measure biologically relevant chemicals in tissue, including various types of assay procedures for determining the presence or concentration of different compounds.

biogenic amines. Group of neurotransmitters that includes norepinephrine, dopamine, and serotonin.

bipolar cells. Neurons having processes at both poles; characteristic especially of retinal cells.

birthdate effect. Effect of birthdate on subsequent success at sports or school (some entrants will be older and some younger than average, producing differential advantages due to age).

bitemporal hemianopsia. Loss of vision in both temporal fields due to damage to the medial region of the optic chiasm.

blood-brain barrier. Functional barrier produced by the glial cells and cells in the walls of the capillaries in the brain, which prevents the passage of many substances into the brain.

brain abscess. Localized collection of pus in the brain

formed from tissues that have disintegrated as a result of infection.

brain hypothesis. Idea that the brain, rather than some other body organ such as the heart, produces behavior.

brain scan. *See* **radioisotope scan.**

brainstem. Hypothalamus, midbrain, and hindbrain. (Some authorities also include the thalamus and basal ganglia.)

Broca's aphasia. Expressive, or nonfluent, aphasia; chiefly a defect of speech; results from a lesion to Broca's area.

Broca's area. Region of the left frontal lobe (frontal operculum) believed to be involved in the production of language. Damage results in Broca's aphasia.

Brodmann's map. Map of the cerebral cortex devised by Brodmann; it is based on cytoarchitectonic structure and labels anatomical areas by number. (It conforms remarkably closely to functional areas based on lesion and recording studies.)

Brown-Sequard syndrome. Condition of unilateral paralysis and loss of joint sensation and contralateral loss of pain and temperature sensation caused by damage to one half of the spinal cord.

butyrophenones. A class of drugs that block dopamine receptors.

calcification. Accumulation of calcium in various brain regions after brain damage.

catecholamine. Class of neurotransmitters that includes epinephrine, norepinephrine, and dopamine.

caudate nucleus. Nucleus of the basal ganglia.

cell assembly. Hypothetical collection of neurons that become functionally connected; proposed by Hebb to be the basis of ideation, perception, and memory.

cell body. *See* **soma.**

central sleep apnea. Sleep disturbance in which individuals stop breathing when they fall into deep sleep; may be associated with muscle relaxation that occurs during dream sleep.

central sulcus. Fissure running from the dorsal border of the hemisphere near its midpoint, and obliquely downward and forward until it nearly meets the lateral fissure, dividing the frontal and parietal lobes. Also called *fissure of Rolando.*

cerebellum. Major structure of the hindbrain specialized for motor coordination.

cerebral arteriosclerosis. Condition marked by loss of elasticity and by thickening and hardening of the arteries; eventually results in dementia.

cerebral compression. Contraction of the brain substance due to an injury that has caused hemorrhage and the development of a hematoma.

cerebral contusion. Vascular injury resulting in bruising and edema and hemorrhage of capillaries.

cerebral cortex. Layer of gray matter on the surface of the cerebral hemispheres composed of neurons and their synaptic connections, which form four to six sublayers.

cerebral hemorrhage. Bleeding into the brain.

cerebral hypoxia. Deficiency in the amount of oxygen getting into the brain via the bloodstream.

cerebral ischemia. Deficiency in the amount of blood getting to the brain. It may be restricted to limited regions, and may be caused by an obstruction or constriction of cerebral arteries.

cerebral laceration. Contusion severe enough to breach the brain substance.

cerebral palsy. Group of disorders that result from brain damage acquired prenatally.

cerebral trauma. Injury to the brain, usually resulting from a blow to the head.

cerebral vascular accident. *See* **stroke.**

cerebral vascular insufficiency. Deficiency in the amount of blood getting to the brain.

cerebrospinal fluid (CSF). Clear solution of sodium chloride and other salts that fills the ventricles inside the brain and circulates around the brain beneath the arachnoid layer in the subarachnoid space.

channel. Narrow passageway across the neuron membrane that allows the passage of different ions, which subsequently influence the membrane potential; different channels are opened by different ions or by voltage changes in the membrane.

choroid plexus. Tissue that lines the cerebral ventricles and produces cerebrospinal fluid.

chromatolysis. Loss of protein in a damaged cell resulting in loss of its ability to absorb stain; literally, the breakdown of its ability to be colored.

chromosome. Strands of DNA combined with protein in the nucleus of each cell that contain the genetic code determining the structure and function of the individual.

cingulate cortex. Strip of limbic cortex lying just above the corpus callosum along the medial walls of the cerebral hemispheres.

cingulate sulcus. Cortical sulcus that is located on the medial wall of the cerebral hemisphere just above the corpus callosum.

class-common behaviors. Behaviors and behavioral capacities common to all members of a phylogenetic class.

cognition. General term for the processes involved in thinking.

cognitive set. Tendency to approach a problem with a particular bias in thought; for example, when searching for a mailbox, one will have a cognitive set for mailboxes but not for cats.

cognitive space. Space or time about which a person has knowledge.

collaterals. Side branches of axons that may be necessary for neuron survival (essential collateral) or secondary and not essential (sustaining collateral).

color agnosia. Inability to associate particular colors with objects or objects with colors.

color amnesia. Inability to remember the colors of common objects.

color anomia. Inability to name colors; generally associated with other aphasic symptoms. Also called *color aphasia.*

column. Hypothetical unit of cortical organization, believed to represent a vertically organized intracortical connectivity that is assumed to reflect a single functional unit. Sometimes used as a synonym for a *module.*

commissure. Bundle of fibers connecting corresponding points on the two sides of the central nervous system.

commissurotomy. Surgical disconnection of the two hemispheres by cutting the corpus callosum.

complex partial seizure. Focal seizure that most commonly originates in the temporal lobe; characterized by subjective feelings, automatisms, and motor symptoms. Sometimes referred to as a *temporal lobe seizure.*

computerized tomography (CT) scan. X-ray procedure in which a computer draws a map from the measured densities of the brain; superior to a conventional X ray because it provides a three-dimensional representation of the brain. Also called by the trade name *EMI-Scan.*

computerized transaxial tomography. Technique by which a series of brain X rays are used to construct a three-dimensional representation of the brain.

concentration gradient. Difference in the concentrations of an ion on the two sides of a membrane.

concussion. Condition of widespread paralysis of the functions of the brain that occurs immediately after a blow to the head.

conduction aphasia. Type of fluent aphasia in which, despite alleged normal comprehension of spoken language, words are repeated incorrectly.

cones. Highly specialized conical or flask-shaped cells in the retina that are maximally sensitive to light of particular wavelengths. These cells form the basis of color vision.

conjunction search. Concept in attentional theory that assumes there is a mechanism whereby the sensory system searches for particular combinations of sensory information.

constructional apraxia. Inability to perform well-rehearsed and familiar sequences of movements involved in making or preparing something; deficit is not attributable to an inability to move or to perform the individual acts required for the task.

contralateral. Residing in the side of the body opposite the reference points.

contralateral neglect. Neglect of part of the body or space contralateral to a lesion.

contrast X ray. Radiographic procedure using the injection of radiopaque dye or air into the ventricles, or of dye into the arteries, for purposes of diagnosis.

convergent thinking. Form of thinking in which there is a search for a single answer to a question (for example, 2 + 2 = ?); in contrast to divergent thinking in which there are multiple solutions.

corollary discharge. Transmission by one area of the brain to another, informing the latter area of the former's actions; commonly used more specifically for a signal from the motor system to the sensory systems that a particular movement is being produced.

corollary discharge theory. Theory that when an individual initiates a movement, the nervous system keeps a record of the intended movement to which it compares the actual movement; the intended movement is the corollary discharge. Also known as *reafference theory.*

corpus callosum. Fiber system connecting the homotopic areas of the two hemispheres. Split-brain patients are those whose corpus callosum has been severed.

cortex. External layer; in this text, synonymous with *neocortex. See also* **neocortex.**

cortical quotient (CQ). Measure of the relative size of the cortex; analogous to encephalization quotient but applied only to the cortex.

corticobulbar fibers. Traditionally, pertaining to or connecting the cerebral cortex and the medulla oblongata; in more common usage, refers to connections between the cerebral cortex and lower brainstem.

corticospinal fibers. Pertaining to or connecting the cerebral cortex and the spinal cord.

corticospinal tract. Bundle of fibers directly connecting the cerebral cortex to the spinal cord.

cranial nerves. A set of 12 pairs of nerves conveying sensory and motor signals to and from the head.

Creutzfeldt-Jakob's disease. Form of senile dementia in which there is generalized cortical atrophy; the cause is unknown, but a slow-acting virus is suspected.

crossed aphasia. Aphasia that results from damage to the right hemisphere.

cross-modal matching. Ability to match sensory characteristics of objects across sensory modalities; for example, the ability to recognize visually an object that was previously handled tactilely.

cue response. Navigational behavior in which an animal locomotes to a position on the basis of its location relative to a single cue; as distinguished from place or position response.

cytoarchitectonic map. Map of the cortex based on the organization, structure, and distribution of the cells.

cytochrome oxidase. Enzyme made by mitochondria. Increased enzyme activity is thought to represent heightened neural activity; tissue can be stained for this enzyme in order to estimate which areas of the brain display high levels of activity.

deafferentation. Process of removing the afferent input to a structure or region of the nervous system.

decerebrate. Elimination of cerebral function by transecting the brain stem just above the superior colliculi; an animal so prepared is said to be decerebrate.

decerebrate rigidity. Excessive tone in all muscles, producing extension of the limbs and dorsoflexion of the head because antigravity musculature overpowers other muscles; caused by brainstem or cerebellar lesions.

decerebration. Disconnection of the cerebral hemispheres from the brainstem, resulting in deprivation of sensory input and the ability to affect behavior.

declarative memory. Type of memory that is illustrated by the ability to recount the details of events, including time, place, and circumstances, as compared with the ability to perform some act or behavior. Literally, it refers to the ability to recount what one knows, which is lost in many types of amnesia.

decortication. Removal of the cortex of the brain.

decussation. Crossing of pathways from one side of the brain to the other.

deep dyslexia. Reading impairment characterized by a peculiar constellation of errors suggesting that the reading is being performed by the nondominant hemisphere.

degeneration. The death of neurons or neuronal processes in response to injury in the degenerating neuron or, in some cases, in other neurons.

delayed-nonmatching-to-sample (DNMS) test. Behavioral test in which the subject is presented with a sample stimulus and then, after some delay, is presented with the same stimulus and another, novel stimulus. The subject's task is to choose the novel stimulus to obtain reward.

delusion. Belief opposed to reality but firmly held despite evidence of its falsity; characteristic of some types of psychotic disorders.

dendrite. Treelike process at the receiving end of the neuron.

dendritic spine. Protuberence on the dendrites of excitatory neurons; also, the location of most synapses on such neurons.

denervation supersensitivity. Condition of increased susceptibility to drugs, resulting from proliferation of receptors after denervation (removal of terminations) of an area.

2-deoxyglucose (2-DG). Sugar that interferes with the metabolism of glucose. A radioactive marker (such as ^{14}C) can be attached to the 2-DG. When this compound is taken up by the blood it is transported to the brain and will stay in the brain regions that have been most active, which provides a method to measure metabolic activity.

deoxyribonucleic acid (DNA). Long, complex macromolecule consisting of two interconnected helical strands. Strands of DNA, along with their associated proteins, constitute the chromosomes, which contain the genetic information of the animal.

dependence. State of an animal in which doses of a drug are required to prevent the onset of abstinence (that is, withdrawal) symptoms.

depolarization. Inward transfer of positive ions erasing a difference of potential between the inside and the outside of the neuron.

depth-of-processing effect. Improvement in subsequent recall of an object about which a person has thought as to its meaning or shape. It is presumed that some structure deep in the brain is involved in improving the memory for the object.

dermatome. Area of skin supplied with afferent nerve fibers by a single spinal dorsal root.

desynchronization. Change in EEG activity from a high-amplitude slow pattern to a low-amplitude fast pattern.

developmental dyslexia. Inability to learn adequate reading skills even when opportunity and appropriate instruction are given.

diaschisis. Special kind of shock following brain damage in which areas connected to the damaged area show a transitory arrest of function.

dichaptic test. Procedure for simultaneously presenting different objects to each hand to determine which hand is most effective at identifying the object.

dichotic listening. Procedure of simultaneously presenting a different auditory input to each ear through stereophonic earphones.

diencephalon. Region of the brain that includes the hypothalamus, thalamus, and epithalamus.

diplopia. Perception of two images of a single object; double vision.

disconnection. Severing, by damage or by surgery, of the fibers that connect two areas of the brain such that the two areas can no longer communicate; also, the condition that results.

discourse. Highest level of language processing in which there is a stringing together of sentences to form a meaningful narrative.

disinhibition. Removal of inhibition from a system.

dissolution. According to an unproved theory, the condition whereby disease or damage in the highest levels of the brain would produce not loss of function but rather a repertory of simpler behaviors as seen in animals that have not evolved that particular brain structure.

distal. Being away from, or distant to, some point.

divergent thinking. Form of thinking in which there is a search for multiple solutions to a problem (for, example, how many ways one can use a pen?); contrasts with convergent thinking in which there is a single solution.

dorsal columns. Cells in the dorsal spinal cord, which, in upright humans, can be thought of as forming a column from the bottom to the top of the spinal cord, as contrasted with *ventral columns*.

dorsal root. Nerve, composed of fibers carrying sensory information, that enters each segment of the dorsal (posterior in humans) portion of the spinal cord.

dorsal root ganglion. Protuberance produced by the aggregation of cell bodies of the sensory fibers, which are located adjacent to the portion of the spinal cord into which their axons enter.

dorsomedial thalamus. Thalamic nucleus providing a major afferent input to the prefrontal cortex; degenerates in Korsakoff's disease, leading to a severe amnesic syndrome.

double dissociation. Experimental technique whereby two areas of neocortex are functionally dissociated by two behavioral tests, each test being affected by a lesion to one zone and not the other.

dream sleep (D-sleep). Stage of sleep in which muscles are paralyzed, sensory input to the brain is blocked, the brain shows a waking state of activity, and during which vivid dreaming takes place.

dura mater. Tough, double layer of collagenous fiber enclosing the brain in a kind of loose sac.

dysarthria. Difficulty in speech production caused by incoordination of the speech apparatus.

dyscalculia. Difficulty in performing arithmetical operations.

dyseidetic. Pertaining to difficulty in recognizing words by their visual configurations.

dyskinesia. Any disturbance of movement.

dyslexia. Difficulty in reading.

dysphagia. Impairment of speech caused by damage to the central nervous system.

dysphonetic. Pertaining to the inability to decode words or to recognize them using phonic or sound principles.

dystonia. Abnormality of muscle tone, usually excessive muscle tone.

echolalia. Condition in which a person repeats words or noises that are heard.

efference theory. Theory that it is the sensations produced by an act that provide the conscious perception of the act.

efferent. Conducting away from higher centers in the central nervous system and toward muscle or gland.

electroconvulsive shock therapy (ECT or **ECS).** Application of a massive electrical shock across the brain as a treatment for affective disorders.

electroencephalography or **electroencephalogram (EEG).** Electrical potentials recorded by placing electrodes on the scalp or in the brain.

electromyography or **electromyogram (EM).** Recording of electrical activity of the muscles as well as the electrical response of the peripheral nerves.

electron microscope. Microscope that creates images of very small objects by bouncing electrons off the object and creating a picture via the object's resistance to electrons.

electrostatic gradient. Gradient between an area of low electrical charge and an area of high electrical charge, which occurs across the membrane of a cell or between two parts of the same cell.

embolism. Sudden blocking of an artery or a vein by a blood clot, bubble of air, deposit of fat, or small mass of cells deposited by the blood current.

encephalitis. Inflammation of the central nervous system as a result of infection.

encephalization. Process by which higher structures such as the cerebral cortex have taken over the functions of the lower centers; may imply either a phylogenetic or an ontogenetic shift of function.

encephalization quotient (EQ). Ratio of the actual brain size to the expected brain size for a typical mammal of that body size.

encephalomalacia. Softening of the brain, resulting from vascular disorders caused by inadequate blood flow.

encephalopathy. Chemical, physical, allergic, or toxic inflammation of the central nervous system.

encorticalization. Process by which the cerebral cortex has taken over the functions of the lower centers; may imply either a phylogenetic or an ontogenetic shift of function.

endoplasmic reticulum (ER). Extensive internal membrane system in the cytoplasm. Ribosomes attach to part of the ER to form what is known as the *rough ER*.

entorhinal cortex. Cortex found on the medial surface of the temporal lobe that provides a major route for neocortical input to the hippocampal formation; often shows degeneration in Alzheimer's disease.

ependymal cells. Glial cells forming the lining of the ventricles; some produce cerebrospinal fluid.

epilepsy. Condition characterized by recurrent seizures of various types associated with a disturbance of consciousness.

epithalamus. Collection of nuclei forming the phylogenetically most primitive region of the thalamus; includes the habenulae, pineal body, and stria medullaris.

equipotentiality. Hypothesis that each part of a given area of the brain is able to encode or produce the behavior normally controlled by the entire area.

ergotamine. Drug used in the treatment of migraine and tension headaches that acts by constricting cerebral arteries.

ethology. Study of the natural behavior of animals.

Euclidean space. Real space, with three dimensions, according to the laws of Euclid.

event-related potential (ERP). Complex electroencephalographic waveform that is related in time to a specific sensory event; composed of a series of specific subunits that are related to specific aspects of cerebral processing (for example, P_3).

evoked potential (EP). A short train of large, slow waves recorded from the scalp, reflecting dendritic activity.

excitatory neurotransmitter. Transmitter substance that decreases a cell's membrane potential and increases the likelihood that it will fire.

excitatory postsynaptic potential (EPSP). Small change in the membrane potential of a cell that leads to depolarization and increased likelihood that the cell will fire.

explicit memory. Memory in which subjects can retrieve an item and indicate that they know the item (that is, conscious memory). In contrast to implicit memory.

extension. Movement by which a limb is straightened.

extensor reflex. Advancement of a limb to contact a stimulus in response to tactile stimuli that activate fine touch and pressure receptors. The response is mediated by a multisynaptic spinal reflex circuit.

external imagery. Third-person imagery in which an individual imagines that it is another who engages in an act.

exteroceptive. Sherrington's term for the external surface field of distribution of receptor organs; for example, the skin and mucous membranes.

extinction. Term used in learning theory for the decreased probability that a behavior will occur if reinforcement is withheld.

face amnesia. Inability to remember faces.

factor analysis. Statistical procedure designed to determine if the variability in scores can be related to one or more factors that are reliably influencing performance.

fasciculation. Small local contraction of muscles, visible through the skin, representing a spontaneous discharge of a number of fibers innervated by a single motor nerve filament.

feature search. Cognitive strategy in which sensory stimuli are scanned for a specific feature, such as color.

festination. Tendency to engage in behavior at faster and faster speeds; usually refers to walking, but can include other behaviors such as talking and thinking.

fissure. A cleft, produced by folds of the neocortex, that extends to the ventricles.

flexion. Movement by which a limb is bent at the joint, bringing the limb toward the body.

fluent aphasia. Speech disorder in which a person articulates words in a languagelike fashion, but what is said actually makes little sense; usually results from damage to the left posterior cortex. *See also* **Wernicke's aphasia.**

focal seizures. Seizures that begin locally and then spread; for example, from one finger to the whole body.

forebrain. Cerebral hemispheres, basal ganglia, thalamus, amygdala, hippocampus, and septum.

frontal lobes. All the neocortex forward of the central sulcus.

frontal operculum. Upper region of the inferior frontal gyrus.

functional map. Map of the cortex constructed by stimulating areas of the brain electrically and noting elicited behavior, or by recording electrical activity during certain behaviors. Such maps relate specific behaviors to brain areas.

functional MRI (fMRI). Magnetic resonance imaging in which changes in elements such as iron or oxygen are measured during the performance of a specific behavior; used to measure brain activity during rest or behavior. *See also* **magnetic resonance imaging (MRI).**

functional validation. According to theory, the need of a neural system for sensory stimulation if it is to become fully functional.

ganglion cells. The cells of the retina that give rise to the optic nerve.

generalized seizures. Bilaterally symmetrical seizures without a local onset.

geniculostriate system. System consisting of projections from the retina of the eye to the lateral geniculate nucleus of the thalamus, then to areas 17, 18, 19, and then to areas 20, 21; involved in perception of form, color, and pattern.

genu. The bulbous part of the anterior portion of the corpus callosum.

germinal cells. Cells from which particular tissues are formed during development.

Gerstmann syndrome. Collection of symptoms due to left parietal lesion, alleged to include finger agnosia, right-left confusion, acalculia, and agraphia (a source of some controversy).

glial cells. Supportive cells of the central nervous system.

glial sheath. Glial cells, such as oligodendrocytes and Schwann cells, that wrap themselves around the axons of neurons, thus forming a sheath.

glioblastoma. Highly malignant, rapidly growing brain tumor; most common in adults over 35 years of age; results from the sudden growth of spongioblasts.

glioma. Any brain tumor that arises from glial cells.

gliosis. The migration and proliferation of glial cells in areas of neural tissue where damage has occurred; their presence serves as a sign of tissue damage.

globus pallidus. Part of the basal ganglia that receives projections from the caudate nucleus and sends projections to the ventral lateral nucleus of the thalamus; literally, pale globe or sphere.

glycoproteins. Class of proteins consisting of a compound of protein with a carbohydrate group.

Golgi apparatus. Complex of parallel membranes in the cytoplasm that wraps the product of a secretory cell or a protein manufactured by a nerve cell.

graded potential. Electrical potential in a neuron or receptor cell that changes with the intensity of the stimulus. Also known as a *generator potential.*

grand mal attack. Seizure characterized by loss of consciousness and stereotyped, generalized convulsions.

granulovacuolar bodies. Abnormal structures in the brain characterized by granules (small beadlike masses of tissue) and vacuoles (small cavities in the protoplasm of cells).

grapheme. Refers to the pictorial qualities of a written word that permits it to be understood without being sounded out; a group of letters that conveys a meaning.

graphemic reading. Reading in which the meaning of a word is derived from the picture that it makes as a whole rather than by sounding out the syllables.

graphesthesia. Ability to identify numbers or letters traced on the skin with a blunt object.

gray matter. Any brain area composed predominantly of cell bodies.

gyrus. A convolution of the cortex of the cerebral hemispheres.

habituation. Gradual quantitative decrease of a response after repeated exposure to a stimulus.

hallucination. Perception for which there is no appropriate external stimulus; characteristic of some types of psychotic disorders.

Hebb synapse. Hypothetical synapse that is formed when two neurons are concurrently in the same state of activity; named after Donald Hebb who postulated such a mechanism in 1949.

hebephrenic schizophrenia. A form of schizophrenia characterized by silly behavior and mannerisms, giggling, and shallow affect.

hematoma. Local swelling or tumor filled with effused blood.

heme group. Nonprotein, insoluble, iron protoporphyrin constituent of hemoglobin, a constituent of blood.

hemianopia. Loss of pattern vision in either the left or right visual field.

hemiballism. Motor disorder characterized by sudden involuntary movements of a single limb.

hemiparesis. Muscular weakness affecting one side of the body.

hemiplegia. Paralysis of one side of the body.

hemisphere. In the brain, either of the pair of structures constituting the telencephalon; sometimes also used to refer to either side of the cerebellum.

hemispherectomy. Removal of a cerebral hemisphere.

Heschl's gyrus. Gyrus of the temporal lobe of humans that is roughly equivalent to auditory area I. Also known as the *transverse temporal gyrus.*

hierarchical organization. Principle of cerebral organization in which information is processed serially, with each level of processing assumed to represent the elaboration of some hypothetical process.

high decerebrate. Preparation in which an animal has an intact midbrain, hindbrain, and spinal cord. *See also* **decerebrate** and **decerebration.**

hindbrain. Region of the brain that consists primarily of the cerebellum, medulla oblongata, pons, and fourth ventricle.

hippocampus. Primitive cortical structure lying in the anterior medial region of the temporal lobe.

histochemical techniques. Various techniques that rely on chemical reactions in cells to mark features of a cell for microscopic visualization.

histofluorescent technique. Literally, cell fluorescence, a technique whereby a fluorescent compound is used to label cells.

homeostasis. Maintenance of a chemically and physically constant internal environment.

hominid. General term referring to primates that walk upright, including all forms of humans, living and extinct.

homonymous hemianopsia. Total loss of vision due to complete cuts of the optic tract, lateral geniculate body, or area 17.

homotopic areas. Corresponding points in the two hemispheres of the brain that are related to the midline of the body.

horseradish perioxidase (HRP). A compound that, when introduced into a cell, is then distributed to all its parts, allowing the cell to be visualized.

Huntington's chorea. Hereditary disease characterized by chorea (ceaseless, involuntary, jerky movements) and progressive dementia, ending in death.

hydrocephalus. Condition characterized by abnormal accumulation of fluid in the cranium, accompanied by enlargement of the head, prominence of the forehead, atrophy of the brain, mental deterioration, and convulsions.

6-hydroxydopamine (6-OHDA). Chemical selectively taken up by axons and terminals of norepinephrinergic or dopaminergic neurons that acts as a poison, damaging or killing the neurons.

hyperactive child syndrome. Syndrome characterized by low attention span and poor impulse control, which results in disruptive behavior.

hyperactivity. More activity than normally expected.

hyperkinesia. Condition in which there is an increase in movements of a part or all of the body.

hyperlexia. Condition in which a person is given to excessive reading or is a precocious reader, often without understanding the meaning of what is read.

hypermetamorphosis. Tendency to attend and react to every visual stimulus, leading to mental distraction and confusion.

hyperpolarization. Process by which a nerve membrane becomes more resistant to the passage of sodium ions and consequently more difficult to excite with adequate stimulation; during hyperpolarization, the electrical charge on the inside of the membrane relative to that on the outside becomes more negative.

hypothalamus. Collection of nuclei located below the thalamus; involved in nearly all behavior including movement, feeding, sexual activity, sleeping, emotional expression, temperature regulation, and endocrine regulation.

ideational apraxia. Vague term used to describe a disorder of gestural behavior in which the overall conception of how a movement is carried out is lost; emerges when a person is required to manipulate objects.

ideomotor apraxia. Inability to use and understand nonverbal communication such as gesture and pantomime.

idiopathic seizure. Seizure disorder that appears to arise spontaneously and in the absence of other diseases of the central nervous system.

illusion. False or misinterpreted sensory impression of a real sensory image.

immunohistochemical staining. Antibody-based label that, when applied to tissue postmortem, will reveal the presence of some specific molecule or close relatives of that molecule.

implicit memory. Memory in which subjects can demonstrate knowledge but cannot explicitly retrieve the information (for example, a motor skill). In contrast to explicit memory.

infarct. Area of dead or dying tissue resulting from an obstruction of the blood vessels normally supplying the region.

inferior colliculus. Nucleus of the tectum of the midbrain that receives auditory projections and is involved in whole-body orientation to auditory stimuli.

inhibitory neurotransmitter. Neurotransmitter that increases the membrane polarity of a cell, making it less likely that an action potential will occur.

inhibitory postsynaptic potential (IPSP). Small localized change that increases a membrane's potential, making it less likely that an action potential will occur.

insomnia. Inability to sleep.

intermediate zone. The layer of cells in the spinal cord that lie immediately above the motor neurons of the ventral horn.

internal carotid artery. Branch of the carotid artery that is a major source of blood to the brain.

internal imagery. First-person imagery in which a person imagines that it is himself or herself who engages in an act.

interneuron. Any neuron lying between a sensory neuron and a motor neuron.

interoceptive. Sherrington's term referring to the internal sensory receptors, such as those in the viscera.

invariance hypothesis. Hypothesis suggesting that the structure of each cerebral hemisphere ensures that it will develop a set of specialized functions; for example, the left hemisphere is specialized at birth for language.

ipsilateral. Located on the same side of the body as the point of reference.

isolation syndrome. *See* **transcortical aphasia.**

Jacksonian seizure. Focal seizure that has consistent sensory or motor symptoms such as a twitching in the face or hand.

Kennard principle. Idea that early brain damage produces less severe behavioral effects than brain damage incurred later in life; coined after Kennard reported this phenomenon in a series of papers based on the study of neonatally brain-damaged monkeys.

kindling. Production of epilepsy by repeated stimulation; for example, by an electrode in the brain.

kinesthesis. Perception of movement or position of the limbs and body; commonly used to refer to the perception of changes in the angles of joints.

Klüver-Bucy syndrome. Group of symptoms resulting from bilateral damage to the temporal lobes; characterized especially by hypersexuality, excessive oral behavior, and visual agnosia.

Korsakoff's syndrome (or **Korsakoff-Wernicke disease).** Group of symptoms resulting from degeneration of the dorsomedial thalamic nucleus; produced by chronic alcoholism. Metabolic disorder of the central nervous system due to a lack of vitamin B_1 (thiamin); often associated with chronic alcoholism.

landmark test. Behavioral test in which the subject must learn the association between a specific cue (the landmark) and the location of reward.

lateral fissure. A deep cleft on the basal surface of the brain that extends laterally, posteriorly, and upward, thus separating the temporal and parietal lobes. Also called *Sylvian fissure.*

lateral system. One of the two major motor groups of tracts in the motor system; includes the lateral corticospinal tract, which originates in the neocortex, and the rubrospinal tract, which originates in the red nucleus in the brainstem.

laterality. Pertaining to the side of the brain that controls a given function; hence, studies of laterality are devoted to determining which side of the brain controls various functions.

lateralization. Process whereby functions come to be located primarily on one side of the brain.

learning disability. Generally defined by work performance in a specific school subject that falls significantly below average; for example, a reading disability is sometimes defined as reading 2 years below the class average.

lesion. Any damage to the nervous system.

letter-by-letter reading. Reading in which the meaning of a text is determined by extracting information from each letter, one letter at a time.

lexicon. Dictionary, or memory store, in the brain that contains words and their meanings.

light microscope. Microscope that relies on shining light through tissue to visualize that tissue through an eyepiece.

limbic lobe. Term coined by Broca to refer to the structures between the brainstem and telencephalon; in modern usage, equivalent to the limbic system, which includes the hippocampus, septum, cingulate cortex, hypothalamus, and amygdala.

limb-kinetic apraxia. Form of apraxia in which the person is unable to make voluntary movements of the limbs in response to verbal commands; presumed to result from a disconnection of the motor program from language.

limbic system. Elaboration of the structures of the limbic lobe to form a hypothetical functional system originally believed to be important in controlling affective behavior. Neural systems that line the inside wall of the neocortex.

lipofuscin granule. Dark-pigmented substance that accumulates in brain cells as they age.

localization of function. Hypothetically, the control of each kind of behavior by a different specific brain area.

long-term enhancement (LTE). Long-lasting change in the postsynaptic response of a cell that results from previous experience with a high-frequency stimulation. Also known as *enhancement* or *long-term potentiation (LTP).*

long-term memory. Form of memory postulated by Broadbent in which it is assumed that information is stored for longer than about 15 minutes.

long-term potentiation (LTP). *See* **long-term enhancement (LTE).**

low decerebrate. Preparation in which both the hindbrain and spinal cord of an animal remain intact. *See also* **decerebrate** and **decerebration.**

lysome. Small body containing digestive enzymes seen with the electron microscope in many types of cells.

macular sparing. Condition in which the central region of the visual field is not lost, even though temporal or nasal visual fields are.

magnetic resonance imaging (MRI). Imaging procedure in which a computer draws a map from the measured changes in the magnetic resonance of atoms in the brain. Also known as *nuclear magnetic resonance (NMR). See also* **functional MRI (fMRI).**

magnetoencephalogram (MEG). Magnetic potentials recorded from detectors placed outside the skull.

magnocellular layer. Layer of neurons composed of large cells.

mass action hypothesis. Hypothesis that the entire neocortex participates in every behavior.

massa intermedia. Mass of gray matter that connects the left and right thalami across the midline.

maturation hypothesis. Theory arguing that both hemispheres are initially involved in language but the left hemisphere gradually becomes more specialized for language control.

maturational-lag hypothesis. Explanation of a disability suggesting that a system is not yet mature or is maturing slowly.

medial longitudinal fissure. Fissure that separates the two hemispheres.

medulla oblongata. Portion of the hindbrain immediately rostral to the spinal cord.

medulloblastoma. Highly malignant brain tumor found almost exclusively in the cerebellums of children; results from the growth of germinal cells that infiltrate the cerebellum.

meninges. Three layers of protective tissue—the dura mater, arachnoid, and pia mater—that encase the brain and spinal cord.

meningioma. Encapsulated brain tumor growing from the meninges.

meningitis. Inflammation of the meninges.

mental rotation. Ability to make a mental image of an object and imagine it in a new location relative to its background.

mesencephalon. Middle brain; term for the middle one of the three primary embryonic vesicles, which subsequently comprises the tectum and tegmentum.

metastasis. Transfer of a disease from one part of the body to another; common characteristic of malignant tumors.

metastatic tumor. Tumor that occurs through the transfer of tumor cells from elsewhere in the body.

metencephalon. Anterior portion of the rhombencephalon, composed of the cerebellum and pons.

microfilaments. Small tubelike processes in cells, the

function of which is uncertain but that may be involved in controlling the shape, movement, or fluidity of the cytoplasm or substances within the cell.

microtubules. Fiberlike substances in the soma and processes of nerve cells that are involved in transporting substances from the soma to the distal elements of the cell or from distal portions of the cell to the soma.

midbrain. Short segment between the forebrain and hindbrain, including the tectum and tegmentum.

middle cerebral artery. The cerebral artery that runs along the length of the Sylvian fissure and sends blood to the ventral part of the frontal lobe, most of the parietal lobe, and the temporal lobe.

migraine. Type of headache characterized by an aching, throbbing pain, often unilateral; may be preceded by a visual aura presumed to result from ischemia of the occipital cortex induced by vasoconstriction of cerebral arteries.

migraine stroke. Condition in which a cerebral vessel constricts, cutting off the blood supply to a cortical region; if the constriction is severe enough and lasts more than a few minutes, then neuronal death may occur, leading to an infarct.

mitochondrion. Complex organelle within the cell that produces most of the cell's energy, through a number of processes.

module. Hypothetical unit of cortical organization, believed to represent a vertically organized intracortical connectivity that is assumed to reflect a single functional unit. Sometimes used as a synonym for a *column*.

monoamines. Group of neurotransmitters, including norepinephrine and dopamine, that have an amine (NH_2).

monoclonal antibody. Antibody that is cloned or derived from a single cell.

monocular blindness. Blindness in one eye caused by destruction of its retina or optic nerve.

monocular deprivation. Removal of visual stimulation to one eye by closure or bandaging.

morpheme. Smallest meaningful unit of speech.

morphological reconstruction. Reconstruction of the body of an animal, often from only skeletal remains.

motoneurone. Sherrington's term for the unit formed by motor neurons and the muscle fiber to which their axon terminations are connected.

motor aphasia. Disorder in which the affected person is unable to make the correct movements of the mouth and tongue to form words; as contrasted with sensory aphasia in which speech is fluent but without content; a form of nonfluent aphasia.

motor apraxia. Inability, in the absence of paralysis, to execute the voluntary movements needed to perform a goal-oriented action.

motor neuron. Neuron that has its cell body in the spinal cord and that projects to muscles.

motor program. Hypothetical neural circuit so arranged that it produces a certain type of movement; for example, walking.

multimodal cortex. Cortex that receives sensory inputs from more than one sensory modality; for example, vision and audition.

multiple sclerosis (MS). Disease of unknown cause in which there are patches of demyelination in the central nervous system; may lead to motor weakness or incoordination, speech disturbance, and sometimes to other cognitive symptoms.

myasthenia gravis. Condition of fatigue and weakness of the muscular system without sensory disturbance or atrophy; results from a reduction in acetylcholine available at the synapse.

mycotic infection. Invasion of the nervous system by a fungus.

myelencephalon. Posterior portion of the rhombencephalon, including the medulla oblongata and fourth ventricle.

myelin. Lipid substance forming an insulating sheath around certain nerve fibers; formed by oligodendroglia in the central nervous system and by Schwann cells in the peripheral nervous system.

myelin stains. Dyes that stain glial cells, particularly those that wrap themselves around axons.

myelination. Formation of myelin on axons; sometimes used as an index of maturation.

myoclonic spasms. Massive seizures consisting of sudden flexions or extensions of the body and often beginning with a cry.

narcolepsy. Condition in which a person is overcome by uncontrollable, recurrent, brief episodes of sleep.

nasal hemianopsia. Loss of vision of one nasal visual field due to damage to the lateral region of the optic chiasm.

natural selection. Proposition in the theory of evolution that animals with certain adaptive characteristics will survive in certain environments and pass on their genetic characteristics to their offspring, while less fortunate animals, lacking those characteristics, die off.

necrosis. Tissue death, usually as individual cells, groups of cells, or in small localized areas.

neglect dyslexia. Misreading errors that are usually confined to a single half of a word.

neocortex. Newest layer of the brain, forming the outer layer or "new bark;" has four to six layers of cells. In this text, synonymous with *cortex*.

neotony. Fact that newly evolved species often resemble the young of their ancestors.

nerve growth factor (NGF). Protein that plays some role in maintaining the growth of a cell.

nerve impulse. Movement or propagation of an action potential along the length of an axon; begins at a point close to the cell body and travels away from it.

nerve net hypothesis. Idea that the brain is composed of a continuous network of interconnected fibers.

neuritic plaques. Areas of incomplete necrosis that are often seen in the cortex of people with senile dementias such as Alzheimer's disease.

neuroblast. Any embryonic cell that develops into a neuron.

neuroendocrine. Pertaining to the interaction of the neural and endocrine (hormonal) systems.

neurofibril. Any of numerous fibrils making up part of the internal structure of a neuron; may be active in transporting precursor chemicals for the synthesis of neurotransmitters.

neurohumoral. General term for the action of hormones upon the brain.

neuroleptic drug. Drug that has an antipsychotic action principally affecting psychomotor activity and that is generally without hypnotic effects.

neurologist. Physician specializing in the treatment of disorders of the nervous system.

neuron. Basic unit of the nervous system; the nerve cell; its function is to transmit and store information; includes the cell body (soma), many processes called dendrites, and an axon.

neuron hypothesis. Idea that the functional units of the brain are neurons.

neuropsychology. Study of the relationships between brain function and behavior.

neurotoxin. Any substance that is poisonous or destructive to nerve tissue; for example, 6-hydroxydopamine, placed in the ventricles of the brain, will selectively destroy the norepinephrine and dopamine systems.

neurotransmitter. Chemical released from a synapse in response to an action potential and acting on postsynaptic receptors to change the resting potential of the receiving cell; transmits information chemically from one neuron to another.

neurotropic viruses. Viruses having a strong affinity for cells of the central nervous system. *See also* **pantropic viruses.**

nightmares. Terrifying dreams.

Nissl stains. Cells that are selectively taken up by the protein (Nissl substance) in the cell body.

Nissl substance. Large granular body that stains with basic dyes; collectively forms the substance of the reticulum of the cytoplasm of a nerve cell.

node of Ranvier. Space separating the Schwann cells that form the covering (or myelin) on a nerve axon; because the nerve impulse jumps from one node to the next, its propagation is accelerated.

nonfluent aphasia. Impairment of speech that follows brain damage, particularly to the frontal part of the hemisphere dominant for speech, and that is characterized by difficulty in articulating words.

norepinephrinergic neurons. Neurons that contain norepinephrine in their synapses or use norepinephrine as their neurotransmitter.

nuclear magnetic resonance (NMR). *See* **magnetic resonance imaging (MRI).**

nucleolus. Organelle within the nucleus of a cell that produces ribosomes.

nucleus. Spherical structure in the soma of cells that contains DNA and is essential to cell function; also, a group of cells forming a cluster that can be identified histologically.

nystagmus. Constant, tiny eye movements that occur involuntarily and have a variety of causes.

object constancy. Perceptual experience that objects are identified as being the same regardless of the angle of view.

obstructive sleep apnea. Constriction of the breathing apparatus that results in loss of breath during sleep; also thought to be a major cause of snoring.

occipital horns. Most posterior projections of the lateral ventricles that protrude into the occipital lobe.

occipital lobe. General area of the cortex lying in the back part of the head.

olfaction. Sense of smell or the act of smelling.

oligodendrocytes. Specialized support, or glial, cells in the brain that form a covering of myelin on nerve cells to speed the nerve impulse. Also called *oligodendroglia.*

optic ataxia. Deficit in the visual control of reaching and other movements and in eye movements.

optic chiasm. Point at which the optic nerve from one eye partially crosses to join the other, forming a junction at the base of the brain.

orbital-frontal cortex. Cortex that lies adjacent to the cavity containing the eye but that, anatomically defined, receives projections from the dorsomedial nucleus of the thalamus.

organic brain syndrome. General term for behavioral disorders that result from brain malfunction attributable to known or unknown causes.

organicity. General term (of limited value in neuropsychology) used to refer to abnormal behavior that is assumed to have a biological (organic) basis.

orientation. Direction.

orienting reaction. Process whereby an animal's attention is engaged by a novel stimulus.

otolith organs. Bodies in the inner ear that provide vestibular information.

paired helical filaments. Two spiral filaments made of chains of amino acids.

paleocortex. Portion of the cerebral cortex forming the pyriform cortex and parahippocampal gyrus. Also called the *paleopallium*.

pantropic viruses. Viruses that attack any body tissue. *See also* **neurotropic viruses.**

papilledema. Swelling of the optic disk; caused by increased pressure from cerebrospinal fluid; used as a diagnostic indicator of tumors or other swellings in the brain.

paragraphia. Writing of incorrect words or perseveration in writing the same word.

paralimbic cortex. Area of three-layered cortex that is adjacent to the classically defined limbic cortex and has a direct connection with the limbic cortex; for example, the cingulate cortex.

parallel-development hypothesis. Proposition that both hemispheres, by virtue of their anatomy, play special roles, one for language and one for space.

paraphasia. Production of unintended syllables, words, or phrases during speech.

paraplegia. Paralysis of the legs due to spinal cord damage.

paresis. General term for loss of physical and mental ability due to brain disease, particularly from syphilitic infection; a term for slight or incomplete paralysis.

parietal lobe. General region of the brain lying beneath the parietal bone.

parieto-occipital sulcus. Sulcus in the occipital cortex.

Parkinson's disease. Disease of the motor system that is correlated with a loss of dopamine in the brain and is characterized by tremors, rigidity, and reduction in voluntary movement.

parvocellular layer. Layer of neurons containing small cells.

peptide. Any member of a class of compounds of low molecular weight that yield two or more amino acids on hydrolysis. Peptides form the consistent parts of proteins.

perception. Cognition resulting from the activity of cells in the various sensory regions of the neocortex beyond the primary sensory cortex.

perforant pathway. Large anatomical pathway connecting the entorhinal cortex and subiculum with the hippocampal formation.

peripheral nerves. Nerves that lie outside the spinal cord and the brain.

perseveration. Tendency to emit repeatedly the same verbal or motor response to varied stimuli.

petit mal attack. Seizure characterized by a loss of awareness during which there is no motor activity except blinking or turning of the head and rolling of the eyes; of brief duration (typically 10 seconds).

phagocytes. Cells that engulf microorganisms, other cells, and foreign particles as part of the lymphatic system's defenses.

phenothiazines. Group of major tranquilizers (for example, chlorpromazine) that are similar in molecular structure to the compound phenothiazine.

pheromone. Substance produced by one individual that is perceived (as an odor) by a second individual of the same species and that leads to a specific behavioral reaction in the second individual; acts as a chemical signal between animals of the same species.

phoneme. Unit of sound that forms a word or part of a word.

phonological. Pertaining to sound, as in theories of reading that emphasize the role of sound in decoding the meaning of words.

phonological reading. Reading that relies on sounding out the parts of words.

phrenology. Long-discredited study of the relationship between mental faculties and the skull's surface features.

pia mater. Moderately tough connective tissue that clings to the surface of the brain.

piloerection. Erection of the hair.

pineal body. Asymmetrical structure in the epithalamus, thought by Descartes to be the seat of the soul, but now thought to be involved in circadian rhythms.

pituitary gland. Collection of neurons at the base of the hypothalamus.

place response. Navigational behavior in which an animal locomotes to a position on the basis of its location relative to multiple cues; as distinguished from cue or position response.

place task. Task in which an animal must find a place that it cannot see by using the relationship between two or more cues in its surroundings.

planum temporale. Cortical area just posterior to the auditory cortex (Heschl's gyrus) within the Sylvian fissure.

plasticity. According to theory, the ability of the brain to change in various ways to compensate for loss of function due to damage.

pneumoencephalography. X-ray technique in which the cerebrospinal fluid is replaced with air introduced through a lumbar puncture.

poliomyelitis. Acute viral disease characterized by involvement of the nervous system and possibly paralysis; there may be atrophy of the affected muscles, leading to a permanent deformity.

polymodal cortex. Cortex that receives sensory inputs from more than one sensory modality; for example, vision and audition.

polyribosome. Structure formed by the combination

of mRNA and ribosomes that serves as the actual site for protein synthesis.

pons. Portion of the hindbrain; composed mostly of motor fiber tracts going to such areas as the cerebellum and spinal tract.

position response. Navigational behavior in which an animal locomotes to a position on the basis of movements (for example, left or right) previously made to arrive at the same location; as distinguished from cue or place response.

positron emission tomography (PET). Imaging technique in which a subject is given a radioactively labeled compound such as glucose, which is metabolized by the brain, and the radioactivity is later recorded by a special detector.

postconcussional syndrome. Constellation of somatic and psychological symptoms including headache, dizziness, fatigue, diminished concentration, memory deficit, irritability, anxiety, insomnia, hypochondriacal concern, hypersensitivity to noise and light, all of which are typical after suffering a brief period of disturbed consciousness, usually after a blow to the head.

posterior cerebral artery. Cerebral artery that supplies blood to the posterior part of the cerebral hemispheres, including the occipital lobe and hippocampal formation.

posterior parietal cortex. Nonspecific term pertaining to tissue beyond the primary somatosensory areas; usually includes areas PE, PF, and PG.

postsynaptic membrane. Membrane lying adjacent to a synaptic connection across the synaptic space from the terminal.

posttraumatic psychosis. Psychotic reaction that occurs after head trauma.

praxis. Action, movement, or series of movements.

precentral gyrus. Gyrus lying in front of the central sulcus.

preferred cognitive mode. Use of one type of thought process in preference to another—for example, visuospatial instead of verbal; sometimes attributed to the assumed superior function of one hemisphere over the other.

prefrontal cortex. Cortex lying in front of the primary and secondary motor cortex; thus, the association, or tertiary, cortex in the frontal lobe.

premotor cortex. Cerebral cortex lying immediately anterior to the motor cortex; includes several functional areas, especially the supplementary motor area and Broca's area.

presynaptic membrane. Terminal membrane adjacent to the subsynaptic space.

primary motor cortex. Neocortical area corresponding to Brodmann's area 4; forms the major source of the corticospinal tract.

primary projection area. Area of the brain that first receives a connection from another system.

primary sensory cortex. Neocortical areas that receive the projections of the principal thalamic regions for each sensory modality; corresponds to Brodmann's areas 17 (vision), 41 (audition), and 3-1-2 (somatosensation).

primary zones. Areas of the cortex that first receive projections from sensory systems or that project most directly to muscles. Also known as *primary sensory areas.*

priming task. Task in which subjects are presented with information that will subsequently influence their behavior but which they may not subsequently consciously recall; for example, given a list of words, a subject may be more likely subsequently to use a word on the list than some other word that would also be appropriate.

proactive interference. Interference of something already experienced with the learning of new information.

procedural memory. Memory for certain ways of doing things or for certain movements; this memory system is thought to be independent from declarative memory (that is, memory used to "tell about" some event).

projection map. Map of the cortex made by tracing axons from the sensory systems into the brain and from the neocortex to the motor systems of the brainstem and spinal cord.

proprioceptive. Term referring to sensory stimuli coming from the muscles and tendons.

prosencephalon. Front brain; term for the most anterior part of the embryonic brain, which subsequently evolves into the telencephalon and diencephalon.

prosody. Variation in stress, pitch, and rhythm of speech by which different shades of meaning are conveyed.

prosopagnosia. Inability, not explained by defective visual acuity or reduced consciousness or alertness, to recognize familiar faces; very rare in pure form and thought to be secondary to right parietal lesions.

proximal. Being close to something.

pseudodepression. Condition of personality following frontal lobe lesion in which apathy, indifference, and loss of initiative are apparent symptoms but are not accompanied by a sense of depression in the patient.

pseudopsychopathy. Condition of personality following frontal lobe lesion in which immature behavior, lack of tact and restraint, and other behaviors symptomatic of psychopathology are apparent but are not accompanied by the equivalent mental or emotional components of psychopathology.

psychedelic drug. Any drug that induces behavior characterized by visual hallucinations, intensified perception, and, sometimes, behavior similar to that observed in psychosis.

psychoactive drug. Any chemical substance that alters mood or behavior by altering the functions of the brain.

psychometrics. Science of measuring human abilities.

psychosis. Major mental disorder of organic or emotional origin in which the individual's ability to think, respond emotionally, remember, communicate, interpret reality, and behave appropriately is sufficiently impaired that the ordinary demands of life cannot be met; applicable to conditions having a wide range of severity and duration—for example, schizophrenia or depression.

psychosurgery. Surgical intervention to sever fibers connecting one part of the brain with another or to remove or destroy brain tissue with the intent of modifying or altering disturbances of behavior, thought content, or mood for which no organic pathological cause can be demonstrated by established tests and techniques (for example, lobotomy).

ptosis. Drooping of the upper eyelid from paralysis of the third nerve (oculomotor).

pulvinar. Thalamic nucleus that receives projections from the visual cortex and superior colliculus and sends connections to the secondary and tertiary temporal and parietal cortex.

punctate evolution. Evolution that appears to occur suddenly, rather than in gradual steps; sometimes referred to as *punctuated evolution*.

putamen. Nucleus of the basal ganglia complex.

putative transmitters. Chemicals strongly suspected of being neurotransmitters but not conclusively proved to be so.

pyramidal cells. Cells that have a pyramid-shaped cell body; they usually send information from one region of the cortex to some other brain area.

pyramidal tract. Pathway from the pyramidal cells of the fifth and sixth layers of the neocortex to the spinal cord.

pyramidalis area. Brodmann's area 4.

pyriform cortex. Old cortex; subserves olfactory functions.

quadrantic anopsia. Blindness in one quadrant of the visual field due to some damage to the optic tract, lateral geniculate body, or area 17.

quadraplegia. Paralysis of the legs and arms due to spinal cord damage.

quasi-evolutionary sequence. Hypothetical ancestral lineage of a contemporary species that is composed of the currently living species that most closely resemble the ancestors; for example, for humans, it would include hedgehogs, tree shrews, bush babies, rhesus monkeys, and chimpanzees.

radioisotope scan. Scanning of the cranial surface with a Geiger counter, after an intravenous injection of a radioisotope has been given, to detect tumors, vascular disturbances, atrophy, and so forth.

reading disabled. Pertaining to the inability to read, irrespective of the cause.

reafference. Confirmation by one part of the nervous system of the activity in another. *See also* **corollary discharge.**

reafference theory. *See* **corollary discharge theory.**

real space. Space that one sees around oneself; three-dimensional space.

receptive field. Area from which a stimulus can activate a sensory receptor.

receptors. Proteins on a cell membrane to which other molecules can attach.

reciprocal inhibition. Activation of one muscle group with inhibition of its antagonists.

red nucleus. Nucleus in the anterior portion of the tegmentum that is the source of a major motor projection.

reentry. Process whereby cortical regions send projections back to regions from which they receive afferents; proposed as a mechanism for solving the binding problem.

referred pain. Pain that is felt in a body part other than that in which the cause that produced it is situated.

regeneration. Process by which neurons damaged by trauma regrow connections to the area that they previously innervated.

resting potential. Normal voltage across a nerve cell membrane; varies between 60 and 90 mV in the cells of various animals.

reticular activating system. Diffuse neural system located in the brainstem that functions to arouse the forebrain.

reticular formation. Mixture of nerve cells and fibers in the lower and ventral portion of the brainstem, extending from the spinal cord to the thalamus and giving rise to important ascending and descending systems. Also known as *reticular activating system*.

reticular matter. Area of the nervous system composed of intermixed cell bodies and axons; has a mottled gray and white, or netlike, appearance.

retrograde amnesia. Inability to remember events that occurred prior to the onset of amnesia.

retrograde degeneration. Degeneration of a nerve cell that occurs between the site of damage and the cell body and includes the cell body and all its remaining processes.

retrograde transport. Transport of material by neurons from their axons back to the cell body. Labels or dyes can be placed at the termination of an axon, picked up by the axonal arborization, and transported to the cell body, which makes it possible to trace pathways.

rhinencephalon. Alternative term for the limbic system; literally, smell brain.

rhombencephalon. Hindmost posterior embryonic part of the brain, which divides into the metencephalon and myelencephalon.

ribonucleic acid (RNA). Complex macromolecule composed of a sequence of nucleotide bases attached to a sugar-phosphate backbone; messenger RNA (mRNA) delivers genetic information from a portion of a chromosome to a ribosome (ribosomal RNA, or rRNA), where the appropriate molecules of transfer RNA (tRNA) assemble the appropriate amino acids to produce the polypeptide coded for by the active portion of the chromosome.

righting reflex. Reflex whereby an animal placed in an inverted posture returns to upright; survives low decerebration, hence a reflex.

rods. Light-sensitive retinal receptor cells that contain rhodopsin; together with cones, they form the receptor layer of the retina.

roentgenography. Photography using X rays.

rubrospinal tract. Pathway running from the red nucleus to the spinal cord; involved in the control of the limbs.

saccule. One of two vestibular receptors of the middle ear; stimulated when the head is oriented normally; maintains head and body in an upright position.

saltatory conduction. Propagation of a nerve impulse on a myelinated axon; characterized by its leaping from one node of Ranvier to another.

savant syndrome. Syndrome characterized by various degrees of retardation along with some special, sometimes supranormal, skill.

scanning electron microscope (SEM). Special kind of electron microscope that can produce three-dimensional images of an object.

schizophrenia. Type of psychosis characterized by disordered cognitive functioning and poor social adjustment; literally, splitting of thought and emotive processes; probably due to brain malfunction.

Schwann cells. Glial cells that form myelin in the peripheral nervous system.

sclera. Tough white outer coat of the eyeball.

scotoma. Small blind spot in the visual field caused by small lesions, an epileptic focus, or migraines of the occipital lobe.

second messengers. Diffusible molecules that may influence a variety of cellular constituents, including ion channels. When a transmitter is released and binds to a receptor, an intermediate protein (known as a G-protein), which is bound to the receptor, releases the second messenger molecule.

secondary cortex. Cortex that Fleshig found to develop after the primary motor and sensory regions; Luria proposed these regions to be involved in perception (secondary sensory) and in the organization of movements (secondary motor).

secondary projection area. Area of the cortex that receives projections from or sends projections to a primary projection area.

sedative-hypnotic. Any drug that acts to depress neural activity (and behavior) by either decreasing noradrenergic activity or increasing GABAergic activity.

semicircular canals. Structures in the middle ear that are open on one side and act as part of the receptor unit for balance.

sensation. Result of activity of receptors and their associated afferent pathways to the corresponding primary sensory neocortical areas.

sensitization. Condition in which subsequent exposures to a drug (or other agent) induces a stronger behavioral response than the original exposure.

sensory aphasia. *See* **Wernicke's aphasia.**

sensory neglect. Condition in which an individual does not respond to sensory stimulation.

septum. Nucleus in the limbic system that, when lesioned in rats, produces sham rage and abolishes the theta EEG waveform.

serial lesion effect. Term used to describe the observation that slowly acquired lesions, or lesions that occur in stages, tend to have less severe symptoms than equivalent size lesions that are acquired at one time.

sexual selection. Mechanism of evolution in which the processes involved in determining who mates with whom also determines the characteristics of the offspring that will be produced.

short-term memory. Form of memory postulated by Broadbent in which it is assumed that information is stored for no more than about 15 minutes.

silent synapses. Synapses that do not appear to be functional until other, dominant synapses are removed.

simultagnosia. Symptom in which a person is unable to perceive more than one object at a time.

simultaneous extinction. Second stage of recovery from contralateral neglect; characterized by response to stimuli on the neglected side as if there were a simultaneous stimulation on the contralateral side.

single-photon emission computerized tomography (SPECT). Imaging technique in which a subject is given a radioactively labeled compound such as glucose, which is metabolized by the brain; the radioactivity is later recorded by a special detector; similar to PET, but less accurate, it has the advantage of not requiring a cyclotron to produce the isotopes.

sleep apnea. Condition in which an individual stops breathing when they fall into deep sleep.

slow-wave sleep (S-sleep). Stage of sleep characterized by an EEG dominated by large-amplitude slow waves.

soma. Cell body, including the cell membrane, nucleus, and cytoplasm.

somatic muscles. Muscles of the body that are attached to the skeleton.

somatosensory system. Neural system pertaining to the tactile senses, including touch, kinesthesia, pain, and proprioception.

somatosensory zone. Any region of the brain responsible for analyzing sensations of fine touch and pressure and possibly of pain and temperature.

somnolence. Sleepiness; excessive drowsiness.

sparing. Phenomenon whereby some brain functions are saved from disruption after the occurrence of a lesion early in life, usually before the particular function has developed.

spatial summation. Tendency of two adjacent events to add; hence, two adjacent postsynaptic potentials add or subtract.

specifically reading-retarded. Pertaining to individuals who have adequate intelligence to read but cannot read.

spinal cord. Part of the nervous system enclosed in the vertebral column.

spinal reflex. Response obtained when only the spinal cord is functioning.

spiny neurons. Class of neurons that have dendritic spines; most are excitatory.

splenium. Generally, a bandlike structure; used to refer to the posterior rounded end of the corpus callosum.

spongioblasts. Immature cells that develop into glial cells.

spreading depression. Condition in which a wave of depolarization spreads across the cortical surface, leading to a period in which the tissue is functionally blocked.

sprouting. Phenomenon following partial damage whereby remaining portions of a neuron or other neurons sprout terminations to connect to the previously innervated area.

stellate cell. Nerve cell that is characterized by having a star-shaped cell body. Such cells serve largely as association cells whose processes remain within the region of the brain in which the cell body is located.

stereognosis. Recognition of objects through the sense of touch.

stimulation. Act of applying a stimulus or an irritant to something; the occurrence of such a stimulus or irritant.

stimulus. Irritant or event that causes a change in action of some brain area.

stimulus gradient. Gradient along which the salience of a cue increases or decreases; for example, odors get stronger as the source is approached.

storage granules. Vesicles in the terminal that are presumed to store neurotransmitters.

strephosymbolia. Disorder of perception in which objects seem reversed, as in a mirror; disability in which there is confusion between similar but oppositely oriented letters (for example, *b* and *d*) or words and a tendency to reverse direction in reading or writing.

stretch reflex. Contraction of a muscle to resist stretching; mediated through a muscle spindle, a special sensory receptor system in the muscle.

stroke. Sudden appearance of neurological symptoms as a result of severe interruption of blood flow.

study-test modality shift. Process by which subjects, when presented with information in one modality (reading) and tested in another modality (aurally), display poorer performance than when they are instructed and tested in the same modality.

subarachnoid space. Space between the arachnoid layer and the pia mater of the meninges.

substantia nigra. Nucleus area in the midbrain containing the cell bodies of axons containing dopamine; in freshly prepared human tissue, the region appears black, hence the name (Latin, meaning black substance).

sulcus. Small cleft produced by folding of the cortex.

superior colliculus. Nucleus of the tectum in the midbrain that receives visual projections and is involved in whole-body reflexes to visual stimuli.

supplementary motor cortex. Relatively small region of the cortex that lies outside the primary motor cortex but that will also produce movements when stimulated.

surface dyslexia. Inability to read words on the basis of their pictographic or graphemic representations while the ability to read using phonological, or sounding-out, procedures is retained.

Sylvian fissure. *See* **lateral fissure.**

symptomatic seizures. Seizures that have specific symptoms that may aid in localizing the seizure origin.

synapse. Point of contact between two cells. Classically, this refers to the junction between an axonal terminal and another cell, but other types of contacts are also found.

synaptic cleft. Space between the end foot of a neuron and the cell to which it connects.

synaptic knob. Also called *bouton termineau, end foot, synapsis, synapse, terminal knob. See* **synapse.**

synaptic vesicles. Small vesicles visible in electron-microscopic pictures of terminals; believed to contain neurotransmitters.

Syndenham's chorea. Acute childhood disorder characterized by involuntary movements that gradually become severe, involving virtually all movements, including speech. Also known as *St. Vitus' dance.*

synesthesia. Ability to perceive a stimulus of one sense as a sensation of a different sense, as when sound produces a sensation of color.

syntax. Way in which words are put together, following the rules of grammar, to form phrases, clauses, or sentences; proposed as a unique characteristic of human language.

tachistoscope. Mechanical apparatus consisting of projector, viewer, and screen by which visual stimuli can be presented to selective portions of the visual field.

tactile. Pertaining to the sense of touch.

tardive dyskinesia. Slow, abnormal limb or body-part movements.

tectopulvinar system. Portion of the visual system that functions to locate visual stimuli. Includes the superior colliculus, posterior thalamus, and areas 20 and 21.

tectum. Area of the midbrain above the cerebral aqueduct (the roof); consists of the superior and inferior colliculi, which mediate whole-body response to visual and auditory stimuli, respectively.

tegmentum. Area of the midbrain below the cerebral aqueduct (the floor); contains sensory and motor tracts and a number of nuclei.

telencephalon. Endbrain; includes the cortex, basal ganglia, limbic system, and olfactory bulbs.

teleodendria. Fine terminal branches of an axon.

temporal lobe. Area of the cortex found laterally on the head, below the lateral sulci adjacent to the temporal bones.

temporal memory. Memory for the order of events in time.

temporal summation. Tendency of two events related in time to add; hence, two temporally related postsynaptic potentials add or subtract.

terminal degeneration. Degeneration of the terminals of neurons; can be detected by selective tissue staining.

tertiary projection area. Area of the cortex that receives projections from or sends projections to a secondary projection area. *See also* **association cortex.**

thalamus. Group of nuclei of the diencephalon.

thermoregulation. Ability to regulate body temperature.

theta rhythm. Brain rhythm with a frequency of 4 to 7 Hz.

threshold. Point at which a stimulus produces a response.

thrombosis. Plug or clot in a blood vessel, formed by the coagulation of blood.

tolerance. Ability to endure unusually large doses of a drug without ill effect as a result of continuing use of a drug.

topographic map. Map of the neocortex showing various features, projections, cell distributions, and so on.

topographical agnosia. Inability to recognize one's location in space, such as a failure to recognize one's own neighborhood.

topographical amnesia. Inability to remember the location of things or places.

topographical disorientation. Confusion regarding one's location in space.

Tourette's syndrome (TS). Disease characterized by involuntary movements of body parts and involuntary utterance of words and sounds.

tract. Large collection of axons coursing together within the central nervous system.

transcortical aphasia. Aphasia in which people can repeat and understand words and name objects but cannot speak spontaneously, or can repeat words but cannot comprehend them.

transient global amnesia. Condition in which individuals suffer a short-lived neurological disturbance that is characterized by memory loss; may result from transient episodes of ischemia.

transient ischemia. Short-lived condition of inadequate supply of blood to a brain area.

transmitter substance. Substance that allows neurons to communicate with one another and with glands, muscles, and other body organs.

transneuronal degeneration. Degeneration of cells that synapse with or are synapsed onto by a damaged cell; for example, sectioning of optic tracts results in the degeneration of lateral geniculate body cells.

tumor. Mass of new tissue that persists and grows independently; a neoplasm; it surrounds tissue and has no physiological use.

Turner's syndrome. Genetic condition in which a female has only a single X chromosome. Women with Turner's syndrome have severe spatial deficits.

uncinate fasciculus. Fiber tract connecting the temporal and frontal cortex; a hooked or curved tract.

unilateral visual neglect. Neglect of all sensory events of one or more modalities of stimulation when the stimulation is restricted to one half of the world as defined by the central axis of the body.

unit activity. Electrical potential of a single cell.

utricle. Largest of the subdivisions of the labyrinth of the middle ear; major organ of the vestibular system, which provides information about the position of the head.

ventral root. Tract of fibers leaving the spinal cord, hence motor; on the ventral portion of the spinal cord of animals and on the anterior portion of the spinal cord of humans.

ventricles. Cavities of the brain that contain cerebrospinal fluid.

ventriculography. X-ray technique whereby the contours of the ventricles are highlighted using an opaque medium introduced into the ventricle through a cannula inserted through the skull.

ventromedial system. One of the two major groups of tracts in the motor system; made up of the vestibulospinal tract, reticulospinal tract, and tectospinal tract, which originate in the brainstem, and the ventral corticospinal tract, which originates in the neocortex.

vertebral artery. Major artery that supplies blood to the hindbrain and spinal cord.

vestibular system. Sensory system with receptors in the middle ear that respond to body position and movement.

visual agnosia. Inability to combine visual impressions into complete patterns—therefore an inability to recognize objects; inability to perceive objects and to draw or copy them.

visualization. Ability to form a mental image of an object.

voltage-sensitive channel. Narrow passageway across the neuron membrane that is opened and closed in response to changes in the voltage across the membrane.

voluntary movement. Any movement that takes an animal from one place to another; can be elicited by lower level sensory input or executed through lower level postural support and reflex systems. Also called *appetitive, instrumental, purposive,* or *operant movement.*

Wallerian degeneration. *See* **anterograde degeneration.**

Wernicke's aphasia. Inability to comprehend speech or to produce meaningful speech; follows lesions to the posterior cortex. Also called *sensory aphasia. See also* **fluent aphasia.**

Wernicke's area. Posterior portion of the superior temporal gyrus, roughly equivalent to area 22.

white matter. Those areas of the nervous system rich in axons covered with glial cells.

Wilson's disease. Genetic disease characterized by the failure to metabolize copper, which is concentrated in the brain.

withdrawal reflex. Withdrawal of a limb in response to applied stimuli that activate pain and temperature fibers. The reflex is mediated by a multisynaptic pathway in the spinal cord.

word salad. Term used to refer to fluent aphasia in which a person produces intelligible words that appear to be strung together randomly.

Index of Names

Index of Topics

Note: Page numbers in *italics* indicate illustrations; page numbers followed by t indicate tables.